NELSON'S NEW
CHRISTIAN DICTIONARY

The Authoritative Resource
On the Christian World

Editorial Board

NELSON'S NEW
CHRISTIAN
DICTIONARY

The Authoritative Resource
On the Christian World

George T. Kurian, Editor

THOMAS NELSON PUBLISHERS
Nashville

© 2001 by Thomas Nelson, Inc.

Published in Nashville, Tennessee, by Thomas Nelson, Inc.

Unless otherwise indicated, Scripture quotations are from the New King James Version of the Bible, © 1979, 1980, 1982, 1990, Thomas Nelson, Inc., Publishers.

Book design and composition by Mark McGarry, Texas Type and Book Works, Dallas, Texas

Library of Congress Cataloging-in-Publication Data available from Library of Congress

Kurian, George Thomas (ed.)
Nelson's new Christian dictionary
ISBN 0-7852-4300-3

Printed in the United States of America

1 2 3 4 5 6 7—06 05 04 03 02 01

DEDICATION

To the memory of 67,000,000 Christian martyrs
who during the past 2,000 years were beheaded, hanged,
burned at the stake, dismembered, mutilated, disemboweled, drawn
and quartered, tortured, speared, shot, flayed alive, bludgeoned,
or thrown to the lions for their faith in Jesus Christ

Oh that my head were [an ocean], and mine eyes a fountain of tears,
that I might weep day and night for the slain . . . of my people!

JEREMIAH 9:1 KJV

And when he had opened the fifth seal, I saw under the alter the
souls of them that were slain for the Word of God, and for the testimony that they held.
And they cried with a loud voice, saying, How long, O Lord, holy and true, does
Thou not judge and avenge our blood on them that dwell on the earth?

REVELATION 6:9–10 KJV

The blood of the martyrs is [the] seed [of the Church.]

TERTULLIAN

Contents

Preface

Nelson's New Christian Dictionary (NNCD) stands as an authoritative, comprehensive, and the most current resource on the entire Christian world. It provides up-to-date information on a host of topics, including its doctrines, creeds, key events and people, worship, music, literature, history, arts, and much more. In short, the reader will find this work a treasury of information.

The NNCD is a celebratory work. It celebrates 2,000 years of Christianity since the Incarnation and heralds its third millennium. With 10,000 entries, over 500 illustrations and charts, and 22 appendices, it is one of the most comprehensive portraits of the Christian church at the outset of the third millennium. It attempts to capture the entire universe of the Christian church and chronicle the lives of the men and women who built up, stone by stone, the majestic edifice of faith.

It is an inventory of the great Christian achievements in art, architecture, and music and a record of the traditions, doctrines, literature, and missions that make up the legacy of all Christian churches. The vocabulary covers the depth of Christian experience over 2,000 years, 100 generations, and over 260 nations and territories. This is what St. Paul calls the inheritance of the saints, an inheritance that has grown over 20 centuries and will continue to grow in the future, should the Lord tarry.

This dictionary is evangelical, interdenominational, and ecumenical, emphasizing the lordship of Jesus Christ. It has tried to maintain the highest lexical standards in its definitions, which are written from an unabashedly Christian perspective. In keeping with the ecumenical nature of the work, a number of terms relating to the Lesser Eastern churches have been included. These are the endangered churches of the Christian world that have borne the brunt of Islamic oppression and persecution for fourteen centuries. These are also the churches in which Christianity flowered early, and many of their picturesque traditions, institutions, and terms find an appropriate home in this dictionary.

It is also important to note what has not been included. We have not included secular persons and movements that have little or no Christian significance. Thus readers will not find here entries on Darwin or Marx or Napoleon. This is also not a Bible dictionary. There are a number of excellent Bible dictionaries on the market, and there seemed no particular reason why biblical terms should be duplicated here.

The statistical data (such as the number of Christian martyrs) in the dictionary as well as in the Appendix, "Christian Centuries," are drawn from the World Christian Encyclopedia (second edition edited by David Barrett, George Thomas Kurian, and Todd Johnson, 2 vols., Oxford University Press, 2000). They were compiled by David Barrett, the world's foremost authority on missiometrics (the science of statistics relating to missions and evangelism), and a distinguished futurist and Christian scholar.

The NNCD does not include articles on countries, except in the case of national churches, such as the Russian Orthodox Church or the Serbian Orthodox Church. As a result, there are fewer entries on Third World Christianity than would have been desirable, given the phenomenal growth of Christian churches in Africa and in some countries in Asia. However, it may be many more decades before this monumental demographic shift is reflected in Christian vocabulary and thus can be included in a dictionary. Long, overview articles are suitable in an encyclopedia, but not in a dictionary where the definitions need to be short, taut, and linked to lexically valid headwords.

This resource is designed primarily for the lay Christian, though the scholar will find much of value here. Its style and tenor, however, are directed more to the level of the laity. To paraphrase Gregory the Great, this dictionary provides "water in which lambs may walk and elephants may swim," that is, it is useful for the scholar and the minister as well as those, Christian or non-Christian, who know little or nothing about the history of Christianity and the people and ideas that shaped it.

Acknowledgments

My biggest debt of gratitude is to the folks at Thomas Nelson who have worked closely with me in the creation of this work. They include Philip P. Stoner, executive vice president, to whom I brought this project back in 1994; Mark Roberts, director of reference, who doggedly propelled this project through the publishing channels and successfully oversaw the negotiations; and Jim Weaver, who took over from Mark when the latter moved to the Holy Spirit Center at Oral Roberts University in 1999. All of them have played a part in the successful completion of the work in a relatively short period. Jim Weaver was the laboring oar at Thomas Nelson toward the end of the project, along with Lee Hollaway. George Knight was in charge of copyediting, a particularly onerous job involving many hours of cleaning and sandpapering the manuscript. Working with Thomas Nelson was a happy experience for which I am grateful.

The project was privileged to have the assistance, counsel, and support of the six advisory board members and four associate members, all of whom reviewed the final manuscript. Worthy of particular mention are David Wright of the University of Edinburgh and John Thompson of Fuller Theological Seminary, who spent countless hours poring over the manuscript entry by entry, making changes and noting comments in longhand on almost every page. Many of the entries bear the impress of their skill and knowledge. I am grateful to James D. Smith III, not merely for his painstaking review of the manuscript but also for his pastoral solicitude and care. I must also mention Mark Galli, managing editor of *Christianity Today,* the one I would turn to whenever I needed any special help or counsel.

Finally, I must acknowledge the support, help, and encouragement of Annie, my beloved wife, companion, encourager, counselor, and fellow soldier in life's battles. Above all, for these 34 years we have shared the same faith and loved the same Lord.

How to Use This Dictionary

FEATURES AND BENEFITS

Nelson's New Christian Dictionary (*NNCD*) provides the most up-to-date information on everything related to Christianity: its movers and shakers, theology, music, architecture, liturgy, art, missions, history, and more. Since it contains approximately 10,000 articles, it is also exceptionally comprehensive. It covers the entire Christian world as expressed in the traditions of Protestantism, Catholicism, and Orthodoxy.

Further, the *NNCD* has been reviewed and critiqued by a distinguished editorial board. All of these scholars are on the cutting edge of scholarship and are recognized for their expertise. Their role has been invaluable to ensure accuracy and authoritativeness.

Moreover, it is presented in easy-to-understand language. Great care has been used to ensure that the user will be able to understand this dictionary and benefit greatly from it.

Finally, the *NNCD* also boasts an attractive, winsome design. It features more than 500 illustrations, charts, and other graphics. Its design is intended to make the dictionary visually appealing and enjoyable to use.

In sum, this dictionary is more than a glossary of words. In addition to being introduced to all the various elements of the Christian church, the user will be reminded of the great legacy of the Christian faith as expressed in all its various strands. It helps Christians recover their past and become aware of the infinite riches of their heritage in Christ, including the glorious work of the missionaries, saints, and martyrs of the church.

Organization

The *NNCD* has three parts. The first part, particularly the Preface and Introduction, sets the stage for the entries. The Preface explains the purpose and rationale for the dictionary and the ways in which it fills an unmet need for authoritative information on the Christian church. The Introduction is a synoptic and interpretive overview. It is an essential part of the dictionary. It provides a broad-brush portrait of the Christian church that will serve users well before exploring the alphabetical entries.

The second part is the dictionary proper, arranged in alphabetical order.

The third part consists of 22 appendixes and a bibliography. The appendixes themselves may be divided into six segments:

Chronologies
- Christian Centuries
- Evangelization
- Christian Music
- English Versions of the Bible
- Electronic Church

Lists
- U.S. Denominations
- World Council of Churches Membership

- Popes of the Roman Catholic Church
- Patron Saints of the Roman Catholic Church
- Feast Days of Saints and Other Notables of the Church
- Liturgical Books
- Most Important Books and Authors in Christian Literature
- Major Theologians
- Notable Christian Missionaries

Rankings
- 100 Most Important Events in Christian History
- 100 Greatest Christians
- 300 Great Hymns of the Christian Church

Charts
- Major Creeds of the Christian Church
- Comparative Denominational Chart

Comparative Glossary
- Greek and Slavonic Churches: A Comparative Liturgical Glossary
- Lesser Eastern Churches: A Comparative Liturgical Glossary

List of Abbreviations in Evangelism

Bibliography

HOW TO USE *NNCD*

To derive the maximum benefit from this dictionary, the user needs to be familiar with the conventions and techniques used in defining the entries.

- All headwords appear in boldface and are placed in alphabetical order.
- A word within the text marked by an asterisk (*) refers to an entry on that subject elsewhere in the dictionary. In order to avoid cluttering the text with the constant use of an asterisk, the *NNCD* does not use an asterisk when referring to generic words such as "theologian," "pope," etc.
- Definitions are numbered serially when a term may be used in more than one sense.
- Non-English words appearing in parentheses as part of the headwords are italicized. For example, **act of trust** (Lat., *actus fiduciae*).
- See References that refer the user to variant readings or related entries are set in small caps as "Acathistos." (See AKATHISTOS.)
- When a main entry is followed by a word or name with another spelling, both are variants, but the preferred form appears first.
- In some entries, denominational qualifiers appear, such as "mainly in the Roman Catholic Church."
- Most common words begin with a lower case letter. When an entry begins with an upper case letter, it means that it is generally capitalized.
- Etymologies are provided for most words of foreign origin and where such etymologies serve to illustrate the original sense of the term.
- Dates are provided with parentheses for all biographical entries and for most book titles or works of art or monuments.

Abbreviations

Arab.	Arabic	Heb.	Hebrew
Aram.	Aramaic	Ital.	Italian
Arm.	Armenian	Kor.	Korean
b.	born	Lat.	Latin
c.	circa or about	lit.	literally
Celt.	Celtic	masc.	masculine
d.	died	Old Eng.	Old English
e.g.	for example	pl.	plural
esp.	especially	Russ.	Russian
fem.	feminine	sing.	singular
Fr.	French	Span.	Spanish
Ger.	German	Syr.	Syriac
Gk.	Greek		

Introduction

Christianity is more than a religion in the conventional sense. It is a kingdom of its own, a spiritual kingdom it is true, but nevertheless a kingdom with its own monarch, laws, language, institutions, intellectual currencies, culture, and civilization. It is a kingdom that coexists with the kingdoms of this world with which it has always been in conflict. *Nelson's New Christian Dictionary (NNCD)* is an effort to present the vocabulary of this kingdom and its peoples in a proper dictionary format. It provides an overview of the whole procession of Christian history, and it is also a more detailed look that portrays the contemporary Christian church and its various branches and confessions. Like a pointillist painting, it uses the entry words as dots or points to construct a portrait of the church as it evolved through the centuries.

A classification of Christian ideas and traditions has never been attempted, but a dictionary is a good place to make a start. Such a classification is important because the various influences that shaped Christian history are not apparent to casual observers or even to believers. Making the task even more difficult is its sheer immensity. The landscape of the Christian world would be similar to the great Amazon River with its vast network of interlocking tributaries and branches. To separate and identify the various strands that make up the whole is one of the most important functions of a dictionary. It will reveal those areas where Christianity is strong, and those areas where Christianity is lagged, and the contributions that each branch has made to the universal church.

THE THREE CONSTANT THEMES

There are three constant themes in Christian history: defense of orthodoxy, evangelism, and persecution. The defense of the faith has been one of the principal tasks of the church. The definition of true faith began with the Epistles of Paul and continued through the first seven Ecumenical Councils and through the many denominational councils held in every century since. Sound doctrine is like oxygen to the believer, and Paul himself warned of strange doctrines and the seductions of false teachers.

The church has been remarkably successful in its efforts to defend orthodoxy. The majority of the churches in the modern world subscribe to the principal tenets of orthodoxy including the divinity of Christ, the Trinity, virgin birth, the resurrection of Christ, plenary inspiration of the Bible, baptism, last judgment, and Jesus' second coming. Many entries in *NNCD* deal with the evolution of these theological concepts as well as the evolution of the canon of the Scriptures.

The second constant theme is evangelism and the fulfillment of the Great Commission. Every Christian is called upon–in fact commanded–to proclaim the gospel, convert, teach, and baptize. The great bimillennial question is: Why is it that after 2,000 years Christians make up only one-third of the human race?

To answer this question, it is important to look at both the nature of the enemy and the nature of conversion. Christ did not use the term *harvest* along with or as part of the Great Commission, yet the two have become closely associated. However, the term *harvest* suggests that there are millions of stalks out there patiently waiting for the imminent sickle. True, the stalks are out there–"white unto harvest" and perishing–but the ground is the enemy's.

Before the harvest can take place, the ground has to be seized from the enemy and the "strong man" has to be bound. The gospel is not marching into a vacuum or virgin land; it is going into enemy-held and enemy-owned territory. The Great Commission is as much a declaration of war against the prince of this world as it is a call to duty to Christians. The Great Commissioners–as all Christians should properly be called–are conscripts in a war that has lasted 2,000 years.

The nature of conversion also determines the success of evangelism. No human being is ever born saved. Through original sin, every person at the point of birth is already a chattel of the enemy. His or her mind is not a *tabula rasa*, but is already written over with the message of the anti-gospel and the vessel of his or her being is brimming full with the spirit of disobedience. As everyone knows, it is not possible to pour water into a full cup. The cup has to be emptied first before the refilling can take place.

Similarly, it is not possible to write on a slate that has been written over. The original writing has to be erased first and then a new message can be written on it. Indeed, the degree of erasure is quite important; otherwise, as in many ancient parchments, the old writings tend to resurface after a few years, an unfortunate phenomenon with many spiritual parallels. Again, it is relatively easy to fish in the open sea, yet it is never possible to catch fish that are already in someone else's net. That net has to be cut first; the captives have to be set free before the gospel can be preached to them.

The third constant theme in Christian history is persecution. Persecution and martyrdom began at the time of the Incarnation with the Massacre of the Innocents, and it has continued to the present day. According to the *World Christian Encyclopedia*, there have been over 67 million martyrs over the course of the past 2,000 years. The river of blood that runs through Christian history has never run dry.

In fact, there were more Christian martyrs in the twentieth century than in any of the preceding centuries. Christians have faced considerable opposition in modern times and millions of Christians were murdered by the Communists in the twentieth century. But the gates of hell have not prevailed, and the church has survived its tormentors. As John Buchan said, the church is an anvil that has worn out many hammers.

THE SIX LEVELS OF CHRISTIANITY

Christianity is a multifaceted, many-splendored faith. It operates on many levels simultaneously. Any classification of the Christian church must begin by identifying the principal levels of this living faith.

1. The first and most primary level is the vertical. Above everything else, Christianity is a way of salvation, working with one person at a time. "The Son of Man came to seek and to save that which was lost" (Luke 19:10) encapsulates the entire gospel in fourteen words. Christianity is first of all a vast universal search and rescue mission, a lifeline thrown to those who are drowning in a stormy sea.

It is important to visualize Christianity not in the abstract but in concrete terms and in numbers. Over two millennia, more than 8 billion persons have lived on planet earth as Christians and every one of them had direct access to salvation. Christianity is the sum total of the spiritual lives of these 8 billion persons. More than 67 million died for their faith. More than 120 million dedicated their lives to the Lord as priests, pastors, missionaries, and monks.

2. The next three levels are lateral or horizontal. Of these the most important is the local church. The local church may mean either the physical building or other facility where Christians meet or the bond that binds believers together. Christianity is a relational religion in which horizontal relationships are critical in

maintaining the integrity of Christian testimony in a hostile world. The local assembly is the focal point of all Christian activities, whether it be Sunday school, the transmission of Christian values across generational divides, evangelism and hospitality, or scripturally sanctioned sacraments such as baptism, marriage, and communion. There are over 1 million such local churches and assemblies throughout the world, where on every Sunday the divine service is celebrated and believers reaffirm their faith.

3. The third level is the denomination, which overlaps with the tradition or confession. It is sometimes contended that Christianity should be denominationless, but denominations have played a useful role in Christian history in defining creeds, mobilizing evangelistic efforts, and providing a home for varieties of doctrinal emphases. There are over 22,000 denominations in the world today. While this large number gives the impression that Christians are disunited and disorganized, it has historically helped to enlarge the Christian presence in every country.

In a sense, denominations are comparable to the large land masses, continents, and islands that make up the planet. Since the fifteenth century, the Roman Catholic Church, Protestants, and Eastern Orthodox churches have made up the largest "continents" of the Christian world. The fact that there are various branches of the Christian church does not make it disunited, just as the fact that there are over 2,000 land masses of various sizes does not make the earth a divided planet.

4. The fourth level is the Universal Church, which is the proper Body of Christ. The individual believers, local assemblies, and denominations are all part of His body. The Universal Church is a mystical concept in which all human beings who confess Jesus Christ as Lord and Savior are members. Because the Universal Church is an organic and living entity, whatever affects an individual member affects the whole body and whatever affects the whole body affects individual members. In theological terms, the Universal Church on earth is the Church Militant, which has carried the torch for her lord and bridegroom for the past 2,000 years.

The four marks of the Universal Church are stated in the Nicene Creed: one, holy, catholic,

and apostolic. The Universal Church consists of both the visible church and the invisible church. The invisible church comprises those millions of Christians who for some reason are not formal members of a local assembly or denomination. It also includes millions of silent and underground Christians in countries where open profession of the Christian faith is proscribed.

Interestingly, the word *church* may properly be applied in the English language to any of the four preceding levels. This may lead to some confusion in the entries as readers of the dictionary will discover.

5. The final two levels on which the Christian church functions are ancillary, but these have nothing to do with its purpose or goals. The first is as a folk religion and the other as a civil religion. In many countries, Christian presence is mainly as a folk religion (like any other religion). It is encrusted with myths and popular traditions associated with rites of passage marking life events, such as births, marriages, and funerals. Human beings are innately religious, and folk religion satisfies their limited spiritual needs. Even here there are wide variations. Some nominal Christians are openly pagan in their beliefs and practices, while others retain some Christian identity in their lives.

Associated with the folk religious aspect of Christianity is cultural Christianity. Christian influences on contemporary civilization are still very strong. An example is the Christian calendar that is now the global calendar followed by almost all nations of the world. Modern legal, educational, and political systems owe much to biblical and Christian values and ideas. Cultural Christianity has also helped to change the social landscape. For example, the dominance of monogamy as the norm in marriage is due solely to Christian influence, since virtually all other religions sanction, approve, or condone polygamy. Christian contributions to literature, architecture, and music are enormous.

6. Lastly, Christianity functions as a civil or state religion in many countries. This is the role in which the church is most uncomfortable. It has had to make compromises and seek accommodation with state authorities to survive as a secular institution. Especially since the time of Constantine, Christianity has become a handmaiden to

society and state and performs functions that are designed to advance not itself, but the larger civil community. The church is heavily involved in social welfare, the education of children and youth, hospitals and health care, and it also offers prayers and invocations on state occasions and inaugurals.

THE CONFLICTS

Even though a classification of the various levels of Christianity is extremely helpful, it does not reveal internal conflicts within the Christian church. The most important are the conflicts between law and grace, between works and faith, between predestination and free will, and between tradition and renewal. These conflicts, which go back to the first century, have led to many of the schisms and divisions within the church. They were also responsible for the development of the three major doctrinal traditions in Christian history: the Petrine tradition represented by the Roman Catholic Church and the Eastern Orthodox Church, the Pauline tradition represented by the Protestant churches, and the Johannine tradition represented by the Pentecostal churches.

There is also the dichotomy between Christianity as a religion that affirms the world system and a faith that defies the world system. The term *world system* refers to the entire order of the *physical* universe–the river of life into which human beings are thrown at birth and in which they have to swim until they sink. It does not refer to the world system in its evil sense, but rather to the social order of things.

As a formal religion, Christianity affirms the world order, and it undergirds the social and moral order of the universe. Almost all modern denominations and theologians belong to this school. There are Christian pastors and psychologists whose message is exclusively "positive," on how to have a successful marriage or how to manage money, and so on. They emphasize virtues such as order, discipline, ambition, and obedi-

ence, all affirming the legitimacy of the world system.

But it was not always so. Christianity was in the beginning a world system-defying, incendiary faith, designed not so much to buttress as to overcome the world, ultimately destroy it, and replace it with a heavenly kingdom. Even in the first century, both Jews and Romans recognized the subversive nature of the Christian faith; the pagans said that Christians had turned the world upside down. Hatred for the world system and contempt for the god of this world were strong themes running through the writings of the early church fathers and ascetics. For them the world system was not merely illegitimate but also represented everything that they hated–sex, power, greed, money, and inhumanity.

This hatred reached a crescendo in the Revelation of St. John in which the immediacy of the second coming emboldened Christians to thumb their noses at the world. Even death did not hold any terrors for these Christians because they placed a low value on "the present life."

By the fourth century hundreds of thousands of monks and stylites (pillar saints) in Palestine, Syria, Asia Minor, and Egypt represented the triumph of this strain of Christianity. For them, mortification of the flesh, fasting, and asceticism became articles of faith. Like the monks, heretics–especially Marcionites and Gnostics–regarded all matter as evil.

After the fifth century, as the eschatalogical timetable receded, defiance of the world became muted in Christian theology. It survived in small pockets like Bogomils in the Balkans and the Cathari in France and Italy and finally died out in the early Middle Ages. Interestingly, opposition to the world system has resurfaced in many of the modern-day millennial movements, but in a more subdued form.

Thus the *NNCD* is published with the prayer that it fully captures and communicates the richness of Christianity in all its multifaceted aspects.

GEORGE THOMAS KURIAN
DECEMBER 2000

a capella (Lat., in chapel style) Singing without instrumental accompaniment.

a parte ante Scholastic term for the eternal past of God before the creation of the world.

Aachen City in Germany, site of the octagon cathedral with a sixteen-sided dome, built by Emperor Charlemagne* around 789. It was the earliest completely vaulted building north of the Alps. The name of the architect was Master Odo of Metz. From the center of the high-vaulted dome hangs a magnificent circular chandelier of gilded copper which the goldsmith Wibert made in 1160 as a symbol of the Celestial City. In the center is the Octagon of Charlemagne consecrated in 805 by Pope Leo III*. The cathedral is surrounded by a necklace of chapels.

Aba I, Mar (d. 552) Nestorian* catholicos* from 540. A convert from Mazdaism, he studied and later taught at Nisibis*. As catholicos, he opened a school at Seleucia-Ctesiphon*. The Magi persecuted him and later imprisoned and exiled him.

abba (Syr., father) 1. In the New Testament, God as heavenly Father. 2. Term of address, especially for Desert Fathers* and revered pioneers of asceticism*.

Abba Salama 1. The first bishop of Axum*, Ethiopia, generally identified with Frumentius*. He is often surnamed Kasate Berhan, or "the Illumina-

tor." 2. Title of the abuna* (patriarch*) of the Ethiopian Orthodox Church*, meaning "Father of Peace."

abbas Title of a Coptic bishop or metropolitan*.

abbateia In the Byzantine Church*, abbey or monastery.

abbe Originally the abbot of a monastery in France, but often applied to anyone who wears clerical dress.

abbess Superior* of certain autonomous houses of nuns.

abbey 1. Monastery or nunnery that houses a religious community. It generally ranks above a priory*. 2. A church connected with a monastery.

abbey nullius Abbey whose abbot is exempt from diocesan control and is under direct papal jurisdiction.

Abbo of Fleury, St. (945–1004) Monastic reformer and abbot of Fleury. He helped Oswald*, archbishop of York*, to introduce into England the reforms of the Monastery of Cluny*. On return to France, he was elected abbot of Fleury (Saint-Benoit-sur-Loire*). His writings cover canon law*, ecclesiastical history, the lives of the Fathers of the Desert*, logic, and grammar. He was killed in 1004 by dissident monks. Feast day: November 13.

abbot In the Western Church*, the official title of the superior* of certain monasteries of monks or monastic congregations* belonging to the Benedictine*, Cistercian, or Trappist* families or of houses of certain orders of canons regular*. The abbot is the father of his monastic community, and he determines the rules that apply to the monks. He is generally elected in accordance with the constitution of the order or congregation.

abbot primate Leader of the Benedictine Order.

abbreviator Official who, until 1908, drafted the pope's ecclesiastical writings as a member of the college of abbreviators at the Vatican*.

ABCFM American Board of Commissioners for Foreign Missions.

Abecedarians Sixteenth-century German group founded by Nicolas Storch, who held that human knowledge hinders religious understanding and that knowledge of even the alphabet is unnecessary.

Abeel, David (1804–1846) Pioneer American missionary to China. He was appointed as a missionary to China by the American Board of Commissioners for Foreign Missions* in 1830. From 1835 to 1838, he actively promoted interest in missions in the Dutch Reformed Church* in the Dutch East Indies. He returned to China in 1841 and established a mission station in Kolangsu, small island at Amoy, one of the five ports open to missionaries. Amoy later became a major mission station.

abegha (Arm., monk) In the Armenian Church*: 1. title of celibate priests who have not been made vartabeds*. 2. a monk-priest.

Abel, Charles William (1863–1930) English missionary to Papua New Guinea. Converted through the preaching of Dwight L. Moody*, he went to New Zealand at age 18 to work among the Maori. In 1890 he was sent by the London Missionary Society to Papua New Guinea on the small island of Kwato. Here Abel and his wife, Beatrice, taught the natives technical and vocational skills, language, and sports along with strong personal faith.

Abelard, Peter (1079–1142/3) French ecclesiastic. He achieved fame as a young teacher with his brilliant refutation of the Realism of William of Champeaux. His lectures were attended by large audiences, but the tragic scandal of his illicit love affair with Heloise forced him to retire to the Monastery of St. Denis* in 1117/18. He established a small oratory* called Paraclete, near Troyes, where Heloise was later to become the abbess of a house of nuns. In 1127 he became abbot of St. Gildas, and in 1136 he was back as a teacher in Paris. His teachings were twice condemned: first at the Council of Soissons* in 1121 where he was made to burn his book on the Trinity*, and then at the Council of Sens*. Before his death he was reconciled to Bernard of Clairvaux*, who had earlier denounced him, and restored to communion.

Abelard's fame rests on *Sic et Non**, a collection of apparently contradictory statements from the Bible and the Church Fathers* on a large number of questions to force the reader to resolve the differences. His other major works included *Scito te Ipsum, Dialectica, Theologia,* and *Dialogus.* He was also the author of a collection of hymns, including the well-known *O What the Joy and the Glory Must Be,* written at the request of Heloise for the nuns of the Paraclete. Most of his philosophy dealt with the problem of universals and the relation of language to reality. Rather than pitting reason against faith, Abelard questioned the content of faith to make it more lucid and viable. In his exemplarist theory of the Atonement*, he stressed the suffering and death of Christ as a supreme example for his followers without denying the salvation purchased on the cross.

abemnat Abbot of an Ethiopian Orthodox monastery.

Abendmusik (Ger., pl., *Abendmusiken*) Music of evening church service.

Abercius Inscription of Greek epitaph of Abercius, bishop of Hierapolis (c. 200), now in the Vatican Museum. It testifies to the universal celebration of the Eucharist* in the early church.

Abgar King of Edessa*, who being ill, according to a legend recounted in the *Doctrine of Addai,* wrote to Christ asking him to come and heal him.

Christ wrote back to the king in Syriac*, according to the *Pilgrimage of Egeria**, that he could not come himself but promised to send, after his ascension, a disciple to cure the king and preach the gospel to his people. According to Eusebius*, the letter was followed by Thaddaeus*, one of the Seventy, who healed the king and converted the inhabitants of the city. Both Christ's letter written on parchment* and an accompanying portrait of Christ were reputed to have been preserved at Edessa* for centuries.

abjuration (Lat., *abjurare,* to deny an oath) Act of renouncing a false doctrine or heresy formerly held or adhered to.

ablutions (Lat., *ablutio,* cleansing) In the Roman Catholic tradition, ritual washing of the chalice* and other objects with wine and water prior to the Eucharist*, and the washing of the fingers and the chalice after the Eucharist.

Abode of Love Religious community founded by Henry James Prince at Spaxton, England, about 1850.The group held all their possessions in common and believed in the imminent return of Christ. The group disbanded after a scandal and a lawsuit in 1860.

Abraham Echellensis (1605–1664) Birth name: Ibrahim al-Haqilani. Maronite scholar who was instrumental in introducing European scholars to the languages and literatures of the Christian Orient. From 1635 to 1645 he was interpreter for the Congregation for the Propagation of Faith, from 1645 to 1660 at the College de France, and from 1660 scriptor for Syriac* and Arabic at the Vatican Library*.

Abraham Malpan (1796–1845) Mar Thoma Church* founder. Ordained in 1915, Abraham was elevated as a malpan* or teacher in the Syrian Orthodox Church* in Kerala, India. However, he developed Protestant sympathies as a result of contact with the Church Missionary Society* and broke with the Syrian Jacobite tradition. Later he and his nephew Matthew formed the Mar Thoma Church. He revised and translated the liturgy and prayers into Malayalam, the local language, and dispensed with prayers to the Virgin Mary* and the saints.

Abraham of Kashkar (d. 588) Nestorian anchorite* who founded the Great Convent on Mount Izla near Nisibis*, for which he composed the Rule.

Abraham of Phou (d. 580) Superior general* of Pachomian monasteries under Justinian*, living in the Convent of Phou in the Thebaid*. He was forced to leave his monastery because he would not adhere to the Confession of Chalcedon.

absolution (Lat., *absolvere,* to set free) Formal act of forgiving sins by an ordained priest by virtue of the power granted to him in John 20:23. Mortal sins* are absolved only in the sacrament* of penance* or reconciliation. Sins may be forgiven by the priest by reciting the formula*, "I absolve you" or, as in the Russian Church, "May God forgive you."

Absolutions for the Dead Medieval service after a Requiem Mass* consisting of prayers for the dead.

Abstemii In the early church, persons who abstained from drinking wine at the Eucharist*.

A.B.Th. Bachelor of Arts in Theology.

abudiyakun In the Coptic Church*, subdeacon. Subdeacons are ordained by the bishop by placing one hand on each of the candidate's temples with the thumbs meeting on the forehead while the candidate holds a lighted candle.

abu-halim In the Church of the East*, book of collects* used at the conclusion of night prayers on Sundays. It was compiled by Patriarch Elias III Abu-Halim (1176–1190).

abuna (Arab. and Ge'ez, Our Father) (*noun*) Title of the patriarch* of the Ethiopian Tewahdo Church. (*adjective*) Abuna.

abyss 1. In the New Testament, the abode of Satan* and his demons. 2. In Gnosticism*, one name for the supreme deity.

Acacian Schism 1. Fourth-century division over Arianism*, named for Acacius of Caesarea, who maintained that the Son is *like* the Father. 2. Fifth-century division between the Eastern and Western churches caused by the publication of the Henotikon (482), a formula* for union between the Chalcedonian and Orthodox churches. It was named after Acacius of Constantinople (471–489). The schism* lasted until 518.

Acarie, Mme Barbe (1566–1618) "Mary of the Incarnation," one of the founders of the Reformed Carmelites*. Their first house was founded in 1604. She also helped to bring the Ursulines* to Paris. She was beatified in 1791.

Acathistus See AKATHISTOS.

accentus Plainsong* of the simple recitation type as sung by the celebrant.

acceptance Acceptance of humans by God based on the redemptive work of Jesus Christ.

acceptilation (Lat., *acceptilatio,* formal discharge of a debt) God's acceptance of the death of Jesus Christ as satisfaction* of the penalty for human sin.

accident Nonessential quality of a work or thing, as opposed to its essence. In the Roman Catholic Church, bread and wine consecrated in the Mass* retain their accidents or their outward appearance, color, and shape, but in essence are transubstantiated into the body and blood of Christ.

accidie (Lat., *akedia,* fatigue) State of restlessness and inability to work or pray, a sin particularly affecting monks or hermits because of the outward monotony of their lives; lethargy or torpor often identified with the noonday devil referred to in Psalm 91. See also ACEDIA.

acclamation Short formulae spoken by the congregation in response to the clergy, as Kyrie eleison* and hallelujah,* sometimes with raising of arm, as in Charismatic worship.

accommodation (Ger., *Herablassung,* condescension) 1. God condescending to the level of human understanding in communicating the message of salvation and clothing eternal truths in transitory words, symbols, and forms. Incarnation is the supreme instance of accommodation. 2. Adaptation of the gospel to local situations by omission or suppression of certain Christian traditions or customs regarded as offensive to non-Christians. Matthew Ricci in China and Robert de Nobili* in South India are examples of accommodation.

acedia The deadly sin of sloth; spiritual torpor and apathy. See also ACCIDIE.

acephali (lit., without a head) Monophysites of Egypt who refused to accept the Chalcedonian patriarch* imposed on them by Byzantium*.

Achaia Province of Greece whose capital was Corinth* and whose Christian converts aided the poor in Jerusalem*.

acheiropoietos (Gk., not made by hands) Images, usually portraits of Christ, of miraculous or unexplained origin.

acmam Liturgical cuffs worn by Catholic Ethiopian clergy.

Acoemetae Order of monks founded in the fifth century by the Syrian monk Alexander. The order was divided into three groups who worked in continuous relays and performed divine service* without interruption day and night. They were also bound by vows to absolute poverty and banned from manual work. They were condemned by a synod* in Rome* in 534 for holding that Mary was not the mother of God.

acolouthia In the Byzantine Church*, the fixed arrangement of the Divine Office*.

acolyte (Gk., *aklouthos,* follower) Assistant or novice* in a religious group. In Roman Catholicism*, an assistant at a Mass* or a member of the highest of the four minor orders*.

Acosta, Jose de (1540–1600) Jesuit missionary to Peru. He arrived in Lima in 1572 and was named provincial superior* of his order in 1576. He served as adviser to the Third Lima Council and was instrumental in preparing the catechism* for use among priests in Indian parishes. Returning to Spain, he wrote two influential works, *De*

Procuranda Indorum Salute (*On How to Bring About the Salvation of the Indians,* 1588) and *Historia Natural y Moral de las Indias* (*A Natural and Moral History of the Indies,* 1590). The former was one of the most influential guides for missionaries in the New World.

Acre Harbor on the west coast of Palestine, also known as Ptolemais. It was a center of the Crusaders and the scene of many battles during the Crusades*, including the last decisive battle in 1291.

act of faith (Lat., *actus fidei*) Appropriation of the redemptive power of Jesus Christ and the actualization of his promises through the exercise of will and intellect.

Act of Supremacy Law enacted by the British Parliament in 1534 under Henry VIII, repealed by Mary Tudor and reenacted under Elizabeth I, making the English monarch the head of the Church of England* with the power to appoint bishops.

act of trust (Lat., *actus fiduciae*) Placing one's trust in Jesus Christ as Lord and Savior.

Act of Uniformity Law enacted by the British Parliament in 1549 making the new prayer book mandatory in all religious services and requiring conformity to its prescribed rites. Its distinctive features were the use of the vernacular, Communion in both kinds*, and transformation of the Mass* into Communion service*. A Second Act of Uniformity was passed in 1552, accompanying the revised *Book of Common Prayer** which reflected a Zwinglian interpretation of the Lord's Supper*. A Third Act of Uniformity was passed in 1559 at the accession of Elizabeth I, reflecting her desire for a *via media** regarding liturgical vestments and the Communion. A Fourth Act of Uniformity was passed in 1662 during the reign of Charles II, accompanied by another revision of the *Book of Common Prayer*. It resulted in the ejection of two thousand dissenting clergy from the Church of England*. Heavy penalties for nonconformity* and strict enforcement of the act failed to achieve religious uniformity, and in 1689 the Toleration Act exempted Protestant dissenters from its purview.

act of union (Lat., *actus unionis*) Union of the divine and human natures in the person of Jesus Christ.

Acta Apostolicae Sedis Official publication of the Vatican*, founded in 1908.

Acta Martyrum (Acts of the Martyrs) A record of the acts and lives of the early Christians who were killed for their faith. Very few of the early acts have survived. Among those that are official shorthand reports of the trials and executions is the *Acta Proconsularia* of St. Cyprian*. A second category, the *Passiones,* are stories of martyrdoms based on eyewitness accounts. To this type belongs the Martyrdoms of St. Ignatius, St. Polycarp*, the Martyrs of Lyons, the Passion of St. Perpetua* and St. Felicitas, and the Passion of St. Irenaeus*. The later accounts of these martyrdoms are embellished with miraculous and legendary materials. A third category of purely legendary accounts includes the martyrdoms of St. George* and St. Catherine of Alexandria*. Eusebius* of Caesarea compiled the first collection of Christian martyrs, but it survives only in fragments. Many Acts of the Martyrs were included in the liturgy of the early church.

Acta Sanctorum A collection of the lives of saints begun in the seventeenth century by the Jesuit order known as the Bollandists*. It is arranged according to the calendar.

action Ancient name for the Mass*.

action sermon In Scottish Presbyterianism*, a sermon before the Lord's Supper*.

active life Life devoted to works of mercy and charity. Sometimes divided into corporal works of mercy*, such as nursing; and spiritual works, such as preaching and evangelization. Distinguished from contemplative life*.

active order Religious order or congregation engaged in charity, preaching, or teaching. Distinguished from contemplative order.

Acts of John Apocryphal account, dating from the second or third century, of the life and death of the apostle John.

Acts of Pilate Apocryphal account, probably dating from the fourth century, of the trial, execution, and Resurrection of Jesus Christ.

Acts of St. Paul Apocryphal account, dating from the second century, of the life and work of the apostle Paul*.

Acts of St. Peter Apocryphal account, dating from the second century, of the miracles and martyrdom of the apostle Peter*. It includes the story of Quo Vadis and the crucifixion of Peter head downwards.

actual grace See GRACE, ACTUAL.

actual sin Rebellion against God and deliberate disregard of His will.

Acuna, Cristobal de (1597–c. 1676) Spanish Jesuit missionary and explorer of the Amazon.

A.D. See ANNO DOMINI.

ad fontes (Lat., to the sources) Returning to the original source of Christian faith, such as the Scriptures* and the early Church Fathers*. It was the slogan of the Protestant Reformers.

ad limina apostolorum (lit., to the thresholds of the apostles) 1. Pilgrimages* to the tombs of St. Peter and St. Paul in Rome* in the Middle Ages. 2. Obligation, imposed on all Roman Catholic bishops, to visit the tombs of the two apostles and report on the state of their dioceses* to the pope. This custom originated with a decree of the Roman Synod in 743. The 1983 Codex Iuris Canonici* requires a diocesan bishop to travel to Rome every five years for presenting himself to the pope.

ad majorem dei gloriam (Lat., to the greater glory of God) Motto of the Society of Jesus*.

ad sanctos Custom of burying Christians near the tombs of saints. Many churches of late antiquity and the Middle Ages were located on top of burial grounds or graves of martyrs.

Adalbert, St. (?–741) English saint who built a church in Egmont, Holland, and became Utrecht's* first archbishop.

Adalbert, St. (c. 950–997) "Apostle of the Prussians" who was bishop of Prague* and later missionary in Germany and Poland. He founded the Benedictine abbey of Brevnov. He met with opposition and was exiled twice, and undertook a mission to Pomerania and the Baltic coast. According to tradition, he was martyred at Königsburg.

Adaldagus (c. tenth century) Archbishop of Hamburg and Bremen who established three episcopal sees in Jutland and sent missionaries to Scandinavia.

Adam, Karl (1876–1966) Roman Catholic theologian. Ordained in 1919, he was professor at Tubingen* from 1919 to 1949. He was noted for his liberal and ecumenist views, which he expounded in a number of influential works, including *Das Wesen des Katholizisimus* (1924), *Christus unser Bruder* (1926), *Jesus Christus* (1933), *Una Sancta in Katholischer Sicht* (1948), and *De Christus des Glaubens* (1954).

Adam of St. Victor (c. 1110–1180) One of the greatest Christian poets of the Middle Ages. He was the Augustinian canon* of the Abbey of St. Victor in Paris. He is sometimes identified with the Adam who was the precentor of the cathedral of Notre Dame* and thus known as Adam Precentor. He is the author of some 60 sequences or hymn-like rhythms sung as part of the liturgy, of which the most famous are "Zima Vetus," "Ecce Dies Celebris," "Mundi Renovatio," "Lux Iocunda, Lux Insignis," "Heri Mundus," "Prunus Datum," and "Laudus Crucis."

Adamites 1. A sect of the second and third centuries in North Africa whose adherents sought to return to the purity of Adam before the fall by rejecting the use of clothing. They are sometimes identified with the Capocratians (mentioned by Clement of Alexandria*), who advocated sexual promiscuity and community of wives. 2. A thirteenth-century group in Europe whose communistic beliefs included a belief in cleansing from sin and the coming of a savior called Marokan.

Adamnan, St. (c. 624–704) Irish historian and saint who wrote the *Life of St. Columba* and *Concerning Holy Places*. He was elected abbot of Iona* in 679. Feast day: September 27.

Adamson, Patrick (1537–1592) Scottish Calvinist who was archbishop of St. Andrews, but was twice excommunicated by the Presbyterian Church. He translated Job, Lamentations of Jeremiah, and the Book of Revelation. He is considered one of the most learned writers in sixteenth-century Scotland.

Addai (first century) Traditional founder of the church at Edessa*, sometimes identified with Thaddaeus*. He was one of the 70 disciples sent to heal King Abgar*.

Addai and Mari, Liturgy of Syriac* liturgy used in the Church of the East* and by the Chaldeans, dating back to the third century. Its most notable features are the fact that it is addressed to Christ, not God the Father, and the absence of the institution narrative.

Addams, Jane (1860–1935) American social worker who founded Hull House and was a strong advocate of women's suffrage and world peace. She was awarded the Nobel Prize for Peace in 1931.

Address to the Roman Catholics of the United States First Roman Catholic publication in the United States by Bishop John Carroll* in 1784.

Adelphos Theos (Gk.) Title of St. James the Less*, brother of our Lord.

Adeste Fideles Famous Latin hymn, translated into English as "O Come All Ye Faithful." The hymn first appeared in *Cantus Diversi*, written by John F. Wade in 1743, although the Latin text was attributed to various medieval figures, including St. Bonaventura*. Frederick Oakeley rendered the famous and beloved English translation in 1841.

Adhemar de Monteil (?–1098) Bishop of Le Puy and crusader who led the First Crusade*. He was closely associated with Raymond of Toulouse. He died soon after the capture of Antioch*.

adherent (Lat., *adhaerere*, to cling to) Believer who attends church services regularly but is not a formal member.

adiaphora (Gk., things indifferent) Things or actions that in themselves are neither immoral nor moral, or neither commanded nor forbidden by Scripture, and thus may be permitted for Christians.

Adiaphorists Sixteenth-century group that favored a plan, known as the Leipzig Interim* (1548), to reunite Catholics and Lutherans by permitting such things as votive candles, confirmation* and extreme unction*, the Mass* without transubstantiation*, and the veneration* of saints, in the interests of peace. The controversy continued until after the Peace of Augsburg* (1555) and was brought to an end only by article 10 of the Formula of Concord* in 1577 which declared that no such concessions were to be made to the Catholics.

adjuration (Lat., *adjurare*, to bind earnestly) Solemn or earnest plea in the name of God or a holy thing or person.

Ado (c. 800–874) Archbishop of Vienne in France who compiled a martyrology* between 853 and 860 based on an ancient Roman work, *Martyrologium Romanum Parvum*. Ado's work was the basis of most later martyrologies.

adoption The process of making a person a son or daughter and a heir. It is one of the first works of grace by which a believer becomes a child of God, is given his name as a Christian, grafted on to the divine stock, and promised his inheritance (Rom. 8:15–17; Gal. 4:6–7).

Adoptionism 1. Heresy of the second and third centuries that Jesus was purely human until divinity was conferred on him through baptism*. 2. Eighth-century Spanish heresy that Christ is the Son of God only through adoption. Its chief spokesmen were Elipandus, archbishop of Toledo*, and Felix*, bishop of Urgel. A synod* at Rome* in 798 anathematized Felix and he recanted. The heresy was revived in the twelfth century by Abelard*, Gilbert de la Porree*, and others and later by Duns Scotus*. The historian Adolf Harnack* is among those who tried to revive the term in the nineteenth century.

Adoration of the Cross Part of Good Friday* services in which the priest uncovers the cross which is then adored by the congregation by kneeling before it, kissing it, and singing hymns to it.

Adoro Te Devote (lit., Thee I Adore) Medieval eucharistic hymn, sometimes attributed to Thomas Aquinas*.

Adrian, St. (?–303) Praetorian guard who became a Christian martyr* and was executed and dismembered. He is considered the patron saint* of soldiers. Feast day: September 8.

Advent (Lat., *adventus,* coming) 1. The coming of Jesus Christ. 2. In the Western Church*, the season prior to Christmas* honoring the birth of Christ, the traditional beginning of the ecclesiastical year. Advent begins with the Sunday nearest to St. Andrews Day on November 30. Four Sundays in Advent thus always precede Christmas. In the Eastern Church*, Advent is a much longer season, beginning the middle of November. Originally, the sixth-century *Gelasian Sacramentary** called for five Sundays in Advent. Formerly, believers fasted during Lent*, but the season is still observed as a solemn time for preparation for the mystery of the Incarnation*. The season's liturgical color* is purple, except on Gaudete Sunday* (or third Sunday), when it is rose.

Advent wreath Circle of evergreen set with four candles, one of which is lighted every week of the season, beginning Advent Sunday.

Adventism Belief in the imminent and literal return of Jesus Christ to the earth. It is related to millenarianism* and apocalypticism, and was widely held by the early Church Fathers* including Polycarp*, Ignatius, Papias*, Hermas*, and Justin Martyr*. It was a key tenet of Montanism* which predicted between 150 and 175 that a new age would begin with the descent of a heavenly Jerusalem near Papuza in Phrygia. The belief was dormant in the Middle Ages but was revived in the thirteenth century by Joachim of Fiore*, in

the fourteenth century by the Hussites*, and in the nineteenth century by William Miller* and the Seventh Day Adventists*.

Adventists Christian denominations which believe that the Second Coming* of Christ is imminent. The primary group that holds this doctrine was founded by William Miller* (1782–1849), who made the prediction that Christ would return in 1843–1844. When this prediction did not come to pass, Miller suggested other dates which also proved illusory. See also SEVENTH DAY ADVENTISTS.

advocatus dei (Lat., advocate of God) The defender in a canonization* procedure who supports the evidence brought forth on behalf of a candidate for sainthood*.

advocatus diaboli (Lat., devil's advocate) The prosecutor in a canonization* procedure who tries to critically examine the evidence brought forth on behalf of a candidate for sainthood*. Also known as *promotor fidei*, or promoter of the faith, he is the foremost theologian of the Congregation for the Causes of Saints*. The first formal mention of the office was in connection with the canonization* of St. Lawrence Justinian.

advocatus ecclesiae (Lat., advocate of the church) Caretaker of a church or abbey in medieval times.

advowson In the Anglican Church, the right of appointment to a vacant parish* or other ecclesiastical office. Advowsons are of two kinds: collative when they are held by the bishop of the diocese*, and presentative when they are held by a corporate or individual patron who may present a nominee for induction into the office. In English law, advowson is a property right which can be passed on by gift, inheritance, or sale.

aedicule (Lat., small shrine) Niche* or opening framed by columns on either side, with an entablature and pediment above. Early Christian aedicules held funerary urns or statues.

aeiparthenos Title of the Virgin Mary*, meaning "ever virgin," adopted by the Second Council of Constantinople* (553). The term first appears in

Epiphanius* and was endorsed by the Council of Constantinople.

Aelfric (c. 955–1021) Abbot of Eynsham in England, known as "the Grammarian." In 987 he issued two sets of homilies, dealing with the events of the liturgical year*. These homilies are said to have denied the immaculate conception* as well as the doctrine of transubstantiation*. His writings include an abridgment of the *Regularis Concordia,* a Latin life of Ethelwold, and an English translation of Bede's* *De Temporibus.*

aer (Gk., cloud) In the Byzantine Church*, large veil used in the Eastern Church* to cover the chalice* and paten* during the Eucharist*. It is folded according to a set pattern and placed on the altar. When the creed is being sung, the priest takes the aer gently and fans the oblation* symbolizing the Holy Spirit*.

Aetius (d. 365) Extreme Arian bishop who maintained that God, being above all causality, is above generation, and that the Son is a generated being who does not share in the substance or the divinity of the Father.

aetos In the Byzantine Church*, the mat on which the bishop stands while celebrating the liturgy.

affection 1. Usually affections. Emotions. 2. Emotional attachment whether toward temporal things or "on things above" (Col. 3:2).

affective prayer Form of prayer in which the emphasis is on adoration of God rather than on formal petitions or spiritual discourse.

affirmation Simple attestation of the truth of a matter in place of a formal oath*.

afflatus Supernatural or divine inspiration or revelation.

affusion Method of baptism*, now practiced in most mainline churches*, in which water is poured over a candidate's head. It supplanted in the later Middle Ages the earlier method of immersion* and submersion*.

Africa Inland Mission (AIM) Largest mission in East Africa, founded in Philadelphia* in 1895 by Peter Cameron Scott*. It was at first sponsored by the Philadelphia Missionary Council. Under Charles Hurlbert, AIM's first general director, it made considerable progress assisted by Lee Downing, Albert Barnett, and John Stauffacher. It is now headquartered in Bristol, England, and has missionaries in 15 countries.

African Methodist Episcopal Church (AMEC) The largest African-American Methodist denomination founded by Richard Allen* in Philadelphia* after leaving the white St. George's Methodist Episcopal Church. Allen held services in a rented blacksmith shop, later renamed Bethel. Bishop Francis Asbury* dedicated the Bethel Church in 1793. In 1801 Daniel Coker established another Bethel Church in Baltimore. In 1816 representatives from the many Bethel churches met in Philadelphia to found the African Methodist Episcopal Church, with Allen as its first bishop. After Reconstruction the church grew. Foreign missions were established in the Caribbean, South America, and Africa. Today it has a membership of over 2.5 million in 13 districts.

African Methodist Episcopal Zion Church (AMEZC) Second-largest African-American Methodist denomination, founded in 1796 by Peter Williams, James Varick, George Collins, and Christopher Rush. The first church called Zion was built in 1800. In 1821, 19 preachers representing six African-American congregations in New York, New Haven, Newark, and Philadelphia*, organized AMEZC, with Varick as the first bishop. After the Civil War, AMEZC spread rapidly throughout the South. Home missions were established in Louisiana, Mississippi, and Oklahoma and foreign missions in Caribbean, Africa, and South America. AMEZC sponsors three colleges, including Hood Theological Seminary and Livingstone College. Today, AMEZC has over 1.3 million members and over 6,000 churches.

Afscheiding Separation of conservative Calvinists from the Dutch Reformed Church* in 1834.

afterglow Youth gathering after an evening worship service as a time of fellowship.

agape (Gk., love) 1. Selfless or spiritual love as revealed in Christ, especially as distinguished from *eros,* or carnal love. 2. Love feast or fellowship meal among the early Christians in close relation to the Eucharist*. Love feasts* are mentioned by St. Ignatius in his letter to the Smyrnaeans, St. Hippolytus* in his *Apostolic Tradition*, and Tertullian* in his *Apology.* 3. By the fourth century, a charity supper no longer connected with the Lord's Supper*.

Agapemonites Members of the Abode of Love* community who described themselves as Children of the Resurrection.

Agapetae 1. Nuns and monks of the early church who lived together ascetically. Also known as *virgines subintroductae*, a controversial practice opposed by Chrysostom*. 2. A fourth-century Gnostic group.

Agapetus, St. (d. 536) Pope from 535. A strong defender of orthodoxy*. In 536 he visited Constantinople* and deposed Anthimus, the Monophysite patriarch* of Constantinople. Feast day: September 20.

agapic Having or expressing the qualities of agape* love.

Agatha, St. Sicilian virgin who was martyred in 251 in Catania in Sicily after being imprisoned, tortured, and set on fire. She is the patron saint* of bell founders and wet-nurses. Feast day: February 5.

Agathangelos (fourth century) Armenian historian, reputed author of the *History of the Armenians,* which gives the first account of the life of St. Gregory the Illuminator* and the conversion of Armenia.

Agatho (c. 577–681) Pope from 678. He held a council at Rome* against the Monothelites and furthered the spread of the Roman Liturgy in England.

agathology Branch of theology dealing with goodness.

agbiah In the Coptic Church*, a Breviary* in Arabic containing the Divine Office*.

Agde, Council of Council held in 506 at Agde in France under the presidency of St. Caesarius of Arles*. Its 47 canons deal with clerical celibacy, the age for ordination, relation of a bishop with his diocesan synod*, church property, and the religious obligations of believers.

age In Scripture, a long indeterminate period of time associated with a person, event, or movement.

age, canonical Age at which a person becomes eligible to receive special privileges, undertake specific functions, or enter into certain official duties. Generally used in connection with ordination.

Age of Faith Period of the Middle Ages up to 1500 during which the church dominated European society, life, and learning.

Age of the Martyrs Period of church history before Constantine* (313) when Christians were persecuted in the Roman Empire.

agenda Liturgical uses and the books prescribing them. In the seventeenth century, English theologians distinguished between agenda, matters of religious practice, and credenda*, essentials of belief. The Council of Carthage* in 390 applied the term to the entire eucharistic service, but others limited it to the anaphora*.

aggiornamento (Ital., renewal) Fresh presentation or modernization of the faith associated with the Second Vatican Council*, whose purpose was to "bring the church up to date."

aggoi In the Byzantine Church*, small cups holding wheat, wine, and oil blessed on some major feasts.

Aghtamar Island in Lake, in modern-day Turkey, originally the see* of an Armenian catholicos*. It is the site of the abandoned Church of the Holy Cross.

agia trapeza In the Byzantine Church*, the holy table* or altar.

agiasmatarion (Gk., book of blessings) The small euchologion*.

agiasmos In the Coptic Church*, the three anaphoras*.

agios athanatos (Gk., holy immortal) In the Byzantine Church*, the third part of the Trisagion*.

agios ischyros (Gk., holy strong) In the Byzantine Church*, the second part of the Trisagion*.

agios o theos (Gk., holy God) Anthem sung in the Eastern Church*, so named from its opening words.

Aglipay, Gregorio (1860–1940) Former Catholic priest who, along with Isabilo de los Reyes, founded the Philippine Independent Church, known as the Aglipayans, in 1902 after seceding from the Roman Catholic Church. The church retained many Catholic traditions and practices with the exception of celibacy and confession*. Aglipay was an unsuccessful candidate for the presidency of the Commonwealth of the Philippines in 1935.

Agnellus of Pisa (c. 1194–1236) Founder of the English Franciscan Province. He was sent by St. Francis to Paris to erect a convent and later to England in 1224. He arrived at Dover, England, with eight other friars*, four of them English, and established friaries at Canterbury*, Oxford, and London. He died at Oxford, where his remains were venerated until the Reformation*.

Agnes of Montepulciano, St. (1268–1317) Founder of the Santa Maria Novella Convent, a Dominican abbey in Montepulciano, Italy. Feast day: April 20.

Agnes, St. (c. 291–304) Roman virgin beheaded for her chastity*. A basilica* was built about 350 on the Via Nomentana on the site of her remains. Her symbol is the lamb*. Feast day: January 21.

agnetiz In the Byzantine Church*, the square portion of the bread called the lamb* which is re-

moved from the first loaf as part of the prothesis*, or rite of preparation. The priest uses a lance* (kopyo) for this purpose.

Agnoetae 1. Fourth-century sect which held that God's omniscience was limited. 2. Sixth-century Monophysite sect founded by Themistius, a deacon from Alexandria, which held that Christ was not omniscient, on the basis of such Scriptures as Mark 13:32.

Agnus Dei (Lat., Lamb of God*) 1. Canticle* beginning with the words, "O Lamb of God," said or sung in the Latin Liturgy shortly before Communion.* Drawn from Scripture, the phrase was first used in Mass* under Pope Symmachus*. In the

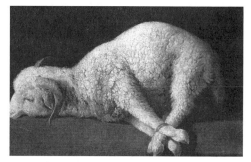

Agnus Dei

Middle Ages, the Agnus, like the kyrie*, was extensively interpolated. 2. Symbolic representation of Christ as a lamb*.

Agonistici (Gk., *agon,* martyr's contest) Also, Milites Christi. Roving bands of Donatist terrorists in North Africa in the fourth century, more commonly known as Circumcellions*.

agonizant (Lat., *agonizo,* to be at the point of death) Roman Catholic fraternity ministering to the sick and dying. Founded by St. Camillus de Lellis* in 1586. Also known as Camillians.

agony Image of Christ in Gethsemane* as he faced the prospect of death and prayed that the cup might pass from him.

agrapha (lit., unwritten sayings) Sayings attributed to Jesus not recorded in the four canonical

Gospels or other sources but found in the apocryphal gospels.

Agreda, Maria (1602–1665) Spanish abbess noted for her visions. She was the author of *The Mystic City of God*.

Agricola, Johann (c. 1494–1566) German Protestant reformer and early associate of Martin Luther*. He studied theology at Wittenberg* under Luther, whom he accompanied later to the Disputation of Leipzig*. He taught theology at Wittenberg and Eisleben. His antinomian views brought him into conflict with Luther and Melanchthon*, but he later recanted. In 1540 he moved to Berlin as general superintendent and preacher at the court of John II, elector of Brandenburg. He was associated with the preparation of the Augsburg Interim* of 1548 and supported the traditional Lutherans against the Adiaphorists*.

Agricola, Mikael (c. 1510–1557) Finnish reformer, called the father of Finnish literature. He studied at Wittenberg*, where he met Luther*. He became principal of the theological school at Abo and later bishop of Abo. He translated the Scripture into Finnish.

agrypnia In the Byzantine Church*, the night vigil* which follows the ceremony of artoklasia*.

ahl al dhimma In Islamic countries, People of Protection whose religious freedom was theoretically guaranteed on payment of a poll tax. However, in practice, Christians were brutally persecuted and forced to convert.

ahl almantal-kah (Arab., people of the girdle) Copts and Jacobites in Egypt and Syria from the girdle* they were forced to wear by the Muslims as a sign of humiliation.

Aidan, St. (?–651) Irish monk and bishop of Lindisfarne*. He was sent about 635 from the Iona* monastery to evangelize England at the request of St. Oswald*, king of Northumbria. The Christian practices that he taught were those of the Celtic Church*. Feast day: August 31.

Ailred, St. (1109–1167) Also, Aelred; Bernard of the

North. He entered the Cistercian house of Rievaulx in about 1133 and became its abbot in 1147. In 1142–1143, at the invitation of Bernard of Clairvaux* he wrote *Speculum Caritatis*, his most important work. He also wrote a life of Edward the Confessor*. Over 100 homilies attributed to him are extant. Feast day: January 12.

AIM Africa Inland Mission.

Ain Karim Village about five miles west of Jerusalem*, the birthplace of John the Baptist.

ained In the Ethiopian Church*, the paten*.

ainoi (Gk., praise) In the Byzantine Church*, service equivalent to the Western lauds*, part of the morning service or the orthros*. Psalms 148–150 form the main body of the service.

Ainsworth Psalter Psalter with 39 tunes published in Amsterdam in 1612 by Henry Ainsworth (d. 612) under the title *The Book of Psalmes: Englished both in Prose and Metre*. Brought to the New World by the Pilgrims, it was the principal psalter in America before the publication of the *Bay Psalm Book**.

aisle (Fr., *aile*, wing). 1. Passage between pews in a church. 2. Extension of the nave* of a church, or less commonly, of a transept* or chancel*.

aitesis In the Byzantine Church* Liturgy, a series of invocations* interspersed with congregational responses.

akathistos (Gk., not sitting) Hymn during which the congregation stands, written probably by Romanos* the Melodist in honor of the Theotokos* or the Virgin Mary*.* It consists of 12 long and 12 short *oikoi* (houses). The long ones begin with *chaire* or hail and end with the refrain, "Hail Bride without Bridegroom." The short oikoi is followed by hallelujah*. The akathist form part of the mattins* on the fifth Saturday of Lent*. In Athonite monasteries, the whole akathist is recited nightly at apodeipnon*.

akaz In the Coptic Church*, the crozier carried by the patriarch* and bishops. It is about a man's height, with its upper end terminating in a cross with two short symmetrical branches in the shape of a serpent's neck.

Akhmim Fragment Greek fragment containing portions of apocryphal writings, including the Apocalypse of St. Peter* and the Gospel of St. Peter*, discovered at Akhmim in Egypt in 1886.

akmam In the Ethiopian Church*, a pair of richly ornamented cuffs fastening the sleeves of the priestly sticharion*.

akoimetona In the Byzantine Church*, the light that burns before the reserved sacrament*.

akoimetos lychnia (lit., watchful light) In the Byzantine Church*, the perpetually lit lamp that faces the royal doors* of the iconostasis*.

akolouthia (Gk.) Order of service or the service itself. Complete akolouthia exist for all canonized and some noncanonized saints. It includes text for the hesperinos*, orthros* and the divine liturgy, and an akathistos* or paraklesis* of the saint.

Aksum Also, Axum*. Ancient religious capital of the Abyssinians and the home of the Queen of Sheba and her son, Menelek. Aksum was a powerful kingdom in northern Ethiopia, and it reached the zenith of its power from the third to the sixth centuries. The kingdom extended into South Arabia after the Aksumite emperor Kaleb crossed the Red Sea and rescued the Christians of Nagran in Yemen from the rule of Dhu Nuwas, the Judaic king of Hymiar, in 525.

akuatea qurban (Ge'ez, thanksgiving sacrifice) In the Ethiopian Church*, the Eucharist*, especially the section of the liturgy between the Preface* and the Epiclesis*.

alabanza (Span., I will praise) Seventeenth-century hymnody* on the theme of Christ's passion* popularized by Franciscan missionaries.

Alabare (Span., I will praise) A theme song of Latin American Charismatics.

alabastron In the Byzantine Church*, glass or metal vessel holding the holy chrism*.

aladura (Yoruba, prayer people) Prophetic and healing church in Nigeria, founded about 1930.

Alain de Lille (c. 1128–1202) French scholastic*, theologian, poet, philosopher, and preacher. He taught at Paris for about 35 years from 1150 but later moved to the south of France, where he joined in the struggle against the Catharists. He is considered one of the so called "Porretani" or disciples of Gilbert de la Porree*. Among his important works are *De Planctu Naturae,* a mixture of prose and verse; *Summa Quoniam Homines* and *Regulae Caelestis Iuris,* both theological works; *Anticlaudianus,* an allegorical poem; *Distinctiones,* a dictionary of biblical terms; and *Liber Poenitentialis,* the earliest of the medieval manuals for confessors. Toward the end of his life he entered the abbey at Citeaux*.

alapa Light blow formerly delivered by a bishop on the cheek of a person being confirmed.

alaqa Head or chief of an Ethiopian Orthodox* parish church.

Al-'Assal Coptic family of learned and prolific scholars during the Ayyubid Dynasty in early thirteenth-century Cairo. The family includes **Abu'l-Fadl ibn Abi Ishaq Ibrahim ibn Abi Sahl Girgis ibn Abi al-Yusr Yuhanna ibn al-'Assal;** his two sons, **al-Safi Abu'l-Fada-'il ibn al-'Assal** and **As'ad Abu'l Farag Hibat-Allah ibn al-'Assal;** and their two step brothers, **al-Mu'taman Abu Ishaq Ibrahim ibn al-'Assal** and **Amgad Abu'l-Magd ibn al-'Assal.** The four made significant contributions to theology and biblical studies, prepared Coptic-Arabic grammars and dictionaries, and wrote many homiletic works.

alb Long white linen liturgical vestment reaching from the neck to the ankles, with tight-fitting sleeves held at the waist by a girdle* worn by priests celebrating the Mass*. It is sometimes embroidered near the hem. The alb symbolizes innocence or purity.

Alban and St. Sergius, Fellowship of St. Organization founded in England in 1928 for promoting better understanding between the Anglican Church and the Eastern Orthodox Church*.

Alban, St. (third or fourth century) First British martyr*, killed in 303. The place where he was martyred, Verulamium, was renamed in his honor as St. Albans*. Later a church and a monastery were built there. Feast day: June 17.

St. Alban

Albanel, Charles (1616–1696) Jesuit missionary who came from France to Canada in 1649 and explored the New World.

Albanenses Thirteenth-century Cathari* group in Italy, especially in Lombardy and in the vicinity of Verona*, so called from the town of Albi*, a Cathari stronghold.

Albanian Orthodox Church The Albanian branch of the Eastern Orthodox Church*. Long persecuted by the brutal Turks, it became autocephalous* in 1922. It underwent another period of persecution under the Communists from the end of World War II to 1991. In 1992 the first exarch* and archbishop of Tirana was appointed by the ecumenical patriarch*.

Albans, St. British town noted for its Romanesque cathedral built on the spot where St. Alban*, the first English martyr*, was martyred in 303. It was part of the Benedictine abbey founded around 793 by Offa, king of Mercia. Soon after the Norman Conquest in 1066, a large church was built here, and it quickly became a center of pilgrimage*. Built largely of stone from Roman ruins, the cathedral was completed by the twelfth century, but the choir was extended in the thirteenth century. The cathedral is 550 feet long, the

transept* is 216 feet long, and the tower is 140 feet high.

Alberic, St. (d. 1109) Abbot. Cofounder, with Stephen Harding* and Robert of Molesme,* of the Monastery of Citeaux*, from which the Cistercian Order developed. When Robert returned to Molesme, Alberic took his place. Feast day: January 26.

Alberti, Leon Battista (1404–1472) Florentine architect, sometimes described as the purest Renaissance man—writer, painter, musician, sculptor, athlete, Latinist, philosopher, and mathematician. Together with Brunelleschi*, he laid the foundations of church design for the Renaissance. Among his buildings are San Sebastiano, the first modern use of the Greek cross* plan; Sant Andrea, the first long-nave church to have side chapels opening off the nave* instead of the aisles; and San Francesco in Rimini.

Albertus Magnus, St. (d. 1280) Dominican theologian. He entered the Dominican Order in 1229. He taught at various stages of his life in Paris (where Thomas Aquinas* was his student), Cologne*, and Strasbourg*, and also served as a papal emissary and arbitrator in ecclesiastical disputes. Of his many theological works, the most influential were *De Natura Boni* and *Summa de Creaturis* (1249). He was the foremost authority on Aristotle in his day. Beside his influence on Aquinas*, his neo-Platonism was popular among his German Dominican followers, such as Ulrich of Strasbourg*, Dietrich of Freiburg, and Berthold of Moosburg who constituted the Albert School. He was beatified in 1622 and canonized and declared a doctor of the church* in 1931. In 1941 he was proclaimed patron of natural scientists. Feast day: November 15.

Albi Fortified church built in Albi, the town in Languedoc, the scene of the Albigensian Crusades*. It is built in the tradition of the hall church. The foundation stone was laid in 1282, but the work was not completed until 1480.

Albigenses/Albigensians Medieval heretics, a branch of the Cathari*, concentrated in the south of France during the twelfth and thirteenth centuries. They were condemned by successive councils at Lombers in 1165 and at Verona* in 1184. So called from the city of Albi*, one of their centers.

Albigensian Crusade Crusade authorized by Pope Innocent III* after the assassination in 1208 of the papal legate* Peter of Castelnau by the Albigensians*. The expedition led by Simon de Montfort was long and bloody, even by the standards of medieval warfare. In 1245 in Montsegur, 200 were

The Albigneses

burned in one day. By 1300 only a few heretics survived in remote outposts.

Albright Brethren See EVANGELICAL ASSOCIATION.

Albright, Jacob (1759–1808) Founder of the Evangelical Association*. Born in Pennsylvania, he became a successful businessman when he experienced conversion and entered the ministry.

Albright, William (1944–) American pianist, organist, and composer of religious music. He has maintained a balance between the new and the traditional and between the tonal and the atonal. Among his vocal works are *Alleluia Super-Round* (1973) for eight or more voices; *Mass in D* (1974) for chorus, congregation, organ, and percussion; *Chichester Mass* (1974) for chorus; Psalm settings entitled *David's Songs* (1982) for soloists and chorus; and an oratorio*, *A Song to David* (1983), for soloists, two choruses, and an organ.

Alcantara, Order of Military and religious order founded in the twelfth century by St. Julian de Pereiro to combat the Moors in Spain and to defend Alcantara.

Alcobaca Cistercian abbey at Alcobaca in the province of Estremadura in Portugal, founded by the first Portuguese king, Alfonso Henriquez, after his victory over the Moors in 1147. The building, dedicated to the Virgin Mary*, was begun in 1178 and completed by 1222. The Gothic* building on a square ground plan comprises the massive church and five cloisters*. The monastery was inhabited by 999 monks, and its abbot was a counselor to the king. Its library was a precursor of the University of Coimbra.

Alcuin (c. 740–804) Scholar and abbot and a major figure in the English Carolingian age. He spent most of his life in France, where he was the abbot of St. Martin's at Tours*. Besides his theological works, he wrote the lives of many saints, manuals of grammar and rhetoric, orthography, mathematics, and poems. He supervised the production of several editions of the Bible, revised the Roman

Alcuin

lectionary*, and adapted the Gregorian Sacramentary* for use in Gaul. Feast day: May 20.

Alcuin Club English group, founded in 1897, which promotes the study and use of the *Book of Common Prayer**.

Aldersgate Street in London where in a religious meeting in 1738 the heart of John Wesley* was "strangely warmed." It is considered the birthplace of the Methodist Church.

Aldhelm, St. (c. 640–709) English churchman, scholar, and musician. In 705 he became the bishop of Sherborne. He took a prominent part in the reforms initiated by Archbishop Theodore* and the monk Hadrian, and founded churches and monasteries. He gained a reputation as a notable singer and poet and is regarded as the father of Anglo-Latin poetry.

Aldrich, Bess Streeter (1881–1954) American religious novelist, author of *A Lantern in Her Hand* and *Journey into Christmas.*

Aleandro, Girolamo (1480–1542) Italian churchman who opposed Luther* at the Diet of Worms*. He was one of two papal envoys appointed by Pope Leo X* to present Luther with the bull*, *Exsurge Domine*, and to request the emperor to condemn him.

aleiptron In the Byzantine Church*, small brush or cotton wand used to anoint the faithful with oil burning in a lamp before a holy icon*.

Alenio, Giulio (1582–1649) Italian Jesuit missionary to China. He wrote a life of Christ in Chinese.

Alesius, Alexander (1500–1565) Scottish Protestant theologian and reformer. In 1532 he visited Germany, where he became a friend of Luther and Melanchthon*, and signed the Augsburg Confession*. In 1535 he returned to England, where he was warmly received by Thomas Cranmer*. At various times he lectured at Cambridge*, England, and at Frankfurt-on-Oder. He is the author of many exegetical and controversial writings.

alethiology Branch of theology dealing with the doctrine of truth.

Alexander II (d. 1073) Pope from 1061. Birth name: Anselm of Lucca. As pope he headed the reforming party and renewed decrees against simony* and enforced clerical celibacy. He insisted on personal attendance at Rome* before conferring the pallium*. He blessed the successful invasion of England by William the Conqueror in 1066.

Alexander III (d. 1181) Pope from 1159. Original name: Orlando Bandinelli. As pope, he imposed penance* on Henry II of England for the murder of Thomas a Becket*. In 1179 he presided over the Third Lateran Council*, which decided on papal election by the cardinals.

Alexander V (c. 1339–1410) Pope from 1409. Original name: Peter of Candia. A Cretan by birth, he became a Franciscan and later studied at Oxford and Paris. He is the author of *A Commentary on the Sentences.*

Alexander VI (1451–1503) Pope from 1492. Original name: Rodrigo Borgia. A Spaniard by birth, his own election as pope was secured through bribery. As pope, he divided the New World between Spain and Portugal by the Treaty of Tordesillas in 1494, prosecuted and executed Savonarola*, organized the jubilee* in 1500, and decreed a crusade against the Moors in 1499–1500. He rebuilt the Leonine City* and the Castle of Sant' Angelo.

Alexander VII (1599–1667) Pope from 1655. Original name: Fabio Chigi. A native of Siena by birth. As pope, he condemned Jansenism*, signed the humiliating Peace of Pisa with the French king Louis XIV in 1664, and secured the readmission of the Jesuits* into Venice*.

Alexander VIII (1610–1691) Pope from 1689. Original name: Pietro Ottoboni. A Venetian by birth. As pope, he condemned Gallicanism* although he maintained good relations with Louis XIV, helped Venice* against Turkey, and enlarged the Vatican Library* by acquiring valuable manuscripts from Queen Christina of Sweden.

Alexander, Archibald (1772–1851) Presbyterian theologian and educator. In 1794 he assumed the presidency of Hampden-Sydney College and held that position for over a decade. In 1812 the General Assembly* of the Presbyterian Church (whose moderator* he had been) established a theological seminary at Princeton and named him as its first professor. He taught over 1,800 candidates for the ministry during the next 40 years.

Alexander Nevski, St. (1219–1263) Russian prince of Novograd, Vladimir*, and Kiev*, called Nevski following his victory over the Swedes at the River Neva. Shortly before his death he became a monk at the monastery of Vladimir-Kljazma, where he was buried. He was canonized in 1381. Feast day: November 23.

Alexander of Alexandria (d. 328) Bishop of Alexandria from 312. He led the opposition to his deacon, Arius*, whom he excommunicated in 319. He found a faithful and intelligent ally in a young deacon, Athanasius*, who succeeded him.

Alexander of Hales (c. 1186–1245) English theologian and scholar who won his reputation in France as the "Unanswerable Doctor." In 1236 he joined the Franciscan Order* while remaining professor at the University of Paris. He is regarded as the founder of the Franciscan School of Theology, and his unfinished *Summa Theologica* had great influence on Thomas Aquinas*. He also contributed to the "Expositio in Regulam St. Francisci" (1242), popularly known as "The Four Masters."

Alexandre, Noel (1639–1724) French church historian. He was one of the leading theologians of his day and the author of a number of works, including *Theologia Dogmatica et Moralis* (ten vols., 1694) and *Selecta Historiae Ecclesiasticae Capita* (26 vols., 1676–86). The latter work was placed on the *Index* of banned books, but a revised version was published with ecclesiastical imprimatur* in 1734 and 1749.

Archibald Alexander

Alexandria Egyptian city founded by Alexander the Great on the Mediterranean coast, the second most important city in the Roman Empire as well as in Egypt under Muslim rule. According to tradition, the Egyptian Church was founded here by Mark the Evangelist. Between the first and sixth centuries, Alexandria became a major Christian center, and counted among its native sons Clement*, Origen*, Athanasius*, and Cyril*. The Council of Nicaea* assigned Alexandria a place of honor as the seat of a patriarchate second only to Rome* and superior to Antioch*, but its importance diminished through the rise of Constantinople*. Alexandria lost much of its Christian character after the Islamic conquest of Egypt in the seventh century.

Alexandrian Rite Liturgical and canonical system of the Patriarchate of Alexandria.

Alexandrian School School of philosophy founded in Alexandria* by Pantaenus* combining Greek, Jewish, and Oriental thought, and emphasizing the allegorical interpretation of the Scriptures. The leaders of the Alexandrian School were Clement*, Origen*, and Cyril*. The great task of the school was to reconcile Christian faith with pagan learning.

Alexandrian Text Early form of the Greek text of the New Testament, also known as the Egyptian, represented by the Codex Vaticanus*, the Bodmer Papyri*, and the Chester Beatty Papyri*.

Alexandrian theology Christological and exegetical approaches developed by Church Fathers* in Alexandria*, such as Athanasius*, Apollinaris*, and Cyril*. Its principal focus was on the unity of the person of Christ and the hypostatic union* in which the godhood and manhood of Christ were regarded as indistinguishable. See also ANTIOCHENE THEOLOGY.

Alfonsi, Petrus (1062–1110) Jewish convert to Christianity, author of a book against the Jews.

Alford, Henry (1810–1871) English scholar and churchman. In 1857 he became the dean of Canterbury*, a position he held until his death. He is noted as the editor of the Greek New Testament and a number of biblical commentaries, and he also wrote a number of well-known hymns, such as "Ten Thousand Times Ten Thousand."

Algardi, Alessandro (c. 1598–1654) Italian sculptor who made a statue in bronze of Pope Innocent X* and designed a monument for Leo XI. He also carved the marble *St. Philip Neri* with an angel in Sta Maria in Vallicella. Among his other works were *Magdalene* and *St. John the Evangelist* in San Silvestro al Quirinale. His mastery of bronze is shown in his *Urn for the Magdalene* and *Ecstasy of the Magdalene,* both in St. Maximin, southern France, as well as *Pope Innocent X*. His first major works in marble were the *Beheading of Paul* and *Pope St. Leo the Great Repelling Attila from the Gates of Rome.*

alien priory Priory* which was dependent upon a monastery in a foreign country.

Alipy, St. (d. c. 1114) Father of Russian iconography*. Monk and priest, he created the genre of Russian icons, studying under Greek masters.

aliturgical days Days of fasting* and penance* on which the Eucharist* may not be celebrated, including Good Friday* and Holy Saturday*.

All Hallows Day See ALL SAINTS' DAY.

All Saints' Day Feast day held on November 1 in commemoration of the saints. Its universal observance was ordered by Pope Gregory IV.

All Souls' Day Feast held on November 2 or November 3 when prayers are offered for the faithful suffering in purgatory*. Its observance became universal through the influence of Odilo of Cluny*, who in 998 ordered its annual celebration in all Benedictine* houses.

Allaci, Leone (1586–1669) Greek theologian and writer and Vatican librarian.

Allamano, Joseph (1851–1926) Founder and first superior general* of the Consolata* Missionary Fathers (1901) and Consolata Missionary Sisters (1910). The Consolata Fathers and Sisters were active in Kenya. He was responsible for persuading

the pope to establish a day of prayer and support for all Catholic missions.

Allan, George and Mary (1871–1941 and 1871–1939, respectively) Founders of the Bolivian Indian Mission (BIM). Born in New Zealand, they set out in 1899 for Argentina. But they felt a growing burden for the Quechua Indians of Bolivia and relocated to Cochabamba, Bolivia, in 1903. In 1909 they moved to San Pedro, 350 miles north of Cochabamba. George translated the New Testament and the Psalms into Quechua. By 1990 BIM had over 600 churches in Bolivia. In 1992 BIM merged with SIM*.

allegory Symbolic and nonliteral representation of truth. The Jews of the Diaspora, influenced by hellenistic culture, adopted the allegorical canon of exegesis* in the interpretation of the Scripture. In biblical usage, there is a distinction between allegory as a medium of revelation and as a method of interpretation. Allegory was the method of choice in the Alexandrian School* represented in the West by Jerome*, Hilary*, Ambrose*, and Augustine*. Bernard of Clairvaux* was the supreme allegorist of the Middle Ages, while Aquinas* made use of it in Catholic hermeneutics*. Reformed* theologians generally reject allegory as a theological exercise.

Allegri, Gregorio (1582–1652) Italian priest, singer, and composer of the *Miserere.*

Allelouarion In the Byzantine Rite*, Psalm verses with a triple hallelujah* as a refrain, generally sung between the Epistle and the Gospel.

alleluia (Heb., let us praise the Ya or the lord) Cry of praise and joy used at the Mass* and all liturgical services throughout the year, except in penitential times. In the Eastern Church*, it is used in all services. See also HALLELUJAH.

Alleluiatic Sequence Latin sequence ascribed to Notker Balbulus*, translated into English by J. M. Neale*, and set to Anglican chant by A. H. Dyke Troytte.

Allen, Asa Alonso (1911–1970) Healing evangelist. Licensed as an evangelist by the Assemblies of God* in 1936, he established in 1951 his own ministry with headquarters in Dallas. He began broadcasting the Allen Revival Hour on the radio from 1953 and publishing *Miracle Magazine* from 1954. He suffered a setback when he was arrested for drunken driving in 1955 and had to surrender his Assembly of God credentials. In 1956 he started the Miracle Revival Fellowship, which he continued to lead for the remainder of his life. He also began a revival training center in Arizona.

Allen, Richard (1760–1831) Minister who was the first African-American to be ordained in the Methodist Church. He later organized the first black church in the United States and was a bishop in the African Methodist Episcopal Church*.

Allen, Roland (1868–1947) Missiologist. In 1895 he was sent by the Society for the Propagation of the Gospel* to its North China Mission. In Beijing he witnessed the Boxer Rebellion* of 1900. This experience led him to reassess the theology and missionary methods of Western churches. He was an early advocate of the Nevius Plan to make the churches in mission regions self-supporting, self-propagating, and self-governing; adapted to local cultural conditions; and led by the Holy Spirit. In 1912 he published his most famous work, *Missionary Methods: St. Paul's or Ours?* Later he worked in India and Kenya as a volunteer priest, although he continued to be an Anglican.

all-night vigil In the Byzantine Rite*, monastic vigil* of Palestinian origin comprising vespers* and orthros* along with the entire Psalter and all nine canticles*.

allocution 1. Address by the pope in secret consistory*. 2. The pope's remarks to a public audience. 3. Brief formal address to the congregation, as an address to the sponsors in baptism*.

Allouez, Claude Jean (1622–1689) French Jesuit missionary to Canada. He became bishop of Quebec and founded several missions to the Great Lakes area. He wrote important parts of the *Jesuit Relations.*

Alma Redemptoris Mater Loving Mother of the Redeemer, one of the four antiphons to the Virgin Mary*.

almoner Church official vested with the duty of distributing alms. The person who distributes alms on behalf of the king of England is known as the lord high almoner.

alms basin/dish Large plate for the presentation of the congregation's offering before the altar.

Richard Allen

almuce Hooded fur or fur-lined cape used as a choir vestment. Its use may be traced to the twelfth century. In France almuce* is worn by canons over the left arm as a mark of dignity. See also AMICE.

Alogi (lit., people without the Logos) Obscure heretical group led by Gaius in Asia Minor about 175. It rejected the Gospel of St. John and the Apocalypse and the theology of the Logos*.

Alombrados Sixteenth-century Spanish mystic sect that rejected the sacraments, the ministry, and good works*. The name was first applied in 1492 to a group led by Antonio de Pastrana, religious of Ocana, who promoted pure contemplation that merged the human with the divine. They claimed visions and prophecies, followed strange practices of piety, and undertook severe mortifications*. They were exterminated in 1623 in the Spanish Inquisition*.

Alopen (c. seventh century) First known Christian missionary in China. An Assyrian, he arrived in China in 635, according to the Nestorian Tablet first erected in 781. He was received with honor by

Emperor T'ai-tsung, who allowed him to build a monastery and translate the Scriptures into Chinese.

Aloysius Gonzaga, St. See GONZAGA, ST. ALOYSIUS.

Alpha Ten-week cross-denominational, videotaped Bible study course developed by Nicky Gumbel, a minister in the Holy Trinity Anglican Church in Brompton, London, in the 1970s. It is designed to introduce newcomers to the Christian faith. Alpha courses are now taught in many English-speaking countries.

Alpha and Omega First and last letters of the Greek alphabet designating God and Christ as the beginning and the end, following Revelation 1:8; 21:6; 22:13.

Alphabetos Series of 24 hymns in the Byzantine office, each beginning with a consecutive letter of the Greek alphabet.

Alphege, St. (954–1012) English archbishop who was martyred after he was captured by the Danes and refused to ask his parishioners* to ransom him. Feast day: April 19.

Alphonsus Liguori, St. (1696–1787) Founder of the Redemptorists*. He abandoned a legal career to be ordained as a priest in 1726. He moved to Scala in 1731, reorganized a convent of nuns there as the Redemptoristines*, and next year founded Congregation of the Most Holy Redeemer or Redemptorists*, with seven postulants* dedicated to pastoral work among the poor. In 1743 he was elected superior general* of the order and in 1745 he wrote the first of his many devotional works. He outlined his system of moral theology* in *Annotations* (1748) recast as *Theologia Moralis* (1753 and 1755). His many devotional writings were very popular and included *Visits to the Blessed Sacrament and the Blessed Virgin* (1745), *The Glories of Mary* (1750), *Novenas of Christmas* (1758), *Novena of the Heart of Jesus* (1758), *The Great Means of Prayer* (1759), *The True Spouse of Jesus Christ* (1750), and *The Way of Salvation* (1757).

altar (Lat., *altare*, place of sacrifice) Block, mound, table, or platform used for religious sacrifice. In Christian tradition, it is used for the Eucharist* or the Lord's Supper*. The earliest altars were made of wood, but the custom of celebrating the Eucharist on the tombs of the martyrs caused stone altars to come into use. The bodies of martyrs were placed under the altars, but later, as available relics* grew fewer, altars were required to be dedicated by bishops. For centuries there was only one altar in each church but additional altars were permitted, the original being then known as the high altar. Reformed* Protestants replaced the altar with a table.

altar boy Server* or acolyte* during liturgical service.

altar bread Bread or wafers used in Holy Communion* or Eucharist*.

altar call Practice of inviting congregants at the end of a worship service to gather at the altar rails to confess their sins and to rededicate their lives to Jesus Christ. The practice grew out of camp meetings* and became popular during the first half of the nineteenth century.

altar cross Cross, usually metal or wood, standing on the altar to symbolize the crucifixion.

altar curtain Curtain hanging above each end of the altar.

altar desk Movable support consisting of a book plate on a short stem or pillar to hold the missal during the Eucharist*.

altar fellowship In the Lutheran Church, participation in the Communion.

Golden Altar

altar guild Women's association organized to care for the altar and chancel* furnishings.

altar light Candle at either side of the cross on the altar.

altar linen A cloth covering the altar during worship.

altar of repose Elevation on which the Communion sacrament is placed from Maundy Thursday* to Good Friday*.

altar, people's Movable altar placed close to the congregation in a church in which the high altar is far removed from them, as in a Gothic* cathedral with a long choir.

Altar Table

altar prayers Prayers offered by those who responded to an altar call*, usually in a kneeling position near the altar rails.

altar rail Rail to protect the altar from profanation. Worshipers may kneel here to receive the Communion.

altar screen 1. Piece of embroidered needlework, cloth of gold, or tapestry suspended above the altar. 2. Back panel, raised above the altar. Above the permanent or movable base, which may be as high as the altar, is a decorative panel, which serves as a frame to a picture, bas-relief, or statue. Movable screens* are made of hammered silver or other precious metal. See also DORSAL.

altar society Group of parishioners* who care for

the altar and sanctuary. Such societies are usually composed of women who are charged with cleaning and decorating the altar, the sanctuary area, the sacristy*, church vestments, candles, and flowers.

altar stone Table of the altar, either fixed or movable, made of a solid slab of stone, containing the relics* of saints.

altar, stripping of Ceremonial removal of ornaments, candles, and cloths from the altar at the end of the Eucharist* on Maundy Thursday*.

altar wine Wine used at the altar for the celebration of the Eucharist*.

altar-cloth Cloth covering, symbolizing the shroud of Christ, consisting usually of three pieces of which the top one is long enough to touch the ground on each side.

altarpiece Decorative image or representation of a titular* saint, painted or carved in the round or relief. It may hang on the wall behind an altar, or above it. It may be a single picture called the pala* or a large diptych* (two panels), triptych* (three panels), or polyptych* with several panels on a single frame, called the ancona*. Altarpieces may also be made of metal like the pala* d'oro of St. Mark's, Venice*. Frequently the size and importance of the altarpiece overshadowed the altar it-

Decorative Altarpiece

self. Some altarpieces may tell a complex story through a series of representations, using predellas* to extend the altarpieces.

altar-tomb Free-standing tomb with a flat stone slab on top, found in the catacombs, for memorial celebrations of the Eucharist*.

Altenberg Cistercian monastery in Altenberg in the Bergisch land east of Cologne* founded in 1133 by Count Everhard von Berg. It was completed in 1379. The west facade is sumptuously decorated with stained-glass windows in red, blue, and yellow, set in frames of gold. It was destroyed by a fire in 1815.

Althaus, Paul (1888–1966) Lutheran theologian whose studies have restored Luther's influence as a theologian. His *Dogmatics, Die Christliche Wahrheit* (Christian truth) offers an alternative to Barth's Christocentric* understanding of revelation.

Altichiero da Zevio (c. 1330–1395) Italian painter noted for his frescoes in the churches of St. Antonio and St. Georgio.

Altotting Important site of pilgrimage* in honor of the Virgin Mary* in Bavaria. Its chapel goes back to the eighth century and became a center of pilgrimage under the patronage of the dukes of Bavaria.

altum dominium In ecclesiastical law*, supreme control of church property by the pope.

Amalric of Bena (?–1207) French mystic and heretic. He held that the Trinity* was revealed in successive historical epochs, that God is in everything, and that those who love God cannot sin. His teachings were condemned at a synod* in Paris in 1210 and five years later at the Fourth Lateran Council*.

Amalricians Pantheistic followers of Amalric of Bena*, also known as Brethren of the Free Spirit*. Seven of them were burned at the stake.

Amana Community Christian sect also known as the Community of True Inspiration and as the Amarites. It originated in Germany in 1714 under the influence of two Pietists, E. L. Gruber and J. F. Rock. A large part of this body emigrated to America in 1842 and 13 years later settled at Amana, Iowa, where they were incorporated as a community in 1859. They had very little contact with the outside world until the mid-twentieth century. The society, now a joint stock corporation, runs farms, woollen mills, and other industries. The Amana Church Society is a separate legal entity.

Amandus, St. (d. c. 675) Merovingian apostle of Flanders and Danubian Slavs. In 628 he was consecrated bishop without any fixed see* and began active missionary work in Flanders and Carinthia. He founded two monasteries in Ghent and a large monastery at Elnon, near Tournai, later known as St. Amand in his honor. It is possible he was bishop of Mastricht from 649 to 652. Feast day: February 6.

Amazing Grace Hymn, a perennial favorite, written by John Newton* and William Cowper* in 1779 and included in their *Olney Hymns*. Its first stanza runs, "Amazing Grace, how sweet the sound, That saved a wretch like me. I once was lost but now am found, Was blind but now I see."

amba In the Coptic Church*, the title of the patriarch*, "the Most Holy Pope and Patriarch of Alexandria . . . and all the Preaching of St. Mark."

ambo (pl., ambos/ambones) In the early church, a raised platform or a reading desk* for the reading of the Epistles and the Gospels and the singing of the liturgical portions of the service. It was larger than a pulpit because it had to accommodate the preacher as well as his candle-bearing attendants. It was reached by a flight of stairs. In later Christian basilicas*, it was replaced by the lectern* and the pulpit.

Ambrose (1708–1771) Russian archbishop who was strangled by a mob as he tried to help them in time of plague.

Ambrose, Isaac (1604–1664) English Puritan whose *Looking to Jesus* has been compared to *Pilgrim's Progress*.

Ambrose, St. (c. 339–397) Bishop of Milan* and, with St. Jerome*, St. Augustine*, and St. Gregory*, one of the four doctors of the Latin Church. He succeeded Auxentius*, the Arian bishop of Milan, in 373 or 374. He was a powerful preacher and was revered by St. Augustine* who was converted by him. He had great influence on the civil authorities and maintained the independence of the church against their incursions. He wrote extensively on Christian ethics in *De Officiis Ministrorum* and on the sacraments in *De Sacramentis*. He also wrote many hymns and was instrumental in making hymns a part of liturgical worship. He encouraged asceticism* and the cult of the martyrs. Feast day: December 7.

Ambrose the Camaldulian (1386–1439) Ambrogio Traversari, Italian churchman who translated Greek theological texts, including the sermons of Chrysostom*.

Ambrosian Chant Liturgical music of the Milanese Rite, attributed to St. Ambrose*. It is classified under four, rather than eight, modes. The psalm tones*, which lack the mediation, are grouped in four corresponding series, with variable reciting notes or tenors.

St. Ambrose

Ambrosian Rite Non-Roman Rite that was once used in the province of Milan*. It differs widely from the Roman Rite*. Among its peculiarities is that the offertory takes place before and not after the creed and is accompanied by a procession.

Ambrosiana Famous library in Milan* founded in 1609 by Cardinal Federico Borromeo, a cousin of Charles Borromeo*.

Ambrosians 1. Fourteenth-century Catholic order of Milan* whose members followed the Ambrosian Rite*. 2. Sixteenth-century Anabaptist* sect which rejected the clergy and claimed direct communication with God through the Holy Spirit*.

Ambrosiaster Name for the unknown author of a fourth-century Latin commentary on the Pauline Epistles, long attributed to St. Ambrose* or Hilary of Poitiers*.

ambry See AUMBRY.

ambulatory Covered walkway outside a church or a processional aisle around the sanctuary.

amcha In the Ethiopian Rite, the gesture of peace by bowing to one another.

AMDG (Lat.) *Ad Majorem Dei Gloriam*, "For the Greater Glory of God," the motto of the Jesuits*.

AME African Methodist Episcopal Church.

amen Hebrew word meaning "verily or truly," or "so be it." In the Bible it is used as an affirmation indicating trust at the end of a statement or prayer. In Revelation 3:14 Christ is called "the Amen" who is faithful and true.

amen corner Corner in a church near the pulpit occupied by those leading in the responsive amens.

American Baptist Association Group of conservative Baptist churches, sometimes called Missionary Baptist Churches, descended from the Landmark Baptists based in Texarkana, Arkansas.

American Baptist Churches in the USA (ABC-USA) Major Baptist denomination, formerly known as the American Baptist Convention (1950–1972) and the Northern Baptist Convention (1907–1950), founded in 1907. Its first president was Charles Evans Hughes, governor of New York. The driving force behind all Baptist churches was foreign missions. The General Baptist* Missionary Convention was soon joined by the Baptist General Tract Society, later the American Baptist Publication and Sunday School Society in 1824, and the American Baptist Home Mission Society started in 1832. Women's Missionary Societies were started in the 1870s.

In 1972, when it assumed its present name, ABC-USA had over 60 regional, national, and general organizations. Today ABC-USA has over 1.5 million members, close to 6,000 churches of which 800 congregations are dually aligned with one or more African-American churches or other Protestant mainline churches*. Theologically, American Baptists are broadly Evangelical. They operate 15 universities or colleges, six theological seminaries, and 122 homes, children's centers, and hospitals. Its official periodical, *The American Baptist,* is the oldest Christian magazine in continuous publication in North America.

American Bible Society Nondenominational organization, founded in 1816, with headquarters in New York City, dedicated to the translation of the Bible and its distribution. Elias Boudinot* served as its first chairman of the board, composed mostly of Christian laymen. It has printed the Bible in more than 1,000 languages.

American Board of Catholic Missions Standing Committee of the National Conference of Catholic Bishops* founded at Notre Dame* in 1919. It was restructured in 1924 when it merged with the Society for the Propagation of the Faith. Its grants are specifically targeted to ministries serving blacks, Hispanics, Asians, and the handicapped.

American Board of Commissioners for Foreign Missions First foreign missions society organized in the United States in 1810. It resulted from the Haystack Prayer Meeting* at Williams College in 1806. Later in 1961 it became the United Church Board for World Ministries.

American Board of Missions to the Jews Independent mission agency* engaged in evangelism to the Jews, founded as the Williamsburg Mission in 1894 by Leopold Cohen, a Jewish immigrant from Hungary. His magazine, *The Chosen People,* spread news of Jewish evangelism. In the 1920s, Cohen's missions expanded into several North American and European cities, leading to the adoption of the present name in 1924. Leopold's son, Joseph, succeeded him in 1937.

American Friends Service Committee (AFSC) Quaker* philanthropic agency, founded in 1917, dedicated to the promotion of peace and justice and assistance to those in need in developing countries. It supports conscientious objectors*, illegal immigrants, refugees, homeless, starving, and unemployed. In 1947 AFSC and its British counterpart were jointly awarded the Nobel Peace Prize.

American Lutheran Church (ALC) One of the denominations that merged with other Lutheran churches to form the Evangelical Lutheran Church in America*. It was itself the union of several churches: Evangelical Joint Synod of Ohio and Other States (1818), Buffalo Synod (1818) and Iowa Synod (1854), all of German origin; Evangelical Lutheran Church (1817) and the Lutheran Free Church (1897), of Norwegian origin; and United Evangelical Lutheran Church (1896), of Danish origin. ALC was strongest in the Midwest. Its membership in 2000 was estimated at 2.4 million.

American Prayer Book Authorized liturgical book of the Protestant Episcopal Church adopted by the General Convention* of the Protestant Episcopal Church in 1789 following the establishment of the United States. It replaced the Anglican BCP*. Its principal innovation was the inclusion in the consecration of the Eucharist* an oblation* of the elements* and an invocation* of the Holy Spirit*.

American Standard Version U.S. version of the English Revised Version*, based on a new international translation of the Bible, published in 1901.

American Sunday School Union Primary agency for development of Sunday schools*, founded in 1824 as an outgrowth of the Sunday and Adult School Union in Philadelphia*. It has published a significant collection of instructional materials for Sunday school* students, including a 100-volume library. In 1974 the name was changed to the American Missionary Fellowship to reflect its new mission of assisting new ethnic groups to form churches in rural and inner-city areas.

American Tract Society (ATS) Chief publisher of religious material founded in 1825. By the late 1820s, ATS was annually printing and distributing over 5 million tracts. It was also an innovator in the use of traveling salesmen called colporteurs*. Today ATS is publishing over 30 million tracts per year.

Americanism Nineteenth-century Roman Catholic movement in the United States to modernize the church and adapt it to democratic and humanitarian ideals. It was initiated in 1891 by I. T. Hecker*, who laid emphasis on "active" values, such as humanitarianism, eugenic reform, and democracy while deemphasizing traditional values such as humility and obedience. It was condemned by Pope Leo XIII* in 1899 and disappeared soon thereafter.

Ames, William (1576–1633) Calvinist moral theologian and controversialist. He sought exile in Holland, where he took part in the Remonstrant controversies. As professor of theology at Franeker, he was recognized by Calvinists as one of their best theologians. Among his important theological works are *De Conscientia eius Jure et Casibus* (1632) and *Medulla Theologiae* (1627). Among his controversial and polemical works were *Bellarminus Enervatus* (1628) and *Animadversiones in Synodalia* (1629).

Amharic Semitic language spoken in Ethiopia used primarily for secular purposes, compared to Ge'ez*, the liturgical language.

amice (Lat., *amictus,* that which is wrapped around) Linen cloth with strings attached, worn around the neck along with the alb* by ministers presiding at the Eucharist*. Described in the prayers when it is put on as the helmet* of salvation, it is a head covering and hood.

Amiens Largest cathedral in France, with a ground area of 82,885 square feet, an internal

length of 438 feet, and a height of 139 feet. Construction work began in 1220 under the direction of architect Robert de Luzarches. The south tower was not topped out until the nineteenth century, or after seven centuries of construction. Its design is known as Radiant Gothic*. The statue of the Golden Virgin on the central pier* of the south doorway, once completely gilded, is one of the finest sculptures of the thirteenth century.

amillennialism In eschatology*, the symbolic and nonliteral interpretation of the millennium* and other related concepts which states that the millennium is not a literal future event, but symbolizes Christ's presence in the church between his first and second advents*.

Amish Conservative sect which grew out of a split among the Swiss Brethren*. A group under the leadership of Jakob Ammann, an elder of Erlenbach in the Canon of Berne, broke away from the main body because of their practices, including the more frequent observance of the Lord's Supper*, the practice of washing one another's feet during service, wearing plain dress, and shunning* those who had been excommunicated. They gained adherents in Alsace and Switzerland, most of whom migrated to the United States in the eighteenth and nineteenth centuries.

Most Amish are members of the Old Order Amish* Mennonite Church. In doctrine and practices they differ little from the Mennonites*,

Amish Buggies

except that they worship in private houses and use Pennsylvania Dutch (Deutsch or German) in their services. They shun publicity, but have become quite well-known and even admired for their crafts, educational methods, and traditional dress as well as their use of horse and buggies as a means of transportation. They practice mutual aid rather than using commercial insurance. In some states they are exempt from taxes and Social Security.

Ammon, St. (d. c. 350) One of the most famous ascetics of the Nitrian Desert* and an associate of St. Anthony. Feast day: October 4.

Amnos 1. Byzantine icon* representing the Christ child lying on a paten*, sometimes covered by an asteriscos, symbolizing the Eucharist*. 2. Sacrificial lamb* as the symbol of Christ. 3. Portion of the prosphora*, the loaf of pure wheat bread prepared for liturgical use.

amphibalum 1. Chasuble*-like garment worn by Gallican priests. 2. Birrus*, or a garment put on first to cover the head, similar to the amice*.

Amplified Bible, The English translation of the Bible that features expanded meanings of words within parentheses, brackets, or italics. The Old Testament was prepared by Frances E. Siewert in 1958, and the New Testament was prepared by a committee.

ampulla (pl., ampullae) Narrow-necked vase used to hold holy oil* consecrated by a bishop. It symbolizes consecration. Some of them, called ampullae sanguinis, were bottle-shaped vessels made of glass and have been found in the catacombs with the blood of the martyrs. A second category made of baked clay often bore the image of a saint and were used to preserve oil from the lights in a martyr's tomb. A third category was used to preserve sacramental oils in a church.

Amsdorf, Nikolaus von (1483–1565) Lutheran theologian, associate of Martin Luther*, and author of numerous theological works. He accompanied Luther to the Disputation of Leipzig* in 1519 and to the Diet of Worms* in 1521. He led the opposition to Catholicism* in Wittenberg* and Goslar. He quarreled with Melanchthon* and Bucer* and alienated the emperor during the Colloquy of Ratisbon*. He opposed the Leipzig Interim* and became the leader of the Gnesio-Lutheran* Party against the Adiaphorists*.

Amsterdam Assembly Assembly at Concertgebouw, Amsterdam, from August 22 to September 4, 1948, which formally created the World Council of Churches*.

amvos Raised step in front of the holy doors* of the iconostasis*.

Amyot, Joseph (1718–c. 1795) French Jesuit missionary to China.

Amyraldus/Amyrald, Moise (1596–1644) French Protestant theologian, professor, and later principal of the Protestant Academy of Saumur. In 1634 he published *Brief Traitte de la Predestination,* which led to a controversy over universal grace. He held a neo-Arminian position, known as Amyraldianism, or hypothetical universalism*, that the Son had been sent into the world to redeem* all people provided they had faith. For these views he was strongly criticized by Calvinist theologians and was tried for heresy in 1637 at the Protestant Synod of Alencon, but escaped condemnation. His *Le Morale Chrestienne* (1652) was the most important work of Calvinist ethics.

Anabaptists (Gk., *ana,* again and *baptein,* to dip in water) Continental sect which refused to baptize their infants and reinstituted the baptism* of believers. The name was applied mainly to six groups with slightly different emphases. 1. Zwickau Prophets*, led by Thomas Muntzer*, who taught a doctrine of Inner Light*. 2. Swiss Brethren*, who additionally believed in non-resistance and non-participation in politics. 3. Moravian Hutterites* under Jacob Hutter, who practiced communal ownership of property. 4. South German Anabaptists, led by Pilgram Marpeck. 5. Melchiorites or Hoffmanites, influenced by Melchior Hoffman*, who taught a Docetic and apocalyptic Christianity. 6. Mennonites*, led by Menno Simons*. Anabaptists were severely persecuted by both Protestants and Roman Catholics, and many of them were drowned for heresy. The Anabaptist Confession of Schleithem is the closest thing to an Anabaptist creed or doctrine.

In 1534 an Anabaptist sect led by John of Leyden captured the town of Munster, expelled the local bishop, and instituted the Old Testament practice of polygamy. This discredited the movement among the other denominations. Initially the Anabaptists were fired with a revolutionary zeal for changing the world; only later did they accept the role of a pacifist minority, separate from the world. Millennial expectations were central to the movement, as was church discipline*, which meant keeping the church pure as the bride of Christ*.

anabathmoi In the Byzantine Church*, short hymns composed by Theodore the Studite, based on the Psalms of Ascents (119–133) sung at mattins* on Sunday and on feasts with a Gospel. They form part of a series of eight troparia.

anagnosmata Excerpts from the Old and the New Testaments read in the liturgy and other divine services* in the Eastern Orthodox Church*.

anagnostes In the Eastern Rite*, a reader* who has received the first of the minor orders*.

anagogical (Gk., *anago*, to lead) One of the modes of biblical interpretation* adopted by the Alexandrian School* in which scriptural texts have a secret, spiritual meaning.

anakephalaiosis (Gk., summary, recapitulation*) Christ's life and work as summing up God's redemptive activity in history. It is tied to Ephesians 1:22 as developed by Irenaeus*.

anakomide Ceremony transferring relics* from one place to another.

analabos In the Byzantine Church*, linen monastic band forming a cross. It consists of two oblong pieces joined at the shoulder and falling in front and behind like the scapular* in the West.

Analecta Bollandiana Quarterly review of hagiographical studies issued since 1882 by the Bollandist Fathers.

analepsis In the Byzantine Rite*, the Feast of the Ascension on the Thursday of the sixth week after Easter*.

analogion In the Byzantine Church*, stand on which icons are placed for worship, or a lectern* used by singers.

anology of faith (Lat., *analogia fidei*) Principle derived by Karl Barth* from Romans 12:6 emphasizing comparisons of scriptural texts for hermeneutical purposes.

Analogy of Religion Famous apologetic work by Joseph Butler*, published in 1736, showing the reasonableness of the Christian faith. Its full title was *The Analogy of Religion, Natural and Revealed, to the Constitution and Course of Nature. Designed as a Refutation of Deism.* Butler held that religious truths are attested by natural truths and that both are based on probability rather than certainty.

analysis fidei (Lat., analysis of faith) Theological investigation of faith.

anamnesis (Gk., lit., memorial) Commemoration* of the passion, Resurrection, and ascension of Christ in the liturgy, with reference especially to his charge to the disciples, "Do this . . . in remembrance of Me" (1 Cor. 11:24–25; Luke 22:19). The idea has been subject to reinterpretation, especially in the sense of reenactment rather than merely remembering.

anamphiasis In the Byzantine Rite*, preparation of the altar on Holy Thursday* before it is washed.

anaphora (lit., offering) Central prayer of the eucharistic liturgy over the bread and the wine. Among the oldest anaphoras* are those of the *Apostolic Tradition** of Hippolytus*, the Liturgy of Addai and Mari*, and the Egyptian form of the Liturgy of St. Basil*.

anarchism, Christian Religious-political ideology associated with Leo Tolstoy*, based on his rejection of the state.

anargyroi (Gk., healing saints) Saintly physicians who healed the sick without charge. The most famous of the anargyroi were Sts. Cosmas and Damian*.

Anastasia, St. (c. 304) Martyr. According to some accounts, she was a Roman matron of noble birth and disciple of St. Chrysostom* who was martyred on the Island of Palmaria. According to other accounts, she was martyred in Sirmium in Pannonia and her relics* were transferred to Constantinople* by St. Gennadius and interred in the Church of Anastasis, founded by St. Gregory of Nazianzus*. Feast day until 1969: December 25.

Anastasimatarion Byzantine liturgical book containing text and music for Sunday offices, especially orthros* and hesperinos*, all of which are resurrection hymns.

anastasimon In the Byzantine Rite*, the troparion* that commemorates the Resurrection.

anastasis (Gk., resurrection) Any church dedicated to the Resurrection of Christ.

Anastasis

anathema (Gk., something set up above). In the Old Testament, used of votive offerings* or things dedicated to God and thus banned from common use. Used in the New Testament by St. Paul* to denote being accursed and separated from the Christian community for such sins as preaching a different gospel. In the post-apostolic church, anathema became a regular procedure against heretics, the earliest recorded instance being that at the Council of Elvira* in 306. In 431 St. Cyril* of Alexandria issued his famous 12 anathematizations against Nestorius*. By the fifth century, anathema meant complete separation from the body of believers as distinguished from excommunication*, which meant only exclusion from

sacraments and worship. Gregory IX* described anathema as major excommunication limited to the solemn ritual in which the bishop pronounced excommunication, surrounded by 12 priests carrying lighted candles which were thrown to the ground when the sentence had been uttered. The 1983 Codex abolished the distinction between anathema and excommunication so that the former has no official application.

anathema maranatha Expression in 2 Corinthians combining one Greek word and two Aramaic words meaning: "Let him be accursed. Our Lord come."

anathematization Pronouncement of an anathema upon.

anatolika Byzantine Sunday resurrection hymn attributed to Patriarch Anatolios of Constantinople (449–458).

anbero ed In the Ethiopian Church, prayer of blessing recited at the end of the liturgy.

Anchieta, Jose de (1534–1597) Spanish Jesuit missionary, called the father of Brazilian literature. He was the first Brazilian writer who composed the first grammar and dictionary in the Tupi language and canticles*, dialogues, and religious plays in Latin, Spanish, Portuguese, and Tupi as well as autosacramentals*, as *No festa de Sao Lourenco*. Together with Manoel de Nobrego, he helped found Sao Paulo and Rio de Janeiro.

anchor Christian symbol of hope, based on Hebrews 6:19. The crossbar of the anchor was a symbol of the cross. It is also the symbol of Pope Clement I, who is said to have been tied to an anchor and cast into the sea, and of Nicholas* of Bari, the patron saint* of sailors.

anchor-cross Christian symbol combining an anchor representing strength and security and a cross.

anchorite (Gk., to withdraw, take to the bush; fem., anchoress) Hermit who lives alone in a cell. Generally, a person who withdraws from the world to live a solitary life of silence, prayer, and mortification*.

Ancient Christian Fellowship Group belonging to the Apostolic Episcopal Church* with doctrines similar to the Eastern Orthodox Church*, but using English in its services.

ancona Multipaneled altarpiece on a single frame.

Ancrene(e) Riwle/Ancrene Wisse Anonymously written thirteenth-century rule or guide for anchoresses, a classic of English devotional literature. Originally written for three young ladies, it was later expanded to include all women religious. The eight parts of the rule deal with devotional routine, custody of the senses and of thoughts, temptation, confession*, penance*, love of God, and external regulations. Most of the material is taken from Dominican and Franciscan sources, St. Bernard of Clairvaux*, Gregory I*, St. Augustine*, and Ailred of Rievaulx's treatise *De Vita Eremetica ad Sororem.*

Ancyra, Council of Name of two councils held in Ancyra, Asia Minor. The first, in 314, dealt with the question of the lapsi*, and the second, a semi-Arian one, in 358 rejected both the Arian and the Nicene positions and asserted that the Son was like in substance to the Father.

And Can It Be That I Should Gain? The text, by Charles Wesley* (1707–1788), was written shortly after his conversion in 1738, and was published that year in *Psalms and Hymns*. In his journal, Wesley sensed the spiritual opposition associated with it was a "device of the enemy to keep God

from receiving the glory due Him." Set to Thomas Campbell's* (1825) tune published in *The Banquet,* this has long been a worship favorite when celebrating the Lord's Supper.

Andachtsbild (Ger., devotional picture; pl., *Andachtsbilder*). German devotional image intended for devotion and meditation with a flexible iconography* expressed in narrative cycles. The most popular themes were the man of sorrows*, the Pieta*, and the sorrows of Mary.

Andechs Benedictine monastery on the eastern shore of Lake Ammer, southeast of Munich* on the family seat of the counts of Diessen and Andechs. It was the home of a number of relics*, including the Sacrament of St. Gregory, objects of pilgrimage* in the twelfth century. The Reformation* and the Thirty Years' War brought the monastery to near extinction, but around 1755 architect Lorenz Sappel and decorator Johann Baptist Zimmermann began a restoration that transformed the monastery into an "earthly paradise." A picture of the Virgin Mary* enthroned and surrounded by a blaze of light is an object of veneration*.

Andel, Huibert Antonie van (1875–1945) Dutch pioneer missionary in central Java and one of the founders of the Javanese Christian Church. He served as a missionary from 1912 to 1942 in central Java. In *Een Grootsche Poging om de wereldzending in de macht van het Modernisme te Brengen,* he warned against the rising tide of modernism*.

Anderson, Rufus (1796–1880) American missionary statesman. He was foreign secretary of the American Board of Commissioners for Foreign Missions* for 34 years from 1832 to 1866. His *Foreign Missions: Their Relations and Claims* (1869) influenced missionary practice for over a generation. He wanted missions to be self-governing, self-supporting. and self-propagating. His visit to India in 1855 resulted in the dispersion of central stations, organization of village churches, and the ordination of native pastors.

Andover Controversy Late nineteenth-century dispute among Congregationalists at Andover Theological Seminary* in Massachusetts who believed

Anchor-Cross

that persons who die without hearing the gospel have a second chance after death (future probation) and others who insisted that no salvation is possible for those who reject the gospel while alive.

Andover Theological Seminary Congregational* seminary founded in 1808 on the campus of the Andover Academy in northwest Massachusetts by Old Calvinists and New Divinity men, such as Timothy Wright, Jedidiah Morse*, and Leonard Woods, in response to the takeover of Harvard by Unitarians. Although the seminary produced a number of orthodox theologians during the next 75 years, Romanticism, Unitarianism*, and Rationalism eroded Andover's commitment to biblical truth. By 1881, its faculty openly embraced liberalism*. After a failed merger with Harvard in 1908, the seminary's operations were suspended until 1931 when it became affiliated with a local Baptist seminary, Newton Theological Institute, to form Andover-Newton Theological Institute.

Andrade, Antonio de (1580–1634) Jesuit missionary. In 1624 he became the first Western missionary to cross the Himalayas into Tibet. The following year, he and four associates established a mission in Tsaparang which was destroyed by angry Buddhist monks in 1631.

Andrae Laurentius (c. 1470–1552) Churchman who translated the Bible into Swedish and helped Swedish king Gustavus to strengthen the Swedish Church.

Andre, Brother (1845–1937) Catholic mystic of Montreal to whom many miraculous healings are attributed.

Andrea, James (1528–1590) Lutheran scholar. He became professor at the University of Tubingen* in 1561 and later chancellor. He participated in many of the religious colloquies of his time, among them the conference with Farel* and Beza* in 1557. He belonged to the Center Party among Lutherans. He probably formulated the Strasbourg Formula of Concord* (1563) and the Swabian Concordia and was responsible in part for the Torgau Book and the Belgic Book. He wrote over 200 works.

Andrew, Acts of St. Apocryphal book dating from the second century, parts of which have survived in Coptic and Armenian translations and in a summary by Gregory of Tours*. It describes the apostle's imprisonment at Patras and his defense of ascetic practices. The Martyrdom of St. Andrew, a variant text, describes the apostle's death by crucifixion.

Andrew Kim Taegon, St. Korean Catholic martyr*. He was the first native Korean Catholic priest, martyred in 1846.

Andrew of Crete (c. 660–740) Byzantine hymnographer and theologian. After 690 he became archbishop of Gortyna in Crete. His *Great Canon,* a lengthy penitential poem, is sung on the fifth Thursday of the Great Lent*. His hymn, "Christian! Does Thou Still See Them," is still sung. Feast day: July 4.

Andrew of Longjumeau (thirteenth century) French Dominican who served as a messenger from Pope Innocent IV* to the Mongols, and who wrote an account of Mongol Christianity.

Andrew, St. Apostle, brother of Peter*. Patron saint* of Scotland, Greece, and Russia. He was originally a disciple of St. John the Baptist. According to tradition, he was crucified at Patras on a cross in the form of an X.

Andrewes, Lancelot (1555–1626) English churchman and bishop of Winchester*. A dedicated scholar, he was a master of 15 languages who was highly regarded by both Elizabeth I and James I. In 1604 he attended the Hampton Court Conference which appointed him as one of the translators of the Authorized (or King James) Version. He was largely responsible for the Pentateuch and the historical books of the Old Testament. He defended King James and the Oath of Allegiance against St. Robert Bellarmine*. His *Ninety-Six Sermons* and *Preces Privatae* remain classics of Anglican spirituality*. Feast day: September 25 or 26.

Andrew's Cross, St. A cross in the form of the letter X, on which St. Andrew* is reputed to have been crucified. It is the official symbol of Scotland and thus appears on the Union Jack.

Andrews, Lorrin (1795–1868) American Protestant missionary to Hawaii who became an educator and judge.

Andronicus Jewish convert to Christianity at Rome*, mentioned in Romans 16:7.

anemone In Christian art, a symbol of the Trinity*, because of its three leaves.

Anerio, Felice (1516–1614) Italian composer who succeeded Palestrina at St. Peter's*. His principal output consisted of madrigals, magnificats, Masses, and motets.

anestenaria Custom of dancing barefoot on coals, holding an icon or Gospel book, common in certain villages in Thrace and Macedonia* on May 21, the Feast of Constantine and Helena*. The dancers, called Anestinarides, keep their portable icons in a special shrine (konaki) hung with bells and red shawls.

angel (Gk., *angelos,* herald or messenger) 1. Supernatural spirit serving as God's messenger and divine intermediary or as a special guardian of an individual or place. 2. Member of the lowest order of the heavenly hierarchy*. 3. One of an order of fallen spirits who were former angels of God.

Angela Merici, St. (1470–1540) Italian nun who founded the order of Ursulines* and who was canonized in 1807. After devoting some years to the education of young girls and the care of sick women, she made a pilgrimage* to Palestine in 1524–1525 during which she became blind. As a result of her visions, she founded in Brescia, her native town, a community for women named after her patron, St. Ursuline. Feast day: January 27.

Angela of Foligno (c. 1248–1309) Italian nun who had many visions and was beatified in 1693. Feast day: January 4.

Angelic Brothers Community founded by J. G. Gichtel in the seventeenth century. Its members believed that they had already achieved an angelic state.

Angelic Doctor Epithet of St. Thomas Aquinas* in reference to the angelic quality of his intellect.

Angelic Hymn The hymn, "Gloria in Excelsis*," based on the song of the angelic host at the birth of Christ.

angelic salutation Salutation, "Hail Mary*, the Lord is with you," with which Gabriel greeted the Virgin Mary*.

Angelica, Mother (1923–) American religious broadcaster and founder of EWTN (Eternal Word Television Network). She is a member of the Franciscan Nuns of the Most Blessed Sacrament.

Angelico, Fra See FRA ANGELICO.

angelology Branch of theology dealing with the study of angels.

Angelus In the Western Church*, thrice-daily devotion in honor of the Virgin Mary* consisting of the repetition of three Ave Marias* with versicles and a collect* as a memorial of the Incarnation. A bell is rung three times for each Ave* and nine times for the collect*.

Angelus Clarenus (c. 1245–1337) Birth name: Peter of Fossombrone. Leader of Franciscan Spirituals. He entered the Friars Minor* in 1270, but soon came into conflict with the ecclesiastical authorities over his opposition to any mitigation of the Franciscan rule in regard to poverty. He assumed leadership of a group of Franciscans who came to be known as Clareni.

Angelus Silesius (1624–1677) Pseudonym of the German mystic Johannes Scheffler*, one of the forerunners of Pietism*. See SCHEFFLER, JOHANNES.

Angelus Temple Headquarters of the International Church of the Four Square Gospel, in Los Ange-

Angelus Temple

les, founded by Aimee Semple McPherson*. It is a semicircular building that can seat over 5,000 people.

Angers Church, named Notre Dame et Saint Maurice, dedicated to the Virgin, originally a small church in Angers, France, that burned down twice in 1001 and 1032. It was rebuilt in the twelfth century by Henry II. The 44.6 feet hall-nave is the widest of any church in France. Over the next few centuries, several new features were added: twin doors in the seventeenth century, two chapels in the fifteenth century, and two spires* in the nineteenth century. Between these two spires rises a third topped by a cupola, built in 1535. The cathedral is a unique monument in Romano-Gothic* style.

Anglican Chant Music of the Psalms, widely used in the Anglican Church, that developed from the plainchant psalm-tones of the seventeenth century. Anglican chant is based on short formulas harmonized in four voices to which the text of a psalm or a canticle* is adopted. The first part of each half-verse is sung on a reciting note, and the concluding words are fitted to a tune in a metrical rhythm.

Anglican Church of Canada The first Anglican worship service on Canadian soil was conducted on Baffin Island in 1578. The first Anglican bishop in Canada, then British North America, was appointed in 1787. The Constitution Act of 1791 reserved one-seventh of all crown lands as an endowment for Protestant clergy, but the Clergy Reserves* Act of 1840 recognized religious pluralism and rejected the principle of an established church*. In 1860 Bishop Francis Fulford was elected as the first metropolitan* of the self-governing Ecclesiastical Province of Canada. In 1893 Archbishop Rupert Machray was elected primate* of all Canada at the inaugural General Synod of the Church of England* in Canada. There are now 30 dioceses* grouped into 4 ecclesiastical provinces.

Anglican Communion The Church of England* in fellowship with Anglican churches throughout the world. It consists of the See of Canterbury* or the Church of England as the only established

church*, and the following churches: the Church of Ireland*, the Church in Wales*, the Scottish Episcopal Church, the Episcopal Church in the U.S., the Anglican churches of Australia, Canada, Papua New Guinea, and the Southern Cone of America, the Anglican Church in Aotearoa, New Zealand, and Polynesia, the provinces of Southern Africa, the West Indies, West Africa, Central Africa, Uganda, Kenya, Myanmar, Tanzania, the Indian Ocean, Melanesia, Nigeria, Sudan, Burundi, Rwanda, Congo, Korea, Mexico, and South East Asia, the Nippon Sei Ko Kai, the Church of Sri Lanka, the Episcopal Church of Brazil, the Episcopal Church of Jerusalem and the Middle East, and the Philippines Episcopal Church.

The Lusitanian or Portuguese Episcopal Church and the Spanish Reformed Episcopal Church are also members. The United Churches of South India, North India, Pakistan, and Bangladesh are members of the Anglican Consultative Council, the Lambeth Conference*, and the Primates' Meeting. The Philippine Independent Church, the Old Catholic churches, and the Mar Thoma Syrian Church* of Malabar are in communion with most Anglican churches.

Anglicanism Distinctive organization and teachings of the Church of England* and the ecclesiastical bodies within the Anglican Communion. It claims to be catholic, scriptural, and reformed and seeks to maintain the best elements of both Catholicism* and Protestantism*. As a doctrinal system, its formularies include the *Book of Common Prayer**, the Ordinal, the Thirty-Nine Articles*, and the two Books of Homilies*. The seventeenth century was the golden age of Anglicanism and was reflected in the writings of the Caroline Divines*, including Andrewes,* Cosin, Ken*, Laud*, Taylor*, and Thorndike*. Classical Anglicanism steered away from the confessional* systems of the continent and rejected any form of external authority. While the historic institution of the episcopacy* was preserved, it was not regarded as divine. Scripture was acknowledged as sufficient for salvation, but the role of reason was affirmed. The rise of secular learning in the eighteenth century led to the rise of the Cambridge Platonists* with their emphasis on devotional religion. The emergence of Evangelicalism* did much for the spiritual life of Anglicanism, but its appeal to the emotions and its emphasis on the primacy of the Scriptures and preaching of the Good News* did not sit well with the main body of Anglicans. Evangelicals, however, still form a sizeable group within Anglicanism.

The beginning of the nineteenth century saw a resurgence of the High Church* tradition through the Oxford movement* in 1833. It began as a scholarly movement led by Keble*, Pusey*, and Newman*, who issued the series known as *Tracts for the Times*. The Catholic movement, as it is called, sought to restore to Anglicanism the sacramental traditions of the Catholic Church. A parallel movement saw the development of the Broad Church* or liberal theological movement which drew its core beliefs from German scholarship. The second half of the twentieth century has witnessed great changes within Anglicanism, particularly in the form of liturgical experimentation, so that diversity rather than unity is the rule. Almost every province has its prayer book and those outside the English-speaking world have their own cultural and spiritual mores. The ordination of women and inclusion or exclusion of homosexuals have produced new controversies that have strained the homogeneity of the Anglican communion.

Anglo-Catholicism Movement within the Church of England* emphasizing the catholic and universal aspects of Anglicanism. It specifically refers to the party that sympathized with the Tractarian movement of the 1830s and held a high view of the sacraments and attached great importance to the apostolic succession*. The original Tractarians were concerned with reviving personal discipline through confession* and fasting*, but they grew increasingly preoccupied with external rituals of worship and came to be known as ritualists. Through their influences many traditional Catholic practices, such as votive candles and the wearing of stoles*, spread throughout the Anglican Church. In the latter part of the nineteenth century, Anglo-Catholicism was split between liberals and conservatives. Christian socialists under F. D. Maurice* also had a formative influence on the movement. Anglo-Catholicism reached its acme in the interwar years when several Anglo-Catholic conferences were held. The movement crested during the 1930s and, since then, has been on the wane. It is particularly opposed to the ordination of women and any alliance with free churches*. In some countries Anglo-Catholics have formed secessionist churches.

Anglo-Israelism Movement based on the hypothesis that the British peoples are descendants of the ten tribes of Israel and that the biblical prophecies relating to Israel will be fulfilled in them.

anhypostasis In Christology*, description of the human Christ as not an individual human being but as hypostasis* (person) without an individual mode of existence.

Ani Ruined churches of Ani in eastern Turkey, near the Armenian border, once the capital of the Bagratids, reminders of the golden age of Armenian Church* architecture. The cathedral of Ani was built during 989–1001 by the Armenian architect Trdat.

anida In the East Syrian Rite, book used for conducting funerals.

Anima Christi (lit., soul of Christ) Eucharistic prayer beginning, "Soul of Christ, sanctify me, Body of Christ, save me," ascribed to Ignatius* of Loyola.

anjil In the Coptic Liturgy, Gospel sung by the senior cleric.

Annacondia, Carlos (1944–) Argentine evangelist. Converted in 1979, he founded the Church of the Salvation Message which became identified later with Pentecostalism*. Many of his crusades last from 20 to 60 days and are held in open fields.

annaphuro In the Jacobite Rite, large veil covering the paten* and the chalice*.

annates (Lat., *annus*, year) In the Middle Ages, the first year's revenues (or firstfruits) of an ecclesiastical benefice*, paid to the king or the pope, usually in the form of a tax on appointments to bishoprics* and monasteries.

Annexed Book Original manuscript of the *Book of Common Prayer**, which was annexed to the Act of Uniformity* in 1662.

annihilationism Doctrine that the souls of the wicked are not immortal but are destroyed at death or after the final judgment. It entails a denial of the immortality* of the soul. Thus, annihilationist, one who holds such a doctrine. See also CONDITIONAL IMMORTALITY.

Anno Domini (lit., in the year of our Lord*) Designation of any year after the birth of Jesus Christ according to the system devised by Dionysius Exiguus*. Usually A.D.

Annuit Coeptis (lit., He [God] has smiled on our undertaking) Motto on the reverse of the Great Seal of the United States.

annulment Declaration by a Roman Catholic tribunal that a marriage was not canonically valid. A marriage may be invalid for two reasons: because of a disqualifying or invalidating law or because of a consent that was in some ways defective. A disqualifying law is known as an impediment, and the church recognizes 12 impediments* to marriage. For example, being a first cousin is an impediment to marriage. An invalidating law renders the wedding ceremony invalid because it was not conducted properly by a priest. Lack of consent applies to marriages in which one of the parties is mentally impaired or where consent has been obtained under false pretenses.

Annunciation Announcement of the archangel* Gabriel to the Virgin Mary* that she will bear the Son of God. The Feast of the Annunciation is observed on March 25 or Lady's Day*. Also known as Annunciation of Our Lady or Annunciation of the Lord.

anointing 1. Ceremonial pouring of oil on a person to consecrate him or her to the Lord. 2. Infusion of a person with the Holy Spirit* to symbolize sanctity*. In the New Testament usage, anointing is part of the rites of baptism*, confirmation*, and ordination as well as the dedication of churches and altars. Anointing is also used as a means of Charismatic healing and combined with prayer in extreme unction*.

anointing of the sick Ceremonial application of consecrated oil on a sick person for the purpose of healing and restoration. The New Testament speaks of two types: the apostolic ministry of healing (Mark 6:13) and the presbyterial rite of anointing. Prayers for this purpose are found in the early liturgical sources of both Eastern and Western churches*, especially the *Apostolic Tradition* of Hippolytus*, the Prayer Book of Serapion, and the Gelasian* and Gregorian* sacramentaries. In the Eastern Church*, the rituals are based on the Euchologion*.

anoixis Ceremony opening a church after its consecration or its rededication.

Anomoeans (lit., dissimilar ones) Radical Arians of the fourth century who taught that Jesus Christ was a created being and was neither fully human nor fully divine. They also taught that Christ bore no resemblance to God, and was totally unlike him. They were also known as Aetians, Eunomians, and Exoucontians*. Anomoeanism was condemned in 381.

anomy That which cannot be explained in terms of natural laws; a miracle.

anonymoi In the Byzantine Rite*, saints who have no proper kontakion* for their office.

Anqasa Amiln (Ge'ez, Gate of Faith) Sixteenth-century theological discourse written by an Ethiopian monk named Enbaqom*, a Muslim convert.

Anselm of Laon (d. 1117) Theologian. He was influential as a teacher of liberal arts and theology at the cathedral school at Laon*. After his death, his lectures were collected and published in two textbooks, *Sententiae Divinae Paginae* and *Sententiae Anselmi*.

Anselm, St. (c. 1033–1109) Archbishop of Canterbury*. He entered monastic orders in 1059 and succeeded Lanfranc* as prior* in 1063 and on Lanfranc's death in 1089, was appointed archbishop of Canterbury in 1093. Anselm's tenure as archbishop of Canterbury was marked by conflicts with the crown and with York*. But Anselm was one of the most outstanding medieval thinkers, and his body of theological writings place him on the same rank as St. Thomas Aquinas* and St. Augustine*. As prior* of the monastic school at Normandy, he wrote *Monologion* and *Proslogion* (1078–79), followed by *De Veritate, De Libero Arbitrio, De Grammatico,* and *De Casu Diaboli.* He completed *De Incarnatione Verbi* in 1095 and his greatest work, *Cur Deus Homo,* a treatise on the Atonement*, in 1098. He defended the Double Procession* in *De Processione Sancti Spiritus.* In 1720 he was declared a doctor of the church*. Feast day: April 21.

Ansgarii Synod Swedish denomination that merged with the Mission Synod in 1885 to form the Swedish Evangelical Mission Covenant of America.

Anskar, St. (801–865) Also, Ansgar. "Apostle of the North." Missionary to Sweden and Denmark. A native of Picardy in France, he proselytized both Denmark and Sweden and built the first Christian church in Sweden. He became the first bishop of Hamburg and did much to mitigate the horrors of the slave trade. Feast day: February 3.

antechapel Part of the chapel on the western side of the choir screen* separating the choir from the congregation.

antecommunion The early part of a Communion service*, up to and including the Prayer for the

St. Anskar

Church Militant. It is similar to the Prayer of the Catechumens in the early church.

antelapsarianism See SUPRALAPSARIANISM.

Ante-Nicene Fathers Fathers of the Church* who lived before the Council of Nicaea*. A complete collection of their writings was issued by Jacques Migne* in Paris in 383 volumes (1844–1866). Its English translation was first published as the Ante-Nicene Christian Library in Edinburgh* (1857–1871).

antependium Ecclesiastical vesture or frontal* hanging in front of the altar.

Antependium

anterion In the Byzantine Church*, the outdoor dress of the clergy consisting of a long cassock* without buttons, open in the front, crossed over the chest, and secured at the neck with a hook. Monks wear black while secular clergy may use blue, grey, or green.

anthem Anglicized form of antiphon*. Sacred choral composition with words from Scriptures. Sometimes it refers to a canticle*, as in an Easter* anthem. Until the nineteenth century anthems were divided into full anthems, sung by the whole choir; and verse anthems, sung by one or more solo voices. Leading anthem composers were Christopher Tye (c. 1500–1572) and Thomas Tallis* (c. 1505–1585). Toward the latter part of the sixteenth century, a new form called verse anthem was created by William Byrd* (1543–1623), Thomas Morley (c. 1557–1602), Thomas Tomkins*

(c. 1572–1656), Thomas Weelkes (c. 1575–1623), and Orlando Gibbons* (1583–1625). Henry Purcell* created 63 anthems of which 50 were verse anthems. Anthems were introduced into America in the eighteenth century. Among the many American composers, Lowell Mason* and George F. Root were the most prominent. In the twentieth century Gordon Young and Jane Marshall have continued the tradition.

Anthemius of Trallus (sixth century) Greek builder of the Church of Hagia Sophia* in Constantinople*.

Anthim the Iberian (?–1716) Romanian churchman and scholar who promoted the use of Romanian in church services.

Anthing, Frederik Lodewijk (1818–1883) Dutch evangelist. After serving as vice president of the Supreme Court of the Dutch East Indies in Batavia, he began evangelizing by training and sending Christian workers throughout Java, using Javanese cultural means for spreading the gospel. He established the Depok Seminary, the first mission-run training school for Indonesian evangelists (1878–1926). In 1879 he was ordained apostle for the East Indies by the Restored Apostolic Mission Church.

Anthony of Padua, St. (1195–1231) Also, Antony. Franciscan monk, preacher, theologian, and saint, called "Hammer of the Heretics." Born Ferdinand, he changed his name to Anthony when he received the Franciscan habit* in the chapel at St. Antonio at Olivares, near Coimbra. In 1220 he sailed to Morocco but was forced to return because of illness and was sent to the hermitage of San Paolo* near Forli. His eloquence made him a popular preacher, and he was appointed lector* in theology to the Franciscan order. He taught at Bologna*, Montpelier, and Toulouse. After 1227 he devoted himself entirely to preaching. During his life and after his death, he was widely venerated as a worker of miracles, and he is now one of the most popular saints in the Catholic calendar. He is chiefly invoked for the return of lost property, and he is also the protector of the poor, the pregnant, and the travelers. In art he is usually represented with a book or lily* or holding the Holy Child. The huge basilica* of Sant'Antonio in Padua, known as Il Santo, was built about 1350, modeled on St. Mark's, Venice*, with a central dome and six smaller domes and nine radiating chapels. Feast day: June 13.

Anthony, St. (c. 251–356) Also, Anthony the Great; Antony. Egyptian hermit and father of monasticism*. At the age of 17 Anthony gave up all his possessions and became a hermit, retiring at the age of 34 to the Outer Mountain at Pispir, a desolate desert, where he is reputed to have fought with demons who appeared in the guise of wild beasts. His holiness* attracted a number of disciples, and he came out of his retirement for a few years to organize them into a community of hermits. In 310 he retired again to the Inner Mountain, now called Der Mar Antonios, near the Red Sea. He was closely associated with the Orthodox party under Athanasius* in the Arian controversies. His utterances are found in the Sayings of the Fathers. Knowledge of his life depends largely on the biography written soon after this death by Athanasius and translated twice into Latin by 379. His life was that of the ideal anchorite*, one of severe—almost superhuman—austerity, incessant prayer, supernatural healings, and perpetual warfare with demons. Feast day: January 17.

St. Anthony of Padua

St. Anthony the Great

anthropology, theological Also, the doctrine of man. Study of human beings in relation to God in the context of theology. Since God is not fully knowable except in his dealings with human beings, theological anthropology is concerned with the existential or human response to divine acts and purposes.

Antibaptists Group who, like the Quakers*, oppose water baptism*, holding that it has been replaced by spirit baptism.

Antiburghers In Scottish church history, opponents of the Burghers* who seceded from the Church of Scotland* and refused to take an oath* called the Burgess Oath which certified that church as the true religion.

anti-Catholicism Prejudice toward Catholicism* and its doctrines. Anti-Catholicism is closely related to the rise of rationalism and Deism* and is often a cloak for prejudice against Christianity as a whole. In history, anti-Catholicism has manifested itself in many forms: as legislation against the church, such as the prohibition against wearing of clerical garb in Mexico in 1929 and the expulsion of religious orders, as the Jesuits*, from Spain in 1767 and from Portugal in 1759. Sometimes it stemmed from nationalism as in post-Reformation England and nineteenth-century United States. More anti-Catholicism has developed among leftists and feminists in opposition to the positions advocated by the church on issues like abortion and homosexuality.

Antichrist 1. Person who will appear in the last days* in fulfillment of apocalyptic prophecies to destroy the church and slaughter the saints of God. 2. Spirit of opposition to Christ as expressed in persecution of Christians or restrictions on the free expression of Christian faith.

anti-Christian Hostile to the Christian faith or working to undermine it.

anticlericalism Opposition to Catholic and clerical influence in politics and society. It was generally strong throughout Europe and Latin America during the nineteenth and early twentieth centuries, fueled by the apparent identification of the church with reactionary regimes and rich social elites. Its manifestations include the French Revolutionary excesses of 1793–1799, the 1830 revolution in France and Belgium, the liberal coups in Portugal (1834) and Spain (1836), the Paris Commune of 1871, the Spanish Republic of 1873, the radical and republican regimes in France in 1879 and 1902, the liberal regime of Belgium in 1879, and the Liberal regime in Spain in 1885. Anticlericalism rose to rabid levels during the Mexican Revolution of 1910 and Portuguese Revolution of 1910. In almost all countries where there was a drive toward national unification, there was a strong anticlerical faction. This was the case during the German Kulturkampf* of 1872–1887 and the Italian Risorgimento.

anticreedalism Opposition to any creed as a rule of faith*, shared by many Protestant churches, as Friends, Baptists, Seventh-Day Adventists, and the Salvation Army*.

antidoron (Gk., instead of the gift) In the Greek Church, the bread distributed after the Mass*. It is cut from the prosphora* left after the prothesis* and offered after the apolysis*. See also PAIN BENIT.

antilegomena (Gk., disputed things) New Testament books not considered as canonical or genuine. Eusebius* divided them into two classes: those generally recognized, such as Jude and 2 Peter, and those considered spurious, including the Acts of St. Paul*, *The Shepherd*, Apocalypse of St. Peter*, the Epistle of Barnabas*, and Didache*. Distinguished from homologoumena*, or books universally accepted as genuine.

antimension/antiminsion (Gk., instead of a table) In the Greek Church, portable altar consisting of a cloth, about 18 inches square, containing relics* and usually decorated with representations of the Passion. It was originally used when there was no consecrated altar.

antimissionism Protestant movement in the nineteenth century, particularly between 1820 and 1840, hostile to the formation of national mission societies. It was particularly strong among certain Baptist groups, such as the Primitive Baptists*. The opposition stemmed from a fear that national organizations might militate against the identity of smaller denominations and impose a homogeneous rule of faith*.

antinomianism (Gk., against the law) Rejection of the authority of the Mosaic Law on the grounds that it has been superseded by Christian grace and freedom, based partially on Romans 3:8. Some Gnostic sects, such as the Carpocratians, interpreted this freedom as a license to sin because only the spirit, and not the body, mattered. During the Reformation*, antinomianism was revived by the Anabaptists and Agricola as an extension of the Lutheran doctrine of justification* solely by grace. This was a major issue in Puritan New England regarding Anne Hutchinson* and John Cotton*.

Antinomistic Controversy Dispute between Luther* and Agricola and others on the degree to which Christians are subject to the Mosaic Law.

Antioch 1. City in Pisidia with a large Jewish population, visited by St. Paul* (Acts 13:14; 14:21). 2. City formerly in Syria, about 300 miles north of Jerusalem*, on the Orontes River, an important center of commerce in Roman times. It was founded by Seleucus about 300 B.C. and was the capital of Syria until 300 A.D. Called the "Crown of the East," it vied with Rome* and Alexandria* as a city of great splendor and influence. It was here that the term *Christians* was first applied to the followers of Jesus Christ (Acts 11:26). According to tradition, St. Peter* and St. Ignatius were among its bishops. In 387 it was the scene of a serious riot. The Dedication Council, also known as the Council of Antioch, was held here in 341 on the occasion of the consecration of Constantine's Golden Church. By the fourth century it ranked as one of the patriarchates of the Christian world and until the fourteenth century was the residence of the Latin patriarch. It passed to the Turks in 1516. Now called Antakya, it is a minor town in Turkey.

Antioch, Canons of Twenty five disciplinary canons formulated by the Council of Antioch in 340.

Antioch Chalice See CHALICE, ANTIOCH.

Antioch, Synod of Any one of several synods held in Antioch, Syria, during the early centuries of the church. The first three condemned the heresies of Paul of Samosata*. Two synods in 341 deposed Athanasius* the Great and attempted to replace the Nicene Creed* with Arian confessions. The Dedication Council of 341 was held on the occasion of the consecration of Constantine's Golden Church. It was attended by 97 bishops besides Emperor Constantius.

Antiochene Rite Rite associated with or followed by the Patriarchate of Antioch during the first six centuries.

Antiochene Theology/Antiochene School System of theology associated with the Church Fathers* of Antioch, especially as distinguished from Alexandrian theology. Broadly, it opposed the allegorical interpretations of the Alexandrian School* and emphasized historical exegesis*. Emphasis was laid on the humanity of Christ and the free moral agency in man. Its Christology* was expressed in looser terms than in Alexandrian theology. Its most famous exponents were Diodorus of Tarsus, Theodore of Mopseustia*, John Chrysostom*, Nestorius*, and Theodoret* of Cyrrhus.

Antiochus 1. (?–408) Bishop of Ptolemais in Palestine, noted for his eloquent preaching. 2. (sixth to seventh century) Monk at St. Saba near Jerusalem*, at the time of the capture of Jerusalem* by the Persians in 614.

antipashka In the Byzantine Church*, the second Sunday of the Paschal* Feast, commonly called St. Thomas's Sunday.

antiphon (Gk., *antiphonos,* responsive) 1. Literally, something sung alternatively by two choirs. Short phrase sung before and after a psalm or canticle* in the Divine Office*. 2. In the Eastern Church*, three anthems sung antiphonally in the early part of the eucharistic liturgy. 3. Psalm or anthem sung by alternating choirs. 4. Four anthems of Our Lady sung, according to the season, at the close of compline*. There are also antiphons at vespers* and matins*. Thus antiphony, the mode for singing antiphons.

antiphonary/antiphonal Also, chorale or office book. Liturgical book in the Western Church* containing the choir office* sung by the choir antiphonally.

antipope Claimant to the office of the supreme pontiff* of the Catholic Church in opposition to the person already holding the office and whose claim is not acknowledged officially or is invalid. There have been 35 antipopes in church history. See also POPE.

Antiremonstrants Dutch Calvinists of the early seventeenth century opposed to the Arminians.

anti-Romanism Opposition to the doctrines or influence of the Roman Catholic Church.

antisabbatarian 1. One who rejects the observance of the Jewish Sabbath. 2. One who opposes blue laws prohibiting various activities on Sundays.

antitrinitarianism Opposition to the orthodox Christian doctrine of or belief in the Holy Trinity* as the Godhead, especially as an element of a heresy. Antitrinitarianism was based partly on the fear that it involved the abandonment of monotheism*. In early church history, anti-Trinitarians included Ebionites*, Gnostics, Monarchists, Modalists, and Arians who subordinated

Jesus Christ to a less than coequal role in the Godhead. In the early modern period, Unitarianism*, Socinianism*, and other heresies promoted more radical forms of antitrinitarianism.

antitype Person in the Scripture who prefigures or symbolizes another. Many Old Testament objects, rites, and personalities are considered types of Christ or New Testament events, these being antitypes of realities.

Antoine, Pere (1748–1829) Spanish Capuchin priest who was empowered to begin the Inquisition* in the United States, although he never did so.

Antonella da Messina (c. 1430–1479) Italian painter who was noted for his paintings of Jesus, Madonna*, Jerome, and others.

Antonians Any of the orders claiming special dedication to St. Anthony the Great*, such as the Disciples of St. Anthony; the Hospitalers of St. Anthony;the Antonians, founded by Abram Poresigh; the Congregation of St. Anthony; and the Chaldean and Armenian Antonians.

Antoninus, St. (1389–1459) Italian Dominican theologian and archbishop of Florence*. He joined the Dominican Order in 1404–1405 and rose quickly to prominence. He was prior* successively in Cortona, Fiesole, Naples, Rome*, and Florence*, vicar general* in Tuscany, and prior of the former Dominican monastery of San Marco* in Florence. In 1446 he was made archbishop of Florence by Pope Eugenius IV*. He did pioneer work in theology and was the author of *Summa Theologica Moralis,* several treatises on Christian life, and a general history of the world. He helped his people during several disasters, plagues, and earthquakes.

anxious seat Penitents' bench in American revivalist meetings. It was introduced by Charles Finney* in his meetings.

apatheia (Gk., apathy; passionlessness or impassibility) In the ascetical theology* of the Eastern Church*, dispassion or extinction of lust or sin and the control of evil passions, leading to serenity.

Apellites Sect founded by Apelles, a disciple of Marcion*, in the second century. He was closely associated with a female visionary, Philumene, whose visions he recorded. He rejected the Old Testament more strongly than Marcion and maintained that all that was necessary for salvation was Jesus crucified.

Aphraates (fourth century) Also, Aphrahat. First Church Father* of the early Christian church in Syria. A monk who was probably a bishop, he wrote extensively and composed 23 treatises known as *Demonstrations,* the first 10 of which were completed in 337, the next 12 in 344, and the last one in 345. His writings exalt asceticism* and celibacy and also throw light on early Christianity in Persia under the Sassanid king, Shapur II (310–379). Later writers have called him the "Sage of Persia."

Aphthartodocetae (Gk., *aphthartos,* imperishable) Monophysite sect of the first half of the sixth century founded by Julian of Halicarnassus* which regarded Christ's body as impassible, immortal, and imperishable from the moment of conception. Condemned as heresy because it was incompatible with belief in Christ's true humanity.

Apocalypse (Gk., revelation or unveiling) 1. The Book of Revelation, the last book of the New Testament, attributed to St. John the Apostle. 2. Any of various apocryphal books, such as the Apocalypse of St. Peter*. 3. Vision that reveals things normally hidden and unveils the future or deals with the end of the present world order and the coming of a heavenly kingdom.

Apocalypse of St. Peter The most important of the noncanonical apocalypses, written in the second century, and similar to 2 Peter.

apocalyptic literature Prophetic writings, such as Daniel and the Book of Revelation, dealing with future events, the destruction of evil, messianic expectations, and the fulfillment of biblical prophecies. Among the surviving post-New Testament apocalyptic works are the Apocalypse of Peter*; Apocalypse of James*; Apocalypse of Paul*; Apocalypse of Thomas*; Apocalypse of

Stephen; and Apocalypse of Mary, Bartholomew*, Daniel, and Zechariah.

apocalypticism Preoccupation with end times, the Antichrist*, and with the interpretation of the Book of Revelation. It includes the identification of the Antichrist with an evil ruler and the relation of contemporary events to biblical prophecy. In recent years, popular writers such as Hal Lindsey*, Mary Stewart Rolfe, and Constance Cumbley have made apocalypticism a subject of intense interest in some Christian circles, especially in America.

apocatastasis (Gk., reestablishment or return to a former place or condition) 1. Theological heresy that all free moral agents, including human beings, devils, and angels, will eventually achieve salvation. Propounded by Origen*, Clement of Alexandria*, and St. Gregory of Nyssa*, it was formally condemned by the Council of Chalcedon* in 543 in the first anathema against Origenism. In modern times, the doctrine has found favor in the theology of certain Moravians, Anabaptists, and Christadelphians* and among certain theologians such as F. D. E. Schleiermacher*. Also known as Universalism*, it is a creed of the Unitarian-Universalist Association. 2. In hellenistic philosophy, the restoration of the constellations at the end of a cosmic cycle.

apocrisarios Ecclesiastical official of high rank, especially envoys used by the patriarchates to other patriarchiates or, formerly, senior chaplains* of the Frankish courts.

Apocrypha (Gk., hidden things) Biblical books that are part of the Greek version of the Old Testament, but are excluded from the canonical books. They have an ambiguous status in modern translations. The Septuagint incorporates all of them (with the exception of 2 Esdras), and they are not differentiated in any way from the other books of the Old Testament. The Vulgate* retains them, but they are excluded from almost all non-Roman modern versions and in others form a separate section where they are accorded less validity. They comprise 1 and 2 Esdras, Tobit, Judith, the Rest of Esther, the Wisdom of Solomon, Ecclesiasticus*, Baruch with the Epistle of Jeremiah, the Song of the Three Holy Children, the History of Susanna, the Bel and the Dragon, the Prayer of Manasses, and 1 and 2 Maccabees.

Although no book of the Apocrypha is quoted in the New Testament, the early Church Fathers*, including Clement of Rome*, Clement of Alexandria*, and Origen* cite them frequently. Christians made considerable use of them for apologetic purposes, because some of the texts referred to the Incarnation, Logos*, and the Son of God. But the Reformation* leaders were instrumental in completely rejecting them, and they refused to ascribe to them the status of inspired Word of God*. Luther*, nevertheless, included the apocryphal books (except 1 and 2 Esdras) as an appendix to his translation of the Bible as "useful and good to be read," while the Geneva* translators acknowledged their value for "knowledge of history and instruction of godly manners."

However, Puritan opposition to the Apocrypha combined with the decision of the British and Foreign Bible Society* to omit them from its printed Bibles led to their being finally relegated in the Protestant world to writings outside the place of Scripture. Roman Catholics continue to uphold the validity of the Apocrypha in their translations. The Council of Trent* and the First Vatican Council* confirmed the full canonicity* of the Apocrypha (with the exception of 1 and 2 Esdras and the Prayer of Manasses). See also PSEUDEPIGRAPHA.

Apocryphal New Testament Christian writings outside the canon of the New Testament, but claiming in different ways to be by apostolic authors or about them or otherwise contemporary with the beginnings of the church. They include among others: Gospel of St. Thomas*, Gospel of the Ebionites, Gospel of Philip*, Infancy Gospel of St. Thomas*, Gospel of Peter*, Gospel of Nicodemus*, Dialogue of the Redeemer*, Apocryphon of John*, Testament of Our Lord in Galilee, Protevangelium or Book of James, History of Joseph the Carpenter, Acts of Peter*, Acts of Paul*, Acts of John*, Acts of Andrew*, Acts of Thomas*, Epistle of Barnabas*, and Epistle to the Laodiceans. Some of these apocryphal writings are heretical.

apodeipnon (Gk., after supper) In the Eastern Church*, the late evening liturgical service, similar to the compline* in the Western Church*. The smaller form is normal, and the longer one, called "great," is used on weekdays in Lent*.

apodosis (Gk., return or giving back) Byzantine Rite* liturgical closure or concluding day of festive periods.

apokoukoulismos In the Byzantine tradition, ceremony when a monk of the highest degree, the megaloschemos*, lays aside his monastic cowl* after wearing it for eight days.

apokreos In the Byzantine Church*, week preceding a period of abstinence.

Apollinarianism Theological doctrine developed by Apollinaris* of Laodicea* which held that Christ's human nature was so completely eclipsed by the divine Logos* that he was not completely human. It was a forerunner of Monophysitism*.

Apollinaris of Laodicea (c. 315–390) Also known as Apollinaris the Younger, and Apollonarius. He collaborated with his father, Apollinaris the Elder, a grammarian, in paraphrasing the Bible along Greek classical lines when Emperor Julian* forbade Christians from reading pagan classics. A vigorous defender of orthodoxy* and a friend of Athanasius*, he became bishop of Laodicea* in Syria. His Christology*, later called Apollinarianism*, emphasized the divinity of Christ at the expense of his humanity and was condemned by synods of Rome (374–380) and by the First Council of Constantinople* in 381. Apollinaris seceded from the church in about 375 and was excluded from public worship from 381.

Apollos Alexandrian Jew who became a Christian teacher and preached the gospel at Ephesus* and Corinth* and who is cited by St. Paul* (Acts 18–19; 1 Cor. 1:10–12; 3:4–6, 16–22). He was trained in Ephesus by Priscilla* and Aquila*. Martin Luther* argued that he was the author of the Epistle to the Hebrews.

apologetics (Gk., *apologetikos*, suitable for defense) Systematic and logical defense of Christianity against its detractors and unbelievers backed up by evidence of its credibility. Sometimes it is replaced with more contemporary terms, such as "missionary theology or eristics*" or "fundamental theology" and sometimes it is treated as a branch of systematic theology*. It addresses unbelievers rather than believers, and it argues primarily from reason rather than revelation. St. Peter* on the day of the Pentecost* and St. Paul* in Athens* provide the classic examples of apologetics. St. Peter calls on every Christian to be ready to give a reason (apologia) for the hope that is in him (1 Pet. 3:15). The earliest apology is *Apologia* by Quadratus* addressed to Emperor Hadrian around 130. Justin Martyr* left two apologiae. St. Augustine* in his *City of God* defended Christianity against pagan allegations that it was responsible for the fall of Rome* and St. Thomas Aquinas* in *Summa Contra Gentiles* defined apologetics as making known the truth that the Catholic faith professes and setting aside the errors that are opposed to it. Contemporary apologists like C. S. Lewis*, Emil Brunner*, Wolfhart Pannenberg*, Charles Hodge*, Francis Schaeffer*, Josh McDowell, and Paul Little have had a great impact on the resurgence of conservative Christian theism* in the West.

There are three principal types of apologetics. The first is apologetics as a defense of religion and the concept of God directed toward atheists and agnostics; the second is apologetics as a defense of Christianity against non-Christian religions, and the third is apologetics as a defense of a Christian denomination or sect, such as Roman Catholicism*, against other denominations and sects. Distinguished from polemics* which seeks to defend Christianity against internal dissent and protreptics which invites readers to lead a good and moral life.

Apologia pro Vita Sua (Lat., Defense of [My] Life) Autobiography of John Henry Cardinal Newman*, published in 1864. It also contains a history of the Oxford movement* which sought to restore Anglo-Catholicism* to a dominant role in the Anglican Church.

apologist Person who engages in apologetics. Applied especially in the early church to a class of writers who defended the faith against pagans and Jews. The outstanding apologists in the early and medieval church were St. Augustine*, Justin Martyr*, Tatian*, Athenagoras*, Theophilus*, Minucius Felix*, Tertullian*, Origen*, Eusebius*, Athanasius*, and St. Thomas Aquinas*.

apologue Short story or fable with a moral, favored by Luther* as an aid to virtue.

Apology of the True Christian Divinity Declaration of Quaker* beliefs written by Robert Barclay* (1678). Written in scholastic style, it consists of 15 propositions among which were inner revelation as a source of faith, justification*, perfection*, perseverance*, and spiritual worship.

apolousis In the Byzantine Church*, custom of leaving those parts of an infant that were anointed with chrism* at baptism* unwashed for eight days. At the end of the period the child is taken once again to the church where a priest washes the chrismated parts with a sponge while reciting a prayer after which the priest cuts the hair in the form of a cross.

apolysis (Gk., dismissal) Concluding benediction in the Eastern Church* liturgy.

apolytikion In the Eastern Church*, the principal troparion* or religious stanza of the day sung at the end of the vespers* in honor of the saint or feast day according to the calendar. It is repeated in the orthros*, the liturgy, and other offices.

apophatic theology Also, apophasis. Negative theology* that begins by denying that human categories are capable of conceptualizing God. It affirms that God is essentially ineffable and unknowable and that he cannot be an object of knowledge at all. The term was first used by Dionysius the Areopagite*, who distinguished it from cataphatic* or affirmative theology or symbolic theology.

apophthegm Narrative woven around a particular saying of Christ in order to drive its teaching home. Also called paradigm.

Apophthegmata Patrum Anthology of the sayings of the Egyptian monks, also known as Sayings of the Desert Fathers*, dating from the fourth century. They are arranged alphabetically by speaker and thematically by subject. A large segment of these collections is ascribed to Poemen.

apostasy (Gk., *apostasia*, falling away) Total renunciation of the Christian faith by a baptized person or a desertion by a professed religious who had taken perpetual vows.

apostate One who is guilty of apostasy*.

aposticha In the Byzantine Church*, series of hymns and alternating Psalm verses sung toward the end of the hesperinos* and daily orthros*.

apostil Explanatory note on a text of Scripture or a commentary on a Scripture lesson.

apostle (Gk., one who is sent) 1. One of the 12 disciples chosen by Christ: Peter*, James, John, Andrew, Thomas*, James the Less*, Jude*, Philip*, Bartholomew*, Matthew, Simon, and Judas (replaced by Matthias*). Paul* claimed the title for himself on the basis of a direct commission from the risen Christ (Rom. 1:1; Gal. 1:1) and used it also of James, the Lord's brother (Gal. 1:19).

2. The highest of the five ecclesiastical offices or titles in the New Testament, the other four being prophet*, teacher, evangelist, and pastor.

3. The leader of a first Christian mission to a country, such as: Patrick*, the apostle of Ireland; Cyril and Methodius*, the apostles of the Slavs; Frumentius*, apostle of Abyssinians; Felix Naif, apostle of the Alps; Juan de Avila*, apostle of Andalusia; Hubert*, apostle of Ardennes; Gregory the Illuminator*, apostle of Armenia; Jose de An-

chieta*, apostle of Brazil; Augustine*, apostle of England; Denis, apostle of France; Willibrord*, apostle of Frisians; Martin of Tours*, apostle of Gaul; Paul*, apostle to the Gentiles; Boniface*,

Traditional Missions of the First Apostles

apostle of Germany; Columba*, apostle of Scotland; King Stephen, apostle of Hungary; John Eliot*, apostle to the Native Americans; Francis Xavier*, apostle to the Indies; Ansgar, apostle to the North; Alonso de Barcena, apostle of Peru; Ninian*, apostle to the Picts; James the Great, apostle of Spain; and David, apostle of Wales.

Apostle of England Epithet of St. Augustine* of Canterbury*.

Apostle of Rome Epithet of St. Philip Neri*.

Apostle of the Gentiles Epithet of the apostle Paul*.

apostle spoon Silver spoon having the figure of an apostle at the top of the handle, formerly given at christenings.

The Apostles' Creed

I believe in God, the Father Almighty, creator of Heaven and Earth
And in Jesus Christ, His only Son, our Lord
who was conceived of the Holy Spirit, born of the Virgin Mary
suffered under Pontius Pilate
was crucified, died, and was buried.
He descended into Hell;
On the third day He rose again from the dead.
He ascended into Heaven, sits on the right hand of God, the Father Almighty;
From thence He shall come to judge the living and the dead.
I believe in the Holy Spirit, the Holy Catholic Church, the Communion of Saints,
the forgiveness of sins, the resurrection of the body, and life everlasting. Amen.

Apostles' Creed One of the shortest confessions* of the Christian faith, an elaboration of the Old Roman Creed*, used widely in Western churches at baptism* and at matins* and evensong*, except for 13 days in a year when the Athanasian Creed* is recited in its place. It has three sections dealing with God, Jesus Christ, and the Holy Spirit*, and includes such distinctive phrases as "descent into hell*" and "communion of saints." Despite its name, it does not have an apostolic origin but dates from the eighth century, although portions of it date from the third and fourth centuries.

Apostles, Doctrine of the Twelve See DIDACHE.

Apostles, Epistle of the See TESTAMENT OF OUR LORD IN GALILEE.

apostles, symbols of In Christian art, symbols assigned to each of the apostles: Andrew: X-shaped cross because was crucified on one; Bartholomew*: knife because he was flayed alive with one; James the Great: scallop shell, pilgrim staff, or a gourd bottle because he is the patron saint* of pilgrims; James the Less: fuller's pole because he was killed with one; John: cup with a winged serpent because he drank poison after making a sign of the cross; Judas Iscariot: bag because he kept money in it; Jude*: club because he was martyred with it; Matthew: hatchet or halberd because he was killed with it; Matthias: battleaxe because he was beheaded with it; Paul*: sword because he was beheaded with one; Peter*: bunch of keys because Christ gave him the keys of the kingdom*; Simon: a saw because he was sawn to death; Phillip: long staff surmounted with a cross because he suffered death by being suspended by the neck from a pillar; and Thomas*: lance* with which he was pierced through at Mylapore, India.

Apostleship of Prayer Roman Catholic pious association initiated by the Jesuit Order with special devotion to the Sacred Heart of Jesus*, founded in Vals, France, in 1844 by F. X. Gautrelet.

apostolate 1. Office or mission of an apostle. 2. Participation of the Christian faithful in the sav-ing mission of Christ through different roles and functions.

Apostolic Age The first century of Christian history, corresponding to the lifetime of the 12 apostles. The Apostolic Age is regarded as the model for Christian activity and church growth.

Apostolic blessing Papal blessing* pronounced at the end of a Mass* or on other occasions.

apostolic canons A series of 85 canons attributed to the apostles, forming the last chapter of the Apostolic Constitutions*. Most of the canons deal with ordinations and the official and moral conduct of the clergy. About 20 of the canons are drawn from the Canons of Antioch*.

Apostolic Christian Church An association of Holiness churches* in United States, Germany, and Switzerland. It originated from a movement started by S. H. Froehlich in 1832. Its ministers and pastors are unpaid and are gainfully occupied in other professions.

apostolic Christianity Christianity as practiced in the Apostolic Age*.

Apostolic church 1. Church of the Apostolic Age*. 2. Any of different Apostolic churches that have introduced the office of apostle. The most prominent among them are the Catholic Apostolic Church*, founded by Edward Irving* (1792–1834); and the New Apostolic Church*, founded by Heinrich Geyer (1818–1896), which is led by 230 apostles, who are in turn led by the chief apostle. Only apostles can administer the sacraments. The church expects the imminent return of Jesus Christ and the first resurrection*.

Apostolic Church Order Egyptian Christian document dating to about 300 and containing regulations on ecclesiastical practice and moral discipline. It is purported to have been drafted by the apostles themselves. See also APOSTOLIC TRADITION.

apostolic college Transmission of the authority of Jesus Christ through Peter* as the rock* and as the first pope and through subsequent popes as his legitimate successors.

apostolic constitution Solemn papal document, legal in content, dealing with matters of faith, doctrine, and discipline that apply to the universal church.

Apostolic Constitutions Fourth-century collection of rules governing Christian life, faith, and worship for both laymen and clergy. Possibly of Syrian origin, it is arranged in 8 books and concludes with the 85 apostolic canons*. Its full title is "Ordinances of the Holy Apostles through Clement." The Trullan Synod* believed it to be work of an Arian.

Apostolic Council First council of the Christian church described in Acts 15. It made the important decision that Gentiles may be admitted to the church on the basis of faith, without keeping all the Jewish dietary laws and other regulations.

apostolic decree Decision of the Apostolic Council* granting Gentiles liberty from most of the Mosaic rituals and restrictions.

apostolic delegate 1. Representative of the pope in a country without diplomatic ties to the Vatican*. 2. An official papal representative to the local church.

Apostolic Episcopal Church Autonomous American Catholic denomination that claims apostolic succession* through Chaldean orders.

Apostolic Exhortation Papal document or letter published from the Vatican*, hortative and pastoral in purpose, rather than dogmatic or legal. Occasionally issued by popes since 1917.

Apostolic Faith Mission U.S. denomination emphasizing holiness, faith healing*, speaking in tongues*, and foot-washing*. It grew out of the work of a lay Methodist preacher, Charles F. Parham*, who taught divine healing* as well as Spirit-baptism that sealed Christ's bride for the rapture*. In 1900 he opened Bethel Bible School in Topeka, Kansas, with some 40 pupils whom he taught to speak in tongues* as evidence of Spirit-baptism. One of Parham's proteges, William Seymour*, a one-eyed black, carried the message to Los Angeles, where the Pentecostal movement was born at Azusa Street. Another worker, Florence Louise Crawford, carried the message to Portland, Oregon, in 1907.

Apostolic Fathers Title applied since the seventeenth century to those Fathers of the Church* immediately succeeding the New Testament period whose works are extant either in part or in whole. They are Clement of Rome*, Ignatius, Hermas*, Polycarp*, Papias*, and authors of the Epistle to Barnabas* and Epistle to Diognetus*, 2 Clement, and the Didache*. Sometimes fragments of the Quadratus of Papias* of Hierapolis are also included.

Apostolic Letter 1. Any of the New Testament letters of Paul*, Peter, John, and others. 2. A papal letter from the Vatican*.

Apostolic Majesty Also, Apostolic King. Title conferred on Stephen*, the first Christian king of Hungary, in 1001 and held by all his successors until the twentieth century.

apostolic nuncio Permanent ambassador from the pope to a foreign government.

Apostolic See 1. The see* of Rome* headed by the pope, with reference to its founding by St. Peter*. 2. A church founded by one of the apostles, such as the church at Jerusalem* or Ephesus*.

apostolic succession Doctrine of an unbroken transmission of the Holy Spirit* conveyed by properly ordained bishops through the laying on of hands* going back to the first apostles and to Christ himself. The continuity of the succession is considered a sign of the validity of all ordinations and is taught in the Roman Catholic, Orthodox, and Episcopal churches.

Apostolic Tradition Document known as the Egyptian Church Order believed to be the work of St. Hippolytus*. It contains a detailed account of the rites, including baptism*, ordination, and eucharistic prayer, as practiced by the Christian church of the third century or earlier.

apostolic tradition 1. Reception and transmission of the gospel by the apostles and the practices and rites through which the gospel is received and transmitted. 2. The faith that has been entrusted (1 Tim. 6:20; 2 Tim. 3:16–4:16) to the apostles and to the church as a whole which is guarded and kept pure and unsullied.

Apostolici Also, Apostolic Brethren. 1. Medieval heretic groups who practiced vegetarianism, and celibate cohabitation and rejected oaths, the veneration* of saints, prayers for the dead, and infant baptism*. 2. Lay Evangelical movement begun at Parma about 1260 by Gerard Segerelli* as a return to the apostolic life of poverty, penance*, and preaching. Members adopted a distinctive garb, but took no vows and followed no rule, being bound together by what Segerelli called interior obedience. Men and women lived together as companions. Later under Fra Dolcino in 1300 it espoused a form of millenarianism. The movement was extirpated in a crusade summoned by Nicholas V* in 1305. Segerelli was burned at the stake and Dolcino was captured and executed. 3. Manicheaen heretic group in twelfth-century Europe.

apostolicity 1. One of the four marks of the church set forth in the Nicene Creed*, the others being one, holy, and catholic. 2. Nature of ecclesiastical office or doctrine transmitted through the apostles and fidelity to such office or doctrine. It expresses the continuity of the church as it has evolved from apostolic times.

apostolicum Continental term for the Apostles' Creed*.

Apostolius, Michael (fifteenth century) Greek theologian who copied manuscripts and helped preserve early Christian literature.

Apostolos In the Eastern Orthodox Church*, book containing lessons from the Acts of the Apostles and the Epistles together with the Prokeimena or graduals, sung before the Epistle at the liturgy.

Apostool, Samuel (1638–c. 1695) Mennonite preacher who taught the importance of right doctrine in contrast to the emphasis on practical living made by Hans Galenus. Apostool's followers were called Apostoolians.

Apotactici/Apotactites Variant term for Apostolici*.

Apotome (Gk., cutting off) Commemoration* of the beheading of John the Baptist.

apparel Embroidery on an alb* or amice*.

Apparition of the Virgin Appearance of the Virgin Mary*.

apparitor/apparator Ecclesiastical official who summoned people to appear before a church court and executed church decrees. Also called summoners.

appellant Priest who appeals from an ecclesiastical decision or a papal bull*.

Apphia Christian woman from Colossae* (Philem. 2) who, according to tradition, was martyred with Philemon in the first century.

Appian Way Roman high road from Rome* to Capua along which the apostle Paul* is reputed to have walked (Acts 28:15). Many catacombs and tombs flank the highway. It was built by the Censor Appius (hence the name) Claudius Caecus in 312 B.C. The Appii Forum or Market and the Three Taverns where Paul met some believers is on the Appian Way about 40 miles east of Rome*. Among the Christian landmarks near the highway are the Domine Quo Vadis Chapel, the catacombs of St. Callistus* and of Praetextatus, and the basilica* of St. Sebastian*.

appropriation 1. Acceptance of the offer of salvation by Jesus Christ. 2. In ecclesiastical law*, annexation of a benefice*, as in the assignment of parish funds to a monastery. 3. Designating to one person of the Trinity* an attribute that belongs to the whole Godhead.

approved supply pastor In the Methodist Church, a ministerial candidate* who fills a pulpit in a church on a temporary basis.

apron Short cassock* extending to the knees used in the Church of England*.

apse Semicircular or polygonal end of a sanctuary or chancel* covered by a half dome, found in the basilican type of church architecture. The altar was in the chord of the apse, with the seats for the clergy in the curved space behind.

apsidiole Small chapel grafted on to the apse, east of the transept.

aquamanile Basin to hold the water proffered by the subdeacon for the priest's ablutions during the Mass*.

Aquarians 1. Third-century sect that refused wine and used only water in the Eucharist*. 2. A fifth-century group that abstained from alcohol entirely.

Aquaviva, Claudio (1534–1615) Italian Jesuit, the fifth general* of the order, elected in 1581. During his tenure, membership increased from 5,000 to 13,000. He established the famous Jesuit system of education through the "Ratio Studiorum"* outlining teaching procedures and his guidelines or directory for the use of *Spiritual Exercises**. The Jesuits* encountered considerable external and internal difficulties during this period, including expulsions from France and Venice*, persecutions in England and Japan, and theological controversies involving free will* and the temporal power of the pope.

Aquila Jewish Christian who, with his wife Priscilla*, was a companion of the apostle Paul* (Acts 18:2–3; Rom. 16:3–4).

Aquileia Village on the Adriatic coast, now in Croatia, once an important Roman city and the seat of a Western patriarchate. An anti-Arian synod* was held here in 381 presided over by St. Ambrose*.

Aquinas, Thomas See THOMAS AQUINAS, ST.

Ara Coeli (Lat., Altar of Heaven) Sta Maria in Aracoeliis, a church on the Capitoline Hill in Rome*.

arabonismos Byzantine betrothal service in which rings are exchanged, sometimes combined with the wedding service.

aradchenord In the Armenian Church*, a vartabed* or prelate* who exercises episcopal jurisdiction but who is not in episcopal orders.

Aramaic The language of Aramaeans which became the lingua franca of Palestine at the time of Christ. Jesus and his disciples are recorded as having spoken in Aramaic. Parts of Daniel are in Aramaic. Because common folk did not know Hebrew in this period, the Scriptures were issued in the form of Aramaic paraphrases, known as Targums. Syriac* and Mandaic are both dialects of Aramaic.

araray One of the three modes of chanting in the Ethiopian Church. On major religious feasts, it is chanted by a church choir led by a dabtara*.

Arason, Jon (1484–1551) Poet and bishop of Iceland who brought printing to the island.

Arator (sixth century) Christian Latin poet, born in Liguria. He left imperial service to join the ministry in Rome*, where he enjoyed the friendship of Pope Vigilius*. He completed his major work, *De Actibus Apostolarum*, a hexametrical version of the Book of Acts which was a symbolic interpretation and exegesis* of the biblical narrative. It was widely studied until the twelfth century.

aratshavoratz In the Armenian Church*, week following the tenth Sunday before Easter*.

Arbousset, Jean Thomas (1810–1877) French Protestant pioneer missionary in Lesotho and Tahitian church leader. He preceded Livingstone* in combining mission with exploration and set up a home missionary society in Lesotho in 1848. After the death of his wife, Katherine, he left for Tahiti, where he ministered from 1860 to 1865.

arca (Lat., coffer, chest, coffin) Richly decorated, free-standing tomb usually borne on columns or caryatid figures, serving as both a shrine and a tomb.

Arcana Coelestia *Heavenly Secrets*, best known work of Emanuel Swedenborg*.

arcani disciplina See DISCIPLINA ARCANI.

archangel Title given to an angel of high rank in the celestial hierarchy*, including Michael, Gabriel, Raphael, Uriel, Chamuel, Jophiel, and Zadkiel.

archbishop Chief bishop generally of a group of dioceses* or a province. See also METROPOLITAN; PRIMATE.

archchaplain The chief chaplain*.

archdeacon Originally, the chief among the deacons of a church, but in later times a priest ranking only slightly below a bishop. In Anglican churches, an archdeacon may administer part of a bishop's diocese* and enjoys the title of venerable*. His duties may include supervision of the clergy, care over the temporal administration of church property, and the examination and presentation of candidates* for ordination.

archdiocese Ecclesiastical district governed by an archbishop.

arche (Gk.) Beginning; foundational principle, authority, or source.

Arche, L' (Fr., ark) Hospices for mentally ill started in France by Jean Vanier.

archetype The original pattern or model, especially Christ as the model for all Christians.

Archieratikon (Gk., Book of the Bishop) In the Eastern Orthodox Church*, book corresponding to the Pontifical* in the Latin Church, containing services and blessings.

archiereus In the Byzantine Church*, the episcopacy* representing the highest order of priesthood.

archimandrite (lit., the ruler of a mandra or fold) In the Eastern Church*, the head monk or superior* of a large monastery or of a group of monasteries, the equivalent to a hegumenos* or an abbot. Compare Greek *hegumenos* and English abbot.

Archippus Christian leader of Colossae* referred to in Colossians 4:17. Paul* called him a "fellow soldier" in Philemon 2.

archon In the Byzantine Church*, cleric who directs a special function or a special part of a service. It was originally a Gnostic term.

archpriest The chief priest. In the early church, the title was applied to the senior presbyter* who performed many of a bishop's administrative and liturgical functions. Gradually the archpriest's functions were taken over by the archdeacon, the vicar general*, or the rural dean.

arcosolium/arcosolia Arched burial niche* or recess in a catacomb* used as a tomb. They were recessed in the galleries and cubicula* of the catacomb. Bodies were placed in the loculi cut into walls or floors. They were also placed sometimes on or under a stone slab known as mensa* which, in the case of saints, served as altars. In some cases a stone sarcophagus or solium was used.

Areopagus Mars Hill, a sacred meeting place in Athens* where the apostle Paul* preached to the Athenians (Acts 17:19).

Aresson, Jon (c. 1484–1550) Catholic bishop and poet of Iceland who was executed for opposing the Reformation*.

Arethas (c. 860–940) Byzantine scholar and theologian noted for his commentary on the Book of Revelation.

Argue, Andrew Harvey (1868–1959) Canadian Pentecostal preacher. Born into a Methodist family, he became a Pentecostal under the ministry of William Durham. He founded Winnipeg's Calvary Temple, for many years Canada's largest Pentecostal church, and was a key figure in the emergence of the Pentecostal Assemblies of Canada.

Arianism Heresy, named after Arius*, which denies the full divinity of Christ. Arius held that the Son of God was not eternal but was created before the foundation of the world by the Father. He was therefore not God by nature, but a creature. His dignity as Son of God was bestowed on him as a gift. Full divinity and the worship that goes with it belongs uniquely to the Father.

The teachings of Arius, initially condemned by his bishop Alexander, found many sympathizers until the Emperor Constantine*, eager to restore peace to the church, convened the Council of Nicaea* in 325 to define the faith. There the champions of orthodoxy* were victorious in defining the Catholic faith as postulating the coeternity and coequality of the three persons in the Trinity*, using the term *homoousios** to express their consubstantiality. Arius and the bishops who supported him, especially Eusebius* of Nicomedia, were banished. Constantine* began to waver, and within three years the Arians were restored to their office, while Athanasius and his supporters were exiled.

However, Constantius, who succeeded Constantine as emperor, embraced Arianism, and a council at Antioch* convened by him tried to water down the decrees of the Nicaean Council. After 346, Constantius renewed his persecution of the orthodox party, again exiling Athanasius*, Pope Liberius*, and St. Hilary of Poitiers*. Meanwhile the Arian party had split into three: an extreme party called Anomoeans* (dissimilar), also known as neo-Arians; a middle party called Homoeans* (similar); and a third party called Semi-Arians, who favored the term *homoiousios** as expressing both the similarity and the distinction between the first two persons of the Trinity*. The Homoean Formula, drawn up at the Council of Sirmium*, was found acceptable by bishops of both Eastern and Western churches* who met at the synods of Seleucia and Ariminum* in 359.

This was the zenith of Arianism, but thereafter it declined. With the death of Constantius, Arianism lost its major supporter. Athanasius returned to Alexandria*, where a council was held in 362 marking the resurgence of orthodoxy. In the First Council of Constantinople* in 381, the orthodox party under the three Cappadocian Fathers*—St. Basil*, St. Gregory of Nazianzus*, and St. Gregory of Nyssa*—finally put to rest Arianism as a major threat to the church. After being ousted from the Roman Empire, Arianism survived for a while among the Teutonic tribes through Ulphilas's* Gothic Bible and liturgy, but the conversion of Franks to Catholicism* in 496 led to its gradual disappearance from Europe. It resurfaced many centuries later as Socinianism*, Unitarianism*, and other deviant theologies, and continues to this day in various heretic cults.

aridity In mysticism, dryness of the soul which makes worship and communion with God difficult.

Arimathea Town in Palestine, possibly Rama or Ramathaim-Zophim northwest of Jerusalem*. It was the home of Joseph of Arimathea (Matt. 27:57).

Ariminum (Rimini) and Seleucia, synods of Two synods, convened by the Emperor Constantius II to bring together the bishops of the Eastern and Western churches in 359 for settling the Arian controversy. The councils were forced to accept the Arianizing Creed drawn up at Nice in Thrace.

Aristides, St. (second century) Christian Greek philosopher, author of *Apology,* a treatise defending the Christian faith and protesting the persecution of Christians by Emperor Hadrian and his predecessors. A Syriac* copy of the *Apology* was found in the Monastery of St. Catherine* in Sinai in 1889, and an Armenian translation was published in Venice* by the Mechitarist Fathers.

Aristion (first century) According to Papias*, contemporary of John the Elder, and one of the principal authorities on the traditions about Jesus.

Aristobulus Person to whose household St. Paul* sent greetings in Romans 16:10. He was probably either the grandson of Herod the Great and friend of Emperor Claudius or one of the 70 disciples and the brother of St. Barnabas*, whose daughter married St. Peter*. He was consecrated bishop by St. Paul*. He is named in the *Roman Martyrology**. Feast day: March 15 or 16.

Arius (c. 256–336) Heresiarch*. A presbyter of the Church of Alexandria and a pupil of Lucian of Antioch*. He formulated the heresy known as Arianism*. He was excommunicated by the Council of Nicaea and spent a few years in banishment in Illyria, but was recalled and reinstated in 334. He died in 336.

arkidyakna In the Church of the East*, an archdeacon, comparable to a vicar general*, who exercises liturgical rather than administrative functions.

Arles City in southeastern France, an archepiscopal see* from the fourth to the eighteenth centuries. Founded in the sixth century B.C., it was an important Roman city with a population of over 100,000 in its heyday. In the later Roman Empire, it was the third most important city after Rome* and Constantinople*. In the tenth century, it became the capital of Provence. Local Provencal traditions link the advent of the gospel in the city with Sts. Martha and Mary Magdalene, whose legendary boat landing at Les Saintes Maries de la Mer is said to have begun the spread of the gospel into Provence.

Near Arles Martha is said to have tamed the mythical pagan creature the Tarasque. Here the first church was built in 606 in memory of St. Trophimus, a Greek from Ephesus*, who brought the gospel before the sixth century. The church underwent several renovations until the fifteenth century when it was completed with a Gothic choir. The west front of the cathedral is in the form of a Roman arch. Its cloister*, though small, is one of the most beautiful in the world. The tympanum* represents the day of judgment, with Christ surrounded by the symbols of the Gospels. On the bas-relief there are scenes from the life of Mary.

Arles, synods of Fifteen general synods were held at Arles between 314 and 1275. The first general council in the Western Church* was convened by Constantine I in 314 in Arles to settle a dispute between the Donatists and the Catholics of North Africa. It passed 22 canons against the Donatists. The other important councils were: an Arianizing Council in 353, Second Council of Arles in the fifth century, council on preaching and the education of the clergy in 813, council against the Albigensians in 1234, and council against Joachim of Fiore* in 1263.

arma Christi (Lat., arms of Christ) Weapons of Christ's victory over death, principally the cross, crown of thorns, nails, and lance*.

Armageddon In Revelation 16:16 the last great battle between Christ and Antichrist* on the Mount of Megiddo, a promontory on the Plain of Esdraelon, near Mount Carmel.

Armagh Town in northern Ireland where St. Patrick* founded a church in 445. From the seventh century it was the most powerful church in Ireland. It has two cathedrals and is the seat of both Catholic and Protestant archbishoprics*.

Armagh, Book of See BOOK OF ARMAGH.

armarium Cupboard in the sacristy* of a basilica*.

Armenian chant Monophonic music of the Armenian Church* in an eight-mode system sometimes accompanied by percussion instruments. The principal hymn types include sharaknotz, gandz, tegh, erg, and meghedi*.

Armenian Church The first national church in history. Armenia became Christian about 301 when King Tiridates III or IV (298?–330) was converted by St. Gregory the Illuminator*, and therefore the Armenian Church is sometimes called the Gregorian Church*. Gregory established the patriarchal see* at Ashtishat* in Taron, and for many years the catholicate or primate* of Armenia was hereditary in his family. When Armenia became divided between the Persian and Roman empires in 390, the patriarchal see was moved to Etchmiadzin*, near Mount Ararat. By 428 Armenia ceased to become independent and was subjected to various oppressive rulers until the latter half of the twentieth century.

Armenian Church

In 374, after the death of St. Nerses*, the church achieved full autonomy after breaking earlier links with the church of Caesarea* in Cappadocia*. In the early part of the fifth century, St. Isaac the Great* (catholicos* from about 389 to 438) and St. Mesrob greatly strengthened the church by the invention of a national script and the translation of the Bible and the liturgy into Armenian. Armenians repudiated the Council of Chalcedon* (to which they were not invited) and are therefore considered as Monophysite.

Persecution during the next seven centuries resulted in the breakup of Armenia into two kingdoms: Greater Armenia and Little Armenia or Cilicia*. The latter accepted union with Rome* at the Council of Sis in 1307, confirmed at the Council of Florence* (1438–1439). Greater Armenia, however, did not accept the uniat status, and established an independent patriarchate at Etchmiadzin*. In the nineteenth and twentieth centuries, Armenians suffered severe persecutions in which more than 1.5 million Armenians perished. As a result there is a vast Armenian diaspora, most of whom live in North America.

The Gregorian Church* is organized in two catholicates, one at Etchmiadzin*, and the other at Sis, whose catholicos* is resident in Antelias, a suburb of Beirut. Under them there are two classes of priests: unmarried vartabeds* and married parish priests. Armenians follow the Liturgy of St. Basil*, and the priestly vestment is the shurjar* or chasuble*, shaped like a cope*. In the Eucharist* they use unleavened bread* and do not mix water with wine. Communion is in both kinds by intinction*. Christmas* is not observed as a separate feast but is celebrated as part of the Epiphany* from January 5 to 13.

Armenian Rite The systems and forms of worship in the Armenian (Gregorian) Church*, based on the Liturgy of St. Basil*.

Armenian Version Translation of the Bible from Syriac* and Greek into Armenian by Sahak* and Mesrob, in the early part of the fifth century.

Arminianism Theological system, named after Jacobus Arminius*, Dutch Reformed* theologian, emphasizing freedom of the will and opposing the Calvinistic creed of unconditional election* and

irresistible grace*. The Arminian position was formally set forth in the Remonstrance* of 1610. Arminians hold that freedom of human will is not incompatible with the sovereignty of God and that Jesus Christ died for all, not merely the elect*.

The 15 major tenets of Arminianism are: 1. Human beings are free agents and human events are mediated by the foreknowledge of God. 2. God's decrees are conditional, not absolute. 3. God created Adam as innocent. 4. Sin consists in acts of the will. 5. Only the pollution, not the sin of Adam, is imputed to his descendants. 6. Man's depravity is not total, and his will is inclined toward God and good. 7. The Atonement* was not necessary but once offered is available to all. 8. The Atonement does not actually effect the salvation of human beings but merely makes it possible. 9. Salvation becomes effectual only when accepted voluntarily by penitent sinners. 10. Regeneration* is determined by the human will, not divine decree. 11. Faith itself is a good work. 12. There is no distinction between common grace* and special grace*. 13. Grace may be resisted. 14. The righteousness of Christ is never imputed to the believer. 15. A believer may attain full conformity to divine will in this life, but may also fall from grace and be lost eternally.

Initially Arminians were charged with the heresies of Pelagianism* and Socinianism* and condemned at the Synod of Dort* (1618–1619). It was only in 1795 that they were restored to full toleration. Gradually Arminianism came to be viewed as a more liberal theology and thus more in tune with the times. It had considerable influence on modern European and U.S. theology, particularly on Wesleyanism and General Baptists*.

Arminius, Jacobus (1560–1609) Birth name: Jakob Hermansz or Harmensz. Dutch theologian. He was ordained in 1588. Studies in the Epistle to the Romans led him to doubt the prevailing Calvinism* of his day. For the rest of his life, he waged a lifelong struggle against Calvinism. He taught at the University of Leiden until his death.

armorium In the Catholic Church, the recess over the altar containing the pyx*.

Armstrong, William Frederick and Hannah Maria (Norris) (1849–1918 and 1842–1919, respectively) Canadian

Maritime Baptist missionaries in Burma. They worked from 1873 among the Tamil and Telugu Indians as well as the Karens of Burma. They established schools and orhpanages and were frequent speakers at mission conferences.

Jacobus Arminius

Arnaud, Henri (1641–1721) Waldensian leader who was both a pastor and a general*. For two years he successfully led their struggle in the Swiss mountains against France.

Arnauld, Antoine (1612–1694) French theologian, known as the "Great Arnauld." He entered the holy orders* in 1641 and retired to Port-Royal*. In 1643 he published *De la Frequente Communion* justifying the Jansenist positions which provoked such a strong opposition from the Jesuits* that he withdrew from public life. Next year he published *Apologie de M. Jansenius*, a Jansenist manifesto that made Arnauld the unofficial leader of the Jansenist party. The publication of two anti-Jesuit treatises led to his censure by the Sorbonne* in 1656. However, in 1669 he was restored to his position and treated as a popular hero. When the Jansenist controversy revived in 1679, he left France for the Netherlands, where he remained actively engaged in polemics* until his death. A friend of Pascal*, he was the first noted theologian to accept the philosophy of Descartes.

Arnauld, Jacqueline Marie Angelique (1591–1661) Cistercian abbess and sister of Antoine Arnauld*.

She became abbess of Port-Royal* in 1602. She introduced a number of reforms, such as community of goods, regular office, uniformity of dress, and abstinence and silence, placing great emphasis on inner discipline of the spirit. In 1618 she carried out similar reforms at Maubuisson. Under the influence of Saint-Cyran*, she became a strong Jansenist.

Arnauld, Robert Arnauld D'Andilly (1588–1674) Brother of Antoine and Marie Arnauld.* Poet and translator of the works of Josephus*, the *Confessions of St. Augustine**, and the New Testament into French.

Arndt, Johann (1555–1621) German theologian and mystical writer much revered by the Pietists. A follower of Melanchthon* and Luther*, he was opposed by the Calvinists in the controversies of the age. His best known work is *Vier Bucher vom Wahren Christentum* (1606).

Arne, Thomas Augustine (1710–1778) English composer. He is best known for his oratorios, as *Abel* (1744) and *Judith* (1733). He also composed beautiful melodies, including "This Is the Day the Lord Has Made" and "Am I Soldier of the Cross."

Arnobius (fourth century) Christian in the time of Diocletian (284–305) and teacher of Lactantius*. He was converted to Christianity in a dream. In his *Adversus Nationes*, he offered a defense of

Jacqueline Marie Angelique Arnauld (kneeling)

Christian beliefs and refuted the charges that Christianity was the cause of various disasters that befell the Roman Empire.

Johann Arndt

Arnobius the Younger (fifth century) African monk who held semi-Pelagian views and attacked Augustine's* doctrine of grace. He wrote an allegorical commentary on the Psalms.

Arnold, Eberhard (1883–1945) Founder of the Bruderhof* movement at Sannerz in 1920. A pacifist, he incurred the hostility of the Gestapo. In 1930 he went to western Canada and established links with the Hutterian Brethren. *God's Revolution* is a selection of his writings and addresses.

Arnold, Gottfried (1666–1714) German Protestant theologian, hymn writer, and devotional writer. After his conversion, he wrote his first important work, *Die Erste Liebe* (1696), followed by his principal work, *Unparteiische Kirchen- und Ketzer-Historie* (1699–1700). He moved into devotional literature with *Geheimnis der göttlichen Sophia* (1700), *Historia et Descriptio Theologiae Mysticae* (1702), *Geistliche Gestalt eines Evangelischen Lehrers* (1704), and *Wahre Abbildung des inwendigen Christentums* (1709).

Arnold of Brescia (c. 1090–1155) Italian reformer who preached against the worldliness of the church. He was condemned at the Council of Sens* (1140), excommunicated by Eugenius III* in 1148, and executed.

Arnot, Frederick Stanley (1858–1914) Missionary to Africa. Inspired by David Livingstone*, he answered a call to serve God in Africa, going there as a Christian Brethren missionary in 1881. He worked with the Barotse tribe and also in Garenganze in Zaire. Two missionary societies owe their existence to his direct influence.

arrachealch In the Armenian Church*, the Epistles which are read on the north side of the bema*.

Arrupe, Pedro (1907–1991) Thirty-first general* of the Society of Jesus*. After serving as superior* of the Jesuits* in Japan, he was elected general in 1965. His strong belief in social justice became the cornerstone of Jesuit policy for many years under his leadership. In 1967 he was elected president of the union of superiors general* of major orders, a post he held until 1981. His influence was felt in important church assemblies, as Medellin* (1968). His major contribution to missiology* was his letter on inculturation* (1978).

Ars Moriendi (lit., the art of dying) Guide to the clergy who minister to the dying. Usually there were 11 illustrations, 5 pairs of faith, despair, impatience, vainglory, and avarice with angels and devils contending for the dying person's soul. The 11th illustration showed the final triumph of the guardian angel*.

Ars Praedicandi (lit., the art of preaching) Medieval book of instruction on the art of preaching. Although most of the early Church Fathers* were great preachers as well, it was not until the twelfth century that preaching came to be regarded as an art with well-defined rules. The earliest manuals were Guibert of Nogent's *Quo Ordine Sermo Fieri Debeat,* Alain of Lille's *Ars Praedicandi,* Humbert of Romans' *De Eruditione Praedicatorum,* Robert of Basevorn's *Forma Praedicandi* (1322), and Thomas Waleys' *De Modo Componendi Sermones* (c. 1340). There were also sermon collections of Honorius of Autun*, Maurice of Sully, and Peter the Chanter*. Most manuals offered guidance on choice of themes and prothemes, the technique of division and subdivision, and mode of delivery.

ars sacra (lit., sacred arts) Music and art designed to glorify God, particularly in a worship setting.

Arsenius the Great, St. (c. 354–c. 450) Roman scholar who became famous as a monk in Egypt. From 383 to 394 he was tutor to Arcadius and Honorius, sons of Theodosius the Great, but hearing a divine call, went to Egypt as a hermit under St. John the Dwarf, first at Scetis, and then at Troe and the island of Canopus. He is particualrly venerated in the Russian Orthodox Church*. Feast day: May 21.

Arta Metropolitan town in Thessaly noted for its Byzantine churches, especially the Panagia Parigoritissa; Our Lady the Comforter, built between 1286 and the thirteenth century; St. Basil Church; and St. Theodora Church.

Artemon (third century) Heretic who taught Sabellian and adoptionist views that held that Christ was a mere man. His followers, among whom Paul of Samosata* was the most important, were known as Artemonites.

article of faith A statement of core Christian belief.

Articles Declaratory Statement setting forth the distinctive claims of the Church of Scotland* as a national church, enacted by Parliament in 1921 and approved by the General Assembly of the church in 1926.

Articles, Forty-Two Document drafted in 1553 by Thomas Cranmer* embodying the doctrinal positions of the Church of England* which formed the basis of the later Thirty-Nine Articles*. See also FORTY-TWO ARTICLES.

Articles, Irish The 104 articles of faith adopted by the Irish Episcopal Church in 1615 at its first convocation. Calvinistic in its creedal form, they teach absolute predestination*, ignore episcopal ordination, and affirm that the pope is the Antichrist*. See also IRISH ARTICLES.

Articles, Lambeth See LAMBETH ARTICLES.

Articles of Religion Twenty-four doctrinal articles of the Methodist Church prepared by John Wesley* on the basis of the Thirty-Nine Articles*. Wesley kept most of the Thirty-Nine Articles including the Trinity*, councils, the unique authority of the Scripture, original sin*, the redemptive work of Christ, justification* by faith, baptism*, and the Lord's Supper*. He dropped the articles on predestination* and election*.

Articles, Organic The provisions of Napoleon in 1802 to regulate public worship and church-state relations. They modified the Concordat of 1801 by giving the government power over ecclesiastical councils and synods*, seminaries and clergy, processions and clerical dress, stipends, and parish* boundaries. The pope objected to these provisions which were never strictly enforced, and they were finally repealed in 1905.

Articles, Six Pro-Catholic English law of 1539 designed to reverse the Reformation*. See also SIX ARTICLES.

Articles, Ten The first articles of faith adopted by the English church at the Convocation of 1536. They upheld the three sacraments of baptism*, penance*, and Eucharist*; prohibited the worship of images but not their representation; and permitted the intercession of saints and prayers and masses for the dead. It also held that justification* is the result not only of faith but also of charity and contrition*.

Articles, Thirteen Statement drawn up in 1538 by Lutherans and Anglicans modeled on the Augsburg Confession*. It was the basis for the later Forty-Two Articles*.

Articles, Thirty-Nine The principal doctrinal confession* of the Church of England* and the Protestant Episcopal Church, first adopted by a convocation in 1563. They are not in the form of a creed but rather short summaries of dogmatic tenets. Though not vague, the articles avoid narrow definitions. Acknowledgment of the Thirty-Nine Articles is required of all Anglican clergy. See THIRTY-NINE ARTICLES.

Articles, Thirty-Seven Calvinistic creed prepared in

1561 and adopted by the Synod of Dort* in 1619. It has been adopted by many Reformed* denominations. See also BELGIC CONFESSION.

Articles, Twenty-Five See ARTICLES OF RELIGION.

articuli fidei fundamentalis Fundamental doctrines that a Christian must hold to gain salvation. Principal among them is the deity of Christ.

articuli fidei puri Doctrines of faith derived either from the Bible or from supernatural revelation, as the Trinity*.

articulus stantis vel candentis ecclesiae (Lat., article of a standing or falling church) Doctrine of justification* by faith, as the pillar of Protestant churches.

artoklasia Byzantine Rite* of Blessing of Loaves performed before the apolytikion* at vespers* when there is a vigil*. In the ceremony, wheat, wine and oil are blessed together with five loaves of bread. The bread and wine are taken together with the antidoron*.

artophorion In the Eastern Church*, the tabernacle on the altar in which the Blessed Sacrament* is reserved or a small portable altar in which Communion* is taken to the sick.

artzeburion In the Armenian Church*, the Fast of Nineveh* that precedes Lent*.

Arundel, Thomas (1353–1414) Archbishop of Canterbury* who severely suppressed the Lollards*. In 1408 he established an inquisition against heresy. He also prohibited the circulation of the Scriptures in English. He was twice chancellor under Richard II (1386–1389 and 1391–1396), but in 1397 he was impeached in Parliament and banished. Restored to Canterbury* in 1399, he became three times chancellor under Henry IV.

Asam, Cosmas Damian and Egid Quirin (1686–1739 and 1692–1750, respectively) German architects and decorators. Cosmas was a fresco painter and Egid a stucco sculptor. The chief examples are the churches at Einsiedeln*, Rohr, Weingarte, and Weltenburg.

asbadikon In the Coptic Liturgy, the central and largest square of the consecrated bread.

Asbury, Francis (1745–1816) English-born leader of American Methodism*. As a tireless evangelist, he used circuit riders* who traveled thousands of miles on horseback every year. Setting an example, Asbury traveled 300,000 miles, preached over 16,000 sermons, and ordained 4,000 preachers in

Francis Asbury

45 years. He had no place he could call home, and letters to him from England were addressed simply, "in America." When American Methodists became a separate organization, he and Thomas Coke* became joint superintendents. He later became the first Methodist bishop in the United States. Asbury College is named after him.

Asbury Theological Seminary Founded by Herbert Clay Morrison in 1923 to train students in historic Wesleyanism with the motto, "Standing Firm; Moving Forward." It has two physical campuses in Kentucky and Florida and a virtual campus, with a total enrollment of over 1,200.

ascension Departure of Jesus Christ to his heavenly home on the right hand of the Father, at the close of his earthly ministry. This event recorded in Acts 1:12 took place on the Mount of Olives and marked the end of his post-resurrection appearances. The angelic message at this event was that he will come back in the fullness of time in majesty and glory.

Ascension Day Feast, observed since the fourth century, honoring the ascension* of Christ. It is celebrated 40 days after Easter*.

ascetical theology Branch of theology dealing with the spiritual war against the flesh and the development of Christian perfection* through active and disciplined self-denial.

asceticism (Gk., exercise or training) In monastic tradition, the discipline of self-denial for the purpose of refining the soul by denying the flesh. Christian asceticism is drawn from the biblical commandment to deny oneself and follow Christ. Self-abnegation took many forms, such as fasting*, chastity*, celibacy, constant prayer, physical separation from the world, and renunciation of worldly possessions. In asceticism these forms were carried to their limits, involving self-deprivation, flagellation*, and the wearing of hair shirts* and chains. Ascetics perceived a correlation between these practices and the acquisition of holiness and miraculous powers. It was seen as a work of supererogation*, doing more than the minimum demands of the gospel in order to attain perfection* on earth.

The Fathers of the Desert* found in asceticism a means of loving and uniting with Godhead more perfectly and for attaining unbroken union with a holy God. Penitential and devotional asceticism was popularized by mendicant orders* who produced some of the classics of ascetic literature. Even after the Reformation*, asceticism was embraced by both Catholics and Protestants. Among the former, ascetic champions, such as St. John of the Cross*, Peter of Alcantara*, and Cure d'Ars* continued the tradition of the Fathers of the Desert. Among Protestants, both Puritans* and Methodists upheld the basic ascetic impulse and there was a widespread revival of religious communities in England and the United States.

ascription Offering of praise, particularly in prayer or following a sermon.

aseity (Lat., *aseitas,* being from itself) Self-created and self-sustaining existence, a quality belonging to God alone.

Ash Wednesday First day of Lent*, 40 days before Easter*. It is symbolized by the placing of ashes of the palm leaves from the past year's Palm Sunday* on the foreheads of believers, as a mark of penitence and mourning.

Ashland Brethren Group in the Brethren Church or progressive Dunkers*, subscribing to the Arminian theology, that holds an annual conference in Ashland, Ohio.

Ashmun, Yehudi (1794–1828) American Congregational* missionary to Liberia who helped save freed African-Americans from extinction in their new homeland.

ashram, Christian Religious community of monks, modeled on ancient Indian institutions, founded by Christian missionaries in India. The earliest were Protestant foundations, as Christu-Kula Ashram (1921) and Christa Prema Seva Ashram (1922). Later ashrams like Santivanam (1950) and Kurisumala* (1958) were associated with the Benedictine monks, Abhishiktananda, and Bede Griffiths. The Fellowship of Catholic Ashrams, the Ashram Aikiva, was formed in 1978. Members follow a simple lifestyle and devote themselves to *sadhana* (spiritual exercises*).

Ashtarak Town in Armenia with a fifth-century church and a seventh-century martyrium*.

Ashtishat One of the oldest cities of Greater Armenia, on the left bank of the Euphrates* where the earliest Christian buildings arose. It became an episcopal see*, and a synod* was held there in about 345.

Asinou Church of the Panagia Phorbiotissa, Our Lady of the Pastures, in Asinou in the foothills of the Troodos Mountains in Cyprus*. It was built in the twelfth century, with a narthex* added around 1200.

Askew, Anne (1521–1546) English Protestant martyr*. Turned out of her house by her husband for her Protestant beliefs, she was arrested and stretched on the rack and burned.

Asmatike Akolouthia In the Byzantine Church*, the sung order of service, consisting mainly of orthros* and hesperinos*. It was gradually displaced by the monastic office.

asotos In the Byzantine Rite*, the Sunday of the Prodigal Son on the Sunday that falls nine weeks before Easter*.

aspasmos In the Byzantine tradition, the kiss of peace*, or the kissing of an icon* or the priest's hand or the Gospel.

asperges Ceremony of sprinkling of holy water* over the altar and people after the entrance rite at Mass* on Sundays. During the ceremony, a verse from Psalm 51:7, beginning "Cleanse me, Lord," is sung.

aspergillum Brush or instrument used to sprinkle holy water*.

aspersion Method of baptism* in which water is sprinkled on the baptizee*, variant of affusion* in which water is poured.

aspersorium 1. Small broom made of dried plants used in the Eastern Church* to sprinkle blessed water. 2. Vessel for holding holy water*.

aspirant Person who plans or trains to enter the holy orders* or any ecclesiastical vocation*.

aspiration Short prayer.

ass Symbol of humility in Christian art. It was also a symbol of the apostle Thomas* among Westphalian Germans because of his slowness to believe.

Ass, Feast of the Medieval French festival, held on January 14, now discontinued, commemorating the flight of the holy family* into Egypt on a donkey.

Assemani Family name of four noted Maronite Orientalists of the eighteenth century. 1. Joseph Simonius (1687–1768). As prefect of the Vatican Library*, he collected a vast library of manuscripts relating to the early Syrian Church. Besides *Bibliotheca Orientalis* (4 vols., 1719–1728), his principal work, he edited the works of Ephraem Syrus in six volumes (1732–1746), and compiled *Kalendaria Ecclesiae Universae* (6 vols., 1755), a collection of texts on saints, *Italicae Historiae Scriptores* (4 vols., 1751–1753) and *Bibliotheca Juris Orientalis Canonici et Civilis* (5 vols., 1762–1776). 2. Stephen Evodius (1707–1782), nephew, whose principal work was *Acta Sanctorum Martyrum Orientalium et Occidentalium* (2 vols., 1748). 3. Joseph Aloysius (1712–1782), who edited *Codex Liturgicus Ecclesiae Universae* (13 vols., 1749–1766), *Commentarius Criticus de Ecclesiis* (1766), and *Commentaria de Catholicis seu Patriarchis Chaldaeorum et Nestorianorum* (1775). 4. Simon (1752–1821), who was professor of oriental languages at Padua.

Assemblies of God The largest and strongest Pentecostal denomination in the United States, formed in 1914. The formation of the Assemblies of God (AG) was the result of efforts initiated by Eudorus N. Bell, Howard Goss, Daniel C. O. Opperman, Archibald P. Collins, and Mack M. Pinson who issued a call for a general council to form a Pentecostal denomination. The first headquarters was in a small Bible school in Findlay, Ohio. In 1915 it moved to St. Louis and in 1918 to Springfield, Missouri, where it has remained since. The general council held at St. Louis in 1916 adopted a Statement of Fundamental Truths identifying acceptable doctrines. This statement, as expanded over the years, has come to include speaking in tongues*, healing, and baptism of the Holy Spirit*. A weekly paper, *The Pentecostal Evangel,* founded in 1918, is still being published. Among its able leaders have been Eudorus Bell, Archibald P. Collins, J. Roswell Flower, Ernest S. Williams, Ralph Riggs, Thomas F. Zimmerman, and G. Raymond Carlson. The Assemblies of God in Britain and Ireland were organized in 1924.

Assemblies of God services are informal and nonliturgical. Vestments are not worn by the officiating clergy. There may be three or more regular services every week: a Sunday morning service emphasizing worship, Sunday evening service mainly for unbelievers emphasizing regeneration*, and the mid-week service for Bible study, prayer, and testimony. The order of service usually includes congregational singing accompanied by a variety of musical instruments, public prayer, and the ministry of the Word*. Personal testimonies intersperse the service. Enthusiastic congregational participation is an important aspect of worship. Special features of the Assembly of God worship include united audible prayer, speaking in tongues, interpretation of tongues* and prophecy, and prayer for the sick. The needs of the congregation are remembered during public prayer. Most services end with an invitation to those present to kneel at the altar.

The Assemblies of God recognizes only two ordinances*—baptism* and the Lord's Supper*— and both are considered symbolic rather than inherently efficacious. Baptism is by total immersion* as an act of obedience and an outward sign of the believer's identification with Christ in his death, burial, and Resurrection. Infants are dedicated. The Lord's Supper is celebrated monthly as a memorial of Christ's substitutionary death and as a reminder of his Second Coming*. Communion* is open to all who profess faith in Christ. Communicants* partake of both elements*, usually at their seats, served by laymen. The Bible is accepted as infallible and authoritative as the rule of faith* and conduct.

assemblies of the French clergy Meetings of the Catholic clergy of France at five-year intervals from the sixteenth through the eighteenth centuries to consider ecclesiastical matters.

assembly Gathering or congregation of Christians.

Assent, Declaration of A formal declaration accepting the three historic formularies of the Church of England*, the *Book of Common Prayer*, Thirty-Nine Articles*, and the Ordinal, legally required of all clergy, bishops, deacons, readers*, registrars, chancellors, and lay workers.

Assisi Central Italian city in the Umbrian Hills, noted as the birthplace of St. Francis*. Its principal landmarks are the St. Francis Basilica, partially destroyed in an earthquake in 1997; Sta Maria degli Angeli Basilica, the Portiuncula*

chapel where the Franciscan Order* originated; and the church where St. Clare* is buried. The double church is built above the saint's tomb on a cruciform* plan and consists of an upper and

Sta Maria Degli Angeli Basilica

lower church, built between 1228 and 1263. The lower church is a crypt with a single nave*. The upper building built as a hall church* is the earliest Gothic* ecclesiastical building in Italy. The 1997 earthquake destroyed priceless frescoes by Giotto* and Cimabue*, including the Twenty-Eight Episodes from the Life of St. Francis, which Giotto began in 1298.

Association of Baptists for World Evangelization Foreign mission society founded in 1927 as the Association of Baptists for Evangelism in the Orient under the leadership of Raphael C. Thomas after breaking away from the American Baptist Foreign Mission Society. In 1939 it expanded its work to Peru and changed its name to the present form. After World War II, it entered new mission fields* in Latin America, Africa, Australia, and Europe. It is primarily engaged in church planting*, theological education, medical relief, and Bible translation.

Association of Evangelical Lutheran Churches One of the constituent groups in the Evangelical Lutheran Church of America. They broke away in 1969 from the Lutheran Church-Missouri Synod when the conservatives took over that denomination and joined the Evangelical Lutheran Church in America* in 1987.

assumption Roman Catholic doctrine that the Virgin Mary* was physically taken into heaven*. The doctrine of corporal assumption was first formulated in the Western Church* by St. Gregory of

Tours*, based on account by Melito* of Sardis, and in the Eastern Church* by Dionysius the Areopagite* who recorded that he had witnessed the assumption.The date of the Virgin's death is variously assigned, from 3 to 50 years after the ascension. Declared as a dogma* by papal decree in 1950.

Assumption, Feast of the Commemoration* of assumption of the the Virgin Mary* observed on August 15.

Assumptionists Also called Augustinians of the Assumption*, a Roman Catholic educational and missionary order founded at Nimes, France, in 1845. The order was suppressed in France in 1900 but has spread to other parts of the world where they are engaged in the care of the poor, asylums, and spread of the gospel.

assurance of salvation Conviction of believers that now and in the future they are in an unbreakable and covenantal fellowship with God. It is the central theme of Protestant doctrine and is an offshoot of trust in the faithfulness of God and the inerrancy of the Bible* as well as the inner witness of the Holy Spirit* (Rom. 8:38–39; 2 Cor. 1:18–20; 2 Tim. 2:13). Theologically, assurance is grounded on the character of God and the finality of his revelation in Jesus Christ.

Assyrian Church Properly, the Church of the East*. Church whose members claim to be descendants of the ancient Assyrians. It is Nestorian by faith, although its Christology* is strictly Antiochene, derived from Theodore of Mopsuestia* rather than Nestorius*. The church flourished in the time of the Persian Empire when its schools at Edessa* and Nisibis* were centers of theological learning. Its greatest theologians were Barsumas*, bishop of Nisibis*, and Babai the Great* (d. 628), author of the *Book of the Union*.

By the time of the demise of the Sassanian Empire, Assyrian Christians formed the most important religious minority under a catholicos-patriarch at Seleucia-Ctesiphon* and ten metropolitans*. The most notable of the catholicos-patriarchs was Mar Aba I* (540–555). Following a monastic revival under Abraham of Kashkar* (d. c. 580), numerous monasteries were founded,

some of them described by Thomas of Marga* in his *Book of the Governors*. By the seventh century Assyrian missionaries had founded outposts in Malabar, India, and in Central and East Asia.

After the Arab conquest the fortunes of the church declined, and the patriarchate moved to Baghdad, where Syriac* scholars such as Hunayn ibn Ishaq (d. 873) played an important role in transmitting Greek knowledge to the West. After the conversion of the Mongols to Islam and the rise of Chengiz Khan, the church was wiped out in Central Asia, and Assyrian Christians were reduced to a tiny group centered on the mountains of Kurdistan. They were further divided by the creation of a separate Uniat body called the Chaldean Christians*. During World War I they suffered reprisals from Turks and Kurds, and the survivors fled to the protection of the British Mandate in Iraq.

At the end of the mandate in 1933, many members, including the catholicos*, emigrated to other parts of the world, especially the United States. Only a few thousand remain in the Middle East. Its patriarch* is officially styled catholicos-patriarch of the Assyrian Church of the East and resides in Chicago, while a dissident catholicos remains in Baghdad. The liturgical language is Syriac*. The Assyrian Jacobite Apostolic Church is a group which accepts the Nicene Creed*. Its members emigrated from Turkey to the United States in 1907.

asterisk/asteriskos (Gk., star) Vessel consisting of two metal strips crossed and bent and placed over the eucharistic bread used in the Eastern Church* to keep it from touching the veil.

astvatzashounch (Arm., inspired by God) Holy Bible.

Astvatzatzin (Arm., Bearer of God) Theotokos*, the Virgin Mary*.

ASV American Standard Version.

ataba In the Ethiopian Liturgy, the rite of consignation in which the priest takes the central square of consecrated bread.

Athanasian Creed One of the most important professions of faith* in the Christian Church, also known from its opening words as Quicunque Vult*, originally believed to have been composed by St. Athanasius*. Later research has established that it was composed in Latin, not in Greek, and until modern times, has circulated mostly in the Western Church*. It differs from the Apostles' Creed* and the Nicene Creed* in form as well in its inclusion of anathemas or damnatory clauses. It is dated variously; some attributing it to a date between 381 and 428 and others to a date later than 428. The creed has two parts: one dealing with the Trinity* and the other with the Incarnation*. It begins and concludes with the assertion of the truths necessary for salvation. It runs as follows:

Whosoever will be saved: before all things it is necessary that he hold the Catholic faith, which faith except every one do keep whole and undefiled, without doubt he shall perish everlastingly. And the Catholic faith is this:

That we worship one God in Trinity, and Trinity in Unity; Neither confounding the Persons, nor dividing the Substance. For there is one person of the Father, another of the Son: and another of the Holy Ghost. But the Godhead of the Father, of the Son and of the Holy Ghost is all one: the Glory equal, the Majesty co-eternal. Such as the Father is, such is the Son; and such is the Holy Ghost. The Father uncreate, the Son uncreate: and the Holy Ghost uncreate. The Father incomprehensible: the Son incomprehensible: and the Holy Ghost incomprehensible. The Father eternal, the Son eternal: and the Holy Ghost eternal. And yet there are not three eternals: but one eternal. As also there are not three incomprehensibles nor three uncreated: but one uncreated and one incomprehensible.

So likewise the Father is Almighty: the Son Almighty: and the Holy Ghost Almighty. And yet there are not three Almightys: but one Almighty. So the Father is God, the Son is God: and the Holy Ghost is God. And yet there are not three Gods: but one God. So likewise the Father is Lord, the Son Lord: and the Holy Ghost Lord. And yet not three Lords: but one Lord. For like as we are compelled by the Christian verity: to acknowledge every Person by Himself to be God and Lord: so are we forbidden by the Catholic Religion to say there be three Gods, or three Lords. The Father is made of none: neither created nor

begotten. The Son is of the Father alone: not made nor created but begotten. The Holy Ghost is of the Father and of the Son: neither made, nor created, nor begotten, but proceeding.

So there is one Father, not three Fathers; one son, not three Sons; one Holy Ghost, not three Holy Ghosts. And in this Trinity, none is afore, or after other: none is greater, or less than another; but the whole Three Persons are co-eternal together: and co-equal. So that in all things, as is aforesaid: the Unity in Trinity, and the Trinity in Unity, is to be worshiped. He therefore that will be saved: must thus think of the Trinity.

Furthermore, it is necessary to everlasting salvation: that he also believe rightly the Incarnation of our Lord Jesus Christ. For the right Faith is, that we believe and confess: that our Lord Jesus Christ, the Son of God, is God and Man; God, of the Substance of the Father, begotten before the worlds, and Man, of the substance of His Mother, born in the world; Perfect God, and Perfect Man: of a reasonable soul and human flesh subsisting. Equal to the Father, as touching His Godhead: and inferior to the Father, as touching His Manhood. Who although He be God and Man: yet He is not two but one Christ; One: not by conversion of the Godhead into flesh: but by taking of the Manhood, into God; One altogether; not by confusion of Substance: but by unity of Person.

For as the reasonable soul and flesh is one man: so God and Man is one Christ; who suffered for our salvation; descended into hell; rose again the third day from the dead. He ascended into Heaven, He sitteth on the Right hand of the Father, God Almighty: from whence He shall come to judge the quick and the dead. At Whose coming all men shall rise again with their bodies: and shall give account of their own works. And they that have done good shall go into life everlasting: and they that have done evil into everlasting fire.

This is the Catholic Faith, which except a man believe faithfully he cannot be saved.

Glory be to the Father, and to the Son, and to the Holy Ghost. As it was in the beginning, is now, and ever shall be, world without end, Amen.

Athanasius, St. (c. 296–373) Bishop of Alexandria*. He attended the Council of Nicaea* as deacon and secretary to Bishop Alexander, whom he succeeded in 328. As the principal defender of orthodoxy*, he incurred the enmity of the Arians, who had him deposed at the Council of Tyre* in 335 and exiled to Trier* in 336. He was restored in 337, deposed again in 339, and forced to flee to Rome, which supported him throughout his life. He was restored a second time in 346 and driven out again in 356. On the accession of Julian* in 363, he returned once more, only to be exiled later in the year. He came back from his last exile in 365–366 and thereafter sealed his career by building up the orthodox party. He died in 373. Seven years later, the orthodox won their final victory over Arianism* at the First Council of Constantinople* in 381.

Athanasius the Athonite, St. (c. 920–1003) Monastic founder. In 961 he established the first monastery on Mount Athos*. By the time of his death it had grown to 58 communities. Feast day: July 5.

Athenagoras (second century) One of the earliest and ablest Christian apologists, who with his lucid style and forceful logic, was the first to elaborate a philosophical defense of the Trinity*. Among his works was *Apology* or *Supplication* (c. 177), addressed to Emperor Marcus Aurelius and his son Commodus refuting pagan charges of incest and cannibalism brought against Christians. A treatise on the *Resurrection of the Dead* also has

St. Athanasius

been attributed to him. He held that marriage is indissoluble even by death.

Athenagoras (1886–1972) Patriarch of Constantinople*. Trained at the theological school at Halki, he became the Greek archbishop of North and South America in 1930 and the ecumenical patriarch* in 1948. His achievements included the Panorthodox Conferences at Rhodes since 1961, his meeting with Pope Paul VI* at Jerusalem* in 1964, and the revocation of the anathemas between Rome* and Constantinople in 1965.

Athenogenes (second century) Christian martyr* who composed "Hymn for the Lighting of the Lamps."

Athens Capital of Greece, named for its patron goddess, Athena. St. Paul* visited it on his second missionary journey in A.D. 50 (Acts 17:15–18). Among the most famous Christian Athenians were Dionysius the Areopagite*; Publius, bishop of Athens*; St. Basil*; and Gregory of Nazianzus*. It is the metropolitan see* of the Church of Greece.

Athonitissa Icon of the Theotokos* or the Mother of God, as the protector of Mount Athos*.

Athos, Mount Also known as the Holy Mountain* (Hagion Oros*). Greek peninsula known as Chalkidiki projecting from the coast of Macedonia* into the Aegean Sea, the site of 20 Basilian* monasteries of the Orthodox Church. The earliest of these monasteries was founded in 961. In 963 St. Athanasius the Athonite* founded the greatest of the monasteries, Magisti Lavra. Twenty fortified monasteries were built on terraced slopes at five different levels, including the Great Lavra of Athanasios (963), Vatopedi (972–980), Agiou Paulou (tenth century), Xeropotamou (tenth century), Ephigmenou (tenth century), Panteleimon (eleventh century, Russian), Docheiariariou (eleventh century), Xenophontos (tenth century), Constamonitou (eleventh century), Caracallou (eleventh century), Philotheou (twelfth century), Hilander* (twelfth century, Serbian), Koutloumousiou (twelfth century), Pantokrator (twelfth century), Simonos Petras (thirteenth century), Dionysiou (thirteenth century), Gregoriou (thirteenth century), Zographou (thirteenth century, Bulgarian), and Stavronikita (sixteenth century). Each of these massive complexes, looking more like castles than monasteries, have only one entrance.

Monastery on Mount Athos

Although each monastery is independent, a common council legislates matters of common concern. Women are excluded from the peninsula.

Atonement Redemption* of the human race by God through the full payment of the penalty of sin. The ransom theory of atonement, common among Church Fathers*, states that Christ died as an expiatory sacrifice to ransom human beings from the power of the devil (Mark 10:45; 1 Tim. 2:6). Anselm* taught the satisfaction* theory of atonement by which Christ paid the infinite debt owed by the human race to God as a result of sin. This, however, precludes forgiveness, because if a debt is paid in full it cannot be forgiven.

The Calvinist penal satisfaction theory is that God's claims against the elect* were satisfied by Christ's death being a vicarious* punishment. The emphasis is not on debt but on justice. The governmental theory emphasizes that Christ died for all men as a provisional substitute for penalty. In Wesleyan theology the idea of atonement as propitiation* dominates. According to Wesley*, the Atonement is God's method of becoming immanent in a sinful race. Calvinists teach limited atonement for the elect*, while Arminians teach unlimited atonement for all.

Atonement, Friars of the Franciscan group founded

at Graymoor, Garrison, New York, in 1899 as a Protestant Episcopal organization. In 1909 it was received into the Roman Catholic Church.

atrium Entrance court in ancient churches consisting of a colonnaded triangle with a fountain* in the middle and connected with the interior of the church by a narthex* or portico which ran the length of one side.

atsh (Arm., right arm) The right arm of St. Gregory the Illuminator* laid on the head of the catholicos* designate during ordination.

attrition Imperfect repentance which proceeds from the fear of punishment, as distinguished from contrition* which proceeds from love of God.

Auburn Affirmation Affirmation signed by 1,274 Presbyterian ministers in 1924, rejecting the attempt to define Christianity in terms of the five points of Fundamentalism*, known as the Fundamentals.

Auburn Declaration Statement of doctrine issued in 1837 which eventually led to the reunion of the "Old School" and "New School" Presbyterians. The declaration affirmed a moderate but generally orthodox Calvinism*.

Auca Five Also, Ecuador Martyrs. Five young American missionaries—Jim Elliot, Peter Fleming, Ed McCully, Nate Saint, and Roger Youderian—who lost their lives along the Curaray River in the jungles of Ecuador in 1956 when they were speared by Auca Indians. Their martyrdom is described in Elizabeth Elliott's *Through Gates of Splendor*.

audientes (lit., hearers) In the early church, persons in the first stage of catechetical instruction. Those who wished to move to the next stage of prebaptismal instruction were admitted to the second order of competentes.

audientia episcopalis Resolution of disputes among Christians within the community, by using one of them as judge, a course recommended by the apostle Paul* (1 Cor. 6:1–8).

auditor (lit., hearer) 1. Official in an ecclesiastical case who listens to and records the evidence. 2. Ordinary adherent* (non-elect) in Manichaeism*.

auditory church Preaching church developed by the Calvinists in sixteenth-century France, Switzerland, and the Netherlands. Centrally planned, it is circular, square, or octagonal to enable the preacher's voice to be heard everywhere. Galleries may add to the available space.

Aufklarung (Ger., Enlightenment) Period of European history embodying the spirit of Rationalism and freethinking, represented by H. S. Reimarus, G. E. Lessing, and J. G. Herder. It was opposed to all supernatural religion, particularly Christianity in both Catholic and Protestant forms, and believed in the all-sufficiency of human reason to promote human welfare. One of its principal tenets was religious toleration and pluralism. Extended into theology, it subverted faith in the Bible and fostered biblical criticism*.

Augouard, Prosper Philippe (1852–1921) Holy Ghost Fathers* missionary to Central Africa. He arrived in the Congo five days after Henry Stanley and charted the Congo and Ubangi Rivers, establishing mission stations* along their length of 1,300 miles. In 1915 he became archbishop of the region.

Augsburg, Confession of The great creed of Lutheranism*, formulated by Melanchthon*, and presented to the Diet of Augsburg in 1530. It is the doctrinal standard in the Lutheran Church. Its 21

Augsburg

articles in the first part define the early Lutheran position, elaborating the doctrine of faith and good works*. The second half reviews and suggests remedies for Roman Catholic "abuses," such as celibacy, compulsory confession*, private masses, communion in one kind, and monastic vows. In the years following, a number of variant confessions were issued, such as the *Variata* of 1540. The Augsburg Confession exerted a significant influence on English Protestantism* by informing the Thirteen Articles* of 1538 and the Thirty-Nine Articles* ultimately adopted by the Church of England* under Elizabeth I.

Augsburg Friends Group in the United States that seceded from the United Norwegian Lutheran Church. In 1897 it was organized as the Lutheran Free Church.

Augsburg, Interim of Provisional doctrinal formula* prepared at the Diet of Augsburg of 1548, accepted as the basis of settlement between Roman Catholics and Protestants. It consisted of 26 articles. The chief concessions to the Protestants were clerical marriage and Communion in both kinds*. After being accepted by the Diet of Augsburg, it was promulgated in parts of south Germany. However, it failed to receive approval in the more Protestant regions where the less pro-Catholic Leipzig Edict, put forth by the elector Maurice, was adopted.

Augsburg, Peace of Settlement of the Catholic-Protestant conflict at the Diet of Augsburg in 1555. It recognized the coexistence of both Roman Catholicism* and Protestantism* in Germany, providing that in each region the subjects should follow the religion of its ruler. Those who did not accept the religion of their ruler were free to emigrate. In the imperial cities, both religions were allowed to flourish. The Augsburg Confession* of 1530 was recognized as the official standard of the Lutheran faith. The Peace of Augsburg remained the basis of the ecclesiastical settlement of the empire until the Edict of Restitution (1629) and the Treaty of Westphalia (1648).

Augusta, John (Jan) (1500–1575) Leader of the Bohemian Brethren* who tried to form an evangelical interdenominational Protestant group in Bohemia. During the persecution of the Brethren, he was imprisoned from 1547 to 1564 by Ferdinand of Hapsburg.

Augustana Evangelical Lutheran Church Denomination, first known as Augustana Synod, formed by Swedish immigrants in 1860. Its doctrines were based on Swedish Lutheranism and Pietism*. In 1962 it merged with the Lutheran Church in America.

Augustine of Canterbury, St. (d. between 604 and 609) First archbishop of Canterbury*. He was prior* of St. Andrew's monastery in Rome* when he was sent by Pope Gregory* the Great to refound the church in England. Within months of his landing in Kent in 597, King Ethelbert* became a Christian (his queen Bertha had been a Christian before marriage). Feast day: May 26 (Anglican Church); May 27 (Roman Catholic Church).

Augustine of Hippo, St. (354–430) Bishop of Hippo. Regius and doctor of the church*. Born to a pagan father and a Christian mother, St. Monica*, he had a restless adolescence and took a concubine with whom he lived for 15 years and who bore him a son. For a decade thereafter he was a Manichaean while he taught in Carthage*, Rome*, and Milan*. At Milan he underwent a spiritual crisis* as he abandoned Manichaeism*, left the mother of his son, and came under the influence of St. Ambrose*. He retired from his teaching position in Milan at the age of 32 and was baptized on Easter eve 387 by Ambrose. He moved to Rome and after the death of his mother, returned to Africa where, at Hippo Regius, he was consecrated priest and later bishop, succeeding Valerius.

In his early years, Augustine produced a series of works against Manichaeans, Donatists, and Pelagians. He condemned Manichaeism because of its emphasis on the power of darkness, although his later teaching against Pelagians on sexuality and original sin* probably reflected persistent Manichaean influence on his thought. He was conciliatory toward Donatists and urged the Catholic Church to recognize the orders conferred by them, making an important distinction between the validity and the efficacy of sacraments*.

Against Pelagians he wrote some of his most important works: *The Merits and Remissions of Sins and Infant Baptism, The Spirit and the Letter, Nature and Grace, The Perfection of Human Righteousness, The Grace of Christ and Original Sin, Marriage and Concupiscence, Against Two Letters of Pelagians, Against Julian, Grace and Free Will, Correction and Grace, The Predestination of Saints,* and *The Gift of Perseverance.*

Augustine maintained that because of Adam's fall there could be no faith or good works* without grace. Augustine held that grace is available only to the elect* who are predestined to receive it and who are granted the gift of perseverance*, although he conceded that grace can be given temporarily. While he was engaged in the Pelagian controversy, he wrote a vindication of Christianity against pagan critics who indicted it as the reason for the fall of Rome* in 410.

The 22 installments of the *City of God* appeared between 416 and 422. It contrasted the earthly city, represented by Rome, with the heavenly city in which alone true justice, humanity, and forgiveness prevailed. Augustine prescribed asceticism* as the cure for the ills of society. His

St. Augustine of Hippo

ethic dealt with the dehumanization of a society driven by lust, greed, and power. Between 399 and 419 he wrote the 15 books of *On the Trinity,* comparing the three persons of the Trinity* to three components of a personality: memory, intellect, and will. He also described the Holy Spirit* as the bond of love between the Father and the Son and thus laid the foundation of the Filioque*.

Augustine's profound sense of the ecclesial community* is brought out in his *Tractates on the St. John's Gospel,* sermons, and rules for monks and nuns. Among his other works are *De Doctrina Christiana* on biblical exegesis*; *Harmony of the Evangelists,* rebutting pagan charges regarding inconsistencies of the Bible; *Enchiridion,* a handbook of theology; and *Retractationes,* a review of his writings. His *Confessions,* a record of his spiritual and intellectual development, is one of the great classics of all time. Augustine has been a towering figure in Christian theology. He laid the foundations of the school that bears his name, and he exercised strong influence on the Roman Catholic Church* and on the Reformers and Jansenists. Feast day: August 28.

Augustine, Rule of Three main monastic texts attributed to St. Augustine of Hippo*, the basis of the constitutions of the Augustinian Canons*, Augustinian Friars or Hermits*, Servites*, Ursulines*, the Dominicans*, Visitation Nuns, and other Catholic orders. The *Ordo Monasterii* was a book of regulations for monasteries. The *Praeceptum* (Precept) was a manual for male monks, and Epistula 211, paragraphs 5–16 was its counterpart addressed to women. The Ausgustinian regulations were simple, emphasizing common prayer, poverty, charity, and unity.

Augustinian Canons Also known as Austins; Black or Regular Canons. Communities of clerks* inspired by the Gregorian Reform in North Italy and South France who in the middle of the seventh century sought to live together bound in vows of poverty, celibacy, and obedience. They received formal papal approval at the Lateran synods of 1059 and 1063, and by the twelfth century had spread all over Europe. They followed the Rule of St. Augustine*; hence their name.

From the twelfth century a number of independent congregations following the Rule of St. Augustine were established, such as the Victorines* and the Premonstratensians*, showing Cistercian influence. The Augustinian Canons suffered considerable depradations during the Reformation* and many were suppressed. Augustinian Canons had some parochial* duties. The rule was flexible enough to allow them to follow active or contemplative vocations. Many were involved in medical services in hospitals.

Augustinian Friars/Hermits Also called Augustinians. Catholic order, based on the Rule of St. Augustine*, founded in 1256 through the union of various monastic groups. They have three branches: the Calced*, Discalced*, and the Recollects, the latter two being Reformed* congregations. Their garb is black tunic with hood, cowl*, and·girdle*.

Augustinian Nuns Female religious affiliated with the Order of Hermits of St. Augustine.

Augustinianism The body of theological doctrines associated with or derived from St. Augustine of Hippo's* writings and treatises, especially his anti-Pelagian works. He was the first to clearly formulate the orthodox Christian doctrines of sin, salvation, predestination*, free will*, and ethics. Augustine argued that without grace, there could be no faith or salvation. The 22 books of the *City of God* were a massive vindication of Christianity against pagan critics and laid the framework of an ecclesiology* founded on justice. Augustine's ascetic ethic called for the renunciation of the selfish quest for power, honor, wealth, and sex. Augustine's 15 books *On the Trinity* laid the foundation for the later Filioque* clause.

The hallmarks of Augustinianism are a yearning for God and a profound sense of ecclesial community*, the body being the church and the head being Christ. The influence of Augustinianism on the development of later Christianity was immense. Augustine's legacy was carried forward by the monastic movements that followed his rule. All Protestant reformers, particularly Luther* and Calvin*, were indebted to Augustine, who became a Protestant icon in the sixteenth century.

Augustinians of the Assumption See ASSUMPTIONISTS.

Augustinus Title of a book by Cornelius Jansen* (1638) on grace and human nature based upon the works of St. Augustine*. It is considered the classic exposition of Jansenism*.

Auld Lichts See BURGHERS.

Aulen, Gustaf Emanuel Hildebrand (1879–1977) Swedish theologian and bishop. He was professor of dogmatic theology from 1913 to 1933 and bishop of Strangnas from 1933 to 1952, contributing significantly to the liturgical renewal movement within the Swedish Lutheran Church. He became an exponent, along with Soderblom* and A. Nygren*, of the Lundensian school of liberal theology and also participated actively in the emerging ecumenical movement*. Among his works are *Christus Victor* (1931) and *The Faith of the Christian Church* (1948).

aumbry/ambry Receptacle in the wall of a church in which holy oils* and objects were kept in the Middle Ages. In the Anglican Church, the reserved sacrament* is kept in the aumbry*.

Aumbry Lamp

aura/aureole (Lat., *aureolus,* golden) Glorious radiance or luminous cloud surrounding the whole figure of a saint, angel, or divine being in Christian art. Distinguished from the nimbus* or halo* which surrounds only the head.

Aurelius of Carthage (d. 430) Elected bishop between 390 and 393, he was a friend of Augustine and he dedicated his *De Opere Monachorum* and other works to him. Orosius places Aurelius among the great defenders of the faith, and Fulgentius* calls him one of the great doctors of the church* for his vigilance against heresies. Feast day: July 20.

auricular confession (lit., confession to the ear) Practice of confessing sins to a priest authorized to forgive them in the name of the Lord.

Aurora Mass Mass* of Christmas dawn, celebrated in Rome* at the Church of St. Anastasia*.

Ausculta Fili (Lat., Listen, My Son) Papal encyclical* of Pope Boniface VIII* in 1301, affirming papal authority over temporal powers.

Austin Short form of Augustine or Augustinian.

authority of the believer Power granted to the children of God* over the works of the enemy, especially sickness, and to break the bonds of sin and death.

Authorized Version See KING JAMES VERSION.

auto da fe (lit., act of faith). Public ceremony in the Spanish Inquisition* at which, after a procession, Mass*, and sermon, the sentences were read and executed. Heretics were dressed in the ceremonial sanbenito* crowned by a yellow mitre*. Those sentenced to death were handed over to the secular power.

autocephalous (lit., himself the head) 1. Independent, autonomous or self-governing, bishop, especially as applied to the bishops of Cyprus*, Armenia, Ravenna*, and Iberia. 2. In the Eastern Orthodox Church*, a national church in communion with Constantinople* but governed by its own national synod*. The monastery of St. Catherine* is also autocephalous. Autocephalous offices of the Eastern Church* illustrate an important distinction between Roman and Byzantine branches of Christianity.

autocephaly State or condition of being autocephalous*, especially as applied to national autonomous Eastern Orthodox* churches.

autopistic Faith that is not in need of a sanctioning authority for authentication, such as that based on personal revelation.

autosacramental Spanish play similar to the medieval morality plays*. It was based on religious themes and was preceded by a procession of the host* through the streets of a town. Most often it was associated with the feast of Corpus Christi* and dealt with the mystery of the Eucharist*. The best known writers of autosacramentals were J. de la Enzina and Pedro Calderon* (1600–1681).

autosoterism Doctrine associated with Pelagianism* that human beings can achieve their own salvation through good works* and obedience.

Autun Cathedral of St. Lazare built in Autun in Burgundy between 1120 and 1140 to house the relics* of St. Lazarus. It is a Gothic* structure built by Master Gislebertus. It was from the first a unique pilgrimage* church mainly visited by lepers who came in hope of being miraculously healed. They were corralled by horsemen who kept them at a safe distance with their spears. In the cathedral the lepers saw a vision of terror and damnation in the last judgment*, a reflection of their hopeless existence.

Auxentios the Persian, St (c. 420–470) Founder of one of the most influential Byzantine monastic communities which bore his name. Feast day: February 14.

Auxentius (fourth century) Arian bishop and theologian of Milan* who was appointed by Constantius and who remained in office until his death despite orthodox efforts to dislodge him.

Auxerre Cathedral of St. Germain in Auxerre in central France, built between thirteenth and sixteenth centuries. It is dedicated to St. Stephen* or St. Etienne. The doorways date from the thirteenth and fourteenth centuries and are admired for their fine sculptures. Among its most impressive features are the soaring nave*, the rose windows* adorning the transept*, and the elegant choirs.

auxiliary bishop Bishop who assists another in the same diocese*.

auxiliary saints See FOURTEEN HOLY HELPERS.

auxios (Gk., worthy) Acclamation by the congregation during the ordination of a bishop or high ecclesiastic.

AV Authorized Version*.

avagueretz In the Armenian Church*, an archpriest in charge of the spiritual administration of a church.

avandatoun In the Armenian Church*, the sacristy* where the priest puts on his liturgical vestments.

Cathedral of St. Lazare at Autun

avathran In the Armenian Church*, the Gospel book.

Ave Ave Maria.

Ave Maria See HAIL MARY.

Ave Maris Stella (Lat., hail star of the sea) Popular Marian* hymn dating from the ninth century and attributed to Paul the Deacon*. It is sung during the second vespers* of the Common of Feasts of the Blessed Virgin Mary*.

Ave Regina Coelorum Hail, Queen of the Heavens. Second antiphon* of the Virgin used in Roman Catholic services from the Feast of the Purification until Maundy Thursday*.

Ave Verum Corpus (Lat., hail, true body) Short anonymous eucharistic hymn dating from the fourteenth century sung during Mass* after the Preface* and during the Consecration* and at the Benediction.

Averbode Premonstratensian abbey in Averbode, situated to the north of Zichem in Belgium and dedicated to John the Baptist, founded in 1174. It was rebuilt between 1664 and 1672 by Jan van den Eynde the Younger. The tower was finished in 1700.

Avignon Provencal city in France, once the center of the Albigenses*. During the Middle Ages, it was the residence of the Avignon popes from 1309 to 1377, the period labeled by the Italian poet Petrarch as the "Babylonian Captivity of the Papacy." From 1378 to 1415 Avignon also housed the anti-popes of the Great Schism*. The papacy first moved to Avignon in 1309 when the city was technically in the Holy Roman Empire, on the border with France. In 1377 Pope Gregory XI* finally moved the papacy back to Rome*. However, a pro-French faction of cardinals elected an alternative pope, who promptly moved his office back to Avignon. This Great Schism lasted until 1415. The city remained a major ecclesiastical center throughout the rest of the Middle Ages and well into the early modern period.

Papal Avignon and its environs were confiscated by the French government in 1791. Among the city's landmarks are the Romanesque church of Notre Dame des Doms housing the tomb of John XXII* and the fortress-like Palais des Papes.

Palais des Papes, Avignon

Avila, Juan de (1500–1569) "Apostle of Andalusia." Spanish priest beatified in 1893. One of his followers was St. Theresa.

avoidance Mennonite practice of ostracizing church members who have been placed under the ban. Obbe Philips introduced the practice among the Dutch Anabaptists* in 1533, and Menno Simons* continued it. See also SHUNNING.

Avvakum (c. 1620–1681) Martyr and conservative leader of the Russian Orthodox Church* who, as an Old Believer, refused to accept the revised Greek form of the Russian ritual. He was exiled to Siberia in 1653 and burned at the stake in 1681.

awakening Religious renewal or revival.

Awakening, Great See GREAT AWAKENING.

ax Symbol of St. Boniface* and Thomas of Canterbury*.

axiology Branch of philosophy dealing with an ethic of values by which right and wrong actions are determined.

Axum Also, Aksum*. Town in northern Ethiopia, capital of a medieval kingdom from the second to the seventh centuries. It emerged as a major Christian power under King Kaleb.

Ayacucho Peruvian city famous for its churches and convents*.

Aylward, Gladys (1902–1970) Independent British missionary to China. With no educational background and few skills, she was turned down by the China Inland Mission*, but nevertheless headed for China on the Trans-Siberian Railway, settling in remote Yangcheng in Shansi (Shanxi) province in northwest China. She learned Mandarin and became a Chinese citizen in 1936. Together with Jeannie Lawson, she opened an inn for muleteers where guests heard Bible stories in Chinese. Later, she became inspector of feet to enforce the government's edict against binding the feet of young girls. When the Japanese forces reached the region, she led one hundred children on a long journey to safety—an epic story that was the basis of the film, *Inn of the Sixth Happiness*.

Azariah, Vedanayakam Samuel (1874–1945) First Indian-born bishop of the Anglican Church. In 1909 he went to Dornakal, in the Telugu-speaking sector of Hyderabad and labored there for the

Azusa Street

best part of his life. He hosted the World Missionary Conference* at Tambaram, Madras, in 1938.

Azusa Street Revival Revival at 312 Azusa Street, a dilapidated warehouse in Los Angeles, that became the founding event of modern Pentecostalism* in 1906. See also PENTECOSTALISM.

azyme (Gk., unleavened) In the Roman Catholic Church, unleavened bread* used in the Eucharist*.

Bb

Baader, Franz Xavier Von (1765–1841) German Catholic mystic who was influenced by Jakob Boehme* and Friedrich Schelling. He viewed God as an evolving process and history as the unfolding of his grace.

Babai bar Nesibnaye (the Less) (563–629) Persian hermit and miracle worker. At Mount Izla he built a monastery of over 1,000 monks.

Babai the Great (d. 628) Persian monk, third superior* of the Great Convent at Mount Izla founded by Abraham of Kashkar*. Abdiso of Nisibis's *Catalog of Church Writers* attributes to him more than 83 works, most of them lost.

Babylas (third century) Bishop of Antioch*. He is credited with having refused Emperor Philip the Arabian entry into his church until he had done penance* for a murder. He was imprisoned during the Decian persecutions* and died in bonds. He became the object of a widespread cult. Feast day: January 24 (Western Church*); September 4 (Eastern Church*).

Babylon 1. Ancient Akkadian city of Mesopotamia. 2. In the New Testament, a metaphor for a corrupt, decadent, and immoral world, drawn primarily from Revelation 17:1–6.

Babylonian Captivity 1. Captivity of the Jews in Babylon* under Nebuchadnezzar (604–562 B.C.). 2. Period when the popes were exiled from Rome* to Avignon* from 1309 to 1377. 3. Term used metaphorically by Luther* to suggest the church in bondage.

Bach, Johann Sebastian (1685–1750) German composer. He was court organist and koncertmeister at Weimar (1708–1717), kapellmeister* at Cothen (1717–1723), and cantor* at Thomaskirche in Leipzig (1723–1750). During his life he wrote more than 200 cantatas; two great oratorio-passions, in which the Gospel narrative is interspersed with arias and chorales; a series of six cantatas for the Christmas* season called the Christmas Oratorio; the Mass* in B Minor; and the Magnificat*.

Bachkovo Monastery in southern Bulgaria founded in 1083 by Georgian Gregory Bokouriani, a general* under Emperor Alexis Comnenos. Known as Theotokos Petritsoni, the monastery was largely populated by Georgian monks until the fourteenth century when it became Bulgarian.

Back to God Hour Radio program founded in 1939 as the radio voice of the Christian Reformed Church*. It was hosted for many years by Peter Eldersveld, whose clear biblical message had a wide audience.

backslide (verb) To regress spiritually and to begin a process that leads ultimately to apostasy*. Viewed as a process rather than as a state, it includes broken fellowship with God, sin, defiled conscience, spiritual indifference, hardness of heart, and unbelief.

Backus, Isaac (1724–1806) New England minister and evangelist. He was converted during the Great Awakening* and became a Separatist and New Light, then a Congregationalist, and finally a Baptist*. He was strong advocate of religious freedom and the separation of church and state*.

Bacon, Benjamin W. (1860–1932) American Congregationalist and biblical scholar.

Bacon, Leonard (1802–1881) American Congregational* minister and antislavery leader. Author of "Pilgrim Hymn."

Bacon, Roger (c. 1214–c. 1294) Also known as "Doctor Mirabilis." English Franciscan scientist and philosopher. About 1257 he entered the Franciscan Order,* where he came under the influence of Adam of Marsh. Under the direction of Pope Clement IV, Bacon prepared an encyclopedic work in seven parts, called *Opus Maius,* followed by two briefer works known as *Opus Minus* and *Opus Tertium.* The work was a summa* of theology, philosophy, natural sciences, mathematics, and optics. Bacon wrote four other works, *Communia Naturalium, Communia Mathematica, Compendium Studii Theologiae,* and *Compendium Studii Philosophiae.* In 1277 he was condemned by the general* of the Franciscan Order for "dangerous doctrines" and "suspect novelties."

bad faith (Lat., *mala fides*) In Catholic theology, those who remain outside the church even though convinced of its authority.

badarakamaduitz (Arm., Book of the Sacrament) Armenian book containing the full text of the liturgy but not the Epistles or Gospels.

Baillie, Donald Macpherson (1887–1954) Scottish theologian and brother of Robert Baillie. His acclaimed work, *God Was In Christ* (1948), used the Pauline* paradox of grace to study Christology*. He was a prominent figure in the Faith and Order* Conferences in Edinburgh* (1937) and Lund (1952).

Baillie, John (1886–1960) Scottish theologian. He was moderator* of the General Assembly* of the Church of Scotland* in 1943 and joint president of the World Council of Churches* from 1954 and professor of theology at the University of Edinburgh. Among his numerous works are *Invitation to Pilgrimage* (1942), *And the Life Everlasting* (1934), *Our Knowledge of God* (1939), and *The Sense of the Presence of God* (1962).

Bainie, Giuseppe (1775–1844) Italian composer of sacred music and composer of *Miserere.*

Bainton, Roland Herbert (1894–1984) American church historian. He was a congregational minister and an affiliated member of the Society of Friends* with whose service committee he worked to relocate refugees from the Nazis. His greatest contributions, however, were in the fields of writing and teaching. Among his many popular books were *The Church of Our Fathers* (1941) and *The Reformation of the Sixteenth Century* (1952).

baion In the Byzantine tradition, palm branches and leaves blessed and distributed on Palm Sunday*.

Baius, Michel (1513–1589) Flemish theologian and forerunner of Jansenism*. Along with John Hessels, he asserted views on sin* and grace* which earned him the censure of the University of Louvain* and the archbishop of Malines. In 1560, 18 of his propositions were condemned by Sorbonne*. In 1579 Baius formally recanted but continued to write expressing the same opinions.

Baker, Henry Williams (1821–1877) English writer and compiler of hymns. He was the vicar* of Monkland and a dedicated supporter of the High Church* movement. Among his popular hymns were "The King of Love My Shepherd Is," "Lord, Thy Word Abideth," and "O, Praise Ye the Lord." He was also the compiler of the first edition of *Hymns, Ancient and Modern*.

Bakker, Dirk (1865–1932) Dutch missionary and founder of Gereja Kristen Jawa (Church of Central Java). He arrived as a missionary in Central Java in 1900. In 1906 he set up a theological teaching program in Yogyakarta. He wrote in Javanese a textbook of dogmatics*, a summary of Christian doctrine, and a guide for ministers.

Bakker, James (1940–) Television evangelist and erstwhile head of PTL* Television. Along with his wife, Tammy Faye, Bakker launched his career by hosting a children's puppet show on the Christian Broadcasting Network*. During the 1980s the couple rose to fame and fortune as neo-Charismatic evangelists. He resigned in 1987 amid charges of sexual impropriety and financial irregularities. In 1989 he was convicted on fraud and conspiracy charges. After serving a prison term and after being divorced by his wife, he publicly acknowledged his sins in his book, *I Was Wrong* (1998).

baldachino (From Baghdad, from where the materials were obtained) Canopy over an altar or tomb, made of wood, stone, or metal supported on pillars, or of silk and velvet when suspended from a ceiling. It was originally surmounted by a cross. Also used of the canopy over a bishop's throne, statues, and of the movable canopy* carried in processions. The most famous example of a baldachino is Bernini's* baldachino at the altar of St. Peter's* Basilica in Rome*.

Baldachino

Baldovinetti, Alesso (c. 1425–1499) Italian painter of altarpieces and frescoes.

Bale, John (1495–1563) English bishop and dramatist. A Carmelite*, he was converted to Protestantism* about 1533 and thereafter became a vigorous defender of the Reformation*. He wrote 21 plays, most of which are lost. His scholarship is attested by his *Illustrium Maioris Britanniae Scriptorum, hoc est, Angliae, Cambriae, ac Scotiae Summarium* (1548).

Balfour, Arthur James (1848–1930) British statesman and prime minister (1902–1905). He was a noted defender of theism* and published an apology for religious faith, *A Defense of Philosophic Doubt* (1879). Further development of his thought is to be found in *Foundations of Belief* (1895) and in his Gifford Lectures*, *Theism and Humanism* (1915), in which he opposed naturalistic positivism and the idealism that identified man with God.

Ball, John (?–1381) English priest who preached doctrines of social equality and was implicated in the Wat Tyler peasant rebellion of 1381. He was excommunicated for promoting "errors and schisms and scandals" and executed. He is the author of the famous couplet, "When Adam dalf and Eve Span, Who Was then a Gentilman."

Ball, John (1585–1640) One of the early leaders of Presbyterianism* and Puritan* divine whose views on the covenant of grace* are enshrined in the Westminster standards of the Presbyterian churches. He wrote two catechisms.

Ballou, Hosea (1771–1852) Clergyman, known as the father of American Universalism*. He wrote a number of works attacking Trinitarianism. He was the first president of Tufts College.

balokole (Luganda, save one) East African revival dating from 1927.

Balthasar, Hans Urs von (1905–1988) Swiss Roman Catholic theologian, noted for his magisterial work, the seven-volume *Glory of the Lord* (1982–1991), *Theologik* (1985), and *Theodramatik* (1973–1983). Balthasar's theology, like Barth's, is Christocentric*. Through his association with the mystic Adrienne von Speyr (1902–1967), he has developed a remarkable theology of Holy Saturday*, in which Christ's descent into hell* becomes a leading motif in Christology*. Among his other works are *Das Betrachtendes Gebet* (1955), a work on prayer, and *Heart of the World* (1979).

Baltimore Catechism Catechism* approved in 1885 by Cardinal James Gibbons*, archbishop of Baltimore, as the official text for the religious instruction of Catholic children. It remained the standard catechism in the United States until the Second Vatican Council*.

Baltimore, councils of Series of Roman Catholic ecclesiastical councils, including three plenary ones (1852–1884) and ten provincial synods (1829–1869), held in Baltimore concerning education, sacraments, books, secret societies, and other topics, but not matters of faith. The Third Plenary Council* launched the Baltimore Catechism* and the Catholic University of America*.

Bamberg Magnificent cathedral in Bamberg, Germany, erected by Emperor Henry II, consecrated in 1012. The cathedral was gutted by fire in 1081, and a new building was completed in 1237. The twin-choired church, dedicated to St. Peter* at the west end and to St. George* at the east end, rises on four towers in one of the finest squares in Germany. The Bamberg Horseman, created in 1230, is a monument to King Stephen of Hungary who is said to have been converted after seeing the cathedral.

bambino Artistic representation of the baby Jesus, commonly used during Christmas* in nativity scenes.

Bampton Lectures Lectures delivered biennially at the University Church at Oxford for the exposition and defense of the Christian faith. The first lecture was given in 1780. The lectures are funded by an endowment established by John Bampton, canon* of Salisbury* (d. 1751).

ban 1. Excommunication*, especially as practiced by the early Anabaptists* and by Mennonites*. There are two kinds of ban, exclusion from Communion (Kleiner Bann) and exclusion from church membership (Grosser Bann). 2. An ecclesiastical fine. 3. A curse.

Bancroft, Richard (1544–1610) Archbishop of Canterbury* (1604–1610). A strong opponent of Puritanism*, he shepherded the King James Version* of the Bible and was prominent in the Hampton Court Conference. He was also instrumental in the passage of the canons of 1604 and 1606 by the convocations of Canterbury* and York*.

bands 1. Small Wesleyan cells that promoted personal holiness* and good works*. 2. White collar clerical pendants often known as preaching bands.

Bamberg Cathedral

Banez, Domingo (1528–1604) Spanish Dominican theologian, founder of Banezianism*. From 1552 until his death, he taught theology in various places, especially at Salamanca*, Avila, and Alcala. He was one of the greatest commentators on the *Summa Theologiae* of Aquinas*.

Banezianism Theological system explaining the cooperation between divine grace* and free will*, developed by Domingo Banez*. Banez maintained that prevenient grace* or actual grace* is intended to be sufficient to bring about human consent, but added another element called efficacious grace* which reconciles the apparent contradiction between predestination* and free will.

Bangor 1. Bangor Fawr in Caernarfonshire and Merionethshire, a see* founded by St. Deiniol. Its cathedral was rebuilt by Bishop Anian (1267–1305) and again by Bishop Thomas Skevington (d. 1533). 2. Bangor Iscoed in Wrexham, the site of a great Welsh monastery which at one time had 2,000 monks. 3. Bangor in Ireland where St. Comgall* founded an abbey in 555 or 559 from which many daughter monasteries were established. It was the home of St. Columbanus* and St. Gall*. In the Middle Ages, it was occupied by the Franciscans and Augustinians.

Bangor, Antiphonary of Antiphonary written in the Monastery of Bangor* in Ireland between 680 and 691. It contains the familiar hymn, "Draw Nigh and Take the Body of the Lord."

Bangor, Use of Ancient ritual use in Bangor*, Wales, before the Reformation* illustrating Celtic influences.

Bangorian controversy Dispute within the Church of England* between those who held the view that Christ had delegated his authority to the church and the Erastian position advocated by Benjamin Hoadly, bishop of Bangor*, that Christ's kingdom was not of this world and that his authority cannot thus be delegated.

bankers Church curtains or coverings.

Banneaux, Our Lady of Apparitions of the Virgin Mary* to Mariette Beco in Banneaux, Belgium, in 1933. Banneaux became a popular pilgrimage* site.

banner Flag or standard adorned with sacred or ecclesiastical symbols, such as crosses, used especially in processions.

banns (lit., proclamation) Public announcement in church of a forthcoming wedding. Originally, it was designed to prevent clandestine marriages as well as marriages that violated restrictions on consanguinity.

Banz Cathedral and monastery in Banz in Germany, originally established in 1069 when Margravine Alberada built a Benedictine* monastery at the site of their castle with nine towers. The monastery had a tempestuous history marked by fires, the Peasants' War, and the Thirty Years' War. In the eighteenth century, the complex was replaced by imposing Baroque buildings and a new church.

baptism One of the most important sacraments* in the Christian church. It was instituted by Christ himself who was baptized by John the Baptist. In the writings of Paul*, it represents the believer's union with Christ through participation in his death and Resurrection (Rom. 6:4), and it is efficacious in cleansing from sins (1 Cor. 6:11). According to St. Augustine, baptism removed the stain of the original sin*, and it produced a royal character and a mark which set the baptizee* apart as God's. The baptismal character created the Christian in the image of Christ and made him a participant in Christ's royal priesthood.

From the end of the first century, baptism was in the name of the Father, the Son and the Holy Spirit*, although some passages in the Acts (2:38; 10:48; 19:5) speak of baptism in the name of (the Lord) Jesus (Christ). The rite of adult baptism was administered in any one of two ways: triple (or double) immersion* and affusion*. Tertullian* in his *De Baptismo* and *De Corona* describes other elements of the rite, such as preparatory fast and vigil*, the confession* of sins, the renunciation of the devil, anointing with chrism*, lighting of the candle, clothing with a white garment, and a symbolic meal of milk and honey. In

Baptistry at Ephesus

the early church, baptism was performed only on mature adults or those on their deathbeds.

The Catholic doctrine of baptismal regeneration* was accepted by Luther* but not by the other Reformers. Zwingli* held that it was only a sign of admission to the Christian community, while Calvin* held that it was only for the elect*. According to the Thirty-Nine Articles*, baptism is "a sign by which the promises of forgiveness of sin and of our adoption to be the Sons of God by the Holy Ghost* are visibly signed and sealed."

baptism, believer's Baptism administered only to adults or those who have reached the age of accountability on personal confession* of faith in Jesus Christ.

baptism for the dead Practice by which a living Christian was baptized on behalf of a dead believer (1 Cor. 15:29). In the early church it was practiced by Marcionites*, Montanists*, and Cerinthians. Among modern cults, it is practiced by the Mormons*.

baptism, infant Baptism of infants sponsored by Christian parents or others, usually by sprinkling water on the head. One of the most vigorous proponents of infant baptism* in the early church was St. Augustine*, who saw in it an antidote to original sin*. See also CHRISTENING; PAEDOBAPTISM.

baptism of blood Martyrdom, especially as a substitute for baptism* when an unbaptized person is martyred. Used by Tertullian* and other early Christian writers.

baptism of desire Act of perfect contrition* or pure love of God considered the equivalent of baptism* in the case of an unbaptized person, who for some reason is unable to undergo water baptism.

baptism of fire Spiritual baptism as the third blessing of the Holy Spirit. In camp meetings those receiving baptism of fire would see balls of fire or feel fire burning in their bodies. It is a key tenet of the Fire-Baptized Holiness Church.

baptism of/in the Holy Spirit Outpouring of the Holy Spirit* on confessing believers, as distinct from sacramental or water baptism*. A unique Pentecostal doctrine, it draws on Acts 2:4 and 11:15

where the apostles were filled or baptized with the Holy Spirit*. Glossolalia* or speaking in tongues* is considered one of the outward signs of this baptism.

baptismal bowl/font Vessel holding the water in which the baptizee* is immersed or from which the water is sprinkled.

Baptismal Font

baptismal formula Trinitarian* formula uttered during baptism*: "in the name of the Father, the Son and the Holy Spirit*" or "in the name of the Lord Jesus Christ."

baptismal garment White clothing placed on the baptizee* after baptism*.

baptismal name Christian name* bestowed on the baptizee*.

baptismal regeneration Doctrine that a person is born again* at baptism*, based on Scriptures (Titus 3:5 and John 3:3).

baptismal shell Metal shell from which baptismal water is poured on the baptizee*.

baptismal vow Promise made at baptism* by the candidate, if an adult, or by the sponsors or parents, if a child, usually swearing allegiance to Christ and renouncing the devil.

Baptist General Conference Church, once known as Swedish Baptists, founded in 1852 by Gustav

Palmquist (1812–1857). It is a voluntary fellowship of autonomous Baptist churches that affirm inerrancy of the Scriptures, Trinity*, and Christ's vicarious* Atonement*. It is divided into 14 districts, with historic roots in the northern central U.S. It maintains Bethel College and Seminary in St. Paul, Minnesota, and owns Harvest Publications.

Baptist Mid-Missions Independent Baptist foreign missions agency founded by William C. Haas and others in 1920 as the General Council of Cooperating Baptist Missions of North America. Its principal focus was Central Africa, especially the Congo region, where Haas worked for many years with the Heart of Africa Mission (later the World Evangelization Crusade*). After World War II, the agency expanded its work in Africa and also opened new stations in Central and South America, the Caribbean, Europe, Asia, Australia, and the Pacific Islands. It received its present name in 1953.

Baptist World Alliance International fellowship of Baptists* organized in 1905. It is headquartered in Washington, D.C., and holds a world congress every five years. About 71 percent of all Baptist congregations are in North America. In the United Kingdom, the Baptist Union represents nearly 2,000 churches, including Particular and General Baptists*. Baptist churches are found in nearly every European country and owe their origins and spread to Johann Gerhard Oncken, assisted by Julius Kobner, a Jewish convert, and Gottfried Lehmann. Baptists are also very strong in Russia, where it was introduced through the efforts of Lord Radstock, an English peer who had served in the Crimea.

baptisterion In the Byzantine Church*, the baptismal font* with three lit candles on its brim.

baptistery/baptistry Part of the church set apart for baptisms. In the early church, it was a building set apart for this purpose. In Baptist churches, it is a tank large enough for immersion* or a font sometimes placed below floor level. In other churches, it may be a place within the church containing the baptismal font*.

Baptists Christian denomination related to the Anabaptists* or Antipaedobaptists whose signature doctrine was believer's baptism* or the immersion* of adults in water upon personal profession of faith*. Baptists enlarged their doctrinal base by including among their tenets the sole authority of the Bible, religious liberty and freedom of conscience, and the primary authority of the local church. The Anabaptists to whom the Baptists are related were persecuted by the Lutherans and the established churches*. As a result, Baptists were associated with radical political and social movements in the seventeenth century. In England they became one of the three denominations of Protestant Dissenters. John Bunyan* was one of their outstanding leaders.

In America, Baptist history begins with the settlement of Roger Williams* at Providence, Rhode Island, and the church he formed there in 1639. The Great Awakening* in New England witnessed the rapid growth of Baptists in the United States. Driven by their missionary zeal, the Baptists have become the largest Protestant denomination. Among African-American churches, about two-thirds of the members are Baptists. They are organized in several conventions of which the Southern Baptist is the largest and most conservative. Among their distinguished members are Billy Graham* and Martin Luther King*. They also form the largest Protestant community in many of the former republics of the Soviet Union. Historically, Baptists have spawned a number of varieties, such as General Baptists*, Particular Baptists*, Separatists, and Sandemanian Baptists. Baptist theology emphasizes calling*, conversion*, and regeneration* and the priesthood of all believers*. Church discipline* is consistently practiced.

Baptists have no required orders for public worship and the responsibility lies with the congregation. Therefore, Baptist worship is characterized by great variety. Some Baptist churches have formal services and have set prayers read from printed orders distributed to the congregation beforehand. Choirs and clergy are robed, and there are lamps, candles, and crosses often set upon altars, backed by reredos* and decked out in seasonal liturgical colors*. Other Baptist churches, especially black churches, may have completely informal and spontaneous services. In the West, Baptist churches have the flavor of revival meetings with lively singing, testimonies preceding the preaching of the Word, and the call to repentance*. In Germany and Scandinavian countries, Baptist services have a strong Pietistic overtone, with meditation and introspective hymns making it a solemn affair.

The central place in the worship service is the reading and the proclamation of the Word. Baptist emphasis on the importance of preaching has produced a number of the greatest preachers of modern times, including Charles Spurgeon*, John Bunyan, and Billy Graham*. The sermon is the climactic point of the service. The Lord's Supper* is regarded highly but only observed monthly (in the United Kingdom, often weekly). Communion* is generally closed to non-Baptists. Laymen may officiate at Communion and baptism services. Communion is essentially a memorial meal by which the believer renews his or her faith and fellowship in Jesus Christ. Its value lies in the symbolism of the act rather than in the actual elements*. Both bread and wine are distributed by the deacons to the congregation as they sit in their seats.

Baptists have no official manuals of worship or books of common prayer. But there are unofficial ones, such as John E. Skoglund's *Manual of Worship*. The most commonly used hymn books are *The Baptist Church Hymnal* and the *Baptist Hymn Book*. Baptism, which is by full immersion*, is a purely symbolic rite, a dramatic affirmation of what had already taken place in the life of the candidate. Baptism always follows the Trinitarian formula* after the candidate confesses faith in the Holy Trinity*, accepts Jesus Christ as Lord and Savior, and pledges to follow and serve him. Baptists have no creeds* or sacraments*, but only ordinances*.

baptizand Candidate for holy baptism*. See also BAPTIZEE.

baptizee Person being baptized; baptisand*.

Baraca-Philathea Bible classes Movement featuring Bible classes for men (Baraca, or blessing) and women (Philathea, lover of the truth), popular in many countries in the early part of the twentieth century.

Baraga, Frederic (1797–1868) Catholic missionary to the Indians of the upper Michigan peninsula who was ordained a bishop.

barakka (Arab., blessing) Blessed bread that is brought to the offertory but not used.

Barat, St. Madeleine Sophie (1779–1865) French nun who founded the Society of the Sacred Heart* and was canonized.

Barbara, St. Christian martyr* who, according to tradition, was a native of Nicomedia in the third or fourth century. Her martyrdom is recorded in the *Golden Legend**. She is one of the Fourteen Auxiliary Helpers, and the patron saint* of artillerymen and firemen. Feast day: December 4.

barbe (lit., the bearded one) Waldensian title for pastor.

Barberini, Francesco (1597–1679) Scion of a noble Roman family of Tuscan descent. One of his relatives was Maffeo Barberini, who was elected pope as Urban VIII*. Francesco built the Palazzo Barberini in Rome* and founded the Biblioteca Barberini, containing the famous collection of manuscripts which passed into the Vatican Library* in 1902.

Barbour, Clarence A. (1867–1937) American clergyman who was also an educator and author. He was secretary of the YMCA*, president of the Rochester Theological Seminary, and president of Brown University.

Barclay, John (1734–1798) Scottish clergyman and founder of the Bereans. His theology, expressed in his book, *Rejoice Evermore, or Christ All in All,* was censured by the General Assembly of the Church of Scotland*. He and his adherents, known as Barclayites*, seceded and formed their own church known as the Berean Assembly, from its zeal for the study of the Bible (Acts 17:11).

Barclay, Robert (1648–1690) Scottish Quaker* leader whose *Apology for the True Christian Religion, as the Same is Set Forth and Preached by the People Called in Scorn, Quakers* (1678) explained the Friends' doctrine of Inner Light*. A formidable theologian, he published a *Catechism and Confession of Faith* for his fellow Quakers. A favorite of James II, he became governor of East New Jersey and helped William Penn* in the establishment of Pennsylvania.

Barclay, William (1907–1978) Scottish New Testament scholar. He was ordained in the Church of Scotland* in 1933 and ministered as a pastor before joining the University of Scotland as a lecturer in 1947 and professor in 1964. His *Daily Study Bible* (New Testament) series sold 1.5 million copies. In addition to being a preacher, he was a successful television personality. Among his more than 50 books was *A Spiritual Biography* (1975) in which he rejected substitutionary atonement*, regarded miracles as only symbols, and expressed serious doubts about the Virgin Birth* and the inerrancy* of Scripture. He described himself as a "liberal evangelical" but urged Christians to confront the living Christ and to set aside a time for prayer every day.

Barclayites Mild Calvinist followers of John Barclay* who later merged with Congregationalists.

Bardesanes (154–222) Also, Bar-Daisam. Syrian poet, hymn writer, and missionary to Armenia. His theology, which later influenced Mani*, was dualistic. Although called "the last of the Gnostics," his teachings hewed to the orthodox line in most respects. He lived for some time at the court of Abgar VIII at Edessa*. Of his many books, only *Dialogue of Destiny, or the Book of the Laws of the Lands,* is extant in fragments preserved by Eusebius* and other writers. He is considered one of the founders of Syriac* literature.

Bar-Hebraeus, Gregorius (1226–1286) Birth name: Abu-l-Faraj. Syrian Jacobite scholar, bishop, and Maphrian (primate*) of the Jacobite Church* from 1264. Of Jewish descent, he was converted and consecrated bishop in 1246. In 1264 he became primate of the East with residence at the Monastery of Mar Mattei near Mosul. A polymath and encyclopedist of prodigious output, his works include: *The Candelabra of the Sanctuary, The Storehouse of Mysteries* on the Bible, *The Cream of Science* on Aristotelian philosophy, the

Book of the Dove on monastic life, *Book of the Conversation of Wisdom, Book of Splendors* on grammar, *The Ascent of Reason* on astronomy, and two books on church discipline* and life, *Nomocanon** and *Ethicon* as well as numerous translations, chronologies, and poetry.

Baring-Gould, Sabine (1834–1924) English rector* and hymn writer, noted for his hymn, "Onward Christian Soldiers." His best literary legacy was the *Lives of the Saints* in 15 volumes which was banned on the Roman Catholic Index.

Bar-Jesus Also, Elymas. Sorcerer and false messiah who was stricken with blindness for his opposition to St. Paul*. (Acts 13:6–12).

Barmen Declaration Influential statement of the German Confessing Church* in 1934 under the leadership of Karl Barth and Martin Niemoller*, declaring that the allegiance of the church is to Jesus Christ and not to Nazism or any other political or cultural order.

Barnabas, Epistle of Deuterocanonical epistle attributed sometimes to St. Barnabas*. It was probably written in Alexandria* early in the second century. It contains a strong attack against Judaism and the Mosaic Law and purports to find allegorical meaning in the Old Testament upholding the Christian faith.

Barnabas, Gospel of Fifteenth-century work in Italian by an apostate* or Gnostic.

Barnabas, St. Jewish Levite of Cyprus* and one of the earliest Christian disciples of Jerusalem*. He was the companion of St. Paul* on several missionary journeys, and is sometimes called an apostle. He parted from St. Paul over a dispute involving St. Mark* and sailed for Cyprus*. Tertullian* attributes the authorship of the Epistle to the Hebrews to him. He is reputed to have been martyred at Rome* or in Cyprus. Feast day: June 11.

Barnabites The Clerics Regular of St. Paul*, founded in 1530 at Milan* by Antonio Maria Zaccaria, for education, relief of the sick, and mission work.

Barnes, Albert (1798–1870) American Presbyterian minister whose sermon, "On the Way of Salvation," led to heresy charges against him by the strict Calvinists. His *Notes on the Bible* were popular commentaries. He became a leader of the New School* revivalist party.

Barnes, Robert (c. 1495–1540) English reformer and friend of Martin Luther* who was burned without a trial.

Barnett, Samuel Augustus (1844–1913) English cleric and social reformer. As vicar* of St. Jude's Whitechapel, he began to work with the poor and the disenfranchised of London. From 1884 to 1896 he was the first warden of Toynbee Hall. In 1884 he helped to form the Education Reform League. In 1906 he was made a canon* of Westminster. Barnett House for the Study of Social Problems at Oxford University was founded in his honor.

Barnett, Tommy J. (1937–) Assemblies of God* pastor and evangelist. He became pastor of the First Phoenix Assembly of God in 1979 and led its growth from 250 members to 9,000. within nine years. His creative approaches to evangelism include dramatic presentations, specialized ministries to the homeless and to drug addicts, and a program known as Masters Commission.

Barnhouse, Donald Grey (1895–1960) American Presbyterian preacher and writer. Ordained in 1918, he became an early opponent of liberalism* and a leading figure in the Fundamentalist-Modernist ontroversy within the Presbyterian Church. His fiery defense of Fundamentalism* led to a reprimand by the presbytery* of his church in 1932. From 1928 until his death he was the host of a nationally syndicated radio Bible program in which he expounded on biblical themes in a measured and stately tone. Later in his life, his attitude mellowed and he sought to heal the breach with the liberals.

Baronius, Cesare (1538–1607) Italian cardinal and church historian. In 1596 he was made cardinal and in 1597 the Vatican librarian. His most important work is the *Annales Ecclesiastici* (12 folio vols., 1607), a year-by-year chronicle of the church. The work was left unfinished at his death.

He also published two new and corrected editions of the *Roman Martyrology**.

Baroque Catholicism Renewal within the Catholic Church that extended from the sixteenth to the nineteenth centuries. It was expressed by figures like Teresa of Avila* and Melchior Cano* in Spain and Pierre de Berulle*, Margaret Mary Alacoque*, Vincent de Paul* and Louis de Marillac in France. In theology it led to an interest in the mystical and a veneration* of Christ in his humanity and redemptive love. It represented a shift toward the personal, as Catholics began to pursue intense spiritual lives through prayer. The principal theme of Baroque Catholicism was grace*.

Barratt, Thomas Ball (1862–1940) Norwegian Pentecostal leader. He was ordained as a pastor in the Methodist Episcopal Church of Norway. In 1906 on a visit to the United States, he came into contact with the Pentecostal movement and returned to Norway as its most ardent promoter. He was a key figure in the establishment of indigenous Pentecostal churches throughout Europe and the Third World. In 1916 he left the Methodist Church to found the Filadelfia Church in Oslo.

Barreira, Balthazar (1531–1612) Portuguese Jesuit missionary in Angola and Sierra Leone. Arriving in Angola in 1579, he claimed 20,000 converts within a decade. In 1605 he moved to Sierra Leone, where he converted a local chieftain, King Philip. He opposed the slave trade and respected local peoples and languages.

Barrow, Henry (c. 1550–1593) English Puritan whose defense of separation from the established church* led to his being charged with the circulation of seditious books. Three years later he was sentenced to be hanged.

Barrow, Isaac (1630–1677) English theologian and mathematician. His scholarly credentials were impressive. He was appointed professor of Greek in Cambridge in 1660, professor of geometry at Gresham College, London, and the first Lucasian professor of mathematics at Cambridge in 1663. Isaac Newton* was his pupil and successor as Lucasian professor. Charles II made him his chaplain* and master of Trinity. His *Treatise on the*

Pope's Supremacy is a theological work that reflected his outstanding ability.

Bar-Salibi, Jacob (twelfth century) Syrian Jacobite bishop and writer.

Barsanuphius, St. (d. 540) Ascetical writer who spent most of his life as a hermit in the region south of Gaza. His correspondence with a fellow hermit called *Questions and Answers* represents the best of desert spirituality*. Feast day: February 6.

Barsoum, Ignatius Afram (1887–1957) Patriarch of the Syriac Orthodox Church* (1933–1957). He became a monk in 1907 at Deir al-Zaafaraan and later became its abbot. He was ordained bishop in 1918 and elected patriarch* in 1933. He moved the patriarchal see* from Mardin to Homs and helped to establish St. Ephraem Seminary.

Barsumas (d. c. 457) Archimandrite* and saint* of the Syrian Jacobite Church*. He defended Eutyches* at the Second Council of Ephesus* (Latrocinium*, 449). Feast day: February 3.

Barsumas (d. 496) Bishop of Nisibis* and the Church of the East*. He actively defended Theodore of Mopseustia*. At the Synod of Beth Lapat in 484 he secured the deposition of Babowai, the catholicos* of Seleucia. He was instrumental in founding the influential theological school in Nisibis*.

Barth, Karl (1886–1968) Swiss Protestant theologian. After serving as pastor at Geneva* and Safenwil, he taught at Gottingen, Munster, and Bonn. With his *Commentary on the Romans* (1918–1922) he led the reaction against the liberal theology of the eighteenth and nineteenth centuries and heralded the resurgence of the classic themes of Christocenrtic orthodoxy*. Barth maintained that knowledge of God can be based only on the Bible and the revelation of Jesus Christ as Savior and Redeemer. He thus clearly rejected natural theology* and all non-Christian religions of the world. His *Church Dogmatics* published in 1932 without the final volume is his crowning work. It is the most comprehensive exposition of Protestant Christian doctrine published in the twentieth cen-

tury, tying together such doctrines as the Trinity*, Incarnation*, and Christ's humanity.

Influenced by Dostoevsky* and Kierkegaard*, Barth in turn influenced a whole generation of theologians in the 1940s and 1950s. His influence has been diffused since, but he still has a large following. Almost singlehandedly he stemmed the liberal tide in Continental theological circles. Among his other books are *Credo* (1935), *The Knowledge of God and the Service of God* (1938), *Das Wort Gottes und Die Theologie* (1924), *Die Kirchliche Lehre von der Taufe* (1943), *Dogmatik und Grundriss* (1946), and *Die Protestantische Theologie im 19. Jahrhundert* (1947).

Bartholomew, Gospel of Apocryphal gospel apparently written by a Gnostic writer.

Bartholomew, St. One of the 12 apostles, also called Nathanael, mentioned only in the Synoptic Gospels*. According to Eusebius*, he is reported to have visited India. He is traditionally said to have been flayed alive in Armenia. He is therefore represented by three flaying knives. Feast day: June 11 (Eastern Church*); August 24 (Western Church*).

Bartholomew's Day Massacre, St. See ST. BARTHOLOMEW'S DAY MASSACRE.

Bartleman, Frank (1871–1936) Pentecostal evangelist and author. Called to the ministry in 1894, he moved in 1903 to Los Angeles, where he came

Karl Barth

under the influence of William J. Seymour* and the Azusa Street Revival*. Thereafter he became a strong Pentecostal voice and took the message of Azusa Street around the country and the world as an itinerant preacher. Most popular among his six books is *How Pentecost Came to Los Angeles* (1925).

Bartolommeo, Fra (1475–1517) Also, Baccio di Paolo del Fattorino; Baccio della Porta. Florentine painter. In 1500 he entered the Dominican Order and became the most important painter from Florence* after Leonardo da Vinci* and Raphael*. He painted numerous magnificent altarpieces. Among his best known works are *The Last Judgment, Lamentation, Vision of St. Bernard, Madonna in Glory with Saints and Donor,* and the *Holy Family*.

Bascom, Henry B. (1796–1850) Methodist clergyman and circuit rider* who became president of Madison College and of Transylvania University. He helped to found the Methodist Episcopal Church and became one of its first bishops.

base communities Small lay Roman Catholic communities found among the urban poor and in isolated rural areas of Latin America. They function with or without clergy. They have often represented the grassroots of liberation theology*.

Basel City in Switzerland, site of an old Carolingian cathedral built in 917, rebuilt in 1019, and consecrated in the presence of Henry II, who came to be venerated as the patron saint* of the cathedral and the protector of the city. It was almost entirely destroyed by fire in 1185 and by earthquake in 1356. It was completely rebuilt in 1500 when the finial cross was placed on St. Martin's Tower. Its sculptural decorations include the tympanum* showing Christ judging the world and the Wheel of Fortune. Basel was an important center of the Reformation* and of Christian humanism. See also ERASMUS, DESIDERIUS; OECO-LAMPADIUS, JOHANNES.

Basel/Basle, Confession of Reformation* statement of 12 articles promulgated at Basel, Switzerland, in 1531. It was compiled by O. Myconius* on the basis of a formula devised by J. Oecolampadius*. It adopted a position midway between Luther* and Zwingli*, and described the Lord's Supper* as food for the soul.

Basel/Basle, Council of Roman Catholic reforming council, 1431–1449. It was convened by Martin V* and opened in 1431. When its deliberations became hostile to Pope Eugenius IV*, he denounced it as heretical and dissolved it but was forced to revoke his decision and allow the council to continue. The council thereupon reasserted the decrees of the Council of Constance*, imposed restrictions on papal legates, prescribed an oath* to

Basel Cathedral

be taken by the pope on his election, and regulated the affairs of the Curia*. In 1439 the council deposed Eugenius IV* as a heretic and elected Amadeus VIII of Savoy as Antipope Felix V. The council's action was denounced by the pope as well as the great princes, and it was forced to close down in 1449. The council then continued in Ferrara and then Florence*.

Basel Mission Missionary sending organization founded in Basel* in 1815 by members of the Deutsche Christentumsgesellschaft (German

Christian Fellowship). Its mission seminary (1816–1955) trained over 2,500 missionaries who were sent to Ghana, India, China, Cameroon, Togo, Borneo, and Nigeria. In 1914 when World War I put an end to the work, its staff consisted of 450 missionaries. Work was restarted in 1925 but was again suspended during World War II. After the end of the war, the mission was resumed in 1954.

bashak In the Armenian Church*, the chalice*.

Basham, Don Wilson (1926–1989) Pentecostal Bible teacher. He was ordained in 1955 and pastored churches in Washington, D.C., Toronto, and Sharon, Pennsylvania. He left the pastorate* in 1967 and began a freelance writing and teaching ministry with emphasis on the Holy Spirit*. He joined Bob Mumford*, Derek Prince, and Charles Simpson in founding Christian Growth Ministries and served as editor of its monthly publication, *New Wine Magazine*. He was among the first in the Charismatic movement to teach on deliverance. He is the author of *Deliver Us From Evil* and 15 other books.

Basil, Liturgy of St. Liturgy that exists in two forms: a shorter and a longer one. The shorter liturgy, used in the Coptic Church*, contains an Antiochene anaphora* and is brief and simple, comparable to the Liturgy of Addai and Mari*. The longer form is used in the Orthodox Church on the first five Sundays in Lent*, Maundy Thursday*, and the eves of Eastern Christmas and Epiphany*, and on the Feast of St. Basil*.

Basil of Ancyra (fourth century) Moderate Arian bishop. Elected bishop of Ancyra, modern Ankara, in 336, he was deposed by the Council of Sardica* in 343, reinstated in 348, and then removed and banished in 360. He took part in the Arianizing synods of Sirmium (351), Ancyra (358), and Seleucia (359).

Basil Preobrazhenski (1875–1945) Russian martyr*. He taught at Voronezh Theological Academy from 1901 and became a missionary preacher. He continued to preach after the Russian Revolution, defying the Bolsheviks. He was ordained priest in 1920 and consecrated bishop of Kineshma in 1921.

He was jailed from 1923 to 1940 and rearrested again after refusing to sign a declaration of loyalty to the Soviet regime. Feast day: July 29.

Basil, Rule of St. Two works of Basil the Great* that were part of his ascetical theology* and which, because of his authority, became highly influential in Eastern and Western monasticism*. The *Moral Rules* (*Regulae Morales* or *Moralia*) composed by him in 358–359, contains 80 rules, each supported by a quotation from the Bible. The second and more important treatise is the *Asceticon,* a collection of questions and answers on monastic life. The shorter version of the *Asceticon* was used by St. Theodore of Studios* and through him came to establish the norms of monastic life. The more widely used form of the *Asceticon,* known as the Vulgate or the *Great Asceticon,* was compiled in the sixth century. In this version, the questions and answers are divided into 55 detailed rules or principles and 313 short rules giving instruction on the application of these rules to monastic life.

In the Middle Ages, the *Great Asceticon* was expanded by the addition of an ascetical constitution and a treatise on baptism*. Hours were laid down for liturgical prayers and manual and other works and set chores. Poverty and chastity* were enjoined. The monks were also required to care for the poor.

Basil the Great, St. (c. 330–379) One of the three great Cappadocian Fathers* and the brother of St. Gregory of Nyssa* and St. Macrina*. In 358 he abandoned a worldly life and became a hermit by the River Iris in Neocaesarea, but came out of his retirement at the request of Eusebius* of Caesarea to defend orthodoxy* against the Arian Emperor Valens. In 370 he succeeded Eusebius as bishop of Caesarea*. As bishop he was responsible for infusing Eastern monasticism* with its deep spirituality* and for establishing hospitals and hostels for the poor. His writings represent his great legacy to the church. They comprise a large collection of letters, a treatise on the Holy Spirit*, three books against Eunomius*, and *Philocalia* which he compiled with Gregory of Nazianzus*. Through his efforts the Arian controversy was laid to rest at the First Council of Constantinople* (381–382), held shortly after his death. Feast day: January 1 (Eastern Church*); January 2 (Western Church*).

Basilian In the Eastern Church*, a monk.

Basilian monks In the Eastern Orthodox Church*, cenobite monks in the monasteries on Mount Athos*, Sinai, and elsewhere from whose ranks the hierarchs are chosen. So called because they are governed by the Rule of St. Basil* the Great.

basilica Place of Christian worship built on the same plan as Roman buildings of the same name that were used as a law court or a commercial exchange. A basilica was often approached by an atrium* or outer courtyard with a colonnaded cloister*. Entry into the main building was through a narthex* or narrow porch. The church itself was built with a nave* and two or four aisles with pillars or arches supporting the horizontal architraves. The building faced east, with the east end completed by an arch and semicircular apse*, with mosaic on its vaults. The altar stood apart from the wall on the chord of the apse, on a raised platform surmounted by a canopy. Underneath the altar and below the floor level was the confessio* or chapel which in earlier times contained the body of the patron saint*. During worship, the bishop sat on the throne in the center of the apse wall with the clergy on a semicircle on either side.

The title "basilica" is given by the pope only to certain privileged churches. The four major basilicas are the Roman churches of St. John Lateran, St. Peter's* at the Vatican*, St. Paul's Outside the Walls*, and Santa Maria Maggiore*. Minor basilicas are found on every continent.

St. John Lateran

Basilides (second century) Gnostic theologian of Alexandria*, whose doctrines have survived only in the works of his detractors, such as Hippolytus*, Clement of Alexandria*, and Irenaeus*. According to Irenaeus, he taught Gnostic dualism in which there are 365 heavens, the ruler of the lowest of which is the Yahweh of the Old Testament. The universe is ruled by archons who are ignorant of the Supreme God. Christ is a messenger of the supreme God who did not actually die on the cross. According to Hippolytus*, Basilides was a monist for whom Christ is an enlightened being who leads the elect* back to an ineffable God. His followers were called Basildeans, whose rituals included magic.

basilikos (Gk., royal) Central door of the iconostasis*, so called because it was reserved for the emperor.

Basnage, Jacques (1653–1723) Huguenot scholar. After Louis XIV revoked the Edict of Nantes*, he settled in Amsterdam as the pastor of a Walloon church. His most important work was *Histoire de la Religion des Eglises Reformees* (1690).

bason Ecclesiastical basin, particularly a receptacle for offering plates.

Bassano, Jacopo (c. 1515–1592) Venetian painter of religious scenes.

Bassendyne Bible Earliest edition of the Bible to be published in Scotland, printed by Thomas Bassendyne in Edinburgh. The New Testament appeared in 1576 and the entire Bible in 1579. It was a version of the Geneva Bible*.

Bassett, James (1834–1906) American Presbyterian missionary who founded the first mission in Iran as head of the Eastern Mission in Persia.

bastagarios In the Byzantine Church*, a cleric who carries the icon of the saint* during procession.

Batalha Town in Beira in Portugal, site of a Dominican monastery, built by King Joao I in fulfillment of a vow made in 1385, just before the Battle of Aljubarota. It was built by Huet, the master builder, who created a Gothic* masterpiece with minuscule towers and finials, pillars, tracery and delicate balustrades. The six panels of the main portals are the setting for 100 statues. The interior of the monastery church is 262 feet long and 105 feet high. The Claustro Real, the Royal Cloister, was built between the fourteenth and fifteenth centuries around a spacious quadrangle. On the east side of the cloister* is the chapterhouse decorated with stained glass, approached through a massive gateway. On the northwest side is a second cloister. The monastery is one of the crowning achievements of Portuguese architecture.

Bath Qol/Kol (Heb., lit., daughter of the voice) Audible voice of God as heard during Christ's baptism, the transfiguration, and before the passion*.

Battle-Axe Experiment Religious community founded by Theophilus Gates near Philadelphia* in 1837 that practiced free love according to "the principle of holiness."

Bauer, Walter (1877–1960) German evangelical theologian* and lexicographer and professor at Gottingen (1916–1945). In his *Rechtglaubigkeit und Ketzerei im altesten christentum* (1934), he held that heresies were legitimate variants of Christianity in the early church. His masterwork was *Griechischdeutsches Woirterbuch zu den Schriften des NT und der ubrigen urchristlichen Literatur*, a lexicon of the New Testament which was the basis of the Greek-English Lexicon (1957).

Baur, Ferdinand Christian (1792–1860) German Protestant theologian and leader of the Tubingen* school of theology. A Hegelian, he interpreted the New Testament from a dialectical standpoint and rejected those books that did not reflect a conflict between St. Paul* and St. Peter*. He considered only the Epistles to the Romans, Galatians, and Corinthians as genuine. He is the author of a number of books on biblical exegesis*, including *Die christliche Gnosis* (1835), *Die christliche Lehre von der Versohnung* (1838), *Die christliche Lehre von der Dreieinigkeit und Menschwerdung Gottes in ihrer geschichlichten Entwicklung* (3 vols., 1841–1843), *Die Christuspartei in der korinthischen Gemeinde* (1831), *Die Sogenannten Pastoralbriefe des Apostels Paulus* (1835),

Kritische Untersuchungen uber die kanonischen Evangelien (1847), and *Church History of the First Three Centuries* (1878–1879).

bautha dniwage In the Church of the East*, the three-day Fast of Nineveh* observed on Monday, Tuesday, and Wednesday of the third week before Lent*.

Bavinck, Johan Herman (1895–1964) Dutch Calvinist writer and missiologist. He spent two decades from 1921 in the Dutch East Indies as a missionary. In 1939 he became professor of missions at Kampen and the Free University. After World War II, he founded the Calvinist Center for Missions at Baarn. His best known works are *Gereformeerde Dogmatiek* and *An Introduction to the Science of Missions* (1960).

Baxter, Richard (1615–1691) English nonconformist leader and pastor, author of over 200 books, including *Gildas Salvianus: The Reformed Pastor* (1656) and the *Saints' Everlasting Rest* (1650). *The Call to the Unconverted* shows Baxter's evangelistic concern. He also wrote several hymns, including "Ye Holy Angels Bright" and "He Wants Not Friends Who Hath Thy Love." Although a moderate Presbyterian, he accepted modified Episcopalianism and promoted ecumenism*.

bay Division of a Gothic* cathedral.

Bay Psalm Book (1640) Full title: *The Whole Book of Psalmes Faithfully Translated into English Metre*. The first book to be printed in the English colonies of North America, compiled by John Eliot*, Richard Mather*, and Thomas Weld, and printed by Stephen Day at Cambridge. It was the approved hymnal of the Massachusetts Bay Colony.

Bayeux Cathedral One of the finest examples of Romanesque architecture in Normandy, severely damaged by fire in 1105 and 1160. Work on restoration began immediately but was interrupted by the Hundred Years' War, during which time it served as a fortress. Work resumed in 1477 and was completed within two years. In 1652 the church was plundered by the Huguenots* and its roof-truss was destroyed by fire in 1676.

Bayeux Tapestry Beautifully embroidered strip of linen, 321 feet by 20 inches, preserved in France depicting the Norman invasion of England. It was made for the use of the Cathedral of Bayeux at the

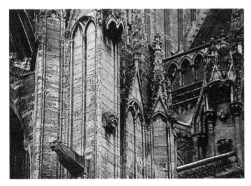

Bayeux Cathedral

instance of Bishop Odo, who himself appears in the tapestry. It has 626 humans and 506 symbols. It may have been made at Canterbury*, Kent, one of Europe's leading embroidery schools.

bazpan In the Armenian Church*, a pair of richly ornamented cuffs fastening the sleeves of the priestly sticharion*.

B.C. Before Christ, designation for time before the birth of Christ. See A.D.

BCMS Bible Churchmen's Missionary Society*.

BCP *Book of Common Prayer*.

B.D. Bachelor of Divinity.

Be Thou My Vision The most beloved of all Irish hymns, it began as an eighth-century "lorica" or protection prayer. First translated into English by Mary Byrne in 1905, it was put into verse by Eleanor Hull in 1912. The traditional Irish tune is called "Slane," the name of a hill in County Meath, where St. Patrick* reportedly challenged the Druid priests.

Bea, Cardinal Augustin (1881–1968) President of the Secretariat for Promoting Christian Unity* in Rome. He was responsible for drafting the Dogmatic Constitution on Divine Revelation, the De-

claration on the Relationship of the Church to Non-Christian Religions, and the Declaration on Religious Freedom at the Second Vatican Council*. He was rector* of the Pontifical Biblical Institute, 1930–1949, editor of *Biblica* for 20 years, and confessor* to Pope Pius XII* (1945–1958). He also was influential in founding the Sophia University in Tokyo.

Beachy Amish Mennonite Church Group, less strict in ecclesiastical standards, that seceded from the Old Order Mennonites*.

beadle Church official in Scottish churches, called a "minister's man." He is the custodian of church buildings; he carries the mace* in ecclesiastical processions; and he bears the books to the pulpit before the service begins.

beadroll Roll of dead persons for whom prayers are to be said.

beatific vision The ultimate privilege of a Christian to see God directly and clearly rather than through knowledge. It is often accompanied by indescribable joy and bliss as recorded by Paul* (1 Cor. 13:12), by John* (1 John 3:2), and by mystics such as St. Therese of Lisieux.

beatification Formal declaration in Roman Catholic Church that a person is "blessed" and may be venerated. The veneration* is limited to a particular locality and is not binding on the whole church. It is often a step toward canonization*. Normally, one attested miracle is required for beatification.

beating of the bounds Medieval English ceremony associated with Rogationtide procession around the parish* when the boundaries were beaten with willow rods as a means of keeping away poachers.

beatitude Title applied to patriarchs of any of the autocephalous* Eastern Orthodox* churches.

Beatitudes (Lat., *beatitudo,* blessedness, happiness) In the Sermon on the Mount, nine states of blessedness mentioned in Matthew 5:3–12 and four states of blessedness mentioned in Luke 6:20–23.

Beatus (d. 798) Spanish presbyter* and abbot of the Benedictine* monastery of St. Martin's at Liebana, near Santander. He is the author of *Commentary on the Apocalypse,* a work compiled in expectation of the end of the world in 800. He was also a hymn writer.

beatus (pl., beati; fem., beata, blessed) Title of a beatified person.

Beatus page First page of a psalter, from the first word of Psalm 1. The initial B is decorated and in some manuscripts occupies the whole page.

Beatus Page

Beauduin, Lambert (1873–1960) Pioneer of the liturgical movement* in Europe. He was a Benedictine* of the Abbey of Mont-Cesar in Louvain, Belgium. His *Manifesto* of 1909 is believed to be a landmark in the liturgical movement.

Beaulieu, Abbey of Cistercian abbey in Hampshire founded and endowed in 1204 by King John for 30 monks from Citeaux* and dedicated in 1246.

Beauraing, Our Lady of Apparitions of the Virgin Mary* in 1932–1933 to children in Beauraing, Belgium.

Beauvais Cathedral of Saint-Pierre in Beauvais in France. It was designed to be the greatest cathedral ever, but it remained only a dream and is only half finished. Its building began in the middle of the thirteenth century under the direction of Bishop Milon de Nanteuil. Financial problems and the Hundred Years' War delayed the construction, and it was 1500 when the foundation stone for the transept* was laid. In 1569 the four-storied central tower reached a height of 492 feet, the tallest in the Christian world. In 1573 the tower collapsed. Resumption of the work became difficult because financial resources had become exhausted. After the religious wars of the sixteenth century, all hopes of completing the cathedral disappeared. During the French Revolution, the church was plundered. Only the choir with its clerestory* windows remains as evidence of the great dream.

Bec, Abbey of Celebrated Benedictine abbey between Rouen* and Lisieux, in Normandy, France, founded by the Blessed Herluin and consecrated in 1041. It was rebuilt a number of times, especially in 1060, 1263, and 1626. Among its abbots were Lanfranc* (1045–1063) and St. Anselm* (1078–1093).

Beck, Johann Tobias (1804–1878) German Protestant theologian who saw the Bible as the progressive work of the Holy Spirit* and the revelation* of the kingdom of God* as the climax of human history. He influenced Adolf Schlatter* and later theologians.

Becket, St. Thomas See THOMAS A BECKET, ST.

Beckx, Pierre Jean (1795–1887) Belgian Jesuit who became general* of the Society of Jesus*. Author of the *Month of May.*

Beda College at Rome* where English candidates* for priesthood are trained.

Bede, St. (c. 673–735) "The Venerable." The father of English history. Anglo-Saxon scholar and historian. For nearly 53 years he was a monk at Jarrow, where he devoted himself to reading and teaching. His literary labors resulted in one of the great works of medieval historiography, *Historia Ecclesiastica Gentis Anglorum* (731). His interest in hagiography* is reflected in his two lives of St. Cuthbert* and his revision of the *Hieronymian*

Martyrology*. He also wrote a dictionary of Latin and treatises on science and computing. In 1899 he was declared a doctor of the church*. Feast day: May 25.

The Venerable Bede

Beecher, Henry Ward (1813–1887) American Congregational* preacher, brother of Harriet Beecher Stowe, the antislavery novelist. He was a political activist and reformer and champion of the abolition of slavery and women's suffrage. A Charismatic and witty preacher, he emphasized love rather than Calvinist morality. His later life was clouded by an adultery charge that led to a drawn-out trial. His sermons were collected in *The Plymouth Pulpit* (10 vols.). He is also the author of *Yale Lectures on Preaching* (1872–1874).

Beecher, Lyman (1775–1863) American Presbyterian preacher and a major figure in Evangelical Protestantism* before the Civil War. Converted during the Second Great Awakening*, he became pastor of Presbyterian churches in Ohio, New York, Connecticut, and Massachusetts. In Cincinnati, he was the president of the Lane Theological Seminary and he was also a founder of the American Bible Society*. He was a champion of social reform, including temperance, abolition of slavery, and women's suffrage, and a staunch foe of Unitarianism* and Roman Catholicism*. All his seven sons, including Henry Ward Beecher*, en-

tered the ministry. His daughter Harriet Beecher Stowe wrote *Uncle Tom's Cabin*.

beehive Symbol of religious eloquence and of St. Ambrose*.

Beethoven, Ludwig van (1770–1827) German composer, one of the greatest in the history of music. He began his career as an organist in the Bonn Cathedral, but later moved to Vienna*, where he achieved fame. While he was not strictly a religious composer, his sacred compositions include an oratorio*, *Christ on the Mount of Olives*, the Mass* in C and *Missa Solemnis**, a monumental choral work. The chorus of his Ninth Symphony, based on a 1785 text by Frederick Schiller, *An Die Freude* (Ode to Joy) is a classic Christian hymn sung in English-speaking churches as "Joyful, Joyful, We Adore Thee."

Begbie, Harold (1871–1929) English religious writer, author of *Twice-born Men* and *The Life of William Booth*.

Beguines/Beghards Lay Christians who formed a loose association without a common rule or hierarchy*, lived in austerity without vows, except chastity*, emphasized manual work, and were free to hold private property and to marry. Women in the group were known as Beguines and men as Beghards. The groups were founded in the Netherlands in the twelfth century and soon spread to other countries. Called extra-regulars, they were neither lay nor monastic, but they cared for the sick and the poor and spent time in communal prayer. Suspected of heresy and immorality, they were harried and persecuted by both Protestants and Roman Catholics. They were condemned by the Council of Vienne in 1311. The Beghards reformed and survived until the French Revolution. The Beguines have adopted the Austin rule and are still active in Belgium and other countries. Beguine authors, such as Mechthild of Magdeburg* and Hadewijch, have left an important body of mystical writings, known as bridal mysticism.

Beissel, John Konrad (1690–1768) Rechristened as Gottrecht Friedsam. Mystic, hymn writer, and founder of the Ephrata Society*. Born in the

Palatinate in Germany, he emigrated to America in 1720 and settled in Pennsylvania, where he joined the Seventh-Day Baptists*. His piety gained him many followers whom he rebaptized into a new group called the Ephrata Society. One of his best-loved hymns is *Turtle Dove* (1747).

belfry Tower or steeple with one or more bells.

Belgic Confession Calvinistic creed with 37 articles prepared in 1561 and adopted by the Synod of Dort* in 1619. It was originally drawn up in French by Guido de Bres* (1522–1567) on the basis of the Gallican Confession* of 1559. Its adoption in synod* at Antwerp in 1566 marked the triumph of Calvinism* in the Netherlands.

belief Trust and assurance in a person, thing, or idea which is held to be true; emotional and intellectual assent to a set of values and ideas; conviction about the reality of the object of a religious faith.

believer Synonym for Christian, especially one who believes in Jesus Christ as Lord and Savior.

believer's baptism See BAPTISM.

bell Metallic device used in public worship in Christian services for centuries, particularly to summon the faithful to prayer or worship or some special occasion. It was first mentioned by Gregory of Tours* in 585. Bells are used at Mass*, funerals, and the angelus, and small bells are used in the Eucharist*. Very large bells known as carillons are musical instruments in their own right. The three largest bells in the world are at Notre Dame* (1680), 17 tons; the "Great Paul" of St. Paul's Cathedral* in London (1716), 16.25 tons; and the Cathedral of Milan, 15 tons. The custom of blessing bells with holy water* and chrism* is known as the Baptism of the Bells.

bell, book, and candle Ceremonial excommunication* or anathema in the Roman Catholic Church. After pronouncing the sentence, the officiating cleric closes his book, quenches the candle by throwing it to the ground, and tolls the bell as for one who has died.

bell cote/cot Turret, gable, or group of arches where bells are hung.

Bell, Lemuel Nelson (1894–1973) Presbyterian medical missionary in China. Responding to a call* to overseas mission, he arrived in 1916 in Tsingkiangpu (now Huaiyin) to serve in the Love and Mercy Hospital which, under his leadership became the largest of the Southern Presbyterian overseas medical missions. He returned to the United States in 1941 and founded *The Presbyterian Journal*. He is the father of Ruth Graham, wife of Billy Graham*.

bell, passing Bell rung at the time of death to notify the parish* of the passing away of a member.

bell tower Church tower containing bells; companile.

Bellarmine, St. Robert (1542–1621) Full name: Roberto Franceso Romolo Bellarmino. Roman Catholic cardinal and theologian. He entered the Jesuit order in 1560 and studied at Padua and Louvain*. Ordained in 1570, he taught at the New Roman College (later the Gregorian University*), where he produced his famous *Disputationes de Controversiis Christianae Fidei* (1586–1593)—a clear and systematic exposition of the Roman Catholic faith. He also took a prominent part in the revision of the Vulgate*, known as the Sixto-Clementine, in 1592. In 1589 the pope sent him on an important diplomatic mission to France and in 1597 he became personal theologian to the pope. He was canonized in 1930 and made a doctor of the church* in 1931. Feast day: September 17.

Bellini, Giovanni (c. 1430–1516) Venetian painter. He was the greatest of the group known as Madonnieri, or Madonna Painters, painting seemingly endless variations on the simple theme of the Madonna* holding the child in an upright position. In these paintings the Madonna is always of a serious mien, with a white coif covering her hair beneath a blue hooded mantle. She is the corporeal ciborium*, the earthly bearer of the Godhead. The child appears in various positions, in her arms or standing, and appears robust and lively. He also created deeply devotional images of the Pieta*. His other works include *Transfigura-tion, Agony in the Garden,* and *St. Francis on Mount Avernus.*

Belloc, Hilaire Pierre (1870–1953) English Catholic writer. A pupil of John Henry Newman*, he was a well-known figure in English journalism for his advocacy of economic liberalism* combined with a deep and abiding respect for the traditional values of Christian civilization. He was the author of many books, marked by their brilliant and provocative style, including his principal work, *Europe and the Faith* (1912), histories of *The French Revolution* (1924) and *England* (1925–27), and biographies of Joan of Arc* (1929), Richelieu (1930), Wolsey (1930), Napoleon (1932), Charles I (1933), Cromwell (1934), and Milton* (1935). With G. K. Chesterton* he issued a series of political broadsides known as "Chesterbellocs."

belothyron In the Byzantine Church*, curtain that is drawn across the holy doors* concealing the mysteries* from the congregation.

Beloved Disciple Epithet of the apostle John.

Beloved Physician Epithet of the apostle Luke.

Belvedere Vatican* museum containing priceless classical art and statuary.

bema (lit., platform) In the Eastern Church*, the sanctuary, usually a raised space containing the altar and shut off from the iconostasis*. Sometimes used for the altar itself.

Bembo, Pietro (1470–1547) Italian cardinal and humanist and theologian.

bemothyra In the Byzantine Church*, the altar door.

Benedic Anima Mea (Lat., Bless the Lord, O, My Soul) Beginning of Psalm 103 and an anthem based on it.

Benedicamus Domino (Lat., Let us bless the Lord) Formula used in the Roman Rite* to mark the end of the choir office* or, sometimes, of the Mass* at Advent* or other special times. It is now

used at the conclusion of the Office of Readings* and the midday office. It was a favorite chant of medieval composers.

Benedicite (Lat., bless ye) Canticle* or song of praise based on Psalm 148 that also forms part of the "Song of the Three Children," sung by Shadrach, Meshach, and Abednego while in the fiery furnace before King Nebuchadnezzar. It was widely used in the morning office of lauds* on all Sundays and festivals. In the *Book of Common Prayer*, it was sung as an alternative to the *Te Deum** at matins* in Lent* and Advent*. In the Byzantine orthros*, it is sung as the eighth daily canticle.

Benedict XII (d. 1342) Pope from 1334. Original name: Jacques Fournier. A Frenchman by birth, he was the third of the Avignon popes. He was a zealous reformer of the religious orders and improved the training of novices*. He also started the building of the papal palace at Avignon*.

Benedict XIV (1675–1758) Pope from 1740. Original name; Prospero Lorenzo Lamberini. A native of Bologna*. As pope, he was an exemplary administrator and he did much to strengthen the papacy. He wrote a number of works, including a classic treatise on beatification* and canonization*, and also authoritative works on diocesan synods, canon law*, and sacrifice of the Mass*.

Benedict XV (1854–1922) Pope from 1914. Original name: Giacomo P. G. B. della Chiesa. A native of Genoa, he was elected pope at the outbreak of World War I and he made several efforts to bring about peace. In 1917 he promulgated a code of canon law*. To promote relations with the Eastern churches*, he established the Congregation of the Oriental Church and the Pontifical Oriental Institute at Rome*.

Benedict Biscop, St. (c. 628–690) English ecclesiastic who was Bede's* superior* and who erected the monasteries of Wearmouth and Jarrow*. He brought precentors from Rome* to teach Gregorian chants* to the English. He is reported to have introduced into England glass windows and the use of stone in church buildings.

Benedict of Aniane (c. 750– 821) Benedictine abbot and monastic reformer. Of Visigothic noble descent, he entered the monastery of St. Seine in Burgundy and later established a monastery at Aniane, Languedoc, where he gained fame by enforcing the Rule of St. Benedict,* emphasizing manual labor more than study. Emperor Louis the Pious made him his ecclesiastical adviser at Aix-la-Chapelle, where he founded a new monastery.

Benedict of Nursia, St. (c. 480–c. 550) Patriarch of Western monasticism*. He withdrew from the world and retired as a hermit to a cave in Subiaco where he eventually set up 12 small monastic communities. In 529 he moved to Monte Cassino*, where he established the now famous monastery and where he drew up his rule for the reform of monasticism. The Benedict Rule became one of the most followed rules of medieval monasteries. He was buried in the grave of his sister Scholastica* in the chapel dedicated to St. John the Baptist at Monte Cassino*. Feast day: March 14 (Eastern Church*); July 11 (Western Church*).

St. Benedict of Nursia

Benedict, Rule of Monastic rule governing the spiritual and administrative life of a monastery drawn up by St. Benedict of Nursia* (c. 540) for the use of his monks at Monte Cassino* but adopted by many monastic orders during the following centuries. It was based on earlier rules of John Cassian*, Basil of Caesarea*, as well as from the Egyptian Fathers of the Desert* and St. Augustine. The core of the rule is the Divine Office*, the opus dei, followed by private devotions, spiritual reading, and some forms of manual work. It is directed by the abbot who functions as a patriarch*, elected by his monks. Monks may not hold private property, but the monastery may. The goal of the rule is perfect obedience to the Word of God*.

Benedict the Black, St. (?–1589) Black Sicilian slave who rose to become a Franciscan superior* and was canonized in 1807. Feast day: April 4.

Benedictine Liqueur originally made by French Benedictine monks, each bottle of which is initialed with the letters, D.O.M.* for *Deo Optimo Maximo* (To God, Most Good, Most Great).

Benedictines One of the most ancient monastic orders in the West, following Rule of St. Benedict of Nursia* in the sixth century. The original monastery at Subiaco was followed in Benedict's lifetime by another at Monte Cassino* and by 11 others with 12 monks each. The Benedictines wear black and follow the Rule of St. Benedict*, which became the constitution for each monastery. Each monk is attached for life to one monastery. Each monastery is economically self-supporting. The order consists of congregations, each of which is autonomous, and there is no common superior* other than the pope himself. Each monastery has an abbot who is elected for life and other officers elected for limited terms. The monks take a vow of poverty, chastity*, and obedience in perpetuity. Monks remain novitiates* for one year, but may be expelled for serious offenses.

The first attempt to bring some uniformity to the Benedictine monasteries was made by Benedict of Aniane* under the reign of Charlemagne* and Louis the Pious. The major center for reform of the order was Cluny* (founded 910) which in the twelfth century embraced 314 monasteries throughout Europe. In 1893 Leo XIII* united all the Benedictine congregations of monks into the Benedictine Confederation, with an abbot primate* resident at Rome*. In the twentieth century many small orders that followed the Rule of St. Benedict*, such as the Vallumbrosans*, Olivetans*, Camaldolese*, Celestines*, Sylvestrines*, and Cistercians*, have joined the Benedictine Confederation.

In England, the first Benedictine congregation was established at Canterbury* by St. Augustine* about 597. But with the dissolution of the monasteries during the Reformation*, they were suppressed. Benedictines were in the van of the revival of learning in Europe after the Dark Ages*. The Benedictine Rule became the basis of all Western monasticism* because of its adaptability, its moderate asceticism*, and its balance of prayer, work, and study. They preserved classical learning by their care and copying of manuscripts and by their teaching. They have fostered scholarship and have played a key role in the development of liturgical worship and the Gregorian Chant* in church service.

Benedictine nuns have existed since the seventh century and some of them, such as Hildegard of Bingen*, St. Gertrude the Great*, and Mechthild of Magdeburg*, have made great contributions to monastic culture.

benediction (Lat., *benedictio*, blessing) 1. Blessing, especially the ritual concluding the Eucharist* and other church services. In Protestant services, it is generally a verse from the Scriptures such as 2 Corinthians 13:14. 2. In Roman Catholic usage, the service where, at the climax, the congregation is blessed by the consecrated host*. 3. Imparting of divine favor to things, objects, and people either informally or formally. 4. In the Roman Catholic Church, the reserved sacrament*.

Benediction of the Blessed Sacrament In the Roman Catholic Church, blessing by a priest during which the host* is placed in the ciborium* or exposed in a monstrance*.

Benedictionale 1. Book of personal blessings to be pronounced personally by a bishop during Mass* on feast days. 2. Liturgical book containing various blessings.

benedictory Of or relating to a benediction*.

Benedictus 1. Thanksgiving hymn of Zacharias over the birth of his son, John the Baptist. 2. Choral statement based on Matthew 21:9. In the Western Church*, it is sung liturgically at lauds* or in the morning service. In the Eastern Church*, it is sung at the morning office or orthros*, except in Lent*.

Benedictus Es Anglican canticle* based on "Song of the Three Children."

Benedictus Qui Venit (Lat., Blessed is he who comes [in the name of the Lord]) Canticle* based on Matthew 21:9 sung immediately after the Sanctus*.

benefice (Lat., *beneficium*, grant of land for life as a reward for service) In canon law*, ecclesiastical income or a church office with attached property.

beneficiatus One who holds a benefice*.

benefit of the clergy Medieval clerical privilege entitling all clergy (including monks and nuns) to be tried for offenses against common law by an ecclesiastical rather than civil court where the

Illuminated Benedictionale

penalties were likely to be more severe. It was abolished in England in 1827 and in the United States by 1855.

Benezet, St. (c. 1165–1184) Shepherd who helped to build a bridge across the Rhone at Avignon* beginning 1177. He is buried in a small sanctuary atop one of its piers. Feast day: April 13.

Bengel, Johann Albrecht (1687–1752) Lutheran minister, theologian, and New Testament scholar. A Pietist and premillennialist, he prepared a Greek text of the New Testament which became the starting point for modern biblical criticism*, and *Gnomon Novi Testamenti* (1742), an exegetical New Testament commentary, admired by John Wesley*.

Benjamin, St. (d. c. 422) Persian martyr* who defied the king's order to stop preaching the gospel. Feast day: March 31.

Bennett, Dennis Joseph (1917–1991) English-born American Charismatic preacher. Ordained into the Congregational Church*, he became a priest in the Episcopal Church* in 1952. In 1959 he received the baptism of the Holy Spirit* and thereafter moved to St. Luke's Episcopal Church in Seattle, Washington. Within a few years, it became one of the strongest churches in the Northwest. He was one of the founders of Episcopal Renewal Ministries. His wife, Rita (1934–), is a popular speaker and the author of *The Holy Spirit and You* (1971).

Benno, St. (1010–1106) German bishop, known as the "Apostle of the Wends." Many miracles are recorded at his tomb in the Meissen Cathedral*. He is the patron of fishermen and drapers. Feast day: June 16.

Benoit, Peter Leonard (1834–1901) Belgian composer of a number of sacred works and the opera *Drama Christi.*

Benoit-sur-Loire, St. Romanesque basilica* of Saint Benoit near the River Loire in France founded in 672 as the Benedictine abbey of Fleury, the resting place of the relics* of St. Benedict* and his sister Scholastica*. The Normans sacked the monastery three times, but the Benedictines* rebuilt it each time and fortified it with walls. In the tenth and eleventh centuries the small church was replaced by a massive basilica built in three phases between 1004 and 1218 when it was consecrated. The monastery buildings were broken up and sold during the French Revolution and have disappeared. Only the church stands.

Benson, Edward White (1829–1896) Archbishop of Canterbury* (1883–96). He sought closer association between the Anglican Church* and the Russian and Assyrian churches. To give the laity more institutional recognition in church affairs, he helped to create the House of Laymen, with consultative status in 1886. He was the author of a life of St. Cyprian*, a book on the Apocalypse and some hymns.

Benson, Richard Meux (1824–1915) He was ordained in 1848 and appointed vicar* of Cowley. Inspired by a sermon by John Keble*, he founded the Society of St. John the Evangelist in 1865 and remained its superior* until 1890.

berakah (Heb., blessing) 1. Divine endowment of blessings and gifts on his children. 2. Human response to divine blessings through the gift of praise.

Berceo, Gonzalo de (c. 1180–1265) Benedictine deacon and priest who was Spain's first poet. He wrote more than 13,000 devotional verses, including 25 on the miracles of Mary. He also composed the lives of St. Oria, St. Dominic*, and other saints*.

Berdyaev, Nikolai (1874–1948) Russian Orthodox philosopher and theologian. After the Russian Revolution he moved to Paris and Berlin as an emigre and moved from Marxism to Orthodox mysticism. His studies in orthodoxy began with *The Meaning of the Christian Act,* published in Russian in 1916. In *Freedom and the Spirit* (1927), he formulated his existentialist sense of divine transcendence. He continued his philosophical explorations with his major work, *The Destiny of Man* (1931), *The End of Our Time* (1924), *The Fate of Man in the Modern World* (1934), and *Slavery and Freedom* (1939). His autobiography was published in 1949 as *Dream and Reality*. He was particularly concerned with religious ethics and the dehumanization of modern society.

Berengar of Tours (c. 1010–1088) French churchman and theologian who was criticized for his teachings on the Eucharist*. He held that the elements* of the Eucharist became the body and blood of Christ only in the spiritual sense. He later recanted, but the controversy led to a further clarification of the doctrine of transubstantiation*.

Bergamo Episcopal see* in Lombardi in northern Italy. Site of a twelfth-century Romanesque church and the beautiful Renaissance Colleoni chapel.

Bergamo Sacramentary One of the two surviving sacramentaries of the Ambrosian Rite*, dating from the ninth century.

Berggrav, Ervind (1884–1959) Norwegian Lutheran primate* and ecumenical leader who led the resistance to the Quisling government during World War II.

Bergson, Henri Louis (1859–1941) French philosopher. Born of Jewish parents, he became a Catholic of intent, although never baptized. A brilliant lecturer and writer, he wrote extensively on psychology, biological evolution, and sociology of religion. His major work, *Creative Evolution* (1907), appeared at the time of the Roman Catholic modernist controversy with which many of his friends and students were associated. His books were therefore placed on the Index in 1914. In his last book, *The Two Sources of Morality and Religion* (1932), he maintained that the Christian saint* is the highest development within humanity.

Berkeley, George (1685–1753) Irish bishop and philosopher. After four years in North America as a missionary, he was made bishop of Cloyne, a position he held until his death. Berkeley is known as a philosopher more than as a theologian. His metaphysical ideas were contained in his major works, *Alciphron* (1732), *A New Theory of Vision* (1709), *Principles of Human Knowledge* (1710), and *Hylas and Philonous* (1713). In them he

developed the idea of subjective idealism according to which all material things are real only in so far as they are perceived. The only things that are real are spirits, and material objects exist only in the mind of God.

Berkeley, Xavier (1861–1944) Catholic missionary in China, known as "mother of the orphans and the poor." She spent 54 years in China, first in Kiangsi (Jianxi) Province and then at Ningpo in Chekiang (Zhejiang) Province. In 1911, on Choushan (Zhou-shan) Island, she developed House of Mercy, a model mission of charity.

Berkhof, Louis (1873–1957) Reformed* theologian. At the age of nine, Berkhof came to the United States from his native Holland and spent much of his remaining life in Grand Rapids, first as professor (1906–1931) and later as president (1931–1944) of the Grand Rapids (later Calvin) Seminary. An arch opponent of modernism* and higher criticism*, Berkhof wrote his monumental *Reformed Dogmatics* (1932) that explored the scriptural roots of Reformed faith and tradition.

Berlioz, Hector (1803–1869) French Romantic composer, generally regarded as the leading French composer of the nineteenth century. He made use of liturgical texts in some of his music, as *Grande Masse des Morts* (1837), which was commissioned by the government minister of the interior and not by the church, and *Te Deum* (1849) for the Exposition Universelle of 1855. A third composition was *L'Infance du Christ* in three parts. Berlioz's music, however, has found little place in the church.

Bernadette, St. (1844–1879) Birth name: Marie Bernarde Soubirous. French peasant girl of Lourdes* in France. At the age of 14 she received 14 apparitions of the Virgin Mary* at Massabielle Rock near Lourdes in 1858 between February 11 and July 16. She later joined the Sisters of Notre Dame* at Nevers, where she lived until her death. Canonized in 1933. Feast day: February 18.

Bernanos, George (1888–1948) French Catholic author whose masterpiece, *The Diary of a Country Priest* (1936), established his reputation. Shortly before his death he completed *Dialogue des*

Carmelites, a film script telling the story of 16 nuns martyred during the French Revolution.

Bernard, John Henry (1860–1927) Archbishop of Dublin, Ireland, from 1915. He was the author of over 20 books, including a commentary on the Pastoral Epistles* and an anthology of Irish hymns.

Bernard of Clairvaux, St. (1090–1153) Abbot of Clairvaux. Monastic reformer, mystic, and theologian. In 1112 he entered the recently founded Monastery of Citeaux*. Three years later, at the request of his abbot, St. Stephen Harding*, he established a house at Clairvaux that became one of the great Cistercian monasteries. As abbot, he was influential in both political and ecclesiastical affairs of his day. As secretary to the Synod of Troyes in 1128, he obtained recognition for the rules of the new order of Knights Templar. Bernard developed intimate relations with Innocent II*, whom he helped against the antipope, Anacletus, and Eugenius III*, his former pupil. He led the attack on Peter Abelard* at the Council of Sens* in 1140. Bernard is noted for his devotional works, a series of sermons on the Song of Songs, *De Consideratione, De Gradibus Humilitatis et Superbiae* on humility, and *De Diligendo Deo* on love. Feast day: August 20.

St. Bernard of Clairvaux

Bernard of Cluny (c. 1100–1150) Also, Bernard of Morlas. Monk, noted as the author of *De Contemptu Mundi,* contrasting the transient pleasures of this life with the peace and glory of heaven*.

Bernard of Menthon (?–c. 1081) Italian churchman who founded the famous hospices of St. Bernard* in the Alps.

Bernard of Tours (twelfth century) Medieval Christian Platonist scholar who interpreted Genesis.

Bernardino of Siena, St. (1380–1444) Italian Franciscan preacher. A popular preacher, he was an early member of the Observants*, a reform group within the Franciscans opposed to usury and party strife. Using the monogram HIS*, he emphasized devotion to the holy name of Jesus*. In 1438 he was elected provincial* of the Friars of the Strict Observance. His works include sermons and tracts on asceticism* and morals. Feast day: May 20.

Berne, Theses of Ten statements of faith drawn up by Francis Kolb and Berchtold Haller* with the aid of Zwingli* after a disputation* held at the city council of Berne* in 1528. The core statement was the first thesis against the papacy: "The Holy Christian Church whose only head is Christ is born and nourished out of God's Word and hears not the voice of a stranger." The other nine theses were directed against tradition, satisfaction*, the real presence* in the Eucharist*, the sacrifice of the Mass*, mediation through the saints*, purgatory*, images, and celibacy*. The publication of the theses marked an important stage of the Reformation* in Switzerland.

Berneuchen Circle Lutheran liturgical movement* held since 1923 at a German estate from which, later in 1931, the Michaelsbruderschaft originated. From the Berneuchen Spiritual Weeks of Prayer, new orders of the liturgy have been developed.

Bernini, Gianlorenzo (1598–1680) Italian Baroque artist. His first major work was the triumphal gilt-bronze baldachino* over the high altar of St. Peter's* (1624–1633), inspired by the twisted marble columns of Constantine's Old St. Peter's, modeled on the columns of the Beautiful Gate of the Temple in Jerusalem*. He was also responsible for the Cathedra Petri (1657–1666) in the apse* of the basilica* showing four fathers of the church—Ambrose*, Augustine*, Athanasius*, and John Chrysostom*—upholding the throne of St. Peter* illumined by brilliant gold stained glass with the image of the dove*. *The Ecstasy of St. Theresa of Avila* in the Cornaro Chapel in Sta Maria della Vittoria and *Blessed Ludovica Albertoni* shows ecstatic devotion in marble.

His grand papal tombs in St. Peter's* of Urban VIII* and Alexander VII* shows a bold use of polychrome marble and gilded bronze. His equestrian statue of Constantine the Great* appears on the landing at the junction of the staircase from St. Peter's with the Scala Regia of the Vatican Palace. Bernini built three churches, San Tommaso di Villanova in Castelgandolfo, the Assunta in Ariccia, and Sant'Andrea al Quirinale in Rome*—the novitiate* church of the Jesuits*.

Bernward/Berward, St. (?–1022) German bishop who promoted ecclesiastical craftsmanship. He was canonized in 1193. Feast day: November 20.

Berthold of Regensburg (c. 1210–1272) Franciscan monk known as "Chrysostom of the Middle Ages." He preached against heresy throughout Bavaria, Germany, Switzerland, Czech lands, and Hungary.

Bertolucci, John (1937–) Catholic Charismatic leader. Ordained priest in 1965, he was baptized in the Spirit in 1969. From 1981 to 1987 he was the host of a weekly television series, "The Glory of God." He is the author of *On Fire with the Spirit* (1984) and *Healing: God's Work Among Us* (1987).

Bertram, St. Luis (1526–1581) Dominican priest, noted as a preacher and counselor. He went to Latin America as a missionary but deplored the cruelty of the conquistadores. He is the patron saint* of Colombia.

Berulle, Pierre de (1575–1629) French Jesuit priest called by Urban VIII* as the "apostle of the incarnate Word." In 1611 he founded the Congregation of the French Oratory similar to the one established by St. Philip Neri*. Made cardinal in 1627, he initiated a cult of devotion to child Jesus and took a vow of spiritual servitude to Jesus and Mary. He also established the Reformed Carmelites* in France. His principal work is *Discours de l'Etat et des Grandeurs de Jesus* (1623).

Beschi, Constanzo Giuseppi (1680–1747) Italian Jesuit missionary to the Tamils in India. Arriving in the Madurai Mission in 1710, he donned the robe of the Indian holy man or sannyasi and spent the next 36 years in active ministry. What set him apart from others was his mastery of the Tamil language to which he contributed many Christian classics, such as *Thembavani* (The Unfading Garland), an epic of 36 cantos considered a masterpiece of Tamil literature. His other Tamil works include *Thirukavalur Kalambagam* in praise of Mary, *Kitheriammal Ammani,* two books of grammar, and two dictionaries.

Bessarion, John (1403–1472) Greek theologian. He became a Basilian* monk, taking the name of Bessarion in 1423 and was made abbot of St. Basil's Monastery. His work for the union of Greek and Latin churches made him unpopular in Constantinople*. Thereafter he resided in Italy. Pope Eugenius IV* made him cardinal in 1439, and in 1463 he received the title of Latin patriarch* of Constantinople. He was an enthusiastic scholar and patron of learning and helped to promote neo-Platonism. He left his large library to the Senate of Venice where it became the foundation of the Marciana, the library of St. Mark's.

bestiary Popular medieval books describing real and imaginary animals and drawing moral lessons from their behavior.

bet lechem (Ge'ez, house of bread) In the Ethiopian Church*, place where the eucharistic bread is prepared by the clergy.

beth gazza In the Church of the East*, treasury* built into the north wall of the sanctuary in which the paten* is placed.

beth kaddishe In the Church of the East*, a reliquary* or a memorial to a saint* located on the south side of the sanctuary.

beth mada In the Church of the East*, the baptistery on the right of the east end of the sanctuary.

beth qurbana In the Church of the East*, tabernacle in which the reserved sacrament is kept after the liturgy.

beth shamasa In the Ethiopian Church*, oven in which the eucharistic bread is baked.

beth slotha In the Church of the East*, covered part of a courtyard outside a church in which the office may be recited from the Feast of the Ascension until the Feast of the Hallowing of the Church.

Beth Yaldo In the Syrian Church, Christmas*.

Bethany Fellowship Organization founded in 1945 to train and support missionaries, with its headquarters at Bethany Campus in Bloomington, Minnesota. It also runs an extensive printing and publishing program.

bethel (lit., house of worship) 1. Place of religious worship among certain Methodists and Baptists. 2. German institution dedicated to charitable work founded in 1867. Its first director was Johannes Unsold (1843–1934), who was followed by Friedrich von Bodelschwingh* (1831–1910) and his son, Fritz von Bodelschwingh (1877–1946) It operated hospitals and schools and took care of epileptics, mentally retarded, and the learning disabled.

Bethel Mission Missionary-sending organization founded in Berlin in 1886 as the Evangelical Missionary Society for German East Africa. Its first mission field* was Zanzibar and Dar es Salaam. Later it expanded to Usambara, Rwanda, and Bukoba. After World War II, American and Scandinavian missionaries took over the work as trustees.

Bethlehem Town, five miles south of Jerusalem*, the native city of King David and also the birthplace of Christ. It contains one of the oldest churches in the world, the Church of the Holy Nativity, built by Constantine* in 330.

Bethlehemites Name of several orders of religious. 1. Thirteenth-century English friars*. 2. Knights and Hospitallers*, a military order dedicated to the Virgin Mary*. 3. A military order dedicated to Our Lady of Bethlehem in 1257. 4. A nursing order established in 1655 in Guatemala. 5. A Carthusian order founded in 1976 in France with a special interest in religious art.

Beulah Beautiful region beyond the river of death in *Pilgrim's Progress**.

Beuno, St. (sixth century) Welsh saint* who founded the monastery at Clynnog Fawr where he was buried. His relics* were later transferred to Eglwys y Bedd. Many miracles were reported at his tomb. Feast day: April 21.

Beuron, Abbey of The mother abbey of the Beuron Congregation of Benedictine monks of Hohenzollern on the upper Danube. The present abbey was built in 1863, and the monastic congregation* was established in 1873. It is famous for its work on liturgical reform.

Bevan, (Emma) Francis (1827–1909) Hymn writer. She published several collections of hymns, mostly translations from German.

Beverly Minster English church which stands on the site of a Saxon church founded by St. John of Beverley*. It is one of the finest examples of early Gothic* architecture. It was restored in 1713.

Beyzym, Jan (1850–1912) Polish Jesuit missionary in Madagascar. From 1899 he worked among the lepers in Madagascar. He created a shelter and hospital for them at Ambatuwuri in 1911. Eventually, like Father Damien*, he contracted leprosy and died within a year.

Beza, Theodore (1519–1605) French Protestant theologian who was a spokesman for the Reformed* churches in France. He wrote a biography of Calvin* and succeeded him as chief pastor in Geneva*. He wrote and taught extensively as professor of Greek and theology at the Genevan Academy*. In 1551, at Calvin's suggestion, he completed Marot's translation of the Psalms into

French. In 1556 he published an annotated Latin translation of the Greek New Testament. In 1565 and 1582 he followed with the Greek text of the New Testament, to which he added the Vulgate* and his own translation. After Calvin's death, he continued to engage in vigorous polemics* with Ochino*, Arminius*, Castellio*, and Petrus Ramus. His strong defense of Calvinistic ideas, such as double predestination*, biblical literalism*, and church discipline*, had a permanent impact on the Reformed* tradition.

Theodore Beza

BFBS British and Foreign Bible Society.

Bhengu, Nicholas Bhekinkosi Hepworth (1909–1986) African evangelist known as "the black Billy Graham." He entered full-time evangelism in 1938 and conducted "Back to God" crusades under the auspices of the South African Assemblies of God*. At the time of his death there were 1,700 assemblies, with 450 ministers.

Bible (Gk., books) Holy Scriptures containing the Old Testament and New Testament. The Old Testament is also the Jewish Scriptures divided into three classes: the Law, the Prophets, and the Writings. The canon* of the Old Testament was settled about the first century. The canon of the New Testament was settled much later, around 382. The Apocrypha* is not included in most Protestant Bible versions, but was included in the Septuagint.

Bible and Medical Missionary Fellowship International and interdenominational evangelical fellowship, recently renamed Interserve, which began in 1852 as the Zenana Bible and Medical Mission, the pioneer mission among women in the Indian subcontinent. It became BMMF in 1952, when it began sending out men also. It is now active in Nepal, Middle East, and Central Asia.

Bible Belt Region roughly encompassing the southern and midwestern states of the United States where Evangelical Christianity is strongest and where biblical commandments and injunctions are taken seriously.

Bible bigots/moths Students who gathered around John and Charles Wesley* for Bible reading and prayer at Oxford University in 1729.

Bible Christians One of the bodies which constitute the United Methodist Church of 1907, founded by

Chinese Bible

William O'Bryan (1778–1868), who left the Methodist Church* in 1815 out of a desire to extend his evangelism to unreached* peoples in the west of England, including Kent, Northumberland, Devon, and Cornwall. In 1831 missions were founded in Canada and Prince Edward Island, in 1846 in the United States, and in 1850 in Australia. Opposition to O'Bryan's autocratic ways led to his withdrawal from the movement in 1829. Bible Christians were sometimes called "Quaker Methodists." The influence of Quakerism was reflected in their simple style, reliance on Inner Light*, and the importance of women in the ministry. After O' Bryan, the great leaders of the movement included James Thorne, who succeeded the founder; Billy Bray; William Read; and F. W. Bourne.

Bible Churchmen's Missionary Society (BCMS) British society, recently renamed Crosslinks, formed in 1922 by a split within the Church Missionary Society*. It is a cross-cultural mission manned by Evangelicals.

Bible Communism Communal life based on Christian principles, as practiced in the Oneida Community* under the direction of its founder, John Humphrey Noyes*.

Bible lands Countries prominent in the Bible, including Palestine, Egypt, Arabia, Syria, Asia Minor, Greece, Assyria, and Babylonia.

Bible school School specializing in providing Bible-centered training for pastors and missionaries. The first Bible school was the Grossner Mission, started by Johannes Grossner in 1842. It was followed by the East London Institute for Home and Foreign Missions in 1872 and the American Bible School, later the Nyack College, founded by A. B. Simpson* in 1882. In 1886 the Moody Bible Institute* began as the Chicago Evangelization Society to provide what D. L. Moody* called training for "gap men," to fill the gap between the laity and the clergy. Two-thirds of the over 300 Bible schools are denominational. Unlike seminaries, they accept high school graduates and train for lay church vocations and Christian ministries rather than for the professions.

Bible society Association dedicated to the translating, printing, and dissemination of the Bible. Two of the earliest Bible societies were formed in New England in 1649 and in Germany in 1710. Among the largest Bible societies are the American Bible Society*, based in New York; the British and Foreign Bible Society*, based in London; and the Netherlands Bible Society. The United Bible Societies* is an umbrella group of national Bible societies.

Bible study Personal or group study of the Scriptures, usually focused on biblical implications of contemporary living and Christian devotion.

Bible, Versions of and Translations into English Before the Reformation*, the Latin Vulgate* was the only authorized version available in the West. The Vulgate was first printed in 1456. It was followed by Erasmus's* Greek New Testament (1516) and the *Complutensian Polyglot** (1522). In the immediate pre-Reformation period, new translations by William Tyndale* and Matthew Coverdale appeared. Tyndale depended greatly on Luther's German translation which had appeared in 1522. Miles Coverdale* published the first complete Bible in 1535. In 1537 a revised English Bible known as Matthew's Bible* appeared, edited by John Rogers*. The Great Bible* of 1539 was issued under Thomas Cromwell's patronage and printed in Paris. In 1559 the Geneva Bible* was published in Geneva*, based on the French versions of Olivetan* and Lefevre. In 1566 Archbishop Parker* undertook a revision of the Great Bible*. This new translation, known as the Bishops' Bible*, was published in 1568 and revised in 1572. Meanwhile, the Roman Catholic Church also initiated a new translation by members of the English College at Reims*. Both the Old Testament (translated at Douai*, 1609–1610) and the New Testament (Reims*, 1582) were translated from the Vulgate. The resulting Bible was known as the Douai-Reims Bible*.

The next landmark was the creation of the Authorized Version* or the King James Version* by 54 divines under the authority of King James I. Although known as the Authorized Version (AV), it was never formally authorized, although the statement, "Appointed to be read in churches," appeared on the title page. The growth of biblical scholarship made a revision of the Authorized Version necessary by the nineteenth century. In 1890 the Convocation of Canterbury* appointed a committee of revisers including non-Anglicans. The result of their labors was the Revised Version (RV) which appeared in 1895. Parallel companies of translators in the United States produced the American Standard Version* (ASV) in 1901 without the Apocrypha*. In the twentieth century there have been numerous complete translations of the whole Bible or of the New Testament: John Eliot's* Algonquin Bible (1663), King James Bible (R. Aitkin's first American printing; 1777), Revision of Authorized Version by F. W. Grant (1891–1931), American Standard Version* (1901), Scofield Reference Bible* (1909), Moffat Bible (1926), The Bible: An American Translation by J. M. P. Smith and Edgar J. Goodspeed* (1931), Revised Standard Version* (1946–1952), New American Standard Bible* (1963–1971), Amplified Version (1965), American Bible Society Revision of the Authorized Version (1966), Good News Bible* (1966–1976), New American Bible* (1970), New English Bible (1970), Living Bible* (1971), New American Standard Bible (1971), RSV Common Bible (1973), New International Version of the New York Bible Society* (1973–1978), New King

James Version of the United Bible Societies (1982), Reader's Digest Bible (1982), Revised English Bible* (1989), Revised Standard Version* (1989), and New Living Translation (1998).

On the Roman Catholic side, there have been three new versions: The Westminster Version of the Holy Scriptures by C. Lattey and J. Keating (1935) and the Jerusalem Bible* produced by the Dominican Ecole Biblique* in Jerusalem and first published in France (1948–1954). A revised edition, The New Jerusalem Bible, appeared in 1985 under the chairmanship of Dom Henry Wansbrough and was revised in 1999. The New American Bible (1970) was made by members of the Catholic Biblical Association of America under the patronage of the Bishop's Committee of the Confraternity of Christian Doctrine*.

Biblia Medieval Romanceada Published in Buenos Aires in 1927, this edition presents manuscripts from the Royal Library of San Lorenzo de El Escorial in Madrid, Spain. The three Old Testament texts probably originated in the thirteenth century, placing them among the oldest medieval Spanish-language biblical manuscripts. One represents the famed polylingual Biblia Alfonsina, developed through the patronage of King Alfonso X "el Sabio" (d. 1284), under whom the language was standardized, and cultural forms developed, amid recurrent church-state controversies.

Biblia Pauperum (Lat., "The Bible of Poor People") Medieval picture book in which on each page a group of figures illustrates a New Testament antitype flanked by two corresponding Old Testament types with short explanatory texts from the Bible and mnemonic verses. It was very popular

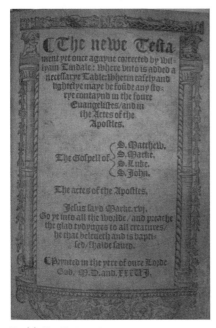

Tyndale New Testament

Luther's Translation of the Bible

on the Continent soon after the invention of printing.

Illuminated Biblia Pauperum

Bibliander, Theodor (c. 1504–1564) Swiss theologian who succeeded Zwingli* at Zurich University as professor of theology and biblical literature. A master of 30 languages, he was an accomplished philologist and one of the most brilliant biblical exegetes of his day. His works include a Hebrew grammar. His opposition to Calvinism* cost him his job in 1560.

biblical archeology Branch of archeology concerned with excavations in and study of archeology in the Holy Land*.

Biblical Commission Committee of five cardinals assisted by 39 consultors appointed in 1902 by Pope Leo XIII* to publish biblical studies, defend the authority of the Scriptures and Catholic exegesis*, and decide points of critical dispute. Its essential role was redefined in "Dei Verbum" of the Second Vatican Council*. Pope Paul VI* reorganized the commission, making it a counterpart of the International Theological Commission, a part of the Congregation for the Doctrine of the Faith. It is now composed of 20 biblical scholars.

biblical criticism Study of the text, authorship, date, form, and meaning of the Bible and its parts. Lower criticism* deals with the narrative or the text, while higher criticism* deals with questions of authorship, sources, and other weightier issues.

biblical interpretation See HERMENEUTICS.

biblical theology Branch of theology describing spiritual doctrines in non-dogmatic terms. It studies the inner coherence and evolution of biblical ideas, centered upon certain key concepts. It deals particularly with the distinctive stream of human history known as salvation history. It establishes the historical trustworthiness of biblical events and documents and examines the choice, sequence, and arrangement of biblical texts. It was especially influential in the mid-twentieth century.

biblicism Strict adherence to the literal truth of the Bible.

bibliolatry Worship of the Bible, particularly among Protestants, as reflected in their saying, "the Bible and Bible only."

bibliomancy The use of the Bible as a divining tool, especially by opening it at random and taking directions from the verses or words that first meet the eye.

biblion (Gk., *biblia,* book) Scroll long enough to contain one of the Gospels.

Biblioteca Apostolica Vaticana Also, Vatican Apostolic Library*. Official library of the Vatican* founded in 1450 by Pope Nicholas V* and provided with a staff and a structure by Sixtus IV* in 1475. At the present time it contains some 65,000 manuscripts, 130,000 archival files, 100,000 engravings, 7,000 incunabula, and 1 million other volumes. Among the famous collections that helped to build the library are those of the dukes of Urbino (1657), Queen Christina of Sweden (1690), the Florentine Marquis Capponi (1745), Barberini (1902), Chigi (1923), and Borghese, the last of which included many items housed in the papal library at Avignon*. The Sistine Chapel* collection is one of the most priceless for music historians. Among the many rare and precious manuscripts in the library are a Greek Bible of the fourth century, Virgils of the fourth and sixth centuries, a palimpsest* of Cicero's Republic, and autographs of St. Thomas Aquinas*, Tasso*, Petrarch, Boccaccio, Michelangelo*, and Luther*.

Bickersteth, Edward (1786–1850) English rector* and secretary of the Church Missionary Society* who wrote a number of hymns. His *Christian Psalmody* comprised 700 hymns to which he later added 200. It went through 59 editions in seven years. He was one of the founders of the Parker

Society* and was active in the foundation of the Evangelical Alliance*. His piety and scholarship are reflected in his books, particularly *A Treatise on Prayer* (1818), *A Treatise on the Lord's Supper* (1822) and *A Treatise on Baptism* (1840).

bidding prayer Form of prayer interceding for the universal church, persons in authority, and deceased persons, uttered by a preacher before a sermon. In the Liturgical Constitution of the Second Vatican Council* it is called community prayer or prayer of the faithful. It says, "By this prayer, in which the people are to take part, intercession will be made for the Holy Church, for the civil authorities, for those oppressed by various needs, for all mankind, and for the salvation of the entire world."

Biddle, John (1615–1662) English heretic who founded Unitarianism* in England. In 1647 he published his anti-Trinitarian views in *Twelve Arguments*. He spent most of his life in and out of prison.

Biel, Gabriel (c. 1420–1495) German theologian who is considered the last of the great scholastic philosophers. He was instrumental in founding the University of Tubingen*, where he held the chair of theology from 1484. Later in life he joined the Brethren of the Common Life*. He systematized the nominalistic theology of William of Occam* and introduced Martin Luther* to theology. His best known works are *Epitome* (1495), *Sermons* (1499), and *Exposition* (1499).

Bigg, Charles (1840–1908) English church historian and classical scholar. Among his works are a commentary on Peter and Jude* (1901), *The Christian Platonists of Alexandria* (1886), *The Origins of Christianity* (1909), and editions of several classics of Christian spirituality*.

Billing, Einar Magnus (1871–1939) Swedish theologian and bishop of Vasteras. He was a leader in the so-called "Luther Renaissance" which followed the publication of his book on Luther (1910). He also contributed to the cause of religious freedom.

Billings, William (1746–1800) Outstanding American composer of the eighteenth century. He composed over 350 works, the majority of them settings of Psalms and hymns. In 1770 he published 120 vocal settings of the Psalms in *The New England Psalm-Singer*. *The Psalm-Singer's Amusement* (1781) offered Billings' most outstanding anthems.

Billy Graham Center Agency of Wheaton College* devoted to research, strategy, and training for evangelism and missions, founded in 1970. It includes the Billy Graham* archives, library, and museum and a cluster of programs including workshops, conferences, prison ministries, and an institute of evangelism.

Billy Graham Evangelistic Association (BGEA) Nonprofit religious corporation which conducts the ministries of Billy Graham*, his associate evangelists, and affiliated agencies, founded in 1950 and headquartered in Minneapolis, Minnesota. Among the activities and subsidiaries of the association are telecasts of Graham's crusades, the Hour of Decision radio program, Worldwide Pictures, which produces documentary and dramatic evangelistic films, *Decision* magazine, counseling, Grason/Worldwide Publications which publish Graham's books, and radio stations in North Carolina and Hawaii. BGEA supports and was responsible for the founding of *Christianity Today**, the World Congress on Evangelism* (1966), Lausanne International Congress on World Evangelism*, the Evangelical Council on Financial Responsibility, the Billy Graham Center* of Wheaton College*, the International Conferences for Itinerant Evangelists (1983 and 1986), and The Cove, near Asheville, North Carolina—a lay retreat* center.

Bilney, Thomas (c. 1495–1531) Protestant martyr*. After his conversion, he became a central figure in a theological group that met at the White Horse Inn. Among those who came under his influence were Hugh Latimer* and Matthew Parker*. His opposition to the worship and mediation of saints* led him to be charged with Lollardism, arrested, and burned at the stake.

bilocation Being in more than one place at a time, an attribute of certain saints*, such as Anthony of Padua*, Alphonsus Liguori*, and Philip Neri*.

Bimeler, Joseph Michael (1773–1853) German separatist* who helped the disciples of Barbara Grubermann found the communal settlement at Zoar, Ohio.

bination Celebration of two masses on the same day by the same priest. In the Roman Catholic Church, bination is permitted only on special occasions or with special dispensation*.

Binchois, Gilles de (c. 1400–1460) Flemish composer of masses and other ecclesiastical music.

binding and loosing Power of the keys of the kingdom* bestowed on the representatives of Christ in Matthew 16:19 and 18:18. It is generally represented as the power to exercise ecclesiastical and spiritual oversight.

Bingham, Hiram (1789–1869) Pioneer American Congregationalist missionary who founded the first Christian mission in Hawaii. He helped to create a written language for the people and set up schools. He completed a translation of the Bible in 1839. He built the first church in Honolulu in 1821. His son, **Hiram Bingham, Jr.** (1831–1908) was a missionary to Micronesia. He worked in the Gilbert Islands, reduced their language to writing, and published the first Bible in Gilbertese. For two years he skippered the brig, *Morning Star,* that maintained contact among the scattered islands.

Bingham, Joseph (1668–1723) English church historian. His masterpiece was the *Origines Ecclesiasticae: The Antiquities of the Christian Church* (10 vols, 1708–1722), the fruit of 20 years of labor. He was an authority on the hierarchy*, organization, rites, discipline, and calendar of the early church.

Bingham, Roland (1872–1942) Canadian founder of the Sudan Interior Mission (SIM)*. Converted through the Salvation Army*, he left for the Sudan in 1893 along with Walter Gowans and Tom Kent. Forced to return to Canada, he made two more attempts to return to the Sudan. In 1901 on his third attempt he established a mission station in Patigi. Within 50 years, the mission had a staff of over 1,300 engaged in medical work, education, Bible translation, and printing. Its Nigeria Press published the *African Challenge* from 1951. Bingham was responsible for a number of other ventures beside SIM, including the *Evangelical Christian,* the Gowans Home for Missionaries' Children, and the Canadian Keswick Conference.

biretta Square cap with ridges worn by Roman Catholic and Anglican clergy. It is coded by color: black for priests, purple for bishops, white for canons and abbots, and red for cardinals.

biritualism Use of more than one liturgical tradition or rite in the celebration of liturgical services.

Biro, Matyas Devai (c. 1500–1545) Hungarian reformer, sometimes called the "Hungarian Luther." Originally a Franciscan, he was a student at Wittenberg* and lived in Luther's home. He returned to Hungary where, after 1541, he changed to Calvinism*. His *Orthographia Ungarica* was published posthumously in 1549.

birrus See AMPHIBALUM.

birthright church membership Right of membership for children of believers based on the Half-Way Covenant* in the New England Puritan churches of the seventeenth century.

birun In the Church of the East*, a small embroidered hood worn by bishops.

bishop (Gk., overseer) Higher order of ministers, called episkopos or superintendent in the early church. Bishops are the chief pastors of the church in most Christian traditions, with the exception of the Congregationalists and Presbyterians, and they are consecrated to rule a particular diocese* or part of a church within an ecclesiastical province. They are elected in the case of Protestant denominations or selected by the pope in the case of the Roman Catholic Church or by the metropolitan* or patriarch* in the case of Eastern churches*. In the Roman Catholic Church, a bishop is required to visit Rome* every five years and to report to the pope on the state of his diocese. The diocesan bishop may be assisted by other subordinate bishops, known as suffragans, auxiliaries, bishop coadjutors*, or assistants. In both the Roman Catholic Church and in the Eastern churches, bishops must be unmarried and are generally recruited for that reason from the monastic orders. Among the traditional insignias of a bishop are the cathedral throne, mitre*, pastoral staff*, pectoral cross, and ring. In Protestant circles, he is addressed as "right reverend" and in Catholic and Orthodox usage as "his grace."

bishop coadjutor (Lat., *adjutare,* to help) Assistant bishop in a diocese* with right of succession.

bishop in ordinary Residential or diocesan bishop.

bishop in partibus Bishop without a diocese* who is named as titular* bishop of an ancient diocese that has become extinct. See IN PARTIBUS INFIDELIUM.

bishop of Rome The pope.

bishop suffragan A bishop who serves in a similar capacity as the bishop coadjutor*.

Bishop, William Howard (1885–1953) American founder and superior general* of the Glenmary Home Missioners, a religious community of rural missionaries, founded in 1937 to evangelize the unchurched* in rural areas where there are no priests. He also founded the National Catholic Rural Life Conference in 1923 and the League of the Little Flower in 1924.

bishopric The office of a bishop.

Bishops' Bible Official English version of the Bible from 1568 to 1611, so called because many of the translators were bishops. It was replaced by the King James Version*.

Bishops' Book Compromise* doctrinal statement of the English bishops in 1537, known as *The Institution of a Christian Man.* It is an exposition of the creed, the seven sacraments*, the Decalogue, the Lord's Prayer*, and the Ave Maria*. It never received royal authority.

bit qanki In the Church of the East*, the baptistry* on the south side of the sanctuary including the font or gurna*.

Bithynia Province near the Black Sea where the Councils of Nicaea* and Chalcedon* were held.

bi-Trinitarianism Heretical teaching that the Godhead consists of only the Father and the Son and excludes the Holy Spirit*.

bl Blessed, used in the Roman Catholic Church for those who have been beatified.

black books Bibles, missals, and similar books bound in black and sold in religious stores, distinguished from other types of books.

Black Canons Epithet of the Augustinian Order of Canons Regular in medieval England.

Black Christ Ancient statue of Christ in Panama, a carved and painted representation of Christ that has darkened over the years.

black fast Severe fasting practiced in the Middle Ages in Lent* and before ordination.

Black Fathers Epithet of the Holy Ghost Fathers* and the Immaculate Heart of Mary*.

Black Friars Epithet of Dominican monks who wear black.

black genevan Black preaching gown worn formerly by Anglican priests. So called from Geneva*, where Calvin* preached in such a robe.

black letter days Minor holy days in the ecclesiastical calendar* printed in black in contrast to the major days which are printed in red.

Black Madonna Icon of the Virgin Mary* in Czestochowa*, Poland, believed to have been painted by St. Luke*.

Black Monastery Augustinian monastery in Wittenberg*, Germany, in which the monks wore black. Martin Luther* was a monk in this monastery at one time.

Black Monks Epithet of Benedictine monks.

Black Pope Epithet of the superior general* of the Jesuit Order.

Black Sisters Alexian nuns.

Black Sunday Passion Sunday*, the second before Easter*.

black theology Form of theology that developed in the late 1970s as a response to the dilemma of racism and as a means of reconciling the eternal truths of Christianity with the needs of the black community. Like liberation theology*, it attempts to break away from the traditional European concepts and empower blacks to transcend and transform a negative sense of oppression into a message of hope. It does so by emphasizing the African heritage of Christianity and interpreting anew the African religious experience. Among the seminal works of black theology are *Black Theology and Black Power* (1969) by James H. Cone, *Liberation and Reconciliation* by J. Deotis Roberts, *Is God a White Racist?* by William R. Jones, and *The Identity Crisis in Black Theology* by Cecil Cone.

Blackstone, William Eugene (1841–1935) Christian Zionist. Converted at the age of 11, he wrote the widely popular *Jesus Is Coming* (1908), predicting the imminent return of Christ. His millennial belief led him to found the Chicago Hebrew Mission and to advocate the settlement of Russian Jews in Palestine.

Blackwell, Antoinette (1825–1921) The first ordained woman minister in the United States and pastor of the Congregational Church of South Butler, New York. She eventually became a Unitarian and a champion of abolitionism and women's rights.

Blaesilla (fourth century) Female acquaintance of St. Jerome*, at whose request he wrote his commentary on Ecclesiastes.

Blair, James (1655–1743) Scottish-born Episcopalian* minister who served in Virginia as pastor of the Henrico parish church, Jamestown, and Bruton parish church. He obtained the charter for the College of William and Mary and served as its first president.

Blaise, St. (?–c. 316) Armenian bishop and martyr*. He is invoked in cases of sore throats and cattle diseases. Feast day: February 11.

Blake, Eugene Carson (1906–1985) American ecumenical leader. From 1966 to 1972 he was general secretary of the World Council of Churches*, in which position he sought to advance his vision of Christian unity.

Blake, William (1757–1827) English metaphysical poet and artist best known for his *Songs of Innocence* (1789) and *Songs of Experience* (1794). Most of his works were a reaction against the Rationalism of the day, and he sought the mystical experience in which his imagination could soar toward a divine vision and unite his spirit with the divine. But he rejected the narrow morality of traditional religion. Although he emphasized the uniqueness of Christianity, he rejected the Atonement* and the idea of Christ as a personal savior.

Blandina, St. (second century) Virgin slave girl martyred in 177 at Lyons together with Bishop Pothinus*. Feast day: June 2 (Western Church*); July 26 (Eastern Church*).

Blasein, St. Benedictine abbey of St. Blasein in the upper Alb Valley south of Freiburg* in Germany, one of the oldest in the Black Forest. It was originally inhabited by monks called "brothers on the Alb." In 915 they started work on a large pillared basilica* with a transept* and twin towers. The church was consecrated in 1108. Beginning in 1728, the old building was replaced by a new one built in the Baroque style, but in 1768 a fire destroyed most of it. In 1771 the French architect Pierre d'Ixnard began the rebuilding of the new church and continued until 1783, based on the model of St. Peter's* in Rome* and the Church of the Tomb in Jerusalem*.

blasphemy 1. Insult or mockery of God or his messengers and prophets. 2. Presumption of divinity by a human being. 3. Attribution of the works of God to the devil or of the works of the devil to God.

blasphemy against the Holy Spirit Unforgivable sin mentioned in Matthew 12:31, Mark 3:28–29, and Luke 12:10.

Blaurock, Georg (c. 1492–1529) Birth name: Jorg Cajakob. Also known as "Blue Coat" and "Sturdy Georg." Early Anabaptist* evangelist. He initiated the practice of believer's baptism* in Zurich* and founded the first Anabaptist congregation in Zollikon in 1525. Expelled from Zurich in 1527, he became an itinerant preacher and spread the Anabaptist faith over much of central Europe and founded Anabaptist colonies in Moravia. He was finally burned at the stake as a heretic.

blended worship Worship service in which multiple styles of worship are mixed, such as the use of traditional and contemporary hymns.

blessed In the Catholic Church, person who is beatified.

Blessed Sacrament Eucharist* or Communion.

Blessed Virgin Mary, the mother of Jesus.

blessing 1. Benediction*, the invoking of divine favors through gestures and words. 2. Manifestation of God's grace, as in Proverbs 10:22: "The blessing of the LORD makes one rich, and He adds no sorrow with it." 3. State of being blessed. 4. Papal blessing* urbi et orbi*.

Blessing of the Waters In the Eastern Church*, custom of blessing lakes, rivers, and seas, commemorating Christ's baptism* in the Jordan River. It takes place on the twenty-fifth day of Easter*.

Blickling Homilies Sermons and homilies from the time of Aelfred and Aelfric* preserved at Blickling Hall, Norfolk, England.

Bliss, Daniel (1823–1916) American missionary to Syria who founded in 1920 what is now the American University in Beirut.

Bliss, Philip Paul (1838–1876) Baptist hymn writer. Gifted with a bass voice of great range and beauty, he served as D. L. Moody's* lead singer during revivals. Among his best known hymns are "Jesus

Loves Me," "Hold the Fort" (which also was his epitaph), "Free from the Law," "Man of Sorrows," "Sing Them Over Again to Me," "The Whole World Was Lost in the Darkness of Sin," "I Will Sing of My Redeemer," "Almost Persuaded," and "Hallelujah, What a Savior."

Blondel, Maurice (1861–1949) French Catholic philosopher. He was acknowledged as an original thinker with his publication of *L'Action* (1893). He amplified his ideas in his later works, as *History and Dogma* (1904), *The Process of Intelligence* (1922), *The Problem of Catholic Philosophy* (1932), and *La Pense* (2 vols., 1934). Many of his ideas have had considerable influence on later philosophers.

blood Generally, the blood of Christ. Sacrificial death of Christ as the symbol of redemption* (Eph. 1:7, 1 Pet. 1:18–19, Rev. 1:5), propitiation* (Rom. 3:25), reconciliation (Eph. 2:13, Col. 1:19–20), cleansing (Heb. 9:11–14), sanctification* (1 John 1:7, Eph. 5:25–26), and victorious living (Rev. 12:11).

blue The color of Scottish Covenanters*, Virgin Mary*, Presbyterians, the Nativity of St. John the Baptist*, All Souls' Day*, funerals, and requiems*.

blue laws Laws regulating private conduct, so called from the blue paper on which the New Haven Puritan Community printed its laws governing dress, Sabbath, and other matters.

Blue Nuns Sisters of the Temple and other Roman Catholic sisterhoods who wear a blue garb.

Blumhardt, Johann Christoph (1805–1880) Swiss pastor. In 1838 he became pastor at Mottlingen in Wurttemberg where his evangelistic work was accompanied by miraculous cures. From 1852 until his death he worked at Bad Boll, which became a center of missionary outreach*.

boat Ancient Christian symbol for salvation.

boat, incense Small liturgical vessel used for holding incense.

Bobbio Small town in the Appennines northeast of Geneva*, seat of a former abbey founded in 612 by St. Columbanus* whose collection of early manuscripts has passed on to the Vatican Library*, the Ambrosiana* at Milan, and the Bibliotheque Nationale in Paris.

Bobbio Missal Important collection of liturgical texts dating from the eighth century. It is of Gallican provenance with Irish influences.

bobeche Metal receptacle around a candle to catch wax drippings.

Bodelschwingh, Friedrich von (1831–1910) German founder of the Bethel Center. In 1872 after several years of pastoral work, he was appointed head of a home for epileptics that grew to become the world-famous Bethel Center.

bodiki In the Maronite Church, prayer recited in a low voice by the deacon on behalf of the living and the dead.

Bodmer Papyri Collection of important Christian manuscripts on papyrus* or parchment* acquired by Martin Bodmer of Geneva* in 1956 from a find in Nag Hammadi* or Akhmim in Egypt. The earlier manuscripts are in Greek and the later ones in Sahidic*. The collection includes the third and fourth Gospels and the Acts.

body evangelism Evangelism* undertaken by all members of a congregation rather than missionaries alone, and that which results in measurable growth in the church as the body of Christ*.

body ministry Congregational life, especially in Pentecostal and Charismatic churches, in which the gifts of ministry are exercised not only by the pastor or minister* but by each member of the congregation. These gifts may include teaching, music, healing, prophecy* or exhortation, and evangelism.

body of Christ Community of believers who constitute the chronological extension of Christ's earthly Incarnation* and who, because of their commitment and obedience to him, serve as his organs of ministry.

Boehler, Peter (1712–1775) Moravian missionary and bishop from Germany to Georgia who founded the cities of Bethlehem and Nazareth in Pennsylvania. He influenced Wesley* in 1738, although they later split.

Boehm, Martin (1725–1812) American Methodist bishop. After being expelled from the Mennonite Church, he joined in 1768 with Philip Otterbein* to found the Church of the United Brethren in Christ* with an Arminian and perfectionist theology.

Boehme, Jakob (1575–1624) German mystic. At the age of 25 he began having mystical visions, which he set on paper and published in *The Beginning of Dawn* (1612) followed by *The Way to Christ* (1623). Some of his ideas were heterodox and tinged with theosophy. He saw God as a mixture of contradictions, at once the abyss and the urgrund, or the ground, of all being. Christian life is a mystical imitation of Christ's suffering and triumph. The Pietist, Romantic, and Idealist movements drew from his teaching. His followers, the Boehmenists, eventually became Quakers*. His other books included *Die Drei Prinzipien Gottlichen Wesens,* an inquiry into divinity, *Mysterium Magnum* on the Book of Genesis, and *Von Christi Testamenten* on the Baptism and the Eucharist*.

Boethius, St. Anicius Manlius Torquatus Severinus (c. 480–524) Roman theologian and philosopher. His *The Consolation of Philosophy,* written in prison near Pavia* while awaiting execution for alleged treason, had great influence in the Middle Ages. Feast day: October 23.

Boff, Leonardo (1938–) Liberation theologian, born in Brazil. His liberation theology*, expressed in Marxist terms, brought him into conflict with the hierarchy*, and he resigned from the priesthood in 1992. Among his books are *Jesus Christ, Liberator* and *The Base Communities Reinvent the Church.*

Bog (Slavonic) God.

Bogomils (Literally, those beloved of God) Medieval heretical sect in the Balkans founded by Bogomil or Theophilus. Their beliefs combined Gnostic, Paulician, and Manichaean elements. They rejected all of the Old Testament as the work of Satan*. The creation of the world and of human beings was ascribed to Satan, only the soul being the work of God. Birth was the incarceration of the good spirit in evil flesh as punishment for sins in a preexistent state. To escape Satan's net, the true Bogomil abstained from marriage, meat, and wine and renounced all earthly possessions. This ideal was attained only by the perfect; the ordinary faithful might fall into sin, but were required to obey the perfect and receive spiritual baptism* on their deathbeds. They held the Docetic belief that Christ did not have a material body and that his death was an illusion. They rejected the sacraments, baptism, saints, miracles, and images. Baptism and the Lord's Supper* were practiced spiritually without any material props. They refused to obey all civil and ecclesiastical authority, and were as a result persecuted heavily.

Bogomilism spread rapidly in the Balkans in the eleventh century, and its influence spread as far as France where the Cathari* were an offshoot of the heresy. Its adherents were concentrated in Dalmatia, Herzegovina and Bosnia where, under the name of Patarenes, they became the dominant group. When the Turks conquered Bosnia in 1463 and Herzegovina in 1482, many of them converted to Islam.

bogoroditchni In the Byzantine and Slavonic churches, hymns in honor of the Virgin Mary*.

bogoyavlenie In the Byzantine and Slavonic churches, feast commemorating the baptism* of Christ by St. John the Baptist.

Bohairic One of the principal dialects of Coptic spoken in the northern Nile delta region. By the ninth century its use became widespread throughout Egypt, supplanting Sahidic*. It is the official dialect of the Coptic used in the Coptic Church*.

Bohemian Also, Moravian Brethren*. Czech Christians of the fifteenth century, also known as Unitas Fratrum. They were inspired by the biblical simplicity advocated by Archbishop Rokycana, Brother Gregory, and Peter Chelcicky* to band together to practice primitive Christianity. They rejected oaths, military service, and urban

life as well as private property. They were organized as a church under Lukas of Prague* under whom they spread rapidly. At various times, they were allied with the Lutherans and the Calvinists. Concentrated in Moravia (hence their name), they became the leading branch of Bohemian Protestantism*. Following the Battle of the White Mountain (1620) they were exiled together with their last bishop, the educational pioneer, J. A. Comenius*. Moravian schools were admired, and they made substantial contributions to Czech literature, especially the translation of the Bible in six volumes (1579–1593). They survived for over a hundred years until 1721, when they accepted an invitation by Count Zinzendorf* to join the Herrnhutter.

Bohm, Dominikus (1880–1955) Influential German church architect.

Bollandists Jesuit editors of the *Acta Sanctorum**, the multivolume critical edition of the lives of the saints*. They were so named after John van Bolland (1596–1665), the founder and first editor of the work. The work was conceived by Heribert Rosweyde (1569–1629). The work was suspended by the suppression of the Jesuits* in 1773, and it was not resumed fully until 1837. Since 1882 the *Analecta Bollandiana* is published as a supplement to the work.

Bologna Ancient city in northern Italy, known formerly as Bononia. Its university, founded in the twelfth century, was the chief center for the study of canon law*. Its patron saint* is St. Petronius (d. c. 450). The first general chapter* of the Dominican Order was held here in 1220, and St. Dominic* is buried in its Church of St. Dominico.

Bologna, Concordat of Pact between Pope Leo X* and Francis I of France in 1516, giving the French church considerable independence in choosing candidates* for bishoprics*, abbeys, and priories*.

Bolsena, the miracle of Apocryphal story of the institution of the Feast of Corpus Christi* by Pope Urban IV when a German priest on a pilgrimage* to Rome saw blood issue from the elements* that were being consecrated and bathe the corporal*.

Bolshakoff, Sergey Nikolaevich (1901–1991) Russian theologian. His works include *In Search of True Wisdom: Visits to Eastern Spiritual Fathers* (with Basil Pennington, 1979) and *The Doctrine of the Unity of the Church in the Works of Khomyakov and Moehler* (1946).

Bonald, Louis (1754–1840) French philosopher who founded the traditional school of Roman Catholic theology. He saw Christianity as a means of holding society together. In his book, *Theory of Political and Religious Power in Civil Society* (1796), he defended the divine right of kings and the ultimate authority of the pope.

Bonar, Andrew Alexander (1810–1892) Scottish preacher. He was the brother of Horatius Bonar*. He belonged to the Non-Intrusion movement which led to the Disruption* of 1843. He took part in the revival which led to the Kilsyth Revival of 1838–1839. His *Diary* is a devotional classic.

Bonar, Horatius (1808–1889) Scottish Presbyterian minister who was among the early leaders of the Free Church. Among his many hymns are the celebrated "What A Friend We Have in Jesus" and "I Heard the Voice of Jesus Say."

Bonaventura/Bonaventure, St. (1221–1274) Birth name: Giovanni di Fidanza. "Prince of Mystics." In 1238 or 1243 he entered the Friars Minor* and received the doctorate for his commentary on the Sentences of Peter Lombard* and his treatise, *De Paupertate Christi*. At the age of 36 he was elected minister general* of the Friars Minor*. In 1263 he was made cardinal bishop of Albano. His last act was to attend the Council of Lyons* in 1274 and contribute to the short-lived reunion with the Greek schismatics. His theology, as stated in *Itinerarium Mentis in Deum,* was Christocentric* and emphasized the folly of human wisdom when measured against mystical illumination*. His meditation on the Passion, *Lignum Vitae,* was illustrated by the Tree of the Cross with 12 branches. He believed contemplative prayer to be the ultimate form of spirituality*. He denied the immaculate conception* of the Virgin Mary*. Feast day: July 15.

Bonhoeffer, Dietrich (1906–1945) German theologian and martyr*. He began his pastoral work in Berlin in 1931. A strong opponent of the Nazis, he joined the Confessing Church* and signed the Barmen Declaration* in 1934. He was forbidden by the Nazis to teach, banned from Berlin, and

Dietrich Bonhoeffer

dismissed from his teaching position in 1936. He was arrested in 1943, imprisoned in Buchenwald, and hanged at Flossenburg in 1945. His principal works are *The Cost of Discipleship* (1948), and *Letters and Papers from Prison* (1953).

Boni Homines Name given to the perfecti among the Albigenses* and other medieval sects.

Boniface VIII (c. 1243–1303) Pope from 1294. Birth name: Benedict Gaetani. He was one of the great upholders of the secular power of the papacy in the tradition of Gregory VII* and Innocent III*, but his efforts ended in failure. Among his achievements were the compilation of the Sext, the decoration of Roman churches, and the foundation of the university Sapienza. He was the author of *Unam Sanctam*. He also proclaimed the first Holy Year* in 1300.

Boniface/Bruno of Querfurt, St. (?–1009) "Apostle of the Prussians." German missionary. He preached the gospel among the heathen of the eastern coast of the Baltic and Ukraine*. He was martyred by pagans on the Lithuanian border. Feast day: June 19.

Boniface, St. (c. 675–754) "Apostle of Germany." English Benedictine priest who was sent by Pope

Boniface VIII

Gregory II* as a missionary to the pagan Germans beyond the Rhine. In Thuringia and Bavaria, he saw thousands of Hessians baptized and at Geismar he cut down the sacred oak of Thor to symbolize the fall of paganism. After consecration as a bishop at Rome, he returned to Hesse and later became archbishop of Thuringia in 732 and papal legate* in 739. He divided Bavaria, Hesse, and Thuringia into dioceses and founded Benedictine monasteries, including Fulda*, Fritzlar, Tauberbischofscheim, Ohrdruf, Ochsenfurt, and Kitzingen. After the death of Charles Martel*, he convened a series of councils to reform the Frankish church and became archbishop of Mainz* in 746. After a few years, he re-

St. Boniface

signed his see* to return to Frisia, where he met his martyrdom. Feast day: June 5.

Bonifatiusverein (Ger., Boniface Society) Society founded in 1849 for the support of Catholics living in Protestant areas of Germany.

bonitas In Roman Catholic theology, ethical value of good deeds, as distinguished from dignitas* or religious value.

Bonn Reunion conferences Conferences held in Bonn, Germany, in 1874 and 1875 to promote unity between the Old Catholics* and other churches faithful to historic Christianity, such as Greek-Oriental and Russian churches. It was presided over by Johann Joseph Ignaz von Dollinger.

Bonnke, Reinhard Willi Gottfried (1940–) International evangelist. In 1967 he moved to Africa and worked for many years in Lesotho. In 1974 he received a call* to minister to the whole of Africa with the assurance that Africa would be saved. His first mass healing crusade* took place in Gaberones, Botswana, in 1975. Thereafter he began preaching to tens of thousands in every meeting, and his preaching was accompanied and confirmed by signs and wonders. His crusades have attracted the largest crowds in the history of evangelism, up to 250,000 in one service in Nigeria in 1986. He uses the largest gospel tent ever built that can hold up to 34,000 people. In 1987 he set up his headquarters in Frankfurt for his organization, known since 1972 as Christ For All Nations.

Bonosus (d. c. 400) Bishop of Naissus in Yugoslavia. He was excommunicated for having denied the perpetual virginity* of the Virgin Mary*. His followers, known as Bonosians, survived for many centuries, especially among Goths, in Spain and Gaul.

Book of Advertisements Book entitled *Advertisements, Partly for Due Order in Public Administration of Common Prayers and Using the Holy Sacraments, and partly for the Apparel of All Persons Ecclesiastical by virtue of the Queen Majesty's Letters Commanding the Same,* issued in 1556 by

Archbishop Matthew Parker*. Among its 39 "advertisements" were ones that required the use of the surplice* in the Eucharist* and kneeling at the reception of the Communion.

Book of Armagh Ninth-century vellum codex* containing a number of documents, partly in Latin and partly in Irish. It includes the non-Vulgate text of the Latin New Testament, the Pauline Epistles, the Catholic Epistles* and Acts, a Life of St. Martin of Tours*, and documents on St. Patrick*. It is currently in Trinity College* Library in Dublin.

Book of Cerne Ninth-century collection of nonliturgical Celtic prayers, now in Cambridge University Library.

Book of Common Order The directory of worship first drawn up by John Knox* in 1556 for the English Protestant congregations in Geneva* and taken back to Scotland by him. Commonly known as John Knox's Liturgy, it included a collection of metrical psalms*. It was not a prayer book, but a guide to the conduct of services. It was approved for use in Scotland by the General Assembly* in 1562 and continued in general use among the Scottish Calvinists until 1645 when it was replaced by the Directory of Public Worship* compiled by the Westminster Assembly*. In 1994 a new service book was issued, entitled *Common Order*.

Book of Common Prayer (BCP) Anglican service book produced under Edward VI in 1549. Official service book of the Church of England* containing the daily offices of morning and evening prayer, the forms of administration of the sacraments*, the Psalter, and the Ordinal. It replaced three of the five main Latin service books: the Breviary*, the missal, and the manual, and abolished the other two: the processional and the pontifical*. It also increased the vocal participation of the congregation. Originally compiled by Archbishop Thomas Cranmer*, it was designed to supplement the Sarum Breviary (1543), the Litany in English (1544), and the Order of the Communion* (1548).

It was revised and reissued a number of times, most notably in 1552, 1559, and 1662, and, except for a few minor changes, remained substantially the same for the next three centuries. In 1955 the archbishops of York* and Canterbury* appointed a Liturgical Commission to prepare a revision which led to the publication in 1980 of the Alternative Service Book. Anglican churches outside England have produced their own revisions of the BCP, especially Scotland (1637 and 1929), United States (1789 and 1928), Canada (1922 and 1962), Ireland (1877), South Africa (1954), and India, Pakistan, Myanmar, and Sri Lanka (1960). In the 1960s modern English was introduced into the liturgy, such as addressing God as you rather than thou.

Book of Concord Collective Lutheran confession* of faith including the Nicene*, Athanasian*, and Apostles'* creeds, the Augsburg Confession* and its Apology, the Smalcald Articles* and the "Tract Concerning the Power and Primacy of the Pope," Martin Luther's Small and Large Catechisms, and the Epitome and the Thorough Declaration of the Formula of Concord*. It was published in German at Dresden in 1580. An extensive catalog of testimonies from the Scriptures and the writings of the early Church Fathers* appeared as an appendix. Adherence to the *Book of Concord* varies among Lutheran groups. Among some it is considered *quia* (because) or in conformity with the Scriptures, while among others it is considered *quatenus*, or in so far as they are. Modern versions have used the same title.

Book of Confessions Collection of 11 creeds and confessional* documents fom the early church, the Reformation* period, and the twentieh century that is the confessional standard of the Presbyterian Church, USA.

Book of Deer Irish manuscript of the four Gospels written in Gaelic, dating from the ninth century. So called because its Gaelic notes describe the foundation and grants of land made to the Monastery of Deer in Aberdeenshire in Scotland. It contains a corrupt text. It is now in the Cambridge University Library.

Book of Discipline 1. Collection of the doctrinal and procedural norms of the United Methodist Church, revised every four years by the General

Conference. 2. Scottish book of ecclesiastical organization, a blueprint for the newly reformed Church of Scotland*.

Book of Durrow First Irish manuscript with elaborate decoration, dated 675. Written possibly in Northumbria, it was preserved at Columba's* monastery at Durrow and is now in Trinity College* Library, Dublin.

Book of Hours Form of devotional book developed in the fourteenth century containing prayers and meditations appropriate to the seasons, months,

Book of Hours

dates, and hours. Many are masterpieces of illumination*, such as *Tres Riches Heures* (1415) made by the Limbourg Brothers and other artists for the renowned collector, Jean, duc de Berry.

Book of Kells Ornamented and illuminated Latin manuscript of the Gospels, originally from the monastery at Kells in Ireland, and now at the Trinity College* Library in Dublin. The book has 340 leaves, each 13 by 9.5 inches of thick glazed parchment*. The copy is made of brownish-black ink. The work was probably begun at Iona* and finished at Kells. The illumination is of extraordinary intricacy and richness.

Book of Lismore Fifteenth-century manuscript found in Lismore Castle, now in the Chatsworth House. It includes a collection of the lives of saints* in Middle Irish.

Book of Mormon Scriptures of Latter-Day Saints, supposedly written on golden tablets and discovered and translated by Joseph Smith* in the early nineteenth century.

Book of Remembrance Memorial book, recording various gifts and donors, often kept in a church narthex* or vestibule.

Book of Rituals Guide to worship in the Evangelical United Brethren Church*, authorized by the General Conference in 1954.

Book of Sports Controversial declaration of King James I of England in 1617/18, defining the kind of activities permitted on Sunday.

Boos, Martin (1762–1825) German Pietist leader and Roman Catholic priest who preached "Christ for us and in us" and justification* by faith. He was put on trial for heterodoxy* and forced to flee.

Booth, William (1829–1912) Founder and first general of the Salvation Army*. Of partly Jewish de-

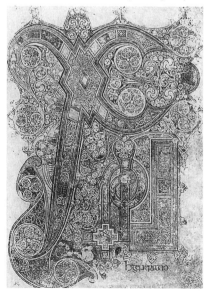

Book of Kells

scent, he was converted in 1844 at the age of 15. Within two years he became a Methodist New Connection revivalist preacher. In 1861 he left the Methodists to undertake evangelistic, social, and rescue work known at first as the "Christian mis-

William Booth

sion." Out of this effort in 1878 the Salvation Army was born with Booth as its first general. In 1879 the first Salvation Army band was formed and next year the now familiar uniform was devised.

By the first decades of the twentieth century the Salvation Army had spread to the Commonwealth countries and India. To the end of his life Booth worked tirelessly among the poor and outcast, setting up new methods for reaching and helping them: cheap meals, night shelters, unemployment exchange, farm colonies, missing persons bureau, poor man's bank, legal aid for the poor. He continued to tour many countries on evangelistic crusades*. In a lifetime that spanned eight decades, he traveled five million miles, preached 60,000 sermons, and appointed 16,000 officers to serve in the Salvation Army. When he died, 150,000 people filed past his coffin and 40,000 attended his funeral. Poet Vachel Lindsay celebrated the occasion with his poem, "General William Booth Enters into Heaven."

His wife, **Catherine Booth** (1829–1890), known as the "mother of the Salvation Army," married her husband in 1855. They had eight children. She was active in the women's branch of the Salvation Army. William's son, **William Bramwell Booth** (1856–1929), succeeded his father as general of the Salvation Army. Another son, **Ballington Booth** (1859–1940), commanded the Salvation Army in Australia and the United States and founded the Volunteers of America*. Daughter **Evangeline Cory Booth** (1865–1950) was commander-in-chief, USA, from 1904 and general from 1934 to 1938.

Bordeaux Pilgrim The earliest known Western pilgrim* in the Holy Land* in 333–335. He left an account entitled *Itinerarium Burdigalense*.

Borgia, St. Francis (1510–1572) Jesuit general*. Grandson of Pope Alexander VI*, he entered the Society of Jesus* in 1551 and became the third general of the order in 1565. He did much to improve the Gregorian University*. He was canonized in 1671. Feast day: October 10.

Boris and Gleb Russian Christian princes, two of the 14 sons of the Grand Duke St. Vladimir*. They were murdered by their elder brother, Svyatapulk. Their incorruptible bodies are now at the Church of St. Basil at Novgorod*. In the Russian Orthodox Church*, they are considered as strastoterptsy or passion bearers*.

Boris, St. (d. 907) Khan (king) of Bulgaria. Boris was converted to Orthodox Christianity and baptized about 864. He succeeded in gaining autonomy for the Bulgarian church. In 889 he abdicated and entered St. Panteleemon Monastery. Feast day: May 2.

born again Of or relating to a Christian who is reborn of the Spirit and transformed into a new person, and has experienced conversion* and regeneration*, given his or her heart to Christ, and pledged to serve Christ for the rest of his or her life. It is the central act in the spiritual life of an Evangelical Christian. Based on John 3:3, "Unless one is born again, he cannot see the kingdom of heaven."

Bornholmers/Bornholmians Danish Lutheran Mission, an Evangelical layman's home mission movement and a society of foreign missions in the Danish national church, originating from a revival movement on the island of Bornholm in the 1860s. It was inspired by Pietist leaders such as P. C. Trandberg and C. O. Rosenius who preached the new birth*, justification* by the free and unmerited grace* of God, and sanctification* as the result of salvation.

Borromeo, Charles (1538–1584) Archbishop of Milan*. He was ordained in 1563. When his uncle, Pius IV*, became pope, he was called to Rome* and named archbishop of Milan, cardinal secretary of state and Protector of the Low Countries, Portugal, the Swiss Catholic cantons, and several religious orders. He played an active role in the final session at Trent* and helped to reform the College of Cardinals* and revise the missal* and the Breviary*. As a bishop, he reformed his diocese* by enforcing discipline and creating a constitutional framework. He founded six seminaries for the education of the clergy and established the Confraternity of Christian Doctrine* to help the education of the young. Priests were encouraged to join the Oblates of St. Ambrose* to raise the standards of pastoral care. He also established orphanages and havens for deserted wives. During the plague of 1576, he personally ministered to the sick. He was canonized in 1610. Feast day: November 4.

Borromini, Francesco (1599–1667) Italian sculptor and architect who worked in Rome* all his life. Among his buildings were San Carlo alle Quattro Fontane for the Trinitarians*, the Oratory of St. Philip Neri*, the Chapel of St. Ivo* for the Sapienza, the chapel of the Spada family in San Girolamo della Carita, and Sant'Agnese in Piazza Navona.

Borrow, George Henry (1803–1881) English writer and friend of the Gypsies. As an agent of the British and Foreign Bible Society*, he translated the Gospels into European languages. His *The Bible in Spain* (3 vols., 1843) is a classic.

Bosch, David Jacobus (1929-1992) South African missiologist. He served as missionary* and theological teacher in the Transkei and then as professor of missiology* at the University of South Africa (1971–1992). *Transforming Mission: Paradigm Shifts in Theology of Mission* (1991) was his most significant work.

Bosch, Hieronymous (c. 1450–1516) Dutch painter of religious and mythological themes. His best known works are *The Garden of Earthly Delights, The Last Judgment, The Mocking of Christ, St. Jerome in the Desert, The Temptation of St. Anthony, The Haywagon,* and *The Ship of Fools* which contain dreamlike vista filled with fantastic figures in vibrant color.

Bosco, St. John (1815–1888) Birth name: Giovanni Melchior Bosco. The founder of the Salesian Order. Ordained priest in 1841 in Turin*, he established technical schools and workshops for destitute youth. With the goal of creating similar schools in other parts of Italy and the world, he founded the Society of St. Francis of Sales* (the Salesians*). He was beatified in 1929 and canonized in 1934. Feast day: January 31.

Bossey, Ecumenical Institute of Ecumenical training center founded under the aegis of the World Council of Churches* in 1946 at Bossey, near the foothills of the Jura Mountains near Geneva*.

Bossuet, Jacques Benigne (1627–1704) French churchman and preacher, considered one of the most eloquent of all time. His orthodoxy* combined with oratorical skills made him a formidable controversialist. He conducted theological skirmishes with Fenelon*, the Quietists of Madame Guyon*, the Jesuits*, and the Protestants. His most important work was *Discours sur l'Histoire Universelle* (1681), a Christian philosophy of history. He defended Catholic orthodoxy in *Exposition de la Doctrine Catholique sur les Matieres de Controverse* (1671), while his *Meditations sur l'Evangile* (1731) and *Elevations sur les Mysteres* (1727) rank as classics of devotional literature.

Boste, St. John (1543–1594) English Roman Catholic martyr*. Converted to Roman Catholicism*, he went to the English College at Reims and was ordained priest. He returned to England and carried out an active missionary campaign until he was betrayed, arrested, imprisoned, tortured, hanged, drawn, and quartered. He was canonized in 1970 and included among the forty martyrs* of England and Wales. Feast day: October 25.

Boston, Thomas (1677–1732) Scottish preacher and theologian whose *Notes to the Marrow of Modern Divinity,* suggesting special grace* and limited atonement*, was condemned by the General Assembly* of the Church of Scotland* in 1720. His other books included *A View of the Covenant of Grace* (1734), *An Illustration of the Doctrines of the Christian Religion* (1773), and the best known, *Human Nature in Its Fourfold State* (1720).

Botticelli, Sandro (1445–1510) Birth name: Alessandro di Mariaco Filipepi. Florentine painter, noted for his Madonna* pictures and altarpieces. His *Adoration of the Magi* shows a blending of resurgent pagan culture and biblical truth. His most imaginative works were *Lamentations, Mystic Nativity,* and *Mystic Crucifixion.* He is remembered for his many Madonnas: *Madonna of the Pomegranate, Madonna of the Magnificent,* and the *Chigi Madonna.* He was deeply influenced by Savonarola's* ideas. His works adorn a number of churches.

Botulph, St. (mid-seventh century) Founder and first abbot of a monastery at Icanhoe in Eastern England in 654. Feast day: June 17.

Boudinot, Elias (1740–1821) American revolutionary and first president of the American Bible Society* and the Continental Congress.

boun barekendan (Arm. great carnival) In the Armenian Church*, Shrovetide*, or the last day before the beginning of Lent*.

boundary situation (Ger., *Grenzsituation*) In existentialism*, point in human life when a person becomes aware of a transcendent dimension to existence. Boundary situations are normally times of crisis caused by illness or death of a loved one. They generally lead to the search for an authentic existence.

Bourdaloue, Louis (1632–1704) French Jesuit preacher known as "the king of orators and the orator of kings." He was the court preacher to Louis XIV.

Bourgeoys, Marguerite (1620–1700) French nun, founder of the Congregation of Mount Royal. She arrived in the frontier settlement of Ville Marie, in New France (Canada) in 1653 and erected a school for the education of girls. It later expanded into a facility for vocational training as well as for the training of Native Americans.

Bourges Saint Etienne Cathedral in Bourges, France, one of the great cathedrals of France, begun in the twelfth century. The cathedral was finished about 1260, but was consecrated only in 1324. Between the fourteenth and sixteenth centuries chapels were added and a huge rose window* installed above the west door. In 1506 the north tower collapsed, destroying a large part of the vaulted roof. The tower was rebuilt in 1542. It escaped destruction during the French Revolution and was fully restored in the nineteenth century.

Bourignon, Antoinette (1616–1680) Dutch mystic who left her Roman Catholic convent to preach a heresy, denying the Atonement* and the Scriptures. Attacking all established churches, she taught direct contact with God through the inner light of the spirit. Her writings are published in 21 volumes.

Bourne, Hugh (1772–1852) English founder of the Primitive Methodist Church*, a movement which, at the time of his death, had 110,000 members.

Bousset, Johann Franz Wilhelm (1865–1920) German professor of New Testament theology. His researches into the hellenistic world helped to found the branch of theology known as Religionsgeschichte Schule (History of Religions School). His principal works include: *Die Antichrist* (1895), *Die Religion des Judentums im Neutestamentlichen Zeitalter* (1903), *Die Hauptprobleme der Gnosis* (1907), and *Kyrios Christos* (1913).

boutistes Official in the Byzantine Church* who immerses an infant in the font as part of the baptismal rite.

Bouts, Dieric (c. 1415–1475) Dutch painter. His most important painting is the altarpiece of the Mysic Meals in St. Peter's* in Leuven. He also painted two grisly martyrdoms, those of St. Hippolytus* and St. Elmo*.

Bow Church The Church of St. Mary-le-Bow, in Cheapside, London. It was built by Christopher Wren* after the great fire of 1666.

Bowden, John William (1798–1844) Tractarian and hymn writer. He was a close friend of John Henry Newman* and a supporter of the Oxford movement*. He wrote some of the *Tracts of the Times* and contributed six hymns to *Lyra Apostolica* (1836).

Bowen, George (1816–1888) "The White Saint of India." American missionary who was converted when his dying sweetheart gave him a Bible as a parting gift. He trained as a missionary and was appointed to the Marathi Mission by the American Board. From 1848 to 1888 he served in India, living a life of self-denial and as a self-supporting missionary.

bowing Physical gesture, including kneeling, genuflection, and prostration, used to express reverence or worship. Bowing is usually directed toward the cross, images of Christ, or the saints*, or during specified times in a service. Distinguished from profound bow, kneeling, genuflection, and prostration.

bowotho In the Jacobite Liturgy, a hymn divided into four strophes, the last of which included the doxology*.

Bowring, Sir John (1792–1872) English diplomat and hymn writer. A member of Parliament and governor of Hong Kong, he was an able linguist and a fellow of the Royal Society. He is chiefly remembered for his hymns, "In the Cross of Christ I Glory" (1825), made famous in Stainer's oratorio* *The Crucifixion* (1887) and "Watchman! Tell Us of the Night."

Boxer Rebellion Anti-Western Chinese rebellion in 1899/1900 during which many foreigners, especially Christian missionaries, were killed.

Boxing Day Day after Christmas*, in England and some Anglophone countries. So called because the day was devoted to the disposition of gift boxes received on Christmas.

boy bishop In the Middle Ages, a boy elected to perform some of the symbolic duties of a bishop from the Festival of the Holy Innocents* (December 6) to St. Nicholas Day (December 25).

Boyce, William (1710–1779) English composer and organist. He was the organist at the Chapel Royal from 1758 to 1769. Forced to retire because of loss of hearing, he spent his remaining years compiling the great anthology, *Cathedral Music*.

Boyle Lectures Lectures founded under the will of Robert Boyle* to prove the truth of Christian religion "against notorious infidels*, viz. atheists, deists, pagans, Jews, and Mohammedans." Eight lectures are delivered annually.

Boyle, Robert (1627–1691) Scientist and philosopher who sought to reconcile science and religion. A violent storm in Geneva* led to his conversion, and thereafter he combined his scientific pursuits with a deep devotion to God. His book, *Seraphic Love* (1660), is a classic of devotional literature.

Boys' Brigade Uniformed voluntary organization for Sunday school* boys that combined Bible study with physical sports and related activities. It was founded in 1883 in Glasgow, Scotland, by William A. Smith for "the advancement of Christ's kingdom among boys and the promotion of habits of obedience, reverence, discipline, self-respect and all that tends towards a true Christian manliness."

brachium saeculare (Lat., secular arm) In canon law*, the power of the civil government to intervene in cases dealing with the church.

Bradbury, William Batchelder (1816–1868) American hymn writer who composed such hymns as "Just As I Am," "He Leadeth Me," "Savior, Like a Shepherd Lead Us," and the famous tune to "Jesus Loves Me." A protégé of Lowell Mason*, he was also influenced by Felix Mendelssohn*. His gospel music publishing company, Bigelow and Main, founded in 1867, was later acquired by Hope Publishing Company in 1922.

Bradford, John (c. 1510–1555) Popular English preacher and Reformation martyr*. In 1551 he was named a royal chaplain*. Two years later he was imprisoned for his Protestant sympathies and burned at Smithfield. He wrote *The Hurt of Hearing Mass* and other works of a devotional nature.

Bradford, William (1589?–1657) Second governor of the Plymouth Colony in Massachusetts. Cotton Mather* described him as the "Moses who brought the Pilgrims out of England to the New Canaan," and admired "his exemplary, holy, prayerful, watchful and fruitful walk with God." He governed the colony for 34 years and was re-elected 30 times. He wrote the *History of Plymouth Plantation,* a valuable historical chronicle.

Bradley, Dan Beach (1804–1873) American pioneer medical missionary in Thailand. He began work in 1835 under the American Board of Commissioners for Foreign Missions* and later the American Missionary Association. As dean of Protestant missionaries in Thailand, he became a friend of King Mongkut. He supported his extensive medical activities through a commercial printing operation which also produced voluminous Christian literature. He imported the first Thai printing press and published the first newspapers in English and Thai.

Bradwardine, Thomas (c. 1295–1349) Archbishop of Canterbury*, known as "Doctor Profundus." He was a foe of Pelagianism* and champion of Augustinianism*, especially predestination*. Appointed archbishop of Canterbury* in 1349, he died of the Black Death within 40 days of consecration.

Braga, Rite of Form of the Latin rite used in the Cathedral of Braga in Portugal. It was revised in 1924 and 1971.

Brahms, Johannes (1833–1897) German composer. He was one of the few major composers in the nineteenth century to create a significant body of music suitable for church use. He composed a considerable number of motets, as well as part-songs set to biblical or to chorale texts. Among them are *Gestliches Lied* (Sacred Song) and *Gestliches Choere* (Sacred Choruses). They reveal his thorough knowledge of the music of J. S. Bach* and included such motets as "The Grace of God Has Come to Man," "Create in Me," "When We Are in Deepest Need," "Why Light Is Given," and "O Savior Rend the Heavens Apart." In his "Burial Song," the composer came to terms with the theme of death and resurrection. Foremost among Brahms' music is *Ein Deutsches Requiem* (A German Requiem) shaped from Martin Luther's translation of the Bible. Its composition occupied Brahms for over a decade. His last composition was a chorale setting of "O World, I Must Leave Thee."

Brainerd, David (1718–1747) Missionary to the American Indians, sent by the Scottish Society for the Propagation of Christian Knowledge. His selfless devotion, zeal, and life of prayer inspired Henry Martyn* and other missionaries. By 1745

David Brainerd

he had ridden over 3,000 miles by horseback, but he died of tuberculosis in his thirtieth year. His *Journal* is a devotional classic.

Bramante, Donato (c. 1444–1514) First great Italian architect of the High Renaissance. He emerged as an architect with the reconstruction of Sta Maria Presso St. Satiro in the late 1470s. He went about 1499 to Rome*, where he built the cloister* of Sta Maria della Pace and the Tempietto in the courtyard of San Pietro in Montorio, commemorating the site of St. Peter's* martyrdom. He was appointed architect for the rebuilding of St. Peter's* by Pope Julius II* but did not live to see it completed.

bramble In religious art, a symbol of the purity of Mary.

Branch Davidians American Adventist group, originally the Davidian Seventh-Day Adventist Association, led by a Mrs. Houteff, who predicted that God would restore the Davidic monarchy in 1959. When this failed, the association was dissolved but a splinter group, the Branch Davidians, took over under Vernon Howell, who assumed the name of David Khoresh or Cyrus. They settled in Mount Carmel, near Waco, Texas, and stockpiled arms for a final world conflict. After being besieged by federal forces, the settlement was destroyed in 1993 in a fire that killed all but a few of its members. A rival group still lives at the site.

branch theory View that although the church is now divided, its many segments that retain the historic apostolic succession* continue as living branches of the church.

brandea Cloth placed on the stone slab covering the tomb of a martyred Christian.

Branham, William Marrion (1909–1965) Leader of the post-World War II healing revival. He began preaching in the early 1930s, carrying a prophetic message of healing and deliverance. Toward the end of his career, he began to preach some outlandish doctrines, proclaiming himself as the angel of Revelation and predicting that the rapture* would take place in 1977.

Brant, Joseph (1742–1807) Indian name: Thayendanegea. Christian Mohawk chief who converted to Christianity. He translated the Gospel of Mark and the *Book of Common Prayer** into the Mohawk language. He sided with the royalists during the Revolutionary War and, when the war ended,

moved to upper Canada, where he built the first church.

Brauweiler Benedictine abbey of St. Nicholas in Brauweiler, Germany, west of Cologne*. Originally a tiny wooden chapel built in 970, it became a monastery church in 1028. The abbey church was consecrated in 1061. An earthquake in 1117 and later arson and war in the thirteenth century caused considerable damage to the buildings. The restoration began in 1135 and lasted for over a century and included the west towers, side aisles, central nave*, and the east end. The Romanesque crypt with seven naves in the earlier church was incorporated into the later church.

Bray, Thomas (1656–1730) English clergyman who helped to organize the Anglican Church* in Maryland and founded the Society for the Propagation of the Gospel* (1701) and the Society for Promoting Christian Knowledge* (1698). Through his efforts, hundreds of parochial* libraries were built and endowed with books.

bread box Receptacle for the wafer* in the Eucharist*.

bread plate Plate for the distribution of bread or wafers in the Eucharist*.

breaking of bread Sharing the Lord's Supper*.

Breastplate of St. Patrick Old Irish hymn, beginning "I bind unto myself today the strong name of the Trinity*." In it the hymn writer invokes the Trinity*, angels, prophets, the powers of heaven* and earth, and Christ himself against the forces of evil.

Brebeuf, St. Jean de (1593–1649) French Jesuit missionary and martyr*. After evangelizing the Huron Indians of Quebec, he and others were massacred by the Iroquois. He left an account of his missionary travels in *Jesuit Relations*. He was canonized in 1930. Feast day: September 26 or March 16.

Bredeson, Harald (1918–) Pastor and leader in the Charismatic movement. Ordained as a Lutheran minister in 1944, Bredeson received the baptism

Martyrdom of St. Jean de Brebeuf

of the Holy Spirit* in 1946 and thereafter was instrumental in bringing the Charismatic renewal* to mainline churches*. He and Jean Stone are credited with coining the term, *Charismatic renewal.* He traveled widely and took the Charismatic message to campuses and media centers. He played a role in the creation of the Full Gospel Businessmen's Fellowship International*. His life is chronicled in his autobiography, *Yes, Lord* (1963).

Bremond, Henri (1865–1933) Roman Catholic scholar, elected to the Academie Francaise in 1924. He was a member of the Society of Jesus* from 1882 to 1904, but he had a running battle with his superiors because of his modernist views. His greatest work was *Histoire Litteraire du Sentiment Religieux en France, Depuis les Guerres de Religion Jusqu'a Nos Jours* (11 vols., 1915–1933). He also wrote a life of John Henry Newman*, whom he admired.

Brendan, St. (c. 484–578) Irish Benedictine abbot of Clonfert. A navigator, his *Navigatio St. Brendani* recounts his visit to a number of mythical islands in the Western Ocean in search of an earthly paradise. Feast day: May 16.

Brent, Charles Henry (1862–1929) Canadian bishop and ecumenist. He was chief of chaplains* of the American Expeditionary Force in Europe in World War I. He was president of the World Conference on Faith and Order* at Lausanne* in 1927. His works included *The Mind of Christ in the Church of the Living God* (1908), *Presence* (1914), and *The Mount of Vision* (1918).

Brenz, Johann (1499–1570) German reformer who left the Roman Catholic Church under the influence of Luther* and Oecolampadius*. His *Syngramma Suevicum* (1525) explains the Lutheran teaching on the presence of Christ in the sacrament*. He was a reformer of Halle in Swabia.

Bres, Guido de (1522–1567) Belgian Protestant martyr*. He helped to draft the Belgic Confession*. During the Wars in the Netherlands between the Spaniards and the Dutch, he was executed for rebellion.

Bresee, Phineas F. (1838–1915) Founder of the Church of the Nazarene*. Converted at 17 in a Methodist meeting, he became a full-time Methodist minister in 1858. From 1866 he became a leading figure in the Holiness movement*. In 1895 he left his denomination to start the Church of the Nazarene and presided over the church until his death.

Brethren in Christ Sect founded between 1775 and 1788 in Lancaster County, Pennsylvania. Initially known as Brethren, the sect was led by two Swiss Mennonite leaders, Jacob and John Engel. The three principal elements of their beliefs were conscious experience of a new birth*, discipleship and restoration of the church, and Wesleyan perfectionism*. In the latter part of the nineteenth century they experienced a surge of missionary

Church of the Brethren

activity at home and abroad. After merging with River Brethren*, they expanded into Canada, where they are known as Tunkers. Brethren in

Christ are affiliated with the Mennonite Central Committee, the National Association of Evangelicals*, and National Holiness Association

Brethren of the Common Life One of the most important spiritual associations in the Middle Ages, founded in the fourteenth century to foster Christian devotion and mystical piety. The original leader was Gerard Groote*, a canon* of Utrecht*, who, when the church banned him from preaching, retired to Deventer, his home-

Illuminated Breviary

town, and gathered a group of people dedicated to the higher life*. The group consisted of clerics and laymen, bound by no vows, who continued in their own vocations. They emphasized education and teaching, promoting books, copying manuscripts, and printing. Members were self-supporting, pooled their resources, using their surplus for charity.

On the death of Groote* in 1384 the leadership passed to Florentius Radewijns, who converted the commune into a formal association known as Brethren of the Common Life. The movement spread to Germany and other countries in Europe. Out of this group rose many of the influen-

tial leaders of the time, such as Nicholas of Cusa*, Erasmus*, and Thomas à Kempis*, whose *The Imitation of Christ** remains one of the all-time classics of devotional literature. See also DEVOTIO MODERNA.

Brethren of the Free Spirit Any one of the medieval pantheistic sects of the thirteenth century. They believed they could attain union with God and liberate themselves from moral laws. Among them were the Amalricians*, founded by Amalric of Bena*.

Breughel/Bruegel, Peter (1524/30–1569) Dutch painter. Also known as "Peasant Bruegel." Although sometimes considered a painter of drolleries, he was a serious painter whose work was didactic, concerned with human follies. Among his religious paintings, the largest was *Christ Carrying the Cross* (1504) which presented biblical events in a contemporary frame. The same format was used in the *Census at Bethlehem* (1566) and the *Massacre of the Innocents* (1566).

Breviary Roman Catholic liturgical book containing the Psalms, hymns, lessons, and prayers to be recited in the Divine Office* and for each day's canonical hours*. Originally called Ordo, it came to be called Breviary from its opening words, *Breviarium Sive Ordo Officiorum per Totam anni Decursionem* (Short Conspectus or Order for the Offices of the Whole Year). For centuries referred to as the Divine Office*, it is known today as the Liturgy of the Hours. The first Breviary was prepared for the papal chapel in the twelfth century. In medieval England the Breviary was known as the portiforium or portuise.

Brewster, William (1567–1644) Founding member of the Plymouth Colony. He was a prominent member of the Separatists*, small Puritan congregation in Scrooby, which migrated to Holland in 1608 with Brewster as their elder. In 1620 he sailed on the *Mayflower* and helped to establish the Plymouth Colony. Until 1629, he was the ruling elder, lay teacher, and also an able administrator of the colony.

Briant, St. Alexander (c. 1556–1581) English martyr*. Converted to Roman Catholicism*, he went to the English College at Douai*, but returned to England on a mission, making many converts. He was arrested, tortured, tried on false changes, and executed. He was canonized in 1970 as one of the forty martyrs of England and Wales*. Feast day: October 25.

bride of Christ 1. The church as the expectant bride of the coming Lord (Eph. 5:22–32). The eschatological union will be the occasion of the marriage supper* of the Lamb (Rev. 19:7–9). Some Pentecostal churches* interpret this metaphor as applying to each individual believer on the basis of Matthew 22:1–14. 2. The soul.

Bridges, Robert (Seymour) (1844–1930) English poet laureate and anthologist of hymns. His interest in church music led to his compilation of the *Yattendon Hymnal* (1895–1899) for which he wrote, adapted, or translated 44 hymns. His selections were later used in the *English Hymnal* (1906) and the *Oxford Hymn Book* (1908). In 1913 he was made poet laureate.

Bridget (Birgitta) of Sweden, St. (c. 1303–1373) Swedish nun. Of noble birth, she withdrew into a contemplative life* after the death of her husband. With the help of the Cistercians* and one of her daughters, who later became St. Catherine of Sweden*, she founded the Bridgettine Order. She had visions and revelations from Jesus and Mary and worked tirelessly to reform the church. Her private devotions were highly esteemed in the Middle Ages. Feast day: July 23.

Bridget, St. (c. 455–523) Also, Brigit. Irish patron saint* of mercy. She founded a church and monastery at Kildare. Later her cult spread to Scotland and England. After St. Patrick*, she is the second patron saint of Ireland. Feast day: February 1.

Bridgettines Also, Brigittines. Catholic order of Augustinian canonesses formed by St. Bridget of Sweden* about 1350. Its members devote themselves to meditation, prayer, and literary activities. Its members are organized in double (i.e., male and female) monasteries, strictly segregated and with separate liturgical obligations. The male order died out in 1842. The order was re-

vived in Spain and Belgium after the Reformation*.

Bridgman, Elijah Coleman (1801–1861) First American missionary to China. On graduation from seminary in 1829 he was appointed to China by the American Board. An authority on the Cantonese dialect, he translated the Bible into Chinese.

brief 1. Papal epistle signed by the papal secretary and less formal than a bull*. It is sealed with the pope's so called fisherman's ring*. 2. In the Middle Ages, warrants for collections for specific charitable purposes.

Bright Week In the Eastern Church*, the Holy Week*.

Bright, William Rohl ("Bill") (1921–) Evangelist and founder of Campus Crusade for Christ*. Converted in 1945, he experienced in 1951 a call* from God to enter full-time evangelistic work. He founded Campus Crusade for Christ which has grown into one of the largest faith mission* organizations in the world. It developed the *Four Spiritual Laws* as part of an evangelization technique and also produced the film *Jesus* in 1979.

Brigittines See BRIDGETTINES.

Brill, Mattys (1550–1583) Dutch painter who did frescoes in the Vatican* for Pope Gregory XIII*.

British and Foreign Bible Society Largest and oldest Bible society*, formed in 1804 with the purpose of encouraging "the wider circulation of the Holy Scriptures, without note or comment." It is directed by an international committee of 36 members of which 15 are British Anglican.

British Council of Churches A national association of British churches associated with the World Council of Churches*, formed in 1942. It describes itself as "a fellowship of churches in the British Isles which confess the Lord Jesus Christ as God and Savior according to the Scriptures and therefore seek to fulfill together their common calling to the glory of the one God, Father, Son and Holy Spirit." Its 112 members represent over 700 local councils of churches and 25 larger or regional bodies. The Roman Catholic Church sends observers to its meetings. Since 1990 it was replaced by the Council of Churches for Britain and Ireland* which then changed its name to Churches Together in Britain and Ireland (CTBI*).

Britten, (Edward) Benjamin (1913–1976) British composer who combined operas and art songs with outstanding religious music. Functional church music, as *Te Deum* (1934) and *Missa Brevis** (1959), is rare among his large number of concert works on religious texts. Cantata-like compositions are particularly prominent in Britten's early years. These included *A Boy Was Born* (1933), *A Ceremony of Carols* (1942), *Rejoice in the Lamb* (1943), *Saint Nicolas* (1948), and *Cantata Misericordium* (1961). In his later years he employed dramatic music effectively and revived the medieval liturgical drama as in *Curlew River* (1964), *The Burning Fiery Furnace* (1966), and *The Prodigal Son* (1968).

Britto, John de (1647–1693) Portuguese missionary and martyr*. After joining the Society of Jesus*, he was appointed to the Madurai Mission in India in 1673 to work with the lower castes. Beset by wars and disorders, he was imprisoned, beaten, tortured, and condemned to death, but was reprieved by the local raja on condition that he would no longer preach. He returned to Portugal in 1687 but was back in Madurai within a few years. Here he was imprisoned by the ruler and beheaded in 1693.

Broad Church The liberal branch of the Church of England* that interprets its creeds with a greater degree of latitude than the conservatives. They hold positions that are midway between Low Church* and High Church*. The description is used also of other churches that occupy a similar place on a theological scale.

broad stole Broad band of cloth, generally a folded chasuble*, worn by the deacon during part of the High Mass* in certain penitential seasons.

Broadus, John Albert (1827–1895) Professor of New Testament for 36 years (1859–1895) and president of the Southern Baptist Theological Seminary (1889–1895). He was converted at 16 and served as pastor for many years at the Baptist church at Charlottesville. His reputation as a scholar and teacher is based on his numerous books, especially *On the Preparation and Delivery of Sermons* (1870), *Commentary on the Gospel of Matthew* (1886), and *Harmony of the Gospels* (1893).

Brompton Oratory The house and church of the Oratorians* in London. The original oratory* was built in 1849 through the efforts of John Henry Newman*.

Bronson, Miles (1812–1883) Pioneer American Baptist missionary to Assam, India. Reaching northeast India in 1837, Bronson built up the Christian church in the region. He was the first to live among the Naga, first to organize a Garo congregation, the first to build a Baptist church and the first to ordain indigenous pastors in the northeast. He established the first coeducational school in the northeast and produced the first Anglo-Assamese dictionary.

Brookes, James Hall (1830–1897) Presbyterian minister. Ordained in 1854, he served as pastor at the Sixteenth and Walnut Street Church in St. Louis. Best known as a conference speaker, he was active in the International Prophetic Conferences and the Niagara Bible Conferences which he helped to found. A prolific author, he wrote over 17 books, 250 tracts, and dozens of sermons and pamphlets. From 1875 until his death he was the editor of *The Truth*, an influential premillennial journal. Among his disciples was C. I. Scofield*.

Brooks, Phillips (1835–1893) Episcopal preacher and bishop who wrote the hymn, "O Little Town of Bethlehem," and delivered the eulogy for President Lincoln. In 1877 he published his *Yale Lectures on Preaching*. In 1891 he was consecrated bishop of Boston.

Brorson, Hans A. (1694–1764) Danish bishop and writer of several outstanding hymns.

brother 1. In the Protestant churches following the New Testament, a term of address for a fellow believer. 2. In the Roman Catholic Church, term of address for a member of a religious order or a congregation.

Brother Lawrence of the Resurrection (c. 1614–1691) Birth name: Nicholas Herman. French mystic and Carmelite* lay brother*. After a short stint in the army, he entered the Discalced* Carmelite monastery in Paris in 1649 and was placed in charge of the kitchen. As a cook he spent his time absorbed in meditation even while carrying out his mundane tasks. His maxims and prayers were collected after his death by Abbe de Beaufort and published in 1694 as *The Practice of the Presence of God.*

brothers of Jesus Jesus' half brothers, sons of Mary and Joseph*. First Corinthians 9:5 mentions in passing the ministry of the brothers of the Lord. In Galatians 1:19 Paul calls James the Lord's brother. The Gospel mentions four brothers in all —James, Joses or Joseph, Simon, and Judas (Matt. 13:55) in addition to unnamed sisters. Roman Catholics who argue that the Virgin Mary* was a perpetual virgin take the word *brothers* to mean either sons of Joseph by a prior marriage or cousins of Jesus.

brotherhood Fraternal unity of those sharing a common bond of faith.

Brotherhood movement Organization founded in England in 1875 by John Blackham as a Sunday Bible class for men.

Brotherhood of St. Andrew Episcopal organization in the United States.

Brotherhood of the New Life Communal religious group founded in New York in the nineteenth century by the mystic Thomas Lake Harris.

Brotherhood Week Week ending February 22 dedicated to the promotion of interdenominational and interreligious dialogue, sponsored by the National Conference of Christians and Jews*.

Brothers Hospitallers Lay organization founded by John of God* at Granada and continued with the support of Philip II with hospitals in many Spanish cities. In 1572 Pope Pius V* approved the order under the Augustinian Rule*. The order is governed by a prior general* at Rome and divided into provinces.

Brothers of Charity Catholic order founded in Germany in the nineteenth century to care for orphans and the needy.

Brothers of Christian Schools Religious community founded by St. John Baptist de la Salle* in 1682 in Rheims, France, and approved by the Vatican* in 1725. The community flourished until the French Revolution, and was revived afterwards, reaching 1,000 members by 1820 and 16,000 by 1960.

Brothers of the Holy Cross Religious institute founded by Basil Anthony Moreau in 1837 in Le Mans, France. It merged with the Brothers of St. Joseph, founded in 1820 by Canon Jacques Francois Dujarie. In 1946 it split into two societies, brothers* and priests.

Brothers Penitent/Penitentes Group founded in the southwestern United States whose members carry heavy crosses and carts and flog and crucify one of their members on Good Friday* and resurrect him on Easter*. Its practices were condemned by the Roman Catholic Church in 1869.

brown In religious art, color used as a symbol of degradation or renunciation.

Brown, Raymond (1928–1998) Scripture scholar. A member of the Society of St. Sulpice, he taught for many years at St. Mary's Seminary and Union Theological Seminary*. He was a member of the Pontifical Biblical Commission*. He is the author of more than 25 books on the Bible, including two notable works on the birth and death of the Messiah.

Browne, George (?–1556) Promoter of the Reformation* in Ireland. An English Augustinian friar*, he joined the royalist side and was appointed archbishop of Dublin. He worked hard to establish royal supremacy and bring about the union of the Irish church with the Church of England*. He took part in the suppression of the Irish monasteries.

Browne, Robert (c. 1553–1633) English separatist* leader. He is often called "the father of English Congregationalism"* and his followers were known as Brownists. He called the authority of the bishops unlawful and held that the true authority lay in the gathered church. Imprisoned several times and persecuted by the authorities, he went abroad and settled at Zeeland. Here he set forth his doctrines in his *Treatise of Reformation Without Tarrying for Anie* and *Booke which Sheweth the Life and Manners of all True Christians,* in which he denounced "ungodlie communion with wicked persons." He died in jail after a fight with the local parish constable.

Browne, Sir Thomas (1605–1682) English physician and writer. He attempted to reconcile religion and science in *Religio Medici* (1642) and *Pseudodoxia Epidemica* (1646) and other works. A man of encyclopedic knowledge, he was knighted by Charles II in 1671. Among his posthumous works is *Christian Morals* (1716).

Browning, Robert (1812–1889) English poet whose religious poems included "Christmas Day," "Easter Eve," "A Death in the Desert," and "Cleon."

Brownsville Revival A movement originating at the Brownsville Assembly of God Church in Pensacola, Florida, on June 18, 1995. Following three years of weekly prayer for revival, and kindled by the preaching of visiting Texas-based evangelist Steve Hill, that Father's Day there was a singular sense of the Holy Spirit* at work. Expressed initially in weeping, dancing, shaking, tears, and other forms, Pastor John Kilpatrick's exultant words, "Folks, this is it—the Lord is here—get in, get in!" were soon heeded by thousands who, almost nightly in the months to come, would gather to share in the revival. In the years since, an estimated two million guests have been hosted at Brownsville, whether at worship services, conferences, or other events. Kilpatrick's book, *Feast of Fire,* describes the revival's beginnings.

Brubeck, David Warren (1920–) American composer and jazz pianist. His many sacred publications include *Light in the Wilderness* (1968), *Beloved Son* (1978), *Voice of the Holy Spirit, La Fiesta de la Posada,* a Christmas carol pageant, *Pange Lingua*,* and *Mass of Hope.*

Bruce, Alexander Balmain (1831–1899) Scottish theologian. In 1875 he was appointed professor of apologetics and New Testament exegesis at Glasgow College. His reputation as a scholar rests on *Training of the Twelve* (1871), *The Humiliation of Christ* (1876), *The Kingdom of God* (1889), and *St. Paul's Conception of Christianity* (1894). He was also an active hymn writer.

Bruce, Frederick Fyvie (1910–1990) Scottish theologian and writer. A scholar in Greek, Hebrew, and German, he was chair of biblical studies at Sheffield University (1947–1959) and of biblical criticism and exegesis at Manchester (1959–1978). He was president of both the Society for Old Testament Study and for New Testament Study and editor of the *Evangelical Quarterly* and *Palestine Exploration Quarterly.* He was an active member of the Christian Brethren. Apart from numerous commentaries on the New Testament, he wrote *Second Thoughts on Dead Sea Scrolls* (1956), *The Spreading Flame* (1958), *Paul and Jesus* (1974), *The Pauline Circle* (1985), and the autobiographical *In Retrospect* (1980).

Bruckner, Anton (1824–1896) Austrian composer of church music. His masterpieces are *Te Deum* (1884), *Psalm 150* (1892), and three great masses for soloists, chorus, and orchestra: *Mass in D Minor, Mass In E Minor, and Mass in F Minor.* He created symphonic type of church music that advanced the Catholic Cecilian movement*.

Bruderhof Anabaptist* communal group founded by Jacob Hutter in the sixteenth century. They first emerged in Moravia in 1529 and were reorganized by Jacob Hutter in 1533. After the martyrdom of Hutter in 1536, they continued to grow and develop their unique ideas about pacifism and communal living. They expanded into Slovakia, building about 100 bruderhofs or farm colonies. Following the triumph of Catholicism* after the Battle of White Mountain in 1620, they moved into Transylvania, where they produced some of their best devotional literature. When the Hapsburgs persecuted them, they moved in 1770 into Ukraine*, where they flourished for a century. But the introduction of military conscription in Russia forced them to migrate once again, this time to the United States and Canada. Also known as Hutterian Brethren. See also HUTTERITES.

Bruegel, Pieter See BREUGHEL, PETER.

Brugglers Heretical sect led by two imposters, Christian and Hieronymous Kohler, who, along with one of their disciples, Elizabeth Kissling, asserted that they were the three persons of the Trinity* and that the world would end in 1748. Hieronymous Kohler was burned.

Brunelleschi, Filippo (1377–1446) Florentine sculptor and architect. His early works included the two basilicas* of San Lorenzo and Sta Spirito, the Pazzi Chapel in Sta Croce, and the Sta Maria degli Angeli, all noted for his strict adherence to mathematical proportions. He pioneered the concept of the centrally planned chapel. His crowning achievement is the dome of Florence Cathedral*, the duomo*, which took 16 years to build.

Brunner, Heinrich Emil (1889–1966) Swiss theologian. From 1922 to 1953 he taught at Zurich and thereafter until 1956 at the International Christian University at Tokyo. He was a Barthian in his opposition to theological liberalism*, but he parted company with Barth* in his ideas on natural theology*. Among his early books was *Die Mystik und das Wort* (1924), which highlighted the supremacy of divine revelation over human knowledge and reason. He followed it with *The Mediator* (1927), in which the gospel was presented in terms of dialectical theology* and Christ was revealed as the mediator* and the reconciler who fulfills the two great commandments. He made the good a reality rather than a philosophical abstraction. Faith* is essentially obedience to Christ in whom divine will is manifested as love.

Brunner was influenced by both Kierkegaard* and Martin Buber. He interpreted Christian experience as a personal encounter* with God who is himself the message and not merely the messenger. Brunner opposed both the theological liberals and the orthodox Evangelicals. He also departed from conventional orthodoxy* in his belief that hell* has no place in Christian theology and in his opposition to institutional forms. He held that there is a mythical element in the Christian revelation because myth is a necessary language, given the incommensurability between the Creator and the creature. Among his other books were *Divine Imperative* (1932), *Revelation*

and Reason (1942), *Dogmatics* (3 vols., 1946–1960), *The Philosophy of Religion from the Standpoint of Protestant Theology* (1937), *Man in Revolt* (1939), and *Christianity and Civilization* (1947–1948).

Bruno, Giordano (1548–1600) Italian freethinker. A Dominican monk, he turned apostate* and abandoned the order in 1576. He opposed all the core Roman Catholic doctrines, such as immaculate conception*, transubstantiation*, monasticism*, miracles, and Scriptures. Although idealized by later secularists as a freethinker and rationalist, he was a devotee of the ancient Egyptian hermetic tradition which used magic and worshiped the occult. After wandering through Europe from 1576 to 1592, he returned to Rome* and was arrested by the Inquisition*. After eight years of imprisonment, he was sentenced as a heretic and burned.

Bruno, St. (c. 925–965) Archbishop of Cologne*, brother of Otto I. He was a patron of learning with a deep concern for clerical and lay education. He also established three foundations and reformed many of the monasteries. Feast day: October 11.

St. Bruno

Bruno, St. (c. 1030–1101) German monk who founded the Carthusian Order. About 1082 he retired to the Chartreuse* as a solitary hermit. His fame led to the founding of the Carthusian Order in 1084 with the aid of Hugh of Grenoble. The first Carthusians* did not follow a rule but took vows of silence and poverty. In 1090 he founded a second hermitage at Santa Maria of La Torre in southern Italy. His works include commentaries on the Psalms and the epistles of Paul. Feast day: October 6.

Bryan, William Jennings (1860–1925) American political leader and defender of Creationism*. In 1891, the age of 30, he was elected to the U.S. Congress from Lincoln, Nebraska. An orator of rare eloquence, he became the leader of the emerging Populist movement and the spokesman for cheap money policy. He won the Democratic nomination for the presidency three times (1896, 1900, and 1908) but was defeated every time. In 1912 he was appointed secretary of state by Woodrow Wilson, but resigned in 1915 in disagreement over the administration's violation of strict neutrality in World War I. Undeterred, he launched into a new career as a reformer. He gave his powerful support to women's suffrage, prohibition, and graduated income tax. Toward the very end of his life, he engaged in his last battle in defense of the biblical account of creation at the Scopes trial* in Tennessee. He won the day in court, but died five days later.

Bucer/Butzer, Martin (1491–1551) German reformer. He entered the Dominican Order at 14, but was released from it at 30 when he became a Protestant after hearing Luther*. He soon became one of the chief statesmen among the Reformers, combining diplomatic skills of a rare order with theological agility. A prolific compiler of church orders*, he prepared the constitutions of several Reformed* churches. Calvin* was a pupil of his at Strasbourg*.

On the question of the Lord's Supper*, a major dividing line between Luther on the one hand and Zwingli*, Carlstadt*, and Oecolampadius* on the other, Bucer adopted a middle path. He believed in the real presence* of Christ's body representing the sacramental union of earthly and heavenly realities. Alone among the Reformers, Bucer showed an openness on the issue of divorce. After 1530 he was the chief Protestant negotiator with the Roman Catholic Church and participated in the conferences at Leipzig (1539), Hagenau and Worms* (1540), and Regensburg* (1541). Refusing

to accept the Augsburg Interim* compromise, he left for England, where he spent the rest of his life. As regius professor at Cambridge, he participated in the revision of the *Book of Common Prayer** (1549) and the Ordinal (1550) and influenced a generation of Protestant leaders, including John Bradford*, Matthew Parker*, and John Whitgift. His bones were burned by Mary Tudor.

Buchanites Heretical community founded in the eighteenth century in Scotland by Elspeth Buchan. She believed herself to be the woman clothed with the sun of Revelation 12 and her paramour, Hugh White, to be the manchild who ruled with a rod of iron.

Buchman, Frank (Nathan Daniel) (1878–1961) British founder and director of the Oxford Group* and later founder of the Moral Rearmament movement. After a few years in the Lutheran ministry, he was converted in 1908 after attending a Keswick convention*. He took up evangelism, founding the Oxford Group* in 1920. He traveled extensively, promoting the group which later became the Moral Rearmament. The movement declined after his death.

Buck, Dudley (1839–1909) American composer of anthems, hymns, and vocal solos. He is best known for his large-scale cantatas, as *The Forty-Sixth Psalm* (1874) and *The Golden Legend* (1880).

Martin Bucer

Buckfast Abbey Benedictine abbey in Devon, England, founded in 1018 by Earl Aethelweard. It was Cistercian until the dissolution of the monasteries in 1539. It was revived and rebuilt in 1922 and reconsecrated as a Benedictine monastery in 1932.

Bugenhagen, Johann (1485–1558) Also, Pomeranus. German reformer and associate of Martin Luther* who helped to spread the Reformation* to Denmark at the invitation of Christian III. He assisted Luther in translating the Bible, and is well-known for a commentary on the Psalms and a history of Pomerania. He delivered the eulogy at Luther's funeral.

bugia Also, palmatorium*; scotula*. Portable candlestick containing a lighted candle, used in Roman Catholic liturgy.

Bulgakov, Makarii (1816–1882) Metropolitan* of Moscow* (1879–1882). Historian. He was professor at the Petersburg Theological Seminary and later a member of the Academy of Sciences. He is best-known for his 13-volume *History of the Russian Church* (1857–1882) and for the five-volume *Dogmatic Theology* (1851–1853).

Bulgakov, Sergei Nikolaevich (1871–1944) Russian theologian. He became a priest shortly after the Russian Revolution. Expelled from Russia by the

Makarii Bulgakov

Communists, he was dean of the Orthodox Theological Academy at Paris (which he helped found) from 1925 till his death. Theologically, he helped to develop a body of doctrines called Sophiology, or the study of divine wisdom. His work was condemned by the Communist-influenced Moscow Patriarchate. He was also a strong but critical supporter of ecumenism*. His principal works are: *The Unfading Light* (1917), *Jacob's Ladder* (1929), *Agnus Dei, The God-Manhood* (1933), *The Orthodox Church* (1935), *The Comforter* (1936), and *The Wisdom of God* (1937).

Bulgarian Orthodox Church The Bulgarian national church, founded 864–865 with the baptism* of Prince Boris*. Clement of Ochrid (d. 916), one of the disciples of Sts. Cyril and Methodius*, helped to establish a Slavonic church under Byzantine auspices. The reign of Tsar Simeon (893–927) was the golden age of the church when its Slavonic literature reached full flowering. After the defeat of Bulgaria by the Byzantines in 1018, the church lost its autonomy and did not fully regain it until 1953, when it became an autocephalous* church under a patriarch*.

bull (From Latin, seal) Apostolic letter* of the pope bearing the papal seal. Only the most important papal pronouncements are treated as bulls*. Consistorial bulls, signed by the pope and the cardinals, are sealed; others are merely stamped in red.

bullarium (pl., bullaria) Collection of papal bulls* and other documents.

bulletin Printed order of church service, often displayed on the bulletin board or distributed to the congregation.

Bullinger, Johann Heinrich (1504–1575) Swiss Protestant churchman and reformer who led Swiss Protestantism* after Zwingli* died. He was one of the most influential of the second-generation Reformers. His literary output was impressive. It included *The Decades* (50 sermons on Christian doctrine), *The Diary,* and *A History of the Reformation.* He helped to draft the Consensus Tigurinus* (1549) and the Helvetic Confessions* (1536 and 1566). Although he accepted the doctrine of predestination*, he opposed Calvin's* theory of two polities and his ecclesiastical discipline. He took a deep interest in the Church of England* and corresponded with Henry VIII, Edward VI, and Elizabeth I. He opposed the Lutheran doc-

Johann Heinrich Bullinger

trine of the Eucharist* and engaged Johann Brenz* in controversies on this subject. His main contribution to theology was his doctrine of the covenant that he developed in his book, *De Testamento* (1534).

Bultmann, Rudolf (1884–1976) German theologian. From 1921 until his retirement he was professor of New Testament studies at Marburg. A follower of the history-of-traditions method, he challenged the authenticity of the Gospels in his *History of the Synoptic Tradition* (1963). In *Jesus and the Word* (1934), he presented his Christology* in which Jesus' mission was interpreted as calling his hearers to a decision (*Entscheidung*), accepting his proclamation, and obeying his commands. Developing independently the dialectical theology* of Karl Barth* in the Lutheran context of saving faith, Bultman reduced Christianity to the bare fact of the Crucifixion, stripping the religious mythology as totally irrelevant to the believer. In *Theology of the New Testament* (1952–1955), he accepted St. Paul* and St. John's* Gospel as the only genuine elements in the gospel necessary for personal salvation. It was this effort to demythologize Christianity that earned Bultmann his undeserved notoriety in the 1950s and 1960s. Bultmann's existential theology was essentially

kerygmatic, presenting individual salvation in terms of life changes produced by the kerygma* or proclaimed Word.

Buntain, Daniel Mark (1923–1989) Canadian Pentecostal missionary to India. He went to India in 1953 and started the Calcutta Mission of Mercy and also pastored the Assembly of God church in Calcutta. His mission feeds over 22,000 people a day. These projects are highlighted in the publication *The Cry of Calcutta*.

Bunting, Jabez (1779–1858) Wesleyan Methodist minister, called the "second founder of Methodism*." He completed its detachment from the Church of England* and was elected president of the conference four times.

Bunyan, John (1628–1688) English author of *Pilgrim's Progress**. Few details are known about him, except that he was a tinker who became a Baptist and was imprisoned for 12 years for preaching without a license. In jail he turned to writing both poetry and prose. Of his prose works, the most famous is *Pilgrim's Progress** (1678 and 1684), one of the classics of devotional literature. He also wrote *The Holy War* (1682) and his autobiography, *Grace Abounding to the Chief of Sinners* (1666). As a master of allegory*, he is unsurpassed in Christian literature.

John Bunyan

Burckard/Burchard, John (d. 1506) Papal master of ceremonies. He was made a cardinal in 1504. He assisted in the revision of *Pontificale Romanum* (1485) and the creation of the new *Caeremoniale Romanum** (1488). He prepared a detailed set of rubrics for the Low Mass*, the *Ordo Servandus* per *Sacerdotem in Celebratione Missae* (1502), which was the basis of the *Ritus Celebrandi* of 1570.

burctho In the Jacobite Liturgy, blessed bread distributed by the deacon during Lent*.

Burghers Also, Associate Synod. Members of the Secession Church of Scotland who interpreted the Burgess Oath upholding "the true religion presently professed within this realm" to be the Protestant faith, and were prepared to take the oath*. In 1799 the Burghers split into Auld Lichts* and New Lichts. The latter joined the United Secession Church in 1820. The Auld Lichts rejoined the Church of Scotland* in 1839. See also AN-TIBURGHERS.

Burgos Cathedral in Burgos, Spain, built in the thirteenth century. It is a three-aisled basilica* boxed in by chapels and other later additions. The walls of the nave* comprise three stories, with arcades, triforium*, and clerestory*. The central tower was added in the sixteenth century.

Burnand, Eugene (1850–1921) Swiss artist, noted for his biblical scenes, such as *Peter and John*

Burgos Cathedral

Running to the Tomb, Come Unto Me, and *The Talents.*

Burned-Over District Area in New York State, bounded by the Catskills in the East and the Adirondack Mountains to the north, known for its concentration of eclectic religious enthusiasts. It was the scene of frequent revivals of religion, including that of Charles G. Finney*.

Burne-Jones, Edward (1833–1898) English painter who designed stained glass for many churches. Among these works are "The Star of Bethlehem" and "The Morning of the Resurrection."

Burns, William Chalmers (1815–1868) Scottish missionary to China. In 1846 he went to China as the agent of the Presbyterian Church of England, studied Chinese, adopted Chinese dress, and labored in the region around Amoy and in Manchuria. He helped Hudson Taylor* in his early years and translated *Pilgrim's Progress** into Chinese.

Burroughs, Bob Lloyd (1937–) American composer of over 1,000 compositions and arrangements. His hymns include "He is Risen." With his lyricist wife Esther Milligan Burroughs, he has written eight musicals, including *A Celebration of Gifts, Daybreak in the Kingdom, Resurrection Celebration,* and *The Word Became Flesh.*

bursar Treasurer of a cathedral or a monastic community.

bursary Funds of a cathedral or religious order.

burse Stiff square box in which the corporal* for the Eucharist* was kept. Its color changed with the liturgical season.

Bursfield Union German order of Benedictine monasteries that existed from the fifteenth to the eighteenth centuries.

burshanah (lit., firstfruits) In the Maronite* and Jacobite* tradition, leavened bread.

Bushnell, Horace (1802–1876) American liberal Calvinist leader. He was a pioneer in liberal theology. He interpreted the doctrine of the Trinity* that while human beings perceived God in three aspects, there was no such distinction in the inner nature of the Godhead. He further explained miracles and atonement* in terms of their moral influence. His principal works included *Christian Nurture* (1847), *God in Christ* (1849), *Christ in Theology* (1851), *Nature and Supernatural* (1858), and *Vicarious Sacrifice* (1866).

buskins Stockings worn by a bishop or a mitred abbot during pontifical Mass*.

Buswell, James Oliver, Jr. (1895–1977) Presbyterian educator. Ordained in 1918, he pastored several Presbyterian churches until 1926. He was dismissed from the Presbyterian Church in 1936 for his Fundamentalist sympathies. He was president of Wheaton College* from 1926 to 1940 and helped to build its reputation as a conservative bastion. His most significant contribution to theology was *A Systematic Theology of the Christian Religion* (2 vols., 1962–1963).

Butler, Alban (1710–1773) Hagiographer. Ordained priest in 1735, he served as a chaplain* in Paris. He completed his monumental four-volume *Lives of the Fathers, Martyrs, and Other Principal Saints* (1756–1759), covering 6,000 lives arranged according to the church calendar.

Butler, Eugene Sanders (1935–) American composer. His works include two music dramas, *Samuel, the Promise* (1970) and *God's Word in Their Hearts* (1973), and a number of anthems,* including *How Excellent Is Thy Name* (1967) and *Go Ye into all the World*.

Butler, Joseph (1692–1752) Theologian and apologist of the Church of England* whose *Analogy of Religion** attacked the Deists and explained the rational foundations of Christianity.

Butler, William and Clementina (1818–1899 and 1820–1913, respectively) Founders of American Methodist missions in India and Mexico. They described their experiences in *The Land of the Veda* (1871) and *Mexico in Transition* (1892). Clementina was a founder of the Women's For-

eign Missionary Society of the Methodist Episcopal Church.

butterfly Ancient symbol of the soul. In Christian art, a symbol of the Resurrection.

Buxheim Carthusian foundation of Mariae Saal, Cella Beatae Virginis, in Buxheim in southwest Germany, founded in 1402. It was especially noted for the rich treasures of its library. The monastery was wrecked and desecrated during the Peasants' War of 1525 and the Reformation* that followed, but by 1548, it came under imperial protection and was restored. In 1631 Sigmund Schalk created the high altar, and between 1684 and 1700 Ignaz Waibel created the choir stalls*.

Buxtehude, Dieterich (1637–1707) Most influential composer of organ music in the seventeenth century. For 40 years he was organist at the Marienkirche in Luebeck. Nearly all of his nearly 125 extant vocal works were composed on sacred texts. They are generally referred to as church cantatas, although they were composed for one solo voice. In his 40 free organ works, toccato-like passages alternate with structured fugal sections. His 50 settings of chorale melodies constitute his most clearly functional organ compositions.

B.V.M. Blessed Virgin Mary*.

Byrd, William (1543–1623) English composer, considered the finest in Tudor England. Although a Roman Catholic, he served as organist and choir master in the Lincoln* Cathedral and the Chapel Royal. For the Anglican rite Byrd composed two services, two settings of the Magnificat* and Nunc Dimittis*, various litanies, preces*, responses, and nearly 60 anthems. His Latin church music consisted of three masses and two books of motets*, among which are some of his masterpieces.

Byzantine Style of architecture developed in the Eastern Roman Empire characterized by low cruciform* churches with a central dome.

Byzantine Chant See BYZANTINE MUSIC.

Byzantine Church The Eastern Orthodox Church*, so called because the ecumenical patriarch* lives in Byzantium* or Constantinople*. Used chiefly of the period between the founding of Constantinople in 330 to its fall to the Turks in 1453.

Byzantine music Liturgical music of the Greek Orthodox Church. It has no fixed rhythm but fuses song and accompaniment, threading hymns among the verses of a Psalm.

Byzantine Rite Greek Liturgy of the Eastern Orthodox Church*.

Byzantine Text Form of text of the Greek New Testament from which the early English versions are drawn. The standard text is related to the Syriac* manuscripts, and is distinguished by a smooth literary style. See also LUCIANIC TEXT.

Byzantium See CONSTANTINOPLE.

Cc

Cabanilles, Juan Bautista Jose (1644–1712) Organist, composer, and priest, acknowledged as the greatest of the seventeenth-century Spanish organ masters.

Cabasilas/Cavasilas, Nicolaus (1320–1390) Byzantine churchman and mystic. His best known works are *Life in Christ,* a set of seven discourses, and *Interpretation of the Divine Liturgy,* a text on sacramental worship. He defended Gregory Palamas*, author of a classic work on the Hesychast. Feast day: June 20.

Cabrera, Don Miguel (1695–1768) Mexican Baroque painter. His pictures decorate many churches and convents, especially the Church of Santa Prisca, Taxco, Mexico.

Cabrini, St. Frances Xavier (1850–1917) Italian-born nun who founded the Missionary Sisters of the Sacred Heart of Jesus*. Although physically frail, she had indomitable will and energy and established a number of schools, hospitals, and charitable organizations. She was the first American to be canonized as a Catholic saint. She is the patron saint* of emigrants and displaced persons. Feast day: December 22.

Cabrol, Fernand (1855–1937) French liturgical scholar and Benedictine monk. Together with M. Ferotin and H. Leclercq* he launched the *Monumenta Ecclesiae Liturgica* and *Dictionnaire d'Arch-* *eologie et de Liturgie,* begun in 1903 and completed in 1953.

cachel In the Ethiopian Church*, the paten*.

Cadbury, Henry Joel (1883–1974) American New Testament scholar of Quaker* descent. He was one of the founders of modern Lucan scholarship and a pioneer of redaction criticism* with an encyclopedic knowledge of the Greek and Graeco-Roman world. His principal works include *The Making of Luke-Acts* (1927), *The Style and Literary Method of Luke* (1929), *The Peril of Modernizing Jesus* (1937), and *Jesus, What Manner of Man* (1947).

Caedmon, St. (seventh century) The first known English Christian poet. He was a laborer at the monastery at Whitby who received in a vision the gift of composing verses of praise to God, and thereafter became a monk. He is believed to have turned the Bible into verse, but only one hymn on Genesis survives.

Caeremoniale Episcoparum In the Roman Catholic Church, the book governing the liturgical celebrations of a bishop. The first version was promulgated by Clement VIII* in 1600, and it remained in force until the Second Vatican Council*. A new *Caeremoniale Episcorum* was issued in 1984. Divided into three parts, of which part one provides general rules, part two is devoted to the stational Mass* (formerly the pontifical Mass*) and part three covers ordinations, confirmations, the blessing of abbots and abbesses*, the dedication or blessing of churches, and the general councils and local synods*.

Caeremoniale Romanum Latin service book dealing with the ceremonies of the papal court originally compiled about 1273 at the command of Gregory X*. It contained the ceremonial for the election, ordination, and enthronement of the pope. In 1341 it was expanded to cover canonizations* and general councils. A revised edition was published at Venice* in 1516.

caeremoniarius Master of ceremonies of a religious service.

Caesarea 1. Properly, Caesarea Maritima to distinguish it from Caesarea Philippi*. Important port and city in Palestine built by Herod the Great between 22 and 10 B.C. halfway between Joppa and Dor on the Mediterranean coast and named after the Roman emperor Caesar Augustus. It had a large circular artificial harbor, a magnificent forum, theater, and amphitheater. It was particularly famous for its aqueduct that brought water from springs in the hills several miles away. It was here that Pontius Pilate lived, Peter* preached, Cornelius was converted, and Paul* was imprisoned. It was the home of the Church Father, Eusebius*. 2. Capital of Roman province of Cappacodia* and an important early Christian bishopric, especially under Basil*.

Caesarea

Caesarea Philippi City near Mount Hermon, north of the Sea of Galilee*, now Banias, at the foot of Mount Hebron. Here Peter* confessed that Jesus was the Christ or Messiah (Matt. 16:13–16), and the woman with the issue of blood approached Jesus.

Caesarean Text Family of manuscripts of the Greek New Testament related to the text used by Origen at Caesarea*. Its leading representative is the Koridethi Codex* and two families of minuscules, family 1 and family 13, which contain characteristics similar to the Western Text* in some instances and to the Alexandrian Text* in others.

Caesarius of Arles (c. 470–542) French monk and bishop of Arles*, France. Educated in the monastery of Lerins*, he founded a monastery for women and wrote rules for men and women. He encouraged daily attendance at worship, congregational singing, memorization of Scriptures, and the involvement of laymen in church affairs.

Caesarius of Heisterbach (c. 1180–c. 1240) German Cistercian monk and prior* of the House of Heisterbach, near Cologne*. He employed his considerable literary talent in writing lives of St. Elizabeth and St. Englebert. His *Dialogue on Visions and Miracles* (c. 1223) is a delightful anthology of religious anecdotes illustrating medieval religious events and beliefs.

Caesaropapism The control of the church by a secular ruler, such as existed in Byzantium and medieval England after the Reformation*.

Cajetan, St. (1480–1547) Birth name: Gaetano de Thiene. Founder of a congregation of priests called Theatines* for priests bound by vows and living in common, but engaged in pastoral work. Feast day: August 8.

Cajetan, Tommaso de Vio (1469–1534) Dominican cardinal and philosopher who presided over the Diet of Augsburg and drew up the bull* that excommunicated Luther*. A wide-ranging writer, he is credited with 115 books, including commentaries on most of the Bible, of which the best known is *De Ente et Essentia* directed against Averroism. His *Commentary on St. Thomas*

Aquinas led to the revival of Thomism* in the sixteenth century and is one of the great classics of Scholasticism*. As general* of the Dominican Order, he was responsible for sending the first Dominican missionary for the conversion of American Indians.

Luther Standing Before Cardinal Cajetan

Calasanz, St. Joseph (1556–1648) Spanish founder of the Clerks Regular of Religious Schools in 1621. Later its name was changed to Order of the Pious Schools. Feast day: August 15.

Calced (Lat., shod) Descriptive of members of certain religious orders who wear shoes, as distinguished from the Discalced*, or those who walk barefoot.

Calderon de la Barca, Pedro (1600–1681) Spanish writer and playwright of religious themes. Among his best-known plays are *Life Is a Dream* and *To God for Reasons of State*.

calefactory (lit., warming place) Room in a medieval monastery heated by a fireplace.

calendar See GREGORIAN CALENDAR.

calendar, ecclesiastical Listing of the events of a church year* consisting of two cycles. Christmas* cycle has five events: Advent*, Christmas Eve*, Christmas*, Circumcision, and Epiphany*. The Easter* cycle has 16 events: Septuagesima*, Sexagesima*, Quinquagesima*, Ash Wednesday*, Quadragesima*, Passion Sunday*, Palm Sunday*, Maundy Thursday*, Good Friday*, Holy Saturday*, Easter*, Low Sunday*, Ascension*, Pentecost* (Whitsunday*), Trinity Sunday* and Corpus Christi*.

calf, winged In Christian art, symbol of St. Luke*.

Calixtines Moderate Hussites* or Utraquists of Moravia and Bohemia who held that communicants should receive both the wine and the bread during Mass*.

Calixtus, Georg (1586–1656) German Lutheran theologian who sought to unite Lutherans, Calvinists, and Roman Catholics on the basis of the Apostles' Creed* and other documents of the early church. He had little success in these efforts. In 1614 he was appointed professor of theology at Helmstedt, where he served as the most influential representative of Melanchthon*. He took part in the Colloquy of Thom in 1645. Among his books were *Epitome Theologiae, Theologia Moralis,* and *De Arte Nova Nihusii.*

call 1. Divine summons to salvation. Sometimes it is used in the sense of conversion. Calvinists hold that call is irresistible, but other Protestants hold that it requires a voluntary response. 2. A congregation's formal invitation to a person to become its minister. In this sense it has been important since the Reformation* in Reformed* churches, especially in relation to a congregation's right to elect a minister.

call and response Responsorial and antiphonal songs of African origin. They have an echo-like effect between solo passages and choral refrains or repetitions.

calling 1. Vocation*, especially to a sacred ministry, expressing consecration of one's talents and gifts to service of the Lord in a specified area. 2. Invitation to salvation*. In the Reformed* tradition, there is a distinction between general calling* applied to the universal offer of the gospel made without distinction and effectual calling* or the event or process by which this calling is made available to individuals.

Callistus II (d. 1124) Pope from 1119. Birth name: Guido. He was elected pope at Cluny*. His papacy was marked by a long struggle with Emperor Henry V, whom he excommunicated at the Council of Reims in 1119. The struggle was ended with the Concordat of Worms* in 1123.

Callistus III (1378–1458) Pope from 1455. Birth name: Alfonso de Borgia. The main effort of his papacy was directed to the organization of a crusade against the Turks who had conquered Constantinople* in 1453, but his plans met with little success. He annulled the sentence against Joan of Arc*, declared her innocence, and rehabilitated her.

Callistus/Calixtus I, St. (d. c. 222) Bishop of Rome* from 217. Originally a slave, he became chief secretary to Pope Zephrynus, whom he succeeded. His pontificate* was marked by conflicts over doctrine and discipline with the first antipope, Hippolytus, who thought Callistus too lax.

calogers (Gk., good old men) Monks who follow the Rule of St. Basil*. There are three orders of calogers: archari or novices*, microschemoi or ordinary monks, and megaloschemoi or monks of the highest order.

Calovius, Abraham (1612–1686) German Lutheran churchman and theologian. He was a vigorous defender of Lutheran orthodoxy and an opponent of Georg Calixtus's* plan to reunite the denominations. He also opposed Socinianism* and liberalism*. His principal dogmatic work, *Systema Locorum Theologicorum* (12 vols., 1655–1677), is a monument of Protestant Scholasticism*.

caloyer (lit., venerable*) Term of address for a Greek monk.

calpas Armenian ecclesiastic headwear lined with fur.

Calvary Chapel Fellowship of Congregations growing out of an original church in Costa Mesa, California, founded in the 1960s by Chuck Smith*. Through its inclusion of societal dropouts, hippies, and drug addicts, the congregation soon became a vibrant center for worship, including Christian rock* concerts, such as the Maranatha Singers. By the 1970s the church registered 900 conversions a month and 8,000 baptisms over a two-year period. As it grew, it spawned 300 other Calvary chapels throughout the United States. In 1983 a small group of Calvary chapels under John Wimber* broke away to form the Vineyard Ministries.

Calvary Cross Ecclesiastical cross with a three-step base symbolizing faith, hope, and charity. Also known as the graded cross, it has the general form of a Latin cross.

Calvary, Gordon's See GORDON'S CALVARY.

Calvert, George (c. 1580–1632) Lord Baltimore. English politician and secretary of state under James I who converted to Roman Catholicism* and was granted the American territory that became Maryland.

Calvin, John (1509–1564) French reformer and founder of Calvinism*. Educated at the College de Montague, Calvin became a Protestant while still a student. By the 1530s he was caught up in the Reformation* movement. He was forced to leave Paris along with his friend, Nicholas Cop, rector* of the University of Paris, because of their attack on the church and a call for Lutheran reform. For the next three years he was on the run, but he used his literary talents during this time on behalf of the Protestant cause. In 1534 Olivetan's* French translation of the Bible appeared with a preface by Calvin. In 1535 he fled to Basel, where

John Calvin

he published one of his most important works, *Christianae Religionis Institututio* (1536), a short summary of the Christian faith and an able exposition of Reformers' doctrines.

On passing through Geneva*, Calvin was persuaded by Guillaume Farel* to assist in organizing the Reformation in that city. The articles they drew up organizing worship met with considerable opposition because they imposed ecclesiastical discipline and used excommunication* as an instrument of social policy. Forced to leave the city, Calvin spent the next three years at the invitation of Martin Bucer* as pastor to the French congregation at Strasbourg*. Here he expanded the *Institutes**, wrote a *Commentary on Romans* (1539), and took part in the colloquies with Lutherans and Roman Catholics at Worms* and Regensburg*. In 1541 he returned to Geneva at the invitation of the city council. His ecclesiastical ordinances for establishing a Christian social and political order were approved by the city council. They established four ministries within the church—pastors, doctors, elders, and deacons—introduced vernacular catechisms and liturgy, and set up a consistory* of 12 elders to enforce morality. His goal was to make Geneva a "holy city," a Christian commonwealth in practice as well as doctrine.

In 1559 Calvin established the Genevan Academy* for the training of his followers. Although there was constant opposition from the pleasure-loving Genevans against Calvin's measures, he was not deterred from his mission. At the same time, Calvin helped to make the civil laws more humane, established a universal system of education for the young, and promoted the public care of the old, the poor, and the infirm. Geneva gained a reputation as a haven for all persecuted Protestants who flocked in from many countries. From Geneva they returned home as missionaries for the propagation of Calvinist ideas and reforms. Thus the name of Calvin was scattered all over Europe, and he became one of the dominant figures of the Reformation in the mid 1600s. Meanwhile, Calvin was busy producing commentaries on 23 books of the Old Testament and on all books of the New Testament except the Revelation in addition to pamphlets and collections of sermons. By 1559 the *Institutes* had been revised five times and expanded from a book of six chapters into four books with a total of 79 chapters. It was also translated from Latin into French, and its French edition became a literary classic.

Calvin left a legacy that transcended theology. Calvinism* was a complex set of ideas whose ramifications extended into society, politics, and economics as well as theology. He was a warm and humane person fully committed to the Word of God* in everything he did. As a religious statesman, a logical and seminal thinker, a formidable controversialist, and a biblical exegete, he had few peers in his generation or in the centuries since.

Calvinism System of Protestant Christian doctrine expounded by Calvin* in his commentaries on the Bible and in his *Institutes*. Calvin himself held that the term *Calvinism* was a misnomer because what he taught was entirely biblical and not his creation. The bedrock of Calvinism is the Bible which, he averred, along with all other Protestant Reformers*, was the inspired Word of God*. It was also an infallible rule of faith and practice, the standard by which everything is judged and measured. The authority of the Scripture is based objectively in its divine inspiration* and subjectively in the "internal testimony" of the Holy Spirit*. The Bible is the only source of human knowledge of God, which comes through the direct revelation* in Jesus Christ.

Calvinism rejects natural theology* because creation is corrupt and conceals rather than reveals God's redeeming love. Because of the discontinuity between the Creator and the creature, man's knowledge of God is partial and clouded in mystery. Faith* is the only bridge across this chasm. Implicit in this belief is the material principle* of Calvinism, the sovereignty of God. Everything in the universe exists only through his providence and according to his purpose. His purpose is manifested in his sovereign will according to which he allowed sin to enter into the world and permitted Adam to fall while, at the same time, he planned the redemption* and reconciliation of the elect* through Jesus Christ, the incarnate Son of God.

Calvin initially treated predestination* as a mystery, but later theologians, such as Theodore Beza*, made it a central aspect of the doctrine of salvation*. As the struggle between the Son of perdition and the Son of God intensifies, God calls his people, the elect* of God, out of the kingdom of this world into his kingdom. God bestows upon his elect the gift of the Holy Spirit*, who brings them to a saving faith in Christ as Savior and Lord. After conversion*, the elect grow in grace* and in the likeness of Jesus Christ to be more and more conformed to his image in this life. This work is all of God and not of human beings. Thus the elect can never be lost, but shall persevere till the end.

As regards the Lord's Supper*, Calvin took a middle position between Luther's concept of real presence* and Zwingli's* characterization of it as mere symbolism. Whereas Luther made a sharp distinction between the law and the gospel, Calvin emphasized the continuity of the Old Testament and the New Testament, retaining the law as a moral guide for believers. From this position of God's sovereignty, Calvinist ethics emphasizes human responsibility as a corollary. Human beings are the stewards of creation, and they also have the responsibility to serve and worship God. In a state of alienation from God, this responsibility becomes perverted and corrupted into a search for self-gratification, riches, and power.

After Calvin's death, Calvinism was developed and more elaborately defined by a number of Calvinist theologians and councils. Perhaps the most authoritative document on Calvinist doc-

trines is the Second Helvetic Confession* of 1566. It was summarized at the Synod of Dort* (1618) in what are known as the five points or TULIP*: 1. Total depravity* of human nature, 2. unconditional election, 3. limited atonement*, 4. irresistible grace*, and 5. perseverance* of the saints. Calvinism spread in the seventeenth and eighteenth centuries throughout the Protestant world. In England and Scotland it formed the core of Puritan thought and the basis of the Westminster Confession* (1648), and it was the basic doctrine of the Reformed* churches in other parts of western Europe. It became the state religion of the Netherlands. Controversy over predestination led to the emergence of factions, such as sublapsarians and supralapsarians and antagonistic theological schools, such as the Arminians.

Among the great Calvinistic theologians have been Theodore Beza*, John Owen*, Thomas Boston*, Jonathan Edwards*, Abraham Kuyper*, Charles Hodge*, B. B. Warfield*, and J. Gresham Machen*. Extending beyond theology, Calvinism has exercised a formative, if often unacknowledged, influence on science, politics, poetry, visual arts, and capitalism.

Camaldolese Strict religious order founded by Romuald* in 1012 near Florence*. They observed two Lents in a year, abstained from meat, and lived on bread and water for three days in the week.

Camara, Helder Pessoa (1909–1999) Brazilian theologian and former archbishop of Olinda and Recife. He founded the National Conference of Brazilian Bishops in 1952 and served as its secretary for 12 years and also served as vice president of the Council of Latin American Bishops from 1959 to 1965. In 1961 he initiated the Movement for Basic Education. His nonviolent resistance to the military rulers brought him worldwide renown. He was awarded the Martin Luther King* Memorial Award in 1970.

camarin (Span., small room) Small chapel above and behind the high altar of a Spanish church, normally visible from the nave*.

Cambridge City and municipal borough in east central England on the River Cam. It is the site of

Theodore Beza

one of Britain's two leading universities. It was a center of the English Reformation*. The round church of the Holy Sepulchre dates from the Norman period.

Cambridge Platform A statement of Congregational polity* for the New England Puritans* formulated by a synod* authorized by the general court of the Massachusetts Bay Colony in 1646.

Cambridge Platonists Group of theologians, philosophers, and mystics in Cambridge University in the seventeenth century. Among them were Benjamin Whichcote, Ralph Cudworth, Henry More, John Smith, and Nathanael Culverwel. They sought to combine the idealism of Plato with Christian mysticism. Reacting against the Rationalism of Hobbes and the dogmatic Calvinism* of the Puritans*, they sought to promote humanistic ethics, tolerance in religion, and reason in philosophy.

Cambridge Seven Seven Cambridge students who gave up everything to go to China to join J. Hudson Taylor* and the China Inland Mission* in 1885. They were: Montagu Beauchamp, W. W. Cassels, D. E. Hoste, A. T. Polhill-Turner, C. H. Polhill-Turner, S. P. Smith, and C. T. Studd*.

camelaucum Original name of the papal tiara*.

camera Ecclesiastical treasury department at the Vatican*, as in Camera Apostolica.

Camerarius, Joachim (1500–1574) German scholar who assisted Melanchthon* in preparing the Augsburg Confession*. An outstanding Greek scholar and humanist, he translated the Augsburg Confession into Greek, and wrote a biography of Melanchthon. He participated in the religious colloquies and imperial diets at Speier (1526 and 1529) and Augsburg (1530).

camerlengo Chamberlain* of the papal court. His duties include presiding over the apostolic camera, oversight of the Vatican* during a papal vacancy, and assembling and directing the conclave*.

Cameron, John (1579–1625) Scottish theologian who spent much of his life in the Reformed*

church in France, and as a professor at the universities of Sedan, Saumur, and Montauban. He originated the semi-Arminian variety of French Calvinism* known as Amyraldianism.

Cameron, Richard (1648–1680) "The Lion of the Covenant." Scottish Covenanter* from whom the Cameronians* took their name. He was one of the chief authors of the Sanquhar Declaration which tried to depose Charles II. The royal dragoons killed him in an ambush.

Cameronians Followers of Richard Cameron* who fought for religious liberty against the Stuart dynasty. Since 1743 they are known as the Reformed Presbyterian Church.

Cameronites Followers of John Cameron* who maintained his Amyraldian theology.

Cambridge Seven

Camillus of Lellis (1550–1614) Founder of the Ministers of the Sick and patron saint* of the sick and of nurses. He worked with the Capuchins* and the Franciscan Recollects, but was forced to leave because of an incurable disease in his legs. Later he became a nurse and about the same time established an order called the Camillians, who took a fourth vow to serve the sick. The congregation was approved by the pope in 1586 and made an order by Pope Gregory XIV* in 1591. The order is also called Fathers of a Good Death or Agonizantes. He was canonized in 1886, and named patron saint* of the sick in 1746 and patron saint of nurses (1930). Feast day: July 14.

Camisards French Huguenot resistance fighters who fought the attempt to make them Catholics after the revocation of the Edict of Nantes* in

1685. So called from the camise or white shirt worn by them. Led by Roland LaPorte and Jean Cavalier and inspired by Pierre Jureau, they numbered over 3,000, and their guerrilla warfare lasted until 1709. Many were tortured, and many who surrendered were exiled.

camp meeting Nineteenth century religious institution associated with revivals* and crusades*. It was a fervent religious revivalist meeting held outdoors, lasting several days, and marked by considerable emotional display. James McGready* held the first camp meeting at Gasper River in Logan County, Kentucky, about 1800. The most famous camp meeting was in 1801 at Cane Ridge* in Bourbon County, Kentucky, directed by Barton W. Stone*, attended by 25,000 people.

Camp Meeting

campagus Ancient type of boot worn by the popes and others.

campanarion In the Byzantine Church*, a building for housing the bells, similar to the campanile*.

campanile Italian belfry and watchtower connected with the main building, but sometimes detached. The most famous campaniles are those at San Francesco in Assisi*, St-Front in Perigueux, San Marco* in Venice*, San Zeno Maggiore in Verona*, Siena Cathedral*, and the Leaning Tower of Pisa*.

Campanius, John (1601–1683) Swedish Lutheran missionary to the Indians on the Delaware.

campanology 1. Art of bell ringing. 2. Science of making bells.

Campbell, Alexander (1788–1866) Scots-Irish Presbyterian minister who cofounded the Disciples of Christ* and the Churches of Christ* with Barton W. Stone*. After emigrating from Scotland to the United States, he and his father, **Thomas Campbell**, settled at Bethany, West Virginia. He left the Presbyterian Church and joined the Baptist church in 1812. He led a revival on the Western Reserve and in 1832 joined with Stone's Christian Connection in Kentucky to form the Disciples of Christ or Campbellites. By the mid-nineteenth century it was one of the largest denominations in the United States. In 1840 he founded Bethany College. He preached a simple form of Christianity in which baptism* and confession of Jesus Christ as Savior were the only requirements.

Campbell, Isabella and Mary (1807–1827 and 1806–1839, respectively) Scottish intercessors and visionaries who were instrumental in the spiritual revival known as the West of Scotland Manifestations*. Although Isabella died at 20 as a result of pulmonary illness, the publication of her biography, *Peace in Believing*, memorialized her life. Mary claimed miraculous healing of her pulmonary illness and thereafter embarked on a ministry of healing accompanied by speaking in tongues* and prophecy. The movement spread to London where, under the leadership of Edward Irving*, an international restorationist movement was founded as the Catholic Apostolic Church*.

Campbell, John McLeod (1800–1872) Scottish theologian noted for his *The Nature of the Atonement and Its Relation to the Remission of Sins and Eternal Life* (1856) which had considerable influence on Barth*. Campbell's thesis was that the Incarnation* was "the primary and highest fact in the history of God's relation to man." Campbell was deposed by the Church of Scotland* in 1831 for heresy.

Campion, St. Edmund (c. 1540–1581) Anglican divine who was converted to Catholicism* in 1571 and admitted to the Jesuit Order. He was selected by the Jesuits* to go to England on a mission in 1580. In

Alexander Campbell

Cana conferences Spiritual and educational program for Roman Catholic married couples. The movement traces its origin to family renewal days conducted by John Delaney, S.J., in New York City in 1943 and a retreat* held in St. Louis during October 1944 by Edward Dowling, S.J., in honor of Our Lady of Cana. Out of Cana conferences emerged a premarital course of instruction known as pre-Cana.

Canadian Baptist Federation Loose confederation of four autonomous Baptist conventions or unions: The United Baptist Convention of the Maritime Provinces, the Baptist Convention of Ontario and Quebec, the Baptist Union of Western Canada, and the Union d'Eglises Baptistes Francaises au Canada.

cancelli Latticed screen* before the chancel* of a church, marking the space reserved for the clergy.

candidate Person who is eligible and considered for priesthood or pastorate*.

candle Symbol associated in Christian liturgy with light, truth, prayer, and sacrifice. It is generally placed on the altar or table and lit during service. Votive candles are lit before statues in churches or shrines as personal offerings.

England he secretly published a pamphlet called *Ten Reasons* against Protestantism*. Over a year later he was arrested and racked, hanged, drawn, and quartered. He was beatified in 1886 and canonized in 1970 as one of the forty martyrs.*

Campus Crusade for Christ Interdenominational Christian organization for the evangelization of college-age youth, founded by Bill Bright* at the University of California, Los Angeles, in 1951. It developed the Four Spiritual Laws* as an evangelistic tool.

Candle

St. Edmund Campion

Portable candles are permitted in Eastern and Roman Catholic churches. In the Western Church*, two candles are lit for all services. Two floor candles, one on either side of the altar, are also customary. Two altar candles are used for the Low Mass* and six for the High Mass*. At Holy

Communion* four candles may be lighted at a low celebration by a bishop, seven at a high celebration. Two altar lights symbolize the two natures of Christ and six the day and the hour of the Crucifixion.* Multibranched candlesticks, or candelabra, with three, five, or seven branches or more may be used for special services.

candlelight service Christian service at Advent* and Epiphany* symbolizing the coming of Christ as the Light of the World*.

Candlemas Christian festival held February 2 commemorating the purification of the Virgin and presentation of the infant Jesus in the temple (Luke 2:22–38). Eastern churches* call it the meeting (of Jesus and Simeon) and honor the Virgin Mother. In the West the infant Jesus is honored, and candles of beeswax are blessed and distributed to the singing of Nunc Dimittis*.

Candlish, Robert Smith (1806–1873) Scottish minister who was one of the most prominent of those who at the Disruption* of 1843 left the established church*, to form the Free Church of Scotland. He was one of the founders of the Evangelical Alliance*.

Cane Ridge Revival Largest and most famous camp meeting* of the Second Great Awakening* in 1801, held by Barton W. Stone* at Cane Ridge in Bourbon County, Kentucky. The crowd estimated at 25,000 defied the heat to listen to Baptist, Methodist, and Presbyterian preachers for six or seven days. Stone described six types of bodily responses: falling, jerking, dancing, barking, running, and singing. The effects of Cane Ridge

Cane Ridge Meeting House

spread through the West and changed the course of American Protestantism*.

Canisius, Peter (1521–1597) Roman Catholic reformer. He became a Jesuit in 1543 and helped to establish the Catholic Reformation* in South Germany and Austria. His three catechisms* went through 130 editions. As provincial* of Upper Germany he was responsible for founding the colleges of Augsburg, Munich*, and Innsbruck and for extending Catholic influence into Poland. He was canonized in 1925 and declared to be a doctor of the church*. Feast day: December 21.

Cano, Melchior (?1509–1560) Spanish Dominican theologian. He taught at the universities of Alcala and Salamanca*. He took an active part in the Council of Trent*. His reputation rests on the 12 books of his *De Locis Theologicis* (1563).

canon (Gk., straight rod of measurement against which another could be measured) 1. Person holding a particular ecclesiastical office, as a regular* canon or a secular canon. Also, a cathedral chapter* under a dean, originally advisory to a bishop. 2. Ecclesiastical decree. 3. List of saints*. 4. List of inspired books comprising the Holy Scriptures. See also CANON OF THE SCRIPTURE. 5.Ecclesiastical regulations, as in canon law*. 6. Central portion of the Mass*. 7. In the Eastern Church*, eight hymns of the orthros*. 8. Authoritative summary of church doctrine, as in rule of faith* in the early church.

canon Title applied to all clergy on the staff of a diocese* (excluding monks and private chaplains*) and secular clergy belonging to a cathedral or collegiate church. Originally they lived together and shared in the revenues of the church, but later two classes emerged: secular canons or nonresident clergy who owned private property and Augustinian or regular* canons who lived under a monastic rule. In the Church of England*, there are residentiary and non-residentiary canons. The latter receive no pay but have certain privileges and responsiblities. Together with the dean, the residentiary and non-residentiary canons form the general cathedral chapter*. Minor canons* are clerics who sing in the services.

canon In the Eastern Church*, the hymns, odes, or canticles* that form part of the orthros*, or morning service. They were introduced into the liturgy by St. Andrew of Crete*. Other famous authors of the odes were St. Cosmas Melodius, St. John of Damascus*, and St. Theodore of Studios*. In the early centuries, biblical canticles* were sung by themselves, but later stanzas of poetry, or troparia*, were inserted between the verses of each canticle* and now these stanzas constitute the entire canon. The text of the Magnificat* is included in full.

Canon Episcopalis In the Latin rite before 1970, a liturgical book for bishops containing the Ordinary of the Mass* with the form of episcopal blessing and other prayers.

canon law Body of ecclesiastical laws* or rules imposed by authority in all matters of faith, morals, and discipline. The corpus of law was built slowly through the decisions of councils. Of these the 20 canons promulgated at Nicaea* were accepted universally. A large body of rules came from the councils of the African Church which met frequently. The Council of Chalcedon* cites 330 Antiochene canons. There were also private collections of canons by John Scholasticus and Dionysius Exiguus*. Additional canons were promulgated by the decrees of influential bishops, such as Dionysius* of Alexandria, Gregory Thaumaturgus*, Basil of Caesarea*, and Amphilochius of Iconium*.

Beginning with Pope Siricius* in 385, popes issued decretals* that carried great weight. A number of fictitious or forged decretals were also in circulation. A landmark was the decretum issued by Gratian* in about 1140. Gratian's work was the dividing line between *ius antiquum*(old law) and *ius novum* (new law). The canon established later than the Council of Trent* is called *ius novissimum*. Gratian's collection was supplemented by a series of later collections and incorporated in the *Corpus Iuris Canonici**, which remained the authoritative basis for canon law until it was completely overhauled and codified in Codex Iuris Canonici* in 1917. The codex was revised in 1983. There is a separate code for Uniat churches*. In the Orthodox Church, the Code of Justinian* served as a digest of canon law. There are other collections of canon laws, such as the Nomocanon*.

Canon of the Mass Ancient consecratory prayer in the Roman Mass* and in all eucharistic liturgies. In the Roman Catholic Church, the original canon goes back to the fourth century. It was modified slightly by St. Gregory* the Great. It is found in more or less its present form in the *Gelasian Sacramentary**, the Bobbio Missal*, and the Missale Francorum*. The Canon of the Mass* originally began with the Preface* and is followed by 11 prayers, named from their opening words as "Te Igitur*," "Memento Vivorum," "Communicantes*," Hanc Igitur*," "Quam Oblationem," "Qui Pridie" (accompanied by the elevation* of the host*), "Unde et Memores*," "Supra Quae*," "Supplices Te Rogamus," "Memento Defunctorum," "Nobis Quoque Peccatoribus," and "Per Quem Haec Omnia," the concluding doxology*. Until 1967 nine of the 11 prayers of the canon were recited silently. In its revised form the canon appears as the first of the four eucharistic prayers in the 1970 Roman Missal.

canon of the Scripture Collection of inspired writings, determined by the tradition and authority of the church as well as the order, authenticity, and sequence of the books of the Bible. The Christian church accepted *in toto* the Old Testament Scriptures in the Septuagint version, including the Apocrypha*. However, the Roman Catholic Church, at the Council of Trent*, accepted the authenticity of the Apocrypha and imposed their acceptance as a matter of faith on all Roman Catholics, a decision confirmed by the First Vatican Council*.

Determination of the authenticity of the books of the New Testament was slower. By the second century the four Gospels, the Acts, and Pauline Epistles had come to be accepted. One of the earliest canons of the New Testament came from a heterodox source, the heretic Marcion*, who excluded everything except the 10 Pauline Epistles and the Gospel of Luke. During the third century, various books of the New Testament, such as Hebrews, James, 2 Peter, 2 and 3 John, Jude, and the Revelation, were excluded at various times. In the Eastern Church*, the canon was established in its current form by 367 and is set out in Athanasius's* Easter Letter listing the 27 books. Other early lists of the New Testament Scriptures are included in the Muratorian Canon* and in the fourth-century Canon of the Council of Laodicea*. However, certain other books, as Hermas'* *Shepherd* and the Didache*, are permitted for private reading. A similar list was drawn up by the Synod of Carthage* (397) and the Council of Rome (382). The latter list was included in the Gelasian Decree* (495).

During the Reformation* the canonicity of the Old Testament and the New Testament became a major theological issue. Luther* created a deuterocanon* (books of the Bible whose canonicity is questionable) by suggesting that Hebrews, James, Jude, and Revelation had less value than the others and placing them at the end of the Bible. The Orthodox and Roman Catholic churches hold that only the church has the right to set the canons of the Bible. In recent years the canonical approach or canon criticism has introduced scholarly considerations into the question.

canonarch In Greek monasteries, monk designated to ensure that the correct texts are sung in the correct tone.

canoness Member of a religious order for women bound by the vows of the order. Formerly, member of an order of women, known as canoness regular, who did not renounce their own property although living in a community. Later, the female counterpart of a canon regular*.

canonical hours The seven periods of the Divine Office*: matins* (including nocturn* and lauds*), prime*, terce*, sext*, nones*, vespers*, and compline*.

canonical marriage Marriage in accordance with church law.

canonicals Vestments worn by the officiating clergy according to canonical prescriptions.

canonicity 1. Status or character of belonging to the biblical canon*. 2. Authority or genuineness when measured against the standards of the biblical canon.

canonization Papal decree commanding veneration* by the faithful of a member previously beatified by the church. It creates a universal and obligatory cultus*. In the Orthodox churches, canonization is usually made by a synod* of bishops of a member church. In the early church, martyrs* were publicly venerated without any formal procedure. From the fourth century this cultus was extended to confessors. Initially, the cultus was controlled by each individual diocese*. However, papal intervention was found necessary when the veneration* of certain saints spread beyond the limits of a diocese or when abuses occurred.

The first historically attested canonization was that of Ulrich of Augsburg by Pope John XV in 993. In 1634 Urban VII published a bull* which reserved to the Holy See* the right of canonization. The process of canonization is spelled out in canon law* as well as the apostolic constitution, "Divinus Perfectionis Magister," of 1983. The process begins at the diocesan level and continues in Rome* in the Congregation for the Causes of Saints*. After the investigation, the evidence is assessed by historical and theological experts under

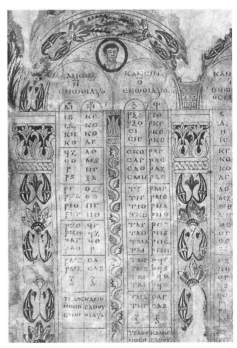

Canons of Eusebius

the presidency of the Promotor Fidei*. Their findings are then considered by the cardinals and bishops who advise the pope. Normally, canonization requires proof of at least one miracle since beatification*.

Canonization confers a sevenfold honor. First, the name is inscribed in the catalogue of saints. Second, the new saint* is invoked in the public prayers of the church. Third, churches may be dedicated to God in the saint's memory. Fourth, Mass* and office are publicly offered in the saint's honor. Fifth, festival and feast days are celebrated in the saint's memory. Sixth, the saint is represented in pictures in which the saint is surrounded by a heavenly light of glory. Seventh, the saint's relics* are enclosed in precious vessels and publicly honored.

Canons of Dort See DORT, SYNOD OF.

Canons of Eusebius Tables devised by Eusebius* of Caesarea that connect a passage in one Gospel with a similar passage in the others.

Canons of Hippolytus Fourth-century Syrian adaptation of the *Apostolic Tradition**.

Canons of Hippolytus Sixth-century collections of canons, written in Greek and wrongly attributed to St. Hippolytus, relating to disciplinary and liturgical matters. The Greek text is lost, but it survives in thirteenth-century Arabic and Ethiopian manuscripts.

canons regular Canons living under the Rule of St. Augustine*. See also AUGUSTINIAN CANONS.

canons secular Non-residential canons in a church or cathedral who may own private property.

Canons, the The principal body of canonical legislation in the Church of England*, a collection of 141 canons, drawn up in Latin and passed by James I and by the Canterbury Convocation of 1604 and by the York Convocation of 1606. Many of these canons were taken from Matthew Parker's* *Book of Advertisements** and the Thirty-Nine Articles*. A revised code was promulgated in two parts, the first in 1964 and the second in 1969. The canons were again revised by the general synod* in 1993. Among other things, the canons deal with the conduct of divine service*, the administration of sacraments*, the duties of clerics, and the care of churches.

canopy Awning supported by four poles, one at each corner, and carried over the Blessed Sacrament* or High Church* dignitaries, during processions.

cantata Mutisectional choral composition extending from an anthem to an oratorio*. It involves arias and recitatives for solo voices as well as choral sections. It is sung in the Communion and ante-communion services of the Lutheran Church especially as a commentary on the Gospel reading. J. S. Bach* has left over 200 cantatas.

Cantate Fourth Sunday after Easter*, from the first word of the introit* for the day.

Cantate Domino (lit., Sing unto the Lord) Title of Psalm 98, a canticle* for evening prayer in the Western Church*.

cantatorium (Lat., of the singers) Early medieval liturgical book containing chants sung between the readings during Mass*, often by a soloist or cantor*.

Canterbury Borough in Kent, in southern England, the seat of the archbishop of Canterbury* and the primate* of All England, the cradle of English Christianity, and the site of the primary see* of the Church of England*. The principal palace of the archbishop of Canterbury* is Lambeth Palace* in London, but he also has a palace at Canterbury. Canterbury was the royal capital of Ethelbert*, the king of Kent who was converted by St. Augustine* in 597. The church stands on the site of a Roman basilica* consecrated by St. Augustine as the Cathedral Church of Christ. It was rebuilt by archbishops Lanfranc* and Anselm* in Norman style and reconsecrated in 1130 after being destroyed by the Danes in 1067. Archbishop Becket* was murdered in the cathedral in 1170. The choir was reconstructed in transitional style with a magnificent shrine for Becket and dedicated in 1220. From 1376 the Norman nave* was reconstructed and transepts* were added. The

Bell Harry Tower was added about 1495. It is the pride of the cathedral and is rung only on the death of a British monarch or the archbishop of Canterbury.

The Chichele (or Oxford or Dunstan) steeple was erected by Archbishop Chichele. The beautiful stained-glass windows in the transept, the so-called "King's Windows," date from 1070 to 1130. The great crypt with its pillars and capitals is the oldest part of the cathedral, dating from Norman times. The archepiscopal throne, or St. Augustine's chair, is built of Purbeck marble. A monastery was attached to the cathedral until the Reformation*.

Canterbury

Canterbury cap Soft flat cloth cap worn by English clerics.

cantharus (Lat., bowl, basin) Fountain placed in the atrium* of Old St. Peter's* and used for ritual ablutions by pilgrims.

canticle (Lat., song) Song or prayer, other than a Psalm, derived from the Bible, used in the liturgy. In the Eastern Church*, it refers to the nine odes from the Bible of which eight are from the Old Testament. They are the two songs of Moses, the Song of Hannah, the Song of Habakkuk, the Song of Isaiah, the Song of the Three Children, and the Benidicite. The New Testament canticles* are the Magnificat* and Benedictus*. The Nunc Dimittis* is used daily at vespers*. In the Roman Catholic Church, the Benedictus is said daily at lauds*, the Magnificat at vespers, and the Nunc

Dimittis at compline*. Forty-four Old Testament and nine New Testament canticles* are used, including Te Deum*. In the Church of England*, it refers to the Benedicite*, Jubilate*, Cantate*, and Deus Misereatur*.

Canticle of the Blessed Virgin The Magnificat*, the song of the Virgin Mary* (Luke 1:46–55). It was given a beautiful musical setting in Johann Bach's* Christian Oratorio.

Canticle of the Sun Hymn of St. Francis beginning, "Be thou praised, my Lord, with all thy creatures, above all brother sun," traditionally believed to have been composed in 1225 in the garden of San Damiano in Assisi*. The 1925 English translation by William H. Draper is the hymn, "All Creatures of Our God and King."

Canticles, Book of The Song of Solomon.

cantiga (Span., song) Medieval song about or in praise of the Virgin Mary*.

cantillation Chanting, intoning, and reciting in a musical monotone.

Cantionales Books of Lutheran music service for the minister, choir, and congregation, first prepared in the sixteenth century. The basic format was set by Lucas Osiander's* Fifty Sacred Songs and Psalms (1586) followed by similar collections by Hans Leo Hassler and Michael Praetorius.

cantique Popular folk hymn, similar to a Negro spiritual.

cantor Church singer or choir master who leads and directs the liturgical or worship music. He generally sings the opening words and the solo parts of a chant. In the Church of England*, he is also known as precentor*. In the Eastern Church*, the cantor belongs to the minor orders*.

cantoris/cantoria (Lat., the place of the cantor) Place of the cantor* on the north side of a choir or cathedral, generally leading the antiphonal singing. Those on the south side are known as decani*.

cantus firmus Use of a pre-existing melody, often a Gregorian Chant* in the Catholic Church and chorale melodies in the Protestant churches, as the basis for a new polyphonic composition.

canzona Instrumental song played in either secular or sacred contexts, such as a composition by Giovanni Gabrieli* or Girolamo Frescobaldi*.

Capernaum Town near the Sea of Galilee*, one of the centers of Jesus' ministry, now identified with Kefar Nahum (Tell Hum). The town synagogue has been excavated and partially restored.

Capgrave, John (1393–1464) English Augustinian friar* who wrote the *Chronicle of England, Liber de Illustribus Henricis,* and *A Guide to the Antiquities of Rome.* He is best known for his *Nova Legenda Angliae,* the first English hagiology*.

capillas posas Early sixteenth-century Mexican open chapel designed to hold the tabernacle and sacred host* during open-air processions.

Capistrano, John of (1386–1456) Franciscan preacher who condemned the Hussites* and raised an army that defeated the Turks in Hungary. He was canonized in 1690. Feast day: March 28.

capitalavium (Lat., washing of the head) Name of Palm Sunday* in the Middle Ages, in reference to the custom of washing the heads of children.

Capito, Wolfgang Fabricius (1478–1541) Protestant reformer and Old Testament scholar. A friend of Erasmus* and Luther*, he settled in Strasbourg*, where he became the leading reformer with Bucer*. He drew up the Tetrapolitan Confession* of 1530 and signed the Concord of Wittenberg* in 1536.

capitular Of or belonging to an ecclesiastical chapter*.

Capitular Mass Public Mass, sung or said, in cathedrals or collegiate church, attended by the whole chapter*.

capitulary 1. Compilation of laws made by the bishops for the clergy and the laity. 2. In biblical manuscripts, a brief summary of the contents preceding the actual text.

capitulations Agreement with a bishop or pope in which he promises to do certain things after his election.

capitulum 1. Chapter house* in a monastery. 2. Verse or brief passage of Scripture read at certain daily offices.

cappa 1. Vestment used in the Ethiopian Rite resembling a small cloak that reaches from the neck to the knees, secured at the top, and decorated with small bells. 2. Ecclesiastical cape.

cappa magna In the Roman Catholic Church, violet cloak with a long train and large hood used by bishops. In the Middle Ages, it was also used by cardinals whose cloaks were scarlet.

cappa nigra Hooded black cloak worn by clergy during choir offices*.

Cappadocia Region north of Cilicia* in Asia Minor, home of the celebrated Cappadocian Fathers*.

Wolfgang F. Capito

Cappadocian Fathers The three great Fathers of the Church—Basil the Great*, Gregory of Nyssa*, and Gregory of Nazianzus*—all of whom hailed from Cappadocia*.

Capreolus, John (c. 1380–1444) "The Prince of Thomists." A Dominican theologian who helped to revive Thomism* through his ardent defense in *Four Books of Defenses of the Theology of St. Aquinas* (1409–1433).

capsula Short, round, metal vessel used in Roman Catholic churches to reserve the consecrated bread.

Captain of Our Salvation Jesus Christ (Heb. 2:10).

Captivity Epistles Letters written by St. Paul* in prison: Ephesians, Philippians, Colossians, and Philemon.

capuce Hooded cowl* worn by Capuchins*.

Capuchins Reformed branch of the Franciscan Order* whose 1529 rule emphasized the ideals of poverty, prayer, and austerity and who devoted themselves to charity. The official title of the order is Ordo Fratrum Minorum Capuccinorum. It was founded in 1525 by Matteo da Bascio (1495–1552), a Friar Observant at Montefalcone who desired to return the Franciscans to their original simplicity. He adopted the pointed cowl* or capuce* from which the name of the order was derived, together with brown* robes, sandals, and a beard. They received papal approval in 1528. The movement nearly died when their third general*, Bernardino Ochino*, became a Protestant, but it survived through the efforts of Cardinal Sanseverino and Vittoria Colonna, the duchess of Amalfi, and helped to advance Counter-Reformation*. Capuchins are among the strictest Franciscans, but the severity of their rule has been softened in recent years. A female branch of the order, whose members are called Capuchinesses, was founded in 1538.

Caput Jejunii Ash Wednesday* in the *Gelasian Sacramentary**.

Caputiati (Lat., *caputium*, hood or cowl) Name applied to several monastic orders wearing a cowl* or hood.

Caravaggio, Michelangelo Merisi da (1571–1610) Italian artist. His earliest religious work was *Flight into Egypt* (1595/7), painted for Cardinal del Monte, who obtained for him his commission for his first major work, a series of three pictures in San Luigi dei Francesi, Rome, depicting the *Calling of St. Matthew, Martyrdom of the Saint,* and *Saint Inspired by an Angel.* These works introduced his vivid realism and his down-to-earth portrayal of his subjects in common settings, quite unlike the artificial grandiloquence of religious art. The same realism appears in *Madonna di Loreto* (1604/5), *Madonna dei Palafrenieri* (1605), *Death of the Virgin* (1606), and the *Entombment of Christ* (1602/4). His brief stay in Malta produced the *Decollation of St. John the Baptist* (1607/8). Caravaggio's influence was immense, mainly outside Italy.

carbuncle Symbol of martyrdom or of the suffering Christ.

Cardijn, Joseph-Leon (1882–1967) Belgian cardinal, founder of the Jocists* or Jeunesse Ouvriere Chretienne* (Young Christian Workers). He became a priest in 1912 and was put in charge of social work among the disaffected workers in industrialized society. He organized young factory workers in a Catholic movement which was approved by Pope Pius XI* in 1925. He attended the Second Vatican Council* as a peritus* and was made a cardinal in 1965.

cardinal (Lat., *cardo,* hinge) Highest ecclesiastical official in the Roman Catholic Church, below the pope. Cardinals are considered as princes of the church and serve as counselors of the pope when assembled in a consistory*. There are three ranks among cardinals: Cardinal-priests, cardinal-deacons, and cardinal-bishops. Since 1962 all cardinals are cardinal-bishops. The present functions of the cardinals are administrative. They are nominated by the pope. Their number, originally fixed at 70 in 1580, has now no ceiling. Those resident in Rome* head ecclesiastical commissions, curial offices, and congregations. Sometimes cardinals represent the pope personally (legatus a latere). The red hat* they wore formerly has been abolished, but their present insignia include the biretta*, red skull cap, the sacred purple, ring with a sapphire stone, pectoral cross, and the use of the ombrellino* or canopy* during processions. Together, cardinals form the electoral college of the pope whenever there is a vacancy in the Apostolic See*. Only those below the age of 80 may vote. They are addressed as "your eminence*."

cardinal virtues The seven qualities of character on which human conduct hinges: prudence, justice, self-control, courage, faith, hope, and love. The first four are called natural virtues, and the latter three theological virtues*.

cardinalate The office or rank of a cardinal.

CARE Cooperative for American Relief Everywhere, an arm of several U.S. religious and philanthropic organizations for providing food and other essentials for those in need in any part of the world.

Carey, William (1761–1834) The father of modern missions. Pioneer British missionary to India. Converted at 18, he became a preacher and received a call* to convert the unevangelized in heathen lands. In 1792 he published the pamphlet, *An Enquiry into*

William Carey

the Obligations of Christians to Use Means for the Conversion of the Heathens. To achieve this goal, he formed the first missionary society. In 1792 he preached his famous missionary sermon, "Expect Great Things from God, Attempt Great Things for God." In the same year he helped to form the Baptist Society for Propagating the Gospel Among the Heathen, now the Baptist Missionary Society.

In 1793 Carey set sail for India in a Danish vessel (as missionaries had been banned from British ships) and reached Bengal, then a British East India Company possession. Combining the work of a pastor and the manager of an indigo factory at Malda, he mastered Bengali and Sanskrit and translated the Bible into Bengali, the first in any Indian language. To print the Bible he set up a printing press. In 1800 he moved to the Danish colony of Serampore, where he remained for the rest of his life. Despite his wife's increasing mental illness, he continued to work tirelessly in Bible translation, medical relief, evangelism, church planting*, and education. He served as professor of Sanskrit, Bengali, and Marathi at the College of Fort William for 30 years and supervised and edited the translation of the Scriptures into 36 languages and produced dictionaries and linguistic manuals of Sanskrit, Marathi, Punjabi, and Telugu.

carillon Set of fixed bells, usually 25 to 40 in number, with hammers designed to play polyphonic music from a keyboard, found in wealthy churches.

Carissimi, Giacomo (1605–1674) Italian composer who played an important role in the development of oratorio* or sacred opera. From 1629 he was maestro di cappella* st the Church of Sant'Apollinaire in Rome*. His works presented episodes from the Bible in dramatic style. The actors sang solo without costumes and scenery. The chorus sang in simple chordal style.

Caritas (Lat., love) International Catholic social welfare organization. The American branch of Caritas International is Catholic Relief Services (CRS) based in New York.

Carlile, Wilson (1847–1942) Founder of the Church Army*, the Anglican equivalent of the Salvation

Army*. After the failure of his business, he was converted and began evangelizing the downtrodden in the poorest areas of England. His efforts to train lay preachers led to the founding of the Church Army.

Carlstadt (c. 1477–1541) Original name: Andreas Rudolf Bodenstein von. German Protestant reformer. Originally a Thomist professor of theology in Rome*, he was converted to Protestantism* around 1515 after reading Augustine's doctrine of grace*. He attacked the Catholic theologian Eck* and defended Luther*. He was mentioned by name in the papal bull*, *Exsurge Domine*, that excommunicated Luther in 1520.But he soon fell out with Luther over matters of doctrine and became a Radical Reformer*. He opposed infant baptism*, the sacraments*, clerical dress, monasticism*, liturgical music, and Communion in both kinds*. He claimed direct revelation of the Holy Spirit* in his doctrinal statements. In 1524 Luther called him a Judas, and he was forced to flee to Switzerland, where he lived for the rest of his life as preacher of the university church and professor of Hebrew at Basel*.

Andreas Carlstadt

Carmelites The Order of the Brothers of Our Lady of Mount Carmel, founded by Berthold* about 1154 on Mount Carmel, a high ridge in Palestine near the port of Haifa. Their main church was dedicated to the Virgin Mary*. In 1208 they adopted the Rule of St. Albert under which each hermit lived in a cave-dwelling, praying continually day and night. It also prescribed a daily Eucharist* and recitation of the psalter, abstinence from meat, and a fast that lasted eight months. By the middle of the thirteenth century, political conditions in the Middle East and the fall of the crusader states forced them to spread to Europe, where they became less eremetical. Permission to accept alms brought them into the class of mendicant friars. They grew rapidly when communities of lay people became affiliated with the order. They wore either white (from which they were known by the name of White Friars*) or a brown scapular*.

In the later Middle Ages many reforms tried to renew the order. The best known of the reforms were begun by St. Teresa of Avila*, who founded 16 convents following the Primitive Rule* of Carmel and her Constitutions for Discalced Nuns. The Carmelites now comprise three orders for men: the Carmelite Friars of the Ancient Observance, the Discalced Friars who follow the Teresian reform, and the Carmelites of Mary Immaculate, founded in India. They have in common a strong devotion to the Virgin Mary*, particularly to Our Lady of Mount Carmel.

Carmichael, Amy (1867–1951) Missionary to India and devotional writer. She went to India as a member of the Church of England Zenana Missionary Society. In 1901 she began the Dohnavur Fellowship* with the purpose of rescuing young girls dedicated to prostitution in Indian temples. She left behind a body of devotional literature marked by an intense and mystical spirituality*. Among her best known books is *Things as They Are* (1903).

Carnell, Edward John (1919–1967) Evangelical theologian and educator. In 1948 he joined the faculty of the newly founded Fuller Theological Seminary* and served there for the next 14 years as professor and five years as president (1954–1959). Carnell shaped neo-Evangelicalism* through his nine books, especially *An Introduction to Christian Apologetics* (1948), *Christian Commitment* (1957), and *Kingdom of Love and Pride of Life* (1960).

carnival (Lat., *caro vale*, goodbye, flesh) The period before Lent*, especially the three days before Ash Wednesday*, marked in most cities by unbridled and raucous festivities.

carol (Fr., carole, song) Traditional, popular religious song, similar to a folk song or ballad, sung on joyous occasions. Unlike hymns, carols are informal. Carols are sung generally at Christmas*, but they may be sung on other festivals. Most of them are of unknown authorship.

Caroline Books Document compiled about 790–792 attributed to Charlemagne* but probably written by Alcuin* or Theodulf of Orleans. It was an attack on the Iconoclastic Council of 754 that banned images and Nicaea II* of 787 that sanctioned veneration* of images. The Caroline Books approved the use of images but not their veneration.

Caroline Divines Anglican divines of the reign of Charles I and Charles II, who generally favored the High Church*. Its leaders were Lancelot Andrewes* and William Laud*.

Carolingian Renaissance Revival of learning in western Europe during the reign of Charlemagne*.

Carolingian schools Schools founded during the reign and at the initiative of Charlemagne*. In 787 he issued the Capitulary* of Bangulf, ordering all monasteries and bishops' houses to conduct classes in Psalms, notes, chants, computus*, and grammar. This document is called "the charter of modern education." Charlemagne himself founded a palace school at Aix-la-Chapelle for instruction in the seven liberal arts for members of the nobility and the laity. He staffed it with some of the great scholars of the day, such as the historian Paul the Deacon*. Some of the cathedral and monastery schools attained great distinction, including that of Alcuin* at Tours*; Orleans under Theodulf; Reims under Hincmar* and Remigius* of Auxerre*; Fulda under Rabanus Maurus*; Corbie under Adalhard and Paschasius Radbertus*; and Ferrieres under Lupus Servatus, St. Wandrille, St. Gall*, and St. Riquier.

Carpocrates (second century) Alexandrian Gnostic heretic whose followers were called Carpocratians. He was accused by his orthodox critics of preaching licentious living, transmigration of souls, and the creation of the world by demiurges*. He honored Jesus as only one of several saviors.

Carpzov Family of German theologians, including **Benedikt** (1595–1666), founder of the earliest complete system of ecclesiastical law* in *Jurisprudentia Ecclesiastica seu Consistorialis* (1649); his brother **Benedikt I** (1607–1657), who systematized Lutheran creeds in his *Isagoge in Libros Ecclesiarum Lutheranarum Symbolicos* (1665); his sons **Johann Benedikt II** (1639–1699) and **Samuel Benedikt** (1647–1707), Pietist controversalists; **Johann Gottlob** (1679–1767), son of Samuel Benedikt, outstanding Old Testament scholar; and **Johann Benedikt III** (1720–1803), son of Johann Gottlob, authority on the New Testament and patristics*.

carrel Niche* in a cloister* where monks gathered to study.

Carroll, John (1735–1815) First Roman Catholic archbishop of North America. The French-educated Jesuit came to America in 1773 on the dissolution of the Jesuit Order in France and became the leader of the colonial Catholics. After the revolution, which he supported, he was appointed by Pius VI* as the first prefect apostolic of the United States in 1784 and as the first Roman Catholic archbishop in 1790. He defended the right of his flock to the religious freedom guaranteed in the U.S. Constitution. His *Address to the Catholics of the United States* (1784) was the first Roman Catholic writing to be printed and published in the new republic. He founded Georgetown College*, which has become a premier American Catholic university.

Carta Caritatis The Charter of Love, the constitution of the Cluniac Order* presented in 1119 to Pope Callistus II*. It provides for a general chapter* with legislative and judicial powers with instructions on elections and correction of delinquent abbots and monasteries.

Carter, James ("Jimmy") Earl (1924–) U.S. president. Elected president in 1976, Carter served for a single term. After leaving the presidency, he continued to be active as an international troubleshooter and humanitarian. Carter was the first U.S. president to confess publicly his faith as a committed born-again Christian. He had first professed faith in Christ as his personal Savior at the age of 11 and recommitted himself to Christ again after a spiritual crisis in 1967. He is active in his Southern Baptist church as a Sunday school teacher and deacon.

Carthage Ancient city in North Africa, near modern Tunis, originally Phoenician (Punic) and later, Roman. It was the ecclesiastical capital of North Africa until the Arab conquest of the seventh century. Twelve councils were convened here, and Donatism flourished here. Famous Carthaginian Christians included Tertullian*, Cyprian*, Felicity*, and Perpetua*.

Carthage, synods of At least 12 important church synods were held in Carthage between the third and sixth centuries. They were held in 251, 252, 254, 255, 256, 348, 390, 393, 411, 414, 419, 424, 525, and 534.

Carthusians Roman Catholic monastic order founded at the Grande Chartreuse* in France in 1084 by St. Bruno*. It is an austere and strictly contemplative order in which members live in separate cells and practice mortification* and renunciation of the world. They are bound to constant prayer and silence and speak to one another only once a week, except for daily services. They wear white with a white belt. Between 1121 and 1128 Guigo I, the fifth prior* of the order, compiled their Rule, *Consuetudines Cartusiae*, which received the approval of Innocent II in 1133. Further revisions to the rule were made in 1271, 1509, and 1581 and were collected together as the *Statuta*.

Their property was confiscated during the French Revolution but restored in 1816, and they were driven from Grande Chartreuse in 1901 but allowed to return in 1904. The Carthusians are governed by a general* who is the prior* of Grande Chartreuse, elected by the monks of his house and assisted by the general chapter*. They have produced a number of mystics and devotional writers, including St. Hugh, the founder of the first English charterhouse* at Witham in 1175–1176. They are famous for the liqueur they make from their vineyards.

cartouche Wall tablet popular in seventeenth-century English churches as memorials for the dead.

Cartwright, Peter (1785–1872) American Methodist preacher and circuit rider*. Ordained by Bishop Asbury* and McKendree, he served in two Illinois legislatures but lost when he ran against Abraham Lincoln for Congress. He baptized 12,000 converts, preached 14,000 times, and founded the Illinois Wesleyan University.

Cary, Phoebe (1824–1871) Christian poet, famous for the hymn, "Nearer Home."

Casalis, Eugene (1812–1891) French Protestant pioneer missionary in Lesotho. He entered the Paris Evangelical Missionary Society* in 1830. Ordained in 1832, he went to Lesotho, where he worked for the next 20 years. He translated the Gospel of Mark into Sotho and helped to convert King Moshoeshoe.

Case, Shirley Jackson (1842–1947) Church historian. From 1908 to 1938 he taught New Testament and early church history at the University of Chicago Divinity School, becoming dean in 1933. He contributed to the development of the liberal Chicago School of Theology* which rejected the supernatural element of Christianity. Among his books were The *Evolution of Early Christianity* (1914) and *Christian Philosophy of History* (1943).

Casel, Odo (1886–1948) Benedictine scholar and liturgist*. His writings dealt with the mystery of the Eucharist*, which he interpreted as a reenactment of the mysteries* of Christ. His teachings were summarized in English in *The Mystery of Christian Worship* (1962).

Cashel, Synod of Meeting of Irish bishops in 1172 with a representative of Henry II of England to reform the Irish church. All native liturgies were replaced by that of the Church of England*. The archbishop of Armagh* was recognized as the primate* of Ireland.

Casimir, St. (1458–1484) Prince of Poland, second son of King Casimir IV, who served as viceroy during his father's absence. He was buried at Vilna, where miracles were reported. In 1602 he became the patron saint* of Poland. Feast day: March 4.

Caspari, Carl Paul (1814–1892) Jewish Christian missionary to the Jews. Born of Jewish parents, he was converted to Lutheran Pietism* and baptized at age 24. As professor of the University of Christiania (now Oslo), he became a leading authority on the Old Testament and the Apostles' Creed* and the Nicene Creed*. From 1861 to 1892 he was chairman of the Norwegian Mission to the Jews.

Cassander, Georg (1513–1566) Catholic theologian. In his writings he sought to mediate between the Catholics and Protestants by requiring concessions from both. To support Emperor Ferdinand I's official attempt at reunion, he wrote his *Consultatio de Articulis Religionis inter Catholicos et Protestantis Controversis* (1577), seeking to make Protestant doctrines palatable to the Catholics. He was condemned by both sides. A complete edition of his works was placed on the Index in 1616.

Cassian, St. John (c. 360–435) Scythian monk who introduced monasticism* in the West. As a young man, he joined a monastery at Bethlehem*, and went to Egypt to study monasticism under Evagrius Ponticus*. He later settled in the West. About 415 he founded two monasteries near Marseilles and wrote two of the earliest monastic manuals: the Institutes and the Conferences. The former was the basis of all later Western monastic rules, such as that of St. Benedict*. The latter was a record of his conversations with the great monks of the East. In it he also expressed his differences with the Augustinian doctrine of grace*, espousing a form of semi-Pelagianism*. The Eastern Church* considers him a saint. Feast day: July 23.

Cassinese Congregation Monastic congregation of Benedictine monks founded by Ludovico Barbo at Padua in 1409. It spread throughout Italy under the name of Congregation of Santa Giustina or Congregation of Unity. After the accession of Monte Cassino* in 1504, it changed to its current name. At one time it had 70 houses. It suffered loss of property during the French Revolution and the Italian Unification. Now it includes a number of monasteries, including Monte Cassino*, Cava, and St. Paul's Outside the Walls*. As a result of a split in the nineteenth century, some monasteries separated to form Cassinese

St. John Cassian

Congregation* of the Primitive Observance, now the Subiaco Congregation*.

Cassiodorus, Flavius Magnus Aurelius (c. 477–570) Roman writer who founded a monastery at Vivarium on his ancestral estate at Calabria on the shores of the Gulf of Squillace, in southernmost Italy. There he built up a large library of biblical manuscripts. He encouraged his monks to copy manuscripts and helped to create the monastic tradition of preserving classical culture. Among his religious books were *Historia Ecclesiastica Tripartita* and *Institutionis Divinarum et Saecularium Litterarum*. He promoted the fusion of Christian and secular learning.

cassock Long-sleeved garment, usually black, worn by the clergy. It symbolizes devotion. The

Cassock

cassocks of Catholic bishops are purple, those of cardinals red, and that of the pope white.

Castagno, Andrea del (c. 1423–1457) Italian Renaissance religious painter. The *Last Supper* and *David* are among his paintings.

Castel Gondolfo Town in the Alban hills, southeast of Rome*, the site of the pope's summer residence since the seventeenth century. Under the Lateran Treaty* of 1929, the papal palace and gardens are part of the Holy See*.

Castellio, Sebastian (1515–1563) French Protestant reformer, colleague and later opponent of Calvin*. In Geneva* he attacked many Calvinist doctrines, such as predestination*, insisted that the Song of Songs should be expunged from the canon* as obscene, pleaded for religious freedom, and denounced the burning of Servetus*. After leaving Geneva, he published French and Latin translations of the Bible.

Castrati Eighteenth-century cult of men who mutilated themselves with reference to Matthew 19:12. Castrated men sang in the choirs during the early modern period.

Castro, Emilio (1927–) Uruguayan ecumenical leader. He was director of the Commission on World Mission and Evangelism of the World Council of Churches* and editor of the *International Review of Missions* from 1973 to 1983 and general secretary of the World Council of Churches and editor of the *Ecumenical Review* from 1985 to 1992. His published works include *Amidst Revolution* (1975), *Freedom in Mission* (1975), and *When We Pray Together* (1989).

Castro, Jose Damian Ortiz de (1750–1793) Mexican architect noted for introducing the use of plaster in architecture, as in the Old Church at Tulancingo and the Church of San Hippolito and the Cathedral of Mexico in Mexico City.

casuistry Application of standards of ethics, or moral principles, to particular situations, usually in accordance with an established code of ethics. It acquired a pejorative meaning from its association with various systems, such as probablism*,

probabiliorism*, and equiprobabilism*, to justify a course of conduct patently unjustifiable.

Caswall, Edward (1814–1878) Hymn writer. An Anglican curate* from 1840 to 1847, he converted to Roman Catholicism* under the influence John Henry Newman*. Among his many hymns, the most popular was "Jesus, the Very Thought of Thee." He published *Lyra Catholica* (1849) and other devotional collections.

catabasia In the Byzantine Liturgy, an irmos* placed at the end of a hymn or a short hymn sung by the choir.

catabasion In the Byzantine Rite*, place beneath the altar where relics* are stored.

catacomb (Gk., at the ravine) Subterranean burial place consisting of labyrinths of galleries, often two to five stories high, with connecting stairs. Shafts admitted light and served as ventilators. Bodies were placed in niches in the walls or in floor graves, each holding sometimes more than one body, and sealed by stone slabs or tiles. Family tomb-chambers became popular from the third century. Larger niches had curved arches or a sarcophagus. The walls were painted with icons or symbols, such as the dove*, anchor, cross*, palm branch, fish*, bread, and basket. Since burial grounds were sacred under Roman law, Christians were able to worship here in peace during times of persecution. In the case of a martyr*, the Eucharist* was often celebrated at his grave on anniversaries. In course of time basilicas* were built above ground over the site of a martyr's grave and

Catacomb

relics* were moved up from the catacombs.

Catacombs are found mostly at Rome*, but they also exist in other Italian cities, including Sicily, Malta, Milos in Syria, Roman North Africa, Jerusalem*, and Alexandria*. About 70 catacombs of different lengths are known with a total length of 105 miles and an estimated 800,000 graves. Among them are those of Sts. Callistus*, Praetextatus, and Sebastian, all on Via Appia; St. Domitilla Aurelia Vetus, St. Agnes, St. Pancras, St. Commodilla, all on the Via Ostiensis; and Sts. Marcellinus and Peter* on the Via Labicana.

catacomb church Underground church in modern times in countries where Christianity is proscribed.

catafalque Funeral stand or bier covered with a pall* used at requiem* masses.

cataphatic theology Branch of theology that describes God positively on the basis of divine self-revelation. Distinguished from apophatic theology*.

Cataphrygians Montanists*, so named because they were mostly Phrygians.

catastroma In the Jacobite Church*, section between the sanctuary and the nave* reserved for the choir, separated from the nave by one step and a railing.

catechesis 1. Instruction in matters of Christian faith and practice given to catechumens* preparing for baptism*. Sometimes used, by extension, of the book containing such instruction, such as the *Catecheses* of Cyril of Jerusalem. 2. Responsibility of every Christian to bear witness to the gospel and to communicate it to others.

Catechetical School of Alexandria Celebrated Christian school in Alexandria* headed by Clement*, Origen, Heraclas, Achilles, and other leaders in the Alexandrian church.

catechism (Gk., *katecheo,* to teach) Summary or manual of doctrine for the instruction of the catechumens*, often arranged in the form of questions and answers. The earliest catechisms ex-

plained Christian doctrines in simple terms. Some of them, such as Gerson's* *ABC des Simples Gens,* the catechism of J. Colet, and *Christenspiegel,* were very popular in the Middle Ages. The Protestant Reformers found the catechism a useful tool. Most catechisms are based on the Lord's Prayer*, the Apostles' Creed*, the Decalogue, and the sacraments.

Luther* himself issued a *Shorter Catechism* (1529) which is still used in the Lutheran Church. In the Calvinist denominations, *Heidelberg Catechism* (1563) and *Calvin's Geneva Catechism* (1541) occupy a similar position. The Church of England* uses the catechism in the *Book of Common Prayer*, Westminster Larger Catechism*,* and *Westminster Shorter Catechism**. The post-Tridentine Roman Catholic Church has produced a number of catechisms, such as the Catechism of Trent (1560s), in addition to the Roman Catechism*. In 1554, St. Peter Canisius* published *Summa Doctrina Christianae.* In England Catholics use the *Catechism of Christian Doctrine* (1898) based on R. Challoner's* *Abridgment of Christian Doctrine* (1759). In 1992 the Roman Catholic Church produced for universal use the official *Catechism of the Catholic Church** which has superseded all others.

Catechism, Larger See LARGER CATECHISM.

Catechism, Larger See WESTMINSTER CATECHISM.

Catechism of the Catholic Church Official catechism* of the Roman Catholic Church published in 1992 and translated into English in 1994. In addition to the Apostles' Creed*, the Ten Commandments*, and the Lord's Prayer*, it includes Hail Mary*, the three theological virtues*, commandments of the church, and the sacraments*. In size and comprehensiveness it amounts to a summa* of Catholic theology.

Catechism, Prayer Catechism* included in the *Book of Common Prayer* of the Church of England*. It includes teaching about baptism*, Trinity*, the Apostles' Creed*, the Ten Commandments*, the Lord's Prayer*, and Holy Communion*.

Catechism, Shorter Name of the catechism* prepared by the Westminster Assembly* (1647) for those of "weaker capacity." It begins with the question, "What is the chief end of man?" and gives the answer, "Man's chief end is to glorify God and enjoy him forever." See also SHORTER CATECHISM.

Catechism, Smaller Name of Luther's catechism* for children.

catechist Person who conducts the catechism* or gives instruction to new Christians or children. In the primitive church, the term was applied to a lecturer in a catechetical school.

catechumen One receiving instruction in the fundamentals of the faith while preparing for baptism* or confirmation*.

catechumenate The institution of the training of catechumens* and the process by which they are admitted into full membership in the church. Catechumenate has become necessary in the mission field* where new Christian converts have to be initiated into the mysteries* of the faith. It begins with Bible reading, followed by a time of purification and enlightenment, recitation of the creed and the Lord's Prayer*, anointing with oil, and finally, Holy Communion*.

Catechumens, Mass of the The first part of the Eucharist* or Communion service*. This was the only part of the service that catechumens* were permitted to attend in the early church.

Catena Aurea (Lat., golden chain) Famous catena of the Gospels written by Thomas Aquinas*.

catena/catenae (Lat., chain) Series of scriptural citations or doctrines explained by means of chains of sentences or paragraphs from biblical commentaries without any comments. Sometimes used for any collection of passages from different authors on a single subject.

cathanar In the Syro-Malabarese Church, a priest.

Cathari (Gk., pure) Any of a group of heretics, including the Novatianists, Bogomils*, Manichaeans, Bulgari, Albigenses*, and Patarenes, but most properly applied to a group in France in the twelfth and thirteenth centuries. In the thirteenth

century the word *heretic* was applied exclusively to the Cathari, who were bent on restoring the purity of the early church by dispensing with most of the later dogmatic and liturgical accretions. Their dualist theology bears a marked resemblance to the Bogomils, Manichaeans, and Gnostics. They rejected the flesh and the material world as evil. Their dualism was absolute, good and evil being equally matched, and mitigated, with good triumphing over evil in the end.

Humans thus lived in a mixed state, and the purpose of redemption* and the Incarnation* was to bring an end to this mixed state and liberate the flesh from the devil. Both the Old and the New Testaments were allegories. Christ was an angel with a phantom body who consequently did not die or rise again and whose only accomplishment was his teaching of the true doctrine. The Catholic Church in so far as it worshiped the corrupt and evil Old Testament God was doing the work of the devil. The Cathari rejected the sacraments, doctrines of hell* and purgatory*, and the resurrection of the body. Because all flesh was evil, they condemned marriage and the use of animal produce, such as meat and milk.

Such an austere and rigorous doctrine was intended only for the elite, or the *perfecti,* who received the *consolamentum* or the baptism of the Holy Spirit* by the imposition of hands*. The ordinary believers, the *credentes,* received the *consolamentum* only on the point of death, when the *endura*, or ritual suicide, was recommended or permitted. See also ALBIGENSIAN CRUSADE.

Catharinus, Ambrosius (c. 1484–1553) Birth name: Lancelot Politi. Dominican theologian. By age 30 he was professor at the Sapienza in Rome*, and in 1517 he entered the Dominican Order. He became an apologist for the Catholic Church, writing two controversial books: *Excusatio Disputationis Contra Lutherum* (1521) and *Apologia pro Veritate Catholica* (1520). He was elected prior* in Siena, but was soon embroiled in a controversy over the doctrine of immaculate conception* which he defended strongly against his provincial superiors* and Thomas Cajetan. For this Catharinus was deposed as a prior in 1530, and he moved to France. In 1545 Paul III* summoned him to the Council of Trent*, where he played an active role. From 1549 he lived in Rome* until he was named archbishop of Conza a year before his death. On many points of his teaching he was at variance with official Dominican Thomism*.

cathedra (Lat., chair) 1. Official church teaching, set forth by a bishop or pope. 2. Official throne or chair of a bishop or pope. Originally, it was in the center of the apse* behind the high altar.

cathedra, ex Infallible character of a formal pro-

Cathedra

nouncement defining a doctrine by the pope as the guardian of the faith. The right was first asserted at the First Vatican Council*.

cathedral The mother church of a diocese* where the bishop has his cathedra* or chair. Cathedrals are generally large, and they have a long tradition of high musical performances in their services. The great cathedrals, such as those of Chartres*, Amiens* and Cologne*, represent the triumph of Christian architecture.

cathedral chapter Body of diocesan priests, known as canons*, responsible for the spiritual and temporal concerns of the diocesan cathedral.

cathedral music Relatively elaborate style of Anglican and Catholic church music, traditionally

played in cathedral settings.

cathedral priory Building attached to a cathedral and often used as a residence.

cathedral school School attached to a cathedral.

Catherine of Alexandria, St. (fourth century) Virgin and martyr*. She was tied to a spiked wheel* and tortured to death for her faith under Emperor Maxentius, or Maximian. According to legend, her body was transported by angels to Mount Sinai. She was one of the most popular saints in the Middle Ages. Her symbol is a spiked wheel, and she is the patron saint* of young women, attorneys, wheelwrights, and scholars and is one of the 14 auxiliary saints*. Because she referred to herself as the "bride of Christ," she is shown in Christian art as receiving a ring from the Christ child, seated on his mother's lap. Feast day: November 25.

Catherine of Bologna, St. (1413–1463) Italian nun and patron of Bologna. She became a nun in 1426/28 and abbot of the Convent of Poor Clares* in 1456. She wrote a book of prophecies, published in 1511. Feast day: March 9.

Catherine of Genoa, St. (1447–1510) Italian noblewoman and mystic. She was released from her marriage in 1474 and entered the Ladies of Mercy to work with the terminally ill in the Hospital of St. Lazarus in Genoa. Her spiritual life is recorded in her *Dialogues on the Soul and the Body*. Canonized in 1737. Feast day: September 22.

Catherine of Siena, St. (1347–1380) Dominican tertiary*. The twenty-third of 25 children born to a dyer, she vowed perpetual virginity* as a young

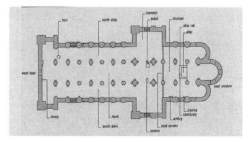

Cathedral

girl. She joined the Dominican Order of Penance as a tertiary in 1364 and lived in Siena from 1368 to 1374. At the age of 28 stigmata* appeared on her, and she had mystical visions. With her attractive personality and sanctity* she attracted a large band of followers. She also had great influence with popes Gregory XI* and Urban VI* and helped to end the Great Schism*. Her spiritual wisdom comes across in her *Dialogue* of four treatises that she dictated because she could not write. Some 400 of her letters have survived. In 1939 Pope Pius XII* declared her a copatron saint* of Italy along with St. Francis of Assisi*. She was canonized in 1461. Feast day: April 30.

Catherine of Sweden (1331–1381) Daughter of St. Bridget of Sweden*, she succeeded her mother as head of the Bridgettine* Order.

Catherine Tekakawitha (1656–1680) American Indian girl of the Mohawk tribe, baptized at age 5. Ascetic, missionary, and miracle worker, she was stoned to death for her faith.

catholic (Gk., general, universal) 1. Worldwide and universal. Distinguished from sectarian. 2. Belonging to the "One True, Holy, Catholic" church. According to Ignatius, "Wherever Jesus Christ is, there is the Catholic Church." According to Cyril of Jerusalem, "The Church is called Catholic because she is throughout the whole world, from one end of the world to the other; because she teaches universally and without fail all the doctrines that ought to be preached to the knowledge of men concerning the visible and the invisible, in heaven and on earth; because she subjects to her faith the whole of mankind . . . because she is the universal physician and healer of sins of every kind, sins of soul or body, and possesses in herself every form of excellence that can be named in deeds, and words in spiritual gifts* of every kind." 3. Catholic. Of or belonging to the Roman Catholic Church, distinguished from the Orthodox Church and Protestant churches. See also ROMAN CATHOLICISM.

Catholic Action Lay Roman Catholic organization seeking to influence public and social policy, inspired by Pope Pius XI's* encyclical* "Ubi Arcano" (1922).

Catholic Apostolic Church Sect, also called Irvingites, founded under the inspiration of Edward Irving* in London in the early nineteenth century. It grew out of the annual prophecy conferences conducted by Henry Drummond*. It was governed by 12 apostles, and each congregation by an angel (bishop), priests, deacons, and acolytes*. It practiced glossolalia*, and believed in the real presence* of Christ in the Eucharist* and in his Second Coming*. They adopted many Roman Catholic practices, such as anointing of the sick, holy water*, vestments, and incense. The last apostle died in 1901, and the sect slowly died out.

Catholic emancipation Legislation in the United Kingdom removing some of the discriminatory laws against Roman Catholics in the statute books. They included the Papists Act of 1778, the Roman Catholic Relief Act of 1791, the Roman Catholic Relief Act of 1829, and the Roman Catholic Relief Act of 1929. Among the few restrictions that remain is the one that bars Roman Catholics from being the king or queen of England.

Catholic Epistles General or universal epistles of the New Testament: James; 1, 2, and 3 John; 1 and 2 Peter; and Jude. These epistles, unlike the others, are not addressed to a specific individual or church but to the church in general. See also GENERAL EPISTLES.

Catholic Evidence Lay Catholic movement or guild engaged in outdoor witnessing.

Catholic Foreign Mission Society of America Society founded in Maryknoll*, New York, by James A. Walsh* and Thomas F. Price in 1911. Modeled on the foreign missionaries of Paris, Maryknoll priests are secular priests who do not take religious vows. A parallel society of women religious, known as Maryknoll Sisters of St. Dominic*, was founded in 1912 by Mother Mary Joseph. Maryknoll is active in South America, where it entered in 1942, and Africa, where it entered in 1946. In the 1970s and 1980s Maryknoll was identified with liberation theology* which was promoted by its publication arm, Orbis. See also MARYKNOLL.

Catholic Majesty Traditional title of the king of Spain granted by Alexander VI* to Ferdinand of

Aragon in recognition of the conquest of Granada*.

Catholic Truth Society Roman Catholic society formed in 1884 by Henry Cardinal Vaughan for the printing and distribution of inexpensive devotional tracts and leaflets.

Catholic truths In the Roman Catholic Church, truths taught by the church as authentic but not infallible. Distinguished from dogma*.

Catholic University of America University in Washington, D.C., founded in 1889, originally for the training of Roman Catholic clergy. Its ex-officio chancellor is the archbishop of Washington, D.C. Presently, the university consists of ten schools, including theology and canon law*.

Catholic Worker Lay Catholic movement founded during the Great Depression by Dorothy Day* and Peter Maurin. It is an intentional community with volunteers from all walks of life. Some practice voluntary poverty, and some have formed communes. It was the first Catholic pacifist movement to emerge in the United States. There are satellite houses in England, Canada, Australia, and Mexico.

Catholicism Body of traditions, tenets, beliefs, and practices that distinguish the Roman Catholic Church.

catholicity 1. Universal quality of the Christian church, as expressing the essential unity in doctrine and practice professed by believers. 2. Such universality as pertaining to the Roman Catholic Church. 3. Breadth of faith and belief.

catholicon In the Greek Orthodox Church, the main church of a monastery.

catholicos Title or designation of the head of the Armenian Church*, the Georgian Church, the Nestorian Church of the East, and the Syrian Orthodox Church* of Malankara, India.

Caton, William (1636–1665) One of the earliest Quakers* and associate of George Fox*. His *Journal* (published 1689) occupies a prominent position in Quaker devotional literature.

Cauchon, Pierre (?–1442) French bishop who presided over the trial of Joan of Arc* in 1431. He was posthumously excommunicated.

cauldron In Christian art, symbol of the apostle John.

Causes of Saints, Congregation for the Congregation established by Paul VI* in 1969 by splitting the Congregation of Sacred Rites*. It deals with beatification* and canonization*, procedures for declaring the doctors of the church*, and the authentification and preservation of relics*.

Caussade, Jean Pierre de (1675–1751) French ascetic writer. He joined the Jesuit Order in 1693. He tried to rehabilitate mysticism and Quietism* through his books, *Instruction Spirituelles en forme de Dialogue sur les Divers Etats d'Oraison* (1741) and *L'Abandon a la Providence Divine* (published 1867).

cautel Direction in the Roman Missal for the correct administration of the sacraments*.

CBN Christian Broadcasting Network*.

CCBI Council of Churches in Britain and Ireland*.

CCD Confraternity of Christian Doctrine*.

Cecilia, St. (second century) Martyr whose relics* were discovered in a Roman catacomb*. There is a church in her name in Rome*. She is the patroness of church music. Feast day: November 22.

Cecilian movement Movement in the Roman Catholic Church against the adoption of secular musical idiom in church music. The movement began in the nineteenth century and has continued into the present. The Allgemeine Caecilien-Verein was founded by Franz Witt in 1869 and sanctioned by Pope Pius IX*. It supports the needs for authentic editions of chant, congregational singing, musical education for the clergy, and church music in the vernacular.

cedana'awed In the Ethiopian Liturgy, veil used to cover the paten*.

CEF Child Evangelism Fellowship*.

Cefalu Romanesque cathedral built on the north coast of Sicily by the Norman king, Roger I. Its foundation stone was laid in 1131, and the facade was completed in 1240, but the whole building was finished only in the fifteenth century. The architects were perhaps Benedictines, but the structure betrays Nordic influences and gives the building an impression of impregnability.

CELAM Consejo Episcopal Latino-Americano, Conference of Latin American Bishops, established in 1956.

celebrant Priest or pastor who administers the Mass* or the Eucharist*. The title is an unhappy usage, since celebration* is the calling* of all God's people.

celebration Communion or the observance of sacraments.

celebret (Lat., let him celebrate) Document or commendatory letter authorizing a priest to celebrate the Eucharist* in a church not his own.

celestial hierarchy Order of celestial beings consisting of three groups of three choirs each. The first choir consists of seraphim, cherubim, and thrones; the second of denominations, virtues, and powers, and the third of principalities, archangels, and angels. See also DIONYSIUS THE PSEUDO-AREOPAGITE.

Celestine I, St. (d. 432) Pope from 422. He was a firm defender of orthodoxy* and condemned Pelagianism* and Nestorianism*.

Celestine III (c. 1106–1198) Pope from 1191. Birth name: Giacinto Babone. He was elected pope in his eighty-fifth year. Although his reign was marked by his inability to control the recklessness and cruelty of King Henry VI, he worked hard to organize another crusade and approved many military orders, including the Knights Templars*, the Hospitallers*, and the Teutonic Order.

Celestine V, St. (1215–1296) A celebrated ascetic, he founded the Celestine Order. When nearly 80 he

was elected pope in July 1294 but after a disastrous pontificate* of four months he abdicated in December of the same year. Boniface VIII*, his successor, had him arrested and imprisoned in the castle of Fumone, where he died.

Celestines Formerly, an ascetical congregation of the Benedictine Order, founded in Monte Morrone in central Italy by Peter of Morrone, who later became Pope Celestine V*, in 1294. It had a very severe discipline. At one time, it had as many as 120 monasteries. It was closed in 1785.

Celestius (fifth century) British heretic and friend of Pelagius*. He not only rejected the doctrine of grace* in favor of free will*, but denied original sin* itself. He was condemned by the Council of Carthage* in 411 and 414 and by the Council of Ephesus* in 431.

celibacy of the clergy Practice of ordaining only unmarried men as priests, followed most notably in the Roman Catholic Church. The requirement was spelled out at the Council of Elvira* (303) and became an ecclesiastical law* at the Lateran Council* of 1139 and was confirmed at the Council of Trent*. The Second Vatican Council* reaffirmed the law. The biblical sanction for celibacy is found in Matthew 19:12, 29 and 1 Corinthians 7:26–35, especially the latter, which states that celibacy is a condition for the more fervent consecration to God because it avoids earthly entanglements. It has become the subject of intense debate within the Catholic Church since the Second Vatican Council*.

cell 1. Small room in a monastery 2. In Evangelical churches, a small group that meets periodically for prayer, Bible study, and fellowship.

cella Small Christian chapel in a cemetery, used either as a place of worship or for commemorating the dead.

cellarer The official or obedientiary* responsible for catering in a medieval monastery. He was responsible for most of the shopping for materials, such as wood, iron, coal, and wax, as well as foods, and keeping the accounts for such purchases.

Celsus (second century) Greek pagan philosopher against whom Origen* wrote his classic apology, *Contra Celsum*. He debunked Christianity as a religion and certain Christian practices and doctrines. In his book, *The True Doctrine*, he blamed Christianity for undermining the Roman Empire.

Celtic Church Organized British Christianity that flourished in British Cambria, Wales, Cornwall, Brittany, Ireland, and Scotland between the second century and the arrival of St. Augustine* in the sixth century. Its two main characteristics were evangelism and monasticism*. St. Columba* founded the celebrated monastery at Iona*, Columbanus* monasteries at Luxeuil* and Bobbio*; St. Samson churches in Ireland and Cornwall; Dubricius, Illtyd, and David churches in Wales; and Comgall churches in Bangor*. In the fifth century St. Patrick* converted the Irish chieftains and founded churches and monasteries. Under the Celtic Church, the monastery rather than the diocese* was the basic unit of ecclesiastical organization, and the abbot was superior* to the bishop. Each monastery served a single tribe. The Celtic Christians had a distinctive tonsure* and their own method of calculating Easter*. These differences were settled at the Synod of Whitby* (663/64) which favored the Roman practices.

Celtic Cross Latin cross with a ring around the intersection of the two arms, now also used in Presbyterian churches.

Celtic Cross

cemetery (Gk., sleeping place) Burial place for the dead. Until the twentieth century, cemeteries were found in or close to churchyards*.

cenacle 1. Roman dining room. 2. The upper room in Jerusalem* where the Last Supper took place (Mark 14:15; Luke 22:12) and the Holy Spirit* descended on the day of the Pentecost* (Acts 1:13). 3. Retreat house.

cenae Also, cewa'e. In the Ethiopian Rite, the chalice*.

cenobite See COENOBITE.

censer Covered metal incense burner dangling from four chains, handled by the priest or deacon. See also THURIBLE.

censure Ecclesiastical penalty ranging from a reprimand, suspension, and exclusion from the sacrament* to interdiction and excommunication* and removal from office. Canon law* recognizes two kinds of censures, one in which the individual is notified while the other requires no such admonition.

Censer

centering prayer Also, prayer of quiet*; prayer of the heart*. Ancient form of Christian prayer in which the person who is praying concentrates, with eyes closed, on a single word representing some aspect of divine love. It is a deeply healing prayer similar to Hesychasm*.

centrally planned church Church with parts equal or nearly equal about the center. It may be square, round, octagonal, or of other geometrical form and is often shaped like a Greek cross*.

Cerdonians Heretical sect founded by Cerdo, the Syrian heretic who was a forerunner of Marcion*. It rejected most of the Bible with the exception of the Gospel of Luke and the epistles of Paul. It maintained that the God of the Old Testament and the Father of Jesus Christ were distinct and separate.

cere cloth Cloth impregnated with wax laid on the surface of the altar to prevent the linen cloths from being soiled by the holy oil* or wax drippings. See also CHRISMALE.

ceremonarius Master of ceremonies in a church.

ceremonial Ritualized performance of divine worship.

Cerinthus (c. 100) Heretic who was an enemy of St. John of the Book of Revelation. His heresy appears to have been a mix of Ebionitism and Gnosticism*. He taught that the world was created by an inferior demiurge* and that Jesus, a mere man, was chosen at the time of his baptism* by the supreme God to be Christ and to proclaim the kingdom of God*. Christ left Jesus just before the Crucifixion. Cerinthus envisioned the millennium* as a 1,000-year orgy of carnal pleasure.

Cerularius, Michael (d. 1059) Patriarch of Constantinople* (1043–1058) who precipitated the Great Schism* between the Greek and Latin churches. He disputed the papal assertion of authority and forced Latin churches in Constantinople to use Greek language and practices.

cessationism Belief that the charismata*—the supernatural gifts of the apostolic church—ceased

with the death of John, the last apostle, by the end of the first century or with the completion of the canon* of the Scripture. It was expanded influentially by B. B. Warfield*.

CEZMS Church of England Zenana Missionary Society.

Chabenel, Noel (1613–1649) French Jesuit missionary to the Indians of North America. He was martyred by the Iroquois Indians. Feast day: September 26.

chaburah (Heb., friend) In Talmudic Judaism, an informal band of friends who gathered together for devotional purposes. Jesus and his disciples have been described as a chaburah.

Chafer, Lewis Sperry (1871–1952) American Presbyterian clergyman who founded the Dallas Theological Seminary* in 1924. He served the seminary as president and professor of theology until his death. He is best known for his eight-volume *Systematic Theology* (1948) expounding dispensational premillennialism*.

Chair of St. Peter The authority of the pope as the successor of St. Peter*.

Chair of Unity Octave Period of prayer for Christian unity held annually from January 18 to 25. It was founded in 1908 by Lewis Thomas Wattson, an American Episcopalian* clergyman. Its distinctive purpose was the corporate reunion of the Anglican Church* with the Roman Catholic Church*.

Chalcedon, Council of Fourth Ecumenical Council held in the town of Chalcedon in Asia Minor (near Byzantium*) in 451. It was convened by the Emperor Marcian to deal with the Eutychian heresy. It was attended by between 400 and 500 bishops. After annulling the decisions of the Latrocinium* and condemning Eutyches*, the council drew up the Chalcedon Definition*. All of its enactments were accepted by the pope except the one that made the patriarch* of Constantinople* second only to Rome with exclusive right to ordain bishops in the eastern provinces of the Roman Empire.

Chalcedon, Definition of The statement of the Catholic faith made by the Council of Chalcedon*. It reaffirmed the definitions of Nicaea* and Constantinople and repudiated the Eutychian and Nestorian positions as heresies. Specifically, it rejected confusion or mixture of two natures in Christ. Christ is declared to be one person in two natures, divine, of the same

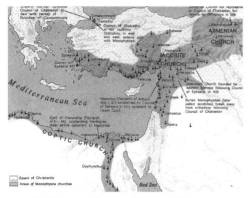

Map of Christianity at the Time of the Council of Chalcedon

Definition of Chalcedon

Therefore, following the holy fathers, we all with one accord teach men to acknowledge one and the same Son, our Lord Jesus Christ, at once complete in Godhead and complete in manhood, truly God and truly man, consisting also of a reasonable soul and body; of one substance with the Father as regards His Godhead, and at the same time of one substance with us as regards His manhood; like us in all respects, apart from sin, as regards His Godhead, begotten of the Father before the ages, but yet as regards His manhood, begotten, for us men and for our salvation, of Mary the Virgin, the God-bearer; one and the same Christ, Son, Lord, Only Begotten, recognized in two natures, without confusion, without change, without division, without separation; the distinction of natures being in no way annulled by the union, but rather the characteristics of each nature being preserved and coming together to form one person and subsistence, not as parted or separated into two persons, but one and the same Son and Only-Begotten God the Word, Lord Jesus Christ; even as the prophets from earliest times spoke of Him, and Our Lord Jesus Christ Himself taught us, and the creed of the Fathers has handed down to us.

substance as the Father and human as the same substance as us, united inseparably, unconfusedly, indivisibly, and unchangeably. His two natures are preserved in one *prosopon** and one *hypostasis**. Even though the definition was neither exact nor final, it was not universally accepted except in the Roman Catholic and Eastern Orthodox* churches. Many of the Lesser Eastern Churches* continued to espouse—and still do—the cause of Eutyches* and his follower, Jacob Baradeus*.

Chaldea Southern part of the valley of the Tigris and Euphrates* rivers.

Chaldean Christians Members of the Church of the East* in communion with Rome. They are found in Iraq and also in Malabar, India. The Uniat branch of the church arose out of a dispute over succession to the patriarchate* in 1553. There were two lines of patriarchs, one named Simeon and the other named Elias. In 1681 another line of patriarchs was admitted to the Uniat family. Since 1830 the patriarchate of Babylon*, as it is called, has been located in Baghdad. They follow the Syriac* liturgical tradition and language.

chalice Cup holding the wine of the Eucharist*. The earliest types of chalice were bowls with two handles, but without a stem. Later, the stem was elongated and the bowl made smaller. Originally made of glass or earthenware, they were fashioned of gold and silver in the Middle Ages.

Chalice, Antioch Silver and silver-gilt chalice*, now in the Metropolitan Museum, New York, found near Antioch* in 1910. It featured two figures of Christ, one bearded and one beardless, with ten other figures, perhaps apostles, a lamb*, an eagle*, and a symbolic vine. It dates from the fifth century.

chalice, mixed Eucharist* chalice holding wine mixed with water.

chalice veil Cloth, sometimes made of silk, for covering the empty chalice* and the paten* in the Eucharist*.

Challoner, Richard (1691–1781) English Roman Catholic devotional writer. Born to Protestant parents, he became a Catholic at the age of 13. He was consecrated a bishop at Hammersmith in 1741 and vicar apostolic* in 1758. He produced a revised version of the Douai* Old and New Testaments and two popular devotional works, *The Garden of the Soul** (1740) and *Meditations for Every Day of the Year* (1753). He also translated the *Imitation of Christ** and prepared a history of Catholic martyrs.

Chalice

Chalmers, James (1841–1901) Scottish Congregational* missionary to New Guinea. In 1867 he sailed for the Cook Islands in Polynesia under the auspices of the London Missionary Society, and ten years later he moved to New Guinea to work among the cannibals. He opened up the island to the gospel. He vigorously opposed attempts to westernize the native dress or customs. He was murdered by the cannibals he served while on an expedition into the interior. His two books, *Work and Adventure in New Guinea* (1885) and *Pioneering in New Guinea* (1887), are records of his mission.

Chalmers, Thomas (1780–1847) Scottish theologian and churchman. At the Tron Church in Glasgow he pastored to over 10,000 people. In 1832 he became moderator of the Church of Scotland* and the leader of spokesmen for the Evangelical party. During the next decade he helped to build 216 churches. After the Disruption* of 1843 he became the leader of the Free Church assembly and the first principal of the New College, Edinburgh,

the Free Church's first theological college. His *Institutes of Theology* was published posthumously in 1849.

chamberlain 1. Cardinal who administers the Vatican* properties. 2. Secretary-treasurer of the College of Cardinals*.

Chamberlain, Jacob (1835–1908) Dutch Reformed Church* missionary to India. In 1859 he joined the Arcot Mission in South India and founded two hospitals in Telugu country. From 1873 to 1894 he chaired the committee to revise the Telugu Bible and also compiled a Telugu hymnbook. He became the first moderator* of the Synod of South India in 1902.

Chambers, Oswald (1874–1917) Bible teacher and writer. Converted by Charles Spurgeon*, he trained for the Baptist ministry. From William Quarrier, founder of Orphan Homes, he learned a life of prayer and became a traveling missioner for the Pentecostal League of Prayer. He became principal of the Bible Training College at Clapham Common (1911–1915) and superintendent of YMCA* in Egypt during World War I. His book, *My Utmost for His Highest,* is a devotional classic.

chambre ardent (Fr., burning chamber) Extraordinary session of a French court in the seventeenth and eighteenth centuries to pass final judgment on heretics.

Chaminade, Guillaume Joseph (1761–1850) Founder of the Marianist Sisters and of the Marianists (Society of Mary). After being expelled from France in 1797, he returned in 1801 and began to found various Marian* sodalities and religious societies which developed into the Marianist Sisters (or Daughters of Mary, 1816) and Marianists (1817). They take a fourth vow of stability requiring daily consecration to the Virgin Mary*.

Champagnat, Marcelin (1798–1840) Founder of the Marist Brothers of the Schools in 1817. The Marists* received papal approval in 1863 and soon spread rapidly throughout the world.

Champmol Carthusian charterhouse* near Dijon in Burgundy. The foundation stone was laid in

1383 by Margaret of Flanders and Philip the Bold. The plans were drawn up by the architect Drouet de Dammartin. The dramatic carvings were done by Nicholas Sluter, also called Celoistre, who also did the Well of Moses, between 1385 and 1406. Almost 30 feet high, it is surrounded by statues of Moses, David, Isaiah, Jeremiah, Zacharias, and Daniel.

chancel Sanctuary of a church including the main body of the church east of the nave* and the transepts*, including the choir and the altar or communion table and sometimes the baptistery. Sometimes a screen* separates the chancel* and the nave.

chancel, split Front of a church sanctuary that features a pulpit on one side and a lectern* on the other side of the chancel.

chancellor 1. In the Roman Catholic Church, the head of the papal chancery*, or the priest who cares for the diocesan archives. 2. In the Church of England*, official who presides over the bishop's consistory* court and advises the bishop on legal matters and administers his temporal affairs. He issues marriage licenses, hears applications for dispensations*, and hears complaints against clerics. He also serves as the bishop's vicar general* and principal official with wide educational functions. The title is also applied to certain residentiary canons in cathedrals.* Originally the chancellor was the head of the cathedral school.

chancery, apostlic/papal In the Roman Catholic Church, Vatican* office, headed by a cardinal, which issues bulls* establishing new dioceses*.

chancery, diocesan Department of a bishop's* court in charge of a diocesan documents. It is headed by the chancellor.

Channing, William Ellery (1780–1842) American Unitarian leader. He set forth the tenets of Unitarianism*, such as the rejection of the Trinity* and the divinity of Christ. In 1820 he organized the Berry Street Conference of Liberal Ministers out of which the American Unitarian Association developed in 1825.

chanson spirituelle (Fr., sacred song) Song created by replacing the original secular text of a chanson with a religious text. Both Claude Le Jeune and Orlando Lassus contributed to this genre.

chant Melodic recitation of prose, especially the Psalms. Throughout the Middle Ages the Psalms were chanted in unison to a series of short, plainsong* melodies known as tones. See also AMBROSIAN CHANT; ANGLICAN CHANT; BYZANTINE CHANT; GREGORIAN CHANT; MOZARABIC CHANT; PLAINSONG.

chantry 1. Part of a church set apart for the offering of Mass* for the founder or some special person, or a small chapel where masses are chanted for the soul of the founder or persons designated by him. 2. Endowment for the priests to sing or say Mass* for the soul of the founder or others nominated by him.

Chao Tzu-ch'en (Zhao, Zichen) (1888–1979) Chinese theologian. His earlier theology was influenced by Confucian models without any supernatural elements, but later, especially after his imprisonment by the Japanese, he become more conservative and Barthian. Among his later works is the *Life of Paul* (1947).

chapel 1. Originally, a shrine containing a relic*. By extension, a place of worship that is distinct from a parish church belonging to a school, college, military installation, hospital, embassies, or any similar institution. 2. Part of a cathedral or parish church where there is a separate altar or communion table, called the "Lady Chapel*." 3. A nonconformist place of worship. 4. In Ireland, a Roman Catholic place of worship. 5. On the Continent, chancel* of a church and, by extension, the musical choir.

chapel of ease A building in a parish church subordinate to the mother church for the use of parishioners*.

chapel, proprietory Place of worship built by subscription and maintained by private individuals but without parochial* rights.

chapel royal A place of worship attached to a royal court under the direct control of a monarch.

chaplain Priest or minister in charge of a chapel serving kings, bishops, and other dignitaries. Originally, they were custodians of sacred relics* in a royal chapel*. The military services of most Christian countries have chaplains* attached to their units. In the army, they hold a rank equal to a captain or above. There are chaplains in prisons, campuses, legislative bodies, hospitals, and athletic teams.

chaplet Any one of the three parts into which the rosary is divided, each corresponding to a set of 5 of the 15 mysteries*. It contains five decades, each devoted to one mystery. Sometimes applied to the string of beads constructed to count the prayers of one complete chaplet of the rosary and sometimes to the devotion itself.

Chapman, John Wilbur (1859–1918) Presbyterian evangelist who devoted more than half his ministry to missions. He was for some time an associate of D. L. Moody* and director of the Winona Lake Bible Conference. He wrote *The Surrendered Life*, a devotional classic.

Chappotin de Neuville, Helene de (1839–1904) Also, Maries de la Passion. Founder of the Franciscan Missionaries of Mary. In 1864 she entered the Congregation of Marie Reparatrix and was sent to Madura, India, where she worked until 1876. She then left for Rome*, where Pius IX* approved in 1877 the new missionary congregation, the Missionaries of Mary, dedicated exclusively to universal mission. In 1882 it became part of the Franciscan family as the Franciscan Missionaries of Mary.

chapter 1. Division of the Bible. 2. Division of the rule of a monastery. 3. Membership of a religious house. 4. Assembly of the members of a religious house. Meetings of a whole province or order of monks are known as provincial chapters or general chapters. 5. Branch of a religious house. 6. Assembly of monks or canons in a cathedral or collegiate church presided over by the dean and responsible for its administration and worship. 7. Clergy of a rural deanery* under the chairmanship of a rural dean.

chapter, greater Prebendaries* and honorary canons* in a cathedral or collegiate church.

chapter house Building used for meetings of a cathedral or monastic chapter*. They are rectangular or polygonal in shape with vaulted roofs. They were often built off the eastern end of the cloister* with a low vestibule and a double entrance.

chapter, lesser Residentiary members of the assembly of canons* in a cathedral or collegiate church.

chapter, little Short lesson from the Breviary*. Also called *Lectio Brevis*, short reading.

chapter of faults Meeting of members of a monastery in which each member engages in self-accusation for weaknesses and failures.

character, sacramental In Roman Catholic theology, the permanent imprint of divine grace* left by the sacraments*, such as baptism*, comfirmation, and ordination, which may not therefore be repeated.

Chardin See TEILHARD DE CHARDIN.

Chardon, Louis (1595–1651) French Dominican mystic and theologian. He spent most of his life as a spiritual director* at the Annunciation Priory. His principal work is *The Cross of Jesus* (1647) in which he argued that suffering is an integral part of grace. He also wrote *Meditations on the Passion of our Lord Jesus Christ* (1650) and translated the works of Catherine of Siena* and John Tauler*.

charge In the Methodist Church, a local church (station charge) or a group of local churches (circuit charge). The charge conference involves an annual meeting with the district superintendent, who reviews budgetary and administrative matters.

charisma/charismata (Gk., gift) In the New Testament, a special gift bestowed by the Holy Spirit* according to his will in proportion to the recipient's faith for the profit of the whole fellowship and for the work of the ministry to enable a Christian to fulfill certain assigned functions or to follow a spiritual vocation* (1 Cor. 12:4, 6–7,

11). Among these gifts are word of wisdom*, word of knowledge*, faith*, healing, the working of miracles, prophecy, speaking in tongues*, and the interpretation of tongues*.

Charismatic renewal Worldwide renewal and revival* movement, also known as neo-Pentecostalism*, emphasizing the charismata*, or the gifts of the Holy Spirit*, demonstrative worship, theological Fundamentalism*, and evocative music. Among the Protestants, it has found a natural home among independent churches with Pentecostal antecedents, but the classical Pentecostals have often been cautious. In the Roman Catholic Church, it is a lay movement recognized by the Vatican*. The term was coined by H. Bredesen and J. Stone in 1963 to describe a growing trend that later developed in three separate sectors: mainline Protestant churches from 1950, Roman Catholic Church from 1967 and independent churches from the late 1960s.

Key people and institutions in the movement were Nights of Prayer for Worldwide Revival and London Healing Mission in the United Kingdom; The Full Gospel Business Men's Fellowship International*; and the ministries of Dennis Bennett*, T. L. Osborn*, and Michael Harper*. The movement resembled in many respects the earlier Pentecostal movement because both had a strong lay character with an emphasis on every-member ministry. Their assemblies were characterized by vocal praise, long prayers, and personal testimonies.

The Charismatic Roman Catholic movement has given rise to intentional or covenant communities such as the People of Praise, Servants of the Lord and Word of God* (now Sword of the Spirit*), and centers for ministry and healing. There are Charismatic Catholic television personalities, such as Mother Angelica* and John Bertolucci*, and specialized ministries, such as FIRE, SHARE, LAMP, Calix, Centurions, and Families in Christ. The Charismatic renewal has had strongest impact among the Mennonites* and the Episcopalians but has significantly and widely influenced all major denominations except Orthodoxy. Independent and nondenominational Charismatic groups came into prominence in the early 1970s with the impact of Christian Growth Ministries led by Derek Prince,

Bob Mumford*, Charles Simpson, Ern Baxter, and Don Basham*, who introduced discipleship into Charismatic circles.

Soon there were large networks, including the International Convention of Faith Ministries, Liberty Fellowship, People of Destiny, Vineyard churches, and the Abbot Loop Fellowship in the United States; Pioneer, New Frontiers, Salt and Light, and Ichthus in the United Kingdom; Emmanuel, Chemin Neuf, Lion de Juda (now Beatitudes), and Pain de Vie in France. The movement has produced several megachurches, including Charles Green's Word of Faith Temple in New Orleans; Lester Sumrall's Cathedral of Praise in South Bend, Indiana; Wally and Marilyn Hickey's Happy Church in Denver, Colorado; Billy Joe and Sharon Daugherty's Victory Christian Center in Tulsa, Oklahoma; Ron Tucker's Grace World Outreach Center in Maryland Heights, Missouri; and John and Anne Jimenez's Rock Church in Virginia Beach, Virginia.

Among the more prominent individual ministries are those of Kenneth Hagin* in Tulsa and Kenneth Copeland* in Fort Worth, Texas. A number of groups have become quasi denominations. These include Chuck Smith's Calvary Chapels*, Bob Weiner's Maranatha Christian churches, Larry Lea's Churches on the Rock, and John Wimber's* Vineyard Christian Fellowships*. Since 1994 the Charismatic renewal has been boosted by the so-called Toronto Blessing*, which has introduced holy laughter* into the Christian lexicon. Since the 1990s the movement has had to face some points of tension, particularly over the role of apostles and prophets, signs and wonders, healing and prosperity, the "positive confession"* teaching of certain televangelists and the question whether Christians can be troubled or possessed by demons.

Charlemagne (742–814) First emperor of the Holy Roman Empire, who dominated the religious and political life of Europe in the early Middle Ages. A wise and benevolent ruler, he sponsored schools and monasteries. Through his encouragement of letters, he inspired the Carolingian Renaissance*. He encouraged Alcuin* to revise the text of the Bible and promoted the Roman Mass* and liturgical uniformity within the church. He made provision for a standard homiliary* and an authorized collection of canon law*. His palace school and library were remarkable institutions that brought together Christian intellectuals like Alcuin of York* and Theodulf.

Charlemagne

Charles Borromeo, St. See BORROMEO, CHARLES.

Charles Martel (c. 688–741) Also known as "Charles the Hammer." Frankish ruler who saved Christian Europe from the onslaught of the Muslim barbarians at the Battle of Poitiers in 732. He was the grandfather of Charlemagne*.

Charles, Thomas (1755–1814) Welsh Methodist churchman, a founder of the British and Foreign Bible Society*. He was converted to Evangelical Christianity under the ministry of Daniel Rowland. He was a pioneering organizer of Sunday schools* and wrote a popular catechism*, *Yr Hyffordwr*, and a Bible dictionary, both of which had great influence on Welsh Christians. The need for Welsh Bibles* led to his participation in the efforts that founded the British and Foreign Bible Society* (BFBS). He himself edited the Welsh version of the Bible for BFBS. Charles is considered the greatest Welsh Calvinist Methodist leader after Williams Pantycelyn and Daniel Rowland.

Charpentier, Marc-Antoine (1645–1704) French composer of sacred music. From 1688 he was music director at the Jesuit Church in Paris and Saint-Chapelle*. His output consisted of 11 masses, 207 motets*, including 36 oratorios*, 84 psalm settings, 10 Magnificats*, 54 lessons and responsories for tenebrae*, 37 antiphons*, 19 hymns, 9 settings of the Litany of Loreto*, 4 settings of *Te Deum**, and 4 sequences.

charterhouse Carthusian religious house.

chartion In the Byzantine Rite*, authorization for the consecration of an altar written on a piece of parchment* and placed inside the pillars of the altar.

chartophylax In the Byzantine Church*, the diocesan chancellor under the bishop.

Chartres Town about 50 miles south of Paris famous for its Gothic* cathedral built between 1130 and 1230. Described as the "Acropolis of France," Chartres is the radiant queen of all cathedrals. Since 876 Chartres has preserved a supposed robe of the Virgin Mary* which Charlemagne* received as a gift on his crusade to Jerusalem*. In 1020 a fire destroyed the original Carolingian building. Rebuilding of the main church was completed in the twelfth century and of the two towers in the thirteenth century. One of Chartres's towers is Romanesque, the other Gothic*, reflecting the cathedral's construction during a transitional period between architectural styles. However, in 1194 a fire destroyed the cathedral again, and it was rebuilt again accord-

Chartres Cathedral

ing to the original plans. Beside the sculptures, the chief glory of Chartres is its stained-glass windows. Originally there were 186 of them of which 152 have survived. Chartres was miraculously saved from the plundering mob during the French Revolution and survives as a miracle of Gothic* art.

Chartreuse, La Grande Chartreuse monastery in Grenoble, in the Dauphine Alps, where the Carthusian Order originated and where Chartreuse liqueur was made by the monks.

Grande Chartreuse Monastery

chartsveratz In the Armenian calendar, Feast of the Exaltation of the Holy Cross between September 11 and 17.

chastity (Lat., *castitas*, purity) 1. Abstinence from sexual misconduct; freedom from immorality and lewdness. 2. Moral and spiritual purity.

chasuble Sleeveless outer garment worn by the celebrants of the Eucharist* as the symbol of charity. In the Eastern Church*, it is known as phelonion*.

Chateaubriand, Francois Rene, Vicomte de (1768–1848) French statesman, writer, and Christian apologist. He was converted in London and wrote the famous defense of his faith in *The Genius of Christianity* (1802). He tried to discredit the rationalist

opponents of Christianity by transferring the debate from the plane of reason to that of feeling. He demonstrated that Christianity was the fountain of art and civilization in Europe. He also wrote *Les Martyrs, ou le Triomphe de la Religion Chretienne* (1809).

Chaumonot, Joseph Marie (1611–1693) French Jesuit missionary to Quebec and New York.

Chautauqua movement American movement to promote universal education, begun in 1874 at Chautauqua, New York, as a summer course for Sunday school teachers. It holds an annual assembly marked by outstanding lectures and artistic presentations, and provides home study courses as extension programs.

chazranion (Gk., walking stick) In the Byzantine tradition, a bishop's* staff, usually a decorated ebony stick, with a knob of silver or ivory at the tip.

cheap grace See GRACE, CHEAP.

Cheese, John Ethelstan (1877–1959) Independent missionary in Somalia, described as the "holiest man in Somalia." Although he did not convert anyone, he established the presence of Christ in the horn of Africa for 33 years.

cheirotonia (Gk., extending the hand) Sacramental ordination of deacon, priest, or bishop by episcopal laying on of hands*.

Chelcicky, Peter (c. 1390–1460) Czech founder of the Chelcic Brethren. Under the influence of John Wycliffe*, he condemned the worldly power of the church and anticipated the Anabaptists* in his pacifism and rejection of oaths. His ideas are contained in the *Net of Faith* (1440). The Bohemian Brethren* movement (later the Unitas Fratrum or Moravians) grew out of the Chelcic Brethren.

Chemnitz, Martin (1522–1586) Lutheran theologian. A friend of Melanchthon*, he became interested in theology about 1553 and drew up the Formula of Concord*. He defended the Lutheran doctrine of the real presence* of Christ in the Eucharist* and was one of the main influences on Lutheran doctrine and practice. His most important theological treatises are the *Examen Concilii Tridentini* in four volumes, an attack on the Council of Trent*, *De Duabus Naturis in Christo,* and *Loci Theologici.* He took part in the Adiaphorist dispute and persuaded the Saxons and the Swabians to accept the Formula of Concord*.

Cherubicon The Cherubic hymn sung at the Great Entrance* by the choir in the Eastern Liturgy since 574: "We who in a mystery represent the cherubim and sing the thrice-holy hymn to the life-giving Trinity, let us now lay aside every care of this life, for we are about the receive the king of all, invisibly escorted by the king of hosts."

Chester Beatty Papyri Portions of three New Testament manuscripts designated P45, P46, and P47 comprising 126 leaves, found near Memphis, on the banks of the Nile, and acquired by Chester Beatty from an Egyptian dealer in 1930. They are a century or more older than the earliest vellum manuscript. Most of the papyri are in the Chester Beatty Library in Dublin.

Chester Beatty Papyri Fragment

Chesterton, Gilbert Keith (1874–1936) Catholic essayist and writer. His literary reputation rests on his defense of Christian orthodoxy* and medieval culture in *Heretics* (1905) and *Orthodoxy* (1908). He created Father Brown, a portly Catholic priest, as detective in his Father Brown stories. He was a Catholic parallel to C. S. Lewis*, and is still widely appreciated in Catholic circles.

Chevalier, Jules (1824–1907) French founder of two Roman Catholic missionary societies, Society of the Missionaries of the Sacred Heart of Jesus (1854) and Congregation of the Daughters of Our Lady of the Sacred Heart (1883).

chevet In European churches, eastern end of an ambulatory with radiating apsidal chapels.

Chevetogne Benedictine community now at Chevetogne founded in 1925 at Amay-sur-Meuse by Lambert Beauduin* in response to Pope Pius XI's* call for Christian unity. It seeks to establish closer relations with the Anglican churches* on the one hand and Eastern churches* on the other. The community is divided into two groups: one following the Latin rite and the other the Greek rite.

Chicago Call Appeal signed by 42 leading Evangelicals in 1977 reaffirming the historical roots of Evangelical Christianity, such as creedal identity and fidelity to the Bible.

Chicago School of Theology Liberal theology associated with Shailer Mathews and others of the Divinity School of the University of Chicago. They interpreted theology less from a moral than from a social, cultural, and psychological basis. The central themes of the Chicago School were a sociological focus, use of the German historical-critical method, and an appropriation of Darwinism and the philosophies of William James and John Dewey. Among its leaders were George Burman Foster, Gerald Birney Smith, Henry Nelson Wieman, Bernard M. Loomer, Daniel Day Williams, and Bernard E. Meland.

Chicago-Lambeth Articles Also, Chicago Quadrilateral; Lambeth Quadrilateral*. Four principles on which Christian churches could agree to bring about unity, drawn up by William Reed Huntington. They are: adherence to the holy Scriptures as the ultimate standard of faith; adherence to the Apostles' Creed* and the Nicene Creed*; adherence to the two sacraments of baptism* and the Lord's Supper*; and adherence to a belief in the historic episcopate*.

Child, Brevard Springs (1923–) American Old Testament scholar who taught at Yale. He is best known for his canonical criticism which held that a critical study of the books of the Bible must be based on their final form. He tried to stem the tide of minute dissection of the texts.

Child Evangelism Fellowship International organization working with children founded by Jesse Irwin Overholtzer in 1937. It is based in Warrenton, Missouri. It originally focused on Bible classes (Good News Clubs) to which were later added prayer programs, Radio Kids Bible Club, the magazine *Evangelizing Today's Child,* summer programs, overseas summer missions program, a children's television program (The Treehouse Club), telephone outreach (Tel-A-Story), video training, and a summer camping program.

Childermas Feast of the Holy Innocents* on December 28, commemorating the children slain by Herod at the birth of Christ.

children of God 1. Believers redeemed and adopted as his children by Jesus Christ. 2. Cult, established in the 1968 by David Berg, later known as Moses David or Mo. In the 1970s its name was changed to Family of Love. It was an offshoot of the Jesus movement*, but later degenerated into a promiscuous group with communes of followers living together and practicing prostitution.

Children of the Light An early name of Friends or Quakers*.

Children's Crusade A peasant movement led by a boy named Stephen of Cloyes with the ostensible purpose of recovering Jerusalem* from Muslim rule. The crusade began in 1212 in France and Germany and went as far as Genoa when the children were dispersed. Some were sold into slavery, while others died of disease and hunger.

chiliasm (Gk., *chilioi,* one thousand) Doctrine that anticipates Christ's return to earth to rule for 1,000 years. Also known as millenarianism*.

chimere Long sleeveless satin garment worn by a bishop over his rochet*.

China Inland Mission (CIM) Mission to China, founded by Hudson Taylor* in 1866 as successor to the China Evangelization Society. By 1895 CIM had 40 percent of all Protestant missionaries in China and by 1935 it had 1,368 expatriate missionaries working in every province. CIM suffered during the Boxer Rebellion* of 1900 and the Communist takeover in 1949. After the fall of China to the Communists, the name was changed to Overseas Missionary Fellowship*.

China Rites controversy Debate about the degree to which non-Christian religious practices and superstitions, such as ancestor worship, should be tolerated or permitted by Christian missionaries. The controversy arose from the methods of Matteo Ricci*, a Roman Catholic priest who worked in China from 1582 to 1610, and who tried to incorporate Confucian ideals into the Christian message. These rites were condemned by Clement XI* in 1704 and 1715.

Chionadites School of folk icon* painters operating from the Chionadi village in Epiros, Greece. Their icons represented unusual incidents from the Scriptures and the lives of the saints.

Chi-Rho Greek initial letters of the name of Christ symbolizing his name. They have the form of X interposed on P. See also CHRISMON.

Cho, Paul Yonggi (1936–) Korean pastor. Raised as a Buddhist, he was converted after receiving a physical healing. After graduating from an Assemblies of God* Bible school, he started a tent church in Seoul in 1958. Named Full Gospel Central Church in 1962, its membership grew from 2,000 in 1964 to 500,000 by 1990. The membership is sustained and promoted through thousands of believers' cells. Cho espouses a form of positive confession* in which his followers are asked to visualize, dream, incubate, and hatch.

choir 1. Organized group of singers in a worship service. 2. Place set apart for such a group and the clergy in a church, formerly in the apse* behind the altar and later at the eastern end of the nave* or in the chancel*. Derived from the *schola cantorum** in Rome and the choral foundations of the Reformation*. In churches outside the Roman Catholic and mainline Protestant tradition, the trend is to give the congregation fuller scope for participation in singing. Choirs are generally mixed, including both men and women.

choir gown The traditional dress of the choir, a surplice* worn over the cassock*.

choir loft Elevated portion of a church where the choir sings.

choir office Worship service conducted in the choir portion of the chancel*.

choir screen Division between the nave* and the choir. See ROOD.

choir sisters Formerly, nuns who were obliged to attend all choir offices*.

choir stalls Pews set apart for the choir.

chorale 1. Metrical congregational hymn introduced into the worship service at the time of the Reformation*. Melody for a chorale was often taken from a folk song and then given a sacred text, a process called contrafactum*. Many chorales were composed by Luther* himself. 2. Simple hymn tune sung in unison.

chorale cantata Cantata in which several, or all, of the movements are based on the same melody. An example is Luther's "A Mighty Fortress Is Our God."

chorale fantasia Composition, usually for the organ, freely based on the inventive use of a chorale melody, as in Bach's* "Fantasy on Christ Lay in the Bonds of Death."

chorale motet Elaborate treatment of a chorale melody in which each phrase is treated successively as a point of imitation.

chorale partitia Set of variations for organ on each verse of a chorale melody.

chorale prelude Organ piece based on a chorale melody.

chorepiscopus A rural bishop who exercised limited episcopal functions. They were present at the Council of Nicaea* (325), Council of Antioch (341), Council of Ephesus* (431), and Council of Chalcedon* (451). The office has died out in the West, but survives as a title in the Syrian Orthodox Church* of Antioch and Malankara, India.

Chorin Cistercian abbey in Chorin, north of Berlin, founded in 1258. In 1278 it was moved to the shores of Lake Chorin and consecrated in 1334. It is a cruciform* pillared basilica* with three naves, a gallery, and a two-tiered transept*. It is the most outstanding example of brick Gothic*. The Cistercians* were bound by a vow of poverty, and there were no costly gold or silver furnishings or costly carpets. The massive nave* of the church was bare, devoid of decoration. The Thirty Years' War and the Reformation* dealt a death blow to the monastery. In 1542 the buildings were taken over by the state, and they lay in ruins for centuries. In the nineteenth century, the entire complex was restored to its former glory.

chorister 1. Choir boy or singer. 2. Choir leader.

chorrock Black gown of the European clergy, also called talar*.

chosen people Christians as the elect* of God, chosen according to his purpose and for his glory (1 Pet. 1:1–2; 2:9).

chosiac In the Coptic tradition, a 45-day fast prior to Advent*.

chrism (Gk., *chrisma,* anointing) Mixture of oil and balsam used in both Roman and Eastern Orthodox* churches in certain liturgical ceremonies, especially, baptism*, confirmation*, and ordination, and in the consecration of churches, altars, chalices*, patens*, and church bells. The use of special oils for the consecration of kings and priests was practiced in the Old Testament, and it was taken over by the early church as a mystical symbol of salvation*. Olive oil symbolizes strength and balsam the sweet fragrance of virtue. The consecration of chrism is an impressive ceremony conducted at a special Mass* celebrated in cathedral churches on Maundy Thursday* in the Roman Catholic Church. In the Greek Church, the ceremony is conducted by the patriarch*.

chrismale/chrismatory 1. Small cylindrical metal jar for keeping three kinds of holy oils*, oil for the catechumens*, oil of the sick, and chrism*. One set of these vessels is kept in the sacristy* and the other in the chancel*. 2. Cloth wrapped around relics*, or the wax-soaked linen cloth used on a newly consecrated altar. 3. White robe of the newly baptized.

chrismation 1. The liturgical rite of applying chrism*. 2. In the Eastern Church*, anointing a newly baptized person with oil and the sign of the cross as the seal of the gift of the Holy Spirit*.

chrismon 1. Chi-Rho* as a monogram, used almost universally as a Christian symbol. 2. Any of various Christian three-dimensional symbols. They include: (a) Crowned fish*, iota chi, HIS* in a circle or cross. (b) Eight-pointed star, cornerstone, eye of God. (c) Trinity*. (d) Nativity. (e) Celtic, Eastern Latin, and Jerusalem cross*, crown of thorns, shepherd's crook, omega* and cross, alpha and cross. (f) Iota chi with lilies (resurrection). (g) Butterfly*, orb, and cross (eternity*).

chrisom White cloth or robe thrown over a baptized child especially to cover the head where the baptismal oil was placed, to symbolize innocence. It was later given as an offering at the mother's purification or churching*.

Christ (Gk., the Anointed One) Derived from the Hebrew concept of Messiah, the title was applied to Jesus of Nazareth (Matt. 16:13–17; Gal. 1:6; Heb. 9:11). See also JESUS CHRIST.

Chi-Rho

Christ candle Small candle, decorated with Chi-Rho* or other symbol of Christ, sometimes added to the Advent* wreath.

Christ

Christ child Picture or image of Christ as a child.

Christ Church, Oxford One of the largest constituent colleges of the University of Oxford founded in 1525 on the site of the monastery of St. Frideswide under Henry VIII. It also included the cathedral of the Anglican diocese of Oxford. See also OXFORD CATHEDRAL.

Christ mysticism Believer's mystical union with Christ as described by Paul* (2 Cor. 5:17).

Christ of faith Christ as proclaimed in the Gospels as distinct from the Jesus of history* as presented by scholars.

Christ the King Feast observed in the Roman Catholic Church on the last Sunday before the beginning of Advent*. It was instituted by Pope Pius XI* in 1925.

Christadelphians Heretical, anti-Trinitarian sect founded by John Thomas in 1848. It has branches in the United States and the United Kingdom. Their churches are known as ecclesia*, and they have a democratic organization with no clergy. Most of their doctrines are set forth in *Christendom Astray from the Bible* by Robert Roberts, the influential British leader of the sect. They accept the Bible as their sole authority and look forward to the imminent return of Christ, but reject the Trinity*, immortality* of the soul, the divinity of Jesus Christ, and redemption* through the cross.

Christe eleison 1. Words of an invocation* in Latin litanies preceded and followed by Kyrie eleison*, each of the three petitions being said three times. 2. The musical setting for this prayer.

Christendom The realm of Christ, in the temporal sense of countries where Christians live in substantial numbers, and where Christian values and traditions are dominant, especially with a national or state church, or in a spiritual sense of constituting the kingdom of God* with Christ as its monarch. In the Middle Ages, it was the dream

Christ in Majesty

of a united Christian realm under one temporal or spiritual ruler. It is often used of the church-dominated order that prevailed in the Western world for centuries until the latter half of the twentieth century.

christening Rite of baptism*, especially the act or ceremony of naming a child.

Christ-event Neo-Orthodox term for the eternal redemptive work symbolized by the death and Resurrection of Jesus Christ.

Christian (*noun*) 1. Person who believes in Jesus Christ and follows or tries to follow his teachings. 2. Name by which a follower of Jesus Christ is known, first used at Antioch*, between 40 and 44 (Acts 11:26). In the New Testament, it occurs only in two other places: Acts 26:28 and 1 Peter 4:16. Originally a pejorative epithet used by pagans, it replaced the earlier terms by which Christians were known, as disciples (Acts 11:26), brethren (Acts 1:16), saints (Acts 9:13; Rom. 12:13), the elect* (Rom. 8:33; Col. 3:12), Nazarenes* (Acts 24:5), and believers (Acts 2:44). 3. In Roman usage, person belonging to, or the property or slave of, Christ. (*adjective*) Of or relating to Christ, Christianity, or the Christian Church.

Christian Action 1. Lay apostolate* in the Roman Catholic Church. 2. Interdenominational movement for the application of Christian ideas and principles in public life.

Christian Aid Major British relief agency, now an arm of the Council of Churches for Britain and Ireland*.

Christian and Missionary Alliance Worldwide denomination founded in 1881 by A. B. Simpson* (1844–1919). It traces its roots to the American Holiness movement* and upholds historically orthodox and conservative doctrines, and is Fundamentalist, premillennial, and evangelistic with elements derived from Calvinism* and Wesleyanism. It acknowledges Christ as savior, sanctifier, healer, and coming Lord, is unswervingly loyal to the inerrancy of the Holy Scriptures, and the role of the Holy Spirit* in leading and empowering Christians. There are over 4,000 congregations in

North America with over 5,000 ministers, and over 1,000 missionaries serving in nearly 40 countries in six continents. The missionary emphasis has been historically strong in the CMA. Its missionaries planted the first churches in Hunan and Kwangsi in China, Vietnam and Cambodia, and the first Protestant churches in Venezuela and Ecuador. Its theological seminary is located in Nyack, New York.

Christian Booksellers Association (CBA) Group of over 3,000 Christian booksellers in the United States, nine international chapters, and over 650 suppliers, founded in 1950 and headquartered in Colorado Springs, Colorado.

Christian Broadcasting Network (CBN) Christian television network located in Virginia Beach, Virginia. It was founded in 1959 by Pat Robertson* in a small UHF station. At the time of the sale of its commercial division to Rupert Murdoch in 1997, it had 30 million subscribers. The primary Evangelical thrust of the network is the daily broadcast "700 Club," a talk show and news program. Supporting ministries include Regent University and Operation Blessing.

Christian Brothers Order of Brothers of Christian Schools*, founded in 1684 by St. John Baptist de la Salle*, as the first Catholic order devoted to the advancement of education.

Christian Brothers, Irish Institute for Christian education founded by Edward Ignatius Rice in 1802. It operates Christian schools* in various countries.

Christian Catholic Church Denomination founded as a theocracy* in 1896 in Chicago by John Alexander Dowie*, who called himself Elijah III, "the restorer." In 1901 he moved his community to Zion, Illinois. As first apostle after 1904, he enforced strict codes of conduct on members of the church and banned pork, alcohol, tobacco, and drugs. He was deposed in 1906.

Christian Century Ecumenical Protestant journal of news and opinion, founded in 1884 as the *Christian Oracle,* published by the Disciples of Christ*. It assumed its present name in 1900 and began to gain prominence about 1908 when Charles Clayton Morrison* became editor, dropped the denominational affiliation, and made it an ecumenical weekly. *Christian Century* reflects the liberal wing of mainline churches* and over the years has covered liberal issues, such as social gospel*, pacifism, and civil rights.

Christian Churches 1. Churches of Christ*. American denomination founded in the nineteenth century by Alexander Campbell* and other dissidents who broke away from Presbyterian, Methodist, and Baptist churches. A product of the Restoration movement*, its major doctrinal thrust is to align faith and practice with the Word of God*, which is accepted as "the perfect constitution for the worship, discipline and the government of the New Testament church." It affirms belief in the Trinity*, Christ as Messiah and Savior, virgin birth*, vicarious atonement*, spiritual rebirth, and baptism by immersion*. Their worship service is distinguished by liturgical practices of the Reformed* type. Sacraments* may be administered by local lay elders and even eucharistic prayers are ex tempore and not read from a book. They eschew musical instruments in worship music. The Lord's Supper* is the most significant act in public worship, and it is held every Sunday but in commemoration only. However, eucharistic theology is closer to Calvin* than Zwingli*. The unofficial service book is that by G. Edwin Osborn which emphasizes the centrality of the Lord's Supper* in worship.

2. Christian Church/Churches of Christ is an independent group that is more Evangelical in outlook. They hold Scripture as divinely inspired and maintain strong opposition to theological liberalism*. They believe in the need for baptism by immersion* for the remission of sins as a condition of church membership.

Christian Communities of Christ See DOUKHABORS.

Christian Endeavor Society Interdenominational youth association, founded in 1881 in Portland, Maine, by Francis E. Clark*. With the motto, "For Christ and the Church," it encourages young people to confess and to serve Christ in fellowship with their peers. It is affiliated with the World Christian Endeavor Union.

Christian Era Period of human history beginning with the birth of Christ, or Anno Domini*.

Christian flag Banner* adopted by a number of Protestant denominations and displayed in churches with a body of white and a blue field bearing a red Latin cross*.

Christian Knowledge, Society for the Promotion of Church of England* outreach* dating back to 1698 that has as its goal the distribution of Bible and Christian literature in various languages. Usually abbreviated as SPCK.

Christian Library Collection of 50 spiritual books selected by John Wesley* and issued between 1749 and 1755.

Christian Literature Crusade (CLC) Nondenominational foreign missionary and literature distribution agency founded by Kenneth and Bessie Adams in Colchester, England in 1939. They developed close ties with Norman P. Grubb and the World Evangelism Crusade. Today CLC operates in 45 countries on all continents.

Christian Majesty Title of the kings of France.

Christian Methodist Episcopal Church African-American denomination in southern USA with a Methodist structure, founded 1870 as the Colored Methodist Episcopal Church.

Christian name Name assumed at baptism*, or more loosely, of given name(s) as distinct from family name (surname).

Christian Nurture Title of book by Horace Bushnell* (1802–1876), published in 1846, emphasizing spiritual growth and maturity rather than rebirth itself. Reacting against the revivalism* of his day, which regarded a dramatic adulthood conversion as essential, Bushnell maintained that "a child is to grow up a Christian, and never know himself as being otherwise." His concept was developed in the twentieth century into an extremely humanistic type of religious education seeking to establish a perfect democratic society which was equated with the kingdom of God*.

Christian Radicals Term applied to the so-called "atheistic theologians" of the 1960s who wrote on the death of God theology*. Its leaders were Gabriel Vahanian, author of *The Death of God* (1961) and *Wait Without Idols* (1964); Harvey Cox, author of *The Secular City*; Thomas J. J. Altizer, author of *The Gospel of Christian Atheism* (1967); and Paul van Buren, author of *Secular Meaning of the Gospel* (1963).

Christian Reformed Church American Calvinist denomination, headquartered in Grand Rapids, Michigan, that was born of a secession, *Afscheiding**, of conservative Christians from the main Dutch Reformed Church* in the Netherlands. They emigrated to the United States, settling in what is now Michigan, in 1846. They were joined by more emigrants from Holland in the last decades of the nineteenth century. By World War I, Calvin College was founded, the first of three under its auspices. Its doctrinal standards are the Synod of Dort*, the Belgic Confession*, and the Heidelberg Catechism*.

Christian rock Contemporary Christian music combining Christian lyrics with rock tunes and styles. It is not used in traditional Christian worship except in churches targeting young people. The first all-Christian rock radio station was founded in 1975.

Christian Schools movement Evangelical movement promoting the establishment of schools based on Christian values and learning as alternatives to public schools. Most Christian schools are in the elementary and middle grades.

Christian Science Officially, Church of Christ, Scientist*. Heretical cult* founded by Mary Baker Eddy*, headquartered in Boston. Its core doctrine is physical healing through the manipulation of prayer. She set out her teaching in *Science and Health, with a Key to the Scriptures**, which she claimed was written under divine inspiration, although it is flawed by poor grammar and many inaccuracies. She promoted her book heavily, and its sales helped her to establish Christian Science as a church devoted to her ideas in 1879. It was reorganized on a permanent basis in 1892. The church is governed by a board of five directors in accordance with the *Church Manual* prepared by the founder. The church has no preachers and no sermons. Instead, each church has two readers who read portions of the Scriptures to the assembly followed by hymns and a selection from *Science and Health*. Interpretation of the Scriptures, outside the founder's comments, is forbidden. The divinity of Jesus is denied, although the historicity of the Gospels is accepted. One of the chief assets of the church is the newspaper, *Christian Science Monitor*.

Christian Socialism An idealist movement combining socialism with Christian ethics and values, founded by a group of Anglicans in England, especially, J. M. F. Ludlow*, F. D. Maurice*, and Charles Kingsley*. The purpose of Christian Socialism was, in the words of Maurice, to "Christianize socialism and to socialize Christendom." It was a reaction against the dominant materialism of the age, laissez-faire economics, and Anglican indifference to social issues. Christian Socialism did not have a significant impact on church or society, but inspired later groups such as the Guild of St. Matthew.

Christian year 1. Ecclesiastical calendar* of the seasons and holy days and feasts of the church. Beginning with Advent* and Christmas*, the Christian year proceeds through Epiphany*, Lent*, Holy Week*, Easter*, Whitsuntide* or Pentecost*, and Kingdomtide*. See CHURCH YEAR. 2. A collection of hymns, *The Christian Year,* by John Keble* published in England in 1827.

Christianity 1. The Christian gospel. 2. Christendom*. 3. The totality of belief in and commitment to Jesus Christ as Redeemer and Lord. 4. The condition of being a Christian; Christian spirit, and character.

Christianity Today Leading Evangelical periodical in the United States, founded in 1956, on the initiative of Billy Graham* and his father in law, Nelson Bell*. Under its able editors, such as Bell (1956–1973), Carl Henry* (1956–1968), and Harold Lindsell (1968–1978), it became the most influential Christian journal in the United States. Its par-

ent company publishes a number of sister publications, including *Leadership, Christian History, Books and Culture,* and *Christian History.*

Christianize To make Christian or to convert to Christianity.

Christians Awake, Salute the Happy Morn Hymn of the nativity of Jesus by John Byrom (1691–1763), an English poet deeply influenced by William Law*. Sung to the tune "Stockport," it combines narrative and theology in verse that makes it one of the finest Christian hymns.

Christians of St. John See MANDAEANS.

Christians of St. Thomas Christians belonging to the Syriac Church of Kerala, India, which traces its origins to the apostle Thomas* in the first century.

Christian's Secret of a Happy Life Popular devotional book by Quaker Hannah Whitall Smith* published in 1833.

Christingle Decorative candle used in Christmas celebrations. It is fastened inside an orange with four small sticks and a red ribbon. Also used of service of worship using it.

Christmas Feast of the Nativity of Christ observed on December 25 by the Western Church* and 13 days later by the Eastern Church*. The Armenians observe it on January 6, on the Feast of the Epiphany*. The earliest mention of the observance on December 25 is in the Philocalian calendar* in 336. The day is celebrated in the Latin Rite* by three masses, at night, early dawn, and morning, symbolizing the threefold birth of Christ, eternally in the bosom of the Father, from the womb of the Virgin Mary*, and mystically in the soul of the faithful.

Christmas card Ornamental card with a greeting sent at Christmas. The creator of the Christmas card was John Callcott Horsley, an English illustrator, who designed the first card in 1843. It showed three generations of an English family celebrating Christmas and carried the message,

"A Merry Christmas and a Happy New Year to You." By 1870, the custom of exchanging Christmas cards had spread to the United States. It was promoted by Louis Prang, a Boston printer, who is known as the father of the American Christmas card.

Christmas Eve The night before Christmas, on which the Vigil of the Nativity is kept and watch-night services are often held. In popular lore, this is the time when children hang their stockings by the chimney.

Christmas tree Cut tree, such as spruce or fir, or an artificial tree, erected within a house or outside, with lights and decorations, now almost universally done during Christmastide*. The custom is of German origin and was introduced into Britain by Prince Albert, husband of Queen Victoria. Martin Luther* is reputed to have been the first to place candles on trees.

Christmastide The twelve days of Christmas* from Christmas to Epiphany* eve or Twelfth Night*.

Christocentric 1. Christ-centered, as in a curriculum or instructional program. 2. In theology, concept that maintains that God has never revealed himself to human beings except through Jesus Christ.

Christogram Symbol of Christ* with the first two Greek letters in his name superimposed.

Christotokos (Gk., Christ-bearer) Nestorian title for the Virgin Mary*, inferior to the Theotokos* (God-bearer), used by the orthodox.

Christology Study of the person and work of Christ, especially as the branch of theology dealing with the divinity and the humanity of Christ and the definition of the Logos* or the Word of God*. It answers the question, Who is Christ? Is he a teacher (Mark 1:27), a prophet* (Matt. 21:11; Luke 24:19; John 4:19), wisdom itself (1 Cor. 1:24), or the Son of God (Matt. 3:17; 11:27; John 3:16)? In patristic theology, Christology was developed in the councils of the early church in response to various heresies and were incorporated in the creeds formulated by these councils. The Creed of Nicaea* (325) and Creed of Constantinople* (381)

reaffirmed Christ's divinity, and the Council of Chalcedon* reaffirmed Christ's humanity, insisting that only a person who is fully divine and fully human can redeem* humanity. In the Christological controversies of the early church, the Ebionites*, Cerinthians, Adoptionists, Monarchians, and Nestorians erred about Christ's divinity, and the Docetists, Monarchians, Apollinarians, and Eutychians erred about Christ's humanity.

At the Reformation*, Christological studies shifted from a discussion of the two natures in Christ that had occupied most of the early councils to his redeeming work. The Lutheran tradition developed a new Christology that emphasized Christ's humiliation through kenosis* or self-emptying, and exaltation through his Resurrection. The nineteenth-century German liberal theology of Friedrich Schleiermacher* and Albert Ritschl* tried to reduce Christology to a system of ethics, but Barth* rescued it in the twentieth century by reviving incarnational Christology. The most important modern Christologists, outside Barth, are Wolfhart Pannenberg*, Karl Rahner*, Hans Kung*, Hans Urs von Balthasar*, and Edward Schillebeeckx*. At the end of the twentieth century, Christological controversies are as vigorous as ever.

Christomorphic Christ-shaped, and Christ-centered, as a believer, system of theology, or doctrine.

Christopher, St. (third century) Syrian Christian saint martyred in Asia Minor under Emperor Decius. According to legend, he ferried the child Jesus across a river. He is the patron saint* of travelers and ferrymen and one of the 14 auxiliary saints*. Feast day: July 25 (Western); May 9 (Eastern).

Christophers, the Roman Catholic organization founded by Father James Keller in 1945. It seeks to enlist Catholics from all walks of life to become Christophers or Christ-bearers and to overcome evil with good.

Christophoria (Gk., the carrying of Christ) In the Ambrosian Rite*, feast on January 7, the day following Epiphany* and commemorating the return from Egypt.

Christos (Gk.) Anointed One, Messiah or Christ.

Christus, Petrus (?–c. 1473) Flemish painter of religious subjects.

Christus Rex (Lat., Christ the king) Ancient form of the crucifix, showing Christ on the cross as priest and prophet* and crowned as king.

Chrodegang, St. (d. 766) Bishop of Metz and ecclesiastical reformer. As chancellor to Charles Martel*, he played a formative role in both church and state*. In 748 he founded the Abbey of Gorze*, near Metz, and furthered monasticism* by drawing up rules for communal religious life. These rules shored up monastic discipline but did not enforce poverty or unquestioning obedience.

Chronicon Edessenum Anonymous Syriac* chronicle of events in Edessa* from 132 B.C. to 540. It is a chronicle of ecclesiastical history written about 550.

Chronicon Paschale Sourcebook and chronology of history of the Christian world ending in 627. It is based on the Easter* reckoning. The principal copy of the manuscript is at the Vatican*.

Chronographer of A.D. 354 Name given by historian Theodore Mommsen to the compiler, believed to be Dionysius Philocalus, of an almanac for the use of Roman Christians. The almanac includes, among other things, an illustrated list of Roman holidays, a description of the 14 districts of Rome*, Easter* tables from 312 to 354, a chronicle of the world, anniversaries of the Roman bishops from 255 to 352, a list of martyrs*, and a list of the bishops of Rome* from Peter* to Liberius*.

chronos (Gk., time) Time, in the sense of duration.

chrysography (Gk., writing in gold) Linear hatching in gold leaf on Christ's garment to indicate the presence of divinity.

chrysom See CHRISOM.

Chrysostom, John (c. 347–407) Bishop of Constantinople* and doctor of the church*. Educated in

law under the pagan orator Libanius and trained in theology under Diodore of Tarsus*, Chrysostom entered monastic life and lived as a hermit between about 373 and about 381. He was made deacon in 381 and priest in 386. Immediately, his eloquence made him one of the most powerful preachers of his day, earning him the sobriquet, "golden-mouthed." His sermons, many of them preserved in their original form, reveal him to be one of the greatest biblical expositors*, using both the moral and literal interpretation effectively. Against his wish he was made patriarch* of Constantinople in 398, and he immediately set upon the task of reforming the corrupt court and church.

St. John Chrysostom

However, his zeal proved to be his undoing. His enemies included Empress Eudoxia, who took his crusade for reform as directed against herself, and Theophilus, the patriarch* of Alexandria, who was angered by Chrysostom's welcome for the Tall Brothers* who had fled Egypt after the condemnation of Origenism. At the Synod of Oak of 403, carefully packed by the supporters of Theophilus, Chrysostom was condemned on 29 charges. He was removed from his see*, allowed to return, and then banished again in 404, despite the support of the people of Constantinople, the Western Church*, and the pope. Forced to move from his first place of exile in Antioch* to Pontus on the Eastern Black Sea, he died of the rigors of the journey.

Almost all of his writings have survived. Besides hundreds of sermons, they include 236 letters and practical treatises, including *On the Priesthood*. Feast day: September 13 (Western Church*); November 13 (Eastern Church*).

Chrysostom, Liturgy of St. See LITURGY OF ST. JOHN CHRYSOSTOM.

Chrysostom, Prayer of St. Prayer in the *Book of Common Prayer** drawn from the Liturgy of St. Chrysostom*, part of the concluding prayers at mattins* and evensong*.

church (Gk., *kuriakon*, the Lord's) 1. Fellowship or convocation of all believers and people of God who confess Jesus Christ as Lord and Savior. Used in this sense in Matthew 16:18: "On this rock I will build My church." It is the historical and earthly manifestation of the kingdom of God*. It consists of the visible church and the invisible church. 2. Also, ecclesia*. Universal ecclesiastical institution governed by a hierarchy* of elders, priests, and bishops and sustained by historically sanctioned sacraments*, the proclamation of the Word, and the partaking of Holy Communion*. The four notes of the church are "One, Holy, Catholic, and Apostolic," as in the Nicene Creed*, but Protestants have emphasized the essential marks of the church, namely, proclamation of the scriptural Word of God* and the administration of the two sacraments, often including church discipline*. 3. Local group of believers meeting in assembly under a pastor and emphasizing their fellowship and brotherhood*. 4. Building set apart for Christian worship. 5. A sect or denomination that subscribes to biblical teaching, such as the Church of England* or the Methodist Church. 6. Public worship or religion in general, as in church and state*.

Church Age In dispensationalist theology, period of time between Pentecost* and the Second Coming* of Jesus Christ.

church and state Term used to describe the relationship between secular authorities and Christian churches collectively, or the protocols governing this relationship.

Church Army Church of England* group founded by Wilson Carlile* in 1882 to train laymen in evangelism. It is also engaged in welfare work among the poor and homeless.

Church Assembly The former National Assembly of the Church of England, established by the convocations in 1919, superseded since 1990 by the General Synod. It was composed of a house of bishops, a house of clergy, and a house of laity elected every five years by the representative electors of the diocesan conferences.

Church Commissioners Body of 95 commissioners formed in 1948 by the merger of the Ecclesiastical Commissioners* and Queen Anne's Bounty. It is responsible for the management of most material and real estate assets of the Church of England* used to pay the clergy. They also recommend the scale of fees for marriages, funerals, and other rites.

church discipline In Reformed* churches, the procedure by which God's Word is applied on the basis of Matthew 18:15–18 to exhort individual members who have gone astray. The faults of erring members are dealt with first by fraternal conversation, then by a small group of pastors and elders, and then by the whole church. It is part of what Calvin* called "the right order," one of the marks of a true church. According to the Westminster Confession*, church censures are necessary for "the reclaiming and gaining of offending brethren, from the deterring of others from the like offenses, for the purging out of that leaven which might infect the whole lump, for vindicating the honor of Christ and the holy profession of the gospel, and for preventing the wrath of God, which might justly fall upon the church, if they should suffer his covenant and the seals thereof, to be profaned by notorious and obstinate offenders."

church expectant Body of Christians in purgatory*, as distinguished from the church militant* and the church triumphant*.

Church Fathers See FATHERS OF THE CHURCH.

Church Growth movement Movement begun by Donald A. McGavran* (1897–1990) in the early

1960s studying conditions and factors that helped the planting of new churches and their growth. McGavran's *Bridges of God* has been called the "Magna Carta" of the movement and his *Understanding Church Growth* as its textbook. According to McGavran, mission is "an enterprise devoted to proclaiming the Good News* of Jesus Christ and to persuading men and women to becoming His disciples and responsible members of His church." In practice, church growth is designed to lead to a numerical growth of congregations. A major contribution of the Church Growth movement to missiology* has been the people-movement concept which emphasizes the sociological and anthropological dimension of conversion designed to make the transition to Christianity less disruptive. The movement also investigates the resistance or receptivity of any culture to the gospel as well as cultural barriers that need to be overcome by the missionaries as well as converts. Critics have attacked the movement for its excessive concern for numerical growth as against a broader goal of spiritual growth.

Church House The headquarters of the Church of England* in Westminster where the Convocation of Canterbury* and the General Synod generally sit. It was designed by Sir Herbert Baker and opened in 1940.

Church Hymnary Authorized British Presbyterian hymnal containing nearly 700 hymns, first published in 1898.

Church in Wales Autocephalous* Church of the Anglican Communion* in Wales with six dioceses, founded in 1920. It is organized as a single province with no fixed metropolitan see*, the bishops electing one of their numbers to serve as metropolitan.

church invisible Body of believers in Jesus Christ whose membership is known only to God.

church militant The church of Jesus Christ on earth in the Church Age* engaged in warfare against the principalities and powers of evil.

Church Missionary Society Leading missionary soci-

ety within the Church of England*, founded in 1799.

Church of Christ, Scientist See CHRISTIAN SCIENCE.

Church of England Official and established church of England, known also as the Anglican Church. Christianity was established in England first through the labors of Celtic missionaries from Ireland and later through St. Augustine* sent by Rome to evangelize* the island in 597. At the Synod of Whitby* in 664 Roman traditions triumphed over Celtic. Theodore of Tarsus*, sent from Rome, unified the ecclesiastical organization, created dioceses*, and summoned ecclesiastical councils. After an interregnum* when England was isolated by Danish raids and internal unrest, the Norman Conquest of 1066 brought the country back into the European mainstream. For several centuries that followed, the English Church experienced a revival of religious life through its monasteries, cathedrals, and schools. The Catholic era came to an end with the conflict between Henry VIII and Rome* which led to the dissolution of the monasteries and the establishment of Protestantism* as the official and national church.

From the beginning, the Church of England embraced a middle way between Roman Catholicism* and Protestantism*. The Elizabethan reign marked the consolidation of Protestantism and the publication of the *Book of Common Prayer** and the Thirty-Nine Articles*. In the nineteenth century there was a distinct resurgence of Anglo-Catholicism* spearheaded by the Oxford movement*. In the twentieth century, the Church of England had to redefine itself and accept a more quiescent role in national life. Increasing pluralism and secularism* have eroded much of its base, but it still adheres to the doctrinal framework laid down in the sixteenth century. The focus of worship is predominantly eucharistic. Although women have been ordained since 1994, the structure of episcopal government has remained unchanged. See also ANGLICANISM.

Church of God, Cleveland, Tennessee One of the oldest and largest Pentecostal bodies in the United States, with congregations in all 50 states and mission outposts in over 100 countries. It was founded in 1866 as Christian Union by R. G. Spurling, a Baptist preacher, with the purpose of "restoring primitive Christianity." Under the leadership of Spurling's son, it changed its name to Holiness Church and five years later to its present name. From 1906 onward it became more aggressive in preaching Holy Spirit* baptism and healing. In 1923, the denomination suffered a split when a dissident group under A. J. Tomlinson* broke away. It conducts a vigorous overseas ministry and operates a number of colleges and seminaries, of which Lee College is the most prominent.

Church of God in Christ Largest African-American Pentecostal group, founded by Charles H. Mason* and Charles P. Jones in 1895, and originally called Church of God (Holiness). Mason experienced glossolalia* in 1907 at Azusa and thereafter introduced Pentecostal doctrines into his congregation. Mason and Jones parted company over the baptism of the Holy Spirit*, and Mason founded the Church of God in Christ* in 1907. It is biblical, Trinitarian*, and Pentecostal in doctrine and practice. The Church of God in Christ (International) split off as a separate group in 1969.

Church of Illumination Denomination founded in 1908 by Swinburne Clymer that revived the priesthood of Melchizedek.

Church of Ireland Autocephalous* Church of the Anglican Communion* in both Eire and northern Ireland. It is organized in 14 dioceses* in two provinces of Armagh* and Dublin. It was the established church* in Ireland until 1869.

Church of Jesus Christ of Latter-Day Saints See MORMONS.

Church of New Jerusalem See SWEDENBORG.

Church of North India Church founded in 1970 through the union of six older Christian bodies: the Anglican Church of India, Pakistan and Ceylon; the United Church of North India, itself a merger of Congregational* and Presbyterian* churches, Baptists*, Church of the Brethren*, Methodists*, and the Disciples of Christ*. It is in full communion with the Church of England* and is a member of the Anglican Consultative Council, although not formally a member of the worldwide Anglican Communion.

Church of Scotland National Presbyterian Church of Scotland, the mother church of Presbyterian churches around the world. As founded by John Knox* in the sixteenth century, its doctrinal bases are the Scots Confession* and the First and Second Books of Discipline, later superseded by the Confession, Catechism, and other standards of the Westminster Assembly*.

Church of South India Denomination formed through the merger on Indian independence in 1947 of the Anglican Church in India and the Methodists, Presbyterians, and Congregationalists. Its counterpart in North India is called the Church of North India*. Church services are held in vernacular, Tamil, Malayalam, Telugu, or Kannada and are sometimes sung to Carnatic ragas, or melodic system. The Holy Eucharist* follows a classical pattern with adoration, confession*, a liturgy of the word*, and a liturgy of the sacrament*. Anglican collects*, lections, and prefaces* have been retained. The Indian handclasp is passed by each member of the congregation before the offertory. Responses derived from the Eastern liturgies are said or sung after the narrative of institution and the anamnesis*. Three alternative orders are specified: the antecommunion, mattins*, and evensong*. The Trisagion*, Benedictus*, and the *Te Deum** are said or sung during the service. Baptism by immersion* is encouraged but is not mandatory, and infant baptism* is normative. Baptism*, confirmation*, and Communion are linked closely together. The principal service book is the revised Book of Common Worship.

Church of the Brethren Major "peace" church founded in 1708 at Schwarzenau, Germany, as a Pietist*, Anabaptist* movement. Its leader was Alexander Mack, Sr.* Brethren beliefs included baptism* by triune immersion*, love feast*, washing of the feet, anointing of the sick with oil, laying on of hands*, and opposition to war, oaths, secret societies, and worldly clothes and habits. Persecuted in Germany, the Brethren fled to the United States, where they eventually established their headquarters in Elgin, Illinois.

Church of the East Often referred to in misleading fashion as the Nestorian Church*. Its doctrinal position is based largely on the Antiochene theology of the School of Nisibis as developed by Theodore of Mopsuestia*, Barsumas, and Babai the Great*, author of *The Book of the Union*. Under Roman and Seleucid rule, the church was based in Seleucia-Ctesiphon* on the River Tigris with about ten metropolitan sees*. A monastic revival under Abraham of Kashkar* (d. c. 580) on Mt. Izla led to the establishment of many monasteries described by Thomas of Marga* in his *Book of the Governors* and by monastic writers, such as Sahdona, Isaac of Nineveh*, John Saba, and Joseph the Seer.

By the seventh century, the church included the Christians of St. Thomas*, in Malabar, India. After the Arab Conquest in 651, the patriarchate* moved to Baghdad, and the church became Arabized. Before the Mongol Conquests, the church with its vigorous missionary activity spread throughout central Asia with thousands of bishoprics* from Persia to China. It was virtually wiped out by the Mongols under Chengiz Khan and his successors and by the mid-sixteenth century was reduced to the mountains of Kurdistan. It was further weakened by internal divisions, resulting in the establishment of a Uniat patriarchate.

The church fared even worse in the twentieth century. Because it sided with England during World War I, it suffered reprisals from both Turks and Kurds. After the war, most of the surviving Assyrians fled to the British Mandate in Iraq. At the end of the war, the catholicos* was deported and eventually settled in the United States. A rival catholicos is resident in Baghdad. Assyrians are now scattered throughout the world.

The liturgical language of the Church of the East is Syriac*, properly East Syriac. There are three main eucharistic liturgies: Addai and Mari*, Theodore of Mopsuestia*, and Nestorius*. In addition to the various lectionaries, one for the Gospels, the second for the apostle Paul*, and the *qaryana** which contains the first two lessons for the liturgical office, from the Old Testament and the Acts, the Church of the East has the *Turgama** or homilies on the lessons in the form of hymns to be chanted with the aid of the *Dawida* or psalter, prayers for ferial days, marriage, ordination, etc. The offices are chanted with the aid of the *hudra**, which contains the propers of the office, antiphons, hymns, and prayers, the *gazza* which contains the offices of the feasts of the Lord and the saints*, and other books for the choirs.

The words of the institution are absent in the Liturgy of Addai and Mari*. The Liturgy of the Presanctified* is used on Good Friday*. The Liturgy of the Catechumens begins with the Trisagion* and continues with two lections read from the bema*, the *Turgama**, sung as the priest ascends the altar, followed by lections from the Pauline Epistles and the Gospels. The Liturgy of the Faithful begins with a litany* of intercession, as in the Byzantine Liturgy. The Virgin Mary* and the 318 Church Fathers* are commemorated as well as Byzantine emperors. The priest censes his hands after a lavabo* before proceeding to the fraction*. Leavened bread is used and Communion is generally in both kinds by intinction*. See also ASSYRIAN CHURCH.

church of the poor In liberation theology*, the poor as an oppressed class, constituting a fellowship of their own with different needs and hopes than the rich.

Church of the United Brethren in Christ 1. Protestant denomination founded by Philip Otterbein* and Martin Boehm* in 1800. 2. A splinter group, known as Old Constitution, founded in 1889 in York, Pennsylvania, that split from the original denomination as a protest against their toleration of secret societies and lodges. It is Arminian in theology and conservative in doctrine.

church officer In the Anglican Church, caretaker of church buildings, often with ceremonial role in services and other duties.

church order 1. Church polity* or structure of governance. Historically, the three basic forms of church order are: episcopal, congregational, and presbyterial. Originally church order was exclusively episcopal, but congregational and presbyterial polities emerged out of the Protestant Reformation*. 2. Document or book setting out arrangements for the ordering of a church's corporate life.

Church Pastoral Aid Society (CPAS) British society, created in 1836, to promote home missions within the Church of England* based on Evangelical principles.

church planting Establishment of new church congregations in areas without a strong Christian presence through gathering a core of believers in a Bible study group which later develops into a full-fledged congregation.

church rate Tax formerly collected in England and Ireland to support established churches*.

church school School associated with a church or denomination, such as Bible school, Sabbath school, or Sunday school*. In Britain, normally used of an ordinary primary or secondary school sponsored by a church.

church session Lowest court in a Presbyterian church consisting of a pastor or minister and the ruling elders of a particular church or congregation, charged with ecclesiastical administration.

church sisters In the Church of Scotland*, women who assist parochial* work in industrial areas as deaconesses.

Church Slavonic Ecclesiastical language based on a ninth-century Bulgarian dialect, used in the liturgy of the Russian and other Orthodox churches.

Church Society Society formed in 1950 from the union of the Church Association (1865) and the National Church League (1906), devoted to the defense of the Reformation* principles in the Church of England*, at first by lawsuits, and more recently by advocacy and publications, including the quarterly *Churchman*.

church triumphant Church in heaven* when it is finally victorious over the power of evil.

church visible Institutional church of Jesus Christ constituted by the clergy and the laity as well as the church buildings and organizations.

Church World Service Agency of the National Council of Churches engaged in relief and philanthropic work, founded in 1946. Over 30 Protestant and Orthodox churches support the agency in its worldwide mission "to carry on works of Christian mercy, relief, technical assistance, rehabilitation and inter-church aid."

church year Also Christian year*; liturgical year*. Liturgical unit of time based on the annual recurrent cycles of Sundays and festivals. Each denomination has its own church year*:

The **Eastern Orthodox*** church year begins on September 1 and comprises four Sundays before Lent* (called the Sunday of the Pharisee and the Publican, the Sunday of the Prodigal Son, the Meat-Fast Sunday, and the Milk-Fast Sunday), five Sundays of Lent*, followed by Holy Week*, followed by six Sundays of Easter* with readings from John (known as the Sundays of Thomas, the women with the anointing oil, paralytic man, the Samaritan woman, the man born blind, and the fathers of Nicaea). The Feast of the Ascension is 40 days after Easter and the seventh Sunday after Easter is Pentecost*. Depending on the date of Easter, there are between 32 and 37 Sundays after Pentecost, 17 of them Matthew Sundays (with readings from Matthew), ending with the Sundays before and after the Feast of the Elevation of the Cross on September 14. Then come as many as 19 Luke Sundays (with readings from Luke) up to Epiphany*. There are four Sundays after Epiphany with readings from Luke and Matthew and then four Sundays before Lent. The major feasts include Circumcision (January 1), Presentation (February 2), Annunciation (March 25), John the Baptist (June 24), Peter* and Paul* (June 29), Transfiguration (August 6), Dormition of the Blessed Virgin Mary* (August 15), Beheading of John (August 29), Birth of Mary (September 8), Elevation of the Cross (September 14), and Mary's Visit to the Temple (November 21). Since the Orthodox Church uses the Julian calendar*, 13 days must be added to convert these days to the Gregorian calendar*.

The **Roman Catholic*** church year begins with

the four Sundays of Advent*, followed by the Christmas* season, which lasts until Epiphany. The season includes Christmas, the Feast of the Holy Family, the Feast of Mary (January 1), Epiphany, and the Feast of the Baptism of Our Lord (the first Sunday after Epiphany). The season of Lent* begins on Ash Wednesday*, followed by five Sundays of Lent, and then Holy Week*. The Triduum Sacrum* includes Maundy Thursday*, Good Friday*, and Holy Saturday*. The Easter season lasts for 50 days from Easter to Pentecost. Ascension Day* is celebrated on the Thursday following the sixth Sunday of Easter. In between there are 33 ordinary Sundays per year. The last Sunday before the first Sunday of Advent is the Feast of Christ the King*. Special days commemorate Stephen (December 26), Holy Innocents* (December 28), Conversion of Paul (January 25), Presentation of the Lord* (February 2), Annunciation of the Lord (January 25), John the Baptist (June 24), Michael (September 29), and All Saints (November 1). Other celebrations include Trinity Sunday* (first Sunday after Pentecost), Corpus Christi* (Thursday after Trinity Sunday), Sacred Heart of Jesus* (third Friday after Pentecost), the Chair of St. Peter* (February 22), Joseph* (March 19), Transfiguration (August 6), St. Lawrence* (August 10), Assumption (August 15), Birth of Mary (September 8), Triumph of the Cross (September 14), Dedication of St. John Lateran (November 9), and immaculate conception* of Mary (December 8).

In the **Lutheran churches***, there are four Sundays in Advent until Epiphany, and up to six Sundays (depending on the date of Easter) after Epiphany, followed by the prepassion season with three Sundays known as Septuagesima*, Sexagesima*, and Quinquagesima*, also called Estomihi*, the last exactly 50 days before Easter. Passiontide* includes Ash Wednesday* (40 days before Easter) followed by six Sundays known as Invokavit, Reminiscere, Oculi*, Laetare*, Judica*, and Palm Sunday*, followed by Holy Week*, Easter, and six Sundays after Easter named Quasimodogeniti, Misericordias Domini, Jubilate*, Cantate*, Rogate*, and Exaudi. Ascension Day* falls on the Thursday after Rogate (or 40 days after Easter). Pentecost, Trinity Sunday, and 22 Sundays after Trinity complete the cycle. Special days commemorate apostles, evangelists, the Vir-

gin Mary*, Michael (September 29), John the Baptist (June 24), and Reformation (October 31). Certain celebrations are observed only when they fall on a Sunday, such as John (December 27), Peter* and Paul* (June 29), Presentation (February 2), Stephen (December 26), Holy Innocents* (December 28), and Augsburg Confession* (June 25). Local churches may also commemorate Andrew (November 30), Thomas* (December 21), Matthias* (February 24), Mark (April 25), Philip* and James the Less* (May 3), James (July 25), Bartholomew* (August 24), Matthew (September 21), Luke (October 18), Simon and Jude* (October 28), Annunciation (March 25), Visitation (July 2), Circumcision (January 1), All Saints (January 11), and Conversion of Paul (January 25). There are new feast days in some countries, such as Judgment Sunday in Sweden and Name of Jesus (January 1) and Confession of Peter (January 18) in the United States.

In the **Anglican Communion***, the church year begins at the end of October with the ninth Sunday before Christmas*. It continues to the fifth Sunday before Christmas and is followed by the four Advent Sundays, six Sundays after Epiphany, seven to nine Sundays before Easter, Ash Wednesday*, the six Sundays of Lent, including Palm Sunday*, Easter, the six Sundays after Easter, Pentecost, Trinity Sunday, and 18 to 23 Sundays after Pentecost. The *Book of Common Prayer** adds feasts, such as Barnabas* (June 11), Mary Magdalene (July 22), Transfiguration (August 6), Birth of Mary (September 8), and Holy Cross (September 14).

In the **Syriac Orthodox Church***, the liturgical year* begins with the eighth Sunday before Christmas with Church Sanctification Sunday and ends with the Sundays following the Feast of the Holy Cross (September 14). The year is divided into three periods: Church Sanctification Sunday to Lent, Lent to Easter, and Easter to Sunday before Church Sanctification Sunday. The first period includes the Sundays of Advent Christmas, Circumcision of Our Lord, Epiphany, Baptism (January 6), the Presentation of Jesus in the Temple and Blessing of the Candles (February 2). The second part begins with the Sunday of Cana and moves through Lent, Holy Week*, and Easter. The third part begins with Easter and runs through Sundays of the Holy Cross, Ascension,

Pentecost, and Transfiguration of Christ. There are six periods of fasting: Nineveh Fast of three days, three weeks before Lent, the Great Lent of 40 days and the Holy Week*, three-day Fast of the Apostles (June 26–29), Fast of the Virgin Mary* (August 10–15), and Christmas (December 15–24). In addition, Wednesdays and Fridays are fast days throughout the year. The major Marian* feasts in a church year are Annunciation (fourth Sunday), Visitation (fifth Sunday), Glorification of the Mother of God (December 26), Our Lady of Sowing (January 15), Our Lady of the Harvest (May 15), Assumption of the Virgin Mary* with the Blessing of the Grapes (August 15), and the Birth of the Virgin Mary* (September 8).

Churches of Christ 1. In Great Britain, known also as Disciples. Derived from eighteenth-century sects, such as Baptists*, Haldaneites, and Sandemanians*, organized since 1842. They practice weekly breaking of bread* and believer's baptism* and have a congregational form of government. Most have united with the United Reformed Church*. 2. United States. Church, associated with the Disciples, founded in 1832 by Alexander Campbell* and Barton Stone*.

Churches of Christ in Christian Union Denomination that withdrew from the Christian Union because of its tenet that sanctification* is a second definite work of grace* subsequent to regeneration*. It is Fundamentalist in doctrine and has a congregational* form of government.

Churches of God Group of over 200 Christian bodies in the United States. The name was first adopted by a revival group within the German Reformed Church in 1825. It consists of four groups of churches:

1. **Pentecostal group** consisting of the Original Church of God* (founded in 1886 in Tennessee by R. G. Spurling), the Church of God of Prophecy founded by Bishop A. J. Tomlinson* in 1903, the Church of God of All Nations (1957), the Church of God by Faith (1923), Church of God in Christ* (1895), Church of God in Christ (Mennonite) founded by John Holdeman in 1859, and Church of God and Saints in Christ, founded by Bishop William S. Crowdy in 1896.

2. **Holiness Church of God** founded in Atlanta in 1914 by K. H. Burress. It believes in perfection* and divine healing* and practices feet washing. It includes The Church of God, Anderson, Indiana, and the Church of God (Apostolic) founded by Elder Thomas J. Cox in 1896.

3. Church of God (Seventh Day), which keeps the Sabbath and its sister body, The Church of God General Conference (Abrahamic Faith), founded about 1825 in Pennsylvania under the leadership of John Winebrenner. The church government is Presbyterian, headed by a general eldership.

4. See WORLDWIDE CHURCH OF GOD. In addition, there are hundreds of small storefront churches that use the name Church of God but belong to no denomination.

churching Rite of thanksgiving offered by a mother after the birth of her child. It follows the Old Testament custom of ceremonial purification of the mother and child on the fortieth day after delivery.

churchwarden Lay officer in the Church of England* responsible for the business and financial side of parish* administration. They kept order in church, distributed alms, and cared for the pews. Two churchwardens were generally elected by the laity in every church.

churchyard Consecrated ground attached to a church, often used for burial.

ciborium 1. Chalice-shaped vessel with a lid used as a container for the sacramental bread of the Eucharist*. 2. Formerly, the canopy resting on four pillars over the altar of Christian basilicas*. See also BALDACHINO.

cidaris In the Coptic tradition, cap decorated with small crosses, made from crimson velvet material, bound on the upper and lower hems by a circlet of silver lace and divided into four parts by vertical bands of lace.

CIDSE Cooperation Internationale pour le Developpement et la Solidarite, a federation of 14 Roman Catholic development organizations in

Europe and North America. Its general secretariat is in Belgium.

cilice/cilicium (Gk., goat's hair garment) Hair shirt* worn under clothing by monks as a form of self-mortification.

Cilicia Province in Asia Minor where St. Paul* spent his youth.

CIM China Inland Mission*.

Cimabue (c. 1240–1300) Birth name: Cenni di Pepo. Florentine painter, considered one of the finest in the thirteenth century. His religious works include *St. John the Evangelist* in the Pisa* Cathedral, *St. Trinita Madonna* in Uffizi, Florence*, Crucifxions in the churches of St. Domenico, Arezzo, and St. Croce, Florence, *Virgin and Child with Angels* in the Louvre, and frescoes in the lower and upper churches of San Francisco at Assisi.

cincture Cord worn around the alb* or cassock*.

cippus altar Altar supported by a massive stone block with a niche* cut out for a reliquary*.

circuit of the lamb In the Coptic Liturgy, procession carrying the bread or the lamb* wrapped in a veil. Some clergy precede the lamb while another bears the wine and yet another a lighted taper.

Ciborium

circuit rider Eighteenth-century Methodist preacher who traveled over an extensive circuit on horseback. Circuit riders, under Francis Asbury*, advanced Methodism* in the American West.

Circumcellions Fanatical anti-Roman peasant bands who flourished in North Africa, especially Numidia in the fourth century, so-called from the *cellae* or martyr's shrines around (*circum*) which they met. Their Donatist beliefs were combined with rigorous asceticism* and a passion for fighting injustice. They considered themselves as religious warriors (*agonistici*) of Christ.

circumincession/circuminsession (Gk., *prichoresis*) Interpenetration of the three persons of the Trinity*, first used by St. John of Damascus*. It describes the seamless Trinity of God while maintaining the personal distinctions of the Father, the Son, and the Holy Spirit*.

circumscription An ecclesiastic jurisdiction.

Ciseri, Antonio (1821–1891) Italian painter of religious scenes.

Cistercians Benedictine order founded at Citeaux* in 1098 by St. Robert* of Molesme and Stephen Harding* who sought to establish a strict form of Benedictinism emphasizing poverty, simplicity, and solitude. It was approved by Pope Paschal II* in 1100. Cistercians are also known as "white" or "grey" monks because of their habit*, which is a cowl*. Except in the choir the monks wear a black scapular*, a shoulder garment with hood. A unique feature of the order is that the monks worked to earn their food and board. Cistercians grew rapidly, as a result of the leadership of Bernard of Clairvaux*, who was responsible for founding 65 new houses. By the time of his death (1115), the order had over 300 houses and by 1200 over 740. Cistercians followed a life of continual intercession and adoration. Their churches were plain, and the vestments and ornaments were not made from precious metals. The strictest rules related to diet and silence. The Cistercians were agricultural pioneers in many countries where they had houses.

According to the monastic constitution, the founding abbeys had permanent oversight of the abbeys it founded through periodical visitation* by the abbot. Daughter abbeys could make foundations of their own, making it easier for the houses to multiply. Hurt by the Reformation* and the civil wars of the sixteenth century, the Cistercians revived through reform spearheaded by congregations like Feuillants* and Common and Strict Observance communities. Strict Observants* was transformed into the Trappists*, while Common Observants (or Reformed Cistercians) took on pastoral and teaching functions. Nuns of the Cistercian Order, also called Bernardines, were organized by Stephen Harding in 1120. They lead a completely secluded life. Jansenism* developed at their famous convent at Port Royal, France.

After the Second Vatican Council*, new constitutions were finally approved in 1990. Abbots are no longer elected for life; regional conferences have wider powers; the dietary prescriptions are no longer mandatory although abstention from meat is recommended; and Divine Office* has been simplified.

Citeaux French village, 16 miles south of Dijon, where the Cistercian Order developed, and the site of a famous Cistercian abbey and the mother house* of the Cistercian Order. Today it consists of nothing but ruined walls.

Abbey of Citeaux

City of God 1. Title of a book by St. Augustine* describing the emergence of a divine order from the dissolution of earthly kingdoms. The heavenly city is the true people of God both in its earthly pilgrimage* and in its heavenly destiny. 2. Title of Jerusalem*, described as the dwelling place of God, or metaphorically of the church.

Clairvaux Fourth house of the Cistercian Order near Bar-sur-Aube, founded in 1115 by Bernard of Clairvaux*. It was the wealthiest house until it was confiscated by the state during the French Revolution.

Abbey of Clairvaux

Clapham sect Group of politically powerful and rich Anglican Evangelicals, including Hannah More*, the banker Henry Thornton, the rector John Venn*, Charles Grant, Lord Teignmouth, James Stephen, Zachary Macaulay, Isaac Milner, Charles Simeon*, and William Wilberforce* who sought to abolish the slave trade, improve social conditions for the poor, and expand missions and Sunday schools*. So called because most of the members lived in a suburban area of London called Clapham. The sect was responsible for the founding of the British and Foreign Bible Society* (1804) and the Church Missionary Society* (1709).

Clare, St. (c. 1193–1253) First abbess of the Poor Clares*. Born in Assisi* and drawn by the sanctity* of St. Francis, she was named by him the abbess of a community at St. Damian which later became the Poor Clares. Many daughter houses were founded in Europe in the thirteenth century, including 47 in Spain. She was canonized by Alexander IV* in 1255. Feast day: August 11.

Claretian Member of the Congregation of the Missionary Sons of the Immaculate Heart of Mary*, instituted in 1849 by Anthony Mary Claret (1807–1870).

Clari, Giovanni Carlo Maria (c. 1669–1745) Italian composer of religious music.

Clark, Francis Edward (1851–1927) Founder of the Christian Endeavor movement in 1881. He was a Congregational* minister in Portland, Maine, and South Boston.

class meeting Informal weekly church meeting, originated by Wesley* and continued by later Methodists. It served the same purpose as mid-week prayer meetings* or cells in other Protestant denominations.

Classical Pentecostals Traditional or older Pentecostal groups, including Pentecostal-Apostolic, Oneness Pentecostal, Baptist-Pentecostal, Holiness-Pentecostal, Perfectionist-Pentecostal, as contrasted with neo-Pentecostal, Charismatic Pentecostal, and other later groups.

classis Governing body of a group of Reformed* churches, made up of clergymen and ruling elders, corresponding to a synod* or presbytery*.

Claudel, Paul (1868–1955) French Catholic poet and diplomat. Converted at the age of 18, he combined a distinguished diplomatic career with literary pursuits. His complete works, published in 29 volumes, included plays, such as *Le Soulier de Satin* (1931), canticles*, such as *L'Annonce faite a Marie* (1916), prose works, such as *Figures et Paraboles* (1936), and *Art Poetique* (1907), biblical commentaries, such as *Les Aventures de Sophie*, and collections of poems, such as *Visages Radieux* (1947), *Cinq Grandes Odes* (1910), and *Feuilles de Saints* (1925).

clausura (lit., closure) 1. Portion of a religious house from which members of the opposite sex are excluded. 2. Practice of such exclusion in a monastery.

Claver, Peter St. (1580–1654) "Apostle of the Negroes." Jesuit missionary to the New World. In 1610 he went to Cartagena, Colombia, where he began ministering to the black slaves. In 1615 he was ordained, declaring himself to be the slave of slaves. He is said to have instructed and baptized over 300,000 people. He was canonized in 1888 and in 1896 became patron of Catholic missionary activities among blacks. Feast day: September 9.

Peter Claver

CLC Christian Literature Crusade*.

Clemens non Papa Epithet of Jacques Clement (c. 1500–c. 1556), Dutch composer of church music, so called to distinguish him from Pope Clement VII*, his contemporary.

Clement V (1264–1314) Pope from 1305. Birth name: Bertrand de Got. He inaugurated the 70 years of Avignon* captivity by moving papal residence to that French city. For most of his pontificate* he was subservient to the interests of Philip the Fair of France. However, he did much to further scholarship, especially the study of medicine and Oriental languages, and founded the universities of Orleans (1306) and Perugia (1308).

Clement VI (1291–1352) Pope from 1342. Birth name: Pierre Roger. Although he was a typical Renaissance pope, he was generous to the poor and a friend of the Jews. He bought the city of Avignon* from Joanna of Naples and embarked on a spectacular building program.

Clement VII (1478–1534) Pope from 1523. A Medici by birth, he was a patron of many great artists, including Cellini, Raphael*, and Michelangelo*. Although he was personally of blameless character, his irresolute policies encouraged the spread of Protestantism* through northern Europe.

Clement VIII (c. 1536–1605) Pope from 1592. Birth name: Ippolito Aldobrandini. He was largely responsible for the Treaty of Versailles (1598) which brought about peace between France and Spain. His interest in the revision of service books led to the issue of new editions of the Vulgate*, the Missal, the Breviary*, and the Pontifical*.

Pope Clement VII

Clement XI (1649–1721) Pope from 1700. Birth name: Giovanni Francesco Albani. During his papacy he had to contend with the heresies associated with Jansen and the Chinese Rites, both of which he condemned. He was a generous patron of arts and scholarship and instigated Joseph Assemani* to assemble the Assemani manuscripts in the Vatican Library*.

Clement XIII (1693–1769) Pope from 1758. Birth name: Carlo della Torre Rezzonico. During most of his papacy he was engaged in a losing struggle against the efforts of France, Spain, and Portugal to suppress the Society of Jesus* which he defended until his death.

Clement XIV (1705–1774) Pope from 1769. Birth name: Vincenzo Antonio Ganganelli. He tried to restore good relations with Spain, France, and England by suppressing the Society of Jesus*, but failed to do so.

Clement of Alexandria (c. 150–c. 215) Theologian and philosopher. He was an Athens-born pagan who converted to Christianity and presented Christian theological concepts in philosophical terms familiar to the Greeks. He fled from Alexandria* during the persecution of 202. Of his many works mentioned by Eusebius*, a few survive, including *Protrepticus,* an exhortation to the

Clement of Alexandria

Greeks, *Paedagogus* on Christian manners, eight books of *Stromateis* or Miscellanies, a homily*, and several fragments. Some of his ideas were borrowed from the Gnostics and the Platonic philosophers. He wrote "A Hymn to Christ the Savior," one of the earliest extant hymn texts. It is often sung today as the "Shepherd of Tender Youth."

Clement of Rome, St. (d. c. 96) Fourth bishop of Rome, according to some ancient lists, and author of the First and Second Epistles of Clement. He is the subject of many legends. Feast day: November 23 (Western Church*); November 24 or 25 (Eastern Church*).

Clement Slovensky, St. (d. 916) One of the seven apostles of Bulgaria who worked with St. Methodius* as a missionary in Moravia, until he was driven out. He then worked among the Bulgars and founded the see of Velico. He also founded the monastery of Ohrid*.

Clementine Edition Edition of the Vulgate* revised in 1592 under Pope Clement VIII*.

Clementine literature Writings ascribed to Clement of Rome*, including two epistles to the Corinthians, two epistles on virginity, an epistle to James, Apostolical Constitutions, Apocalypse of Clement, Homilies, and Recognitions. Only the first epistle to the Corinthians is acknowledged as true.

Clementines Also, Liber Septimus. In canon law*, collection of decretals* issued by Clement, including the decretals of Boniface VIII*, Urban IV, and Clement himself.

clerestory High part of a church with windows to admit light. In English and French churches, there is a passageway inside at this level.

clergy (Gk., *kleras,* chosen by lot) Collective term for ordained ministers or pastors, especially as distinguished from the laity.

clergy reserves One-eighth of crown lands once set apart in England for the support of the clergy of established churches*.

clergyman Ordained minister or pastor.

clerical collar Stiff white collar buttoned behind, used by both Roman Catholic and Protestant clergy.

clericalism 1. The secular powers of the church and their application to strengthen the ecclesiastical establishment vis a vis the secular powers, used in a negative or pejorative sense. 2. The professional interests of the clergy as a class.

Clerics Regular of St. Paul Order founded at Milan* in 1530 by Antonio Maria Zaccaria for education, relief of the sick, and mission work. See also BARNABITES.

clerisy 1. Formerly, the clergy. 2. Intelligentsia or the learned class.

clerk Person who has received holy orders*, especially one in minor or lay orders as distinguished

from one in major orders*, such as a bishop, a priest, and a deacon.

clerks regular In the Roman Catholic Church, those bound by religious vows who live communally and engage in active pastoral work. The more important of these communities were founded in the sixteenth century, such as the Clerks Regular of St. Paul*, Theatines* (1524), the Society of Jesus* and Clerks Regular of the Good Jesus, founded in Milan* in 1526.

Clermont, Council of Council summoned by Urban II* at Clermont in 1095 for planning the First Crusade*. It also passed reform measures, such as the prohibition against eating flesh at Lent*.

clinical baptism (Gk., *kline,* bed) Baptism during illness or on the deathbed.

clinical communion Communion received by a sick person at home.

clinical theology Study of psychological, mental, and emotional factors in a person's spiritual development. It is an approach to pastoral caring and healing developed by Frank Lake (1904–1982), author of *Clinical Theology* (1986) and *Tight Corners in Pastoral Counselling* (1981). He grafted Christian concepts on Freudian principles of psychiatry.

clinici (sing., clinicus) Persons who receive clinical baptism*.

Clitherow, Margaret (1556–1586) Martyr. Daughter of the sheriff of York*, she was converted to Roman Catholicism* and sheltered fugitive priests. Charged with treason, she refused to plead in her defense and was crushed to death. She was beatified in 1929.

cloister (Lat., *claustrum,* closed place) 1. Covered walkway connecting the buildings of a monastery, often forming a colonnaded open court surrounded on all four sides by broad covered alleys with roofs supported on their inner sides by arcades and on their outer sides by the walls of the church. 2. Synonym for religious life.

Cloister

close Area of a cathedral enclosed by walls or buildings.

closed communion Restriction of the Eucharist* to only those in good standing in a particular congregation or denomination.

closed time (Lat., *tempora clausa*) Period in Lent* during which marriages are not performed.

cloth Usually "men of the cloth." The clergy, so called because of their distinctive dress.

Clotilda, St. (474–545) Queen of the Franks who converted her husband King Clovis* to Christianity. She helped to build the Church of the Holy Apostles in Paris, and as a widow entered the Abbey of St. Martin in Tours*. Feast day: June 3.

cloud Ancient symbol for God.

Cloud of Unknowing Fourteenth-century mystical treatise, a guide to contemplation of the divine, sometimes attributed to a contemporary of Walter Hilton*. According to the author, God cannot be grasped by human intellect because there is a "cloud of unknowing" between the two which can be pierced only by "the sharp dart of love." Prayers* should be directed to God without any discourse or any other intention beside simple worship and adoration and should be limited to an ejaculatory or monosyllabic utterance.

clover Symbol of the Trinity*.

Clovis (c. 406–511) King of the Franks, converted and baptized as a Catholic in 496, 503, or 506. His

baptism* is a milestone in Christian history because it ensured the spread of orthodox Christianity on the Continent.

Clowes, William (1780–1851) Primitive Methodist leader. Converted in 1805, he began emotional open-air meetings that alarmed Methodist leaders, who expelled him. Together with Hugh Bourne*, he founded the Primitive Methodist Connexion. He devoted the rest of his life to spreading the gospel in the midlands and north of England.

CLS Christian Literature Society.

Cluniac Order Catholic monastic order founded by William the Pious of Aquitaine and the monk Berno in 910 at the Benedictine abbey at Cluny*. Under Berno's successor, St. Odo* (927–942), many Italian and French houses reformed themselves on the Cluniac model. Under three later abbots—Majolus (954–994), Odilo* (994–1048), and Hugh (1049–1109)—the influence of Cluny reached its height, with the number of Cluniac houses reaching 1,000. During the next two centuries, it was one of the most powerful orders in Christendom* and a force for reform. The new church at Cluny, whose altar was consecrated by Urban II* in 1095, was then the largest church in Europe, 555 feet long. In the later Middle Ages, the order declined and it was dissolved in 1790.

Cluny Site in Paris where the abbey of Cluny (a museum since 1833), the Church of St. Marcellus, and the Notre Dame* Cathedral are located. It was

Clovis

once the largest basilica*, after Rome*, in Europe. Today it is in ruins, but for the high transept*, the Holy Water Tower, a smaller clock tower, ten capitals from the columns of the choir, and the abbot's palace. The foundation stone was laid in 1088, and it was consecrated by Pope Urban in 1095. The massive basilica* was finished in the thirteenth century. The church was dominated by seven steeples at varying levels. The interior was lighted with 300 windows. During the French Revolution the building was sold to a demolition firm which made sure that little remained of the place once called "worthy of angels."

Abbey of Cluny

CMA Christian and Missionary Alliance*.

CMS Church Missionary Society*, originally called the Society for Missions in Africa and the East, founded in 1799. It was the first Anglican society to send missionaries to Asia and Africa, fostering the development of indigenous and autonomous churches.

coadjutor bishop See BISHOP COADJUTOR.

Cocceius, Johannes (1603–1669) Also, Koch. German dogmatic theologian. His moderate Calvinism* was outlined in his major work, *Summa Doctrinae de Foedere et Testamento Dei* (1648). He was among the first to use the terms *covenant of works*★ to describe the Old Testament and *covenant of grace*★ to describe the New Testament. He thus was a pioneer in the branch of theology known as federal theology*, inspired the Pietist

movement, and introduced the history of salvation and millennialism into Reformed* theology.

coconsecrator Bishop who assists the presiding bishop in the consecration of a new bishop.

codex Manuscript with leaves bound in book form as distinguished from a scroll. See also PAPYROLOGY.

Codex

Codex Alexandrinus Fifth-century manuscript of the Greek Bible (including the Epistles of Clement) written in vellum on two columns, now in the British Library.

Codex Amiatinus ("A") The oldest extant manuscript of the Latin Vulgate*, one of the three Bibles written at either Wearmouth or Jarrow* in North Britain under Abbot Ceolfrith between about 690 and 700. In the ninth or tenth century,

Codex Amiatinus

the manuscript was at the Monastery of Monte Amiata from which its name is derived. One copy is in the Laurentian Library at Florence*, and fragments of the other two are in the British Library. Its illustrations include a full-page picture of Christ in Majesty.

Codex Bezae ("D") Sixth-century bilingual (Lat. and Gk.) manuscript of the gospel, including the four Gospels (presented in a different order, Matthew, John, Luke, and Mark), and parts of Acts and 3 John, gifted to the Cambridge University by Theodore Beza*. It is a small codex* (ten inches by eight inches). There are numerous mistakes and certain additions in the Acts.

Codex Canonum Ecclesiae Universae Collection of the official canon laws* of the church, sanctioned by the Council of Chalcedon* and the Emperor Justinian*. It contains the canons of Nicaea*, Ancyra, Neocaesarea, Gangra*, Antioch, Laodicea*, Constantinople*, Ephesus*, and Chalcedon, published in 1610 by C. Justel.

Codex Ephraemi ("C") Fifth-century Greek manuscript of the Bible now at Paris containing every book of the New Testament except 2 Thessalonians and 2 John. Its name derives from Ephraem Syrus, the scribe, whose writings were written over the original text.

Codex Fuldensis Latin manuscript of the New Testament written in 541–546 at the order of Victor, bishop of Capua. The four Gospels are arranged in harmony*, as in Tatian's* *Diatessaron**, but the text is that of the Vulgate*.

Codex Iuris Canonici Code of canon law* in force in the Roman Catholic Church. The first codex* was produced at the instance of Pope Pius X* by a commission under the direction of Cardinal Gasparri*. The resulting volume, consisting of 2,414 canons, was promulgated in 1917. It was revised by the Second Vatican Council* and promulgated in 1983 in seven books divided into 1,752 canons. Book I (canons 1–203) deals with general norms. Book II entitled "The People of God" (canons 204–746), deals with constitutional issues and groupings of churches, such as the rights and duties of all Christians, the laity and the clergy, the

hierarchical constitution of the church and institutions of the dedicated life. Book III (canons 747–833), entitled "The Teaching Office of the Church," formulates the law of the church's ministry of proclamation in preaching, catechesis*, mission, education, media, and literature.

Book IV (canons 834–1253), entitled "The Office of Sanctifying in the Church," deals with sacraments, sacramentals, worship, saints, relics*, sacred places, and feasts. Book V (canons 1254–1310) deals with church property and finances. Book VI, entitled "Sanctions in the Church" (canons 1311–1399), deals with the church's penal law, offenses, and punishments. Book VII (canons 1400–1752), entitled "Processes," deals with judicial processes. A separate codex was published in 1990 for the Uniat churches*.

Codex Sinaiticus The most famous Greek manuscript of the Bible, discovered in 1859 by Constantine Tischendorf* in the Monastery of St. Catherine* on Mount Sinai, and now in the British Library. Written in the fourth century, it is written on vellum, two columns to a page. It contains half of the Old Testament, the complete New Testament, the Epistle of Barnabas*, and part of *The Shepherd**.

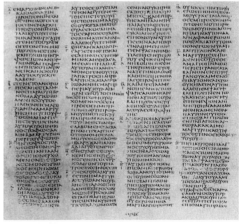

Codex Sinaiticus

Codex Sinopensis Fifth- or sixth-century manuscript found at Sinope in Turkey and now in Paris. It contains part of the Gospel of Matthew with illustrations. It is written in gold and silver on purple vellum.

Codex Vaticanus ("B") Fourth-century manuscript of the Greek Bible, without the Pastoral Epistles*, now in the Vatican Library*. It was extensively restored in the fifteenth century. Like the Codex Sinaiticus*, it is based on the Neutral or Alexandrian Text*.

Coe, Jack (1918–1957) Pentecostal healing revivalist*. Ordained by the Assemblies of God* in 1944, he developed a tent ministry by 1947 in what was considered to be the world's largest tent. He was expelled from the Assemblies of God in 1953. Next year he opened the Dallas Revival Center as an independent ministry. In 1956 he was arrested for practicing medicine without a license, but after a two-day trial, the case was dismissed.

coenobite (Gk., living in a community) Monk or nun who lives in a community or separately, but within a common enclosure. See also CENOBITE.

coenobium Common-life monastery.

Coerper, Heinrich Wilhelm (1863–1936) Founder of the Liebenzeller Mission. In 1899 he founded a German branch of the China Inland Mission* in Hamburg, moving it to Liebenzell, southwestern Germany. Overseas work was begun in the Chinese provinces of Hunan (1901) and Guizhiu (1906) and then in Micronesia and Japan.

coetus Church assembly or governing body, especially in the Reformed* churches.

Coke, Thomas (1747–1814) Methodist preacher and missionary. As John Wesley's* associate, he was the first Methodist bishop and the superintendent who set up the Methodist Episcopal Church of America. He was a tireless promoter of overseas ministries and helped to send out missionaries to the West Indies, Ceylon, India, Cape of Good Hope, and Sierra Leone.

Colette, St. (1381–1447) Franciscan superior*. She became a Franciscan tertiary* at an early age and had visions and dreams in which she was exhorted to reform the Poor Clares*. She eventually became superior general* of the order and established 17 convents in her lifetime. Feast day: March 6.

Colettines Poor Clare nuns who embraced the reform of St. Colette*.

Colin, Jean-Claude Marie (1790–1875) Founder of the Marist Fathers and Sisters, a four-branched order of laypeople, sisters*, brothers*, and priests who worked in Oceania, particularly New Caledonia and Melanesia.The order received papal approval in 1836, but administrative and financial difficulties hampered the work for the order until the late 1850s.

collation 1. Light meal allowed on days of fasting in addition to one full meal. 2. Lives of the Fathers arranged for reading by monks, after John Cassian's *Collationes Patrum*. 3. Ecclesiastical consultation.

collect Short opening prayer in a service of worship before the Epistle is read. It may be an invocation*, petition*, or an affirmation of God's glory. The term is derived from the gathering of private petitions from several members of a congregation into a single public prayer.

collectar Medieval liturgical book containing the collects* used in Divine Offices*.

collection Part of the divine service* when a plate, bag, or box is passed around for the congregation to present their tithes and offerings.

college, apostolic The 12 apostles collectively.

Thomas Coke

College of Bishops 1. Bishops elected by a Methodist Conference. 2. In the Roman Catholic Church, bishops collectively.

College of Cardinals Body of cardinals, known as princes of the church, who advise and elect the pope. Formerly limited to 70, they now number over 100.

Collegiants Also, Rynsburgers. Dutch religious group, an offshoot of the Remonstrants, founded in the Netherlands about 1619, so called because their communities were called colleges. They believed that the church was an invisible society and all external forms were corrupt. Although they acknowledged Christ as Messiah and the literal truth of the Bible, they had no creed or ministry. Their theology was very liberal and influenced by Spinoza, the Jewish philosopher.

collegiate church Church served by a group of clergymen or a group of churches administered jointly by several ministers. It is distinguished from a cathedral which is a bishop's see*.

collegium See SACRED COLLEGE.

colloquy 1. Informal theological meeting. 2. Presbytery* or classis* in the French Reformed Church.

colobium/colobion Long ankle-length tunic, an early form of sticharion* with close-fitting sleeves.

Cologne German city, the seat of an important archbishopric in the Middle Ages. Its main cathedral dates from the thirteenth and fifteenth centuries and contains the Shrine of the Magi. Its other famous churches are St. Maria in Kapitol and St. Gereon's, both built in the eleventh century.

Cologne Cathedral Cathedral dedicated to St. Peter* and the Virgin Mary* in Cologne*, Germany, a five-aisled basilica* with a three-aisled transept* and a raised choir at the east end, enclosed by a ring of seven chapels. The west front with its two slender towers is the largest facade of any Christian building. The neo-Gothic* exterior sculpture

was designed in 1854 by Sulpice Boisserie. According to tradition, Gerhard, the main architect, died when he fell from the scaffolding. The building towers remained unfinished for centuries until it was completed in the nineteenth century and consecrated by Kaiser Wilhelm I in 1880. The

Cologne Cathedral

cathedral was built on the site of Hildebold Church, which stood there in the tenth century. Among the cathedral's greatest art treasures is the Gero Cross of Oak dating from 976. In the Middle Ages, it was a center of pilgrimage* as the reputed resting place of the bones of the three Magi.

Colombini, Blessed Giovanni (1304–1367) Founder of the Gesuati*. Converted when he was 50, he separated from his wife and, together with his friends, led a life of poverty, prayer, and works of mercy*. He visited several Italian towns and converted many by his example and preaching. In 1367 he and his group were formally admitted into the Congregation of the Gesuati* by Urban V*. Beatified by Gregory VIII. Feast day: July 31.

colors, liturgical Association of particular colors with the liturgy and worship services, vestments, and vessels. Originally only white was used in Christian services, but after 1000, various colors were introduced, depending on the availability of richer and more varied textiles. By 1570 Pope Pius V* tried to standardize the practice in a missal. According to this missal, the following colors were to be used in the sequence of seasons:

Advent to Christmas eve*: Violet/Blue/Black; Christmas to Epiphany*: White/Gold; Sundays after Epiphany: Green; Septuagesima* to Ash Wednesday*: Violet/Blue/Black; Throughout the Lent*: Veiling of colors; Passion Sunday* to Easter eve*: Red*/Rose; Easter*: White/Gold; Pentecost*: Red*; Trinity*: White/Gold; Sundays after Trinity: Green; Ordinary weekdays: Green; Virgin Mary*: White/Red*; Apostles, evangelists, martyrs: Red*; Saints other than martyrs: White/Yellow; Baptisms/Confirmation: White/Red; Ordination/Marriage: White; Funeral: Violet/Blue/Black; Dedication of a church: White.

Colossae City in the Roman province of Asia, in the Lycus Valley. It was reputed to have been evangelized by Epaphras, a member of Paul's* missionary team and a native. Paul's epistles to the Colossians were addressed to its citizens.

Colosseum Roman amphitheater built by Flavian emperors in 72–82 in which Christians were thrown to the wild beasts.

Colossian heresy Heretical first-century sect of Judaic Christians in the Asia Minor town of Colossae*, rebuked by Paul* in Colossians 2:16–18. Their practices involved celebration of pre-Christian festivals and worship of angels.

colportage Work of a colporteur*.

colporteur In the eighteenth and nineteenth centuries especially, distributor of Bible tracts and books.

Colson, Charles ("Chuck") W. (1931–) Founder of Prison Fellowship Ministries*. Charged with obstruction of justice as an aide to President Nixon in the Watergate affair, Colson was in prison for seven months. He emerged from the ordeal as a committed Christian* and dedicated his life to reform of prison conditions and prison evangelism. The Prison Fellowship Ministries which he founded has become an international movement and now encompasses the Angel Tree program

for the families of offenders and Neighbors Who Care, a ministry to victims of crime. In 1993 he was awarded the Templeton Prize for Progress in Religion. Colson also is a prolific writer whose works include *Born Again* (1976), *Kingdoms in Conflict* (1987), and *The Body* (1992).

Columba, St. (521–597) Irish churchman known as Colum Cille, "Dove of the Church," and as "Apostle to Caledonia." Born in Ireland, he founded a monastery at Durrow, but left Ireland in 563 as a "Pilgrim for Christ" for Iona*, an island off the coast of Scotland. Here he established a church and later a monastery, followed by numerous monasteries on the Scottish mainland. He converted the Scottish and Pictish notables. Feast day: June 9.

Columbanus/Columban, St. (c. 540–615) Irish saint* and missionary to Europe. He established monasteries at Annegray and Luxeuil in the Vosges in Gaul. However, he aroused much opposition among the local clergy because of his adherence to Celtic traditions, such as the dating of Easter*, and also at the royal court because of his attacks on the king's polygamy. He was expelled from Gaul but began missionary work among the Alemanni near Lake Constance, and later settled near Bobbio* in Italy where he established a great school. He was also a noted poet and an able commentator on the Bible. Feast day: November 23.

columbarium Vault in a cemetery or crypt where the ashes of the dead are interred.

Columbus, Christopher (1451–1506) Discoverer of the New World. Born in Genoa, Italy, and brought up by pious Catholic parents, Columbus was a devout Catholic all his life. Obsessed with the idea of finding a westward sea route to India, he secured the patronage of and funds from Queen Isabella of Spain, and became the first Christian to see the New World in 1492. He made four further voyages, but never realized that the lands he had discovered were not part of Asia. Columbus established the first church in the New World on Isabella, Haiti, where the first Mass* was celebrated on January 6, 1494, and the first baptism* on September 21, 1494.

Comboni, Blessed (Antonio) Daniele (1831–1881) Founder of the Verona Fathers* and Roman Catholic missionary to Africa. As a priest for the Africa Mission, he went on missionary journeys to Egypt and Aden. In Rome* he conceived his plan for the regeneration* of Africa, and three years later founded the Missionary Institute for Africa, now officially called the Comboni Missionaries of the Sacred Heart, or more commonly as the Verona Fathers*. In 1870 he presented a Petition on Behalf of the Black Populations of Central Africa to the First Vatican Council* and was entrusted by Pius IX* with the mission to Central Africa as vicar apostolic*. He was actively involved in the struggle against slavery. He was beatified in 1996. Feast day: October 10.

comediatrix Unofficial title of the Virgin Mary* in Marian* devotions of the Roman Catholic Church, representing her as a mediator, along with Jesus Christ, before God the Father. See COREDEMPTRIX.

Comenius, (Komensky) Jan (Johannes) Amos (1592–1670) Bohemian reformer. He belonged to the Bohemian (Moravian) Brethren* and learned theology at the Calvinist universities of Heidelberg and Herborn*. As a Moravian minister in Lissa, Poland, he wrote his first important work, *Didacta Magna* (1657). From 1641 to 1648 he traveled in England, Sweden, and Germany, promoting the Protestant cause and studying educational systems. Between 1650 and 1654 he lived in Hungary, where he founded a school at Sarospatak. After the Catholic victory in Poland in 1656, he took asylum in the Netherlands, where he completed his final work, *Unum Necessarium* (1668). His pedagogical ideals, founded on Christian love, have had considerable influence on the development of education in the West.

Jan Comenius

Comes Book containing passages to be read at Mass*, including the Gospels and Epistles.

Comfortable Words Four passages of the New Testament (Matt. 11:28; John 3:16; 1 Tim. 1:15; 1 John 2:1) recited by the celebrant during Holy Communion* after absolution*.

Comforter, the In the King James Version*, title of the Holy Spirit* (John 14:16, 26; 15:26; 16:7).

Comgall (517–c. 601) Irish monk. In 558 he founded at Bangor* the famous monastery which became an important seat of learning in Ireland, with an enrollment of over 3,000 students. Feast day: May 10.

coming great church Ecumenical ideal of a reunited church without any denominational divisions.

commandments of the church Also, precepts* of the church. Regulations prescribed by a church group for its members. *The Catechism of the Catholic Church** (1992) lists five, including regular attendance at Mass*, confession* at least once a year, Holy Communion* during the Easter* season, observance of the feasts of obligation, and observance of the days of fasting and abstinence. To these is sometimes added the provision of the material needs of the church.

commemoration 1. Prayer of remembrance. 2. Celebration of a minor feast that occurs on the same date as a major feast.

commendation of the soul (Lat., *commendatio animae*) Prayers offered on behalf of a dying person. Also called commendation of the dying.

commendatory prayer Prayer commending a dying person's soul to the Lord.

commentary Detailed passage-by-passage interpretation or explanation of the Holy Scripture.

Commination Service In the Anglican Sarum rite*, service for the blessing of ashes on Ash Wednesday*.

commingling Placing a piece of consecrated bread in the chalice* containing the consecrated wine to indicate the unity of the body and blood of Christ and, when the bread comes from a previous Mass*, the unity of all sacraments.

commissary Church official representing a bishop.

commission Charge or command, as in the Great Commission*.

committal Laying a corpse into the grave and commitment of its soul to God in a burial service.

committed Christian Believing, active, and practicing Christian who has a personal relationship with Jesus Christ.

commixture Mixing bread and wine in the Eucharist* symbolizing the Resurrection.

common grace Grace shared by all persons as distinguished from the special grace* known only by the elect* of God.

Common of the Saints In the Western Church*, parts of the Missal* and the Breviary* containing office for those saints* who do not have a proper or office of their own.

Common Order, Book of See BOOK OF COMMON ORDER.

common places See LOCI COMMUNES.

Common Prayer, Book of See BOOK OF COMMON PRAYER.

Communaute (Fr.) In the Congo, a Protestant denomination.

communicant One who partakes of the Holy Communion*.

Communicantes Section of the Canon of the Roman Mass* which comes before the words of the Institution. It consists of a memorial of the saints mentioning by name the Virgin Mary*, St. Joseph*, the 11 apostles, St. Paul*, 11 Roman martyrs*, and 1 African martyr.

communicate (*verb*) To partake of the Holy Communion*.

communicatio essentiae Doctrine that the Son receives his essence from the Father and the Spirit his essence from the Father and the Son, although this takes place within the single essence of God. It safeguards the monarchy of the Father as the source of the whole Trinity* while at the same establishing the full divinity of Christ.

communicatio idiomatum (lit., commonness or sharing of the attributes) The inextricable unity of the divine* and human natures in Christ so that the attributes of one nature are shared by the other. In Lutheran theology, it was held to establish the ubiquity* of Christ's body known as Ubiquitarianism.

communicatio in sacris Catholic participation in the worship services of other churches, permitted by Vatican Council II*.

communicatio operationum Belief expounded by Lutheran theologians, as Chemnitz*, to express the presence of Christ in the bread and wine of the Holy Communion*. It speaks of the transference of ubiquity* from the divine* to the human nature of Christ.

communio Verse, usually from the Scripture, as an element of the proper sung during or after the Communion.

Communio Sanctorum In the Apostles' Creed*, the Communion of Saints or the Communion of Holy Things.

Communion See COMMUNION, HOLY.

Communion and Liberation (Ital., *comunione e liberazione*) Catholic renewal movement founded and led by Father Luigi Guissani and directed mostly at students. It is a loosely organized movement without formal membership.

communion anthem (antiphon) In the Roman Mass*, a short passage said or sung during the administration of the Holy Communion*, by the reader*, choir, or the people. If it is sung, it is accompanied by a psalm, hymn, or chant, commonly Psalm 34.

communion bread Bread or wafers served at Holy Communion*, whether leavened or unleavened.

communion, closed Practice of restricting participation in Holy Communion* to a particular group, such as those in good standing in a denomination.

communion, corporate Participation in the Holy Communion* as a group.

communion cup Cup used in the Holy Communion* to hold wine and from which it is drunk by the communicant.

Communion, Holy Also, breaking of bread*; Eucharist*; Lord's Supper*; Love feast*. Central act of Christian worship service in imitation of the Last Supper and in remembrance of Jesus' sacrifice at the cross, when the priest or pastor consecrates and distributes and believers partake of the bread and wine, representing the body and the blood of Jesus Christ in a prescribed sacramental manner. Holy Communion represents the full fellowship of Jesus Christ with his followers and the authentic reminder of his continuing presence in their midst. It is also a token of the eternal feast that awaits believers on Christ's return to establish his glorious kingdom.

Theologians have struggled to establish the real significance of the act of Holy Communion. On one level it is a memorial of the Paschal lamb* and on another level it is the means by which the power of the death and Resurrection of Jesus is applied to successive generations for all time. The elements* themselves become a sacramental and/or symbolic food enabling creatures to assimilate the essence of the Creator. In this spirit, Paul* uttered a warning to those who ate and drank "in an unworthy manner . . . not

discerning the Lord's body" (1 Cor. 11:29). In the doctrine of transubstantiation*, officially accepted by the Roman Catholic Church in 1215, the substance of the bread and the wine are actually changed into the body and blood of Christ. The Reformers adopted a different view that harked back to Augustine's* teaching and distinguished between the sign and the thing signified. They held that the change took place not in the elements* but through the faith* of the communicant. Luther* adopted the more moderate position and Calvin* and Zwingli* the more radical one.

Communion in both kinds Serving Holy Communion* of both bread and wine to all communicants, a practice common to all Protestants. Variants of this practice include that of restricting the wine to the celebrants or the dipping of the bread into the wine (intinctio panis*).

Communion of the Apostles The Last Supper.

communion, open Participation in the Holy Communion* by all believers present, irrespective of their denominational affiliations.

Communion, Order of the (1548) Form of administering Holy Communion* in the Sarum (Lat.) Mass* translated into English. It consisted of a brief address to the intending communicants, confession*, absolution*, the Comfortable Words*, the Prayer of Humble Access*, the words of administration* (for both kinds), and the Blessing.

communion plate 1. Plate of silver held under the chin of the communicant during the intake of the Holy Communion*. 2. Vessels used for the celebration of the Holy Communion.

Communion service Communal distribution of Communion outside the context of a Mass*, a practice common in parishes without a regular priest.

Communion Sunday Special Sunday set apart in some Protestant denominations for the observance of the Lord's Supper* and the administration of the Holy Communion*.

communion table Table or altar from which Holy Communion* is administered.

communion wafer Thin cracker or crackerlike bread served at Holy Communion*.

communion ware Vessels, cups, and other receptacles used during Holy Communion*.

community church Independent non-denominational congregation serving a local community.

Community of the Resurrection Anglican community founded at Oxford in 1892 by Charles Gore* and the brotherhood of the Epiphany* in Calcutta, India. In 1893 the group moved to Radley, and five years later to Mirfield. The main feature of the community was a simple communal life, but it soon began to develop its own distinctive mission, to train ordinands*, conduct retreats*, and serve as warden to communities of women. It conducts the College of the Resurrection in Mirfield.

Compactata Agreement of the Council of Basel* in 1436 that pacified Hussites* by various concessions, including permission to take Holy Communion* in both kinds.

companation (Lat., *cum,* with; *panis,* bread) See CONSUBSTANTIATION.

comparative symbolics Branch of theology dealing with Christian creeds and public confessions of faith.

compelle intrare (lit., compel them to enter) Phrase in the Vulgate* (Luke 14:23) used as a scriptural charter for the Inquisition*.

completuria Brief post-communion prayer of thanksgiving.

compline The last hour of prayer in the Daily Office, after the vespers*. It included recitation of the Psalms and the canticle* Nunc Dimittis*. In the Eastern Church*, it is called the Apodeipnon*.

Complutensian Polyglot The first complete Bible printed in the original languages under the direc-

tion of Cardinal Jimenez de Cisneros* and dedicated to Pope Leo X*, published in 1521 or 1522 in six volumes. It was produced at the newly founded University of Alcala de Henares, near Madrid. It contained the text in Hebrew, Greek, and Latin.

Compostela See SANTIAGO DE COMPOSTELA.

comprecation Intercessory prayer by the saints* for the universal church.

compromise In ecclesiastical law*, the transfer of a legal right.

computus Collection of rules by which the date of Easter* is calculated.

concelebration Joint celebration of the Eucharist* simultaneously by several priests together.

concern In Protestant worship service, the mentioning of persons about whom or situations about which the congregation is asked to pray or assist.

concha Apse, or the semidome over an apse*.

conciliar fellowship Model of ecumenical unity bringing all local churches and denominations together in such a way as to exclude confessional* differences.

conciliar theory Doctrine that emphasizes the collegiality of ecclesiastical government and that vests the supreme authority in the church in the general councils rather than in the pope. It held that the general councils derived their authority directly from God and that all Christians, including the pope, were bound by their decisions. Thus, conciliarism, a movement in the Western Church* during the thirteenth to fifteenth centuries.

conciliarity In the Eastern Orthodox Church*, the principle of ecclesiastical government in which supreme authority rests with representative councils.

concision (lit., cutting off [the male member] or sexual mutilation) Derisive term used by St.

Paul* to describe the practice of the rite of circumcision as a requirement for salvation*.

conclave (Lat., *cum clave,* with a key) Secret meeting of the cardinals as princes of the Roman Catholic Church to elect a new pope. Also, the locked room or set of rooms in which they meet for this purpose.

concomitance Roman Catholic eucharistic doctrine that both the body and the blood are intaken even when the communicant receives only one of the elements*.

Concord, Formula of Lutheran confession* prepared by Martin Chemnitz* and James Andreae in 1577 based on the Swabian-Saxon Concordia, the Torgau Book, and the Bergen Book. It is made up of an Epitome and a Thorough Declaration, each with 12 articles. The formula* was designed to settle the doctrinal controversies between Philippists and Flacians regarding Majorism, or the place of good works* in salvation*; synergism, or the role of freewill* in conversion*; Antinomianism, or the role of Mosaic Law; the Lord's Supper*; Christ's descent into hell*; and predestination*.

Concord of Wittenberg Agreement in 1536 between Zwinglian and Lutheran theologians on the disputed doctrine of the Lord's Supper*. It was signed by Luther*, Melanchthon*, and Bucer*.

concordance Thesaurus or reference guide to the Bible consisting of topically arranged word lists. There are Bible concordances for most languages and most versions. The first concordance to the Vulgate* was produced by the Dominican Order in Paris in the thirteenth century and compiled by St. Jacques. The first English language concordance for the whole Bible was that by J. Merbecke* in 1550. However, the most famous are those by Alexander Cruden* and James Strong for the Authorized (or King James) Version*. R. Young's *Analytical Concordance to the Bible* (1879) offers Hebrew and Greek equivalents of English words.

concordat Agreement between the Holy See* and a national government establishing the rights and limits of the Roman Catholic Church in that country.

concurrence 1. Simultaneous or consecutive occurrence of holy days. 2. Harmony between divine actions and the actions of human beings working in tandem.

concursus divinus The cooperation between divine grace* and human will, manifested in God's endowment of certain gifts for the performance of human tasks and human dependence on God for the actual exercise of these gifts and the conditions under which they are exercised. Sometimes applied to the writing of the Scriptures under divine inspiration*.

condign merit (Lat., *con dignus,* worthy) Distinguished from meritum de congruo*, reward given solely out of divine generosity without reference to human activity. See also CONDIGNITY.

condignity In scholastic theology, grace of God merited through good works* performed by a Christian acting in conscious reliance on the Holy Spirit*. The New Testament example of condignity is Cornelius*, whose prayers and alms came up as a memorial before God.

conditional baptism In Roman Catholic and Anglican traditions, baptismal rite administered when it is uncertain whether the candidate has been previously baptized.

conditional election Doctrine that saints* are elected by God based upon his foreknowledge of their faith.

conditional immortality Doctrine that immortality* is the privilege of regenerate persons who have accepted Jesus Christ as Lord. Nonbelievers cease to exist but escape eternal punishment*. It was formally condemned at the Fifth Lateran Council* in 1513. See also ANNIHILATIONISM.

conductus Medieval Latin song, not set on liturgical texts, but used in processions and on ceremonial occasions.

conference Governing body of the Methodist Church.

Conference of European Churches Regional ecumenical organization for Europe, representing 118 churches.

Confessing Church Protestant movement in Nazi Germany founded in 1933 by Martin Niemoller* in opposition to Hitler and the state-supported church headed by Ludwig Muller. Its basis was the Declaration of Barmen* (1934) and the Synod of Dahlem (1934). It included such leaders as Dietrich Bonhoeffer* and Karl Barth*. After World War II, the movement folded into the Evangelical Church.

confessio See CONFESSION NO. 4.

confession 1. Act of acknowledging sin or wrongdoing to a priest or a group of fellow believers (*exomologeo*). 2. Profession of faith*. 3. Statement of faith or belief subscribed to by an ecclesiastical body, especially an acknowledgment and acceptance of Jesus Christ as Lord and Savior through the recitation of the Nicene Creed*, the Apostles' Creed*, or similar formulas, often used of the Reformation* and post-Reformation statements in distinction from the early creeds. 4. Tomb of a martyr* or confessor*; the structure built over a tomb, crypt, or shrine in which relics* are placed; the church in which a martyr is buried.

Confessio

confession ad auriculam (lit., confession into the ear [of a priest]) Individual acknowledgment of sin to a priest as part of the ancient ritual of absolution* and penance*.

Confession of Dositheus (1672) Eastern Orthodox* confession* of faith, drawn up by a synod* presided over by Dositheus*, patriarch* of Jerusalem* (1641–1707).

Confession of 1967 Statement of faith drawn up by the United Presbyterian Church of North America and the Presbyterian Church in the USA as part of their merger. It emphasizes the work of reconciliation in Christ and the church's ministry of reconciliation in matters relating to racial discrimination, peace, war, poverty, and social injustice. Conservatives resisted the confession because of its supposedly weak position on the authority of the Scripture, the deity of Christ, the virgin birth*, and predestination*.

confessional 1. In Roman Catholic churches, a place—as a room or stall—set aside for the administration of penance*, furnished with two chairs, a table, and a kneeler. 2. Act or practice of confessing sins to a priest. 3. Denominational adherence to a confession of faith.

confessionalism Adherence to a creed or normative standard of beliefs.

Confessions of St. Augustine Spiritual autobiography of St. Augustine dating from 398–400, considered one of the great classics of religious literature. Near the beginning comes the celebrated sentence: "You have made us for yourself, and our heart is restless, until it rests in thee." The first nine autobiographical books deal with his Manichaean past, his conversion at Milan*, and an account of St. Monica*. The remaining four sections deal with memory, time, creation, and the church.

confessor 1. Priest who hears confessions. 2. In the early church, believer who was persecuted for confessing the faith but did not suffer martyrdom. Later, applied to holy men so named by the pope.

confided In Roman Catholic usage, given to the care and charge of a missionary society or religious order or congregation.

confirmand Candidate for confirmation*.

confirmation In Catholic sacramental theology*, one of the seven sacraments*, a one-time-only consecration of a baptized person for a fuller endowment of the Holy Spirit*. In Eastern Orthodoxy it is administered immediately after baptism*. In some Protestant churches, confirmation* initiates young people into the privileges of the church. Generally, confirmation is by laying on of hands*, anointing with oil, or both. Confirmation as a sacrament separate from baptism dates from the twelfth century.

confirmation in grace In Roman Catholic theology, state of sinlessness bestowed by God on certain individuals, such as the Virgin Mary*, John the Baptist, and the apostles.

confirmation of bishops Ecclesiastical approval of the election of new bishops.

confiteor (lit., I confess) A form of confession* of sins, addressed to God, used in Roman Catholic and Anglican churches. It runs as follows: "I confess to Almighty God, and to you my brothers and sisters, that I have sinned through my own fault, in my thoughts and in my words, in what I have done and what I have failed to do; and I ask Blessed Mary, ever Virgin, all the angels and saints, and you, my brothers and sisters, to pray for me to the Lord our God."

confractoria Anthems sung during the fraction* or breaking of bread in the Eucharist*.

confraternity Roman Catholic brotherhood*. Most parishes have a Confraternity of Christian Doctrine* and one of the Blessed Sacrament*.

Confraternity of Christian Doctrine (CCD) Official organ for the catechetical instruction of the laity established by Pope Pius X* in 1905 through his encyclical* *Acerbo Nimis*. CCD was established in the United States in 1935 as an independent apostolate* and is coordinated by the Office of U.S. Bishops.

Confraternity of Unity Anglican society founded in 1926 and seeking the reunion of Anglican and Roman Catholic churches.

Congar, Georges-Yves (1904–1995) French Dominican theologian. He entered the Dominican Order in 1925 under the name of Marie-Joseph. He developed an early interest in ecclesiology* and ecumenism*, on which he wrote his first book, *Divided Christendom* (1939). At the end of World War II (during which he was a prisoner of war), he made a bold appeal for a structural reform of the church. He was forbidden to teach in 1954, but on the election of Pope John XXIII* in 1958 he was appointed a peritus* to the Second Vatican Council* and he helped to write the Message to the World delivered at its opening. In 1969 he was named a member of the Pontifical International Theological Commission. He was created a cardinal in 1994, a year before his death. Among his other works were *Esquisse du Mystere de l'Eglise* (1960), *L'Eglise de Saint Augustin a l'Epoque Moderne* (1970), and *Je Crois en l'Esprit Saint* (3 vols., 1979–1980).

conge d'elire (Fr., permission to choose) In the Church of England*, royal authorization for election of a bishop or an archbishop.

congregation 1. Assembly of worshipers or the membership of a church. A congregation is a specific local assembly, while the church is the people of God*. 2. Roman Catholic religious organization devoted to a particular cause. 3. Roman Catholic religious order or branch of an order. 4. Committee of bishops at a general council. 5. Also, Sacred Congregation. Administrative committee of the College of Cardinals*, one of the agencies of the Roman Curia* that exercises administrative powers. They are composed mainly of cardinals with some bishops and each is presided by a cardinal prefect (except those of the Doctrine of Faith, Bishops, and Oriental Churches, where the pope reserves the prefecture to himself). They are nine in number as follows: 1. Congregation of the Doctrine of the Faith. 2. Congregation of Oriental Churches. 3. Congregation for Bishops. 4. Congregation for Divine Worship and Sacraments. 5. Congregation for the Causes of Saints*. 6. Congregation for the Clergy.

7. Congregation for Religious and Secular Institutes. 8. Congregation for Catholic Education and 9. Congregation for the Evangelization of Peoples.

Congregation of the Holy Cross Roman Catholic religious order founded in 1837 by Basil Moreau. It is a union of two previously existing institutes, the Brothers of St. Joseph and the Auxiliary Priests of Le Mans. The new community's center was Sainte-Croix (Holy Cross), a suburb of Le Mans, from which it took its name. An institute of women, the Marianite Sisters of Holy Cross*, was added in 1841. In 1841 seven members, under the leadership of Edward F. Sorin*, were sent to work in Notre Dame* in the diocese* of Vincennes, Indiana. Here, in 1842, they opened a school which later became the University of Notre Dame du Lac in 1844. The congregation started seven other colleges and universities, including St. Joseph's College, Cincinnati, Ohio; Holy Cross College, New Orleans; University of Portland, Portland, Orgeon; and King's College, Wilkes-Barre, Pennsylvania. In addition, the community directs more than 20 high schools.

congregational (*adjective*) 1. Of or belonging to a form of ecclesiastical government in which each church is independent and self-governing. 2. Practicing Congregationalism* or belonging to a Congregational church. 3. Performed or sung by a whole congregation, as in congregational singing.

Congregationalism Presbyterian form of unregimented ecclesiastical government favoring autonomy for local congregations. Congregationalism was first formulated by Robert Browne* (1553–1603), separatist* leader, who asserted in his treatise, *Reformation Without Tarrying for Anie* (1582), that each Christian believer has made a separate covenant with God and is not subject to bishops or magistrates. Ordination is not vested in leaders but is in the hands of the whole church. The Pilgrim fathers* who emigrated to America in 1620 were Congregationalists, and Congregationalism became the established order in Connecticut and Massachusetts for the next two centuries. The officers of the Congregational church are a minister, deacon, and secretary-treasurer. The governing body is the church assembly. Historically, Congre-

gationalism has been actively involved in ecumenism* and missionary work. The latter was undertaken through the London Missionary Society, founded in 1795, which in 1966 became the Congregational Council for World Mission*. Great LMS* missionaries include David Livingstone*, John Williams*, and James Chalmers*.

Congregational worship is similar to that of the Presbyterians* and the Quakers* in that it is both biblically-based and Spirit-led. Public prayer is not from any prescribed form. Although there is no prescribed manual, worship practices are shaped by *The Directory of Public Worship of God Throughout the Three Kingdoms,* published in 1644, which set some objective standards for Congregational service. Nevertheless, until the twentieth century, Congregationalism was marked by the absence of creeds as doctrinal anchors, the infrequent celebration of the Lord's Supper*, prolix sermons, and the lack of color and ceremony. Some of these failings have been corrected with the publication of *The Book of Congregational Worship* in England and *A Book of Worship for Free Churches* in the United States.

congregations, monastic Group of monasteries united under an abbot general* or an abbot president. The best known of such congregations is the Cassinese Congregation*.

congregations, religious Religious institutes* within the Roman Catholic Church whose members do take simple vows, but not solemn vows.

congruism Grace conferred by God for the performance of good works, especially by the unregenerate and unsaved.

connectional/connexional Of or relating to a Methodist form of polity*, or one similar to it, based on a system of conferences. It was later replaced by the term *conference.* Connectional* polity is more centralized than the congregational*. Unlike the presbyterian*, it allows for episcopacy* as a function, although not as a sacred order.

connexion/connection John Wesley's* term for Methodism* or the association of Methodist societies.

Conques Benedictine abbey of Sainte-Foy founded by Charlemagne* in the town of Conques on the great pilgrimage* road to Santiago de Compostela*. It was completed around 1000, destroyed by the Huguenots* in 1561 and restored in the nineteenth century at the urging of author Prosper Merimee. The church's greatest treasure is the statue of St. Fides (Sainte-Foy in French), a girl who was martyred at the age of 12. Another treasure is the Last Judgment on the west tympanum* of the church.

Conrad of Marburg (c. 1180–1233) German monk who became Germany's first inquisitor in 1231. In 1225 he became the confessor* and spiritual director* of Elizabeth of Hungary*.

conscience clause Legal provision exempting people from taking oaths on grounds of religious scruples* or conscience.

conscientious objector Person who refuses to serve in the military on grounds of religious convictions or pacifism. Among Christian pacifist groups are Quakers*, Brethren, and Doukhbbors. Many cults, such as Jehovah's Witnesses*, also reject military service.

conscientization In liberation theology*, the process of becoming aware of the suffering and oppression caused by social and economic bias and discrimination.

consciousness theology School of theology and anthropology associated with Friedrich Schleiermacher* which replaced the Bible with human consciousness as the source of the knowledge of God, and God's self-revelation with human search for and discovery of God. In consciousness theology, human consciousness is the final arbiter of theological truths.

consecration 1. Act by which a person or thing is separated from secular and profane use and dedicated to the service of God. Among the material objects that are generally consecrated to God in Christian usage are altars and eucharistic vessels and elements*. 2. Ordination or elevation of a person to a higher ecclesiastical office, especially that of a bishop, through proper rituals and ceremonies.

Consecration, Prayer of Central prayer in the eucharistic rite of the *Book of Common Prayer** corresponding to the middle of the canons of the Roman Mass*.

consensus fidelium (Lat., consensus of the faithful) Also, sensus fidelium. General agreement on theological doctrines and liturgical practices among members of a denomination.

Consensus Genevensis (lit., the Geneva Agreement) Calvin's* doctrine of predestination* presented to the Council of Geneva in 1552.

consensus patrum (lit., agreement of the fathers) Collective agreement of the fathers of the early church as a basis for determining orthodoxy* of a doctrine or creed.

consensus quinquesaecularis Term applied by Georg Doisch to the conciliatory theory of the Lutheran theologian Calixtus*, who proposed a distinction between fundamental and nonfundamental teachings. The first were those concerning which there was universal agreement during the first five centuries. Most Lutherans repudiated Calixtus.

Consensus Tigurinus (Lit., the Zurich Agreement) Formula of faith agreed upon in 1549 by Calvin*, Farel*, and Bullinger*. Its 26 articles set forth a Calvinist doctrine of the Eucharist*.

consequence, theology of Teaching that makes baptism* or filling by the Spirit a second-stage experience subsequent to conversion* and regeneration*.

Conservative Baptist Association Association of 1,200 Baptist churches founded in 1947 in response to the Fundamentalist-Modernist controversy within the Northern (now American) Baptists. Closely affiliated with the Association are the Conservative Baptist Foreign Mission Society, the Conservative Baptist Home Mission Society, Southwestern Bible College in Phoenix, Arizona, Western Seminary, Denver Seminary*, and Conservative Baptist Seminary.

Conservative Dunkers Common name for Church of the Brethren*.

consignatorium Also, chrismatorium. Part of the church building where the newly baptized were confirmed on Holy Saturday* and the Vigil of Pentecost by signing them with the chrism*.

consilia evangelica (Lat., gospel counsels) Christian ideals of poverty, celibacy, and obedience, as instruments or counsels of perfection*.

Consistent Calvinism Also, Edwardsianism; Hopkinsianism; New Theology. Modified Calvinism* as developed by Samuel Hopkins* (1721–1803) and Joseph Bellamy (1719–1790).

consistory (Lat., consistorium) 1. In the Roman Catholic Church, the College of Cardinals* or a meeting of the cardinals headed by the pope. 2. In the Presbyterian and Reformed* churches, a kirk-session* or governing body of a local church consisting of the ministers and the elders concerned particularly with discipline. 3. In the Lutheran Church, a board of clerical overseers.

consistory court In the Church of England*, a bishop's court that administers ecclesiastical law*.

consolamentum Among the Cathari*, spiritual baptism or baptism of the Holy Spirit*.

consolation 1. Comfort or relief, especially after a loss or tragedy. 2. In a monastery, compensation, as an evening meal, for a sacrificial effort or labor.

Consolata Missionaries Institute of the Consolata for Foreign Missions, a Roman Catholic missionary organization founded by Blessed Giuseppe Allamano at Turin*. The Consolata Fathers were founded in 1901 and the Consolata Sisters in 1910. The group is dedicated to the Virgin of Consolation.

Constance, Council of Sixteenth Ecumenical Council convened from 1414–1418 by Pope John XXIII* and the Holy Roman Emperor Sigismund to end the schism* among rival popes. The council ended the schism by deposing all rival popes and electing Martin V*. It also tried to end the Hussite heresy by burning John Hus*. Its efforts to reform the church resulted in two decrees, one affirming authority of the councils over the church and an-

other which set the intervals at which the councils should meet. Much of the work of Constance unraveled at the Council of Basel-Ferrara-Florence.

Constantine the Great (c. 274/280–337) First Christian emperor of Rome. He was proclaimed emperor in 306 on the death of his father Constantius Chlorus. In the ensuing contest for supremacy, he defeated Maxentius in 312 in the fateful Battle of Milvian Bridge*, north of Rome. Before the battle he received a vision assuring him of victory if he adopted the Christian labarum* as his standard. In 313 he and Licinius, master of the Eastern Empire, issued the Edict of Milan*, granting full legal toleration for Christianity. As sole emperor after defeating Licinius in 324, Constantine intervened in the Arian dispute by convening the Council of Nicaea* and was instrumental in including homoousios* in its creed. However, under the influence of the Arianizing Eusebiuses of Caesarea* and Nicomedia, he exiled the orthodox Athanasius*. In 330 he founded Constantinople* as a second Rome. He was baptized shortly before his death and was buried amid the apostles in the basilica* he founded in their honor in Constantinople. He regarded himself as the servant of God and, with his mother, Helena*, is revered in the Eastern Church* as one of the greatest figures in Christian history.

Constantine the Great

Constantinism Church-state alliance ushered in by Constantine's conversion to Christianity in about 312. It was a mixed blessing; while the church enjoyed state support and some privileges, it also experienced state interference.

Constantinople City on the Bosphorus, formerly Byzantium*, named by Constantine as the capital of the Eastern Empire in 330. It remained the capital of he empire until the Turkish conquest in 1453, except for a brief period (1204–1261) when it was the seat of the Latin empire. Byzantium* was a Christian city from the very beginning. By the fourth century, it had become the see* of one of the four major patriarchates, second in preeminence after only Rome*. Since the sixth century, the patriarch* of Constantinople was acknowledged as the ecumenical patriarch* of all Orthodox Churches. After the Turkish conquest, the city was renamed Istanbul.

Constantinople, councils of Four general councils held at Constantinople in 381, 553, 680, and 869–870.

Constantinople, First Council of General council convened by Emperor Theodosius in 381 to unite the Eastern Church* and attended by 150 orthodox bishops. It confirmed the work of the First Council at Nicaea* by condemning Apollinarianism* and by drawing up the Niceno-Constantinopolitan Creed*.

Constantinople, Fourth Council of In the Eastern Church*, the general council which met under the presidency of Patriarch Photius* of Constantinople in 879 and in the Western Church* the general council which met under the presidency of Patriarch Ignatius in 869. The latter council reaffirmed opposition to the Filioque* (and from the Son) clause added to the Nicene Creed* by the Western Church*.

Constantinople, Second Council of General council convened in 553 by Emperor Justinian* to decide the controversy over the so called "Three Chapters"* and to settle the conflict with the Monophysites who had opposed the decrees of the Council of Chalcedon*. The Three Chapters, Theodore of Mopsuestia*, Theodoret* of

Cyrrhus, and Ibas of Edessa were condemned as tainted with Nestorianism*. Under the influence of Empress Theodora*, a secret Monophysite, the council moved closer to Monophysitism*. In another decision regarding the Virgin Mary*, the council added aeiparthenos* (ever virgin) to the earlier title of Theotokos* (God-bearer), thus confessing her perpetual virginity*.

Constantinople, Third Council of The sixth general council convoked by Emperor Heraclius in 680 to discuss Monothelitism*, which stated that in Christ there were two natures, but not two wills and that therefore he was a single person who acted with one will. The council rejected this doctrine and reaffirmed the Chalcedonian definition which stated that Christ had two wills and two natures. The council also anathematized Pope Honorius* and Macarius, the patriarch* of Antioch, as Monothelites.

constructive theology Branch of theology that relates Christian precepts* and doctrines to the contemporary world, often related to systematic theology*.

consubstantial Sharing identical nature, as an attribute of the Trinity*, a theological term at the heart of the Arian controversy. In the Nicene Creed* the Athanasian party defined the Son as *homoousios*, of the same essence or substance as the Father, to be distinguished from the later Arianizing term, *homoiousios*, like or similar in essence or substance. Thus, consubstantiality.

consubstantiation Lutheran doctrine of the Lord's Supper* which maintains that while the wine and bread of the Holy Communion* retain their physical qualities, the body and blood of Christ are substantially inherent in them. According to Luther*, Christ's body and blood are present "in, with, and under" the sacrament*, and yet not visible. Distinguished from transubstantiation*, since it claims no change of the substance of the elements.

consuetudinary Manual of the ritual of a religious order or cathedral.

consultor 1. Authority whose advice and consent is solicited or required. 2. Member of an official papal study commission. 3. In a Catholic diocese*, member of a college of consultors, a diocesan body of 6 to 12 priests.

contakion (Gk., pole or shaft, hence a vellum roll wound around a piece of wood) In the Eastern Church*, a liturgical hymn composed in a series of strophes. In current usage, only the first strophe of the contakion* is read or sung after the sixth ode of the canon*, after the Little Entrance*.

contemplative life Life of prayer and meditation followed by those who live apart from the world either as solitaries or in religious houses. It is one of the three elements of an intense love of God, the other two being prayer and meditation. Contemplative meditation consists of supernatural or infused contemplation in which the soul receives illumination* and revelation*, although the mind and will still exercise their natural functions. It is often contrasted with the active life.

contemplative orders Monastic orders following the contemplative life*, such as the Carthusians*, Cistercians*, and Carmelites*.

Contemporary English Version (1995) English translation of the Bible in modern English, published by the American Bible Society*.

Contestatio (Lat., a supplication) Also, Illatio or Immolatio*. Preface of the Eucharist* in the Gallican and Spanish Missals.

contextual (Lat., *contexere*, to weave together) Relating to a particular historical setting or culture.

contextual theology Branch of theology that places emphasis on the social, cultural, and economic settings in which the gospel in general and specific theological doctrines are applied in practice. It owes its origins to the concept of indigenization* developed by the early mission strategists, Henry Venn* (1796–1873) and Rufus Anderson* (1796–1880) whereby a universal church could be translated into indigenous traditions and accepted by peoples who were non-Christians for generations. The term *contextualization* was coined by Shoki Coe and Aharoan Sapsezian of WCC's* Theological Education Fund in their 1972

report, *Ministry and Context*. It has implications for evangelization of non-Christian societies as well as in the proclamation of the gospel to the poor and oppressed.

Contextual theology holds that in the Incarnation* God contextualized the gospel to the human race and that the process needs to be developed further to the various human geographical, racial, and gender divisions, without destroying the universality of Christ's message. Liberation theologians have used contextualization extensively, arguing that since all Scripture is culturally and historically conditioned, its message is relative and situational. Further, they hold that contextualization is a means of aligning truth and practice, thought and action and that all authentic theology must be participatory. Its opponents argue contextual theology, although an inescapable task, runs the risk of syncretism and compromise and mutes the revolutionary content of the Christian message and ignores the Holy Spirit's* role in evangelization.

contrafactum In sacred music, substitution of a new text for an old one, such as the replacement of the secular text of a composition by a sacred text.

Contra-Remonstrants Dutch defenders of Calvinist orthodoxy against the followers of Arminius*. In 1610 Arminians had issued the Remonstrance* to which the Calvinists responded with the Counter-Remonstrance. Supported by the stadtholder (viceroy), William of Orange, the Contra-Remonstrants gained control at the Synod of Dort* in 1618. The Canons of Dort* became one of the official standards of the Dutch Reformed Church*.

contrition (Lat., *contritio,* a wearing away of something hard) Form of repentance* defined by the Council of Trent* as "sorrow of heart and detestation of sin committed, with the purpose of not sinning in future." See also ATTRITION.

convalidation Ratification of canonically invalid marriage.

convent (lit., coming together) 1. Nuns living as a religious community under a single superior*.

Formerly, it was applied to male religious communities as well. 2. By extension, the place or the buildings set apart for this purpose.

conventicle Unauthorized religious assembly, or the place where such an assembly is held. In England, it is applied to the meeting place of the Dissenters, in Scotland used of gatherings of Covenanters*, often in the open.

convention 1. Ecclesiastical meeting. 2. In the Protestant Episcopal Church, a legislative body, such as the General Convention* and the District Convention.

conventual Mass Public Mass sung or said in religious communities where public choir office is recited. The Mass* is attended by the whole community. See also CAPITULAR MASS.

Conventuals 1. Branch of Franciscan Order*, sometimes called Black Friars* or Friars Minor Conventual*, who are permitted to hold private property. 2. Members of an order following a revised rule. 3. Members of a convent.

conversation Old English term for lifestyle or conduct (1 Pet. 1:15).

conversi Lay brothers* in a monastery.

conversion 1. Experience or act leading to an abandonment of a undesirable lifestyle, spiritual outlook, or religious belief system and the adoption of and commitment to a new lifestyle, spiritual outlook, and religious belief system. 2. Radical turnaround or transformation characterized by repentance* (turning from) and faith* (turning to). It is often seen as the first step in a process that includes spiritual rebirth, baptism*, and regeneration*.

Conversion of St. Paul, Feast of Feast on January 25 commemorating the conversion of St. Paul* on the road to Damascus*.

converso Also, Marrano. Christianized Jew or Moor in medieval Spain.

convert Person who undergoes or experiences conversion.

conviction Profound sense of sin, personal unworthiness, and need for salvation through the working of the Holy Spirit*, as a preliminary step toward conversion.

convocation 1. Provincial assembly in the Church of England* The two most important of such assemblies are the convocations of Canterbury* and York*. 2. Special assembly in the Protestant Episcopal Church*.

Conybeare, Frederick Cornwallis (1856–1924) English scholar in Armenian. He spent most of his life discovering and collating Armenian manuscripts. He wrote *Myth, Magic and Morals: A Study of Christian Origins* (1908) and *The Historical Christ* (1914).

Cook, A. Robert (1913–1981) American radio evangelist and educator. He served for several years in the pastorate before joining Youth for Christ* International as director, and later as president for nine years. From 1962 to 1985 he served as president of The King's College, Briarcliff Manor, New York, and then as chancellor of the college until his death. His radio program, "Walk with the King," reached thousands for over two decades. He wrote nine books of which *Now That I Believe* sold more than a million copies.

Priest Wearing a Cope

Cook, David C. (1850–1927) Sunday school* curriculum author and publisher. In 1875 he founded the David C. Cook Publishing Company in Lake View, Illinois. He led Sunday school educators in producing age-graded curricula, developing the "I Am His" circles for youth, and promoting the adult Bible class movement.

Coonen Cross (lit., crooked cross) Cross outside the church at Mattancherry in Cochin, India, at which a group of Christians of St. Thomas* took an oath* in 1653 to resist the imposition of Roman Catholicism* on them. Eventually, more than half of them went back to the Syrian Church and now follow the Jacobite tradition.

cope Long, sleeveless cloak of rich materials, fastened at the chest with a clasp, worn by priests.

Copeland, Kenneth (1937–) Evangelist and Bible preacher prominent in the Charismatic and Positive Confession* movements, emphasizing faith, divine healing*, and prosperity. His theology and ministry methods were influenced by E. W. Kenyon*, Oral Roberts*, and Kenneth Hagin*. In 1973 he and his wife, Gloria, began the "Believer's Voice of Victory," a radio program that now reaches millions.

Coptic (Arab., *kibt,* Egyptian) Form of the ancient Egyptian language, comprising 24 letters of the Greek alphabet in uncial form and seven Demotic characters expressing consonantal sounds not in Greek. It was a spoken and literary language until the seventh century, and it remains the church language of the Coptic Church*. Its four main dialects are Sahidic* (Upper Egypt), Fayumic, Akhmimic, and Bohairic* (Lower Egypt). The earliest Bible translations were in Sahidic. Most of the known Gnostic writings, such as those discovered in Nag Hammadi*, were written in Coptic.

Coptic calendar Calendar used in the Coptic Church* with its starting date in 284, the year of the accession of Diocletian. It is often known as the Era of the Martyrs*. It has 12 months of 30 days each.

Coptic Church Ancient Christian church reputedly founded, according to tradition, by St. Mark* in

Alexandria*, in Egypt, the birthplace of Christian monasticism*. As one of the four major patriarchates* of the Christian world, it played an active role in the defense of orthodoxy* through its great sons, Clement*, Origen*, Dionysius*, Athanasius*, and Cyril*. It adopted the Monophysite creed in the fifth century, and, at the Council of Chalcedon*, championed the Monophysite cause through Patriarch Dioscorus*. The Coptic Church has faced a long night of persecution since the Arab conquest of the seventh century. The Arab conquerors used taxation and open repression to lure Christians to turn apostate* and induce mass conversions. The massacre of Christians and the destruction of over 3,000 churches and monasteries under Caliph El Hakem biamr Allah (c. 1000) sparked the Crusades*. The persecution continued under Turks until the early twentieth century, and even now the Coptic Church is a suffering church, facing severe persecution both from official authorities and from Islamic fundamentalists.

Coptic Christians follow the Alexandrian Rite* and use the Liturgy of St. Basil*. The Eucharist* is offered in one kind and baptism* is combined with confirmation* as one sacrament*. They practice circumcision and refrain from pork. Masses are lengthy, often lasting two hours or more. The Coptic Church observes five important fasts: The Pre-Lenten Fast of Nineveh*, the Great Fast* of Lent* (55 days), the Fast of the Nativity before Christmas* (28 days), the Fast of the Apostles after the Ascension, and the Fast of the Virgin after the Ascension (15 days). The Coptic patriarch*, called the Pope of Alexandria, Pentapolis, and Ethiopia, is chosen by a religious tribunal, subject to approval by the government. There are 24 bishoprics*, most of them in Lower Egypt. Outside Egypt, there is a large Coptic diaspora, with dioceses* at Jerusalem*, Sudan, South Africa, and North America.

Since the 1960s there has been a dramatic revival in monastic life. Membership in the church is estimated at about 10 million. The official liturgical language is the Bohairic* dialect of Coptic, but Arabic is commonly used for the audible parts of the service. Three eucharistic prayers are in use: The anaphora of St. Cyril used in Lent*, the Syro-Byzantine anaphora of St. Basil, and the anaphora of St. Gregory used at Christmas*,

Epiphany*, and Easter*, which has the unusual feature of being addressed only to the Son. The eucharistic bread is in small leavened loaves, stamped with a design including the Trisagion* in Greek, and the wine is made from the fermented juice of raisins. Baptismal and other sacramental rites resemble the Greek Orthodox. Baptism begins with exorcism*. Unction*, with seven lighted

St. Bishoi Monastery

lamps, is administered as a public healing service on the Friday before Palm Sunday*. There are foot-washing ceremonies on Maundy Thursday* and the Feast of St. Peter and St. Paul. There are seven daily offices: midnight, dawn, third, sixth, and ninth hours, vespers*, and compline*. Incense is offered morning and evening. A traditional Coptic church has a solid sanctuary

Coptic Museum Cross

screen* with a central door flanked by windows and side doors and lighter screens to mark off the choir and the men's and women's sections of the nave*.

In modern times, three events have infused new vigor into the Coptic Church: the apparitions of the Virgin Mary* at Zaytun, near Cairo; the return of the relics* of St. Mark* from Venice* to Egypt; and the dedication of the gigantic cathedral of St. Mark in Cairo. The flourishing Coptic diaspora, mostly in the United States, has also helped the Coptic Church to be more assertive against the constant threat from Islamic fundamentalists.

Coptic Rite Liturgical traditions of the Coptic Church developed after the post-Chalcedonian break with the Western and Orthodox churches. It is essentially the monastic usage of Scetis, as modified by later reforms. It has three anaphoras: St. Mark, St. Basil*, and St. Gregory. The liturgical language is Bohairic*. Reflecting its monastic origins, the rite is solemn and long, and has less splendor and sumptuous ceremonial than the Orthodox.

Corbie Celebrated monastery, ten miles east of Amiens*, founded about 660. It also had one of the most important Carolingian theological schools.

Cordeliers Franciscan Observatines, so-called from the knotted cord they wore around the waist as a pledge of their strict observance of the Rule of St. Francis.

Cordoba Cathedral known as Mesquita, converted from a mosque in Cordoba, Spain. Built between the eighth and eleventh centuries, on the foundations of a Roman temple to Janus and a later Visigothic church, it had 11 aisles and 36 transepts*, including the Orange-tree courtyard. After the Reconquest, when it was converted into a church, the 19 portals opening on to the courtyard were all sealed up, with the exception of the central one. The interior is only 36 feet high but the 850 pillars—it is said that originally there were 1,000—made from marble, jasper, breccia, and other stone lend the room a delicate weightlessness. At one time, the church was illuminated by 1,000 lamps. The central area is surrounded by chapels, including the Capilla Real (royal chapel*) and the Capilla de Villaviciosa.

coredemptrix In Roman Catholic theology, the Virgin Mary* understood to be an effective agent of redemption* along with her Son and thus worthy of veneration*. See COMEDIATRIX.

Corinth Greek city where St. Paul* established a church about A.D. 50 and where he lived for 18 months (Acts 18:11). St. Paul wrote two canonical letters to the Corinthians as well as possibly a third letter, now lost.

Corinthians, Third Letter to the Apocryphal letter, attributed to St. Paul*, accepted as canonical by the Armenian Church*.

Cornelius (d. 253) Bishop of Rome* from 251. He was elected pope after the see* had been vacant for 14 months after the Decian persecution*. He himself died in exile as a martyr*. Feast day: September 16.

cornerstone The capital letter or gammadion L in the Latin alphabet, used as the symbol of Christ as the cornerstone. It was first used in the Roman catacombs* in the fourth century, and the practice continued into the Middle Ages.

cornet White headdress of the Sisters of Charity.

cornice Top edge of a pulpit.

corona 1. Five mysteries* of the Rosary*. 2. Circle of candles in a church. 3. Narrow band of hair left around the head of a tonsured* monk.

coronation of the Virgin The crowning of the Virgin Mary* in heaven* by her Son, subject of the Fifth Glorious Mystery of the Rosary.

corporal White linen on which the bread and the wine of the Eucharist* are placed for consecration. See also ANTIMENSION; BURSE; EILETON; PALL.

corporal works of mercy Seven Christian duties of feeding the hungry, quenching the thirsty, clothing the naked, giving shelter to the homeless, aid-ing the sick, ministering to prisoners, and burying the dead.

corpus Figure of Christ on a crucifix.

Corpus Christi Catholic festival of the Eucharist* celebrated on the Thursday or Friday following Trinity Sunday* by carrying the host* in procession around the streets. First established in 1246, it was made universal by Pope Urban IV in 1264 and became very popular in later Catholicism*.

Corpus Iuris Canonici Collection of canon law* in the Western Church* in force until the promulgation of the Codex Iuris Canonici* in 1917. It included the Decretum of Gratian, the Liber Extra or the six books of the Decretals* of Gregory IX*, the Liber Sextus of Boniface VIII, the Clementines*, collection made by Clement V*, the Extravagantes* of John XXII*, and the Extravagantes Communes, or the decrees of various popes between 1261 and 1484.

correctoria Medieval books with readings to correct the text of the Vulgate*.

Correggio, Antonio (1489–1534) Painter of the High Renaissance, probably a pupil of Mantegna*. Much of his work shows the influence of Leonardo*, Raphael*, and Michelangelo*. His finest works are *The Madonna of St. Francis* (1514–1515), *St. John the Evangelist* (1520–1522), *Assumption of the Virgin* (1526–1528), *Lamentation over the Dead Christ* and *Martyrdom of Four Saints* (1524–1526), *Madonna of St. Jerome* (1527–1528), *Nativity* (1529–1530), *Day and Night,* and *Madonna and Child with Sts. George and John the Baptist* (1531–1532).

corrody Right of those who have performed some service to a monastery to receive board or lodging or other benefit.

Corvey Benedictine monastery on the left bank of the Weser, between Hanover and Kassel, Germany, founded by monks from Corbie, France, in 816. The monastery received the patronage of Louis the Pious, Charlemagne*, and his son. Anskar*, the apostle of Norway, lived here as a monk, and from here he set out on his missions to North Germany and Scandinavia. The old church was replaced by a Baroque edifice in the eighteenth century.

Cosmas and Damian, Sts. Fourth-century martyrs* and patron saints* of physicians. A number of miraculous healings have been ascribed to them. A famous church was constructed in Rome* in their honor. Feast day : July 1 (Eastern Church*); September 26 (Western Church*).

Cosma e Damiano

Cosmas Melodus, St. (c. 675–c. 751) Also, Cosmas of Jerusalem; Cosmas of Maiuma. Author of Greek liturgical hymns. Among his most famous works are his canons, or odes in praise of the great Christian feasts. He was also a poet whose poems are distinguished by their metrical design.

cosmocrator (lit., the ruler of the world) The devil as the prince of this world. In Gnostic thought, the Old Testament creator-god.

cosmogony Theological speculation about the origin or creation of the universe.

coso In the Syrian Rite, the chalice*.

cotta Shorter form of the surplice* reaching to the waist or a little lower, with tighter sleeves, and a square-cut yoke at the neck.

Cotton, John (1584–1652) Puritan leader of the Massachusetts Colony in New England, grandfather of Cotton Mather*. Through his influence, dissenters*, such as Roger Williams* and Anne Hutchinson*, were driven out of the colony. He helped to establish the pattern of church govern-

ment in his book, *The Way of the Churches of Christ in New England* (1645).

Coudrin, Pierre Mary Joseph (1768–1837) Founder of the Congregation of the Fathers of the Sacred Hearts of Jesus and Mary and of the Perpetual Adoration of the Most Holy Sacrament of the Altar. The purpose of the group was to emulate the four ages of Christ: his infancy by the instruction of children; his hidden life by the adoration

Sts. Cosmas and Damian

of the Eucharist*; his public life by missionary works; and his crucifixion by exercises of mortification*. The group is also known as the Picpus Fathers, since their main building is located on Rue Picpus in Paris. Picpus Fathers are active in Vanuatu and South America.

council Formal ecclesiastical assembly participated in by bishops and members of the hierarchy*. General and ecumenical councils are held for the purpose of defining doctrine or ritual. The first such general council is often held to be the meeting in Jerusalem* (Acts 15). Provincial councils are now called synods*.

Council for World Mission Council formed in 1966 as successor to the London Missionary Society and the Commonwealth Missionary Society. It has 22 member churches in all continents.

Council of Churches for Britain and Ireland Successor organization that replaced the British Council of Churches*. It includes the Roman Catholic Church, Pentecostal and Holiness churches*, and Russian, Greek, and Oriental churches as well as the older Anglican and mainstream Protestant churches. In 1999 it changed its name to Churches Together in Britain and Ireland (CTBI*).

Council of the Twelve Apostles In the Church of Jesus Christ of Latter-Day Saints* (Mormons*), a body subordinate to the First Presidency that oversees the church and ordains its ministers.

counsel 1. Spiritual or moral guidance. 2. Practice of prudence. 3. Purpose or plan (Ps. 33:11). 4. Divine directive (Matt. 19:21).

counsels of perfection Three monastic obligations of poverty, chastity*, and obedience which, taken collectively, approximated perfection*. They are seen as instituted by Christ as instructions beyond his general commandments and thus as a rule for Christian ascetics. See also CONSILIA EVANGELICA.

Counter-Reformation Revival, renewal, and reform of Roman Catholicism* in response to the Reformation*. It was spearheaded by the new religious orders, including the Jesuits*, Capuchins*, Theatines*, Somaschi*, Ursulines*, Oratorians*, and Barnabites*. Its high point was the Council of Trent*, which defined the doctrines and practices of the Catholic Church and also legislated reforms eliminating the most glaring clerical abuses and thus taking the wind out of the Reformers' sails. The theological groundwork of Counter-Reformation was laid in Robert Bellarmine's* *Controversiae* (1586–1589). Also contributing to the triumph of the papacy was the dominant temporal power of Spain and other Catholic princes in the Continent. It was a time marked by the emergence of strong Catholic leadership, especially monastic leaders such as St. Francis de Sales and St. Charles Borromeo*, mystics such as Teresa of Avila* and St. John of the Cross*, and theologians such as Robert Bellarmine* and Peter Canisius*.

Pius V* (1565–1572) initiated a series of internal reforms within the Curia* and issued edicts against simony*, blasphemy*, sodomy, and concubinage. He reformed the Breviary* and encouraged the reading of Scripture. Among the other weapons of Counter-Reformation were the Inquisition* and the *Index Librorum Prohibitorum**. The Counter-Reformation succeeded in halting

the progress of Protestantism* and created a firewall against its spread to Southern Europe and France. Its success was complete in Spain and Italy, partially successful in Ireland, France, and Poland. In Germany, Switzerland, Austria, Hungary, and Bohemia, it managed to regain some of the population. Its failure was most complete in England, Scotland, Scandinavia, and the Netherlands. See also TRENT, COUNCIL OF.

Countess of Huntingdon's Connexion Religious body founded by Selina Hastings, the Countess of Huntingdon (1707–1791). She became a Calvinist Methodist in 1739 and a prominent leader in the Evangelical revival and a friend of John Wesley* and George Whitefield*. She opened chapels in Brighton, Tunbridge Wells, Bath, and London and established a college for the training of Evangelical clergy in South Wales. Her interest in the evangelization of the Americas led to the founding of Dartmouth College and Princeton University.

Couperin, Francois (1668–1733) Leading French composer of the eighteenth century. In 1693 he succeeded Jacques Thomelin as maitre de chapelle and organist of the Chapelle Royal. Although his fame rests on his secular works, he composed a large body of church music, including two organ masses. The larger one, *Mass for Parish Services,* was intended for use on principal feasts. Most of Couperin's vocal church music was not published during his lifetime; at least 21 motets* belong to this category. Among the published works are three collections of versets, 18 cantata-like motets, and one collection of lamentations.

Courts of the Church In the Reformed* tradition, the kirk-session*, synod*, and general assembly as seats of governing and judicial authority in the church.

Coutances Cathedral in Coutances, France, built between 1218 and 1548. The transept* and choir were completed in 1274, the first of the vaulted roofs in 1250, the Gothic* choir in the fourteenth century, and the triforium* in the fifteenth. In 1548, the cathedral was formally consecrated, even though it was still incomplete.

covenant Solemn agreement or bond between two parties, by which each pledges to do or acknowledge something of value to the other. When the covenant is pledged in blood, it is called the blood covenant. In theology, divided into the new covenant* or the covenant of grace* and the old covenant or the covenant of works* or the law. It is a major theme in the theology of the Bible and of much later Protestant theology, especially in the Reformed* tradition.

Covenant churches Protestant churches, especially in Scotland, based on special covenants or based on covenant theology*.

covenant of grace 1. Covenant that forms the basis of the new dispensation* in the New Testament. It is governed by mercy, love, forgiveness, and salvation* through the working of the Holy Spirit* and through the intercession of Jesus Christ. 2. In reformed theology, there is no discontinuity between the Old and New Testament, and the covenant of grace begins with the protoevangelium (Genesis 3:15) rather than with the New Testament.

covenant of works 1. Covenant that forms the basis of the old dispensation* in the Old Testament. It is governed by an inflexible Mosaic legal system, punishment for sins, and the inaccessibility and impassibility* of God. 2. In Reformed theology, the covenant of works remained in effect from the Creation to the Fall (Genesis 2:16–17)

Covenant Service Special Methodist service, usually held on the First Sunday of the year, at which church members rededicate themselves to God.

covenant theology Branch of Reformed* theology dealing with covenants and that explains relations between God and his creation on the basis of the making and keeping of covenants. It was one of the distinguishing features developing the Puritans* and Reformed churches. The covenant of works was in effect from the creation of Adam until the Fall. The terms of the covenant are found in Genesis 2:16–17, where the tree is prohibited. The covenant of grace was instituted after the Fall; its terms are first described in Genesis 3:15, the Protoevangelium*. This covenant had various administrations from Adam to Christ,

but its terms were the same. Covenant theology holds that man is a sinner and has no right or plea before a sovereign and righteous God except through the blood of Christ. Major theologians of this school were Caspar Olevianus*, Zacharias Ursinus*, and Johannes Cocceius* in Germany, William Ames* in England, and A. A. Hodge* in the United States. See also FEDERAL THEOLOGY.

Covenanters Scottish Presbyterians who, after the Restoration of 1660, pledged themselves to maintain Evangelical Presbyterianism* and resist Catholicism* and the established church. They signed the National Covenant* of 1638 and the Solemn League and Covenant of 1643. As a result of their efforts, Presbyterianism was restored to Scotland by William III in 1690.

covenanting Concept of church unity that permits a diversity of traditions within a unity of faith. In covenanting, each member church maintains its ecclesiastical structures, forms of worship and organization, but accepts common sacraments*, mission, and confession*. Covenanting is an incremental process and moves slowly, and is often hobbled by historical and nontheological factors.

Coventry City in England, site of a Benedictine house founded in 1043 by Leofric, Earl of Mercia, and his wife, the famous Lady Godiva. In the twelfth century it became an ecclesiastical see*. In 1918 the Collegiate Church of St. Michael, completed in 1433, became a cathedral, but was largely destroyed by air raids in 1940. A new cathedral, designed by Sir Basil Spence, was built at right angles to the old cathedral, and consecrated in 1962. Its outstanding feature is the majestic 72-foot high tapestry of Christ in Glory, designed by Graham Sutherland, behind the altar. Other architectural features include the Chapel of Unity, Chapel of Industry, the bronze sculpture of St. Michael and the Devil by Jacob Epstein, and the huge glass screen* at the south end of the nave*, allowing an unimpeded view of the ruins of the old cathedral. The charred cross in the old cathedral remains an emblem of the work of reconciliation with Germany.

Coverdale, Miles (1488–1569) Bible translator. An Augustinian friar* ordained in 1514, he left his order and became a Lutheran, and an associate translator for William Tyndale*. In 1535 he brought out his version, the first printed English Bible, printed in Zurich*. It was followed by his Great Bible* in 1539 and Cranmer's Bible in 1540. After a few years of exile in Europe, he was named bishop of Exeter* by Edward VI. Exiled again under Mary, he spent a year in Geneva*, where he worked on the Geneva Bible*. He returned to England in 1559 and became a leader of the Puritan party.

cowl Wide-sleeved garment with a hood, or a cloak with hood and mantle, worn by a monk.

Cowley Fathers Members of the Society of Mission Priests of St. John the Evangelist, an Anglican order founded by R. H. Meux Benson* in 1865 at Cowley St. John, Oxford, England.

Cowper, William (1731–1800) English poet. A master of religious poetry and imagery, he worked with John Newton* to produce the *Olney Hymns* (1779). Cowper's contributions included "O for a Closer Walk with God," "God Moves in a Mysterious Way," "Hark My Soul! It Is the Lord," "Jesu, Where'er Thy People Meet," and "There's a Fountain Filled with Blood." He also wrote a number of secular poems. His latter days were clouded by bouts of depression and suicidal melancholy.

Cox, Richard (c. 1500–1581) Bishop of Ely* (1559–1580) who was chancellor of Oxford University (1547–1552). He helped to compile the "Order of Communion" of 1548 and the prayer books of 1549 and 1552. He also translated Acts and Romans for the Bishops' Bible*.

Craig, John (1512–1600) Scottish reformer. A Dominican prior* and rector* of the Dominican Convent in Bologne, he converted to Protestantism*. Condemned to death by the Inquisition* in Rome, he escaped to Vienna* to become the favorite preacher of Emperor Maximilian II. In 1560 he returned to his native Scotland, where he joined John Knox*. In 1570 he became chaplain* to James VI, drafting the first Scots Catechism and helping to produce the King's Confession* in 1581, later incorporated into the National Covenant*.

Cranach, Lucas (1472–1553) German "Painter of the Reformation" and a friend of Martin Luther*. He produced numerous woodcut illustrations of Bible events, Luther's works, and Reformation* tracts as well as paintings of Luther himself. His most famous paintings include *Crucifixion* (1500) and *Rest on the Flight* (1504).

Lucas Cranach

Cranmer, Thomas (1489–1556) Archbishop of Canterbury* (1533–1556). As the primate* of England, he spearheaded moderate doctrinal reform and supported an official English translation of the Bible. In 1544 he produced the first of his vernac-

William Cowper

Thomas Cranmer

ular services, the English litany. In 1549 he sponsored the first *Book of Common Prayer*, followed in 1552 by the second *Book of Common Prayer*, breaking away from the Latin Mass* entirely. He defended the new communion service* in his *The True and Catholic Doctrine of the Lord's Supper*. Under Mary, whose accession he had opposed in favor of Lady Jane Grey, he was tried and convicted and condemned to death for treason. He went to the stake as a martyr*.

Crashaw, Richard (1612–1649) English religious poet. As a Roman Catholic subcanon in Loretto, he wrote religious poetry, including *Steps to the Temple* (1646), *The Delights of the Muses,* and *Carmen deo Nostro*. He is linked to the group of metaphysical poets, of which John Donne* was a member.

Crawford, Percy B. (1902–1960) American Evangelical preacher and broadcaster. Converted in 1932, he was a key figure in mid-century Evangelicalism*. In 1930 he launched the Saturday night youth rallies which became models for later Youth for Christ* rallies. In 1931 he began one of the first national Christian radio broadcasts, "the Young People's Church of the Air," which was heard on 450 stations. In 1950 he started the first Fundamentalist coast-to-coast television program with an audience in the millions. He also established the Pinebrook Bible Conference and in 1938 the King's College in Briarcliff, New York.

Crayer, Gaspard de (1584–1669) Flemish painter of altarpieces and religious scenes.

Creationism 1. Cosmogonical theory holding that matter, the various forms of life, and the world were created by God out of nothing as described in the Book of Genesis; opposed to Darwinian theory of evolution. 2. Doctrine that God creates a fresh soul for each human being at conception, as opposed to Traducianism*, which holds that the soul is formed naturally in the body through procreation.

creche Representation of the nativity scene showing the Holy Infant and Mother, surrounded by angels, shepherds, Joseph*, and animals.

credence 1. Acceptance or belief. 2. Small side table where the eucharistic elements* are placed before consecration.

credenda Articles of faith or set of beliefs.

credo (lit., I believe) Creed, especially the Nicene Creed*.

credo quia absurdum (Lat., I believe because it is absurd) Misquotation of a statement by Tertullian* ("I believe because it is foolish"), illustrating the antithesis between faith* and reason, glossing Paul's comment on the folly of the gospel (1 Cor. 1:18).

credo ut intelligam (Lat., I believe that I may understand) Teaching of St. Augustine* and St. Anselm* that faith* should precede knowledge.

creed Also, confession*; articles of faith; articles of religion. Concise and formal statement encapsulating a doctrine or system of belief requiring personal commitment. Creeds are brief, authoritative doctrinal formulas for confession and hallmarks of the faithful, distinguishing them from nonbelievers and heretics. They are also used as tests of orthodoxy*, as evidenced by their recitation during service. Creeds are used at baptism*, worship, and instruction. The best known creeds are the Nicene*, Athanasian*, and Apostles'*. Creeds serve many functions. They play a role in the liturgy and the teaching of the church, and they have a hermeneutical function as well. In the Eastern Orthodox Church*, the creed is *kanon aletheias,* the standard of faith or the *symbolum*, a password by which the faithful would identify themselves.

Creed of Pius IV Also, Professio Fidei Tridentinae. Creed published by Pius IV* in 1564, to which all ecclesiastical officials in the Roman Catholic Church were required to subscribe. It contains a summary of the doctrines promulgated at the Council of Trent* and reaffirms Tridentine* doctrines on Scripture, original sin*, justification*, Mass*, sacraments*, saints*, indulgences*, and the primacy of the Roman See*. The decrees of the First Vatican Council* were added to it in 1877. It was replaced in 1967 by a shorter formula*.

creeping to the cross Veneration of the cross on Good Friday*.

crescent Symbol of the Virgin Mary*.

Cripps, Arthur Shearly (1869–1952) Anglo-Catholic missionary in Rhodesia. Sent to Rhodesia in 1901 by the Society for the Propagation of the Gospel*, he spent the next half century as a maverick missionary. Acquiring 7,700 acres of farmland, he welcomed blacks to farm it without rent. He fought a lifelong battle for African rights and, after 1930, formally cut his links to the Anglican Church, becoming simply a "Christian missionary in Mashonaland."

crisis Encounter with the divine as a result of which human beings are forced to acknowledge their dependence on God.

crisis theology Also, dialectical theology*. Branch of theology associated with Karl Barth* and the neo-Orthodox theologians. Born out of the disillusionment of World War I, it emphasized the separation between time and eternity*, divine judgment on human sin and imperfection as well as the futility of human search for righteousness, and "catastrophe," or the suddenness and finality of divine judgment. The resulting crisis is resolved only by God's mercy, or "God's yea," leading human beings out of the negative dialectics and paradoxes. It emphasizes the Word of God* in Christ and Scripture, the centrality of proclaiming the gospel, the necessity of justification* by faith*, and social compassion. Crisis theology is grounded in the theology of the Reformation*, especially Calvinism*. It has had great influence on the development of Evangelical and Reformed* thinking.

Crispin and Crispinian, Sts. (third century) Two Christian brothers from a noble Roman family who were martyred during the Diocletian persecution*. Patron saints* of leather workers and shoemakers. Feast day: October 25.

criticism, canonical Study of biblical texts according to their final form in the canonical texts in relation to the other portions of the Scripture, particularly associated with the American scholar, Brevard Childs.

criticism, form (Ger., *Formgeschichte*) Biblical criticism* that studies texts, especially the Gospels, according to their pre-history in oral and written forms, classifying them in their literary forms or genres.

criticism, historical Study of biblical texts according to their historical settings, time and place of composition, circumstances, authors, and audiences.

criticism, literary Study of biblical texts according to the meaning of their final form, especially focusing on language, style, genre, and form.

criticism, narrative Study of biblical texts as narrative stories with a beginning, middle, and ending.

criticism, redaction Study of biblical texts according to the ways in which they have been edited, the manner of editing, and the scope and extent of changes.

criticism, rhetorical Study of biblical texts that analyzes them as typical modes of communication and discourse, focusing on their arguments, motifs, metaphors, and parables by which essential truths are conveyed to the readers.

criticism, source Study of biblical texts according to their source origins. It is a subdiscipline of historical criticism, and it focuses on sources used by their writers and the extent of borrowing and revision.

criticism, structural Study of biblical texts that focuses on linguistic structures and idiosyncracies and narrative grammar as revealing the biases and intentions of their writers.

criticism, textual Study of biblical manuscripts and papyri* to determine which reading is authentic.

croce dipinta (Ital., painted cross) Painted crucifix, varying in size between one foot and ten feet, with a painted representation of a crucified cross.

Croft, William (1678–1727) English composer. Organist in the Westminster Abbey* and composer to the Chapel Royal, noted for his Psalm tunes. Many of his tunes were later used by Handel* and Bach*.

Crosby, Fanny (1823–1915) Mrs. Fanny J. Van Alstyne. Blind American poet and hymn writer. Between 1864 and her death, she produced over 2,000 hymns of which some 60 are still sung. For some time she was associated with Ira D. Sankey*. Her most famous hymns include "Safe in the Arms of Jesus," "Blessed Assurance," "Pass Me Not, O Gentle Savior," "All the Way My Savior Leads Me," "I Am Thine, O Lord," "To God Be the Glory," "Tell Me the Story of Jesus," "Rescue the Perishing," and "Saved by Grace."

crosier/crozier Bishop's staff, resembling a shepherd's crook, symbolizing his pastoral role as a shepherd of the flock*. In earlier times, it was shaped in the form of a T. In the Eastern Church*, the crosier is surmounted by a cross between two serpents.

Priest with Miter and Crozier

Crosier Fathers and Brothers Also, Canons Regular* of the Order of the Holy Cross. A community founded in Belgium in 1210 by Theodore de Celles.

cross 1. Ancient instrument of execution, used especially in Roman times. 2. Universal symbol of Christianity commemorating Christ's death on a cross at Golgotha. The principal forms of the cross include the Greek cross* or crux quadrata with four equal arms; the Latin cross or crux im-

missa with base stem longer than the horizontal arms and the vertical intersected at about two thirds of the way up; the crux commissa or Tau cross* of Egyptian origin, used by St. Anthony and the Fathers of the Desert* that resembles the Latin cross with the head cut off; and the crux decussata or an X-shaped saltire*, commonly known as St. Andrew's cross.

Variations of these four basic types of cross include: anchor, cross in an anchor shape; avellan, similar to a bulb-less botonee, a circle within a center intersection. Its beams are curved like a stair railing with ends flaring into a crown shape; fleury or gable, similar to a pommee except that the ends are the three-pointed fleur-de-lis; Y-shaped cross, as in the Siena Cathedral* pulpit, also called the forked cross or the pestilence cross; budded cross or botonee, a Latin or Greek cross* with trefoil* ends; formee, bell-shaped, horn-like equal arms, intersecting in center to form a square area; fourchee plain, slender equal arms with v-shaped ends;

Huguenot cross, cross with a suspended dove*; tear-drop cross with opening arms; Jerusalem cross* that carries the suggestion of the five wounds of Christ; cross of light (crux radiata), gold in color, with four beams radiating from it; graded cross, a Latin cross with three steps at the base. Variants of the Latin cross have additional horizontal bars with a shorter bar or bars above the normal one. That with three bars of diminishing width is the papal cross, the shorter short arm being called the titulus*. The one with only one short bar is the cross of Lorraine or the patriarchal cross;

Moline cross, similar to the fleury, except horizontally shorter and vertically longer. It has only two points on fleur-de-lis ends; papal or triple cross, single vertical standard intersected by three cross bars, each ascending bar diminishing in length to form a tree-shape. In the East, the bottom arms are shorter and slants upward left to right. In Russia, the bottom arm slants upward right to left; cross pattee, square cross with arms curving outward and straight outer edges; cross of Constantine*, combination of cross and Chi-Rho*, seen by Constantine in the sky; pommee, thin, equal braced center-intersection with circular bulbs on four ends; potent*, square area, plain, central intersection beams with intersecting equal

Greek Cross   Tau Cross   St. Andrew's Cross   Patriarchal Cross

Latin Cross   Budded Cross   Graded Cross   Papal Cross

Celtic Cross   Fleury Cross   Jerusalem Cross   Maltese Cross

Cross Pattee   Anchor Cross

length beams at end of each arm; Eastern Ortho-dox Church cross, a patriarchal cross with an oblique bar beneath, representing the suppeda-neum*, or the piece of wood to which Christ's feet were nailed;

Celtic or Irish cross with a circle around the arms of a Greek or Latin cross; Maltese cross that has four arrowheads with their points meeting in the center like a Greek cross; processional cross, a cross or crucifix on the end of a long pole carried in processions accompanied by two acolytes car-rying candles; trophy cross, surmounted by a Chi-Rho*, encircled by a wreath.

Crosses appear on altars and communion ta-bles and at the top of steeples on many churches. Elaborately carved standing crosses dotted the countryside in the Middle Ages. Where they have sculptured scenes, they have didactic as well as symbolic significance and may be read as ser-mons in stone.

Cross, Frank Leslie (1900–1968) Anglican patristic scholar. He was Lady Margaret professor of divin-ity at Oxford from 1944 and editor of the *Oxford Dictionary of the Christian Church* (1957). He founded the quadrennial International Confer-ence on Patristic Studies held at Oxford*.

cross in square Architectural plan of certain churches in which a centrally planned cross is en-closed within a triangle. The central crossing* may be a cross-vault or a dome. The corners be-tween the arms of the cross and the rectangle may be used as chapels or sacristies.

cross, pectoral Cross made of wood or precious metal worn by bishops and abbots on their chest and suspended by a chain around their neck. Some Eastern priests also wear such a cross.

cross, theology of the (Lat., *Theologia Crucis**) Term coined by Martin Luther*. Opposed to the-ology of glory*. Theology dealing with the cross as the focal point of the Atonement*. According to Luther, the cross alone is Christian theology. The cross shatters human preconceptions of di-vinity and human illusions of how God may be known. God is hidden in this revelation and may be perceived only by faith*. Natural reason looks for divinity in power and glory, but the cross represents the opposite: humiliation, suffering, disgrace, and death. But in the cross God comes closest to a sinner in a sense of abandonment, weakness, and foolishness. It also establishes the passibility and humanity of Christ.

cross-bearing Suffering and sacrifice as a sign of Christian discipleship (Matt. 10:38; 16:24; Mark 8:34; Luke 9:23; 14:27).

crossing Intersection of the nave* and transepts* in a traditionally constructed church.

crosslet Small cross.

Crouch, Paul Franklin (1934–) Evangelist and founder of Trinity Broadcasting Network (TBN*). In 1973 he and his wife Jan, along with Jim and Tammy Bakker*, established TBN's flagship station in Santa Ana, California. This network has now become the largest Christian television network in the world with close to 1,000 stations.

crown rights of Christ See KINGSHIP OF CHRIST.

Crowther, Samuel Adjai (c. 1806–1891) African slave who became the first African Anglican bishop. He translated the Bible into a number of African languages, including Yoruba.

Samuel Crowther

crucifer Cross-bearer in a church procession.

crucifix (Lat., *crux*, cross + *figo*, I fix) Figure of Christ on a cross. Earlier crucifixes showed a victorious Christ, alive, standing, head erect, clothed and crowned. Later, about the tenth century, crucifixes showed a suffering Christ realistically and were widely used as objects of devotion. It was the central object of the rood screen*. Protestants have generally preferred a box cross to symbolize Christ's Resurrection.

Crucifix

crucifixion Execution by being nailed to a cross, frequently used as a punishment for slaves or non-Romans. It was usually preceded by scourging.

Isenheim Altar

cruciform In the shape of a cross, as the nave* and transepts*.

Cruciger, Kaspar (1504–1548) Associate of Martin Luther* who helped him translate the Bible into German. He preserved in shorthand many of Luther's lectures and sermons.

Cruden, Alexander (1701–1770) Eccentric British bookseller who prepared the famous concordance* to the King James Version* of the Bible, which is still used.

cruet Vessel of glass or precious metal for the wine and water of the Eucharist*.

Cruger, Johann (1598–1662) German church organist and composer of hymns and concertos. His works include "Jesu Mein Freude" and "Nun Danket Alle Gott."

crusade Evangelistic meeting held by peripatetic evangelists for preaching the gospel and inviting persons to make a personal decision of faith in Jesus Christ as their personal Savior. It is a characteristic feature of modern Protestantism*.

Crusades 1. A series of seven major and several minor campaigns in the Middle East by Christian powers between 1095 and 1291, all with the avowed purpose of recovering the Holy Lands* and Asia Minor from the infidel* Muslims. The **First Crusade** (1095–1099) followed the defeat of the Byzantine forces by Seljuk Turks at the Battle of Manzikert (1071). Pope Urban II* inspired the crusade in a sermon at the Council of Clermont* (1095) at the end of which he issued the rallying cry, "God wills it." With 5,000 soldiers, supported by Emperor Alex Comnenus, the Crusaders took Antioch* and Jerusalem* and established several Christian states in the region. The **Second Crusade** (1147–1149) was organized by Bernard of Clairvaux*, but it ended in defeat at Damascus* at the hands of Saladin.

The **Third Crusade** (1189–1192) was provoked by Saladin's seizure of Jerusalem. It was called "the Crusade of Kings" because its leaders were Frederick I, Richard I, and Philip II. It resulted in a three-year truce and the grant of free access to Jerusalem for Christian pilgrims. The **Fourth Crusade** (1202–1204) was launched by Pope Innocent III*, and it ended in the establishment of a Latin empire at Constantinople* under Count Baldwin of Flanders. The two largest crusades were the international crusade of 1217–1221 and the French crusade under Louis IX, both directed against Egypt and both of which failed. The **Fifth Crusade** (1228–1229) under Emperor Frederick II,

the **Sixth Crusade** (1248–1250) under Saint Louis of France and the **Seventh Crusade** (and last, 1270–1272) were all unsuccessful. In 1291, Acre*, the last Christian stronghold in the Holy Land*, fell to the Muslims. See also CHILDREN'S CRUSADE.

Pope Urban Calls for a Crusade at Clermont

2. Campaign against heretics, as for example the Albigensians. See also ALBIGENSIAN CRUSADE.

Crutched Friars Augustinian mendicant order* founded by Gerrard, prior* of St. Mary of Morello at Bologna*, and confirmed by Alexander III* at Bologna. Initially, they carried a cross fixed to a staff and were therefore called fratres cruciferi or "Crossed Athos*." Later, they wore a cross of red on their backs or chests. One branch of the order was suppressed in 1656 by Pope Alexander VII*. Others have survived in Flanders, France, Germany, England, Belgium, Austria, Brazil, and the United States.

crux ansata Cross in the form of a T with a loop above.

crux interpretatis Text of Scripture whose interpretation is a matter of keen dispute among scholars.

crypt Underground cell, chamber, or vault, generally used as a burial place beneath a church floor. The crypts of martyrs served as altars and as centers of pilgrimage*.

crypto-Christian Secret believer in Christ, not professing publicly nor publicly baptized or enumerated as Christian in censuses.

Crystal Cathedral Large glass cathedral in Orange Grove, California, built by architect Philip Johnson for Robert Schuller*.

CSC Holy Cross Fathers.

CSI Church of South India*.

CTBI Churches Together in Britain and Ireland.

c'thobko teshmeshto (lit., Book of the Ministry) In the Maronite Church, collection of rubrics governing the celebration of the Divine Office*.

cubicula Family tomb chambers in a catacomb*.

cubicularius Person attached to the household of the pope, generally a cleric or a monk, who looked after the holy father's* personal needs.

cuius regio, eius religio (Lat., whose the region, his the religion) Principle accepted at the Peace of Augsburg* and giving each ruler the right to choose his country's religion.

Culdees (lit., companions of God) Irish and Scottish religious between the eighth and twelfth centuries. They did not owe allegiance to Rome* and maintained a separate and independent existence until the Reformation*. They have been called Pre-Reformation Evangelicals*. About 1100, they abandoned their monastic habits and became a college of secular priests who married and were somewhat lax in discipline.

Cullmann, Oscar (1902–1998) Biblical theologian and patristic scholar. He was professor of New Testament and ancient church history at the University of Basel from 1938. He developed the theory of salvation history (*Heilsgeschichte**) which maintains that the gospel is not metaphysical speculation but the proclamation of concrete historical events that occurred at a particular time and place. Salvation history is a succession of redemptive acts of which Christ is at the center and it connects his earthly work with his preexistence and his present and future work. He also wrote extensively on the pseudo-Clementine Literature* and the meaning of the Eucharist* in primitive Christianity.

cult 1. Deviant and heretical pseudo-religious group. Cults may originate either within the host Christian society, as Jehovah's Witnesses*, Mormonism and Christian Science*, or be imported from another hostile culture, as Hare Krishna, Unification Church, Bahaism, and Scientology. Pseudo-Christian cults have extrascriptural source of authority, deny justification* by grace*, brainwash their members, devalue Christ, and maintain punitive disciplinary practices for members who question their scriptural legitimacy. 2. Religious rites. 3. Sect. 4. Also, cultus*. Adoration or devotion.

cultus 1. Cult. Heretical sect that practices a form of pseudo-Christianity. 2. (Lat., devotion) Form and practice of worship. 3. Devotion addressed to a particular saint*.

cumdach Case of precious metal enclosing a Bible.

cumm In the Coptic Rite, cuffs that cover the forearm, broad at the elbow and narrow at the hand, highly ornamented and embroidered. Also, cummin.

cup Communion chalice*.

Cur Deus Homo (lit., Why Did God Become Human?) Title of Anselm's* treatise on the Atonement* in 1098, explaining the death of Christ on the cross as full repayment of the debt a sinful mankind owed to a just God.

curate 1. Person with the care of souls; rector* or vicar* of a parish*. 2. In English-speaking countries, assistant to a parish priest.

cure Parish priest in France.

Cure d'Ars See VIANNEY, ST. JEAN-BAPTISTE MARIE.

Curetonian Manuscripts Syrian manuscripts from the Nitrian monasteries catalogued by William Cureton (1808–1864), a librarian on the staff of the British Museum. Among his discoveries were the Epistles of St. Ignatius, the Old Syriac* text of the Gospels, and the festal letters of Athanasius*.

Curia/Curia Romana Body of nine congregations, pontifical* councils, five offices, and three tribunals through which the pope governs the Roman Catholic Church.

curialism The system of papal government under the authority of the supreme pontiff*.

Cursillo (Span., little course) Renewal movement within the Roman Catholic church consisting of a weekend retreat* from sundown Thursday to sundown Sunday in which a group of 30 to 40 Catholics participate as a spiritual exercise to gain heightened religious and social awareness. It originated in Spain in 1949 when Eduardo Bonin, a layman, and Bishop Juan Hervas decided to make Catholic Action* retreats more meaningful. At first opposed by the church, it was approved in 1966 and now operates in many countries, including the United States. The course includes a series of *rollos* or lectures delivered by trained leaders. The weekends result in the formation of small groups or *cursillistas* who share common interests and who meet weekly to build upon the spiritual renewal achieved through the initial cursillo. It has also been widely accepted in Anglican churches.

Cursor Mundi English poem on the history of the world, dating from the early fourteenth century. It has seven books. The first four deal with the Old Testament, the fifth and sixth with Jesus Christ, and the seventh with the Last Judgment*.

cursus Regular course of divine service*, or directions for its conduct.

cushapa In the Church of the East*, private prayers said in a low whisper while kneeling.

custodia Elaborately designed tabernacle for housing the host*.

customary Also, Liber Ordinarius*. Book containing ecclesiastical rites and ceremonies and the rules and customs of discipline of a particular monastery, cathedral, or religious order.

Cuthbert, St. (c. 635–687) Celtic bishop of Lindisfarne* and Hexham in northern England. He retired to a solitary life toward the end of his life and lived as a hermit on Farne Island. A cult* developed around his relics* that lasted for many centuries. Feast day: March 20.

cuthino In the Syrian Church, an alb* worn by the celebrant, usually embroidered with many crosses.

cutty stool Seat or gallery in Scottish churches where alleged immoral persons were forced to sit.

Cynewulf (ninth century) Anglo-Saxon religious poet. Four poems have been attributed to him: *Juliana, Ascension, Elene,* and *Fates of the Apostles.* The poems reveal great devotion to the mysteries* of Christianity and its saints* and have passages of remarkable and evocative power.

Cyprian, St. (d. 258) Bishop of Carthage*. Birth name: Thascius Caecilianus Cyprianus. He was a pagan rhetorician converted to Christianity about 246. Within two years, he was elected bishop of Carthage. He fled during the Decian persecution*, but on his return he opposed the easy readmission to the church of those who had lapsed from their faith. The *libellatici*, or those who had merely purchased certificates from the civil authorities that they had sacrificed to the idols when they had not, were readmitted with lighter punishment but the the *sacrificati*, or those who had actually sacrificed to the idols, were required to submit to severe penance*, which led to a clash with Stephen, bishop of Rome, over the baptism* of schismatics. Cyprian was also involved in conflicts with some disaffected clergy led by Novatus and Felicissimus. During this time the Valerian persecution broke out. Cyprian surrendered to the authorities and was beheaded.

Cyprian's writings enjoyed great popularity. His principal works include *Ad Quirinum* or *Testimonia* (248), *De Habitu Virginum* (249), *De Lapsis* (251), *De Catholicae Ecclesiae Unitate* (251),

De Dominica Oratione (c. 252), and *De Opere et Eleemosynis* (253). Feast day: September 14.

Cyprus Island in the Mediterranean evangelized by Paul* and Barnabas*. At the Council of Nicaea* in 325, Cyprus was represented by three bishops and its independent status was affirmed at the Council of Ephesus* in 431. The Cypriots suffered under Arab and later Turkish rule until the establishment of British rule in 1878. Archbishop Makarios led the island to independence in 1960. The church in Cyprus is governed by a holy synod* with four dioceses*. After the Turkish invasion in 1974, nearly 40 percent of the island was occupied, most of the Greeks were expelled from the Turkish part, and churches and monasteries were closed, demolished, or turned into mosques.

Cyril V (1824–1927) One hundred and twelfth Coptic patriarch* of the See of St. Mark* from 1874. Birth name: Yuhanna al-Nasikh. He convened the Coptic Congress of Assyut in 1911 and founded the Clerical College in Cairo in 1894. His love of books and learning earned him the monastic name of John the Scribe.

Cyril VI (1902–1971) One hundred and sixteenth Coptic patriarch* of the See of St. Mark*. Birth name: Yusuf Ata. Monastic name: Mina. He strengthened the relations between the Coptic Church* and other Monophysite churches, including the Ethiopian Church* and the Syrian Orthodox Church*, from 1959. As a former monk, he promoted monastic life and established the Monastery of Mar Mina in Maryut, Egypt.

Cyril and Methodius, Sts. (826–869 and c. 815–885, respectively) Apostles of the Slavs and patrons of Europe. Greek brothers from Thessalonica who were sent in 862 by Emperor Michael III to what is now Moravia. Cyril invented an alphabet called Glagolitic* and thus founded Slavonic literature. He also adopted Slavonic for the celebration of the liturgy and produced a Slavonic version of the Scriptures. The memory of Cyril and Methodius is treasured by Czechs, Croats, Serbs, and Bulgars. Feast day: February 14 (Western Church*); May 11 (Eastern Church*).

Cyril, St. (c. 315–387) Bishop of Jerusalem* from about 349. He is the author of a series of catechetical instructions known as *Catecheses* and *Procatechesis* which illustrate the Palestinian liturgy of his times.

Cyril, St. (d. 444) Patriarch*of Alexandria*. In 412 he succeeded his uncle Theophilus as patriarch* of Alexandria. Cyril is remembered as the champion of orthodoxy* against Nestorius*. When Nestorius, the patriarch of Constantinople*, objected to the use of Theotokos* (God-Bearer) in reference to the Virgin Mary*, Cyril persuaded Pope Celestine* to summon a synod* in Rome and condemn Nestorius. He held a synod at Alexandria, where the condemnation was re-

St. Cyril of Alexandria

peated and Nestorius was anathematized. At the Council of Ephesus*, Nestorius was condemned before the pro-Nestorius Antiochene bishops arrived. The Antiochenes retaliated by holding a separate council to depose Cyril in turn.

Cyril was the most brilliant Alexandrian theologian of his day. He formulated with clarity and skill the orthodox teachings on Christology* and the Trinity*, although the Monophysites later viewed him as their great authority. Among his works that have survived are biblical commentaries, an apology against Julian the Apostate*, about 20 sermons, and many letters. His Christology is developed most forcefully in *On Worship in Spirit and in Truth, Treasury, That Christ Is One,*

Czestochowa Monastery

and *Dialogues on the Holy and Consubstantial Trinity.* Feast day: June 27 (Western Church*); June 9 (Eastern Church*).

Cyrillic Slavonic language devised by St. Cyril*.

Czestochowa Town in Poland, site of a monastery famous for its icon* of Black Madonna*, alleged to have been painted by St. Luke*. The monastery stands on a hilltop known as Clear mountain on the River Warta, close to the German border. It was founded by Wladislaw of Oppelin as a Pauline monastery in 1382 in honor of Paul the Hermit. The monastery was heavily fortified. Between 1690 and 1693 the church was transformed into a Baroque basilica*. The altar, with its Assumption of the Virgin, is the work of Jacopo Buzzini and Adam Karinger. The celebrated miracle painting of the Black Madonna, crowned in gold and painted in black and brown on a panel of cypress wood, is believed to be the work of Luke. It was once the property of St. Helena*, mother of Emperor Constantine*.

Dd

Da Costa, Isaak (1798–1860) Jewish-born poet and theologian, converted to Christianity through the witness of Dutch poet Willem Bilderdijk. He edited the works of Bilderdijk. His *Collected Work* was published in 1861–1863. Of his translations, the best known are *Israel and the Gentiles* and *The Four Witnesses*.

Da Todi, Jacopone (1228–1306) Italian Franciscan monk and mystic.

Dabney, Robert (1820–1898) Theologian of the Southern Presbyterian Church. In 1853 he became a professor at Union Seminary*, first of ecclesiastical history and later of systematic theology. In 1881 he took a prominent part in the founding of the Southern Presbyterian Church. In 1870 he published the influential *Syllabus and Notes of the Course of Systematic and Polemic Theology Taught in the Union Seminary in Virginia*.

Dabra Matmaq, Council of Council convened by Ethiopian emperor Zara Yakub (1434–1468) which approved the observance of Saturday Sabbath.

dabtara In the Ethiopian Church*, a learned deacon or layman who administers a local church.

dagharan In the Armenian Church*, a hymnbook.

D'Ailly, Pierre (1350–1420) French scholastic, theologian, and cardinal. He was chancellor of the University of Paris from 1389 and soon afterwards confessor* and almoner* to Charles VI. He worked hard to heal the Great Schism* and to this end he attended the Council of Pisa* in 1409. At the Council of Constance*, he supported the theory of the supremacy of the general council over the pope without, however, entirely approving the Decrees of Constance. He maintained that bishops and priests received their authority directly from Christ unmediated by the pope and that neither the councils nor the pope were infallible. This theory was later developed by Martin Luther* and the Reformers.

dair (Arab.) 1. Ringed wall that enclosed a monastery. 2. By extension, the monastery itself.

daktylios In the Byzantine tradition, a ring worn by a bishop.

Dabtaras

Dallas Theological Seminary Professional graduate-level seminary founded in 1924 as the Evangelical Theological College by Lewis Sperry Chafer*, a popular evangelist and Bible teacher. Chafer designed its curriculum with three goals in mind: an intense study of each book of the Bible, promotion of spiritual development of each student, and teaching of dispensationalism* and premillennialism*. In the 1930s it became one of the leading Evangelical seminaries, offering a four-year Th.M program. As the liberal climate in the nation intensified, the school became a major training center for the nondenominational separatist movement. Since the death of Chafer in 1952, Dallas Theological Seminary has had three presidents, John F. Walvoord* (1952–1986), Donald K. Campbell (1986–1995), and Charles Swindoll (1995–).

dalmatic Colored silk vestment with wide sleeves worn over the alb* by deacons during High Mass*. It is embroidered with two clavi or colored strips running from front to back over the shoulders. Compare sakkos* in the Eastern Orthodox Church*.

Dalmatic

Damasus I, St. (c. 305–384) Pope from 366. He was very active in suppressing heresy, especially Arianism*, Donatism*, Macedonianism*, and Luciferianism. He strengthened the papacy, placed the papal archives in their own building, and adorned the monuments of martyrs* with marble inscriptions by Filocalus. At a council con-

vened in Rome*, he promulgated a canon* of scriptural books and commissioned his secretary, St. Jerome*, to revise the biblical text which led to the Vulgate*. Feast day: December 4.

Pope Damasus I

Damascus Capital of Syria, on the road to which St. Paul* was converted. It is the seat of a Greek Orthodox, Greek Catholic, and Syrian (Jacobite) patriarchate*.

Damian, St. Peter (c. 1007–1072) Italian reformer and doctor of the church*. As a Camaldolese* monk and prior* of the Benedictine hermitage at Fonte Avellana, he reformed old monasteries and founded new ones. Made cardinal of Ostia, he attacked clerical corruption, including concubinage and homosexuality. He sided with Pope Alexander II* against antipope Honorius II. He enjoyed great influence in the church of his day on account of his learning, zeal, and integrity. Feast day: February 21.

Damien, Father Birth name: Joseph de Veuster (1840–1889) Belgian Catholic missionary to lepers in Hawaii. Trained for the priesthood by the Fathers of the Sacred Heart (Picpus Fathers), he was sent to Hawaii in 1864. In 1873 he joined the leper colony at Molokai as a superintendent and priest. Eventually, he became a leper himself but continued to serve the colony until his death.

dance of death Allegory of death leading a dance to the grave, a common motif in morality plays* in the Middle Ages.

dandelion Symbol of Christ's suffering and death.

Daniel the Stylite (409–493) Syrian ascetic, a contemporary of Simeon the Stylite*. He lived on a platform at the top of his pillar and did not descend for 33 years except once. Thousands flocked to his pillar to see and hear him.

Danielou, Jean (1905–1974) Roman Catholic theologian. He held for many years the chair of the history of Christian origins at the Institut Catholique de Paris. As a peritus* at Vatican II*, he devised a theology of religions and of the church's mission. In 1969 he was made a cardinal. His theological position is called the Fulfillment Theory, by which Christianity has superseded all other religions and represents God's self-revelation and not merely a human quest for God.

Daniel-Rops, Henri (1901–1965) Born Henri Jules Charles Petiot. French Catholic writer, elected to the French Academy. His prodigious literary output included 70 books, of which 20 were novels. His novel, *Death, Where is Thy Victory?* (1946) was very popular and was made into a film. His 12-volume *Biblical and Ecclesiastical History* included *Jesus and His Times* and *The History of the Church of Christ.*

Daniil of Moscow (1261–1303) Son of Aleksandr Nevskii who inherited the principality of Moscow*. He took the monastic habit* before his death and was buried in the St. Daniil the Stylite Monastery which he had founded.

Danner, David (1951–1993) American composer. Among his 120 compositions are musicals, such as *Joy Comes in the Morning* (1981), *Praise* (1985), and *And We Beheld His Glory* (1984) and choruses such as *Holy Is His Name* (1985), *He Is Worthy of Our Praise* (1986), and *Jesus Is the Song* (1979).

Dante Alighieri (1265–1321) Italian poet. The death of his beloved Beatrice Portinari in 1290 led to a spiritual crisis and he turned to poetry and philosophy. He studied under the Dominicans* of Florence*. In 1294 he entered politics, but took the losing side in the struggle against Pope Boniface VIII* and was exiled for life from Florence. His greatest achievement was the epic *Divine Comedy*, one of the greatest literary classics of all time. Composed of 100 cantos, it is divided into

Dante Alighieri

The Inferno, The Purgatory, and *The Paradise.* Written in *terza rima,* this "Cathedral in Words" begins with the poet in a dark wood (sin) at Eastertide*. The poet Virgil, representing philosophy, acts as his guide through hell* and up to Mount Purgatory. Then Beatrice, representing theology, leads him up to Paradise, where he beholds the ineffable glory of God.

Darby, John Nelson (1800–1882) English leader of the Plymouth Brethren* and of the Darbyites. In 1827, soon after writing his tract *On the Nature and Unity of the Church of Christ,* he joined the Brethren, but upon the breakup of that sect in 1848 into the Open and Exclusive groups, led the stricter Brethren into a separate body called the Darbyites. His evocative hymns are still sung and are expressive of his mystical devotion. Darby's influence has been greatest in two areas: eschatology* and ecclesiology*. Traveling extensively, Darby propagated his ideas in Europe as well as the United States, where his disciples included Dwight L. Moody*, A. J. Gordon*, and James H. Brookes*. One lasting legacy of his work was the Bible conference movement of 1870 through which dispensationalist premillennialism* gained a large constituency. It led to Cyrus I. Scofield's Scofield Reference Bible* published in 1909.

daretha In the Nestorian Church*, covered area in the eastern part of a church courtyard, forming an entrance to a church building.

Dark Ages The centuries in Western Europe from the sixth to the twelfth, so called because of the supposed decline in religion and culture.

dark night of the soul As used by the Fathers of the Desert*, dry period that alternates in the life of a mystic with ecstatic experiences; synonymous with aridity*. Term also used by St. John of the Cross*.

datary Roman Catholic official who investigates the qualifications of claimants to papal benefices*.

Daughters of Charity of St. Vincent de Paul Religious community of women founded in France in 1603 by Vincent de Paul* and Louise de Marillac. Unlike other religious communities, the Daughters of Charity profess their vows for only a year at a time.

Daughters of Isabella Women's counterpart of the Knights of Columbus*, founded in 1904.

Daughters of Our Lady Help of Christians Order of nuns founded by St. John Bosco* to aid Salesians*.

Daughters of the Cross Catholic Order of nuns founded in 1833 by Mere M. Therese Haze, who wear black habits* and visit schools, hospitals, and prisons.

Daughters of Wisdom Order of nuns with grey habits founded in 1703 by St. Louis Grignion de Montfort* and Marie Louise Trichet in France.

David, Christian (1691–1751) Moravian Brethren* leader and missionary. Converted in 1717, he became a lay evangelist. Together with Count Zinzendorf* he founded the Christian community at Herrnhut*. In 1733 he led a group of mis-

sionaries to Greenland to assist the pioneer Hans Egede*.

David, Johann Nepomuk (1895–1977) Austrian composer. The bulk of his creative output comprises organ music. Although born a Roman Catholic, he used the Protestant chorale in much of his church music. He also did some Catholic settings of the Mass*, a Stabat Mater*, a Requiem*, and works based on plainchants. His *Choralewerk* is published in 21 volumes.

David, St. (sixth century) Missionary and monastic founder and patron saint* of Wales, commemorated at St. David's. Feast day: March 1.

Davidson, Randall Thomas (1848–1930) Scottish archbishop of Canterbury* from 1903 to 1928. Davidson exercised considerable influence as adviser to Queen Victoria before he became the primate* of England. He presided over the disestablishment* of the church in Wales and supported the revision of the Prayer Book.

Davies, Samuel (1723–1761) Founder of the Presbyterian Church in the United States. Ordained as a Presbyterian evangelist in 1747, he became an active promoter of the Great Awakening*. He succeeded Jonathan Edwards* in 1753 as president of the College of New Jersey, later Princeton.

Davies, Walford (1869–1941) English musician and organist who composed numerous cantatas and hymns.

Davis, Katherine Kennicott (1892–1980) American composer. *The Little Drummer Boy* is the best known of her 800 compositions and arrangements.

dawah In the Syrian Liturgy, epiclesis* in the anaphora* after the words of the institution* and the anamnesis*.

dawidha In the Assyrian Liturgy, the Psalter, divided into 20 hulali, each consisting of two or more marmitha or sittings.

Dawson, Christopher (1889–1970) English Roman Catholic historian. A convert to Roman Catholicism* in 1914, he became an outstanding Christian apologist and intellectual. Among his books are *Religion and the Rise of Western Culture* (1950), *The Formation of Christendom* (1967), and the *Dividing of Christendom* (1965, 1971).

Day, Dorothy May (1897–1980) American social activist and founder of the Catholic Worker* movement. Born and raised in the Episcopalian Church, she abandoned religion and became a

Dorothy Day

radical socialist. In 1927, however, she gave up her bohemian lifestyle to become a Catholic. Still concerned over social injustice, she joined with Peter Maurin to found a movement known as Catholic Worker* that expressed her radical social vision. The movement's newspaper of the same name attracted like-minded Catholic thinkers, such as Thomas Merton*, Daniel and Philip Berrigan, Claude McKay, J. F. Powers, and Helene Iswolsky. Day's social activism ranged from picketing unfair labor practices to civil disobedience and pacifism during World War II. Her testimony is contained in her many books, such as her autobiography, *From Union Square to Rome* (1938) and *The Long Loneliness* (1952).

day hours Seven services of the Breviary* other than the matins*: lauds*, prime*, terce*, sext*, none*, vespers*, and compline*. The order of service for them is contained in the diurnal*.

day of the Lord Second Coming* of Jesus Christ (2 Pet. 3:10).

Day Star Christ as the Morning Star (2 Pet. 1:19).

Day Thou Gavest, Lord, Is Ended, The Beautiful evening hymn by John Ellerton (1826–1893), an Anglican vicar*. Best sung to "St. Clement," it conveys a moving sense of the church worldwide praising God in unbroken succession.

Dayro d-Za'faran Also, Dayro d-Kurkmo. Ancient Syriac Orthodox monastery founded in 439 at Murdin in modern-day Turkey. It is known as the Saffron Monastery from the yellowish rock from which it is built. Between 1166 and 1932, with some interruptions, it was the residence of the Syriac Orthodox patriarchs*.

D.D. Doctor of Divinity*.

de fide (lit., of the faith) Essential article of faith*, defined by the church as true, to contradict a heresy.

De Foucauld, Charles Eugene (1858–1916) French explorer and "Hermit of the Sahara." After a distinguished career in the army exploring the Sahara, he entered a Trappist monastery in France in 1890. He spent many years in Syria and Palestine before returning to France for ordination as a priest in 1901 and then went to Algeria, where he led a hermit's* life in Beni Abbes and the remote Hoggar Mountains. Here his sanctity* and charity made an impression on the native Muslims as well as the French Foreign Legion. He also became an authority on the Tuareg language and compiled dictionaries and language aids. In 1916 he was assassinated in obscure circumstances, but probably by Senoussi fanatics.

De Foucauld did not make any converts or establish any religious order during his lifetime. But his life inspired Rene Voillaume and four other priests to adopt the rule by which he lived and to establish a community at El Abiodh Sidi Cheikh, on the edge of the Sahara. After World War II, it became the Little Brothers of Jesus, who, while maintaining a contemplative discipline, worked in ordinary professions and mingled with the people around them. Other offshoots of the order include Little Sisters of the Sacred Heart (1933), Little Sisters of Jesus (1939), Little Brothers of the Gospel (1958), and Little Sisters of the Gospel (1965).

de Nobili, Robert (1577–1656) Jesuit missionary to India. He arrived in India in 1605 and moved to Madura in South India where he lived for 36 years. He dressed in saffron like a Hindu sanyasin or monk, lived in the Brahmin quarter, learned Sanskrit and studied the Vedas and other Hindu scriptures. His first convert, Sivadarma, was baptized in 1609 but was permitted to retain his Brahmin caste-marks. He was condemned for his tolerance of pagan customs and banned from performing his ecclesiastical functions. De Nobili appealed to the pope and was upheld. By adapting and incorporating native customs, many of which have no Christian content, he launched a missiological controversy that has not yet been resolved. He wrote numerous books in Indian languages and is credited with more than 100,000 converts.

De Rance, Armand-Jean le Bouthillier (1626–1700) Trappist* founder. Born into a noble French family, he renounced worldly life in 1663 and joined the Cistercian Order and became abbot of La Trappe*. He set himself to reform the monastery according to the principles laid down in his *Traite de la Saintete et des Devoirs de la Vie Monastique*. The Trappist Rule that he established is one of the most austere of all monastic rules.

De Sacramentis Short liturgical treatise on the sacraments* most probably by St. Ambrose*. It has six homilies or books dealing with baptism*, confirmation*, and the Eucharist*.

De Smet, Pierre Jean (1801–1873) Belgian Jesuit missionary to the American Indians in the northwestern United States.

de tempore hymns (Lat., hymns of the time) Hymns sung at specific times, seasons, or certain Sundays of the church year*.

deacon (Gk., *diakonos*, servant) Assistant and auxiliary to bishops or overseers, a rank in the Christian ministry below a priest or pastor. The office was instituted in apostolic times with the appointment of the Seven (including Stephen* and Philip*) in Acts 6:3–4, although deacons were not called such. Their earliest functions were the distribution of alms and service of the poor. In 1 Timothy 3:8 one of their qualifications was noted as a lack of greed. In the Clementine age, they commonly read or chanted the Epistles and the Gospels, received the offerings of the faithful, inscribed the names of the donors in the diptychs*, assisted the bishop in the distribution of the consecrated elements* to the people, directed the prayers of the laity during the service, and gave the signal to penitents* and catechumens* to leave the church before the eucharistic prayer.

In the Western Church*, the diaconate is only a stage in the preparation for priesthood. The vestments of the deacon are the dalmatic* and the stole* worn over the left shoulder. In the Eastern Church*, the diaconate is permanent and they wear the orarion*. In some countries older married men may be ordained as deacons, although young men ordained as deacons are bound to celibacy*. In some Protestant churches, such as the Lutheran Church, the title *deacon* is applied to assistant pastors. Among Baptists*, deacons are generally elected by the church meeting for a limited period.

deaconess Female deacon, an office cited in the Acts and in Romans 16:1, where Paul* mentions Phoebe as a deaconess (NRSV). The office developed in the third and fourth centuries. She was charged with the visitation of the sick and the poor and was required to be present during interviews of women with bishops, priests, and deacons. She instructed women catechumens*, kept order in the female part of the congregation, and assisted in the baptism* of women. By the early Middle Ages, the office had died out. There were attempts by some Reformed* churches to revive the office in the seventeenth and eighteenth centuries. In the Lesser Eastern Churches*, she also administered Holy Communion* to women. In the nineteenth century the office was revived in Protestant churches.

The first Protestant community of deaconesses was that established by Theodor Fliedner at Kaiserswerth*, near Dusseldorf, Germany, devoted to nursing. In 1969 deaconesses were admitted to the diaconate in the Church of England*. In the United States, the deaconess movement gained strength from the mid-nineteenth century. In 1850 Katherine Louisa Marthens became the first consecrated American deaconess.

By 1855 both Lutherans and Episcopalians had established deaconess houses. The movement was introduced into the Methodist Church in 1883 when the Women's Home Missionary Society started the first of many schools to prepare women as home missionaries. In 1888 the General Conference sanctioned deaconess as a ministerial order. Deaconesses ministered particularly to the sick, the dying, the displaced, and the disadvantaged. They wore a distinctive navy blue or black dress with a white collar and a black hat, and so were sometimes called "Protestant nuns."

Dead Sea Scrolls Scrolls belonging to the Jewish sect of Essenes, preserved in the caves of Qumran* and other sites and discovered by Bedouin goatherders in 1947 and later years. The scrolls throw considerable light on Jewish ascetic life and practices at the time of Christ.

Archbishop Samuel and the Dead Sea Scrolls

deambulatoria Covered walkway surrounding the body of a church, sometimes with altars.

dean (Lat., *decanus,* ultimately from *decem,* ten) Official in the Roman Catholic and Anglican churches. He may preside over a cathedral, assist a bishop, or preside over a church court. In earlier times, it was the title of a monk supervising ten novices*. In the Anglican Church, the term is applied to the heads of the collegiate churches* of Westminster, Windsor, or other churches; the bishop of London as the dean of the province of Canterbury*; or a lay judge. In the Roman Catholic Church, the term is used for the high office of the head of the Sacred College*, who is the cardinal bishop of Ostia. Rural deans assist the bishop in administering his diocese*.

deanery Office or residence of a dean.

Dearmer, Percy (1867–1936) Anglican hymnologist who edited several hymnals and wrote on various aspects of worship. He was coeditor of the *English Hymnal* (1906) and *Songs of Praise* (1925).

death of God theology Quasi-theological idea that God has ceased to be transcendent in the conventional sense and that he has become the creator emeritus, who, having accomplished his creation, has ceased to be active and remains unengaged in the affairs of mankind. In the nineteenth century, the idea was expressed in nontheological terms by the German poet Jean Paul, Hegel, and Nietzsche. In the 1960s the idea was revived in theological works, such as *The Death of God* (1961) and *Wait Without Idols* (1964), by Gabriel Vahanian, *The Secular City* (1965) by Harvey Cox, *The Gospel of Christian Atheism* (1966) by T. J. J. Altizer, and *Secular Meaning of the Gospel* (1963) by Paul van Buren. They believe that God is no longer relevant to theology or that God is wholly other* and can never be objectified.

death, the second Lake of fire*, into which, according to Revelation, sinners are placed after the last judgment*. It is the eternal punishment* for those outside of God's salvation*.

decade Each of the five divisions into which each chaplet* of the Rosary* is divided, because each contains ten Hail Marys*, one Lord's Prayer*, and a Gloria Patri*. Also, of a set of ten, as in Bullinger's* *Decades*.

decani Church singers who sit on the dean's* side of the chancel*.

Decani The Pantocrator* church built between 1327 and 1335 at Decani in Kosovo* region of southern Serbia, founded by King Stefan Uros III Decanski and his son, Tsar Dusan. Its frescoes illustrate Serbian liturgical practices as well as material culture.

Decapolis League of ten cities, east of Jordan, all of which had Greek-speakers in biblical times.

Decian persecution The first large-scale persecution of Christians under Decius, Roman emperor from 201 to 251. In 249 he commanded all his subjects to sacrifice and to obtain certificates showing they had done so. When Christians refused, many were martyred, including Fabian, bishop of Rome*; Alexander, bishop of Jerusalem*; and Babylas*, bishop of Antioch*.

Pope Fabian

decision card Printed card filled in by a new convert at an evangelistic campaign.

decision for Christ In Evangelical theology, a public or private act by which one accepts Jesus Christ as personal Lord and Savior and commits oneself to his service.

Declaratory Act Enactment by the highest court of the Presbyterian Church clarifying or adjusting doctrinal standards.

declension Decline of the spiritual foundations of the Holy Puritan Commonwealth in New Eng-

land in the seventeenth century. Increased moral laxity and lower standards for participation in the church, such as the Half-Way Covenant*, were seen as evidence of a spiritual decline, compared to the dedication of the first generation.

decretals Papal epistles having the force of canon law*. They are generally drafted in response to questions.

decretive will of God (Lat., *voluntas decreti*) The ultimate or hidden will of God as distinct from the revealed will of God.

Decretum Gelasianum Document mistakenly attributed to Pope Gelasius (492–496), also known as Decretum de Libris Recipiendis. It has five divisions: 1. Christ and the Holy Spirit. 2. Books in the biblical canon*, including the Apocrypha*. 3. Statement on the claims of the Roman See* to supremacy over the universal church. 4. List of writings from the Fathers of the Church* and councils. 5. List of non-canonical books.

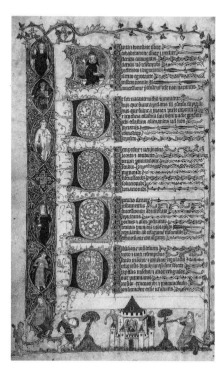

Illuminated Decretals

dedication 1. Consecration*, as of a church or building. The Feast of the Dedication is an annual celebration of the day of the dedication of the church. 2. In some Protestant churches, consecration of an infant in lieu of infant baptism*.

Deer, Book of See BOOK OF DEER.

Deesis (Gk., humble petition) Representation of Christ seated, with the Madonna* on his right hand and St. John the Baptist on his left, with their hands outstretched, interceding for the human race.

Deesis

Defender of the Faith (Lat., *Fidei Defensor**) Title given Henry VIII by Pope Leo X* on the basis of an anti-Lutheran royal treatise on the sacraments*.

definition Clear and precise definition of truth as approved by a church council or synod*.

deggua In the Ethiopian Church*, antiphonal chant for the whole liturgical year*, except Lent*. The chant was introduced in 534 by a chorister named Yared.

DeHaan, Martin Ralph (1891–1965) Radio preacher and founder of Radio Bible Class. DeHaan started a local radio ministry in the mid-1920s. By the 1940s it was heard on several hundred stations, and its devotional booklet, *Our Daily Bread,* was used in millions of homes. He was a powerful speaker whose anecdotal style rendered the Bible in folk terms and metaphors.

Dei gratia (Lat., by the grace of God) Phrase acknowledging the sustaining power of God in human activities.

deification See THEOSIS.

Deipara (Lat., God-bearer) Title, equivalent of the Greek *Theotokos**, applied to the Virgin Mary* at the Council of Ephesus* in 431.

deisis In the Byzantine Church*, icon* of Jesus in royal robes over the royal doors* of the iconostasis*.

Deism An often anti-Christian philosophy substituting natural religion for revealed religion and disbelieving all miracles and supernatural events in the Bible. Deists believe that God created the world but does not actively participate in its running or in human affairs and is simply irrelevant. As a philosophy, it espoused an intermediate position between Renaissance humanism and hardcore Marxist materialism, which denied the existence of God altogether. The eighteenth century was the heyday of Deism when its popular spokesmen, Thomas Paine, Elihu Palmer, and Ethan Allen, made it the fashionable ideology of the elite classes.

Deissman, Adolf (1866–1937) German New Testament scholar. His studies showed that the New Testament was written in popular rather than classical Greek and described the evolution of Christian doctrine in terms of a popular cult*. Deissman wrote a life of the apostle Paul* and other biblical studies. The more important of his books were *Light from the Ancient East* (1910) and *The Religion of Jesus and the Faith of Paul* (1923).

dekanikion In the Byzantine Church*, a staff with a crosspiece on the top on which the clergy support themselves during long services.

delegate, apostolic See APOSTOLIC DELEGATE.

Delehaye, Hippolyte (1859–1941) Bollandist hagiographer. He entered the Jesuit Order in 1879 and joined the Bollandists* in 1891, becoming their president in 1912. He contributed regularly to the *Acta Sanctorum** and *Analecta Bollandiana.* His many hagiographical works included: *Les Legendes Hagiographiques* (1905), *Les Legendes Grecques des Saints Militaires* (1909), *Les Origines du Culte* des Martyrs (1912), *Les Passions des Martyrs et les Genres Litteraires* (1921), *Les Saints Stylites* (1923), and *Sanctus* (1927).

Della Robbia, Andrea (1435–1525) Florentine artist. Nephew of Luca Della Robbia*. He did a series of altars for the Franciscan church at La Verna and a large number of Madonnas*.

Della Robbia, Luca (1399/1400–1482) Master sculptor and artist in terra cotta. His masterpiece is the la Cantoria di Santa Maria del Fiore (the singing and dancing boys) done in marble in Florence*. His most famous bronze work, which took him 30 years to compete, is the north sacristy* door in the cathedral divided into several panels. From 1442 he began to work in enamelled terra cotta in which his white figures on a pale blue background were framed by brilliantly colored borders of fruits and flowers. The finest examples of his terra cotta are found in the Bargello at Florence, the Chapel of the Crucifix at San Miniato, and the Tabernacles at Impruneta.

Demetrios, St. (280–303) Christian martyr* who was killed by the sword under Emperor Galerius during the Diocletian persecution*. According to his biographers, his body was thrown into a deep well "whence a spring of sanctified water issues always."

Demetrius of Rostov, St. (1651–1709) Bishop of Rostov. He was a noted scholar and preacher who left a mark on Russian religious literature with his *Spiritual Alphabet* and dramas and verses. He accompanied Mazeppa, the Cossack leader, to Moscow*. He was canonized in 1857. Feast day: October 28.

demission Relinquishment of the ministry with the approval of the denominational authorities.

demiurge Inferior or malevolent, not absolutely intelligent deity who is the creator of the material world, identified in Gnostic theology with the Yahweh of the Old Testament. See COSMOCRATOR.

demythologization (Ger., *enmythologisierung*) Stripping away the overlay of fiction or myth to gain access to the kernel of historical and redemptive truth of the gospel, a term popularized by Rudolf Bultmann*. It is driven by a desire to make Christianity more relevant to the modern mind by removing the mythical substructure, such as miracles and angels*, but retaining the anthropological and existential insights. Central to Bultmann's theology is his distinction between *Historie,* or the facts of history, and *Geschichte,* or the significance of an event in history. For Bultmann, many New Testament events are *Geschichte,* but not *Historie*—that is, they are only significant legends. Bultmann insisted that he was only interpreting rather than eliminating myths, but many of his followers have used it as a reductionist tool to do violence to the message of the New Testament. Bultmann emphasized the kerygma* as a call to authentic existence, but said this could be meaningful only when it had been demythologized.

denomination Religious group or sect holding common beliefs or principles, composed of local congregations, subscribing to common creeds, and acknowledging the authority of a common body or head.

denominationalism Exclusive adherence to or advocacy of denominational principles and beliefs and allegiance to denominational bodies; used often in an unfavorable sense as synonymous with sectarianism*.

Denver Seminary Evangelical school in the Baptist tradition in Denver, Colorado. Founded in 1950, it was first named Conservative Baptist Theological Seminary. Under the leadership of Vernon Grounds in the 1960s and 1970s, the school participated in and contributed to the Evangelical renewal.

Denys, St. See DIONYSIUS OF PARIS.

Deo favente With divine favor.

Deo gratias "Thanks be to God." Liturgical acclamation used in the early church.

Deo volente "God willing." Often d.v.

deodand (lit., given to God) That which is set apart and surrendered to God.

deontology Branch of ethics dealing with duty or moral obligation.

deoosculatorium Also, pax brede*. Small plate of ivory, metal, or wood with a crucifix on the face and a projecting handle at the back, used in the Mass* for conveying the kiss of peace*.

deposit of faith Body of truths entrusted by Christ to the apostles and by the apostles to the church. The church guards this deposit as a sacred trust and may not add to it or subtract from it. The church is also required to preserve it without change or corruption. Faith* is thus an objective fact independent of subjective human need. The magisterium* of the church is seen as the guardian of this objective faith.

depositio (Lat., burial) Birthday of a martyr*, formerly known as natalitia*.

deposition Permanent removal of a church official from his office and title.

deprecation (Lat., averting by entreaty) Prayer that evil may be removed or turned away.

deprogramming Process of reversing the programmed indoctrination and brainwashing imparted by a cult*, thus restoring an individual to orthodox faith.

deputation Solicitation of prayer and financial support by missionaries before embarking for the mission field* or during furloughs.

Der Balyzeh Fragments Pages of a Greek papyrus* codex* containing liturgical prayers and a creed discovered by W. Flinders Petrie and W. Crum at Der Balyzeh in Egypt in 1907. It throws light on the liturgies of St. Mark* and St. Serapion*.

derder In the Armenian Church*, a married priest.

Des Prez, Josquin (c. 1440–1521) Belgian composer who helped to define the Renaissance musical style. His greatest music is in his motets*, of which there are over 100, as well as 20 masses. He also helped to establish the contrapuntal texture of choral music.

descent into hell/hades Statement in the Apostles' Creed* and in Acts 2:31, commonly understood as Christ's visit to the world of the dead between His Crucifixion and His Resurrection. It is not found in the Nicene Creed* or in the Old Roman Creed*.

Desert Fathers Early Christian monks, such as St. Anthony the Great*, who lived in the Nitrian Desert* and other places in Egypt, Syria, and the Holy Land*.

Desert Fathers

Despoina In the Byzantine Church*, a title of the Virgin Mary*.

Despotes (Gk., master, sovereign) Also, Despotikos. In the Byzantine Church*, a descriptive title of God or of Jesus Christ.

Deus a se (Lat., God as he is in himself) God who cannot be known by human beings.

Deus absconditus (Lat., the hidden God) Divine condition of anonymity that can be broken not by reason but only by self-revelation. Distinct from Deus revelatus*, or the God revealed in Jesus Christ. Suggestively developed by Martin Luther*.

Deus misereatur "God be merciful," title of Psalm 67.

Deus pro nobis (Lat., God for us) God as he is revealed to human beings.

Deus revelatus (Lat., the revealed God) God as he is revealed in Jesus Christ.

Deus vult "God wills it." Slogan with which Pope Urban II* rallied the Christian West in the First Crusade*.

deuterocanon Apocryphal books of the Bible outside the received canon*. Their authenticity is doubtful or has not been fully established.

Deutsche Messe (Ger., German Mass) Luther's vernacular version of the Eucharist*, called the German Mass and Order of Service, 1526.

devil's advocate See ADVOCATUS DIABOLI.

devotio moderna (Lat., modern devotion) Revival and deepening of the spiritual life beginning in the fourteenth century, associated with the Brethren of the Common Life*. It found its finest expression in the teachings of Gerard Groote* and Thomas à Kempis* and in the Winchester* canons. Marked by a pronounced preference for affective spirituality*, it was Christocentric* rather than theocentric* and cultivated devotion to the Eucharist* and meditation on the Scriptures.

devotion 1. Earnestness and fervor in the performance of religious duties and obligations. 2. Usually, devotions, nonliturgical prayer, and personal worship.

Devout Life, Introduction to the (1608) Work on spiritual life by St. Francis of Sales*, a classic of devotional literature.

devshrimi Turkish policy of kidnaping the healthiest Christian children, converting them forcibly to Islam, and training them as Janissaries.

Deyneka, Peter (1898–2000) Founder of the Slavic Gospel Association. Immigrating in 1914 to the United States from Belarus, he was converted through the ministry of Paul Rader*. The Slavic Gospel Association was founded in 1934 to evangelize* east Europeans in their homelands as well as in other parts of the world.

diaconicon/diakonikon 1. Chamber in the south side of a Greek church, in charge of the deacons, where the sacred vessels are kept. It corresponds to the sacristy* in the Western Church*. The corresponding area on the north side is called prothesis*. 2. Book containing the deacon's portion in the liturgy.

Diadochus (fifth century) Bishop of Photike in Western Greece after 451. He was the author of *Capita Gnostica* on spiritual perfection* which was very popular with Christian readers. He was also one of the earliest practitioners of the Jesus Prayer*.

Diakainesimos In the Byzantine Rite*, the Easter* Week, or the Week of Renewal.

diakonia (Gk., *diakoneo,* serve) Responsible service of the gospel by deeds and words performed by Christians in response to the needs of people. It is the practical expression of Christ's command to feed the hungry, minister to the sick, clothe the naked, and act as the Good Samaritan in caring for human beings in need.

dialectical theology Also, crisis theology*; neo-Orthodoxy*. School of theology associated with Karl Barth*. It transcends traditional orthodoxy* to apprehend God dialectically, that is, as an absolute without the constraints of formulas. God comprehends all paradoxes and contradictions, as Yes and No. Thus God is both mercy and judgment, working within history while outside of time. In addition to Barth, the leading exponents of dialectical theology were Friedrich Gogarten* (1887–1967) and Eduard Thurneysen* (1888–1974).

dialogue of the Mass Also, dialogue Mass. Mass* in which the congregation responds to the prayers of the priest.

Dialogue of the Redeemer A fragmentary document found in Codex III of the Nag Hammadi* Library in which Christ talks with Matthew, Judas, and Mary Magdalene.

dialogue sermon Sermon presented jointly by two preachers in two pulpits.

Diamper, Synod of A diocesan synod* of the church of St. Thomas Christians* in 1599 held by Alexis Menezes, archbishop of Goa, at Diamper

(Udayamperur, south of Cochin) creating a Malabar Uniat Church. The synod renounced the earlier Nestorianism* of St. Thomas Christians and imposed complete submission to Rome. As the Portuguese power waned, about half the Christian population left the Catholic fold and embraced the Jacobite (Syrian Orthodox*) Church based in Syria.

diastyla In the Eastern Orthodox Church*, a cancello or partition, separating the bema* from the nave*.

Diatesseron (Gk., of four) Harmony* of the four Gospels composed by the Assyrian Christian Tatian* about 150. It was very popular among Syriac Christians for many centuries. There are no extant manuscripts of the whole book, but portions of it in Arabic, Greek, Persian, and Armenian have been discovered.

Diatesseron

dibampoulos In the Byzantine Liturgy, a two-branched candlestick carried in front of a patriarch*.

Dibelius, Otto (1880–1967) German pastor and ecumenical leader, bishop of the Berlin-Brandenberg Church. He gained prominence in 1933 when he refused to acknowledge a Nazi appointee as church overseer. He was also a strong supporter of the Barmen Declaration*. He was in jail three times during World War II. After the war he was instrumental in the formation of the German Evangelical Church. He was as fearless in resisting the Communists as he had been the Nazis. He was president of the World Council of Churches*

from 1945 to 1961, and also participated in the World Congress on Evangelization*.

dicastery One of the 28 departments of the Roman Curia*.

Didache 1. The earliest church order document, of unknown authorship, dated roughly 100, "The Teaching of the Lord to the Gentiles through the Twelve Apostles," containing ethical precepts*, guidance for conducting sacraments, and directives for bishops and deacons. Of its 16 chapters, chapters 1 to 6 describe the "Way of Life," and "The Way of Death"; chapters 7 through 15 contain instructions on baptism, prayer, fasting, the Eucharist, and general protocols of conduct; and the last chapter deals with the Antichrist* and the Second Coming*. The book also gives the full text of the Lord's Prayer*. The much-debated treatise throws light on the early organization of the church. 2. (Gk., teaching) Instruction in the Christian faith as distinguished from kerygma* or preaching.

Didascalia Apostolorum Latin title of a Syriac* treatise, originally in Greek, called "Catholic Teaching of the Twelve Apostles and Holy Disciples of our Redeemer," included in the Apostolic Constitutions*. It describes the order of the early church, bishop's duties, penance*, liturgical worship, the administration of offerings, and the settlement of disputes. The author denounces the observance of the ceremonial rituals of the Old Testament.

Didymus Hebrew form of Thomas*.

Didymus the Blind (313–398) Alexandrian theologian. Although blind from childhood, he became the head of the celebrated Catechetical School of Alexandria*, where Antony, Rufinus*, Palladius*, and Jerome* were among his pupils. Jerome praised his "luminous thought and simplicity of words." Among his extant works are *On the Holy Spirit, On the Trinity,* and *Against the Manichaeans.*

Dies Irae (Lat., day of wrath) Medieval Latin hymn about the last judgment* written by Thomas of Celano, sung in the Requiem Mass*.

Dies Luminum (Lat., day of lights) Ancient name for Epiphany*.

Diet of Spires See SPEYER, DIET OF.

Dietrich of Nieheim (1340–1418) Secretary of Pope Gregory XII, called the greatest journalist of his age and an able pamphleteer. He wrote tracts to end the Great Schism* and a history of the Council of Constance*.

Dieu avec nous (Fr.) "God with us."

Dieu defend le droit (Fr.) "God defends the right."

Dieu et mon droit (Fr.) "God and my right," the motto of the British monarch.

difnari In the Coptic Liturgy, an antiphonary* containing two alternative hymns for each day of the year.

digamy Second marriage, especially after the death of the first wife, widely condemned in the early church, partly through an interpretation of 1 Timothy 3:2.

dignitas In Roman Catholic theology, religious value of any work, as distinguished from bonitas* or ethical value.

dikaios (Gk., just or righteous) In the Byzantine Church*, the superior* of a skete*.

dikanikion In the Byzantine Church*, the crosier* with two curved branches decorated with serpents' heads.

dikerion Also, dikeretrikera. Byzantine double candlestick, used in the blessing of the congregation, symbolizing the two natures in Christ. Compare trikerion*.

dime Tenth or a tithe*, paid as tax to the church.

dimissory letter Letter authorizing the transfer of a church member or official from one parish* or diocese* to another.

Dinkha/Beth Dinkha In the Assyrian Church*, the Epiphany*.

diocese (Gk., *dioikesis,* administration) 1. Most common geographical unit of ecclesiastical administration in Episcopal churches. 2. In the Roman Catholic Church, "a portion of the people of God entrusted for pastoral care to a bishop." It was generally divided into parishes and subdivided into rural deaneries* and subdeaneries. Dioceses* may be grouped into provinces.

Diocletian persecution Persecution of Christians initiated by Emperor Diocletian from 303 to 305, known as the Great Persecution. An edict issued at Nicomedia enjoined the destruction of churches and the burning of Christian books. The next two edicts were directed against the clergy, punishment for resistance being imprisonment, torture, and death. The fourth edict imposed the duty of sacrifice to pagan gods on all subjects.

Diocletianic Era Reckoning of time from the time of Diocletian's accession in 284. From 303, it is also called the Era of the Martyrs*.

Diodore of Tarsus (?–394) Bishop of Tarsus and an influential teacher in Antioch* among whose pupils were Theodore of Mopsuestia* and John Chrysostom*. Although generally orthodox, he was condemned by a synod* at Antioch as author of the Nestorian heresy, and his books were destroyed. He wrote many commentaries on the Scriptures, defending the faith against heretics.

Dikerion

Diognetus, Epistle to Anonymous work, sometimes attributed to Quadratus* or Pantaenus*, dated approximately 180. It attacked pagan idolatry and Jewish ritualism* and described Christians as the salt of the earth. Often included among the Apostolic Fathers*, it is widely admired as a winsome essay on apologetics*.

Dionysius bar Salibi (d. 1171) Syriac Orthodox metropolitan* of Diyarbakir in modern-day Turkey, exegete and polemicist. He was one of the most prolific Syriac Orthodox writers of the Middle Ages and the first to write a commentary of the entire Syriac Bible. His works include a treatise on baptism*, two anaphoras, several homilies, a compendium of theology, poems on the Muslim capture of Edessa* in 1144, and commentaries on the *Centuries* of Evagrius.

Dionysius Exiguus (c. 500–c. 545) Scythian monk and chronologer who changed the calendar of the modern world and established Anno Domini* as the dividing line of history. He settled the controversy on the dating of Easter.* Dionysius drew up a new system of dating the calendar on a 19-year cycle, beginning with the birth of Christ, rather than the founding of Rome*. He was also the author of a sixth-century decretal collection and translations into Latin of the works of the early Greek Fathers*.

Dionysius of Paris, St. (d. ?250) Also, Denys*. Patron saint* of Paris. Traditionally believed to be one of the seven bishops sent to convert Gaul. He was martyred at Montmartre. Feast day: October 9.

Dionysius Telmaharensis (?–848) Monk who became patriarch* of the Syrian Jacobite Church* (818–848). He is best known as the author of a history from 582 to 842. The original work was composed in two parts, one on church history and the other on secular history.

Dionysius the Areopagite Convert of St. Paul* as recorded in Acts 17:34, and later, according to tradition, the first bishop of Athens*. Feast day: October 9.

Dionysius the Carthusian (1402/3–1471) Mystic and writer, known as Doctor Ecstaticus. He wrote commentaries on Scripture and books on moral theology* and ecclesiastical discipline. He helped to inspire a crusade* against the Turks. His major work on contemplative life* was *De Contemplatione*. He also published a compendium of Aquinas's* *Summa*.

Dionysius the Great (c. 190–c. 264) Bishop of Alexandria, a pupil of Origen* who endured both the Decian* and Valerian persecutions. Fragments of his writings have survived in the commentaries of Eusebius* and Athanasius*. As an apologist, he attacked Sabellianism*, Paul of Samosata*, and Epicureanism. He welcomed back to the church those who had lapsed during the persecutions. He served as an influential adviser and arbitrator in disputes. Feast day: November 17.

Dionysius the Pseudo-Areopagite (fifth century) Unknown author, believed to be a Syrian, of ten epistles and four treatises. His extant writings include *The Celestial Hierarchy, The Ecclesiastical Hierarchy, Divine Names,* and *Mystical Theology,* all of which helped to shape mystical and Byzantine theology and synthesize Christian truth and neo-Platonism. He described the soul's ascent, through a series of graded illuminations, to a full knowledge of God. Among those who were influenced by his books were Gregory* the Great, Martin I*, Hugh of St. Victor*, Albertus Magnus*, Thomas Aquinas*, Dante, and John Milton*. His influence derived from his claim to be Paul's convert at Athens, which went unchallenged until the Reformation*.

diophysite Person who believes in two natures, divine and human, united in Jesus Christ.

Dioscorus (d. 454) Patriarch* of Alexandria* who succeeded Cyril* in 444. He supported the Monophysite doctrines of Eutyches* and was deposed at the third session of the Council of Chalcedon* in 451 and banished by civil authorities. He is reckoned a saint* in the Coptic Church*. Feast day: September 4.

diphros In the Byzantine tradition, the abbot's* chair in a monastery.

diptych (Gk., two tablets) Pair of tablets hinged together to form a book. Originally the two inner leaves were covered with wax and used to list names of Christians for whom prayer was offered.

Diptych

Directory for the Public Worship of God Manual prepared by the Westminster Assembly of Divines and adopted by the General Assembly* of the Church of Scotland* and the English Parliament in 1645 as a replacement for the Church of England's* *Book of Common Prayer**. Its purpose was to provide a direction but not to prescribe a set form or liturgy to be followed exactly.

dirge Office or church service for the dead, derived from the first word of the former antiphon*, *Dirige Domine Deus*. It is set to music as in *Mattutino di Morti* by David Perez (1752). It includes the morning office and the vespers* of the night before.

diriment impediment In canon law*, circumstance or fact that nullifies a marriage; distinguished from an impedient that made a marriage unlawful but not null and void. Such impediments may include age differential, impotency, existing marriage, vows of chastity*, holy orders*, consanguinity, and difference in religious beliefs.

dis aliter visum (Lat.)"The gods decreed otherwise."

Discalced (Lat., without shoes) Of a monastic order whose members go without shoes, wearing sandals instead, or go barefoot, following Matthew 10:10. First introduced by John of Guadalupe about 1500 among the Friars Minor* of Strict Observance. The major discalced orders are the Discalced Carmelites, Trinitarians*, and Passionists*.

discernment Spiritual gift that enables a believer to distinguish between good and evil and between right and wrong, and to recognize what is hidden or obscure to the spiritually immature.

disciple (*noun*) 1. One of the 12 chosen followers of Jesus Christ. 2. Any follower or student of a spiritual teacher. 3. An apostle. 4. A Christian. 5. (*verb*) To assist and mentor new believers to mature in the knowledge of the Lord through continual oversight of their life and through edification* and discipline. It is based on Christ's injunction to teach [new converts] "all things whatsoever I have commanded you." The discipling approach is seen by its advocates as the quickest way not only to multiply but also to develop disciples who will also be soul-winners.

discipler In a discipling church or program, the person who mentors another spiritually.

Disciples of Christ American denomination founded by Thomas Campbell, his son Alexander Campbell*, and Barton W. Stone* in 1809. It became a separate communion in 1832, but split into three main groups: the Christian Church (Disciples of Christ*), Christian Churches/Churches of Christ, and the Churches of Christ*. Disciples have an active missionary program and have spread to over 20 countries worldwide. They are also committed to the ecumenical movement*.

disciplina arcani (Lat., discipline of secrecy) Practice in the early church of concealing certain theological doctrines and practices from catechumens* and pagans and revealing them only to the baptized. It was expressed in the custom of excluding catechumens from the central part of the Eucharist*.

discipline 1. Teaching of precepts* and commandments that help Christian growth and discipleship and contribute to the life and witness of the whole body. 2. Punishment. 3. Rigorous training, as that of an ascetic or monk. 4. Rites and activities of a denomination. 5. Scourge of knotted cords, chain, or other instruments used by penitents*. 6. In Reformed* and other Protestant traditions, such as the Anabaptists*, practice of correction of serious faults of faith or life by the congregation or its leaders. It is a third essential mark* of the church in some Reformed* churches.

Discipline, Book of 1. Manual detailing the rites and activities of a church or denomination. 2. Doctrine, worship, and government of the Reformed Church of Scotland set out in the *Book of Common Order** and *The First Book of Discipline** (1560), and in *The Second Book of Discipline** (1580). They were an adaptation of Genevan Ordinances to meet the needs of the Church of Scotland*. They were divided into nine heads: 1. doctrine, 2. sacraments*, 3. election of ministers, 4. abolition of idolatry, 5. provision for the ministers, 6. rents and patrimony of the kirk*, 7. ecclesiastical discipline, 8. election of elders and deacons, and 9. church policy.

discipling movement See SHEPHERDING MOVEMENT.

discrimination 1. Spiritual gift enabling its recipient to distinguish the promptings of grace* from the Holy Spirit* from human delusions or demonically inspired ideas. 2. A spiritual gift enabling a person to discern the spiritual state of another (1 Cor. 12:10).

discursive prayer Mental prayer based on a fixed chain of thought, usually stimulated by reading.

discus Plate on which the communion bread* is placed in the Eastern Church*, corresponding to the paten* in the Western Church*.

disestablishment Delinking the bonds between a state and an established church, making the church independent of state control and the state neutral in religious affairs.

dishallow (*verb*) To profane, violate, sully, or deconsecrate.

diskelion In the Byzantine tradition, a lectern* made up of two long shafts in the shape of an X.

dismissal *Ite, missa est**, in the Roman Mass*.

dispensation 1. Exemption granted by ecclesiastical authorities from fulfillment of a vow or compliance with a law. 2. Exemption from a penalty for breaking a rule or permission to do an act normally illegal.

dispensation 1. Divine plan or economy (oikonomia) as in 1 Corinthians 9:17, Ephesians 1:10; 3:2, and Colossians 1:25. 2. Covenant. 3. Period of history or era in which God deals with his creation in a characteristic manner or, according to one of its chief proponents, C. I. Scofield*, "period of time during which man is tested in respect of obedience to some specific revelation of the will of God." Scofield outlines seven dispensations: innocence (before the Fall), conscience (from the Fall to Noah), human government (from Noah to Abraham), promise (from Abraham to Moses), law (from Moses to Christ), grace (the Church Age*), and kingdom (the millennium*). Thus, dispensational.

dispensationalism Theology based on a dispensational interpretation of history. J. N. Darby* is considered the founder of dispensationalism, although St. Augustine* prefigured some of its elements. According to Darby, the Church Age* is a parenthesis* between the sixty-ninth and seventieth weeks of Daniel 9:25–27 and there would be a rapture* of believers from earth to heaven* by Christ before the seventieth week when the Great Tribulation* of divine wrath will be poured out on human wickedness and unbelief. Darby also developed the idea that the organized church is an apostate* church and that the true church is heavenly and invisible. Dispensationalism was fostered by an emphasis on prophecy. All dispensationalists are premillenialists, although the reverse is not true. Dispensationalists hold that the gifts of the Spirit*, especially the "sensational gifts," or sign gifts, such as speaking in tongues*, healing, and the working of miracles, were confined to the Apostolic Age* and should be forbidden.

Dispensationalism was advanced in the works of L. S. Chafer* and E. W. Bullinger who coined the term *ultradispensationalism**. Chafer's *Systematic Theology* (8 vols., 1948) is the most classic statement of dispensationalism. Chafer's students, J. F. Walvoord*, J. D. Pentecost, and C. C. Ryrie* all made significant contributions as well as modifications to dispensationalism. In the twentieth century dispensationalism was popularized by C. I. Scofield* through his Scofield Reference Bible*. In recent years a further modification called Progressive Dispensationalism has emerged. It holds that God did not reveal all truth at one time but through various periods and stages of revelation* and that God's revelation is constantly unfolding.

disputation Theological controversy or argument, especially in formal setting in centers of scholastic theology or in controversy during the Reformation*.

Disruption Schism* in the Church of Scotland* in 1843 resulting in the formation of the Free Church.

dissent Disagreement with the doctrines of, and separation from, an established church.

dissenter 1. In seventeenth-century England, a Puritan, Presbyterian, or a non-Anglican Protestant. 2. In seventeenth-century Scotland, an Episcopalian.

dissident Member of a dissenting church who upholds doctrines contrary to those accepted by the established church*.

dissolution of the monasteries The royal takeover of Roman Catholic monasteries in England by Henry VIII and his advisor Thomas Cromwell. It was accomplished through acts of Parliament. In 1536, 243 smaller monasteries were taken over and between 1537 and 1540 the larger abbeys and houses of the Athos* were appropriated through a process of surrender. By 1540 there were no more English religious houses. The spoils of the Dissolution passed first to the crown and then to the nobility, but some went to the foundation of six new sees*.

Distler, Hugo (1908–1942) German composer of church music, the most influential in the interwar years. In 1932 he composed musical vespers* and later, under the influence of Buxtehude* and Hindemith, composed functional church music in modern idiom. Toward the end of his life, he became conductor of Staats und Domchor. He committed suicide in 1942 to avoid conscription in the Nazi army. His sacred works include a German Mass*, chorale motets*, chorale cantatas, and an incomplete Passion.

distribution of the elements Administration of the bread and wine to communicants during Holy Communion*.

district superintendent Official in the Methodist Church as well as in some Evangelical churches, directly under a bishop or in lieu of a bishop.

diurnal Servicebook containing the day hours* or all traditional canonical hours* except the matins*.

divided chancel Chancel* in which rows of choir stalls* or pews face each other.

divine (*adjective*) Of or relating to God; godlike. (*noun*) A clergyman or theologian.

divine afflatus Inspiration of God imparted through special wisdom, insight, or prophecy.

Divine Comedy Literary masterpiece written by Dante Alighieri* between 1305 and 1310. A sacred poem in three parts, it is divided into *Inferno, Purgatory,* and *Paradise.*

Scene from Dante's Divine Comedy

divine healing See FAITH HEALING.

Divine, Major J. (1880–1965) "Father Divine." African-American founder of the Peace Mission movement. Born George Baker into a poor Georgia family, he changed his name about 1919 while claiming to be God. He established a cult* that grew rapidly with the help of a cooperative and employment agency that provided in communally owned "heavens" low-cost meals and lodging to thousands. He enforced a strict discipline on his members, including prohibition of alcohol, tobacco, cosmetics, obscene language, and promiscuity. His white widow and heir, "Mother Divine," continued his work.

Divine Office See OFFICE, DIVINE.

divine praises In Roman Catholic Church, series of praises, beginning with the words, "Blessed be God, blessed be His holy name," said or sung after the Benediction of the Blessed Sacrament before the host* is placed back in the Tabernacle.

divine service 1. Public worship. 2. In Anglican churches, the choir office*.

Divine Word, Society of the See SOCIETY OF THE DIVINE WORD.

divinity 1. Quality or state of being divine; nature or essence of Godhead. 2. Theology.

divinity school Seminary or comparable institution teaching theology and training ministers of the gospel.

Dix, Dom Gregory (1901–1952) Anglican scholar. He left a teaching position at Oxford University to enter the Anglican Benedictine monastery at Nashdom Abbey, becoming its prior* in 1948. His contributions to the study of Christian worship include *The Shape of the Liturgy* (1945), *The Treatise on the Apostolic Tradition of St. Hippolytus of Rome* (1937), *The Apostolic Ministry* (1946), and *Jew and Greek: A Study in the Primitive Church* (1953).

Dix, William Chatterton (1837–1898) English poet and hymn writer. His hymns appear in *Hymns of Love and Joy* (1861), *Altar Songs, Verses on the Holy Eucharist* (1867), and a *Vision of All the Saints* (1871). His Christmas* carol, *What Child Is This* (1865), is used even today. He also wrote two devotional books, *Light* and *the Risen Life*.

diyaqoniqon In the Jacobite Church*, the southern apse* in a church where the sacred vessels are stored.

djachotz (lit., Book of Noon) Armenian lectionary* containing the Epistles and the Gospels.

DNJC Dominus Noster Jesus Christus ("Our Lord Jesus Christ").

Doane, George Washington (1799–1859) American Episcopal bishop, author of "Softly Now the Light of Day" and other hymns.

Doberan Cistercian monastery founded in Doberan, east of Lubeck, Germany, by Heinrich Borwin I. The first brick basilica*, consecrated in 1232, was burned to the ground. Between 1295 and 1368, it was rebuilt. The monastery was pillaged in the Thirty Years' War and secularized in 1552. For a few years it served as a princely hunting lodge and then fell into ruins.

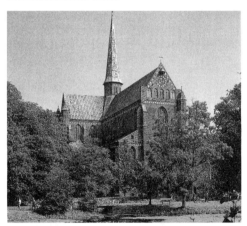
Doberan Monastery

Dobson, James (1936–) Founder and president of Focus on the Family. He was a physician and psychologist when he gained national attention through his book, *Dare to Discipline* (1970). The public response to this book led to a series of workshops which developed in 1977 into Focus on the Family, one of the largest Christian national organizations in the United States with a strong political agenda.

Docetism (Gk., *dokein,* to seem) Heretical theological beliefs held by some, called Docetae, in the early church that Christ did not have a real physical body and that his humanity and suffering as well as his crucifixion and Resurrection were illusory and not real. The Docetae shared with the Gnostics the idea that all matter was inherently evil. They held that death was an ignominy unfit for God and that Christ was spared such an ignominy by Judas Iscariot or Simon of Cyrene taking his place or by the separation of the divine Christ from the human Jesus. Among those who championed Docetism were Cerinthus* and Serapion, bishop of Antioch*, who was the first to use the term. Later heresies, such as Apollinarianism, Eutychianism*, and Monophysitism*, had some Docetic elements in them.

Doctor of Divinity Theological degree from an academic institution. Abbreviated D.D.

doctors of the church Title given over 30 outstanding theologians who combined sound learning with holiness*. Among them are Gregory the Great*, Ambrose*, Augustine*, Jerome*, Athanasius*, Chrysostom*, Basil the Great*, Gregory of Nazianzus*, Aquinas*, Teresa of Avila*, and Catherine of Siena*.

doctors, scholastic Theologians acknowledged by the church as outstanding teachers of the gospel.

James Dobson

The best known scholastic doctors are: St. Thomas Aquinas*, doctor angelicus; Gregory of Rimini*, doctor authenticus; John Gerson, doctor christianissimus; Jan van Ruysbroeck* or Dionysius the Carthusian*, doctor ecstaticus; William of Ockham*, doctor invincibilis or singularis; Alexander of Hales*, doctor irrefragabilis (or doctorum); St. Bernard of Clairvaux*, doctor mellifluus; Roger Bacon*, doctor mirabilis (or admirabilis); Thomas Bradwardine* or Jacobus de Esculo, doctor profundus; St. Bonaventura*, doctor seraphicus (or devotus); Richard of Middleton*, doctor solidus (or copiosus); Duns Scotus*, doctor subtilis; and St. Albert Magnus, doctor universalis (or venerabilis or expertus).

doctrine (Lat., *doctrina,* teaching) Codified belief of a denomination and one of the elements of a creed.

Dodd, Charles Harold (1884–1973) British New Testament scholar. He was one of the most influential New Testament scholars in the mid-twentieth century. He was Rylands Professor at Manchester (1930–1935) and Norris-Hulse professor of divinity at Cambridge. From 1950 he was in charge of the New English Bible* and played a major role in the translation of the New Testament. His works include *The Authority of the Bible* (1928), *The Epistle to the Romans* (1932), *The Parables of the Kingdom* (1935), *The Apostolic Preaching and Its Developments* (1936), *History of the Gospel* (1938), *The Interpretation of the Fourth Gospel* (1953), and *The Historical Tradition in the Fourth Gospel* (1963).

Doddridge, Philip (1702–1751) English Presbyterian clergyman and hymn writer, author of many hymns, including "O God of Bethel," "Hark, the Glad Sound," and "Awake My Soul." His *Rise and Progress of Religion in the Soul* (1745) is considered the last great Puritan autobiography.

dodecaorton In the Eastern Orthodox Church*, a series of 12 representations of the great feasts of the Byzantine Church*, usually displayed on an iconostasis*. The 12 feasts are Annunciation, Nativity, Presentation in the Temple, Baptism, Transfiguration, Raising of Lazarus, Entry into Jerusalem, Crucifixion, Harrowing of Hell*, Ascension, Pentecost*, and Koimesis* or Dormition of the Virgin*.

dogma (Gk., opinion, that which seems good) 1. Definitive belief or group of tenets held by a religious group; total creedal system of a denomination identifying the key doctrines collectively. 2. Religious truth or authoritative teaching established by divine revelation* and defined by the church. It is essentially a corollary and test of orthodoxy*. All dogmas have a central focus in Jesus Christ and are deduced from revelation.

dogmatics Branch of theology dealing with the systematic study of the history and meaning of Christian doctrine.

dogmatikon/dogmatika (Gk., doctrinal hymn) Sticheron* sung to the Mother of God at the end of Psalm 141 in the Byzantine hesperinos*.

Dohnavur Fellowship Missionary work founded in 1901 by Amy Carmichael* at Dohnavur in South India that rescued and rehabilitated young girls dedicated to ritual prostitution in Hindu temples. It was the first mission supported by the Keswick Convention*.

Doleanle Exodus of conservative Calvinists from the Dutch Reformed Church* in 1886.

Dollinger, Johann Joseph Ignaz von (1799–1890) Roman Catholic church historian, teacher, and theologian. He was a pioneer in setting the standards and methods of church history as an academic discipline and influenced both Lord Acton and Felicite Robert de Lamennais*. A liberal in theology, his opposition to the political power of the papacy grew after the First Vatican Council* promulgated the doctrine of papal infallibility*.

Johann Joseph Ignaz von Dollinger

His further attacks on immaculate conception*, the *Syllabus of Errors*, and the Jesuits* led to his excommunication*. He took a part in the founding of the Old Catholics* but disagreed with them when they cast away such practices as clerical celibacy* and auricular confession*.

Among Dollinger's large body of writings are *Reformation* (3 vols., 1845–1848), *Luther* (1851), *Hippolytus und Kallistus* (1853), *Heidenthum und Judenthum* (1857), *Christentum und Kirche* (1860), *The First Age of the Church* (1866), *Die Pabstfabeln des Mittelalters* (1863), *Geschichte der Moralstreitigkeiten in der romisch-katholischen Kirche seit dem 16 Jahrhundert* (2 vols., 1889), and *Briefe und Erklarungen uber die Vaticanischen Dekrete* (1890).

D.O.M. Deo Optimo Maximo ("to God, the Best and the Greatest").

dom (Lat., *dominus,* lord) Title accorded to certain ecclesiastics, especially in the Benedictine, Carthusian, and Cistercian orders and also to certain canons regular*.

dome Also, kubbah*. In the Coptic Liturgy, an asterisk* made of two loops of silver crossed and riveted together and placed over the paten* and diskos.

domine Informal title for a clergyman in the Netherlands.

Domine quo vadis? (Lat., "Lord, where are you going?") According to legend, Peter* was fleeing Rome* to escape martyrdom when he encountered the Lord going toward Rome. When asked, "Domine quo vadis?" Jesus answered reproachfully, "I am going to Rome to be crucified." Peter thereupon turned back. The Church of Quo Vadis is located on the site of this incident on the Appian Way*, near Porta San Sebastiano.

Dominic de Guzman, St. (1170–1221) Founder of the Order of Preachers*, commonly known as the Dominicans* or Black Friars*. Challenged by the need to combat heresy, he preached in Languedoc, affected at that time by the Albigensian conflict. He began a new style of itinerant, mendicant preaching that was very effective. In 1206, with the help of Fulk, the bishop of Toulouse*, he opened the first Dominican convent, followed by the first monastery for men in 1215. In 1216 Honorius III* recognized the new mendicant order*, devoted to preaching and the conversion of heretics. There-

St. Dominic

after Dominic traveled tirelessly in Italy, France, and Spain organizing his order. The first general chapter* of the order was held in Bologna* in 1220 and the second one in 1221, the year of his death. He was canonized in 1234.The intensity of his zeal for souls and his dedication to prayer and preaching have rarely been equalled. Feast day: August 8.

dominica in albis In the Western Church*, former name for Low Sunday* when those newly baptized at Easter* put aside their white robes.

dominical (Lat., of the Lord) Used of acts or words of Jesus Christ the Lord.

dominical injunctions Commands of Jesus Christ in the New Testament as binding on his followers.

dominical sacraments See SACRAMENTS, DOMINICAL.

dominicale Veil or napkin used as a head covering when receiving the Holy Communion*.

Dominicans Official name: Ordo Praedicatorum. Order of preachers or black friars* founded by St. Dominic*. The members dress in white with black mantles and take vows of poverty, chastity*, and obedience and refrain from eating meat.The order insists not only on individual poverty, but also corporate poverty so that the order itself is supported by alms and not by revenues from properties. They are champions of orthodoxy* devoted to the defense of the faith. In order to emphasize study and preaching, the order abolished manual labor and shortened its Divine Office*.

Authority in a general chapter* is assigned to a master general* chosen for life to whom members vow obedience. Each house is ruled by a prior* chosen by its members. A number of houses make up a province. Each province has its prior and is represented in the general chapter. The government of the order is much admired by constitutional scholars because of the efficient distribution of power between the central government under the master general and the local government in the provinces and the priories. A second order of nuns and a third order* of lay people are attached to the order.

Because of their zeal for preaching, the Dominicans were particularly useful to the pope for preaching crusades and for accompanying the Spanish and Portuguese conquerors in the Americas, Asia, and Africa. They also chose established intellectual centers, such as Paris and Bologna*, for their activities, with the result that by the middle of the thirteenth century each province had its own Dominican university.

Many of the intellectual leaders of Europe in the Middle Ages, including St. Thomas Aquinas* and St. Albert Magnus, were Dominicans, and their literary and scholastic output was impressive. Several Dominican houses contained public schools of theology. In their role as crusaders against heresy, they were actively involved in the Inquisition*, which was often staffed by Dominicans.

dominus vobiscum (Lat.) Liturgical salutation meaning "the Lord be with you."

dona (Lat., gifts) Alms offered at a religious service.

Donatello (c. 1386–1466) Full name: Donato di Niccolo di Betto Bardi. Italian sculptor, considered the greatest Florentine sculptor before Michelangelo*. He was apprenticed to Ghiberti*. His heroic style is evident in *St. Mark* (1411–1412), *St. John the Evangelist* (1413–1415), *St. George and the Dragon* (c. 1417), and *Herod Presented with the Head of John the Baptist* (1427). From 1443 to 1453 he was in Padua, where he made the high altar of Santo and the first major equestrian monument since antiquity—the statue of the condottiere of Gattamelata. His *Baptist* (1438) and *Magdalene* (1455) are powerful examples of his ability to evoke passion from stone.

Donation of Constantine Eighth-century forgery in which Constantine gives certain territories and rights to Pope Sylvester*, including primacy over the patriarchs* of Antioch*, Alexandria*, Constantinople*, and Jerusalem*. The letter, which was used to bolster the claims of the papacy in the Middle Ages, was included in the False Decretals*. It was exposed as a forgery in the fifteenth century by Lorenzo Valla.

Donatism African separatist church that originated in opposition to the ordination of Caecilian as bishop of Carthage* in 312, because one of his consecrators had committed *traditio* (abjured his faith under persecution) by handing over copies of the Scripture. The anti-Caecilian party, composed mostly of Numidians, elected Majorinus, and then Donatus*, as rival bishops in 313. The Numidians constituted the anti-imperial and anti-Catholic party, and they grew rapidly under Donatus and his successor Parmenian. Eventually the Catholics regained ascendancy after the Imperial Edict of Unity (405), but Donatism survived until the Moorish conquest in the seventh century.

Theologically, Donatism was uncompromising in its puritan ecclesiology*, adoration of martyrs*, apocalyptic rejection of state and society, and opposition to traditors*. Politically, it represented a reaction to imperial repression and led to violent incidents under the bands of marauders called *Circumcellions** and during the revolts of Firmus (372–375) and Gildo (397–398).

Donatus (270–355) Bishop of Carthage*. From 315 to 355 he led and inspired the Donatist schism* in North Africa. None of his writings has survived except in the citations by his opponents. His personal prestige was immense, and he was considered a prophet*.

donatzvitz In the Armenian Church*, a directory of festival days, similar to the Byzantine Typikon*. It also notes the Epistles and Gospels to be read and the hymns to be sung on a festival day.

Donne, John (1572–1631) English poet and dean of St. Paul's. He was the first and the greatest of the metaphysical poets whose songs, sonnets, sermons, and elegies are filled with an intense religious imagery and permeated by a deep sense of sin. According to T. S. Eliot*, "he was much possessed by death." He was a regular preacher at court and a favorite of both King James I and Charles II. A few years before his death he wrote *Devotions upon Emergent Occasions* (1624) and the famous "Hymn to God the Father."

door money Small contribution made voluntarily on entering a church.

doorkeeper (Lat., *ostiarius*) Lowest of the minor orders* of the church. One of his functions was keeping unauthorized persons from attending the Eucharist*. His place was taken by the verger* in modern times.

Dooyeweerd, Herman (1894–1977) Dutch Calvinist philosopher. Dooyeweerd spent his entire teaching career (1926–1965) at the Calvinist Free University of Amsterdam. He taught that religion is at the heart of all human activities, that Christians need to be guided by the Holy Spirit* in their efforts to be engaged in social reforms, and that diversity of gifts must be respected and encouraged. He set forth these ideas in *A New Critique of Theoretical Thought* (4 vols., 1953–1958), *The Twilight of Western Thought* (1960), and *Roots of Western Culture* (1979).

Dordrecht, Synod of See DORT, SYNOD OF.

Dore, Paul Gustave (1832–1883) French artist who made hauntingly beautiful illustrations and woodcuts for the Bible, *Paradise Lost**, *Divine Comedy**, and other books.

Dormition of the BVM Also, Transitio; Koimesis*. In the Eastern Church*, the Feast of the Falling Asleep of the Blessed Virgin, corresponding to the Assumption of the Virgin in the West. It is one of the Twelve Great Feasts* celebrated on August 15.

dormitorium Sleeping room or dormitory in a monastery.

Dorner, Isaak August (1809–1884) German Lutheran theologian, author of a history of the doctrine of the person of Christ, first published in 1839. In 1867 he issued his *Geschichte der Protestantischen Theologie* (2 vols., 1871) and was the founder and editor of the *Jahrbuch fuer Deutsche Theologie.*

doron (Gk., gift) In the Byzantine Liturgy, the offering of consecrated bread in the Communion.

Dorotheus, St. (sixth century) Ascetical writer. He founded a monastery near Gaza of which he became an archimandrite*. His instructions for his monks, *Didaskaliai Psychopheleis,* are an important resource in ascetical literature.

Dorothy, St. (d. c. 313) Also, Dorothea. Legendary martyr*. Christian maiden of Caesarea*, in Cappadocia*, some of whose miracles happened on the way to her martyrdom. Feast day: February 6, suppressed 1969.

dorsal Piece of embroidered cloth hung at the back of an altar in place of a reredos*. See also DOSSAL.

Dorsey, Thomas A. (1900–1993) American songwriter and publisher. He was a blues singer known for his off-color lyrics when he was saved and turned to writing religious songs. He has been credited with coining the term *gospel music**, and he became known as the father of gospel music. He was also a strong influence in the life of Mahalia Jackson*. Among his more than 1,000 gospel songs, the better known compositions are "Peace in the Valley" and "Precious Lord, Take My Hand."

Dort, Synod of Assembly of the Dutch Reformed Church*, convened at Dort (Dordrecht*) to deal with the Arminian controversy in 1618–1619. Five sets of articles were passed which reaffirmed a limited atonement*, unconditional election*, total depravity*, irresistibility of grace*, and the final perseverance* of the saints. At the final session, the synod drew up 93 canonical rules and confirmed the authority of the Belgic Confession* and the Heidelberg Catechism*. It also approved a proposal for an official translation of the Bible.

dorter Dormitory in a monastery, usually on the first floor of the east range of the cloister*, and thus adjacent to one of the transepts* of the conventual church.

Dositheus (1641–1707) Patriarch of Jerusalem*, a defender of Greek orthodoxy, and an opponent of Western Catholic and Protestant influences. He presided over the Synod of Jerusalem in 1672 that rooted out all Protestant influences from the Greek Church. He also tried to limit the rights of Western religious orders in the landmarks of the Holy Land*. He wrote a history of the Jerusalem patriarchate* in *History of the Patriarchs of Jerusalem* (2 vols., 1715).

dossal Ornamental cloth hung behind and above an altar.

dossal cross Cross attached to a dossal* in place of a cross resting on the altar. See also DORSAL.

Dostoevsky, Feodor Mikhalovitch (1821–1881) Russian writer, one of the greatest in the history of literature. Beginning life as an atheist, he ended up, after four years of forced labor in Siberia, as a committed Christian. His large body of works includes *Memoirs from the Underworld* (1864), *Crime and Punishment* (1865–1866), *The Idiot* (1869), *The Possessed* (1871), and *The Brothers Karamazov* (1880). Dostoevsky's religious experience was characteristically Slav in its primeval intensity. For him human beings are a battleground between good and evil and suffering is the road to salvation. In his story, "The Grand Inquisitor" in *The Brothers Karamazov,* he pitted Christ against the institutional church. His influence on modern theology was phenomenal for a non-theologian.

Feodor Mikhalovitch Dostoevsky

Douai Abbey English Benedictine community of St. Edmund* the Martyr, founded in Paris in 1615. It was an important Jacobite center. In 1818 it moved to Douai in Spanish Netherlands, the seat of a university founded by Philip II serving, from 1562, Roman Catholic students from Britain. Members of the college translated the Douai-Reims Bible*. The college was suppressed during the French Revolution and transferred to England.

Douai-Reims Bible Roman Catholic translation of the Bible begun in 1578 at the instance of William Allen. The Old Testament was translated at the University of Douai in France in 1568 and the New Testament at Reims* in 1582. The chief translator was Gregory Martin assisted by Allen and Richard Bristow, and they used the Latin Vulgate*. The entire Bible was revised by Bishop Richard Challoner* in 1749–1750 and 1763–1764 and completely modernized in 1941.

double church 1. Church in two tiers, one above the other, like the upper and lower churches of St. Francis at Assisi or the Ste Chapelle in Paris. 2. Double-ended church with an apsidal projection at both ends.

double feast Important feast at which antiphon* is sung both at the beginning and the end of the canticles*.

double justice Theological distinction between gracious justice acquired through sanctifying grace* or the imputed righteousness of Christ and inherent justice acquired through good works*.

double monasteries Separate houses used by nuns and canons* of the Order of Sempringham, founded by Gilbert of Sempringham*. The only common portion of the monasteries was the church in which the nuns and canons could neither see nor hear each other.

double predestination Doctrine that God by parallel acts chooses the elect* to eternal life* and rejects the damned to everlasting hell*. See also PREDESTINATION, SINGLE.

Double Procession See PROCESSION OF THE HOLY SPIRIT.

doubling Practice in India and Africa of having two preachers for a sermon, one as an echo of the other. The second repeats every sentence of the first louder and with more emphasis.

douillette (lit., padded gown) Long cloak with cuffs for outdoor wear, worn over a cloak.

Doukhobors (Russ., lit., spirit-wrestlers) Heterodox sect* of dissenting believers in eighteenth-century Russia, also known as Christians of the Universal Brotherhood. Their tenets included pacifism, agrarianism, hostility to secular government, and opposition to war, taxes, ceremonies, and registration. Their theology also was suspect of being tinged with heresy. They rejected all rituals, the Bible, hierarchy*, sacraments*, and dogma*. They believed that death was insignificant because the soul migrates after death, that God is present in all human beings, and that Christ was only one of many inspired leaders. They had no sacraments and worshiped in meetings called *sobranyas*. Doukhobors were fiercely persecuted in Tsarist Russia and by the Orthodox Church and were exiled first to Siberia, and then allowed, through the influence of Leo Tolstoy*, to emigrate to Canada. Here also they came into conflict with the authorities over private land ownership and registration of births, deaths, and marriages. They split into three groups: Union of Doukhobors, Christian Communities of Christ*, and the Sons of Freedom.

dove Symbol of the Holy Spirit*. The medieval pyx* was in the shape of a dove.

Dowie, John Alexander (1847–1907) Scottish founder of the Christian Catholic Apostolic Church* in Zion in 1896 in Chicago, Illinois. Earlier he had founded the Divine Healing Association in Australia and New Zealand. As the first apostle of the Chicago church, he ruled with an iron hand, calling himself Elijah III, the restorer. In 1906, he was accused of polygamy and deposed. His followers were called Doweites.

Dowland, John (1563–1626) English composer. He contributed musical settings for Thomas Este's *The Whole Booke of Psalmes* (1592) and Thomas Ravenscroft's *The Whole Booke of Psalmes* (1621).

Downside Abbey St. Gregory's Abbey, Downside, near Bath, the premier English Benedictine congregation. It is a successor to the Douai* Monastery which was transferred to England after being suppressed by the French Revolution. In 1899 it was raised from the status of a priory* to that of an abbey. The abbey church, consecrated in 1935, is one of the finest examples of Modern Gothic* in England. The abbey maintains a school and a journal, *The Downside Review*.

doxa (Gr.) Religious opinion. Hence, orthodoxy*, right opinion; heterodoxy*, different opinion; pseudodoxy*, false opinion; and homodoxy*, same opinion.

doxastikon In the Byzantine Rite*, a hymn normally sung after the short doxology* and followed by the verse, "Now and ever and to the ages of ages, Amen" and a theotokion*.

doxology (lit., speaking praise) 1. Offering of worship in wonder, love, and praise. 2. Praises of God, usually sung during divine service*. Gloria in Excelsis* (derived from Luke 2:14) is the greater doxology and Gloria Patri* (a Trinitarian* hymn) is the lesser doxology. 3. Concluding prayer of worship, normally in Trinitarian form, based on 2 Corinthians 13:13.

dpir In the Armenian Church*, an acolyte* who wears the shapik*, a vestment covered by a heavily embroidered cloak with three crosses.

Dracontius, Blossius Aemilius (fifth century) Christian Carthaginian poet, author of *Concerning God.*

dread Emotion that arises in the face of profound awareness of freedom that promises both new possibilities as well as the uncertainty of the unknown. Distinguished from fear, which focuses on a particular situation or object.

Dream of the Rood Old English poem of unknown authorship consisting of 156 lines describing the feelings of the cross during Christ's crucifixion. Fifteen lines of the poem are carved on the eighth-century Ruthwell Cross and two of its verses appear on the Brussels Cross, a reliquary* in the cathedral at Brussels.

Drew, Daniel (1797–1879) American speculator who founded the Drew Theological Seminary and many Methodist churches*.

Drexel, Katherine (1858– 1955) American founder of the Sisters of the Blessed Sacrament for Indians and Colored People. Drexel was born to a prominent Philadelphia* banking family of immense wealth. On her parents' death, she inherited an estate of over $14 million which she decided to use to help Native Americans and African-Americans. In 1887 she asked Pope Leo XIII* for missionaries to Native Americans, but he challenged her to become one herself. Following the pope's advice, she founded the Sisters of Mercy* in Pittsburgh, professing vows as a sister*. She served as superior general* of the order until her health failed in 1937. She established numerous missions and schools for African-Americans and Native Americans including, in 1915, Xavier University in New Orleans. She was beatified in 1988.

Drummond, Henry (1786–1860) Founder of the Catholic Apostolic Church*, also known as Irvingites, because meetings for the study of biblical prophecy* were held at the home of Edward Irving*. In 1834 Drummond moved the headquarters of the movement to his country estate in Albury which served as the international headquarters of the Catholic Apostolic Church.

Drummond became the apostle and "angel" of the new church for Scotland.

Drummond, Henry (1851–1897) Revivalist* and preacher. He was an associate of D. L. Moody* and I. D. Sankey* in their crusades in the British Isles in 1882. In 1883 he published his *Natural Law in the Spiritual World,* illustrating the relationship between the natural and the spiritual. In his later life Drummond acquired a reputation as a powerful revivalist.

dry Mass Abbreviated form of the Mass* from which the offertory, canon*, and Communion are omitted. It is used only on certain occasions, such as a second Mass, in rough seas on board ship, or on hunting expeditions.

Dryden, John (1631–1700) English essayist, playwright, and poet considered the father of English criticism. His religious beliefs led him from Anglicanism* which he defended in *Religio Laici* (1682) to Roman Catholicism* which he defended in *The Hind and the Panther* (1686).

d'sh-heeme In the Assyrian Church*, a dry Mass* in which the priest reads the prayers of the liturgy without a prayer of consecration.

D.Th. Doctor of Theology.

Du Plessis, David (1905–1987) Pentecostal leader, known as "Mr. Pentecost." A native of South Africa, he served as pastor and general secretary of the Apostolic Faith Mission* Church in South Africa. In 1947 he became the organizing secretary of the World Pentecostal Fellowship, now the World Pentecostal Conference. He emigrated to the United States in 1949. Du Plessis was also a committed ecumenist who braved Pentecostal criticism to work with Roman Catholics and the World Council of Churches*, thus fulfilling Smith Wigglesworth's* prophecy that Du Plessis would take the Pentecostal message to all denominations. The Assemblies of God* revoked his ministerial credentials in 1962 but restored them in 1980. He spent his later years associated with Fuller Theological Seminary*, where he founded the Du Plessis Center for Christian Spirituality.

Duccio di Buoninsegna (c. 1255/60–1315/18) Sienese painter. His style is Byzantine as in the *Rucellai Madonna* at Uffizi, a 14-foot high altarpiece, and the even larger altarpiece of Maesta at Siena. This painting has 14 panels devoted to the Passion* of which 12 are divided into two, making 26 narratives in all.

Duchesne, Louis (1843–1922) French priest and church historian. He was professor at the Institut Catholique at Paris (1877–1885), professor at the Ecole Superieure des Lettres (1885–1895) and director of the French School at Rome* (1895–1922). His works include *Christian Worship* (1903), *L'Histoire ancienne de l'Eglise chretienne* (3 vols., 1906-1910) and *L'Eglise au sixieme siecle* (1925).

Duchesne, Rose Philippine (1769–1852) French-born Catholic nun, beatified in 1940, missionary to the Indians and the destitute in the United States. In 1804 she joined the Society of the Sacred Heart*, founded in 1800 by St. Madeleine Sophie Barat* for the education of girls. In 1818 she left for the United States, where she established academies in St. Charles and St. Louis. In 1841 at Sugar Creek, Kansas, she joined a Jesuit mission to the Potawatomi Indians.

Dudley-Smith, Timothy (1926–) English hymn writer and president of the Church of England Evangelical Council. His collections of hymns include *Youth Praise I* (1966), *Songs of Deliverance* (1988), *A Flame of Love* (1987), and *Lift Every Heart* (1983).

Dufay, Guillaume (c. 1400–1474) Franco-Flemish composer. His contributions to church music included 90 motets* and hymn-settings and eight complete settings of the Mass Ordinary. The custom of basing a Mass* on a secular tune may have begun with Dufay.

Duff, Alexander (1806–1878) The first Church of Scotland* missionary to India, he founded an English school in which the Bible was the main textbook. During the Disruption* in 1843, he joined the Free Church and had to rebuild his missionary enterprises. He was one of the founders of the University of Calcutta. Back in

Scotland, he was an influential advocate of missions, becoming the first professor of missions at New College, Edinburgh*.

duhovnek In the Nestorian Church*, a commemoration of a saint*.

dukhrani In the Nestorian Church*, a class of memorials of saints* that normally falls on Fridays except during Lent*.

dulia (Gk., service) In Orthodox and Catholic belief, veneration* that is due to the saints*, as distinguished from hyperdulia*, that is due to the Virgin Mary* and latria*, that is due to God alone.

Dumb Ox Epithet of St. Thomas Aquinas*, from his great bulk and taciturn appearance.

Dunkers (Ger., dippers) Popular name of the Brethren, a sect originating in Germany in 1708 under Alexander Mack*. Emigrating to Pennsylvania, they followed the New Testament to the letter, practicing triple immersion*, foot-washing*, the holy kiss*, and anointing the sick with oil.

Duns Scotus, John (c. 1264–1308) Scottish-born scholastic philosopher who defended the immaculate conception* of Mary. He entered the Franciscan Order* at the age of 15, became a priest in 1291, and taught in Europe. His philosophy was so

John Duns Scotus

intricate that he was given the title, the "Subtle Doctor," and his name from his hometown of Duns entered the dictionary eponymously as "dunce." Unlike Thomas Aquinas*, he held that faith* was a matter of will and that will was superior to the intellect. Thus, the Incarnation*, as the central event in history, was the result not so much of original sin* but of the love and grace* of God. There has been renewed interest in his thought in modern times because of his emphasis on the non-intellectual element in human thought. His principal work is a *Commentary on the Sentences*. He was beatified in 1993.

Dunstable, John (c. 1390–1453) English composer whose output included 50 compositions on sacred texts, including Latin motets*.

Dunstan, St. (c. 909–988) English abbot of Glastonbury* and archbishop of Canterbury* who reformed the English church and served as an able adviser to three kings: Eadred, Edgar, and Edward* the Martyr. Under Dunstan, Glastonbury became a major center of learning. Feast day: May 19.

duomo (Ital.) Cathedral.

Durandus, William (c. 1230–1296) French bishop of Mende, canon jurist and liturgist*. He was the author of *Mirror of Law,* a study of canon and civil law, and *Rationale of the Divine Office,* a study of the liturgy.

Durandus of Saint-Pourcain (c. 1275–1334) Scholastic philosopher known as "Doctor Modernus" and "Doctor Resolutissimus." He was a Dominican who taught at Paris and became a bishop in 1317. He was one of the earliest exponents of Nominalism.

Durer, Albrecht (1471–1528) German artist and engraver, a native of Nuremberg. He is considered the greatest master of etching, woodcut, and copper engraving. The best known of his works are the Paumgartner altarpiece, *Nativity Between St. George and St. Eustace* (before 1505), *Four Apostles* (1526), and *Adoration of the Magi* (1504) among his religious paintings; *Four Horsemen of the Apocalypse, Large Passion, Small Passion, Engraved*

Passion, and *Life of the Virgin* (all 1511) among his woodcuts; and the *Virgin and the Monkey* (1498), *St. Eustace* (1501), and *St. Jerome in his Study* (1514) among his engravings. He produced a continuous stream of single prints of ever-mounting technical virtuosity, such as *The Prodigal Son* (1497), *Adam and Eve* (1504), *Knight, Death and the Devil* (1513), and *Melancholia* (1514). His prints, with their vivid imagery and layers of iconographic meaning, spread all over Europe and had great influence. In Venice*, he painted

Albrecht Durer

Madonna of the Rose Gardens and *Christ Among the Doctors.* Toward the end of his life he became a sympathizer with the Lutheran cause and was eulogized by Luther* himself.

Durham See in England with a cathedral built in 1093. It was the seat of a Benedictine community until the dissolution of the monasteries in 1540. The cathedral, which began as a shrine for the relics* of St. Cuthbert*, has the Galilee Chapel built in Norman style and the famous Chapel of Nine Altars, with rose windows* and elaborate carving in Early English style. Together with London and Winchester*, it is among the most important sees in England, next to Canterbury* and York*.

Durufle, Maurice (1902–1986) French organist who composed a number of works for the church. His first major work for organ was prelude, adagio,

and chorale variations on the chant, Veni Creator* (1930). It was followed by *Suite* in three movements and *Requiem for Soloists, Choruses, Orchestra and Organ* (1948). There are also four Latin motets* for Gregorian melodies for unaccompanied chorus and a Mass*.

Durham Cathedral

Dutch Reformed Church Dutch denomination formed in 1946 through the merger of the Dutch Reformed Church (Hervormde Kerk) with the Reformed churches in the Netherlands. It is the major Protestant church in the Netherlands. It is Calvinist in theology and presbyterian* in church government. In the nineteenth century the church underwent cycles of conservatism and liberalism*. The awakening* opposed the increasing modernism* of the church. Some conservatives left the church in what is known as *Afscheiding** or Separation. The tension between Evangelicals* and modernists led to the Groningen School* which bridged the gap between the two and controlled most of the seminaries. In the 1880s Abraham Kuyper* led another exodus of conservatives (Doleante*) in a revival of dogmatic Calvinism*, and they soon joined the earlier separatist* group to form Gereformeerde Kerk. The Reformed Church exists wherever the Dutch emigrated or colonized: South Africa, Indonesia, the United States, and Suriname.

Dwight, Timothy (1752–1817) American Congregational* minister and president of Yale University from 1795 to 1817. A grandson of Jonathan Edwards*, he was active in the Great Awakening*. His sermons were posthumously published as *Theology, Explained and Defended* (5 vols., 1818–1819). He was a member of the New Divinity Movement which included Samuel Hopkins* and

Joseph Bellamy. His grandson, Timothy Dwight (1828–1916), was a member of the committee that produced the American Standard Version* of the Bible.

Timothy Dwight

Dykes, John Baachus (1823–1876) Vicar* of St. Oswald, Durham* and English hymn writer, author of many well-loved hymns, such as "Jesu, Lover of My Soul," "The King of Love, My Shepherd Is," "Holy, Holy, Holy," and "O Come and Mourn."

Dyophysites Those who adhered to the canons of the Council of Chalcedon* in affirming two natures in Christ, as opposed to Monophysites.

Dyothelites Those who adhered to the Third Ecumenical Council of Constantinople* (680) in affirming two separate wills, one human and the other divine, in Christ. See also MONOTHELITISM.

dysteleology Purposelessness, opposite of teleology*.

dzairaakouyn In the Armenian Church*, a major grade of vartabed* who is in charge of instructing the faithful.

dzoum In the Armenian Church*, a fast from sunrise until 3:00 P.M.

Ee

Eadmer (c. 1055–1128) English monk and historian. His *Historia Novorum* is an important source for the ecclesiastical history of his age. He was also the author of *Vita Anselmi,* a life of St. Anselm*, of whose household he was a member and *Tractatus de Conceptione St. Mariae,* a defense of the immaculate conception* of the Virgin Mary*.

eagle In Christian art, attribute of St. John the Evangelist. It is a symbol of divine inspiration* and thus appears on lecterns*. It also appears as a symbol of Christ. An eagle with a serpent in its beak is symbolic of Christ's victory over Satan*.

Easter (from Eostre, the Teutonic goddess of spring) The Feast of the Resurrection of Christ, the grandest and oldest feast in the Christian calendar, celebrated on a Sunday between March 21 and April 25, on the day of the first full moon after the vernal equinox. In the Eastern Orthodox Church*, the day can fall as much as five weeks later. It is preceded by the most prolonged season of preparation that includes Lent*, Passiontide*, and Holy Week*. In the early church it was the day when the catechumens* who had watched for a whole night were baptized and received Holy Communion*. The popular custom of exchanging Easter eggs* is of a later origin.

Easter candle Large ornamental candle kept lit from Easter eve* to Ascension Day*.

Easter duty Obligation of a Roman Catholic or Anglican to receive Holy Communion* between Ash Wednesday* and Trinity Sunday*.

Easter egg Colored, hard-boiled egg or chocolate egg rolled down slopes or across a lawn as an Easter* game for children.

Easter eve/even Saturday preceding Easter*.

Easter Monday The day after Easter*, a statutory holiday in some countries.

Easter offering Special church offering taken on Easter*.

Easter sepulcher Recess in a church wall where the sacrament* is kept until Easter eve*.

Eastern Catholic Generic term used to designate Christians outside Western Europe in full communion with Rome but who follow any of several Eastern rites. The principal Eastern Catholic churches are: **Ukrainian Catholic Church,** the largest of all Eastern Catholic churches; **Ruthenian Catholic Church,** united to Rome since the Union of Uzhorod of 1646; **Melkite Catholic Church; Romanian Catholic Church; Greek Catholic Church** under the Byzantine Catholic archdiocese* of Athens*; **Slovakian Diocese of Presov** established in 1937. It follows the Byzantine Rite*; the **Byzantine Rite Diocese** of Hajdudorog in Hungary founded in 1912; **Russian Catholic Church** founded in 1893 following the conversion to Catholicism* of the Russian priest Nikolai Tolstoy; the **Chaldean Church;** the **Syro-Malabar Church** in Kerala, India. Part of this church follows the East Syrian Rite and part of it the West-Syrian Rite; **Maronite Church; Syrian Catholic Church,** Kerala, India; **Armenian Catholic Church; Coptic Catholic Church;** and **Ethiopian Catholic Church.** See also UNIAT CHURCHES.

Eastern churches Eastern Orthodox* and Lesser Eastern Churches* collectively.

Eastern Orthodox Church Federation of a number of autocephalous*, or self-governing, churches in communion with one another who honor the primacy of the ecumenical patriarch* of Constantinople. The principal churches in this third largest grouping of Christian churches, after the Roman Catholic and Protestant churches, are the four ancient patriarchates of Constantinople*, Antioch*, Jerusalem*, and Alexandria*. The other member churches are the Russian, Romanian, Serbian, Greek, Bulgarian, Georgian, Cypriot, Czech, Polish, Albanian, Moldovan, and Sinaian.

The heads of the Russian, Serbian, Bulgarian, and Romanian churches are called patriarchs*. The head of the Georgian Church is called catholicos-patriarch, and the heads of the other churches are called metropolitans* or archbishops. In addition there are smaller autonomous, but not autocephalous*, churches such as those of Finland, China, Japan, and in some countries belonging to the former Soviet Union. In West Europe, North America, South America, Africa, and Australia, there are provinces of some of the autocephalous churches.

Orthodox Christians are concentrated in South and East Europe. Orthodoxy is the dominant faith in Russia, Greece, Cyprus*, Serbia, Bulgaria, Romania, Moldova, and Georgia. It is estimated that one-sixth of all Christians are Orthodox and that two-thirds of the Orthodox live in Russia. Unlike the Roman Catholic Church, the Eastern Orthodox Church is not bound by a common organization or head but rather by a common faith, theology, and praxis*.

The Orthodox Church calls itself the Church of the Seven Councils. These seven councils are Nicaea (325), Constantinople (381), Ephesus* (431), Chalcedon* (451), Constantinople (553), Constantinople (680–81), and Nicaea (787). The Orthodox also accept the two councils of Constantinople (1341 and 1351), the Council of Jassy* (1642), and the Council of Jerusalem* (1672). Icons flourished in the Orthodox Church after a bitter struggle between the iconodules*, or venerators of icons, and iconoclasts, who saw iconography* as a form of idolatry. Byzantium* itself was described as "the icon of the heavenly Jerusalem." Orthodox monasticism* found its finest flowering in Mount Athos* and in the Hesychast movement which gave birth to the Jesus Prayer*.

The Orthodox Church and the Roman Catholic Church separated from each other in 1054 through the Great Schism*. The major doctrinal issues behind the schism* were the Filioque* clause and the claim of universal supremacy by the pope. There are also minor differences, such as Roman Catholic insistence on

Orthodox Symbol

priestly celibacy* while the Orthodox permit married clergy, different rules of fasting, and the use of unleavened bread* in the Eucharist* by the Latin Church whereas the Orthodox use leavened bread. The Orthodox also do not subscribe to the dogma* of the immaculate conception* of the Virgin Mary* and the doctrine of purgatory*. The fall of Constantinople to the barbarian Turks in 1453 completed the separation of the two churches.

The Orthodox Church has not undergone any major reform movements, but they have had to face proselytizing pressures from both the Roman Catholic and Protestant churches. Orthodoxy is renowned for its magnificent liturgy. The Orthodox Church uses the vernacular in its services rather than a common lingua franca. All services are sung or chanted. Singing is unaccompanied, and instrumental music is uncommon. Normally worshipers stand during services, although they sit or kneel occasionally. The sanctuary is separated from the congregation by a solid screen* known as the iconostasis*, with three doors, the central holy door* that gives a view of the altar, the left door that leads into the chapel of preparation, and the right door that leads into the diakonikon* or the vestry*.

Patriarch Bartholomew I

Eastern Rite Liturgical rites followed by Eastern Orthodox* churches in communion with Rome. The sign of the cross is made from right to left, the priests are permitted to marry, and Holy Communion* is received in both kinds.

Eastertide Period of 40 days between Easter* and Ascension Day*.

Ebedjesus (?–1318) Birth name: Abdisho bar Berikha. Nestorian theologian and metropolitan* of Armenia. Of the many works that he wrote, most are lost except for two collections of canon law*, a theological work entitled *Margaritha* (the Pearl), and a series of 50 poems.

Ebenezer Society Pietist commune in the nine-

teenth century near Buffalo, New York. They later moved to Iowa to form the Amana Society in 1855.

Ebionites (Heb., poor) Jewish-Christian groups in Palestine* and elsewhere after the fall of Jerusalem*. They denied the divinity of Christ while accepting him as prophet*, teacher, and Messiah, rejected the Pauline Epistles, showed some Gnostic tendencies, and kept the Jewish rituals and commandments, including the Sabbath. They were vegetarians, like most of the community at Qumran*. Their gospel, called the Gospel of the Ebionites, has survived only in quotations in Epiphanius*. Some information on them is available in the Journeys of Peter. They suffered heavily in the Bar Kochba revolt but survived until the Islamic conquest, when they were wiped out.

Ebrach Former Cistercian monastery in Ebrach, Upper Franconia, Germany, founded in 1127. It was rebuilt in 1200, consecrated twice in 1218 and 1221; but it was not until 1285 that the sacred rite was performed. The Romanesque basilica* has no towers. Under Abbot Wilhelm Rosshirt, the church was refurbished in the Baroque-Classical style.

Ecce Homo (Lat., Behold the Man) Painting of Jesus Christ crowned with thorns and bound with ropes, shown to the people by Pilate, who then said, "Ecce Homo" (John 19:5).

ecclesia (Gk., assembly) 1. Popular assembly, translation of the Hebrew *qahal,* or assembly of the people of Israel on ceremonial occasions. 2. In Christian parlance, the church.

ecclesia discens (Lat.) The learning church, consisting of the laity.

ecclesia docens (Lat.) The teaching church, consisting of the clergy who are commissioned to teach and proclaim the gospel.

ecclesial community Term, often used in papal encyclicals*, to describe denominations whose doctrinal orthodoxy* is less complete than that of either Roman Catholicism or Eastern Orthodoxy.

ecclesiarch High Church* official or ruling prelate*.

ecclesiastic (*noun*) Clergyman.

ecclesiastical Of or relating to the church.

Ecclesiastical Commissioners Body which managed the estates and revenues of the Church of England* from 1835 to 1948. It consisted of the archbishop of Canterbury* and York* and the bishops of England, the deans of St. Paul's, Westminster and Canterbury, the lord chancellor, the lord president of the council, the first lord of the treasury, the chancellor of the exchequer, a secretary of state, the lord chief justice, the master of the rolls, and some lay members. In 1948, they were replaced by the Church Commissioners* for England.

ecclesiastical court Church court with jurisdiction over church personnel and affairs.

ecclesiastical law Canon law*.

ecclesiastical name Christian name taken by popes, patriarchs*, and other dignitaries, usually one in a series.

ecclesiasticism 1. Excessive dedication to the external details of church administration and practice. 2. Concern with the interests of the church to the exclusion of the interests of other institutions within a society.

Ecclesiasticus Apocryphal Old Testament book, also known as The Wisdom of Jesus, the Son of Sirach. It is reckoned among the so called Wisdom Books.

ecclesiography Descriptive analysis of churches and denominations.

ecclesiola (little church) Church within a church, or small groups of Christians living a distinct and separate existence without breaking away from the institutional church.

ecclesiology 1. Branch of theology concerned with the church and its polity*. 2. Branch of theology concerned with church buildings and decoration.

echage Formerly, the chief administrator of the Ethiopian Orthodox Church*, generally selected from the monastery of Dabra Libanos. The offices of the echage* and the abuna* (or patriarch*) were merged in 1951.

echoi In the Byzantine Church*, one of the eight modes. The singing is traditionally unaccompanied.

Echternach Monastery founded in Luxembourg in 698 by St. Willibrord*. It adopted the Rule of St. Benedict* in 673. From the eighth to the eleventh centuries, its scriptorium* produced a number of fine manuscripts of which the *Codex Aureus Epternacensis* (1055) is the most magnificent. This copy of the Gospel, with its letters resplendent in gold, was remarkable for its illustrations. Today it is in the German National Museum in Nuremberg. The monastery was dissolved in 1797. The buildings were destroyed during World War II but have been subsequently restored. Every year on the Tuesday of the Pentecost*, the celebrated

Echternach Monastery

Procession of the Leapers take place here, a festive act of thanksgiving that celebrates the deliverance of the people from St. Vitus's Dance.

Eck, Johann Maier (1486–1543) Birth name: Johann Mayr. German Roman Catholic theologian who condemned Luther*, Zwingli*, and the Augsburg Confession*. A vigorous polemicist, he opposed

Andreas Carlstadt* and Martin Luther in the famous Disputation of Leipzig* in 1519 and was responsible for procuring the papal bull* *Exsurge Domine** against Luther in 1520. In 1530 he presented 404 propositions against Luther and composed the *Confutatio* against the Augsburg Confession. He participated in the colloquies at Hagenau (1540), Worms* (1541), and Ratisbon* (1541). Besides a translation of the Bible into German, he wrote *Enchiridion Locorum Communium Adversus Lutherum et Alias Hostes Ecclesiae* (1525) against the Reformers and *De Primatu Petri Adversus Ludderum* (1520) in defense of the papacy.

Eckhart, Meister (c. 1260–1327) Birth name: Eckhart von Hochheim German mystic and scholastic theologian. Entering the Dominican Order as a young man, he became prior* in Erfurt*, vicar* of Thuringia, provincial* of Saxony, and vicar general* of Bohemia. A noted preacher, he left 110 sermons, 18 tracts, and 60 brief notices. In 1326 he was accused of heresy, tried by the archbishop of Cologne*, and convicted. He appealed to Rome, where 28 of his propositions were posthumously condemned as heretical. It is generally admitted that he was a pantheist who believed that there was a divine remnant called funck or funcklein ("spark") in every soul. The soul gives birth to the Word, making God and the soul inextricably one. Among those influenced by Eckhart were Henry Suso*, John Tauler*, and Nicholas of Cusa*.

Ecole Biblique Roman Catholic research institute that opened in 1892 in Jerusalem* on the site of St. Stephen's* martyrdom. Its first director was Marie-Joseph Lagrange*, who also founded the quarterly *Revue Biblique*. The institute is under the direction of the Dominican master general*. In 1920 it became also Ecole Francais Archeologique de Jerusalem.

economic Trinity Trinitarian* doctrine proposed chiefly by Hippolytus* and Tertullian* that differentiates the Father, Son, and Holy Spirit* in terms of their roles in the divine economy, God's unfolding purposes in creation, revelation, and redemption, rather than their external relationship and natures.

economy (Gk., *oikonomia,* plan, dispensation) 1. God's plan or system for the government of the world 2. Special divine dispensation* suited to the needs of a nation or era. See DISPENSATION.

ecophonesis The concluding words, uttered in an audible voice, of a silent prayer.

ecstasy (Gk., being beside oneself) Supernatural state of joy and rapture produced by the union of the human and divine during certain stages of a mystic's life, when the mind is inflamed with love and illuminated by grace and knowledge. Some of the external signs of ecstasy are incoherent speech, insensibility to pain, wild contortions and jerking, and speaking in tongues*.

ectene (Gk., earnest prayer) In the Eastern Church*, a prayer in the form of a litany* for use in the liturgy. It consists of short prayers recited by the deacon to which the congregation responds with Kyrie eleison*.

Ecthesis (Gk., statement of faith) Formula issued in 638 by Emperor Heraclius forbidding the mention of energies or modes of activity in the person of Christ and asserting that the two natures were united in one will, thus conceding the Monothelite position. It was accepted by the councils of Constantinople* held in 638 and 639, but was later disowned by Heraclius and withdrawn by Emperor Constans in 648.

ecumenical (Gk., *oikoumene,* the inhabited world) 1. Of, relating to, or representing the whole church. 2. Promoting or tending toward worldwide Christian unity or cooperation.

ecumenical conferences Any of the 36 major conferences held between 1910 and 2000 under the auspices of the World Council of Churches*, its predecessors or affiliated organizations. The most important of these conferences were: Life and Work*, Stockholm (1925); Oxford (1937); Faith and Order*, Lausanne* (1927); Edinburgh* (1937); St. Luke* (1952); Montreal (1963); Bristol (1967); Louvain (1971); Accra (1974); Bangalore (1978); Lima (1982); Stavanger, Norway (1985); Budapest (1989); International Missionary Council*, Edinburgh* (1910); Jerusalem (1928); Tambaram*, India, (1938); Whitby* (1947); Willingen,

Germany (1952); Accra, Ghana (1958); Mexico City (1963); Bangkok (1973); Melbourne (1980); San Antonio, Texas, (1989); Christian Youth, Amsterdam (1939); Oslo (1947); Kottayam (1952); Church and Society, Geneva (1966); Bucharest (1974); Cambridge, Massachusetts (1979).

ecumenical councils Church councils representing the whole church. According to canon law*, an ecumenical council must be convoked by the pope, must be attended by all the diocesan bishops, and its decrees must be ratified by the pope. In the early church, after the conversion of Constantine*, universal councils were convoked by the emperor, who ratified their decrees. The Roman Catholic Church recognizes 21 councils; the Coptic, Armenian, and Syrian churches accept only the first three, the Eastern Orthodox Church* and many Protestant churches accept the first six or seven, while Lutherans accept only the first four.

The first eight councils convened by emperors were: Nicaea (325), Constantinople (381), Ephesus* (431), Chalcedon* (451), Constantinople II (553), Constantinople III (680–681), Nicaea II (787), and Constantinople IV (869–870). The ten medieval councils were: Lateran* I (1123), Lateran II (1139), Lateran III (1179), Lateran V (1215), Lyon I (1245), Lyon II (1274), Vienne (1311–1312), Constance (1414–1418), Basle-Ferrara-Florence (1431–1437), and Lateran IV (1512–1517). The three modern councils were all convened by the pope: Trent* (1545–1563), First Vatican* (1869–1870), and Second Vatican* (1962–1965).

ecumenical creeds Creeds accepted by the whole church, as the Apostles'*, Athanasian*, and Nicene*.

Ecumenical Institute Center founded at Bossey, near Geneva, in 1946 by the World Council of Churches* for studies promoting Christian unity.

ecumenical movement Twentieth-century movement toward unity among the various denominations of the Christian church. It dates its active phase from the Edinburgh Missionary Conference* of 1910, which explored avenues of unity extending from cooperation and convergence to merger on the basis of Christ's prayer that "they

might be all one." The next step was the establishment of the International Missionary Council* (1921), the Universal Christian Conference on Life and Work* (1925), and the First World Conference on Faith and Order* at Lausanne* (1927). From these efforts sprang the World Council of Churches*, which formally took shape in 1948. During this period there were also calls for "closer intercourse and mutual cooperation" from the ecumenical patriarch* and the archbishop of Canterbury*.

Ecumenism* challenged the notion of exclusivity embedded in many historic denominations, and thus collaboration was limited initially to areas of common interest. Many denominations struggled to be a part of the movement without compromising their own beliefs and to conduct dialogue with other denominations without losing their identity. In 1960 the archbishop of Canterbury visited the pope, and in 1961 Vatican observers were permitted to attend the third assembly of the World Council of Churches in New Delhi. Observers from non-Catholic churches were invited to attend the Second Vatican Council*, which issued a decree on ecumenism describing other communions as "separated brethren" rather than as heretics. In 1965 the ecumenical patriarch* Athenagoras and Pope Paul VI* nullified the anathemas in force since 1054. Although Evangelicals* remain divided on the issue, the Eastern Orthodox* churches have become fully involved in the movement, and the Roman Catholic Church is participating in various ways short of actual unity. Even separatist Pentecostal denominations and the Salvation Army* have accepted the need for ecumenism.

Ministerial order and apostolic succession* have proved the most intractable hurdles on the road to unity. Evangelicals also have criticized ecumenical theology for its imprecise language, overuse of words—such as peace, love, salvation*, and renewal—quest for consensus rather than truth, the subtle pervasiveness of universalist assumptions, lack of commitment to evangelism so as not to interfere with inter-religious dialogues, and excessive deference to Marxism, feminism, and liberation theologians. These criticisms have been partly shared by Orthodox churches, a few of which have suspended or revoked their membership. At the national and regional levels there have been more dramatic ecumenical activities, and there are now forums for continuous interdenominational dialogue in most countries.

ecumenical patriarch The patriarch of Constantinople* as the first among equals in the hierarchy* of patriarchs in the Eastern Orthodox Church* with the right to determine certain theological doctrines or disputes and to represent the church in universal councils. His official residence is the Phanar* on the Golden Horn, Constantinople* (Istanbul).

ecumenicity Quality or state of being drawn close to one another without loss of identity, through common or shared action.

ecumenics Study of the nature, mission, and strategy of the Christian church as a whole or of the forces working toward unity of the various denominations and bodies constituting the universal church.

ecumenism Practices and ideals tending to produce or promote unity in the Christian church.

Eddy, George Sherwood (1871–1963) American student missionary leader and evangelist. Inspired by Dwight L. Moody's* appeal, he joined the Student Volunteer Movement* in 1893 and worked in the United States and India. From 1911 he served as the chief YMCA* evangelist in Asia. After the war he led the influential Fellowship for a Christian Social Order, a liberal organization dedicated to finding Christian solutions to the problems of industrial capitalism. Among his 36 books is *A Pilgrimage of Ideas: or the Re-education of Sherwood Eddy* (1934).

Eddy, Mary Baker (1821–1910) Founder of Christian Science*. After years of ill health and bad marriages, she finally discovered a system of spiritual healing* that she named Christian Science. She parlayed this doctrine into a cult* and established a mother church in Boston for which she wrote a manual in *Science and Health, with a Key to the Scriptures*.

Edersheim, Alfred (1825–1889) Biblical scholar. Born in Austria, of Jewish parents, he was con-

verted to Christianity in Budapest under the influence of John Duncan, a Scottish missionary. He entered the Presbyterian ministry and became a missionary to Romanian Jews. Subsequently, he became an Anglican vicar*. His book, *Life and Times of Jesus the Messiah* (1883–1890) was widely read.

Edessa Ancient Mesopotamian city, center of Syriac Christianity. It is now Urfa in Turkey. It is the home of the Old Syriac* and Peshitta* versions of the New Testament and also the *Diatesseron**. For many centuries, it was the home of the Persian School that trained generations of Nestorian clerics and missionaries. Until the expulsion of Christians from the area by the Turks in the early twentieth century, it was the residence of a Syrian Orthodox metropolitan*.

edicule Small structure surrounding the tomb of Christ under the Church of the Holy Sepulcher in Jerusalem*.

edification Building up of faith* through preaching or reading; state of being uplifted in spirit.

Edinburgh Capital of Scotland, site of St. Giles's* Cathedral dating from the twelfth century. In ecclesiastical history, it is associated with John Knox* and the Scottish Reformation, from which derive most Presbyterian Reformed churches. Two major conferences were held here in the twentieth century: the World Missionary Conference* in 1910 and the Second World Conference on Faith and Order* in 1937.

Edinburgh Conference Second World Conference on Faith and Order* in 1937 attended by 504 delegates representIng 123 churches. The discussions centered on four areas: grace*, ministry and sacraments*, church of Christ and the Word of God*, and church's unity in life and worship. The conference called for the formation of a World Council of Churches*.

Edinburgh Missionary Conference Ecumenical conference (1910) attended by 1,355 delegates and chaired by J. R. Mott*. All churches, except the Roman Catholic Church, were represented. Discussion ranged over a wide range of subjects, including education in relation to the Christianization of nations, relation to non-Christian religions, preparation of missionaries, and promotion of ecumenical unity.

Edmund of Abingdon, St. (c. 1175–1240) Archbishop of Canterbury* from 1233. He preached the crusade in England from 1227. He unsuccessfully challenged papal exactions and encroachments and also opposed King Henry III's wrong conduct. His influence waned after the pope named a legate* as his direct contact with the king. Considered one of the most saintly figures in the early English church, he was canonized in 1247. Feast day: November 16.

Edmund, St. (c. 840–869) King of East Anglia martyred in the Danish invasion of 869. He was buried at Bury St. Edmunds. Feast day: November 20.

Edward, St. (c. 962–978) English king and martyr*, eldest son of King Edgar the Peaceful, who was murdered at the age of 16 by his stepmother. Feast day: March 18.

Edward the Confessor (c. 1005–1066) English king (1042–1066). He was displaced as king in 1066 by his brother-in-law, an action that led to the Norman Conquest. He gained a reputation for sanctity* and was canonized in 1151. Feast day: October 13.

Edwards, Jonathan (1703–1758) American Congregational* minister and New England's most brilliant Calvinist theologian whose Evangelical preaching was one of the contributory causes of the Great Awakening* in New England. His legendary style of preaching, as reflected in his celebrated sermon, "Sinners in the Hands of an Angry God," has left a mark on the annals of preaching.

His theology is set forth in a number of classics: *Freedom of the Will* (1754), *Faithful Narrative of the Surprising Works of God* (1737), *Justification by Faith Alone* (1738), *Original Sin* (published posthumously), *Thoughts Concerning the Revival* (1743), and *Treatise Concerning Religious Affections* (1746). He emphasized the sovereignty of God and the need for a personal Christian awareness of sin, forgiveness, and grace*. He combined a highly intellectual and speculative spirit with a personal devotion to the person of Christ. In *Freedom of the Will,* he resolved to "cast and venture my whole soul on the Lord Jesus Christ, to trust and confide in him, and consecrate myself wholly to him."

Edwards pastored at Northampton (1724–1750) and at Stockbridge (1751–1757), where he also served as a missionary to the Indians. He was elected president of Princeton in 1758 but died of smallpox within a month. Edwards has exercised considerable influence on the course of American religious history through the development of New England theology* and the expansion of the Evangelical movement in the nineteenth century represented by Andew Fuller*, Thomas Chalmers*, Robert Hall, and others. His defense of Calvinism* delayed the rise and dominance of Arminianism* in New England for over a hundred years.

Jonathan Edwards

eedah In the Assyrian Church*, one of the seven feast days dedicated to the Lord. Thus, eedah gorah, the great Feast of the Resurrection.

effectual calling Leading of a person by the Holy Spirit* to repentance*, faith*, and salvation*.

efficacious grace See GRACE, EFFICACIOUS.

efiskufa In the Assyrian Church*, a bishop. He is required to be unmarried and bearded. He wears a sudra* (or kuthino*), a garment like an alb*, a zunara (a belt or stole*), a kafila* or ma'apra*, paina or pakila* (a hoodless cope*). He also wears a birun* (or amice*) over the head.

Egbert, St. (639–720) English monk from Lindisfarne who was largely responsible for arranging the mission of St. Willibrord* and others for the evangelization of Germany. He lived the last years of his life at Iona*, where he persuaded the monks to accept the Roman method of calculating Easter*. Feast day: April 24.

Egede, Hans (1686–1758) "Apostle of Greenland." Norwegian missionary to the Eskimos of Greenland and superintendent of the Greenland Mission. His sons, Poul and Niels, carried on the work. Poul (1708–1789) published a catechism* and translated the New Testament into the Eskimo language.

Egeria, Pilgrimage of See PILGRIMAGE OF ETHERIA.

Egerton Papyrus Two imperfect leaves and a scrap of papyrus* in the British Library containing passages from a Greek variant of the Gospels. It is dated about 150 and is thus the oldest known specimen of Christian writing.

Egyptian Versions of the Bible Versions of the Bible in four dialectal forms of Coptic: Sahidic* (Upper or southern Egypt), Bohairic* (Lower or northern Egypt), Akhmimic (from Akhmim in Upper Egypt), and Fayumic (Nile Valley or West Bank, including Asyutic, from Asyut in Upper Egypt).

Egyptian Book of Acts

Egyptians, Gospel According to the Apocryphal second-century gospel believed to be of Encratite origin. It is different from the Gospel of the Egyptians found in the Nag Hammadi* Library, called the Holy Book of the Great Invisible Spirit.

Eielsen, Elling (1804–1883) Founder of the Norwegian Evangelical Lutheran Church who convened the first Norwegian Synod in 1846.

eiletarion (Gk., wrapper) Manuscript scroll that unrolls vertically rather than horizontally.

eileton (Gk., something wrapped) In the Eastern Church*, the silk altar cloth, similar to the corporal*, used under the antimension*.

Einmaligkeit (Ger., onceness) That which has happened only once in human history, as the Incarnation.

Einsiedeln Benedictine abbey and place of pilgrimage* and former dwelling place of St. Meinrad*, in Switzerland, founded by St. Benno*, bishop of Metz and Eberhard in 934. Between the tenth and twelfth centuries, its chapel, known as Our Lady of the Angels or the Mary Chapel, was one of the most important places of pilgrimage in Europe. In 1466 the monastery's annals record that there were 133,000 pilgrims. During the Counter-Reformation*, a new building program reconstructed the abbey and the monastery. The Baroque interior was the work of a monk, Moosbrugger. Cosmas Damian Asam* and his brother Egid Quirin Asam* painted the ceiling and did the stucco decoration. Cosmas painted the Christmas* picture in the dome, while Egid cre-

Einsiedeln Abbey

ated the completely gilded pulpit by the pillar in the central nave*. The abbey library has a large collection of valuable manuscripts. Zwingli* was once a parish priest at the monastery. A religious play called "The Great World Theater" is performed here annually.

eirenika (Gk., peace thing) Opening litany* in the Byzantine Rite* sung by the deacon at the end of the liturgy of the word* during orthros* and hesperinos*. The congregation responds three times with "Lord, have mercy."

Eirmologion In the Greek Church, book containing the text of anthems known as eirmoi sung at the beginning of the odes or canticles* of mattins*.

eisegesis Interpretation of Scripture according to personal ideas and biases read into the text rather than on textual meaning read out of it. Distinguished from exegesis*.

Eisenach German city famous for its many medieval churches, notably the Church of St. Nicholas*. It was founded in about 1150 and chartered in 1283. Martin Luther* studied here.

eisodikon (Gk., entry) In the Byzantine Rite*, anthem or hymn sung during the Little Entrance*.

eisodos In the Byzantine Rite*, a processional entrance from the sanctuary through the north door of the iconostasis* to the center of the church and the return to the sanctuary through the royal doors*.

ejaculation/ejaculatory prayer Very short prayer, also called aspiration*, such as "Jesus, have mercy."

ekphonesis (Gk., lifting of the voice) Doxological conclusion of a prayer which is recited aloud.

ekplusis In the Byzantine Rite*, washing of the altar on Holy Saturday*.

ektene In the Byzantine Liturgy, a litany* consisting of petitions sung by the deacon to which the choir or congregation responds with Kyrie eleison*.

El Greco See GRECO, EL.

elder Official in certain Christian churches and denominations, originally corresponding to the presbyter*. In the Presbyterian Church, there are two types of elders: the teaching elder, who moderates the session which governs each congregation, and ruling elders, who are laity ordained to assist the pastor as members of the session* in church government.

elect, the Persons chosen and sanctified by God for eternal salvation, adopted as children of God* and sealed by the Holy Spirit*.

election Divine choice determining salvation*. Augustine*, Aquinas*, Luther*, and Calvin* all held a doctrine of unconditional election*, in which the divine choice is a function of God's sovereignty in no way dependent on the person chosen or not chosen. Arminius* and Wesley* held that election was conditional upon the individual's faith*. In New Testament theology, believers are chosen in Christ and all those who believe in him are saved. But even here there is an element of divine foreknowledge determining those who will believe in him and thus become candidates for salvation*. The six main features of election are: 1. Election is a sovereign, eternal decree of God. 2. The human race is fallen, and election is God's gracious rescue plan. 3. Election is in Christ and through Christ. 4. Election involves both the elect's salvation and the means to that end. The means include faith and sanctification*. 5. Election is individual and personal. 6. The ultimate goal of election is the glory of God.

electronic church Religious broadcasting that proclaims the gospel and sometimes serves as surrogate ministries reaching into people's homes. It began in the 1920s with the rapid development of radio broadcasting. American Evangelicals* began purchasing air time on commercial stations and paying their bills through contributions from listeners. During the 1930s and 1940s Charles E. Fuller* and Walter A. Maier* had radio audiences in the millions. Fuller's "Old Fashioned Revival Hour"* was one of the first to combine good gospel music* with preaching and listener-oriented programs. In the 1940s and 1950s the electronic church continued to grow as television became another potent medium. Oral Roberts*, Bishop Fulton

Sheen*, Billy Graham*, and Rex Humbard* were among the early pioneers in this field, venturing into prime time and combining some elements of popular entertainment with evangelism.

By the 1970s the electronic church became a powerful institution in its own right with three major networks, the Trinity Broadcasting Network (TBN*) begun by Paul Crouch*, the 700 Club or the Christian Broadcasting Network* begun by Pat Robertson*, and PTL* begun by Jim and Tammy Faye Bakker*. Many hosts of Christian television, like Jimmy Swaggart* and Jerry Falwell* became media celebrities, with their influence extending far beyond religion. Pentecostalism* gained as a result of these programs, as most of the electronic church leaders were Pentecostal. Even in Canada, the major religious satellite television program, *100 Huntley Street,* was Charismatic. Annual budgets of the largest religious broadcasters often exceeded $100 million.

However, in the late 1980s, scandals brought down the ministries of Jimmy Swaggart and Jim and Tammy Faye Bakker and left a permanent stain on some of the practices of the religious broadcasters as celebrities. Despite this setback, the electronic church has continued to grow and has become a worldwide phenomenon. The Roman Catholic*, Orthodox*, and mainline* denominations also have entered the field with several national and international radio and television networks and channels.

eleison (Gk., have mercy on us) Antiphonary chant or response during service.

element Either the bread or the wine as part of the Holy Communion*.

Eleousa (Gk., compassionate) Iconographic type of the Virgin, showing her and the Christ child cheek to cheek.

elevation At the Eucharist*, lifting of the sacred elements* to exhibit them for the adoration of the people by the celebrant immediately after he has recited the Words of Institution* over them. Both elements are elevated together or successively.

Elgar, Sir Edward (1857–1934) English composer of choral and orchestral music. Among his religious

works are his setting of Newman's* *Dream of Gerontius** (1900) and the oratorios *The Apostle* (1903) and *The Kingdom* (1906).

Elias III (1867–1932) Syriac Orthodox patriarch* (1917–1932) and saint*. He entered monastic life in the Monastery of Dayro d-Za'faran* and became bishop of Mosul in 1908 and patriarch* in 1917. He shepherded the church during the Turkish massacres of 1895 and 1917. In 1930 he called the Synod of Mar Mattei. In 1930 he went to India to bring peace to the divided church there but died during his stay, in 1932. He was canonized as a saint in the Malankara Syriac Orthodox Church* in 1982. Feast day: February 13.

Elias, John (1774–1841) Birth name: John Jones. Greatest of all Welsh preachers. He was ordained as a Calvinist Methodist minister in 1811 and succeeded Thomas Jones* as leader of Calvinistic Methodists.

Elim The Elim Foursquare Gospel* movement or alliance founded by George Jeffreys* at Belfast in 1915. The movement preached the imminent return of Jesus Christ as savior and healer. It became, with the Assemblies of God*, the leading Pentecostal denomination in the United Kingdom.

Eliot, James (1928–1956) American Plymouth Brethren* missionary to Ecuador who was martyred with four other young men by Auca Indians in 1956. *Through Gates of Splendor* by his widow, Elizabeth, presents the story of his martyrdom. Eliot is remembered for his quote, "He is no fool who gives up what he cannot keep to gain what he cannot lose."

Eliot, John (1604–1690) "Apostle to the Indians." Born in England, he was ordained in the Church of England*, but was drawn into nonconformism. He emigrated to the New World in 1631 and became a teacher in a church at Roxbury in Massachusetts. He began working as a missionary among Native Americans in 1646 after learning their languages. By 1674 he had converted over 3,600 Native Americans, and helped them establish their own church at Natick. His work was set back during King Philip's War when the Native

Americans turned against the settlers, but in 1689 he gave 75 acres of land in Roxbury for the education of Native Americans and African-Americans.

In addition to his missionary efforts, Eliot was active in Bible translation and publishing. With Richard Mather* and Thomas Welch, he prepared for printing in 1640 *The Bay Psalm Book**, the first book printed in the American colonies. He trans-

John Eliot

lated the Bible into the Algonquin language (1661–1663), the first Bible produced in the colonies. His translation of the *Larger Catechism** followed in 1669. His other works included *The Christian Commonwealth* (1659), the *Harmony of the Gospels* (1678), and an Indian grammar. His learning, piety, and missionary zeal were admired by all his contemporaries.

Eliot, Thomas Stearns (1888–1965) American-born British poet, dramatist, and critic whose writings reflected the spiritual desolation of his age. Of Unitarian origin, he moved toward orthodoxy* and by 1928 defined himself as an Anglo-Catholic in religion and a defender of order and authority in society. He was deeply influenced by medieval Christian writers and mystics, such as Dante, Julian of Norwich*, and St. John of the Cross*. He tried to deal with the dilemmas of faith* in prose works such as *The Idea of a Christian Society* (1939) and poetic works such as *The Waste Land* (1922), *Hollow Men* (1925), *Ash Wednesday* (1930), *Four Quartets* (1935–1942), and *The Rock* (1934). The best known of his plays were *Murder in the Cathedral** (1935), *The Cocktail Party* (1950), and *The Confidential Clerk* (1954). The recurring themes in his works were human haplessness, isolation, and dysteleology*, all of them descriptive

of twentieth-century civilization. His influence as a poet on his generation was immense.

Elizabeth of Hungary, St. (1207–1231) Royal ascetic. She was the daughter of King Andrew II of Hungary. She was married at the age of 14 to Ludwig IV, the landgrave of Thuringia. In the early years of her marriage she came under the influence of the Franciscans and began to show ascetic tendencies. On her husband's death in the Crusade of 1227, she was driven from the court by his brother, Henry Raspe, on the pretext that her charities were bankrupting the treasury. In 1228 she settled at Marburg and became a member of the Third Order of St. Francis under the spiritual direction of Conrad of Marburg*. In addition to her severe austerity and physical punishments, she was active in visiting and caring for the sick and poor. After her death, numerous miracles were recorded at her tomb and she was canonized in 1235. Feast day: November 17.

Elizabeth of the Trinity, Blessed (1880–1906) Birth name: Elizabeth Catez. Carmelite* nun of Dijon whose spirituality* is strongly Trinitarian* and Christocentric*. Feast day: November 8.

Elliott, Charlotte (1789–1871) English hymn writer who wrote the perennial favorite, "Just As I Am" (1834). She assisted in the compilation of *The Invalid's Hymn Book* (1834–1854) in which 112 of her hymns appear.

T. S. Eliot

Ellul, Jacques (1912–1994) French Reformed sociologist and theologian who explored the interface between technology, culture, and spirituality* in a number of books, including *The Technological Society* (1964), *The Meaning of the City* (1970), and the *Ethics of Freedom* (1976). He always maintained a strong Christian witness in his writings, even though his nontraditional ideas offended both liberals and conservatives.

Elmo, St. (c. 1190–1246) Birth name: Peter Gonzalez. Dominican preacher. As chaplain* to Ferdinand III of Leon, he helped Ferdinand in his crusade against the Moors. Subsequently, he left the court and began to preach among the poor and sailors of Galicia and the Spanish coast. After his death, he became the patron saint* of Portuguese and Spanish sailors. The electrical discharge seen on the decks, mastheads, and yardarms of ships is known as "St. Elmo's fire" in his honor and as a sign of his protection. Feast day: April 14.

Eloquent Doctor Epithet of Peter Aureolus, eleventh-century scholastic.

Elvira, Council of Church council held in Spain about 306. It passed 81 canons imposing severe disciplinary penalties, including lifelong excommunication*, for apostasy* and adultery.

Ely Third largest cathedral in England on the island of Ely in the Fens marshland. The monastery island was the last piece of Anglo-Saxon soil to fall into Norman hands in the eleventh century. The monastery can be reached only by a causeway. It is built in Norman-Romanesque style with a wealth of sculpture. The central tower collapsed in 1322. The Lady Chapel*, added in the fourteenth century, is in High Gothic* style.

embades In the Byzantine tradition, heelless slippers worn by monks in church.

ember days Special days of abstinence and prayer, such as Wednesday, Friday, and Saturday after St. Lucy's Day (December 13), the first Wednesday in Lent*, Whitsunday*, and Holy Cross Day (September 14).

embolism (lit., intercalation) 1. Variation in the liturgy resulting in the insertion of a special prayer between the Lord's Prayer* and the Prayer for Peace. 2. Difference of days between a 364-day lunar calendar and a 365-day solar calendar, also known as epact*.

Embury, Philip (1728–1775) Founder of the first Methodist church in America. Born in Ireland of German Palatinate parentage, he was converted by John Wesley* in 1752. He migrated to New York in 1760 and began preaching to migrants in 1766. He erected the first Methodist chapel in New York in 1768.

eminence Term of address and title of honor for the cardinals of the Roman Catholic Church and the grandmaster of the Order of Malta.

emip'oron In the Armenian Church*, the great stole* corresponding to the pallium* or the Byzantine omophorion*.

Emmerick, Anna Katharina (1774–1824) German mystic and Augustinian nun who received the stigmata* of the Passion on her body. Her *Meditations on the Passion* were published in 1833.

emotionalism Excessive emphasis on feeling in the practice of religion. It is manifested mostly in Protestant revivalism* and includes demonstrative acts, such as crying, shouting, weeping, and laughing.

empirical theology Branch of theology concerned with experience. It holds that valid knowledge of God is based on human experience. It emerged in the nineteenth century as part of a broader movement of theological liberalism* and in response to the challenge of atheism and humanism. Although apologists in intention, empirical theologians sought to reinterpret Christian theology in terms that would make sense to a scientific-industrial age, rejecting any appeal to religious authority. Empirical theology was developed at the University of Chicago under the leadership of Shailer Matthews (1863–1941), author of *The Growth of the Idea of God* (1931). The later leaders in empirical theology were Henry Nelson Wieman (1884–1975), a student of John Dewey, and author of *The Source of Human Good* (1946); Douglas Clyde McIntosh (1877–1948), author of *Theology as an Empirical Science* (1919); and Eugene W. Lyman (1872–1948), author of *The Meaning and Truth of Religion* (1933). Empirical theology died out in the 1930s.

Emser, Hieronymous (1478–1527) German Catholic polemicist who opposed Luther* and Zwingli*. He issued a revised translation of the Bible in 1527 to counteract Luther's December Bible of 1522.

enarxis (Gk., lit., the beginning) In the Byzantine Liturgy, the section between the Proskomide* and the Little Entrance* consisting of three diaconal litanies, each followed by psalms or antiphons* sung by the choir and ending with the Beatitudes* while the celebrant silently recites the prayers of the antiphon.

Enbaqom (abu-l-Fath) (d. 1561) Eleventh abbot of the monastery of Debre Libanos in Shewa, Ethiopia. He was originally a Muslim merchant from Yemen who was converted to Christianity. He helped to preserve the church against the onslaughts of the Muslim invader Ahmad ibn Ibrahim al-Ghazi (Ahmad Gran). He is remembered for his compilation of the *Gate of Faith* in Ge'ez* and his translation of Chrysostom's* commentary on the Epistle to the Hebrews.

encaena Festival commemorating the dedication of a church.

enclosed order Religious order which sequesters its members from the outside world.

encolpion (Gk., worn on chest) Also, panagia*. In the Eastern Church*, an oval medallion worn by bishops, suspended from the neck by a chain, with the figure of Christ or the Virgin Mary* depicted on it. It may also enclose relics*.

encomion Mournful composition of a number of troparia* sung on Holy Saturday* at lauds*.

encounter Concept in contemporary theology associated with Emil Brunner*, for whom the source of religious truth was the divine-human relationship rather than objective knowledge. It is derived from existentialism* and Martin Buber's *I and Thou* (1923). It is contrasted with the traditional view that knowledge of God is propositional based on objective revelation in the Bible and on the creeds and dogmas of the church.

Encratites (Gk., self control) Early Christian group sometimes considered heretical because of the extremity of their ascetic practices. They rejected the use of wine and flesh and remained celibate. Many of the apocryphal gospels were produced by them.

encyclical 1. Circular letter on matters of faith or church discipline* from an apostle or a bishop to local Christian churches under his jurisdiction. 2. Such a letter from the ecumenical patriarch* to all autocephalous* churches in communion with him. 3. Papal letter to all dioceses* worldwide or within a country on matters of doctrine or faith. The first recorded modern papal encyclical was *Ubi Primum*, issued by Benedict XIV* in 1740. Like other pontifical* documents, encyclicals are indexed by their opening words. Encyclicals are issued by the pope as the shepherd of the church and head of the episcopal college, and thus are part of his ordinary magisterium* as distinct from his extraordinary infallible magisterium which he exercises only when defining dogma* approving the decrees of an ecumenical council. The most significant modern encyclicals are as follows:

Benedict XIV*: *Allatae Sunt*, 1755, on Oriental rites. Clement XIII*: *A Quo Die*, 1758, on Christian unity. Pius VI*: *Inscrutabile*, 1775, on the problems of the church; *Caritas Quae*, 1791, on the civil oath* in France after the French Revolution. Gregory XVI: *Mirari Vos*, 1832, on liberalism*; *Singulari Nos*, 1834, condemning the liberal ideas of F. de Lamennais*; *Probe Nostis*, 1840, on the propagation of the faith. Pius IX*: *Ubi Primum*, 1849, on Mary's immaculate conception*; *Quanta Cura*, 1864, on the religious errors of the age; *Aeternus Pastor*, 1870, on papal infallibility*; *Respicientes*, 1870, on the unification of Italy.

Leo XIII*: *Quod Apostolici Muneris*, 1878, on socialism; *Aeterni Patris*, 1879, on St. Thomas Aquinas*; *Immortale Dei*, 1885, on the Christian constitution of states; *Libertas Praestantissimum*, 1888, on Christian liberty; *Rerum Novarum*, 1891, on capital and labor; *Providentissimus Deus*, 1893, on the study of Scriptures; *Divinum Illud Munus*, 1897, on the Holy Spirit*; *Graves de Communi Re*, 1901, on Christian democracy.

Pius X*: *Acerbo Nimis*, 1905, on Christian doctrine; *Pascendi Dominici Gregis*, 1907, on modernism*. Benedict XV*: *Ad Beatissimi Apostolorum*, 1914, on peace; *Quod Iam Diu*, 1918, on a fair settlement after World War I. Pius XI*: *Casti Connubii*, 1930, on Christian marriage; *Quadragesimo Anno*, 1931, on the fortieth anniversary of *Rerum Novarum; Mit Brennender Sorge*, 1937, on the church in Nazi Germany; *Divini Redemptoris*, 1937, on Communism. Pius XII*: *Summi Pontificatus*, 1939, on Christian idea of the state; *Mystici Corporis*, 1943, on the church as the body of Christ*; *Divino Afflante Spiritu*, 1943, on biblical studies; *Deiparai Virginis Mariae*, 1946, on the Virgin Mary*; *Mediator Dei*, 1947, on liturgy; *Humanis Generis*, 1950, on subversive doctrines; *Evangelii Praeconis*, 1950, on missions; *Ad Caeli Reginam*, 1954, on the queenship of Mary; *Musicae Sacrae*, 1955, on sacred music; *Haurietis Aquas*, 1956, on devotion to the Sacred Heart*; *Luctuosissimi Eventus*, 1956, urging prayers for believers in Hungary; *Laetamur Admodum*, 1956, urging prayers for believers in Hungary, Poland, and the Middle East; *Datis Nuperrime*, 1956, on persecution in Hungary; *Fidei Donum*, 1957, on African missions; *Invicti Athletae*, 1957, on martyr, St. Andrew Bobola; *Le Pelerinage de Lourdes*, 1957, on the centenary of the visions at Lourdes*; *Miranda Prorsus*, 1957, on morality and the media; *Ad Apostolorum Principis*, 1958, on the church in Communist China; *Meminisse Iuvat*, 1958, on prayers for the persecuted church.

John XXIII*: *Ad Petri Cathedram*, 1959, on truth, unity, and peace; *Sacerdotii Nostri Primordia*, 1959, on French saint, St. John Vianney; *Princeps Pastorum*, 1959, on missions, native clergy, and lay participation; *Mater et Magistra*, 1961, on Christianity and social progress; *Aeterna Dei Sapientia*, 1961, on St. Leo I*; *Paenitentiam Agere*, 1962, on penance*; *Pacem in Terris*, 1963, on peace, truth, justice, charity, and liberty.

Paul VI*: *Ecclesiam Suam*, 1964, on the church's duties; *Mense Maio*, 1965, on peace; *Mysterium Fidei*, 1965, on the Holy Eucharist*; *Christi Matri*, 1966, on prayers for peace; *Popularum Progressio*, 1967, on human development; *Sacerdotalis Caelibatus*, 1967, on priestly celibacy; *Humanae Vitae**, 1968, on birth control.

John Paul II*: *Octogesima Adveniens*, 1971, on the social problems of the poor; *Redemptor Hominis*, 1979, on the redemption* and dignity of the human race; *Dives in Misericordia*, 1980, on the mercy of God; *Laborem Exercens*, 1981, on the dignity of labor; *Slavorum Apostoli*, 1985, on the apostles to the Slavs, Sts. Cyril and Methodius*; *Dominum et Vivificantem*, 1986, on the Holy Spirit*; *Redemptoris Mater*, 1987, on the Virgin Mary*; *Solicitudo Rei Socialis*, 1987, on social concerns; *Centisimus Annus*, 1991, on a free and just society; *Redemptoris Missio*, 1991, on evangelization; *Veritatis Splendor*, 1993, on the objectivity of moral truth; *Evangelium Vitae*, 1995, on human dignity; *Ut Unum Sint*, 1995, on ecumenism*; *Fides et Ratio*, 1998, on faith and reason.

Endo, Shusaka (1923–1996) Japanese Christian writer. He became a Roman Catholic at the age of 11. His best known work is *Silence*, a historical novel of Portuguese missionaries and the slaughter of Christian martyrs* in seventeenth-century Japan.

endowments Secret temple rites among the Mormons* in which only Mormons in good standing are allowed to participate.

endura Among the Cathari*, secret suicide as the highest act of virtue, liberating the spirit from the body.

energumen Demoniac or person whose body is possessed by an evil spirit.

England, John (1786–1842) Irish-born Roman Catholic priest who fought for religious liberty in Ireland and was later appointed bishop in the United States, where he ministered to African-Americans.

English College College founded in Rome* in 1362 as a hospice for English pilgrims and converted in 1578 into a seminary. It was directed by Jesuits* until 1763 when it was taken over by secular priests. In 1818 it was returned to the English clergy.

English Ladies The Institute of the Blessed Virgin Mary*, founded by Mary Ward* in 1609, approved by the pope in 1703.

enhypostasia (Gk., in-personhood) Doctrine first

set forth by the sixth-century theologian, Leontius of Byzantium*, that the personhood or hypostasis* of the Incarnate Christ was drawn from the Logos*, yet unified with its human nature in the manner of a fire and a torch.

Enlightened Doctor Epithet of Ramon Llull* of Palma.

enosis (Gk., union) Also, henosis. 1. Commixture* of the consecrated bread and wine in the chalice* after the fraction*. 2. Mystical union with God, usually used pejoratively.

enstar In the Armenian Rite*, the oblation*, especially the bread.

enthronization Public ceremony in which a newly consecrated bishop or archbishop is elevated to his throne and given possession of his diocese*.

enthusiast (Gk., *enthousiasmos,* possessed by the divine) Believer possessed or driven by intense devotion to God.

entire sanctification In Wesleyan and Holiness traditions, belief that a Christian can attain full perfection* and holiness* in this life. It is an extension and interpretation of John Wesley's* idea of Christian perfection. Wesley did not believe, however, that perfection meant that one would never commit mistakes or sins of ignorance. It was prominent in nineteenth-century revivalism*. Charles Finney* taught that the sanctified "habitually live without sin or fall into it at intervals so few and far between that it may be said that they do not sin." Sanctification is called entire because while justification* takes away or covers the guilt of voluntary, sinful actions, sanctification takes away inbred sin and fills the believer with holiness.

Entrance, Great See GREAT ENTRANCE.

Entrance, Little See LITTLE ENTRANCE.

entsaiaran In the Armenian Rite*, the credence* table on the north side of the sanctuary.

E.O. Eastern Orthodox*.

epact Excess of days of the solar year over the lunar year.

epanokamelavchion Veil placed on top of the kamelavchion* and hanging down on the back, by monks and bishops of the Eastern Church*. It is usually black, except in the case of the Russian Church, where it is white.

eparchy Ecclesiastical province of the Eastern Church*. Thus, eparch, the metropolitan* in charge of an eparchy*.

ephemerios In the Greek tradition, local parish priest.

Ephesus Chief city of the Roman province of Asia at the crossroads of the coastal route between Smyrna and Cyzicus and the interior route up the Meander and the Lycus valleys. The temple of Artemis in the city was one of the great wonders of the ancient world. At its zenith it had over half a million inhabitants. Paul* took Christianity to Ephesus (Acts 18:18–19) and stayed there for two years on his third missionary journey (Acts 19:8, 10).

Ephesus, Council of The third general council summoned by Emperor Theodosius II in 431 to settle the Nestorian heresy. Attended by 60 bishops, it was presided over by Cyril of Alexandria*. It was not attended by the Nestorian bishops of Syria or by the Western delegates. The canons of the council deposed and excommunicated Nestorius* and condemned his heresy, affirmed the Nicene Creed*, approved Theotokos* (God-

Theater at Ephesus

bearer) as a title for the Virgin Mary*, and anathematized Pelagianism* and chiliasm*.

Ephesus, Robber Council of Also called Latrocinium*. Council of 130 bishops in 449, presided over by Dioscorus*, patriarch* of Alexandria, and convened by Emperor Theodosius II to condemn Nestorianism* and approve Monophysitism*. Eutyches*, the Monophysite leader, who had been deposed from his position of archimandrite*, was cleared of heresy charges and reinstated. The council was not recognized by Pope Leo I*, who demanded another council. Its decisions were reversed by the Council of Chalcedon* in 451.

ephor In the Eastern Church*, a lay guardian or custodian in charge of monastic property from the tenth century onward.

ephphatha (lit., be opened) 1. Jesus' command in Aramaic to the deaf and dumb man (Mark 7:34). 2. Ceremony in the Roman Catholic baptismal rite in which the celebrant consecrates to the service of the Lord the ear and mouth of the candidate and pronounces the word, "Ephphatha, be opened."

Ephraem the Syrian, St. (c. 308–373) The greatest writer of the Syrian Church, called "the Lyre of the Holy Spirit" and declared a doctor of the church* in 1920. Born in Nisibis*, he was baptized as a young man and entered a monastery. After the Persian occupation of Nisibis*, he fled to Edessa*, where he spent the remainder of his life. He left a large of body of writings, including commentaries and exegesis* and a harmony of the Gospels*. His poetry is divided into hymns (*madrashe*) and verse homilies (*memre**). Over 500 of his poems survive. Arranged in cycles, they have had significant influence on the development of Syriac hymnography. He defended the orthodox faith against Bar-Daisan, Marcion*, and Mani*. But his fame rests chiefly on his ascetic writings and hymns. Many of his works in Syriac* have been lost, but they have survived in fragments in Greek, Armenian, and Latin. Feast day: January 28 (Eastern Church*); June 9 (Western Church*).

Ephrata Society/Ephrata Cloister Cloistered Protestant commune founded in the early 1700s at Ephrata, Pennsylvania, by German Pietist mystic Johann Konrad Beissel* and his Dunker disciples. They practiced celibacy* and pacifism, kept the Sabbath, pooled their resources, and held all property in common. The society had an active program of publishing books and music and brought out the first American edition of *Pilgrim's Progress** and the first music book. The society was dissolved in 1934.

epiclesis (lit., invocation*) Prayer in the anaphora* in the liturgy that the Holy Spirit* might descend upon the elements* and transform them into the blood and body of Christ or sanctify them for use in the sacraments.

epieikeia Canon law* that may not be strictly enforced when enforcement may cause such hardship that it violates natural law or equity.

epigonation In the Eastern Church*, a lozenge-shaped vestment made of a cardboard covered with cloth. Decorated with a cross with elabo-

St. Ephraem the Syrian

rately embroidered icons, it is suspended from the girdle*, hanging from the right side. It is used by bishops, archimandrites, and archpriests. It probably originated as a handkerchief. It is a symbol of the spiritual sword of justice.

epimanikia (Gk., the sleeve) Cuffs, usually made of embroidered silk, worn in the Eastern Church* by bishops and priests over the ends of the sleeves of the sticharion* and by deacons over the end of the sleeves of the cassock*.

Epiphanius (c. 315–403) Bishop of Constantia, later Salamis, in Cyprus* who was a vigorous defender of monasticism* and orthodox faith, denouncing Origen* and John of Jerusalem. Jerome* called him "the fire tongued." Of his writings, the most important is the *Panarion* (Medicine Box) commonly known as the *Refutation of All Heresies* in which he catalogued all the heresies in the first three centuries. It was intended to heal those Christians who had been poisoned by heresies. He was also the author of *Anchoratus,* a compendium of Christian doctrines.

Epiphany (Gk., manifestation) Festival, on January 6 commemorating the manifestation of Christ to the Gentiles in the persons of the Magi. It is one of the three principal feasts of the church. Originally, it was a celebration of the baptism* of Christ. In the Eastern Church*, baptismal water is blessed on this day.

episcopacy (Gk., *episkopos,* overseer) 1. System of church government based on ecclesiastical authority exercised by bishops. 2. The rank or office of a bishop.

episcopal Of or relating to the authority of bishops.

Episcopal Church of the United States U.S. church in communion with the Anglican Church, known until 1979 as the Protestant Episcopal Church. The first Anglican church in the American colonies was built in 1607, and all congregations remained for the next 170 years under the jurisdiction of Canterbury*. After the American Revolution, the church broke its links with the Church of England* and elected Samuel Seabury* as its

bishop. Seabury was consecrated by the Episcopalian Church of Scotland. At a general convention in 1789 the constitution and canons were drawn up and the *Book of Common Prayer** adopted with some modifications. Further revisions to the prayer book were made in 1892 and 1928, and a new prayer book was authorized in 1979. The official hymnal also has been revised a number of times, most recently in 1982.

The Episcopal Church has 11 theological seminaries, of which the oldest is the General Theological Seminary in New York, established in 1817. The governing body of the church is the general convention, which meets every three years. There are no archbishops, but a presiding bishop is elected by the general convention. In recent years it has been deeply divided by disputes over doctrine and ethics, fostered by radical liberal leaders.

Episcopalian Member of an Episcopal Church or adherent of the episcopal* system of church government.

episcopate 1. Group of bishops. 2. Bishop's term or office.

episcopi vagantes (lit., wandering bishops) Bishops who have no see* of their own, or were consecrated in an irregular or clandestine manner, or were excommunicated, after being legitimately consecrated.

episqupo In the Maronite Church, a bishop who is not a monk.

Epistle 1. Letter written by one of the apostles in the Bible. 2. In church liturgy, reading of a lesson from one of the New Testament epistles.

epistle side The right side of the altar, where the New Testament epistles are read or sung.

epistle sonata Movement in sonata form intended for performance after the reading of the Epistle during the Mass*.

epistler Writer or reader of an epistle.

Epistles, Catholic See CATHOLIC EPISTLES.

epistles of captivity Letters believed to have been written by St. Paul* from his prison cell in Rome* or perhaps elsewhere, such as Ephesus: Ephesians, Philippians, Colossians, and Philemon. See also PRISON EPISTLES.

Epistles, Pastoral See PASTORAL EPISTLES.

epitaphion (Gk., belonging to burial) In the Eastern Church*, a richly embroidered veil representing the scene of Christ's burial. It is carried in procession at the end of vespers* on Good Friday* and then decorated with flowers and placed at the center of the church. It is again carried in procession at the end of the orthros* of Good Saturday* and either placed on the altar, as in the Greek Liturgy, or returned to the center of the church and placed on the altar at the end of the Midnight Office of Easter Day, as in the Russian Liturgy. It remains on the altar until the eve of Ascension Day*.

Epitaphion

epitimion In the Byzantine tradition, an imposed penance* that must be discharged before absolution*.

epitrachelion (Gk., neck) In the Eastern Church*, a stole* worn by priests and bishops in the form of a long strip of material, buttoned or sewn into a double scarf, hanging down to the ankles, fastened in front, and decorated with crosses and a fringe.

epitropoi In the Byzantine tradition, leading monks of a monastery who elect the abbot.

eqbo In the Jacobite Liturgy, a short liturgical anthem or verse.

equiprobabilism Moral system developed by St. Alphonsus Liguori* in the 1760s that held that a stricter interpretation should be applied in cases where the Mosaic Law is deemed to have lapsed after New Testament times and a laxer interpretation in cases where the law is deemed to have never existed.

erakhah In the Armenian Church*, a catechumen*.

Era of the Martyrs In Ethiopian and Coptic churches, time of persecution of Christians beginning with the accession of Diocletian (284), although actual persecution did not begin until 303.

Erasmus, Desiderius (c. 1466–1536) Christian humanist and scholar. Born the illegitimate son of a Dutch priest, he was educated by the Brethren of the Common Life*. He became an Augustinian canon in 1487 and was ordained in 1492. He soon left for Paris to study at the College of Montaigu. For the next 40 years he lived in various places, including Oxford, Paris, Louvain, Turin*, Bologna*, Cambridge, Venice*, Rome*, and finally Basel, where he died. He influenced some of the brightest and most powerful men of his age, including King Henry VIII, Charles V, Archduke Ferdinand, William Blount, the Fourth Baron Mountjoy, Aldus Manutius, Leo X*, the Vatican librarian, Tomasso Fedra Inghirami, and St. John Fisher*, as well as most of the Protestant Reformers who were trained as humanists.

Epitrachelion

Erasmus was the most renowned scholar of his age; his intellectual prowess fascinated his friends as well as detractors. He was also the first best-selling author of the new Gutenberg age. His *Praise of Folly* appeared in 600 editions and the *Colloquies* in more than 300 editions. He was also a noted biblical scholar, publishing a critical edition of the New Testament based on Greek manuscripts, a paraphrase of the New Testament, numerous editions of the Greek and Latin Fathers, *Adages,* a collection of sayings from Greek and Latin classics, and theological works, including *Enchiridion Militis Christiani* (Handbook of a Christian Knight, 1504).

Although considered a forerunner of Luther*, he conducted a running battle with the reformer. His *Diatribe De Libero Arbitrio* (1524) was an attack against Luther's position on free will*. Luther responded with *De Servo Arbitrio*

Desiderius Erasmus

(1525) to which Erasmus responded with *Hyperaspistes* (1526). As a polymath, Erasmus tried to reconcile a number of contradictions within himself. He was a Catholic, Protestant, and humanist rolled into one, although he never left the Catholic Church. He was also a scholar who valued Christian traditions and heritage, but distrusted partisanship for fear of compromising his integrity.

erechsrbeann In the Armenian Liturgy, the Trisagion* sung while the Little Entrance* is made around the altar.

eremite Solitary religious hermit.

eretz In the Armenian Church*, a priest. The feminine form is eretzkin, wife of a priest.

erfa maskal In the Ethiopian Church*, a cross spoon used to administer the wine from the chalice*.

Erfurt Dominican monastery founded in Erfurt, Germany, in 1229. Work on a hall basilica* with three aisles began in 1270 and continued into the fourteenth century. The monastery's most famous inhabitant was Meister Eckhart*, who began here as a novice* and ended as prior* and vicar* of Thuringia. In 1521 it was one of the first monasteries to fall into Protestant hands. Although many of the monastery's precious treasures were sold off, the church itself was saved

Erfurt Monastery

from pillage. The city took over the monastery and repainted its vaulting* and interior. The building was fully restored in 1960. Between the north transept* and the choir is the Late Gothic* triangle in which two portals meet each other at a sharp angle. Among the cathedral's ancient treasures is the Wolfram, a Romanesque candelabrum figure which originally served as a lectern* stand, and an enthroned Madonna*.

eristics Practice of disputation* and polemics* on specious grounds involving hairsplitting and casuistry*.

Eritrean Orthodox Church New Monophysite church created in 1991 when Eritrea became independent of Ethiopia. In 1994 Pope Shenouda III*, the Coptic patriarch, created an Eritrean Holy Synod* and also consecrated Abuna Philipos as the first patriarch* of Eritrea. As a result of the creation of a separate Eritrean church, relations between Alexandria and the Ethiopian Church have become strained.

Eriugena (c. 810–877) Also, Erigena. John the Scot. Irish scholar and theologian who was condemned by the church for his pantheism*. In his major work, *Periphyseon* or *De Divisione Naturae,* he wrote of nature as the equivalent of God. He was an original thinker and scholar in Greek. His teachings were condemned at Paris in 1210, and again at Sens in 1225. He translated the works of Dionysius the Pseudo-Areopagite*, St. Maximus the Confessor*, and Gregory of Nyssa*.

Erlangen School Theologians of the University of Erlangen in the nineteenth century who based their theology on personal experiences rather than on scriptural authority.

erphei In the Coptic Church*, sanctuary in the east end with three altars, each altar dedicated to a saint*. There is usually a screen*, the equivalent of an iconostasis*, with three doors that swing into the sanctuary. These doors have curtains with hems which are kissed by those who enter.

Erskine, Ebenezer (1680–1754) Scottish minister who founded the secession church in 1733. His sermons have been described as "probably the finest religious literature that Scottish Protestantism* has produced." He was deposed from the established church of Scotland* for insisting on the right of a congregation to choose its own minister.

Erskine of Dun, John (1509–1591) Scottish reformer and friend of John Knox* and George Wishart*. He helped to prepare the *Second Book of Discipline*.

Erskine, Thomas (1788–1870) Scottish lay theologian whose books influenced a generation of thinkers. Among his books are *Internal Evidence for the Truth of the Christian Religion, The Brazen Serpent,* and *The Unconditional Freeness of the Gospel.* In opposition to the prevalent Calvinism* of his day, he progressively developed liberalizing views. For a time he supported Edward Irving* and the Catholic Apostolic Church* and he backed John McLeod Campbell* after his deposition* for heresy. Erskine himself embraced universal salvation* and an understanding of Christianity as an education of humanity into a filial relationship to God through the indwelling* Christ. His *Letters* are considered a minor classic.

Escalante, Silvestre (eighteenth century) Pioneering Spanish Franciscan missionary to the American West.

eschatological sign Missionary preaching of the gospel among all nations as the sign of the imminent return of Jesus Christ (Matt. 24:14; Mark 13:10).

eschatology (Gk., last discourse) 1. Doctrine of last things* and end times, covering not only the destiny of the individual, but also that of all creation. It is related to the Second Coming*; millenarianism*; the four last things* mentioned in Ecclesiasticus* (death, judgment, heaven*, and hell*); apocalypticism; and messianic hopes. 2. Branch of theology that deals with hope and the "not yet" part of messianic prophecy*.

eschatology, consistent Albert Schweitzer's* theory that Jesus embraced death in order to consummate his eschatological goals. When the wheel of history did not respond to his hand, he threw himself on it and was broken by it.

eschatology, inaugurated Kingdom of God* inaugurated by Jesus' death and Resurrection. Before the Resurrection, the kingdom of God was anticipated but did not exist.

eschatology, realized Interpretation of Jesus' proclamation of the kingdom of God* as the reign of God fully present or realized in the person and work of Jesus Christ. It was first proposed by the British scholar C. H. Dodd*. It is opposed to the consistent or thoroughgoing eschatology of Albert Schweitzer*, who argued that Jesus was mistaken in his expectation of an apocalyptic cataclysm that would establish the kingdom of God* and bring history to an end.

eschatology, symbolic Belief that the eschatological events mentioned in the New Testament are to be interpreted symbolically, not literally.

eschatology, teleological Belief that the eschatological events mentioned in the New Testament will not occur at the end of history but rather are being fulfilled currently.

eschaton (Gk., the last thing) The Second Coming* as the final event of history.

Escorial, El Huge, austere complex of buildings, near Madrid, Spain, dedicated to St. Lawrence*, erected by Philip II of Spain. The complex includes a monastery, palace, library, and infirmary centered on a large church with a high dome and a royal mausoleum under the high altar. Its general form is that of gridiron in memory of St. Lawrence's* martyrdom. Called the eighth wonder of the world, it is 787 feet long by 623 feet wide, with seven gates, 15 towers, and 1,110 windows. The dome is 350 feet high and there are 48 altars. It was planned by Juan Baptista and supervised by Juan de Herrera, and among its artists were Federigo Zuccaro* and Pellegrino Tibaldi.

El Escorial Monastery

Behind the upper choir is a marble crucifix by Benvenuto Cellini.

eskhim In the Jacobite tradition, the monastic hood, the holy schema*, worn by monks and bishops. It consists of a long black strip, shaped like a hood at one end with the other end hanging down the back. It has two white stripes with white crosses covering the intervening space.

Espousals of the Blessed Virgin Mary* Feast of the Latin Church on January 23.

espugo In the Jacobite tradition, sponge used to clean the chalice* and paten* at the end of the liturgy after the ablutions.

essential Trinity Trinity as an eternal union of the Godhead as distinct from economic Trinity that refers to the respective roles, offices, and functions of each of the three persons in the Trinity.

established church Official church in a country where the religious establishment and political establishment are closely interlinked and where the church receives special recognition and perhaps other benefits from the state. The Church of England* is one of the most notable established churches, but unlike several European churches, it receives no financial support from the state.

estates of Christ Two states in which Christ appears in the Gospels: humiliation (as a suffering servant*) and exaltation (ascension and return in majesty as judge and ruler).

estavromenos In the Byzantine tradition, crucifix with the body of Christ either painted directly on the cross or painted on a tablet attached to the cross.

Estienne (Stephanus) Family of Christian printers originally in Paris, including **Henri Estienne** (d. 1520) and **Robert Estienne** (1503–1559), printer to Francis I, famous for his Latin Bibles, Eusebius*, and Justin Martyr*. Robert's most important edition of the Greek New Testament was that of 1550. Faced with Catholic strictures against his biblical annotations, he moved from Paris to Geneva* and became a Calvinist. He was the first to introduce the division into verses of the New Testament which is still used today. **Henry Estienne** (1528–1598) was the publisher of editions of the early Church Fathers*.

Estomihi Quinquagesima* Sunday, 50 days before Easter*.

esychia In the Coptic Liturgy, a rubric* in a prayer book directing that the prayer be recited silently.

etcheghie In the Ethiopian Church*, principal or senior bishop with administrative functions.

Etchmiadzin Seat of the catholicos* of the Armenian Church* and its spiritual center, 12 miles west of Yerevan. It was the capital of the ancient kingdom of Armenia (184–344).

eternal city Rome* as the central city of the Roman Empire and later of the Christian church and as the seat of the pope.

eternal generation The relation of the Son to the Father in the Trinity*, being eternally begotten of him, an eternal relationship, not a specific act of generation.

eternal life Life everlasting with Christ and all his saints, as distinct from biological life, which is terminated in death.

eternal punishment Final and permanent punishment of the wicked after the last judgment* (Matt. 25:46).

eternal security Also, perseverance* of the saints. Doctrine that once saved, a believer is always saved (John 10:27–29; Rom. 8:35–39; Phil. 1:6; 1 Pet. 1:5), derived from Calvin* and his doctrine of unconditional predestination*. It states that salvation* cannot be lost as a result of human actions because he who saves is also able to keep.

eternity State of timeless duration without beginning or end, or infinite time not subject to the chronological progress of years, months, weeks, days, hours, minutes, and seconds. 2. (Gk., *aion*, age) Everlasting divine state that is shared by the children of God*.

Ethelbert, St. (d. 616) King of Kent and the first Christian English king. His marriage with Bertha, daughter of Charibert, the Frankish king, introduced Christianity into the Anglo-Saxon kingdom. Through Bertha's influence, he welcomed St. Augustine in 597, and was himself converted in the same year. Feast day: February 25.

Etheldreda, St. (d. 679) Also, St. Audrey. The daughter of Anna, Christian king of the East Angles, she became a nun about 672. About a year later, she founded the double monastery at Ely and was its abbess until death. Feast day: October 17.

Etheria See PILGRIMAGE OF ETHERIA.

Ethiopian calendar Calendar used in the Ethiopian Orthodox Church*, based on the Coptic calendar* which is eight years behind the Gregorian calendar*.

Ethiopian Orthodox Church Properly, Ethiopian Orthodox Tewahdo Bete Church. Ancient church founded in Ethiopia, also known as Abyssinia, by Frumentius* in the fourth century. According to Rufinus*, Frumentius was a Syrian from Tyre. At the end of the fifth century, nine Syrian monks, now known as the "nine saints," helped to establish the Coptic and Syrian Orthodox traditions in Ethiopia. A great revival* took place in the fifteenth century under King Zara Yakub (1434–1468). Like other Lesser Eastern Churches*, the Ethiopian Church has been wrongly labeled as Monophysite. It describes itself as miaphsyite after a Christological doctrine known as miaphysis which holds that Christ had divine and human natures. As formulated by Dioscorus* and Cyril*, miaphysis maintains that "Christ is perfect God and perfect man, at once consubstantial with the Father and with Humankind; the divinity and the humanity continuing in him without mixture or separation, without confusion or change." In 1959 the Ethiopian Church* became independent of the See of St. Mark* in Alexandria* under its own abuna* or patriarch*.

Most parishes worship in the ancient classical language of Ge'ez*, although the vernacular Amharic* was introduced in the 1960s. The main sources of worship are *Sunodos* (Apostolic

Canons), *Mets'hafe-Kidan* (The Testament of Our Lord), *Didaskalia, Feteha Negest* (Nomocanon*), *Ser'at-we-tezaz* (Ordinances and Instructions), *Mets'hafe Bahr'i* (The Book of Nature), and *Te'aqebe Mestir* (Stewardship of the Mystery). The seventeenth-century liturgical revision resulted in four major books: *Mets'hafe Qeddase* (Missal), *Mets'hafe Nuzaze* (Manual of Penitence), *Mets'hafe Taklil* (Matrimony), and *Mets'hafe Qandil* (Manual of Unction of the Sick).

The Missal* has two parts, one containing 16 to 20 anaphorae (*Quaddase*) and another with the psalmody* for the Eucharist* (*Zemmare*), chanted by specially trained choirs. In addition, there are four books for the canonical daily offices: *Deggua**, containing antiphonal chants for the whole year except Lent*; *Tsomedeggua**, containing chants for the Lent but not for the Holy Week*; *Mawase'et*, an alternate form of the daily offices; and *Me'eraf*, the common order for the daily office. There are also paraliturgical works such as *Waddase Mariam* or Praises of Mary and *Anqetse Berhan* (Gate of Light). Twenty different anaphorae are known, including those by Basil*, Gregory*, Cyril*, Athanasius*, St. Mark*, and Chrysostom*. Most of them are of Syrian rather than Egyptian origin. The Liturgy of St. Mark is not widely used. The father of Ethiopian hymnody* and musicology is Yared, a disciple of the Nine Saints. He devised the system of Ethiopian chant called the *zema* with its three different chants, *ge'ez**, *'ezl*, and *araraye*.

Ethiopian priest

The Ethiopian Church follows the Julian calendar*. The liturgical year* has 97 feasts, 9 major feasts of the Lord, 6 secondary feasts, 32 Marian* feasts, and 50 main feasts of the saints*. In addition to Wednesdays and Fridays of every week, there are 6 major fast cycles: the great Lent* fast for 55 days, Advent fast of 40 days, the Fast of the Apostles, the Fast of Mary, and the Fast of Nineveh*. The main manual for the daily offices is the *Me'eraf*.

ethnarch (lit., head or ruler of an ethnic group) Under the Ottoman Empire, office assigned to the Orthodox patriarchs* or ecclesiastics of autocephalous* churches who served as civil and religious rulers. Known in Turkish as milletbashi, they enjoyed wide jurisdiction over their flock and represented and defended them before the sultan.

etimasia Also, hetoimasia*. In Christian iconography*, representation of the empty divine throne of the last judgment* with the royal insignia placed on the cushion. Various symbols were added to the representation in course of time, especially a cross, diadem or crown, the four evangelists, the scroll of the seven seals, lamb*, and the dove*. In Byzantine iconography*, a book of the Gospel is placed on the cushion.

Eto, Silas (1905–1984) Prophet-leader of an Melanesian independent church, marked by ecstatic utterances and glossolalia*, a rich hymnology, idiosyncratic prayer techniques, and a mixture of indigenous and Methodist iconography*.

etro In the Syrian Church, prayer of incense recited by the bishop during pontifical* liturgies.

Ettal Benedictine monastery in Ettal in Bavaria, Germany, founded by Emperor Ludwig on his return from Italy, after being anathematized by the pope. As a token of penitence, he set up as a pilgrimage shrine a white marble statue of the Virgin Mary*, about 6 pounds in weight and a little more than a foot high, that a monk in Rome had given him. In 1522 the troops of Prince Elector of Saxony vandalized the monastery, as did the Swedes in 1632, and a fire totally consumed it in 1774. The entire complex was rebuilt in Baroque style by Enrico Zuccalli and Josef Schmuzer.

Ettwein, John (1721–1802) German Moravian missionary and bishop of the Moravian church for 17 years.

Eucharist (Gk., *Eucharistia,* thanksgiving) Also, Divine Liturgy; Holy Communion*; Lord's Supper*; Mass*. The central act of Christian worship and thanksgiving instituted by Christ. In the New Testament there are four accounts of its institution (Matt. 26:26–28; Mark 14:22–24; Luke 22:17–20; 1 Cor. 11:23–25). There are also notices of its celebration in the New Testament, in Jerusalem* (Acts 2:42, 46) and by St. Paul* on his visits to Troas (Acts 20:7). The eucharistic doctrine was developed in the early church by the Church Fathers*, especially St. Chrysostom*, St. Cyril of Jerusalem, St. Gregory of Nyssa*, St. Cyril of Alexandria, Theodoret*, St. Ambrose*, St. Augustine*, and St. John of Damascus*. Eucharist is the inauguration of the new covenant*, and because of its close association with the Crucifixion, an epitome of Christ's life and death, humiliation, and glory. It resonates with the great Christological doctrines, as the Incarnation*, Atonement*, and Resurrection. It also proclaims the unity of the body of Christ*, united as grains of wheat in a loaf of bread.

It was generally accepted by most early Christians that the elements* of the Eucharist were the body and blood of Christ and not symbols or antitypes. But the doctrine was not clearly defined until certain theologians, especially Berengar of Tours* and some heretic sects, as the Cathari*, raised doubts about the real presence*. The Fourth Lateran Council* of 1215 was the first to use the term *transubstantiation** in its current sense. It maintained that consecration changed the substance of the bread and wine, without altering its accidents or outward appearance. At the same time, Urban IV instituted the Feast of Corpus Christi* as a means of reinforcing eucharistic devotion.

During the Reformation*, the Roman Catholic definition was challenged by Luther*, Zwingli*, and Calvin*. Luther replaced it with what has been called consubsantiation*, while Zwingli considered it as only a memorial rite without any change in the elements whatsoever. Calvin* took an intermediate position, called later virtualism*, which held that while there was

no change in the elements, the faithful partook of the virtue and power of Christ through eating in faith. Since then, Protestant churches have held conflicting and ambiguous definitions of the Eucharist, ranging from the Roman Catholic to Zwinglian positions.

In the Second Vatican Council*, Roman Catholic theologians used other terms, including *transignification** and *transfinalization**, to describe the change in the elements. Some theologians also explain the Eucharist as a sacrifice without detracting in any sense from the ultimate and final sacrifice at Calvary. Bread and wine are sacrificial elements drawn from Judaism where the blood is poured forth in a covenantal act. The Council of Constantinople* in 1157 upheld the Eucharist as an eternal sacrifice. Thus developed the doctrine of the sacrifice of the Mass* as a propitiatory act for the living and the dead.

The Constitution of the Second Vatican Council on the Sacred Liturgy declared that at the Last Supper, "Our savior instituted the eucharistic sacrifice of His Body and Blood in order to perpetuate the sacrifice of the Cross throughout the centuries until He should come again and so to entrust to His beloved spouse, the Church, a Memorial of His Death and Resurrection." Protestant churches, on the other hand, continue to express the significance of the Eucharist in various ways as a sacrament* or ordinance*, an anamnesis* or memorial, a fellowship meal, and a spiritual feeding on Christ.

Eucharistia Eucharistic prayer or the prayer of consecration.

eucharistic congress Any one of many international Roman Catholic assemblies for promoting devotion to the Blessed Sacrament*. The first one was held in 1881 at Lille, France.

eucharistic fast Abstinence from food and water for a period preceding the reception of the Holy Communion*. In the Eastern Church*, the fast is observed from bedtime on the previous day. In the Roman Catholic Church, it is one hour before the reception of the Holy Communion*, with an exception being made for water and medicine. There are also exceptions for the elderly and the sick and those caring for them, and priests celebrating a second or third Mass* on the same day.

eucharistic lights Candles used only during the Eucharist.

eucharistic prayers Any of the central prayers offered during the Eucharist, such as the anaphora* in the Eastern Orthodox Church* and Canon of the Mass* in the Roman Catholic Church. In the great liturgies of the church, those of St. Basil*, St. John Chrysostom*, the Gallican, Mozarabic, and Ambrosian, it consisted of several short prayers. During the Reformation*, the Lutherans chose only Preface* and the Words of Institution* from the Mass of the Canon, while the Church of England* retained the Preface*, the Prayer of Humble Access*, the Prayer of Consecration*, and the Words of Institution.

Almost all eucharistic prayers have some common elements: Thanksgiving, sanctus*, the words of Christ at the Last Supper, anamnesis* or prayer of oblation*, epiclesis* or invocation* of the Holy Spirit*, intercessory prayer, and a final doxology*. In 1968 the Congregation of Sacred Rites* provided three additional eucharistic prayers for use in the Roman Catholic Church as an alternative to the Canon of the Mass*. They are drawn from a variety of sources, including the *Apostolic Tradition** and the anaphora of St. Basil*.

eucharistic vestments Priestly vestments worn while celebrating the Mass*, including the alb*, amice*, chasuble*, girdle*, maniple*, and the stole*. They all derive from the costume of Roman citizens in the second century. In the Roman Catholic Church, it is forbidden to celebrate Mass without vestments. In the Anglican Church, the main vestments are cope*, cassock*, and surplice*.

euche opistombonos (Gk., prayer behind the ambon) Dismissal prayer in the Byzantine Rite*.

Euchelaion In the Greek Church, the sacrament* of the holy unction*.

Euchologion Usually, the Great Euchologion*. In the Eastern Orthodox Church*, liturgical book,

containing the text and rubrics of the three main liturgical rites (of St. Chrysostom*, of St. Basil*, and the Liturgy of the Presanctified*), the invariable parts of the Divine Office*, and the prayers during the administration of the sacraments* and the sacramentals. It corresponds to the Missal*, Pontifical*, and Rituale in the Roman Catholic Church. The Small Euchologion* or Agiasmatarion contains funeral offices and occasional blessings. See also GREAT EUCHOLOGION.

Eudes, St. John (1601–1680) French missioner and pastor. He became an Oratorian in 1623 and was appointed superior* of the Caen Congregation in 1639. In 1641 he founded the Order of Our Lady of Charity of the Refuge for the rehabilitation of reformed prostitutes. He promoted devotion to the Sacred Heart of Jesus* and the Sacred Heart of Mary* through his books, *Le Coeur Admirable de la Mere de Dieu* (1670) and *La Vie et la Royaume de Jesus* (1637). The Congregation of Jesus and Mary, called Eudists, after their founder, was reconstituted in 1826 after the revolution in France and is now active in South Africa, Canada, and the United States. Eudes was beatified in 1909 and canonized in 1925. Feast day: August 19.

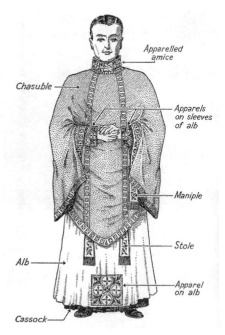

Eucharistic Vestments

Eugenius III (d. 1153) Pope from 1145. Birth name: Bernardo Pignatelli. Cistercian from Pisa. He worked for the Second Crusade*, which he commissioned Bernard* to preach. He presided over synods at Paris in 1147, Trier* in 1147, and Reims* in 1148 which excommunicated many heretics, including Gilbert de la Porree* and Arnold of Brescia*. In 1153 he concluded the Treaty of Constance with Frederick Barbarossa. Bernard wrote for him the ascetical treatise, *De Considerazione.*

Eugenius IV (1383–1447) Pope from 1431. Birth name: Gabriel Condulmaro. Venetian Augustinian. Throughout his papacy he was embroiled in a dispute with the Council of Basel. In 1434 a revolt in Rome* forced him to flee to Florence*, where he remained until 1443. In 1439 he claimed a major victory when the Council of Florence initiated the union between the Latin and Greek churches. In 1444 he organized a crusade against the Turks which ended in defeat of the Christians at Varna. He was a man of great piety who tried to root out nepotism.

eulogia (Gk., blessed) 1. In the Eastern Church*, blessed but not consecrated bread distributed after Holy Communion*. 2. Bread distributed after Mass* to catechumens* and others. 3. Consecrated gifts associated with pilgrimage* or made holy by contact with a holy place or object.

Eulogitaria In the Byzantine Church*, a series of short hymns introduced with the refrain, "Blessed are you, O Lord, teach me your statutes," sung at the end of Psalm 118 at the orthros* service on Sundays.

Eulogius (d. 859) Defender of Christians against Muslim oppression in Spain. He developed a theology of confrontation with the infidel* Arabs that drew heavily upon biblical apocalyptic accounts. In two books, *Memoriale Sanctorum* and *Liber Apologeticus Martyrum,* he vindicated Cordoban Christians who courted death by publicly defaming Muhammad. He was executed by the Muslims in 859, and his remains were reinterred on the pilgrimage* route to Santiago de Compostela*. Eulogius inspired the Christian reconquest of Spain.

Eunomius (c. 333–394) Arian bishop of Cyzicus on the Hellespont. Banished several times because of his Arian sympathies, he wrote two works, defending his Anomoean positions, *First Apology* (to which St. Basil* responded) followed by a *Second Apology* (to which St. Gregory of Nyssa* responded). Eunomius taught that the Father and the Son were different in substance and unequal in power. The Father produced the Son who, in turn, produced the Holy Spirit*. Eunomius baptized in the name of the Creator, not in the name of the Trinity*.

Euphemia, St. (fourth century?) Virgin and martyr*, patroness of the church at Chalcedon. Feast day: September 16.

Euphrates River in Mesopotamia, originating in modern-day Turkey. It is believed to be one of the rivers of Eden. On its banks were some of the great cities of antiquity, such as Ur and Babylon*.

Eusebian Canons Thesaurus devised by Eusebius* of Caesarea that highlighted sections in the Gospels parallel to the one being read or that contained similar subject matter. It was used in Greek and Latin manuscripts of the Bible until the thirteenth century before the Bible was divided into numbered chapters and verses. The sections are numbered consecutively in the margins of the Gospels in red ink and, sometimes, illuminated.

Eusebius (c. 260–c. 340) Generally known as Eusebius of Caesarea in Palestine*. The father of church history and the bishop of Caesarea from 315. During the Arian controversy he supported Arius, and was condemned by the Council of Antioch (324–325). However, he moved gradually to a more orthodox position and was reinstated by Emperor Constantine* after he accepted, although half-heartedly, the Nicene Creed*. He remained an opponent of Athanasius* throughout his life. He presided over the Council of Caesarea in 334 and took part in the condemnation of Athanasius at Tyre* in 335. He delivered in 336 the triennial oration in honor of Constantine's accession to power. He was the chief prosecutor of Marcellus of Ancyra at the Synod of Constantinople in 336. Throughout the Constantine era, he was the spiritual voice of the Byzantine court and the heir and master of the Origen* legacy.

Eusebius is remembered chiefly for his *Ecclesiastical History* (325), the principal source for the history of Christianity from the earliest times to

Eusebius

his day. It consists of ten books, of which the last three deal in great detail with his own time. It survives in Greek, Latin, Syriac*, and Armenian versions. His apologetic books include *Contra Hieroclem, Praeparatio Evangelica and Demonstratio Evangelica* (on the Old Testament), and *Theophania* (on the Incarnation*). Among his other writings are: the *Martyrs of Palestine, Life of Constantine, Against Marcellus, Church Theology, Onomasticon* (a biblical topography), a collection of the letters of Origen*, a biography of Pamphilius*, his mentor, and commentaries on Isaiah and the Psalms.

Eusebius (fifth century) Bishop of Doryleum in Asia Minor from 448. He accused Nestorius* of denying the divinity of Christ and later defended orthodoxy* against Eutyches* before the Synod of Constantinople. He was deposed and exiled by the Robber Council of Ephesus*. He was restored to his see* by the pope and Emperor Marcion in 451 and took part in the Council of Chalcedon*, and helped to draft its Definition of Faith.

Eusebius of Nicomedia (d. 341/2) Bishop of Nicomedia in Asia Minor and patriarch* of Constantinople. A fellow student of Arius under Lucian of Antioch*, he rose to the defense of his friend when Arius was deposed in 320. Although he

signed the Nicene Creed*, he engineered the reaction against it, leading to the deposition of Athanasius. His leadership of the anti-Nicene party was so relentless that the group was called Eusebians. He baptized Constantine* just before the emperor's death in 337 and exercised great influence over Constantine's son, Constantius.

Eusebius of Samosata (d. 380) Champion of the Nicene Creed* and bishop of Samosata from 361. He was a member of the synod* held under Melitus of Antioch in 363 that drew up the orthodox formula* of faith, incorporating the word *homoousios*. An associate of Basil of Ancyra* and Gregory of Nazianzus*, he was banished in 374, first to Cappadocia* and then to Thrace.

Eusebius, St. (d. 371) Bishop of Vercelli in Italy from 340. A strong supporter of orthodoxy* against the Arians, he accompanied St. Lucifer* of Cagliari on his embassy to Constantius in 354. He was exiled after the Synod of Milan in 355. Feast day: August 2.

Eustathius (c. 280–c. 335) Bishop of Berea and patriarch* of Antioch (324–326). A prominent and eloquent opponent of Arianism* and Eusebius* of Caesarea, he was deposed and exiled for insulting Helena*, the emperor's mother. He was also accused of Sabellianism*. His followers were called Eustathians.

Eusthathius Bishop of Sebaste. He was a famous exponent of severe asceticism* and influenced St. Basil the Great*. At the Synod of Ancyra in 358, he supported the Arians and was consequently deposed.

Eustochium, St. Julia (370–c. 419) Roman virgin who, with her mother, was inspired by St. Jerome* to visit the Holy Land*. In Bethlehem*, they founded four monasteries. Feast day: September 28.

Euthalius (fourth century?) Reputed biblical editor credited with redaction of the text in short lines, a system of references and reading aids, a division of the Bible into chapters, with summary headings of their contents. He is also the author of a lengthy sketch of Paul's* life, writings, and martyrdom, and a chronology. Nothing is known about him except that he was a deacon.

Euthymius, St. (377–473) Armenian monk. In about 426 he established near Jerusalem* a lavra* or a colony of anchorites at present-day Khan el-Ahmar. He was one of the founders of Palestinian monasticism*, among whose many disciples was St. Saba. Feast day: January 20.

Euthymius Zigabenus (eleventh or twelfth century) Byzantine monk and exegete. He was commissioned by Emperor Alexis Comnenus to write a work against the heresies. The result was *Panoplia Dogmatica*, a work in 28 chapters. He also wrote commentaries on the Psalms, the Gospels, and the Pauline Epistles.

Eutropius, St. (d. 250) One of the missionaries sent along with St. Denys* to evangelize* Gaul. He was martyred in Saintes in southwest France, where his relics* are housed.

Eutyches (c. 380–c. 456) Heresiarch*, archimandrite*, and exponent of Monophysitism*. In 444 he led the opposition to the compromise of Cyril*, which, he felt, leaned toward Nestorianism*. But his emphasis on a single nature in Christ offended the orthodox party, and he was condemned by Patriarch Flavian*. Eutyches refused to accept the condemnation and engineered the Robber Council of Ephesus* in 449 to retry and acquit him. However, the Council of Chalcedon*, meeting two years later, condemned his heresy and deposed and exiled him.

Eutychianism Heresy, first put forth by Eutyches*, that there was only one divine nature in Christ after the Incarnation*, his human nature being swallowed up in the divine nature.

Evagrius Ponticus (345–399) Monastic writer. A native of Pontus, he became a noted preacher in Constantinople*, but left in 382 for the Nitrian Desert*, where he remained until death as an ascetic. He was a disciple of St. Macarios and, in turn, trained and influenced Palladius*, Rufinus*, Heraclides, Cassian, Diadochus* of Photike, and Maximus the Confessor*. His writings covered the monastic traditions and include *Monachos* or *Practicos, Gnostic Chapters,* a treatise, *On Prayer,* and a collection of apophthegms.

Evagrius Scholasticus (c. 536–600) Syrian historian whose *Ecclesiastical History* is a treasury of information on the church in the fifth and sixth centuries. His history updated Eusebius* and brought it down to 590.

evangel (Gk., *eu angelos,* good news) 1. The gospel. 2. The messenger of the gospel or good tidings.

evangeliary Volume containing the four Gospels or portions of them.

Evangelical (*noun*) Member of a Bible-based Protestant church emphasizing personal salvation* solely through being born again* and through uncompromising commitment to the person of Jesus Christ. (*adjective*) 1. Of or relating to the gospel. 2. In the spirit of New Testament Christianity. 3. Belonging or relating to a Bible-based Protestant church emphasizing personal salvation solely through being born again and through uncompromising commitment to the person of Jesus Christ. 4. Emphasizing the doctrine of sin*, repentance*, grace*, salvation, and saving faith*. 5. Lutheran, as opposed to Reform. 6. Generally, Protestant, as opposed to Catholic.

Evangelical Alliance Union of Evangelical churches formed in 1846 in London to "associate and concentrate the strength of an enlightened Protestantism* against the encroachments of Popery* and Puseyism and to promote the interests of Scriptural Christianity." The alliance holds conferences and sponsors crusades, promotes a week of prayer annually, defends biblical Christianity, and supports missionary work. Its affiliate, Evangelical Missionary Alliance* (recently renamed Global Connections), was founded in 1958. It is one of the founding members of the World Evangelical Fellowship*. In recent years, the Evangelical Alliance has grown rapidly to become a prominent force in British Christianity.

Evangelical Association Group founded by Jacob Albright*. The first general conference of Albright's followers was held in 1816.

Evangelical Church in Germany Federation of autonomous Protestant territorial churches in Germany. Its member bodies include the Evangelical Church of the Union which goes back to 1817 and the United Evangelical Lutheran church of Germany formed in 1948. It is governed by a council, a conference of churches, and a synod. The Evangelical Church is very active in politics, often espousing more leftist positions on controversial issues.

Evangelical counsels Virtues recommended rather than mandated to achieve perfection* in the Christian life, so called because the call to their practice is found in the Gospels and is addressed to some but not all Christians. They consist of the three virtues of chastity* (1 Cor. 7:25–35), poverty (Mark 10:17–22), and obedience (Luke 10:16). See also CONSILIA EVANGELICA; COUNSELS OF PERFECTION.

Evangelical Covenant Church of America Continuation of a lay Lutheran movement that developed in Sweden in the nineteenth century and was brought to the United States by Swedish immigrants. Organized as a denomination in 1885, the Covenant is noncreedal, but subscribes to the article of faith that the "Bible is the only sufficient rule for faith and conduct." The church emphasizes a pietistic "growing in faith" and "being born again unto a living hope." Typical of the Mission Friends, as the early Covenant people were called, were mission meetings, often held outdoors.

Evangelical Doctor Epithet of John Wycliffe*.

Evangelical Fellowship of Canada National alliance of Canadian Evangelicals* founded in 1964 to defend evangelism and orthodoxy*. It includes more than 20 denominations with a total membership of more than 1 million. It is affiliated with the World Evangelical Fellowship* and publishes *Faith Today*.

Evangelical Foreign Missions Association (EFMA) Fellowship of 87 Evangelical missionary organizations, affiliated with the National Association of

Evangelicals*, founded in 1974. In 1963 it joined with the Interdenominational Foreign Mission Association to form a publishing arm called Evangelical Missions Information Service. It produces the *Evangelical Missions Quarterly*.

Evangelical Free Church Denomination with roots in the Scandinavian Free Church movement and a conference of free churches held in Boone, Iowa, in 1884. In 1950 the Evangelical Free Church of America (Swedish) and the Evangelical Free Church Association (Norwegian-Danish) merged into the Evangelical Free Church of America. Doctrinally, it is committed to the absolute authority of the Scriptures, and the Second Coming*, but allows latitude in regard to "non-essentials," as predestination*, baptism*, and spiritual gifts*. The denomination runs two divinity schools* in the United States and one in Canada.

Evangelical frontier Religious or cultural barrier or obstacle to evangelism in a country or region.

Evangelical Lutheran Church in America The largest Lutheran denomination in America, founded in 1988. It represents the merger of the Lutheran Church in America, the Association of Evangelical Lutheran Churches*, and the American Lutheran Church*.

Evangelical Missionary Alliance British association, recently renamed Global Connections, founded in 1958 as a subsidiary of the Evangelical Alliance*. Its membership includes about 100 missionary societies and training colleges.

Evangelical Theological Society Association of North American theologians and biblicists, founded in 1949. Its members promote conservative biblical scholarship and the doctrine of the inerrancy of Scriptures.

Evangelical United Brethren Church formed in 1946 based on the teachings of Jacob Albright*. In 1967 it merged with the Methodist Episcopal Church to create the United Methodist Church.

Evangelicalism One of the main strands of Protestant Christianity. Its distinguishing marks are acceptance of scriptural authority as binding on

Christians, personal commitment to Jesus Christ, and adherence to historic Trinitarianism. In almost all countries, Evangelicals are pitted against the liberals, and there are divisions between conservatives and liberals even within Evangelicalism. The Laodicean character of the liberal churches, as contrasted with the earnestness of the Evangelicals, has helped the latter gain an edge in terms of converts and growth.

Evangelicals have been in the forefront of the missionary movement. The Church Missionary Society* in England and the British and Foreign Bible Society* owe their origin to Evangelicals. In the nineteenth century, Evangelicalism received a boost from the revivalist movements and from the Keswick Convention*. With Evangelicalism's twin focus of world missions and personal consecration, the social gospel* has disappeared from its horizon. In the post-World War II period, the conservative Evangelicals have spearheaded a revival under the leadership of John Stott*, Martyn Lloyd-Jones*, Carl Henry*, and others. The crusades of Billy Graham*, the Charismatic movement, the impact of Inter-Varsity Fellowship* among students, the popularity of theology as an academic discipline, and experiments in new forms of worship and evangelism have contributed to the phenomenal growth of Evangelicalism.

Evangelicals and Catholics Together Initiative begun in the United States in 1994 by Evangelicals* led by Charles Colson* and Roman Catholics led by Richard Neuhaus. Its initial joint statement, subtitled "The Christian Mission in the Third Millennium," was followed by a volume of essays (1995) and a second statement, "The Gift of Salvation." It was born out of a growing recognition of the importance of forming a common front against liberalism*.

Evangelico In Latin America, a Protestant.

Evangelion (Gk. gospel) In the Greek Church, book containing the text of the four Gospels arranged in the order required for liturgical use. It is treated with great reverence and is usually bound in a cover decorated with or made of silver and gold.

Evangelion da-Maparreshe Syriac* translation of the four Gospels dating from the second to the fourth centuries. See OLD SYRIAC VERSION.

evangelism Fulfillment of the Great Commission* (Matt. 28:19–20) through proclamation of the gospel of Jesus Christ and witnessing to the unsaved in order to win disciples for him and the church. Evangelism encompasses the message, the methods, and the goal. The message is the Good News* that "Jesus Christ died for our sins, and was raised from the dead according to the Scriptures, and that as the reigning Lord now offers the forgiveness of sins, and the liberating gift of the Spirit to all who repent and believe." The methods are varied and include personal, mass, and saturation evangelism. The goal is to bring people into a new relationship with God through Jesus Christ and to enable them to commit their lives to him.

Evangelism in Depth Cooperative mass evangelistic effort started in 1960 by R. K. Strachan* of the Latin American Mission. It attempts to impact a country in an all-out, year-long campaign that mobilizes the entire Christian community in a country under local leadership. It includes neighborhood prayer cells, training classes for witnesses, and evangelistic rallies and crusades.

evangelist 1. One of the four Gospel writers, Matthew, Mark, Luke, or John, represented by man, lion*, ox, or an eagle*, respectively. 2. Traveling missionary or one who is engaged in evangelism. 3. In the New Testament, a fisher of men who is called to the ministry of preaching the gospel.

Evangelistarium In the Eastern Orthodox Church*, a book of tables showing the Gospel lections for each year in accordance with the movable date of Easter*.

evangelistics Branch of theology dealing with evangelism.

Evangelium Veritatis "The Gospel of Truth," Gnostic treatise found among the Nag Hammadi* Coptic texts. It recounts aspects of the gospel story with fewer distortions than most Gnostic texts. It is generally attributed to Valentinus*.

evangelize 1. To preach the gospel. 2. To convert to Christianity.

Evans, Christmas (1766–1838) Welsh Baptist preacher. Ordained in 1789, he ministered for most of his life in Anglesey and Caernarvon. He had a passion for souls, preached tirelessly, and was able to communicate his fervor to his largely working-class Welsh audiences. Together with John Elias* and William Williams*, he is considered one of the three greatest preachers in Wales.

Evanston Assembly Second international meeting of the World Council of Churches* held in 1954 at Evanston, Illinois, on the theme, "Christ, the Hope of the World." It was attended by 132 member denominations.

evening communion Celebration of the Eucharist* in the evening.

evensong/evening prayer Worship service held in the evening; vespers*. It includes recitation of the psalter and the canticles*, Magnificat*, and Nunc Dimittis.

Everard, John (c. 1575–c. 1650) English nonconformist mystic and preacher who preached to the "lowest of men." He was always in trouble with the established church* and was jailed and fined many times. In 1653 he published a collection of sermons under the title, *Some Gospel Treasures Opened*.

every member canvass Solicitation of all members of a parish for financial support.

every member visitation Campaign to visit every home in a parish, generally for evangelistic purposes.

Everyman Character in medieval morality plays* who finds that everything will fail him except his good deeds.

ewer Large metal pitcher used to carry water to the baptismal font*.

Ewostatewos (1273–1352) Monastic founder in Ethiopia, known as the "Ethiopian Sun." He taught a rigorous observance of the Jewish Sabbath which was later legislated into law.

ex opere operantis (Lat., from the work of the worker) In theology, the efficacy of a sacrament* as dependent on the spiritual goodness of the person administering or receiving it; subjective validy.

ex opere operato (Lat., from the work worked) In theology, the efficacy of a sacrament* irrespective of the merits or qualities of the person administering or receiving it. It defines a sacrament as an instrument of God that will operate and accomplish its purpose without reference to the worthiness of the recipient or administrator; objective validity.

ex voto Object, usually a candle, offered in fulfillment of a vow and placed near the altar or in a sanctuary.

exaltation of Christ Christ's glorification at his Father's right hand after the Resurrection prefigured by the transfiguration, when Christ's human body was transformed into his original glory.

Exaltation of the Cross Also, Holy Cross Day. Feast in honor of the cross of Christ observed on September 14. It celebrates the exposition of the True Cross at Jerusalem* in 629 by Emperor Heraclius after its recovery from the Persians into whose hands it had fallen in 614.

exapostelarion (lit., one who is sent forth) In the Eastern Church*, troparion* occurring at the end of the canon of orthros*, immediately before ainoi*. It is also called "the hymn of light" because it is usually sung at daybreak.

exapsalmos In the Byzantine Liturgy, six psalms recited at the start of orthros*: Psalms 3, 37, 62, 87, 102, and 142.

exapteryga In the Byzantine tradition, liturgical fans* set on poles and carried during processions. They have a large image of a seraphim inscribed on them.

exarch Greek military term applied to metropolitan*, provincial bishop, or the superintendent of a council or monastery.

exaudi Sunday after Ascension Day*.

excardination In the Roman Catholic Church, process by which a cleric loses canonical attachment to a particular diocese*, as when he joins a religious order. Opposite of incardination*.

exclaustration Permission given by a superior* allowing member of his or her congregation to live outside the community for up to three years. However, the religious remains bound by vows, although he or she may dispense with the religious habit*.

Exclusive Brethren Group of the Plymouth Brethren* led by J. N. Darby* that broke away from the Plymouth Brethren because of disagreements on the nature of Christ and church government. Exclusive Brethren observe infant or household baptism*. They exclude other Christians from Communion. Their moral outlook is conservative, and they maintain strict biblical standards in matters of faith and practice. See also OPEN BRETHREN.

exclusive language Words or phrases used for a class or group that are in the opinion of some not strictly applicable to all its members, as, for example, the use of "men" for "human beings." The use of exclusive language is often construed as gender bias. See also INCLUSIVE LANGUAGE.

excommunication Exclusion from the community of the faithful or particulary from the Lord's table* because of an error in doctrine or lapse in morals or both. It is an act of discipline exercised by the whole body or by the pastor or other leaders and is defined in the New Testament as a sanction (2 Cor. 2:5–11; 2 Thess. 3:10, 14). In the primitive church, excommunication meant complete isolation from the church and even handing over to Satan* (1 Cor. 5:5). In the early and medieval church, there were four kinds of excommunication: 1. Minor excommunication or temporary exclusion from Holy Communion*. 2. Excommunication with ecclesiastical censure* in which the

guilty party is not only excluded from Holy Communion but also barred from communal activities. 3. Major excommunication or complete exclusion from the church. 4. Break of ecclesiastical communion imposed on a segment of a church.

The two purposes of excommunication are to ensure that the good is not corrupted by communication with evil and that the sinner may be ashamed and thus led to repent. But by the fifteenth century, a distinction was tolerated between the vitandi* (those excommunicated for gross error) and the tolerati* (those excluded from the sacraments* only). Excommunication does not affect a person's standing with God, making it possible for an excommunicated person to remain within a state of grace*. Calvin* expected those excommunicated to be present during the preaching of the Word so that it might effect correction.

exedra Niche* or semicircular recess in a church behind the altar.

exegesis (Gk., explanation) Critical exposition or explanation of the meaning of a scriptural passage in the context of the whole Bible. Often used to apply biblical text to contemporary or personal problems and situations. Its rules are governed by hermeneutics*, or interpretation. The main types of exegesis are allegorical exegesis and literal exegesis. The Scholastics favored a fourfold method of literal, allegorical, mystical or anagogical, and moral exegesis, dividing the Word of God* by logical categories. The Reformation* recovered the primacy of the literal sense. That is the plain grammatico-historical meaning, which was itself viewed as the historical sense.

exegetical preaching Preaching in Christian churches based on interpretation and explanation of biblical text with close attention to their context and relevance to the congregation.

exemplarism View of the Atonement* as limited in its value to a moral example of love and self-surrender.

exemption 1. Release from a spiritual obligation or from the penalty for failing to meet it. 2. Release of a cleric from the control of his or her normal superior*, as a bishop, and transfer of such control to another, as an abbot. A common practice in the Middle Ages, its abuse led to the restoration to the bishop by the Council of Trent* of control over all religious orders within his jurisdiction. The 1983 Codex Iuris Canonici* modified this provision by granting all institutes of consecrated life autonomy of governance and discipline.

exequatur (Lat., he may perform) Also, Regium Placet. Right claimed by certain rulers in the Middle Ages to decide whether papal decrees should take effect within their dominions. This right was condemned by Pope Pius IX*.

exequial Mass Requiem Mass said at a funeral, followed by absolution* and procession to the grave.

exercises, spiritual 1. Forms of prayer and meditation prescribed for the religious as part of spiritual regimen. 2. *Spiritual Exercises*. Book by Ignatius Loyola* containing prayers and meditations suitable for Jesuits*.

Exeter Site of an ancient English monastery founded or restored by Kings Athelstan in 932, Edgar in 968, and Canute in 1019. A Norman cathedral was erected here, dedicated by John Grandison and completed by Thomas Brantingham. Among its notable treasures are its miserere seats, the bishop's throne installed by Walter de Stapledon, and Edward the Confessor's* charter.

Exeter Hall Building in the Strand, London, used by Evangelicals* in the nineteenth century, and hence used as a term to describe all Evangelicals.

exhort To admonish, entreat, encourage, or comfort through formal preaching. Thus, exhortation.

existentialism, Christian System of philosophy with Christian overtones in which the starting point and the end are individual experiences. The main themes of existentialism are anxiety and dread*, being and existence, authenticity, interiority, absurdity, choice, and the individual. Modern existentialism goes back to Soren Kierkegaard*, who stated that God is a subject and hence subjectivity or inwardness is the fountain of knowledge

and faith. Translated into theology, existentialism calls for an authentic existence, a "leap of faith*," by which one crosses the chasm between the human and the divine, and an encounter* between a hidden God and a tragically sinful and vulnerable creature. It represents a radical reaction against the rule of reason and liberalism* in European philosophy. Beside Kierkegaard, the most important Christian existentialist was Gabriel Marcel.

exokamelavchion In the Eastern Orthodox Church*, a veil hanging behind the headdress of a priest.

exokklesiai In the Byzantine tradition, wayside shrine that may contain an altar.

exomologesis (Gk., confession) Series of steps by which a penitent is restored to communion with the church, including confession*, satisfaction*, and absolution*. The emphasis is on demonstrating penance through works of satisfaction.

exonarthex The outer narthex* or porch in Eastern churches*.

exorcism The rite of casting out evil spirits, based on the example of Christ and the apostles (Matt. 10:1; Luke 11:14; Acts 16:18–19). The manual for the Roman Catholic Rite is in the *Rituale Romanum*. It can be done only with ecclesiastical permission.

Exorcism Sunday Third Sunday in Lent*, also called oculi*.

exorcist Person who conducts exorcism*, sometimes formally set apart for this ministry. In the Roman Catholic Church, the second of the traditional minor orders* until 1972 when it was abolished.

exordination (Lat., to unhinge) Removal of a cleric from his ordinary diocese before enlisting him again under a new superior*. Opposite of incardination*. See also EXCARDINATION.

Exoucontians (Gk., from nothing + ians) Also Aetians; Anomoeans*. Radical Arians who claimed that the Son was a created being.

expectant Formerly, a candidate* for the Presbyterian ministry in Scotland before being licensed to preach the gospel.

Expectation Sunday Sunday between Ascension Day* and Whitsunday*, in reference to the apostles' expectation of the descent of the Holy Spirit* after Christ's ascension.

experiential church Church or denomination that places more emphasis on a personal experience or encounter with God than on historical dogma*.

expiation Payment of full price or penalty for an offense against God or man. Christ's death on the cross was full payment and atonement* for the sins of all humankind.

explicit faith Faith grounded in knowledge and understanding of the meaning of the teachings of the church.

exposition of the Blessed Sacrament Elevation of the host* during Mass*, either when it is exposed to view in a monstrance*, placed on or above the altar, surrounded by flowers, lights, and incense or when the ciborium* containing the host for the Communion is shown at the open doors of the tabernacle. The rite concludes with the blessing of the people with the host*.

expositor One who explains the meaning of and interprets scriptural passages.

expository preaching Type of preaching, popular in Protestant churches, in which an extended passage of the Scripture, particularly a book of the Bible, is explained and interpreted over a number of weeks.

Exsurge Domine Bull* issued by Leo X* in 1520 to excommunicate Martin Luther*, listing as heretical, scandalous, false, and offensive 41 propositions attributed to Luther. Luther burned the bull at Wittenberg*.

extent of atonement Issue whether Christ's death was intended to secure the salvation* of the elect* or to make salvation available to all who believe of their own free will*.

extern sister Member of a cloistered order who lives within a nunnery but outside the cloister*.

extra ecclesiam nulla salus Traditional Christian teaching as formulated first by Cyprian* but later endorsed by Calvin* that outside the Church there is no salvation*.

extra-liturgical Of or relating to services without any fixed form in the authorized liturgies.

extraordinary minister of the Eucharist Nonordained Catholic who distributes Holy Communion* to the faithful or takes the Eucharist* to the sick or the dying.

Extravagantes Officially recognized papal decretals* excluded from the Decretum of Gratian but included in two collections of decretals of John XXII* and various popes from Urban IV to Sixtus IV*.

extreme unction See UNCTION.

Exultet In the Western Liturgy, the Paschal* proclamation or Paschal praise sung by the deacon standing near the Paschal candle on Holy Saturday*, so called from its opening word.

exultet rolls Long strips of parchment* or vellum with the prayers, canticles*, and lessons of the liturgy of the midnight Mass* of Easter eve, accompanying the blessing and lighting of the Paschal candle. On Easter eve* the deacon carries the roll in procession to the pulpit while chanting the words, *Exultet iam Angelica Turba Coelorum* ("Now let the Heavenly Angelic Host Exult").

Luther Burning the Papal Bull

Eymard, St. Peter Julien (1811–1868) Founder of two religious communities, the Blessed Sacrament Fathers (1856) and the Servants of the Blessed Sacrament (1858). Feast day: August 1.

Ezana (fourth century) First Christian king of Axum* or Ethiopia. Converted by Frumentius*, he evangelized the Ethiopian nation.

ezli In the Ethiopian Church*, one of the three modes of chant used from September 26 through November 6, from the first Sunday of Advent* until the vigil* of the season of Lent*, and from Easter* until June 16.

Eznik (fifth century) Armenian bishop of Bagrevand who translated the Bible into Armenian. He also wrote a *Confutation of the Sects*.

Ff

Faber, Frederick William (1814–1863) English poet, hymn writer, and theologian. A friend of John Henry Newman* and a convert to Catholicism*. His *Hymns* (1861) contained over 150 hymns, including "Faith of Our Fathers," "My God, How Wonderful Thou Art," "O Come and Mourn with Me Awhile," and "Hark, Hark, My Soul." He is also remembered for his devotional writings, including *All for Jesus, The Blessed Sacrament, The Foot of the Cross,* and *The Precious Blood.*

Faber, Johannes (1478–1541) Bishop of Vienna* and Dominican theologian called the "hammer of the heretics." Despite his friendship with Erasmus* and sympathy with Zwingli* and Melanchthon*, he became a staunch opponent of the Reformation* and defended Catholicism* in writings, conferences, and disputations.

Faber Stapulensis, Jacobus (c. 1455–1536) Also, Lefevre d'Etaples. French humanist and Bible translator. Commentaries on the Epistles and Gospels appeared in 1512 and 1523–1528 followed by his French translation of the Bible in 1530.

Fabricius, Johann Philipp (1711–1791) German missionary and Bible translator. He arrived in South India in 1740 to take charge of the small Tamil Lutheran congregation and helped it to grow from 300 to 2,200 members during the 30 years of his ministry. He is remembered for his linguistic achievements: a collection of 335 hymns translated from German, the first Tamil-English dictionary and Tamil-English grammar, and his translation of the Bible into Tamil, called the "golden version."

faculty A dispensation* or license from an ecclesiastical superior* permitting an action to be done or a position to be held.

faino In the Jacobite tradition, the chasuble* split up the center in front and secured by a loop or button at the neck.

fair linen Topmost cloth that covers the top of the altar and hangs down at either end, commonly embroidered with five white crosses in the center and at each of the corners of the mensa*, to represent the five wounds of Christ.

faith 1. Objective body of truth in the Bible, the creeds, the definitions of the universal councils, and/or the teachings of the church. 2. Positive, subjective, and personal allegiance to and trust in Jesus Christ as Lord and Savior. Faith exists in constant tension with three other elements: works, reason, and knowledge. In Protestant scholastic theology, faith is viewed as a threefold process: *notitia** (knowledge of what is to be believed), *assensus* (intellectual acceptance of the truth of what is believed), and *fiducia* (personal commitment to that truth).

The first involves reception* of the message of the gospel. The second involves objective acceptance of certain theological concepts and historical events. Theologians call this *fides quae creditur** (the faith that is believed), comprising *erkennen* (recognition) and *assensus* (assent). *Assensus* includes confidence in God's promises and trust in the events recorded in the Scripture. Peter Lombard* pointed out that assensus alone is *fides informis* (incomplete faith).

Authentic faith must include a second aspect—a personal commitment to Jesus Christ. Theologians variously call this *fides qua creditur** (faith by which one believes), *fides formata caritate* (faith formed by love), *bekennen* (acknowledgment), and *fiducia* (trust in what is believed). *Fiducia* also involves obedience to God's Word, perseverance* in God's will, and love for God's people (John 3:36; Rom. 5:1–5; 1 Cor. 13:2; 1 John 3:10). Thus Christians not only live because of faith but they also live according to the faith (Rom. 1:16–17). Faith is in one sense a human act, but it is also at the same time a divine gift.

Faith and Order Branch of the ecumenical movement* dedicated to the resolution of differences in doctrine and church order and to the reunion of churches. It sponsored the 1927 Conference at Lausanne* and the 1937 Conference in Edinburgh*. It is now part of the World Council of Churches*.

World Conference on Faith and Order, 1937

faith healing Physical healing caused directly through an act of prayer or indirectly through intercession and the laying on of hands*. It is part of the doctrinal foundation of Holiness and Pentecostal groups and holds that physical healing is the "children's bread" and that good health and freedom from sickness are among the prerogatives that accompany salvation*. In Europe, faith healing has a long history, going back to Dor-

othea Trudel of Switzerland, Johann Blumhardt* and Otto Stockmayer of Germany, and Edward Irving* and William Boardman of England. In America, faith healing was introduced by such early Evangelicals* as A. B. Simpson* (in whose Christian and Missionary Alliance* healing is

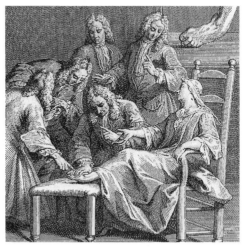

Faith Healing

part of the fourfold gospel*), R. A. Torrey*, John Alexander Dowie*, R. Kelso Carter, and Maria B. Woodworth-Etter*.

Early Pentecostals believed that healing grace* was part of the Atonement* and that people should expect to be healed by faith just as they were saved by faith. Almost all modern faith healers have been Pentecostals, including Kenneth Hagin*, Kathryn Kuhlman*, T. L. Osborn*, A. A. Allen, John Wimber*, Gayle Jackson, O. L. Jaggers, Oral Roberts*, Smith Wigglesworth*, Stephen Jeffreys* and George Jeffreys*, and Benny Hinn. A ministry of healing through prayer and, often, of laying on of hands* and sometimes anointing, is also practiced in many mainstream denominations.

faith mission Evangelical mission that operates in faith that God will provide. It does not generally solicit funds and does not guarantee the salaries of missionaries. Its original inspiration is the China Inland Mission* founded by Hudson Taylor*. Among the missions that were founded on this principle are the Evangelical Alliance Mission (1890), Central American Mission (1890), Sudan

Interior Mission* (1893), and the Africa Inland Mission* (1895).

faith movement Charismatic movement emphasizing the power of faith and positive confession* in obtaining the double blessing of physical and financial wellbeing. The patriarch of the movement is Kenneth Hagin*, whose Rhema Bible Training Center* has trained hundreds of ministers and whose books are considered the manuals of the movement. Other leaders include Kenneth and Gloria Copeland, Frederick Price of Ever Increasing Faith Ministries, Charles Capps, Marilyn Hickey, Lester Sumrall, and Bob Tilton. Oral Roberts* is closely associated with the movement. Drawing on the writings of E. W. Kenyon*, the faith movement teaches that God's promises of health and prosperity are obtained through positive confession based on God's Word. The movement has spread largely through independent Charismatic churches, many of them founded by Rhema alumni. The movement is known by many names, including the Prosperity Gospel and the Word of Faith movement.

Faith, St. (d. c. 287) Virgin and martyr*. She was martyred, together with St. Caprasius, in Aquitaine under Maximian Hercules and the procurator* Dacian. Her relics* were translated to a basilica* named in her honor, and many miracles were credited to her. Her relics were brought in about 855 to the Abbey of Conques*, which became a famous place of pilgrimage*, and her cult* was very popular in the Middle Ages. St. Paul's Cathedral* in London was built on the site of her church.

faithful One who is worthy of faith or keeps promises. Applied to both God and humans.

Faithful, Mass of the Part of the Mass* extending from the offertory to the end. So called because in the early church the unbaptized catechumens* were dismissed before the offertory and only the baptized were permitted to remain during the remainder of the service.

faithful, the Body of baptized and practicing believers who are part of the visible church or invisible church.

falda White vestment worn by the pope on solemn occasions.

faldstool Folding stool without a back used by Roman Catholic bishops when not sitting on a throne or as a prie-dieu*.

fall Pendant paraments* on the altar, pulpit, and lectern*.

fall of Jerusalem Capture and sack of Jerusalem by the Romans in A.D. 70, ending the Jewish revolt begun in 66. The event had important influence on the development of the Christian church.

false christ Counterfeit religious leader who deceives many believers by assuming the role of a messiah.

false decretals Ninth-century collection of canon law* documents, some of which were probably fabricated to legitimize the supremacy of the pope over other patriarchs*. It contains three sections, the second and third of which are genuine canons of councils. The first section is spurious and includes letters in the names of pre-Nicene popes from Clement I to Militiades and includes the Donation of Constantine*. This conferred upon Pope Sylvester I* primacy over all other churches and dominion over Rome and over all provinces and places in the West.

Falwell, Jerry (1933–) Baptist pastor and founder of the Moral Majority. Converted in 1952, he became in 1956 the founding pastor of Thomas Road Baptist Church in Lynchburg, Virginia, whose congregation grew to 18,000 in three decades. He also began a popular radio and television ministry called "Old-Time Gospel Hour." In 1971 he founded Liberty University, one of the largest Christian universities in the United States. In 1979 he gained national attention when he founded the Moral Majority to serve as a rallying point and catalyst for Christian conservatism opposed to the liberal agenda. The movement was dissolved in 1989, but he remains a controversial lightning rod for conservative social and political issues.

fama clamosa (Lat., bad report) Rumors of bad ministerial conduct as grounds for investigation.

Familists Sixteenth-century sect called "Family of Love" founded by Henry Nicholas* in 1540 in Friesland, and later in England. A mystical and antinomian group, they believed in the Inner Light* and birth of Jesus Christ in their own souls and rejected all sacraments*. They survived well into the seventeenth century.

fan, liturgical Fan used at the Eucharist* to keep the flies and other insects away from the oblations*. It was also used when the pope was carried on his sedia gestatoria* during processions.

fanon 1. Maniple; the white linen cloth in which the congregation brought their offerings; strings of the mitre*; humeral veil of the subdeacon or processional banner*. 2. Collar-shaped liturgical garment worn by the pope over his amice* when celebrating solemn pontifical Mass*.

farcing Filling in between verses of a psalm with scriptural texts in singing.

Farel, Guillaume (1489–1565) French reformer of French-speaking Switzerland. At Basel, he prepared the first Protestant liturgy in French and a declaration of Protestant belief. He introduced the Reformation* to Neuchatel in 1530 and to the Canton of Vaud and Geneva* in 1534–1536. He was a lifelong friend of Calvin*.

Guillaume Farel

farmery Infirmary in a monastery in the charge of an infirmarian*.

Farrar, Frederic William (1831–1903) Dean of Canterbury*. He gained recognition with his *Life of Christ* (1874) which went into 12 editions. He wrote a similar *Life and Works of St. Paul* (1879). He provoked great controversy by questioning eternal punishment* for the wicked in *Eternal Hope* (1877).

farse Interpretation of the reading from the Epistle at Mass*.

Fast of Nineveh Three days' fast, also known as the Rogation of the Ninevites, or the Supplication of Nineveh, in Eastern churches*, commemorating the fast undertaken by the Ninevites as a mark of their contrition*. It begins 70 days before Easter* and leads into Lent*. It was instituted in the sixth century because of a devastating plague whose spread was halted by a fast.

fasting Penitential practice recommended for believers by Jesus Christ by example and teaching (Matt. 6:16–18; Mark 2:20; Luke 4:2) and observed by the apostles (Acts 13:2; 14:23; 2 Cor. 11:27). It is designed to weaken the flesh and, correspondingly, to strengthen the spirit. In the early church, believers fasted regularly on Wednesdays and Fridays. In addition, the fast of Lent* gradually extended to 40 days in honor of Christ's fast in the desert. In the Eastern Church*, three more periods of fasting were observed: Advent* (from November 15), from the Monday after Pentecost* to the Feast of Sts. Peter and Paul, and the fortnight before Assumption. Fasting is also mandatory in the Roman Catholic Church before reception of the Eucharist*.

Fasting may mean abstention from all food for the whole or part of a day or a restricted diet. In the latter case, only one meal is taken, generally in the middle of the afternoon. Or, it may mean abstinence from certain types of food, such as meat and animal products. Days of abstinence have been distinguished from fasting. In the Roman Catholic Church, the two universally obligatory fast days are Ash Wednesday* and Good Friday*. Children, the elderly, and the sick are exempt from fasting.

fasting communion Reception of the Holy Communion* after a stipulated period of fasting.

Fastnacht In Switzerland and Germany, Shrove Tuesday*.

Fat Thursday (Ger., *Fetter Donnerstag*) Thursday preceding Ash Wednesday* in which quantities of food are consumed.

Fat Tuesday (Ger., *Fetter Dienstag*) German name for Shrove Tuesday* from the practice of consuming fatty foods, prohibited in Lent*.

father 1. God, as abba*. 2. Title of certain mendicant friars, now generally used as a term of address for all Roman Catholic and Eastern Orthodox* priests.

father of Christian monasticism St. Antony the Great.

father of ecclesiastical history Eusebius* of Caesarea.

Father of Fathers Title of Gregory of Nyssa*.

father of heresies Simon the Sorcerer who tried to bribe Peter* (Acts 8:9–24), from whose name simony* is derived.

Fathers of the Church Ecclesiastical leaders and teachers who are accepted as authorities in matters of doctrine. In the early church, orthodoxy* was determined by the so-called consensus patrum* that showed general agreement among a set of Christian leaders distinguished by purity of faith, holiness of life, approval of the church, and antiquity. The authority of the Fathers was binding only when there was complete unanimity, because any one of them might be liable to error. The patristic period is often defined as between the first century and St. Isidore of Seville* in the West and St. John of Damascus* in the East.

Church Fathers are generally divided geographically into Eastern and Western and chronologically into ante-Nicene and post-Nicene. They are held in higher regard in the Eastern Church* than in the Western Church*, because in the absence of a pope they provided a source of magisterium*. In a wider sense the Father is used of all early Christian sources, including writings of those condemned as heretics, texts produced by councils, and other documents which cannot be ascribed to an individual.

Fathers of the Desert Monks and hermits in the Nitrian and other Egyptian deserts and in Palestine and Syria from the late third century. The most celebrated of the Fathers of the Desert are St. Antony the Great, St. Pachomius*, and St. Hilarion*.

Fatima Small town in Portugal where the Virgin Mary* appeared six times to three children on May 13, 1917. It is a famous place of pilgrimage* and the site of the Basilica and Shrine of our Lady of Fatima.

Faustinus and Jovita, Sts. (second century) According to legend, martyrs* of Brescia who were imprisoned by Emperor Trajan and executed by Hadrian.

Fayum Gospel Fragment Brief papyrus* fragment written in the third century and discovered in Egypt in 1882. It is preserved at Vienna* among the Rainier Papyri.

Fathers of the Church

First century: Clement of Rome

Second century: Ignatius of Antioch, Clement of Alexandria, Justin, Irenaeus, Polycarp

Third century: Cyprian, Dionysius, Origen, Tertullian, Gregory Thaumaturgus

Fourth century: Hilary, Cyril of Jerusalem, Gregory of Nyssa, Gregory of Nazianzus, Basil of Caesarea, John Chrysostom, Eusebius of Caesarea, Jerome, Epiphanius, Athanasius

Fifth century: Rufinus, Augustine, Pope Leo I, Cyril of Alexandria, Vincent of Lerins

Sixth century: Caesarius of Arles

Seventh century: Isidore, Pope Gregory the Great (although Bernard of Clairvaux has sometimes been viewed as the last of the Fathers)

Eighth century: John of Damascus, Venerable Bede

Fayumic Dialect of Coptic* spoken in early Christian times in Middle Egypt.

feast (Lat., *festum*) Obligatory day of celebration, less important than *solemnitatas* or solemnities and more important than *memoria** or memorial. They are observed by a Proper in the Eucharist and Offices. There are three kinds of feasts: 1. Sundays, the weekly commemoration of the Resurrection. 2. Movable feasts* of which the most important are Easter*, Pentecost* or Whitsuntide*. 3. Immovable feasts*, including Christmas* and the Epiphany*, Ascension, Corpus Christi*, Assumption, Immaculate Conception*, and the anniversaries of saints* and martyrs*.

Feast of Dedication Formerly a feast of obligation, such as Purification or Finding of the Cross.

Feast of Fools Medieval European burlesque of the church. It began with the election of a pope of fools, a cardinal of numbskulls, and a boy bishop. Sometimes a donkey was brought into the church as a ribald gesture.

Feast of Our Lord Day of worship honoring some event in the life of Christ.

Feast of Weeks Pentecost*.

Febronianism Catholic movement in Germany and Austria in the late eighteenth century to limit the power of the papacy. It was the German counterpart to French Gallicanism*. Its main tenets were developed by J. N. von Hontheim, writing under the pseudonym of "Justinus Febronius," in his *The State of the Church and the Legitimate Authority of the Roman Pontiff, a book Composed for the Purpose of Uniting in Religion Dissident Christians* (1763). Hontheim held that the keys of the kingdom* were given not to the pope but to the whole church represented by the general councils of all bishops. Although Hontheim did not advocate secular supremacy, Febronianism was used by the secular rulers to buttress their power. The Synod of Pistoia* (1786) and the Congress of Ems (1786) adopted Febronianist principles. Later Hontheim was condemned and forced to recant.

Federal Council of Churches Organization of 33 U.S. Protestant denominations founded in 1908. It was renamed as the National Council of Churches in 1950.

federal theology Branch of theology that studies God's two covenants (foedus; pl., foedera) with human beings, the covenant of works*, and the covenant of grace*. Among the principal federal theologians are Andreas Musculus (1514–1581), Stephanus Kis (1505–1572), Johannes Cocceius* (1603–1669), William Ames* (1576–1633), and Charles Hodge* (1797–1878).

Fedotov, George P. (1886–1951) Orthodox historian. He taught church history at the Paris Orthodox Theological Institute (1925–1949). He came to the United States in 1941 and taught at St. Vladimir's Russian Orthodox Seminary* at Crestwood, New York, until his death. Among his many books in English are *The Russian Religious Mind* (1947) and *Treasury of Russian Spirituality* (1949).

Felicity, St. (?–203) Carthaginian martyr*, who was killed by Roman authorities together with St. Perpetua*. Feast day: March 7.

Felix (1127–1212) Founder of the Order of the Redemptionists to redeem Christians captured by Saracens.

felix culpa (Lat., happy fault) In the *Exsultet*, Adam's fall, considered as fortunate, because it was the cause for the Redeemer's Incarnation* and the salvation* of Adam's descendants.

fellowship Communion of believers in the common bond of their faith.

Fellowship of Reconciliation Peace organization founded in 1914 during World War I in England by Henry Hodgkin, a Quaker*. It emphasized the oneness of all humanity and proclaimed love as "an effective force for overcoming evil and transforming society."

Fellowship of St. Alban and St. Sergius Organization, an offshoot of the British and Russian Student Christian Movement*, dedicated to the promotion of understanding and cooperation between the Church of England* and the Russian Orthodox Church*. In 1943 it established a permanent base in London at St. Basil House. The fellowship makes an annual pilgrimage* to St. Albans*.

Fellowship of St. Andrew Scottish society, named after the common patron saint* of Scotland, Russia, and Greece, to promote mutual understanding among the churches of the three countries.

felon In the Byzantine tradition, a short tunic, or chasuble*, worn by a reader* over his shoulders during ordination. It symbolizes the yoke of Christ.

felonion In the Coptic tradition, a cruciform chasuble* resembling the cope*, but without a hood. The sides of the vestment are secured by a hooked clasp.

felsata In the Ethiopian Church, the Assumption of the Blessed Virgin Mary* into heaven*, commemorated August 22.

feminist theology Branch of theology developed by feminists who reinterpret the Scriptures and church traditions in the light of their opposition to male dominance and bias in history and society. The feminist agenda rests on a twofold analysis: 1. Women were excluded from ordained ministry throughout much of Christian history and given a subordinate role in shaping theological doctrines. 2. Christianity has confirmed rather than weakened traditional patriarchal social structures.

Feminist theologians therefore seek to recover the rightful role of women in Christianity, known as covenant mutuality, and to establish alternative theological traditions. Even traditional feminine concepts in theology, such as mariology*, are perceived as deficient because they only buttress male domination by showing women as subservient and passive. Some feminists also object to the exclusive language* of traditional theology in which God is always presented in masculine terms. Feminist theologians also question such concepts, as humility, because it suggests an extension of patriarchal society.

Three general divisions of feminist theology

are: radical feminism, revisionist feminism, and biblical feminism. Radical feminists seek their theology in sources beside the Scripture whereas revisionist feminists limit themselves to the Scripture. Radical feminists include Mary Daly and Rosemary Radford Reuther, and revisionist feminists include Sallie McFague, Elizabeth Schussler Fiorenza, and Letty Russell. Biblical feminists, on the other hand, believe that the Bible, when correctly interpreted, is neither sexist nor oppressive. But they stand for inclusive language* and the ordination of women as pastors and deacons. This group includes Elizabeth Achtemeier, Aida Besancon Spencer, Stanley Grenz, Patricia Gundry and members of Christians for Biblical Equality.

fencing the table Restricting access to Holy Communion* by forbidding those who are not fully confirmed or those living in open sin.

Fenelon, Francois de Salignac de la Mothe (1651–1715) Mystic, archbishop of Cambrai. He was ordained in 1675 and three years later became superior* of the Nouvelles Catholiques, a school for girls. Based on his experience, he wrote *Traite de l'Education des Filles* (1687), at the request of the duchess of Beauvillier. Two years later he was appointed tutor to Louis XIV's grandson, the duke of Burgundy, for whom he wrote the novel, *Telemachus*. In 1688 he met Madame Guyon* and was attracted to her mystical teachings on love and passive prayer. He became her principal defender even after she was censured in 1693.

In 1694 he was elected a member of the French Academy. In 1695 he was appointed archbishop of Cambrai and signed the Thirty-Four Articles of Issay which condemned Madame Guyon* and Quietism*. He continued to defend Madame Guyon, nevertheless, in his *Explication des Maximes des Saints sur la Vie Interieure* (1698). The controversy flared once again and led to his banishment. In 1699 Pope Innocent XII* condemned Fenelon's book. His last book, *Traite sur l'Existence de Dieu* (1718), was a defense of orthodoxy*.

fenqith In the Jacobite Liturgy, a festal office.

Fenwick, Edward Dominic (1768–1832) American Dominican clergyman and missionary, the first bishop of Cincinnati, and founder of Xavier University, the first Dominican institution in the United States.

feretory 1. Shrine holding the relics* of a saint*. 2. Movable reliquary* shrine behind an altar.

feria (lit., feast day) Day in which there is no religious festival. Thus, ferial.

fermentarian Priest who celebrates Communion with leavened bread.

fermentum (lit., leaven) Portions of bread from the bishop's Eucharist* sent to other places of worship in the early church.

ferraiola Brief cape which is worn with the cassock* and which reaches halfway to the elbows.

ferraiolone Long black cloak worn over the cassock* by secular priests at a papal audience.

Ferrar, Nicholas (1592–1637) English theologian who established a monastic community at Little Gidding*, emphasizing ascetic devotion, austerity, religious instruction, and charity. They were also active in book production. Little Gidding was destroyed by the Puritans* in 1646.

ferula (Lat., rod) In the early church, a staff with a short cross-piece at the top on which a clergyman or a layman may lean during church services. See DEKANIKION.

festival of the tank In the Coptic Liturgy, the celebration of Epiphany* in the narthex* of a church beside a large tank filled with water. Psalms and hymns are sung around the tank, and a candlestick with three branches is lit beside it. The water is blessed, censed, and stirred. Then those present are sprinkled with its water.

fetate In the Ethiopian Church*, the fraction* of the consecrated bread during which the priest divides the bread into 13 parts and arranges the portions in the form of a cross.

fethe neghest In the Ethiopian Church*, the church calendar, as revised by King Zara Yakub.

Feuillants Reformed Cistercians of Le Feuillants founded in 1577 by Abbot J. de la Barriere (1544–1600) in the neighborhood of Toulouse as a strict order. It was approved by Gregory XIII* in 1581. In 1588 a related order for women was begun, called the Feuillantines. Soon the order spread to Italy, where they were called Reformed* Bernardines. The order did not survive the Napoleonic Wars.

Fey, Clara (1815–1894) German religious. In 1837 she opened a school in Aachen*, Germany, which became Sisters of the Poor Child Jesus in 1844. For the next 50 years she served as superior*, although she was forced to leave Germany during the Kulturkampf*.

Fiacre, St. (seventh century) Irish hermit, patron of Brie, France, and founder of a monastery.

fidei defensor See DEFENDER OF THE FAITH.

Fideism Doctrine promoted by the French theologians Auguste Sabatier and E. Menegoz that holds that human reason and intellect are incapable of comprehending God and that salvation* is based on faith* alone to the exclusion of reason.

Fides Damasi Creedal formula formerly attributed to St. Damasus. It is a Trinitarian* creed resembling the Athanasian Creed* and including the Filioque* clause.

Fides Hieronymi Early form of the Apostles' Creed* dating back to the fourth century, attributed to Jerome* or St. Gregory of Elvira*.

fides historica Traditional faith passed on from generation to generation. For Luther*, it was the act of assent.

fides qua creditur (Lat., faith by which one believes) Also, fides quae intellectum. Act of faith* in itself; actual trust of the believer in Jesus Christ.

fides quaerens intellectum (Lat., faith seeking understanding) Search for deeper truth by a committed believer. Classic definition of theology provided by Anselm* of Canterbury.

field preaching Preaching out of doors begun by George Whitefield* in 1739 and continued by John Wesley* and the early Methodists.

Fifth Monarchy Men Apocalyptic movement during the Commonwealth and Protectorate in seventeenth-century England. They believed in the imminence of the kingdom of Christ as the fifth monarchy prophesied in Daniel 2—succeeding the Assyrian, Persian, Greek, and Roman empires. In successive uprisings in 1657 and 1661, they tried to hasten the coming of the fifth monarchy. Its leaders, Maj. Gen. Thomas Harrison, Maj. Gen. Robert Overton, and Thomas Venner, were arrested by Cromwell.

fig Sunday Sixth Sunday in Lent*, when the lessons record the cursing of the fig tree (Mark 11:14).

Figurovskii, Innokentii (1894–1931) Russian Orthodox missionary to China. He was sent to Beijing in 1897 with the task of revitalizing Russian missionary outreach*. During the violently anti-Christian Boxer Rebellion* in 1901, Russian missionaries suffered more than the numerically larger Roman Catholics and Protestants. Utilizing reparation* payments from the Chinese government, he opened 32 mission centers. His clergy baptized over 5,000 people, and a seminary was opened to train native clergy.

Filarete (1400–1469) Birth name: Antonio Averlino. Italian architect. His best known work is the bronze door for St. Peter's* showing the martyrdom of Sts. Peter and Paul.

filiation Relation of the eternal Son to the eternal Father.

Filioque (Lat., and from the Son) The interpolation, "and from the Son" added by the Western Church* to the Niceno-Constantinopolitan Creed* immediately after the words, "the Holy Spirit . . . who proceedeth from the Father." The addition reflected the dogma* on the Double Procession* of the Holy Spirit*. It was first added at the first council of Toledo* (589). Filioque was opposed by the Orthodox Church, and it remains one of the principal disagreements between the Western and Eastern churches.

filled with the Spirit State of a Christian who has received the baptism and the infilling of the Holy Spirit*, resulting in the displacement of the carnal spirit. In Holiness*, Pentecostal*, and Charismatic* circles, the term is used to describe a post-conversion baptism in the Spirit but others understand it differently (Eph. 5:18).

Filofei, (Leshchinsky) (1650–1727) Russian Orthodox missionary in Siberia*. After the death of his wife, he joined the famous Kiev-Pechery Lavra (Monastery of the Grottoes), taking the monastic name of Filofei. In 1701 he was appointed abbot of the Svensk Dormition Monastery and a year later consecrated metropolitan* of Siberia and Tobolsk. In 1702 he set off for Tobolsk with a group of monks to evangelize* the Siberians. In 1715 he sent an Orthodox mission to Beijing under the archimandrite* Hilarion*. At the age of 70 he left his official duties and devoted himself to traveling, teaching, and baptizing. It is claimed that he and his fellow missionaries converted 40,000 persons and founded 288 new parishes.

Finan (d. 661) Second bishop of Lindisfarne* from 652. He worked hard to convert all of England and baptized the kings of East Saxons and Mercia. In the controversy over the date of Easter*, he took the side of the Celtic tradition.

Finney, Charles Grandison (1792–1875) American preacher and evangelist. Trained as a lawyer, he was converted in 1821 and thereafter devoted his life to preaching the gospel. For the next eight years he preached widely as an itinerant revivalist*, and the revivals that followed his crusades were among the most sweeping in the history of Christian evangelism. Finney pioneered the art of revivals*, introducing such features as protracted meetings (when all non-religious activities ceased in a place during the crusade), the anxious bench, prayer meetings*, and public prayer for individuals by name. From 1832 to 1835 he was a pastor in the Second Presbyterian Church in New York City and from 1835 to his death, professor of theology (president from 1851 to 1866) at Oberlin College. His unique theological perspective, known as "Oberlin theology*," was a synthesis of Calvinism* and Arminianism*, although he emphasized human responsibility in obedient Christian life.

Together with Asa Mahan*, he held that Christians could reach a state of perfection* through consecration to God in this life.

Charles Finney

Finnian, St. 1. (d. 549) "Tutor of the Saints of Ireland" who founded the Irish monasteries at Rossacurra, Drumfea, and Kilmaglish before going to Wales with David. He returned to Ireland to found the monastery of Clonard of which be became abbot and where his disciples included Columba*. Feast day: December 12. 2. (d. 579) He founded the monastery at Moville and another at Dromin and became the patron saint* of Dublin. Feast day: September 10.

Fioretti (Lat., Little Flowers) *The Little Flowers of St. Francis*, an anthology of legends about St. Francis and his fellow monks.

fire Symbol of the Holy Spirit*.

Fire-Baptized Holiness Movement Early radical Holiness movement* espousing a "third-blessing" theology, founded in 1895 by Benjamin Harding Irwin of Lincoln, Nebraska. He was an ardent advocate of crisis experience of sanctification* subsequent to new birth*, a baptism of burning love or a baptism with Holy Ghost* and fire*. Irwin's preaching led to the formation of a number of state Fire-Baptized Holiness associations. A national association was formed in 1898 with Irwin as the overseer. Irwin was later removed from leadership for open and gross sin and was replaced by John Hillery King. In 1911 the move-

ment was absorbed by the Pentecostal Holiness Church. There are white and black offshoots of the movement in the American South.

first Friday Special observance of first Friday every month to receive Holy Communion* for nine consecutive months. It is based on the supposed promise of Christ to St. Margaret Mary Alacoque* (1647–1690) that those who so observe will receive special favors, especially grace of full repentance* and the assurance of the Sacred Heart* as their refuge at the hour of death.

first Saturday Devotional practice of honoring the Immaculate Heart of Mary* by receiving the Sacrament of Reconciliation* and Holy Communion* on the first Saturday of five successive months, reciting five decades of the Rosary*, and meditating on the sacred mysteries* for at least 15 minutes.

First Wavers Classical Pentecostals*.

Fischer, Johann Michael (1692–1766) German Baroque architect who built 32 churches and 22 abbeys. Among them were the abbey church at Osterhofen, (1726–1728); Church of St. Anna am Lehel, Munich* (1727–1729); Abbey of Furstenzell (1741–1748); Abbey of Zweifalten (1742); Abbey of Ottobeuren*, west of Munich*; and the Abbey of Rott am Inn, south of Munich (1759–1763), arguably his finest.

Fischer von Erlach, Johann Bernhard (1656–1723) Austrian Baroque architect. Most of his works were secular, but he built three great churches: Dreifaltigkeitskirche (Trinity Church) in Salzburg, begun 1694; the Kollegienkirche (University Church; 1696–1707) in Salzburg; and Karlskirche in Vienna,* dedicated to Borromeo*, begun in 1715.

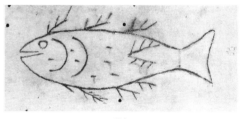

Fish

fish Symbol of Christ in Christian art and literature. The symbol is found in the earliest Christian writings, as that of Tertullian* and *The Shepherd*. The Greek word is an acrostic of the first letters of "Jesus Christ, Son of God, Savior."

Fisher, Geoffrey Francis (1887–1972) Archbishop of Canterbury* (1945–1961). In 1932 he became bishop of Chester and was translated to London in 1939. He succeeded William Temple* as archbishop of Canterbury in 1945. He managed to hold together the Anglo-Catholic* and Evangelical wings of the Anglican Church. Driven by a strong devotion to the cause of Christ and a strong sense of duty, he presided over the church during some of its most critical years after World War II. During his time, the British Empire dissolved, and he was largely responsible for the orderly transition of colonial churches to independent status. He was chairman of the World Council of Churches* in 1948. He traveled widely and was the first archbishop of Canterbury to meet the pope since 1397. He also met the ecumenical patriarch* of Constantinople*. At home, he created the Church Commissioners* in 1948 to replace the Ecclesiastical Commissioners* and initiated the revision of the canon law*.

Fisher, St. John (c. 1469–1535) English cardinal and martyr*. An admirer of Erasmus* and a proponent of moderate reform, he strongly opposed Lutheranism*. Fisher was one of the great scholars of his day and the owner of one of the finest libraries in England. As Catherine of Aragon's confessor*, he protested Henry VIII's divorce from her and the royal attempt to overthrow the church in England. He was removed from his office and put in the tower for refusing to take the oath* relating to the Act of Succession. Thereupon the pope made him cardinal. The enraged king brought Fisher to trial. Charged with treason, he was found guilty and executed. He was canonized in 1936. Feast day: July 9.

Fisherman, the St. Peter*.

fisherman's ring Signet of the pope.

fishing Street evangelism among people who pass by.

Fiske, Fidelia (1816–1864) Missionary to Persia and founder of the Nestorian Female Seminary. In 1843 she was chosen as a missionary to the Assyrians of Persia by the American Board of Commissioners for Foreign Missions*. She opened a boarding school for girls at Urmia patterned after Mount Holyoke Seminary in Massachusetts. She also led numerous revivals among the Assyrians.

fistula Silver or gold tube through which communicants received Holy Communion* from the chalice* at the Eucharist* in the Middle Ages. Replaced since 1969 by a calamus (reed*).

five articles of Arminianism Five points differentiating Arminianism* from Calvinism*: 1. Election* based on divine foreknowledge of the sinner's faith. 2. Universal atonement*. 3. Salvation* only by grace*. 4. Grace necessary but not irresistible. 5. Possibility of falling from grace.

five points of Calvinism Five distinctive Calvinist doctrines, known as TULIP* from their first letters, outlined at the Synod of Dort* in 1619: 1. Total depravity*. 2. Unconditional election*. 3. Limited atonement*. 4. Irresistible grace*. 5. Perseverance* of the saints.

five sacred wounds Five wounds experienced by Christ during his crucifixion, on his two hands, two feet, and side.

Fjellstedt, Peter (1802–1881) Pioneer of the Swedish missionary movement. After serving as a missionary in India, Turkey, and Malta from 1828 to 1843, he returned to Sweden in 1843 and spent the remainder of his life as a missionary organizer. In 1845 he helped to found the Lund Missionary Society, one of the forerunners of the present-day Church of Sweden Mission and the missionary training institute which in 1862 became the Fjellstedtska School in Uppsala*.

flabellum Fan of ostrich plumes carried on each side of the pope during processions.

Flacius, Matthias Illyricus (1520–1575) Birth name: Vlacic. Croatian-German Lutheran theologian. He attended the universities of Basel, Tubingen*, and Wittenberg*, where he was converted to

Protestantism* through contact with Melanchthon* and Luther*. He became a professor of Hebrew at Wittenberg (1544). Subsequently he fell out with Melanchthon over the Augsburg Interim*. In his later years he wandered from Jena to Regensburg, Antwerp, Strasbourg*, and Frankfurt. His fame rests on *Clavis,* a key to the Scriptures and the *Magdeburg Centuries*,* an antipapal survey of Christian history. The Flacians, or Gnesio-Lutherans*, were named for him.

flagellants Bands of men who scourged themselves to the accompaniment of psalms in public procession, in penance* for the sins of the world. The phenomenon was common in Europe in the late Middle Ages from the thirteenth to the fifteenth centuries. It may have been associated with the Black Plague, strife, anarchy, famine, and other troubles during this period. The church withdrew its earlier approval of this practice, and they were repressed by Pope Clement VI* and condemned by the Council of Constance*.

flagellation Whipping and flogging as a means of penance* and as an ascetic practice for punishing the flesh. Self-flagellation is required of some monastic orders, as the Cistercians*. Latin American penitentes still practice flagellation, especially on Good Friday*.

flagon Large silver container in which wine for the Holy Communion* is brought to the credence* table.

Flavian (d. 449) Patriarch* of Constantinople* who took an active role in the condemnation of Eutyches* and presided over the Synod of Constantinople convened for that purpose in 441. The Robber Council of Ephesus* overturned this condemnation and removed Flavian* from office and had him killed.

fleche Slender spire* on the ridge of a church roof. It intersects the transept* and nave*.

Flemal, Bertholet (1614–1675) Flemish religious painter whose *Mysteries of the Old and New Testaments* is in the Louvre.

Fleming, Paul William (1910–1950) American missionary and founder of the New Tribes Mission. He died in a tragic air crash of a missionary transport plane.

flesh 1. Human nature alienated from God and devoted to sensual self-gratification and pursuit of worldly pleasures and possessions. 2. Human body, as distinguished from the soul. 3. Human race.

Fletcher, John William (1729–1785) Birth name: de la Flechere. Swiss-born Methodist bishop of Bangor*. A strong defendant of Arminianism*, he became superintendent of the Countess of Huntingdon's ministerial training college at Trevecca. His main contribution to the controversy over Arminianism was his Five *Checks to Antinomianism* (1771–1775). He also attacked Priestley's Unitarian doctrines. He was an advocate and exemplar of Christian holiness* and was widely admired as a model of Christian reconciliation.

fleur de lis (Fr., lily*) Symbol of the Virgin Mary*.

Fleury Also, Saint-Benoit-sur-Loire*. Site of an ancient French monastery where the relics* of St. Benedict* and St. Scholastica* were transferred in the seventh century from Monte Cassino* after the Lombard invasion of Italy. In 1790 the abbey was suppressed and most of the buildings demolished, but a new abbey was built in 1944.

Fleury, Claude (1640–1723) French church historian. A confessor* to King Louis XV, he wrote a 20-volume *Histoire Ecclesiastique* (1691–1720), one of the first large encyclopedic histories of the church. It was censured for its Gallican views.

floating parish Group of Christians who form their own worship community apart from the local parish*. The group is usually made up of whole families. Liturgical experimentation and spontaniety are prominent features of such groups.

flock Congregation of a church or members of a parish* in relation to the pastor or priest as a shepherd.

Florence City in Italy, the heart of the Renaissance. It was the home of some of the world's greatest Christian artists, including Cimabue*, Giotto*, Aretino, Brunelleschi*, Ghiberti*, Donatello*, Luca and Andrea Della Robbia*, Ghirlandaio*, Lippi*, Andrea del Sarto, Raphael*, Fra Angelico*, and the two universal geniuses, Leonardo de Vinci* and Michelangelo*. It was also the residence of Boccaccio, the birthplace of Dante, and the center of Medici glory. Its great cathedrals include Santa Maria del Fiore, started in 1296 by Arnolfo di Campio, whose original cupola erected by Brunelleschi* is a familiar landmark. The campanile* was started by Giotto in 1334. The baptistry* has bronze gates by Andrea Pisano and Lorenzo Ghiberti*, sculptures by Donatello, murals by Giotto, and a pulpit by Benedetto da Maiano.

Other religious buildings include Capella Pazzi by Brunelleschi; the Santissima Annunizata (1250) with murals by Andrea del Sarto; San Lorenzo, founded in the fourth century and rebuilt in the fifteenth, which contains in the Capella Medici the famous statue of *Day, Night, Morning and Evening* with other sculptures by Michelangelo; the Capella dei Principi, containing the tombs of the grand dukes of Tuscany; and the Church of Or San Michele (1248–1412), with works by Ghiberti*, Donatello, and Verrocchio*. Other churches are Santa Trinita, San Marco*, Santa Maria del Carmine, and San Miniato al Monte.

Florence Cathedral The Santa Maria del Fiore enclosed by Piazza del Duomo and the Piazza San Giovanni built between 1420 and 1434 in Florence, Italy. It is a three-aisled basilica* in the form of a Latin cross about 502 feet long and 295 feet wide. The crossing* is in the form of an octagon. Beyond the crossing, there are three large apses*, each enclosing five chapels. The cathedral

Piazza del Duomo

has a gloomy interior because of the absence of large windows. The most notable feature of the cathedral is the Brunelleschi dome.

Florence, Council of Council that met in Florence from 1438 to 1445 and proposed a union between the Western and Eastern churches and an end to the Great Schism*. The council, numbered sixteenth or seventeenth, was convened at the request of the Greek emperor John VIII Paleologus, to unite all Christian churches against the Turkish infidels*. It met first at Basel, and then later at Ferrara and Florence before moving to Rome* in 1443 to conclude its sessions. The discussion centered around the main points of theological differences, including the Double Procession* of the Holy Spirit*, the use of unleavened bread* in the Eucharist*, the doctrine of purgatory*, and the primacy of the pope. The decree of union beginning with the words, *Laetentur Coeli*, was signed July 5, 1439.

On July 6, in the Cathedral of Florence, a divine service* was held to celebrate the union when the pope celebrated the Mass*. However, the decree unraveled after Constantinople* fell to the Turks and the Greek Church turned it down. Despite its ultimate failure, the council established the principle that has governed twentieth-century ecumenism*: unity of faith with diversity of practices and rites.

Florensky, Pavel (1882–1937) Russian theologian. He took holy orders* in 1911 and thereafter devoted himself to teaching and writing. In 1914 he published his most famous work, *The Pillar and Ground of Truth*. He was imprisoned by the Bolsheviks in 1933 and died in a labor camp.

Florentinus Radewijns (1350–1400) One of the earliest members of the Brethren of the Common Life* and its head after the death of Gerard Groote*. The monastery of Winchester* was founded under his guidance in 1387. He also wrote several devotional works.

Florian, Monastery of St. Monastery south of Linz in upper Austria, on the site of the shrine erected above St. Florian's grave. The shrine was replaced by a monastery in the eighth century. Between 1686 and 1726 a new complex was constructed here by the great Baroque masters, Carlo Carlone and Jakob Prandtauer. The massive church has two domed towers 262 feet high. Its interior is 245 feet long, 46 feet wide, and 82 feet high. The sumptuous rooms, elegant staircases, and ceiling frescoes make St. Florian one of the finest monasteries in Austria.

Florian, St. (fourth century) Austrian martyr* drowned in the Diocletian persecution* for confessing his faith. A monastery named after him stands on the site of his tomb. He is the patron saint* of firefighters. Feast day: May 4.

florilegium (pl., florilegia) Collection or anthology, especially of the Church Fathers*.

Florovsky, Georges (1893–1979) Russian theologian. He taught theology at the Orthodox Theological Institute of St. Sergius in Paris, St. Vladimir's Russian Orthodox Seminary* at Crestwood, New York, Harvard Divinity School, and Princeton University. He wrote extensively on Russian theology, and his study of the Russian religious mind in *The Ways of Russian Theology* (1937) is considered a classic. Florovsky's vision of the church is eschatological, mystical, and catholic*. The church is fuller than the Scriptures, since it embodies Christ's victory and it is his body. God's truth is given to human beings, not in their isolation, but in their unity or sobernost. Orthodoxy is the true manifestation of the living tradition of the universal church. Florovsky is considered the most important Russian theologian in the twentieth century.

Focolare (Ital., the hearth) Lay movement, originally Roman Catholic, but now ecumenical. Officially styled Opera di Maria (Work of Mary), it was founded during World War II by Chiara Lubich in Trent, Italy. It received papal approval in 1962, and its statutes were sanctioned by Pope John Paul II* in 1990. Its membership includes celibates and married people, priests and lay people of all denominations. Its mission is to bring to reality Christ's prayer, "May they all be one," and to this end engages in dialogue with other denominations and secular people. In 1977 Chiara Lubich received the Templeton Prize.

folded chasuble Priestly vestment rolled or pinned up in front for wear by deacons and subdeacons in penitential seasons.

Folk Catholicism Roman Catholic practices that incorporate popular pietistic traditions or pre-Christian religious customs.

folk church Church or denomination limited to a particular nationality or tribe.

folk Mass Mass with participation of the congregation in singing.

follow-through evangelism Mass evangelistic campaigns in which converts who give their heart to Jesus Christ are followed up, taught, and trained in discipleship in affiliated local churches.

font (Lat., *fons,* spring of water) Metal or stone basin for baptismal water. It varies in size from a large basin below ground level for adult baptisms to medium basins slightly raised above ground for child baptisms and cup-shaped receptacles, smaller and higher and richly ornamented, for baptism by affusion*. In some churches, the font stands in a separate chapel or is railed off in a locked enclosure. See also BAPTISTERY.

Fontenoy Former Cistercian monastery in Fontenoy, France, founded in 1118. The building was sold after the French Revolution and converted into a paper factory. It was restored in the early twentieth century. Fontenoy is a cruciform* basilica* without a clerestory*. Its is one of the best preserved monasteries in Burgundy.

Fontevrault A double order of monks and nuns, based on the Benedictine Rule*, living under the direction of an abbess, though in separate convents. It was founded by Blessed Robert d'Arbrissel (d. 1116) at Fontevrault, southeast of Saumur in France. The order had houses in England and France, and was reformed by successive abbesses between 1475 and 1502. It disappeared during the French Revolution, but was restored as an order for women only in 1806.

footpace Also, pedella. Upper step before an altar, on which the celebrant stands while celebrating the Eucharist*.

foot-washing Also, pedilavium*. Rite on Maundy Thursday* during Passion Week*, reenacting Christ's washing of the disciples' feet. Many denominations, such as the Dunkers*, Mennonites*, and Moravians, wash one another's feet as a church ordinance*. During the ceremony, 12 unshod men are led into the sanctuary, where the celebrant washes and dries the feet of each in turn. It begins with a reading of John 13 as the Gospel basis of the rite.

forbidden times Days between the beginning of Advent* and Christmas* and between the beginning of Lent* and Easter* when nuptial Mass* may not be celebrated in the Roman Catholic Church.

Ford, Leighton Frederick Sandys (1931–) American evangelist. He married Jean Coffey Graham, sister of Billy Graham*, in 1953 and two years later joined the Billy Graham Evangelistic Association* (BGEA). In 1986 he left BGEA to become founder and president of Leighton Ford Ministries. He chaired the program committee of Lausanne International Congress for World Evangelization* in 1974, the Lausanne II Congress in Manila in 1989, and the program committees of the International Conference for Itinerant Evangelists in Amsterdam in 1983 and 1986. His books include *Meeting Jesus* (1988).

Foreign Missions Conference of North America Former name of the Division of Foreign Missions of the National Council of Churches of Christ in the USA*. It began officially in 1893 under the leadership of Robert E. Speer and John R. Mott*.

forensic justification Act or process by which sinners are declared righteous in God's sight by his forgiving mercy alone, interpreted as acquittal of the guilty by the judge. It was an essential tenet of the Reformation*.

form criticism (Ger., *Formsgeschichte,* form-history) Textual study of the Scriptures with the purpose of peeling away the accretions of myth and legend and arriving at the original germ of the story or narrative and the facts as they understood them. Form critics are taxonomists who classify the forms that underlie written documents and literary detectives who reconstruct the process by which the writings reached their present shape. The most important pioneers of biblical form criticism were Hermann Gunkel* and Julius Wellhausen, but their application to New Testament studies was the work of K. L. Schmidt, Martin Dibelius, and Rudolf Bultmann*. Form-critics also have tried to find the setting in life (*Sitz im Leben**) of the Gospel accounts in order to reconstruct the original context and purpose of the document. The assumptions under which form criticism developed and the indiscriminate use of the words *myth* and *legend* to suggest historical unreliability of biblical accounts give form criticism a negative cast.

formae Floor graves in a catacomb*.

formal sin Sinful act which the person committing it knows to be wrong. Compare material sin.

formula 1. Doctrinal statement. 2. Prescribed verbal formulation used in a religious ceremony.

Formula Missae et Communionis The Lutheran Communion Service* prepared by Martin Luther* in 1523. It kept Latin as the language of service and altered only slightly the Roman Mass*. But the Mass of the Faithful* was radically revised. The prayers were eliminated from the Offertory, which became merely a preparatory rite, and the Words of Institution* were included in the Preface*, followed by the singing of the Sanctus* and the Benedictus Qui Venit* during which the host* was elevated. The rest of the Canon was omitted altogether. Communion was in both kinds, and accompanied by the singing of Agnus Dei*.

formulary Book of prayers or creedal statements.

Fortescue, Adrian (1874–1923) Roman Catholic scholar and priest, author of *The Orthodox Eastern Church* (1907), *The Lesser Eastern Churches* (1913), *The Uniate Eastern Churches* (1923), *The Mass* (1912), and *The Ceremonies of the Roman Rite* (1918).

Forty Hours Devotion Also, Quarant' Ore. Modern Roman Catholic devotion in which the Blessed Sacrament* is exposed for a period of about 40 hours and the faithful pray before it by turns. The practice originated in Italy in the sixteenth century. The period of 40 hours corresponds to the time Christ's body rested in the tomb.

Forty Martyrs of England and Wales Forty English and Welsh Roman Catholics put to death during the Reformation* in England between 1535 and 1680. They included 13 secular priests, 20 monks, and 7 laypeople. They were canonized in 1970. Their names are: John Almond, Edmund Arrowsmith, Ambrose Barlow, John Boste*, Alexander Briant*, Edmund Campion*, Margaret Clitherow*, Philip Evans, Thomas Garnet, Edmund Gennings, Richard Gwyn, John Houghton, Philip Howard, John Jones*, John Kemble, Luke Kirby, Robert Lawrence, David Lewis, Anne Line, John Lloyd, Cuthbert Mayne*, Henry Morse, Nicholas Owen*, John Payne, Polydore Plasden, John Plessington, Richard Reynolds, John Rigby, John Roberts, Alban Roe, Ralph Sherwin, Robert Southwell*, John Southworth, John Stone, John Wall, Henry Walpole, Margaret Ward, Augustine Webster, Swithun Wells, and Eustace White. Feast day: October 25.

Forty Martyrs of Sebaste Forty Christian soldiers of the Thundering Legion who, according to St. Basil of Caesarea*, refused to worship the Roman emperor while stationed at Sebaste in Armenia in 320 and were punished by being left naked on the ice of a frozen lake. The place of one who recanted was taken by one of the pagan guards who was converted by witnessing the devotion of the remaining 39. The martyrs' ashes were recovered by the Empress Pulcheria*. Feast day: March 9 (Eastern Church*); March 10 (Western Church*).

Forty-Two Articles The first truly Protestant confession of faith drawn up by Thomas Cranmer* for the Church of England*. Drafted in 1553 and promulgated, it followed the Augsburg Confession* in matters of Trinity* and justification* and the Calvinistic tradition on predestination* and the Lord's Supper*. It later formed the basis of the Thirty-Nine Articles* Act of 1563. See also ARTICLES, FORTY-TWO.

forum Judicial power of the church as exercised through ecclesiastical courts* or through ordi-

nances* relating to the spiritual welfare of its members.

Fosdick, Harry Emerson (1878–1969) American liberal minister who served as pastor in Montclair, New Jersey, and Riverside Church in New York City, and as professor of theology at Union Theological Seminary* in New York City. He popularized a personal religion in his problem-centered sermons and books. His sermon, "Shall the Fundamentalists Win?" set off the Modernist-Fundamentalist debate in the 1920s in the United States.

fosh In the Coptic tradition, the prayer of the fraction*, one of the six prayers recited aloud in the liturgy.

Fossa Nova Cistercian monastery on the southern edge of the Volscian Hills of Lazio in central Italy. In 1133 the White Canons took over the monastery founded in the ninth century by the Benedictines*. The monastery is constructed in plain, unostentatious style. The triple-aisled basilica* has a towering central edifice and a portal reached by a flight of steps below an immense rose window*. The heavy pillars and the pointed arches are suggestive of Gothic*, but the overall style is Romanesque. From 1812, the church was used as a stable, but later it was acquired by the Franciscan Order*.

fossors/fossarians (lit., diggers) Also, lecticarii; copiatae. 1. Grave diggers in the early church as a lower clergy. 2. Fifteenth-century hermits who lived in caves.

Foundations English theological symposium published in 1912. It consisted of nine essays by theological liberals, including William Temple*.

fountain Symbol of the Virgin Mary*.

Fountains Abbey Cistercian abbey, southwest of Ripon, England, founded in 1132 as a Cistercian abbey by monks from the Benedictine* abbey of St. Mary's, York*. The following year it became a daughter house of Clairvaux*. It soon became one of the richest Cistercian houses in England and established 12 daughter houses by 1150. One of its most prominent features was the Chapel of the Nine Altars. The abbey is now in ruins.

Fountains Abbey

Fouquet, Jean (c. 1415–1485) French artist noted for his illumination* of the Book of Hours and other religious works.

Four Articles of Prague Reform platform of the moderate party of the Hussites*, known as the Utraquists, drafted in 1420. The four articles affirm the freedom of priests to preach, receiving Communion in both kinds*, public punishment for serious offenses, and renunciation by clerics of property and civil office.

Four Crowned Martyrs (Lat., *Quattro Coronati*) Group of four saints* to whom a famous ancient basilica* on the Celian Hill at Rome* is dedicated. They are the patrons of stonecutters. Feast day: November 8.

four horsemen of the Apocalypse In the Revelation of St. John* the Divine, four agents of destruction, two being agents of war and two of famine and pestilence. The first appeared on a white horse, the second on a red horse, the third on a black horse, and the fourth on a pale horse.

four last things Death, judgment, heaven*, and hell*.

Four Spiritual Laws Tool of evangelism formulated by Bill Bright, founder of Campus Crusade for Christ.* They are printed in a tract entitled, "Have You Heard of the Four Spiritual Laws?" The four spiritual laws are: 1. God loves people and has a plan for each person's life. 2. Because people are sinful and separated from God, they are incapable of knowing God's love and plan. 3. Only through Christ can people experience God's love and plan for life. 4. Each individual must accept Jesus Christ as Lord and Savior in order to receive salvation* and God's love.

Fourier, St. Peter (1565–1640) French-born co-founder of the Augustinian Canonesses of Our Lady, an order devoted to the education of poor children. Feast day: December 9.

Foursquare Gospel 1. Part of name of Elim*, Pentecostal, Protestant, Evangelical, and Fundamentalist denomination founded by George Jeffreys* in 1915 in England. 2. Pentecostal denomination founded by Aimee Semple McPherson* in 1922 in the United States. The four squares represented Christ as Savior, Christ as healer, the baptism of the Holy Spirit* with speaking in tongues* as initial evidence*, and the Second Coming*.

fourteen holy helpers Also, auxiliary saints*. Saints designated as providing succor to those in need. They are: George*, Blaise* (sore throats), Erasmus*, Pantaleon*, Vitus*, Christopher*, Denis, Cyriacus, Acacius, Eustace, Giles*, Margaret (troubles in childbirth), Barbara* (death by lightning), and Catherine of Alexandria*. Sometimes Sebastian* is substituted for any one of them.

Fox, George (1624–1691) English founder of the Quakers* or Society of Friends*. Without any formal education, he traveled in search of religious certainty and found enlightenment in 1646 in the Inner Light* of the living Christ. He rejected church attendance, clergy and rituals, embraced pacifism, and took the Holy Spirit* as the only authority and guide for a Christian. He began preaching in 1647 that the truth is found only in God speaking directly to the "inner condition," calling his followers "Friends of Truth," shortened later as "Friends." In 1650 he admonished the judge who sentenced him for blasphemy* to "tremble at the Word of the Lord," and hence gained the monicker "Quaker." He spent six years in different prisons. In 1652 he established the headquarters of his new group in Ulverston. His last years were spent fighting for social justice and against militarism. To promote his sect he traveled extensively to the West Indies, North America, the Netherlands, and Germany. His autobiographical *Journal* was published in 1694.

Foxe, John (1516–1587) English martyrologist. During the reign of Queen Mary he fled to the Continent, where he met a number of other Protestant refugees. In Strasbourg* he published the book that he is famous for: *Acts and Monuments of Matters Happening in the Church,* commonly known as *Foxe's Book of Martyrs.* It was one of the most popular books of his time and went through many editions.

fr. Father.

Fra Angelico (1400–1455) Birth name: Giovanni da Fiesole. Italian religious painter. He entered the Dominican Order and painted his first major work, a series of 50 frescoes, in the Convent of San Marco*. He also painted numerous altarpieces for San Marco* and other convents. From 1445 to 1447 he was commissioned by Pope Eugenius IV* to decorate a chapel in the Vatican*. His last work was the fresco cycle, *The Last Judgment,* at Orvieto Cathedral* in 1447.

fraction Term used in some traditions for the formal breaking of the bread before distribution in

George Fox

Holy Communion*. The act of breaking the bread is referred to as a synonym for the Eucharist*. The practice varies among the various rites. In the Roman Rite*, it comes immediately after the kiss of peace* when the celebrant breaks a small portion from the host* and places it in the chalice* and, during the Agnus Dei*, he divides the host into a number of small portions for distribution to the communicants. In the Byzantine Rite*, the host is divided into four portions which are arranged on the paten* in the form of a cross, and one of them is put into the chalice*. In the Mozarabic Rite*, the host is divided into nine portions, seven of which are arranged in the form of a cross. In the Anglican tradition, the bread is broken immediately before it is consecrated. At the time of the fraction, the koinonikon* is sung in the Eastern Orthodox* Liturgy, the Confractorium in the Ambrosian Rite*, and Agnus Dei* in the Roman Rite*.

fragment Piece from a large piece of bread or wafer used in the Eucharist*.

Frances of Rome, St. (1384–1440) Italian religious. Married in 1397 to Lorenzo de' Ponziani, she founded, while still married, the Oblates of St. Benedict of Tor de'Specchi in 1425 and, after her husband's death, became its superior*. Members of the society were dedicated to good works*, but did not take vows or give up property or live in community. Her visions were recorded by Giovanni Mattiotti, her biographer. She is the patron saint* of motorists. Feast day: March 9.

Franceschini, Baldassare (1611–1689) Italian religious painter of the Florentine school.

Francescon, Luigi (1866–1964) Pentecostal evangelist and founder of the Congregacione Christi in Brazil. He was converted in 1892 and received the baptism of the Holy Spirit* in 1907. In the same year he established the Italian Pentecostal Church in Chicago, followed later by similar churches in New York, Los Angeles, St. Louis, and Philadelphia*. In 1910 he traveled to Argentina and Brazil, where he established the Congregacione Christi. Today it is one of the largest denominations in Brazil with over 2,500 congregations.

Francia (c. 1450–1517) Birth name: Francesco Raibolini. Italian painter, engraver, and goldsmith of the early Bolognese school. In 1508 he came under the influence of Raphael*. Among his paintings are a number on the Virgin Mary*, especially the *Madonna del Terremoto* and *The Judgment of Paris*. Of his frescoes only a few survive, including one on the life of St. Cecilia*.

Franciabigio (c. 1480–c. 1525) Birth name: Francesco de Cristofano Bigi. Italian painter, imitator of Andrea del Sarto, with whom he worked on many commissions. Some of his portraits are in the Uffizi Gallery in Florence*. Among his paintings are *The Marriage of the Virgin* and *The Bath of Bathsheba*.

Francis Borgia, St. (1510–1572) Spanish Jesuit general*. A grandson of Pope Alexander VI*, he entered the Jesuit Order after the death of his wife in 1546. He became an associate of Ignatius* of Loyola, and was sent on the latter's behalf on many diplomatic missions and also given oversight of Jesuit work in the Spanish overseas empire. In 1565 he became the third general of the Jesuits*. He used the society's wealth to build colleges and improve education. He was canonized in 1671. Feast day: October 10.

Francis of Assisi, St. (1181/2–1226) Founder of the Franciscan Order*. In 1204, following a vision, he went on a pilgrimage* to Rome*, where he found himself moved by the plight of the beggars. Returning to his native Assisi*, he sold all his possessions and devoted himself to repairing churches. As a result his friends abandoned him and his father disowned him. One day in 1208 while attending Mass* in the Church of the Portiuncula he heard a call* from the Lord to leave all and follow him (Matt. 10:7–10). He took the call literally, discarded his shoes, put on a dark garment with a cord as girdle*, and gathered 12 men around him. Francis drew up a simple rule for them, the Regula Primitiva, and secured the approval of the pope for his new order of monks called Friars Minor*.

In 1212, with the assistance of St. Clare*, he founded a second order for women, the Poor Clares*. The order grew so fast that by 1217 Francis divided it into provinces. To correct abuses of his rule by the friars, Francis codified his earlier rules into the Regula Prima which received papal approval in 1213. He resigned as minister general* of the Order and handed over the day-to-day administration to others without relinquishing his leadership. At this time, a third order was added to the movement. In 1223 the first Christmas creche* was made at his instance. During this period, he composed his famous "Canticle to the Sun," *Admonitions,* and *Testament.* Two years before his death, he received the stigmata* at Mount La Verna in the Apennines. He was canonized in 1228, and in 1230 his body was moved to the magnificent basilica* in Assisi. Feast day: October 4.

Francis of Paola, St. (1416–1507) Founder of the Order of Minims*. In 1431 he began an ascetic life as hermit, first in a cave and later in a forest. A group of hermits gathered around him, and he became their spiritual guide in 1435, the date of the founding of the order. His reputation for holiness spread throughout Italy and France, many miracles were attributed to him, and kings and emperors sought his counsel and blessings. He was canonized in 1519 and declared patron of Italian seafarers in 1943. Feast day: April 2.

Francis of Sales, St. (1567–1622) A leader of the Counter-Reformation*. Ordained priest in 1593, he made it his mission to convert Calvinists, but always engaged in controversies in a conciliatory spirit. In 1610 he cofounded the Visitation Order*

St. Francis of Assisi

in Annency with St. Jane Frances de Chantal*. In 1602 he was named bishop of Geneva* and achieved considerable success in bringing many Genevans back into the Catholic fold. He was also a devotional writer whose *Introduction to the Devout Life** (1609) and *Treatise on the Love of God* (1616) had deep influence on later spiritual writers. He was beatified in 1661, canonized four years later, and declared a doctor of the church* in 1877 and the patron saint* of Catholic journalists in 1923. Feast day: January 24.

Francis, Prayer of St. Popular prayer said to have been composed by St. Francis of Assisi. It runs as follows:

Lord, make me an instrument of your peace.
Where there is hatred, let me sow love.
Where there is injury, pardon.
Where there is doubt, faith.
Where there is despair, hope.
Where there is darkness, light.
Where there is sadness, joy.
O Divine Master, grant that I may seek
not so much to be consoled as to console,
to be understood as to understand,
to be loved as to love;
for it is in giving that we receive,
it is in pardoning that we are pardoned,
and it is in dying that we are born to eternal life.

                                          AMEN

St. Francis de Sales

Francis, Samuel Trevor (1834–1925) English hymn writer. Converted as a teen, Francis spent 73 years in the service of the Lord, traveling widely. He is best known for the hymn, "O the Deep, Deep Love of Jesus."

Francis Xavier, St. (1506–1552) Jesuit missionary to Asia, named apostle of the Indies. At the University of Paris, he met Ignatius Loyola*, with whom he and six others founded the Society of Jesus* in 1534. He was ordained in 1537 and two years later was sent to evangelize* the heathen in Asia. He arrived in Goa, a Portuguese possession, in 1542 and spent three years preaching and ministering to the natives. From Goa, he went on to the native state of Travancore, Sri Lanka, and the Malacca and Moluccas Islands in the East Indies and to Japan, where he arrived in 1549. He studied Japanese and within two years established a flourishing Christian community of 2,000, but was driven out by Buddhist monks. He returned to Goa briefly before leaving for China, where he was denied entry. He died on his return voyage at Sancian. His body was brought back to Goa, where his body is reputed to remain in an incorruptible state. More than 700,000 conversions have been attributed to him. He was canonized in 1622 and named patron saint* of Foreign Missions. Feast day: December 3.

Franciscan Order Order of Friars Minor* or Grey Friars, the largest religious order in the Roman

St. Francis Xavier

Catholic Church, founded by St. Francis of Assisi in 1209. It has three great divisions: Friars Minor or Observants; Friars Minor Capuchin or Capuchins*; and Friars Minor Conventuals or Conventuals*. There is also a second women's order, the Poor Clares*, founded by St. Clare* with St. Francis, and a third order, the Tertiaries, divided into regular and secular tertiaries. Franciscans follow the Rule of St. Francis, the original of which is now lost. Pope Innocent III* gave the rule his oral approval in 1209. It was recast in 1221 and confirmed by a bull* in 1223.

The rule is unique in that it stipulates complete corporate poverty, not merely for the individual friars. The friars are to live by working with their hands or by begging, and are forbidden to own property or to accept any funds. The practical difficulties of maintaining this vow led to conflict between the Zelanti, or the Spirituals, who interpreted the rule literally and others who were in favor of relaxing it. When Pope John XXII* decided in favor of the latter in 1317–1318, many of the Spirituals became schismatics under the name of Fraticelli*. After a general decline of the order in the fourteenth century, the Spirituals, now called the Observants*, gained recognition in 1415 at the Council of Constance*. In 1453 Pope Eugenius IV* gave them a separate vicar general*, and in 1517 they were separated from the Conventuals and declared the true order of St. Francis.

Early in the fifteenth century, another reform initiated by Matteo di Bassi (1495–1552) led to the establishment of the Capuchins, whose rule was drawn up in 1529. During the seventeenth and eighteenth centuries, new reform movements led to the creation of the Reformati, the Recollects, and the Discalced*, each of whom had their own rules, yet lived under the same general. The order survived the turbulent era of the French Revolution, the Napoleonic Wars, and revolutions in Spain, Poland, and Italy although in a much debilitated form, but regained new vigor at the end of the nineteenth century through a reunification of the different branches.

The order has given the church a number of saints* and scholars, including St. Anthony of Padua*, St. Bonaventura*, Alexander of Hales*, Roger Bacon*, Duns Scotus*, and William of Ockham*. Five of their members became popes: Nicholas IV, Sixtus IV*, Julius II*, Sixtus V, and

Clement XIV*. They have initiated a number of devotions, such as the Stations of the Cross*, the Angelus*, and the Crib. Many Protestant groups have been inspired by Franciscan ideals to form monastic communities in England and elsewhere.

Franck, Cesar (1822–1890) Belgian composer and church musician. Among his sacred choral works are *Solemn Mass* (1858), and a *Mass in Three Voices* (1860).

Franck, Sebastian (1499–1542) German religious writer, historian, and radical reformer. He is noted for his *Cronica, Zeitbuch und Geschichtesbibel* (1531), and *Paradoxa* (1534). He rejected creeds and sacraments* of the institutional church but professed belief in the divinity of Christ.

Francke, Auguste Hermann (1663–1727) German Lutheran preacher, professor, and Pietist. Converted in 1687, he was deeply influenced by Spener*. He was professor of Greek and Oriental languages at the newly founded University of Halle from 1691 to 1698 and professor of theology from 1698 to his death. In 1695 he organized his Institutes for the education of children, followed by a paedagogium, orphanage, publishing house, and dispensary. His Pietism* was distinguished by a strict ethical code as well as an emphasis on an inner religious struggle (Busskampf).

Auguste Francke

Francke, Meister (fifteenth century) German painter, known for his *Christ as a Man of Sorrows, Crucifixion*, and other religious paintings.

Frankfurt, Councils of The 16 imperial councils during the Carolingian epoch. Of these, the most important was the one called by Charlemagne* in
794 to condemn the Adoptionist heresy.

Frankfurt Declaration The Frankfurt Declaration on
the Fundamental Crisis of Christian Mission
(1970) issued by the German Evangelical
churches, reaffirming the New Testament principles of mission. It is modeled on the Barmen Declaration* and has seven affirmations: 1. The sole
authority of the Bible. 2. The primacy of the doxology* over against humanization. 3. Biblical
Christology* over against abstract Christ-pres-
ence in history. 4. Personal salvation* over against
Universalism*. 5. Emphasis on the spirit of the
church over against its functions. 6. The uniqueness of the gospel over against other religions. 7.
The Second Coming* instead of an ideology of
progress.

Franson, Frederik (1852–1908) Founder of The
Evangelical Alliance Mission (TEAM). Born in
Sweden, he emigrated to the United States in 1869
and was converted in 1872. His largely itinerant
ministry produced spiritual awakening* in many
countries.

frater 1. Refectory*, common room, or chapter
house* in a monastery. 2. Brother* or friar*.

fraternal worker In contemporary usage, an inof-
fensive term for a foreign missionary or evangelist.

fraternity In the Roman Catholic Church, association of the faithful for the purpose of providing
mutual support through masses, prayers, alms,
and intercessions in sickness. They also provide
financial and material assistance during emergencies, such as death, sickness, and natural disasters,
and promote fellowship through social gatherings and corporate meals. They sometimes provide a forum for the resolution of disputes.

Fraticelli (lit., little Athos*) Medieval branch of
the Franciscan Order* that left the main body be-

cause they upheld the strict interpretation of the
Rule of St. Francis as demanding poverty from
the members and the corporate order.

Frauenchiemsee Monastery founded in the tiny, remote island of Frauenchiemsee in Germany in
770. It was destroyed in 907 during the Hungarian
raids but was rebuilt in the eleventh and twelfth
centuries. A prominent feature of the building is
the free-standing octagonal tower.

Freckenhorst Monastery in Westphalia, Germany,
founded in 860 by a noble lady called Geva and
her husband Everwood. Its church was consecrated in 1129.

Free churches Generally, churches not formally related to a state or nation, especially Protestant
churches in England and elsewhere outside the
established church*. They were once called dissenters and nonconformists. The most notable of
these free churches are the Methodists*, Baptists*,
Congregationalists*, and Presbyterians*, now
largely represented by the United Reformed
Church*.

Free Methodists Group that left the American
Methodist Episcopal Church in 1860 under the
leadership of Benjamin Roberts. It is a conservative body upholding classic Wesleyanism,
including the deity of Christ and entire sanctification*.

free will The ability to choose between good and
evil without reference to the grace* of God or any
external constraint or imposed necessity. Normally, the issue pertains to the question of free
will after the Fall. The apparent conflict between
the exercise of free will and the sovereign
omnipotence of God is the subject of endless theological debates, between Augustinianism* and
Pelagianism* in the early church and between
Calvinism* and Arminianism* in the latter-day
church. Augustinianism held that after the
Fall the will is inherently enslaved and corrupted
by original sin*. Calvinism held that God has a
predetermined plan for each human being.
In matters of salvation* Calvinism emphasizes
the weakness of the will and the power of sin.
Both taught the liberating power of grace.

Free Will Baptists Two groups that arose in the eighteenth century that rejected the Calvinist doctrine of predestination*. One group began in the 1720s in North Carolina under the leadership of Paul Palmer. The second began in New England under the leadership of Benjamin Randall in 1780. In 1935 both groups joined to form the National Association of Free Will Baptists.

free worship In Pentecostal churches, unstructured, unscripted, and uncoordinated praise and worship by the congregation, each member offering individual praise aloud.

freedom Also, liberty. In Christian theology, liberation from the bondage of sin. Freedom is not a natural state of human beings but is gained through faith* in Jesus Christ and the right relationship with him. Freedom is distinguished from its antithesis: slavery or bondage.

Freer Logion An addition to the words of Jesus in Mark 16:14, appearing in a sixth-century Greek codex*, now in Washington's Freer Museum. It begins with the words, "The limit of the years of the power of Satan is fulfilled."

freewill offering Voluntary offering in Christian churches for some special mission or benevolence, in addition to regular offerings.

Freiburg Cathedral in Freiburg, Germany, with an incomparable tower built between 1200 and 1350. Work on a Romanesque choir began in 1354 and took 200 years to complete. The richly sculpted doorway in the west front opens on to the market square. The high altar with its Coronation of Mary is a masterpiece by Hans Baldung.

Freising Cathedral in Freising, Germany, dedicated to Corbinian, the apostle of Bavaria. After a fire destroyed the original church, construction began on a new three-aisled Romanesque basilica* in 1159. In 1803 the church was secularized.

Frelinghuysen, Theodorus J. (1691–1748) Dutch Reformed minister in Raritan, New Jersey, who was part of the Great Awakening*. He organized the first coetus*, or assembly, of Dutch Calvinist churches in America.

fresco (Lat., fresh) Painting made on fresh plaster.

Frescobaldi, Girolamo (1583–1643) Italian keyboard composer of the early Baroque period. In 1608 he became organist at St. Peter's Cathedral* in Rome*, where he remained for the rest of his life except for six years as a court organist in Florence*. Beside 30 motets* and two masses, all his works were for the keyboard. In 1635 he published *Fiori Musicale*, a collection of his keyboard pieces.

Frey, Joseph Samuel Cristian Frederick (1771–1850) Father of modern Jewish missions. Born in a German rabbinical family, he was converted in 1798 and left for London to train with the London Missionary Society (LMS*) for work in Africa. However, he discovered the plight of the Jews in London's East End and began a mission to them in 1815. When the LMS declined to be involved, he founded the first modern mission to the Jews, the London Jews' Society, now the Church's Ministry among Jews (1962).

friar (Lat., *frater*, brother) Monk in a mendicant order*, such as Augustinians, Carmelites*, Dominicans*, and Franciscans. In England friars are distinguished by the colors of their mantles, the major ones being grey for Franciscans, black for Dominicans, white for Carmelites, and red for Trinity*.

Friars Minor Largest branch of the Franciscan Order*, sometimes called Observants* or Minorites*.

Friars Minor Capuchins See CAPUCHINS.

Friars Minor Conventual Branch of the Franciscan Order* that follows relaxed rules and wear a black tunic and hood.

Friars Preachers See DOMINICANS.

friary Brotherhood of friars or monastery.

Friday Traditionally, day of fasting or abstinence from meat or of acts of penitence and charity, in commemoration of the Crucifixion.

Friends of God Fourteenth-century European mystics led by John Tauler* and Heinrich Suso*. The group was led by Dominicans* but included members of the Franciscan Order* and lay people who lived either alone or in groups. Influenced by Meister Eckhart*, they had links with the Brethren of the Common Life* and cultivated austerity, prayer, and self-renunciation. They were fully orthodox in theology and considered themselves part of the church. Members were concentrated in Bavaria, the Rhineland, Switzerland, and the Low Countries with Basel, Strasbourg*, and Cologne* as their chief centers.

Friends of Light Alternate name of nineteenth-century German Free congregations.

Friends, Religious Society of Also, Quakers*. Originally, Children of the Light*; Friends of the Truth; Friends in the Truth; Friends. Sect founded by George Fox* in England about 1668, emphasizing reliance on Inner Light* or leading as the sole authority in spiritual matters. Friends' worship service is simple and unstructured and includes periods of silence and meditation. In life, they emphasize "plainness of speech, behavior and apparel." During the eighteenth century Quakerism was influenced by Quietism* and in the nineteenth century by Evangelicalism*. They have no elaborate hierarchy*, and the church government is in the hands of the Monthly Meeting, supplemented by Quarterly Meetings and Yearly Meetings.

Quaker theology is set out in Robert Barclay's* *Apology for the True Christian Faith* (1668). The Bible is regarded as secondary to the Inner Light and the direct experience of God's guiding, saving, and empowering spirit. They have no liturgy or creeds and no sacraments*. There is no ordained ministry, although elders are responsible for the nurturing of souls and are overseers for pastoral care, and some officers are named to perform specific tasks for limited periods. Men and women have equal responsibility in worship services. In some parts of the world, spontaneous worship is being replaced by structured worship led by pastors. The society maintains a *Book of Discipline** as a record of the activities of the members.

Quakers are noted for their pacifism, which has often brought them into conflict with civil authorities. They oppose the taking of oaths.

They are also known for their commitment to social progress, penal reform, promotion of peace and justice, and international relief. They have made significant contributions to penal reform and abolition of slavery and were responsible for opening the first asylum in England in 1796. In 1947 the Friends Service Council in Great Britain and Ireland and the American Friends Service Committee* received the Nobel Peace Prize. Notable Quakers in history have included William Penn*, who established the Commonwealth of Pennsylvania, John Woolman, Elizabeth Fry*, John Greenleaf Whittier*, Rufus Jones*, and Richard Nixon. See also FOX, GEORGE.

Frith, John (c. 1503–1533) Protestant martyr and English associate of William Tyndale* who was burned at the stake at Smithfield, London, for denying purgatory* and transubstantiation*.

Froben, Johann (c. 1460–1527) Printer and scholar. He started a press in Basel in 1491 and soon became renowned throughout Europe for his technical and scholarly excellence. He published his friend Erasmus's* Greek New Testament and also editions of Church Fathers*, such as Jerome*, Cyprian*, and Hilary of Poitiers*.

frontal Panel of embroidered cloth, usually in the color of the season, hanging in front of the altar.

frontier religion Christianity as practiced by the pioneers in the Wild West United States in the nineteenth century. It was highly individualistic, emo-

Frontier Religion

tive, and democratic and was bred in camp meetings* and revivals eminently suited to the rough character of frontier inhabitants. Baptists* and Methodists* were the most effective denominations in winning frontiersmen to the Christian faith. Many Baptist ministers were often working-class people who turned preachers on Sundays, and Methodist ministers were circuit riders* who brought a message of free will* and free grace*.

frontlet Narrow band, usually in the liturgical color of the season, extending across the top front of an altar.

Frumentius, St. (c. 300–c. 380) "Apostle of the Abyssinians." According to Rufinus*, Frumentius was a Phoenician who was captured by pirates along with friends on a voyage to India. He was then taken to the court of the Abyssinian king, who treated him well and made him a part of his government. He used his position to evangelize* the country, bringing the new church under the jurisdiction of Athanasius*, the patriarch* of Alexandria*, who consecrated him bishop of Axum*. Feast day: October 27.

Fry, Elizabeth (1780–1845) English Quaker* and pioneer of penal reform. Through her efforts, men and women inmates were separated, women warders were appointed for women, religious and secular education was offered in prisons, and employment opportunities were made available to them. She also established soup kitchens for the poor, night shelters for women, and worked to improve conditions in hospitals and asylums.

fuga mundi (Lat., flight from the world) Separation from the world and its evil, as a monastic ideal.

Fulda Benedictine abbey founded in Hesse Nassau in 744 by St. Sturmius, a disciple of St. Boniface*. Under Rabanus Maurus*, abbot from 822–842, it became one of the most important centers of Christian learning with a fine library. The abbey church was designed by Johannes Dientzenhofer. The twin towers of the cathedral extended by a chapel at either side are impressive for their classic and monumental facade.

Fulgentius of Ruspe, St. (468–532) Bishop of Ruspe (Byzacena) in North Africa from 507. His anti-Arian and anti-Pelagian writings mark him as a strong defender of orthodoxy* and Augustinianism*. Feast day: January 1.

Fulke, William (1538–1589) English Reformation* scholar and controversialist. His *Defence* (1583) of English Bible translations is the best-known of his many writings, which covered also some radical positions and apocalyptic themes.

Full Gospel Business Men's Fellowship International International Charismatic organization of lay people, founded by Demos Shakarian in 1951. Many Pentecostal preachers, including Oral Roberts*, Tommy Hicks*, Jack Coe*, and Gordon Lindsay*, were associated with this group in its early stages. By 1990 it had over 3,000 local chapters, spread over 90 countries.

Fuller, Andrew (1754–1815) English Baptist minister, considered by some the greatest original theologian in the eighteenth century. He developed an evangelistic, milder form of Calvinism* that had great influence on William Carey*. His book, *The Gospel Worthy of All Acceptation* (1785), was well received.

Fuller, Charles E. (1887–1969) American Baptist radio preacher. Influenced by Paul Rader* and R. A. Torrey*, he became a pastor in Calvary Church, Placentia, California, in 1925. He was one of the earliest radio preachers. His "Old Fashioned Revival Hour*" was broadcast nationwide

Charles E. Fuller

over the Mutual Broadcasting System and later CBS, beginning 1937. At its peak in the 1940s it was aired over 625 stations. He was cofounder of Fuller Theological Seminary in 1947.

Fuller Theological Seminary Largest nondenominational seminary in the United States, founded in 1947 by Charles E. Fuller* and Boston pastor Harold John Ockenga*. It began as a school that furthered the post-war Evangelical renaissance, and the neo-Evangelical movement. During the next couple of decades, the faculty included many distinguished scholars, such as Carl H. Henry*, Wilbur Smith*, Harold Lindsell, Everett Harrison, George E. Ladd, Edward J. Carnell*, Paul K. Jewett, Geoffrey W. Bromiley, and Ralph P. Martin. Theologically, the school was identified with the New Evangelicalism*, but its theological stance was clouded by internal conflicts over inerrancy* and eschatology*. However, under David Hubbard's leadership, Fuller became the leading seminary for Evangelicals and Pentecostals. More recently, it has appeared to move toward a broader orthodoxy. It includes a School of World Mission closely associated with the Church Growth movement*.

fundamental theology Branch of theology* dealing with four fundamental issues: 1. The divine revelation of God, its direct and indirect aspects, its operation in the Apostolic Age* and in the present age. 2. The religious dimension in human experience that makes human beings potential hearers of the word and believers. 3. The relation between faith* and reason, the relation between faith and signs, wonders and miracles, and the relation between theology and other disciplines and ideologies. 4. Communication of divine truths through Scriptures, canons, creeds, doctrines, and dogmas. Fundamental theologians are more concerned with the *a priori* religious experience than the *a posteriori* Christian revelation*.

Fundamentalism Conservative theological movement in Protestantism* that developed in opposition to modernism*. It was a byproduct of the revivalism* of the nineteenth century and a backlash against liberal Christianity. It sought to preserve the five central affirmations on which

Christianity is founded: virgin birth*, deity of Christ, substitutionary atonement*, second coming*, and the authority and inerrancy* of the Bible. Fundamentalism initially sought to create a firewall against the encroachments of secular anti-Christian movements, embodied in evolution, biblical criticism*, and the social gospel* of the liberal establishment. In seminaries, many teachers skirted close to heresy as they tried to redefine Christian faith and make it relevant to society.

One of the first shots in this battle was the publication, beginning in 1910, of *The Fundamentals,* a series of books dedicated to the cardinal tenets of the Christian faith. The terms *fundamentalism* and *fundamentalist* were coined by Curtis Lee Laws, the moderate editor of the *Watchman-Examiner.* During a conference in Buffalo in 1920, Laws and his associates formed the group, the Fundamentalist Fellowship. Later, in the 1960s, the Fundamentalists emerged as opponents of the teaching of evolution and abortion, and advocates of prayer in school, and still later, by the 1970s, they began to pursue a political agenda under Jerry Falwell*, founder of the Moral Majority, and Pat Robertson*, founder of the Christian Broadcasting Network*. Their secular enemies from the outside and liberal Christian opponents from the inside joined to brand Fundamentalists as narrow-minded, right-wing bigots.

In the 1990s, Fundamentalists joined battle with the liberals in the culture wars, trying to secure society from a host of social evils and stem the tide of moral decline. Fundamentalism is also opposed to Pentecostalism* and the working of miracles and healing which they, following the dispensationalist tenets, believe are limited to the Apostolic Age*. Despite the accretion of social and political issues, the original concerns based on the five basic doctrines remain the core of Fundamentalism. Many denominations are split into liberals and conservatives, and seminaries are identified as belonging to one or the other of these wings. There is some connection between Fundamentalism and Millenarianism*. Most conservative Evangelicals have distanced themselves from the label of Fundamentalism, especially in its recent usage which embraces militant reactionary movements in other religions, such as Islam and Judaism.

Fundamentals, The Series of 12 books published from 1910 to 1915 outlining the basic doctrines undegirding the Christian faith: virgin birth*, physical resurrection of Jesus Christ, his imminent physical return, substitutionary atonement*, and the infallibilty of the Scriptures. Of the 90 articles in the series, about one-third defend biblical inerrancy*, another third presents basic doctrines or general apologetic works, and the last third presents personal testimonies, practical applications of Christian teachings, as well as attacks on various "isms." It was sponsored by a wealthy oilman, Lyman Stewart, and his brother Milton. Among the contributors were well-known Fundamentalists and scholarly conservatives, such as B. B. Warfield* and James Orr* of Scotland.

Fux, Johann Joseph (1660–1741) Musical composer, considered the greatest German exponent of church music in the eighteenth century. He is remembered for his *Gradus ad Paranassum*.

Gg

Gabarain, Cesareo (1936–1991) Spanish priest and composer whose hymns are widely used in the Hispanic church. Among them are *Camina, Pueblo de Dios* (Walk on O People of God), *Tu Has Venido a la Orilla* (Lord, You Have Come to the Lakeshore [1979]), and *Una Espiga* (Sheaves of Summer).

gabbari sannai In the Ethiopian church, an officiating priest or deacon.

Gabriel, Charles Hutchinson (1856–1923) American gospel song writer. He wrote both text and music for more than 7,000 gospel songs, including "Pentecostal Power" (1913) and "Send the Light" (1890).

Gabrieli, Giovanni (1557–1611) Italian Baroque composer and pioneer in the concertato style based at St. Mark's Cathedral in Venice*. He cultivated the Renaissance polychoral* style and specialized in motets* for two or three choirs. He composed nearly 100 motets, a number of Mass* sections, some organ pieces, and many works for instrumental ensembles. His major vocal works were published in 1597 under the title *Sacred Symphonies*. His brother **Andrea** (c. 1510–1586) was a prolific composer who contributed to all genres. Lively rhythms and melodies are characteristic of his work as in *Sacrae Cantiones* (1565) and *Ave Regina Coelorum** (1587).

Gaebelein, Arno Clemens (1861–1945) American Fundamentalist leader. He had a lifelong interest in Israel and the conversion of Jews. He wrote more than 40 books on dispensationalism* and prophecy*. His son, **Frank Ely** (1899–1983), was editor of *Christianity Today** and *Expositor's Bible Dictionary*.

Gairdner, William Henry Temple (1873–1928) Anglican missionary and scholar who tried to evangelize* Arabs. He went with the Church Missionary Society* to Cairo in 1898, became fluent in Arabic, and wrote a number of hymns, plays, poems, and other Bible-based works in Arabic. He collected some 300 Middle Eastern tunes for use in worship. Among his books is *The Reproach of Islam* (1909).

Gaither, William J. and Gloria (1936– and 1942–, respectively) American composers who lead the touring group, the Gaither Trio. Among their songs are many that have become standard fare in Evangelical meetings, such as "There's Something About That Name" (1970) and "Because He Lives" (1971).

Galatia Region and Roman province in Asia Minor, named after Gauls, a Celtic tribe. In St. Paul's* time, it included Phrygia as well as Cappadocia*.

Galgani, St. Gemma (1878–1903) Italian stigmatic. She experienced frequent ecstasies and received stigmata* and marks of scourging between 1899 and 1901. She was beatified in 1933 and canonized in 1940. Feast day: April 11.

galilaeon In the Coptic tradition, the oil of the catechumens*.

Galilean Geographical appellation of Jesus Christ.

galilee Chapel or porch at the west end of some medieval churches where penitents* waited before admission to the church and where the clergy transacted business with women.

Galilee 1. Roman province of Palestine* in the time of Jesus. Located between the Mediterranean Sea and the Jordan River, it was the northernmost of the three provinces of Palestine. Galilee was the boyhood home of Jesus, and all his disciples, with the exception of Judas, were Galileans. Most of the events of his ministry are set against the backdrop of Galilee. 2.**Sea of Galilee.** Also, Sea of Chinnereth; Lake of Gennesaret; Sea of Tiberias. Freshwater lake fed by the Jordan River. A major fishing industry flourished here in the time of Jesus. Major cities around the lake included Bethsaida, Tiberias, and Capernaum.

Gall, St. (c. 550–c. 640) Irish missionary. One of the followers of Columbanus* who lived in Swabia, now Switzerland. The famous monastery of St. Gallen* was founded in about 719 on the site of his hermitage.

Gallia Christiana Multi-volume documentary account of the French church first published by Claude Robert in 1626 and continued later by Benedictine scholars.

Gallican Articles Four demands made at the instigation of Louis XIV by French Catholic clergy in 1682 for more internal freedom. The first article states that the French king was not subject in temporal matters to the authority of the pope. The second stated that in the exercise of his spiritual authority, the pope was subject to the councils as decreed by the Council of Constance*. The next limited papal authority to canons of the church and the constitutions of the kingdom. The last denied the pope's infallibility*. The articles were denounced by the Intermultiplices of Alexander VIII* in 1690 and by the First Vatican Council* of 1870.

Gallican Confession French Protestant statement of faith with 40 articles drafted by John Calvin*, and adopted by the Synod of Paris in 1559. It is still the confession of the French Reformed Church.

Gallican Psalter One of the three Latin versions of the Psalter made by Jerome*. It was taken to Gaul by Gregory of Tours* and later reached England.

Gallican Rite Rite practiced in Merovingian Gaul. It differed in certain respects from the Roman Rite* which ultimately replaced it. In the baptismal service, the confession of faith preceded immersion* or affusion*, and washing of the feet was part of the ceremony. In the Mass*, the trisagion* was sung in Greek and Latin before kyrie* and the trecanum*, a trinitarian hymn, was sung during the actual Communion.

Gallicanism Nationalist French movement for more internal autonomy and less control by the pope. It recognized the universal spiritual authority of the pope, but with qualifications. Its manifesto was Pierre Pithou's *Les Libertes de l'Eglise Gallicane* which called for a self-governing national Catholic church under the temporal authority of the king.

Gallitzen, Demetrius Augustin (1770–1840) Popularly known as Father Smith, "apostle of the Alleghenies." Russian Catholic missionary who came to the United States in 1792 and founded the settlement of Loreto*.

Galvin, Edward J. (1882–1956) Founder of the Columban Fathers. In 1912 he was drawn to missionary service in China, where, in 1916, he founded St. Columban's* Foreign Mission Society. Formal approval from Rome came in 1918. By 1920 when the Columbans expanded their work to central China, they numbered 40 priests and 60 seminarians*. In 1946 Galvin was appointed bishop of the new Hanyang diocese*. After the Communist takeover of China, he was expelled from the country.

gamos Also, crowning; stephanoma. In the Byzantine Liturgy, matrimony* as one of the sacraments* of the church.

Gang-days Formerly, the three Rogation Days*: Monday, Tuesday, and Wednesday before Ascension Day*.

Gangra, Council of Council held at Gangra in Paphlagonia in northern Asia Minor in about 341. It passed 20 canons directed against the exaggerated asceticism* propagated by Eustathius*, who had attacked marriage and church attendance.

Garabandal, Our Lady of Apparitions of the Virgin Mary* to four children in the mountains of northern Spain between 1961 and 1965. A diocesan investigation did not accept the apparitions as authentic.

Garden of the Soul Book described as the manual of spiritual exercises* and instructions for Christians who, living in the world, aspire to perfection*, written by Richard Challoner*.

Gardiner, Allen Francis (1794–1851) English pioneer of South American missions. Following his wife's death in 1834, he devoted his life to missions, first in South Africa, where he helped to establish the Zulu Mission, and then in South America, Australia, and the Dutch East Indies. In 1844 he founded the short-lived Patagonia Mission which worked in Tierra del Fuego, using two boats. Gardiner died tragically of starvation and scurvy when his party ran out of food. His death inspired the founding of the South American Missionary Society.

Garnier, Charles (1606–1649) French Jesuit missionary to the Huron Indians of Canada who was killed by the Iroquois Indians. Feast day: September 26.

garth (Old Norse) Open space enclosed by the walls of a cloister*.

Gaspar del Bufalo (1786–1836) Italian priest and founder of the Society of Precious Blood, an order dedicated to parish ministry, chaplaincies, and missionary work.

Gasparri, Pietro (1852–1934) Roman Catholic cardinal who directed the codification of canon law* under Pius X* and was secretary of state under popes Benedict XV* and Pius XI*.

Gate of Heaven Title of the Virgin Mary*.

gathered church The church as essentially a local congregation of believers gathering in worship and fellowship in contrast to a church organized on a territorial or parish* basis. The advocates of a gathered church generally emphasize personal commitment of members rather than nominal adherence.

Gaudete Sunday Third Sunday in Advent*, named from the first word of the introit*.

Gaudi, Antonio (1852–1926) Spanish architect noted for his extravagant New Art style. His legacy is the spectacular Church of the Holy Family in Barcelona that was begun in 1883 and is still under construction.

gavazan In the Armenian tradition, staff of office presented to a vartabed* as part of the ordination ceremony. A minor vartabed is given a staff topped with a cross and one entwined serpent, while a major vartabed's staff has two entwined serpents.

gebra hawaryat In the Ethiopian Liturgy, a lesson from the Acts of the Apostles read by an assistant priest.

gebra lelet Night service in the Ethiopian Church in which the sa'aat (hours of the night) are chanted by the dabtaras*.

gedekion In the Byzantine Church*, seat beside a bishop's throne but on a lower level and much less ornate.

Geertgen, tot Sint Jans (c. 1460–1490) Dutch painter to whom is attributed *The Nativity* (1480), a night scene lighted solely by the radiance of the infant Jesus, and *St. John in the Wilderness* (1480) that shows a subtle mastery of landscape.

Ge'ez Ethiopic language, an extinct Semitic language still used as the liturgical language in the Ethiopian Orthodox Church*. It is derived from Old South Arabic and has some similarities with biblical Hebrew. It flourished in the Aksumite Empire, but was replaced by Amharic* as the national language in the thirteenth century.

Geiler von Kaisersberg, Johannes (1445–1510) German Roman Catholic preacher, considered the German Savonarola and the prince of the pulpit. From 1478 to his death he was at Strasbourg*, where his sermons were much admired. Although not a humanist, he emphasized the need for reform.

Geisslerlied Song of flagellants*, a genre cultivated by medieval penitents* in Germany.

Gelasian Decree See DECRETUM GELASIANUM.

Gelasian Sacramentary Liturgical book for the celebration of the Mass* written by the nuns of Chelles, mistakenly attributed to Pope Gelasius.

Gelassenheit (Ger., calmness) In mystical theology*, total dependence, humility, and trust before God.

gelbab In the Ethiopian Orthodox Church*, a veil, cover, or priestly vestment.

Gelineau Method of singing psalms and canticles* to melodic formulas developed by Joseph Gelineau*. It has a regular recurring pulse that accommodates a variable number of syllables.

Gelineau, Joseph (1920–) French Jesuit composer and liturgist. He was professor of liturgical musicology and pastoral liturgy at the Institute Catholique in Paris. He cofounded Universa Laus, and served as a member of the study group for the reform of the Roman Mass* according to the decrees of Vatican Council II*. His versified setting of the Psalms is popularly known as the Gelineau Psalms (1955), and he has composed liturgical music in many other forms, such as cantatas, antiphons*, motets*, and eucharistic prayers. Among his influential books is *Voices and Instruments in Christian Worship* (1964).

Gellert, Christian Furchtegott (1715–1769) German poet. He was a teacher of Goethe and Lessing and was noted for his piety. Besides his popular fables, he wrote a number of hymns, collected and published in *Gestliche Oden und Lieder* (1757). Among

them is the familiar Easter* hymn, "Jesus Lives, Thy Terrors Now."

Gemeinschaftsbewegung Independent German movement emphasizing Bible study, fellowship, evangelism*, and holiness*, founded in 1848 by A. Stoecker and J. H. Wichern*. It combined Pietism* with Evangelicalism*.

general Title of a head of a religious order or congregation, usually combined with a noun. Thus minister general of the Franciscans and Capuchins*, prior general* of the Carmelites*, and superior general* of the Jesuits* and Redemptorists*.

General Assembly Annual national Presbyterian assembly with final legislative and administrative power. It consists of delegates chosen from the ministers and ruling elders in each presbytery*.

General Baptists Baptist churches adhering to the Arminian doctrine of general atonement* which claims that Christ died for all human beings, founded by John Smyth and the separatists* who had followed him into exile in Amsterdam in 1608/09. Also known as Six-Principle Baptists, they opposed singing in worship and required hands to be laid upon new converts. Their theology is based on the Standard Confession of 1660 and the Orthodox Creed of 1678. The earliest American churches resulted from schisms in Particular-General Churches in Newport, Providence, and Swansea. After being almost extinct by 1800, they were revived in 1822 and were numerous enough to form the Association of General Baptists* in 1870.

general chapter Meeting of a religious order to determine policy and to elect leaders. It is generally composed of heads and representatives of constituent communities and may be convoked every three or four years.

General Conference of Mennonite Brethren Churches of North America Mennonite denomination originally made up of congregations of Mennonite immigrants from Russia in the nineteenth century. The first conference of these congregations was organized in 1879. In 1909 the General Conference was divided territorially into district conferences of which today there are 16 in the United States and six provincial conferences in Canada. The conference supports extensive foreign missions programs and operates several Bible colleges and seminaries.

general confession Set form of confession* in the *Book of Common Prayer**, suitable for all persons and all occasions and recited morning and evening by the whole congregation, with the minister kneeling. Based on Romans 7:8–25, it includes a confession of sins to God, a prayer for forgiveness, and a prayer for grace* to live rightly. Distinguished from particular confession* for specific needs.

General Convention Supreme legislative body in the Protestant Episcopal Church in the USA consisting of a House of Bishops* and a House of Deputies*. It is held every three years.

general council 1. See ECUMENICAL COUNCILS. 2. Administrative organ of certain denominations, such as American Baptist Convention and the Presbyterian Church.

General Epistles Epistles in the New Testament addressed to all churches collectively. See also CATHOLIC EPISTLES.

general menaia In the Byzantine Liturgy, general office used on saints' days.

General Presbytery Presbyterian administrative body from 1706 to 1716. It was replaced by the General Synod and later by the General Assembly*.

general superintendent Title of highest office in certain Protestant churches.

general supplication Prayer for all mankind, or "for all conditions of men," as in the Anglican *Book of Common Prayer**.

general synod Highest administrative body in some Reformed* and Lutheran churches.

general thanksgiving Prayer of thanksgiving for di-

vine blessings in general, offered in unison by the congregation.

generalate Headquarters of a Roman Catholic religious institute headed by a general* or superior general*.

genesion (lit., birth) In the Byzantine Liturgy, a nativity feast.

Geneva Swiss city and canton, an episcopal see* from the fourth century. The main cathedral was built about this time. From the twelfth century to the 1530s Genevan bishops bore the title of prince-bishops. Under Guillaume Farel* and John Calvin*, it became a center of Reformed Protestantism*. Church and state* were not separated until 1907. Geneva is the seat of the World Council of Churches*, the World Alliance of Reformed Churches*, and the Lutheran World Federation*.

Reformation Wall at Geneva

Geneva bands Two white stripes hanging from the neck opening of a clerical gown, symbolizing the law and the gospel.

Geneva Bible English translation of the first English Bible published in Geneva* in 1560, sometimes called the "Breeches Bible" because of its mistranslation of Genesis 3:7. It was the first English Bible to be printed with chapters and verses.

Geneva Catechism Reform catechism* by Calvin* in the form of questions and answers published in French in 1542 and in Latin in 1545 at Geneva. It had five sections on faith, law, prayer, the Word of God, and sacraments. It was related to an earlier document, the *First Geneva Catechism,* drawn from the *Institutes**, issued in 1537. It accompanied Articles Concerning the Organization of the Church.

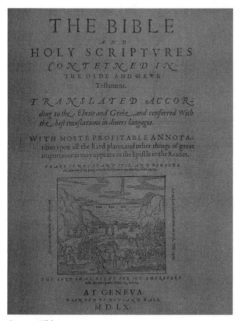

Geneva Bible

Geneva cross Red Greek cross* on a white background.

Geneva gown/robe Black, loose-fitting academic gown with full sleeves, worn first by Genevan preachers to emphasize preaching over the priestly functions of their ministry.

Genevan Academy The Academy of Geneva established by John Calvin* and Theodore Beza* in 1559 for training Protestant ministers and missionaries. It developed into the University of Geneva.

Genevan Psalter Any of several collections of metrical psalmody* published between 1539 and 1551 under the direction of John Calvin*.

Genevieve, St. (c. 422–c. 500) Virgin and chief patroness of the city of Paris. Consecrated to God at the age of 7, she took the veil at 15. Her intercession is credited with saving Paris from the Franks and the Huns and also a fierce pestilence in 1129. Feast day: January 3.

Gentile Christianity Christianity as it developed into a non-Jewish religion in the Roman world.

genuflectentes (lit., those who kneel) In the early church, a class of penitents* who were permitted to be present during the first part of the liturgy, kneeling at the west end of the nave*, but were dismissed together with the catechumens* and energumens* before the Eucharist* proper.

genuflection In the Roman Catholic tradition, religious act of bending the knee in worship with the body erect when passing before the Blessed Sacrament* or before the unveiled cross on Good Friday* or in the presence of an ecclesiastical superior*. Until recently a double genuflection*, made by kneeling on both knees and bowing the head, was made during the exposition of the Holy Sacrament.

genus maiestaticum Explanation of the incarnate person of Christ, whereby his human nature possesses qualitites of his divine nature or majesty, such as omnipresence.

George (c. 640–724) "Bishop of the Arabians." In 686 he became bishop of the Arabian nomads in Mesopotamia, with his see* at Akula. He is one of the principal sources for the history of Syriac Christianity and literature. Among his writings are a commentary on the mysteries* of the church, monastic canons, and prose homilies.

George, St. (c. fourth century) Martyr and patron saint* of England. One of the most popular saints and martyrs* in Christian hagiography*, he was martyred in Lydda, Palestine. He is reputed to have slain a dragon. Feast day: April 23.

Georgetown College/University Oldest Catholic institution of higher education in the United States, founded in Washington, D.C., in 1786 by John Carroll* and others. During the administration of Timothy S. Healy (1976–1989), the university achieved national prominence.

Georgian Version The New Testament in the Georgian language, dating from the fifth century, although the earliest extant manuscript dates from the eighth century and was translated from Armenian with links to the Syriac Version and the *Diatesseron**. Earlier fragmentary manuscripts in the archaic forms of Georgian known as hanmeti and hae-meti contained parts of the Old and New Testaments. Revelation was not included until the tenth century.

Gerard (c. 1040–1120) Founder of the Knights of St. John of Jerusalem.

Gerbillon, Jean-Francois (1654–1707) Jesuit missionary to China. Sent to China in 1677, he found favor with the emperor Kang-Hai and was used by him on many diplomatic and scientific missions. He was placed in charge of the French College in Beijing, and later became superior general* of the mission. In 1692 he received an edict granting freedom for Christian missions and was presented by the emperor with a site for a chapel and residence.

Gerhard, Johann (1582–1637) German Lutheran theologian, considered the third most important after Luther* and Chemnitz*. A prolific writer, his masterpiece was the massive nine-volume *Loci Theologici* (1610–1622) which is the standard compendium of Lutheran theology. His other works included *Confessio Catholica* (1634–1637), a popular anti-Catholic Lutheran apology; *Harmonia Evangelistarum Chemnitio-Lyseriana* (1626–1627), a harmony of the Gospels*; and *Meditationes Sacrae* (1606), a devotional classic.

Gerhard Zerbolt of Zutphen (1367–1398) Prominent member of the Brethren of the Common Life*. A pupil of Gerard Groote* and a close friend of Florentius Radewijns, he became a spiritual adviser and librarian at the headquarters of the Brethren of the Common Life at Deventer in the Netherlands. His is the author of several spiritual works, of which the best known are *De Reformatione Virium Animae* and *De Spiritualibus Ascensionibus*.

Gerhardt, Paul (1607–1676) German Lutheran hymn writer, author of 133 hymns, including "O Sacred Head, Sore Wounded," "Commit Thou All Thy Griefs," "All My Heart This Night Rejoices," "Jesu, Thy Boundless Love to Me," and "The Duteous Day Now Closeth." He is considered one of the greatest hymn writers of German Protestantism*.

Germanus, St. (c. 496–576) Bishop of Paris. Ordained in 530, he became bishop of Paris in 555. He exerted considerable influence on King Childebert, the son of Clovis*, and took part in several councils. The Church of St.Germain-des-Pres stands over his tomb. Feast day: May 28.

Germanus, St. (c. 640–c. 733) Patriarch of Constantinople* and liturgist*. He was elected patriarch* in 716 and shortly thereafter officially proclaimed the Catholic faith and anathematized the Monothelites. He resisted Emperor Leo the Isaurian's efforts against the veneration* of icons and was forced to resign in 730. He was an ardent promoter of the cult of the Virgin Mary*. He is the author of *Historia Mystica Ecclesiae Catholicae,* an important liturgical work and many poems. Feast day: May 12.

gerontika In the Byzantine Church*, parts of the Divine Office* traditionally read by the superior* or elder, or in his absence by the senior monk.

Gerontius, The Dream of Poem by John Henry Newman* narrating the vision of a soul at the point of death conversing with the angels. Two well-known hymns, "Firmly I Believe and Truly" and "Praise to the Holiest in the Highest" are based on the poem.

Gerson, Jean le Charlier de (1363–1429) French churchman and writer known as Doctor Christianissimus. In 1395 he succeeded Pierre d'Ailly as chancellor of Notre Dame* and the University of Paris. His lifework was devoted to reform of the church from within through internal renewal and prayer, and the unity of the church in the time of the Great Schism*. He was responsible for bringing back the Dominicans* who had been expelled from the university. In 1415 he attended the Council of Constance* which affirmed the superiority of the general council over the pope and drew up the Four Articles of Constance, the charter of Gallicanism*. He wrote extensively on the authority of the church, particularly *De Unitate Ecclesiae, De Auferibilitate Papae ab Ecclesia,* and *De Potestate Ecclesiae*. In moral theology* he upheld Nominalism in which nothing was sinful in itself but sinfulness and goodness depended on the will of God.

Most of his treatises, however, were devoted to spiritual life. Among them were *The Mountain of Contemplation* (1397), *Mystical Theology, Perfection of the Heart,* and commentaries on the Magnificat* and on the Song of Solomon. His mystical writings had a great influence on later Roman Catholic mystics.

Gertrude the Great (1256–c. 1302) German mystic. She had her first mystical experience in 1281 and from then on led a life of contemplation. She was one of the first exponents of devotion to the Sacred Heart*. Her two devotional works are classics of Christian mysticism: *Legatus Divinae Pietatis* and *Exercitia Spiritualia.* Although she was never canonized, her cult was authorized in 1606 and extended to the entire Roman Catholic Church by Clement XIII* in 1738. She is the patron saint* of West Indies. Feast day: November 16.

Gervase and Protase, Sts. First martyrs of Milan* whose remains were discovered by St. Ambrose* in 386 as the result of a vision. They were twins who were put to death by Nero.

Gess, Wolfgang Friedrich (1819–1891) German theologian. He came from a Pietist tradition and was professor at Gottingen and Breslau. He was an exponent of kenotic Christology*, which explained the Incarnation* in terms of Christ's emptying himself of his full divinity.

Gesu, Il Mother church of the Jesuit Order in Rome*, begun by Vignola* in 1568. When Vignola died, the work was completed by Giacomo della Porta.

Gesuati Official name: Clerici Apostolici St. Hieronymi. Congregation of laymen founded by Giovanni Colombini* about 1360. Their name was derived from their frequent ejaculations* of "praise be to Jesus" or "hail Jesus" in preaching. Approved by Urban V* in 1367, they established monasteries and adapted a white tunic and greyish brown cloak as their habit*. They spread beyond Italy in the fifteenth century but were dissolved in 1668 by Clement IX. A female offshoot of the order, Jesuatesses (Sisters of the Visitation of Mary) was founded about 1367 and lasted until 1872.

Gethsemane (lit., olive press) Garden on the Mount of Olives, east of Jerusalem, across the Kidron Valley and opposite the temple, where Jesus went often to pray and where he was betrayed by Judas on the night before his crucifixion (Luke 21:37; John 18:1–2).

gethsemane Also, mercy ground. In West Africa, an open plot of ground near a church, often walled, where believers may come for private prayer and often prostrate themselves for whole nights at a time.

Gethsemani, Abbey of Our Lady of Monastery of Cistercians* of the Strict Observance (Trappists*) founded in 1848 near Bardstown, Kentucky. Thomas Merton* lived here.

Geulincx, Arnold (1624–1669) Belgian Calvinist theologian who proposed the theory of Occasionalism*. He resolved the paradox of free will* and God's sovereignty by suggesting that God is the sole cause of all events and man's freedom of will is illusory. His main works were *Metaphysica* (1651) and *Ethica* (1655).

Gesu Church

geza/gaza (lit., treasury) In the Assyrian Church*, book of hymns and anthems proper to the festivals.

g'hantha In the Syrian tradition, either a deep bow made while saying a prayer or a prayer that is said with the head inclined.

Ghelderode, Michel de (1893–1962) Belgian playwright. He continued the tradition of the medieval liturgical drama in *Escurial* (1948), *Fastes d'Enfer* (Chronicles of Hell, 1935), and *Barabbas* (1928). His works are obsessed with a sense of evil and death.

Gheon, Henri (1875–1944) Birth name: Henri Leon Vangeon. French Roman Catholic poet and playwright. After 1912, when he wrote his first play, *Le Fils de M. Sage—Le Pain,* he devoted his talent to the development of a Catholic theater by founding two companies, Les Compagnons de Notre Dame (1924) and Les Compagnons de Jeux (1931). Many of his plays dealt with medieval themes, similar to miracle plays*. His collection of verse, *Chanson d'Aube,* was published in 1897. He also wrote a number of biographies and novels.

Ghiberti, Lorenzo (1378–1455) Italian sculptor whose bronze gates to the baptistery of Florence* were described by Michelangelo* as worthy to be the gates of paradise. He took 49 years from 1403 to 1452 to complete them. He was the first artist to write his autobiography. Ghiberti also did the stained glass windows for the Florence Cathedral*.

Ghirlandaio, Dominico (1449–1494) Florentine religious painter who was a teacher of Michelangelo*.

Gibbons, James (1834–1921) American Roman Catholic archbishop and cardinal. He was instrumental in founding the Catholic University of America* in Washington, D.C. His books, *The Faith of Our Fathers* (1871) and *Our Christian Heritage* (1889), sold widely.

Gibbons, Orlando (1583–1625) English composer and organist of the Chapel Royal and the Westminster Abbey*. He was the first great English Protestant composer. The bulk of his work consists of 40 anthems and two Anglican services. Among his best-known works are "Hosanna to the Son of David" and "Almighty and Everlasting God."

Gideons International Association of Christian professional and business persons that grew out of a chance meeting between two Christian traveling salesmen, John Nicholson and Samuel Hill at Central Hotel, Boscobel, Wisconsin, in 1898. Next year, with W. J. Knights they formed Christian Commercial Travelers Association, popularly known as Gideons as an organization whose pri-

Ghiberti Doors

Gideon Founders, John Nicholson and Sam Hill

mary purpose was to win men and women to Christ through free distribution of Scripture. Their symbol is a two-handled pitcher with a torch, recalling the Old Testament story of Gideon leading Israel to victory over the Midianites with torches and pitchers. Beginning in 1908, they have placed 200 million Bibles in schools, hotels, and prisons.

Gifford Lectures Lectures in the four ancient Scottish universitites of St. Andrew, Glasgow, Aberdeen, and Edinburgh established by Adam Gifford, Lord Gifford (1820–1887), for "promoting, advancing, teaching, and diffusing the study of natural theology*, in the widest sense of that term, in other words, the knowledge of God and of the foundation of ethics." The first lectures were delivered in 1888. Among those who have delivered the lectures are R. B. Haldane, William Inge*, Etienne Gilson*, William Temple*, and Karl Barth*.

gifts of the Spirit (Gk., *charismata*, grace gifts) Divinely ordained means and powers with which Christ endows His church in order to enable it to perform its task on earth. Paul* gives two lists of the gifts of the Spirit (Rom. 12:6–8; 1 Cor. 12:7–11) with only prophecy* common to both. Romans lists seven gifts: prophecy, service (*diakonia**), teaching (*didaskon*), encouragement (*paraklesis**), contributing to the needs of others (*metadidomi*), leadership (*proistemi*), and compassion (*eleeo*). First Corinthians lists nine gifts: word of wisdom*, word of knowledge*, discernment*, faith (pistis), healing, miraculous powers, prophecy, speaking in tongues*, and interpretation of tongues*. Their recovery, especially of speaking in tongues, inspired the Pentecostal and Charismatic movements which now represents a major and fast-growing stream of world Christianity.

Gilbert de la Porree (d. 1154) French Scholastic theologian. A pupil of Bertrand of Chartres, he became chancellor of Chartres* and bishop of Poitiers* from 1142. His *Commentaries* on the Trinity* led to his being summoned before the Council of Reims in 1148. His followers were known as the Porretani.

Gilbert of Sempringham (c. 1083–1189) English founder of the Gilbertine Order. In 1148, he founded the only purely English monastic order. By the time of his death there were 9 houses and 25 at the time of the dissolution of the monasteries.

Giles, St. (c. eighth century) One of the 14 auxiliary saints*. An Athenian by birth, he lived as a hermit in a forest near the mouth of the Rhone. Flavius Wamba, king of the Visigoths, impressed by his holiness*, built a monastery for him. The town of St. Giles grew up around his grave and became a place of pilgrimage*. He was one of the most popular medieval saints*, and more than 160 churches were dedicated to him in England. He is the patron saint* of cripples, beggars, and blacksmiths. Feast day: September 1.

Gill, Arthur Eric Rowton (1882–1940) English sculptor, letterist, and wood engraver. The son of an Anglican priest, he became a Roman Catholic in 1913, joining the Dominican order as a tertiary*. His best-known works are the Stations of the Cross* in the Westminster Cathedral* (1918), ten panels in the New Museum, Jerusalem, and the bas-reliefs in the League of Nations Council Hall at Geneva*. As a stone-carver he revived the art of working directly upon the stone to make small stone objects, such as crucifixes.

Gilmour, James (1843–1891) Scottish missionary to the Mongols. In 1870 he went to Mongolia under the auspices of the London Missionary Society, learned Mongolian, and lived in a tent on the plains to reach the nomads. He worked for almost 15 years without any success and in the face of adverse criticism.

Gilson, Etienne (1884–1978) French Thomist philosopher. He served successively as professor at Lille, Strasbourg*, Sorbonne, College de France, and the Pontifical Institute of Medieval Studies in Toronto, which he helped found in 1929. Of his Christian works, the most important were *History of Christian Philosophy in the Middle Ages* (1955), *Le Thomisme* (1919), *The Christian Philosophy of St. Thomas Aquinas* (1956), *La Philosophie de Saint Bonaventure* (1924), *Introduction a l'Etude de Saint Augustin* (1929), *L'Esprit de la Philosophie Medievale* (1932), *La Theologie Mystique de Saint Bernard* (1934), *Heloise et Abelard* (1938), *L'Etre et l'Essence* (1948), *Jean Duns Scot, Introduction a ses Positions Fondamentales* (1952), *Reason and Revelation in the Middle Ages* (1939), and *God and Philosophy* (1941).

Giorgione da Castelfanca, Giorgio Barbarelli (c. 1475–1510) Italian Renaissance painter and student of Bellini*. Among his best known works is the *Adoration of the Shepherds* (1505–1510).

Giotto (c. 1266–1337) Birth name: Ambrogiotto di Bondone. Italian painter. As head of the Florentine Cathedral school from 1334, he is credited with the development of modern painting. He broke away from the rigid formality and distance of Byzantine art and introduced dramatic realism into his paintings. He painted cycles of frescoes in the Arena Chapel in Padua and the Peruzzi and Bardi chapels of Santa Croce in Florence*; the huge mosaic of the *Navicella* (the ship of the

Uffizi Giotto

church, with Christ walking on the waters) in Old St. Peter's*; and *Ognissanti Madonna* in the Uffizi in Florence. It is possible that he painted the cycle of frescoes on the life of St. Francis in the Upper Church at Assisi*.

Giovanni Capistrano, St. (1386–1456) Franciscan friar*. He entered the Friars Minor* in 1416 and became a priest in 1420. He worked with St. Bernardino of Siena* in the reform of the order and was named vicar general*. In 1451 he was sent by Pope Nicholas V* to preach against John Hus*. He was highly effective in this mission which was ended by the fall of Constantinople* in 1453. He rallied the Hungarians against the Turks, leading

to the defeat of the Turks in 1456 before Belgrade. He died of plague in the same year. Feast day: October 23.

Giraldus Cambrensis (1147–1223) Also, Gerald de Barre; Gerald of Wales. Welsh clergyman and historian who preached the Third Crusade* and whose complete works, published in eight volumes, include *Topographia Hibernica,* an autobiography, biographies, and poems.

girdle Belt, waist cord, cincture*, or ceremonial sash, a symbol of service in Christian art. It is one of six ecclesiastical vestments.

Girling, Mary Anne (1827–1886) English reformer, also known as "Mother Ann," who founded the Shaker group known as Children of God*.

gita In the Maronite Liturgy, the silk veil used to cover the oblation*. The gita absainiyak covers the paten*, and gita alcas covers the chalice*.

Gladstone, William Ewart (1809–1898) British prime minister and Victorian Christian statesman. A committed Christian* activist, he was influenced by the Oxford movement* and also supported Catholic emancipation*. A weekly communicant, a devout student of the Bible, frugal in habits, and generous in giving, he found time in his busy schedule to witness in London's streets. He wrote a number of theological treatises, including *The Impregnable Rock of Holy Scripture.*

Glagolitic Medieval Slavonic alphabet devised by St. Cyril*, the apostle of the Slavs, in the ninth century. It was supplanted in the tenth century by the Cyrillic* alphabet.

Glasites Also, Sandemanians*. Small Scottish sect founded by John Glas (1695–1773) and his son-in-law Robert Sandeman (1718–1771). Glas held that an established church is unscriptural and challenged the Presbyterian state church of Scotland*. He published his teachings in *The Testimony of the King of Martyrs Concerning His Kingdom* (1727). Suspended from the Presbyterian Church, he established independent congregations led by non-ordained elders rather than pastors. Sandeman succeeded Glas as leader of the sect. In his

Letters on Theron and Aspasio (1757), Sandeman rejected the Calvinist teaching of salvation* through the imputed righteousness of Christ, replacing it with reasoned faith*. Among Sandeman's followers was Michael Faraday, the scientist. See also SANDEMANIANS.

Glastonbury Abbey The oldest and the most prestigious of English monasteries, founded in the seventh century. From the time St. Dunstan* became its abbot about 940, it became one of the main spiritual and educational centers of England. Under Norman rule it became a famous place of pilgrimage* because it contained the tombs of King Arthur and St. Dunstan. The many legends relating to the abbey were recorded by William of Malmesbury* in his history, *De Antiquitate Glastoniensis Ecclesie*. The monastery was suppressed in 1509. Partly as a result of legends linking the town to the Holy Grail* and Joseph of Arimathea, it has become a hub of New Age cultic activity.

Glendalough Valley in Ireland noted for its ruins of the Seven Churches, Kevin's cross, and Kevin's Kitchen. The monastery of Glendalough was founded by Abbot Kevin.

Gloria in Excelsis One of the best known hymns in the Liturgy*, also known as the Angelic Hymn* and greater doxology. Of unknown origin, it was a Greek private psalm composed on the model of the biblical Psalms. It is usually sung after the kyries*. Its full text is: "Glory to God in the highest/and on earth peace/to men of good will/we praise you, we bless you/we worship you, we glorify you/ we give thanks to you/because of your great glory/Lord God, heavenly king/God the Father almighty/Son of the Father/only begotten/Jesus Christ/Lord God, Lamb of God/ Son of the Father, you who/take away the sins of the world/have mercy upon us/you who take away the sins of the world,/receive our prayer/ you who sit at the right hand/of God the Father/have mercy upon us/for you only are holy/you only are the Lord/you only are Most High/Jesus Christ, with the Holy Spirit/in the glory of God the Father/amen."

Gloria Patri First two words of the lesser doxology, a Trinitarian* prayer. It is a prayer of praise to the

Father based on Romans 16:27, Philippians 4:20, and Revelation 5:13.

gloria tibi (Lat., glory to you) Acclamation sung in response to the reading of the holy gospel.

glorification Perfect conformity of the believer to the image of Jesus Christ at the final resurrection. Paul* suggests (Phil. 3:21) that a completely sanctified believer will be conformed to the radiance of Christ and John suggests (1 John 3:2) that the believer will be entirely like Christ.

glorified body Resurrection body* possessed by saints in heaven*, as distinct from earthly body.

gloriole Circle of radiant light around the head or figures of Christ, the Virgin Mary*, or the saints*.

Glorious Mysteries, the Five Third chaplet* of the Rosary* consisting of the Resurrection, ascension, descent of the Holy Spirit* at Pentecost*, assumption of the Blessed Virgin Mary*, and the coronation of the Blessed Virgin Mary.

Glossa Ordinaria/Communis Standard medieval commentary on the Bible. It was made up chiefly of extracts from the Fathers and was arranged in the form of interlinear and marginal glosses. It was believed to be the work of many scholars, over a period of time, begun in the school of Anselm of Laon* and continued by Walafrid Strabo* and Gilbert the Universal.

glossolalia (Gk., lit., tongue talking) Speaking in tongues*—a form of spiritual, supernatural, and ecstatic speech—is one of the gifts of the spirit* (Acts 10:46; 1 Cor. 13:8; 14:6, 9, 23). It is often described as an angelic language. It is one of the hallmarks of the Pentecostal churches* and is actively fostered by the Charismatic movement. Glossolalia is of two kinds. One is the talking in foreign tongues, such as Chinese, by a person who is unfamiliar with it. The other is talking in a spiritual language that needs interpretation by the speaker or by another believer. Also used to refer to praying in tongues.

Gloucester Site of the abbey church of St. Peter, founded in 681, and rebuilt in 1089, consecrated in 1100 and given cathedral status by Henry VIII in 1542. It is one of the most beautiful ecclesiastical buildings in England built in Late Gothic* style with prominent Norman features. Its choir has the largest stained-glass window in England,

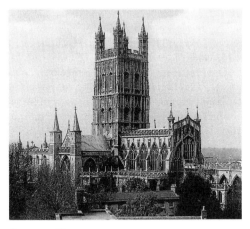

Gloucester Abbey

depicting the coronation of the Virgin Mary*. The cathedral contains the tomb of the saintly Edward II, and it became a place of pilgrimage*. Under Gilbert Foliot, its abbot from 1139 to 1148, it was wealthy and influential. In 1540 the monastery was suppressed. The triennial Three Choirs Festival is held in Gloucester.

Glukharev, Mikhail Iakovlevich (1792–1847) Monastic name: Makarii. A gifted linguist in Latin, French, German, Greek, Hebrew, and Altaian, he translated much of the Bible, *Confessions of St. Augustine**, the *Ladder of St. John Climacus,* the *Discourses of Gregory the Great,* and the works of Teresa of Avila* into Russian. In 1821 he became the rector* of Kostroma Seminary and archimandrite* of a local monastery. Answering a Holy Synod* call to mission, he volunteered to go to Siberia* and established a pioneer mission at Maima in the Altai Mountains in 1830. Glukharev was a visionary whose ideas on evangelism were encapsulated in his *Thoughts on the Means for Successful Dissemination of the Christian Faith* (1839).

glusqomo In the Jacobite tradition, an oblong stone container used to house relics*.

glykophilousa (Gk., sweetly kissing) Icon showing the Theotokos*, the Virgin Mary*, kissing her infant son.

g'murtho In the Assyrian Liturgy, particles* set aside for the communion of the faithful. Adults receive the bread on their right hand while children receive it on their tongue.

Gnesio-Lutherans Strict Lutherans, led by Nikolaus von Amsdorf* and Matthias Flacius*, who opposed the Leipzig Interim* and the followers of Philip Melanchthon*, known as Philippists*. They held that the Philippists's concessions to Calvinists* and Roman Catholics represented betrayal of Luther's* legacy and accused them of being crypto-Catholics and crypto-Calvinists.

gnosis Immediate knowledge of spiritual truth without the mediation of churches or other institutions or rituals.

Gnosticism (Gk., knowledge) Heretic movement in the early Christian centuries that emphasized salvation through a secret gnosis* or knowledge. Originating as perversion of Jewish and Christian truths, it developed into an independent religious phenomenon. The principal patristic sources of knowledge about Gnosticism come from Church Fathers*, such as Justin Martyr*, Irenaeus*, Hippolytus*, Origen*, Tertullian*, and Epiphanius*. The richest source of Gnostic literature is Coptic. They include the Codex Askewianus, containing the Pistis Sophia*; the Codex Brucianus, containing the Book of Jeu; and the Codex Berolinensis, containing the *Gospel of Mary* (Magdalene), *Sophia of Jesus, Acts of Peter**, and the *Apocryphon of John**.

In 1946 a cache of 13 Coptic codices were discovered near Nag Hammadi* in Upper Egypt. Dating from the third to fifth centuries, they contain 53 treatises including *The Gospel of Truth, the Epistle of Rheginos, The Gospel of Thomas**, *The Gospel of Philip**, *The Apocryphon of John**, *The Hypostasis of the Archons,* and *The Apocalypse of Adam.* The discovery has revitalized the study of Gnosticism and provided some support for the theory of its pre-Christian origins. Also related to Gnosticism are texts and manuscripts of Mandaic origin.

The texts and writings of Mandaeans* of modern-day Iraq are the sole remnants of ancient Gnostic literature still in use. These include the *Ginza,* a cosmology; the *Johannesbuch,* containing legends about John the Baptist whom the Mandaeans* revere; the *Qolasta,* a collection of liturgies; and the *Haran Gawaita,* a history. Other sources bearing on Gnosticism include the Syriac* "Odes of Solomon*," the "Hymn of the Pearl," and the writings of Philo of Alexandria.

Many scholars believe that Gnosticism was based in Jewish mysticism encapsulated in the Kabbala and the Dead Sea Scrolls*. There are also many pre-Christian features, especially mythology and cosmology and magical rites, in some Gnostic teachings. Some of these accounts point to Simon Magus as the "fountain" of the Gnostic heresy. He was followed by a fellow Samaritan, Menander, who taught at Antioch* toward the end of the first century. By the middle of the second century some Samaritans had become followers of Gnosticism. Other Gnostic teachers include Saturninus; Cerinthus*; Basilides* and his son, Isidore; and Carpocrates* and his son Epiphanes, the last four of whom taught at Alexandria*. The most famous Gnostic teacher was Valentinus*, whose disciples included Ptolemy and Heracleon in the West and Theodotus in the East.

Gnostic theology was dualistic. It taught that the material world was evil and was created by a malevolent demiurge*, the Old Testament Jehovah, who exists in opposition to a good and benevolent God. However, there is a class of human beings of celestial origin, called pneumatics, who contain sparks of divinity. The good God sent down Jesus Christ as a redeemer and emissary, in the docetic sense, to reawaken the divine spark through imparting gnosis* or knowledge and the rites associated with it. Salvation* is viewed as escape from the earthly bondage and reunion with the deity. Jesus appears in most Gnostic teachings but in a wildly mutated form. Since salvation is through secret gnosis and not moral conduct, some Gnostics found a licentious lifestyle permissible. They believed that they were pearls who could not be sullied by any external mud. However, the majority of the Gnostics held ascetic ideas about marriage and rejected the procreation of children as the multiplication of souls in bondage to the powers of darkness.

Gnosticism survived for many centuries. In the Middle Ages, it reappeared in the Cathari*, Bogomils*, and the Albigenses*, and there are a number of new religious movements in the early twenty-first century that resemble Gnosticism.

God/God the Father 1. In the New Testament, the one triune God including God the Father, God the Son, and God the Holy Spirit*. Each member of the Godhead may be addressed as God. 2. In the Old Testament, Jehovah. 3. In theology, holy, infinite, transcendent, all-knowing, all-powerful sovereign, eternal and spiritual being who is the creator, sustainer, judge, righteous sovereign, and redeemer of the universe. 4. In philosophy, ultimate and infinite reality and unchangeably perfect being that is the first and final cause of the universe.

God of Abraham Praise, The Perhaps the classic example of Jewish piety expressed in Christian hymnody*. One evening in 1770, Welshman Thomas Olivers (1725–1799), an evangelist with John Wesley*, attended Sabbath worship at the Great Synagogue, Duke's Place, London. There, as the "Yigdal" (traditional Hebrew doxology*) was sung by cantor* Meyer Lyon (d. 1796), he was so moved that he requested the tune notations (*Leoni*). Olivers then produced a free rendering of this doxology, which was based on the Thirteen Articles* of Faith stated by the famed Jewish philosopher Moses Maimonides in the twelfth century. The opening word, *yigdal* (Hebrew for "may He be magnified"), inspired the effort. Some time later, Lyon had to resign his post after singing in Handel's "Messiah*"; later he became reader in the Kingston, Jamaica, synagogue.

Godet, Frederic Louis (1812–1900) Swiss Protestant theologian, the founder of the Free Evangelical Church of Neuchatel. Considered one of the most influential Reformed* scholars of the day, his commentaries on John, Luke, Romans, and Corinthians defended orthodoxy* against liberal theologians.

godparents Adults who sponsor infants at baptism* and on their behalf confess the faith* and renounce Satan*. They receive the infant from the hands of the minister and acknowledge their

God, the Son: Christological Controversies

In the fourth and fifth centuries, the burning question not only among theologians but in the marketplace was whether God the Father and God the Son were "identical" or only "similar." Gregory of Nyssa* described the situation in Constantinople* as follows: "In this city if you ask anyone for change, he will discuss with you whether the Son is begotten or unbegotten. If you ask about the quality of bread, you will receive the answer that the Father is greater, the Son is less." There were four contending parties in this debate as follows:

	Watchword	Beliefs	Advocates	Developments
ARIANS	anomoios (dissimilar)	God the Father and God the Son are dissimilar in essence. The Son is divine but not fully divine. Because the Son was begotten by the Father, there must have been a time when the Son did not exist. The Son is subject to the Father and the Holy Spirit is subject to the Son.	Arius*, Eusebius of Nicomedia*.	Arianism* flourished in the East until Theodosius I presided over its demise at the Council of Constantinople* in 381. It survived for another four centuries among the Goths, north of the Danube, and later in countries under Goth domination.
SEMI-ARIANS*	homoios (similar) or homoiousios (of like substance)	The Son is similar to the Father but not in all things. He is not a creature and is higher than angels. The word homoios is in the Bible and is therefore acceptable.	Emperor Constantius; Basil of Ancyra*	Synods in Sirmium*, Ariminum*, and Seleucia* put this party in controlling power in both the East and West for a few years, leading Jerome* to comment that the "whole world groaned in astonishment to find itself Arian." The Semi-Arians* remained influential until 381 when they switched their support to the orthodox Cappadocians.
NICAEANS	homoousios* (of identical substance)	The Father and the Son are of identical substance. The Son is fully divine and is coequal with the Father.	Athanasius* of Alexandria, Hilary of Poitiers*.	The Nicaeans were victorious at the Council of Constantinople* in 381 thanks in part to the backing of Emperor Theodosius I and again in 451 at the Council of Chalcedon.
CAPPADOCIANS	homoiousios (of like substance)	Like the Nicaeans, the Cappadocians believed that God the Father and God the Son were of identical substance, but they also emphasized that the Father and Son were distinct, though equally divine.	Basil of Caesarea, Gregory of Nyssa*, Gregory of Nazianzus*.	Cappadocians and Nicaeans joined forces in 381 to ensure the triumph of orthodoxy*.

responsibility to bring him or her into the Christian faith. Originally, sponsors spoke for candidates for believer's baptism* unknown to the congregation. Reformed* churches have not generally used godparents in infant baptism. See also SPONSOR.

God's acre Cemetery.

godtalk Language of theology and theological sermons and discussions.

godwalk Actual practices and lifestyles of Christians, applying acquired principles of Christian ethics and morality.

Goes, Hugo van der (d. 1482) Flemish artist. One of his most important works is the Portinari Altarpiece, a triptych* 8.5 feet high by nearly 20 feet wide when open. Its central panel is the *Adoration of the Shepherds*. His last work was the *Dormition of the Virgin*.

Goforth, Jonathan (1859–1936) Canadian Presbyterian missionary to China. Converted at age 18, he was influenced by Hudson Taylor* and Charles Finney* to go to Manchuria as a missionary. He was a leader of the Manchurian Revival of 1907. He was a strenuous opponent of liberal theology.

Jonathan Goforth

Gogarten, Friedrich (1887–1967) German theologian who abandoned early liberalism* to adopt neo-Orthodoxy* along with Karl Barth*. In *Demythologizing and History* and *The Reality of Faith* he broke with Barth and advocated a more existential theology in which Christian faith was presented along historical rather than metaphysical lines.

Golden Legend Lives of the saints written by Jacob of Voragine about 1265. Its miraculous stories were popular until the Reformation*.

golden rose Jeweled ornament, in the form of a rose, blessed by the pope on Laetare*, the fourth Sunday in Lent*, also known as Rose Sunday. The golden rose was bestowed on distinguished individuals, churches, or communities.

Golden Sequence The Whitsuntide* hymn, "Veni, Sancte Spiritus*."

goldfinch Symbol of Christ's suffering in Christian art.

golgotha In the Jacobite Liturgy, the stand on which the Gospel rests outside the central door on the top of the steps leading to the altar, slightly to the north.

Gomar, Francis (1563–1641) Dutch Calvinist theologian from Bruges, noted as a skilled defender of Calvinist orthodoxy* against the Arminian Remonstrants. He played a prominent role in the Synod of Dort* which condemned the Remonstrants. His *Opera Theologica Omnia* (1645) was published posthumously.

gomuro In the Syrian Church, the small cushion on which the tarwodho* or spoon rests.

gonuklisia In the Byzantine Rite*, full kneeling, including the making of the sign of the cross.

Gonzaga, St. Aloysius (1568–1591) Spanish Jesuit. Although of noble descent and destined for a military career, he chose to enter the holy orders* and joined the novitiate* of the Jesuits* in 1585. For the next six years, until his early death at age 23, he worked among the sick and plague-stricken. He is the patron saint* of youth. Feast day: June 21.

Gonzalez, Roque (1576–1628) Jesuit missionary and martyr*. Born in Paraguay, Gonzalez dedicated his life to the evangelization of Indians. He founded a number of settlements in Brazil and was martyred in 1628.

Good Book The Bible.

Good Friday Also, Great Friday* (Eastern Orthodox Church*); Long Friday; Day of Preparation; Day of the Lord's Passion; and the Passion of the Cross. The Friday before Easter* commemorating the crucifixion of Christ. Holy Communion* is never celebrated on this day, but devotional services are held. These often focus on the Seven Words of Jesus on the cross. The liturgical color of the day is red. In the Eastern Orthodox Church*, Good Friday services generally end with a symbolic burial service.

Good News Literal English translation of the Greek word *gospel*.

Good News Bible Translation of the Old and the New Testaments in "today's English" version, produced by the American Bible Society*.

Good Saturday Saturday following Good Friday* in the Passion Week*.

Good Shepherd Title of Jesus Christ, one that he claimed himself.

good works 1. Right deeds through which human beings attempt to please God and fulfill his commandments. 2. Fruits of the Holy Spirit* that are the evidence of salvation* in a believer's life.

Goodall, Norman (1896–1985) British missionary statesman responsible for the merger of the International Missionary Council* (IMC) and the World Council of Churches* (WCC). He succeeded William Paton* in 1944 as secretary of the IMC and 17 years later shepherded its integration with WCC at the WCC Assembly in New Delhi.

Goodspeed, Edgar Johnson (1871–1962) American New Testament scholar of Greek. He taught biblical and patristic Greek at the University of Chicago from 1900 to 1937 and pioneered in collating New Testament manuscripts. He translated into American English the New Testament (1923), the Apocrypha* (1938), and the Apostolic Fathers (1950) and was a member of the committee that produced the Revised Standard Version* of the New Testament in 1946. Of his over 60 books, the most important were *An Introduction to the New Testament* (1937), *History of Early Christian Literature* (1942), *How to Read the Bible* (1946), and *A Life of Jesus* (1950).

Gorcum Martyrs Nineteen secular and religious priests, including 11 friars of the Franciscan convent at Gorcum in Holland, who were massacred by Calvinists at Briel in 1572.

Gordon, Adoniram Judson (1836–1895) American Baptist minister and educator. He founded a school for training missionaries and pastors' assistants from which Gordon College in Boston was formed. His works include *The Ministry of Healing* (1882) and *The Ministry of the Spirit* (1894).

The Good Shepherd

Gordon-Conwell Theological Seminary Evangelical seminary founded in 1969 as a merger between Gordon Divinity School (founded in Boston in 1889 by Adoniram Judson Gordon*) and Conwell School of Theology (founded in 1884 in Philadelphia* by Russell Conwell. The school offers masters and doctoral degrees in three campuses at Hamilton (the home campus), Boston, and Charlotte. The school has had three presidents: Harold John Ockenga* (1969–1979), Robert Cooley (1981–1997), and Walter C. Kaiser (1997–). Among the well-known Evangelicals who have served on the faculty are George Ladd, Carl F. H. Henry*, Kenneth Kantzer, and Peter Kuzmic.

Gordon's Calvary Place near Jerusalem's Damascus Gate, sometimes called the Gordon's Tomb, identified by Charles Gordon and Otto Thenius as the site of the Crucifixion. It is a skull-shaped mound with eye-like caves.

Gore, Charles (1853–1932) English bishop and liberal Anglo-Catholic theologian. He was active in the founding of the Christian Social Union and was the founder in 1892 of the Community of the Resurrection*. He was successively bishop of Worcester, Birmingham, and Oxford. He edited the symposium *Lux Mundi** and was the author of many books, including *The Sermon on the Mount* (1896), *The Body of Christ* (1901), *The Ministry of the Christian Church* (1919), *The Holy Spirit and the Church* (1924), and *Christ and Society* (1928).

Goreh, Nilakantha (Nehemiah) (1825–1895) Indian Christian leader. Born in a high-caste Brahmin family in Maharashtra, Goreh was converted in 1848 and took the Christian name of Nehemiah. At first, he was an Evangelical affiliated with the Church Missionary Society*. In 1861 he wrote the work for which he is best remembered, *Saddarshan Darpan* (Rational Refutation of Hindu Philosophical Systems). Gradually he moved from Evangelical to High Church* Anglicanism and was ordained priest in 1870. He was instrumental in the conversion of Pandita Ramabai* in 1888.

Goreme Valley in Cappadocia* in Asia Minor where Christian refugees from Roman persecutions founded villages among the rock formations. Later, hermits, anchorites*, and monks arrived and carved cells* out of solid rock. At one time, 40,000 monks lived in Goreme.

gornoye myesto In the Byzantine and Salvonic tradition, the elevated place behind the altar upon which the bishop's throne stands.

Gorze Benedictine monastery in Mainz* founded in 748 by St. Chrodegang*. It was revived and rebuilt by Adalbert I and became one of the chief seats of monastic reform, comparable in influence to Cluny. Although it did not create a network of daughter institutions, its abbots were invited by lay and episcopal patrons to take charge of and reform monasteries within their jurisdictions. Its influence lasted until the thirteenth century. Then it declined until it was fully secularized in 1572 and suppressed in 1790.

gospel (Gk., lit., Good News) 1. Good News* of the salvation* of mankind through the redemptive work of Jesus Christ and his sacrifice on the cross, or glad tidings of peace and goodwill, announced by the angels to the shepherds at Jerusalem*. 2. The first four books of the New Testament written by the four evangelists: Matthew, Mark, Luke and John. 3. Part of a liturgical service when portions of the four Gospels are read. 4. Gospel music*.

gospel hymn Hymn or liturgical song based on the gospel or using words borrowed from the gospel.

Gospel Missionary Union Evangelical foreign missionary society founded in 1892 in Topeka, Kansas, with A. E. Bishop, R. A. Torrey*, and George Fisher serving as executives. The union is active in evangelism in Africa and Central and South America.

gospel music Religious music of American origin with a strong revivalist overtone that evolved from the Negro spirituals* and Sunday school* hymnody*. Unsophisticated in melody and harmony, it generally focuses on personal salvation* and relies heavily on biblical text. Its characteristic feature is a refrain at the end of each verse. Representative gospel songs have an enduring appeal like "The Old Rugged Cross" and "Blessed Assurance." Gospel music was used heavily by D. L. Moody* and I. D. Sankey* in their revivals—and also by the Salvation Army*—and it continues to be the dominant musical form in many Evangelical churches.

In the black churches, gospel music incorporates elements of ragtime and jazz blues and much call and response interaction between the lead singers and the congregation. Handclapping and dancing may accompany the singing with or without instrumental music, particularly electric organs, drums, and tambourines. The black style of gospel music has been adopted by most Pentecostal churches* and has spread throughout the world. It was founded by Thomas Dorsey*, writer of "Peace in the Valley" (1937), and was popularized by singers like Mahalia Jackson*. It has became the most commercially viable form of Christian music and enjoys a special place in the recording industry, where it is called *gospel*. The Gospel Music Association in Nashville, Tennessee, awards the annual Dove Awards and also administers the Gospel Music Hall of Fame.

Gospel side Left side of the sanctuary, as one faces the altar table, where the Gospel is traditionally read or sung.

gospeler, gospeller 1. In the Roman Catholic Church, reader and singer of the Gospel. The gospeler is traditionally the deacon, who goes to the appointed place accompanied by thurifer* and acolytes*, says "dominus vobiscum*," announces the chapter and verse, and censes the book. 2. Gospel preacher.

Gossner, Johannes Evangelista (1773–1858) German founder of the Gossner Mission. Brought up as a Roman Catholic, he was ordained priest in 1796. Involved in disputes with his superiors, he became a Lutheran in 1829 and served as a pastor in a Moravian Bohemian Brethren* church. Increasing concern for foreign missions led him to found the Gossner Mission as a loosely knit missionary enterprise in 1836. In 1842 the Gossner Mission was chartered. It sent out 141 missionaries during Gossner's lifetime, mainly to North India.

Gothic Dominant architectural style in medieval

Europe, from around 1150 to 1550. The period is customarily divided into Early, High and Late Gothic. Typical features are high pointed arches, large windows, elaborately vaulted roofs, flying buttresses, spires*, and pinnacles.

Chartres Cathedral

Gothic Version Translation of the Bible into the Gothic language in the fourth century by the Arian bishop Ulphilas*. Only the four Gospels and the Pauline Epistles survive in the New Testament and fragments of Ezra and Nehemiah in the Old Testament. The best known manuscript in this version is the Codex Argenteus, written in gold and silver upon purple vellum, now at Uppsala*.

Codex Argenteus

Gothic vestments Medieval eucharistic vestments consisting of long and narrow stole* and maniple* and circular chasuble*, in contrast to the modern eucharistic vestments with broad and short stole and maniple and rectangular chasuble.

goti In the Armenian Church*, richly embroidered cincture* or girdle* that secures the stole* to the alb*.

Gottesfreunde See FRIENDS OF GOD.

Gotthard, St. (960/61–1038) Bishop of Hildesheim*. He joined the Benedictines* in 991 and soon became prior* and abbot. He initiated many reforms in the monasteries of Upper Germany at the instance of Emperor Henry I. St. Gotthard Pass in the Alps takes it name from a chapel on the summit dedicated to him.

Gottschalk of Orbais (c. 804–c. 869) Controversial theologian and Benedictine monk. His study of the works of St. Augustine* led him to a doctrine, known as double predestination*, according to which the chosen are predestined to blessedness and others to eternal fire, thus limiting the universal saving will of God and the universality of offer of redemption*. He was condemned at the Synod of Mainz (848), the Synod of Quiercy* (849), and the Synod of Douzy (860). Gottschalk was also a skilled poet.

Gottweig Benedictine monastery in Gottweig, Austria, perched above the Danube. In 1718 the original church was destroyed by fire. It was rebuilt by Lukas of Hildebrandt, a military architect. The complex was never quite completed. Five courtyards, seven towers, and a colossal dome above the crossing* were constructed in accordance with Lukas's plan. The imperial staircase occupies an entire wing and gives an idea of the monastery's lavish scale and grandeur. Among the monastery's many treasures is the Gottweig Psalter.

Goudimel, Claude (c. 1510–1572) French Huguenot* composer. Under Calvin's* influence at Geneva* he compiled tunes in the metrical psalms* and published them in extended motet* settings. In 1564 he published 150 Genevan psalms in simple four-part settings and again in more elaborate versions in 1568. He also composed masses and secular chansons. He was killed in the St. Bartholomew's Day Massacre*.

Gounod, Charles Francois (1818–1893) French composer and choral conductor who wrote a number of anthems and sacred songs. His best known works include the oratorio*, *Redemption,* and St. Cecilia Mass.

Goupil, St. Rene (c. 1607–1642) French Jesuit missionary to North America who was tortured and tomahawked by Native Americans. Feast day: September 26.

gourd Religious symbol of resurrection.

Gozzoli, Benozzo (1420–1497) Student of Fra Angelico*, a painter of altarpieces, frescoes, and murals. His best known work is the *Journey of the Magi.*

Grabar Classical Armenian, an Indo-European language and the liturgical language of the Armenian Orthodox Church.

Gracanica The Church of the Dormition (1311–1321) at the Monastery of Gracanica, near Pristina, in Kosovo*, province of Serbia, built by King Stefan Uros II. Constructed on a cross-in-square plan with narthex*, it has five domes and is considered an architectural masterpiece. It was deserted after the fall of Serbia in 1459 but was revived through the efforts of Metropolitan Nikanor, who established a printing press there in 1539.

grace Unmerited and free favor and mercy shown to sinners by a sovereign God with a view to their salvation*. It is most effectively demonstrated in certain aspects of God's relationship with his creation, the Incarnation* itself being an act of grace. Grace operates in the calling* of believers to faith as well as in the individual calling of certain believers to the gifts of the ministry. In the Western Church*, a theology of grace emerged in the controversies between Augustinianism* and Pelagianism*, the former holding that some human beings receive the grace of justification* and salvation and that it is irresistible. Human will can neither of itself invoke divine grace nor defy it. Pelagianism* took the exact contrary position. In New Testament theology, the Old Testament is considered the age of law and the New

Testament as the age of grace. In Roman Catholic theology, grace is portrayed as a power conveyed through sacraments* as well as by faith.

grace Usually, "his grace," "your grace." Title of address for bishops in the Roman Catholic* and Eastern Orthodox* traditions.

grace, actual 1. Supernatural help given to avoid sin or accomplish good deeds. 2. Manifestation of divine grace by which a person is drawn toward God. See GRACE, EFFICACIOUS; GRACE, SUFFICIENT.

grace at meals Customary thanksgiving at meals, based on Christ's example.

grace, baptismal Divine grace extended to the baptizee* as part of baptismal regeneration*.

grace, cheap Acceptance of God's grace in salvation* without a corresponding desire to repent of sin or live a life of obedience to the Lord. The term is especially associated with Dietrich Bonhoeffer*.

grace, cooperating Action of the Holy Spirit* working together with human response to God's operating grace*.

grace, efficacious Power of God to effect salvation* working through human will. Such a grace does not force the will and destroy freedom. Distinguished from sufficient grace*.

grace, habitual Sanctifying work of the Holy Spirit*.

grace, illuminating Work of the Holy Spirit* illuminating the mind of the sinner and leading to understanding of the truth of God.

grace, infused Work of the Holy Spirit* that makes an individual desire and then accept the gospel.

grace, irresistible Power of the Holy Spirit* against which no human will can prevail.

grace of office Gift of the Holy Spirit* bestowed on those called into the ministry and that enables them to exercise the functions they have been assigned.

grace, operating God's initiative in offering salvation* to human beings.

grace, prevenient God's preparatory work in the heart of a sinner turning him or her toward conversion.

grace, sacramental Communication of divine grace through the celebration and reception of sacraments.

grace, sanctifying Divine grace that results in the sanctification* and rebirth of the believer. The person ceases to be a sinner and becomes justified and righteous in the sight of God.

grace, sufficient In theology, grace that is adequate for its purpose if it meets with the necessary human response. Contrasted with efficacious grace* which produces the intended result as a result of human cooperation. See also GRACE, ACTUAL.

Gracian, Baltasar (1601–1658) Spanish Jesuit preacher and head of the College of Tarragona. He is noted chiefly as a practitioner of Gongorism, a polished literary style.

gradine Ledge above and behind the altar upon which the cross, candlesticks, and other ornaments are sometimes placed.

gradual (Lat., *gradus,* step) In the Roman Catholic Church, antiphonal verses, usually from the Psalms, sung immediately after the first scriptural

Illuminated Gradual

lesson. Its name is derived from the practice of singing it on the altar steps or while the deacon was ascending the steps of the ambo*. Since 1969 it has been replaced by the responsorial psalm sung by the cantor* or the choir and the people. The term is also applied to the book containing the proper of the Mass*.

Gradual Psalms The group of Psalms, 120 to 134, called Songs of Degrees or Ascents in reference to their step-like literary progression, lifting up the heart in praise.

Graduale Romanum Book with all the chants for the Mass* required in a year.

graffiti Ancient inscriptions on tombs and catacombs* that are scratched and not carved.

Graham, William Franklin ("Billy") (1918–) American evangelist. After conversion and ordination, he served briefly, as a pastor, before becoming in 1943 an evangelist for the newly founded Youth for Christ*. In 1949 his first evangelistic campaign in Los Angeles was an outstanding success promoted by the popular media, especially the Hearst newspapers. In 1950 the Billy Graham Evangelistic Association* was formed. Thereafter he toured almost all countries in five continents and held crusades* in the stadiums of all major world cities, preaching to millions. Like D. L. Moody* before him, he has had an able team which has included songleader Cliff Barrows and singer George Beverly Shea*.

Billy Graham

The Billy Graham crusades are highly organized events, for which planning begins years before the event, with prayers from local evangelistic churches and the support of local ministers and laity. In every crusade he appeals for decisions for Christ, and the thousands that respond are carefully counseled and followed up by trained professionals. Graham's evangelistic ministry extends beyond crusades into books, films, radio, and television. He is a founder of *Christianity Today*, and was the host of the weekly radio broadcast, "Hour of Decision." Many of his books, particularly *Peace with God, Angels,* and his *Autobiography,* have been bestsellers. He has inspired a number of world conferences, such as that on evangelism in Berlin in 1966. His immensely successful ministries have made him the best known religious figure in the second half of the twentieth-century.

grail Cup* or chalice*.

Grail, Holy Legendary chalice* of the Last Supper, filled with the blood of Christ, sought by the knights of the Arthurian legend. In this vessel, Joseph of Arimathea caught the last drops of Christ's blood as he was taken from the cross. It was then brought by angels and entrusted to a body of knights who guarded it on the top of a mountain. When approached by anyone not perfectly pure, it vanished from sight. The search for the grail was the subject of many literary works, including Chrestien de Troyes' *Perceval,* Thomas Malory's *Book of Arthur,* and Wolfram of Eschenbach's *Parsifal.* According to the Gospel of Nicodemus*, the Holy Grail was taken by Joseph of Arimathea to Glastonbury* in England.

Grail, The International Roman Catholic lay women's movement, with its roots in the Women of Nazareth, a spiritual apostolate* established by Dutch Jesuit Jacques van Ginneken in 1921. It offers specialized programs for young women designed to enrich their personal, professional, and spiritual lives. These courses are offered at Grailville, near Loveland, Ohio. A School of Missiology was opened at Grailville in 1950.

Granada, Luis de (1504–1588) Birth name: Luis de Sarria. Spanish spiritual writer. He entered the

Dominican* Order in 1525 and became a disciple of John of Avila*. In 1550/1 he was invited to go to Portugal, where he lived for most of the remainder of his life. He was provincial* of the Portuguese Dominicans* from 1556 to 1560 and was confessor* to many of the nobles, including the Duke of Alba. He refused higher ecclesiastical office and dedicated himself to writing, preaching, and meditation. His many books on the spiritual life were distinguished by their high literary quality and were translated into Spanish, French, Italian, and English. His two chief books were *Book on Prayer and Meditation* (1554) and *Guide for Sinners* (1556–1557). They were placed on the Index in 1559 but have survived in later editions.

Grande See CHARTREUSE, LA GRANDE.

grange Farm buildings belonging to a monastery.

grasshopper Symbol of triumphant Christianity that appears in religious art in the hands of infant Jesus.

Gratian (twelfth century) The father of canon law*. A Camaldolese* monk, he compiled *Concordia Discordantium Canonum,* better known as the Decreta or Decretum, in which 4,000 papal and conciliar decrees and writings of the Church Fathers* are systematically arranged and all contradictions and inconsistencies resolved. It became part of the *Corpus Iuris Canonici**.

gravamen (Lat., grievance) In the Church of England*, memorial sent from the Lower to the Upper House of Convocation with a view to securing the remedy of disorders cited.

graveyard evangelism Preaching and evangelism engaged in during funerals and burials, especially in anti-Christian countries where preaching outside church buildings is prohibited.

Gray, Asa (1810–1888) American botanist. Preeminent botanist of the nineteenth century who combined an outstanding scientific reputation with a strong Evangelical Christian faith. As professor at Harvard, he was the leading advocate for a theistic interpretation of Darwinism.

Gray Friars See FRANCISCAN ORDER.

Great Awakening Series of revivals* in the American colonies between 1725 and 1760. It began in two locations at the same time. In New Jersey, T. J. Frelinghuysen* and Gilbert Tennent* stirred the faithful with their fervent preaching and experienced a fresh influx of converts. To the north, Jonathan Edwards* witnessed the same phenomenon as a result of his fiery call for repentance*. These two regional revivals were linked through the efforts of the one man with whom the Great Awakening is indelibly associated: George Whitefield*. He traveled throughout the colonies and planted the seeds of Evangelical Christianity. In the South, Presbyterians experienced revival through the reading houses of Samuel Davis, while revival was brought to Methodists with the preaching of Devereux Jarratt and to Baptists through the work of Daniel Marshall and Shubal Stearns.

Resistance from the mainline churches* divided some of the churches. In New England the followers of Jonathan Edwards were known as the New Lights* and their opposition as the Old Lights*. The Presbyterians split into New Side* and Old Side groups between 1741 and 1758 and the Baptists into Separate and Regular Baptists*. In his *Some Thoughts Concerning the Present Revival,* Jonathan Edwards described the spiritual and theological fallout of the Great Awakening. Theologically, it led to the birth of New England theology*. It also made a profound impact on education and led to the founding of Princeton University, the University of Pennsylvania, Rutgers University, Dartmouth University, and Brown University.

A similar revival at the end of the eighteenth and the beginning of the nineteenth centuries is sometimes known as the Second Great Awakening*. Beginning in frontier Kentucky, it was spread by the Methodists and Baptists. Another revival in the 1850s is sometimes called the Third Great Awakening.

Great Bible English Bible published by royal authority and edited by Miles Coverdale* in 1539 and distributed to every parish church in England. It appeared in several successive editions in 1540 and 1541 and for several years thereafter.

Great Commandment 1. Great Commission*. 2. Commandment to love God with heart, soul, and strength, the greatest of the commandments according to Jesus (Matt. 22:37; Luke 10:27).

Great Commission Also, Great Commandment*. Mandate given to all believers by Jesus Christ which says: "Go therefore and make disciples of all the nations, baptizing them in the name of the Father and of the Son and of the Holy Spirit, teaching them to observe all things that I have commanded you; and lo, I am with you always, even to the end of the age" (Matt. 28:19–20; Mark 16:15–18; Luke 24:46–49; John 20:21–22; Acts 1:8). The missionary movement of the early church and the modern church is based on this command.

Jesus' Great Commission to His Followers

Great Commissioner Christian engaged in evangelism and who follows and obeys the Great Commission*.

Great Entrance 1. In the Eastern Church*, solemn procession in which the eucharistic bread and wine are carried from the prothesis* to the altar. See also LITTLE ENTRANCE. 2. In the Byzantine Rite*, the name for the procession of priests and deacons who bring bread and wine as gifts to the altar at the beginning of the eucharistic service.

Great Euchologion In the Eastern Church*, book containing the fixed parts, or ordinary, of vespers*, mattins*, the eucharistic liturgy, and the Liturgy of the Presanctified* as well as the remaining six sacraments. See also EUCHOLOGION.

Great Fast In the Eastern churches*, Lent which begins on a Monday, known as the Clean Monday or on the preceding Sunday evening, known as the Sunday of Forgiveness, and lasts for 48 days until Easter*. It is preceded by an eighth week, known as Cheese Week, when no meat may be eaten, but cheese and dairy products are permitted.

Great Festival In the Coptic Church*, Easter*.

Great Friday See GOOD FRIDAY.

Great Intercession Prayer for "the whole state of Christ's church." It is part of all the major rites.

Great Martyr St. George* of Cappadocia* about whom many legends abound.

Great Octave Easter* as an octave* made up of eight Sundays.

Great Prayer In the Presbyterian Church of Scotland*, pastoral prayer in the church service, including adoration of God, confession* of sin, petition* for mercy, supplication for needs, and general thanksgiving*.

Great Revival Religious revival in 1800 and 1801 in states west of the Allegheny Mountains, led by James McGready* and John McGee and accompanied by unusual manifestations.

Great Sabbath Saturday in Holy Week* (John 19:31).

Great Schism 1. Breach between the Western and Eastern churches* beginning in 1054. The break was caused by the excommunication* of the patriarch* of Constantinople* by the Latin legates and the retaliatory expulsion of the Latin legates by the ecumenical patriarch*. The two churches grew further apart after the Latin capture of Constantinople in 1204. Although the Councils of Lyons* (1274) and Florence (1439) tried to mend the breach, it became final when the Union of Florence was repudiated by a Synod of Constantinople in 1484. In the twentieth century, the division has become less bitter, especially after Pope Paul VI* and the ecumenical patriarch*

Athenagoras nullified the anathemas of 1054. 2. Known also as the Great Western Schism. Period of 39 years from 1378 to 1417 when there were two popes in the Roman Catholic Church. It was ended with the Council of Constance* (1414–1418) and the election of Martin V* in 1417. See also POPE.

great silence Period of silence observed from compline* until after prime* next morning.

Great Sobor Russian Orthodox administrative church council.

Great Thursday In the Byzantine tradition, Maundy Thursday*.

Great Week In the Eastern Church*, the Holy Week*.

Grebel, Conrad (c. 1498–1526) Organizer of the first Free Church congregation, also known as Swiss Brethren*, in Zurich* in 1525. An early follower of Zwingli*, he broke with Zwinglianism* after espousing believer's baptism*, rejection of civil oaths* and military service, religious toleration, and the saved status of infants who die before baptism*. On January 21, 1525, the Anabaptist* movement was born when Grebel baptized Georg Blaurock*. He was fined and imprisoned by civic authorities in Zurich*.

greca (lit., Greek) Long overcoat worn by European clergy over the cassock*.

Greco, El (1541–1614) Birth name: Dominikos Theotokopoulos. Born in Crete, he moved to Venice*, where he was a pupil of Tintoretto*. He moved to Rome* about 1570 and then to Toledo* in Spain in 1577. His work in Toledo included a side altar and two side altars in St. Domingo el Antiguo with eight paintings: *Assumption* (over 16 feet high), the *Trinity* (over 10 feet in height), *St. John the Evangelist, St. John the Baptist, St. Bernard, St. Benedict, Adoration of the Shepherds,* and *Resurrection.* El Greco remained in Toledo for the rest of his life, producing huge altarpieces of passionate and ecstatic feeling, heightened by his religious devotion to the Jesuit ideals. He painted only New Testament themes, and one of his char-

acteristics was his fondness for vertical and elongated figures. Among the paintings he produced in his workshop are the *Epolio* (The Disrobing of Christ), *Martyrdom of the Theban Legion,* and *Burial of Conde de Orgaz.*

Greek 1. Native of Greece. 2. Language of Greece in which the New Testament and the Septuagint were written, known to linguists as Hellenistic Greek or Koine*. It was a simplified form of Attic Greek with borrowings from other languages, such as Aramaic and Hebrew. Hellenistic Greek was the lingua franca of Palestine at the time of Christ and for many succeeding centuries. The Septuagint was written in the Alexandrian version of Greek while the New Testament was written in the Palestinian version. Greek style in the New Testament varies from the highly literate Luke to the highly vernacular and ungrammatical Revelation. After Christianity became the official religion of the Roman Empire, most Eastern Church Fathers* tended to adopt Byzantine or Patristic Greek.

Greek cross Cross with all four arms equal in length.

Greek Fathers Church Fathers* of the Eastern Orthodox Church*, such as Basil*, Athanasius*, and Chrysostom*.

Greek Rite Liturgy of the Eastern Orthodox Church*.

Green Thursday Maundy Thursday*, so named from the custom of giving green branches to penitents* who had made confession* at the beginning of Lent*.

Gregoire, Henri (1750–1831) French cleric and revolutionary. Bishop of Blois, who sided with the French revolutionaries and was elected to the States General. He was the first priest to sign the loyalty oath* to the civil constitution of the clergy. In 1792 he was elected president of the National Assembly. At the height of the terror in 1793 he refused to renounce his faith or to give up his clerical robes. He opposed Napoleon's rapprochement with the Vatican* and resigned his office in 1801.

Gregoras, Nicephoras (c. 1295–1360) Controversial Byzantine theologian and historian. He was a prolific writer on a variety of subjects, including theology, astronomy, hagiography*, philosophy, grammar, and history. His masterpiece was *Roman History,* covering the years 1204 to 1359 in 37 volumes. He led negotiations for the reunion of the Western and Eastern churches* and opposed the Hesychasm* movement.

Gregorian calendar The Christian calendar as reformed in 1582 by Gregory XIII* and now in universal use. Its predecessor, the Julian calendar* devised by Julius Caesar, was inaccurate by a few hours every year, and it was determined that an error of ten days had accumulated by the sixteenth century. The difference was corrected by the papal bull* *Inter Gravissimas.* It was further determined that century years were to be leap years only when divisible by 400, for example in 2000. Protestant countries accepted the calendar reform only slowly. Protestant German states adopted it in 1699, Switzerland in 1701, England in 1752, Sweden in 1753, Japan in 1873, China in 1912, the Soviet Union in 1918, and Greece in 1923. Orthodox churches began to accept it only in 1924, but most of them still use the Julian calendar*.

Gregorian Chant Also, plainsong*. Unmetrical and unaccompanied plainsong, the traditional liturgical music of the Roman Catholic Church, so named from Pope Gregory I*, who standardized it. Its tonal organization is based on a system of modes, or scales corresponding to the white notes of the piano and centered for the most part on the notes D, E, F, and G. Its repertory grew enormously in the later Middle Ages, but most additional melodies were eliminated by the Council of Trent*. There was an attempt by the monks of Solesmus under the leadership of Dom Joseph Pothier (1835–1923) to revive the medieval traditions. Since the Second Vatican Council*, the Gregorian Chant* is no longer the standard accompaniment of the Roman Liturgy, but it experienced a commercial revival in the 1990s and has gained more acceptance in Roman Catholic and Anglican churches. Most Gregorian chants are contained in the Gradual for the Mass* and the Antiphonal* for the Choral Office, and others are found in the Manuale, the Pontifical*, and the Processional.

Gregorian Church See ARMENIAN CHURCH.

Gregorian Sacramentary Roman liturgy in use in the Frankish kingdom, traditionally ascribed to Pope Gregory I*. One copy of the Gregorian Sacramentary is known as Hadrianus, because it was sent by Pope Hadrian I* to Charlemagne*, dated 811 or 812. It is preserved at Cambrai, and another copy is preserved in the Chapter Library at Padua. Later it was combined with the Gelasian service books to form the Roman Missal.

Gregorian University Formerly, the Pontifical Gregorian University, a Jesuit institution in Rome*, founded as the Roman College by Ignatius Loyola* and Francis Borgia* in 1551. Closely associated with the university, yet autonomous, are the Pontifical Bible Institute and the Pontifical Oriental Institute.

Gregorian water Solemnly blessed water with a mixture of salt, ashes, and wine, used in the consecration of churches and altars, so named because Pope Gregory I* devised the formula* for blessing it.

Gregorians Armenian Orthodox Christians, from St. Gregory the Illuminator*, the apostle of Armenia.

Gregory I, St. (c. 540–604) Known as Gregory the Great. Pope from 590. He was the fourth and last of the traditional Latin doctors of the church* and also the first monk to become pope. With the breakdown of temporal authority in Italy, he became the virtual civil ruler. A gifted administrator and reformer, he promoted the evangelization of England by sending St. Augustine to Canterbury*. His most enduring work is *Pastoral Care,* which became a textbook for medieval bishops. Gregory was an keen promoter of monasticism* and brought religious orders under direct papal control. He encouraged the veneration* of authentic relics*, and his *Dialogues* on Italian saints fostered a debased popular piety. Some of the prayers in the Gregorian Sacramentary* are believed to be his, and his contributions to the development of liturgical music led to the Gregorian Chant* being named after him. A man of great personal humility, he was the first to use the papal title, Servus Servorum Dei* (Servant of the Servants of God). Feast day: March 12 (Eastern Church*); September 3 (Western Church*).

Pope Gregory I

Gregory II, St. (669–731). Pope from 715. In 719 he sent St. Boniface* to convert the German tribes. In 727 he opposed the iconoclasm* of Leo the Isaurian at the Synod of Rome*.

Gregory III (d. 741) Pope from 731. Syrian by birth, he was elected by acclaim at his predecessor's funeral. He held a synod* in Rome in 731, denouncing iconoclasm* and confirming the worship of images.

Gregory V (d. 999) Pope from 996. Birth name: Bruno of Carinthia. The first German pope.

Gregory VII, St. (d. 1085) Pope from 1073. Birth name: Hildebrand. One of the greatest popes in history, his pontificate* marked the end of the first millennium of the church. Throughout his pontificate*, he worked hard to reform the church by issuing decrees against simony* and clerical immorality. He also insisted that metropolitan* bishops should come to Rome* to receive the pallium*. His last words summed up his papacy: "I have loved righteousness and hated iniquity." Feast day: May 25.

Gregory IX (1148–1241) Pope from 1227. Birth

name: Ugolino, Count of Segni. During his papacy he was embroiled in a struggle with Frederick II. He was a personal friend of St. Francis and assisted in the development of the third order*.

Gregory X (1210–1276) Pope from 1271. Birth name: Teobaldo Visconti. The chief events of his papacy were the deliverance of Jerusalem*, the reform of the church, reunion with the Greeks, and pacification of the German Empire. During his reign the constitution Ubi Periculum was passed in 1274, introducing the conclave* for the election of the pope.

Gregory XI (1329–1378) Pope from 1370. Birth name: Pierre Roger de Beaufort. The last French pope. He terminated the Babylonian Captivity* at Avignon* by moving to Rome* in 1376, at the insistence of St. Catherine of Siena*.

Gregory XIII (1502–1585) Pope from 1572. Birth name: Ugo Buoncompagni. He is remembered for his introduction of the Gregorian calendar*. His pontificate* was notable for his vigorous enforcement of the decrees of the Council of Trent*, especially those dealing with the foundation of seminaries. He founded in Rome* the German College in 1573, the Greek College in 1577, the English College* and the Hungarian College in 1579, and the Maronite College in 1584. He entrusted most of them to the Jesuits* to whom he also gave a monopoly over the missions to China and Japan.

Gregory XIV (1535–1591) Pope from 1590. Birth name: Niccolo Sfondrati. He insisted on a just treatment of Indians in the New World and ordered a revision of the Sixtine Bible.

Gregory XVI (1765–1846) Pope from 1831. Birth name: Bartolomeo Alberto Capellari. Popular insurrections took place in the papal states at the beginning of his reign which were suppressed only through Austrian intervention. He was successful in promoting foreign missions. His apostolic constitution*, *In Supremo* (1839), denounced slavery and the slave trade.

Gregory of Elvira, St. (d. after 392) Bishop of Elvira near Granada. An implacable foe of Arianism*, he became a follower of Lucifer* of Cagliari, who refused to pardon Arians at the Council of Ariminum* (359), and became a leader of the Luciferians. A theologian of note, his writings include *De Fide Orthodoxa,* the so called *Tractatus Origenis,* and *Tractatus de Epithalamio.*

Gregory of Narek, St. (c. 950–1010) Armenian poet, monk, and theologian. He spent most of his life in the Monastery of Narek, south of Lake Van. Best known for his *Book of Lamentations,* he also wrote a number of hymns dedicated to the Virgin Mary*. Feast day: February 27.

Gregory of Nazianzus, St. (c. 330–390) Cappadocian bishop of Constantinople* and one of the four great fathers of the Eastern Church*. A friend and classmate of Basil of Caesarea*, he joined Basil's monastery and was ordained priest and later bishop. He was summoned out of the monastery to Constantinople to defend the Nicene faith against Arianism*. His ministry at the Church of the Anastasis contributed to the final triumph of Nicene orthodoxy. During the council, he was named bishop of Constantinople but resigned his see* and retired to the church at Nazianzus. Although unimpressive in stature, Gregory was a great orator whose famous five *Theological Ora-*

St. Gregory of Nazianzus

tions against Arians and Eunomians were powerful statements of faith. His other writings include *Philocalia,* a selection from the works of Origen* and 242 letters and poems. Feast day: January 2 (Western Church*); January 25 (Eastern Church*).

Gregory of Nyssa, St. (c. 330–c. 395) Cappadocian bishop of Nyssa, one of the four great Eastern Fathers. Younger brother of Basil of Caesarea*, at whose invitation he became first a monk and then bishop of Nyssa. A champion of orthodoxy*, he was deposed by a synod* of Arian bishops in 376, but regained his see* in 378 on the death of Emperor Valens. Within a few years his fame spread throughout the Middle East. He took a leading part in the First Council of Constantinople*. He was tireless in attacking Apollinaris*, Eunomius*, and Jews.

Although lacking in Basil's* immense practical abilities, he was the more gifted theologian and is considered the outstanding theologian of the later fourth century. Such was Gregory's originality and intellectual prowess that the Council of Nicaea* (787) named him the "Father of Fathers*." His chief apologetic work was *Catechetical Oration,* a manual of theology. Many of his sermons, funeral orations, and letters have survived. A defender of the Nicene Creed*, he was among the first to differentiate between *ousia* and hypostasis*. His exposition of the doctrines of the Trinity*, Incarnation*, and redemption* was accepted as theologically expert. Together with Origen* he held that souls in hell* and even the devils will return to God. Feast day: January 10 (Eastern Church*); March 9 (Western Church*).

Gregory of Rimini (d. 1358) Medieval philosopher known as Doctor Authenticus. He joined the Augustinian Hermits and was elected general* of his order in 1357. Between 1329 and 1357 he taught at Bologna*, Padua, and Perugia and in 1345 was made doctor of the Sorbonne*. His philosophy was uncompromisingly Augustinian and held that works done without grace* are sinful. Much interest has focused on his influence on Luther's* early development.

Gregory of Sinai (1255/65–c. 1337) Monk and ascetic. He is credited with the revival of orthodox monasticism* and the Hesychast movement in the fourteenth and fifteenth centuries. He actively promoted the practice of the Jesus Prayer*. Originally from the Monastery of St. Catherine on Sinai*, he lived most of his life on Athos* and, later, Thrace.

Gregory of Tatev, St. (c. 1346–1409) Armenian theologian and monk. He was the author of the *Book of Questions*, a summa* of Armenian theology. Feast day: Third Saturday of Lent*.

Gregory of Tours, St. (c. 538–594) Frankish bishop and historian. Born of a noble Roman family, he was named bishop of Tours in 573. In addition to performing his ecclesiastical duties, Gregory wrote extensively. His writings consist of ten books of histories, seven books of miracles, a book on the lives of the fathers, and a treatise on the offices of the church. His best known work, *Historia Francorum,* covers the history of the world up to 511 in the first two books and the history of the Franks up to 591 in the remaining eight books. His works are an important source for the history of Gaul and the spread of Christianity in the region. Feast day: November 17.

Gregory Palamas, St. (c. 1296–1359) Greek theologian and chief advocate of Hesychasm*. He embraced monastic life as a youth and went to Mount Athos* in 1318 where he became familiar with the Hesychast tradition of mystical prayer. After a brief residence as a bishop in Thessalonica, he returned to Athos as a monk in 1331. In refutation of an attack on Hesychasm by Barlaam, a Greek monk from Calabria, Gregory composed his most important work, *Triads in Defense of the Holy Hesychasts* (1338). His stand was approved by his fellow monks as well as three councils at Constantinople* in 1341, 1347, and 1351. Palamas also wrote *One Hundred and Fifty Chapters,* an exposition of his theological beliefs. Feast day: November 14.

Gregory Thaumaturgus, St. (c. 213–c. 270) "The Wonder Worker," Greek Church Father. At about 233 he went to Caesarea* in Palestine, where he became a disciple of Origen* and was converted by him. After eight years he returned to his native city of Neocaesarea in Pontus in northern Asia Minor, where he was consecrated bishop. Here he acquired his surname of Thaumaturgus because of the many miracles and healings attributed to him. In 264–265 he took part in the Synod of Antioch* against Paul of Samosata*. He claimed the first known apparition of the Virgin Mary*. Among his works is a panegyric on Origen and an

exposition of the doctrine of the Trinity*. Feast day: November 17.

Gregory the Illuminator, St. (c. 240–c. 332) "Apostle of Armenia." A Parthian of royal descent, he converted King Tiridates of Armenia to the Christian faith and thus established the first national Christian church. He was consecrated catholicos*, and the episcopate* remained in his family for a few generations. His son Aristakes attended the Council of Nicaea*. His biography was written by Agathangelos*, the first Armenian historian.

St. Gregory the Illuminator

gremial Lap cloth or silk apron* used by a bishop when seated during Mass* or pontifical* ceremonies.

Grenfell, Wilfred T. (1865–1940) English medical missionary to the fishermen and Eskimos of Labrador who built the first schools and hospitals in the area.

gresaille Church window glass with images in tints of gray.

Grey Friars Friars of the Franciscan Order*. Some Franciscan nuns are called Grey Sisters.

Grey Nuns Full name: Grey Nuns of Charity or Sisters of Charity. Founded by Madame d'You-ville at Montreal in 1937. In addition to the three religious vows, they promise to devote their lives to relief of suffering.

Greyfriars Church

Griesbach, Johann Jakob (1745–1812) German New Testament scholar and professor at Jena (1775–1812). He was the first to systematically apply literary analysis to the Gospels, and his dependence theory placed Mark as the latest of the three Synoptic Gospels*. His edition of the Greek New Testament laid the foundation of modern biblical textual criticism*.

Grignion de Montfort, St. Louis Marie (1673–1716) French missioner. Ordained priest in 1700, he became chaplain* at a hospital at Poitiers, where he founded the Daughters of Wisdom*, a congregation for the relief of the sick and education of poor children. About 1712 he founded the Company of Mary with the same goals. His *Traite de la Vraie Devotion a la Sainte Vierge* was a devotional classic. He was canonized by Pius XII* in 1947. Feast day: April 28.

Grigny, Nicolas de (1672–1703) French composer of organ music. For most of his life he was organist at the Cathedral of Reims. His collection of organ music includes the *First Book of the Organ* (1699) which contained five organ masses and five hymn settings. The mass had five versets for the kyrie*, nine for the gloria, an offertory, three versets for the Sanctus*, an Elevation, two versets for the Agnus Dei*, and a Communion. Grigny's work was distinguished in richness of texture, complexity of counterpoint, expressiveness of melodic embellishment, and intensity of feeling.

Grimke, Sarah Moore and Angelina Emily (1792–1873 and 1805–1879, respectively) Quaker* sisters from South Carolina who were active in the abolitionist and women's rights movements.

Groningen School Theological movement that flourished in the Dutch Reformed Church* in the middle of the nineteenth century, most of the leaders of which were staff members of the University of Groningen. Its leaders were Petrus Hoffstede De Groot and P. W. van Heusde; other prominent members included W. Muurling, H. Muntinge, L. G. Pareau, and J. F. van Oordt. The movement tried to steer clear of the Pietism* and conservatism of the awakening on the one hand and liberalism* on the other, and to develop a humanistic and evangelistic middle way. Its teachings emphasized love and charity rather than dogma*. In its heyday, it was the most dominant influence on the Dutch church.

Groote, Gerard (1340–1384) "Gerard the Great." Dutch founder of the Brethren of the Common Life*. He was drawn to a contemplative life* under the influence of the mystic J. Ruysbroeck* and the Carthusian Hendrik van Calkar. He gained great popularity as a preacher but because of his attacks on clerical abuses, was banned from preaching. In 1380 he joined with a friend Florentius Radewijns to form a group that eventually became the Brethren of the Common Life. He converted his own house into a community of women for whom he wrote a rule.

Grosseteste, Robert (c. 1170–1253) English churchman and philosopher. He was chancellor of the University of Oxford between 1214 and 1221 and later bishop of Lincoln* from 1235. A fearless and dedicated man, he attacked corruption at the papal court as well as the English court, and made proposals for reform which were ignored by the pope. He escaped excommunication*, but the sense of failure clouded his later years. His broad intellectual interests are evident in his scientific and theological studies. Until 1225 he was occupied with scientific studies, especially on light, astronomy, comets, and rainbows.

Among his theological works, the most notable were *Hexaemeron, De Decem Mandatis, De Cessatione Legalium*, commentaries on Psalms and on Galatians. He also initiated and participated in a large translation program from Greek,

including the works of Dionysius the Areopagite*, the *Ethics* of Aristotle, the works of St.
John of Damascus* and St. Basil*, the Testaments
of the Twelve Patriarchs, and the Greek Dictionary of Suidas. He was a teacher of Roger Bacon*
and Adam Marsh and anticipated many of the
earlier reformers, such as John Wycliffe*. He became a cherished figure for the Lollards*. He was
never canonized in the Anglican Church. Feast
Day in the American *Book of Common Prayer**:
October 9.

Grotius, Hugo (1583–1645) Birth name: Huig de
Groot. Dutch statesman, poet, humanist, jurist,
and theologian, best known as the father of international law. He had a checkered career because
of his Arminian sympathies, escaping from the
Netherlands to France and thence to Sweden. His
most important Christian work was *De Veritate
Religionis Christianae* (Concerning the Truth of
the Christian Religion) which set forth the essentials of the Christian faith in nonsectarian terms.

Hugo Grotius

He also proposed the governmental theory of the
Atonement* which anticipated the liberal theologians of the nineteenth century. He envisaged
God as a moral governor and the natural law as
immutable. He sought to interpret the Bible on
the basis of philology without dogmatic assumptions.

Grottaferrata, Abbey of Byzantine Catholic monastery in the Alban Hills, southwest of Rome*,
founded by Nilus of Rossano in 1004. It is the

only surviving Byzantine Catholic monastery in
Italy.

grotto (Ital., cavern) Artificial cave-like structure
where religious statues are placed.

ground of being Term used by Paul Tillich* and J.
A. T. Robinson* to refer to God as the source or
depth of all reality or being.

Groves, Anthony Norris (1795–1853) Plymouth Brethren* leader. In Dublin he associated with a group
that included J. N. Darby*, and that eventually
became the Plymouth Brethren. In *Christian De-
votedness,* he advocated complete dependence on
God for all material needs, a teaching that became
the hallmark of George Muller's* life. Groves
worked as a missionary from 1829 to 1832 in Baghdad and from 1833 to 1852 in India.

Gruber, Franz (1787–1863) Austrian organist who
composed the music for the Christmas hymn,
"Silent Night*."

Grundtvig, Nikolai Frederik Severin (1783–1872) "The
Danish Carlyle." Danish Lutheran pastor, statesman, and poet. Together with Soren
Kierkegaard*, he is one of the most important
figures in Danish Christian history in the nineteenth century. He sought a return to orthodoxy*
and proposed in his pamphlet called *Kirkens Gen-
maele* (The Church's Reply) that the sure foundation of faith* is not the Bible but the living word
in the person of the risen Christ inhabiting his
people. He attacked not only the rationalism and
liberalism* of his age, but also the state domination of the church, and sought to restore the dogmatic orthodoxy reflected in the Apostles'
Creed*. His name is also indelibly associated with
the folk-school movement that he actively promoted. Toward the end of his life, he was made
bishop.

Grunewald, Matthias (c. 1475–1528) Birth name:
Mathis Gothardt Neithardt. German painter. His
most famous work is the altarpiece of Isenheim, a
polyptych* of 11 panels, now in the Colmar Museum, portraying the Crucifixion. It is a huge
work, nearly 9 feet high and 16 feet wide, when
closed, and the total painted surface of all the

panels is over 50 feet in width. It was done between 1512 and 1516 for a chapel.

The central panel is the *Crucifixion*, a vision of horror, agony, and grief with Christ's body twisted, distorted, and blood-stained. No other crucified Christ in all Western art exceeds it as an expression of the ghastly horror of the scene. On either side of the Crucifixion are panels with *St. Sebastian* and *St. Anthony Abbot*, patron saint* of the lazar houses. Below in the predella* is *Lamentation over the Dead Christ*. The predella splits to reveal *Christ and the Apostles*. When the wings are opened, on the left wing is the *Annunciation* and the central part is the *Allegory of the Nativity* where, in a rocky landscape, the Virgin nurses the Holy Child while angelic musicians serenade her. The right-hand wing has a *Resurrection*. The carved centerpiece is flanked on either side by two hermits, *St. Anthony the Great* and *Paul the Hermit*, while on the other side is the *Temptation of St. Anthony*.

Guadalupe, Our Lady of Place of pilgrimage* outside Mexico City where, in 1531, a Mexican Indian peasant, Juan Diego, received an apparition of the Virgin Mary*. She is the national patron of Mexico, and is particularly venerated by Mexican Indians.

guardian Superior* of a Franciscan priory*.

guardian angel Angel believed in popular lore to be assigned to watch and care for individuals (Matt. 18:10; Acts 12:15).

Guardini, Romano (1885–1968) Italian philosopher of religion who taught at Bonn and Berlin before he was dismissed by the Nazis, and at Tubingen* and Munich* after the war. He was a leader in the renewal known as the liturgical movement*. Among his books are *The Spirit of the Liturgy* (1918) and *The Church and the Catholic* (1922).

Guarini, Guarino (1624–1683) Italian Baroque architect. He built his first church in 1660 in Messina. This was followed by Ste-Anne-la-Royale in Paris, Sta Maria da Divina Providencia in Lisbon, San Lorenzo and the Chapel of St. Sindone in Turin*. His architecture is deeply symbolic.

Gueranger, Prosper (1805–1875) French priest who reestablished Benedictine life at Solesmes* and contributed to modern liturgical renewal. He was the author of *Institutions Liturgiques* (3 vols., 1840–1851).

Guide Me, O Thou Great Jehovah The text, by William Williams* (1717–1791), initially appeared in his collection of Welsh hymns, *Alleluia* (1745), entitled "Strength to Pass Through the Wilderness." With various translations into English in the 1770s, the familiar accompanying tune "Cwm Rhondda" was composed by John Hughes (1873–1932) in 1907 for an annual Welsh hymn festival ("Cyman fau Ganu").

Guido d'Arezzo (c. 990–1050) Also, Fra Guittone. Italian Benedictine monk known as the father of church music. His musical innovations include the system of musical notations, known as solmization, which teaches singing by designating the degrees of the scale by syllables, the Guidonian hand or a diagram in the form of an outstretched hand, the Aretinian syllables which are written in regular order on the fingertips and joints, and the four-line staff. He was the first to use the intervals between the lines. He has also been credited with introducing the F clef, and with the invention of the descant and counterpoint.

Guigo Name of two prominent priors of Grande Chartreuse*. Guigo I (1083–1136), fifth prior*, was the author of *Meditationes*, comparable to Pascal's* *Pensees*. Guigo II (d. 1188) was the ninth prior, author of *Scala Claustralium* (Ladder of Monks).

gullta In the East Syrian Church, a priestly headcovering.

Gunkel, Hermann (1862–1932) Protestant theologian. He served as professor at Gottingen, Halle, Berlin, and Giessen. As a member of the Religionsgeschichte Schule*, he pioneered form criticism*. His works include *Zum religionsgeschichtlichen Verstandnis des Neuen Testaments* (1903), *Die Wirkungen des heiligen Geistes nach der popularen Anschauung der apostolischen Zeit* (1888), and *Schopfung und Chaos in Urzeit und Endzeit* (1895).

Gurk Monastery and church in Gurk, Austria, established by St. Hemma, countess of Freisach-Zeltschach about 1043. The building of a new cathedral began in 1140, and in 1200 the high altar was consecrated. It was gutted by fire a number of times and rebuilt each time. The High Romanesque three-aisled basilica* has three apses* and two west towers crowned with onion-domes. Its slender marble columns, capitals, and arches are richly decorated, and there are colorful biblical scenes carved on the doors. The ceilings and walls are decorated with frescoes. The high altar, carved by Michael Honel, depicts the ascension of the Virgin Mary* with a host of angels*. The crucifix altar is by George Raphael Donner.

gurna In the Assyrian Church*, the font.

Gurneyites Branch of the Religious Society of Friends* (Quakers) founded in England by Joseph John Gurney (1788–1847). Gurneyites departed from Quaker traditions by having trained and salaried ministers and evangelists. They emphasized the authority of the Scriptures and the importance of Christ's atonement*. They were also sympathetic to Evangelicalism* and revivals*.

Gutenberg Bible Bible, also known as the 42-line Bible, printed in Mainz* in 1456 by Johann Gutenberg (c. 1398–1468), considered the inventor of modern printing. In 1457 he produced the Psalter, the first dated book to appear in print in Europe. See also MAZARIN BIBLE.

Gutierrez, Gustavo (1928–) Latin American theologian. Ordained in 1959, he began to teach at the Catholic University of Lima. He became a leading exponent of liberation theology*, interpreting Christianity in the light of Marxist dialectics. He is the author of *A Theology of Liberation* and *The Power of the Poor in History*.

Gutzlaff, Karl Friedrich August (1803–1851) First German Lutheran missionary to China. Inspired by Robert Morrison* on a visit to London, Gutzlaff went to the Dutch East Indies, where he learned Chinese. Between 1831 and 1833 he made three journeys along the coast of China which was then closed to missionaries. When Morrison died in 1834, Gutzlaff became the Chinese secretary to British commercial authorities and translated the Bible into Chinese. After the peace of Nanking, he began training native Chinese as evangelists. With a view to evangelizing China in one generation, he formed the Chinese Union which by 1847 had 300 evangelists. After his death in 1851, the Chinese Union was dissolved but his work was carried on by the China Inland Mission*.

Guyard, Marie (1599–1672) Blessed Marie de l'Incarnation, first superior* of the Ursulines* at Quebec. She left her husband and young son to enter the Ursuline convent at Tours*, and later accepted an invitation of the Jesuit Mission to found a convent in Quebec in 1639. The convent flourished despite the cold climate and attacks by Indians. She is the author of *Retraites* (1682) and *L'Ecole Sainte, ou Explication Familiere des Mysteres de la Foi* (1684).

Guyon, Jeanne Marie Bouvier de la Motte (1648–1717). French mystic and friend of Fenelon* and the Spanish mystic Molinos*. A widow at 28, she devoted her life to intensive prayer, but her teachings were deemed heretical and condemned at the Conference of Issy in 1695, and she was imprisoned for long periods. She taught devotion to Child Jesus, mortification*, mystical espousal to Christ, complete detachment from the world, indifference to suffering and pain, and self-abasement. Her books include *Spiritual Torrents, Mystical Sense of Sacred Scripture,* and *Methods of Prayer*. She had lasting influence on the Quakers* and certain Pietists.

gynaeceum/gynaekeion (lit., house for women) In the Eastern Church*, gallery or aisle reserved for women.

Gyrovagi Wandering monks censured in the Rule of St. Benedict* as unstable people.

Hh

habit Distinctive religious garment prescribed for a particular order or function.

habitual sin Condition that results from the repetition of actual sin.

Hadewijch (thirteenth century) Dutch nun and mystic. Her *Visions, Poems in Stanzas,* and *Poems in Couplets* describe her ineffable joy of being united with God. She had great influence on J. van Ruysbroeck*.

Hadrian I (d. 795) Pope from 772. His long pontificate* coincided with the reign of Charlemagne* with whom he maintained amicable relations. The pope enlisted the king's help in suppressing Adoptionism* and in unifying liturgy and canon law*.

Hadrian IV (c. 1100–1159) Pope from 1154. Birth name: Nicholas Breakspear. The only English pope. His papacy was marked by conflicts with Frederick Barbarossa, William I, and the Duke of Burgundy.

Hadrian the African, St. (d. 709/10) Learned African monk who became the head of a monastery near Naples and later went to England, where he became abbot of the Monastery of Sts. Peter and Paul at Canterbury*. He established a number of schools in England.

hagia/hagiasma (Gk., holy) Anything holy, consecrated, blessed, or venerated.

Hagia Sophia See SANCTA SOPHIA.

hagias matarion In the Byzantine Church*, an abridged version of the Euchologion*.

hagiaster/hagiastera In the Byzantine tradition, an aspergil.

Hagin, Kenneth (1918–) Healing evangelist and Bible teacher. He received a call* to ministry after a miraculous healing from tuberculosis as a youth. Influenced by Smith Wigglesworth* and E. W. Kenyon*, he began an independent Charismatic ministry. By 1970 he became the best known leader of the faith healing* as well as the positive confession* ("name it and claim it") movement. He began a daily radio teaching program, known as "Faith Seminar of the Air" which was eventually broadcast in over 100 countries. He founded the Rhema Bible Training Institute* in 1974 in Broken Arrow, Oklahoma, which has trained over 25,000 persons for various types of ministries.

hagiography Branch of religious literature dealing with the lives and cultus* of the saints*. In the Byzantine East, Simeon Metaphrastes was the first to produce a hagiography. Eusebius* is considered the first great churchman to write hagiography. From the seventeenth century, the Bollandists* produced their *Acta Bollandiana* as a classic of hagiography. A comparable work is A. Butler's* *The Lives of the Fathers, Martyrs, and Other Prin-*

cipal Saints. Often used pejoratively to designate uncritical biography idealizing fallible human beings. Thus hagiographer.

hagiology Literature dealing with the lives and legends of the saints* and their cultus*.

hagion oros (lit., holy mountain) Mount Athos*.

hagioscope Opening in the chancel* wall of an ancient church to enable worshipers to view the altar.

Hagiosoritissa Byzantine iconographical theme of the Virgin in prayer, turned toward a bust of Christ or the hand of God* in the upper corner.

Hail Mary Translation of Ave Maria*. 1. Angelic salutation to the Virgin Mary* (Luke 1:28). 2. Prayer based on this salutation. In the traditional form, it runs: "Hail Mary*, full of grace, the Lord is with thee; blessed art thou among women and blessed is the fruit of thy womb, Jesus. Holy Mary, Mother of God, pray for us sinners now and in the hour of our death."

haila/haiklao (lit., temple) In the Syrian Church, the nave* of the church separated into male and female wings.

hair shirt Garment woven of rough hair, worn by ascetics to mortify the flesh or to do penance*.

haitnuthiun In the Armenian Liturgy, the Epiphany* when the celebrant leads a procession carrying a cross and blesses the water in a large metal vessel and pours holy chrism* into it. The congregation may take some of the blessed water home.

haiyimonutho In the Syrian Church, the liturgical creed.

half communion Withholding the cup* from the laity in the Lord's Supper*.

Half-Way Covenant Doctrine of dual membership in American Congregationalism* in the seventeenth and eighteenth centuries by which those church members—often the children of members —who were not committed Christians were deemed to have a lesser covenant with God than those who were committed Christians. The Massachusetts Synod of 1662 stated that baptized adults who professed faith and lived uprightly but were not born again* had a standing in the church that was slightly below that of those who had a real conversion experience.

hall church Simple church design in which there is no transept* and the roofs above the aisles are of equal height.

Hall, Francis Joseph (1857–1932) American Episcopal theologian. He was professor of dogmatics in Western Theological Seminary and later at General Theological Seminary. His *Theological Outlines* (3 vols., 1892–1895) and *Dogmatic Theology* (1907) are classics that have influenced Anglo-Catholic* theology.

hallelujah (Heb., praise ye the Lord) Liturgical expression of praise, sung at all masses and services except in Lent*. See also ALLELUIA.

Hallelujah Chorus High point of Handel's *Messiah**, at which it is traditional for the audience to stand, a custom begun by the English king at its London debut.

Haller, Berchtold (1492–1536) Swiss reformer. He became a Zwinglian around 1521 and was at the center of the Reformation party in Berne. He took part in the Disputation of Baden (1526) and Berne* (1528) and collaborated with F. Kolb in the composition of a Protestant liturgy and the edict of 1528. He became Berne's religious leader after the Synod of 1532.

Halloween Popular name for All Saints' Eve, October 31, a time of vigil associated with the activities of evil spirits and ghosts. In the United States, children visit homes on this day and receive candies and other goodies, after the traditional greeting of "trick or treat."

Hallowmas All Saints' Festival.

halo Circle or disk of light around the head, symbolizing grace, used in paintings of Christ, the apostles, the Virgin Mary*, and saints* of the church. A plain, round halo is used for angels* and saints and a round one with a cross or monogram for Christ. See also AURA/AUREOLE; NIMBUS.

hamartiology (Gk., *hamartia*, missing the mark) Branch of theology dealing with sin.

Hamilton, Patrick (1503–1528) Proto-martyr of the Scottish Reformation*. He was converted to Protestantism* while at Andrews University. At the age of 25 he was summoned before Archbishop Beaton, tried, declared a heretic, and burned.

hampuir srboutian In the Armenian Rite*, the kiss of peace* just before the anaphora*.

Han, Kyung Jik (1902–) Korean Presbyterian preacher. Ordained in 1934, he first ministered in a church in North Korea. In 1945 he escaped to South Korea and with 27 fellow refugees formed Yungnak, the Church of Everlasting Joy. It soon became the largest Presbyterian church in Korea. Yungnak has started more than 350 churches in Korea and abroad and sent missionaries to 21 countries. He has also served as president of Soongsil College (later university) and chair of the Korean National Council of Churches. In 1992 he was awarded the Templeton Prize for Progress in Religion.

Hanc Igitur ([accept]therefore this [offering]) Fourth prayer of the Roman canon* ascribed to Gregory the Great*.

hand of God In Christian art, one of the symbols of God. It is often portrayed with the thumb and the first two fingers extended upward (representing the Holy Trinity*) and two fingers closed against the palm (representing the dual nature of Jesus).

Handel, George Frederick (1685–1759) German-born composer who became a permanent resident in England after 1712. He is considered one of the greatest composers of all time, and his *Messiah** (1741) is the most performed major choral work in history. For the greater part of his career he wrote dramatic music, opera, chamber music,

concertos, and oratorios. His Christian music consists of passions, Latin psalms, and cantata-like anthems. He turned to oratorios based on biblical themes after the failure of his operas. Besides *Messiah*, his outstanding choral works include *Esther* (1732), *Saul* (1738), *Israel in Egypt* (1938), *Judas Maccabeus* (1740), and *Solomon* (1748). Handel could stir an audience and achieve dramatic grandeur using simple but noble melodies. He stopped composing after going blind in 1752 but continued to direct performances of his work to the end of his life.

Hannington, James (1847–1885) Anglican missionary to East Africa and martyr*. In 1882 he was sent to East Africa by the Church Missionary Society* and consecrated the first bishop of Eastern Equatorial Africa in 1884. In 1885 he reached Mombasa and set off on foot to Busoga on Lake Victoria, where he was arrested and killed on the orders of Mwanga, the *kabaka* or ruler of Baganda.

haou inourone In the Jacobite tradition, a short hymn in honor of the Blessed Sacrament* following its reception in Communion.

haplography Omission of portion of text by copyists while transcribing by skipping from one occurrence of a word to a second, often with both at the end of consecutive lines.

Harding, Stephen (d. 1134) Abbot of Citeaux* and founder of the Cistercian Order. He left England in 1098 with 20 men and established a strict and austere religious house at Citeaux, becoming successively its subprior, prior*, and abbot. As the community flourished, Harding added 13 new houses. He drew up the rule, instituted a general chapter*, and introduced the famous white habit.

hard-shell (adjective) uncompromising and unyielding in matters of religious faith.

Hard-Shell Baptists American Baptist group opposed to benevolent societies, Sunday schools*, missionary organizations, payment of salaries to ministers, and other practices that they consider unbiblical.

Harklean Version Revision of the Philoxenian Syriac Version* of the New Testament made by Thomas of Harkel in 616. About 50 manuscripts of this versions have survived, and the version appears in the Peshitta* Syriac New Testament.

harmony Unified text produced from overlapping texts as, for example, harmony of Exodus to Deuteronomy produced by John Calvin*.

Harmony of the Gospels Reduction of the four Gospels to one by harmonization. The earliest of such harmonies was Tatian's* *Diatessaron*. Among modern harmonies, the most important is that of Johann Jakob Griesbach*, who divided New Testament manuscripts into three classes: Alexandrian, Western, and Byzantine.

Harmony Society Pietist communal religious society that flourished from 1805 to 1906 in Harmony, Pennsylvania. It was founded by George Rapp as an experimental celibate group devoted to farming and manufacturing. Rapp held strange ideas, including beliefs that Napoleon was an emissary of God and that the Lord's Supper* and baptism* were works of the devil. The society also founded branches in New Harmony, Indiana, and Economy, Pennsylvania.

Harnack, Adolf (1851–1930) German Lutheran theologian and historian and the most outstanding patristic scholar of his generation. A liberal opponent of traditional orthodoxy*, he emphasized the moral and ethical side of Christianity to the exclusion of its doctrines. The unorthodox opinions that he promoted included doubts about the authorship of the Fourth Gospel, denial of biblical miracles including the Resurrection, and disregard of the institution of baptism*. He adopted a form of Ritschlianism that regarded Pauline* theology as Hellenization and as an alien intrusion. In 1899–1900 he gathered his liberal ideas in a course of public lectures, published as *What Is Christianity?* (1901). In it he portrayed Jesus as a man and the gospel as more concerned with ethical values, such as righteousness, love, and peace.

His other theological works included *Luther's Theologie* (2 vols., 1862–1886), *Das Apostolische Glaubenbekenntnis* (1892), and *History of Dogma* (7 vols., 1894–1899). Although liberal in theology, his historical studies advanced the cause of biblical scholarship. These studies included *Luke the Physician* (1907), *The Sayings of Jesus* (1908), *The Acts of the Apostles* (1909), *The Date of the Acts and of the Synoptic Gospels* (1911), *The Mission and Expansion of Christianity in the First Three Centuries* (2 vols, 1904–1905), *The Constitution and Law of the Church in the First Two Centuries* (1910), *Marcion* (1921), *Beitrage zur Einleitung in das Neue Testament* (1906–1911), and *Briefsammlung des Apostels Paulus* (1926).

Harper, Michael (1931–) Pioneer figure in Charismatic renewal* in Britain. Converted as an undergraduate in Cambridge, Harper was ordained as a priest in 1956. From 1958 to 1964 he worked at All Souls, a major Evangelical church in central London, during which time he experienced a baptism in the Holy Spirit*. In 1964 he became general secretary of the Fountain Trust. From 1978 he began to concentrate on renewal within the Anglican Communion*. In 1984 he became director of SOMA (Sharing of Ministries Abroad) and canon* of Chichester Cathedral. He was a principal organizer of the Acts 1986 European Charismatic Conference in Birmingham. His literary output includes *Power for the Body of Christ* (1964), *Walk in the Spirit* (1968), and *Spiritual Warfare* (1970). In the 1990s he left the Church of England, partly to protest the ordination of women, and became an Orthodox priest.

Harris, Howell (1714–1773) Welsh preacher, considered the principal founder of Welsh Calvinistic Methodism*. He was a revivalist* whose crusades* were accompanied by wild enthusiasm.

Harris, William Wade (c. 1860–1929) West African evangelist, also known as "Prophet Harris." He belonged to the Glebo tribe in Liberia and was a Methodist by background. The white-robed Harris was a powerful preacher. He is reputed to have converted over 100,000 people in Ghana, Ivory Coast, Liberia, and Sierra Leone.

harrowing of hell Descent of Christ into hell* after his crucifixion, a favorite theme of art and drama in the Middle Ages.

Hart, Joseph (1712–1768) English hymn writer and

pastor, one of the most popular independent hymnists in eighteenth-century England. Among his best known hymns is "Come Ye Sinners, Poor and Wretched" (1759).

Harvard, John (1607–1638) Benefactor of Harvard University. Joining the Puritan emigrants to the New World, he settled in Massachusetts. In his will he left half his estate worth 780 pounds and a personal library of 400 volumes to the new college, founded by the Massachusetts Colony in 1636. The gift was dedicated for the education of youth in "godliness." The general court named the college after him in 1638/39 and erected the buildings with his funds.

hasirah In the Coptic Church*, circular mats about five or six inches in diameter, made of silk, on which sacred vessels are placed.

Hastings, James (1852–1922) Scottish Presbyterian minister. Ordained a Presbyterian minister in 1884, he served as a pastor in various Scottish churches until 1911. But his chief claim to fame is as an encyclopedist. He created some of the finest dictionaries and encyclopedias on church history, including *Dictionary of the Bible* (5 vols., 1898–1904), *Encyclopedia of Religion and Ethics* (12 vols., 1908–1921), *Dictionary of Christ and the Gospels* (2 vols., 1906–1908), and *Dictionary of the Apostolic Church* (2 vols., 1915–1918).

Hastings, Thomas (1784–1872) American hymnologist who composed the perennial favorite, "Rock of Ages." He wrote more than 600 hymns and 1,000 hymn tunes and compiled more than 50 collections.

Hauck, Albert (1845–1918) German Lutheran theologian and church historian. He was the author of *Kirchengeschichte Deutschlands* (5 vols., 1887–1920) and coeditor of the *Herzog-Plitt Realencyklopadie* (1896–1913).

Hauge, Hans Nielsen (1771–1824) Norwegian lay preacher, founder of Haugeanism, a movement that emphasized conversion, personal piety, lay preaching, and spiritual brotherhood*. A lay preacher, Hauge was imprisoned and fined by the state church for his unauthorized evangel-

ism. He initiated one of Norway's most fervent revivals*.

Haugeans

havadamk (Arm., we believe) In the Armenian Church*, version of the Nicene Creed* used in the liturgy.

Havergal, Frances Ridley (1836–1879) British devotional writer and hymnologist, noted for such hymns as "Take My Life and Let It Be" and "Lord, Speak to Me That I May Speak." She published several volumes of poems and hymns, the best known of which is *Kept for the Master's Use*.

Haweis, Thomas (1734–1820) Cofounder of the London Missionary Society and trustee-executor of Lady Huntingdon. He was converted and called to the ministry as a young man and served as curate* in various churches. In 1774 he was appointed chaplain* to Lady Huntingdon. He helped to found the London Missionary Society in 1795 and was instrumental in sending missionaries to Tahiti.

Hayastaniaitz The Church of Armenia.

Hayotz Ekeghetzi Church of the Armenians.

Haydn, Franz Joseph (1732–1809) Austrian composer. Haydn was a devout Catholic. "In nomine Domine" ("in the name of God") appears at the beginning of all his works and "laus Deo" ("praise the Lord") at the end. Although more famous for his symphonies and string quartets, he also wrote a dozen masses. He also wrote a variety of Catholic works in the classical, symphonic style, the setting of the *Seven Last Words, Stabat Mater*, and his magnificent oratorio*, *The Creation*.

Hayford, Jack (1934–) Pentecostal pastor. In 1969

he became pastor of the First Foursquare Church in Van Nuys, California, which in time grew to over 10,000 members. He served as president of L.I.F.E. Bible College in Los Angeles and later founded the King's College and King's Seminary in Van Nuys. He has written over 400 songs, including "Majesty" and "We Lift Our Voices Rejoicing," and several devotional books, and was editor of the Spirit-Filled Life Study Bible. In 1999 he retired from pastoring to become president of the seminary he founded.

hayrapet Title of the Armenian patriarch* or catholicos*.

haysmavurk (lit., this day) In the Armenian Church*, a shortened version of the lives of the saints* read during vespers*.

Haystack Prayer Meeting (1806) Meeting held by students in Williams College in Massachusetts out of which grew the American overseas missionary movement and the founding of the American Board of Commissioners for Foreign Missions*. The call* to preach the gospel to all nations first came to Samuel J. Mills* while he was plowing his field in Connecticut in 1802. Thereupon he entered Williams College to prepare for the ministry, and here he met a group of kindred spirits driven by the same passion for souls: James Richards, Francis Robbins, Harvey Loomis, Gordon Hall, and Luther Rice*. One day during a thunderstorm, the group took refuge in the lee of a nearby haystack where they pledged to devote their lives to missionary work. After graduation, several of them went to Andover Seminary*, where they were joined by Adoniram Judson*, Samuel Newell, and Samuel Nott, all of whom formed the Society of Inquiry on the Subject of Missions. In 1810 they presented a memorial to the General Assembly* of Congregational churches* offering themselves as missionaries.

hbst (lit., bread) In the Ethiopian Church*, the eucharistic bread which is leavened, flat, and round and imprinted with a cross made up of nine squares.

heaven 1. Eternal abode of God, the uncreated spiritual realm inhabited by God as well as his angels*. 2. Source of everything that is good and changeless and proceeds from God. Thus, in Matthew the question is asked, "Whence was it from? From heaven or from men?" (Matt. 21:25). Jesus and his work are from "heaven" and from "above" (John 3:13, 31, 35). Accordingly, "every good gift and every perfect gift is from above" (James 1:7), and the Lord's Prayer* is that God's will be done "on earth, as it is in heaven" (Matt. 6:10). 3. Believer's hope and eternal home which "eye has not seen, nor ear heard" (1 Cor. 2:9). It is a place of love (1 Cor. 13:13; Eph. 3:19), rest (Heb. 4:9), joy (Luke 15:7), knowledge (1 Cor. 13:12), and perfect harmony (Rom. 8:17; Rev. 22:3).

Heavenly Father God as abba* or Father, term of address in public prayers.

hebanie In the Ethiopian Church*, a garment roughly equivalent to the Western amice* made of linen and sewn to the cappa* or kaba*.

hebdomadary Priest appointed to officiate at services for a week.

Heber, Reginald (1783–1826) Bishop of Calcutta and hymn writer. He was named bishop of Calcutta, a diocese* which at that time included all of British India. He worked tirelessly to promote the gospel and ordained the first Indian minister. He was also a talented hymn writer, and his 57 hymns were collected and published after his death. His compositions included "Bread of the World," "Brightest and Best," "From Greenland's Icy Mountains," "Holy, Holy, Holy," and "The Son of God Goes Forth to War."

Hebrew 1. A Jew or Israelite. 2. The language of the Jews. It belongs to the northwestern division of Semitic languages. It was the language in which the Old Testament was written, but apart from the Old Testament, there were few literary works in the language until modern times. In the New Testament period, it was largely replaced by Aramaic. The surviving vocabulary of classical Hebrew is small, about 8,000 words, many of them of uncertain meanings. The Hebrew alphabet consists of 22 signs for consonants and none for vowels. Vowels are represented by dots and/or strokes above, within or below the consonants. Like other Semitic languages, Hebrew is written from right to left.

Hebrew Bible The Old Testament.

Hebrews, Gospel According to the Apocryphal Gospel, also called Gospel of the Hebrews. It is cited by Origen*, Clement of Alexandria*, Epiphanius*, Jerome*, and Eusebius*. Some regard it as the original of St. Matthew's Gospel. The surviving fragments include the sayings of Jesus to James not recorded in the canonical Gospels.

Heck, Barbara Ruckle (1744–1804) North American "Mother of Methodism*." Sailing to America in 1760 with her cousin, Philip Embury*, she encouraged him to preach and together they organized the first Methodist society in the American colonies and built the first Methodist church. The family moved to Canada during the Revolutionary War because of their Tory views and she helped to found the first Methodist society in Canada.

Hecker, Isaac Thomas (1819–1888) American founder of the Missionary Priests of St. Paul the Apostle, or Paulist Fathers. A convert from Methodism*, he was for a time a Redemptorist. After a few years of study in England, Belgium, and Holland, he was ordained in 1845 and returned to the United States to work with Roman Catholic German immigrants. He founded in 1858 with papal approval the Missionary Priests of St. John the Apostle to convert Protestants. A proponent of Americanism, he believed that American Catholicism must be distinctive. He founded and edited *Catholic World* (1865) and *Young Catholic* (1870).

Hedberg, Frederik Gabriel (1811–1893) Finnish pastor and founder of the Evangelical movement. Ordained in 1834, he was briefly a Pietist but broke with the Pietists in 1844 with the publication of his *The Doctrine of Faith unto Salvation*. He then founded and became a leader of the Evangelical movement, based on the writings of Luther*.

Heermann, Johann (1585–1647) Silesian hymn writer. Dedicated by his mother to the ministry at an early age, he became pastor of Koben an der Oder in 1611, but suffered during the Thirty Years' War. He wrote over 400 hymns, many of them still sung. Among those translated into English are "Ah, Holy Jesu, How Hast Thou Offended" and "O Christ, Our True and Only Light."

Hegesippus, St. (second century) Church historian of Jewish origin who lived near the time of the apostles. His *Memoirs* survive as quotations in Eusebius*. Feast day: April 7.

hegoumenissa In the Byzantine tradition, the abbess of a cenobitic monastery.

hegumen/hegumenos (Gk., leader) In the Eastern Orthodox Church*, the head of a small monastery. He is usually elected by all the monks.

Heidelberg Catechism Protestant confession* of faith drawn up in 1562 by Zacharias Ursinus* and Caspar Olevianus* at the instance of Frederick III, elector, and accepted as the standard doctrine in the Palatinate. In theology, it represents moderate Calvinism*. It has been widely acknowledged and commented on.

Heiler, Friedrich (1892–1967) German religious thinker. A Roman Catholic at birth, he shifted to Protestantism* under the influence of the Swedish theologian, N. Soderblom*, and became professor of the comparative history of religion at Marburg in 1922. Later, his Roman Catholic sympathies resurfaced and he organized a German High Church* movement and founded an Evangelical order of Franciscan Tertiaries. His work on Catholicism*, *Der Katholizismus* (1923), portrayed the Catholic Church in a favorable light except for the post-Tridentine developments. His most famous works are *Prayer* (1932); *Erscheinungsformen und Wesen der Religion* (1961), a phenomenology of religion; and *Die Ostkirchen* (1971), a study of the Eastern Orthodox Church*.

heileton In the Byzantine Liturgy, a large cloth used to fold over and enclose the antimension*.

Heilsgeschichte (Ger., lit., salvation history) Term coined by J. T. Beck*, German theologian, to describe the stages in the process of God's redemptive work in the world. It is a new teleological approach to history that provides a logical connection between the landmark events in God's transactions with his creation. It was developed especially within the biblical theology* movement in the mid-twentieth century.

Heim, Karl (1874–1958) German theologian and mission spokesman. In his writings he emphasized the transcendence of faith* and an existential apprehension of supernatural truth. His *God Transcendent* (1935) is his best known work in English. He was one of the keynote speakers at the World Missionary Conference* in Jerusalem* in 1928. He defined the purpose of missions in his essays in *Evangelische Missions-Zeitschrift* in 1940.

heirmologion Byzantine Rite* liturgical book containing the text and sometimes the melodies of the heirmoi which provide the metrical and musical models according to which the troparia of the canon* are sung.

heirmos (Gk., chain) The opening stanza in each ode of the canon*. It acts as a link verse joining the theme of the biblical canticle* and the theme of the feast or commemoration.

Helena, St. (c. 248–c. 327) First wife of Constantius Chlorus and mother of Constantine the Great*. Through her son she became a Christian and devoted her life to charity. In her old age, she visited the Holy Land*, where she built many churches and monasteries. In legend, she is associated with the recovery of the true cross. Feast day: May 21 (Eastern Church*); August 18 (Western Church*).

Heliand Old Saxon biblical poem of the ninth century, written in alliterative verse and based on Tatian's* harmony of the Gospels*. It was written by a Saxon bard at the order of King Louis the Pious.

Heligenkreuz Austria's oldest Cistercian abbey, in Vienna Woods, founded in 1133 by the Margrave Leopold III*. The austere monastery church stands in contrast with the light and airy hall-choir consecrated in 1295. It is the finest example of the High Gothic* style in Austria. The cloister* was built between 1220 and 1250. In the seventeenth and eighteenth centuries, the monastic buildings were renovated, and a vast courtyard with twin-tiered arcades by Angelo Canaveles was added between 1637 and 1660. Among the other features of the monastery are the Trinity Column and Joseph Fountain.

hell 1. Place or state where the dead and damned continue to exist and suffer everlasting punishment 2. Spiritual state of lasting separation from God. 3. Nether world inhabited by devils, demons, and fallen angels. 4. The power of evil and wickedness as the opposite of heaven*.

helmet Poetic symbol of salvation (Eph. 6:17).

Helvetic Confession 1. First Helvetic Confession, also known as the Second Confession of Basel, compiled at Basel* in 1536 by Heinrich Bullinger*, Oswald Myconius*, Leo Jud*, and Martin Bucer*. It was an attempt to reconcile Zwingli* and Luther* before the spread of Calvinism*. 2. The Second Helvetic Confession was drawn up by Bullinger and issued in 1566 at the request of

St. Helena

Frederick the Pious. Among the longest of the Reformation* confessions, it is a mixture of Calvinism* and Zwinglianism*. It was accepted by many Swiss cantons. It is regarded as one of the most mature Reformation confessions.

hemamat In the Ethiopian Church, the Holy Week*.

hemnicho In the Syrian tradition, the pallium* or omophorion* worn by bishops, made of white silk, hanging down in the front and back.

henana (lit., holy dust) In the Assyrian Church*, dust taken from the tombs of saints* and used as a sacramental, as potion for the sick, or mixed with wine and given to bridal couples.

Henana of Adiabene (d. c. 610) Superior* of the School of Nisibis*. Firmly linked to Chalcedonian orthodoxy*, he was opposed by the Nestorian patriarchs*. His abundant literary output included commentaries on the Old and New Testaments, homilies, and expositions of the sacraments*.

Henderson, Alexander (1583–1646) Scottish minister. He wrote the National Covenant* of 1638, became moderator* of the General Assembly*, drew up the Solemn League and Covenant, and led the fight opposing the establishment of Episcopalianism in Scotland. He did much to advance the cause of education in Scotland and introduced Hebrew into the regular curriculum at the University of Edinburgh, of which he was rector*.

Hengstenberg, Ernst Wilhelm (1802–1869) German Lutheran theologian and champion of orthodoxy* against the liberals. He wrote many works on Old Testament studies. From 1827 to 1869 he was editor of *Evangelisch Kirchenzeitung*, an influential journal in Evangelical circles.

henosis See ENOSIS.

henotheism Form of faith* midway between polytheism and monotheism*. It recognizes the existence of many gods but regards only one god as the deity of the family or tribe. According to Max Muller and others, the Jewish worship of Yahweh fell into this category.

Henoticon Decree of union issued by Zeno in 482 to settle the Monophysite dispute. It was a letter addressed by the emperor to the bishops, clergy, monks, and faithful of Alexandria*, Libya, and Pentapolis, declaring the sufficiency of the creeds of Nicaea* and Constantinople and the Twelve Anathemas of Cyril*. It denounced any contrary doctrine taught by Nestorius* and Eutyches*. But it offended the Western Church* by ignoring Leo's Tome and the Chalcedon Definition*. Rome responded by excommunicating the patriarchs* of Alexandria and Antioch* and the emperor himself. This was the beginning of the first ecclesiastical schism, known as the Acacian Schism*, between the West and East.

Henry, Carl Ferdinand Howard (1913–) American Baptist theologian and editor. He was professor of theology at Northern Baptist Theological Seminary, Fuller Theological Seminary*, Eastern Baptist Theological Seminary, and Trinity Evangelical Divinity School. As founding editor (1956–1968) of *Christianity Today*, he became the respected voice of Evangelicalism*. His theology emphasized the authority and inerrancy* of the Scriptures, biblical theism*, and ecumenical unity of all believers. Among his works, the six-volume *God, Revelation, and Authority* (1976–1982), is the most magisterial. His *Christian Personal Ethics* is a standard seminary textbook.

Henry, Matthew (1662–1714) English Presbyterian minister and commentator. His *Exposition of the Old and New Testaments* (1708–1710) is a detailed passage-by-passage exegesis* of the Bible still widely used. Among those indebted to him was Charles Spurgeon*.

Henry of Ghent (d. 1293) De Gandavo, Doctor Solemnis. French theologian and philosopher. He taught for many years at Paris, where he condemned certain aspects of Thomism*, defended Augustinianism*, and opposed the privileges of the mendicant orders*. His chief books are *Quodlibeta* and *Summa Theologica*, both of which had a great influence on Duns Scotus*.

Henry of Lausanne (d. mid-twelfth century) Medieval heretic. An itinerant preacher, his strictures on the worldliness of the clergy and his message of poverty and penance* proved very popular, but later he turned radical in his attack on the sacraments* and the institution of the clergy. His teachings were influenced by Peter de Bruys, who preached a similar message. He was condemned by the Council of Toulouse in 1119 and arrested many times. He was in many respects a precursor of the Waldensians.

Henry of Uppsala (d. 1156) Apostle of Finland. English bishop and missionary to Finland, where he was martyred. Feast day: January 20.

Henry Suso, Blessed See SUSO, BLESSED HENRY.

heorti In the Byzantine tradition, feasts.

heortologion In the Eastern Orthodox Church*, the equivalent of a martyrology*. In the absence of a pan-Orthodox compendium of feast days of saints*, each local Orthodox church maintains a heortologion. The Byzantine heortologion is the list of feasts observed by the Patriarchate of Constantinople, and the heortologion of Constantine Platanitis is used in the Greek Church.

heortology Branch of ecclesiology* dealing with festivals, church calendar, and church year*.

Heothina (Gk., of the dawn in the Eastern Orthodox Church) 1. Eleven Gospels of the Resurrection, read in an eleven-week cycle at Sunday orthros*. 2. The eleven idiomela by Emperor Leo the Wise sung as a doxastikon* at the end of Sunday ainoi*.

Herbert, George (1593–1633) English rector*. He forsook a distinguished public career to enter the holy orders* and become rector of Bemerton, near Salisbury*. He is the author of *A Priest to the Temple or Country Parson* (1652) that summed up his advice for pastors. As an Anglo-Catholic he was associated with the Little Gidding* community.

Herborn Protestant institute of higher studies founded in 1584 by Count John VI of Nassau. Modeled after the Genevan Academy*, it flourished under such renowned teachers as Caspar Olevianus*, John Piscator, and William Zepper. Later it became an important publishing center of Reformation* literature.

Here's Life World Global series of urban and rural multimedia multiplication evangelism campaigns, beginning in 1974, through Campus Crusade for Christ*.

heresiarch Leader or founder of a heretical movement or sect*.

heresy (Gk., choice) Doctrinal error or heterodoxy* that deserves censure* and punishment. Originally a school or sect of philosophy, it came to have for the early Christian writers a negative connotation as a false teaching that is destructive of the unity of believers. The church assumed from early times the magisterium*, or the authority, to determine and condemn heresy. In canon law*, heresy is a sin that results in excommunication*, although the church distinguishes two types of heresy: grave heresy and material heresy, the latter involving involuntary heresy. In the early church, heresy mostly involved doctrinal error in relation to the person and work of Christ (such as Nestorianism*, Docetism*, Apollinarianism, Monophysitism*, or Monothelitism*) or in relation to the Trinity* (Monarchianism*, Tritheism*, or Subordinationism*) or both (Arianism*).

In the Middle Ages, heretics rejected the sacraments* or other institutions of the church (as for example, the Bogomils*, Cathari*, and Waldensians), and the church responded by setting up the Inquisition*. The proliferation of heresy led to the creedal definitions by church councils as the best means to combat the spread of heretical ideas and to help believers distinguish between the true and the spurious.

Hergenrother, Joseph (1824–1890) German Catholic scholar. He was professor of canon law* and church history at Wurzburg before becoming a consultant to the First Vatican Council*, cardinal (1879), and the first prefect of the Vatican archives. He was the author of a number of works, including *Liber de Spiritus Sancti mystagogia* (1857), *Handbuch der allgemeinen Kirchengeschichte* (3 vols., 1876–1880), *Anti-Janus* (1870), *Der Zeitgeist* (1861), and *Der Kirchenstaat seit der franzosischen Revolution* (1860).

Herman of Alaska (c. 1756–1837) Russian Orthodox missionary to Alaska. As a monk at Valamo

Monastery on an island in Lake Vadoga, Finland, he was recruited to join a mission to the newly discovered Aleutian Islands. Herman arrived on Kodiak Island in 1794 as the least of ten monks. As the other nine retired from the rigors of life in Alaska, Herman was left alone. Conflict with the Russian fur hunters led to his exile on Spruce Island, where he was followed by a coterie of followers drawn by his radiant personality. In 1970 he was proclaimed the New World's first Orthodox saint*.

Hermann of Reichenau (1013–1054) Hermanus Contractus or Herman the Lame. Chronologist. Although severely handicapped physically, he was considered the most learned man in eleventh-century Germany, proficient in theology, Latin, Greek, Arabic, mathematics, astronomy, and music. His greatest achievement was his *Universal Chronicle,* a chronology of the first millennium.

Hermas One of the Apostolic Fathers*, author of *The Shepherd,* written probably at Rome* in the first half of the second century. The work consists of 5 visions, 12 mandates, and 10 similitudes. Hermas received his visions from a woman representing the church and from an angel of repentance in a shepherd's guise. The major themes relate to purity and repentance. In the Greek Church, Hermas's work was regarded as Scripture, and it was highly valued as a textbook of catechumens*. In the Codex Sinaiticus*, it comes after the New Testament.

Hermeneutics (Gk., *hermeneuo,* to explain, interpret) Branch of theology dealing with principles governing biblical exegesis* and interpretation. It is concerned with various types of interpretation, as allegorical and literal, multiple meanings and senses, and the role of historical criticism. The four principal hermeneutical approaches are romanticist, existential, ontological, and socio-critical. In the romanticist tradition, the goal of the interpreter is to reach behind the text to the mind of its author. Existential hermeneutics interprets the Bible in terms of the interpreter's own life situation. Ontological hermeneutics interprets the meaning of the Bible in the light of the reality it is attempting to create. Socio-critical hermeneutics examines the social traditions and assumptions underpinning biblical narratives.

hermit (Gk., *eremite,* desert dweller) 1. A person who voluntarily adopts a solitary life to please God. 2. A person who lives as a solitary within a religious community, as the Augustinian Hermits.

Hermosillo, Jeronimo (1800–1861) Dominican missionary and martyr* in Vietnam. He worked in Vietnam from 1829 until 1861 during the period when emperors Min Mang and Tu Duc killed some 150,000 Christians in one of the worst persecutions in Christian history. Taken captive, he was beheaded. He was canonized in 1988.

Herrnhut Village in Saxony, south of Dresden, built and settled in 1722 by the Moravian Brethren* under Christian David* on land owned by Zinzendorf*. For many years until 1992 it was the headquarters of the German Moravian Church, and it remains one of the legendary Moravian institutions. John Wesley*, who admired the Moravians, made a pilgrimage* to the settlement in 1738.

Herrnhut

Herzog, Johann Jakob (1805–1882) Swiss Reformed* theologian noted as the editor of *Realencyklopadie fur protestantische Theologie und Kirche* (22 vols., 1854–1868). The English language version was coedited by Philip Schaff* and hence known as the *Schaff-Herzog Encyclopedia of Religious Knowledge.*

hesperinos Byzantine Rite* office of vespers* which opens the liturgical day beginning at sunset.

Hesychasm (Gk., *hesychia,* silence) Practice in the Greek Orthodox Church beginning in the fourteenth century of intense mystical meditation, attempting to dissolve into the divine presence. The practice was particularly associated with the monks of Mount Athos*, each of whom sought to attain a numinous* state by reciting the Jesus Prayer* incessantly and adopting a particular bodily posture: pressing the chin on the chest while focusing their eyes on the navel and holding their breath until vision became dim. This would then lead to a state of ecstatic trance completely isolated from the world. The bodily posture, denounced by Barlaam and others as gross superstition, was not essential to the recitation of the Jesus Prayer*, but it helped to synchronize the prayer with the heart beat.

Hesychasts believed that the union of mind and the heart in prayer enabled them to see the divine light even with their material eyes. This light was held to be identical with the light that surrounded the Lord at his transfiguration on the Mount of Tabor and to be the same as the uncreated energy of the Godhead. The divine light was the object of beatific vision*. Largely through the efforts of Gregory Palamas*, Hesychasm was accepted in the Hagioritic Tome and adopted by the councils of Constantinople* in 1341, 1347, and 1351. It is now an accepted part of the Orthodox tradition. The chief source of Hesychasm is the *Philocalia* of St. Nicodemus of the Holy Mountain*.

Hesychius of Jerusalem, St. (fifth century) Greek writer and exegete. He was the reputed author of a church history that is now lost. He strongly supported the Alexandrian position at the Council of Chalcedon*. He defended the orthodox doctrines against Arians, Manichaeans, and Apollinarians.

heterodoxy (Gk., another opinion) Belief that is contrary to established canons or doctrines and therefore opposed to orthodoxy*.

heteronomy Theological view than human beings are not autonomous but are subject to moral laws established by God.

heteroousian (Gk., another being) In early church history, heretic who maintained that Christ, the Son, was of a different essence or substance from God the Father. See also HOMOOUSIOS.

hetoimasia (Gk., preparation of the throne) Byzantine motif showing preparation of the throne for the last judgment*. It shows an empty throne set up for the Son with Gospel books and other symbols. See also ETIMASIA.

heuristic theology Branch of theology concerned with the discovery of truth in a statement or text.

Heyling, Peter (1607/8–1652) First German Protestant missionary. Influenced by Hugo Grotius*, he volunteered as a missionary and then went on to Malta and Egypt. The Abuna of Ethiopia invited him to come to that country in 1634, and he gained the favor of the court as a tutor of noble children. He translated the Gospel of John into Amharic*. He was martyred by a Muslim fanatic in 1652.

Hexapla Version of the Old Testament produced by Origen* between 231 and 245. Many sections of the Old Testament were presented in six parallel columns, with a Hebrew text, a Hebrew text transliterated into Greek, and the four Greek versions of Symmachus, Aquila, the Septuagint, and Theodotion. For some sections of the Old Testament, three further Greek versions were added.

Origen

hexapsalmos In the Byzantine Rite*, sequence of six Psalms read after the opening prayers of the orthros*. They are the Septuagint Psalms: 3, 37, 62, 87, 102, and 142. During their reading, the priest recites the 12 mattins* prayers.

hexapteryga Also, ripidion*. Fan used in the Eastern Orthodox Church*.

Hicks, Tommy (1909–1973) Pentecostal missionary, evangelist, and faith healer. He conducted successful crusades in Argentina and other countries.

Hicksites Liberal branch of American Quakers*, founded by Elias Hicks (1748–1830), a liberal social activist, who opposed creeds and dogmas and withdrew from the orthodox Society of Friends*.

hidden Christians Also, separated Christians. Crypto-Christians* who remained in Japan after the great persecutions of the seventeenth century.

hierarch (Gk., sacred leader) Supreme leader of a church or sect.

hierarchy 1. System of government in a church or denomination, consisting of councils, synods, convocations, etc. 2. Power structure in a church or denomination consisting mainly of those in holy orders*, such as bishops, priests, and deacons, etc. 3. Order of angels* or other heavenly beings. 4. In the Roman Catholic Church, the organization of clerics according to rank and order of position.

hierarchy of truths Belief that revealed truths are not static propositions but are organized around and point to the center or foundation—the person and mystery of Jesus Christ. Though all Christian beliefs are equally true, they have greater or lesser consequences according to their closeness to the core faith in Jesus Christ. Thus, grace* is more important than sin*, sanctifying grace more important than actual grace, the Resurrection of Christ more important than his childhood, the mystical aspect of the church more important than its juridical, and the liturgy more important than private devotions. This phrase was first used in the Second Vatican Council's* Decree on Ecumenism.

hierateion In the Byzantine Rite*, sanctuary in the eastern side of the church containing the altar.

hieraticon (Gk., priest's book) Byzantine Rite* liturgical book containing the priest's part of the

Liturgy of St. Chrysostom* and St. Basil*, the Liturgy of the Presanctified*, orthros*, and hesperinos*.

hieratike In the Byzantine Rite*, a clerical tonsure*.

hierodeacon In the Eastern Orthodox Church*, a deacon who is also a monk.

hieromonk In the Eastern Orthodox Church*, a priest who was formerly a monk.

Hieronymian Martyrology Fifth-century Italian list of martyrs*. It collated the martyrologies of Rome*, Carthage*, and Syria.

Hieronymites Order of Roman ladies of Bethlehem* who, in the fourth century, placed themselves under Jerome's* direction. The order was revived in Spain in the fourteenth century when Fernando Pecha founded the Hieronymites. In 1389 the Monastery of Our Lady of Guadalupe* passed into their hands and later the Monastery of Belem where the Portuguese kings are buried. The order was dissolved in 1837.

hierurgia The Eucharist*.

high altar Main altar in the church traditionally in the center of the east end.

High Church 1. Episcopal or Anglican Church emphasizing tradition and ritual. 2. Anglo-Catholic groups within the Anglican Church who emphasize apostolic succession*, episcopacy*, and sacraments*. Some of these groups venerate the Virgin Mary* and use Catholic practices during Mass*.

High Mass (Lat., *Missa Solemnis*) Traditional form of the Catholic Mass. Its essential features are the presence of the celebrant assisted by the deacons, thurifer*, and acolytes* chanting the Gospel and *ite, missa est** and subdeacons chanting the Epistle, the choir and the congregation singing the common and proper of saints*, the use of incense, and the kiss of peace*.

higher criticism Critical study of the literary methods and sources used by the writers of the Bible as well as its form, date, and purpose, as distinguished from textual criticism* or lower criticism*. Higher criticism has three main concerns: detecting the presence of underlying sources, identifying the literary types that make up the composition, and determining matters of authorship and dates. Higher criticism includes form criticism* and tradition criticism. It has affinities with the Holiness movement* in Wesleyanism.

higher life Form of Christian holiness* promoted by the Keswick Convention*. It emphasizes actual deliverance from sins, continual cleansing, and the infilling of the Holy Spirit*. It was popularized by the American Presbyterian minister, William Edward Boardman (1810–1886) in his *Higher Christian Life* (1859). It asserted that the work of sanctification* is a distinct second work of grace*, separable from justification*. The message was carried forward by Robert Pearsall Smith, author of *Holiness through Faith* (1870), and his wife, Hannah Whitall Smith*, author of *The Christian's Secret of a Happy Life* (1875).

Hilander Serbian monastery on Athos* founded by Simeon and Saba of Serbia. The chrysobull issued by Emperor Alexios III gave the monastery complete and permanent autonomy. The monastery honors the Virgin Mary* as its abbot. The present Katholicon was built by King Milutin around 1300. Among Hilander's most prominent features is the St. Saba's pyrgos, or fortified tower.

Hilarion, St. (c. 291–371) Eastern ascetic who was a disciple of St. Anthony the Great*. He established several ascetic communities at Maiuma, in Palestine. Jerome* traces the origin of monastic life in Palestine to Hilarion*. He returned to Egypt about 356, but was forced by Julian's persecution to flee to Sicily, Dalmatia, and finally Cyprus*. Feast day: October 21.

Hilary of Arles, St. (401–449) Bishop of Arles*. He was an ascetic who did much to promote the rights of bishops. This brought him into conflict with Pope Leo I*, who deprived him of his see*. He was later called "Hilary of Sacred Memory" and canonized. Feast day: May 5.

Hilary of Poitiers, St. (c. 315–367) "Athanasius of the West." French bishop of Poitiers who converted from neo-Platonism and became a vigorous defender of orthodoxy* and an opponent of Arianism*. He defended the cause of orthodoxy at Seleucia and Constantinople* and was banished for that reason by the pro-Arian emperor, Constantius. He wrote *De Trinitate* on the Trinity*, *De Synodis* on doctrinal history, *Opus Historicum,* several commentaries, and some hymns. He is the earliest Latin hymn writer. He was elevated as a doctor of the church* in 1851. Feast day: January 14.

Hilda, St. (614–680) Abbess of Whitby. She was the grand niece of King Edwin of Northumbria, who was converted through the preaching of Paulinus* and baptized by him. She became a nun and was named abbess of the convent of Hartlepool, and later the abbess of a double monastery at Whitby in Yorkshire. At the Synod of Whitby* in northern England in 653/54 she defended Celtic customs. Feast day: November 17.

Hildegard of Bingen, St. (1098–1179) Abbess of Rupertsberg, near Bingen. In 1136, she succeeded Blessed Jutta as abbess of the Benedictine monastery of Disibodenberg. Subject to supernatural visions from childhood, she began recording, under the direction of her confessor*, some of her visions beginning in 1141. Between 1147 and 1152 she moved her community to Rupertsberg, near Bingen, and founded a daughter house at Eibingen. Her prophetic writings had great influence on her contemporaries, including Emperor Frederick Barbarossa. Her *Scivias* is divided into three books containing 26 visions, her *Liber Vitae Meritorum* (1158–1163) contains six books on the joys that await the believer in afterlife, and *Liber Divinorum Operum* (1163–1173) contains three books. Her musical play, *Ordo Virtutum,* was one of 77 musical compositions. Her other works consists of the lives of saints*, hymns, homilies, theological treatises, and medical textbooks. Feast day: September 17.

Hildesheim Church established as a chapel by Ludwig the Pious. At the end of the ninth century, Bishop Altfried built a massive basilica* over the original church. It was burned down in 1046. A new church built in the eleventh century was completely destroyed in 1945. Between 1950 and 1960 it was rebuilt again as a three-aisled basilica*. Among the church's treasures are the Shrine of St. Godehard and the 12-foot high Christ Column showing in spirally ascending reliefs 23 scenes from the life of Christ.

Hilton, Walter (c. 1343–1396) English mystic and Augustinian canon of Thurgarton. His most famous work is the *Scale of Perfection,* a classic of Christocentric* piety. Among his other works are *De Imagine Peccati* and *Epistola Aurea.*

Hincmar (806–882) Archbishop of Reims* from 845. He was prominent in the controversies with Gottschalk* on predestination*. His tenets were approved at the Synod of Quiercy* (853) but condemned at the Synod of Valence (855). He also wrote extensively on canon law*.

Hinn, Benny (1952–) Healing evangelist. Hinn became a Charismatic in 1972 at the age of 20 under the influence of Kathryn Kuhlman*. He began his public ministry in 1974 in Ontario, soon attracting thousands to his weekly healing meetings. In the early 1980s he moved to Orlando, Florida, and in 1999 to Dallas, Texas. His ministry includes live crusades* and a daily television program. His book, *Good Morning, Holy Spirit,* has sold more than four million copies.

Hippo, Council of Council of the Catholic Church in Latin Africa, held in 393. Its canons have passed into the canon law* of the Western Church*.

Hippolytus, Canons of See CANONS OF HIPPOLYTUS.

Hippolytus, St. (c. 170–c. 236) Theologian and martyr*. As a presbyter*, he opposed Popes Zephyrinus* and Calixtus I*, and was elected as a rival bishop of Rome*. He was deported by Emperor Maximin in 235 and reconciled to the pope. After his martyrdom his body was brought to Rome with honor and he was canonized. His chief work was the *Refutation of All Heresies,* or *Philosophumena,* valuable for its account of Gnostic sects in which he held that Christ as the Word of God* reified the Father's ideas as a creative agent. In the summary of true doctrine at the end of the work, Hippolytus expressed his own Trinitarian* theol-

ogy. Other writings attributed to Hippolytus are commentaries on Daniel and Song of Songs, a historical work entitled *Chronicon,* and an important treatise on the apostolic tradition*, which preserves a picture of Roman church practice and order at the end of the second century. He was the first scholar to construct an Easter* table that was independent of Jewish traditions. Feast day: January 30 (Eastern Church*); August 13 (Western Church*).

Hirsau Former Benedictine monastery at Hirsau in the Nagold Valley in Germany founded in 830 by Count Erlafried. It contained the relics* of St. Aurelius*. The Hirsau monastery school flourished in the tenth century. In 1071 Wilhelm became the abbot of Hirsau and ordered the construction of a new monastery, St. Peter's* and St. Paul's, built between 1082 and 1091. The massive flat-roofed basilica* had columns and towers, a transept* with apses*, and a choir with three aisles. The monastery was destroyed in 1692 by the French general Melac, leaving only the twelfth-century Owls Tower intact.

Hispana Canons Also, Isidoriana. Lengthiest and most authentic recension* of early conciliar and papal decisions from 66 Eastern, African, Spanish, and French councils arranged geographically and chronologically. The 103 papal decretals* extend from the papacy of Damasus I* to Gregory I*. Originally compiled by St. Isidore of Seville*,

St. Hippolytus

it first appeared in seventh-century Gaul. It is recognized as the official corpus of Spanish canon law*.

historia Musical setting of a biblical story, such as the Passion*, Christmas*, or Resurrection.

historical Jesus Jesus as portrayed by scholars who reconstruct his life and teaching according to higher criticism*, as distinguished from the orthodox Christological definitions in dogma* and Scriptures. It is described as a quest, following the title of a seminal digest of the movement, Albert Schweitzer's* *Quest of the Historical Jesus* (1910). The earliest challenges to the historical Gospel accounts began with *Apologie oder Schutzschrift fur die vernunftigen Verehrer Gotte,* by H. S. Reimarus, followed much later by *Leben Jesu* by D. F. Strauss*, and the *Life of Jesus* by Ernst Renan*. The quest was warmly embraced by the liberal Protestants in Germany and the social gospel* theologians in the United States. Martin Kahler in his *Der sogennante Historische Jesus und der geschichtliche biblische Christus* (1892) repudiated the quest, and Karl Barth* and Rudolf Bultmann* succeeded in slowing its progress in diverse ways.

But it has renewed since the 1950s and it has found a forum in the Jesus Seminar* bent on demolition of the Christ of faith* and the Gospels. The revival of the quest, dubbed *The New Quest of the Historical Jesus* (1959) by J. M. Robinson, is buttressed by a new convergence of sociological, literary, and historical methods of investigation. Another quest, called the Third Quest, emphasizing the Jewish milieu in which Jesus lived, has recently emerged as seen in the works of Dominic Crossan, Marcus Berg, and N. T. Wright.

historical theology Branch of theology concerned with the evolution and migration of theological doctrines, concepts, and ideas and with establishing their historical context. Two pioneers in this field of study were John Henry Cardinal Newman* on the Roman Catholic side and Adolf von Harnack* on the Protestant side.

hiuparkiya In the Assyrian Church*, the ecclesiastical province or diocese* under the jurisdiction of a metropolitan* or bishop.

h'mira In the Nestorian tradition, a portion of the dough left over from the last preparation of the eucharistic bread and preserved as a leaven for the new baking.

Hochmann von Hochenau, Ernst Christoph (1670–1721) German Pietist mystic. Converted in 1693 and discipled by Gottfried Arnold*, he taught that the church was primarily spiritual and rejected structures, creeds, and sacraments. He became a peripatetic preacher and was imprisoned many times. He played a major role in founding the Brethren movement and prepared a statement of its beliefs. He eventually broke with the Brethren and spent his last years as a hermit in a small hut named Friedensburg.

Hocktide English holiday, celebrated in the Middle Ages the second Monday and Tuesday after Easter* when rents were due. It was marked by various sports and amusements.

Hodegetria (Gk., she who knows the way) Representation of the Virgin Mary* holding the child in her left arm and pointing to him with her right hand.

Hodge, Charles (1797–1878) Leading American theologian of the nineteenth century. He was professor of theology at Princeton Seminary. He was a tireless defender of the Westminster Confession* and orthodox Calvinism* and became founder of the Princeton (or the Old School) theology. His reputation as a scholar is based on his *Systematic Theology* (3 vols., 1872–1873) as well as New Testament commentaries, such as *A Commentary on the Epistle to the Romans* (1835). His son, Archibald Alexander Hodge, was also a notable theologian.

Hofbauer, St. Clement Mary (1751–1820) Birth name: John Dvorvak. Redemptorist priest. "Apostle of Vienna." He was ordained as a Redemptorist priest in 1785 and two years later went to Warsaw, where he founded many houses, did much pastoral work, and opened schools. He also introduced the Redemptorist order into Switzerland and south Germany and became vicar general* of the order. In his last years, he returned to his native Vienna*, where he served as pastor to St. Ursula's Church and chaplain* to the Ursulines*. The Redemptorists* were established in Austria soon after his death. He was canonized in 1909 and named patron saint* of Austria. Feast day: March 15.

Hofmann, Johann Christian Konrad von (1810–1877) German theologian of the Erlangen School* which represented a modified form of Lutheranism*. He emphasized salvation history which he interpreted within the framework of its ultimate goal of union of God and man in Christ. His writings included *Weissagung und Erfullung im Alten und Neuen Testament* (2 parts, 1841–1844), *Der Schriftbeweis* (1852–1856), and *Die hl Schriften des Neuen Testaments* (8 parts, 1862– 1878).

Hoffmann, Melchior (c. 1498–c. 1543) German Anabaptist mystic who traveled through Europe as a lay preacher. He denounced image worship, proclaimed the imminent end of the world, and held that only the saved should be baptized. He was banished from Denmark for his allegedly Zwinglian views and sentenced to life imprisonment at Strasbourg*. His followers formed themselves into a separate sect of Anabaptists* called Melchiorites.

hogehangist (Arm., requiem) In the Armenian Church, Requiem Mass*, especially on the fortieth day after a death (karasoonk*) and on every anniversary (tarelits).

Holbein, Hans (c. 1465–1524) German painter. He painted many religious altarpieces, church windows, and paintings, such as the *Altar of St. Sebastian* (1516) in Munich*.

Holbein the Younger, Hans (c. 1497–1543) German painter and wood engraver, son of Hans Holbein*. About 1526 he went to England, where he lived from 1532 to the end of his life. He became court painter to Henry VIII about 1536. He also designed cover pages of Coverdale's and Cranmer's Bibles. His Christian paintings Include *The Last Supper, The Dead Christ in the Tomb,* eight Passion pictures, *The Nativity, The Adoration of the Magi, Solothurn Madonna,* and *Madonna and Saints.*

Holden, Oliver (1765–1844) American hymnologist who composed a number of hymns, including "All Hail to the Power of Jesus" (1789).

holiness 1. Moral or spiritual perfection*; sinlessness; entire sanctification*. 2. Quality of being set apart or consecrated to God.

Holiness churches The most important twentieth-century Holiness churches in the United States are: Church of the Nazarene*, Wesleyan Church, Evangelical Church of North America, Holiness Christian Church, Churches of Christ in Christian Union*, Methodist Protestants, Primitive Methodist Church, and Congregational Methodist Church.

holiness, his/your Title and term of address to the pope or any of the patriarchs* and catholicoses* of the Eastern Orthodox Church*.

Holiness movement Movement in the Wesleyan tradition emphasizing a second, distinctive experience of the Evangelical faith subsequent to regeneration* by which the Christian believer is filled with the Holy Spirit* and entirely sanctified. Once a believer is cleansed from inbred sin, he or she may then continue to live without conscious or deliberate sin. The modern movement, which is predominantly American, evolved out of a quest for Christian perfection* in the 1830s in the Calvinistic and Methodist churches* under the leadership of Phoebe Palmer*, Charles Finney*, and Asa Mahan*. Charles Finney's Oberlin theology* provided a further boost to the Holiness movement. The spiritual force of the movement was expressed in promoting a "second blessing* holiness," based on Wesley's call in his book *Plain Account of Christian Perfection* to "the higher Christian life."

In the 1830s two sisters, Sarah Lankford and Phoebe Palmer*, organized a weekly prayer meeting* in New York, known as the "Tuesday Meeting," which spawned a number of similar meetings. By mid-century the movement had rallied support from diverse advocates, as Congregationalist T. C. Upham, Presbyterian W. E. Boardman, Baptist A. B. Earle, and British Methodist William Arthur. The movement reached a wide audience through W. E. Boardman's *The Higher Christian Life* (1858) and Hannah Whitall Smith's* *The Christian's Secret of a Happy Life** (1875). The establishment of the National Camp Meeting Association for the Promotion of Holiness in Vineland, New Jersey, in 1867 marked a new phase in the movement's growth.

Great emphasis was placed on external observance, especially the avoidance of worldly pleasures. John Inskip and other Methodists assumed a leadership in the revival which they maintained for over a quarter of a century. Meanwhile, the movement spread to all major Evangelical denominations and mission fields*, including the British Keswick Convention, the German Heiligungsbewegung, and the Salvation Army*, all indelibly imprinted with the higher life* Christian message. Keswick*, particularly, promoted holiness as a second blessing which may be attained by faith* or by a single act of self-surrender. However, Keswickians cautioned against striving against one's sinful impulses directly. Rather, these impulses were to be remitted to Christ in trustful and expectant passivity. "Let Go and Let God" was a Keswick slogan.

By the end of the nineteenth century, the movement broke with the mainline churches* as large numbers of Methodists joined with other Evangelicals to form what are known as Holiness churches*. New churches, such as the Church of the Nazarene*, Pilgrim Holiness Church, Church of God (Anderson), and the Christian and Missionary Alliance*, were born during this phase of the movement. Two Mennonite bodies, the Missionary Church and the Brethren in Christ*, adopted Wesleyan views and identified with the movement. Some Methodists did not leave their church but continued to support Holiness institutions, such as Asbury College and Theological Seminary*, Taylor University, and Western Evangelical Seminary. Worldwide membership in Holiness churches is estimated at over 2 million with over one-half in the United States. Many of them are members of the Christian Holiness Association and the more conservative International Holiness Convention.

By their denial of glossolalia* (speaking in tongues*), Holiness churches distinguish themselves from Pentecostal churches*, many of which also trace their descent from the nineteenth century Holiness revival and even maintain Wesleyan perfectionism*. However, Pentecostals have appropriated some of the Holiness doctrines, teaching gifts of the spirit* as evidence of personal sanctity*.

holistic evangelism Evangelism involving sociopolitical action.

holy 1. Of God, perfect in righteousness and infinite in wisdom and goodness; commanding adoration and reverence. 2. Of human beings, spiritually perfect and pure in heart; of unimpaired innocence and proven virtue. 3. Set apart or dedicated to the service or worship of God. 4. Of objects and buildings, venerated because of association with God or holy persons. 5. One of the attributes of the universal church.

Holy Apostolic and Catholic Church of the East and Assyrians Assyrian Church. See also CHURCH OF THE EAST.

Holy Atch Right arm of Gregory the Illuminator* laid on the head of the patriarch elect of the Armenian Church*.

holy bread Bread consecrated in the Eucharist*.

holy card Small printed card depicting religious figures, used as a memento of events, as a means of remembrance, and to foster a particular devotion.

Holy Club Association of students formed by John and Charles Wesley* at Oxford University, also called Methodists, because they methodically fasted and prayed.

holy coat Christ's seamless coat (John 19:23), claimed to be in the possession of the Cathedral of Trier* and a church at Argenteuil.

Holy Communion Lord's Supper* or the Eucharist*.

holy door 1. Door in the facade of St. Peter's* in Rome, which is normally closed with bricks, except during the Holy Year* when it is opened for those who wish to gain the Indulgence of the Holy Year by passing through it. There are similar holy doors in each of the other major basilicas*. 2. In the Eastern Church*, central door in the iconostasis* that separates the bema* from the main part of the church.

holy family Infant Jesus, Mary, and Joseph together as a family.

Holy Father Term of address and title of the pope.

Holy Friday Good Friday*.

Holy Ghost Holy Spirit*, the third person of the Trinity*.

Holy Ghost Fathers Also, Spiritans. Roman Catholic congregation of priests and lay brothers* dedicated to missionary and social work, founded as Congregation of the Holy Ghost in Paris in 1703 by Claude-Francois Poullart des Places*. It was destroyed by the French Revolution but revived through the efforts of Jacques Bertout. In 1848 Francois Marie Paul Libermann*, a converted Jew from Alsace, merged the order with his own Congregation of the Immaculate Heart of Mary*.

Holy Grail See GRAIL, HOLY.

holy hour Paraliturgical eucharistic devotion when the Blessed Sacrament* is exposed for one full hour.

Holy Innocents Children of Jerusalem "from two years old and under" killed by Herod the Great (Matt. 2:16–18). Their death as martyrs is commemorated on December 28 in the West and December 29 in the East.

Holy Isle See LINDISFARNE.

holy kiss Kiss of peace* exchanged between believers in a Communion service.

holy lance Lance used by a Roman soldier, later given the name of Longinus, in John 19:34 for piercing the Lord's dead body. One part of it is said to have been taken to Persia at the capture of Jerusalem* by the Persians in 615, from where it

was taken to Constantinople*. In 1241 it was given to St. Louis, who passed it to Saint-Chapelle* where it was preserved with the crown of thorns. It disappeared during the French Revolution. Another part of the holy lance is said to have passed from Palestine to Constantinople, where it fell into the hands of the Turks in 1492. The Turks sent it as a gift to the Vatican*, where it remains at St. Peter's*. Similar relics* were reported in Prague*, Nuremburg, and Vienna*.

Holy Land Palestine.

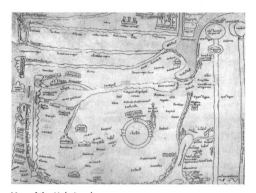

Map of the Holy Land

holy laughter Phenomenon associated with Toronto Blessing* in which believers are overtaken by an uncontrollable spirit of ecstatic laughter accompanied by other physical manifestations, such as as falling down and making noises.

Holy Mountain Mount Athos*, so called because it is open for residence only to monks.

holy mountains Mountains associated with the life of Christ, as Mount of the Transfiguration, or with monastic history. Among the best known holy mountains are Sinai, Tur Abdin* in Syria, Mount St. Auxentios in Bithynia*, Mount Athos* in Greece, Olympos of Mysia in Bithynia*, Mount Galesios north of Ephesus* in Lydia, Mount Ganos or Kalonoros in Thrace, Mount Latros, and Mount Paroria on the Bulgarian border.

Holy Name of Jesus Name of Jesus used as a synonym for Jesus himself to convey his authority. The name of Jesus is venerated above all names

(Phil. 2:9); miracles and exorcisms* are performed and all Christians are baptized in the name of Jesus*, as well as the Father and the Holy Spirit*. Devotion to the Holy Name of Jesus was popularized in the fifteenth century by the Franciscans, St. Bernardino of Siena* and St. Giovanni Capistrano*, and it was approved for the universal church by Leo XIII* in 1886. Until 1969 the Feast of the Name of Jesus* was celebrated on the Second Sunday after Epiphany*.

Holy Name Society Roman Catholic group promoting devotion for the name of Jesus, founded by a Dominican friar, Diego of Victoria, as the Confraternity of the Name of God in fifteenth-century Spain. It was officially approved by Pope Pius IV* a century later.

holy of holies Sanctuary* in Nestorian and Eastern Orthodox* churches.

Holy Office The tribunal of the Inquisition* established by Paul III* in 1542, known as Congregatio Romanae et Universalis Inquisitionis. It went through several reorganizations as its original membership of six cardinals was raised to 13. From 1988 its name was changed to Congregatio de Doctrina Fidei.

holy oil Chrism*.

Holy One Christ, as in Holy One of God (Mark 1:24).

holy orders The major orders* of the Christian ministry: bishop, priest, and deacon.

Holy Rollers Derisive term for Pentecostals and others whose worship services are characterized by physical exuberance such as clapping and dancing.

Holy Rood Holy Cross of Christ.

Holy Saturday The day after Good Friday* and before Easter*, commemorating Christ's full day in the tomb. There is no celebration of the Eucharist* on this day.

Holy See The see* of the pope as the bishop of Rome*.

Holy Sepulchre Rock cave in Jerusalem* where Christ was reputed to have been buried. According to tradition, it was discovered by St. Helena*, the mother of Constantine*, and the first Church of the Holy Sepulchre (or Anastasis or Resurrection) was dedicated in about 335. It was successively destroyed and rebuilt in 614, 626, 1015, 1149, 1310, 1808, and 1810. The main structure of the church consists of two halves: the church proper on the east and the domed building covering the Holy Sepulchre in the west. There are also several chapels and shrines in which many Christian denominations have rights of access.

holy shroud See SHROUD OF TURIN.

Holy Spirit Also, Advocate; Holy Ghost*; Paraclete*. Third person of the Trinity*. He is distinct from, but consubsantial*, coequal and coeternal with, the Father and the Son, and is fully God. His functions are manifold. He is the instrument of divine action in the world. At the time of creation, he brooded on the face of the waters. He was breathed by God on the writers of the Bible. He anoints his prophets through his infilling. He was the baptizer of Jesus Christ. He points people to Jesus Christ, and Paul* calls the Holy Spirit the "Spirit of Christ" (Rom. 8:9; Gal. 4:6; Phil. 1:19).

The Holy Spirit is active in Christian baptism*, worship, proclamation, and instruction, and in moral discernment*. He is the agent of regeneration* and the new birth*. He enables Christians to lead a life of purity and holiness*. He is the Advocate, pleading the cause of Christians before the throne of God. He endows Christians for various ministries and gifts. Finally, he is the means by which Christ was raised from the dead and by which Christians are raised from corruption to eternal life*. He gives gifts as he wills (1 Cor. 12:11), he leads believers and bears witness in them (Rom. 8:14, 16), he has knowledge (1 Cor. 2:1) and mind (Rom. 8:27), he grieves (Eph. 4:30), intercedes (Rom. 8:26), and cries out (Gal. 4:6).

The doctrine of the Holy Spirit evolved through the centuries, and his divinity was fully recognized in the creeds and canons of the ecumenical councils. The major controversies regarding the Holy Spirit were the Macedonian heresy and the dispute regarding the Double Procession* or the Holy Spirit or the Filioque* clause. Both St. Basil* in *De Spiritu Sancto* and Augustine in *De Trinitate* reaffirmed the theology of the Holy Spirit. In the twentieth century, the Pentecostal movement and the Charismatic movement have brought a new vigorous dimension to the Holy Spirit's working in the church.

Dove: Symbol of the Holy Spirit

Holy Synod Supreme organ of the government of the Russian Orthodox Church* from 1721 to 1917. It was an ecclesiastical committee composed of bishops and clergy, established by Peter the Great to replace the patriarch's autocratic powers.

holy table Table or altar from which the Lord's Supper* or Eucharist* is served.

Holy Thursday Thursday of Holy Week*, the day before Good Friday*, also known as Maundy Thursday*, commemorated by Communion services as the day on which the Last Supper was held and the Lord's Supper* initiated.

holy unction 1. In Anglican usage, the rite of anointing the sick with oil (James 5:14–15). 2. In Roman Catholic usage, last rites* or extreme unction* administered to those seriously ill or near death.

holy water Water blessed for religious purposes. In the Eastern Church*, the water is blessed at the Great Blessing of the Waters* on the Feast of the Epiphany* or at the Lesser Blessing of Water on the first day of the month. Holy water is also used at baptisms, blessings, dedications, exorcisms*, and burials. During the Mass*, water is blessed in the asperges*. There are holy water stoups at the entrance of churches.

Holy Week The week beginning Palm Sunday*

and ending with Easter* devoted to the commemoration of the Passion*, suffering, Crucifixion, and burial of Christ. Many of the services during the week recreate the last scenes of the life of Christ in liturgical drama.

Holy Writ Holy Bible.

Holy Year Year during which the pope grants special indulgence*, known as jubilee*, to those who visit Rome and pass through the holy door* and visit the four main basilicas*. It was instituted in 1300 by Pope Boniface VIII* and was originally celebrated every 100 years. Clement VI* in 1343 reduced it to 50, Urban VI* in 1389 to 33, and Paul II in 1470 to 25. Plenary indulgence* granted in these years may absolve most sins. One of the most important ceremonies of the Holy Year is the opening of the holy door* by the pope before the first Christmas vespers* and its walling up again for the next 25 years. Originally the jubilee* indulgence was available only at Rome, but since 1500 it has been extended to all Roman Catholic churches and shrines throughout the world.

In addition to the Holy Years, there have been two special ones in the twentieth century: Holy Years of Redemption and Marian Years*. The former take place in the years 33–34 and 83–84 of a century to celebrate the crucifixion and resurrection of Christ (dated 33) and run from the Feast of the Annunciation to Easter Sunday of the following year. The Marian Years are in honor of the Virgin Mary* and take place from December to December in the years 53–54 and in 87–88 of a century from Whitsunday* to Assumption.

holytide Season devoted to religious activities.

Homberg, Synod of Synod called by Philip of Hesse in 1526 to draw up a constitution for the Protestant church in his state, along the lines of the scheme of Francis Lambert, a former Franciscan. It called for the priesthood of all believers* and congregational government under the general supervision of a synod*. The proposals were abandoned because of Luther's opposition.

home mission Domestic mission as distinguished from foreign mission.

homiletics (Lat., *homiletike,* art of conversation) Art and theology of preaching the gospel. The spoken word and the listening congregation together constitute the ministry of preaching. It includes exposition of the Word of God*, proclamation of the kingdom of God*, and exegesis* of biblical truths. From earliest times, homiletics was based on the homily*, or a text in the Bible, and it was the task of the preacher to explain the mysteries* of the Word, its connection with similar verses, and its practical applications. In the early Middle Ages, collections of the sermons of famous preachers and other homiletic helps were published as an aid to those who wanted guidance in putting together sermons. The art of illustrations also developed. Thematic preaching based on short texts, with introductions, transitions, conclusions, and alliterative headings, was encouraged in seminaries. Homiletic organization follows conventional rubrics, as rhetoric, invention (finding out what is to be said), disposition (arrangement of material), style, memory, and delivery.

homiliarium/homiliary (pl., homiliaria) Medieval collection of sermons or homilies, arranged according to the ecclesiastical calendar* for reading at the office of mattins*.

Homilies, Books of Authorized sermons issued in two books by the Church of England* during the reigns of Edward VI and Elizabeth I. They were designed to serve as models of topical preaching and to conform to Protestant theology.

homily Sermon or discourse on a religious theme delivered to a congregation during a church service.

homodoxy Literally, the same religious belief, generally conforming to orthodox teachings or traditions.

Homoeans Arian party in the theological controversy at Nicaea* who held that Christ was like (Gk., *homoios**) but not of the same substance as the Father. The Homoean party itself qualified their position, ranging from the radical Valens of Mursa and Ursacius of Singidunum, who emphasized the difference in substance, to Acacius of Caesaria, who held that the Son was "like in all things," to Basil of Ancyra,* who held that the Son was "like in substance." The creeds produced by the Arian councils of Nicea (359) and Constantinople (360) use the Homoean formula* qualified by "according to the Scriptures."

Homoiousians Semi-Arians who were opposed to the radical Arians. Initially, they did not recognize the divinity of the Holy Spirit*, and affirmed the reality of Christ's divine sonship in the setting of the doctrine of the three hypostases without recourse to Nicene orthodoxy. They distinguished in the Trinity* three ousiae. Without identifying fully the Son with the Father, they affirmed the Son's likeness to the Father in substance. Father and Son differ from each other by origin; one generates and the other is generated. Their unity is conceived in a dynamic way, as they act and will together always.

homolegetes In the Byzantine tradition, one who has suffered for the faith; confessor*.

homologoumena New Testament writings that are universally acknowledged as authentic, as opposed to antilogomena, about which there is dispute.

homoousios (Gk., of the same substance) Orthodox formula* in the Nicene Creed* stating that the Father and the Son have the same substance or essence, making them coequal and coeternal. Thus Homoousian.

Honegger, Arthur (1892–1955) Swiss composer. He composed extensively in all forms, from Gregorian Chant* to Protestant hymns, jazz, and 12-note atonality. His most famous work was *King David* (1921). His other works include the biblical opera, *Judith* (1926), and *Une Cantate de Noel* (1953).

Honorius I (d. 638) Pope from 625. An admirer of St. Gregory* the Great, he turned the Vatican* into a monastery. He became an unwitting adherent of Monothelitism*, and for this reason he was anathematized at the Third Council of Constantinople* (681).

Honorius III (d. 1227) Pope from 1216. Birth name:

Cencio Savelli. During much of his pontificate*, he was engaged in the implementation of the decrees of the Fourth Lateran Council*. He approved the Dominican, Franciscan, and Carmelite* orders. He is the author of a life of Gregory VII*.

Honorius of Autun (c. 1090–c. 1156) Also, Augustodenensis. Theologian and author of over 500 manuscripts. He wrote extensively on religion, theology, astronomy, astrology, geography, and history. Among his works are *Elucidarium,* an exposition of Christian doctrine; *Sigillum Sanctae Mariae,* on the Assumption and the Song of Songs; *Gemma Animae* on liturgy; *Clavis Physicae,* consisting of extracts from Johannes Scottus Erigena; *Imago Mundi,* a compendium of cosmology and geography; and *De Luminaribus Ecclesiae,* a catalog of Christian writers.

Hooker, Richard (c. 1554–1600) Anglican theologian and apologist. His *Of the Laws of Ecclesiastical Polity* (1593) is a classic of English prose that defined the middle of the road theology of the Church of England*. He is remembered as one of the great apologists for the Church of England whose original ideas on matters like predestination*, assurance, and revelation* make him one of the main architects of Anglican theological tradition.

Hooker, Thomas (1586–1647) Puritan theologian and founder of Connecticut. In 1630 he fled from England to Holland and thence to Massachusetts and later to Connecticut. In 1638 he was responsible for drafting the frame of government for the Hartford Community. He was the virtual dictator of Connecticut for the remaining nine years of his life. He also was a powerful pulpit orator and champion of Puritan orthodoxy. His *Survey of the Summe of Church Discipline* (1648) was an outstanding work on Congregational polity*.

Hoover, Willis Collins (1856–1936) American founder of Pentecostalism* in Chile. Heeding a call* to South America, in 1889, Hoover began working with the Methodist Episcopal Church until 1910 when, influenced by the Azusa Street phenomenon, he broke away from the Methodists. In 1932,

following another division, he founded the Iglesia Evangelica Pentecostal, which is now the second largest Chilean Pentecostal group.

Hopkins, Gerard Manley (1844–1889) English Catholic poet. His Tractarian sympathies led him to join the Catholic Church in 1866 and become a Jesuit. On entering the order he destroyed all the poems he had written until his conversion, and returned to his craft only at the request of his superior* to write a poem on *The Wreck of the Deutschland,* celebrating the death of four nuns exiled from Bismarck's Germany. Hopkins's poems were published not in his lifetime, but 29 years after his death by his friend and literary executor, Robert Bridges*.

Hopkins, Samuel (1721–1803) Congregational clergyman and theologian. Trained in Jonathan Edwards's School for the Prophets, he became one of Edwards's closest friends and most influential disciple. After the death of Edwards in 1758, Hopkins and Joseph Bellamy began to systematize and expand Edwardsean theology that came to be known as "new divinity theology" or Consistent Calvinism*. Hopkins's theological ideas are set forth in his *System of Doctrines* (1793) in which he balanced the radical corruption of humanity through original sin* with the disinterested benevolence of the regenerate convert.

Hopkinson, Francis (1737–1791) American composer. His *Collection of Psalm Tunes with a Few Anthems* contained his religious music.

horarium In the Coptic Liturgy, a type of Breviary*.

Horne, Thomas Hartwell (1780–1862) Biblical commentator. He was the author of more than 40 books on Christian apologetics and bibliography. He is remembered chiefly for his *Critical Study of the Holy Scriptures* (3 vols., 1818).

horns of the altar 1. Corners of the altar (Ps. 118:27). The gospel horn is the northwest corner and the epistle corner is the southwest. 2. In the Old Testament, the shofars or horns made of a ram's horn and placed near the altar.

horologion (Gk., Book of Hours) In the Eastern Orthodox Church*, the liturgical book containing the recurrent portions of the Holy Office*, extending through the ecclesiastical year. It is intended for the use of readers and singers just as the Euchologion* is for the use of priests and deacons.

hortus conclusus (Lat., enclosed garden) Popular motif in Medieval art representing the Madonna* and the Child in a walled garden with well or fountain*. The biblical reference is from the phrase, "I have come to my garden, my sister, my spouse," found in Song of Solomon 4:12.

hosanna (Gk. from Heb.) Praise and beseeching. It was used by the multitude to proclaim Jesus as Messiah on his triumphal entry into Jerusalem* on Palm Sunday*. It is used in all liturgies and rites.

Hosios Lukas Monument in the remote side valley of the Helikon region in Greece built in honor of the hermit St. (Gk., *Hosios*) Lukas of Steiris, who died around 949. The monument included a burial chapel and a monastery in honor of St. Barbara*. About 1011 the great titular* church, the Katholikon, was finished. The church has a small dome. Mosaics from the life of Jesus and 153 paintings cover the walls. The Church of Theotokos, dating from the end of the tenth century, is connected to the Katholikon.

Hosios Lukas Monastery

Hosius/Osius (c. 256–c. 357) Bishop of Cordoba and leader of the orthodox party against the Arians. As bishop he suffered under the imperial persecution. He was present at the Synod of Elvira and gained the confidence of Emperor Constantine*. The emperor sent him as his emissary to Alexandria* to settle the dispute between Athanasius* and Arius* and summoned the Council of Nicaea* on his advice. Hosius presided over the council and was influential in drawing up its creed. He appeared again at the Council of Sardica* in 345 to determine the fate of Athanasius. In 355 he was summoned to Milan* by the Arian emperor Constantius and forced to sign the second creed of the Council known as "the blasphemy." He repudiated the creed before his death.

Hosius, Stanislaus (1504–1579) "Hammer of the Heretics." Polish cardinal and Counter-Reformation* leader. He dedicated his life to the extirpation of Protestantism*, pursuing Reformers such as Johann Brenz* and Jan a Lasco. His *Confessio Fidei Catholicae Christianae* (1553) is one of the polemical classics of the Counter-Reformation*. In 1558 he was called to Rome* and made a member of the Curia*. He played an important role in the final sessions of the Council of Trent*.

Hospitallers See KNIGHTS HOSPITALLERS.

host (Lat., *hostia*, a victim) Bread of the Eucharist*.

houpodiacono In the Syrian Church, a subdeacon who functions as an acolyte* and doorkeeper*.

hours, canonical See CANONICAL HOURS.

house church House in which religious services are held. House churches are common in countries where Christianity is officially banned or discouraged, as in China. House churches were also common in the Roman Empire during the first three centuries before Christians were sufficiently numerous, wealthy, and free from persecution to build churches.

House of Bishops One of the two legislative bodies of the Episcopal Church in the United States that comprise the General Convention*. Each bishop has a seat. The body cannot pass any legislation. There are similar governing bodies in other denominations.

House of Deputies One of the two legislative bodies of the Episcopal Church in the United States that comprise the General Convention*. It consists of four ordained and four lay persons from every diocese*.

house of God Church, cathedral, or chapel.

household baptism Baptism administered to an entire household, as in Acts 16:33.

housel Medieval English term for the Eucharist*.

houseling White linen cloth placed over the altar rail in Swedish churches for communicants.

Hovhaness, Alan (1911–) American composer of sacred music. His abiding love for the music of the Renaissance has found expression in his many unaccompanied works and motets*. His choral works number more than 60 and include *Thirtieth Ode of Solomon* (1948), a cantata for baritone, chorus, and string orchestra plus trumpet and trombone; *Magnificat* (1959) for four soloists, chorus, and orchestra; the anthem entitled "From the End of the Earth"; and the folk mass, *The Way of Jesus* (1974).

How Great Thou Art (1951) Hymn written by Carl Gustav Boberg in Swedish in 1885, translated into English by Stuart Hine, and popularized by George Beverly Shea* and Cliff Barrows during Billy Graham crusades.

Howells, Herbert (1892–1983) English composer. Most of his organ works were composed before World War II, including two sonatas, while most of the sacred choral music were composed afterwards. Among his liturgical texts are a number of canticles*, *Hymn for St. Cecilia, Sequence for St. Michael*, a *Stabat Mater**, several masses, and some anthems and motets*.

hozoh In the Armenian tradition, a garment that is put around the shoulders of the dead.

Hripsime, St. (fourth or fifth century) Early Armenian martyr*. She was a young Roman nun, who, with her superior*, St. Kayane, fled persecution in Rome* and arrived in Armenia, where she and her fellow nuns were killed for resisting King Tiridates. Feast day: second Monday after Pentecost* (Armenian Church); September 29 (Western Church*).

Hrosvit (tenth century) German Christian princess, noted for her learning. Her works in Latin included eight poems on saints*, including Basil*, Dionysius of Paris*, and Agnes*.

Hubert, St. (c. 657–727) "Apostle of the Ardennes." He was active as a missionary in the region that is now Belgium. The monastery housing his relics* was a center of pilgrimage* in the Middle Ages, and many religious houses were dedicated to him. He is the patron saint* of huntsmen, furriers, metalworkers, and butchers. Feast day: November 3.

Hubmaier, Balthasar (c. 1485–1528) German Anabaptist* leader. A friend of Zwingli, he abandoned Zwinglianism* for the Anabaptist confession* and in his *Von dem Tauf der Glaubigen* (1525) asserted the need of personal faith* for baptism* and condemned infant baptism*.

Balthasar Hubmaier

Huc, Abbe (1813–1860) Birth name: Regis Evaniste. Missionary to China who with fellow Lazarist, Father Gabet, undertook a remarkable journey from Beijing through Mongolia and Tibet to

Lhasa and back to Canton in 1844–1846 wearing Mandarin dress. He published an account of this journey in *Travels in Tartary and Tibet*.

Hucusque, Supplement to the Gregorian Supplementary of the eighth to the ninth centuries, from its opening word. The supplement contains the Sunday masses, those of the Common of the Saints*, votive masses*, and other pieces. Its authorship is attributed to St. Benedict of Aniane*.

hudra In the Assyrian Church*, a liturgical book that contains the proper of the liturgy as well as the office for Sundays, feasts, and principal saints' days.

Hugel, Baron Friedrich von See VON HUGEL, BARON FRIEDRICH.

Hugh of Cluny, St. (1024–1109) Abbot of Cluny*. At the age of 21 he became prior* of Cluny and on Odilo's death in 1049 was unanimously chosen abbot. Leo IX* was the first of nine popes whom he served as an adviser. He took part in the condemnation of Berengar of Tours*. Under Hugh, Cluny achieved a preeminent position, and its influence extended beyond its own order. In 1095 he persuaded Pope Urban II* to consecrate in person the high altar of the new basilica* at Cluny, then the largest church in Christendom. In the same year he attended the Council of Clermont*, where he was present during the preaching of the First Crusade*. Feast day: April 29.

Hugh of Lincoln, St. (c. 1140–1200) English Carthusian monk, bishop of Lincoln*, and one of England's most popular saints*. He was invited by Henry II of England to become first prior* of the Carthusian House at Witham, Somerset, as expiation* for the murder of Thomas Becket*. He became much loved for his saintliness, piety, and charity and his defense of the Jews and the poor. He became bishop of Lincoln in 1186 and helped to rebuild the Lincoln Cathedral, occasionally carrying hods of stones and mortar himself. He was canonized in 1220, and his tomb at Lincoln was second only to that of Thomas Becket as a place of pilgrimage*. Feast day: November 17.

Hugh of St. Victor (d. 1142) Theologian and Augustinian monk described by Adolf Harnack* as "the most influential theologian of the twelfth century." About 1115 he entered St. Victor, the House of the Augustinian Canons* founded in Paris by William of Champeaux. Hugh's works cover a wide field, both secular and religious. He wrote on geometry, grammar, and philosophy as well as theology. Among his spiritual works are *De Sacramentis Christianiae Fidei, De Arca Noe, De Vanitate Mundi*, and *De Laude Caritatis*, all of them elevating the contemplative life*. He has been called the "second Augustine."

Huguenots Calvinistic French Protestants who suffered persecution beginning with the Colloquy at Poissy* and during the civil war between Catholics and Protestants that followed. In 1572 in the St. Bartholomew's Day Massacre*, the entire Huguenot leadership was wiped out. The civil war was ended by Henry IV of Navarre, the Huguenot leader turned Catholic, who, in 1598, issued the Edict of Nantes* granting the Huguenots full toleration and civil rights. After Henry IV's reign, the persecution worsened. Louis XIV revoked the Edict of Nantes in 1685 and enforced repressive measures against the Huguenots, forcing thousands to emigrate. The Huguenot peasants of Cevennes, known as the Camisards*, rose in revolt, but they were hunted down and many Protestants went underground. It was not until the Enlightenment and the French Revolution that the Huguenots regained a measure of toleration.

hulala In the Assyrian Rite, one of the 21 divisions of the Psalter, known collectively as the hulali. Each hulala is composed of nine psalms and is further subdivided into three marmitha.

hulolo In the Jacobite Church*, an antiphon* which is sung before the Gospel.

Humanae Vitae Encyclical* issued by Pope Paul VI* in 1968, condemning abortion and all forms of birth control except the rhythm method.

Humbard, Alpha Rex Emmanuel and Maude Aimee (1919– and 1921–, respectively) American itinerant evangelists and radio and television preachers. Although they came from a Pentecostal background, they did not emphasize the baptism of the Holy Spirit* in their ministry. They were pioneers in the field of Christian television broadcasting from their Cathedral of Tomorrow.

Humble Access, Prayer of Prayer before consecration in the Anglican Communion service beginning with the words, "We do not presume to come to this thy table, O merciful Lord, trusting in our own righteousness."

humeral veil Silk shawl, usually 8 by 3 feet, covering the hands worn by the high deacon at High Mass* and by a priest in processions of the sacrament* or other special occasions.

Humiliati Medieval monastic order founded in twelfth-century Italy by Johannes Oldratus (d. 1159). They followed the Benedictine Rule and cared for the poor and the sick and mortified their bodies. One type of members lived at home and were permitted to marry. By the sixteenth century, their discipline and devotion had deteriorated, and they were suppressed in 1571 after Charles Borromeo's efforts at reform led to an attempt on his life.

Humfrey, Pelham (1647–1674) English composer associated with the Chapel Royal. His religious music includes 18 anthems, 5 sacred songs, 1 complete service, and 1 chant for the Anglican service. His verse anthems, such as "By the Waters of Babylon," are considered his finest.

Hunt, William Holman (1827–1910) English religious painter noted for his biblical scenes with authentic local settings. He ushered in a new iconographic representation of Christ in his *Light of the World*. His other paintings include *The Hireling Shepherd, The Shadow of the Cross, The Triumph of the Innocents,* and *The Finding of the Savior in the Temple.*

Huntingdon, Selina Hastings (1707–1791) Countess of Huntingdon. English countess who founded the body of Calvinistic Methodists called the Countess of Huntingdon's Connexion*. After her conversion and her husband's death, she devoted her life to the promotion of Methodism* and evangelism. She retained her Anglican links and appointed Evangelical Anglicans, among them

George Whitefield*, as her chaplains*. She built 64 chapels for the Methodist cause and, in 1768, established at her own expense a college in South Wales for the training of Evangelical clergy. She also sponsored Whitefield's orphanage in Georgia, took an interest in American Indians, and helped the fledgling colleges at Dartmouth and Princeton. On the death of Whitefield*, she became the trustee of his foundations in America.

Huntingdon, William Reed (1838–1909) Protestant Episcopal bishop who helped found the Cathedral of St. John the Divine*, proposed the Lambeth Quadrilateral*, and helped to revise the Order of Deaconesses.

hupath'aqna In the Nestorian tradition, a subdeacon.

huppaoyo In the Jacobite Rite, the veil used to cover the chalice*.

Hus/Huss, Jan (1373–1415) Bohemian reformer. In 1402 he was appointed rector* and preacher of the Bethlehem Chapel in Prague and became the most outstanding champion of reform. When the theological ideas of John Wycliffe* reached the Czech people, Hus became their principal spokesman, defending them against their German critics. In this he was supported by King Wenceslaus and the University of Prague but opposed by the archbishop and the Roman Catholic hierarchy* following their German masters. Hus was then prohibited from preaching. Hus refused

Selina, Countess of Huntingdon

to obey the prohibition and was thereupon excommunicated by Cardinal de Colonna for insubordination.

The conflict worsened in 1411 when Pope John XXIII* issued his crusading bull* against King Ladislas of Naples and appointed a commission for the sale of indulgences*. Hus denounced the sale as heresy, and the citizens of Prague* followed

Jan Hus

his lead by burning a copy of the bull. During the uprising three young men were beheaded for supporting Hus. Prague was declared under interdict*, and Hus himself was forced into exile. He found refuge in Bohemia, where he worked in quiet for two years in writing a number of works, among them *De Ecclesia* (1413), and *Exposition of the Faith, of the Decalogue, and of the Lord's Prayer*.

In 1414 Hus was lured out of his refuge to attend the Council of Constance*. He was arrested and placed in a dungeon to await trial on 42 charges of heresy. Hus refused to recant and was declared an obstinate heretic, a disciple of Wycliffe*, deposed from priesthood, and turned over to the secular arm for execution. He was burned at the stake on the outskirts of Prague on July 6, 1415. The University of Prague declared him a martyr* and fixed his feast day on the day of his martyrdom.

Hussites Followers of Jan Hus who carried on Hus's struggle against the Catholic Church. By the Four Articles of Prague* (1420) Hussites laid down a program of secularization*, antiultramontanism, vernacular liturgy, and ecclesiastical reform. The Hussite War (1420–34) that followed unified the Bohemians and led to the creation of the Bohemian Brethren*.

hussoya In the Jacobite Church*, a solemn liturgical prayer of propitiation* recited during censing.

Hutchinson, Anne (c. 1591–1643) Born: Anne Marbury. New England religious leader. Her belief that salvation* is by faith* alone and that the Holy Spirit* dwells in every believer offended the Massachusetts Puritan leaders, and she was excommunicated "for traducing the ministers." She fled Massachusetts and, after helping to found Portsmouth, Rhode Island, moved to Long Island, where she and most of her family were killed by Native Americans.

hutro In the Jacobite tradition, a pastoral staff*.

Hutterites/Hutterian Brethren Originally, Bruderhof*. Sixteenth-century followers of Jacob Hutter, Anabaptist leader who was burned at the stake in 1536. They grew and prospered in Moravia during the second half of the sixteenth century. After the Catholic victory in the Battle of White Mountain in 1620, they retreated into Slovakia and Transylvania, where they remained for the next 150 years producing a rich devotional liturgy that remains the basis of their worship services. When persecution renewed under the Habsburg Maria Theresa, they were again displaced, this time to Walachia in 1767 and to Ukraine* in 1770. They flourished in Russia until the introduction of military conscription forced them to emigrate to the United States. A second wave of emigration to Canada took place in 1917. Similar to the Amish* and the Mennonites*, they practice farming, hold property in common, and oppose war. See also ANABAPTISTS.

huttomo (lit., the seal) In the Syrian Church, the final prayer recited at the close of the office.

Hyacinth, St. (1185–1257) "Apostle of the North."

Original name: Jacek. Dominican monk who evangelized Poland, and perhaps Sweden, Denmark, and Norway. Most of his missionary labors were centered in Cracow. He was canonized in 1594. Feast day: August 17.

Hybridism, Liturgical Admixture of Eastern and Western rites and customs in worship service.

hymn Song of praise or worship. It is usually metrical and strophic, conveying a Christocentric* and biblical message.

Early Christian Hymn with Musical Notes

hymn anthem Choral arrangement of a hymn text, tune, or both for use by a church choir.

hymnal Book containing hymns for liturgical and devotional use, usually in a public service.

hymnary Medieval liturgical book containing hymns arranged according to the ecclesiastical year.

hymnody 1. Art of singing hymns. 2. Study of hymns and their musical development.

hymnologist Composer of hymns. Contemporary hymnologists include Donald Hustad, William Reynolds, and Eric Routey.

hymnology Study or composition of hymns. The first work on hymnology in English was John Jehan's *Dictionary of Hymnology*, 1892.

Hymns, Ancient and Modern Famous hymnal, product of the Oxford movement*, published in 1861 and edited by H. W. Baker*. It has been revised a number of times.

hymnsing Service composed entirely of hymn singing, Scripture readings, and prayer. It is usually observed during evening worship.

hypakoe (Gk., short hymn) Hymn, normally read, not sung, that replaced the third poetic kathisma* at mattins* on Sundays and some greater feasts in the Byzantine Rite*.

Hypapante (Gk., meeting) In the Eastern Orthodox Church*, the Feast of the Candlemas* commemorating the Presentation in the Temple when the infant Jesus was presented to Simeon and Anna.

Hypatia (c. 370–415) Female neo-Platonic philosopher of Alexandria*, Egypt, noted for her intelligence and beauty. She was burned by a band of monks.

hyper-Calvinism A radical form of Calvinism* that emphasizes the sovereignty of God so completely that it leaves only limited responsibility or choice to human beings. It makes no real distinction between the secret and revealed will of God and obviates the need to evangelize*. The greatest theologian of this school was John Gill (1697–1771), author of *A Body of Doctoral Divinity* and *A Body of Practical Divinity*.

hyperdulia Special veneration* of the Virgin Mary*, on a level lower than latria*, or the worship of God, and above the level of dulia*, or the veneration of saints*.

hyphasma In the Byzantine tradition, four linen strips, each embroidered with the images of one of the four evangelists, attached to the four corners of the altar.

hypodiakonos In the Byzantine tradition, minor order of subdeacon.

hyposis In the Byzantine Rite*, liturgical elevation* of the host* or the raising and Veneration of the Cross* in the morning office.

hypostasis (pl., hypostases) Divine substance, essence, or person. In orthodox creeds, the Trinity* comprises three hypostases in one ousia*.

hypostatic union The union of the divine and human natures in the person of Jesus Christ. The doctrine was elaborated by St. Cyril* of Alexandria and incorporated in the Definition of Chalcedon*. It stated that Jesus Christ was true God and true man, consubsantial* with the Father in all things as to his divinity, yet in his humanity consubstantial with us in all things, sin excepted. He exists in two natures without confusion, without conversion, without severance, and without division, the distinction of natures being in no wise abolished by their union, but the peculiarity of each nature being maintained, and both concurring in one person (prosopon*) and hypostasis*.

hypothetical baptism Conditional baptism* administered to a person who might have been baptized before.

hyssop Shrub mentioned in the Bible. 1. Species of marjoram and a member of the mint family. It was used to sprinkle liquids in purification ceremonies. 2. A reed* of hyssop was offered for Jesus to drink on the cross. In religious art, hyssop symbolizes humility, innocence, and penitence.

Ii

I am Sayings of Jesus in the New Testament beginning with "I am," establishing his equality with God the Father, as in: "I am the Messiah" (John 4:25–26), "I am the Bread of Life" (John 6:35–36), "I am the Light of the World" (John 8:12; 9:5), "I am from above, not of this world" (John 8:23), "Truly, truly I say unto you, before Abraham was born, I am" (John 8:58), "I am the door of the sheep" (John 10:7), "I am the good shepherd" (John 10:11), "I am the Son of God" (John 10:36), "I am the Resurrection and the Life" (John 11:25), "I am the Teacher and Lord" (John 13:13), "You may believe that I am" (John 13:19), "I am the Way, the Truth and the Life" (John 14:6), "I am the True Vine" (John 15:1), "I am the Christ, the Blessed One" (Mark 14:62), "I am the Alpha and the Omega" (Rev. 1:8), "I am the First and the Last" (Rev. 1:17).

I bind unto myself today/the strong name of the Trinity Early Irish hymn known as "Breastplate of St. Patrick," normally sung in Cecil Frances Alexander's translation.

ibrusfarin In the Coptic tradition, a white or colored silk veil or corporal* used to cover the bread and wine. It is about 18 inches square with a cross embroidered in the middle.

IC, ICXC, ICXCNIKA Greek letters standing for Jesus Christ Victor, the Nomen Sacrum*, or sacred name.

ichthus (Gk., fish) Early Christian acrostic for Jesus Christ, Son of God and Savior.

icon (Gk., *eikon,* image) Flat religious paintings, usually painted in egg tempura on wood, and also bas-reliefs or mosaics in the Eastern Orthodox Church*. They usually represent Jesus Christ, the Virgin, or saints. Icons receive full veneration*, including candles, incense, and genuflexion and are associated with miracles. Some icons are very famous, such as the Christ of Edessa*, believed "not to have been made by hands," Theotokos, the acheiropoietos* in the Monastery of the Abramites at Constantinople, Trinity in the Treitiakov Gallery in Moscow*, and our Lady of Perpetual Succor at Rome*.

Iconium Town in Asia Minor visited by Paul* and Barnabas* when it was the center of a thriving Christian community.

iconoclasm (Greek: imagebreaking) Destructive assault on images in Christian churches in the eighth century in the Eastern churches* and at the time of the Reformation in the West.

iconoclastic controversy Dispute between the Eastern Orthodox Church* and the state between 717 and 843 over the presence of icons* in the church and their resulting destruction. Although early councils had banned pictures in churches, icons became widespread in lieu of statues between 400 and 600. Veneration* of the icons and the attribution of miracles to them had also grown among the more illiterate believers. In 717 Leo III*, the Isaurian, acceded to the imperial throne and issued decrees against image-worship. His decrees were rejected by popes Gregory II* and Gregory III* and also by the council of 731 and theologians such as John of Damascus*.

Despite the opposition of Rome*, Leo and his successor Constantine V continued to destroy icons, and their actions were approved by the Council of Hieria, near Chalcedon, in 753. The Seventh Ecumenical Council of Nicaea* in 787 reversed the decisions of Hieria. But Leo the Armenian, who became emperor in 813, restored the actions of Hieria through a council held at Santa Sophia in 815. Iconoclasm continued to be the imperial policy throughout the reign of Michael and Theophilus, but after the death of the latter, his widow, Theodora*, restored the use of icons and permitted the opponents of iconoclasm to return to their sees*. Iconoclasm reappeared during the Reformation* and some of the great Reformers* were iconoclasts.

iconodules Supporters of the use and veneration* of icons* and opponents of iconoclasm*.

iconography Art of making icons*, the study of icons, and the liturgical use of icons.

iconolater One who worships religious images.

iconology Study of icons*; study of the ways in which Christian symbols are transmitted through icons and their theological meanings in the Orthodox tradition.

iconostasis Screen*, with three doors, enclosing the sanctuary in an Eastern Orthodox* church. The screen is generally made of wood or stone and is covered with icons*, from which it derives its name. The central door opens to the altar, and the two side doors open to the diaconicon* on the right and to the prothesis* on the left.

Idea of a Christian Society Lecture series by T. S. Eliot* at Corpus Christi College in Oxford in 1939 advocating the application of Christian principles in a new social order.

idiomelon In the Byzantine Church*, a troparion* or sticheron* with a special melody.

idiorrhythmic Of certain monasteries in Mount Athos, organized with fewer or more liberal regulations than cenobitic houses.

idolothyte Flesh of animals sacrificed to pagan gods which Christians are generally prohibited from eating, although Paul* says that prayer sanctified such foods.

ieratikon In the Byzantine Rite*, a shorter book than the Euchologion* containing the priest's part at vespers*, mattins* and the liturgy. See also HIERATICON.

Iesous Christos Nika (Gk.) Jesus Christ Conquers, usually abbreviated IC, XC, NI, or KA.

Ignatius Loyola, St. (1491–1556) Founder of the Society of Jesus* (Jesuits*). He chose a military career as a young man, but a wound in the right leg that he received during the siege of Pamplona (1521) ended his career as a soldier. While recuperating in the Castle of Loyola, he was inspired by reading Ludolph of Saxony's *Life of Christ* to become a soldier for Christ by taking the vows and entering the monastery at Manresa. Here he spent nearly a year in ascetic practices and experiencing mystical visions and in writing his manual of spiritual warfare* known to later generations as *Spiritual Exercises**.

After a pilgrimage* to Jerusalem*, he went to Paris, where he gathered six colleagues (Francis

Ignatius Loyola

Xavier*, Peter Favre, Nicolas de Bobadilla, Diego Lainez*, Simon Rodriguez, and Alfonso Salmeron) at St. Mary's Church at Montmartre and formed a society dedicated to the service of Jesus and the pope. In 1540 Pope Paul III* officially approved the group as an order of the church. In 1548 he was chosen general* of the society for which he provided its constitution. The key ideas that he instilled in its members were obedience, discipline, and efficiency. The society was to combine evangelization with education and to this end he founded the Roman College in 1551. Canonized in 1622. Feast day: July 31.

Ignatius of Antioch (c. 35–c. 107) The second or third bishop of Antioch after St. Peter*, also called Theophoros, or God-bearer. Little is known of his life except his journey to his martyrdom from Antioch to Rome*. On his way he wrote seven letters, one to Polycarp*, and the remaining six to the churches of Rome, Magnesia, Ephesus*, Tralles, Philadelphia*, and Smyrna. These letters were held in great honor by Christians for many centuries and were included in some canons of the New Testament. They reveal a man passionately serving Christ and seeking martyrdom. He speaks with reverence on the episcopacy*, the church of Rome, and the Eucharist*. Feast day: February 1.

IHS Monogram built by using the first three uncials (capital letters) of Jesus' name in Greek. Sometimes the monogram is held to stand as the first letters of three words, Iesus Hominum Salvator (Jesus, Savior of Men) or Iesum Habemus Socium (We Have Jesus as Our Companion).

ikos In the Byzantine Rite*, a stanza inserted after the kontakion* during the canon* at orthros* or mattins*.

Illatio Also, Contestatio* or Immolatio*. In the Gallican and Spanish Missals, the Preface*.

illuminandi In the early church, those about to be baptized.

illuminated book Handwritten book with decorative work, including embellishment of initial capitals, painted pictures, and designs that frequently spilled over into margins and borders. The embellishments were often of gold and silver and gave the impression that the adorned pages had been lighted up.

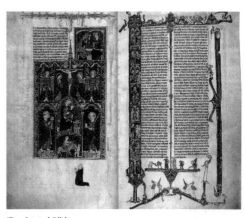

Illuminated Bible

Illuminati (Alumbrados, or the Enlightened Ones) Members of a Spanish mystical group. It was led by Pedro Ruiz de Alcarez, a member of the *dexados* movement. They emphasized freedom in God's love and submission to God's will and lived a life of prayer and meditation through which

Ignatius of Antioch

they communicated with Christ and the Virgin Mary*. The Illuminati left their imprint on the great Spanish mystics, as Ignatius Loyola*, St. John of Avila*, and St. Teresa*. Some Illuminati were later condemned by the Inquisition*.

illumination 1. Decoration of manuscripts, particularly of the Bible, with beautiful colors, designs, and illustrations. 2. Usually, illumination of the Holy Spirit*. Spiritual enlightenment or understanding communicated by or received directly through the action of the Holy Spirit.

illuminative way Intermediate stage in spiritual progress. It succeeds the purgative way and is followed by the unitive way.

Imad ud-din (c. 1830–1900) Indian convert from Islam and evangelist. Born to a family of Muslim notables and scholars, he was converted following an intense study of the Bible. He was baptized and ordained as deacon (1868) and priest (1872). His voluminous writings laid the foundations of Urdu Christian literature and he pioneered the exposition of an inculturated Evangelical faith.

image of God (Lat., imago dei) Phrase in Genesis 1:26 referring to the original condition of human beings before the Fall. For Augustine* the human soul was the direct image of the Holy Trinity* manifested in its threefold structure of memory, understanding, and will. For many of the Reformers, the image of God was lost, damaged, or destroyed as a result of the Fall. Baptism* is seen as the first step in the restoration of the image. Distinguished from likeness, or the final state of glory for all believers.

Imago Pietatis (Lat., image of piety) Devotional image of Christ showing his wounds. The usual form is a half-length figure, upright in the tomb, with eyes open or closed, and arms folded to show the wounds.

Imbomon (Gk., summit) Circular chapel on the Mount of Olives, traditional site of the ascension, built before 378.

IMC International Missionary Council*.

Imitation of Christ All-time devotional classic, attributed to Thomas à Kempis*, a follower of Gerard Groote* and a member of the Brethren of the Common Life*. The book is divided into four parts: the first two contain general counsel for the spiritual life; the third deals with the interior dispositions of the soul; and the fourth with the sacrament* of the Holy Communion*.

Imitation of Christ Ideal pattern of Christian life, especially of Christian monasticism* and mysticism. Paul* suggests that the ideal is not so much the literal imitation of the historical Jesus* but the operation of the Holy Spirit* that brings believers into conformity with the image of Christ as the suffering servant* (1 Cor. 13; 2 Cor. 13:3, 5).

immaculate conception Roman Catholic dogma* embodied in the papal bull*, *Ineffabilis Deus* (1854) which stated that "from the first moment of her conception the Virgin Mary* was, by the singular grace and privilege of Almighty God, and in view of the merits of Jesus Christ, Savior of Mankind, kept free from all stain of original sin*." According to the dogma*, Mary was redeemed at her conception by Christ in anticipation of his atoning death and bestowed with the state of original sanctity*, innocence, and justice. Despite the opposition of some of the great fathers of the Catholic Church, such as Bernard*, St. Thomas Aquinas*, St. Albert, and St. Bonaventura*, it was stoutly defended by the Franciscans, Jesuits*, Carmelites*, and Dominicans* and affirmed by the Council of Basel in 1439. The Council of Trent* explicitly excluded the Virgin Mary* from its definition of original sin. Both the Eastern Orthodox* and the Protestant churches have rejected this dogma*.

The feast of Mary's conception was observed from the seventh century. In the Roman Catholic Church, the Feast of the Immaculate Conception is observed on December 8. In the Eastern Orthodox Church*, the Feast of the Conception of the Virgin Mary* is kept on December 9.

Immaculate Heart of Mary Devotion to the heart of the Virgin Mary*. The first masses in honor of the Immaculate Heart of Mary were authorized in 1648. The festival was universalized in 1944 with a new Mass* and office on August 22.

Immanuel/Emmanuel Heavenly title of Jesus Christ announced by an angel* at his birth. It is translated roughly as "God with us."

immersion Baptism in which the adult candidate is completely submerged in water, a practice followed by most Baptists* and several Protestant sects. Thus, immersionism, belief in such a practice.

Immolatio In the Gallican and Spanish Missals, the Preface*. See also CONTESTATIO; ILLATIO.

immortality 1. Exemption from death or annihilation; everlasting life. 2. In Christian theology, the abiding union with the risen Christ completed by the reunion of body and soul after physical death. The Christian hope of immortality is based on the redemptive work of Christ.

immovable feasts Christian holidays and feast days falling on fixed days in a month, such as Christmas* on December 25 and All Saints' Day* on November 1. They are distinguished from movable feasts*, such as Easter*.

impanation (Lat., *impanere,* to embody in bread) Explanation of the Eucharist* put forth in the Middle Ages and at the Reformation*. It sought to affirm the real presence* of Christ in the elements* in hypostatic union without requiring any physical change in the natural bread and wine. It opposed the Roman Catholic doctrine of transubstantiation*.

imparted/infused righteousness In Roman Catholic doctrine, righteousness intrinsic to a person, gained through faith* and good works*.

impassibility Doctrine that God is immune from emotional feelings, such as a sense of suffering, or pain or happiness, because he cannot be moved by external or internal actions. Theologians distinguish three types of impassibility: external impassibility, internal impassibility, and sensational impassiblity. Because Jesus Christ was God and man, he is both impassible as the former and passible as the latter.

impeccability Freedom from the taint or capability of sin, a trait that applies only to Jesus Christ.

impediment In canon law*, an obstacle to marriage, such as consanguinity or clandestinity.

implicit faith 1. Faith without any reservations or without grasping all the particulars or consequences of an article of revealed truth. Trust in the authority or reliability of the church as teacher. 2. Belief in dogma* or doctrines without concern for its merits.

implicit truth 1. Truth contained within another as a corollary. 2. Truth that undergirds a doctrine even when all its particulars and consequences are not fully understood.

imposition of hands See LAYING ON OF HANDS.

imprimatur (Lat., let it be printed) Ecclesiastical approval in the Roman Catholic church of the publication of a book. It signifies that nothing in the book contradicts the teaching of the church, and it is required for all works dealing with church doctrine, church history, canon law*, morals, and ethics. It was established by the Council of Trent* which also created an index of forbidden and expurgated books.

imprimi potest (Lat., it can be printed) Permission required by a religious to publish writings dealing with faith and morals.

Improperia (Lat., reproaches) Series of chants in Roman Catholic liturgy expressing God's rebuke of human beings, sung at the Veneration of the Cross* on Good Friday*.

imputation Attribution or reckoning of guilt or righteousness on the basis of a prior, extrinsic event or person. The righteousness of Christ is imputed to the believer who is justified on that basis, just as the original sin of Adam was imputed to all later generations who were condemned on that basis. This doctrine is central to Protestant theology in contrast to Roman Catholic theology in which the believer is justified on the basis of infused or imparted righteousness*, intrinsic to a person.

imskaam In the Ethiopian Church*, the start of the church year* on September 11 or 12.

In Coena Domini (Lat., On the Lord's Supper) Series of excommunications* against specified offenders against faith and morals issued in the form of papal bulls* on Maundy Thursday* (hence the name) and also on Ascension Day* and the Feast of the Chair of St. Peter*. The practice was finally suspended in 1869.

In His Steps American novel by Charles M. Sheldon* (1857–1946), published in 1896, about a minister who tried to follow Jesus in various situations in life.

in hoc signo vinces "In this sign you will conquer." Words which, according to tradition, the Emperor Constantine* saw inscribed on the sun, just before the Battle of Milvian Bridge*. Constantine won the battle and went on to support Christianity as an officially tolerated religion in the Roman Empire.

in illo tempore (Lat., at that time) Traditional introductory formula* for the Gospel reading.

in partibus infidelium (Lat., in the countries of infidels) Former title of a Roman Catholic bishop appointed in name only over dioceses* in countries under the heel of Islam. Now designated titular* bishop.

in petto (Ital., in secret) Designation of cardinals appointed at the discretion of the pope but not named in consistory*.

in plano On the same level as the sanctuary floor.

in saecula saeculorum (Lat., unto ages of ages) Eternity*.

incardination 1. Opposite of excardination*. Reception of a priest in a new diocese*. According to canon law*, all ordinands* were bound for life in the diocese in which they had been ordained. Transfers were permitted but only for just causes. A priest who is thus transferred may, after a period of five years, seek incardination in his new diocese by notifying his original superior*. 2. Elevation of an archbishop to the rank of a cardinal.

Incarnation (Lat., *in carne,* in flesh) Doctrine that affirms Jesus Christ is the earthly manifestation

in the flesh of the divine Logos*, and that as a corollary, he is fully God and fully man, that he was born at a specific time and place in history, and that he died and was resurrected at a specific time and place in history. The theological controversies of the early church were concerned with the nature of the Incarnation. The Council of Chalcedon* settled in 451 that the Lord Jesus Christ is "truly God and truly man, consusbtantial with the Father in all things, as to his divinity, yet in His humanity like unto us in all things, sin excepted." He is thus known "in two natures, without confusion, without conversion, without severance and without division, the distinction of natures being in no wise abolished by their union, but the peculiarities of each nature being maintained, and both concurring in one person and subsistence." This mystery of the Incarnation* is known as the hypostatic union*.

incarnational In ministry of servanthood, descending to the level of the group being ministered to, adopting their lifestyles, struggles, and aspirations and totally identifying with them.

incarnational theology Branch of theology that emphasizes the mystical body* of Christ built up by Christian involvement in all phases of human activity. It was particularly active during the years from 1935 to 1955 when its major exponents included M. I. Montuclard, Y. Congar*, H. de Lubac, and G. Thils.

incarnatus Latin designation of the words of the Nicene Creed* which affirm the Incarnation* ("was made flesh by the Holy Spirit"*).

inclination Bowing or kneeling during a worship service.

inclusive language Use of language, particularly in Bible translations, that is considered to be bias-free in usage and style. It may involve the use of pronouns referring to God that are not gender-specific. It may also necessitate text changes in traditional choral literature, as from "He is the King of glory" to "God is the ruler in glory."

incubation Practice of sleeping in churches or chapels or their precincts in the hope of receiving healing or other benefits and receiving visions and revelations. The practice was borrowed from paganism.

inculturation Process of adapting the liturgy, language, rituals, and symbols of the church to the cultural norms of the local people. Through inculturation, the church tries to reformulate Christian doctrine and practice so that they reflect established cultural patterns and do not offend local sensibilities.

incumbent In the Church of England* and Episcopal Church of Scotland, a rector*, vicar*, or curate-in-charge.

indefectibility Incorruptibility or freedom from failure or sin, as a characteristic of Christ and his church.

independency State of a local congregation in which it is answerable only to Christ and is free from all external controls. Applied to the Congregational* churches in the seventeenth and eighteenth centuries.

Independent Fundamental Churches of America Organization founded in 1930 to "unify those that have separated from denominations which include unbelievers and liberal teachers and to encourage one another in world evangelism." Its 16-point doctrinal statement lists the cardinal tenets of Fundamentalism*, such as verbal and plenary inspiration* of the Bible, virgin birth*, deity of Christ, bodily resurrection, and Christ's premillennial and pretribulational return. They oppose ecumenism*, ecumenical evangelism, neo-Orthodoxy*, and neo-Evangelicalism*.

Index Expurgatorius List of books that may be read by Roman Catholics after the deletion of certain objectionable passages and after being amended to meet certain standards of faith and morals.

Index Librorum Prohibitorum List of books that Roman Catholics are prohibited from reading except with special permission. The index was established in the sixteenth century as part of the Inquisition*. The first general index was issued in 1559 and the second in 1564 after the Council of Trent*. In 1571 Pope Pius V* established a special Congregation of the Index to be in charge of the list and to revise it as needed. This Congregation survived until 1917 when its duties were transferred to the Holy Office*. Further revisions were issued in 1590, 1596, 1664, 1751, 1897, 1900, and 1948. At the Second Vatican Council* of 1966, it was decided that no further indexes would be issued.

indigenization See INCULTURATION.

Indre Mission Popular name for the Kirkelig Forening for Indre Mission i Danmark (the Danish Church Home Mission Society), an Evangelical movement within the Danish national church founded in 1861 by Pietistic clergymen. It spearheaded a national revival movement toward the end of the nineteenth and the beginning of the twentieth centuries. Thousands of colporteurs* and lay preachers joined the movement, which retained its vigor until the end of World War II.

induction Ceremony giving actual possession of an ecclesiastical living to a clergyman; formal inauguration after a pastoral charge.

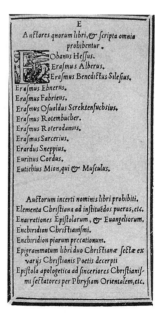

Index of Forbidden Books

indulgence (Lat., *indulgentia,* kindness) In the Roman Catholic Church, pardon* for temporal punishment still due to sin after the guilt has been forgiven. The commutation of penance* and the grant of absolution* are based on the principle of vicarious* satisfaction by which the sinner draws on the spiritual treasury formed by the surplus merits of Jesus Christ, the Virgin Mary*, and the saints* to replenish his or her own bankrupt account. The authority for granting indulgences is vested in the pope,* who may delegate this power to others.

Most indulgences granted by the pope are for souls in purgatory*. Indulgences may be plenary, involving full remission, or partial, involving remission of part of the punishment. Apostolic indulgences are generally attached to religious articles, such as crucifixes, statues, medals, and rosaries, the performance of certain works of merit* on feast days, or the recitation of certain holy names or prayers. By the eleventh century, the grant of indulgences came to be based less on penitential acts than on contributions made to a church or monastery. With the advent of the Crusades*, the grant of indulgences was tied to financial support for the crusaders. For the next few centuries, the practice was used as a milch cow for the church, and there were considerable abuses, especially by pardoners* who sold indulgences. It was one of the principal abuses cited against the Roman Catholic Church by the Reformers* in the sixteenth century.

The Second Vatican Council* redefined indulgences in *Indulgentiarum Doctrina,* reduced the number of plenary indulgences, and did away with the former distinction between personal, real, and local indulgences. The purpose of indulgences under the new definition is to induce a total conversion of the heart from all sin through fervent contrition* and charity.

indult Special permission from a papal office to depart from ecclesiastical law*.

Industrial Christian Fellowship Anglican missionary organization working among industrial workers, formed in 1918.

indwelling Belief that the Holy Spirit* inhabits his people and has his abode in their spirit. The term was first used by John Wycliffe* in his English translation of the Bible.

inerrancy (Lat., *inerrans,* not wandering, fixed) Attribute of the Bible that, when correctly interpreted, it is completely truthful and accurate in all and every respect and that its original autographs are free from error.

inerrancy, harmonistic Internal integrity of the Bible that enables reconciliation of apparent discrepancies and resolution of apparent contradictions or inaccuracies.

inerrancy, limited Belief that the Bible is free of error only in its theological content, and not in its historical or scientific statements.

inerrancy of purpose Belief that the purposes of God are free of error and override any narrative or linguistic contradictions in the Bible.

infallibilist Person who holds or defends the infallibility of the pope or of the Bible.

infallibility Freedom from the liability to err or mislead.

infallibility of the Bible Traditional Protestant doctrine based on 2 Timothy 3:16 that the whole Bible is the inspired Word of God* and is free from error in matters of faith and doctrine.

infallibility of the church Traditional Roman Catholic doctrine that the church is the custodian and guardian of the apostolic faith and the possessor of magisterium*, or the right of proclaiming and teaching the gospel. Since the Holy Spirit* indwells the church, it follows that he will empower the shepherds of the flock* to understand and teach aright the divine message of salvation*. In the Eastern Orthodox Church*, the doctrine is limited to the ecumenical councils. In the Roman Catholic Church, the doctrine is tied in with the infallibility of the pope.

infallibility of the pope Dogma* defined by the First Vatican Council* of 1870 as follows: "The Roman Pontiff, when he speaks ex cathedra—i.e., when, in his character as pastor and doctor of all Christians, and in virtue of his supreme apostolic authority, he lays down that a certain doctrine concerning faith and morals is binding upon the universal church—possesses by the divine assistance which was promised to him in the person of the blessed St. Peter, the same infallibility with which the Divine Redeemer thought to endow His church, to define its doctrine with regard to faith and morals." The scriptural basis of this doctrine is found in Matthew 16:18, Luke 22:31, and John 21:15. The infallibility is declared to be "as wide as the divine deposit of faith, which is to be kept as a sacred trust and faithfully expounded." Vatican Council II* reaffirmed this doctrine.

infancy gospels Apocryphal stories about the birth and childhood of Christ prevalent in the early centuries. The two most important are the Book of James (the Protevangelium) and the Gospel of Thomas*.

infant baptism Also, paedobaptism*. Christian baptism* of babies or young children, ordinarily administered by sprinkling of water. It probably began to be practiced only from the second century, with the aid of an adult sponsor*, but it was the exception rather than the rule. It became obligatory about the fifth century, particularly after St. Augustine* provided a theological basis for the practice in his concept of original sin*. According to Augustine, each child is not only born with an inherited tendency to sin, but also shares in the guilt of Adam's sin. As a corollary, it was believed that children who died unbaptized were damned.

After the sixth century, baptism became a rite of passage universally practiced. In the Eastern Orthodox Church*, infant baptism is followed at once by the administration of chrism* and also of the Holy Communion*, while confirmation* and Holy Communion are deferred until later in the Western Church*. After the Reformation*, some Protestant sects, such as the Anabaptists* and Baptists*, rejected infant baptism on the ground that it has no mandate in the New Testament and that it brings no benefit to an unconscious recipient. In Protestant denominations that retain the rite, such as Methodist* and Congregational* churches, many consider it only as a dedication and as a precursor of a full profession of faith* which happens at confirmation*.

infant communion Communion administered to infants in some traditions if death is imminent, but in others routinely. It was part of infant baptism* in the early church.

infant salvation Belief in most Protestant bodies that a child is assured of salvation* if he or she dies before reaching the age of moral accountability. John Calvin* taught the salvation of the children of the elect*. Catholic doctrine excludes unbaptized infants from heaven*, consigning them to *limbus infantium,* the limbo of the infants*.

infidel Person outside the Christian faith; unbeliever.

infirmarian Monk in charge of the sick in a monastery or religious house.

infralapsarianism Also, sublapsarianism*. Doctrine that God, in his decree of predestination*, knew, even before he created man, that man would fall, and when that happened, elected some persons to salvation* in Christ, leaving the rest in enmity to him. Logically, the Fall preceded the decrees of election* of the few and the damnation of the many. See SUPRALAPSARIANISM.

infused knowledge In medieval theology, direct knowledge given to a human being by God. This knowledge may include ideas, concepts, words, feelings, or intuitions that are outside empirical experience or intellectual deduction from sense data.

infusion Baptism by pouring water on the head. Distinguished from immersion* and submersion*. See also AFFUSION.

Inge, William Ralph (1860–1954) The "Gloomy Dean" of St. Paul's Cathedral*, London, from 1911 to 1934. Theologically he was a liberal, but he held strongly to the historical traditions. He was a student of mysticism and wrote *Christian Mysticism* (1899).

ingeneracy In Trinitarian* theology, the quality of God the Father of being ungenerated while the Son is eternally generated and the Holy Spirit* eternally proceeds from the Father and the Son.

initial evidence Speaking in tongues* as the confirmation* and physical evidence of a baptism of the Holy Spirit*.

initial sanctification In Wesleyan theology, first stage of sanctification involving cleansing from acquired depravity, whereas entire sanctification*, the second stage, involves cleansing from inherited depravity.

Initiari Group in the early church which maintained that the second person in the Trinity* is coeternal with the Father and is the Son only in a metaphorical sense.

inner-city church Church in ghettoes and slums and other undesirable parts of a city, often pastored by dedicated evangelists with a special call* to serve the poor.

Inner Light Among the Quakers*, direct guidance and mystical illumination* within a believer.

inner man Soul or spirit.

Innere Mission (Ger., Inner mission) Evangelical mission proclaimed in Germany by J. H. Wichern* in 1848, to show the love of Christ serving practical human needs as the realization of the kingdom of God* on earth. It combined preaching, personal evangelism, and Bible distribution, promoted prison reform, and helped to build hospitals and insane asylums. It expanded later into Scandinavia.

Innocent I, St. (d. 417) Pope from 402. He made more substantial claims for the teaching authority of the Holy See* than any of his predecessors. Feast day: July 28 (dropped in 1969).

Innocent III (1160/61–1216) Pope from 1198. Birth name: Lotario de'Conto de Segni. Rising rapidly in papal service, he was made cardinal while not yet a priest. His pontificate* marked the climax of the medieval papacy. He became one of the most powerful popes in history. His principal concerns were with the first two Crusades*, reform of the clergy and Curia*, and combating of the Albigen-

sian heresy in France. The culminating event of his reign was the Fourth Lateran Council* of 1215.

Pope Innocent III

Innocent IV (d. 1254) Pope from 1243. Birth name: Sinibaldo de' Fieschi. He was an outstanding canon lawyer and the author of a commentary on the decretals*, known as the Apparatus. During the Mongol invasions, he sent friars as emissaries to the Mongol khans.

Innocent X (1574–1655) Pope from 1644. Birth name: Giambattista Pamfili. He opposed the use of Chinese Rites and condemned Jansenism*.

Innocent XI, Blessed (1611–1689) Pope from 1676. Birth name: Benedetto Odescalchi. His piety and zeal led him to introduce many reforms within the church, and he encouraged daily communion. Because of his Jansenist sympathies, his beatification* was long delayed, but he was finally beatified in 1956. Feast day: August 12.

Innocent XII (1615–1700) Pope from 1691. Birth name: Antonio Pignatelli. He was known for his charity and beneficence.

Innocent XIII (1655–1724) Pope from 1721. Birth name: Michelangelo dei Conti. He denounced the Chinese Rites and Jansenism*.

Innocent, Veniaminov (Ivan Popov) (1797–1879) Russian Orthodox apostle to America. In 1828 he arrived on Unalaska with pastoral responsibility for the entire peninsula and the Pribilof Islands. He became a master in the Fox Aleutian dialect to communicate with the natives. For ten years he rowed kayaks and hiked through the mountains to minister to his flock. He also wrote a short devotional pamphlet, *An Indication of the Pathway into the Kingdom of Heaven*. After returning to Moscow*, he was made bishop in 1840 of a new diocese* stretching from California to Yakutsk. In order to prepare an indigenous clergy, he established a seminary in Sitka. In 1868, blind and worn out, he sought retirement, but was made metropolitan* of Moscow, in which capacity he founded the Russian Missionary Society. In 1977 he was honored by the Orthodox Church as the apostle to America and evangelizer of Aleuts.

Innocents, Feast of the Feast in the early church commemorating the male children under two years old slaughtered by Herod at the time of the Nativity. See also HOLY INNOCENTS.

Inquisition Roman Catholic tribunal for the investigation, prosecution, and punishment of unrepentent heretics. In the Scriptures, the only punishment for heresy was excommunication*, and the early fathers disapproved of physical penalties. According to St. John Chrysostom*, putting a heretic to death was in itself "an inexpiable crime." After Christianity became the state religion, the Catholic Church found it possible to use the power of civil authorities to suppress heresies and to discourage their spread. By 1184, under Pope Lucius III, it became the official policy of the Catholic Church to keep a watch on heretics and to hand over to civil authorities those who refused to recant.

In about 1233 Pope Gregory IX* appointed full-time papal inquisitors drawn mainly from the Dominican and Franciscan orders. Inquisitors were appointed only in areas where heresy was rife and civil rulers were willing to assist them. They were never established in the British Isles or Scandinavia. The inquisitors examined suspects *in camera,* in the presence of sworn witnesses. Those accused were not told of the charges against them or allowed to call witnesses in their defense, and lawyers were unwilling to defend them for fear of the church. In 1252 Pope Innocent IV* authorized the use of torture against the more recalcitrant heretics. The accused had the right to appeal to the pope. Heretics who recanted were given penances, such as fasting*, pilgrimage*, or the wearing of special

crosses on their clothes, and these penances were legally enforceable. Serious offenders were placed in prison for indefinite periods of time. Only the most obdurate offenders were handed over to the civil authorities to be burned at the stake.

In 1542 the Inquisition was reorganized and assigned to the Holy Office*. After the fifteenth century the Roman Inquisition was used to prevent Protestantism* from obtaining a foothold in Italy. It was instrumental in the burning of Giordano Bruno* in 1600, but elsewhere Inquisition had become moribund by the seventeenth century. However, Inquisition took on a new life in the Spanish Peninsula where Ferdinand V and Isabella obtained permission from Pope Sixtus IV* in 1477 to set up a new Inquisition backed by royal authority in the territories under their crown. With the appointment of Tomas de Torquemeda* as inquisitor general in 1483, it became a powerful and feared institution, particularly because it was more a royal than a papal agency.

The Spanish Inquisition was concerned primarily with suppressing the Moriscos* (nominally converted Muslims) the Alumbrados, and Protestants, but over the years it expanded its jurisdiction to cover homosexuals, freemasons, witches, blasphemers, bigamists, married priests, mystics, Jansenists, humanists, philosophers, and writers of anti-Catholic books. Although marked by considerable severity in its early years, it was more benign and just than secular courts of the period. But it acquired its unfavorable reputation because of its efficiency and thoroughness and because it spread terror through the public spectacle of the auto-de-fe. The percentage of those who suffered capital punishment dropped from 40 percent in the early years to 1 percent in the sixteenth century. The tribunal was abolished by Joseph Bonaparte in 1808, restored by Ferdinand VII in 1814, abolished again from 1820–1823, restored in 1823, and finally abolished in 1834.

In 1515 the pope turned down the request of Manuel I to set up an Inquisition in Portugal, but despite papal resistance it was set up in 1536 under John III. In 1561 it was extended to Goa. The Portuguese Inquisition was never fully under royal control and there was considerable tension between it and the crown after 1640. It was abolished under the Marquis of Pombal in 1821.

INRI Initials of the Latin words over the cross on which Christ was crucified: *Iesus Nazarenus Rex Iudaeorum* (Jesus of Nazareth, King of the Jews).

inscripturation Fact or process of preserving God's revelation* in the form of the Holy Scriptures.

inspectorate In French Lutheran churches, ecclesiastical territorial unit equivalent to a deanery* or presbytery*.

inspiration Process and result of the special work of the Holy Spirit by which the writers of the Scriptures were enabled faithfully to record the revelation* of God. Inspiration is *verbal* in that it issues in text expressed solely in words; it is *plenary* because it extends to the production of the whole of Scripture, not merely parts of it; and it is *inerrant* in that it is totally free from error and totally true in all that it affirms. Inspiration may take many forms: mechanistic or dictational, personal or verbal, natural, ecstatic or organic, partial or plenary, static or dynamic, direct or interpretative.

installation Placement of a clergyman or other ecclesiastical official in office.

institute, religious Also, religious order. Roman Catholic society, some of whose members consecrate themselves to a life of meditation and prayer and lead a common life. The others take simple vows and are known as congregations. They are distinguished from members of secular institutes who bind themselves to follow Evangelical counsels and dedicate themselves to a sanctified life. They live regular lives and may be single or married.

institutes of consecrated life Ecclesiastical societies in which members profess Evangelical counsels of perfection* and bind themselves to be dedicated to the sanctification* of the world while living in it.

Institutes of the Christian Religion/The Institutes Book written by John Calvin*, first published in 1536, expounding his theology in systematic form. The original edition had only six chapters covering the Decalogue, the Apostles' Creed*, the Lord's

Prayer*, the sacraments*, and church government. It was revised and expanded to 17 chapters in 1539 and to 80 chapters in 1559. The first edition was modeled on Luther's *Kleiner Katechismus;* the structure of the final edition may reflect Lombard's* *Sententiarum Libri Quatuor* but drew inspiration also from Melanchthon*. The book presents Calvin's teachings on God as Creator, God as Redeemer, grace*, and the ministry and sacraments of the church. It remains the most important theological text of the Reformation*, comparable in its influence on Protestantism* to the influence of Aquinas's *Summa* on Roman Catholicism*.

institution Admission of a new incumbent* into the spiritual care of a parish*. Distinguished in some churches from induction*, which refers to the admission to the temporal duties of the office where these exist in state churches.

institution, words of The words of Christ instituting the Eucharist* (Matt. 26:26–28; Mark 14:22–24; Luke 22:19–20; 1 Cor. 11:23–25). It is part of the central prayer of the liturgy in all its forms.

institutional church Term coined by William J. Tucker, president of Dartmouth College, Hanover, New Hampshire, for a church with a well-developed social program, including gymnasiums, libraries, medical centers, youth centers, and welfare services in addition to worship services. Also used more generally of a church's property-owning aspect.

Instituts Catholiques The five free Catholic institutions for higher studies at Paris, Angers, Lille, Lyons, and Toulouse founded as Christian counterparts to the secular state universities and authorized by a law of 1875. The Institut Catholique at Paris was the hotbed of the modernist movement in the late nineteenth century.

instructed Eucharist Holy Communion* service at which the priest explains the service as it progresses.

instrumental ministry Melodic reinforcement of singing and the use of musical instruments to enhance worship.

Instruments, Tradition of the Ceremony, now part of the Latin Rites* of Ordination, accompanied by a charge to those being ordained of their mission and ministry. The ordinands* originally belonged to the minor orders* but now include deacons and priests. The central act of the ceremony is the laying on of hands*, after which the deacons receive a copy of the Gospels and the priests a paten* with the bread and the chalice*. A similar rite is used in parts of the Anglican* Church.

insufflation Breathing upon a person or thing as a symbolic gesture of the incoming inspiration of the Holy Spirit*. Its biblical basis is John 20:22. It is also used in baptisms, both adult and infant.

Integralism Ultraconservative movement in France in the nineteenth and early twentieth centuries that opposed ecumenism* and modern biblical studies and theology. It was condemned by Benedict XV* in 1914.

intention 1. In Catholic sacramental theology*, purpose of administering the sacraments*, as distinguished from their form and method. Such intention may be exterior or interior. Exterior intention exists when a minister performs the customary rites without intending to administer sacraments. Interior intention exists when the minister performs the customary rites with the full intention of administering the sacraments. The requirement of intention was laid down by the Council of Trent*. 2. Special object, whether spiritual or material, for which a prayer of intercession is made. Thus, in a Mass* of intention the celebrant prays that the benefits of the sacrifice may accrue to a special person or cause. 3. Act of free will* directed to the attainment of an end. Such an intention may be actual, if it is conscious; virtual, if not conscious; habitual; or interpretative. The morality of an action is influenced by its intention.

intercession Petitionary prayer or supplication on behalf of one other than the person interceding. In Protestant theology, intercession is only by the living, while in Catholic theology, such intercession may be by the living or by dead saints, including the Virgin Mary*, saints* designated by the church, and angels*.

intercommunion Participation in Holy Communion* or the Eucharist* by members of different denominations, especially among denominations which recognize the validity* of one another's sacraments*.

Interdenominational Foreign Missions Association (IFMA) American organization founded in 1917 which is comprised of faith missions*, that is, groups that rely solely on God through faith* and prayer for the provision of their needs and are not formally affiliated with any denomination. Also, interconfessional.

interdict Ecclesiastical exclusion from the sacraments*, Christian burial, and other benefits of the church. The interdict may be directed against a person, a group, or a region, such as a parish*, diocese*, province, state, or nation. The purpose of the interdict is to bring about desired cessation of an act or condition and to induce atonement for an offense. It resembles excommunication* but is less severe in its consequences.

interfaith 1. Of or relating to a worship service or event in which different religions participate as equals. 2. Occurring between or among peoples or organizations belonging to different religions.

interim Edict temporarily settling ecclesiastical disputes, generally through compromises* on all sides. The three major Reformation* interims were the Interim of Regensburg (1541), Interim of Augsburg* (1548), and the Leipzig Interim* (1549).

interim ethic Term developed by Albert Schweitzer* and Johannes Weiss* to describe the eschatalogical thrust of Jesus' teaching. According to them, Jesus was preparing his followers for an immediate establishment of the kingdom of God*.

Interim Rite Order of Holy Communion* in the Church of England* proposed in 1931 by Bishop Chandler of Bloemfontein where the prayer of oblation* is placed immediately after the consecration and is followed by the Lord's Prayer*.

internal call Effectual call* of the Holy Spirit* directed to the elect*. Distinct from an external call which is addressed to all those who hear the gospel.

International Bible Reading Association Movement to encourage personal Bible study founded in 1882 by the National Sunday School Union under the guidance of Charles Waters, a member of the congregation of Charles Spurgeon at the Metropolitan Tabernacle in London. The movement has spread to a number of countries, including Australia, New Zealand, Canada, United States, France, Germany, Sweden, India, and Nigeria.

International Bible Society Scripture distribution society originally founded in 1809 as the New York Bible Society*. It changed its name to International Bible Society following the publication of the International Version of the Bible under its auspices. Working worldwide from its Colorado Springs, Colorado, headquarters, the society has distributed 150 million Bibles, New Testaments, and Scripture portions. In association with Wycliffe Bible Translators*, it has published Scriptures in over 350 tribal languages.

International Conference of Christians and Jews Interfaith* organization seeking to promote better understanding between Christians and Jews and to remove mutual prejudices and biases.

International Council of Biblical Inerrancy Organization founded in the 1970s to defend the doctrine of biblical inerrancy*. In 1978 it drew up the Chicago Statement on Biblical Inerrancy.

International Eucharistic Conference Biennial gathering to honor Christ in the Eucharist*, started in France in 1881.

International Fellowship of Evangelical Students (IFES) The IFES was founded in 1947 as Christian college students from 10 countries gathered with the professed aim of starting (when necessary) and sustaining (when feasible) student witness in every university worldwide. Today, campuses in over 140 countries are being touched by this equipping ministry, spiritually and financially supported by volunteers.

International Missionary Council Outgrowth of the World Missionary Conference* in Edinburgh* in 1910, founded at Lake Mohonk, New York, in 1921. Its membership was comprised of national Protestant mission councils, and it was a consultative and advisory body, not an administrative body. Its official organ is the *International Review of Missions,* started in 1912. In 1961 it was merged with the World Council of Churches*, becoming its Commission/Division of World Mission and Evangelism.

International Pentecostal Holiness Church Oldest Pentecostal denomination in the United States. With its roots in the nineteenth-century Holiness movement*, it was formed before the advent of the Pentecostal movement, but it was influenced by the Azusa Street Revival*. It was one of the first organized denominations to adopt the Pentecostal statement of faith. The Holiness component of the church is drawn from the National Holiness Association, founded in Vineland, New Jersey, in 1867; the Iowa Holiness Association, founded in 1879; and the North Carolina Holiness Association, founded in 1896. The present church represents the merger of three groups: the Fire-Baptized Holiness Church*, the Holiness Church of North Carolina, and the Tabernacle Pentecostal Church.

The oldest of the three groups, the Fire-Baptized Holiness Church, was founded by Benjamin Hardin Irwin in 1895. It believes in a "third blessing" called "baptism of fire"* that follows the baptism of the Holy Spirit*. The Holiness Church of North Carolina was founded by Ambrose Blackman Crumpler in 1900. The Tabernacle Pentecostal Church was founded in 1898 by Nickles John Holmes.

internuncio Papal diplomat serving between terms of nuncios, or serving in a less important country.

interpretation of tongues Charismatic gift by which one is enabled to make clear to the congregation the significance and meaning of an utterance in tongues*. (1 Cor. 12:10, 30; 14:26).

interregnum In Episcopal churches, the interval between two incumbencies, or between the departure of one vicar* or rector* and the arrival of the other, when the office is vacant.

interstice In canon law*, the period that must elapse between ordination from one rank to the next. In the Roman Catholic Church and in many Eastern Orthodox* churches, there has to be an interval of at least six months between the time when a person is made a deacon and the time he is made a priest. No one is to be made a deacon until he has received and exercised for a suitable period of time the ministries of acolyte* and lector*. Similar intervals are prescribed for higher orders.

Inter-Varsity Fellowship Movement founded in 1927 to foster cooperation between Evangelical Christian unions in the universities and colleges of Great Britain. Its aim is to "present the claims of the Lord Jesus Christ to the members of the university; to unite those who desire to serve him; and to promote the work of Home and Foreign Missions." It changed its name to Universities and Colleges Christian Fellowship to reflect the diversity of its constituency. The fellowship has affiliates in many countries, notably the United States. In the United States, its publishing arm is known as the InterVarsity Press (IVP). It also holds a student missions conference in Urbana, Illinois, every three years.

intinctio panis Dipping the bread in the wine during the Communion service*.

intinction Administration of the sacrament* of Holy Communion* by dipping the consecrated bread into the wine and giving both together to the communicant. In the communion of the sick, it was done to make consumption easier. The bread may be immersed in the chalice* and administered with a communion spoon, as in the Eastern Orthodox Church*.

intra-uterine baptism Baptism of a fetus with water in a syringe in a situation where there is concern that the child may not survive birth.

introit Praise sung at the beginning of worship, normally by a choir, sometimes as a processional. In the Roman Catholic Church it refers to the opening act of worship in the Mass*. It is said or sung as the celebrant approaches the sanctuary. If it is said, the antiphon* is recited and if sung, a psalm and the Gloria Patri* are required. The singing stops when the celebrant reaches the altar. Introit is not an essential part of the service, unlike a gradual*. Also known as Antiphona ad Praelegendum in the Gallican Rite*; Ingressa in the Ambrosian Rite*; and Officium in the Mozarabic Rite*.

Invariata Version (1580) of the Augsburg Confession* based on the original presented to the Diet in 1530. Although it differs in over 450 places from the original, it remains the standard of faith in Lutheran churches. Melanchthon's revised version, the *Variata** (1540), is accepted by only certain Reformed* churches.

Philip Melanchthon

invention of the cross Legend of the discovery in 326 of the three crosses on Calvary by St. Helena*, mother of Constantine*. According to legend, the cross on which Christ was crucified was discovered miraculously. The account of the invention of the cross is found in St. Ambrose*, St. John Chrysostom*, and Paulinus of Nola*. In the Greek Orthodox Church, the Feast of the Exaltation of the Cross* is observed on September 14, formerly the day for the invention. Until 1961 the Roman Catholic Church observed the invention on May 3.

investiture Ceremony of installation* into ecclesiastical office together with the symbols and vestments of office.

investiture controversy Medieval dispute between rulers of Germany, France, and England and the pope over the right to appoint bishops, abbots, and other clerics and to invest them with the symbols of their office, as the ring and the crosier*. The controversy extended from 1076 when the Emperor Henry IV disputed with Gregory VII* at Worms* to the Concordat of Worms in 1122. And it covered also papal disputes with Anglo-Norman and French kings. The pope won a complete victory in this dispute, but the lay rulers retained a varying degree of control over the elections.

Invincible Doctor Epithet of William of Ockam.

invincible ignorance Spiritual ignorance so all-embracing that no counsel can penetrate it and of which the person is not conscious. Because it is involuntary, there is no intentional breaking of the law and no consequent culpability. It is generally used in reference to persons who are unable to understand the teachings of the church because of problems in their upbringing or environment. Distinguished from vincible ignorance* where there is culpability because of partial knowledge.

invisible church Universal church comprised of living and dead believers as well as those who are not official members of any denomination but whose names are known to God.

invitation 1. Call to prayer, confession*, or worship in a service. 2. Summons to sinners to accept Christ as their Lord and Savior or for saints* to receive his blessings.

invitatory/invitation hymn Choral invitation to prayer in public worship, generally by singing Psalms 23, 66, 95, or 99. Bidding prayers are a form of invitatory*.

Invocabit First Sunday in Lent*, from the first word of the introit* for that day.

invocation 1. Prayer at the beginning of a meeting invoking the blessings of God. 2. Trinitarian formula* used to begin a worship service. 3. Summoning the Holy Spirit* for consecration of the elements of the Mass*. 4. Calling on the intercession of the saints*.

Iona Small island of the Inner Hebrides off the western coast of Scotland where Columba* established a monastery in the sixth century and Reginald founded a Benedictine* nunnery in the thirteenth century. After the Reformation*, it fell into ruins until 1899 whens the Duke of Argyll founded a trust to have it rebuilt for general Christian use.

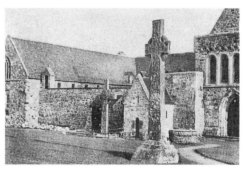

Iona Cathedral

Iona Community Religious brotherhood* founded in 1938 by George MacLeod on the Island of Iona on the site of the ancient monastery and nunnery. Its members include craftsmen who worked to rebuild the Benedictine abbey. In 1951 the community was recognized by the Church of Scotland*.

Iota Chi (IX) Greek letters symbolizing Jesus Christ, *IHSOUS XPISTOS*.

ipsissima verba (Lat.) "The very words" (of Jesus or of the Bible).

Irenaeus, St. (c. 130–c. 200) Church Father, martyr and bishop of Lyons in Gaul. He was probably a native of Smyrna in Asia Minor and a pupil of Polycarp*. He formed a link between the Eastern and Western churches*, and he was the first great Catholic theologian. He systematized theology in his two works, *Against Heresies* and *The Demonstration of Apostolic Preaching. Against Heresies* was an attack on Gnosticism* which was becoming a serious threat to the nascent church. He developed a theory of recapitulation*, or summary, of the human evolution of the Incarnate Christ, according to which Jesus' life "recapitulated" the career of Adam, reversing by his perfect obedience the curse Adam had brought on mankind. He stated that "Christ made the circuit of all the stages of human life, to redeem and sanctify all." Feast day: June 28 (Western Church*); August 23 (Eastern Church*).

Irene of Chrysobalanton (d. 991) Byzantine seer. Although chosen as the bride of Emperor Michael III, she preferred the ascetic life and fled to the Chrysobalanton convent in Constantinople*, where she became an abbess. She gained fame as a seer and as a miracle worker who levitated in prayer.

irenics Branch of theology dealing with Christian unity by highlighting points of agreement among the various sects and denominations and minimizing their differences.

iris Flower symbolizing the Virgin Mary* in religious art.

Irish Articles Articles of religion, 104 in number, largely prepared by James Ussher, approved by a convocation of the Episcopal Church of Ireland*, and ratified by the lord deputy in 1615. They were replaced 20 years later by the Thirty-Nine Articles*. Although in general agreement with the Lambeth Articles* of 1595 and the Twelve Articles of 1566, they had a strong Calvinistic and Puritan flavor. They had considerable influence on the Westminster Confession*. See also ARTICLES, IRISH.

irmologion See HEIRMOLOGION.

irmos (lit., chain) In the Byzantine Rite*, the opening stanza in each of the canticles* of the canon* that is linked to the theme of the feast or celebration.

Ironside, Henry Allen ("Harry") (1876–1951) Canadian Bible teacher and author. Although never ordained, he started preaching at 14. He joined the Plymouth Brethren* in 1896 and for the next 50 years traveled widely as a missionary and evangelist. He wrote over 60 books, the best known of which are *In the Heavenlies* (1939), *Lamp of Prophecy* (1939), and *The Great Parenthesis* (1943).

irresistible grace See GRACE, IRRESISTIBLE.

Irving, Edward (1792–1834) Scottish founder of the Catholic Apostolic Church*. A friend of Thomas Carlyle, Henry Drummond*, and Samuel Coleridge, he served as pastor in Glasgow and London. He became involved in glossolalia*, healing, and prophecy* and was deposed by the Church of Scotland* for Christological heresy. Hundreds of his followers, known as Irvingites, left with him to found the Catholic Apostolic Church. His writings include *For the Oracles of God* (1823) and *The Doctrine of the Incarnation Opened* (1828).

Isaac, Heinrich (c. 1450–1517) Dutch musical composer. He created a cycle of polyphonic compositions for the proper of the Mass* for the whole church year, known as the *Choralis Constantinus,* so named because it was commissioned by the diocese* of Constance. Among his Masses is the *Missa Carminum* based on secular songs of which "Innsbruck" was included by Bach* in his *St. Matthew Passion.*

Isaac of Nineveh (d. c. 700) Also, Isaac the Syrian. Monk and writer. Originally from present-day Qatar, he became a monk about 676 in the monastery of Beth Abe in present-day Kurdistan and was made bishop of Nineveh, but shortly afterwards he retired to the Monastery of Rabban Shabur. His writings were translated into Greek, Arabic, Georgian, and Ethiopic. His *Homilies* have influenced Egyptian and Greek monasticism*. Feast day: January 28.

Isaac of Stella (c. 1100–1178) Cistercian monk of English origin. By 1147 he was abbot of Stella, south of Poitiers, France, but he left Stella in 1167 to found the monastery of Notre Dame* des Chateliers on the Ile de Re. Fifty five of his sermons and two of his treatises survive. Borrowing from the Platonic tradition, he described how the soul ascends toward God through love and attains union with the Godhead in an act of intuitive knowledge.

Isaac the Great, St. (c. 350–438) Armenian catholicos*, son of Catholicos Nerses*. He became a monk after the death of his wife and in 390 became the tenth catholicos. He secured the independence of the Armenian Church* from the See of Caesarea in Cappadocia*. He was also active in the creation of Armenian literature and in the translation of the Bible. He also was the author of many hymns. Feast days (St. Sahak*): September 9 and November 25.

Isakovich, Nikolai Feodorovich (Nil) (1798–1874) Russian Orthodox missionary to the Buryat people. In 1825 he became a monk with the name of Nil. After serving as rector* of the seminary at Yaroslavl and archimandrite*, he was made archbishop of Irkutsk in 1840. For the next 34 years he gave himself to missionary work among the Buryat Buddhists, baptizing more than 20,000 people between 1838 and 1850.

ishkeem Thin leather straps worn by Coptic monks to form a diagonal cross on the chest and back, symbolizing Christ carrying the cross.

Isho'dad of Merv (ninth century) Nestorian bishop of Hedatta on the Tigris. He is a key figure in the Eastern Christian tradition. His fame rests on his biblical commentaries in Syriac*.

Ishu'yab III (600–658) Patriarch of the East from 650. He was the head of the Nestorian Church* during the Arab conquest, and his letters provide eyewitness accounts of the history of the fall of the Arabian Peninsula to the Muslims. He is credited with the ordering of the Hudra, the variable texts for Sundays, and major feasts and fasts. He promoted four new metropolitan provinces: Samarkand, China, India, and Qatar.

Isidore of Kiev (c. 1385–1464) Greek-born Orthodox metropolitan* of Kiev* from 1436. He was one of the six official representatives of the Greek Orthodox Church at the Council of Ferrara-Florence in 1438/39. He signed the decree of union in 1439. Created a cardinal, he returned to Kiev* and Moscow* and proclaimed the union in 1441. But the union was rejected and Isidore was imprisoned. He escaped and returned to Italy. Sent as a papal legate* to Constantinople*

in the fateful year 1453, he was taken prisoner by the Ottoman Turks after the fall of the imperial capital.

Isidore of Pelusium, St. (c. 360–c. 440) Ascetic and theologian. He was for 40 years the abbot of a monastery near Pelusium on the eastern estuary of the Nile. He has left a collection of some 2,000 letters that give information on his contemporaries, as Chrysostom* and Cyril of Alexandria*. His Christology* was Athanasian, holding that the Holy Spirit* was consubsantial* with the Father and the Son. He defined the church as an "assembly of saints knit together by correct faith and excellent manner of life and abounding in spiritual gifts*." Feast day: February 4.

Isidore of Seville, St. (c. 560–636) Archbishop of Seville* and encyclopedist, known as "Schoolmaster of the Middle Ages." He was a polymath who excelled in all branches of knowledge. His fame rests on his many encyclopedic works. His *Sententiarum Libri Tres* was the first manual of Christian doctrine in the Latin Church. His *Etymologiarum sive Originum Libri Viginti* was an encyclopedia of 20 books distilling knowledge in all fields, including grammar, rhetoric, mathematics, music, jurisprudence, history, theology, geography, geology, agriculture, and anthropology.

His *Historia de Regibus Gothorum, Vandalorum et Suevorum* is the principal source for the history of the Goths. His biblical works include *Proemiorum Liber Unus, De Variis Quaestionibus, Proemia, De Ortu et Obitu Patrum, Liber Numerorum, De Nominibus Legis et Evangeliorum, De Vita et Morte Sanctorum Utriusque Testamenti,* and *Quaestionum in Vetus Testamentum Libri Duo. De Natura Rerum* interpreted classical cosmology in Christian terms. *De Ecclesiasticis Offiiciis* is a useful source for the Mozarabic Liturgy. *Synonyma* presented spiritual exhortation, and *Chronica Majora* is a historical chronology from creation to 615. His other works include one against heretics, *De Haeresibus,* and one against Jews, *Contra Iudaeos.*

He presided over the Second Council of Seville (619) and the Fourth Council of Toledo* (633). He was responsible for the general acceptance of the Filioque* clause in the West. He is the national hero of the Spanish Church, canonized in 1598 and named a doctor of the church* in 1722. Feast day: April 4.

Issy, Articles of Thirty-four articles issued in 1694– 1695 at Issy, near Paris, after the ecclesiastical investigation of the works of Madame Guyon*, condemning Quietism*. The articles, which rejected the claim that mystical prayer is the only way to salvation*, were signed by Madame Guyon herself who retracted her principles.

istotchniki (lit., fountains) In the Byzantine Rite*, red and white ribbons, sewn horizontally around a bishop's mandyas*. Where the mantle fastens there are four squares representing fountains* or streams of faith.

Itala/Itala Vetus Old Latin* text of the Bible preceding the Vulgate*.

itchagie In the Ethiopian Church, the grand prior* of Debra Lebanos Monastery, near Addis Ababa.

ite, missa est (Lat., go, you are dismissed) Words of dismissal* at the end of the Mass*.

itinerancy Ministry of teaching or preaching not restricted to one local congregation but involving travel over greater or smaller areas. It has been used of a church with extensive rural territory to serve, but is also associated with irregular, unauthorized preaching.

itinerarium Blessing or prayer before beginning a journey.

ius in sacra Right of the church to administer its own affairs without interference from secular authorities.

IVCF Inter-Varsity Christian Fellowship*.

Ivo of Chartres, St. (1040–1116) Bishop of Chartres*. In 1090 he was appointed to the See of Chartres, famous for its school. He was imprisoned briefly for opposing the plan of King Philip I to leave his wife and marry another woman. An authority of canon law*, he paved the way for Gratian* to synthesize the canons. His most important works were *Panormia* (8 books) and *Decretum* (17 books). Feast day: May 20 or 23.

Iwaz, Ignatius Zakka (1933–) Syriac Orthodox patriarch* (1980–). He became a monk in 1954, was ordained priest in 1957 and bishop in 1963 and patriarch* in 1980. He has built a new patriarchal monastery in Maarat Saydnaya, outside Damascus*, that also serves as a seminary.

izobrazitelnaya In the Byzantine tradition, services recited after hours on days when the liturgy is not celebrated. The office consists of hymns, prayers, and readings.

Jj

Jackson, Mahalia (1911–1972) Black gospel singer. Under the guidance of Thomas Dorsey*, she established herself as one of the most powerful gospel singers. She was called the "the most majestic voice of faith." From her first recording, "God Shall Wipe Away All Tears" (1937) through some of her most popular recordings, as "Upper Room" and "Silent Night*," her recordings sold widely. She was also active in the civil rights movement.

Jacob Baradeus (c. 500–578) Monophysite leader who carried on the work of Eutyches* in Mesopotamia and after whom the Jacobite (Syrian Orthodox*) Church is named. He spent 15 years in Constantinople*, where he enjoyed the patronage of Empress Theodora*. In 542 he was consecrated bishop of Edessa*, then under the Ghassanid kings. He spent most of his life clandestinely spreading Monophysite beliefs, establishing churches and monasteries, and ordaining clergy. He received the epithet Baradai (clad in rags) because he would disguise himself as a beggar to avoid arrest by the imperial forces.

Jacob of Edessa (c. 633–708) Jacobite scholar. He was consecrated bishop of Edessa* in 684 but soon retired to the Monastery of Tell Adda, where he devoted his time to writing. An eminent polymath, he was an exegete, historian, and grammarian. He was also one of the most important Jacobite theologians. His works included Syriac* homilies in verse and prose, liturgies, commentaries on the Old Testament and New Testament, and a chronicle of church history. He also translated the Peshitta* Old Testament. He wrote the earliest known Syriac grammar and introduced Greek letters into the Syriac alphabet.

Jacob of Nisibis (fourth century) "Moses of Mesopotamia." Bishop of Nisibis who took a leading part in the Council of Nicaea* on the side of Hosius* and Alexander of Alexandria*. He baptized and was a friend of Ephraem Syrus. He is venerated as a doctor of the church* by the Jacobites and the Armenians. Feast day: July 15.

Jacob of Sarug (c. 451–521) "The Flute of the Holy Spirit." Syriac writer. As a priest he rallied Christians against their Persian oppressors. In 519 he became bishop of Batnae, the main town of Sarug, in Osrhoene. His principal work was a long series of metrical homilies on biblical themes. He also wrote many letters, sermons, funeral orations, hymns, and biographies.

Jacobins French Dominicans* whose first house in Paris was dedicated to St. James* and was located on Rue St. Jacques. When the radical Society of Friends* of the Constitution began using the buildings during the French Revolution, the term, ironically, was applied to them.

Jacobite Church See SYRIAC ORTHODOX CHURCH.

Jacobus da Voragine See JAMES OF VORAGINE.

Jacopone da Todi (c. 1230–1306) Birth name: Jacopo Benedetti. Franciscan poet. About 1278 he became a Franciscan lay brother*, and he and some of his fellow monks were granted permission by Celestine V* in 1294 to live in a separate community. The decision was reversed by Boniface VIII* on his accession in 1298, and Jacopone was imprisoned until 1303 for satirizing the pope in one of his poems. He wrote many devotional poems in Latin and the Umbrian dialect, among them, possibly, Stabat Mater*. Feast Day at Todi: December 25.

Jaffray, Robert Alexander (1873–1945) Christian and Missionary Alliance* (CMA) missionary in China. Son of the owner and publisher of the *Toronto Globe,* Jaffrey was converted under A. B. Simpson*, and sent to Wuzhou, Gulanxi, China, in 1897. This became his headquarters for the next 35 years, and he soon began to serve as leader of all CMA missions in East Asia. He helped to found the Wuzhou Bible School (later the Alliance Seminary in Hong Kong) and served as its principal. He also planted mission stations* in Annam (now Vietnam) and Borneo. In 1931 he moved to Makassar, Celebes, Indonesia, from where he led a growing mission until 1942, when he was arrested and interned by the Japanese. He died of illness and malnutrition.

jamagarkutian (lit., arrangement of the hours) In the Armenian Rite*, book containing all the prayers for the proper of the office and the common of the office.

Jamarkik In the Armenian Rite*, the Book of Hours containing the invariable part of the office.

James, Apocalypses of Two short Gnostic works contained in Codex V of the Nag Hammadi* Library containing a dialogue between Jesus and James, described as "the Lord's brother." The first piece deals with the liberation of the soul from its earthly bondage and the second with meditations on martyrdom.

James, Apocryphal Epistle of Second-century work contained in Codex I of the Nag Hammadi* Library. It begins as a letter but soon becomes a narrative of the final discourse delivered by Jesus to Peter* and James, 550 days after the Resurrection.

James, Book of Apocryphal infancy gospel of the late second century attributed to James, brother of the Lord. It was probably compiled by a Jewish Christian from a variety of sources, including the canonical Gospels, all of them highly embellished. See also PROTEVANGELIUM.

James, Liturgy of Ancient liturgy extant in Greek and in Syriac*, ascribed, by tradition, to James, the brother of the Lord. It is used by the Syrian, Armenian, Georgian, Coptic, and Ethiopian churches.

James of Voragine (c. 1230–1298) Also, James of Varazze. Dominican monk and author of *Golden Legend*. He held high positions in the Dominican Order, including provincial* of Lombardy and vicar* of the order. In 1292, he was named bishop of Genoa. Feast day: July 13.

James, St. The Lord's brother, possibly the son of the Virgin Mary* and an apostle. He was granted a special appearance of the Lord after the Resurrection. He was with St. Peter*, a leader of the

St. James

church at Jerusalem*. He was put to death by the Sanhedrin in 62. Feast day: October 23.

James the Great, St. Apostle. Son of Zebedee, elder brother of John, named Boanerges, that is "Son of Thunder," by the Lord. He was the first of the 12 to suffer martyrdom when he was beheaded by Herod Agrippa in 44. According to Spanish legends, his body was translated to Santiago de Compostela* in Spain. Feast day: April 30 (Eastern Church*); July 25 (Western Church*).

James the Less, St. Son of Alphaeus, one of the 12 disciples. Feast day: May 3 (Western Church*); October 9 (Eastern Church*).

Jane, St. Frances de Chantal (1572–1641) Founder of the Order of the Visitation. She took vows after the death of her husband, and with the help of her spiritual director*, Francis de Sales, founded the first house of the order at Annecy in 1610. By the time of her death, there were 86 houses. She cared for the sick and the dying in the plague of 1628–1629. Feast day: August 21.

Jansen, Cornelius Otto (1585–1638) Roman Catholic bishop of Ypres and founder of Jansenism*. He studied Augustinianism* and became its fervent advocate as well as an opponent of the Jesuits*. He became the director of a college at Lourdes* from 1617 to 1626. His theological reputation is founded on his masterpiece, *Augustinus*, or the Doctrine of Saint Augustine on the Health, the Sickness, and the Cure of Human Nature: Against the Pelagians and those of Marseilles* (1640).

Jansenism Augustinian theology based on *Augustinus*by Cornelius Otto Jansen*. Its five principal doctrines were: 1. It is impossible to fulfill the commandments of God without special grace*. 2. Grace is irresistible. 3. Only freedom from compulsion is needed for merit*, not freedom from necessity. 4. Grace can neither be resisted nor complied with by free will*. 5. Christ did not die for all men. These propositions brought Jansenism into direct conflict with the church and with the Jesuits* because they undercut the sacramental and hierarchical basis of the Counter-Reformation*.

Jansenists held that sacraments* were not efficacious until the Holy Spirit* transforms the inner disposition of the recipient by his grace. In 1653 these five propositions were condemned by Pope Innocent X*, but the defenders of Jansenism evaded this condemnation by drawing a distinction between "fact" and "law." After this distinction was disallowed by Alexander VII* in 1656, Jansenists were forced to recant, but, in fact, they continued to gain adherents particularly among the Oratorians* and Maurists*.

The first generation of Jansenists were all disciples of St. Cyran* and were therefore also called Cyranists. After St. Cyran's death in 1643, Antoine* succeeded him as leader. His *De la Frequente Communion* (1643) and *La Theologie Morale des Jesuites* (1643) defined the directions of the movement, while Blaise Pascal's* *Lettres Provinciales* elaborated on its theological bases. Pasquier Quesnel's* *Reflexions Morales* (1693), which upheld many Jansenist tenets, was condemned by a papal bull* in 1713. The headquarters of the Jansenists at Port Royal was destroyed and Jansenists began to face persecution, which did not end until the expulsion of Jesuits from France in 1762. Many Jansenists took refuge in the Netherlands and Tuscany, where the civil rulers were sympathetic to Jansenism.

Janssen, Arnold (1837–1909) German founder of the Society of the Divine Word* (SVD). Ordained in 1861, he became in 1869 the director of the Apostleship of Prayer* of the Diocese of Munster. In 1875 he moved to the Netherlands, where he founded St. Michael's Mission House in Steyl as a training school for missionaries. It soon developed into the Society of the Divine Word, a missionary order of priests and brothers*. He also founded two missionary congregations of sisters*, The Servants of the Holy Spirit in 1889, and a contemplative order, the Servants of the Holy Spirit of Perpetual Adoration, in 1896. When he died, SVD had 659 members working in Asia, Africa, Latin America, and the United States.

Jansz, Pieter (1820–1904) Pioneer Dutch Mennonite missionary in Indonesia. He arrived in Java in 1851 and served for the next half century as a teacher and lay missionary. His lasting contribution was as a Bible translator. Working with the British and Foreign Bible Society*, he produced the Javanese New Testament in 1888 and the Old Testament in 1892.

Januarius, St. (d. 305) Bishop of Benevento and patron saint* of Naples. He is known to have been a martyr* during the Diocletianic persecution*. He has acquired considerable popularity as a result of the liquefaction of his blood, preserved in a small glass vial, that takes place 18 times a year. Feast day: April 21 (Eastern Church*); September 19 (by Italians everywhere).

Japan, martyrs of Victims of the persecution of Christians initiated by the Shogun Hideyoshi in 1597. They numbered 26 Franciscans, 36 Jesuits*, 21 Dominicans*, and 107 laypeople. A second persecution took place in 1614.

Jaricot, Pauline-Marie (1799–1862) Founder of the Society for the Propagation of the Faith. At the age of 17 she made a perpetual vow of virginity. Thereafter she devoted her life to the promotion of missions. In 1826 she formed the Association of the Living Rosary whose members committed themselves to daily prayer. In 1822 she became one of the founders of the Society for the Propagation of the Faith. She also promoted the Association of the Holy Childhood, which encouraged children to pray for and contribute to the work of missions.

jaschothsgirch In the Armenian Rite*, a lectionary*.

Jasov Premonstratensian monastery in a secluded valley near the River Bolvda, Slovakia, founded by Duke Kolman, king of Halicz, around the year 1230. It was rebuilt in the middle of the thirteenth century, but was in decline by the early seventeenth century. In the eighteenth century, Andreas Sauberer became the abbot of Jasov and began the building of a new monastery which was consecrated by 1766. The Viennese Baroque painter, Johann Lucas Kracker, painted the frescoes in the monastery church.

Jaspers, Karl (1883–1969) German philosopher. He was professor of philosophy at Heidelberg (1921–1937) and at Basle* (1948–1961). He developed a form of Christian existentialism* derived from Kierkegarard*, but he remained essentially a secular philosopher. Although he rejected the exclusive claims of Christ, he was sympathetic to many Christian theological positions.

Jassy, Synod of Council of the Eastern Orthodox Church* in 1642 held in Jassy in Romania, the most important council in Orthodox history next to the Synod of Jerusalem* in 1672. It condemned the Calvinist teachings of Cyril Lucar* and approved the Orthodox Confession of Peter Mogila*, metropolitan* of Kiev*.

Javouhey, Anne-Marie (1779–1851) Founder of the Sisters of St. Joseph* of Cluny*. Actively engaged in the religious education of young children during the French Revolution, she and a small group of women founded the Sisters of St. Joseph* of Cluny in 1807. Although opposed by the hierarchy*, she was invited by the French government to send sisters* to the French West Indies, French Guiana, and West Africa. The sisters continue to be active in teaching, pastoral ministry, nursing, and rural ministry throughout the world.

jebs-jof Also, khuda. In the Coptic Church*, the prayer of inclination* recited by the priest at the end of the Communion.

Jeffreys, George (1889–1962) Welsh Pentecostal evangelist, founder, and leader of the Elim Foursquare Gospel Alliance. He was baptized in the Holy Spirit* in 1911 and began preaching in 1912. He and his brother, Stephen, are ranked among England's greatest evangelists since John Wesley* and George Whitefield*. He held crusades* in Wales, Ireland, England, Netherlands, Canada, the United States, and Sweden.

Jeffreys, Stephen (1876–1943) Welsh Pentecostal evangelist. He drew large crowds wherever he preached. He helped to build the Assemblies of God* in the British Isles.

Jehovah's Witnesses Also, Russellites. Cult* founded by C. T. Russell* in the 1870s as the Watch Tower Bible and Tract Society* and renamed as Jehovah's Witnesses in 1931 under Russell's successor, J. F. Rutherford. Their theology is essentially a revival of Arianism* in which Jesus Christ is regarded as the first and highest created being, slightly above an archangel*. While on earth Christ was only a man energized by the Holy Spirit* as the active force of Jehovah. The Witnesses* do not believe in a soul without a body and hold that Christ's mission is to give immortality* to humans, either through deathlessness or by resurrection. They have no interest in a devotional life. The Lord's Supper* is celebrated only annually at Passover.

Other cardinal tenets of this heresy include a belief that only 144,000 believers will rule in heaven*, while lesser men of goodwill will people the kingdom, which will be established by Jesus Christ at the end of the age on earth. The sect is highly authoritarian and enforces rigid dogmas, such as rejection of blood transfusion and refusal to serve in military forces, or salute national flags. Their churches are called kingdom halls. Active members are called publishers (of the good news) and the less active as pioneers. Members witness from door to door.

Jellesma, Jelle Eeltjes (1817–1858) Dutch missionary known as the apostle of Java. In 1848 he formed the first Javanese Christian congregation, called Damej (Peace) in Wijung. In 1851 he settled in the village of Modjowarno, where he built up another large congregation.

Jeremiad Sermon of fire and brimstone, focusing on moral failures, social disorder, or natural disasters in order to create among the listeners a sense of personal crisis. Jeremiads explicitly warn of God's wrath and impending punishment and are designed to awaken Christians from their complacency and apathy.

Jeremias II (1536–1595) Greek Orthodox leader and patriarch of Constantinople (1572–1595) who organized the Russian Orthodox Church* by raising the metropolitan of Moscow to the rank of patriarch in 1588.

jereundir In the Armenian Rite*, a book of homilies or discourses.

Jerome Emiliani, St. (1481–1537) Birth name: Girolamo Miani. Founder of the Somaschi*, a Counter-Reformation* order of clerks regular*

caring for orphans. In 1532 he founded a society named Somaschi, after the village of Somasca, between Milan* and Bergamo*, where the mother house* was located. Its members worked with orphans, prostitutes, and the sick. He established at Bergamo the first home in Italy for prostitutes. He was canonized in 1767 and made the patron saint* of orphans and abandoned children. Feast day: February 8.

Jerome of Prague (c. 1371–1416) Bohemian reformer and friend of John Hus*. He was an ardent champion of Wycliffism, although he remained orthodox on transubstantiation*. For leading a Wycliffe* movement at the University of Prague, he was excommunicated in 1409 and dismissed in 1410. He was arrested by the Inquisition* in Vienna* but fled. Thereafter he became more radical and led demonstrations in favor of Hus*, and against indulgences* and relics*. In 1413 he was expelled from Cracow. In 1415 he was arrested at Constance and, after a year in jail, was burned at the stake in 1416.

Jerome, St. (c. 347–c. 420) Church Father. Birth name: Eusebius Hieronymus. Baptized at the age of 19, he journeyed to Gaul, where he became steeped in ascetic practices. In 373 he left for the East and spent some time as an ascetic in the desert near Chalcis. He went to Antioch*, where he was ordained, and later in Constantinople* studied with Gregory of Nazianzus* and Gregory of Nyssa*. In 382 he returned to Rome*, where he became a friend and secretary of Pope Damasus. He left Rome after the death of Damasus and in 386 made Bethlehem* his home for the rest of his

St. Jerome

life, serving as the abbot of a monastery for men and spiritual adviser to a convent.

Jerome's greatest contribution was his translation of the Bible into the common Latin, which became the basis of the Vulgate*. He was instrumental in rejecting the apocryphal books of the Bible and accepting the Hebrew canon* of the Old Testament. He wrote many biblical commentaries that were distinguished by sound linguistic and historical scholarship. His literary labors extended to the translation and continuation of Eusebius*, compilation of *De Viris Illustribus,* a bibliography of ecclesiastical writers, and translation

St. Jerome's New Testament Translation

of Origen*. He also engaged in theological controversies over Origen's teaching and with both orthodox and heretic writers, particularly Vigilantius, Pelagius*, Jovinian*, Rufinus*, and Augustine of Hippo*, and his correspondence with them is of great historical interest. He is represented in Christian art with a red hat* and/or a lion*. Feast day: September 30.

Jerusalem Holy city in Israel, former capital of Judah, sacred to Judaism and Christianity. It is the site of the temple of Solomon and later of Herod the Great. Of the latter, only the Wailing Wall survives. After the dispersal of most Christians from the city during the Jewish Revolt (66–70), the city ceased to hold any special importance to Christians until the discovery of the cross by St. Helena* in about 326 when it became

a place of pilgrimage*. Until the fifth century, the city was a suffragan see under Caesarea*, but at the Council of Chalcedon* (451) it was elevated from a bishopric* to a patriarchate*. But it was only in the eighteenth century that it became the home of a resident patriarch*, who is always a Greek. A Latin patriarchate existed intermittently from 1099 to 1291 and from 1847. There is also an Armenian patriarchate. The Christian center of the city is the Church of the Resurrection, known in the West as the Church of the Holy Sepulcher.

Jerusalem Bible English translation of the Bible from the French original by Roman Catholic scholars in 1966.

Jerusalem Conference World Missionary Conference* on the Mount of Olives at Easter* 1928. It was the first globally representative assembly of non-Catholic Christians.

Jerusalem Conference on Biblical Prophecy Evangelical gathering of over 1,500 delegates from all parts of the world in 1971 to discuss eschatological themes.

Jerusalem, Council of First Apostolic Council* of the Christian church, held in Jerusalem headed by St. James the Great*, at which it was decided that Gentiles need not be circumcised or be forced to keep the Mosaic Law (Acts 15).

Map of Jerusalem

Jerusalem Cross Also, Crusaders' Cross. Square cross with four smaller crosses in its four quarters.

Jerusalem Delivered Italian epic poem in 20 books by Torquato Tasso* (1544–1595).

Jerusalem, Patriarchate of The canons of the Council of Nicaea* (325) placed Jerusalem as the fifth in the territorial divisions of the Christian Church, after Rome*, Constantinople*, Alexandria, and Antioch*. The Council of Chalcedon* (451) raised it to patriarchal rank. However, the Arab conquest in the seventh century reduced its power and influence, and the Crusades* disrupted its continuity. From 1291 to 1847 there was no patriarch* in Jerusalem.

Jerusalem Psalter Set of compact disc recordings of all 150 Psalms sung in the musical traditions of major Christian denominations in Jerusalem and made in 1999.

Jerusalem, Synod of Council of the Eastern Orthodox Church* in 1672 at Bethlehem* held by Dositheus*, patriarch* of Jerusalem. It condemned the Calvinist doctrines espoused by Cyril Lucar*, former patriarch. It declared the infallibility of the church and upheld the seven sacraments* and transubstantiation*. This declaration is known as the Shield of Orthodoxy*.

Jesse window Medieval window in churches showing the genealogy of Jesus or Mary in the form of a tree.

Jesu, Dulcis Memoria Twelfth-century poem, translated into English by Edward Caswall* as "Jesu, the very thought of thee with sweetness fills my breast," and by J. M. Neale* as "Jesu, the very thought is sweet! In that dear name all heart-joys meet." It is probably the work of an unknown Cistercian monk. It is sometimes known as the Rosy Sequence* or as the Joyful Rhythm.

Jesuit College Collegio Romano, built by Giuseppe Valeriani in Rome* between 1583 and 1585 to house the principal training college of the Jesuits*.

Jesuits Society of Jesus*, founded by Ignatius Loyola* with nine companions and approved by Paul III* in 1540. The constitution of the society was approved by the membership in 1558. The general goal of the society is the propagation of the faith and the promotion of Christian piety. Ignatius did not design it as a contemplative order (although the *Spiritual Exercises* of Ignatius is a classic devotional manual) but as a proactive educational and training order committed to serving Jesus Christ and prepared to go anywhere in the world in pursuit of its goals. It is also an authoritarian order in which the general* (known as the Black Pope*) has extraordinary powers and demands absolute obedience from members both to himself and the pope.

Jesuits are distinguished from other Roman Catholic orders by a number of features. They do not, unless asked by the pope, accept any position in the hierarchy*; they have no special habit; they are exempt from the obligation to recite the Office in choir; and there is an extended probation for each new entrant. Supreme authority is vested in a representative general congregation. The general is elected for life and holds plenary authority. Under Claudio Aquaviva*, general from 1581 to 1615, the Jesuits achieved a high order of efficiency, for which they are even now noted, with an elaborate code, called *Ratio Studiorum*, to govern its work. Jesuits soon gained a reputation as preachers and teachers, leaders of retreats*, and hospital chaplains*.

In 1539 they formed a Company of Jesus in Rome* dedicated to the education of children. The first Jesuit secondary school was established in Messina in 1548. Soon they founded universities and colleges in many countries, and the society itself became primarily a teaching order and the leading edge in Catholic higher education, noted for their academic programs. They also established orphanages, houses for the rehabilitation of prostitutes, and centers for poor relief. Their missionary work extended to the New World, Asia, and Africa. Among their pioneering missionaries were Francis Xavier* (one of the original members of the society), who took the gospel to India and Japan, and Manuel de Nobrega, who evangelized Brazil.

The society turned out to be one of the strongest bulwarks of the church at the Council of Trent*, and Jesuits were the frontline troops in the struggle against the Reformers. But their success in many Catholic countries proved to be a mixed blessing. They were expelled from Portugal in 1759, from France in 1764, and from Spain in 1767. Pressure from many nations forced Clement XIV* in 1773 to suppress the society, and they were not restored until 1814. In the late twentieth century, Jesuits have succumbed to the liberalizing influences of the secular world, and many of their theologians have been in the forefront of leftist causes. But they remain the largest educational force in the world, responsible for the Gregorian University* in Rome and hundreds of schools, universities, and seminaries throughout the world.

Jesus Christ Son of God conceived of the Holy Spirit* and born in Bethlehem* of the Virgin

Jesuit Insignia

Mary* about 4 B.C. He began an active ministry at age 30 after gathering 12 disciples, all of whom, except Judas Iscariot, stayed with him until the end. He was brought to trial by the Roman rulers in 33, convicted, and crucified, but he rose again on the third day, appeared to his disciples and numerous others, and ascended to heaven*. Christians believe that he will come again in glory and establish his kingdom.

Jesus Full-length feature film produced by Campus Crusade for Christ* in 1979, this feature-length presentation based on Luke's Gospel has been viewed worldwide by an estimated 1.6 billion people. Theater showings, television broadcasts, and the efforts of over 2,000 traveling national film teams sponsored by CCC in more than 100 countries have contributed to this exposure. The *Jesus* Film Project coordinates international

translations (approximately 500) and film use. An audio/radio format has been more recently developed, as has DVD capability. Project director Paul Eshleman states the continued evangelistic goal: to show "the *Jesus* film to everyone in the world in a language that he or she can understand."

Jesus movement A movement of the 1970s without any formal organization or leadership in which vast numbers of young people expressed a personal commitment to Jesus Christ in Evangelical, Fundamentalist, and Pentecostal settings. They combined an unconventional lifestyle associated generally with the secular hippies with strong ethical conduct and millenarian expectations.

Jesus of history Portrait of Jesus Christ derived by scholarly reconstruction by accepting the Gospel accounts as they stand.

Jesus Only Pentecostal movement begin in 1913 which baptized only in the name of Jesus, and not in the name of the Father, Son, and Holy Spirit*. A further development led to the teaching that in the Trinity* only Jesus is truly a person. The teaching came to be called the New Issue and split Pentecostal ranks, especially in the Assemblies of God*.

Jesus People Young converts to Christianity, especially Pentecostal churches*, from the street culture of the 1960s and 1970s. The movement stanched the massive sexual promiscuity, drug addiction, and the lure of Oriental religions by presenting a gospel to which young people could relate. It was a gospel stripped to its essentials, the chief and only tenet being that Jesus is the Way*. Street preaching was introduced in 1966 by Tony and Susan Alamo in 1966. Coffee houses, like the Catacombs, started by Linda Meissner, carried the message across the land. It was joined by Teen Challenge* and its cold-turkey drug rehabilitation program, established by David Wilkerson* in 1958. There were much-publicized mass baptisms. Jesus People helped to create large mega-churches, such as Melodyland Christian Center in Anaheim, California; the Vineyard Christian Fellowship* in Yorba Linda, California; and the Calvary Chapel* in Cosa Mesta, California. Jesus People brought some of their old customs, such as long hair, unconventional dress, and nontraditional music, into the new environment.

Jesus Prayer The prayer, "Lord Jesus Christ, Son of God, have mercy on me, a sinner." The continuous repetition of the prayer was a characteristic of the Byzantine Hesychasm*. It is widely practiced in the Orthodox Church. Formerly it was recited. Sometimes it is reduced to, "Jesus, have mercy."

Jesus Seminar Group of radically liberal and skeptical scholars who began meeting in 1985 in order to critique the authenticity of the Gospels, the narratives of the Gospel writers, and the sayings of Jesus.

Jeunesse Ouvriere Chretienne Also, Jocists*. Roman Catholic organization of young factory workers, farmers, and sailors who wish to apply Christian principles in their workplace and home. It was inspired in the 1920s by the encyclical* *Rerum Novarum* of Leo XIII*. See also JOCISTS.

Jewel, John (1522–1571) Bishop of Salisbury*. Under the influence of Peter Martyr Vermigli*, he became one of the leaders of the English Reformation*. He was consecrated bishop of Salisbury in 1560 and thereafter became a strong apologist for the Anglican settlement. His defense of the Church of England* in *Apologia Ecclesiae Anglicanae* (1562) strengthened the doctrinal authority of the fledgling church.

Jews for Jesus Jewish missionary organization, officially called Hineni Ministries, founded in 1973 by Moishe Rosen in San Francisco. It is the largest and most effective Jewish missionary organization in the world and the largest producer of gospel broadsides and gospel tracts in the United States. There are branches in Canada, the United Kingdom, South Africa, Australia, and India. Its distinctive missionary programs include gospel music* teams, such as the Liberated Wailing Wall, and gospel drama teams.

jhamamout In the Armenian Church*, the introit*.

Jimenez de Cisneros, Francisco See XIMENEZ/JIMENEZ

DE CISNEROS, FRANCISCO.

Jing Jing (eighth century) Persian priest and scholar, believed to be the author of the inscription on the famous Nestorian monument near Sian (Xi'an) in Shensi (Shaanxi) Province, commemorating the "luminous religion," as the Chinese referred to Christianity.

Joachim of Fiore (c. 1135–1202) Italian mystic. In 1192 he founded the order of San Giovanni in Fiore. Two mystical experiences gave him spiritual understanding of the inner meaning of history. He explained his insights in three major works: *Exposition of the Apocalypse, Concordance of the Old and New Testaments,* and the *Psalterium of Ten Strings.* He applied the doctrine of the Trinity* to depict three historical dispensations: the age of the Father or the age of law (covering the Old Testament), the age of the Son or the age of grace* (the current Church Age*), and the age of the Spirit (to begin after the overthrow of the Antichrist*). Joachim's apocalyptic teachings inspired groups such as the Spiritual Franciscans* and the Fraticelli*, and influenced later apocalptic interpretations of history.

Joan of Arc, St. (1412–1431) "The Maid of Orleans" and the national heroine of France. Birth name: Jean la Pucelle. A devout peasant girl, she received visions that urged her to save France from the

Joan of Arc

English. She persuaded Charles VII to give her armor and attendants with which she routed the English who were besieging Orleans. After a second victory in the Loire, she had Charles crowned at Reims* in 1429. Next year, on a campaign to relieve Compiegne, she was taken prisoner by the Burgundians and sold to the English. She was tried by a court presided over by Pierre Cauchon*, the bishop of Beauvais*, and convicted of witchcraft and heresy, and her visions were declared to be of the devil. She was burned as a heretic in the marketplace of Rouen* in 1431. The judgment was annulled in 1456, and she was canonized in 1920. Feast day: May 30.

Jocists Jeunesse Ouvriere Chretienne* (JOC), the organization of Catholic Workers* founded in Belgium in 1924.

Jogues, St. Isaac (1607–1646) Jesuit missionary and martyr*. He arrived in New France in 1636 and worked in missions among the Hurons, but was captured by the Mohawks. He escaped to France, but returned in 1646 to work among the Mohawks. On the day of his arrival he was killed by a hatchet blow from an Iroquois warrior. He and his companions were canonized in 1930 and proclaimed the patron saints* of Canada. Feast day: September 26.

Johannine Of or relating to St. John the apostle or St. John of Patmos.

Johannine comma Words in 1 John 5:7–8: "For there are three that bear witness in heaven: the Father, the Word, and the Holy Spirit*; and these three are one. And there are three that bear witness on earth: the Spirit, the water, and the blood; and these three agree as one" These words are found in some Latin manuscripts and in the Sixto-Clementine version of the Vulgate*. Their authenticity is repudiated by modern scholarship, especially as the context speaks of the Spirit, the water, and the blood as the three witnesses.

John XXI (d. 1277) Pope from 1276. Birth name: Peter Hispanus. A physician by profession, he is the author of several medical treatises as well as *Tractatus* or *Summulae Logicales,* one of the most influential manuals of logic in the Middle Ages.

John XXII (1249–1334) Pope from 1316. Birth name: Jacques Duese. He expanded papal power through the appointment of bishops and the imposition of papal taxes. A Frenchman, he made Avignon* a center of culture and arts. In 1317 he dissolved the Spiritual Franciscans*, accusing them of heresy in their doctrine of absolute poverty. He was an expert canonist, and his own decrees were collected together as *Extravagantes Johannis XXII.* He himself was accused of heresy for his stated belief that the saints* do not see God until after the last judgment*. A capable administrator, he reorganized the Curia* and established the Rota Romana in 1331 as the tribunal of the papal court. In 1334 he introduced the universal observance of Trinity Sunday*.

John XXIII (1881–1963) Pope from 1958. Birth name: Angelo Giuseppi Roncalli. He was 77 when elected pope, but he had served in a number of positions with distinction since 1905. He surprised everyone by taking the name of John XXIII, since that was the name of an antipope. The most important event of his pontificate* was the calling of the Second Vatican Council*, a historic undertaking with the goal of aggiornamento*, or modernization. He was a strong proponent of ecumenism*, social justice, and peace. As an ecumenist, he set up the Secretariat for Promoting Christian Unity* and invited observers from other churches to the council. His many reforms included permission for the use of the vernacular, a new code of rubrics for the Missal and the Breviary*, and the creation of a pontifical* commission to revise the code of canon law*. He

Pope John XXIII

revised the social teaching of the church in *Mater et Magistra* (1961) and pleaded for the end of colonialism and an improvement in the position of women in *Pacem in Terris* (1963). He also sought to improve relations with Jews by removing certain passages from the Good Friday Liturgy.

John, Acts of Legendary document of the early third century narrating the life and work of John the apostle, purportedly written by the Valentinian Gnostic Leucius. The Greek original consisted of 2,500 lines.

John, Apocryphon of Coptic document, in the form of a dialogue between Christ and St. John, the son of Zebedee. It is suspected of being Gnostic in origin.

John Baptist/Jean Baptiste de la Salle (1651–1719) French priest who founded the Institute of the Brothers of Christian Schools*. He is the patron saint* of teachers. La Salle was a pioneer in educational practice. His boarding school at Saint-Yon is considered the prototype of modern secondary schools. Feast day: April 7.

John Capistran, St. (c. 1386–1456) Italian Franciscan friar* and preacher who raised an army that defeated the Turks in Hungary. Feast day: October 23.

John Climacus, St. (570–649) Also, Sinaites; Scholasticus. An abbot of a monastery at Sinai, his name was derived from his book, *Ladder of Paradise** (Klimax tou Paradeisou), a popular guide to ascetic discipline. Feast day: March 30.

John Gualbert (c. 990–1073) Founder of the Vallumbrosan Order*. Originally a Benedictine monk, he founded a monastic settlement at Vallumbrosa, near Florence* about 1300. The Rule of the Vallumbrosan Order was a modified Benedictine, but it eventually included lay brothers*.

John Malalas (490–c. 575) Also, John Rhetor. Byzantine chronicler, author of *Chronography* in 18 books that covered the history of the world from creation to the mid-sixth century. It was widely used by Greek and Syriac writers.

John of Avila, St. (1499/1500–1569) "Apostle of Andalusia." Of Jewish ancestry, he was ordained in 1526 and began preaching throughout Andalusia. In 1531 he was denounced by the Seville Inquisition* on charges ranging from illuminism to undue concern for the poor. He was imprisoned for a year but then found innocent and released. After release, he continued to work in the mission field* by setting up 15 colleges and schools for the laity and two for the clergy, including the University of Baeza. In his *Memoriales* (1551 and 1561) and *Advertencias* (1565) he sought to raise the level of spirituality* of the clergy. In his major work, *Audi Filia,* he expounded the way of perfection* for all Christians. His lasting legacy was his influence on a wide circle of friends, including John of God*, Francis Borgia*, Teresa of Avila*, and St. Peter of Alcantara*. He was beatified in 1894 and canonized in 1970. Feast day: May 10.

John of Beverley, St. (d. 721) English scholar and monk. He was bishop of York* before he retired to the Abbey of Beverley founded by him. He enjoyed a widespread cultus* in the Middle Ages, and many miracles were attributed to him, especially Henry V's victory at Agincourt. Feast days: May 7 and October 25.

John of Damascus, St. (c. 655–c. 749) Greek theologian and last of the great Eastern Fathers. Doctor of the church*. After serving as chief Christian representative at the court of the caliph in Damascus, he entered the monastery of St. Sabas south of Jerusalem. His reputation is based on his two books: *The Fount of Wisdom* (or Sources of Knowledge) dealing with heresies and *Exposition of the Catholic Faith* (De Fide Orthodoxa in Latin). Divided into three parts, the latter presents the teachings of the Greek Fathers* on important doctrines and is used as a textbook in Greek seminaries. His other great work was *Sacra Parallela*, a compilation of scriptural and patristic texts on Christian life, presenting virtues and vices in parallel columns. He also wrote extensively on the ascetic life and on the Pauline Epistles as well as homilies and poems, some of which form the basis of modern hymns. He had great influence on the development of medieval theology, especially mariology*, angelology, icons*, circumincession* of the Trinity*, hypostasis*, and Christology*. Feast day: December 4.

John of Ephesus (c. 507–c. 588) Syriac Orthodox metropolitan* of Ephesus* and writer. He became a monk at the age of 15. In 540 he settled at Constantinople* and received an imperial appointment from Justinian* as a missionary in Asia Minor (542–546). He proved highly successful, making 80,000 converts, building 98 new churches, 12 monasteries, and earning the epithet, "converter of the pagans." He was elected the abbot of the Monastery of Mar Mare at Sycae near Constantinople. He was consecrated metropolitan* of Ephesus by Jacob Baradeus* in 558. For his Monophysite beliefs he was imprisoned and his monastery was suppressed. His works include *Ecclesiastical History* (of which the third and final part covering 571–589 is extant) and the *Lives of Eastern Saints.*

John of God, St. (1495–1550) Founder of the Order of Charity for the Service of the Sick or Brothers Hospitallers. After leaving military service, he was converted by St. John of Avila* to a life of sanctity*, penitence, and devotion. Later he embarked on a life of service to the poor and founded the Brothers Hospitallers*. He was canonized in 1880 and declared to be the heavenly patron of all hospitals and the patron of booksellers and printers. Feast day: March 8.

John of Matha, St. (d. 1213) Founder of the Trinitarian* order for the redemption of captives. Feast day: February 8.

John of Monte Corvino (1247–c. 1330) Founder of the first Franciscan mission to China. He was commissioned by Pope Nicholas IV in 1291 and journeyed through Persia and India, reaching Khanbalik (Beijing) in China in 1294. Khan Timor Olcheitu greeted the missionary warmly. He established his missionary outpost at Tenduk, ruled by a Nestorian prince, George. He is reputed to have converted over 6,000 people in his lifetime, translated the New Testament and the Psalms into Chinese, and organized a boys' choir.

John of Nepomuk, St. (c. 1340–1393) Bohemian martyr* and patron saint* of Bohemia. As vicar general* of the archdiocese* of Prague*, he resisted interference by Wenceslas* in the affairs of the church, and was by royal orders drowned in the Vltava (Moldau) River. He was canonized in 1729. Feast day: May 16.

John of Parma, Blessed (1209–1289) Franciscan minister general*, elected in 1247 but forced to resign his office in 1257 because of his sympathies with the teaching of Joachim of Fiore*. Thereupon he retired to the hermitage of Greccio, where for 32 years he led a solitary life of penance* and contemplation. Feast day: March 20.

John of St. Thomas (1589–1644) Dominican scholar, so named from his devotion to St. Thomas Aquinas*. In 1620 he began lecturing in theology at Alcala, serving also as qualificator of the Spanish Inquisition* and confessor* and adviser to Philip IV. His principal works were *Cursus Theologicus* (1637–1667), a commentary on St. Thomas Aquinas*, *Cursus Philosophicus* (1631), and *Compendium* (1640).

John of the Cross (c. 1505–c. 1560) Dominican writer. In 1538 he was sent with a group of other Spanish friars to help reform the Dominican Order in Portugal and spent the rest of his life there. His main work was *Dialogue on the Necessity of Vocal Prayer.*

John of the Cross, St. (1542–1591) Spanish mystic and doctor of the church*. Birth name: Juan de Yepez y Alvarez. He entered the Carmelite* monastery at Medina del Campo in 1563 and was ordained in 1567. Prompted by St. Teresa of Avila*, he entered the discalced* branch of the Carmelites and became master of the Carmelite College at Alcala de Henares and confessor* of the Convent of the Incarnation at Avila (1572–1577). He and Teresa were joint founders of the Discalced Carmelites. Imprisoned for advocating reform, he began the first of his devotional works, *The Spiritual Canticle*. He was rector of the College at Baeza from 1579 to 1581 and prior* at Segovia from 1588. At Granada he wrote the other works for which he is famous: *A Dark Night of the Soul,* including *The Ascent of Mount Carmel* and *The Living Flame of Love.* In 1591 he was removed from his office, banished to Andalusia, and spent his last months in solitary confinement. He was canonized in 1726. Feast day: December 14.

John Paul II (1920–) Pope from 1978. Birth name: Karol Wojtyla. The first Slav and the first Pole to be elected pope and the first non-Italian since Hadrian VI in 1523. He is also the most traveled pope in history and the most admired. Although committed to the Second Vatican Council*, his pontificate* has successfully contained the fallout from liberationist, homosexual, and feminist movements. For this reason, he has been called a restorationist pope. He also played a key role in the collapse of Communism and has wielded unparalleled diplomatic influence over governments and nations. Since then, he has spoken against the evils of capitalism and materialism as the new dangers facing civilization.

In his encyclical*, *Veritatis Splendor*￼ (1993), Pope John Paul II upheld the traditional teachings of the church, the Eucharist*, and the place of the Virgin Mary*. He has performed the largest number of beatifications* and canonizations* of any pope in modern times. In 1985 he convened a second Extraordinary Synod of Bishops to reassess the reforms of the Second Vatican Council. By his apostolic constitution*, *Pastor Bonus* (1988), he reorganized the Curia* and confirmed new regulations in 1992. He promulgated the new Codex Iuris Canonici* in 1983 and the first ever codex for Uniat churches*. In 1984 he

Pope John Paul II

concluded the revision of the Lateran Treaty*, modifying some of its provisions. In 2000 he formally apologized on behalf of the Roman Catholic Church for its "mistakes" over the course of two millennia.

John, St. Apostle. Traditional author of the Fourth Gospel, the Book of Revelation, and three of the Catholic Epistles*. He was the son of Zebedee (Matt. 4:21) and one of the inner circle of the Twelve*. The Lord called him and his brother James "Boanerges," or "Sons of Thunder." Jesus entrusted his mother to John on the day of the Crucifixion. The words of the Lord at the Sea of Tiberias before the ascension seem to suggest that John would not die. According to tradition, John left Jerusalem* after attending the first council and went to Asia Minor and settled at Ephesus*. Under Domitian he was exiled to the island of Patmos*, where he wrote the Book of Revelation. Under Nerva he returned to Ephesus and there wrote the Gospel and Epistles in his old age. There are also legends that he was killed by the Jews along with James. Feast day: May 6. See also BELOVED DISCIPLE.

John the Divine, Cathedral of St. Episcopalian* cathedral in New York City designed by Heins and Lafarge and Ralph Adams Cram. It is the world's largest cathedral, with a 601-foot nave* and a 162-foot-high dome. The Port of Paradise carvings at the main entrance were carved by Simon Verity and Jean Claude Marchionni.

John the Faster, St. (d. 595) Patriarch of Constantinople* from 582. He was the first to use the title of ecumenical patriarch*, against papal objections. He was surnamed Faster in honor of his ascetic life. A manual for confessors, known as the *Penitential,* is attributed to him. Feast day: September 2 (Eastern Church*).

Jonas, Justus (1493–1555) Original name: Jodocus Koch. German reformer. Professor of law at the University of Erfurt (1519–1523) and dean of theology at the University of Wittenberg* (1523–1533). He took part in the Marburg Conference* (1529), the Diet of Augsburg (1530), and in the reform at Halle (1541). He translated the writings of Luther* and Melanchthon*. At Luther's funeral in 1546 he delivered the sermon.

Jones, Bob (1883–1968) American evangelist and founder of Bob Jones University. Son of a Confederate army veteran, he held his first evangelistic meeting at the age of 14. In 1924 he founded a university to promote his brand of strict Fundamentalism*, first in Florida, then in Tennessee,

St. Paul's Cathedral

and finally in Greenville, South Carolina. He is reputed to have preached over 1,200 sermons to over 15 million people.

Jones, Clarence Wesley (1900–1986) Pioneer missionary broadcaster. After graduating from the Moody Bible Institute*, he founded, in the 1920s, AWANA (Approved Workmen Are Not Ashamed), a youth program. In 1930, at the invitation of Reuben Larson, Jones moved to Quito, Ecuador, where on Christmas* Day, 1931, radio station HCJB (Heralding Christ Jesus' Blessing) began broadcasting. Retiring in 1961, he spent his remaining years promoting Christian radio. In 1975 he became the first inductee into the National Religious Broadcasters Religious Broadcasting Hall of Fame.

Jones, Eli Stanley (1884–1973) American Methodist missionary to India. He went to India as pastor of a church in Lal Bagh, Lucknow, India. Being sympathetic to Indian culture and India's claims to independence, he tried to Indianize the faith by founding a Christian ashram in Sal Tal and by holding annual conventions at Maramon, Kerala, India. Among his 29 books, many were popular, particularly *Christ of the Indian Road* and *Abundant Living*.

Jones, Inigo (1573–1652) British architect of churches. His ecclesiastical buildings included the Queen's Chapel in St. James's Palace, St. Paul's,* and Covent Garden.

Jones, Jim (1931–1978) American cult* leader. He founded the People's Temple in Indianapolis, Indiana, in the 1950s as a Christian mission for the homeless and unemployed. By the 1960s he had attracted over 1,000 followers. In 1965 he and his followers moved to California and then, in 1977, to Guyana, when Jones founded an agricultural commune called Jonestown, named after himself. In 1978 four members of the group were shot dead as they tried to leave the commune. Fearing retribution, Jones and more than 900 followers committed suicide by drinking arsenic-laced koolaid.

Jones, John Cynddylan (1840–1930) Welsh theologian. He served as pastor successively in Calvinist Methodist and Congregationalist churches from 1867 to 1888, when he resigned to join the staff of the British and Foreign Bible Society* in South Wales. His many biblical commentaries maintained the Evangelical perspective in theology and a vigorous opposition to liberal scholarship. His mildly Calvinistic theology was expounded in the four volumes of *Cysondeb y Ffydd*.

Jones, Rufus Matthew (1863–1948) Quaker* scholar. He spent most of his life at Haverford College, Pennsylvania, teaching theology and philosophy. Within his own denomination, he was considered a prophet* and saint. He helped to found the American Friends Service Committee* in 1917 and served as its chairman for 20 years. Among his more than 50 books were *Dynamic Faith* (1901), *Studies in Mystical Religion* (1909), *The Faith and Practice of the Quakers* (1927), and *George Fox, Seeker and Friend* (1930).

Jones, Samuel (Sam) Porter (1847–1906) American evangelist. Methodist circuit preacher, known as the "Moody of the South." With the Union Gospel Tabernacle in Nashville as the center of his ministry, he preached in every major city in America.

Jones, Thomas (1756–1820) Welsh Calvinist Methodist theologian and preacher. By 1814 he became the most outstanding Welsh Calvinist Methodist leader of his generation. His *Hanes Di-*

wygwyr Merthyron, a Chyffeswyr Eglwys Loegr (1813) was a sustained defense of Evangelicalism* and its Augustinian theology. His writings advanced the Welsh literary tradition with their elegant and forceful prose.

Joseph Calasanctius, St. (1556–1648) Founder of the Piarists* and heavenly patron of Christian schools. In 1597 he opened in Rome* the first free public school in Europe and established in 1602 the Piarist order of teachers. The order was approved by Pope Gregory XV in 1621. In the Piarist schools, also known as "pious schools, "children were taught the three R's and grammar as well as Christian doctrine, and Protestant and Jewish children were admitted on equal terms with Catholics. He was opposed by conservatives, who feared that educating the poor would destabilize society. Bowing to these opponents, Pope Innocent X* reduced the order to a federation of independent religious houses, but its original status was restored in 1669 and Joseph was canonized in 1767. Feast day: August 25.

Joseph of Cupertino, St. (1603–1663) Franciscan prior*. Initially a Capuchin, he was dismissed by his order, and he joined the Franciscans. He is chiefly noted for his ability to levitate, or float through the air, a feat he demonstrated to Pope Urban VIII*. This event was witnessed by the Duke of Brunswick, who was so impressed that he converted from Lutheranism* to Roman Catholicism*.

Joseph of Polotsk, St. (1580–1623) Ukrainian ecclesiastic. He started life as a merchant, but left it to enter the monastery. He became abbot of Vilna and later bishop of Polotsk in Lithuania. His efforts to unite Ukraine* with Rome* were unsuccessful. He was murdered by a mob in 1623. In 1867 he became the first Uniat to be canonized by Rome. Feast day: November 12.

Joseph of Volokolamsk, St. (1439/40–1515) Russian saint and founder of the Monastery of Volokolamsk, a large community consecrated to a rigorous life of obedience and worship. He advocated active involvement in social and political affairs.

Joseph, St. Spouse of Mary and the foster father of Jesus Christ, a carpenter by profession, and a descendant of King David. He is not mentioned in the Bible after Luke 2:48–51.

Joseph the Hymnographer, St. (c. 810–886) Greek hymn writer. He was captured by pirates and sold as a slave in Crete. After release he established a monastery in Constantinople*, but suffered two further periods of exile. A prolific hymn writer, he composed more than 200 hymns in the Menaion*. Feast day: April 3.

Josephus Flavius (37–100) Birth name: Joseph ben-Matthias. Jewish historian. A Pharisee, he joined an ascetic group as a priest and led a mission to Nero in 64. He was one of the commanders in the Jewish revolt of 66, but as a Roman captive at the end of the revolt, impressed Emperor Vespasian with his prophetic powers. He accompanied Emperor Titus to Rome*, where he took Roman citizenship and the name of Flavius, after Emperor Flavian. His chief works are *The Archaeology* (or *Antiquities*) *of the Jews* in 20 books (93–94) and *Jewish War* (75–79) in 6 books. In Book XVIII of the former is found the celebrated reference to Jesus Christ ("A wise man, if indeed one should call him a man") which is generally acknowledged as authentic. The latter is an eyewitness account of and a valuable historical source for the events of 93–94 and the reign of Herod Agrippa II.

Josquin de Prez (c. 1440–1521) French composer, considered among the greatest of all time. He composed about 100 motets and 20 masses. His works mark the transition from Early Renaissance to High Renaissance. Among his supremely moving works are *Pange Lingua**, *Malheur me bat*, and *Miserere Mei, Deus*.

Jovinian (d. c. 405) Controversialist. He was a Roman monk and author of *Commentarioli* which is not extant but which has been reconstructed from Jerome's refutation, *Adversus Jovinianum* (392). He held several controversial opinions, especially that virginity is not more blessed than marriage, that fasting is not more blessed than eating with thanksgiving, that heavenly rewards are not based on status in life, and that Mary's virginity was not perpetual. He was condemned by two synods at Rome* (390) and Milan* (391).

Joyful Mysteries of the Rosary, Five The first chaplet* of the Rosary* consisting of the Annunciation, the Visit of the Virgin Mary* to Elizabeth, Nativity, Presentation in the Temple, and Finding of the Boy Jesus in the Temple.

Joys of Mary Events in the life of the Virgin Mary*, varying in number from 5 to 12, usually including the annunciation, visitation, nativity, epiphany, finding Jesus in the temple, resurrection, and ascension.

Juana Ines de la Cruz (1651–1695) Mexican nun and poet.

jube Rood* loft dividing the nave* of a church from the choir, so named from the first words of the prayer, "jube, domine, benedicere," uttered by the deacon standing in the rood loft before the reading of the Gospel.

jubilate (Lat., be joyful) The first word of Psalm 100 used as an alternative to the Benedictus* at morning prayer in the *Book of Common Prayer*.

Jubilee 1. In the Mosaic tradition, year that occurred after seven sabbatical years, that is after 49 years, when Jewish slaves regained their freedom and when certain types of debts were forgiven. 2. In the Roman Catholic Church, the Holy Year or year of remission when a special indulgence is granted to Catholics who visit Rome*. See also HOLY YEAR.

Jud, Leo (1482–1542) Swiss reformer who helped to translate the Zurich Bible. As an ardent Zwinglian, he was an iconoclast who worked to remove images from churches and to suppress monasteries. He also helped Zwingli* put down the Anabaptists*. He introduced a baptismal liturgy (1523), wrote a Protestant catechism* (1538), and translated into German the works of Erasmus*, Thomas à Kempis*, and Augustine*.

Judaizers Early Christians, especially in Jerusalem*, who believed that Christians must keep the Mosaic Law by performing all the rites of Judaism, such as circumcision and the prohibition of certain types of meat. St. Paul* was instrumental in their condemnation.

Jude, St. (first century) Apostle* and martyr*. He is usually identified with Thaddaeus* and Jude, the brother of James. Little is known of his life after Pentecost*, but he is believed to have been martyred in Persia. In art, his usual emblem is a club, the instrument of his death. In modern times he has acquired considerable popularity as a patron of "hopeless cases." Feast day: June 19 (Eastern Church*); October 28 (Western Church*).

judgment Act or process by which God metes out reward or punishment to individuals on the basis of their beliefs and actions in life. Some theologians speak of four divine judgments: judgment of saints*, designed to reward the saints for their faithfulness; the judgment of Israel; the judgment of nations; and the great white throne judgment.

Judica Sunday Fifth Sunday in Lent*, or Passion Sunday*, so called from the introit* based on Psalm 43:1.

Judson, Adoniram (1788–1850) American Congregational-Baptist missionary to Burma. He first went to Rangoon in 1813 and began the first translation of the Bible into Burmese. In 1829 he transferred the seat of his mission to Moulmein. His work among the Karens met with great success. From 1842 to 1849 he worked on a Burmese dictionary. Broken in health, he was returning home when he died at sea.

Julian (sixth century) First known missionary to Nubia*. He was a Monophysite priest from Constantinople* who evangelized Nubia (542–544) with the support of Empress Theodora* and was accompanied by an Egyptian bishop named Theodore.

Julian calendar See OLD CALENDAR.

Julian of Halicarnassus (d. c. 527) Monophysite bishop who was exiled along with Severus* of Antioch* on the accession of Emperor Justin in 518. He held that Christ's body was immune from corruption before and after the Resurrection.

Julian of Norwich (c. 1342–c. 1416) English mystic. She was an anchoress who lived a solitary life in a cell in the Norman church of St. Julian in Norwich. A series of 16 revelations or showings in 1373 gave rise to her work, *Revelations of Divine Love,* which was a masterpiece of devotional literature. The theme of her work was God's love, often expressed in but triumphant over pain. The work had a lasting influence on contemplative life*, equalled only by *The Cloud of Unknowing.* Feast day: May 8 (Anglican Church).

Julian the Apostate (c. 331–363) Birth name: Flavius Claudius Julianus. Roman emperor who tried to restore paganism and to reverse the Christianization of the empire. A cousin of Constantius, he was originally a Christian by conviction who was converted to paganism by his teachers, Libanius the philosopher and Maximus of Ephesus*, who taught him the glories of the classical world. He was proclaimed Augustus by his troops in 360 and acknowledged as Caesar on the death of Constantius in 361. Immediately he set about restoring the old religions, displacing Christianity. He issued an edict of universal toleration, and ordered the revival of old cults, reopened the temples, ordered paganism to be taught in all imperial schools, and revived the sacrifices to the gods. He also tried to rebuild Herod's Temple in Jerusalem*.

Toward the end of his three-year reign he began persecuting Christians, but before he did the church more harm, he was killed by an arrow during his Persian campaign. According to legend, he died with the words, "vicisti Galilaee" (thou hast conquered, [pale] Galilean). Julian also wrote extensively, among them a set of eight orations, 80 letters, some epigrams, and a treatise called *Adversus Christianos.*

Juliana of Liege, Blessed (c. 1192–1258) Champion of the Feast of Corpus Christi*. In 1230 she became superior* of the Augustinian convent of Mont Cornillon, near Liege. As a result of her efforts, Pope Urban IV instituted the Feast of Corpus Christi in 1264. Feast day: April 5.

Julius I, St. (d. 352) Pope from 337. He was a supporter of Athanasius* against the Arians and convoked the Synod of Sardica in 342. Two churches in Rome* were built during his pontificate*: the Church of the Twelve Apostles and St. Maria in Trastevere.

Julius II (1443–1513) Pope from 1503. Birth name: Giuliano della Rovere A warlike pope, his pontificate* was spent mostly in military conflicts. However, he was an important patron of Renaissance art. Among the many immortal works that his generosity inspired are the frescoes of Raphael* and the paintings of Michelangelo* in the Sistine Chapel*. In 1506 he laid the cornerstone of the Basilica of St. Peter.

Pope Julius II

Julius III (1487–1555) Pope from 1550. Birth name: Giovanni Maria Ciocchi del Monte. During his pontificate*, he did much for the Jesuits*. He was a patron of the arts, particularly of Michelangelo*.

Julius Africanus, Sextus (c. 180–c. 250) Christian African writer. He served in many secular roles, particularly as an emissary from Emmaus to the imperial court and as a planner for a new public library at the Pantheon at Rome*. His chief work was the *History of the World* to 217 in five books. His *Embroidered Girdles* was an encyclopedia in 24 books of natural history, medicine, military science, and magic. Only fragments of these works survive.

Jumieges Benedictine abbey on the lower Seine, west of Rouen*. It was founded about 654 by St. Philibert*. In 841 it was plundered by the Normans and completely destroyed. Later, it was restored and, through the patronage of William the Conqueror, it became the richest monastery in Normandy. It was again destroyed by the Huguenots* in 1562, rebuilt in 1573, but finally ruined by 1790. It is now a national historical monument.

Jumpers Epithet of Welsh Calvinistic Methodists or American Shakers* who jumped for joy during religious services.

Jung Codex Codex I of the Nag Hammadi* Papyri, once in the possession of the Jung Institute at Zurich* but now returned to Cairo with the rest.

Junius Bassus (d. 359) Prefect of Rome and one of the first members of a Roman patrician family to become a Christian. His sarcophagus is a major work of early Christian sculpture.

juramentado Muslim Moro in the Philippines who swear to kill Christians to gain merit* before Allah.

Jurieu, Pierre (1637–1713) Calvinist apologist. In 1674 he became professor of philosophy and Hebrew at Sedan. On the suppression of the Academy at Sedan, he became minister at the Walloon church in Rotterdam where he became a confidant of William of Orange and an influential leader of the French refugee community. He was a tireless in his opposition to Roman Catholicism* and defense of the persecuted French Calvinists. Among his published works are *Traite de la Devotion* (1675), *Traite de la Puissance de l'Eglise* (1677), and *L'Accomplissement des Propheties* (1686).

justification (Gk., *dikaiosis*) Gracious and judicial act of God by which he grants the sinner full pardon* of all guilt, release from the penalties of sin, and acceptance as a child of God. It is a Pauline* concept that a sinner is declared righteous or made righteous by God through faith in Christ. The substantive, "justification," occurs only in Romans 4:25 and 5:18 but the verb, "to justify," ap-

pears 27 times in Paul's Epistles. In biblical understanding, a justified person is one who is approved of and is acceptable to God. Righteousness may be imputed, a process by which Christ's righteousness becomes transferred or imparted to the sinner and the sinner is transformed through the Holy Spirit* into a righteous person.

Justin Martyr, St. (c. 100–c. 165) Christian apologist. He was converted from paganism to Christianity about 130. He continued teaching philosophy as a Christian, first at Ephesus*, where he engaged in dispute with Trypho the Jew, and then at Rome*, where he opened one of the first Christian schools* with Tatian* as one of his pupils. In addition to a record of his *Dialogue with Trypho*, he issued two apologies, the first addressed to Emperor Antoninus Pius and his sons and the second addressed to the Roman Senate. He and some of his disciples were denounced by the pagans, scourged, and beheaded on imperial orders. He rebutted the pagan charges of atheism, sedition, and immorality, taught that the Incarnate Word had the power to transform men and women and redeem* them from demons, demonstrated the fulfillment of Old Testament prophecies in Christ, developed the role of the preincarnate Logos (word in reason) in Greek philosophy, and explained the significance of

St. Justin Martyr

baptism* and the Eucharist*. Feast day: June 1.

Justinian I (483–565) Roman Byzantine* emperor. He unified the Roman Empire by codifying its law and issuing the *Corpus Juris Civilis* as its legal code. He, along with his empress, Theodora*, was active in church affairs. He called the Second Council of Constantinople* to settle the Monophysite controversy. A champion of Nicene orthodoxy, he persecuted Arians and Montanists*, closed the pagan schools of philosophy at Athens*, and forced pagans to accept Christian baptism*. He was a great builder and built many basilicas*, including the grandest of all, the Hagia Sophia*, and the Cathedral of Ravenna.

Justinian I

Justinian, Code of Legal code of the Roman Empire, *Corpus Juris Civilis,* drawn up and published by Emperor Justinian* in 529. It was based on the Theodosian Code. It consists of three parts: *Novella, Digest,* and *Institutes.* Together, they became the authority and basis of Roman law which, at one time, extended over all of civilized Europe and had a profound influence on canon law* as well as modern national codes in Western Europe.

Justus of Ghent (c. 1430–c. 1480) Flemish religious painter, noted for the *Adoration of the Magi,* the *Crucifxion,* and other works.

Juvenaly of Alaska, St. (d. 1796) Eastern Orthodox* protomartyr* and patron saint* of America. A monk from Valaam monastery, he joined the Russian Orthodox mission to Alaska and was killed by the Yupik Eskimos. Feast day: July 2.

Juvencus, Caius Vettius Aquilinus (fourth century) Christian Latin poet, author of 3,200-line hexameter verse, modeled on Virgil, on the life of Christ, called *Historiae Evangelicae Libri IV.*

Kk

kaba In the Ethiopian Church*, the principal eucharistic vestment, a hooded cloak resembling a chasuble*, that reaches down to the feet and is secured at the neck. It is highly ornamented with gold and silver balls.

kachico In the Syrian Church, a priest.

kadishat aloho In the Maronite Church, the Trisagion* which is recited three times.

Käehler, Martin (1835–1912) Lutheran theologian, professor of systematic theology and New Testament at Halle from 1879. His chief work was *Die Wissenschaft der Christlichen Lehre* (1883) on the theme of justification* and its dogmatic significance. He is best known for his attack on the quest for the historical Jesus* in his *Der Sogenannte Historische Jesus und der Geschichtliche Biblische Christus* (1892) in which he drew the distinction between the historical Jesus as reconstructed by historical criticism and the historic, biblical Christ who is experienced by believers.

kafila In the Assyrian Church*, a hoodless cope* that is not joined at the front.

Kagawa, Toyohiko (1888–1960) Japanese Christian leader, reformer, pacifist, and poet. He founded the first labor union and the first peasant union in 1921 in Japan and the kingdom of God* movement in 1930. An illegitimate son of a wealthy cabinet minister and a geisha, he was converted at the age of 15 and thereupon was disinherited by his family. He dedicated his life to the poor, living in the slums. In 1923 he organized relief work after the Yokohama earthquake and in 1928 founded the National Anti-War League. Among his many books were *Before the Dawn* (1925), *Christ and Japan* (1934), and *Love, the Law of Life* (1930).

kahana 1. In the Armenian Church*, a priest who is obliged to fast rigorously and is required to be celibate for three days prior to the celebration of the liturgy. 2. **kahuna.** In the Assyrian Church*, a married priest. 3. **kahenat.** In the Ethiopian church, the clergy.

kahanyapet In the Armenian Church*, the archpriest.

kahnutha In the Assyrian Church*, the priesthood including the three orders.

kairos (Gk., occasion, right) The opportune moment when the divine or the eternal intervenes in human history, or when prophecies are fulfilled, as at the time of the Incarnation*.

Kairos Document Declaration against apartheid signed in September 1985 by 152 theologians and lay people. It affirmed that kairos* or the critical time had come for the church to confess its failure to oppose racial segregation.

Kaiserswerth Rhineland town where Theodore

Fliedner founded an institution in 1836 to train deaconesses, as part of the Innere Mission*. The deaconesses serve as nurses and social and educational workers throughout Germany and in many parts of the world.

kalasiris In the Byzantine Rite*, a cassock*.

kallosa In the Syrian Church, clerical headwear, similar to the kamelavchion*.

kalogeros In the Byzantine tradition, a monk, especially of Mount Athos*.

kaluto In the Jacobite Rite, vessels, generally made of silver, in which the holy chrism* is kept in the north apse*.

kalyba In the Byzantine tradition, an isolated monastic dwelling inhabited by only one or two monks.

kalymmata In the Byzantine Rite*, the veils covering the eucharistic vessels, especially the proton kalymma that covers the paten*, the deuteron kalymma that covers the chalice*, and the aer* or nephele that covers both the paten and the chalice.

Kam, Joseph (1769–1833) Dutch missionary to the East Indies, known as the apostle of the Moluccas. In 1813 he and a few friends were sent to the Java as the first missionaries to the Netherlands Indies. As pastor of a large indigenous church in the Moluccas, he labored to spread the gospel in the eastern archipelago, devoting much attention to the training of preachers, the printing and distribution of Bibles, the building of churches, and promotion of church music. Based in Ambon, he traveled extensively, covering thousands of miles by sea, partly in his self-built schooner.

kamasia In the Coptic Church*, a pair of richly ornamented cuffs fastening the sleeves of the priestly sticharion*.

kamelavchion Black cylindrical hat worn by monks and clergy in the Eastern Orthodox Church*. In the Greek Church, the hat has a projecting brim around the top. In the Russian Church, there is no brim but the diameter at the top is greater than that at the bottom.

Kamelavchion

kamision Long-sleeved ungirdled robe worn by Eastern Orthodox* acolytes*.

Kanamori, Tsurin ("Paul") (1857–1945) Japanese evangelist, known as the "Dwight L. Moody of Japan." Converted in 1875, he became a pastor of one of the largest congregations in Tokyo. In the early 1890s he lost his Evangelical convictions and demitted the ministry for 20 years. However, the death of his wife prompted him to resume his ministry. He became a traveling evangelist, preaching to over 300,000 people and converting some 50,000. His booklet in Japanese, *The Christian Belief,* had a wide circulation.

kanion In the Byzantine Rite*, a small glass or metal container with a sleevelike stopper at the end, used for sprinkling liquids.

kanuno In the Assyrian Rite, the audible conclusion to an inaudible prayer, the equivalent of the Greek ekphonesis*.

Kapellmeister (Ger., master of the chapel) Member of a group charged with conducting church musical services in a chapel attached to a royal or princely court.

kaphila Colored headgear worn by the Assyrian patriarch*.

kappa (Ge'ez) In the Ethiopian Orthodox Church*, originally a hooded outer vestment of rich material, divided down the front and clasped at the neck, worn by priests. Later the hood was discarded.

karasnorth In the Armenian tradition, the Great Lent*, lasting 48 days before Easter*.

karasoonk Obligatory 40-day fast required of a newly ordained Armenian priest.

karianjili In the Coptic Church*, a reader*.

Karlstadt, Andreas Rudolf Bodenstein von See CARL-STADT.

Karshuni Also, Garsuni. Arabic written in the Syriac* script. Diacritics are added to represent those consonants which occur in Arabic but not in Syriac.

karuzutha In the Jacobite tradition, litany* that is read on Sundays and some feasts during the recitation of which incensed vessels are placed on a table near the north wall of the sanctuary.

kas In the Jacobite Rite, the chalice*. It is called kasa in the Assyrian Church*.

Kasatkin, Nicolai Ivan Dmitriyevich (1836–1912) Russian Orthodox missionary to Japan. He was chaplain* to the Russian diplomatic mission in Hakodate from 1861. By 1871 when the Russian Orthodox Mission to Japan was formally established under his leadership, he had 12 baptized Christians and 25 catechumens*. His congregation grew to 1,000 by 1875; 5,000 by 1878; 28,000 by 1904; and 33,000 by the time of his death in 1912. Kasatkin celebrated the liturgy only in Japanese. In 1878 he was consecrated as bishop, and the mission was placed under the direct supervision of the Holy Synod*. See also NICOLAI.

kashkul (Syr., containing all) In the Assyrian Church*, a liturgical book that contains selected prayers and antiphons for the liturgical cycles.

kasis zayetrada'e In the Ethiopian Church*, prayer over the cross spoon, so called because its handle ends in a cross.

kasr Tower of a dair* or Coptic monastery.

kassis In the Coptic Church*, a priest. Known as kasha or kashisha in the Assyrian Church*.

kasyo In the Assyrian Church*, the fraction* of the consecrated bread.

katabasis (lit., a descent) In the Byzantine Rite*, a troparion* that follows the ode of a canon* on great feasts, generally sung by the choir in the middle of a church.

katameros Lectionary* used in the Coptic Rite.

katanyktikon Penitential troparion* in the Byzantine Rite*.

katanyxis (Gk., compunction) Repentance* followed by a sense of God's love and forgiveness.

katapetasma In the Greek and Coptic churches, the curtain that separates the apse* from the nave* or the veil of the holy doors*.

katathesis In the Byzantine Rite*, the act of depositing a relic* in the church.

kategoriares In the Greek Church, official who announces major feasts and festivals to the congregation.

kathegoumenos Abbot of a Byzantine idiorrhythmic* monastery.

kathisma 1. In the Eastern Orthodox Church*, each of the 20 sections into which the Byzantine psalter is divided. 2. Brief liturgical hymn sung during the orthros* at the end of each kathisma of the psalter.

kathschoumn In the Armenian Rite*, consecration of the bread and wine.

kathuliki In the Jacobite Rite, lengthy prayer of general intercession for all the faithful, both living and dead.

katzion Perfumed pan used in Byzantine funeral rites.

katzto In the Jacobite Rite, cover similar to the asterisk* that supports the veil over the paten*.

kawok Black silk turban worn as part of the outdoor dress of Jacobite secular priests.

kdam wadathar (lit., before and after) Assyrian liturgical book containing prayers and some extracts from the Psalter.

Keach, Benjamin (1640–1704) English hymn writer and Baptist preacher who introduced singing into Baptist churches. He published over 300 hymns and 42 complete works, including *Spiritual Melody* (1691).

Keble, John (1792–1866) Tractarian leader and hymn writer. In 1827 he published *The Christian Year,* which has influenced hymnology for many generations. Based on the *Book of Common Prayer*,* it includes such favorite hymns, as "Blessed Are the Pure in Heart," "New Every Morning," "Sun of My Soul," "There Is a Book," and "When God of Old." In 1833 he preached his Oxford Assize sermon on "National Apostasy," in which he denounced the liberal trends in the Anglican Church. This sermon is said to mark the beginning of the Oxford movement*.

With Newman*, Keble issued the *Tracts of the Times,* contributing eight of its issues. In 1836 he issued a critical edition of Hooker's *Works,* and two years later, with Newman and Pusey*, he became one of the editors of the Library of the Fathers* to which he contributed a translation of Irenaeus*. He took the High Church* position in his Tract No.89, "On the Mysticism Attributed to the Early Fathers of the Church," a defense of Alexandrian theology, and in his treatise, *On Eucharistical Adoration.* His poetical works include *Lyra Apostolica* (1836) and *Lyra Innocentium* (1846). In 1870 Keble College at Oxford was named in his memory.

Kebra Negast (Ge'ez, Glory of Kings) Masterpiece of Ge'ez* literature compiled by Yeshaq of Axum

in the early fourteenth century. It tells the story of Solomon and the queen of Sheba and Menelek, their son.

keddase (lit., sanctification) Liturgy of the Ethiopian Rite or the anaphora* used in the liturgy.

kedest Innermost sanctuary of an Ethiopian church.

kedush (lit., holy of holies) The inner sanctuary of an Assyrian church elevated on the east end and separated from the nave* by a curtain.

Keith, George (c. 1639–1716) Scottish Quaker* who founded an American branch of the Quakers called Christian Quakers. Later, he entered the Anglican ministry and became one of the first missionaries of the Society for the Propagation of the Gospel* in America.

Keith-Falconer, Ion Grant (1856–1887) British missionary and Arabicist. Born as the son of the eighth earl of Kintore, he was a Hebrew and Arabic scholar and an early bicycle champion. As a student at Cambridge, he helped found the Inter-Collegiate Christian Union in 1877. In 1885 he went as a missionary to Arabia. He and his young wife helped to found the Sheikh Othman Hospital in Aden but died of fever within a few months.

kellion/kellia In the Byzantine and Russian tradition, a single dwelling with a chapel inhabited by three to six monks. A skete* is served by several kellia grouped around a shared church.

Kelly, Thomas (1769–1854) Irish hymn writer. He was converted in 1792 and took holy orders*. He was engaged in Evangelical work for most of his life. He wrote over 765 hymns, of which the best known are "Look Ye Saints! The Sight Is Glorious," "The Head That Once Was Crowned with Thorns," and "We Sing the Praise of Him Who Died."

Kelly, William (1821–1906) Plymouth Brethren* leader. In 1841 he was converted to the Christian faith of the Plymouth Brethren. Beside editing two of their periodicals, *The Prospect* and the *Bible Treasury,* he wrote many devotional works and Bible commentaries and edited the works of J. N. Darby* in 34 volumes (1867–1883). When the Exclusive Brethren* broke up in 1879, Kelly led the more moderate faction.

Kelpius, Johann (1673–1708) Dutch mystic who founded the Colony of the Contented of the God-Loving Soul at Philadelphia* in 1694. Its members were celibate, looked forward to the imminent return of Christ, and practiced Christian communism.

Kemp, Johannes Theodorus van der (1747–1811) Pioneer Dutch missionary in South Africa. The drowning of his wife and only child in a boating accident in 1791 led to his conversion. He applied to the London Missionary Society and was ordained in 1797 for service in South Africa. Before leaving he also helped to found the Netherlands Missionary Society in Holland. From 1801 he worked among the Khoikhoi (Hottentot) people among whom he founded a mission station, Bethelsdorp, in 1803. He was opposed by the Dutch colonists, especially because of his marriage in 1807 to a teenage Malagasy slave girl. Nevertheless, toward the end of his life he won over many Xhosa and Khoikhoi.

Kempe, Margery (c. 1373–c. 1433) English mystic. In 1413 she and her husband took vows of chastity* and went on a pilgrimage* to the Holy Land* and Compostela*. She described her travels and mystical experiences in *The Book of Margery Kempe,* a devotional classic.

Kempener, Pieter de (c. 1503–1580) Flemish religious painter, noted for his *Descent from the Cross.*

Kempis, Thomas à See THOMAS À KEMPIS.

Ken, Thomas (1637–1711) English hymn writer and bishop of Bath and Wells*. Among his hymns, the best-loved are "Glory to Thee, My God, This Night," "Praise God from Whom All Blessings Flow," and "Awake, My Soul and with the Sun." He declined to take the oath of allegiance to William

and Mary and was deprived of his see*. He is the author of *The Practice of Divine Love* (1685).

Kendrick, Graham Born in Northamptonshire, England, in 1950, the son of a Baptist pastor, he was trained as a teacher but emerged as a singer-songwriter in 1972. His best-known song, "Shine, Jesus, Shine" (1987), became the most popular English contemporary worship song, and has been often featured on the BBC's "Songs of Praise." He received a Dove Award from the Gospel Music Association in 1995. Kendrick, who lives in South London with his wife and four daughters, is a member of the Ichthus Christian Fellowship and a cofounder of "March for Jesus" —a prayer, praise, and proclamation event shared by over 12 million people from 177 nations worldwide on June 25, 1994. His music ranges from prayer songs used in liturgical settings to the exuberance of African, Caribbean, and Latin rhythms. His Christ-centered themes of compassion and justice are popular interdenominationally: "What I would like to see is the best of the old and the best of the new used side by side."

kene mahelet Passage that separates the two inner circular divisions of an Ethiopian church, reserved for the use of a choir.

kenfo In the Jacobite Church*, side altars.

Kennedy, Dennis James (1930–) Presbyterian pastor, political activist, and founder of the Coral Ridge Presbyterian Church in Fort Lauderdale, Florida. An authority on evangelism, Kennedy's methodology of church growth was produced as a program entitled Evangelism Explosion and became widely used by churches of various denominations. His national weekly broadcast, "The Coral Ridge Hour," is heard in over 3,500 cities and towns across America. His interest in the preservation and restoration of America's religious heritage led him to form the Center for Reclaiming America which advocates greater Christian involvement in public life. Kennedy also founded the Knox Presbyterian Seminary and the Westminster Academy.

kenosis (Gk., emptying) In the theology of the Incarnation*, doctrine that Jesus Christ emptied himself of, or surrendered voluntarily during his life on earth, all divine attributes, such as omnipotence, omniscience, and cosmic sovereignty in order to take on humanity (Phil. 2:7). It emphasizes the humanity of Christ. Thus, kenotic.

Kentigern, St. (d. 603) Also, Mungo. Celtic missionary to Wales and Scotland. St. Mungo's Cathedral in Glasgow, Scotland, is named after him. He is the patron saint* of the city Feast day: January 14.

Kenyon, Essek William (1867–1948) American evangelist. He began as an evangelist at a very early age and as an adjunct to his ministry founded the Dudley Bible Institute (later Providence Bible Institute) of which he was president for 25 years. In 1923 he founded the Figueroa Independent Baptist Church in Los Angeles, where he became a pioneer in radio evangelism through his "Kenyon's Church of the Air." He later devoted himself more fully to writing, publishing 16 books in his lifetime. His writings have had great impact on Deeper Life, Charismatic, Word of Faith, and Positive Confession* movements and have influenced such diverse people as David Nunn, T. L. Osborn*, Jimmy Swaggart*, Kenneth Hagin*, Kenneth Copeland*, Don Gossett, and Charles Capps.

Kenyon, Sir Frederic George (1863–1952) British New Testament scholar. He was director and principal librarian of the British Museum from 1909 to 1930. He added much to our knowledge of the Greek Bible though his publications, including *Our Bible and the Ancient Manuscripts* (1895), *The Text of the Greek Bible* (1937), *The Bible and Archaeology* (1940), and *The Bible and Modern Scholarship* (1948).

Keratea Monasteries, convents, and sketes* in the Keratea region in northern Greece of which the most important is the Skepi Monastery, founded in 1950.

kerion In the Byzantine tradition, a candlestick designed to hold several candlesticks. Also, keropegia.

keromastikos Paste that cements the table of an altar to its support at the time of its consecration. It contains dust from relics*.

kerostates In the Byzantine Church*, large and usually ornate candlestick on either side of the royal doors* of an iconostasis*.

keryana In the Assyrian Rite, books of the Old Testament and the Acts of the Apostles from which lessons are read during worship service.

kerygma (Gk., preached message) Proclamation of the gospel of Jesus Christ, as distinguished from didache* or teaching. The historical element in kerygma deals with the Incarnation*, death, and Resurrection of Jesus Christ. For the Fathers of the early church, kerygma meant the totality of the mystery of Christ, as preached by the apostles. The seal of kerygma is baptism*.

kerygmatic theology Branch or type of theology focused centrally on the apostolic kerygma*, the core New Testament preaching about Christ.

kerytho In the Jacobite Rite, the epiclesis* which is recited aloud while the priest flutters his right hand over the bread and the chalice*.

kesela Collar-like garment worn by Ethiopian priests.

keshotz In the Armenian tradition, liturgical fans* to which little bells are attached.

Keswick Convention Annual summer convention of Evangelicals* at Keswick in the English Lake district, founded in 1875 through the efforts of the vicar* of Keswick, Canon Harford-Battersby, following the Moody-Sankey revival. Harford-Battersby himself had been influenced by W. E. Boardman, author of *The Higher Christian Life* (1859); Robert Pearsall Smith, author of *Holiness Through Faith* (1870); and his wife Hannah Whitall Smith*, author of *The Christian's Secret of a Happy Life* (1875). With "All One in Christ Jesus" as its motto, Keswick's keynotes are prayer, deeper Christian life, Bible study, invocation of the Holy Spirit*, zeal for foreign missions, and personal holiness*. Similar Keswick conferences are held annually in the United States and Canada.

Keswick also denotes a theological system. It rejects the possibility of sinless perfection* but emphasizes a normative Christian life characterized by fullness of the Holy Spirit*. Such a fullness is received through a definite act of faith* distinct from but associated with regeneration*. It provides for victory over temptation and sin but does not eradicate the tendency to sin. Among those on whom Keswick left a lasting impress were A. B. Simpson*, R. A. Torrey*, and H. A. Ironside*. Keswick's distinctive emphasis on "Let Go and Let God" has been muted in recent years.

kethons In the Jacobite Rite, cloth covering the altar stone, generally heavily embroidered.

Kevin, Mother (1875–1957) Birth name: Teresa Kearney. Founder of the Franciscan Missionary Sisters for Africa. In 1892, as a member of the Franciscan Convent at St. Mary's Abbey, London, she volunteered to go to Uganda as a medical missionary. In 1923, at Nsambaya, she founded the Congregation of the Little Sisters of St. Francis, a community of African nuns for teaching and nursing. She was instrumental in securing a repeal of the church's ban on priests and nuns practicing maternity nursing, medicine, and surgery. In 1952 the Franciscan Missionary Sisters for Africa was established as a separate missionary order.

Key, Francis Scott (1780–1843) Author of "Star Spangled Banner," the U.S. national anthem, and Sunday school* leader. He was one of the founders of the American Sunday School Union* in 1824. He served on its board and presided over the 1830 meeting that launched the Mississippi Valley campaign which took 50 years to complete and which led to the creation of 61,297 Sunday schools.

keys, crossed Symbol of St. Peter*, as the holder of the power of the keys.

keys of the kingdom In Roman Catholic theology, authority granted by Jesus Christ to Peter* as the rock on which he will build his church, based on Matthew 16:19.

keys, office of the Authority to bind and loose and retain or remit sins, granted by Jesus Christ to his representatives and apostles.

khaghordouthiun In the Armenian Church*, the Holy Communion*.

khasvo Title meaning "venerable*" applied to Maronite bishops.

khatchkar Monumental stone crosses found throughout medieval Armenia. They were used as boundary markers, gravestones, monuments, and foundation markers of churches. They were notable for their geometrical and botanical patterns.

khavatamch In the Armenian Liturgy, the creed including the anathemas of Nicaea*.

khazranion Straight ebony walking stick used by Greek clergy.

kherniboxeston In the Byzantine Rite*, basin and bowl offered to a priest or bishop for washing of hands.

khitoniskos In the Byzantine Rite*, the sticharion*.

Khlysts (Russ., flagellants) Seventeenth century Christian ascetics who flogged themselves in ecstasy*. Their leaders were usually called Christ and Mother of God.

khnana In the Assyrian Church*, a relic* from the shrine of the tombs of martyrs*, used in wedding rites.

Khomyakov, Aleksei Stepanovich (1804–1860) Russian theologian. A Slavophile, he believed that Slavs presented an alternative to the decadent and materialist Western civilization and that the Or-

Charge to Peter

thodox Church presented an equally viable alternative to the Roman Catholic and Protestant churches. He emphasized that the unique feature of Orthodoxy was sobornost*, defined as the organic unity of believers with Christ as the head and the Holy Spirit* as the soul. His ideas have exercised considerable influence on twentieth-century Orthodox theology.

khoneuterion In the Byzantine tradition, drain into which water left from baptism*, ablutions*, and ashes from palm leaves may be poured.

khoran Altar in an Armenian church set into a screen* positioned across the apse* with a door on either side.

khorug In the Byzantine Church*, holy banner* or picture mounted on a staff.

khubz moubarak (Arab.) Blessed bread.

khudoto Feast of dedication of a Maronite church.

khudra (lit., the cycle) In the Assyrian Church*, three volumes containing the parts of the liturgy and daily offices proper to Sundays and major feasts and saints' days.

khuthama In the Syriac Rite, a liturgical prayer, especially the final blessings pronounced at the dismissal* of the faithful at the end of the service.

kiborion In the Byzantine Church*, a dome or canopy supported on four pillars forming a roof over a canopy.

kidan In the Ethiopian Rite, the Testament from which lessons are read.

Kierkegaard, Soren Aabye (1813–1855) Danish existentialist philosopher. Melancholy and brooding, Kierkegaard was not a formal theologian, yet few have been more influential on the course of modern theology. His writings attacked both the rationalistic Hegelianism of the academic philosophers and the arid and lifeless Christianity of the established churches.

At the core of his writings is the belief that there is a yawning gulf between time and eternity*, the immanent and the transcendent, the finite and the infinite, the creature and the Creator. There is no bridge between the two, because God is wholly other. This gulf was bridged once and for all by Christ's Incarnation*, but Christ came incognito and he remains hidden except through the eyes of faith*. Without faith neither knowl-

Soren Kierkegaard

edge nor works can lead to Christ. A leap of faith is required of a believer to cross the gulf into a new kingdom, and the temporal life is only an occasion for the finite to grasp the infinite.

Kierkegaard's ideas are sometimes ascetical, and he was among the first to introduce psychological concepts into theology. His oft-repeated statement that "truth is subjectivity" illustrated his opposition to reason and emphasized the relation of the individual to God to the exclusion of the idea of a Christian community.

Kierkegaard's writings, translated into most major languages, fall into two periods. His first period, when he used a number of pseudonyms, includes *Either-Or* (1843), *Fear and Trembling* (1843), *The Concept of Dread* (1844), *Stages on Life's Way* (1844), *Philosophical Fragments* (1844), and *Concluding Unscientific Postscript to the Philosophical Fragments* (1846). His second phase produced more direct Christian books, including *Works of Love* (1847), *Christian Discourses* (1848), *Sickness unto Death* (1849), and *Training in Christianity* (1850).

Kiev Birthplace of the Russian Orthodox Church* and capital of the Ukraine*. It is the location of the famous Kievo Pechyorska Lavra, the Cave Monastery. It is Russia's oldest monastery and has close ties to Mount Athos*. It was founded about 1050 by a Varangian Russian from Lyubetch by the name of Antonii Feodosii, who had been a monk at Athos. The monastery complex covers a total of 54 acres and is located on the left bank of the River Dnieper. The main church, the Cathedral of the Dormition, built between 1073 and 1078, was dynamited by the German army in 1941. In 1108 the Church of the Gate of the Trinity was added. It was followed by the Hospice Church of St. Nicholas* (1615), All Saints Church, the Church of the Birth of Virgin Mary

The Cave Monastery

(seventeenth century), and the Church of the Raising of the Cross (eighteenth century). The Hagia Sophia*, built in 1040, had 13 cupolas symbolizing Christ and the 12 apostles.

Kijne, Izaak Samuel (1899–1970) Dutch missionary, father of the Evangelical Christian Church in Irian Jaya. He went to New Guinea in 1923 and founded a school for teacher-preachers. After internment by the Japanese during World War II, he became the leader of Dutch mission work in New Guinea and rector of the theological school in Serui. He was a gifted musician and composed five books of hymns. He also wrote the church order*, liturgy, and catechism* for the growing church.

Kilham, Alexander (1762–1798) English founder of the Methodist New Connexion*. He became an itinerant preacher in 1785. He took a leading part in the controversies that followed the death of Wesley* about the relation of Methodism* to the Church of England*. Kilham favored lay representation in church government and opposed the appointment of bishops. For proposing total separation from the Church of England, he was expelled in 1796 and thereupon formed the Methodist New Connexion.

Kilian (c. 640–689) Irish apostle of Franconia. With 11 companions, and with papal approval, he evangelized Franconia and Thuringia with his base at Wurtzburg. At Neumunster he was murdered by the wife of Duke Gozbert, and his relics* were transferred to the cathedral.

Kimbangu, Simon (c. 1889–1951) African church founder of Kimbanguism. Baptized at the age of 26, he was a catechist* when he received a calling* to a healing ministry which attracted huge crowds. Opposed by the Baptists* and the Roman Catholics because of his unorthodox practices, he was arrested, tried on a charge of sedition, and sentenced to death, but the sentence was later commuted to life imprisonment. His death in prison in 1951 and the later persecution of his followers led to a vast cult* being formed around him. A legal church was established by Simon's son, Joseph Diangienda, under the name Eglise de Jesus-Christ sur la Terre par le Prophete Simon Kimbangu. Its ritual center is in Nkamba in Congo. It claims millions of members and has been admitted to the World Council of Churches*.

kimesis/Koimesis In the Byzantine Rite*, the dormition*, or falling asleep, of the Virgin Mary*.

kind Of or relating to one of the elements in the Holy Communion*, as in under one kind.

King James Version Title used, especially in the United States, for the Authorized Version* of the Bible prepared under James I of England. It contained the translation of the Bible prepared by a conference of English divines, known as the Hampton Court Conference, over which King

James I presided. The conference appointed 50 revisers who sat in six groups, two at Oxford, two at Cambridge, and two at Westminster. The translation bears the influence of earlier editions, especially, the Douai*, Geneva*, Bishops'*, and Tyndale's*. The work began in 1607 and took two years and nine months. It was published in 1611. Although it was never officially authorized (despite its title), the words, "appointed to be read in churches," appear on the title page. Its evocative cadences and rhythmic prose have influenced generations of Christians. Originally it contained the Apocrypha*, but these are omitted in modern versions.

King, Martin Luther, Jr. (1929–1968) African-American civil rights leader. In 1954 he became pastor of the Dexter Avenue Baptist Church, Montgomery, Alabama, and copastor with his father of the Ebenezer Baptist Church, Atlanta. He rose to international prominence as the leader of the nonviolent civil rights movement beginning with the Montgomery bus boycott in 1956. In 1963 he led a massive march on Washington and delivered a stirring address with the motif, "I have a dream." As the driving spirit behind the Southern Christian Leadership Conference*, he inspired the pas-

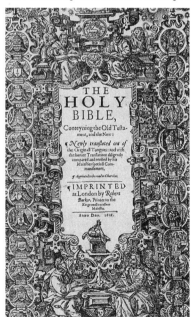

King James Authorized Version

sage of the Civil Rights Acts of 1964–1965. He received the Nobel Peace Prize in 1964. Four years later, he was gunned down by a white racist in Memphis, Tennessee. His birthday is observed as a national holiday in the United States.

kingdom of God Dominion of Christ as distinct from the kingdoms of the world. Augustine* defined it as the city of God, ruled by a different set of laws than the city of man. Paul* defined it as "peace and joy in the Holy Spirit" (Rom. 14:17; 1 Cor. 4:20; Col. 1:13). Since "flesh and blood cannot inherit the kingdom of God" (1 Cor. 15:50; 6:9–10, Gal. 5:21; Eph. 5:5; Col. 4:11; 1 Thess. 2:12; 2 Thess. 1:5; 2 Tim. 4:1, 18), the kingdom of God is a spiritual realm. The kingdom of God is eschatological, i.e., it is a future kingdom, but at the same time it is a present reality. It is also a messianic kingdom in which Christ is *autobasileia,* the kingdom of God in person.

Kingdomtide Season of the Christian year*, beginning with the Festival of Christ the King* on the last Sunday of August and concluding with Thanksgiving Sunday.

King's Confession Protestant confession of faith signed by King James VI of Scotland in 1581. It was drawn up by John Craig* in 1581 under the title, "A Short and General Confession of the True Christian faith and religion according to God's Word and Acts of our Parliaments." Reaffirmed in 1590 and 1595, it formed the basis of the National Covenant of 1638.

kingship of Christ Designation of Jesus Christ as the sovereign of the kingdom of God*. The title affirms his position as the messianic king and redeemer to whom all living things are subject, and in the Reformed* tradition, especially in the phrase often used in ordination services, the "King and Head of the Church." It confesses Christ's supreme authority over his body the church. This is sometimes expressed as the "crown rights of the redeemer."

Kingsley, Charles (1819–1875) English novelist and Christian socialist. Ordained in 1842, he served from 1844 as the vicar* of Eversley, Hants, England. For six years from 1860 to 1869 he was professor of modern history at Cambridge and was also active in the Educational League. He became pamphleteer of the Christian Socialist Movement, which promoted reform in education, health, and manufacturing. He coined the term *muscular Christianity* to suggest a liberal and social gospel*, opposed to all forms of asceticism* and celibacy.

Kino, Eusebio Francisco (1644–1711) Jesuit missionary in Mexico and the American southwest. Born with the family surname of Chino in Tyrol, Italy, he changed his name to Kino on arrival in Mexico in 1681. Assigned to Baja, California, he became apostle to the Pimas. His achievements during the first decade included the founding of many missions and at least 14 expeditions as far as the Colorado River. From 1698 to 1711 he was in Mexico, where he founded nine mission stations*. Kino was a versatile person—missionary, writer, cosmographer, explorer, colonizer, and friend of the Indians. His statue, representing the state of Arizona, is found in the National Hall of Statuary in Washington, D.C.

Kirchenordnung Church order, especially as produced in the sixteenth-century Reformation*.

Kirchentag (Ger., church day) Series of mass Whitsun rallies or festivals of especially the lay membership of German churches held biennially since 1945 and founded by Reinhold von Thadda Triegleff. The Catholic church similarly holds a Katholikentag every other year.

kirk In Scotland, a church. Also, Auld Kirk, the national Church of Scotland*.

kirkman In Scotland, a member of the Church of Scotland*.

kirk-session In Scotland, the corporate body of elders comprising the minister (teaching elder) and ruling elders which governs the congregation's life.

kisarkavag Subdeacon in the Armenian Church*.

kiss of peace Salutation as a token of Christian brotherhood (also known as the holy kiss* in the New Testament (Rom. 16:16; 1 Cor. 16:20; 1 Thess. 5:26; 1 Pet. 5:14). It was mentioned by Justin Martyr* and other Church Fathers* as a greeting, but later it was incorporated into the eucharistic liturgy and was practiced in the Western Church* until the thirteenth century. Originally an actual kiss, it has been modified over the centuries. Sometimes, in lieu of a kiss, each believer places his or her hands on the other's shoulders and then bows. See also PAX/PAX BREDE.

kitab il pasca Coptic Psalter used during Paschal* offices.

KJV King James Version* of the Bible.

klam In the Coptic tradition, a miter* worn by bishops and patriarchs*, generally low and globular, made of silver or velvet embroidered with gold and jewels.

kliros In the Byzantine Church*, parts of the ambo* reserved for the use of the choir.

klitos One of the aisles of a Byzantine Church*.

klobouk In the Byzantine tradition, the veil fastened to a koukoulion, a thimble-shaped cap that serves as a monastic cowl*.

Klopstock, Friedrich Gottlieb (1724–1803) German poet who wrote the first modern epic in German, *Der Messias,* a poem of nearly 20,000 lines in 20 cantos celebrating the Passion and the Resurrection.

Klosterneuburg Celebrated Augustinian monastery near Vienna* founded some time before 1108 by the Margrave Leopold III*. It possesses rich art treasures, including the Verdun Altar as well as a large library of priceless manuscripts. The monastery buildings are built in the Austrian Baroque style.

kneeling Posture of prayer during worship service. Standing and sitting are the normal postures, but kneeling is adopted during certain penitential devotions.

Knights Hospitallers Groups of men and women

who have taken religious vows to care for the sick and the infirm. By the twelfth century there were hospices for the poor and destitute, insane and permanently disabled, most of them in the charge of religious orders. Monasteries sometimes served as hospitals, following Austin*, Benedictine*, and Franciscan rules. Certain orders consisting of laypersons, clerks* in minor orders*, and religious, developed into Knights Hospitallers. During the eleventh and twelfth centuries, such orders grew in numbers and influence. They included the Antonines, Order of the Holy Spirit, Order of St. William of the Desert, Bethlehemites*, Order of St. Catherine*, Beguines*, and Beghards*. Hospitallers also served leper communities, which did not disappear from Europe until 1500.

Knights Hospitallers of St. John of Jerusalem Knights Hospitallers, known after 1310 as the Knights of Rhodes and after 1530 as the Knights of Malta*. The order originated in Jerusalem* in the Benedictine abbey of St. Maria Latina. In addition to the three religious vows, they took a fourth—to be slaves and servants of the sick. They were divided into three classes: knights, sergeants, and priests. Initially founded to care for pilgrims and crusaders in the Holy Land*, it subsequently established and managed hundreds of hospitals and hospices throughout Europe and the Levant. Their conquest of Rhodes in 1309 gave them great military power, which increased after the suppression of the Knights Templars in 1312. From 1530 to 1798 they were based in Malta, and they were relocated in the Malta Palace in Rome* in 1834.

Knights of Columbus Catholic fraternal order organized in the United States in 1882 by Michael J. McGivney. It is a patriotic and benevolent organization closely allied to the Roman Catholic Church.

Knights of Malta See KNIGHTS HOSPITALLERS OF ST. JOHN OF JERUSALEM.

Knights of the Holy Sepulcher Fraternal organization also known as the Equestrian Order of the Holy Sepulchre* of Jerusalem. The order admits both men and women in its various ranks. Membership is bestowed as an honor on influential Catholics who aid in the work of the church. The standard regalia of the confraternity* include a white cape and the red crusader cross of Jerusalem.

Knights Templars Military religious order, officially known as Poor Fellow-Soldiers of Christ and the Temple of Solomon, founded about 1118 by two French knights, Hugh de Payens and Godfrey of St. Omer. Its purpose was to aid and protect pilgrims on their way to the Holy Land*. Its members took the monastic vows of poverty, chastity*, and obedience. From the twelfth century, they expanded in scope and operations and became very wealthy. Their functions included the defense of the Latin states of Palestine. In 1128, at the Council of Troyes, Bernard of Clairvaux* prepared a rule for them under which they were allowed to wear a white mantle to which a red cross was later added. By the middle of the twelfth century, commanderies were established headed by a grandmaster of the temple of Jerusalem.

The knighthood was divided into four ranks: Knights permanent, sergeants consisting of the wealthy burghers, squires, and chaplains*. The Templars grew wealthy from royal bequests, and for a time they functioned as bankers. But with the fall of Jerusalem* in 1187 and the expulsion of all Christians from the Holy Land* after the fall of Acre* in 1291, the Templars lost their raison d'etre, but they continued as a secret organization, independent of secular authority. In 1307 Philip IV of France moved to confiscate their wealth. Pressured by Philip, Pope Clement V* issued a bull* in 1312 formally dissolving the order. Over 120 Templars were executed, and most of their wealth went to the Hospitallers* or other religious orders.

Knock/Cnoc Village in County Mayo, Ireland, the scene of an apparition of the Virgin Mary* along with St. Joseph* and St. John the Evangelist* in 1879. Miraculous cures are reported at the shrine constructed on this spot.

knop Bulbous part of the stem of a chalice* serving as a handle.

knoq (lit., the seal) In the Armenian tradition, the sign of the cross.

knowledge, word of One of the manifestations of the Holy Spirit*, that of knowing what God is doing at any given moment in another person's soul or body, or of knowing the secret of another's heart, so that one may reach out with the gifts of healing or consolation* (1 Cor. 12:7–10).

Knowles, David (1896–1974) Birth name: Michael Clive Knowles. Monastic historian. As professor of medieval and modern history as Cambridge, he wrote magisterial volumes on monasteries and monastic life, including the three-volume *Religious Orders in England (1948–1959), The Monastic Order in England, 943–1216 (1940), The English Mystical Tradition (1961),* and *From Pachomius to Ignatius: A Study in the Constitutional History of the Religious Orders* (1966).

Knox, John (c. 1513–1572) Scottish reformer. He was ordained in 1536 and shortly thereafter was converted to Protestantism*. His theological development owed much to John Rough and George Wishart*, and he appropriated Bucer's* doctrine of the Lord's Supper* and Luther's doctrine of justification*. As a preacher at Berwick he attacked the Mass* and kneeling during Communion as idolatrous practices. In 1551 he was made chaplain* to Edward VI and assisted in the final stages of the

John Knox

revision of the Second Prayer Book. On the accession of Mary to the throne, he was made a galley-slave but escaped and fled to the Continent, where he lived in Geneva*, Zurich*, and Frankfurt, meeting Calvin*, Bullinger*, and other Reformers. In 1558 he wrote a treatise against Mary entitled *The First Blast of the Trumpet Against the Monstrous Regiment of Women.* He returned to Scotland in 1559 and played a major role in drafting the Scots Confession*, which Parliament approved in 1560. He also drafted the *Book of Discipline** as a manual for the clergy of the Presbyterian Church and helped to draw up the *Book of Common Order**. His chief work is the *History of the Reformation of Religion within the Realm of Scotland,* which was published posthumously in 1587.

Knox, Ronald Arbuthnott (1888–1957) Catholic apologist and Bible translator. Son of the Anglican bishop E. A. Knox, a prominent Evangelical, he became one of the leading lights of Anglo-Catholicism* and an opponent of liberals and modernists in the Church of England*. He was received into the Roman Catholic Church in 1917, was ordained priest in 1919, taught at St.Edmund's College, Ware, and was Catholic chaplain* at Oxford from 1926 to 1939. In 1939 he resigned his position at Oxford to devote himself to a translation of the Bible. His books include an autobiography, *A Spritiual Aeneid* (1918), *On Englishing the Bible* (1949), and *Enthusiasm* (1950).

kobe Hood worn as part of the outdoor dress of an Ethiopian cleric.

koboro Drums used as an accompaniment to the Ethiopian chant.

kodi Girdle* worn by an Armenian priest.

kodon Cup-shaped bell used in Mount Athos*, struck three times with a hammer as the liturgy proper is about to start, at the end of the Great Entrance*, and during the Liturgy of the Presanctified*.

kogh 1. In the Armenian Liturgy, silk veil placed over the chalice* during the offertory. 2. Veil used to cover the head of the catholicos* during his consecration.

Koine (Gk., common) Common form of Greek in which the New Testament was written.

koinonia (Gk., fellowship) Sharing, communion, and fellowship as bonds of the Christian community. Its New Testament use does not make it a synonym of congregation or group of believers. It has been much developed in recent ecumenical theology.

koinonikon In the Byzantine Rite*, a troparion* resembling a Western communion anthem.

kokliarion In the Coptic Rite, the communion spoon.

Kolbe, St. Maximilian (1894–1941) Birth name: Raymond Kolbe. Polish martyr*. He joined the Franciscans in 1910. At Rome as a student he founded the Militia Immaculatae to oppose secularism*. Returning to Cracow in Poland, he established a friary, first at Grodno and later at Teresin called Niepokalanow (City of the Immaculate). Another friary was established in Japan. In 1936 he returned to Niepokalanow. When the Germans occupied Poland in 1939, Kolbe was arrested and sent to Auschwitz. Here he took the place of a condemned Jew and was killed by lethal injection. He was canonized in 1982. Feast day: August 14.

kollyva In the Eastern Orthodox Church*, a cake made of grains of wheat or rice, spices, dried fruit, and pomegranate* seeds and covered with sugar, blessed during memorial services and distributed to those present.

Kollyvades Eighteenth-century monks from Athos* whose name derives from their insistence that memorial services at which kollyva* is blessed should be held on Saturday, not on Sunday.

komvologion Form of rosary* used in the Eastern Orthodox Church* when reciting the Jesus Prayer*.

komvoschinion (lit., knotted cord) 1. In the Eastern Orthodox Church*, a knotted cord of wool or other material, comparable to a rosary*, used in reciting the Jesus Prayer*. Monks are expected to make 1500 metanies or prostrations accompanied by prayers and the Jesus Prayer. The komvoschinion is used to count the metanies and the occurrences of the Jesus Prayer. 2. The prayer itself.

konk'er In the Armenian Church*, a flat lozenge of stiffened material, worn suspended from the girdle* by the bishop as a symbolic sword.

kontakion In the Eastern Orthodox Church*, book of prayers or hymns in praise of a saint*.

korban (lit., oblation*) In the Coptic and Ethiopian rites, the liturgy or the bread used in the liturgy.

korhrtadedr In the Armenian Rite*, the veil on which a bishop kneels during the liturgy.

Koridethi Codex Ninth century manuscript of the Gospels written in uncials, so named because it was formerly in the monastery of Koridethi, near the Caspian Sea. It is now in Tbilisi.

Kornelimunster Benedictine monastery at Kornelimunster near Aachen* in Germany established in 814–815 by Louis the Pious, son of Charlemagne*, whose remains are buried in a tomb in the monastery. In the eleventh century, the monastery, now promoted to the status of a free imperial abbey, received the relics* of Pope Cornelius* and henceforward bore the name of Benedictine Monastery of St. Cornelius in Inda. The monastery's first three-aisled basilica* was destroyed by the Normans as was the second one, built in 1310. Starting in the fourteenth century, a new church was built which by 1520 had eight aisles. The chapel has a special significance to pilgrims because it houses linen dress of the Virgin Mary* and the loin cloth of Christ.

Kornthal Pietist settlement northwest of Stuttgart founded in 1819 by Gottlieb Wilhelm Hoffmann and Johann Michael Hahn. It was a millennial community, inspired by Moravian ideals and strictly regulated in matters of food and dress.

Kosmas Aitolos (1714–1779) Greek Orthodox itinerant missionary. He became a monk in Mount Athos* in 1759 but left it the next year to become an itinerant preacher. To stem the tide of conversions to Islam among the poor and illiterate, he established schools in more than 200 villages and towns. He was arrested by the Ottomans and hanged. He was canonized by the Patriarchate of Constantinople in 1961. Feast day: August 24.

Kosovo Region of Serbia, closely associated with Serbian nationalism. It contains the ancient patriarchal church of Pec*, the Gracanica Mon-astery, and numerous shrines as well the Field of Blackbirds where in 1389 the Turks defeated the Serbs and killed Prince Lazar Hrebeljanovic.

kottina In the Church of the East*, alb-like vestment worn by priests.

koubouklion (Gk.) Bier on which the epitaphios, the embroidered icon of Christ, laid out for burial, lies during the orthros* of Holy Saturday*. In Greek churches, they are often canopied, richly carved structures decorated with flowers, but in Slav churches they are plain without a canopy.

koukoulion In the Byzantine Church*, veil or hood worn over the kamelavchion by priests and monks.

koukoulla Baptismal veil in the Byzantine Church*.

koura (Gk., tonsure) Solemn form of tonsure* in the Byzantine Rite* of monastic ordination.

kovsh In the Byzantine Church*, a ladle in which wine and water and pieces of the bread are offered to the communicants after they have received the Holy Communion*.

kovtcheg (lit., the ark) In the Byzantine Rite*, the tabernacle in which the reserved sacrament* is placed.

Kraemer, Hendrik (1888–1965) Dutch missionary and linguist whose *The Christian Message in a Non-Christian World* presented at the Tambaram Conference* in 1938 influenced missionary thinking for over two decades. After many years of service in Indonesia, he was professor of the phe-

nomenology of religion at Leiden and from 1937 he was the director at the Ecumenical Institute* at Chateau de Bossey*.

Krauth, Charles Porterfield (1823–1883) American champion of conservative Lutheranism*. As a teacher in Mount Airy Seminary, Philadelphia, he led the movement in the eastern United States toward a full acknowledgment of the historic Lutheran confessions as a basis for a sound Lutheranism. He was a leading organizer of the General Council in 1867 and later its president. From 1863 to 1868 he was professor of moral and intellectual philosophy at the University of Pennsylvania. His chief work was the *Conservative Reformation and Its Theology* (1871).

Kremsmunster Benedictine monastery in Kremsmunster in Krems Valley, southwest of Linz, Austria, founded in 777 by the Bavarian Duke Tassilo III. The church, a three-aisled basilica*, dates from the thirteenth century, and was remodeled in 1680 by Carlo Carlone. The great ceiling fresco* was painted by Melchior in 1696. The monastery's Tower of Mathematics, Europe's first tower block, was built between 1748 and 1759 and houses a rich scientific collection and an observatory.

Krudener, Barbara Juliana Freifrau von (1764–1824) Russian pietist. After a sudden conversion in 1804, she became a dedicated Pietist. She had great influence on Tsar Alexander I.

kshotz In the Armenian Church*, liturgical fans* to which little bells are attached.

kthobo dkhourobo In the Syrian Rite, the Missal known as Book of the Sacrifice consisting of seven anaphoras.

ktzord In the Armenian Liturgy, an antiphonal refrain.

kubbah In the Coptic Liturgy, dome placed on the paten* to keep the veils from touching the bread.

kuddasha Liturgy of the Assyrian Church*. Assyrians use three anaphoras: the Liturgy of Addai and Mari* or the anaphora of Narsai* as revised by Jesu Yab III of Adiabene: Liturgy of Theodore of Mopsuestia*, or the Second Hallowing: and the Liturgy of Mar Nestorius, or the Third Hallowing. Chaldeans use the Liturgy of the Holy Apostles.

kuddshe ikaddishe Jacobite formula* for the administration of the Holy Communion* to the clergy.

kudshe In the Jacobite Rite, prayer recited at the elevation* of the paten* and chalice*.

Kuhlman, Kathryn (1907–1976) American evangelist and faith healer. She began her itinerant ministry at age 16, but finally settled down at Denver, Colorado, in 1933 at the Kuhlman Revival Tabernacle. Her divorce destroyed this ministry, and she moved away in the 1940s to Pittsburgh, which became her headquarters as she held services in Carnegie Hall and the First Presbyterian Church. In 1965 she also began services at Ralph Wilkerson's Melodyland, the Pasadena Civic Auditorium, and the Los Angeles Shrine Auditorium. She also developed a radio and television ministry. A number of dramatic physical healings have been attributed to her prayers and words of knowledge.

kulagi A Coptic liturgical book used as a missal.

kulich In the Byzantine tradition, rich, spicy cake baked for Easter*.

Kulturkampf Fifteen-year struggle between Bismarck and the Roman Catholic Church in Germany, from 1871 to 1887. It was instigated by Bismarck, who saw the Catholic Church as a threat to German unity. The initial stages of the Kulturkampf were marked by much bitterness on both sides and the passage of anti-Catholic legislation. The Catholic Department of the Prussian Ministry of Public Worship was abolished, the Jesuits* and other religious orders were expelled, Catholic schools were closed, several Catholic bishops were imprisoned, and the German ambassador to the Vatican* was recalled.

Opposition to these measures, and particularly to the May laws, was more than Bismarck had anticipated, and by the end of the 1770s he began to reverse himself. He also realized that the church was a strong ally in the fight against socialism. Peace was made with the new pope, Leo XIII*. By 1887 most of the anti-Catholic legislation, except for the expulsion of the Jesuits, had been repealed. Kulturkampf was a Bismarckian blunder that strengthened the Roman Catholic Church inside Germany and led to a revival among the faithful.

Kumm, Hermann Karl Wilhelm and Lucy Evangeline (1874–1930 and 1865–1906, respectively) Founders of the Sudan United Mission. Karl Wilhelm Kumm met Lucy Evangeline, daughter of the famous evangelist, Henry Grattan Guinness, in 1900 and they were married in Cairo. Next year they founded the Sudan Pioneer Mission, renamed Sudan United Mission in 1904. In 1906 Lucy died and Karl Wilhelm carried on the work until 1924. Today the mission is known as Action Partners—Christians Reaching the World. The Church of Christ in Nigeria and the Sudanese Church of Christ are the fruits of its labors.

kummus In the Coptic tradition, superior* of a cathedral, a senior priest, or an abbot of a monastery.

Kung, Hans (1928–) Roman Catholic theologian. In 1960 he was appointed professor of fundamental theology in the Roman Catholic faculty of the University of Tubingen*. He attended the Vatican Council II* as a peritus*, and made a mark as a progressive, but not radical or liberal, thinker. Most of his books have been translated into English, including *The Church* (1967), *Infallible?* (1970), *On Being a Christian* (1977), *Does God Exist?* (1980), and *Christianity and World Religions* (1984). He is described as an ecumenical or evangelical Catholic. In 1979 his *missio canonica* (or authority to teach as a Catholic theologian) was withdrawn, but he continued to teach at Tubingen*. He has developed in a multifaith direction with a global ethic.

kurban See KORBAN.

Kurisumala Ashram Syro-Malankara Catholic monastery in Kerala, India, founded in 1958 by the Belgian Trappist Father Francis Maheiu, called Acharya (spiritual teacher), and the English

Benedictine* Bede Griffiths. Their ideal was to create an authentic monastic setting in keeping with Eastern Christian traditions in India.

kushapa (Syr., beseeching) In the Assyrian tradition, prayer offered by the kneeling priest in a low voice.

kuthino Black woolen robe of a Jacobite monk or the alb* worn by the regular clergy. It is usually embroidered with many crosses.

kutiya In the Byzantine tradition, a dish of boiled wheat mixed with honey and raisins eaten communally on the day of a funeral, usually at the graveside.

kutmarus In the Coptic Liturgy, a liturgical lectionary* containing the lessons of the day.

Kuyper, Abraham (1837–1920) Dutch Calvinist theologian and statesman. Son of a minister in the Reformed Church, Kuyper embraced orthodox Calvinism* at the age of 30 and became a popular preacher. He moved to Amsterdam, where he came under the influence of Groen Van Prinsterer, founder of the Anti-Revolutionary Party. After Groen's death, Kuyper became leader of the Anti-Revolutionary Party. He was elected in 1874 to the States General, where he drafted a program calling for extension of suffrage, state aid to religious schools, recognition of the rights of labor, reforms in colonial policy, and revitalization of each of the pillars (or spheres) of national life. He also forged an alliance, called the Monstrous Coalition, with the Roman Catholics to press for state aid to schools.

In 1880 Kuyper started an orthodox Calvinist free university in Amsterday free from church and state control and taught in its seminary. In 1886 he led an exodus of over 10,000 conservatives from the Reformed Church and formed the Gereformeerde Kerk, the second largest Protestant body in the Netherlands. In 1888 the Monstrous Coalition won control of the government, and Kuyper was elected prime minister in 1901. He served until 1905, when his party lost control of the legislature. Kuyper's major political legacies were giving the silent Calvinist middle class a voice in the government and the so called "pillarization of society" whereby each social and religious group had inviolable rights in society. As a theologian he helped to propel orthodox Calvinism* back into the mainstream and to make common grace* a theme in Christian discourse. Many contemporary Christian movements can be traced to his work, and he has influenced a number of Christian thinkers, such as Francis Schaeffer*.

kyriakon (lit., the Lord's House) A Greek or Byzantine church.

Kyriale Service book containing the musical chant for the ordinary of the Mass* in Latin.

kyrie Short form of Kyrie eleison*.

Kyrie eleison (Gk., Lord, have mercy) Prayer for divine mercy used in liturgical worship as a response to the petitions made by the deacon or the priest. Sometimes, Kyrie eleison is supplemented by a similar prayer called Christe eleison* (Christ, have mercy). In the ninefold Kyrie, Kyrie eleison is repeated three times, followed by three Christe eleisons and Kyrie eleisons three more times.

kyros/kyrios (Gk., Lord) Used in the New Testament for Christ as Lord.

Ll

La Salette Village in the Alps, near Grenoble, where in 1846 the Virgin Mary* appeared to a peasant boy and girl and communicated to them a special and secret message. A commission appointed by the archbishop of Grenoble confirmed the authenticity of the apparition, and miracles followed. La Salette soon became a center of pilgrimage* where thousands assembled to claim miracle from the "Virgin of the Alps."

La Salle, Jean Baptiste de (1651–1719) French educational reformer. Concerned over the illiteracy of the poor, he set up charity schools for them and formed in 1684 a religious order of teachers to staff these schools—Brothers of the Christian Schools. He established the first training college for secular teachers first in Vaugirard and later in St. You, near Rouen*. He also founded reformato-

St. John Baptist de La Salle

ries and boarding schools. At his death there were 22 such schools, and they spread around the world in succeeding centuries. Among his innovations were the substitution of French for Latin and the introduction of group teaching.

La Trappe Abbey near Soligne (Orne), base of the Cistercian Order of Strict Observance, from which the Trappists* take their name. Founded in 1122 as a house of the Savigny Order, it joined the Cistercian Order affiliated to Clairvaux* in 1148. After centuries of decline, it was revived by A. J. de Rance*, who introduced Strict Observance in 1662. At the time of French Revolution, the monks were scattered, but they returned in 1815 to rebuild the abbey.

Labadists Protestant sect named after Jean de Labadie (1610–1674), a lapsed Jesuit who joined the Reformed Church and formed a group that settled in the United States, after being rejected by several European towns. They held highly Pietistic views, rarely celebrated the Eucharist*, and held that only marriages between believing spouses were binding.

labarum First Christian military standard designed by Constantine* from his celestial vision on the eve of his victory at the Battle of Milvian Bridge* in 313. From 324 it became the official standard of the Roman Empire. It showed a cross surmounted by a wreath containing the monogram of Christ, Chirho, on which hung a purple banner* inscribed "hoc signo victor eris" (in this sign, you will conquer).

labis In the Byzantine Church*, communion spoon.

laborare est orare (Lat., to work is to pray) Motto of many monastic orders.

Labre, St. Benedict Joseph (1748–1783) Patron saint* of tramps and the homeless. Rejected by the Cistercians* and the Carthusians*, he became a wandering pilgrim*, visiting numerous shrines, sleeping in the open, and spending his days in prayer. He was canonized in 1881. Feast day: November 28.

L'Abri Fellowship Christian organization founded in Huemoz, Switzerland, by Francis and Edith Schaeffer* in 1955, as "a demonstration of the existence and character of God." There are now seven branches in various countries in Europe and North America. See also SCHAEFFER, FRANCIS AUGUST.

St. Benedict Joseph Labre

labyrinth Maze inlaid on the floor of the nave*, used as a substitute for pilgrimage*, by following its winding path on one's knees with suitable prayers. The most famous labyrinths are in the Gothic* cathedrals of Chartres*, Reims*, and Amiens*.

lachrymatory Small container for holding the tears of mourners.

Iachumara Prayer at the start of the Assyrian Liturgy of the Catechumens that runs as follows: "To you, O Lord, we give thanks and glorify our Lord Jesus Christ, for you are the quickener of our bodies and the savior of our souls." The prayer is attributed to St. Simon Bar Sabba'e.

Lacombe, Albert (1827–1916) Canadian Roman Catholic missionary to the Cree and Blackfoot Indians. He translated the New Testament into the Cree language.

Lactantius (c. 240–c. 320) North African Christian apologist. He was appointed by Emperor Diocletian as teacher of Latin oratory in Nicomedia. As a believer, he was ousted from his job during the Diocletian persecution*. Later, Constantine made him a tutor to his son. He turned to writing Christian apologetics in simple Latin, without any theologese, for the educated pagan as well as the wavering Christian. His style is much admired, lending credence to his epithet, "the Christian Cicero." His two chief works are *Divine Institutes,* exposing the hollowness of paganism and the truth of the Revelation, and *The Death of the Persecutors,* on the martyrdoms of Christians and the terrible fate of their persecutors.

lacticinia Milk and milk products, such as cheese and butter, often forbidden on fast days.

Ladder of Ascent Also, Ladder of Paradise. Seventh century treatise by St. John Climacus* on the 30 steps of progress toward complete freedom from passion, as the ideal of Christian perfection*.

ladgari In the Georgian Church, book containing troparia for morning and evening offices and the divine liturgy.

Ladislaus, St. (1040–1095) In Hungarian, Laszlo. King of Hungary from 1077 to 1095. He was instrumental in Christianizing Croatia and Dalmatia, which he annexed in 1091. He built many churches and presided over the Synod of Szabolcs in 1092. His plans to participate in the First Crusade* was cut short by his death. He was canonized in 1192. Feast day: June 27.

Lady Chapel Chapel dedicated to the Virgin

Mary*, often located at the eastern end of a larger church, behind the high altar.

Lady Day Feast of the Annunciation, March 25.

Lady House Chapel or grotto* containing a statue of Our Lady.

Lady, Our Roman Catholic designation of the Virgin Mary*.

lady rod In Christian art, scepter or rod surmounted by a dove* in the hand of the Virgin Mary*.

Laestadians Members of a Scandinavian sect* of Lutheran origin, following the teachings of Lars Levi Laestadius (1800–1861). The movement began in 1844 in Swedish Lapland and was carried to Norway and Finland by lay preachers. Members wear a special costume, oppose baptism* and the Eucharist*, and have lay preachers. Their gatherings were marked by ecstatic manifestations and by laying on of hands*. The Laestadian revival left a powerful imprint on the Scandinavian church.

Laetare Sunday Fourth Sunday in Lent*, so named from the first word of the introit* for that day.

Laetentur Coeli (Lat., Let the Heavens Rejoice) 1. The Greek Formulary of Union agreed between Cyril* of Alexandria and John of Antioch in 433 and formally approved by the Council of Chalcedon*. It formulates the Antiochene Christology* in terms sensitive to Alexandria*, emphasizing the unity of the person of Christ and the distinction of the natures, retaining the term *Theotokos* for the Virgin Mary*. 2. Bull* issued by Pope Eugenius IV* in 1439 incorporating the decree of the Council of Florence settling the dispute between the Western and Eastern churches. Under the decree the Eastern Church* accepted the Double Procession* of the Holy Spirit* and the primacy of the see* of Rome.

lafafah In the Coptic Rite, veil or large corporal* covering the bread and wine, made from white or colored silk with an embroidered cross at the center.

Lagrange, Marie-Joseph (1855–1938) Dominican biblical scholar who founded the Ecole Pratique d'Etudes Bibliques* in Jerusalem* in 1890 and *Revue Biblique* in 1892. In 1903 he was appointed a member of the Biblical Commission*. Until 1907 his chief field of work was the Old Testament, but in that year he was asked by the Holy See* to move into the New Testament. His commentaries on Matthew, Mark, Luke, and John are standard works.

lahma dkudasha (lit., bread of holiness) In the Coptic Rite, the Blessed Sacrament*.

lahn Eight tones used in the Coptic Liturgy.

laicism Separation of church and state and the exclusion of the clergy from the organs of state.

laicization 1. Release of an ordained person from his or her vows, allowing a return to laity standing. In the Roman Catholic Church, this action is necessary to enable priests to get married. Such laicized priests do not cease to be priests, but may fulfill no priestly acts. 2. Process in Protestant church by which the laity are allowed to perform functions historically assigned to the clergy.

Lainez, Diego (1512–1565) Also, James Laynez. Associate of Ignatius Loyola*, one of the six who took vows at Montmartre in 1534 forming the Society of Jesus*. He succeeded Ignatius as the second general* of the order. He was also a leading theologian at the Council of Trent*, where he proved uncompromising on the canons of justification*, sacraments*, purgatory*, and papal absolutism.

laity (Gk., laos, people) Nonordained church members as a group, as distinguished from the clergy.

lake of fire Place of eternal punishment* into which the beast and the false prophet are thrown in Revelation. It corresponds to the gehenna of the Old Testament.

Lalande, St. Jean (?–1646) French Jesuit martyred on a mission tour among the Mohawk Indians. Feast day: September 26.

Lalemant, Gabriel (1610–1649) French Jesuit missionary tortured to death by Iroquois Indians at Quebec. Feast day: September 26.

Lalemant, Jerome (1593–1673) French Jesuit missionary among the Huron Indians and director of the Jesuit missions in Canada. He created the Donnes, an order of laymen dedicated to religious service without entering religious orders.

Lalibela Place in north central Ethiopia where some 12 monolithic churches are carved out of the local red sandstone below ground level. Each rock church is individually named, and is different in size, form, and decoration. The place is named after Lalibela, Ethiopian emperor of the Zagwe Dynasty (1181–1221). The churches are arranged in groups, connected by subterranean passageways. The basilicas* of Emmanuel, Marcorios, Abba Lebanos, and Gabriel are all carved from a single rock hill. The most famous is the Basilica of Qidus Giorgis (St. George) carved from a sloping rock terrace. The largest is the Basilica of Medhane Alem (Savior of the World). Each church is of different design and is adorned with colorful frescos and religious paintings.

Lalibela, Ethiopia

Lalor, Teresa (1769–1846) Roman Catholic found-ress of the Order of Visitation. Born in Ireland, she emigrated to the United States in 1794 and settled in Washington, D.C., where she, with the help of Leonard Neale, president of Georgetown College*, established the Order of Visitation in 1816 and served as its superior* until 1819.

lamb 1. Symbol in Christian art for Christ as the Lamb of God* (John 1:29; Rev. 5:12–13; 19:7–9). In early centuries, the lamb was shown with a cross to symbolize the sacrifice on the cross. The symbolism became less common in the East after the Trullan Synod* forbade the representation of Christ as the lamb. 2. In the Eastern Church*, a portion of the consecrated bread in the liturgy. See also AGNUS DEI; PASCHAL LAMB.

Adoration of the Lamb

Lamb of God Designation of Jesus (John 1:29).

Lambarene Village in Gabon, Africa, where Albert Schweitzer* erected a hospital.

Lambeth Articles Nine Calvinistic theological propositions drawn up in 1595 at Lambeth Palace* by Archbishop Whitgift to clarify the doctrine of predestination*. Queen Elizabeth did not like them, and they were not officially authorized, but they formed part of the 1615 Irish Articles*.

Lambeth Conferences Month-long conferences of Anglican bishops throughout the world held every 10 years, in years ending in 8, beginning in 1867. It is a synodical* conference without legislative powers. The 1888 conference was notable for its endorsement of the Lambeth Quadrilateral*. The last conference was held in 1998, when the conference resoundingly declared its disapproval of homosexuality.

Lambeth Palace London palace of the archbishops of Canterbury* since the beginning of the twelfth century when Archbishop Baldwin acquired the manor of Lambeth and the manor house for use as his residence. The chapel was built in 1245, the Water Tower in 1434, the Great Hall in 1663, and the modern part in 1829–1834. It was partially destroyed in Nazi air raids in 1940 and restored in 1956. It also houses a distinguished library.

Lambeth Quadrilateral Four principles upon which Anglicans insist for church unity, formulated by William Reed Huntington of the Protestant Episcopal Church in 1870. These were: 1. Adherence to the Holy Scriptures as the ultimate standard of faith. 2. Adherence to the Apostles' Creed* and the Nicene Creed*. 3. Adherence to the two sacraments* of baptism* and the Lord's Supper*. 4. Adherence to a belief in a historic episcopate*. These principles were endorsed by the Lambeth Conference* of 1888, and thereafter they came to be known as the Lambeth Quadrilateral. The fourth has generally been resisted by non-Anglican Protestants. See also CHICAGO-LAMBETH ARTICLES.

Lamennais, Felicite Robert de (1782–1854) Influential French writer. He became a priest in 1816, but his ideas on civil polity* and religious freedom came into conflict with Rome. His books were placed on the Index, and he left the Catholic faith by 1841. He is considered a forerunner of modernism*.

Felicite Robert de Lamennais

Lamentabili Decree of the Holy Office* issued in 1907 in which 65 propositions of the modernists and liberals were condemned.

Lammas Day English festival of wheat harvest on August 1 when worshipers offered freshly made loaves in church.

lampada Lamp with a wrapped wick sitting in oil used to illuminate an icon* in an Eastern Orthodox* church.

lampas In the Byzantine Church*, a large candle in the ornate candlestick known as kerostates*.

Lampert of Hersfeld (c. 1025–1085) Benedictine abbot and historian, author of *Annales*, a chronicle of world history from creation to 1077.

lance In the Byzantine Rite*, a small knife shaped like a lance, with a handle ending in a small cross used to cut the eucharistic bread at the Proskomide*.

Landmark movement Nineteenth-century Baptist movement in the South that asserted the ecclesiological validity and unbroken succession of Baptist churches since apostolic times and advocated closed communion* and exclusion of alien immersions not performed by a Baptist minister. Its other key principles were: The church is a local entity, and there is no single church, and only members of properly constituted Baptist churches are Christians. The dominant figures behind the movement were John R. Graves, James Pendleton, and A. C. Dayton.

Lanfranc (c. 1005–1089) Archbishop of Canterbury* from 1070. A pupil of Berengar of Tours*, he opened a school at Avranches, but left it to enter the Benedictine abbey at Bec* in 1042. There he started another famous school among whose pupils were Anselm* of Canterbury and Ivo* of Chartres. He also became a trusted counselor to William the Conqueror, who brought Lanfranc with him to England and had him consecrated archbishop of Canterbury. With the support of William, he reformed the church, rebuilt the Cathedral church, and enforced clerical celibacy*. He prefigured the doctrine of transubstantiation* at the Council of Rome* and Vercelli (1050), and at Tours* (1059), and in his book, *The Body and Blood of the Lord* (1059–1066).

Lang, Cosmo Gordon (1864–1945) Archbishop of Canterbury* from 1928 to 1942. He played a crucial role during the abdication of the wayward King Edward VIII in 1936. In 1932 he helped establish full communion between the Anglicans and Old Catholics*.

Lange, Johann Peter (1802–1884) German Protestant theologian and biblical scholar. He taught dogmatic theology at the University of Zurich and the University of Bonn. He refuted the liberal D. F. Strauss* in *Uber den geschichtlichen Charakter der kanonischen Evangelien* (1836) and wrote a life of Jesus as an answer to Strauss's *Leben Jesu*.

Langlais, Jean (1907–) French organist and composer. His works include orchestral and chamber music and songs, organ music, and vocal music. Blind from birth, he became organist at Sainte Clotilde in 1939. Most of his music is driven by his strong religious faith. His works for organ include three *Paraphrases* Gregorienne (1934), two organ symphonies (1952), eight *Pieces Modales* (1956), *Organ Book* (1956), *Office pour la Sainte Trinite* (1958), *Livres Oecumenique* (1958), *Trois Meditations sur la Sainte Trinite* (1962), three voluntaries (1969), and *Five Meditations sur l'Apocalypse* (1974). Among the vocal works are four masses, three psalms, and a festival alleluia for chorus and organ.

Langton, Stephen (1150/55–1228) Archbishop of Canterbury* from 1207. He was the first archbishop of Canterbury since the Norman Conquest who had not been either a monk or a minister of the crown. Because of the troubled political climate of the times, King John refused to admit Langton as archbishop and excluded him from his see* until 1213. As a friend of the barons against the king, he was influential in the framing of the Magna Carta. He was suspended for his role in this event from 1215 to 1218. For the next ten years, he secured better clerical discipline and raised the standards of clerical conduct. He is credited with the division of the books of the Bible into chapters.

lanqua (Ge'ez) Velvet circular shoulder cape ornamented with five points in the form of a cross, representing the five wounds of Christ, worn by Ethiopian ecclesiastical dignitaries.

Laodicea City in southwest Phrygia in Asia Minor near the junction of the Lycus River with the main Meander Valley, named after Laodice, wife of Antiochus II. It was part of the Roman province of Asia. The Christian church in the city, referred to unfavorably in the Revelation, may have been founded by Epaphras (Col. 4:12–13).

Laodicea, Canons of Sixty canons passed by the Synod of Laodicea held in Laodicea in Phrygia between 341 and 381. Thirty-two bishops were present at this conference, which was presided over by Theodosius. They deal with the relationship of Christians to non-Christians, Jews, and heretics; ordination, worship, fasting*, and penance*; and female presbyters. Interestingly, magicians, enchanters, mathematicians, and astrologers are prohibited from becoming clergy. The concluding canon* lists biblical books, but omits Revelation.

Laon Cathedral in Laon, Aisne, France. Work began in 1160, and the west front was completed in the first quarter of the thirteenth century. The sculptures were mostly destroyed during the French Revolution. Restoration work began in 1853 and continued until World War I. Laon had an influential school of theology in the twelfth century. See also ANSELM OF LAON.

laos The people of God*, the whole body of baptized persons.

lappets 1. Decorative folds or flaps on a garment or hat. 2. Two linen strips that extend from the bottom of the rear panel of the bishop's mitre* often ending in decorative tassels.

lapsi (Lat., the fallen) Sometimes, lapsasi. Those who denied the faith under persecution. Apostasy* was a mortal sin in the early church, but to temper the severity of the imperial persecutions, the church decided to forgive and readmit into the fold those who had abjured their faith through fear so long as they showed true repentance*. The Novatians opposed the readmission of the lapsi, and the resulting schism* lasted for a century.

Larger Catechism 1. Martin Luther's catechism* of 1529 for teachers and clergy. 2. Catechism prepared by the Westminster Assembly* in 1647. Neither has been as widely used as their respective *Shorter Catechism*.

Las Casas, Bartolome de (1484–1566) "Apostle of the Indies." Spanish Dominican missionary who opposed the cruel treatment of the Indians by the Spanish conquistadores and campaigned tirelessly for a more humane policy. He was responsible for the passage of the New Laws of 1542–1543, and worked for their enforcement against the opposition of the Spanish colonists. He was named "Protector of the Indians" by Cardinal Ximenez*. He was bishop of Chiapas from 1544–1547 and played a key role in improving Spanish-Indian relations. His books are invaluable sources for the early history of the Spanish Empire: *Historia de las Indias* (first published in 1875), *Brevisima Relacion de la Destruccion de las Indias* (1552), and *De Unico Vocationis Modo: Apologetica Historia*.

Las Huelgas Royal monastery, Monasterio de las Huelgas, founded near Burgos* in Spain by Alphonso VIII in 1187 along with the church of Santa Maria and the Pilgrim's Hospice. It was a religious house for women, and from the beginning it had strong royal connections. The Romanesque cloister* is among the oldest ecclesiastical structures in Spain. Las Huelgas was on the pilgrim route to Santiago, and the Pilgrim Hospice was a major resting place for pilgrims*.

Laski/a Lasco, John (1499–1560) Protestant reformer. In 1529 he was nominated bishop of Veszprem and in 1538 made archdeacon of Warsaw, but he lost his office when he married in 1540. Two years later he broke with the Roman Catholic Church and became a Calvinist minister at Emden. In 1548 he reached England at the invitation of Thomas Cranmer* and became superintendent of the churches of strangers (foreign Protestants) in London in 1550. He is said to have influenced the *Book of Common Prayer**. He published a book on church discipline*, and also a confession* of faith and a catechism*. He left England on the death of his patron, Edward VI, and returned to Poland, where he ended his days as a superintendent of Reformed* churches.

Lassus, Orlando de (c. 1532–1594) Also, Orlando di Lasso. Birth name: Roland de Lattre. Italian composer. Born in Belgium, he received his musical education in Italy, where he became Maestro di Capella of St. John Lateran in Rome*. In 1556 he went to Munich*, where he became maestro di capella* at the court of Duke Albrecht V of Bavaria. He is considered the peer of Palestrina with a greater range of style. His sacred music consists of 60 masses, 80 settings for the Magnificat*, and some 500 motets*. His chorales and Genevan psalms were favorites of Protestants as well as Catholics.

last days Time prior to the end of history or the Second Coming*. Since the time of the Second Coming is unknown, the whole period from Christ's first coming is the last days.

last judgment Final judgment of all humanity by Jesus Christ (John 5:22; Acts 17:31) from his great white throne, the concluding event in human history.

Last of the Fathers St. Bernard*, abbot of Clairvaux*.

last rites In Roman Catholic practice, prayers and sacramental rites administered to those about to die.

last things 1. In eschatology*, the final events in human history, including the last judgment*. 2. In human life, death, judgment, heaven*, and hell* as the final realities.

latent church Nominal Christians who are not part of organized Christianity, a term coined by Paul Tillich*.

Lateran 1. Cathedral Church of Rome, the Basilica of St. John Lateran, built before 311. So called because it stands on the site of an ancient palace on the Celian Hill at Rome, which belonged to the Laterani family. It was the official residence of the popes from the fourth century until 1309. The basilica* is one of the four major basilicas of the Roman Catholic Church. Originally dedicated to the Redeemer as St. Salvator, it was rebuilt by Pope Sergius III in 896 and dedicated to John the Baptist (and later to John the apostle as well). It was burned down in 1308 and 1361 and rebuilt each time. The major architect of the rebuilt basilica was Dominico Fontana. Feast of the Dedication of the Lateran Basilica: November 9. 2. The palace or group of buildings adjoining the Lateran Basilica. 3. Papacy.

St. John Lateran

Lateran councils Five ecumenical councils held at the Lateran* between 1123 and 1512.

1. The **first** (Ninth Ecumenical Council) was summoned by Callistus II* in 1123 to mark the end of the investiture controversy* and confirm the Concordat of Worms*. It prohibited Roman Catholic clergy from having wives or concubines.

2. The **second** (Tenth Ecumenical Council)was convened by Innocent II in 1139 to heal the schism* that had occurred at the time of his election. It condemned Arnold of Brescia* and the practice of usury and simony*.

3. The **third** (Eleventh Ecumenical Council) was convened by Alexander III* in 1179. It restricted the election of a pope to the College of Cardinals*, provided for a school for clergymen in each cathedral church, and condemned the Waldenses* and Albigenses*.

4. The **fourth** (Twelfth Ecumenical Council) was convened by Innocent III* in 1215. It issued an official statement on the doctrine of the Eucharist* (using the term *transubstantiation** for the first time), made annual confession* and communion mandatory, confirmed the new Franciscan Order*, and condemned the teachings of Joachim of Fiore* and Amalric of Bena*. Other canons banned the creation of new orders or the addition of chapters to existing orders. Abuses of indulgences* were to be curbed.

5. The **fifth** (Eighteenth Ecumenical Council) summoned by Pope Julius II* in 1512–1517. It invalidated the decrees of the anti-papal Council of Pisa* convened by Louis XII of France.

Lateran Treaty Concordat* concluded between the Vatican* and the kingdom of Italy under Mussolini in 1929 which finally and irrevocably settled the Roman question and established Vatican

Signing of the Lateran Treaty

City as a sovereign state. The Holy See* recognized the Italian state with Rome as capital. The Italian state recognized the holy Catholic, apostolic, and Roman religion as the sole religion of its people, agreed to provide religious instruction in schools, and acknowledged the validity of marriages in churches. The concordat was substantially modified in 1984 under which the Catholic religion is no longer the sole religion of the Italian state.

Lathrop, Rose Hawthorne (1851–1926) Daughter of Nathaniel Hawthorne, founder of a community of Dominican tertiaries for the relief of the poor.

Latimer, Hugh (1485–1555) English Protestant reformer and martyr*. Appointed bishop of Worcester in 1535, he supported Henry VIII in his breach with Rome and steadfastly opposed clerical corruption and doctrinal error. He promoted Bible reading with his *A Faithful Exhortation to the Reading of Holy Scripture*. Latimer was a fiery and popular preacher. He was twice imprisoned during the reaction in Henry VIII's later years and with Cranmer and Ridley*, he was burned at the stake at Oxford during the Marian persecution. His last words were his legacy to the Protestant faith: "Be of good cheer, Master Ridley, and play the man; we shall this day light such a candle by God's grace in England as I trust shall never be put out." Feast day: October 16.

Latin Language of the Western provinces of the Roman Empire. It superseded Greek as the official language of the Roman Catholic Church and remained so until Vatican Council II*. Ecclesiastical Latin, as used in the Vulgate*, was more allied to the common speech than to literary Latin. It served as the lingua franca of western Europe until the late Middle Ages. The rise of nationalism and the translation of the Bible into national languages helped to displace it from its dominance.

Latin Christianity Christianity in the Western part of the Roman Empire that used Latin language and expressed itself in Latin thought-forms. It later was led by the bishops of Rome and hence became virtually synonymous with Roman Catholicism*.

Latin Rite Roman Catholic liturgy.

Latinization Imposition or imitation of Latin rites, liturgical customs, and principles to the detriment of Eastern Catholic* liturgical traditions or of vernacular languages and cultures.

Latinize (*verb*) To bring into conformity with the Roman Catholic Church and its rites and practices.

Latitudinarians English churchmen in the seventeenth and eighteenth centuries who pleaded for greater tolerance or latitude in matters of doctrine and who expressed willingness to give up adiaphora or nonessentials not specified or prohibited in the Bible. They generally appealed to

Hugh Latimer

reason as a source of religious authority beside the Bible and ecclesiastical approval. Among their leaders were the Cambridge Platonists* as well as Arminian theologians and Broad Church* advocates like William Chillingworth, Edward Stillingfleet, Richard Whateley, Samuel Coleridge, and Charles Kingsley*.

Latourette, Kenneth Scott (1884–1968) Church historian. He taught at Yale from 1921 to 1953. His masterpiece is the seven-volume *History of the Expansion of Christianity* (1937–1945). He also wrote *A History of Christianity* (1953), *Christianity in a Revolutionary Age* (5 vols., 1958–1962), and *History of Christian Missions in China* (1929).

latria Worship to which only God is entitled. Compare dulia* and hyperdulia*.

Latrocinium See EPHESUS, ROBBER COUNCIL OF.

Latter Rain Charismatic movement based on Joel's prophecy that in the last days God's Spirit will be poured out "on all flesh; Your sons and your daughters shall prophesy, Your old men shall dream dreams, Your young men shall see visions" (Joel 2:28) and on Hosea's prophecy that "He comes and rains righteousness on you" (Hos. 10:12). The movement began at Sharon Orphanage and Schools in North Battleford, Saskatchewan, Canada, among Pentecostals. In one of the most important apologias of the movement, *The Feast of the Tabernacles* by George Warnock, it was explained that of the three great Jewish feasts, the feast of the Passover was fulfilled in Christ's death, and the feast of the Pentecost* in the outpouring of the Holy Spirit* on the day of the Pentecost, but the feast of the Tabernacles had yet to be fulfilled.

Latter Rain was considered a fulfillment of the feast of Tabernacles that will bring the rain of revival* to the dry and parched church. According to J. Preston Eby, Latter Rain will "finally bring the fullness, a company of the overcoming Sons of God who have come to the measure of the stature of the fullness of Christ, dethrone Satan, and bring the hope of deliverance and life to all the families of the earth. This great work of the Spirit shall usher a people into full redemption—free from the curse, sin, sickness, death and carnality."

Laubach, Frank Charles (1884–1970) American Congregational* missionary and literacy expert. In 1914 he was ordained and left for the Philippines as a missionary. In 1929 he began teaching reading by phonetic symbols and pictures, eventually developing literacy primers for some 300 languages and 100 dialects in Asia, Africa, and Latin America. His techniques are embodied in the Laubach method by which each new literate teaches another the language under the slogan, "Each One, Teach One."

Laud, William (1573–1645) Archbishop of Canterbury* from 1633. In 1601 he received holy orders* and ten years later he was made president of St. John's College, Oxford. Opposed to Calvinism*, he sought to restore pre-Reformation liturgical practices to the Church of England*. In 1630 he was named chancellor of the University of Oxford, where he carried out many reforms. In 1633 he was named archbishop of Canterbury. From the beginning of his tenure, he drew the ire of Puritans*. His attempts to enforce a new liturgy in Scotland in 1637 proved disastrous. At the sitting of the Convocation in 1640 he introduced new canons proclaiming the divine right of kings, and requiring all members to swear "never to consent to alter the government of the church by archbishops, deans and archdeacons, etc." This article, ridiculed as the "etcetera oath*," was so offensive that it was withdrawn by the king. Soon after he was impeached by Long Parliament, imprisoned in the Tower, and executed in 1645, after repudiating accusations of popery* and declaring adherence to Protestantism*.

lauda (Ital., song of praise) Nonliturgical musical genre that flourished from the thirteenth to the sixteenth centuries.

lauda sion Opening words of the sequence for the Feast of Corpus Christi* composed by St. Thomas Aquinas*. Sion is identified with the church.

laudi Thirteenth-century mystical poems that dealt with the conflict between spirit and flesh. The greatest among the representatives of this genre was Jacopone da Todi*, a Franciscan writer.

lauds The morning office of the Western Church*, so named because of the frequent use of laudate or "praise ye." In the 1971 Roman Breviary*, it begins with Psalm 95, followed by a hymn, then a psalm, an Old Testament canticle*, another psalm, a short reading from the Bible, a short responsory*, the Benedictus* with antiphon*, intercessions, the Lord's Prayer*, collect* of the day, blessings, and dismissal*.

laura See LAVRA.

Laurence/Lawrence of Brindisi, St. (1559–1619) Birth name: Giulio Cesare de'Rossi. Doctor of the church* and Capuchin friar*. A noted preacher, he was elected vicar general* of the Capuchins* in 1602. From 1606 to 1613 he worked to combat Protestantism* in Bohemia, Austria, and Germany and to rally the German forces against the Turks. In 1618 he retired from public life to a priory* at Caserta. He was canonized in 1881 and made a doctor of the church in 1959. Feast day: July 21.

Laurence/Lawrence, St. (d. 258) Martyr. He was one of the seven deacons of Rome* during the pontificate* of Sixtus II* and suffered martyrdom by beheading along with the pope and others in the

St. Laurence

Valerian persecution. He was one of the most famous of the Catholic saints, with a chapel built
over his tomb in a catacomb* on the Via
Tiburtina. His name is found in the Canon of the
Mass* and in the Litanies. He is the patron saint*
of librarians. Feast day: August 10.

laus cerei (Lat., praise of the candle) Easter*
proclamation known as the Exultet*.

laus perennis (Gk., endless praise) Ancient monastic custom of singing the praise of God continually.

laus tibi (Gk., praise be to thee) Response sung
after the reading of the Gospel in the sacrament*
of the Eucharist*.

Lausanne Conference First conference of the Ecumenical Movement of Faith and Order* held at
Lausanne through the initiative of Bishop C. H.
Brent* and Robert H. Gardner in 1927, attended
by over 90 denominations. Among the subjects
discussed were unity, essence of the church, episcopacy*, apostolic succession*, and sacraments*.
The concluding statement, called the Lausanne
Message, defined the gospel as "the joyful message
of redemption, both here and hereafter, the gift of
God to sinful man in Christ."

Lausanne Congress on World Evangelization Conference convened in 1974 by an international group
of 142 evangelical leaders under the honorary
chairmanship of Billy Graham*, attended by
3,000 participants from 150 countries. It produced the Lausanne Covenant*, and set up a continuation committee to further the biblical mission of the church. It was the culmination of the
World Congress on Evangelization*. One of the
major goals of the Congress was to identify the
unreached peoples and to learn of the various
strategies used by the Holy Spirit* to express
Christ's love in action.

Lausanne Covenant The Lausanne Congress on
World Evangelization* was convened in Switzerland in 1974, gathering hundreds of Christian
leaders representing over 150 nations. The
covenant drafted at this meeting, with British
evangelical John Stott* serving as chair, sought to
present the consensus of faith and practice underlying their call to proclaim the gospel to all
peoples. The document addressed 15 issues: (1)
the purpose of God, (2) the authority and power
of the Bible, (3) the uniqueness and universality
of Christ, (4) the nature of evangelism*, (5)
Christian social responsibility, (6) the church and
evangelism, (7) cooperation in evangelism, (8)
churches in evangelistic partnership, (9) the urgency of the evangelistic task, (10) evangelism
and culture, (11) education and leadership, (12)
spiritual conflict, (13) freedom and persecution,
(14) the power of the Holy Spirit*, and (15) the return of Christ. Delegates, led by Billy Graham*,
were invited to sign this covenant.

Lausiac history History of the Fathers of the
Desert* written by Palladius* (c. 363–c. 461)
around the year 419. It derives its name from
Lausas, the court chamberlain* of Emperor
Theodosius II.

lavabo (Lat., I will wash) Ceremony of washing
the fingers of the celebrant with a towel after the
offertory of the Mass*, so named from the first
word of Psalm 51:4 recited during the washing.

Lavigerie, Charles-Martial Allemand (1825–1892) Cardinal and founder of the White Fathers* and
White Sisters*. After ordination, he was named
professor of church history at the Sorbonne* in
1854. As director of the Oriental Schools, he traveled to Syria in 1860 after the massacre of Chris-

Charles-Martial Allemand Lavigerie

tians by the Druses. In 1863 he was appointed bishop of Nancy and, four years later, archbishop of Algiers. His vision was the evangelization of Muslim North Africa, and to this end he founded the Society of Missionaries of Africa (White Fathers) in 1868 and the Missionary Sisters of Our Lady of Africa (White Sisters) in 1869. In 1868 Leo XIII* placed him in charge of Roman Catholic missions in central Africa and in 1884 revived for him the see of Carthage* with the title of primate* of Africa. Throughout his career he opposed slavery and monarchism and encouraged native Africans to evangelize* the continent.

lavra (Gk., street or alley) Colony of anchorites who are subject to a single abbot although living in separate cells or huts. They flourished in Palestine in the fourth and fifth centuries, the most famous being Mar Saba, directed by St. Sabas*.

law Mosaic law of the Old Testament, especially as distinguished from grace* as emphasized in the New Testament. Although Jesus described his mission as one of fulfilling and not destroying the law and the prophets, Paul* developed a theology of grace as superseding law, also identified with works of the flesh. Later, Marcion* argued that law and grace represented not merely two modes of divine economy, but proceeded from two different gods. Luther* also made the distinction between law and grace the central theme of his movement. See also LEGALISM.

Law, Andrew (c. 1749–1821) Composer and teacher of sacred music. He was one of the first American hymn writers.

law of liberty Law of the spirit of life in Christ Jesus which makes his followers free from the law of sin and death (Rom. 8:2). James calls it the "perfect law of liberty" (James 1:25).

Law, William (1686–1761) Anglican clergyman and devotional writer. His claim as the "English Mystic" was established by his principal work, *A Serious Call to a Devout and Holy Life** (1728) which influenced many Evangelicals*, such as George Whitefield*, the Wesleys*, Henry Venn*, Thomas Scott, and Henry Martyn*. He also wrote *The Spirit of Prayer* (1749) and *The Spirit of Love*

(1752), both of which show the influence of Jakob Boehme*.

lax In the Coptic Church*, the consecrated altar stone set into the altar table. It has a cross in the middle, an alpha* symbol on the north side, and an omega* symbol on the south. It is covered with a silk or cotton cover.

laxism System of moral theology* that excused the performance of certain duties because of their practical difficulties or inapplicability to certain situations.

lay Of or relating to a church member not ordained to special office. See also LAITY.

lay abbot Layman placed in charge of an abbey.

lay baptism Baptism administered by a lay person and admitted as valid when there is no clergyman available to perform it.

lay brother Nonordained member of a religious order who is not required to take vows or recite the Holy Office*. Lay brothers have special habits and serve a novitiate*. There are also lay sisters*.

lay clerk Lay person who leads worship in the absence of a clergyman.

lay confession Confession of one's sins to a nonordained Christian, in situations where a clergyman is not available.

lay reader In the Anglican Church, a layman licensed by a bishop to lead worship services. In the Church of Scotland*, both in the Reformation* period and from the twentieth century, readers* (not called lay) have been used similarly.

lay rector In the Anglican Church, a lay person who receives a church's rectorial tithes, occupies the chief seat in the chancel* of the parish* church, and enjoys the freehold of the church. He also has the duty of repairing the chancel.

laying on of hands Also, imposition of hands*. Rite or action imparting sacramental authority or spiritual blessings by laying hands on a person by an ordained superior* or group of superiors who possess such an authority. It is a rite with various meanings—dedication, commission, confirmation*, consecration, healing, blessing, or ordination. It is sanctioned in both the Old and New Testaments (Gen. 48; Matt. 9:25; Mark 16:18; Acts 8:17; 13:3; 19:6; 1 Tim. 4:14). In the Pentecostal tradition, laying on of hands heals the sick, imparts the Holy Spirit*, and commissions a person for the work of the Lord.

Laynez, James See LAINEZ, DIEGO.

Lazarists Also, Vincentians. Popular name of the Congregation of the Priests of the Mission, a society of secular priests living under religious vows, founded by St. Vincent de Paul* in 1625, so called from the priory* of St. Lazare, the headquarters of the society in Paris. They were once concentrated in France, North Africa, and Madagascar, but now are found all over the world. They preach, conduct retreats*, and run seminaries and have rules based on the Jesuit Order.

Ibaitokh Entrance song sung during the Maronite Liturgy.

LDS Latter Day Saints (Mormons*).

Le Clerc, Jean (1657–1736) "Clericus." Arminian theologian and biblical scholar. In 1684 he was appointed professor at Remonstrant College at Amsterdam In his first work, *Liberii de Sancto Amore Epistolae Theologicae* (1679), he tried to explain the mysteries* of Trinity*, Incarnation* and original sin* in rationalistic terms. In 1699 he published a harmony of the Gospels*, *Harmonia Evangelica,* in Greek and Latin. Between 1699 and 1731 he published numerous commentaries on the Bible and edited a new version of the *Apostolic Fathers.* He also edited three periodical works, *Bibliotheque Universelle et Historique* (26 vols., 1686–1693); *Bibliotheque Choisie* (28 vols., 1703–1713); and *Bibliotheque Ancienne et Moderne* (29 vols., 1714–1730); and the standard edition of Erasmus's works (10 vols., 1703–1706).

Le Mans Cathedral of St. Julien, the unfinished cathedral in Le Mans, France. It was the resting place of the relics* of St. Julien. The choir was built between 1217 and 1254. The ring of chapels was extended around the choir as far as the transepts* on both sides. The choir windows contain the figures of not only saints* but also common people who assisted in the building. After the completion of the north transept in the fifteenth century, work on the cathedral was halted and was never resumed.

Le Seuer, Eustache (1616–1655) French religious painter and founder of the French Academy of Painting and Sculpture.

leap of faith Kierkegaardian concept that faith* is not an act of reason or intellect, but a decision fraught with risk, and thus a leap across a chasm.

Lebuin (d. c. 780) Anglo Saxon Benedictine missionary in Frisia and Westphalia. He is reported to have built the first church in Deventer, Netherlands.

Leclercq, Henri (1869–1945) Belgian-French Benedictine scholar who lived for the last 31 years of his life in London. He was an authority on Christian history, archeology, and liturgy. His works include *L'Afrique Chretienne* (2 vols., 1904), *L'Espagne Chretienne* (1906), *Monumenta Ecclesiae Liturgica* (4 vols., 1900–1913), *Histoire des Conciles* (10 vols., 1907–1938), and the *Dictionnaire d'Archeologie Chretienne et de Liturgie* (15 vols., 1903–1953) which he edited and largely wrote himself.

lectern Church reading desk often placed opposite the pulpit. It is sometimes in the shape of an eagle*.

lectern Bible Bible in large type placed on a lectern*.

lectio continua Practice of reading through the entire book of the Bible, in weekly lections*, usually as a basis for exposition in homilies or sermons—in a system today often called expository preaching*. Lectio continua was common in the early church, practiced by Chrysostom* and Augustine*.

lectio divina Meditative reading of the Scriptures

in private devotion or in worship services leading to prayer. In the Rule of St. Benedict*, it is upheld as a monastic virtue and combined with prayer, liturgy, and labor as the goal of Christian life.

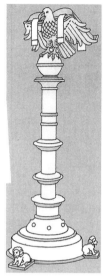

Lectern

lection Bible lesson read in worship service.

lectionary Book of Scripture lessons, or pericopes, to be read during public worship. Originally, incipits (or beginning verses) and explicits (or concluding verses) of the pericopes were noted on the margin of the Bible in the form of a capitulary*, or table, but later they were collected into a book. The Roman Catholic Missal provides for a three-year cycle of three readings for masses on Sundays and a two-year cycle of two readings for weekday masses. Lectionaries are now often produced ecumenically.

lector In the Eastern Orthodox* and Roman Catholic churches, a member of a minor order, corresponding to a reader* in the Anglican Church. His main function is to read the Scriptures, other than the Gospels, and, in the absence of a deacon or cantor*, to announce petitions in the general intercession at Mass*. In the Eastern Orthodox Church*, the lector* serves as the subdeacon.

lecturer Stipendiary minister and deacon com-

mon in Puritan and some Anglican churches to provide regular frequent preaching.

Ledochowski, Vladimir (1866–1942) Twenty-sixth superior general* of the Society of Jesus* (1915–1942). He had a keen interest in missions and required all missionaries to be fluent in the languages of countries to which they were sent. The number of Jesuit missionaries nearly doubled to 3,902 during his tenure in office.

Lee, Ann (c. 1736–1784) English founder of the Shakers*, originally "shaking Quakers." A series of domestic tragedies in which she lost four infants led her to abandon marriage and assume leadership of the local Shaker community. Persecution forced her to emigrate to the United States, where she settled at Watervliet, New York. Now known as Mother Ann, the Word, she shepherded her community to prominence and growth in numbers. She was responsible for shaping the cardinal tenets of the community: celibacy*, confession*, communism, pacifism, millennialism, and ecstatic manifestations through dancing and shaking.

Lee, Jesse (1758–1816) "The Apostle of Methodism* in New England." He was appointed to the first circuit in New England, where he served from 1789 to 1798. Later he served as Asbury's assistant until 1800 and three terms as chaplain* to the House of Representatives and one in the Senate. He wrote the first history of the Methodist Church in his *Short History of Methodism in America* (1810).

Illuminated Lectionary

leeqa dabtara Chief of scribes and ecclesiastical cantors* in the Ethiopian Church.

leeqa memheran Chief of scholars in charge of theological studies in an Ethiopian seminary.

legalism Moral attitude that identifies Christian morality with the literal observance of biblical laws and claims superiority in so doing. The allegation of legalism is often leveled at Christians who believe that God's Word in Scripture gives specific teaching against certain actions and behavior.

legate, papal Personal representative of the pope entrusted with a mission in a nation. Legates may be nuncios, or ambassadors, legati missi or legati a latere, emissary on special missions, and legati nati or emissaries who also hold certain bishoprics*. In modern times, papal legates are ambassadors with plenipotentiary powers.

Legio Maria Church in western Kenya which seceded from the Roman Catholic Church in 1963 under the leadership of a Luo woman, Gaudencia Aoko. By 1967 it was permitted by the newly independent government of Kenya to register as a religious society. It follows conservative Catholic teaching with strong African elements. Latin is retained as the liturgical language, and Mass* is celebrated according to the Latin Rite* with colorful robes.

Legion of Decency Organization established in 1934 by U.S. Catholic bishops to promote quality motion pictures. Since 1968 it has rated motion pictures.

Legion of Mary Lay Catholic association founded in Dublin, Ireland, in 1921 by Frank Duff. It is organized along strict hierarchical lines under its headquarters in Dublin known as concilium. Found in most parts of the Catholic world, the legion emphasizes a Marian* spirituality* inspired largely by the writings of Louis Grignion de Montfort.

Lehrerleut (Ger., teacher people) Hutterite group founded by Jacob Wipf, who established Bruderhof* colonies in South Dakota.

leipsana In the Byzantine tradition, holy relics*.

Leipzig, Disputation of (1519) Debate arranged by Johann Eck*, Roman Catholic theologian, between himself and Luther* and Andreas Carlstadt* representing the Reformers. During the debate Eck was forced to admit that the "power of the keys" had been given to the church rather than to the pope, that church councils may err, and that submission to Rome was not necessary for salvation*. The debate gave Luther's enemies the evidence they needed to condemn him at the Diet of Worms* the following year.

Leipzig Interim Melanchthon's compromise in 1549 between Protestantism* and Catholicism* that was opposed by both the pope and Luther*. It was finally abandoned.

Philip Melanchthon

leitourgikon Byzantine liturgical book containing the texts of the Ordinary of the three liturgies.

lekane In the Byzantine Church*, basin used on Maundy Thursday* for the washing of the altar.

lemon Symbol of faithfulness in religious art.

Lenshina, Alice (c. 1919–1978) African sect* founder. After a near-death experience, she began in Kenya her ministry of preaching and prophecy. In 1955 her movement, estimated over 100,000 strong, was established as a separate sect, known as the Lumpa Church. Conflicts with the tribal chief led to her arrest and death in prison and the suppression of her sect.

Lenski, Richard Charles Henry (1864–1936) Lutheran minister and biblical scholar. After serving several pastorates in Maryland and Ohio, he joined Capital University in 1911 and taught there for the remainder of his life. He is best known for his masterly commentary, the 11–volume *Interpretation of the New Testament*.

Lent (Ger., *lenz,* spring) Also, Quadragesima*. Season of 40 days before Easter* beginning with Ash Wednesday* and ending with Holy Saturday*. The earliest canonical reference is in the fifth canon of the Council of Nicaea* which fixed the number of days at 40, possibly to honor the forty days' fast of Jesus. The fast* may have been part of the preparation of candidates for baptism* on Easter night. The length of the fast varied from three weeks in Rome to seven weeks in the Eastern churches. Originally the fast was rigorous and permitted only one meal a day without white meats, eggs, milk products, and all types of flesh. Gradually the rigors were relaxed until today only Good Friday* and Ash Wednesday* remain fast days and the rest of Lent* is a time of penance* and devotion.

The special character of Lent is also reflected in the liturgy, the use of purple vestments in services, and the omission of hallelujah* and the Gloria in Excelsis* at Mass*. There is a ferial mass for each day in Lent. In the Eastern Church*, the Eucharist* is celebrated only on Saturdays and Sundays, and on Wednesdays and Fridays the Liturgy of the Presanctified* is used.

lenten array Veils of white cloth placed during Lent* before crosses, pictures, and images.

lenten veil Great veil between the chancel* and the nave* in medieval churches during Lent*.

Leo I, St. (d. 461) Known as Leo the Great. Pope from 440. Doctor of the church*. At the Council of Chalcedon*, his *Tome* (449) was accepted as the standard of orthodoxy*. His personal prestige was sufficient to persuade the Huns to withdraw beyond the Danube in 452 and the Vandals to respect people and property when they took Rome*

in 455. Many of the prayers in the Leonine* and Gelasian* sacramentaries have been attributed to him. He was an important systematizer of the theoretical basis of papal authority. Feast day: February 18 (Eastern Church*); November 10 (Western Church*).

Leo III, St. (d. 816) Pope from 795. He crowned Charlemagne* as emperor in 800 and offered him obeisance. However, he resisted the emperor's efforts to add the Filioque* clause to the Nicene Creed* in order not to alienate the Greeks. Feast day: June 12.

Leo IV, St. (d. 855) Pope from 847. He repelled the Saracens, who were threatening Rome*. He built a high wall around the part of Rome now known as the Leonine City* and restored many churches and cities, as Subiaco and Porto, ravaged by war. The asperges* is attributed to him. Feast day: July 17.

Leo IX, St. (1002–1054) Pope from 1048. Birth name: Bruno. His papacy was marked by a reformer's zeal combined with personal humility. At the Easter Synod of 1049 he enforced celibacy* on all clergy and he held more councils at Pavia*, Reims*, and Mainz* in which decrees were passed against simony*. At the Easter Synod of 1050, he condemned the eucharistic doctrine of Berengar of Tours*.

Leo X (1475–1521) Pope from 1513. Birth name: Giovanni de Medici. Elected pope at the age of 38, his eight-year pontificate* was marked by the

Pope Leo X

church's moral and political decline. His only memorable act was his excommunication* of Martin Luther* in 1520.

Leo XIII (1810–1903) Pope from 1878. Birth name: Vincenzo Gioacchino Pecci. On election as pope, he set about improving relations with many of the European powers, as Germany, Belgium, and Great Britain, but relations with Italy and France continued to deteriorate. Social issues played an important part in his pontificate*. His encyclicals upheld the compatibility of Catholic doctrine with modern democracy. In 1891 he issued *Rerum Novarum,* one of the most important papal documents on social justice. His encyclical*, *Aeterni Patris* (1879), helped to revive Thomist studies as the basis of Catholic theology.

In 1883 Leo opened the Vatican archives to researchers and instituted the Biblical Commission* in 1902. His encouragement of the work of missions and the ordination of native clergy led to a vast expansion in Catholic missionary enterprise. In the jubilee* year of 1900, he consecrated the whole human race to the Sacred Heart of Jesus*. He was also the first of modern popes to seriously suggest the possibility of a reunion of Rome with separated churches.

Leofric Missal Tenth-century missal used in Exeter Cathedral in England.

Leon, Luis Ponce de (1527–1591) Spanish mystic and poet. He entered the Augustinian Order in 1544 and became professor in 1561 at Salamanca*, where St. John of the Cross* and Francisco Suarez* were his pupils. He was imprisoned by the Inquisition* for criticizing the Vulgate*. However, he was vindicated of all charges in 1576 and returned to Salamanca, and was named professor of biblical studies in 1579. He is considered one of the greatest lyric poets of Spain. His Latin commentaries on the Song of Solomon, the Book of Job, and other books of the Bible are admired for their lapidary beauty. He is also the author of two spiritual classics: *La Perfecta Casada* (1583) and *De los Nombres de Cristo* (1583–1595).

Leonardo da Vinci (1452–1519) Italian painter and inventor noted for some of the finest religious paintings of all time, including *The Last Supper,* *Virgin of the Rocks, St. Anne,* and *St. John the Baptist. The Last Supper* (1495–1498) was done on the refectory* wall of the Dominican convent of Santa Maria delle Grazie. He was also a scientific genius who has left a large collection of notebooks in which he drew sketches of various machines, anticipating airplanes, tanks, automatic guns, gears, and parachutes.

Leonine City Part of Rome on the right bank of the Tiber River which contains the Vatican* and Castello St. Angelo. It was fortified by Pope Leo IV* in 848–852.

Leonine prayers In the Roman Rite*, prayers ordered by Pope Leo XIII* recited in vernacular by the priest and the congregation at the end of the Mass*, consisting of three Hail Marys*, the Salve Regina*, a collect* *Deus Refugium Nostrum,* an invocation* of St. Michael, and a petition*, "Most Sacred Heart of Jesus, have mercy on us," said for the church. Suppressed in 1964.

Leonine Sacramentary Earliest surviving book of prayers for the Mass* according to the Roman Rite*, attributed to Pope Leo I*. It has no Ordinary or Canon of the Mass* and contains only variable parts of the liturgy arranged according to the civil year.

Leontius of Byzantium (sixth century) Palestinian theologian, noted as an opponent of Nestorians and Monophysites. His Christology* upheld that of Chalcedon, introducing the key clarification of enhypostasia*.

Leontius of Jerusalem (sixth century) Monk and controversialist, considered the most systematic exponent of neo-Chalcedonian orthodoxy. He is probably the author of two works on Chalcedonian Christology*: *Contra Monophysitas* and *Contra Nestorianos.* Sometimes confused with Leontius of Byzantium*.

Leontius the Armenian (d. 454) Martyr*, priest, and disciple of Mesrob and Sahak*. At the Ashtishat* synod, he opposed the de-Christianization order of the Persian king Yezdegerd II. At the Battle of Avarair in 451 he was captured with other Armenian nobles, imprisoned, and tortured to death.

Leopold III (c. 1073–1136) "Leo the Pious." Patron saint* of Austria who founded a number of monasteries.

Lerins Ancient name of two islands off Cannes in South France. On the smaller of the islands St. Honoratus founded in about 410 an abbey from which a long line of bishops and scholars traced their origin: St. Hilary of Arles*, St. Vincent, St. Lupus, St. Eucherius, St. Faustus of Riez, and St. Caesarius of Arles*. It was secularized in 1788, but a Cistercian convent was reestablished here in 1871.

Lesnovo Monastery devoted to archangel* Michael near Kratovo in northeastern Macedonia*, built 1341–1349 by Jovian Oliver, a nobleman at the court of the Serbian Tsar Dusan. The church is built on a cross-in-square plan surmounted by an octagonal dome. It was an important center of learning and housed a scriptorium* well into the Ottoman era. Devastated in the seventeenth century, it was restored in 1728–1730 on the initiative of Arsenije, patriarch of Pec* and again in 1805 through the efforts of a monk, Teodosiji.

Lesser Eastern Churches Collective designation of the non-Chalcedonian churches of Armenia, Syria, Egypt, Ethiopia, and Kerala, India.

lesson Portion of the Scripture read at divine service*.

Lestonnac, St. Jeanne de (1556–1640) Founder of the Congregation, Company of Mary. She became a Cistercian nun on the death of her husband and founded a school and a congregation, The Company of Mary, for the education of girls. The movement spread to 17 countries. Feast day: February 2.

letters commendatory Letters from an ecclesiastical superior* to a cleric on travel as a testimonial of the integrity of his doctrine and morals.

letters dimissory Letters from a bishop permitting a candidate* for holy orders* to be ordained in another diocese* and testifying to his character and doctrinal integrity.

letters of orders Certificate from a bishop attesting the ordination of a person who has entered the holy orders*.

Leuenberg Concord Statement of concord reached between the Lutheran and Reformed* churches of eastern and western Europe adopted in 1973 at Leuenberg, Switzerland. It was signed by more than 60 churches. It affirmed the common faith of the two traditions, revoked earlier disagreements on predestination*, Christology*, and the Lord's Supper*, and expressed toleration of diversity in forms of worship and church order*.

Levellers Seventeenth-century radical group within the Puritan movement who were followers of John Lilburne, so named because they advocated "levelling men's estates." They opposed the established church*, monarchy and nobility, and proposed the complete separation of church and state.

Lewis, Clive Staples (1893–1963) English writer and Christian apologist, one of the most widely read Christian authors of modern times. Raised an Anglican, he became an atheist as a teenager, but moved slowly through Romanticism and Idealism to Theism*, coming full circle back to the Church of England*. His conversion is recorded in *The Pilgrim's Regress* (1933) and his autobiography, *Surprised by Joy* (1955). Lewis was a lifelong opponent of the cant of modern secular intellectuals, but he balanced his apprehension of evil

C. S. Lewis

with a vision of joy derived from faith*. While he valued the clarity that reason brings, he also cherished the power of imagination to create spiritual myths that sustain the human mind and save it from the aridity* of reason.

Lewis had the gift, as C. E. M. Joad wrote, of "making righteousness readable." This gift was most obvious in the satirical *Screwtape Letters* (1941), characterized by wit, effortless elegance, and disciplined logic. He followed it with a number of books, novels, children's books, fantasies, poetry, and literary criticism. But the main body of his works dealt with Christian apologetics in one form or another: *The Problem of Pain* (1940), *Mere Christianity* (1943), *Abolition of Man* (1943), *Miracles* (1947), *Reflections on the Psalms* (1958), *Letters to Malcolm: Chiefly on Prayer* (1963), and *Christian Reflections* (1967).

lex orandi, lex credendi (Lat., the law of prayer is the law of believing). Fifth-century axiom of Prosper of Aquitaine, an affirmation that how Christians pray and worship determines or influences what they believe or should believe.

Liang A-Fah (1789–1855) First ordained Chinese Protestant evangelist, appointed a Bible society* colporteur* by William Milne*, a colleague of Robert Morrison*. He wrote a treatise on Christianity entitled *Good Words Exhorting the Age,* which he distributed among civil service examinees in Canton, one of whom was Hung Hsiuech'uan, the instigator of the Taiping Rebellion.

libellatici Christians who, during the Decian persecution* (249–251) purchased certificates from the civil authorities that they had sacrificed to idols when in fact they had not. The practice was condemned by the church but condoned in practice.

Libelli Missarum Booklets containing formularies for one or more masses for a given period in a particular church, used before sacramentaries came into vogue. They did not include the canons or the fixed and sung parts of the liturgy.

Liber Censuum Official register of the Roman Catholic Church recording the dues payable by

various entities, such as monasteries, churches, cities, and kingdoms to the Holy See*. It also contained a list of the monasteries and bishoprics* directly subordinate to the Holy See.

Liber Comicus (Lat., excerpt book) In the Mozarabic Rite*, a lectionary*, giving complete text of the pericopes.

Liber Gradualis Book for the choir containing text and music of the graduals sung between the Epistle and the Gospel.

Liber Officialis (823) Liturgical book by Amalarius of Metz interpreting the liturgy allegorically.

Liber Ordinarius See CUSTOMARY.

Liber Ordinum Sixth-century Mozarabic book containing a pontifical*, ritual, and some Mass* texts.

Liber Pontificalis Book of biographies of popes from Peter* to the mid-fifteenth century attributed to an anonymous Roman presbyter*. It was periodically updated. It is an important historical source.

Liber Responsorialis Book for the choir, containing responses and psalms.

Liber Vitae (Lat., Book of Life) Lists maintained in the early church of faithful members in good standing. See also DIPTYCH.

liberalism 1. Mode of theological thought that favors an anti-dogmatic and humanitarian reconstruction of the Christian faith and a readiness to subordinate historic Christian traditions and truths to fashionable intellectual and theological compromises. 2. In the Roman Catholic Church, a movement that favors political democracy, less papal control, and ecclesiastical reform. See also MODERNISM.

liberation theology Radical theological movement that had its origins at the Second Conference of Latin American Bishops (CELAM*) held at Medellin* in Columbia in 1968 and the Third Conference held at Puebla in Mexico in 1979. Its ideological basis was first expounded in Gustavo Gutierrez's* *Teologia de la Liberacion* (1979). Other important ideologues included the Brazilian Hugo Assmann and Leonardo Boff*, Argentinian Jose Miguez Bonino and Jan Luis Segundo*, Mexican Jose P. Miranda, and Salvadoran Jan Sobrino. The salient theses of liberation theology are: 1. Preference for the poor is the focus of the church's ministry. 2. Social and political liberation which is based on Marxist analysis of society is as important as salvation*. 3. Social transformation even by violence is a biblical concept. 4. Christ's mission was as political as it was spiritual. 5. Orthodoxy or right belief must be validated by orthopraxy*, or right practice. 6. Physical violence is justified because existing social and political structures are maintained by coercion.

The Roman Catholic Church was concerned that liberation theology's condemnation of all authority included ecclesiastical authority. While accepting some of its premises and even endorsing its "preferential option for the poor," the church rejected its Marxist content. In 1986, Sacred Congregation in Rome issued *Libertatis Conscientia,* which offered a more favorable assessment of the movement, but, as a whole, conservatives dominated the Latin American hierarchy and allowed little room for liberation theologians to extend their influence beyond small pockets. Practical expressions of the movement are found in the growth of *communidades ecclesiales de base,* small communities of 15 to 20 families led by laymen integrating social, political, and spiritual issues. Their goal was *conscientizacion,* or making the disenfranchised people more aware of their situation and rights.

In some countries liberation theologians actively entered politics and government or have led resistance movements to dictators. Two Roman Catholic institutions that have been active in the movement are the Jesuits* and the Catholic Foreign Mission Society of America* at Maryknoll*, New York. Liberation theology stands as much for a new way of doing theology as for its content. Rejecting Western academic-led theology, it insists on starting from social analysis and then moving to praxis*.

Liberian Catalog List of the bishops of Rome* from Peter* to Liberius* compiled by an unknown chronicler named "the chronographer" by historian Theodore Mommsen.

Liberius (d. 366) Pope from 352 to 366. He was ordered by Emperor Constantius to agree to the condemnation of Athanasius* as a rebel. When Liberius refused, he was banished from Rome* in 355, but allowed to resume his see after agreeing under duress to the deposition and to sign the Arian confession* of faith passed at the Council of Sirmium*. He built a famous church on Equiline Hill, the predecessor of the present Santa Maria Maggiore*.

Libermann, Francois Marie Paul (1802–1852) Founder of the Missionaries of the Most Holy Heart of Mary. Born of Orthodox Jewish parents, he was trained to become a rabbi like his father, but was converted at 24. Called to evangelize* Africa, he went to Rome* in 1839 with a plan for a new missionary organization, Missionaries of the Most Holy Heart of Mary, as "a fellowship of priests, who in the name and as envoys of Our Lord Jesus Christ, dedicate themselves entirely to announce His holy gospel, and to establish His reign among the poorest and most neglected souls in the church of God." Ordained to the priesthood in 1841, he opened his first novitiate* at La Neuville, near Amiens*, France. The first missionary was sent to Mauritius and the next to West Africa. In 1848, upon the request of Propaganda Fide, Libermann agreed to take over the Congregation of the Holy Ghost Fathers*, devastated by the French Revolution. The new organization then became known as the Holy Ghost Fathers.

Libertines Two groups of anti-Calvinists in Geneva*. The first opposed the dominance of Calvin* and the "foreigners" in Genevan affairs, and the second were pantheistic spiritualists who rejected formal Christianity.

Library of the Fathers Series of English translations of selected writings of early Church Fathers* beginning with the *Confessions of St. Augustine* in 1838. It was published under the auspices of the Oxford movement*.

liceity In canon law*, determination of the legality of a sacrament*, often used with another juridical term, *valid* or *efficacious*. A sacrament is licit or legal if the provisions of the law regulating its celebration have been followed, irrespective of the status of its celebrant.

licentiate 1. Seminary student who has completed his studies and has received permission to preach the Word of God* but not permitted to administer the sacraments*. 2. In the Roman Catholic Church, a friar* empowered to hear confessions and grant absolution*. 3. Designation of certain academic qualifications, especially in theology.

lich/lych gate Covered gateway in a churchyard wall. Originally so called because coffins were placed there before burial.

Liddell, Eric (1902–1945) Athlete and missionary in China, on whose life the film *Chariots of Fire* was based. He was a Rugby football internationalist and Olympic champion who created a stir because he would not run in the Olympics on a Sunday. In 1925 he joined the staff of the Anglo-Chinese Christian College at Tientsin. He was interned by the Japanese at Weihsien from 1942 to 1945 but died of a brain tumor just before release.

Liddon, Henry Parry (1829–1890) Popular Anglican preacher, canon* of St. Paul's*, London, from 1870. He became a member of the Tractarian group in his youth under the influence of his mentor, Edward Pusey*, and worked hard to restore Roman Catholic institutions to the Church of England*.

Lien-Chou martyrs Four martyrs—Rev. and Mrs. John Peale, their ten-year-old daughter, Ella Machle, and Eleanor Chestnut—killed in cold blood by a Buddhist mob at Lien-Chou, China, in 1905.

Life and Work Branch of the ecumenical movement*, initiated by Swedish bishop Nathan Soderblom*, concerned with the application of Christianity to social, political, and economic issues. World conferences on Life and Work* were held at Stockholm (1925) and Oxford (1937).

lifestyle evangelism Evangelism* based on building friendships and relationships with non-Chris-

tians and sharing their problems and concerns on a personal level.

lifting of hands Gesture of worship generally associated in modern times with Charismatic and Pentecostal believers. The gesture is one of joy, exuberance, gratitude, and devotion and is biblically sanctioned in Psalms 63:4 and 134:2 and 1 Timothy 2:8. See also ORANT.

light Symbol of goodness and truth, as opposed to the darkness of evil. It is associated with divine illumination* or the revelation* of God. In the New Testament, the symbol is used to describe the Incarnate Word ("I am the light of the world," John 8:12) and, in John, Jesus Christ (the true Light which gives light to every man," John 1:9).

light of Tabor See UNCREATED LIGHT.

Light of the World One of the titles of Jesus Christ from John 8:12. It is the subject of a famous painting by Holman Hunt*.

Light of the World

Lightfoot, Joseph Barber (1828–1889) Bishop of Durham* and biblical scholar. He was one of the most learned men of his day, fluent in many languages. His biblical commentaries included *Galatians* (1865), *Philippians* (1868), and *Colossians* with *Philemon* (1875). He wrote extensively on the Apostolic Fathers* and helped to prepare the Revised Version* of the New Testament.

Liguori, St. Alphonsus (1696–1787) Italian theologian considered the father of moral theology*. He abandoned a successful career in law to become a priest in 1726. In 1731 he founded a congregation of the Redemptoristines* for women and in 1732 the Congregation of the Most Holy Redeemer or Redemptorists for men, both dedicated to mission work among the poor. As a theologian he opposed Jansenism*, probabilism*, and Tutiorism*, and developed a middle-of-the-road theology known as equiprobabilism*, which has been accepted by the church. In 1762 he became bishop of a small diocese* near Naples, where he remained until 1775. He was beatified in 1816 and canonized in 1839. Among his writings are many hymns, and popular devotional and mystical writings on the Sacred Heart of Jesus*. His devotional writings include *Visits to the Blessed Sacrament and the Blessed Virgin* (1745), *The Glories of Mary* (1750), *Novena of Christmas* (1758), *Novena of the Heart of Jesus* (1758), *The Great Means of Prayer* (1759), *The True Spouse of Jesus Christ* (1760), and *The Way of Salvation* (1767). Feast day: August 1.

lijkaneat Judge in ecclesiastical matters in the Ethiopian Church*.

lilia Midnight Office in the Assyrian Church*.

lily In Christian art, flower symbolizing purity, immortality*, and the Virgin Mary*.

limbo of the fathers Eternal abode of those just men who died before Calvary but who found salvation* when Christ opened the doors of heaven* to them.

limbo of the infants Everlasting state of those who die unregenerate and under the penalty of original sin*, such as unbaptized infants, but who are not guilty of personal sin.

Limburg Romanesque collegiate church of St. George* and St. Nicholas*, founded in Limburg, Germany, in 910 by Count Conrad Kurzbold, and raised to the rank of a cathedral in 1827. The present building program began between 1215 and 1220, the altar was dedicated in 1235, and work on the seven towers was finished by about 1250.

liminality (Lat., threshold) Sacred rites of passage,

such as baptism*, constituting milestones in religious experience.

limited atonement Also, particular redemption*. Doctrine in Calvinism* that Christ died only for the elect* who are the only recipients of salvation*. Many medieval schoolmen had similar teachings.

Lincoln The largest diocese* in England. The first see* was established by St. Remigius*. The cathedral, begun in 1086, was completed before 1300. The first Lincoln Cathedral was destroyed in an earthquake in 1185. The rebuilding began in 1192, and the vaulted roof was completed in 1233. The star-vaulted chapter house* is the earliest polygonal chapter house in England. The most beautiful part of the cathedral is the choir built between 1256 and 1280.

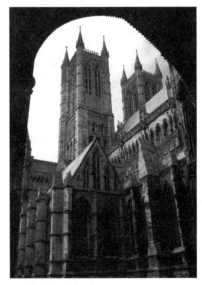

Lincoln Cathedral

Lindisfarne Also called the Holy Isle*. Island in the North Sea off the Northumberland coast. Its history began with the arrival of St. Aidan* from Iona* in 635. In subsequent decades it became a missionary center and episcopal see*. In 793 and 875 the church was pillaged by the Danes, and the monks fled. But monastic life resumed from 1082 and lasted until the dissolution of the monasteries.

Lindisfarne Gospels One of the most splendid of all illuminated manuscripts, written between 698 and 721 by Eadfrith, bishop of Lindisfarne*, in the island monastery—also called Holy Isle*—off the coast of Northumbria. It has features adapted from the Codex Amiatinus*. Among these features are the fine carpet-pages, or purely ornamental pages composed of intricate spirals and interlacings, and a magnificent Chi-Rho* at the beginning of St. Matthew's Gospel.

Lindisfarne

Lindsay, Gordon and Freda Theresa (1906–1973 and 1916–, respectively) Faith healers and founders of Christ for the Nations Institute in Dallas, Texas. Supporters of Pentecostal and Charismatic missions, they pioneered several programs, including Winning the Nations Crusade (1956), Native Church Crusade (1961), and Full Gospel Fellowship of Churches and Ministers International (1962).

Lindsey, Hal (1930–) American author and millennialist. He was with Campus Crusade for Christ* for eight years after graduation from Dallas Theological Seminary*. His *Late Great Planet Earth* (1970) is reported to be the world's best-selling religious book and was extremely popular with students of the Book of Revelation. He later became a radio and television show host.

linobambakoi Crypto Christians in Cyprus* who during the Ottoman period adopted Muslim names and observed Muslim practices while secretly maintaining their Orthodox faith.

Linus, St. (first century) According to unsubstantiated tradition, the successor of Peter* as bishop of Rome*. His term of office is placed at 12 years (68–80). He was supposedly martyred under Emperor Titus. Feast day: September 23.

lion In Christian art, symbol of royalty, associated with Jesus Christ as lion of Judah. A winged lion is the symbol of John Mark.

Lippi, Filippino (c. 1457–1504) Son of Fra Filippo Lippi*. He worked as a young boy with Botticelli*. Among his Madonnas* are ones with new motifs, such as Madonna Lactans, known as the *Intercession of Christ and the Virgin,* in which she bares her breast and he points to his wounds. His frescoes are on St. Thomas Aquinas* and Philip.

Lippi, Fra Filippo (c. 1406–1469) Italian painter. In 1437 he began painting *Madonna and Child with Saints and Angels,* now in the Louvre. He also adopted the motif of the kneeling Madonna* adoring the Christ child, who is lying on the ground, in a series of mystic nativities. Among his principal paintings are the *Barbadori Altarpiece* (1437), *The Coronation of the Virgin* (1441), and his fresco cycles on *St. John the Baptist* and *St. Stephen* (1452–1465).

Lisle, George (c. 1750–c. 1845) The first African-American preacher and missionary in America who sent some of his fellow blacks to evangelize* Africa. He founded the first Negro Baptist church in Savannah and the first Negro Baptist church in Jamaica.

Lindisfarne Gospels

Lismore, Book of Fifteenth-century manuscript found in 1814 at Lismore Castle containing lives of the saints in Middle Irish.

Liszt, Franz (1811–1886) Hungarian composer. A Catholic, he took minor orders* in Rome* and worked to promote the Cecilian movement*.

litany (Gk., supplication) Form of liturgical prayer consisting of a series of petitions or biddings said or sung by the priest, deacon, or cantor* to which the congregation makes fixed responses, such as Kyrie eleison*. The practice originated in fourth-century Antioch* and from there spread to the Western Church* where invocation* of the saints* became a favorite feature. In the Roman Catholic Church, litanies are used in special services, such as Rogationtide processions (litaniae minores) and on St. Mark's Day processions (litaniae majores). In the Byzantine Church*, there are several types of litanies: The Great Litany (velikaya ekteniya*), Little Litany (malaya ekteniya), and the Litany of Fervent Intercession.

litany desk Low movable desk at which the litany is offered.

Litany of Loreto Litany honoring the Virgin Mary*, so named from the famous Italian shrine. It is used in private devotions. It consists of a series of invocations* of Our Lady under a number of honorific titles, such as "Mother of Divine Grace," "Virgin Most Prudent," "Queen of Angels," "Queen of the Most Holy Rosary," "Queen Conceived without Original Sin," "Mother of Good Counsel," "Queen of Peace," and "Queen Assumed into Heaven," each followed by the response, "Pray for us." There is a similar litany of St. Joseph*.

litany of the saints Invocations* of mercy and deliverance addressed to the Father, the Son, and the Holy Spirit* as well as intercession addressed to the Virgin Mary*, prophets, patriarchs, angels*, apostles, confessors*, and the saints*.

lite (Gk., entreaty) In the Byzantine Rite*: 1. Procession of clergy and people to a designated church in celebration of a feast, for intercession, and in thanksgiving. 2. Stichera sung on such occasions. Lites are also sung during the blessing of the bread, wheat, wine, and oil at the end of hesperinos*.

literalism Interpretation of biblical texts in straightforward and nonsymbolic language, using the literal meaning of the original words.

Little Entrance 1. In the Eastern Church*, the procession with the Gospel book in the liturgy. In earlier times, it marked the entrance of the bishop into the service. 2. In the Byzantine Rite*, the procession of priests and deacons who carry the Book of the Gospels at the beginning of the Liturgy of the Word*. It is carried from the altar through the church and back to the altar.

Little Flower of Jesus Epithet of Teresa of Lisieux*.

Little Flowers of St. Francis Book containing stories and legends about St. Francis of Assisi* and his companions. It is based on and derived from *Actus Beati Francisci et Sociorum Eius,* written by Fra Ugolini Boniscambi of Montegeorgio (c. 1335).

Little Gidding Religious community established by the Ferrar family near Huntingdon, England, from 1625 to 1646. It was governed by a systematic rule of devotion, work, and prayer in which there were prayers every quarter of an hour and a night watch from 9:00 P.M. to 1:00 A.M. In addition, the group engaged in works of mercy*, ran a dispen-

Little Gidding

sary, a school, and a study circle called Little Academy. The Ferrars were also skilled bookbinders. The community was dispersed by Oliver Cromwell's Puritans*, but interest in them was revived by *John Inglesant* (1881), a novel by J. H. Shorthouse, and by T. S. Eliot's poem, "Little Gidding," included in his *Four Quartets* (1944). In 1977, a new ecumenical community was founded in the same place with the name The Community of Christ the Sower.

Little Office of Our Lady Brief office in honor of the Virgin Mary*, divided, like the Divine Office*, into seven hours. It also provides for the observance of 28 feasts, of which 12 are Marian*. It was first adopted by the Cistercians* and the Camaldolese* and later spread to the secular clergy. The office was included in many books of hours, often richly illuminated. Although no longer obligatory, it is recommended as a private devotion.

little offices Very short offices intended for devotional recitation. They were compiled, mainly in the vernacular, to meet the needs of those not using existing offices and to provide some liturgical content to their common prayer. In the English language, the book most used is *A Short Breviary for Religious and the Laity,* edited by the monks of St. John's Abbey*, Collegeville, Minnesota.

Little Sisters of the Poor Religious community for women founded in 1839 at St. Servan, France, by Jeanne Jugan and two other companions.

liturgical altar Ecclesiastical altar or table with no shelf or retable* behind it. The cross may rest on the altar or the wall behind it or be suspended over it. The candlesticks and tabernacle rest on the mensa*.

liturgical books Books containing directions for liturgical services. They include Antiphonal, *Book of Common Prayer*, Breviary*, Evangeliary*, Gradual*, Kyriale*, *Liber Responsorialis*, *Liber Usualis*, Martyrologium, Missal, Ordinal, Pontificale, Psalter, Rituale, Sacramentary, Troper, Vesperale.

liturgical colors Colors used at different times in the liturgical year*. They are white, used at Christmastide*, Eastertide*, and Trinity Sunday*; red, used at Pentecost* and on martyr's feasts; green, used in seasons of the Trinity* and Epiphany*; purple, used in Lent* and Advent*; and black, used on Good Friday* and All Souls' Day*.

liturgical lance See lance.

Liturgical Lance

liturgical movement Movement in Roman Catholic and Anglican and other Protestant churches to restore lay participation in worship. The Ritualist movement begun by the Tractarians in Anglicanism* and the Hochkirche movement in Germany are examples in the Protestant church. In the Roman Catholic Church, the movement dates from the directions of Pius X* on church music in 1903 and the promotion of frequent participation in the Eucharist* by the Congress at Malines. It was promoted by several religious orders, particularly in the Benedictine abbeys of Solesmes* in France, Maredsous and Mont-Cesar in Belgium, and Maria Laach* in Germany. At Solesmes, Abbot Prosper Gueranger* (1805–1875) preached a love of worship for its own sake. It spread to England through the writings of Fernand Cabrol* on the liturgy and the publication of his English-Latin missal in 1921. In 1929 the Society of St. Gregory was formed to encourage the active participation of the congregation in worship through plainsong*.

After World War II, the movement spread to parishes and missionary centers. In his encyclical* *Mediator Dei,* Pius XII* blessed the movement with his official approval. There was a parallel movement to make the liturgy relevant to the laity and to restore to it some of its earlier significance. Permission was given to use the vernacular in the administration of all sacraments* except the Eucharist*, and the reform of the rites began with the revision of the Holy Week* Liturgy in 1951 and 1955. This was followed by the publication of a new *Ordo Missae,* lectionary*, and calendar in 1969 and a new *Roman Missal* in 1970 along with new rites prescribed for baptism*, confirmation*, and dedication. The constitution on sacred liturgy at the Second Vatican Council* (1963) initiated a series of legislative reforms of the liturgy, including the use of the vernacular.

liturgical prayer Formal prayer used in the canonical hours*.

Liturgicon Also, hieraticon*. In the Byzantine tradition: 1. Altar book containing the priest's and, sometimes, the deacon's part in the vespers*, mattins*, and the liturgy. 2. Book containing the text of all three Orthodox liturgies.

liturgics Branch of theology concerned with the study of liturgy.

liturgiology Branch of theology dealing with liturgy as an academic discipline.

liturgist 1. Person conducting a liturgical worship service. 2. An authority on or student of liturgy.

liturgy (Gk., *leitourgia*, public duty) Prescribed form for public or corporate worship, but generally restricted to the eucharistic rite. Certain historical texts of the liturgy, as for example, the Liturgy of St. Chrysostom*, are officially used by certain denominations.

Liturgy of Addai and Mari Unique anaphora* that is addressed to Christ and not to God, used by the Assyrians and the Chaldeans, believed to have originated in third-century Edessa*. It was revised by Assyrian patriarch Ishu'yab* III in the seventh century.

Liturgy of Gregory the Great Liturgy of the Presanctified*.

Liturgy of Nestorius Anaphora used in the Assyrian Church* at Epiphany*, the Feast of St. John the Baptist, the Greek Doctors, Wednesday of the Fast of the Ninevites, and Holy Thursday*.

Liturgy of St. Basil One of the three liturgies used in the Byzantine Church*, a revised version of an earlier anaphora* by Basil of Caesarea*. It is Antiochene in style with a long post-Sanctus* section.

Liturgy of St. James Liturgy attributed to St. James*, the brother of our Lord, a modification of the primitive Antiochene Liturgy of the Apostolic Constitutions*. It is used by the Jacobite Church* and the Maronite Church.

Liturgy of St. John Chrysostom The main liturgy of the Eastern Orthodox* churches, used in several languages. It is used on all days except on ten days of the year when the Liturgy of St. Basil* is prescribed.

Liturgy of St. Theodore of Mopsuestia Anaphora used by the Assyrian Church* on Sundays from Advent* until Palm Sunday*. Often called the Second Hallowing.

Liturgy of the Presanctified Liturgy of the Byzantine Rite* that is celebrated on Wednesdays and Fridays during Lent* and on the first three days of Holy Week*. It does not include a prayer of consecration and may be combined with vespers*. St. Sophronius* called it an "apostolic institution."

Liturgy of the Word In the Roman Catholic tradition, part of the Mass* that extends from the first reading of the Scripture to the prayer of the faithful.

lity (lit., entreaty) Litany of the people's needs intoned by the deacon at the end of the Litany of Fervent Intercession.

living In the Anglican Church, benefice*.

Living Bible A paraphrased English translation of the Bible based on the American Standard Version* made by Kenneth N. Taylor*, first published in 1967. It was revised and reissued in the 1990s as the New Living Translation (NLT).

living Christmas tree Christmas production in the form of a large wooden or metal piece in the shape of a Christmas tree on which the choir stands. The tree is usually heavily decorated with only the heads of the singers visible.

Livingstone, David (1813–1873) Missionary and explorer, considered the greatest in modern times, who opened the southern half of Africa to Christianity. Converted at age 17, he decided to devote his life to spreading the gospel. After studying medicine and theology in Glasgow, he went to London and joined the London Missionary Society (LMS*). In 1840, inspired by Robert Moffat*

David Livingstone

(whose daughter he later married), he left for Africa, where he worked for the remainder of his life.

He first worked in Bechuanaland from where he began his great travels that took him some 30,000 miles in what was then a totally unexplored region. He began what has been described as "the greatest journey of exploration ever made by one man" from Cape Town to the Zambesi River, west to the Atlantic Ocean and then east to the Indian Ocean. He discovered Lake Ngami in 1849 and the Victoria Falls on the Zambesi. Reports of his work aroused great interest in England, where he was greeted as a hero when he returned in 1858.

He returned to Africa, no longer as an LMS missionary but as a consul. In 1859 he discovered the Lakes of Shirwa and Nyasa and later explored the basin of the Upper Nile and Lake Bangweulu in 1868. After a second trip home in 1863, he returned once again, but soon lost contact with civilization, and was presumed dead. *The New York Herald* sent out H. M. Stanley to find him, and their celebrated meeting at Ujiji in 1871 has been retold many times. Although sick and exhausted,

Livingstone refused to return home without completing his mission. He died in 1873 at the village of Ilala, while at prayer. He was buried with national honors at Westminster Abbey*. He left an account of his travels in *Missionary Travels and Researches in South Africa* (1857) and *The Zambesi and its Tributaries* (1865).

Llandaff Welsh episcopal see*, north of Cardiff. Its cathedral was built in 1120. It became a Puritan center in the seventeenth century, and, after nearly two centuries of decline, religious life flourished again after the mid-nineteenth century, The cathedral was restored between 1844 and 1869; it was badly damaged in German air raids in 1941 and restored again in 1957. It now has a large statue of *Christ in Majesty* by Jacob Epstein.

Lloyd-Jones, David Martyn (1899–1981) Welsh preacher. He left a promising career as a physician to become pastor in a small Presbyterian church in Wales and later in 1939 at Westminster Chapel in London. He preached there almost every Sunday until his retirement. A powerful expository preacher, he became one of the most influential evangelical leaders in Britain. Among his works was *Studies in the Sermon on the Mount* (2 vols., 1959, 1960) and many volumes of exposition drawn from his sermons.

Llull, Ramon (c. 1233–c. 1315) Also, Lull. Writer and martyr*. At age 30 he had a vision of Christ crucified, and he devoted himself thereafter entirely to his service. His life's mission was the conversion of Muslims. After several years of study of the Muslim mission field, he wrote *The Book of Contemplation* in Arabic. In 1234 he received another vision which he set forth in *Art of Finding Truth*. From 1287 onwards, he was constantly traveling, formulating his plans for converting Muslims, trying to win support for his work, and going on missions in North Africa. He is reputed to have died a martyr's death at Bougie in North Africa, where he was stoned to death. Llull broke the medieval tradition by writing not only in Latin but also in Arabic and his native Catalan. He was prolific, producing some 290 books, of which 240 survive. Many of these works are religious allegories. As a mystic, Llull is regarded as the forerunner of St. Teresa* and St. John of the Cross*.

He was a staunch defender of the dogma of immaculate conception*.

Ramon Llull

Llwyd, Morgan (1619–1659) Welsh Puritan author of *Llyfr y Tri Aderyn* (The Three Birds) (1653), a devotional classic in the Welsh language. He also wrote a number of poems. Two volumes of his works were published in 1899 and 1908.

LMS London Missionary Society, founded in 1795 by a group consisting of Congregationalists, Wesleyans, Anglicans, and Presbyterians. Its first missionary outreach was to Tahiti in 1796. Later it expanded its work to China, India, Southeast Asia, South and East Africa, and South Pacific. Its direction is now in the hands of the Council for World Mission*.

Loayza, Geronimo de (c. 1498–1575) First archbishop of Lima. Named as metropolitan* of all dioceses* in Central and South America, Loayza summoned the first two church councils of Lima in 1551 and 1567. His *Manual* (1549) prescribed norms for working with Indians. He began the building of Lima's cathedral and also helped to found San Marcos University (1551).

lobsh In the Coptic Rite, part of the office of theotokia*, including hymns to the Virgin Mary*.

local preacher Layman licensed to preach in a Methodist conference, as a preliminary to ordination.

loci communes (Lat., common places or common topics) Collection of scriptural references and their interpretations or a representative range of Christian doctrines that together constitute a consistent body of Christian doctrine. Hence commonplaces as the title of such a published collection.

loci theologici Major heads of systematic theology.

loculus (Lat., small place) Most common form of tombs in the catacombs*. It is in the form of a horizontal rectangular niche*, cut one above another, in the sides of the corridors. It is closed at the front by a tile or marble slab bearing the epitaph.

locus classicus (Lat., classical place) Particular text in Scripture considered the source from which a doctrine or biblical concept is chiefly derived.

locus poenitentiae (Lat., place or opportunity of repentance) Interval when it is possible to withdraw from a bargain or a course of action before being fully committed to it.

Logia Collection of the sayings of Christ, generally considered spurious, that circulated independently of the Gospels in the early church. Some of them were discovered at Nag Hammadi* and Oxyrhynchus*.

Logion (Gk., saying) Statement attributed to Jesus, especially when separate from a narrative context.

Logos (Gk., word or reason) Word with Greek and Jewish background, used by John the apostle for Jesus Christ (John 1). In Jewish theology, Logos was the intermediary between the transcendent God and creation. In Greek thought, it was divine wisdom, the rational principle inherent in the universe. In the New Testament, Paul* calls Jesus the "wisdom of God" (1 Cor. 1:24). John ties in the word with its Greek and Jewish usage, but uses the term only once. The Church Fathers* used the term as a bridge between hellenistic philosophy and Christian theology. Theophilus* distinguished between the Logos immanent in God and Logos as the mediator between God and his creation. Athanasius* linked it to the doctrine of redemption*.

Lohe, William (1808–1872) American-German Lutheran leader. He organized the Missouri and Iowa Lutheran synods, established a theological seminary in Australia, and influenced the Lutheran liturgical movement.

Loisy, Alfred Firmin (1857–1940) French modernist biblical scholar. He was ordained priest in 1879 and dedicated himself thereafter to a critical study of the Bible. Although by 1886 he had become alienated from the traditional teaching of the church, he accepted the position of professor of sacred Scripture at the Institut Catholique, but was dismissed from the post in 1893. During the rest of the decade he served as chaplain* to the Catholic School for Nuns at Neuilly and at the Ecole Pratique des Hautes Etudes. In 1902 he published *L'Evangile et l'Eglise* in reply to Adolf Harnack's* *Wesen des Christentums,* and it raised Catholic hackles. It was followed by the publication of *Autour d'un Petit Livre.* Both these works were placed on the Index.

In 1906 Loisy left the priesthood. A final breach with the church came when he was excommunicated in 1908 after the publication of *Les Evangiles Synoptiques* and the papal condemnation of modernism* in 1907. In his later life as an ex-Catholic, he continued to write and produce major works on Christian history and the history of religions, including *Les Actes des Apotres* (1920), *Essai Historique sur le Sacrifice* (1920), *La Religion* (1924), and *La Naissance du Christianisme* (1933).

Lollards Followers of John Wycliffe* in England in the fourteenth and fifteenth centuries. With the Bible as their only authority, they went about the countryside proclaiming salvation* by faith* and denying the validity of indulgences*, pilgrimages*, transubstantiation*, clerical celibacy, oral confession*, the church's temporal power, prayers for the dead, images, and ecclesiastical hierarchy*.

Their beliefs are summarized in the document Twelve Conclusions. Originally, Lollardy was an academic movement led by Nicholas of Hereford, translator of the Lollard Bible. Leadership later passed on to the preacher William Swinderby and later to John Purvey, Wycliffe's secretary.

By 1395, the movement had spread to the middle and artisan classes and had become an organized sect with ordained ministers and representatives in Parliament. The success of the movement prompted many repressive measures: In 1401 Parliament passed a measure branding Lollards as heretics and mandating their burning. In 1414 Sir John Oldcastle led a march on London which was dispersed by the soldiers of Henry V. The abortive uprising shattered the power of the Lollards and forced it to go underground. Thenceforth, until the Reformation*, it was a heterogeneous group of visionaries, knights who coveted church property, and dissatisfied parishioners* and tenants. But it remained a thorn in the side of the church for many years, and there was a Lollard revival in the early sixteenth century in London, East Anglia, and the Chiltern Hills. After 1530 Lollardy merged with Protestantism* and contributed to the anticlericalism*, dissent*, and nonconformity* driving the spread of Lutheran ideas in England.

Lonergan, Bernard (1904–1984) Canadian Jesuit philosopher. He moved from nominalism to critical realism*, from knowing as intuitive to knowing as discursive. He taught at the Gregorian University* in Rome*, Regis College at Toronto, Harvard University, and Boston College. Among his works are *Insight: An Essay on Human Understanding* (1957) and *Method in Theology* (1972).

Longinus, St. The legendary name of the soldier who wounded the side of the crucified Christ with a lance. He is reported to have become a Christian, been baptized by the apostles, and suffered a martyr's death.

Lopez de Mendoza Grajales, Francisco (c. 1525–c. 1569) First Catholic priest in the present-day United States. He was chaplain* of the fleet of Pedro Menendez de Aviles who landed in St. Augustine, Florida, in 1565. Here he celebrated Mass* on the Feast of the Nativity of the Blessed Virgin*.

Lopez, Gregory (1615/6–1691) Birth name: Lo Wentsao. First native Chinese bishop. After studying in Manila, he joined the Dominican Order and was ordained the first Chinese priest in 1654. He was consecrated in 1685 at Canton as vicar apostolic* of Nanking.

Lord, Our Jesus Christ as the center of Christian worship, devotion, and obedience.

Lord's Day Sunday, dedicated to the Lord in commemoration of his Resurrection on Easter* Sunday (Rev. 1:10).

Lord's Prayer Prayer given by the Lord to his followers and disciples, described by Tertullian* as "the epitome of the whole gospel" and by St. Augustine* as "the source of all prayers." It appears in the New Testament in two slightly different forms (Matt. 6:9–13; Luke 11:2–4). The former is one universally used by Christians. A concluding doxology*, which appears in Didache*, is not canonical. There are seven petitions in the Lord's Prayer, three asking for the glorification of God and four asking for physical and spiritual needs. The Lord's Prayer is taught to the catechumens* and is used in services of worship, including Communion*, in virtually all traditions. See also PATER NOSTER.

Lord's Supper See HOLY COMMUNION.

Lord's Table 1. The Eucharist* or the Lord's Supper*. 2. In most Protestant churches, the table from which Communion is served. Some use table or altar interchangeably. The Reformers insisted on table because no service took place in the Supper.

Loreto Town near Ancona, Italy, site of the Holy House, alleged home of the Virgin Mary*, transported by angels first to Dalmatia and later to Loreto.

Loreto Nuns Congregation of the Sisters of Loreto at the Foot of the Cross*, a Roman Catholic order, involved in education in many countries, founded in 1822 in Ireland by Lady Teresa Ball.

Lorsch Benedictine abbey near Worms* founded

in 764. In the middle of the tenth century, it became the center of the Gorze Reform movement under St. Bruno*. It became Cistercian in 1232 and Premonstratensian in 1248. At one time it had one of the largest libraries in Europe.

Lossky, Vladimir (1903–58) Russian lay theologian. Expelled from Russia in 1922, he lived the rest of his life in France, teaching at the Sorbonne*. He is one of the leading theologians of modern orthodoxy*. His published works include *Essai sur la Theologie Mystique de l'Eglise d'Orient* (1944), *Vision de Dieu* (1962), and *A l'Image et a la Ressemblance de Dieu* (1967).

lost 1. Being in an unregenerate and sinful state 2. Being spiritually dead and deprived of the presence of God. 3. Gone astray like sheep.

Lotto, Lorenzo (c. 1480–1556) Venetian painter. His works include large traditional altarpieces, studies of single saints*, and portraits. His few large works are fresco* series at Trescore and Bergamo*.

Lourdes Place of pilgrimage* in the Department of Hautes-Pyrenees, in France, where in 1858 Bernadette* Soubirous had visions of the Virgin Mary* in the grotto* of a rock. In 1862 the pilgrimage was officially approved, and a church was built above the grotto. The crypt of the Basilica of

Loreto

Immaculate Conception and a vast underground church were dedicated in 1958. Since 1907 the Feast of the Apparition of Our Lady of Lourdes has been sanctioned.

Louvain Leading Catholic educational center in central Belgium, famous for its university, the church of St. Peter*, and other medieval churches.

love All-encompassing theological virtue, and one of the defining signatures or hallmarks of God and the Christian as well as the bond between the two. Paul* devotes the entire chapter of 1 Corinthians 13 to this virtue. See also AGAPE.

love feast 1. The agape* or the Eucharist*. 2. Informal. Any of a variety of Christian table fellowships.

Lovedale Missionary educational center in the Eastern Cape, South Africa, founded in 1824 by missionaries of the Glasgow Missionary Society, modeled on the LMS*. Until the 1950s, it was the leading educational institution for Africans, from which a university, a theological school, a nursing school, and a technical college later developed.

Bernadette Soubirous

Lovejoy, Elijah P. (1802–1837) American Presbyterian minister and editor who was killed by a mob for his abolitionist sympathies.

Low Church Originally the liberal wing of the Church of England* consisting of nonconformists opposed to the episcopate*, priesthood, and sacraments*. Later applied to the evangelicals in contrast to the Broad Church* or the liberal group.

Low Mass In the Roman Catholic Church, a simplified and less elaborate form of the Mass* in which the celebrant has only one assistant, where he himself reads the Gospel and the Epistle and no part of the service is sung. In smaller churches, Low Mass is the usual form of celebration except on Sundays and feast days. The current *Ordo Missae* provides for community masses with singing but with a lay person reading the Gospel and the Epistle. See also HIGH MASS.

Low Sunday The first Sunday after Easter*.

lower criticism Textual criticism* of the Bible. See also HIGHER CRITICISM.

Lowry, Robert (1826–1899) American hymn writer. He collaborated with William H. Doane in a number of publications, such as *Royal Diadem* (1873) and *Happy Voices* (1865). Among his hymns, many are sung today, including "Shall We Gather at the River?"(1865) and "Beautiful River" (1851).

Loyola, Ignatius See IGNATIUS LOYOLA.

L.Th. Licentiate in Theology.

Lu, Cheng-hsiang (1871–1949) Chinese statesman and Benedictine monk and abbot. The son of a Protestant catechist*, he rose to become China's foreign minister from 1912 to 1920 (with brief interruptions) and prime minister briefly in 1912 and 1915. He was received into the Roman Catholic Church in 1911, and after the death of his Belgian wife in 1926, he entered the Benedictine abbey of St. Andre, near Bruges, Belgium, under the name of Dom Pierre Celestin Lou.

Lubac, Henri de (1896–1991) French Jesuit theologian. He entered the Jesuit Order in 1913, was ordained priest in 1927, and taught theology from 1929 at Lyons, where Jean Danielou* and Hans Urs von Balthasar* were his pupils. He attended the Second Vatican Council* as a peritus* and was made cardinal in 1983. A prodigious thinker and writer, his vast literary output included *Catholicisme* (1938), on Catholic doctrine; *Corpus Mysticum* (1944); *Surnaturel* (1946), on grace* and the supernatural; *Augustinisme et Theologie Moderne* (1965); *Le Mystere de Surnaturel* (1965); *Histoire et Esprit* (1950), *Exegese Medievale* (1959–1964), and a history of exegesis*. He edited a number of volumes of the correspondence of Teilhard de Chardin* and wrote three books on his ideas. He was also one of the founders of the series of patristic and medieval texts, *Sources Chretiennes*.

luban A variety of incense used in the Coptic Church*.

Lubbertus, Sibrandus (c. 1555–1625) Dutch Calvinist theologian. In 1585 he became professor of theology at the newly founded University of Franeker, where he taught until his death. He was a champion of orthodox Calvinism* against Roman Catholicism*, Arminianism*, and Socinianism*. He played a prominent role in the Synod of Dort*. He took part in the preparation of a new Dutch version of the Old Testament and published a commentary on the Heidelberg Catechism*.

Lubeck Marienkirche in Lubeck, Germany, the most resplendent red-brick Gothic* church in the Baltic region. The building began in 1200 and was completed in 1330. Its pointed twin spires* dominate the city. The cathedral was totally destroyed in World War II and rebuilt shortly thereafter. Inside, two rows of pillars lead up to the light-filled choir and nave* with a ring of chapels and white, red, and green statues. The great composer, Dietrich Buxtehude*, is buried here.

Lucar, Cyril (1570–1638) Patriarch of Constantinople*. He was named patriarch* of Alexandria* in 1601, by which time he had already developed sympathies toward Calvinism*. In 1620 he was elevated as the ecumenical patriarch* of Constantinople, to the alarm of Roman Catholics and conservative Orthodox churchmen. Four times he was

removed from the patriarchal throne, but was restored each time with the help of the English and the Dutch. He supported the translation of the Bible into the vernacular and he also signed the *Confessio Fidei* (1629), restating the traditional Orthodox faith in Calvinistic terms. In 1638 he was accused of inciting the Cossacks against the Ottomans and was put to death. His teachings were condemned by four synods held at Constantinople (1638, 1642), Jassy* (1642), and Jerusalem* (1672).

Lucca San Martino Cathedral in Lucca, one of the oldest and most beautiful cathedrals in Italy where the Volte Santo, the Holy Countenance, is preserved. According to legend, it was carved by Nicodemus and bears the figure of Christ with a narrow face and clad in a long robe. The cathedral was founded in the eighth century and later renovated and consecrated by Pope Alexander II* in 1070. At about the same time, the Tempieto, or Little Temple, was built to house the Volte Santo. Among the other treasures of the cathedral is the equestrian statue of St. Martin.

Luce, Alice Eveline (1873–1955) Anglo-American missionary to India and U.S. Hispanics. Initially, she was sent to India by the Church Missionary Society*, and she labored there until 1912. In 1914 she received the baptism of the Spirit and was ordained as an Assembly of God missionary. In 1926 she founded the Berean Bible Institute in San Diego, California (now the Latin American Bible Institute in La Puente, California) to train Hispanics for the ministry. She was the first missiologist in the Assembly of God. Her books include *The Messenger and His Message* (1925).

lucernarium Ceremonial lighting of candles and lamps at the beginning of vespers* and evening prayer.

Lucian of Antioch, St. (d. 312) Theologian and martyr* who, as the teacher of Arius and Eusebius*, may have inspired the Arian heresy. He was the founder of the Theological School at Antioch. But his ardent devotion to the Christian faith was testified by the tortures he endured before his martyrdom at Nicomedia in 312. Feast day: January 7 (Western Church*); October 15 (Eastern Church*).

Lucianic Text Text of the Greek Bible, as revised by Lucian of Antioch*, which became the accepted standard text in the Middle East. Lucian conflated variant readings and made the text simple and easy to understand by removing obscure words and allusions.

Lucifer (d. 370 or 371) Bishop of Cagliari. He was the most anti-Arian prelate* at the First Council of Milan*, where his diatribes against Arian heresy and spirited defense of Athanasius* earned him the censure* of Emperor Constantius, who first placed him in confinement and later banished him to Palestine and Upper Egypt. During his exile, he continued to write violent letters to the emperor. He is venerated as a saint* in Sardinia.

Lucius According to legend, the first Christian king of England. He is reported to have appealed to Pope Eleutherius (175–189) for Christian teachers, and upon their arrival received baptism* at their hands along with all his subjects and converted the heathen temples into churches.

Lucy, St. (fourth century) Virgin martyr* of Sicily. She was killed in 303 in the Diocletian persecution* for openly proclaiming her faith and distributing her goods to feed the poor. She was highly venerated in the early church and is included in the canons of the Roman and Ambrosian Mass. Feast day: December 13.

Ludlow, John Malcolm Forbes (1821–1911) French-born Anglican who founded Christian Socialism*. Along with F. D. Maurice* and Charles Kingsley*, he gave socialism a respectable religious garb by emphasizing its moral and humanitarian basis. He was responsible for promoting the Industrial and Provident Societies Act of 1852, founding the Working Men's College, and forming cooperative associations.

Ludolf of Saxony (c. 1300–1378) Also, Ludolf the Carthusian. Dominican writer. From 1343 until 1348 he was prior* of the charterhouse* at Koblenz. He wrote the popular *Vita Christi,* a meditation on the life of Christ, which was one of the most widely read book in the Middle Ages. It was translated into many languages and ran into 60 editions. He also wrote a commentary on the Psalms.

Lugo, John de (1583–1660) Spanish Jesuit, described by Alphonsus Liguori* as "the most important theologian after St. Thomas Aquinas*." He entered the Jesuit Order in 1603, taught at several Spanish colleges and at Valladolid, and the Jesuit College* at Rome. He was made cardinal in 1643. His fame as a theologian rests on his chief works: *De Incarnatione* (1633), *De Sacramentis in Genere* (1636), *De Virtute Fidei Divinae* (1646), and *Responsa Moralia* (1651).

Luis of Granada See GRANADA, LUIS DE.

Lukas of Prague (c. 1460–1528) Leader of Unitas Fratrum. His catechism*, liturgies, and theological works shaped the development of the Brethren. The hymnal he edited for his church in 1501 is considered the first Protestant hymnal. His colloquies with Luther* brought the Brethren into the Protestant mainstream.

Luke, St. Evangelist and author of the Third Gospel and the Book of Acts. It is inferred from the "we" sections in Acts that he was a companion of Paul*, from Colossians 4:14 that he was a physician, and from Colossians 4:11 that he was a Gentile. According to tradition, he was unmarried, wrote his Gospel in Greece, and he died of natural causes at age 84, although his *Acta* records his martyrdom. According to legends, he was one of

St. Luke Writing the Gospels

the Seventy and was the unnamed disciple of Emmaus. He is the patron of physicians and painters. Feast day: October 18.

Lully, Jean Baptiste (1632–1687) French composer. Between 1664 and his death he composed 25 motets*, of which 11 are grand motets. His sacred music included *Te Deum* (1677), *De Profoundis* (1683), and *Motets à Deux Pour la Chappelle der Roi* (1684).

lumen fidei (Lat., light of faith) Revealed theological truths known only through God's revelation* and concealed from natural minds.

lumen gloriae (Lat., light of glory) Beatific vision* or supernatural light that illuminates the human mind, in reference to Revelation 22:5, "They need no lamp nor light of the sun, for the Lord God gives them light." It represents the culmination of a threefold process beginning with the light of reason (lumen rationis) and progressing through the light of faith (lumen fidei*).

lumen gratiae (Lat., light of grace) Gift of faith* granted to believers so they may understand the divine mysteries*.

luminaria Shaft admitting light and air in a catacomb*.

Lund An independent archbishopric in Sweden in 1104 and the site of a university founded in 1668.

Lund Cathedral

In the nineteenth century, its faculty represented the High Church* and conservative traditions of Lutheranism* in contrast to the liberal faculty of Uppsala*.

Lund Conference Conference of the Faith and Order Commission of the World Council of Churches* held at Lund, Sweden, in 1952, attended by 225 delegates from 114 churches in addition to Roman Catholic observers. It focused on four areas: church unity; traditions, worship, and institutional practices of the church.

Lundensian theology School of theology developed at the University of Lund focusing on the works of Luther*. Its outstanding representatives were E. Billing*, N. Soderblom*, G. Aulen*, and A. Nygren*.

lunette Circular receptacle within a monstrance* that holds the consecrated host* in an upright position so it may be seen and venerated.

Luther, Martin (1483–1546) German initiator of the Reformation*. In 1505 he entered the monastery of the Augustinian Hermits at Erfurt* and was ordained priest in 1507. In the following year he became professor of moral philosophy at the University of Wittenberg* and in 1511 doctor of theology and professor of biblical exegesis. In 1515 he was made vicar* of his order, supervising 11 Augustinian monasteries. At this time Luther became increasingly concerned over his personal salvation* and the meaning of justification*. The date of his conversion, or the so called "Tower Experience," has been placed between 1514 and 1515. His experience convinced him that 1. the righteousness of God, and not moral works, is the source of salvation; and 2. justification* is solely through the grace* of God, and only the imputed righteousness of Christ cleanses human beings of sin.

Luther's views as yet were not radical and, in fact, paralleled those of St. Augustine*. However, in 1517, he unwittingly fired the first shot of the Reformation by posting his Ninety Five Theses on Indulgences at the door of the Castle Church at Wittenberg*. Considered a manifesto, it aroused much attention among humanists and pro-reform Catholics in Germany. In 1518 Luther defended himself at the Heidelberg Disputation, where he won over a number of Dominicans*, including Bucer*. In the same year he was tried in Rome* on charges of heresy and was summoned before Cardinal Cajetan* at Augsburg and asked to recant. Refusing to do so, Luther fled Wittenberg* and received the protection of Elector Frederick III of Saxony.

In 1519 Luther confronted the Catholic apologist, Johann Eck*, at the Disputation of Leipzig*. In 1520 Luther published three treatises, taking the dispute directly to the German people. The first, *Address to the Christian Nobles of the German Nation,* called for a number of reforms, including the right to challenge the pope's interpretation of Scriptures, and the right of the laity to summon councils and also challenged the celibacy* of the clergy and masses for the dead. The second, *On the Babylonian Captivity of the Church of God,* rejected Communion in one kind, transubstantiation*, and the sacrifice of the Mass*. The third, *Christian Liberty,* called for liberation from the bondage of works. Even before the publication of these three treatises, Luther was condemned by the papal bull* *Exsurge Domine** of 1520. When Luther burned the bull, he was excommunicated and summoned before the Diet of Worms*. Here he is reputed to have made his famous statement, "Here I stand, I can do no other."

In 1521 Luther's teachings were formally condemned by the Edict of Worms*. He hid for the next eight months in Wartburg, near Eisenach*, translating the Bible. The New Testament appeared in 1522. Meanwhile, more radical reformers had emerged, causing confusion and forcing Luther to return to Wittenberg* and issue a pamphlet stating his positions on a number of key issues and explaining the Protestant rite. Next year the *Wittenberg Hymnal* appeared. It included a number of Luther's own hymns. In 1524 Luther discarded his Augustinian habit and in 1525 married a former Cistercian nun, Katharina von Bora. He also sided with the princes against the peasants in the Peasants' War, even though by doing so he alienated the malcontents among the lower classes, and he also attacked Erasmus*, thus causing a rift with the humanists.

Meanwhile, the use of the vernacular in the liturgy, the public reading and distribution of the Bible, and the singing of new hymns proved immensely popular. His cause was also helped by the Diet of Speyer*, which established the right of princes to determine the faith of their subjects and the conciliatory Augsburg Confession* which gave the Lutheran Church a firm doctrinal basis.

Luther's later years were marked by bitter controversies with Zwingli* over the Eucharist* and the rise of new fissures within the Protestant body. As a theologian, Luther tended to be fiercely hostile to his opponents. Beyond theology, he was an important hymn writer. Some of his hymns, such as *A Mighty Fortress Is Our God,* are still sung

Martin Luther

today. He was also a didact who wrote *The Larger Catechism** and *The Smaller Catechism** (both 1529) and genuinely tried to foster education in Christian settings; a biblical commentator and translator, noted for his *Lectures on Galatians* and *Lectures on Genesis;* and a skilled dogmatist who prepared numerous confessional* documents and formularies, such as the Schmalkaldic Articles*. His *Table Talk* records his conversations with friends and students at his home between 1531 and 1544. Many of Luther's ideas were modified by the Lutheran Church after his death, especially through the Formula of Concord*. Nevertheless, Luther stands as a giant whose ideas on justification* and grace set in motion a revolution in Christian history.

Lutheran Scholastics Seventeenth-century Lutheran theologians who used scholastic methods to produce comprehensive theological systems. Among them were Martin Chemnitz*, Johann Gerhard* (1582–1637), Abraham Calovius* (1612–1686), and J. A. Quenstedt (1617–1688).

Lutheran World Federation The most highly organized of global confessional groups, founded in

1947. It is a free association of about 70 autonomous churches based in Geneva*.

Lutheranism Lutheranism is a confession* and an ecclesiastical communion or tradition based on the theology formulated by Martin Luther*. Lutheranism as a confession is based on the Augsburg Confession* (1530), Apology of the Augsburg Confession (1531), Schmalkaldic Articles* (1537), Formula of Concord* (1577), and the Book of Concord (1580), as well as on Luther's Small and Larger Catechisms (1529). On the fundamental articles of the Trinity*, the person of Christ and vicarious atonement*, Lutheranism does not depart from the great creeds or Church Fathers*.

Over the years a form of Lutheran orthodoxy developed in which two beliefs were predominant: the authority of the Bible as the sole guide to doctrine and justification* by faith. *Sola Scriptura* and *Sola Gratia* are two watchwords of Lutheran doctrine. Good works* are the fruit of faith*, not its root. The believer is *simul justus et peccator* (justified but still a sinner). Baptism* is considered the water of regeneration*, by which the new birth* becomes effective. The Lord's Supper* is not merely a memorial meal but is instituted by the Lord for the remission of sins, strengthening of faith*, and as a means of union with him and with fellow believers.

Lutherans believe in the real presence* (although not transubstantiation*) whereby the blood and body of Christ* are present in the wine and the bread. Lutheran theology is strongly Christocentric*, and *Solus Christos* is the third watchword of Lutheranism. Salvation centers in the person and work of Christ. Lutheran Christology* is based on a theology of the cross. As the Word affords the Christian certainty of his doctrine and confession*, the cross affords the Christian certainty of God's grace and his own personal salvation. Regarding predestination*, Lutheranism teaches that God has elected certain human beings for salvation in Christ Jesus before the foundation of the world, but does not teach an election to damnation.

Lutheran Christology is based on the Council of Chalcedon* and is entirely orthodox. Lutherans confess "one and the same Jesus Christ, the Son and Lord, Only-Begotten, in two natures, without mixture, change, division or separation." The Church is one, holy, catholic, and universal. There is a church visible* and a church invisible*. The two marks of the church are the pure preaching of the Word of God* and the correct administration of the holy sacraments. Lutheranism is divided over such issues as original sin*, free will*, good works*, the Lord's Supper, the person of Christ, divine foreknowledge, and predestination. Lutheranism accepts most traditional liturgical forms but places heavy emphasis on preaching. Rites and ceremonies are regarded as adiaphora, or indifferent things, not essential in the principal mission of the church. The Eucharist is celebrated every Sunday. Lutherans do not insist on a uniform church polity*. Some Lutheran churches are congregational, some episcopal, some presbyterian.

The first systematic presentation of Lutheran dogmatics* was *Loci Communes* (1521) by Melanchthon*. The seventeenth century witnessed the development of a Lutheran Scholasticism* which was countered by the emergence of Pietism*. P. J. Spener's* *Pia Desideria* was a reaction against not only the formalism and objectivity of Lutheran teachings, but also the confessional* strife that marked the early centuries of Lutheranism.

Lutheranism spread quickly through much of Germany and all the Scandinavian countries, but it had less success in Eastern Europe, England, and Scotland. In Scandinavia Lutheranism is the official religion. Lutheranism came to North America in the seventeenth century but remained very much a religion of the German immigrants. In 1742, H. M. Muhlenberg* was sent from Halle to Pennsylvania to organize the Lutheran Church. He established the first Lutheran synod*, the Ministerium of Pennsylvania, in 1748. Most of American Lutherans tended to be Pietist. At present there are two main Lutheran bodies in the United States: the Evangelical Lutheran Church and the Lutheran Church-Missouri Synod, both representing the merger of many smaller bodies. In Canada the principal Lutheran Church is Evangelical Lutheran Church in Canada.

Worldwide, the Lutheran World Federation*, founded in 1947, serves as the ecumenical voice of Lutheranism. Lutheran worship retains a great deal of continuity with Western Catholic tradition. The Roman canon* and offertory were cut out and nothing has replaced them. Thus the Words of the Institution, stripped of their context of prayer, has gained a new proclamatory function. Dominating the church service are preaching and music.

Music is one key to the liturgical ethos of the Lutheran Church. From the beginning Lutherans have fostered the use of vernacular hymns, giving impetus to the chorale tradition and generating a superb body of organ literature based on their melodies. Luther's reforms resulted in a new order of service beginning with Preface*, followed by Words of Institution*, Sanctus*, Our Father* (omitting the doxology*), pax*, Communion in both kinds* with Agnus Dei*, collect*, Benedicamus, and Aaronic Blessing.

Lux Mundi 1. Light of the World*, title of Our Lord. 2. *Lux Mundi.* "A Series of Studies in the Religion of the Incarnation" published in 1889 at Oxford under the editorship of Charles Gore. Its purpose was to "put the Catholic faith into its right relation to modern intellectual and moral problems."

Luxeuil Abbey, established by St. Columbanus* in 590 on the site of the Roman Luxovium, France. Here Columbanus ruled his monks with a heavy hand for over 25 years. He introduced the practice of an unceasing song of praise to the Lord under which choirs of monks alternated. The abbey church of St. Peter was built in the thirteenth century. The cloister* built of red sandstone was built between the fourteenth and fifteenth centuries. It was destroyed by the Saracens in 732 and rebuilt by Charlemagne* under the Benedictine Rule. It ceased to exist after the French Revolution in 1790.

LWF Lutheran World Federation.

Lydia Merchant woman of Thyatira* in Asia Minor, the first woman to be converted on the continent of Europe. She opened her home to Paul* (Acts 16:14–40).

Lyons City, important in ecclesiastical history, in east-central France. Irenaeus* was its first well-known bishop.

Lyons, First Council of The Thirteenth Ecumenical Council according to Roman reckoning. It was convoked by Innocent IV* in 1245 to deal with "the five wounds of the church": the bad lives of the clergy and the faithful, the danger from the Saracens, the Greek Schism*, the invasion of Hungary by the Tartars, and the break between the papacy and the Emperor Frederick II. The council deposed the emperor but was unable to do anything about the other four wounds.

Lyons, Lorenzo (1807–1886) American missionary known as "the Isaac Watts of Hawaii." Ordained in 1831, he sailed with the fifth company of the American Board of Commissioners for Foreign Missions* to the Sandwich Islands. For the next 54 years he labored tirelessly in Hawaii without returning home. He was an eloquent preacher in Hawaiian and won thousands of converts. He was also a lyric poet. More than half the hymns in the Hawaiian hymnbook were written by "Makua Laiana," as he was affectionately known.

Lyons, martyrs of Forty-eight martyrs who were killed for their faith in the persecution in 177 at Lyons and Vienne. They included St. Pothinus*, a bishop, and St. Blandina*, a slave girl.

Lyons, Rite of Rite originating in Lyons, approved by the Congregation of Rites in 1904. Its pontifical High Mass* is celebrated by a bishop with six priests, seven deacons, seven subdeacons, seven acolytes*, and seven clerics.

Lyons, Second Council of The Fourteenth Ecumenical Council according to Roman reckoning. It was convoked by Gregory X* in 1274 to bring about a union with the Greek Church, to liberate the Holy Land*, and to reform morals. It was attended by 500 bishops, 60 abbots, and 1,000 other prelates*. At the council the legates of the Emperor Michael VIII Paleologus declared their adherence to the Filioque* clause. It also established new rules for the election of the pope in conclave* and approved the Franciscan and Dominican orders.

Lyra See NICHOLAS OF LYRA.

Lyte, Henry Francis (1793–1847) Anglican clergyman and hymn writer, author of "Abide with Me" and "Praise, My Soul, the King of Heaven."

Izhitza In the Byzantine Rite*, communion spoon.

Ma Di Abbreviation of Mater Dei, Mother of God.

ma'apra In the Assyrian Church*, the chasuble*, a highly ornamented hoodless cope* that is not joined in the front at the neck.

Mabillon, Jean (1632-1707) Maurist scholar. He is best known for grand historical works, such as an edition of the works of St. Bernard* (1667), the *Acta Sanctorum Ordinis Sancti Benedicti* (9 vols., 1668–1701) and the first four volumes of the Benedictine *Annales* (1703–1707). His *Traite des etudes monastiques* (1691) defended the engagement of monks in scholarly pursuits.

Macarius (d. 333) Bishop of Jerusalem* from about 313. He opposed Arius and helped to draft the Nicene Creed*. He is credited with building the Church of the Holy Sepulchre. Feast day: March 10.

Macarius (fourth to fifth century) Also, Simeon. Syrian father. He was the author of 139 spiritual homilies dealing with the sinful nature of human beings and the power of prayer to overcome evil. These homilies have proved influential in Eastern Orthodoxy as well as among Methodists and Pietists.

Macarius of Alexandria, St. (c. 320–c. 404) Desert father*, surnamed Politicus or Junior to distinguish him from Macarius the Great, with whom he was banished during the persecution of the orthodox by Valens. He was the abbot of a monastery of over 5,000 monks, for whom he prepared a monastic rule containing 30 regulations. Feast day: January 2 (Western Church*); January 19 or May 1 (Eastern Church*).

Macarius of Egypt (d. c. 390) Also called the Elder or the Great. He lived in the wilderness of Scete* in Wadi el Natrun, southwest of the Nile Delta, which developed into the center of Egyptian monasticism*. Feast day: January 15 (Western Church*); January 19 or March 9 (Eastern Church*).

Macarius of Moscow (1810–1882) Birth name: Michael Bulgakov. Metropolitan* of Moscow* from 1879. He was a professor of dogmatic theology at the Academy of St. Petersburg. His principal works were *Introduction à la Theologie Dogmatique Orthodoxe* (1845), *Theologie Dogmatique Orthodoxe* (5 vols., 1845–1853), and *History of the Russian Church* (12 vols., 1857–1882).

Macarius, St. (1481–1563) Metropolitan* of Moscow* and all Russia from 1542. He reformed the Russian Church, in both its canon law* and liturgical practice. He was canonized in 1988. Feast day: December 30.

MacArthur, John (1939–) American pastor and teacher. In 1969 he became pastor of Grace Community Church, one of the nation's largest churches in Sun Valley, California. He is also the president of The Master's College and the Master's Seminary in Santa Clarita, California, and president and featured speaker of "Grace to You" radio program. The emphasis of his ministry is the careful study and verse-by-verse exposition of the Bible. Since completing his first best-selling book, *The Gospel According to Jesus* in 1988, he has written more than six dozen books including *The MacArthur Study Bible, Our Sufficiency in Christ, Faith Works, Reckless Faith,* and *The Glory of Heaven.*

MacDonald, George (1824–1905) Scottish Congregational* minister who left the ministry to devote himself to literature. He wrote a number of novels and poems for adults and children that were admired widely and influenced many Christians, including C. S. Lewis*. His Christian works included *Unspoken Sermons* (1867, 1885, and 1905) and *The Miracles of Our Lord* (1886).

mace Short staff borne before an ecclesiastical or other dignitary as a symbol of authority.

Macedonia Province of Greece and later the Roman Empire, now an independent republic, since 1994. In ancient and Christian times, it extended between Epirus and Thrace. To the west it was separated from Epirus by the Pindus chain. Christianity was introduced into Macedonia by the apostle Paul*, who coming from Asia Minor, landed at Neapolis (Acts 16:9–11), and went on to Philippi (Acts 16:12) and other towns (Acts 17:10). Later, the diocese* of Macedonia was part of the administrative district of Illyricum. When the Roman Empire was partitioned, east Illyricum became part of the eastern empire with its administrative center at Thessalonica.

Macedonianism Also, Pneumatomachi*. Fourth-century heresy, attributed to Macedonius, semi-Arian bishop of Constantinople*, deposed in 360. He taught that the Holy Spirit* was a created being and thus subordinate to the Father and the Son.

Machaut, Guillaume de (c. 1300–1377) French composer. His church music consists of his famous Notre Dame Mass and several Latin motets*.

Machen, John Gresham (1881–1937) American conservative Presbyterian scholar. Ordained in 1914, he taught from 1906 to 1929 at Princeton Theological Seminary, where he was leader of the Princeton theology*. As Princeton turned liberal, he resigned in 1929 and founded the Westminster Theological Seminary, serving as its president until 1937. After he was expelled from the Presbyterian Church, he founded the Orthodox Presbyterian Church* in 1936. Toward the end of his life, he emerged as the champion of orthodoxy* in the Modernist-Fundamentalist debate. Among his chief works were *The Origins of Paul's Religion* (1927), *Christianity and Liberalism* (1923), and *The Virgin Birth of Christ* (1930).

John Gresham Machen

machfad In the Ethiopian Rite, veil in which the oblation* is wrapped during the liturgy.

Mack, Alexander (1679–1735) Founder and first leader of the New Baptists, or Brethren, founded in 1708 and known today as Church of the Brethren*. A Pietist and early associate of Pietist leader E. C. Hochmann von Hochenau*, he and eight of his colleagues formed an Anabaptist* community of believers at Schwarzenau. Persecuted and driven out of Germany, the Brethren settled in Pennsylvania in the New World. His son, **Alexander Mack, Jr.,** followed him as leader of the Brethren.

Mackay, Alexander Murdoch (1849–1890) Scottish missionary to Uganda. He arrived in Uganda during a time of persecution, but his engineering skills impressed King Mtesa and helped to save the lives of some missionaries. Mackay withdrew to the south of the Lake Victoria Nyanza, where he translated the Bible into African languages.

Mackay, John Alexander (1889–1983) Scottish missiologist, theologian, and ecumenist. Sent by the Free Church of Scotland, he worked in Peru from 1916 to 1925 and later in Uruguay and Mexico. He was professor and president of Princeton Theological Seminary from 1936 to 1959, chairman of the International Missionary Council* from 1947 to 1957, chairman of the joint committee of the International Missionary Council and the World Council of Churches* from 1948 to 1954, and president of the World Presbyterian Alliance from 1954 to 1959. In 1944 he founded *Theology Today*. His lifework was the restoration of the scriptural roots in theology. His classic, *The Other Spanish Christ* (1932), offered a missiological interpretation of Latin America. His other well-known books included *A Preface to Christian Theology* (1943) and *Christianity on the Frontier* (1950).

Mackie, Robert Cuthbert (1899–1984) Scottish ecumenist. He was general secretary of the World Student Christian Federation*, associate general secretary of the World Council of Churches* from 1948 to 1955, and director (later chairman) of the Inter-Church Aid and Refugee Service. During much of this time he was also pastor of the Scots congregation in Geneva*.

Maclaren, Alexander (1826–1910) Baptist minister, known as prince of expository preachers, who served at Portland Chapel, Southampton (1846–1858) and Union Chapel, Manchester (1858–1903). He was twice president of the Baptist Union and first president of the Baptist World Alliance* (1905). His biblical expositions, especially of the Psalms, are still of use.

Macleod, George Fielden (1895–1991) Also, Lord MacLeod of Fuinary. Founder of the Iona Community*. Born to a noble family, he became a highly decorated veteran of World War I but left military service for the ministry, becoming a minister in the Govan Old Parish Church in the slums of Glasgow. During the interwar years, he became a socialist and a pacifist. In 1938 he re-

founded the Iona Community and as its head became nationally prominent. He became chaplain* to the queen, the moderator* of the General Assembly* of the Church of Scotland*, a peer of the realm and president of the International Fellowship of Reconciliation*.

Macrina, St. (c. 327–380) Elder sister of St. Basil the Great* and St. Gregory of Nyssa*. She was influential in persuading Basil to enter the priesthood. Gregory of Nyssa wrote about her life in *Vita Macrinae Junioris*.

macroecclesiography Descriptive and numerical analysis of the universal church.

macromissiography Descriptive and numerical analysis of global Christian mission.

Madauran martyrs Christian martyrs in Africa, named Namphamo, Miggin, Lucitas, and Samae, who were killed for their faith at Madaura in North Africa probably in the fourth century.

madb'ho In the Jacobite Church*, the sanctuary or altar.

Maderno, Carlo (1556–1629) Italian architect. He became the architect of St. Peter's* in 1603 and converted Michelangelo's centrally planned design into a long nave* church. He also completed the facade of Sta Susanna, creating the first truly Baroque facade in Rome*.

Madonna (Ital., My Lady) Appellation of the Virgin Mary*. In Christian art, she appears in the following forms: Theotokos*, Mother of God; Theotokos Hodegetria*, pointing to the infant Jesus; Dexiotrophousa, carrying Jesus on her right arm; Eleousa*, showing compassionate gestures between mother and child; glykophilousa*, showing affection to infant Jesus; Virgin Orans, standing with no child, with hands prayerfully raised; Maria Deomene or Hagiasotorissa, intercessor standing on the right of Christ; Mater Dolorosa*, Mother of Sorrows; Stabat Mater*, beside the cross; Pieta*, holding the head of the dead Jesus; Madonna of Misericord, devotional posture; Madonna del Latte, feeding Jesus; Madonna Expectans, pregnant; Madonna of Humility, prostrating before the infant Jesus; Madonna of the Rosary.

Madonna del Latte In Christian art, the Virgin Mary* feeding the infant Jesus.

Madonna Expectans In Christian art, pregnant Virgin Mary* of which the most famous example is by Piero della Francesca*.

Madonna lily White lily*, symbol of the Virgin Mary* in art.

Madonna of Humility In Christian art, the Virgin Mary* and St. Joseph* prostrating themselves before the infant Jesus.

madrose Hymn written by Bardesanes*, a Gnostic, but rendered in orthodox terms by St. Ephraem*.

maershooushi In the Coptic tradition, the church as a sanctuary.

maesta Italian form of a painting in which the Virgin Mary* appears enthroned holding the infant on her arm or lap or as Queen of Heaven* surrounded by angels.

maestro di camera Principal chamberlain* at the Vatican*.

maestro di cappella (Ital., master of the chapel) Choir director, known in German as Kapellmeister* and in French as maitre de chappelle.

Magdalenes Religious communities, named after Mary Magdalene, consisting of former prostitutes, established in the thirteenth century in Belgium, Germany, France, Italy, Portugal, and Spain, following the Augustinian, Dominican, and Franciscan rules. They are now extinct except for one convent at Vilsbiburg.

Magdeburg Ottonian cathedral dedicated to St. Maurice and St. Catherine, in Magdeburg, Germany, founded in the sixth century and completed in the fifteenth century. It was completely burned in 1207. It was the first Gothic* cathedral in Germany. The three-aisled vaulted basilica*

was largely completed in the thirteenth century. To the south side is a large cloister*.

Magdeburg Centuries *Ecclesiasticae Historiae Secundum Singulas Centurias,* a Protestant documentary ecclesiastical history, so called because it is divided by centuries. The monumental work contains 13 volumes, one volume for each of the first 13 centuries. It was published in Basel*, 1559–1574. The seven authors, called Centuriators, were led by M. Flacius* Illyricus (1520–1575). The work is marred by a deep anti-Catholic prejudice and by Protestant partisanship.

magh'lonutho Dismissal prayer, also known as commendation, in the Jacobite Church*. It is recited by the priest, who half turns toward the congregation and blesses them with a single sign of the cross.

maghzmah In the Byzantine tradition, the paten*.

magister sacri palatii (Lat., master of the sacred place) Personal chaplain* and theological adviser to the pope, generally a Dominican.

Magisterial Reformation Mainstream Protestant Reformation in which rulers decisively helped to promote, reform, and establish churches. Contrasted with the Radical Reformation* in which the reformers and civil authorities were at odds.

magisterium (Lat., authority of a master) 1. In Roman Catholic theology, teaching authority of the church in matters of faith and morals. 2. Ecclesiastical hierarchy* charged with the definition of faith* and dogma*. They act as judges in matters of faith when there are conflicts on the interpretation of a creed or when new issues arise that demand biblical answers. The supreme teaching authority resides in the episcopacy*, but the pope may exercise this authority on its behalf. He is not above the Word of God*, but it is his duty to guard it faithfully both by virtue of his office and with the help of the Holy Spirit*. The definitive exercise of magisterium is understood to be infallible, because it is believed to be guided by the Holy Spirit*, who will not allow any teaching to be erroneous or lead the whole church into error. Such definitive propositions are termed dogmas of faith. Magisterium can also be exercised in a nondefinitive way in which case it is not infallible.

Magnificat Song of praise sung by the Virgin Mary* (Luke 1:46–55) when she visited her cousin Elizabeth to announce the coming birth of Jesus. So named from the opening word of the Latin text. Its resemblance to the Song of Hannah (1 Sam. 2:1–10) has been noted by many scholars.

Mahan, Asa (1799–1889) First president of Oberlin College, from 1835. He advocated equal rights at Oberlin for women and African-Americans, attainable perfection*, and Scottish commonsense philosophy. He resigned the Oberlin presidency in 1850 and later served as president of Cleveland University and Adrian College. In 1870 he published the *Baptism of the Holy Spirit,* emphasizing the role of the Holy Spirit* in entire sanctification*.

Mai, Angelo (1782–1854) Italian cardinal and paleographer. He was appointed custodian of the Ambrosiana at Milan in 1813, prefect of the Vatical Library* in 1819, and cardinal in 1838. He made great contributions to the study of philology and the study of palimpsests. His published collections include *Classici Auctores* (10 vols., 1828–1838), *Scriptorum Veterum Nova Collectio* (10 vols., 1830–1838), *Spicilegium Romanum* (10 vols., 1839–1844), and *Nova Patrum Bibliotheca* (8 vols., 1844–1871).

maia A variety of incense used in the Coptic Church*.

Maid of Orleans See JOAN OF ARC.

Maier, Walter Arthur (1893–1950) Pioneer Lutheran radio preacher. He was ordained by the Lutheran Church-Missouri Synod in 1917 and served as teacher and editor from 1922. In 1935 he was invited to become the host of the "Lutheran Hour" radio program, and he made it the world's most-listened-to radio program, aired over 1,200 radio stations in 36 languages with a worldwide audience of 750 million. He was also a prolific author, and his devotional guide, *Day by Day,* is still popular.

mainline churches Principal Protestant denominations founded before the twentieth century, characterized by historical traditions, large membership, and a mixture of theological traditions. These include Methodist*, Presbyterian*, Episcopalian*, Reformed*, Congregational*, Baptist*, Lutheran*, Roman Catholic*, and Orthodox churches. Martin E. Marty* defines them as "custodians of religious heritage or standard brand religion and the normative style of passive spirituality." They contribute to and do not challenge society's core values. The word *mainline* is generally used to distinguish the nation's religious establishment from younger and independent, especially Evangelical, Fundamentalist*, and Pentecostal*, churches. Mainline theology tends to be generally liberal and ecumenical. Their social agenda also is different, emphasizing social human rights and feminist issues. They are often called "sunset churches" because of their dwindling influence in society.

Mainz German city where the Cathedral of St. Martin and St. Stephen is located. The original cathedral was burned down in 1009 on the eve of its consecration. Reconstruction began in 1039, but that also burned in 1081. Henry IV again rebuilt it. From the late Middle Ages until the nineteenth century the cathedral underwent constant enlargement and alteration. The nave* is entered through the Market Portal with its fine bronze doors by Master Berengar. It is lined on either side by rows of individual Gothic* chapels.

Majestas Domini Christ in Majesty, the noblest and grandest image of Christ, sitting on a throne surrounded by seraphim.

major orders Higher orders of clerical ordination in the church, consisting of deacons, priests, and bishops, as distinguished from the minor orders*.

Majoristic Controversy Sixteenth-century dispute in Germany over a proposition advanced by George Major (1502–1574) that good works* were necessary in salvation*.

makdas Part of an Ethiopian church set apart for the choir and communicants. Ethiopian churches are generally circular and divided into three concentric circles: the sanctuary or kedest*, the mak-das*, and the kene mahelet* for the congregation.

Makemie, Francis (1658–1708) Chief founder of Presbyterianism* in America. Ordained in Ireland, he was sent to America in 1683. He organized a number of Presbyterian congregations in Maryland, Virginia, New York, North Carolina, and Barbados and formed the first presbytery* in Philadelphia* in 1706. In 1707 he was arrested in New York for preaching without permission but was acquitted after a landmark trial.

Malabar Christians Also, Syrian Christians; Christians of St. Thomas*. Christian community in Kerala, India, claiming descent from 70 families converted by St. Thomas* the apostle in the first century. Tradition holds that Thomas landed at Cranganore in 52 and founded seven churches in Malabar (also called Malankara). It is possible that descendants of the early converts were supplemented by immigrants from Mesopotamia. A separate tradition identifies immigrants from Edessa* in 345 under Thomas of Cana and Syrian immigrants at Quilon (or Kollam) in 823.

The earliest reference to the existence of Malabar Christians is from Cosmas Indicopleustes in the fifth century. At that time they were already in communion with the Nestorian Church of the East; they were ruled by bishops drawn from that rite using Syriac* as their liturgical language. Five extant copper plates record the grant of lands and privileges to Christians by the native rajahs, and five stone crosses also exist with inscriptions in Pahlavi, the extinct language of the Sassanid Persian Empire. One such cross is at Mylapore, in Madras, where St. Thomas is reputed to have been martyred around 53.

When the Portuguese appeared at Goa in the fifteenth century, the ties that bound the Malabar Christians to the mother church in Mesopotamia for 14 centuries had already been broken as a result of the extirpation of the Nestorian Church* by the Mongols under Chengiz Khan and Tamarlane. The Portuguese asserted papal claims over the church and appointed a French Dominican, Jourdain de Severac, as bishop of Quilon. By the mid-sixteenth century the Malabar church submitted to Rome*, and the Synod of Diamper* (1599) completed the transition from Nestorian

to Roman Catholic authority. Syriac*, however, continued to be used in the Romanized liturgy.

But resentment over high-handed Jesuit indoctrination boiled over in an open revolt, resulting in the public demonstration at Coonen Cross* in 1653 when the Malabar Christians repudiated Rome. However, within a decade Rome managed to win back at least half the Malabar Christians, especially in north Kerala. The other half sent a deputation to the Middle East to find remnants of the Nestorian Church. Instead, they found the very opposite: the non-Chalcedonian Syrian Orthodox Church*, better known as Jacobites, whose patriarch*—although known as patriarch of Antioch—resided at Diyar Bakr in Turkey. Thenceforth the non-Catholic Malabar Christians came to be known as Jacobites.

Meanwhile, the British had arrived in India, and the Church Missionary Society* began active work in Kerala from 1816. As a result some Jacobites became Anglicans. It also led to a secession in the Jacobite Church* in which a reform party broke away in 1889 under Abraham Malpan* and formed what is known today as Mar Thoma Church*. In the twentieth century there was a further division within Jacobites between the party of the native catholicos* (headquartered at Kottayam) and the party under the Syrian patriarch of Antioch* (now resident at Damascus*).

Currently, there are eight different groups among Malabar Christians: Syrian Roman Catholics, Latin Roman Catholics, Malankarese Church*, Uniats of the party of Mar Ivanios, Catholic Southists descended from Cranganore immigrants under Thomas of Cana, Jacobites, Mar Thoma Christians, Church of South India* (former Anglicans), and Chaldeans or Nestorians. Of these the Catholics constitute about 50 percent and the Jacobites about 30 percent.

Malachy, St. (1094–1148) Archbishop of Armagh*. Attracted to the monastic system of Gaul, he visited Bernard of Clairvaux* and established the first Cistercian abbey in Ireland at Mellifont in 1142. To bring the Irish church more fully under Rome, he summoned a synod* at Inishpatrick in 1148. The synod appointed him as a delegate to visit Rome and receive the pallium*, but he died on his journey.

Malankarese Church See MALABAR CHRISTIANS.

Malbork Monastery in Malbork (Marienburg in German) on the right arm of the Vistula, east of Gdansk. It was part of a large complex that belonged to the Teutonic Knights. The tall monastery building, constructed around 1290, was built on a rectangular ground plan with a courtyard surrounded by Gothic* arcades. It entered a period of decline after it was captured by the Poles in 1447 and by Prussia in 1772. It was restored to its former glory beginning in 1817.

Malbork Monastery

malca (lit., king) The holy leaven used in the Assyrian Church* in the preparation of the bread. It is kept in a chalice* in a small cupboard, or giuta, above the altar. In addition to flour and salt, it contains particles* of the previous consecrated bread.

malkaa In the Ethiopian Church, hymn chanted on festivals of saints*.

Malleolus/Malleus Haereticorum (Lat., Hammer of the Heretics) Title applied to various defenders of the faith, especially St. Anthony of Padua*, St. Peter Canisius*, and Johann Faber* (1478–1541).

Maleus Maleficarum Hammer of Witches (1487). Treatise on witchcraft and demonology by Henry Kramer and James Sprenger, inquistors to Northern Germany.

malpan In the Indian Christian Jacobite Church*, a cleric who ranks above a priest and below a bishop and who is considered a scholar in Syriac* liturgy.

Maltese Cross Cross with four equal arms, each arm divided into two prongs. It was the symbol of the Knights of Malta*.

Malvern Conference Anglican conference at Malvern, 1941, under the presidency of Archbishop Temple* to consider the application of Christianity to modern society. It was addressed, among others, by T. S. Eliot* and Dorothy Sayers*.

Mamertine Prison Building in the center of ancient Rome* in which, according to tradition, Paul* was incarcerated and where he converted his two gaolers. It consisted of two cells, one above the other. The Church of San Guiseppe dei Falegnami stands above the site.

Mamertine Prison

mamher Abbot of an Ethiopian Orthodox* monastic community.

m'amuditho (lit., house of baptism) In the Jacobite Church*, a baptistery on the south side of the altar.

Man of Sorrows Title of Jesus Christ, a reference to Isaiah 53:3: "He is despised . . . a Man of sorrows and acquainted with grief."

Manalo, Felix (1886–1963) Founder of the Iglesia ni Kristo in the Philippines. He converted to Protestantism* in 1902 at the age of 16, but became an atheist in 1912 and thereafter preached his own gospel, denying the divinity of Christ and justification* by faith*. He declared himself to be the angel* mentioned in Revelation and taught that the only true church was the one he founded called Iglesia ni Kristo. Followers of this heresy number in the millions.

Mandaeans Also, Nasoreans. Gnostic baptizing sect that survives in southern Iraq and southwest Iran. St. John the Baptist plays a large part in their theology, which is borrowed from Jewish, Christian, and other sources and which posits a dualistic opposition between the world of light and the world of darkness. They teach the imprisonment of the soul in human bodies by demons and its eventual liberation by a redeemer called Manda de Hayye (also Hibel or Enos Uthra). Among their rituals is baptism* (one initiatory and the other repeated periodically) and the masiqta by which the souls of the departed ascend to the world of light.

mandarah Guest room in a Coptic church or monastery.

mandate Any one of the seven basic commands in the Great Commission*: receive, go, witness, proclaim, disciple, baptize, train.

mandatum Washing of the feet on Maundy Thursday*, a celebration of its institution during the Last Supper.

Man of Sorrows

Mande, Hendrik (c. 1360–1431) One of the Brethren of the Common Life*. He received a number of visions which he recorded in his tracts.

mandelion In the Byzantine Rite*, towel carried by a deacon on his left shoulder with which a bishop dries his hands after washing them during the Great Entrance*. It is called a mandil in the Jacobite Church*.

Mandeylion In Armenian tradition, image of the features of Christ impressed on a napkin and sent to King Abgar* the Black in Edessa*.

Mandeylion

mandorla (Ital., almond) Oval halo* in Christian art symbolizing divinity and holiness*.

manducation Lat., chewing) In sacramental theology*, the act of eating of the Lord's Supper*, further defined according to the doctrine of the supper in question, e.g., sacramental, spiritual, or oral manducation.

mandyas Cloak worn by monks and priests in the Eastern Church*, black in the case of monks and purple in the case of bishops and abbots. It is called an angelic habit because its flowing lines typified the wings of angels*. Mandyas may have sewn on it the Tables of the Law, squares of velvet at the neck, decorated with the four Evangelists. Additionally, streams of doctrine are represented by red and white ribbons sewn horizontally around it.

Mani (c. 216–c. 276) Also, Manes. Heresiarch* and founder of Manichaeism*. Born near Seleucia-Ctesiphon*, he began his teaching ministry in 240 but was forced by Zoroastrian opposition to flee to India. He returned in 242 and initially received the support of Sapor I, the Persian monarch. He fell out of royal favor and was put to death in the reign of Bahram I by being flayed alive.

Manichaeism Eclectic religion mixing mythological, Gnostic, Mandaean, Buddhist, Hindu, and Christian elements founded by Mani* who called himself "an apostle of Jesus Christ." Mani taught that the two vital eternal principles are light and darkness represented by God and matter. Man is imprisoned in darkness, and Jesus is an example of the suffering of imprisoned light in matter. Salvation* consists in the souls of the elect* (who eat no meat and abstain from sex) being liberated from darkness and reunited with light. For a few centuries, Manichaeism spread rapidly throughout the Roman Empire, Persia, and Central Asia, reaching China by the eighth century. Persecuted everywhere, it eventually died out. The Manichaean canon is made up of six books and letters written by Mani. After more than a millennium, many of these came to light only in the twentieth century in Coptic, Sogdan, Uigur, Chinese, Greek, and Persian documents.

manifest church Organized churches that believe in Jesus Christ as Lord and Savior. A term coined by Paul Tillich*.

maniple Strip of silk decorated with three crosses worn at Mass* on the priest's left arm.

Manning, Henry Edward (1808–1892) Archbishop of Westminster who became a Roman Catholic cardinal. After the death of his wife, he became archdeacon of Chichester, but gradually became a Tractarian and in 1851 was received into the Catholic Church. Two months later he was reordained priest and in 1865 succeeded Cardinal N. Wiseman as archbishop of Westminster. He took part in the First Vatican Council*, where he was a staunch supporter of papal infallibility*. In 1875 he was made a cardinal.

manoualion In the Byzantine tradition, a single candle or lampas* carried in the right hand of the reader* during a procession.

Manresa Cave near Montserrat in Spain to which St. Ignatius* of Loyola retired to write his *Spiritual Exercises**.

manse The residence of a minister, especially in Scotland and English free churches.

Manso, Alonso (c. 1470–1539) First Catholic bishop in the New World. The first three dioceses* in the New World were created by Julius II* in 1511: two on Espanola and the third on San Juan, Puerto Rico. Manso was appointed bishop of the third, and he took up residence in San Juan in 1512. In 1519 he was also appointed apostolic inquisitor of the Indies.

Mantegna, Andrea (1431–1506) Italian Renaissance painter, noted for his frescoes and altarpieces. Among his religious paintings are the fresco*, *Histories of St. James and St. Christopher, Dead Christ,* the altarpieces, St. Luke's Altar, and the triptych*, the *Adoration of the Magi, Madonna della Vittoria* and *Madonna and Child in Glory with Sts. John the Baptist, Gregory the Great, Benedict and Jerome.* His paintings are distinguished by a classic austerity, fidelity to nature, and a concern with perspective. He decorated the Belvedere Chapel in the Vatican for Innocent VIII.

mantelletta In the Western Church*, a short cloak open in the front and reaching to the knees worn by prelates of the Roman Curia* and protonotaries.

mantellone Purple-colored cloak of silk or wool fastened at the neck and reaching to the ground with slits for arms. It was worn until 1969 by certain minor prelates at the papal court.

mantilla Veil-like covering used by women in church in Italy, Portugal, and Spain.

mantum Papal red cloak with which the newly elected popes were invested from the eleventh to the fourteenth centuries.

manual acts Ceremonial handling of the elements* at Holy Communion*.

manuale In the Middle Ages, the equivalent of the Rituale, a book containing prescribed forms of administering the sacraments*.

manuterge Finger towel used during the lavabo* or other times during divine service*.

Manz, Felix (c. 1498–1527) Anabaptist* reformer. He joined Zwingli* but left him to form the original Swiss Brethren* congregation. After disputing with Zwingli on infant baptism*, he began performing believer's or adult baptisms. When such baptisms were declared illegal on pain of death, Manz was arrested in 1527 and drowned in the River Limmat, the first Anabaptist martyr* at the hands of Protestants.

maphorion (Gk., veil) Traditional headcovering of a Greek noble woman. The Virgin Mary* is usually shown wearing a red maphorion.

maphrian (Syr., *mafriano*, one who bears fruit) In the Syrian Orthodox Church*, the title of a bishop who holds a rank only lower than that of a patriarch*. It is borne by metropolitans* of the East, that is, the area formerly under the Persian Empire. Although the first maphrian was enthroned in 629, the term did not come into general use until the eleventh century when the patriarchal authority had to be delegated to a metropolitan resident east of the Euphrates* because of unsettled political conditions. After the Mongol invasions, the post became vacant and was purely honorary until the twentieth century when it was revived in the Syrian Orthodox Church* in Kerala, India.

mappula 1. Linen gremial* used by priests in the Roman Rite*. 2. Portable canopy*.

maqpa In the Assyrian tradition, a monk.

mar (Syr., sir or lord) Term of address, used as a prefix, for a bishop or a saint* in the Syrian Orthodox Church*, as in Mar Ephraem. Mart is applied to the Virgin Mary*.

Mar Thoma Church Neo-Protestant denomination in Kerala, India, an offshoot of the Jacobite Church*. It was founded by a dissident priest, Abraham Malpan*, who was excommunicated by the Syrian patriarch* for his reformist views. His nephew, Mar Athanasios, who sought to become a metropolitan*, was denied the position for the same reason. After lengthy legal battles, the Reformers lost all claims to church properties and began existence as an independent church in 1889. It has kept an evangelistic thrust and close links with the Church of South India*.

maranatha (Aram., our Lord, come) Eschatological expression in 1 Corinthians 16:22 understood as an indicative (Our Lord has/will come) or as an exhortation.

Maranke, John (1912–1963) Founder of the African Apostolic Church in Zimbabwe. Raised and educated as a Methodist, he experienced in 1932 a divine revelation in which he was called to be Christ's apostle. He then founded the African Apostolic Church, which has grown to become the largest initiated church with one million members in southern Africa. For 30 years Maranke traveled throughout the region, often by foot, converting, baptizing, and establishing congregations. His message included opposition to traditional African religion and a ministry of healing and exorcism*. One feature of the Apostolic Church is the annual Paschal* celebration (known as Pende, from Pentecost*) lasting 17 days and attended by thousands.

Marburg Articles Reformation* doctrine drawn up by Luther* for the Colloquy of Marburg.

Marburg, Colloquy of Meeting convened in 1529 by Philip, the landgraf of Hesse, to explore avenues of unity between the Lutherans and Zwinglians. It met at the castle at Marburg-on-the-Lahn with Luther*, Justus Jonas*, Johann Brenz*, Kaspar Cruciger*, Andreas Osiander*, and Melanchthon* on one side and Zwingli*, Oecolampadius*, Wolfgang Capito*, Jakob Sturm, and Martin Bucer* on the other. Accord was reached in 14 of the 15 articles drawn up by Luther but the talks broke down on the fifteenth: the Lutheran doctrine of the Eucharist*. Shortly thereafter, Luther revised the Marburg Articles as the Articles of Schwabach*, the first Lutheran creedal statement and precursor of the Augsburg Confession*.

Marburg, University of University founded by Philip, landgraf of Hesse, in 1527, the first Protestant university in Europe.

Marcan Hypothesis Theory put forward by K. Lachmann in 1835 and later accepted by most scholars that the Gospel of St. Mark* is the earliest of the four Gospels and its narrative is the simplest presentation of facts without embellishment or distortion.

Marcella, St. (c. 325–411) Roman matron and ascetic whose palace on the Aventine Hill was a meeting place and retreat* for Christians. Jerome*, who enjoyed her hospitality for three years, called her "the glory of the ladies of Rome." Feast day: January 31.

Marcellus of Ancyra (d. c. 374) Bishop of Ancyra in central Anatolia. The oldest Greek text of the Old Roman Creed* is preserved in his letter to Pope Julius I* as recorded by Epiphanius*. At the Council of Nicaea*, Marcellus was a supporter of Athanasius* and a defender of the Homoousian position, but was deposed from his see* in 336 because of his notion that the Son and the Holy Spirit* were only emanations from God who became distinct persons at the time of creation and the Incarnation* and in whom they will be reabsorbed at the consummation. The words in the Nicene Creed*, "whose kingdom shall have no end," were added to debar his teaching. In exile, he sought asylum with Julius* in Rome who secured his clearance from charges of heresy at the councils of Rome* (341) and Sardica (343). He was temporarily restored to his see but was deposed again under Constantius. After his death, his teachings were condemned at the First Council of Constantinople in 381.

Marcion (c. 100–c. 165) Heresiarch*, one of the first to challenge the biblical theology* of the early church. Marcion was active in the church at Rome* until about 144 when he was excommunicated because of the heresy now known as Marcionism. His organizers formed a church of their own with branches in many parts of the empire and kept the heresy alive for two centuries. Marcion was a keen intellect who focused on the radical nature of Christianity as preached by St. Paul*,

in contrast to Judaism. His central thesis was that the New Testament was a triumph of the gospel of love and that the God of the Old Testament was a contemptible and capricious demiurge*.

Marcion's theology was built on a series of antitheses: the church stood in opposition to Israel; the New Testament stood in opposition to the Old Testament; law stood in opposition to grace*; flesh stood in opposition to the spirit; and Jehovah, the god of the Old Testament and the creator of the material world, stood in opposition to the Father of Jesus Christ, a God unknown until the Incarnation* and who revealed himself to usher faith*, freedom, grace*, and salvation*. Marcion accepted only Paul*, who was his hero, among the apostles, and his sacred canon* consisted of Luke's Gospel and the ten Pauline Epistles (excluding the Pastorals and Hebrews), edited to delete references to Jehovah as the Father of Jesus Christ and to any continuity with the Old Testament.

In some respects, he was a Gnostic, especially in his rejection of matter and the flesh, his Docetism* and his asceticism*. But in other respects he held traditional beliefs about key elements of the faith. His only known work, *Antitheses,* has not survived, but excerpts from his book appear in Tertullian's* *Against Marcion* as well as writings of other Church Fathers*. His single most important contribution to Christian history was his effort to draw up a canon of the New Testament, a major event in the evolution of the Bible.

Marcionite Prologues Short introductory prologues to each of the Pauline Epistles said to have been written by Marcion, but which were incorporated into the Vulgate*.

Marcionites Followers of Marcion* who existed in various parts of the Mediterranean world until the seventh century.

Mardi Gras (lit., fat Tuesday) Tuesday before Ash Wednesday*, celebrated with revels in many cities. In the United States, the revelry is associated particularly with New Orleans.

Marechal, Joseph (1878–1944) Belgian Jesuit philosopher and founder of transcendental Thomism*. His major work is *Le Point de Depart de la Metaphysique,* which attempted to develop a synthesis between modern thought and Scholasticism*. His work had significant influence on Bernard Lonergan* and Karl Rahner*.

Maredsous Seat of a Belgian Benedictine abbey founded in 1872 as a daughter house of Beuron* in Germany. Its monks are noted for their contributions to scholarship, especially in patristics*.

margarech Old Testament lessons read during the Armenian Liturgy.

Margaret Mary Alacoque, St. (1647–1690) Visitandine, founder of devotion to the Sacred Heart. In 1671 she entered the Convent of the Visitation at Paray-le-Monial* in central France where she received several revelations of the Sacred Heart from December 1673 to June 1675. These visitations* caused her to institute a special devotion, the chief features of which were Holy Communion* on the first Friday of each month, the holy hour* on Thursdays, and the observance of the Feast of the Sacred Heart. She was beatified in 1864 and canonized in 1920. Feast day: October 16.

Margaret of Antioch, St. (d. 303) Also, St. Marina. By tradition a martyr* under Diocletian who became the object of a widespread cult* in the Middle Ages. Hers was one of the voices heard by Joan of Arc*. She is sometimes included among the 14 auxiliary saints*. Feast day: July 17 (Eastern Church*); July 20 (Western Church*).

Margaret of Cortona, St. (c. 1247–1297) Franciscan penitent. Seduced by a knight of Montepulciano, she lived openly as his mistress for nine years and bore him a son. On the murder of her paramour, she entered the Franciscan convent in Cortona and was admitted to the Third Order of St. Francis. She devoted her life thereafter to nursing the sick and the poor. Her personal austerities were extreme and severe but her reputation, fostered by miraculous cures, attracted visitors from all over Italy. Feast day: February 22.

margarites Consecrated particles* given in Holy Communion*.

Maria Deomene In Christian art, the Virgin Mary* as an intercessor.

Maria Laach Benedictine abbey near Andernach, Koblenz, Germany, founded in 1093 by Count Palatine Heinrich II and his wife Adelheid von Orlamunde as the Monastery of Laach on the largest crater lake in the Eifel Mountains, dedicated to the Virgin Mary*. As a branch of Cluny*, its first Romanesque church was consecrated in 1156. Maria Laach is notable for two features. A gateless portal gives access to a circular ambulatory ringed with columns. In the quadrangle within the ambulatory is the tiny Garden of Paradise, a symbolic repre-

Maria Laach Abbey

sentation of the Garden of Eden. The abbey was suppressed in 1802 after the French Revolution, but was acquired by the Jesuits* in 1862/3 as the site of a collegium maximum (institution of higher learning). After the expulsion of the Jesuits in 1872, the abbey passed into the hands of the Benedictines* of Beuron* in 1892. Under Ildefons Herwegen, abbot from 1913 to 1946, Maria Laach became a center of the liturgical revival. Among their many innovations was a crypt Mass* in which a dialogue of the Mass or Missa recitata* was celebrated from a westward position in the abbey.

Mariamne, St. According to tradition, companion of St. Philip* and St. Bartholomew* who helped to evangelize* Asia Minor south of the Taurus Mountains. Feast day: February 17.

Marian (*noun*) One who is a devotee of the Virgin Mary* or belongs to one of the groups devoted to her service. (*adjective*). Of or relating to the Virgin Mary*.

Marian feasts Liturgical celebrations honoring the Virgin Mary*, numbering 15 in the Roman calendar. Among these are four solemnities: Mary, Mother of God, January 1; Annunciation, March 25; Assumption, August 15; Immaculate Conception, December 8; three feasts: Presentation of the Lord*, February 2; Visitation, May 31; Birth of Mary, September 8; four memorials: Queenship of Mary, August 22; Our Lady of Sorrows*, September 15; Our Lady of the Rosary*, October 7; and Presentation of Mary, November 21; and four optional memorials: Our Lady of Lourdes, February 11; Immaculate Heart of Mary*, Saturday after the second Sunday of Pentecost*; Our Lady of Mount Carmel, July 16; and Dedication of the Basilica of St. Mary Major*, August 5.

Marian year Year dedicated to the Virgin Mary*, marked by special events, prayers, penance*, and papal indulgences*. Both 1954 and 1988 were Marian years.

Marianists Roman Catholic order, known also as the Society of Mary, founded in Bordeaux by William Joseph Chaminade* (1761–1850). Both priests and lay persons have equal rights and privileges other than in the administration of sacraments*. Members consecrate themselves to the Virgin Mary* and wear a gold ring on the right hand as a token of their devotion and recite daily the Rosary* and the Little Office of Our Lady*.

Marianus Scotus (c. 1028–1083) Irish monk noted for his *Chronicon,* a world history, and his illuminated Bible commentaries.

Mariavites Polish sect* devoted to the Virgin Mary* founded in 1906 by Jan Kowalski and Maria Felicja Kozlowska, who had been excommunicated by the Roman Catholic Church because of aberrant beliefs. They joined the Old Catholics* in 1909 and remained affiliated with them until 1924 when their excesses led to their expulsion. A split occurred in 1935, and they lost most of their membership during World War II.

marie-gietta In the Ethiopian Church, a dabtara* who acts as a guide during service.

mariolatry Improper or excessive veneration* of the Virgin Mary*, such as that of the Collyridians of the fourth century who were condemned by St. Epiphanius* for offering sacrificial worship to the Virgin Mary*. Strictly speaking, the Roman Catholic Church does not permit latria* or worship of Mary but only hyperdulia*, or veneration* and honor. Special veneration is sanctioned by the Roman Catholic Church on the basis of two dogmas: that of the immaculate conception* of Mary in 1854 and that of her assumption in 1950. She is also the object of special devotions and festivals as a mediatrix*, whose intercessions are a valuable means of receiving grace and help in time of need.

mariology Branch of theology dealing with the Virgin Mary* and her place in the divine plan of salvation*.

Marion Bresillac, Melchior Joseph de (1813–1859) Founder of the Society of African Missions. After serving in India from 1841 to 1849, he petitioned Propaganda Fide to be sent to Africa. On its advice, he founded the Society of African Missions (SAM) for saving "the most abandoned souls in Africa." Bresillac led his society's first missionary venture, arriving in Freetown in Sierra Leone in 1859, but died within six weeks.

Marists Society of Mary founded in 1816 by Jean Claude Courveille and Jean-Claude Marie Colin* and approved by the pope in 1836. Based on the Jesuit Rule, Marists teach school and seminary and do parish, nursing, and missionary work.

Maritain, Jacques (1882–1973) French Thomist philosopher. After studying under Henri Bergson*, he was converted to Roman Catholicism* in 1906. He taught at Institut Catholique in Paris (1914–1933), Institute for Medieval Studies in Toronto (1933–1945), and Princeton (1948–1952). Toward the end of his life, he became a Little Brother of Jesus in Toulouse. His life was primarily devoted to the development of Thomism*. He was a strong opponent of the Vatican council and the neo-modernist movement. He also wrote on moral, social, and political philosophy, as well as education, history, culture, art, and poetry. He wrote over 50 books, of which the most influential are: *The Angelic Doctor, St. Thomas Aquinas*

(1931), *Art and Scholasticism* (1932), *Introduction to Philosophy* (1937), *Degrees of Knowledge* (1938), *True Humanism* (1938), *The Living Thoughts of St. Paul* (1940), *Christianity and Democracy* (1944), *Moral Philosophy* (1960), and *The Peasant of the Garonne* (1966).

Marius Mercator (c. 418–452) Latin Christian theologian who wrote against the Nestorian and Pelagian heresies and helped to condemn them at the Council of Ephesus* in 431.

Mark, Liturgy of St. The traditional Greek eucharistic liturgy of the Church of Alexandria. A modified form of the rite in Coptic is used in the Coptic Church*, and another form of it in Amharic* is used in the Ethiopian Church*. Some of its peculiarities are the great intercessory prayer before the Sanctus* and the absence of the Benedictus* at the end of the Sanctus.

Mark, St. Evangelist. Associate of St. Peter*, traditionally identified with John Mark, the cousin of St. Barnabas*. He accompanied Barnabas on a mission to Cyprus* (Acts 15:39), and was in Rome* with St. Paul* (Col. 4:10; 2 Tim. 4:11; Philem. 24). According to tradition, Mark was the

St. Mark

first bishop of Alexandria* (which is therefore known as the See* of St. Mark*), Venice*, where there is a magnificent cathedral named after him, and claims to have his relics*. Feast day: April 25.

marks of the church In Protestant theology, the marks of the church are the preaching of the pure doctrine of the gospel, the rightful administration of the sacraments*, and also, in some Reformed* churches, the proper administration of church discipline*. Distinguished from notes of the church, which are its unity, holiness, catholicity, and apostolicity, according to the Nicene Creed*.

Marmion, Joseph Columba (1858–1923) Abbot of Maredsous and writer of Christocentric* books, such as *Le Christ, Vie de l'Ame* (1918), *Le Christ dans ses Mysteres* (1919), and *Le Christ, Ideal du Moine* (1922).

marmnakal In the Armenian Rite*, corporal* laid out on the altar prior to the celebration of the liturgy.

Maro, St. (d. 433) Syrian monk. His reputation for sanctity* outlasted him, and many miracles were reported at his tomb near Apamea and Emesa. He was a friend of John Chrysostom* and Theodoret*. The Maronites* are named after him.

Maronite Rite Liturgical usage of the Maronite Catholic Church native to Lebanon. A monastic liturgy by origin, it developed as a branch of the Edessene tradition. Its calendar and liturgy of the hours are closely related to the West Syrian. After coming into contact with the Latin Catholics during the Crusades*, the Maronite Rite underwent progressive latinization, especially in its feasts and vestments. But the latinization did not affect the Divine Office* which remained West Syriac. In the twentieth century, Syriac* has been abandoned in favor of Arabic as the liturgical language.

Maronites Uniat Christian community in Syria and Lebanon in formal communion with the Roman Catholic Church since 1182. They trace their origin and name to St. Maro, who founded a monastery on the Orontes. During the Monothelite controversy in the seventh and eighth centuries, they repudiated the Third Council of Constantinople*. After union with Rome*, a Maronite College was founded in Rome in 1584. Like other Arab Christian communities, Maronites have been decimated by Arab and Turkish persecutions for centuries. They form the largest single Christian community in Lebanon, and thus the president of Lebanon is always a Maronite. Their liturgy follows the Antiochene Rite* in Syriac* with anaphoras* derived from the Liturgy of Addai and Mari*. The Maronite patriarch* resides at Bkerke in Lebanon.

Marot, Clement (1497–1544) French Protestant hymn writer. He wrote 12 out of the 18 hymns that appeared in the Calvinist hymnal published at Strasbourg* in 1539. At Geneva* Marot translated, at Calvin's urging, 20 more psalms for the 1542 *Cinquante Pseaumes,* and in 1562 he contributed 49 hymns to Beza's* hymn book.

Marquette, Jacques (1637–1675) French Jesuit explorer, discoverer of the Mississippi River and missionary in North America. He explored the Mississippi region and founded mission centers among the Huron, Ottawa, Illinois, and Algonquian Indians. He was a man of simple piety who devoted his life to evangelization and the spiritual welfare of Native Americans.

Marranos Christianized Moors or Jews of medieval Spain and Portugal who accepted forced conversion but retained their beliefs and practices in secret. See also CONVERSO.

marriage See MATRIMONY.

marriage supper Apolcalyptic metaphor in the Book of Revelation for the consummation of the union between Christ and his bride, the church, on his triumphal return.

Marrow Controversy Dispute in the Church of Scotland* stemming from the condemnation by the General Assembly* in 1720 of the *Marrow of Modern Divintiy* written by Edward Fisher in 1645. The book promoted an antinomian form of Calvinism*.

Marshall, Peter (1902–1949) Scottish-American Presbyterian minister. Ordained to the ministry in 1931, he became pastor of the New York Avenue Presbyterian Church in Washington, D.C., in 1937 and chaplain* to the U.S. Senate from 1947. He wrote many popular works, including *Mr. Jones, Meet the Master.* His wife, Catherine (1914–1983), wrote a powerful biography, *A Man Called Peter,* that made his name familiar to millions.

Marshman, Joshua (1768–1837) English Baptist missionary to India and Semitic scholar who translated the Bible into Indian languages. He was a colleague of Carey* at Serampore.

Marsilius/Marsiglio of Padua (c. 1275–1342) Italian political philosopher whose tract, *Defender of the Peace,* completed in 1324, presented the thesis that both church and state derive their legitimacy from the people. His book was placed on the Index in 1559.

mart In the Syrian churches, female of mar, used as a title for female saints*.

Martel, Charles See CHARLES MARTEL.

Martin I, St. (d. 655) Pope from 649. He was a vigorous defender of orthodoxy* against Monothelitism*, which he condemned at the Lateran Synod in 649. For this he was imprisoned by the emperor and banished to Crimea, where he died. He is the last of the popes venerated as a martyr*. Feast day: September 20.

Martin IV (c. 1210–1285) Pope from 1281. Birth name: Simon de Brie. He was responsible for the excommunication* in 1281 of Michael Paleologus, thus destroying the union between Latin and Greek churches achieved at the Second Council of Lyons* in 1274.

Martin V (1368–1431) Pope from 1417. Birth name: Otto. His reign marked the end of the Great Schism*. During his 14-year pontificate*, he restored many of the buildings and churches of Rome*. He also strengthened papal power by dissolving the Council of Constance* in 1418.

Martin of Braga (d. c. 579) Apostle of the Suevi.

After the conversion of the Suevian king from Arianism*, Martin was made bishop of Braga in Spain, and he later founded the monastery of Dumium. Among his works is the treatise, *De Ira,* a series of brief catechisms, and a collection of spiritual aphorisms for the use of monks.

Martin, St. (c. 335–c. 400) Bishop of Tours* and patron saint* of France. A soldier by profession, he was converted by a vision of Christ. In 360 Martin joined Hilary at Poitiers* and founded the monastery at Ligugé, where he gained a reputation as a holy man and healer. He was elected bishop of Tours* in about 371, remaining a monk and an active evangelist. After his death and the publication of a biography by Sulpicius Severus, a cultus* built around his name. Feast day: November 11 (Western Church*); November 12 (Eastern Church*).

St. Martin of Tours

Martini, Simone (c. 1284–1344) Sienese painter. His earliest paintings included a *Maesta* (1315 and 1321). In 1324 he became the partner of Lippo Memmi, and together they painted the *Annunciation.* In 1340/41 he went to Avignon*, where he remained until his death. Here he painted *Christ*

Returning to His Parents After Disputing in the Temple. There are also two unfinished frescoes* of his in the Cathedral of Ste-Marie-des-Doms in Avignon, *Christ in Majesty with Angels* and *Virgin and Child with Angels.*

Martinmas Feast of St. Martin of Tours* on November 11.

Marty, Martin Emil (1928–) American church historian. He served on the faculty of the University of Chicago from 1963 and became the unofficial dean of religious commentators and a prolific writer and editor. He bridges the liberal and conservative traditions in American Christianity. He has authored over 50 books of which the best known are *Righteous Empire: The Protestant Experience in America* (1986), and *Pilgrims in Their Own Land: Five Hundred Years of Religion in America* (1984).

Martyn, Henry (1781–1812) Anglican missionary to India. After ordination in 1803, he sailed for India in 1805 as chaplain* to the East India Company. He served at Calcutta, and later, at Dinapore and Cawnpore. An outstanding linguist, he translated the New Testament and the *Book of Common Prayer** into Hindustani and was planning to translate them into Arabic and Persian when he died on his voyage home at the age of 31. His *Journals* reveal a man of rare and intense dedication to the cause of Christ.

martyr (Gk., witness) Blood witness, especially one who dies for his or her faith rather than abjure it. In Christian history, Stephen* was the protomartyr*, or first martyr, as recorded in Acts 7:54–60. According to Tertullian*, "the blood of the martyrs is seed [of the church]." Martyrdom was seen as a baptism of blood. The certainty of Christian resurrection gave the martyrs a power-

Martyrs

ful motive. The anniversary of the martyr's death, called as *natalis,* or heavenly birthday, began to be celebrated from the second century. In hagiography*, martyrs rank after the Virgin Mary* and the apostles but before all saints*. The veneration* of martyrs' bones began with St. Polycarp's* remains, and most of the martyrs are commemorated by special feast days. Special intercessory powers were also attributed to the martyrs.

martyriarius Cleric in charge of a martyrium*.

martyrikon In the Byzantine Rite*, a troparion* or short hymn in honor of a martyr*.

martyrium/martyry Church built to honor a martyr* or as a depository for relics*.

martyrology 1. Study of martyrs* and their martyrdoms, as a devotional aid. 2. List of martyrs, such as the *Hieronymian Martyrology** or the *Roman Martyrology*,* with the lives and deeds of martyrs, arranged according to their anniversaries.

Martyrs' Mirror Chronicle of Anabaptist* martyrdoms written by Tieleman Jansz van Braght, published in 1660. It has had considerable influence on the Mennonites* as a devotional classic.

marwah'tho Fans or metal discs with bells attached to a pole and shaken during solemn moments during the liturgy. They are decorated with seraph's face with wings.

marwebe In the Syrian Rite, antiphons* sung whenever the Magnificat* is recited.

Mary See VIRGIN MARY.

Mary, Gospel of Gnostic work extant only in Greek and Coptic* fragments in different collections. It records a conversation between the risen Christ and his disciples and between Mary Magdalene and Peter*.

Mary of Egypt (c. 344–c. 421) Alexandrian prostitute who was converted on a visit to the Holy Sepulchre* in Jerusalem* and thereafter spent the remaining 47 years of her life as a solitary ascetic.

She miraculously received communion hours before she died. Feast day: April 1 (Eastern Church*); April 2 (Western Church*).

Mary of Egypt

Maryknoll Town in Westchester County, New York, where the Catholic Foreign Mission Society of America*, founded in 1911, is located. Priests trained at the society are known as Maryknoll Fathers and nuns as Maryknoll Sisters.

mas (Arm., portion) Unconsecrated portion of the bread used in the Armenian Liturgy and distributed to congregants who do not receive Holy Communion*. Compare antidoron.

Masaccio (1401–1428) Italian artist, the greatest Florentine painter of the Early Renaissance. His fame rests on five surviving works. The triptych*, *Madonna and Child with Saints; Madonna and Child with St. Anne;* the polyptych*, *Madonna and Child;* the fresco*, *Trinity;* and the fresco cycle in the Brancacci Chapel in Florence* to which Masaccio contributed *Expulsion from Paradise, Tribute Money, Raising of the Prefect's Son,* and *St. Peter Enthroned.* There are other scenes from the Acts on the sides of the altar, including the *Distribution of Goods, the Death of Ananias,* and *St. Peter's Shadow Healing the Sick.*

Masaccio died at a very young age as a result of poisoning.

mashafa/masaheft (Ge'ez;) Book or Scripture, as in Mashafa Qeddusat or the Holy Book of the anaphora*.

mashdotz In the Armenian Rite*, a ritual containing forms of administration of the sacraments*, funeral ceremonies, house dedications, and common blessings.

masn In the Armenian Rite*, a particle* of the consecrated bread separated from the rest of the bread and placed in the chalice*.

masnapto In the Syrian Church, large amice-like hood worn by bishops usually ornamented with the figure of a dove*.

masob In the Ethiopian Rite, a round covered metal or wickerwork box in which bread is brought to the altar before the prothesis*.

Masolino de Panicale (1383/4–1447) Florentine painter and associate of Masaccio*. He worked with Masaccio on the frescoes* for Brancacci Chapel and after Masaccio's death painted a series of frescoes in Castiglione Olona. Among his works are *Crucifixion* and *Madonna and Christ in Glory*.

Mason, Charles Harrison (1866–1961) African-American Pentecostal minister and founder of the Church of God in Christ*, the largest African-American Pentecostal denomination. He was converted in 1880 and received a call* to preach in 1893. With a fellow African-American Holiness preacher, Charles Price Jones, he founded the Church of God in Christ in Memphis. After a visit to Azusa Street in 1906, Mason became convinced of the validity of the Holy Spirit* baptism and received Spirit baptism in 1907. He returned to Memphis, where he parted company with Jones and emerged as the leader of the new Pentecostal movement and bishop of the Church of God in Christ.

Mason, Lowell (1792–1872) American composer, generally acknowledged as the father of church music and music education in America. In 1822 he published his first collection of church music, which proved immensely popular, going into 22 editions by 1858. He inspired a reform of sacred music through nearly 50 publications and composed nearly 1,200 hymn tunes, including the perennial favorites "From Greenland's Icy Mountains," "Nearer, My God to Thee," "Missionary Hymn," "Olivet," "Boyleston," "Bethany," and "My Faith Looks Up to Thee."

masqal Feast of the Discovery of the True Cross, one of the most popular church festivals in Ethiopia.

Mass (Lat., *mitto*, to dismiss) In the Roman Catholic Church, Holy Communion* or the Eucharist*, so called from the concluding words of the Roman Mass, *ite, missa est**. In Roman Catholic doctrine, the Mass is a divine and propitiatory sacrifice and in that sense the consecrated wine becomes the Lord's blood and the consecrated bread, the Lord's body. In Protestant churches, the focus falls on the commemoration of Christ's Passion*, and on spiritual feeding on him.

mass evangelism Also, crusade evangelism. Proclamation of the gospel to a large body of people inviting them to commit their lives to Christ. It involves a series of rallies or services held in a large public facility, as a stadium. Mass evangelism has its roots in the Great Awakening* and the ministry of George Whitefield*. Whitefield's successors include Charles Finney*, Dwight Moody*, Billy Sunday*, and Billy Graham*.

Mass for the People Eucharist* offered for the intentions of the faithful.

Mass of obligation Attendance at Mass* as a duty of every Christian.

Mass of the Catechumens The antecommunion, or the first part of the Eucharist* which catechumens* were permitted to attend.

Mass of the Faithful The second half of the Mass* from the offertory to the end that was open only to the baptized faithful. It contained the most essential parts of the service.

Mass stipend Offering given for the celebration of the Eucharist*.

massah wajh (lit., wipe the face) In the Coptic Rite, the priest's act of wiping his face after sprinkling holy water* over the congregation.

Master of the Sentences Title of Peter Lombard*, author of *Libri Sententiarum*.

masthaba In the Assyrian Church*, the raised platform immediately before the altar.

Mater Dolorosa The Virgin of Sorrows, especially as she appears in Pieta*.

material principle Central doctrine of a denomination. Justification* by faith* is the material principle of the Protestant churches.

material sin In Roman Catholic theology, act that is materially contrary to God's commandments but which does not make the sinner culpable because he or she acted out of ignorance or in response to or fear of external force. Distinguished from formal sin.

Mather, Cotton (1663–1728) Puritan minister. The eldest son of Increase Mather*, he served the Second Church of Boston for many years as pastor. He wrote 469 books. Many of these were very popular in his day, particularly *Magnalia Christi Americana* or *The Ecclesiastical History of New England* (1702), *Wonders of the Invisible World* (1692), *Manuductio ad Ministerium* (1726), *Essays to do Good* (1710), and *Christian Philosopher* (1721).

Mather, Increase (1639–1723) American Congregational* minister, the youngest son of Richard Mather* and father of Cotton Mather*. Born in England, he emigrated to the New World and was ordained minister in the New North Church in 1664. He was president of Harvard College from 1685 to 1701. He was a voluminous writer on historical and theological subjects.

Mather, Richard (1596–1669) English Puritan divine and father of Increase Mather*. He emi-

grated in 1635 to the New World, where he settled at Dorchester, Massachusetts. He was translator of the *Bay Psalm Book** and an advocate of the Half-Way Covenant*.

Matheson, George (1842–1906) Blind Scottish theologian and hymn writer, author of *Sacred Songs* (1890) that included his well-loved hymn, "O Love That Will Not Let Me Go."

Mathias, William (1934–) Welsh composer. Among his choral works are many on sacred texts, including Psalm settings, works on liturgical texts, such as the *Festival Te Deum* (1964), a Communion Service in C (1967), a Magnificat* and Nunc Dimittis* for chorus and organ (1970), a Missa brevis* for chorus and organ (1973), anthems, and hymn tunes.

Mathurin Member of the Trinitarian* order founded for the redemption of Christian captives in 1198 by St. John of Matha*.

matouthsaran In the Armenian Rite*: 1. Prothesis* table on the north side of the sanctuary. 2. Offertory when a curtain is drawn across the sanctuary.

matrimony Marriage as a union for life between a man and a woman. It is one of the seven sacraments* of the Christian church and holds a high

Cotton Mather

place in New Testament teaching where it is compared to that union of Christ and his church (Eph. 5:25–33). Fidelity in marriage is the subject of a number of commandments, particularly

Marriage

those against divorce and unfaithfulness. Traditionally, the rite of marriage consists of two parts: the betrothal and wedding proper. Originally, betrothal took place some time before marriage and at the church door or in the narthex*, not in the church itself, and it consisted of the exchange of rings and the making of vows. The marriage service, a service of blessing, includes the celebration of the nuptial Mass* in front of the altar.

In the Eastern churches*, the couple are given crowns and share a cup of wine. There are limitations on who might marry. Banns are required on three Sundays in the parishes of residence of both parties. In the Roman Catholic Church, restrictions on marriage are spelled out in canon law* and are divided into impedient and diriment impediments. The bride and bridegroom may not be related to each other within the Levitical degrees, both parties must consent to the marriage, and both parties must be above the age of consent. Some churches refuse to marry if either the bride or the bridegroom are divorced or living in adulterous relationships. The sacramental nature of marriage affirms that it is part of the divine plan for human beings and that it confers grace to

both parties. It is unusual among sacraments because the parties themselves are the ministers and the priest or pastor himself is only a witness.

matroneum Area in a church reserved for women, part of the triforium*.

matsahafa In the Ethiopian Church, a liturgical book. Thus, matsahafa qandil is the text for the sacrament of the unction and matsahafa qeddasse is the missal.

Matta al-Miskin (c. 1920–) Coptic orthodox priest and monk, spiritual director* of the Monastery of St. Macarius in the Wadi al-Natrun. He is one of the leaders of the twentieth-century revival of monasticism* in the Coptic Church*.

Mattai, Deyr Monastery founded by Mar Mattai in the fourth or fifth century, near Mosul in modern Iraq. Originally called Djebel Maqlub, it soon became one of the most prosperous and was referred to as the Assyrian Athos. It was the home for so many monks that it was named Tur Alpheph, or "Mount of Thousands." The Jacobites took over the monastery around 540.

Matthew of Aquasparta (c. 1240–1302) Franciscan theologian. He taught in Paris and Bologna*, became general* of his order in 1287, cardinal in 1288, and cardinal bishop of Porto and Rufina* in 1291. His writings include sermons and Bible commentaries, a commentary on the Sentences, *quodlibets,* and *Quaestiones Disputatae.* His theological positions were derived from St. Augustine* and St. Bonaventura* and anticipated Duns Scotus*.

Matthew of Janov (c. 1355–1393) Czech reformer. He was influenced by Milic*, the father of Czech Reform. He began an exhaustive study of the Bible which resulted in the five-volume *Regulae Veteris et Novi Testamenti* and also a new translation of the Bible.

Matthew of Paris (c. 1200–1259) Medieval chronicler and member of the Benedictine monastery of St. Albans*. His principal work was *Chronica Majora,* a history of the world from the creation to 1259. As an annalist he was truthful and did not minimize ecclesiastical abuses.

Matthew, St. Called Levi in Mark 2:14; Luke 5:27. Apostle*, evangelist, and author of the First Gospel. He was a tax collector by profession. He is reputed to have been martyred variously in Ethiopia, Pontus, or Persia. Feast day: September 21 (Western Church*); November 16 (Eastern Church*).

St. Matthew the Evangelist

Matthew's Bible First English authorized version of the Bible in 1537 which served as the basis for later versions, so called because it was dedicated to King Henry and Queen Anne by the pseudonymous Thomas Matthew. It was edited by John Rogers*, a friend of Tyndale*.

Matthias Apostle chosen by the Twelve* by lot to replace Judas. There is no further reference to him in the New Testament. The *Traditions of Matthias* is an apocryphal Gospel attributed to him.

Matthopoulos, Eusebius (1849–1929) Greek Orthodox home missionary. He entered the monastery of Megaspylaeon at age 14 and was ordained priest in 1876. In 1895 he was commissioned by the Holy Synod* to preach throughout Greece. In 1907 with several friends he founded the Zoe (Gk., life) Brotherhood of the Theologians to carry on his work of bringing people back to the church and its sacraments*. The Zoe* movement has had a profound spiritual effect on the Greek Church.

mattins/matins Breviary* office for the night, derived from the practice of vigils* in the early church. Originally said at midnight, it is now said on the preceding afternoon or evening or, as in the Church of England*, in the succeeding morning.

matuniyas In the Assyrian tradition, a deep bow or genuflection*.

Maulbronn Former Cistercian monastery in Maulbronn in northern Wurttemberg, founded by Walter of Lomersheim in 1138. The consecration of the Basilica of St. Mary took place in 1178. The narrow chapel is inset with chapels. A spacious western porch, called Paradise, was built on to the church in 1210. The monastery exhibits a variety of architectural styles, Romanesque, Early Gothic*, and High Gothic*. A fountain* stands in the middle of the fourteenth-century room in the north wing. The vaults above the fountain and the refectory* were painted by Jorg Ratgeb. The monastery was closed down in 1530 and, after Wurttemberg converted to Protestantism*, became a convent school and later a theological seminary.

maumyono In the Syrian Church, an exorcist*.

Maunder, John (1858–1920) English composer. Among his works of enduring appeal are the anthem, *Praise the Lord, O Jerusalem,* and the church cantatas *The Martyrs* (1894) and *From Olivet to Calvary* (1904).

Maundy Thursday Thursday before Easter*, so called from Christ's command (Lat., *mandatum*) that his disciples should love one another (John 13:34). The day is marked in different churches by several commemoratory rites, such as washing of the feet, breaking of the bread in the evening, blessing of oils, and the Reconciliation of Penitents. In the Roman Catholic Church, Mass* is celebrated in the evening when white vestments are worn and the altar is adorned tastefully. Before the Mass, the tabernacle is emptied. After the Mass, the bells are silenced until Easter*, the altars are stripped, and the holy water stoups are emptied.

Mauretania Region comprising various African provinces of the Roman Empire, equivalent to modern Morocco and Algeria, excluding Constantine-Tebessa, which constituted Numidia. It was Christian from the third century to the Arab conquest in the seventh century. By 484 it had over 162 bishops.

Mauriac, Francois (1885–1970) French Roman Cath-olic writer. Educated by the Jesuits*, he published his first novel, *A Kiss for the Leper,* in 1922. It was followed by *The Desert of Love* (1925),

Francois Mauriac

Therese (1928), *Viper's Tangle* (1933), and *A Woman of the Pharisees* (1946). His novels explored the recesses of the human soul, especially sin, greed, lust, hatred, and pride and are dramas of spiritual struggle. He won the Nobel Prize for Literature in 1952.

Maurice Leader of the Theban Legion* and martyr*. According to later accounts, during the Diocletian persecution*, the Theban Legion, consisting of Christians led by Maurice, mutinied at Agaunum (St. Maurice en Valais, Switzerland) and were massacred. There is a sixth-century monastery at the site of the martyrdom.

Maurice, Frederick Denison (1805–1872) Christian socialist. Son of a Unitarian minister, he was converted to Anglicanism* under Coleridge's influence and, later became chaplain* at Guy's Hospital, London. In 1838 he published his most enduring work, *The Kingdom of Christ,* in which he expressed his fundamentally orthodox views on the Incarnation*. In 1848 he helped found the Queen's College and in 1846 was appointed professor of theology at King's College, London, while serving as chaplain* at Lincoln's Inn. In 1848 his desire for a proactive role in social reform led to his joining with J. M. F. Ludlow* and Charles Kingsley* to form the Christian Socialists as a political movement.

Meanwhile, his views on baptism* and eternal punishment were perceived as heterodox. On the publication of his *Theological Essays,* he was expelled from King's College. In 1854 he started the first Working Men's College in London. Subse-

quently, he held positions at St. Peter's*, London, and in Cambridge University. Among his other books were *The Lord's Prayer* (1848), *The Unity of the New Testament* (1854), and *The Gospel of the Kingdom of Heaven* (1864).

Maurists French Benedictine monks of the Congregation of St. Maur, named after St. Maurus (d. 565). It was founded in 1621 as the French branch of a reform movement initiated in the Abbey of St. Vanne, near Verdun. At their peak, the Maurists had over 200 houses. From 1672 to 1818, when they were dissolved by Pius VII*, they devoted themselves to scholarship and produced over 700 works. They included among their numbers some of the outstanding scholars of the seventeenth and eighteenth centuries, such as Jean Luc d'Achery, Jean Mabillon, Edmond Martene, Bernard de Montfaucon, and Thierry Ruinart. Maurists were suspected of Jansenist sympathies. Many of them were executed during the French Revolution.

Mawase'et In the Ethiopian Church, an alternate, less frequently used form of the daily office.

Maximilla (d. c. 179) Prophetess. Leader of the Montanist sect with Montanus* and Priscilla, another prophetess. They proclaimed the imminent return of Christ to establish a new Jerusalem* in Phrygia. She claimed that she would be the last prophetess. Like Montanus, they were gifted with tongues*, ecstatic rapture, and inspired language.

Maximus the Confessor, St. (c. 580–662) Byzantine theologian and opponent of Monothelitism*. During the Persian invasion in 626, he fled to Africa, where he was responsible for the triumph of Chalcedonian orthodoxy at several African synods and at the Lateran Council of 649. For his opposition to Emperor Constans, he was tried for treason and exiled to Thrace and his tongue and right hand were cut off. He wrote over 90 treatises, including Bible commentaries and writings on ascetics and liturgics*. Feast day: January 21 (Eastern Church*); August 13 (Western Church*).

Maximus the Greek, St. (c. 1470–1556) Birth name: Michael Trivolis. He entered the Dominican Order in 1502 but left it two years later to join Mount Athos*. In 1516 he was sent to Moscow* at the request of the tsar to translate works from Greek into Slavonic. In addition to these translations, he produced many works on theology and philosophy. However, he became involved in disputes with the state and was imprisoned from 1525 to 1548. After release from prison, he spent the rest of his life in the Monastery of the Holy Trinity. He was canonized in 1988. Feast day: January 21.

Monastery of the Holy Trinity

May In the Roman Catholic Church, a month dedicated to the Virgin Mary* whose intercession is sought through special prayers and devotions.

May Laws Legislation passed by the Prussian *Landtag* in 1873 and instigated by Bismarck as part of his Kulturkampf* against German Catholicism. They limited the church's powers of excommunication*, placed the supreme ecclesiastical court* under state control, placed seminaries under government supervision, and subjected clerical appointments to state veto. Bitterly opposed by the church, it was modified in 1886/87 after an agreement between Bismarck and Pope Leo XIII*.

Mayflower Compact Agreement signed in 1620 by passengers on the *Mayflower* before disembarking at Plymouth Rock. It provided for a civil government based on the Bible. It remained the pri-

mary constitutional charter of Plymouth Colony until 1691, when that colony was absorbed by Massachusetts.

Signing of the Mayflower Compact

Mayne, St. Cuthbert (1544–1577) Roman Catholic martyr*. He became a Roman Catholic under the influence of Edmund Campion and was ordained at Douai*. In 1576 he became a clandestine priest in Cornwall, but was discovered and sentenced to death. He was beatified in 1888 and was among the forty martyrs* of England and Wales, canonized in 1970. Feast day: November 29.

Maynooth College Also, St. Patrick's College. The principal Catholic seminary in Ireland, located in Maynooth, in County Kildare, 15 miles northwest of Dublin, founded in 1795. Under British rule, it was a center of Irish nationalism.

Mazarin Bible Also, the Gutenberg Bible*; the 42-line Bible. First full-length book ever printed and the first printed edition of the Bible, produced at Mainz* by Johannes Gutenberg, about 1455, acquired by Jules Cardinal Mazarin, French statesman.

Mazenod, Charles-Joseph-Eugene de (1782–1861) French founder of the Missionary Oblates of Mary Immaculate* (OMI). Realizing the deep spiritual vacuum caused by the French Revolution, Mazenod gathered some priests with the aim of undertaking preaching missions and for promoting religious renewal in France, thus laying the foundations of OMI. In 1826 the society received papal approval. From 1841 the society began sending out missionaries abroad, first to Canada and then to Ceylon (1847) and South Africa (1851).

mazmaza kurbana In the Ethiopian Rite, rubbing of the bread at the start of the liturgy.

maznavor In the Armenian Church*, a minor grade of teaching cleric.

m'caprana In the Assyrian Rite, blessed bread distributed at the end of the liturgy during the recitation of the Prayer of Mary when people go forward to kiss the hand cross of the priest.

McAuley, Catherine (1778–1841) Irish founder of the Sisters of Mercy* in 1830. She adopted the presentation rule for the sisters* based on the Rule of St. Augustine*. By the time of her death there were 12 foundations of the Sisters of Mercy* in Ireland and England.

McClintock, John (1814–1870) American Methodist minister who was the first president of Drew Theological Seminary. With James Strong, he edited the ten-volume *Cyclopedia of Biblical, Theological and Ecclesiastical Literature.*

McCloskey, John (1810–1885) American Roman Catholic cardinal who built a number of churches and seminaries in the United States, including St. Patrick's Cathedral* in New York City. He received the papal title, *Sancta Maria supra Minervam.*

McGavran, Donald A. (1897–1990) Missionary to India, father of the Church Growth movement* and founding dean of the School of World Mission at Fuller Theological Seminary*. A third-generation missionary, he became concerned about the lack of conversions and membership growth experienced by his mission during a 50-year period despite a substantial commitment of money and personnel. So he resigned his position in the United Christian Missionary Society and spent the next 17 years as a church planter, analyzing missionary practice so he could identify the causes as well as obstacles to growth. He found that church growth was directly related to dependency on the Holy Spirit* and that stagnation and decline were related to the neglect of evangelism in favor of social action. He was the author of many books, including *Bridges of God* (1955), *How Churches Grow* (1959), and *Understanding Church Growth* (1970).

McGee, John Vernon (1904–1988) Radio evangelist and host of the "Open Bible Hour" and "Thru the Bible." McGee also served as pastor of the Church of the Open Door in Los Angeles. He began the "Open Bible Hour" in the 1940s and "Thru the Bible" in the 1950s. Both were immensely popular, with an audience in the millions.

McGiffert, Arthur Cushman (1861–1963) American church historian and president of Union Theological Seminary* (1917–1926). Among his chief works were *A History of Christianity in the Apostolic Age* (1897), *The Apostles' Creed* (1902), *Martin Luther, The Man and His Work* (1911), *The Rise of Modern Religious Ideas* (1915), *The God of the Early Christians* (1915), and *A History of Christian Thought* (2 vols., 1931–1933).

McGilvary, Daniel (1828–1911) American Presbyterian missionary to Siam (Thailand). In 1858 he joined the American Presbyterian mission to Siam, and in 1867 began the first Christian work in Chiang Mai, where he spent the rest of his life.

McGready, James (c. 1760–1817) Presbyterian pastor and father of the frontier camp meeting*. Licensed to preach in 1788, he moved first to North Carolina and then to Kentucky. At Gaspar River Church in 1800, he organized the first frontier camp meeting.

mchamchono In the Jacobite Church*, the deacon who wears the uroro or stole*, the kuthino* or alb* with its distinctive cuffs.

McKendree, William (1757–1835) First American-born bishop of the Methodist Church (1808–1835). He was converted at the age of 29 and began working with Bishop Francis Asbury*, serving on the circuits in Virginia, Ohio, Kentucky, and parts of Illinois, Tennessee, and Mississippi. He was a leader in the great western revival.

McPherson, Aimee Semple (1890–1944). Canadian-born American Pentecostal evangelist. Her first marriage to Robert J. Semple, missionary to China, ended in his death, and her second marriage to Harold McPherson ended in divorce. Thereafter she devoted herself to evangelism. In 1922 she built the 5,000-seat Angelus Temple* in

Los Angeles and developed her four-square gospel, the four referring to Christ as healer and Savior, the baptism of the Holy Spirit*, speaking in tongues*, and the Second Coming*. In the same year she broadcast what she claims was the first Christian radio sermon. In 1927 she incorporated the International Church of the Foursquare Gospel. In 1926 she disappeared from public view for a while and claimed that she had been kidnapped, but the case was finally dismissed and brought her much ridicule.

Aimee Semple McPherson

Mears, Henrietta Cornella (1890–1963) She was one of the most influential figures in church-based Christian education in the twentieth century. Born the youngest of seven children in Fargo, North Dakota, she graduated from the University of Minnesota in 1913. After over a decade of public school teaching (1915–1928) at Central High School, Minneapolis, Mears moved to California, becoming director of Christian education at Hollywood Presbyterian Church (through 1963). Dissatisfied with the quality of available curricula, she founded Gospel Light Publications in 1933—which remains a major source of non-denominational Christian education resources for all ages. Recognizing the importance of retreat ministries in personal growth, she was instrumental in founding Forest Home Christian Conference Center in 1938. Her 1953 book, *What the Bible Is All About,* has become a classic Bible study intro-

duction—and her gifts as a woman in education and institutional development have made an impact worldwide.

Mechitarists Community of Uniat Armenian monks founded at Constantinople* in 1701 by Mechitar of Sebaste. (1676–1749). Driven from Constantinople, they took refuge in Venice*, where they settled on the Island of San Lazzaro in 1717. Another branch settled in Vienna*. They follow the Benedictine* Rule and devote themselves to study, publishing, education, and missionary work.

Mechthild of Magdeburg (c. 1207–1282) Mystical writer whose *Revelations* record in six books her visions containing dialogue with the risen Christ on eschatology*, mysticism, and theology. They are considered among the most powerful writings by a medieval woman. She left home at 23 to become a Beguine at Magdeburg under the spiritual direction of the Dominicans*. As opposition to the Beguines* became intense, she left the order to become a nun at a Cistercian convent at Helfta, where she worked with two other visionary women, St. Mechthild of Hackeborn and St. Gertrude the Great*.

Medellin City in Colombia, site of the Second General Conference of Latin American Bishops (CELAM*) in 1968. It became synonymous with that conference and its document which adopted liberation theology* as one of its main planks.

Mediator Title of Jesus Christ under the new covenant* (Heb. 8:6; 9:15; 1 Tim. 2:5). It refers to his work in reconciling fallen human beings with God.

mediatrix Also, mediatress; Mediatrix of All Graces. Roman Catholic designation of the Virgin Mary* in her role as a mediator between her Son and the body of believers.

Medina, Bartolome (1527–1580) Spanish Dominican moral theologian. For most of his life he was professor at the University of Salamanca. He is known as the father of probabilism*, a doctrine that he developed in his *Commentaries*. Probabilism held that in a case where two courses of actions are probable, the less probable one favoring liberty rather than the more probable one favoring law should be followed.

meditation 1. Quiet time* spent in contemplating the Word of God* and in fumigating the mind of the toxic thoughts and ideas that infiltrate it every day. 2. Private devotion or spiritual exercise focused on a religious theme. 3. Spoken or written contemplative discourse delving into spiritual things.

Meditationes Vitae Christi *Meditations on the Life of Christ,* by a Franciscan monk, possibly Bonaventura*, one of the most important sources of Western Christian spirituality* in the later Middle Ages. It has 100 meditations arranged in chronological order based on the life of Christ as recorded in the New Testament.

Medjugorje Small village in southern Herzegovina in Bosnia, site of Marian* apparitions since 1981 to six young people. The apparitions are distinctive in that they continued on a daily basis for many years. The young visionaries report seeing the figure of the Virgin Mary* and holding conversations with her without being heard by others present. The messages have consistently emphasized faith in Jesus Christ as the only Savior, repentance* for sins, prayer*, and fasting*. The visionaries have been entrusted with a number of secrets; when the number reaches ten, the visions will cease. These messages have been more evangelical in tone and content than those of previous Marian apparitions, with an emphasis on the love of Jesus and the role of the Holy Spirit*.

me'eraf In the Ethiopian Church, the common order of the daily Mass*.

meetinghouse Building used for worship, especially by nonconformist sects, such as the Quakers*.

megalophonos In the Byzantine Rite*, the recitation of the Nicene Creed* by a bishop being ordained as a test of orthodoxy*.

megaloschemos Highest grade in the Byzantine monastic orders.

megalynarion (pl., megalynaria) In the Orthodox Church, short verse containing the words, "We magnify." On feast days megalynaria are sung with the troparia of the ninth ode of the canon*.

meghedi In the Armenian Rite*, a hymn sung during the prothesis* while the altar veil is drawn. Its text varies according to the feast day.

Meinrad, St. (d. 861) Patron of Einsiedeln*. He became a monk at Reichenau* but left the monastery to become a solitary hermit at Einsiedeln (hermitage) for the last 25 years of his life. He was killed by two persons to whom he had given hospitality. Feast day: January 21.

Meissen Gothic cathedral on the River Elbe. The first cathedral was built here around 968, the second between 1006 and 1073. The present cathedral, including the Chapel of All Saints beside the cloister*, was completed in the second half of the thirteenth century. Of the 50 original altars, only three have survived since it became an Evangelical church in 1581. Of these the triptych altar in St. George Chapel was painted by Lucas Cranach* in 1534.

mekamia Crutches used by Ethiopian clergy and laity to support themselves during the long services.

Melanchthon, Philip (1497–1560) German reformer and associate of Luther*. As professor of Greek at the University of Wittenberg*, he became acquainted with Luther and began promoting his cause. In 1518 he accompanied Luther to the Disputation of Leipzig*, published Luther's *Commentaries on Galatians* and the *Psalms,* and defended Luther against the Parisian theologians. During Luther's eight-month stay at Wartburg Castle, Melanchthon and Andreas Carlstadt* served as leaders of the fledgling Reformation* movement. His *Loci Communes** (1521) was the first systematic treatment of Lutheran theology.

After 1530 Melanchthon was actively involved in drawing up confessions and in negotiating with Protestant bodies. He drew up the Visitation Articles of 1528, the Augsburg Confession* of 1530, Apology of the Augsburg Confession of 1531, Wittenberg Concord* of 1536, and took part in the Ratisbon Colloquy* (1541), Diet of Speyer* (1529), Marburg Colloquy* (1529), and the Diet of Augsburg (1530).

One of the most learned men of his age, Melanchthon was essentially a humane scholar. When Luther died, Melanchthon was his natural successor, but he was not quite equal to the task. For the remainder of his life, he was engaged in a series of conflicts: with Andreas Osiander* over justification*, with Nicholas von Amsdorf* over predestination*, and with other Lutheran theologians over the Lord's Supper*. He died praying for deliverance from the "fury of the theologians." On the one hand, he was closer to some Roman Catholic positions than Luther and, on the other, he was more open than Luther to Calvinist and Zwinglian doctrines on the Eucharist*. Alone among the Reformers*, he objected to the con-

Philip Melanchthon

demnation of the papacy in the Schmalkaldic Articles*. Melanchthon's contributions to theology include his doctrine of synergism, which attempted to combine free will* with predestination.

Melanesian Brotherhood Anglican religious order of evangelists who take for limited periods vows of poverty, chastity* and obedience, founded in 1925. It works in Melanesia, including Solomon Islands, Vanuatu, Fiji, and Papua New Guinea.

Melania the Elder, St. (c. 342–c. 410) Roman lady who, on the death of her husband, left Rome* for the Holy Land* in 372 or 374 and founded a double monastery on the Mount of Olives.

Melania the Younger, St. (c. 385–438/9) Granddaughter of Melania the Elder*, who founded with her husband, Pinian, two monasteries at Tagaste in Africa, joined St. Jerome* and entered monasteries at Bethlehem*, and later founded another monastery on the Mount of Olives. Feast day: December 31.

melisma Practice of singing more than a few notes to one syllable of text.

Melitian Schism 1. Fourth-century dispute associated with Melitius*, bishop of Lycopolis in Egypt. It rose out of his objections to the terms laid down by Peter*, bishop of Alexandria, for the return to the church of those who had lapsed during the Diocletian persecution*. The schism continued until the eighth century. 2. Fourth-century dispute involving an orthodox bishop, Melitius of Antioch (d. 381), who was opposed by another orthodox congregation, the Eustathians, led by Paulinus* and an Apollinarian group. Melitius was twice banished under Valens, but returned under Gratian's Edict of Tolerance in 379 and later presided over the First Council of Constantinople* in 381.

Melitius of Antioch, St. (d. 381) Ordained by Arians, he deserted them and professed the orthodox faith. He was banished from his see* and restored three times, and finally presided over the First Council of Constantinople* in 381. Feast day: February 12.

Melito, St. (second century) Bishop of Sardis in Asia Minor. He was among the first theologians to list the accepted books of the Old Testament, to use the typology of the slain Paschal lamb*, and to name Christ as "both God and Man." He was involved in the problem of the date of Easter*. He was also the first known Christian pilgrim* to Palestine*. Feast day: April 1.

Melk Benedictine*monastery in Melk, on the Danube in Austria. Originally built around 831, it became a Benedictine community from 1089 when the relics* of the martyr* Koloman were transferred here. After a period of decline during the Reformation*, Melk became renowned again as a place of monastic discipline as well as art and scholarship. The present buildings were built between 1700 and 1739 by architect Jakob Brandtauer, and they have been compared to Escorial* and Versailles. Among its outstanding features are the east facade, the prelates' courtyard, Emperor's Walk, the marble hall, and the magnificent two-story library. The monastic church is the most beautiful example of Baroque ecclesiastical architecture north of the Alps, and has been described as "God's audience room."

Melkites/Melchites (Syr., *malkaya,* imperial) Designation of non-Monophysite and non-European Christians who accepted the Definition of Chalcedon* and remained in communion with either Rome* or Constantinople.

Mellifluous Doctor Epithet of Bernard of Clairvaux*, whose writings were called the "River of Paradise."

Melville, Andrew (1545–1622) Scottish reformer. Trained by Theodore Beza*, he had a distinguished career as principal of Glasgow University and later of St. Mary's College, St. Andrews. After the death of John Knox*, he assumed the mantle of leadership of the Scottish Presbyterians, becoming the moderator* of the General Assembly* in 1582. He was instrumental in the ratification of the *Second Book of Discipline** in 1578. After James I became king of England, he had a running battle with the royal efforts to impose the Episcopal system in Scotland. He was imprisoned for four years for resisting these efforts. Toward the end of his life he became professor at the University of Sedan.

memento domini (Lat., remember the Lord) Second section and part of the Roman canon* in which the celebrant prays for the church militant*.

memento etiam (Lat., remember also) Tenth section of the Roman canon* in which the celebrant prays for the dead in Christ.

memento mori (Lat., remember death) Death's head or other symbolic object used by monks as a reminder of death.

Memento Mori

Memlinc, Hans (c. 1440–1494) Flemish religious painter. Among his works are *The Seven Joys of Mary, The Last Judgment, The Adoration of the Magi, The Lamentation Triptych,* and *The Donne Triptych* in the National Gallery, London, as well as several Madonnas.

Memorare (Lat., Remember) Widely used intercessory prayer addressed to the Virgin Mary*, beginning "Remember, O most loving Virgin Mary*, that never was it known that any one who fled to your protection, implored your help, or sought your intercession was left unaided. Inspired with this confidence, I fly to you O virgin of virgins, my mother; to you do I come, before you do I stand, sinful and sorrowful. O mother of the Word Incarnate, despise not my petitions, but in your mercy, hear and answer me. Amen." It is of unknown authorship.

memoria/memoriae 1. The least important of the three categories of feasts, divided into obligatory and optional memoriae. 2. Funerary monument or chapel or a reliquary*.

Memoriale Rituum Also, Rituale Parvum. Latin liturgical book for small churches containing the forms traditionally used in the blessing of candles for Candlemas*, ashes for Ash Wednesday*, and palms for Palm Sunday* as well as services for the last three days of Holy Week*.

memorialism Teaching ascribed to Zwingli* that the Lord's Supper* is only a memorial and that there is only a symbolic presence of Christ in the elements*.

memorion Church erected over the grave of a martyr*.

memre In the Byzantine Church*, rhythmical homilies sung during worship services.

Men, Aleksandr (1935–1990) Russian Orthodox theologian and priest of Jewish descent. In 1955 the institute in which he was studying was transferred to Irkutsk in Siberia*, where he met Gleb Iakunin, the dissident. Both became priests. In 1970 he embarked upon a monumental study, *In Search of the Way, the Truth and the Life,* followed by a multi-volume dictionary of the Bible. Among those he baptized was Nadezhda Mandelstam, wife of the poet, Osip. Father Men was murdered in 1990.

Men of God Russian sect also known as Flagellants or Khlysts*.

Menaion/Menaia (Gk., book of the months) In the Eastern Church*, one of the 12 liturgical books* (one for each month beginning with September) containing the variable parts of the Divine Office* for the immovable feasts*, corresponding to the *Proprium Sanctorum* in the Western Church*.

Menas, St. (third or fourth century) Egyptian martyr*. His birthplace is an important pilgrimage* center for those seeking physical healing. His church was excavated in 1905–1908. He is the patron saint* of merchants. Feast day: November 11.

menbab The four lessons customarily read at an Ethiopian worship service.

Mendelssohn-Bartholdy, Felix (1809–1847) German musical composer. He came from a wealthy Jewish family that had converted to Christianity. Many of his finest works were produced while he was in his teens. At the age of 20, he presented Bach's *St. Matthew Passion*. He spent much of his later life in England, where he wrote one of the greatest nineteenth-century oratorios, *Paulus,* performed in Dusseldorf in 1836, and *Elijah,* for the Birmingham Festival in 1846. He is best known for his choral music, such as Psalm 43 for unaccompanied chorus.

mendicant orders Monastic orders that were not permitted to own property. Its members worked or begged for their living and were not bound to one convent by a vow of stability. They could preach and hear confessions, free from episcopal jurisdiction. The major mendicant orders were the Dominicans*, Franciscans*, Carmelites*, Hermits of St. Augustine, and Servites*.

Menno Simons (1496–1561) Founder of the Mennonites*. A Roman Catholic priest, he was converted to the Anabaptist* sect. By 1536 he had become a leader of the movement, and for the next 25 years traveled through the Netherlands and north Germany, spreading the Anabaptist message.

Mennonites Followers of Menno Simons*. The sect was founded by a disciple of Zwingli* named Conrad Grebel*, whose Anabaptist* ideas were carried to the low countries by Melchior Hofmann*. When Melchior was imprisoned in 1533, his followers broke into two groups, one revolutionary and the other peaceful. The latter, led by Obbe and Dirk Philips*, united with Menno Simons and his followers and the whole movement adopted the Mennonite name. Their principal tenets include believer's baptism* or adult bap-

St. Menas

tism by immersion*, pacifism, community of believers, discipleship, church discipline*, separation from the world, a life of prayer and holiness*, imminent return of Christ, observance of the Lord's Supper* semiannually, foot-washing*, and prohibition of marriage outside the community.

In the course of their migrations, Mennonites came under the influence of Pietism*, which helped to deepen their faith. Suspicious of dogmas, Menno relied on a literal reading of the Scriptures. He thus refused to use terms and doctrines not expressly sanctioned in the Bible, such as Trinity*. The stigma of Socinianism* was therefore sometimes attached to the Mennonites. Mennonites are very active in social and humanitarian work, and they also have a vigorous program of missions. All Mennonite churches are represented in the Mennonite World Conference. The Mennonite Central Committee carries on relief work in many countries throughout the world.

Menno Simons

Menologion/Menology (Gk., book of remembrance; pl., menologia) In the Eastern Church*, liturgical calendar of saints* and martyrs* arranged by month, beginning with September. One of the most celebrated Menologia is that by Simeon Metaphrastes.

mensa (Lat., table) 1. Large tablet of stone, set over or near a grave, and used for receiving food in memory of the deceased. It was a pagan custom condemned by St. Augustine* and others. 2. Top surface of an altar.

meon Concept in theodicy* derived from neo-Platonism that evil does not exist as an independent entity, but only as the absence of good, just as darkness is the absence of light. The scriptural foundation for the view of evil as meonic is Genesis 1:31: "Then God saw everything that He had made, and indeed it was very good." According to Gregory* the Theologian, "Evil is neither substance, nor kingdom, nor without cause nor self-caused, nor created by God."

Merbecke, John (d. 1585) English musician and theologian. He was organist at St. George's Chapel, Windsor, from 1541 until 1565. A Calvinist, he was sentenced to the stake in 1544 for his compilation of the first biblical concordance* in English but was pardoned. In 1550 he adapted the plain chant to Edward VI's first liturgy.

Mercedarians Also, Nolascans. The Order of Our Lady of Mercy (or Ransom) founded in 1218 by Peter Nolasco* to attend to the sick and to rescue Christian captives from the Moors. They are reported to have redeemed 70,000 captives. They follow the Austin* Rule, but added a fourth vow, to pledge themselves as hostages when necessary. Using their white habit, they gained entrance to Muslim countries. As they spread over Europe and the New World, they changed from a military to a clerical order and then to a mendicant order*. There is a second order of nuns and an order of Discalced Mercedarians.

Mercersburg theology School of theology named after the town of Mercersburg, Pennsylvania, where Marshall College and the Theological Seminary of the German Reformed Church were located. Its leaders were Frederick A. Rausch, J. W. Nevin*, and Philip Schaff*, all professors at Mercersburg. They tried to turn back the tide of liberalism* by a return to sacramental theology*, Christology*, and liturgical and doctrinal renewal, all within the matrix of patristic thought and Reformation* teaching. Mercersburg theology has been compared to the Tractarian movement because of its insistence on the mystical presence of Christ in the Eucharist*. Its celebration united the believer with a historical and organic church. Mercersburg theology was strongest from 1840 until the Civil War, but it has been revived in the late twentieth century because of its Christocentric* roots.

Mercier, Desire Joseph (1851–1926) Belgian cardinal and philosopher. Ordained in 1874, he was professor of Thomist philosophy at the University of Louvain* from 1882 to 1906. He was appointed archbishop of Malines and primate* of Belgium in 1907 and made cardinal in 1907. He made Louvain a major center of neo-Thomist philosophy. He was an opponent of modernism* but an advocate of ecumenism*, engaging in the famous Malines Conversations with Anglicans (1921–1926). He wrote extensively on philosophy, psychology, logic, and metaphysics.

merenda Chief meal at noon in a monastery.

meridian Midday rest taken in a monastery.

merit Reward earned as a result of good works* done by a person, or commandments kept and honored. In orthodox Christian doctrine, good works or obedience in themselves do not earn any merit. In Roman Catholic theology, such acts may have bonitas*, or ethical value, but not dignitas*, or religious value.

meritum de condigno Also, condign or full merit. In scholastic theology, merit* earned by due performance of good works*.

meritum de congruo Also, congruous or half merit. In scholastic theology, merit* conferred, not as due by strict desert, but by God's generosity when it is fitting.

Merle d'Aubigne, Jean Henri (1794–1872) Swiss Evangelical minister and historian, author of the classic *History of the Reformation in the Sixteenth Century* (5 vols., 1835–1853) and *History of the Reformation in Europe at the Time of Calvin* (8 vols., 1863–1878). He was professor of church history at Geneva* from 1835.

meron In the Armenian Rite*, the holy chrism* or oil consecrated by a catholicos*. It is made of olive oil and 40 herbs.

Merton, Thomas (1915–1968) Trappist monk and writer. He joined the Trappists* in 1941 and entered the Gethsemani* abbey in Kentucky, taking the monastic name of Louis. Seven years later he was catapulted into fame on the publication of his autobiography, *The Seven Storey Mountain* (1948), which presented in his inimitable style not only the story of his conversion, but also his spiritual evolution. Toward the end of his life, he began to move away from a strict orthodoxy* into a greater acceptance of non-Christian traditions.

mesedi In the Armenian Rite*, the Psalm which follows immediately the reading of the Old Testament and precedes the reading of the Apostles.

meshwa'e In the Ethiopian Church*, the altar as a sanctuary.

mesochoros In the Greek tradition, the choirmaster who conducts and leads the singing.

Mesonyktikon In the Eastern Church*, the Midnight Office, the first office of the day in the Byzantine Rite*, generally celebrated at around 3:00 A.M. On weekdays it has two distinct parts: the first called amomos, contains the verse, "At midnight I arose to confess you for the judgments of your justice." The second is a troparion*, "Behold the bridegroom is coming in the middle of the night."

mesorion In the Byzantine Rite*, the short hours inserted between the day hours* or between vespers* and compline*.

Mesrob (c. 361–438) Birth name: Mashtotz. Armenian patriarch. A pupil of Nerses the Great*, he entered the Armenian royal service and became a monk in 390. He is credited with devising the Armenian and Georgian alphabets and with developing a national Armenian culture. He succeeded Sahak II* as patriarch* in 449. He helped to translate biblical and patristic writings into Armenian. Feast day: February 19 (Armenian Church*); November 25 (Western Church*).

Messalians (Aram., praying people) Also, Euchites. Heretical sect* that originated in Mesopotamia about 360. Mostly vagrants who slept in the streets and prayed continually, they claimed to see evil spirits in everyone, but accepted the indwelling* of the Holy Spirit* in believers. They rejected all rites and rituals. Attempts to suppress them included burning of their monasteries. They survived until the seventh century.

Messiaen, Olivier (1908–) French composer who had a great impact on twentieth-century church music. From 1942 he was professor at the Paris Conservatory. Among his students were some of the more notable composers, including Pierre Boulez, Karlheinz Stockhausen, Luigi Nono, and William Albright. Among his organ works, the favorites are *Le Banquet Celeste* (1928), *Apparition de l'Eglise Eternelle* (1932), *L'Ascension* (1934), *La Nativité du Seigneur* (1935), *Les Corps Glorieux, Sept Visions Breves de la Vie des Ressuscites* (1939), *Messe de la Pentecôte* (1950), *Livre d'Orgue* (1952), *Verset pour le Fête de la Dedicace* (1960), and *Meditations sur le Mystère de la Sainte Trinite* (1969).

Messiah (Heb., *messiach,* anointed; Gk., *Christos*) Title of Jesus Christ, properly Jesus the Christ, or the anointed one. In the Old Testament, the title is applied to the once and future ruler of Israel, a descendant of David, whose throne would be "forever" (Ps. 89:29).

Messiah Oratorio* by George Handel*, first performed in 1742. It is celebrated for its Hallelujah Chorus*.

messianic Of or relating to a church or movement that focuses on the messianic mission of Jesus Christ and is based on expectancy of his immediate return.

Messianic Jews Christians of Jewish ethnic and cultural background who retain their Jewish legacies and heritage as part of the new covenant*. Early Messianic Jewish leaders included Mark John Levy, the general secretary of the Hebrew Christian Alliance of America; Theodore Lukey, editor of *The Messianic Jew;* David Bronstein, who founded the Peniel Community Center in Chicago; and Morris Kaminskey, who started a Messianic congregation in Toronto. In the 1960s and 1970s there was a new surge in Messianic Judaism. It was led by Moishe Rosen, who founded Jews for Jesus*; Manny Brotman, who founded the Young Hebrew Christian Alliance; and Joel Charnoff, who formed the noted musical team called the Lamb. A number of Messianic Jewish congregations were formed at this time, Adat ha Tikvah in Chicago; Beth Messiah in Rockville, Maryland, cofounded by Sid Roth; Beth Messiah in Philadelphia*; and B'nai Macabim in North Chicago. Many visible groups exist in Israel as well, notably Ramat ha Sharon, Nativya in Jerusalem*, and Bet Immanuel in Jaffa. Messianic Jewish congregations in Jerusalem are chiefly of Russian origin, and are predominantly Zionist and Charismatic.

messianic secret Christ's instruction to his disciples not to let any one know until his crucifixion and resurrection that he was the promised Messiah (Mark 8:30; 9:9).

Messihaye East Syrian, Assyrian, or Syro-Chaldean Christians*.

Mestrovic, Ivan (1883–1962) Croatian Roman Catholic sculptor. His masterpiece is the stone cloister* in Split whose walls are decorated with carved scenes from the life of Christ.

metania/metany (Gk., change of mind) In the Byzantine Church*, the reverential bow or prostration used upon entering the church, or in reverence to an icon or relic*.

metanoia (Gk., change of mind) 1. Repentance that indicates not merely sorrow for sin but also a turning from sinfulness to righteousness and obedience. 2. Physical gesture of repentance*, a metany*, made either by making the sign of the cross while bowing with bent knees until the lowered right hand touches the ground or by making the sign of the cross and prostrating onself until the forehead touches the ground.

metatheological Of or relating to the scope, nature, methods, and purposes of theology.

metaxy Place or event where transcendent God touches the human realm.

Meteora Monasteries in Thessaly, Greece, constructed around spectacular rocky pinnacles or holy mountains*. The fourteenth-century skete* of Doupiani is the earliest recorded monastic settlement in the region. Other monasteries founded here in the Ottoman period include Varlaam, Rousanou, and Prodromos.

metheortia (Gk., after the feast) Extension of a feast, such as Easter*, beyond one day.

Methodism Movement in the Church of England* begun by John Wesley* that became a separate denomination in the eighteenth century as an effective "method" for leading Christians toward the scriptural goal of holiness*. According to John Wesley, a Methodist is one "who lives according to the method laid down in the Bible." Wesley's teaching on regeneration* and justification* emphasizes the actual change in the believer and not just a change in standing before God. Righteousness was not merely imputed but imparted through the work of the Holy Spirit*. The end product was holiness perfected in love which radiated to everyone touched by the regenerated saint. The ultimate test of biblical Christianity was whether or not it restored the moral image of God in the believer. In John Wesley's own lifetime it became an aggressive evangelistic movement.

Most Methodist churches, with the probable exception of the Calvinistic Methodists of Wales, are Arminian in their theology. After the death of John Wesley, Methodist theology was developed by a number of theologians. John William Fletcher* (1729–1785), author of *Five Checks to Antinomianism* (1771), defined Methodism in relation to predestination* by retaining human liberty and safeguarding divine control. Adam Clarke (c. 1760–1832) reaffirmed the authority and sufficiency of Scripture. The first systematic outline of Methodist theology was prepared by Richard Watson (1781–1833) in his *Theological Institutes* (1823–24), but it found its classic expression in the *Compendium* (1875–1876) of William Burt Pope* (1822–1903). Other Methodist scholars include John Scott Lidgett (1854–1953), Robert Newton Flew (1886–1962) and Geoffrey Wainwright (1939–).

Methodism, Calvinistic Church established in England through the preaching of George Whitefield* and in Wales through the preaching of Howell Harris* of Trevecca (1714–1773), Griffith Jones (1683–1761), and Daniel Rowland of Llangeitho (1713–1790). By 1795, it was registered as a separate denomination under the Toleration Act, its meeting places were registered as Dissenting Chapels, and its confession of faith was drawn up in 1823. The first seminaries were opened at Bala in 1837 and in Trevecca in 1842. A vast majority of Calvinistic Methodist churches were Welsh-speaking. In the United States, they merged with the Presbyterians in 1920.

Methodist churches Methodist churches make up one of the largest groups of Protestantism* in the world, with an estimated 50 million members, represented by the World Methodist Council with which most Methodist churches are affiliated. All these churches trace their origins back to John Wesley* and the religious societies he founded during his crusades in the eighteenth century. The first society was founded in 1739, the first classes were formed in 1742, and the rules of the society were drawn up in 1743. The first conference met in 1744, and beginning in 1746 the societies were grouped in circuits and later organized into districts. It was not until 1784 that Methodism became a legal denomination, although Wesleyan chapels were registered as dissenting meeting houses under the Toleration Act. In 1795 Methodism parted company with the established church* when it was permitted to administer sacraments* and establish a valid ministerial order.

The fledgling church had its own share of secessions and splinter groups. In 1797 the Methodist New Connexion* broke away, followed by Independent Methodists in 1806, the Primitive Methodist Connexion in 1811, Bible Christians* in 1815, and Tent Methodists in 1822. The United Methodist Free Churches was organized in 1857. The missionary thrust of Methodism began in 1769 when the first evangelists were sent out to North America. Today there are Methodist churches in almost all countries in the world.

Methodist Churches in America Both John Wesley* and George Whitefield* had served as missionaries in the American colonies even before Methodism* was born. But after Methodism became an established denomination, it was introduced into the colonies by lay preachers, including Philip Embury* and Captain Thomas Webb. In 1768 John Wesley* sent the first two official missionaries, Joseph Pilmoor and Richard Boardman. They were followed by Francis Asbury and Richard Wright in 1771 and Thomas Rankin and George Shadford in 1773. The first Methodist conference in America was held at St. George's Church in Philadelphia* in 1773. When the American Revolution broke out, all British missionaries, except Asbury, returned to England.

Asbury worked hard to Americanize the denomination. Together with Thomas Coke*, who was named as general superintendent by John Wesley*, he founded the Methodist Episcopal Church as an autonomous denomination—without the British umbilicals—with its own 25 Articles of Religion, and *Book of Discipline**. At that time, the Methodist church had 18,000 members, 104 circuit riders*, and 60 chapels. By 1844 the church had 4,000 preachers and 1 million members. Asbury, named bishop against John Wesley's* wishes, developed the system of circuit riders to meet the needs of the American frontier. The camp meeting* was the prime instrument of revival, and Methodism rode the crest of the Great Awakening* to bring millions more into its fold.

The nineteenth century also brought a number of rifts as groups split from the main body over both theological and social issues. Of the latter, slavery was the most troubling. In 1816 the first African Episcopal Methodist Church was founded with Richard Allen*, the first Negro to be ordained by Asbury, pastor, and in 1821 the first Methodist Episcopal Zion Church was founded in New York City. In 1845 the Wesleyan Methodists* broke away over the abolition issue, and after the Civil War, it became a holiness church and merged with the Pilgrim Holiness Church to form the Wesleyan Church of America. In the 1840s the Methodist Episcopal Church, South, was formed to represent the slave-owning states, and the Colored Methodist Episcopal Church was formed to represent blacks. As membership grew, the church became more lukewarm in its theology, and the Free Methodist Church was born in 1860 as a protest. The new sect op-

posed slavery, secret societies, rented pews, outward ornaments, and structured worship. The Holiness movement* drained away thousands of members from Methodism. The twentieth century revived the ecumenical tendencies within Methodism. In 1968 the United Methodist Church came into being as the result of the merger of a number of sects that had broken away from the mother church in the nineteenth century.

Early Methodist churches tended to center around preaching and hymn singing, reflecting their formative years in the Western frontier. Most of the historic forms of Christian worship were bypassed in favor of the camp meeting* format. As Methodism became more conventional, choral music came to be a normal part of church service. Orders of worship first appeared in *The Methodist Hymnal* of 1905. In 1944 the Methodist Church published its first *Book of Worship*. Black Methodist churches, however, still retain the spontaneity, rhythmic music, and high degree of participation characteristic of earlier revivals.

The outline of the service is Prelude, Hymn, Scripture sentences, Salutation, Collect for purity, Lord's Prayer*, Gloria in Excelsis*, Invitation, General Confession*, Prayer for Pardon, Comfortable Words*, Prayer for the Church, Epistle, Anthem or Hymn, Gospel, Creed, Sermon, Notices, Hymn, Offertory, Prayer of Dedication, Sursum Corda*, Prayer, *Sanctus**, Prayer of Consecration*, Prayer of Humble Access*, *Agnus Dei**, Communion of Clergy, Communion of People, Peace, Post-Communion Prayer, Hymn, Blessing, and Postlude*.

Methodist New Connexion Breakaway movement of Methodism* in the post-Wesley* church. It was led by a new generation of Methodists, such as Alexander Kilham*, William Thorn, and William Cooke. They called for complete separation from the Church of England*, lay participation in church government, and the elimination of the episcopacy*. In 1907 they rejoined the Methodists under the name, United Methodist Church, and many of their tenets were adopted by the merged denomination.

Methodius of Olympus (c. 260–c. 311) Bishop of Lycia in southern Asia Minor, ecclesiastical writer, and martyr*. Three theological works have been attributed to him. His only complete work extant in Greek is *Symposium, or Banquet of the Ten Virgins,* extolling virginity and concluding with a hymn to Christ as the bridegroom. *Aglaophon, or On the Resurrection,* attacked Origen* and *On Free Will* attacked Valentinian dualism.

Methodius, St. See CYRIL AND METHODIUS, STS.

metochion Daughter house or farm administered by a lavra* or monastery.

metrical psalms Psalms reworded in metrical verse and sung by the whole congregation during worship services in Protestant churches. Luther* was the first to compose metrical versions of the Psalms; he was followed by Clement Marot* in France, Miles Coverdale* in England, the Wedderburn brothers in Scotland, Souter Liedekens in the Netherlands, and John Calvin* in Geneva*. Calvin prepared a collection of Psalms and oversaw the publication in Geneva of a complete psalter versified by Marot* and Theodore Beza*.

metropolia In the Eastern Orthodox Church*, a metropolitan archdiocese* or diocese*.

metropolitan Bishop of the principal city, or metropolis of a province*. Following the Roman imperial administration, early Christian dioceses* (as they were later called) followed the boundaries of the territorial units of the empire. The term was first used in the canons of the Council of Nicaea*. Metropolitans, also known as primates* and archbishops, are under patriarchs* and catholicoses*, but above exarchs*. In the Church of Greece, all diocesan bishops* have the title *metropolitan.*

mets pahk In the Armenian Church*, Lent of 40 days.

Metzger, Bruce Manning (1914–) American New Testament scholar. Ordained by the Presbyterian Church USA in 1939, he taught New Testament at Princeton Theological Seminary from 1938–1985, specializing in textual criticism*. He was chairman of the Revised Standard Version* and the New Revised Standard Version* Bibles committees and contributed to their translations. His prodigious output includes *An Introduction to the Apocrypha* (1957), *The Text of the New Testament* (1964), *The New Testament: Its Background, Growth, and Content* (1965), *Manuscripts of the Greek Bible* (1981), and *The Canon of the New Testament* (1987).

Meyendorff, John (1926–1992) Eastern Orthodox* theologian. A priest and a historical theologian, he was a leading interpreter of Orthodox theology and an authority on the theology of St. Gregory Palamas*. From 1959 he served on the faculty of St. Vladimir's Seminary*, Crestwood, New York, and he was also editor of the newspaper, *The Orthodox Church.* His publications include *St. Gregory Palamas and Orthodox Spirituality* (1974), *Christ in Eastern Christian Thought* (1975), and *Byzantine Theology: Historical Trends and Doctrinal Themes* (1987).

Meyer, Frederick Brotherton (1847–1929) Baptist conference speaker. He began his career in 1869 as assistant pastor at Pembroke Chapel, Liverpool, England, and thereafter served as pastor in various churches in England until his death. In 1873 he became associated with Dwight L. Moody*, who invited him in 1891 to preach in the United States. Meyer made 12 visits to the United States thereafter and addressed hundreds of conferences.

Meyer, Heinrich August Wilhelm (1800–1873) German Protestant New Testament scholar and a founder of the modern historical approach to biblical criticism* and exegesis*. His monumental work, *Kritischexegetischer Kommentar zum Neuen Testament* (16 vols., 1832–1852), is still used in Germany.

Meynell, Alice Christiana Gertrude (1847–1922) English Catholic poet who with her husband Wilfred Meynell encouraged Francis Thompson*. Her verse works include *Preludes* (1875) and *Later Poems* (1901), and her prose works include *Mary, Mother of Jesus,* a collection of essays.

mezhdochasie In the Byzantine Rite*, an intermediate office between the Hours.

Michael the Syrian (1126–1199) Also, Michael the Great. He was elected in 1166 to succeed the Jacobite patriarch* Athanasius VIII. He is the author of the *Chronicle* in 21 books in Syriac*, covering history from creation to 1195. A copy of the work was discovered in the late nineteenth century at Urfa. His other writings include a liturgy with alphabetically arranged prayers and revised versions of the Pontifical* and ritual of ordinations.

Michaelmas Feast day honoring the archangel* Michael on September 29.

Michelangelo Buonarroti (1475–1564) One of the world's greatest artists, his works mark the zenith of the Renaissance. In 1488 he became the pupil of Florentine painters Davide and Dominico Ghirlandaio*, and he was introduced into the court of Lorenzo the Magnificent. In 1496 he went to Rome*, where he did *Pieta* (1500), the first of many religious sculptures. It was followed by *David* (1501–1504), *Madonna Seated on a Step, Christ the Risen Savior,* and *St. John in the Wilderness.* In 1505 Julius II* commissioned him to do the papal tomb for which the grand figure of *Moses* was completed. Between 1508 and 1512 he painted the celebrated frescoes* on the ceiling of the Sistine Chapel*, of which two are considered the finest of all time: the *Creation of Light* and the *Creation of Man.* The ceiling covered 10,000 square feet and included hundreds of figures, some of them 12 feet high. Continuing to work under Pope Leo X*, Michelangelo completed part of the Medici Mortuary Chapel with its four figures of *Night and Day, Morning and Evening.*

From 1534 to 1541 Michelangelo was engaged on *The Last Judgment* in the Sistine Chapel. Just before his death he was entrusted with the building of St. Peter's*. He reworked all the designs and supervised the construction of the supports and lower sections of the giant dome, but did not live to see its completion. In addition to his genius as an architect, painter, and draftsman, he was also a lyrical poet as attested by his sonnets to Vittorio Colonna. He shared with his older contemporary, Savonarola*, a deep brooding melancholy and an austere religious fervor.

Michigan, Papyrus of Fragment containing Acts 18:27–19:6, 12–16 dated 300 and discovered in Egypt, now in the University of Michigan Library.

Middelburg Monastery dedicated to Virgin Mary* in Middelburg, Netherlands, founded in the twelfth century by Norbert* of Xanten. The former abbey church of Middelburg consists of Koorkirk in the east and Nieuwe Kirk in the west. Both churches suffered from fires and had to be rebuilt. The abbey is built around three quadrangles. The oldest part of the monastery still extant is the northeast wing in Flemish Gothic* style.

middle knowledge In Molinarism, the conditional knowledge God has about future human events that leaves some room for human action.

Migne, Jacques Paul (1800–1875) French Roman Catholic priest, patrologist, and publisher. He left his diocese* near Orleans and went to Paris, where he began a monumental publishing program to publish a universal library of all Christian literature in about 2,000 volumes. Included in this library were 221 volumes of the Latin Fathers (1844–1864), and 162 volumes of the Greek Fathers* (1857–1866), in addition to hundreds of volumes on theology, sermons, apologetics, and mariology*.

migrant church Church made up largely or wholly of foreign immigrants from another country.

mikra eisodos (Gk., small entrance) Entrance of the clergy, worshipers, and the Gospel book during the third antiphon* of the enarxis* in the Byzantine Liturgy.

mikrai horai In the Eastern Orthodox Church*, minor hours—prime*, terce*, sext*, and none*.

mikron apodeipnon In the Eastern Orthodox Church*, compline*.

Milan City in northern Italy. According to tradition, St. Barnabas* preached in the city and consecrated its first bishop, St. Anathalon. The Diocletian persecution* claimed its first martyrs* in this city. Ambrose* was its most famous bishop, and it was the scene of Augustine's conversion. Nine councils were held here in 347 or 349, 355,

380, 396, 390, 393, 451, and 679. Its Late Gothic* cathedral is one of the most impressive, if only because of its architectural extravagance. Work on the gigantic cathedral with five aisles and a three-aisled transept* began in 1387. The building material was Candoglia marble. The Tiburio, as the central tower is called, is between a forest of soaring pinnacles. The entire cathedral was finished only in the nineteenth century. Outstanding features of the cathedral include over-lifesize figures placed above the two sacristies, and the Trivulzio bronze candelabra, one of the most celebrated bronze artifacts of the Middle Ages.

The Dominican monastery with its Gothic brick-built church of Santa Maria delle Grazie is also in Milan. Its choir and its massive hexagonal dome were created in early Renaissance style by Donato Bramante*, architect of St. Peter's*. The monastery was founded by Dominico Guzman, a Spanish nobleman. In the refectorium, next to the church, Leonardo da Vinci* painted his *Last Supper* between 1495 and 1497.

Milan, Edict of Circular issued in Bithynia* by Emperor Licinius in 313 extending to the Eastern provinces freedom of worship for all, including Christians, and the restitution* of property lost by the churches since the persecution of 303 in accordance with an agreement he made with Constantine*. The phrase is frequently used of the earlier agreement to this effect covering the whole empire reached between Constantine and Licinius at Milan*.

Mileseva Monastery of the Ascension in the Lim Valley in eastern Serbia founded by King Vladslav, nephew of Sava of Serbia. St. Sava's relics* were interred in the monastery, making it an important place of pilgrimage*. It is renowned for its wall paintings completed before 1228, and its scriptorium* was a cultural center well into the Ottoman period. In 1594 the Turkish grand vizier, quelling a Serbian uprising in Banat, ordered Sava's body removed to Belgrade, where it was burned. By the eighteenth century, the monastery was in ruins, but it was renovated in the nineteenth and twentieth centuries.

Milhaud, Darius (1892–1974) French composer. His sacred compositions include *Miracles of Faith*

(1953), the cantatas *Retour de l'Enfant Prodigue* (1917) and *Job* (1967), and *Sabbath Morning Service* (1947). He was noted for his extensive use of exotic rhythms from Latin America and the West Indies as well as jazz and lyrical melodies.

Milic, Jan (c. 1325–1374) Also, Jan of Kromeriz. Bohemian and Moravian reformer. An officer in the imperial chancery of Charles IV, he left his office to preach against corruption in the church. He was imprisoned by the Inquisition* for a while and later died at Avignon* under the cloud of heresy. Along with Matthias of Janov and Tomas Stitny, he was one of the precursors of the Hussite revolt.

Mill Hill missionaries Roman Catholic missionary society of secular priests and lay brothers*, officially known as St. Joseph's Society for Foreign Missions, founded in 1866 at Mill Hill in London by Herbert Vaughan. It was the first missionary endeavor by English Roman Catholics after the Reformation*. In the United States, they are known as the Josephite Fathers. They are very active in Commonwealth and English-speaking countries.

millenarianism Also, chiliasm*; millennialism. Belief in a 1,000 year period at the end of the age when at his Second Coming* Jesus Christ will reign on earth and establish a perfect world order, based on a literal interpretation of Revelation 20:1–10, and Jewish hopes of a 1,000-year sabbath before the dissolution of the world. Millennialists are divided into premillennialists, postmillennialists, and amillennialists. Premillennialists hold that at the Second Coming* living believers will be caught up to meet the Lord in the air, and they will reign on earth with him for 1,000 years. Satan* will be active again until the final judgment of the great white throne. Postmillennialists hold that the Second Coming will take place after the millennium* which may be a golden age representing the church triumphant* on earth. Amillennialists do not believe in a literal millennium and regard the present age as fulfilling the prophecies of the Revelation.

In the early church, millenarianism was widely prevalent. It was embraced by the Montanists* and accepted by Justin Martyr*, Irenaeus*, Hippolytus*, and other orthodox theologians. In the Middle Ages, millenarian hopes were stoked by Joachim of Fiore*. After the Reformation*, Anabaptists*, Bohemian Brethren*, and Pietists were millenarians. Among the modern millenarian denominations are the Irvingites, Plymouth Brethren*, the various Adventist groups, and cults like Jehovah's Witnesses*.

Millennial Church Name of the Shakers*.

millennium Period of 1,000 years at the end of the present age when Jesus Christ reigns with his people over the earth. Its interpretation has been the focus of intense debates, especially in North America.

Miller, William (1782–1849) American founder of Adventism*. He was converted from Deism* in 1816 and spent the next 14 years in Bible study which convinced him that Jesus Christ would return in 1843. In 1836 he published *Evidence from Scripture and History of the Second Coming of Christ, About the Year 1843*. When the predicted return of Christ did not take place, Miller dropped out of the Adventist movement in 1845.

Mills, Samuel John (1783–1818) American promoter of foreign missions. In college he was a member of the famous Haystack Prayer* Group. He was instrumental in the organization of the American Board of Commissioners for Foreign Missions* in 1810 and in sending out Judson*, Rice*, Nott, Hall, and Newell to India in 1812. He was also influential in the founding of the American Bible Society* in 1816.

Milman, Henry Hart (1791–1868) English historian. A distinguished historian and poet, he was professor of poetry at Oxford and dean of St. Paul's*. He was a Broad Church* advocate whose *History of the Jews* (1830) and *History of Latin Christianity* (1855) were hailed by liberal theologians.

Milne, William (1785–1822) Scottish missionary to China. In 1813 he joined Robert Morrison* in Macao, from where he was expelled. He then moved to Canton and later Malacca in the East Indies, where he established a base for translating and printing the Chinese Bible. In 1815 he cut the first fonts of a Chinese alphabet. He ordained his convert Liang A-Fah* and became principal of the Anglo-Chinese College in Malacca.

Milton, John (1608–1674) English poet. He began writing Christian poetry from the beginning of his career, and his *Ode on the Morning of Christ's Nativity* is a powerful poetic celebration of the Incarnation*. He moved away from the established church* for the rest of his life and became vehemently opposed to the episcopacy*. For a while he joined the Presbyterians but left them

John Milton

because of disputes over the question of divorce. During Oliver Cromwell's Protectorate, he joined the government as latin secretary. The end of the Protectorate and the beginning of the Restoration brought great personal danger to him; he also went blind. Nevertheless, it was a period of great creativity. *Paradise Lost** appeared in 1667, followed four years later by *Paradise Regained* and *Samson Agonistes*. Written to "justify the ways of God to Man," and to show the cause of evil and injustice, *Paradise Lost** was his greatest contribution to English literature and remains one of its most ambitious and heroic masterpieces.

Milton was an Arian in theology, and his posthumously published testament, *De Doctrina Christiana*, denied the coeternity and coequality of the three persons of the Trinity* and the Genesis account of creation. Milton also championed freedom of speech and press in *Areopagitica*.

Milvian Bridge, Battle of Most decisive battle in Christian history on October 28, 312, between the Christian emperor Constantine* and his rival, Maxentius, ruler of Italy and Africa. Maxentius was actually defeated on the Flaminian Way, and he was drowned in the Tiber at the Milvian Bridge. Before the battle Constantine saw a heavenly vision of a cross with the words, *In hoc signo vince* (In this sign, conquer).

Battle of Milvian Bridge

Minims Order of Athos*, *Ordo Fratrum Minimorum,* considered the least of the religious, below the Friars Minor*. Founded as a group of hermits in 1435 by Francis of Paola* and confirmed by the pope in 1474, it adopted its first rule based on the Franciscans in 1493 and its second rule, a more austere one, in 1501. The brothers dressed in black wool habit, cord girdle*, with cape and hood, and abstained from meat and milk products. At its zenith in the sixteenth century, the order had over 400 houses.

minister (Lat., servant) 1. Person ordained to office of leadership in a local church after fulfilling certain conditions of training and vows. A minister's functions include presiding at public worship, the administration of the sacraments*, and other services, such as weddings and funerals, pastoral care, and the general oversight of the congregation. 2. Servant.

ministry 1. Collective term for the clergy. 2. Profession of a minister. 3. Service of any of the fivefold offices enumerated by Paul* in Ephesians 4:11–12 (apostle, prophet*, evangelist, pastor, and teacher) and, by extension, any similar work in the church. 4. Service to which all Christians are called by God.

ministry of the Word Reading and, especially, teaching of the Scriptures in worship. Sometimes used of the whole service, in churches where this is regarded as the central point of worship.

minjung (Kor., mass, people) Form of liberation theology* developed in South Korea. The gospel and the Jesus-event are interpreted from the perspective of the poor and oppressed. Jesus himself was of the minjung and a friend of the minjung. The enemies of the gospel are portrayed as the rich and powerful. It uses liberally the language of liberation theology*, such as God's preferential option for the poor and Jesus the liberator.

minor canon Clergyman who assists in the service of a cathedral although not associated with the cathedral chapter*.

minor orders In the Western Church*, degrees of ministry below that of subdeacon, and generally including lectors and cantors*. Formerly they also included acolytes*, exorcists*, and doorkeepers*. In the Eastern Church*, they include degrees of ministry below that of deacon, including subdeacons, lectors, and cantors. Minor orders* are generally the first step toward full ordination.

Minorite Franciscan.

minster (Old English, munster, monastery) Monastery or monastery church, but applied in England to certain large churches, such as Beverley and Wimborne and to certain large cathedrals, such as York*, Lincoln*, Westminster, Ripon, Southwell, and Lichfield. These are now generally known as cathedrals.

Minucius Felix (third century) African apologist. Author of *Octavius,* a defense of Christianity in the form of a dialogue between a Christian and a pagan.

miracle Remarkable act of god, especially suspension of the normal working of the laws of nature by supernatural intervention, either on divine terms and initiative or as an answer to human supplication. God is the author of miracles since he controls both the natural and supernatural worlds. In some traditions, saints* are often considered as conduits of miracles and are believed to be endowed with the gift of working miracles by interceding with God.

miracle play See MYSTERY PLAY.

Miserere Title of Psalm 51, from its initial Latin word.

misericord 1. Room set apart in a monastery for those who are sick or old and therefore unable to fulfill the rules or duties. 2. Bracket attached to a choir stall* seat to support those incapable of standing for long periods during divine service*. 3. Religious dispensation*.

misrule, lord of Also, abbot or master of misrule. In the Middle Ages, person who presided over Christmas* revels. The custom was associated with the Feast of Fools*, observed in this season, when a precentor of the fools was nominated.

Missa brevis (Lat., short Mass) Form of Mass* including just the kyrie*, Gloria, and Sanctus*.

Missa cantata (Lat., sung Mass) Celebration of the Mass* in which the celebrant and the congregation sing the liturgical parts of the rite set to music for High Mass*, but without the deacon and subdeacon. Since the Second Vatican Council*, singing is encouraged at all masses.

Missa Illyrica Mass Ordo published by Matthias Flacius* "Illyricus" at Strasbourg* in 1557. One of its features was the interpolation of a large number of apologiae, or avowals of personal unworthiness, into the liturgy at several points of the rite.

Missa recitata (Lat., recited, low Mass) Variation of the Missa lecta, or read, low Mass.

Missa solemnis (Lat., solemn Mass) Elaborate form of sung Mass* celebrated with deacon and subdeacon.

missal Book containing everything to be said or sung for the celebration of the Mass* throughout the year with proper directions to the celebrant and the congregation. It is a combination of the antiphonal, gradual*, epistolary, evangeliary*, ordo, and sacramentary*.

Missal, Constance Oldest extant printed book, produced by Johann Gutenberg around 1450 for the diocese* of Constance, Switzerland. It predates the Gutenberg Bible* by six years.

Missale Francorum Eighth-century sacramentary*, now in the Vatican Library*, related to the *Gelasian Sacramentary**. It contains the rites of ordination, the blessings of virgins and widows, the consecration of altars, and 11 masses.

Missale Gallicanum Vetus Manuscript in the Vatican Library* containing fragments of two eighth-century Gallican Sacramentaries. The first contains a Mass for the Feast of St. Germanus* as well as lesser masses. The second contains masses for Advent*, Lent*, Easter*, and the Rogation Days*.

Missale Gothicum Eighth-century Gallican Sacramentary, now in the Vatican Library*, containing masses of the season from Christmas* to Whitsunday*, including saints' days and ferial days.

missale speciale Abridged missal* drawn up for special needs.

missalette Small missal* or booklet to assist the congregation in following the words and actions of the Mass*.

missio Dei (Lat., mission of God) 1. The salvific mission of God toward the world, centering in the sending of the Son in Incarnation*. 2. Missionary work as orchestrated and guided by the triune God, in continuation of the Incarnation. 3. Missionary work as the visible expression of the salvific* work of Jesus Christ.

missiology 1. Branch of theology concerned with the carrying out of the Great Commission*. 2. The science of missions, dealing with the conversion of nonbelievers, and the establishment and expansion of the kingdom of God* in all nations. It includes Bible translation and distribution, production and publication of Christian literature, church planting*, broadcasting, urban strategies for reaching the displaced and the poor in cities, missions, stewardship*, and efforts to reach the unreached*, as well as studies of anthropology and culture. Modern missiology was developed as an academic discipline by two German missiologists: Karl Graul, director of the Leipzig Mission, and Gustav Warneck*, author of *Evangelische Missionslehre* (1892). Warneck influenced the great Catholic missiologist, Josef Schmidlin (1876–1944).

missiometrics Branch of missiology* concerned with the construction, measurement, collection, and publication of statistics relating to the harvest of souls or the results of missionary work.

mission 1. Purpose and task of the church, including evangelization, witnessing, proclamation, teaching, and celebration of the sacraments*, now usually understood as including the service, peace, and justice dimensions of the church's life. 2. Church or parish financially dependent on external sources, a congregation in a missionary phase of development or maintained in an adverse situation (e.g., in an inner city).

mission agency Also, mission board. Sending agency for missionaries within a denomination or a parachurch* organization.

mission field Receiving country or region for missionaries, specifically targeted for missionary operations.

mission station Residence of a missionary or locality in which missionary activities are centered.

missionary 1. Person who carries out the mission of the church, particularly cross-culturally. 2. Evangelist, generally affiliated with a missionary society, who fulfills the Great Commission*.

Missionary Aviation Fellowship (MAF) Service agency that helps evangelical missions with air transport and communications. The American branch of MAF was founded in 1944.

missionary bishop In the Episcopal Church USA*, a bishop appointed to serve in an area not yet organized as a diocese*.

missions mandate The Great Commission*.

mistikos In the Byzantine Rite*, silent priestly prayers.

miter/mitre (Gk., *mitra,* turban) Hat or headdress made of embroidered satin, shaped like a shield, and worn by bishops and abbots in the Western Church* as an insignia of their office, corresponding to the metal crowns in the Eastern Church*. Two fringed lappets* hang down at the back. It is worn at all solemn services and occasions, but taken off during prayers and Canon of the Mass*. The three types of miters are: 1. The precious miter, *mitra pretiosa,* worn on feasts and ordinary Sundays and made of gold and adorned with precious stones. 2. The golden miter, *mitra aurifrigiata,* made of golden cloth, used in penitential seasons. 3. The simple miter, *mitra simplex,* made of plain white silk or linen and worn on Good Friday* and at funerals.

Miter

Mithraism Mystery religion originating in Persia in the second century and popular, especially among soldiers, throughout the Roman Empire until the fourth century. It had a dualistic theology but may have been influenced by some features of Christianity, such as sacred meals and baptism*. The mysteries of Mithras were celebrated by male initiates (of which there were seven grades) in underground temples in which there were representations of their god slaying a bull.

mixed chalice Practice of mixing water with wine in the eucharistic chalice* that was common in many churches, but not the Armenian.

mizmar Flute played during the Coptic Liturgy together with handbells and cymbals.

m'khap ranitha In the Assyrian Rite, a purificator*, used as a chalice* covering. It is also used to wipe around the brim of the chalice and to gather any crumbs of bread into the chalice.

mneme In the Byzantine Rite*, the commemoration of a saint* or other living or dead persons.

mnestra Solemn engagement rite in the Byzantine Church*.

Modalism Also, Patripassianism*; Monarchianism*. Heresy, put forward by Sabellius, Praxeas*, and Noetus that the distinctions among the three persons of the Trinity* are not permanent and that they are not three distinct persons, but rather three modes or forms or names in which God was successively revealed.

moderator In the Presbyterian Church, the presbyter* who presides over the church court, the kirk-session*, presbytery*, and synod*. In the lowest court, the kirk-session, the minister is invariably the moderator ex officio. The moderator of the General Assembly* is often elected for a year. If ordained, he or she may be called for that period "right reverend" and thereafter "very reverend".

modernism 1. Ideology arising out of the Enlightenment, often allied with liberalism*, that hold that all forms of knowledge, including theology, must accept the laws of scientific validity and certitude, conform to the standards of reason, be intellectually coherent, and relate to human experience. 2. Movement within the Roman Catholic Church aimed at revising Catholic theology to conform to the standards and practices of modern culture, especially at establishing the compatibility of intellectual inquiry and faith. It arose independently in various countries as a reaction against dogmatics* and Scholasticism*, and flourished from the late nineteenth century to the early twentieth century. It declined after it was formally condemned by Pius X* in 1907.

The three leading ideas of modernism were: 1. Critical view of the inerrancy* of the Bible* and adoption of considerable scepticism over its miraculous elements. The Bible was to be understood as the partial unfolding of divine plan in history. 2. Subordination of doctrine to practice. Christianity was interpreted as a moral scheme rather than as a creed or theological system. 3. Indifference toward history and skepticism toward Christian origins. Spirituality* and salvation* had less to do with the finished work of Jesus Christ than with the moral development of mankind.

Among the leaders of the modernist movement were Alfred F. Loisy*, Maurice Blondel*, E. I. Mignot, L. Laberthonniere, and Edouard Le Roy in France; Romolo Murri and A. Fogazzaro in Italy; and F. von Hugel* and G. Tyrrell* in England. It was finally condemned as the "synthesis of all heresies," by St. Pius X* in 1907 by the decree "Lamentabili*" and the encyclical* "Pascendi." In 1910 all clerics were required to take an anti-modernist oath* at their ordination. In Protestant churches, modernism has persisted throughout the twentieth century, leading to the reconstruction of the Christian faith as a system of ethics and adoption of a higher critical posture toward the Bible.

In New Testament studies, modernism expressed itself in a quest for a historical Jesus* and in efforts to demythologize Jesus Christ. The leaders of Protestant modernism were F. D. E. Schleiermacher* and A. Ritschl* in Germany, R. J. Campbell in England, and H. E. Fosdick* in the United States. It was embodied in the Broad Church* movement in England and New England theology* in the United States. The two World Wars and the rise of Barthian theology have helped to blunt much of modernism. Liberal theologians now call themselves radicals rather than modernists.

modesty rail Solid partition or textile hung from a rail and placed between the pulpit and the first row of the choir. It may include hinged gates for access to the pulpit area.

Moffat, Robert (1795–1883) Pioneer Scottish missionary in South Africa. He went to Africa as an LMS* missionary in 1816 and nine years later settled at Kuruman, Bechuanaland, which became his headquarters for the next 45 years. He translated the Bible into the Bechuana and Sechwana languages and composed the earliest hymns in those languages. As a result of his work, much of

South Africa was Christianized. He also helped to civilize the natives, introducing new techniques in agriculture, including irrigation, fertilization, forest preservation, and new crops. He was also active in exploration, particularly in the Kuruman River area. By persuading his son-in-law, David Livingstone*, to travel beyond the Zambezi, he helped open the Dark Continent to the gospel.

Robert Moffat

Moffatt, James (1870–1944) Bible translator. Ordained in 1896, he taught at Mansfield College, Oxford, the United Free Church College in Glasgow, and Union Theological Seminary* in New York. While in New York, he took part in the preparation of the Revised Standard Version*. His fame rests on the Moffat Bible, a translation of the New Testament (1913) and the Old Testament (1924), reissued and revised in 1935. It acquired wide readership because of its colloquial style. He also edited a 17-volume commentary on the New Testament.

Moffett, Samuel Austin (1864–1939) Pioneer Presbyterian missionary to Korea. He was one of the earliest Presbyterian missionaries in Korea, arriving there in 1890. Following the Nevius Plan, he emphasized intensive Bible study and evangelism by all believers. In 1901 he began the Presbyterian Theological Seminary in Seoul and served as its president for 17 years. When the Korean Presbyterian Church was organized in 1911, Moffett was elected its first moderator*. From 1918 to 1928 he was the president of Soongsil College in Pyongyang. In 1936 tensions erupted between the church and the Japanese authorities over demand by the latter that Christians should participate in Buddhist temple ceremonies. Moffett was forced to leave the country and to close down the schools. His son, **Samuel Hugh Moffett** (1916–), was Henry Winters Luce professor of ecumenics and mission at Princeton Theological Seminary and editor of the three-volume *A History of Christianity in Asia* (1992–).

Mogila, Peter (1596–1646) Metropolitan of Kiev*. He became abbot of a Kiev monastery in 1627 and was elected metropolitan* in 1633. He initiated several reforms in the education of clergy based on Western educational ideas. His greatest contribution to the Orthodox Church was his *Orthodox Confession of the Catholic and Apostolic Eastern Church,* an authoritative definition of the Orthodox faith. He was also the author of an Orthodox catechism*.

Mohr, Joseph (1792–1848) Composer of *Stille Nacht* (Silent Night! Holy Night!*). He was ordained as a Roman Catholic priest in 1815. While working as a pastor at Salzburg*, he composed *Stille Nacht* in 1818 with guitar accompaniment by the organist and schoolmaster, Franz Gruber*.

Moissac Benedictine abbey founded in Moissac, France. It came under the jurisdiction of Cluny* after being destroyed several times. Its sculptures in the south portal are ranked among the most splendid specimens of Romanesque art. The simplicity of the church interior is relieved only by a large crucifixion dating from the twelfth century. The cloister*, consecrated in 1100, has over 100 columns and is considered the finest in France.

moliebny In the Byzantine Rite*, thanksgiving or intercession before an icon of the Lord, the Virgin Mary*, or a saint*.

Molina, Luis de (1535–1600) Spanish Jesuit theologian. He entered the Jesuit Order in 1553 and later taught at Coimbra and Evora. His major contribution to theology was *Concordia Liberi Arbitrii cum Gratiae Donis* in which he developed the doctrine associated with his name and known as Molinism*. In it he tried to reconcile divine predestination* with human freedom by stating that God foreknows but does not cause human actions. The key element of Molinism is scientia media*, or middle knowledge*, by which God infallibly knows, before he makes an absolute decree creating the free creature, what choices it would make in any given circumstance. God not only knows all possible modes of existence through his intelligence, but also ordains things to exist through his vision. The efficacy of grace* is conditional upon human cooperation. While the Jesuits* accepted this doctrine, Dominicans* and others felt that it detracted from the all-sufficiency of divine grace.

Molinism System of theological thought based on the teaching of Luis de Molina*.

Molinos, Miguel de (c. 1628–c. 1697) Spanish priest whose book *Guida Spirituale* is regarded as one of the founding documents of Quietism*. His controversial book traced the mystic path of perfection* or total submission to the will of God, through annihilation of the human will. The believer progressed from reliance on the church and external rites and observances to devotion to Christ. He described two types of contemplation: acquired or active contemplation that requires no recourse to reason or imagination, and infused or passive contemplation which is a gift of God. Many of his followers gave up the practice of vocal prayer and observance of the sacraments* and were accused of immorality. In 1687 Molinos was arrested, tried, and condemned, and although forced to recant, was imprisoned for the rest of his life. His teaching influenced the Quietists in France and Pietists in Germany.

Moltmann, Jurgen (1926–) German Reformed* theologian. He taught at Wuppertal, Bonn; Duke University in North Carolina; and Tubingen*. He wrote extensively on eschatology* and messianic theology. His major works include *Theology of Hope* (1967), *The Crucified God* (1974), *The Church in the Power of the Spirit* (1977), *The Trinity and the Kingdom of God* (1981), *God in Cre-*

ation (1985), *The Way of Jesus Christ* (1990), *The Spirit of Life* (1992), and *The Coming of God* (1996). In his later works he developed the thesis of divine passibility or a God that is deeply involved with and moved by the suffering of his people.

Monarchianism Second- and third-century heresy centered in Asia Minor and Rome*. The term was coined by Tertullian* and dealt with efforts to reconcile Christology* with conventional monotheism*. There are two varieties of Monarchianism. Adoptionist or Dynamic Monarchianism considers Jesus Christ as a unique man energized by the Holy Spirit* at the time of his baptism and called to be the Son of God for a limited time. This was the heresy associated with Paul of Samosata*, Theodotus of Byzantium*, the Ebionites*, and Cerinthus*. The second variety, called Modalistic Monarchianism, Patripassianism*, or Sabellianism*, held that if Christ is God, he is by the same token also Father and that if Christ died, the Father also died with him. Modalistic Monarchianism also held that God is revealed in different modes, sometimes as the Father, sometimes as the Son, and sometimes as the Holy Spirit*.

monastery House of a community of men voluntarily set apart from the world, dedicated to a life of personal sanctification* through asceticism* and prayer*, generally in subordination to a rule

Monasteries

and discipline under an abbot or superior* and bound by common vows of poverty, chastity*, and obedience. Monasteries are divided into eremetic for solitary hermits and cenobitic for groups.

Monastic Breviary Breviary* formerly used by monks and nuns following the Rule of St. Benedict* as revised by Paul V* on the lines of the Roman Breviary*. Its distinctive features included a different distribution of the Psalms, omission of Nunc Dimittis* at compline*, and different text for some of the hymns. It is replaced by four different alternative forms of the Office prescribed in *Thesaurus Liturgiae Monasticae Horarum* (1977).

monasticism Form of Christian religious life involving asceticism*, celibacy*, prayer*, seclusion from the world, renunciation of private possessions, and some form of regulated manual work. The two main forms of monastic life are eremetical or solitary hermit life and cenobitic or communal life. Christian monasticism had it origins in Egypt, where it had its finest flowering in the fifth century. Male monks and female nuns have separate establishments but may function under similar rules. These rules determined how her-

mits spent their life in prayer; and how cenobites divided their time between celebrating Divine Office* and other works, such as copying, agriculture, teaching, art, and writing. In the Middle Ages, cenobite* monks were the principal agents of civilization, and monasteries were islands of learning in a barbarian society.

The major monastic traditions of St. Anthony and St. Pachomius* in the East were transmitted to the West by Rufinus*, Jerome*, and Cassian. The anonymous *Regula Magistri* had a great influence on St. Benedict*, whose rule dominated Western monasticism for centuries. The thirteenth and fourteenth centuries saw the founding of many new monastic orders, as the Carthusians* and the Cistercians*. Monasticism has an equally strong tradition in the Byzantine Church*. The distinction in the East is between the lavra* or skete* for the hermits on the one hand and monasteries which may be cenobitic or idiorrhythmic* (where the monks are relatively free to follow their own way of life) on the other. Eastern monasticism is governed by the Fathers of the Desert*, the Rule of St. Basil*, the Hesychasm*, and St. Theodore of Studios*. Mount Athos* represents the triumph of monasticism in Eastern Orthodoxy. In Russia, St. Sergius of Radonezh* and St. Anthony of Pechesk founded numerous monasteries, many of which have survived the Communist era.

Monica (331/2–387) Also, Monnica. Mother of St. Augustine* of Hippo, whose conversion is attributed to her prayers. Born of Christian Berber parents, she married Patricius of Tagaste, a pagan who became a Christian shortly before his death. They had three children, of whom Augustine was the eldest, one of whom later headed a women's convent in Hippo for which Augustine wrote the Rule of St. Augustine*. Just before she died at Ostia near Rome*, she shared with Augustine a mystic vision. She is the patron saint* of Christian mothers. Feast day: August 27.

monitum (Lat., warning) Warning regarding a particular teaching or an author suspected of error in matters of doctrine.

monk Member of a monastery or religious community living under a rule and the vows of poverty, chastity*, and obedience.

St. Benedict

Monk, William Henry (1823–1889) English organist. He promoted congregational singing and established a daily choral service at King's College, London. He assisted in the development of the plainchant in Anglican worship. He composed 50 hymn tunes for *Hymns Ancient and Modern* (1861) of which he was the editor.

Monks of St. Hormisdas Antonine Order of St. Hormisdas of the Chaldeans, a Chaldean Catholic monastic congregation* founded in 1880 by Gabriel Dembo beside the ruins of the ancient East Syrian monastery of Rabban Hormuzd near Alqosh in northern Iraq.

Monod, Adolphe (1802–1856) The greatest French Protestant preacher of the nineteenth century and pastor of the Oratoire Church in Paris (1847–1856). He was the leader of *Le Reveil,* an orthodox movement within the Reformed Church.

Monod, Frederic (1794–1863) French Protestant Reformed* pastor and brother of Adolphe Monod*. He was a leader of *Le Reveil* and pastor of the Oratoire Church in Paris from 1832. He was editor for 43 years of the *Archives du Christianisme au Dix-Neuvieme Siecle.*

monoenergism/monenergism/monergism Belief in regeneration* by God alone without human cooperation. Contrasted with synergism in which God cooperated with human beings in effecting regeneration*.

monogenes (Gk., Only Begotten) 1. Christ, the Only Begotten (John 1:18). 2. Hymn or anthem traditionally ascribed to Emperor Justinian*, addressed to the triumphant Redeemer. It forms the conclusion of the second antiphon* in the enarxis* of the Byzantine Liturgy.

monolatry Worship of one god without excluding the possibility of other gods. Distinguished from monotheism*.

Monophysitism Theological doctrine that split the Lesser Eastern Churches* from the Catholic Church after the Council of Chalcedon* set aside the decrees of the Council of Ephesus* (also known as the Robber Council of Ephesus*) and

approved the dogmatic *Tome* of Pope Leo*. The text of the Definition of Chalcedon* reaffirmed that Christ was "truly God and truly man," and that he was "one person in two natures." The Chalcedonian decrees were opposed in Armenia, Egypt, Syria, Ethiopia, and India.

In the tradition of Alexandrian theology, Monophysitism held that Christ had only one divine nature and that his humanity was so sublimated in his divinity that it ceased to exist as an active element or nature. It downgraded Christ's humanity as a means of preserving the unity of his person. This belief was particularly strong in Syria, Palestine, and Egypt where the monks had engaged in constant battle against their own human sinfulness. Humanity was looked upon as an enemy, and to overcome it was the goal of Christian life. Thus, to ascribe humanity to Christ was to destroy the very purpose of Christian faith.

Monophysitism also was a reaction against Nestorianism*, which posited two natures in Christ and made him a double personality. The heretical form of Monophysitism is known as Eutychianism*, after Jacob Eutyches*, who taught that after the Incarnation* there was only one nature in Christ without any human intermixture. Adherents of radical Monophysitism are also known as Julianists, after Julian of Halicarnassus*, who held that after the union of the divine and the human in Christ, his human body was rendered incorruptible. They were thus known as *aphthartodoketai* or "incorruptible Docetists,"or *phantasiastai,* those who declared that Christ's body was only phantasmal.

Moderate Monophysitism taught that in the incarnate Christ there was "one nature out of two." This was promoted by the Severans, following Severus*, the patriarch* of Antioch* (c. 460–538), who closely adhered to Cyril*. They were known as *phthartolatrai,* or worshipers of the corruptible, by their opponents. During the fifth and sixth centuries many emperors attempted to reunite the Monophysites and the Western churches*. Emperor Zeno drew up the Henoticon* to replace the Definition of Chalcedon*, but it was rejected by Rome* and Alexandria* and led to the Acacian Schism*. By this time, the conquest of Egypt, Syria, and Palestine by the Arabs separated the Monophysite churches from imperial control and the separation became permanent.Churches that remain officially Monophysite are often called Oriental Orthodox Churches*.

monotheism Belief in one transcendent God as the creator and ruler of the universe. It is one common link between the three Abrahamic religions, all of which are based on revelation*. Distinguished from pantheism*.

Monothelitism Seventh-century heresy according to which Christ had only one will. The heresy was less theological than political. In 624 Emperor Heraclius produced a formula* that tried to reconcile Monophysitism* with orthodoxy* by asserting two natures in Christ but only one mode of activity called monenergism*. It was similar to the compromise by which the Definition of Chacedon* was accepted but on the basis that "the Word made Flesh had only one nature," using the formula* of Cyril* of Alexandria*. But there was renewed conflict over whether there were two wills or one possessed by the two-natured Christ. Sergius*, the patriarch of Constantinople*, came up with the Monothelitic compromise in an effort to bring the Monophysite churches back into the fold. This formula, however, was opposed by Sophronius*, later patriarch* of Jerusalem*. Sergius thereupon issued a document called *Ecthesis**, the chief manifesto of Monothelitism, giving up the term *energy* and restating his position by affirming that Christ had only one will.

Two councils of Constantinople* (638 and 639) ruled in favor of Monothelitism as being in conformity with the Definition of Chalcedon*. But continuing opposition from the papacy forced Emperor Constans II to withdraw *Ecthesis** in 648 and replace it with another document called *Typos**, rejecting Monophysitism* and Dyothelitism. *Typos* itself was condemned at the Lateran Council of 649. The controversy was finally settled at the Third Council of Constantinople* (681), the Sixth Ecumenical Council, which condemned Monothelitism and proclaimed that there were two wills in Christ, divine and human.

Monreale Cathedral in Monreale outside Palermo in southwest Sicily built where the Virgin Mary* appeared to the Norman king, William II, also known as William the Good, in a dream. The building began in 1174 and was completed in 1189. It is the most important example of Norman architecture in Sicily. The imposing complex is 335 feet long and 131 feet wide and has two massive towers flanking the west facade of the triple-aisled basilica*. Its mosaic murals covering an area of 1.6 acres light up the interior with extravagant colors. Its Romanesque bronze portals were created by Barisanus of Trani and Bonanus of Pisa. The magnificent square cloister* was part of the Benedictine monastery founded in 1174. It has 216 double pillars and decorated arcades.

Monsignor (Ital., my lord) Title or distinction attached to the office of an archbishop or bishop or other high ecclesiastic (abbrev. Msgr.).

monstrance Also, ostensorium. Disc-shaped vessel, framed by gold or silver rays with a glass window in which the consecrated bread is displayed for veneration* in the Mass*. It replaced the earlier closed ciborium* and the later transparent cylindrical container.

Monstrance

Montagna, Bartolommeo (1450–1523) Italian painter. He studied under Andrea Montagna and Giovanni Bellini*. Among his works are *The Presentation of Jesus Christ in the Temple, Madonna and the Two Saints,* and *Ecce Homo**.

Montanes, Juan Martinez (c. 1568–1649) Spanish religious sculptor. He executed a number of altarpieces.

Montanism Apocalyptic movement begun in the middle of the second century by Montanus*, assisted by two women, Prisca and Maximilla*, who proclaimed the imminent return of Jesus Christ and a massive outpouring of the Holy Spirit* in the latter days. The movement had its principal stronghold in Phrygia in Asia Minor. Montanus encouraged his followers to consider themselves as the elect* of God and to prepare for the Second Coming* by separation from the world, fasting*, prayer*, and the exercise of the gifts of the Spirit*. Montanists placed special emphasis on ecstatic prophecy, and Montanus described himself as a prophet*. They welcomed persecution, so that the church would be purified and made a fit bride for the coming bridegroom. From the beginning the sect* was persecuted by the official church, and by 220 it was proscribed. The Synod of Iconium refused to recognize the validity of Montanist baptism*. Thereupon, it went underground but continued to be active for many centuries. One of the most famous Montanists was Tertullian*, who called his fellow members pneumatics or "Spirit-filled" as opposed to Catholics, who were psychics or "animal men."

Montanists Also, Pepuzians*, from Pepuzia in Phrygia. Followers of Montanus*.

Montanus (second century) Phrygian Christian convert who, as the prophet* of God, began the Montanist movement.

Monte Cassino Principal monastery of the Benedictine* Order founded by St. Benedict* about 529. It is located midway between Rome* and Naples. St. Benedict and his sister, St. Scholastica*, are buried there. The main church was consecrated in 1071 when its famed scriptorium* was established. It was destroyed several times in its history, most recently during World War II in 1944 and then rebuilt and reconsecrated. In 1866 it was declared a national monument by the Italian government, and the monks were made its guardians.

Monteverdi, Claudio (1567–1643) "Creator of Modern Music" and the greatest musical genius of the seventeenth century. He composed church music in the older Renaissance style and in the newer Baroque style. He succeeded Giovanni Gabrieli* as maestro di cappella* at St. Mark's in Venice*.

Montfort, St. Louis Grignion de (1673–1716) Mariologist. Ordained in 1700, he became a mission preacher. Not long before his death, he founded the Missionaries of the Company of Mary, known today as the Montfort Fathers. His manuscript, *True Devotion to Mary,* was very popular.

Montgomery, James (1771–1854) English Moravian poet and hymn writer. He contributed over 400 hymns to Thomas Cotterill's *Selection of Psalms and Hymns* (1819). Many of his hymns are still popular, such as "Angels from the Realm of Glory," "Forever with the Lord," "Hail to the Lord's Anointed," "Prayer Is the Soul's Sincere Desire," "The Hour of Trial," and "Stand Up and Bless the Lord."

month's mind Requiem Mass* celebrated a month after the burial or death of the deceased.

Montserrat Mountain near Barcelona, the legendary site of the Castle of the Holy Grail. The Benedictine monastery with its famous image of Our Lady of Montserrat was founded between 1025 and 1035 by Abbot Oliba of Ripoli and raised to the rank of an abbey in 1409. In the fifteenth century it became one of Spain's most famous places of pilgrimage*. St. Ignatius Loyola* visited

Monte Cassino Monastery

the abbey to hang up his sword after his conversion. It is now the principal monastery of the province of Subiaco, and its extensive library promotes research into Catalonian history and sacred music.

Montserrat Monastery

Mont-St.-Michel Abbey and fortress on a rocky island off the north coast of France, near St. Malo. It towers over the Normandy coast over half a mile in circumference and 256 feet high. An oratory* was established there by St. Aubert of Avranches in the eighth century in obedience to the command of an apparition of St. Michael. In 966 it was taken over by the reforming Benedictines* and a monastery was built and a fortress added later. Between the thirteenth and sixteenth centuries a Gothic* building rose here. It has a forbidding, fortress-like appearance. A fortified gateway was added in the fourteenth century, and an imposing wall was built around the base of the hill in the fifteenth. One of the most beautiful features of Mont-St.-Michael is the Merveille, the three-storied abbey built in the thirteenth century. On the top floor is the cloister*. On the second is the Hall of Knights and a thirteenth-century reception hall. At the bottom level are cellars and storage rooms and a hospice for pilgrims. The monastery is now state-owned. The landmark is the subject of many books.

Moody Bible Institute Evangelical training institution originating in the late nineteenth century sponsored and founded by the Chicago Evangelization Society as the Bible Institute for Home and Foreign Missions in 1887. After Dwight L. Moody's death in 1899, the institute was named in his honor in 1900. The institute had a lasting influence on the Fundamentalist movement with which its first two presidents, Reuben A. Torrey* and James M. Gray, were both closely associated. It soon became the model for all Bible institutes that followed its founding. The institute has an active publishing program under the imprint of Moody Press and it also publishes *Moody Magazine.*

Moody, Dwight Lyman (1837–1899) American evangelist. He left his business in 1860 to enter full-time Sunday school* and YMCA* work. After the Civil War he established the nondenominational Illinois Street Church in Chicago. On a trip to a national Sunday school convention, he met Ira D. Sankey*, who became his musical associate. His first major crusade* was in England in 1867, and he followed it up with a second and third crusade in 1872–1875 and 1881–1884. He made three influential visits to Scotland. In 1873 Moody and Sankey produced a *Hymn Book* which was very popular. Moody repeated his English success with similar crusades in Brooklyn, Philadelphia*, New York, and Boston. Over a lifetime as evangelist Moody traveled one million miles and addressed more than 100 million people.

Moody was also active as an educator. In 1879 he established Northfield Seminary, a school for girls, and in 1881 Mount Hermon School, a school

Mont-St.-Michel Abbey

for boys. In 1880 he started a summer conference ministry, in 1886 the Chicago Evangelization So-

Dwight Moody (preaching)

ciety, later known as the Moody Bible Institute*, and in 1895 the Bible Institute Colportage Association for production of cheap religious literature.

Moon, Charlotte (Lottie) Diggs (1840–1912) Southern Baptist missionary in China. In 1872 she was appointed a missionary to China by the Southern Baptist Convention* Foreign Missions Board and she spent the rest of her life in northern China, first in Tengchow and later in P'ing-tu. She established a church, and her first converts were baptized in 1887. Within two decades P'ing-tu became the greatest Southern Baptist evangelistic center in all of China. She wrote books that stirred interest in foreign missions. Her impact on board policy was immense and included her call for more women missionaries, for new missionaries to be involved in mission work immedi-

Lottie Moon

ately (rather than waiting to complete language study), and for establishing regular furloughs for all missionaries. She started the women's Christmas offering, later named in her honor.

Moral Re-Armament See BUCHMAN, FRANK; OXFORD GROUP.

moral theology Branch of theology that deals with moral questions and the foundations of morality in a Christian context. It deals with human nature as distinct from other branches of theology that deal with the nature of God or relations between God and human beings. It emerged as a discipline independent of dogmatic theology in the sixteenth century. The term is more popular with Roman Catholics whereas Protestants prefer the term *Christian ethics*. In the New Testament, Jesus Christ dealt with moral imperatives both as commandments and as directives. This tradition was continued in the Apostolic Age* and by the early Church Fathers*, such as *The Shepherd**, Clement of Alexandria*, Tertullian*, and Cyprian*. With the conversion of pagans in the Roman Empire, moral teaching became the duty of the church. Moral codes were laid down by the Cappadocian Fathers*, Cyril of Jerusalem, St. Ambrose*, and St. Augustine*. By the time of Gregory I*, a system of Christian ethics had been established, summed up in his *Moralia*. The appearance of penitential books* from the fifth to the seventh centuries revealed how far the church's moral teachings had penetrated public practices.

Medieval scholastics tried to link moral actions with divine laws. Aquinas* devoted the second part of his *Summa* to moral theology. During the fourteenth and fifteenth centuries a large number of similar summae, manuals, and treatises on moral theology were produced, including the famous *Summa Theologica Moralis* of St. Antoninus of Florence*. The Counter-Reformation* was a period marked by controversies over contending doctrines of moral theology, such as probabilism*. The most notable Roman Catholic moralists were Bartolome Medina*, Gabriel Vazquez, Francisco Suarez*, and Domingo Banez*. Among the Casuists, both *Aphorismi Confessariorum* (1595) and *Disputationes Scholasticae et Morales* were used as textbooks. Perhaps the most celebrated moral theologian of all was

Alphonsus Liguori*, whose *Theologia Moralis* promoted a theory called equiprobabilism*.

Modern moral theology in the Catholic Church is more focused on using the Bible as the authority for providing positive guidance for Christian living rather than on simple commandments. Moral theology does not loom large in Protestantism* because of its emphasis on grace*. But moral laws were given great weight by Calvinists and Puritans*, who wanted to govern every aspect of human existence through the application of moral directives. The most important Protestant moral theologians were the Anglican Jeremy Taylor* and the Puritan Richard Baxter*. Moral theology, with its clear lines of division between right and wrong, sometimes skirts dangerously close to legalism* and has generally declined in modern times. The rise of twentieth-century culture with its focus on individualism and the growth of new social movements, such as feminism, have complicated the task of the moral theologian.

Morales, Luis de (c. 1520–1586) Spanish religious painter who did many versions of the Pieta*, Ecce Homo*, and other themes based on the life of Christ. He worked on the decoration of the Escorial* in the service of Philip II of Spain.

morality play A form of religious drama that taught moral truths based on a sermon or homily*, popular in the fifteenth to the eighteenth centuries. It portrayed "Everyman's*" quest for salvation* and the cosmic struggle for the soul of man between the forces of good and evil represented allegorically. The earliest known morality play was *The Castle of Perseverance* (1400–1420). Other plays were *The Pride of Life: Wisdom: Mankind, Mundus et Infans,* and the ever popular *Everyman.* During the Reformation*, some morality plays were Protestant in content, as *King Johan* (1538) or Catholic, as *Respublica* (1553).

Moran Mar Term of address prefixed to a name for archbishops and metropolitans* in the Syriac Orthodox Church*.

Moravian Brethren (Lat., *Unitas Fratrum*) Church of the United Brethren, successor to the Bohemian Brethren*. The group consisted of Moravian refugees after the Thirty Years' War who gathered in Herrnhut* on the estates of Count von Zinzendorf* in Saxony and worshiped together with some German Pietists at the Bertholdsdorf Lutheran Church under Pastor J. A. Rothe. Zinzendorf became the superintendent of the group and he led a great spiritual awakening*. The early leaders of the movement were David Nitschmann and A. G. Spangenberg*. Strongly evangelical, the movement acknowledged the Scriptures as the only guide to faith and conduct. The Brethren did not always establish separate churches but often remained within the umbrella of larger denominations. They uphold the episcopacy* with three orders: bishop, presbyter*, and deacon. Infant baptism* and believer's baptism* are both provided, followed by confirmation*.

Moravians emphasize fellowship and service rather than doctrine, but all orthodox creeds are accepted, including the Nicene*, Apostles'*, and Athanasian* and the main Reformation* statements of faith, such as Augsburg Confession*, the *Shorter Catechism* of Martin Luther*, and the Thirty-Nine Articles* of the Church of England*, although some latitude is permitted on nonessentials and adherence to any of them is not a requisite for membership. Church government is presbyterian. The governing body is the Unity Elders' Conference appointed by the General Synod, which is divided into home provinces and mission provinces. Each congregation manages its own affairs subject to the general ordinances of the province. There is a strong emphasis on evangelization. From 1732, itinerant Moravian missionaries established mission centers in all the five continents, covering West Indies, Tanzania, Greenland, North America, Lapland, South America, South Africa, Labrador, Australia, and Tibet. The proportion of missionaries to home communicants is a high 1:60 compared to 1:5,000 for other Protestants. John Wesley* was much influenced by Moravian evangelistic fervor.

The distinguishing features of Moravian worship service are the love feast* and the use of daily texts or watchwords. Love feast consists of the singing of hymns and an informal discourse by the minister during which a simple meal is served and partaken together. The Lord's Supper* is observed regularly and concludes with the covenant hymn during which members of the congregation exchange the right hand of fellowship with one another. Congregational singing is a major part of worship. Moravians have produced some of the greatest hymn writers, including Michael Weisse, Count Zinzendorf*, John Cennick, and James Montgomery*.

More, Dame Gertrude (1606–1633) Benedictine nun and spiritual writer. A direct descendant of Sir Thomas More*, she entered the English Benedictine congregation at Cambrai in 1623. Before she died at the age of 27, she left behind two devotional books of great beauty: *The Holy Practices of a Deuine Lover, or, the Sainctly Ideot's Deuotions* (1657) and *Confessiones Amantis* (1658).

More, Hannah (1745–1833) Religious writer and philanthropist. A friend of William Wilberforce* and John Newton* (who became her spiritual adviser), she established schools for religious and practical education. Between 1793 and 1799 she published a number of tracts known as "cheap repository tracts" which became the inspiration for the later Religious Tract Society*. Toward the end of her life, she joined the Clapham sect*.

More, Sir Thomas (1478–1535) English Catholic humanist, statesman, writer, philosopher, and martyr*, described as a "man for all seasons." In 1504 he entered Parliament and rose to the position of chancellor after the fall of Cardinal Wolsey in 1529. Although a devout Catholic, he remained friends with the leading humanists of the day, such as Dean Colet and Erasmus*. More also was one of the earliest futurists, and his *Utopia* is a visionary book that established a new genre of literature. *Utopia* described a communistic society in which there was no private property or money and there was full religious toleration. More wrote against Luther* and Tyndale* and opposed the royal plans of Henry VIII to make himself the governor of the Church of England*. For his refusal to take the oath* renouncing allegiance to the pope, he was beheaded. He was beatified in 1886. Feast day: June 22.

Morgan, George Campbell (1863–1945) Bible teacher and preacher who preached his first sermon at 13. He served as a Congregationalist pastor. As an itinerant evangelist he attracted large crowds with numerous conversions. He was also an able Bible expositor* whose literary output was enormous.

Morgan, William (1545–1604) Translator of the Welsh Bible*. As parish priest in Llanrhaeadr-ym-Mochnant, he translated the whole English Bible into Welsh. His translation is considered to be on a par with the Authorized English Version, and he is also credited with saving the Welsh language.

Morike, Eduard Friedrich (1804–1875) German minister and poet of the Swabian school whose poems included the much-loved "The Sleeping Christ Child."

Morimond Cistercian abbey founded by Stephen Harding*, third abbot of Citeaux*. It was one of the four sister abbeys of Citeaux, others being La Ferte, Pontigny*, and Clairvaux*. Morimond was destroyed during the wars of religion in 1572 and during the Thirty Years' War in 1636. The church survived but is now in ruins.

Moriscos Spain's native Moors who were converted to the Christian faith after their conquest by the Spaniards.

Mormon 1. Member of the Church of Jesus Christ of Latter-Day Saints*. 2. Apocryphal name of the compiler of the *Book of Mormon**.

Sir Thomas More

Mormon Tabernacle Choir Three-hundred-voice mixed choir that performs in the tabernacle on Temple Square in Salt Lake City. The choir appears on the weekly radio and television program, "Music and the Spoken Word."

Mormons Popular name for the Church of Jesus Christ of Latter-Day Saints* founded in Manchester, New York, in 1830 by Joseph Smith*, who claimed to have received through revelation* *The Book of Mormon**, which, together with the Bible, the *Doctrine and Covenants,* and *The Pearl of Great Price,* form the Mormon scriptures. In 1843 Smith received a further revelation sanctioning polygamy and permitting the president of the church to receive further revelations for the guidance of the church as a whole. By thus adding to the Bible unauthenticated books and revelations, the Mormons have placed themselves outside orthodox Christianity and acquired the characteristics of a cult*.

The group began its exodus to Kirkland, Ohio, then to Jackson County, Missouri, and later to Nauvoo, Illinois, where Smith was killed by an angry mob. Thereafter, the Mormons followed their new leader, Brigham Young*, on a long trek to Salt Lake City, Utah, where the church finally built its temple and established its headquarters. In 1890 the Mormons gave up their doctrine of polygamy in submission to the laws of the land. In 1978 the priesthood was opened "to all worthy male members . . . without regard to race or color," thus ending the bar on blacks from full membership.

Mormon doctrines differ from historic Christianity in many key areas. Mormonism teaches that: 1. God is not merely spiritual, but also physical. 2. There are thousands of gods in some ill-defined order of progression. 3. All gods were once men and all men may become gods. 4. Human beings existed as spirits before being born. Pre-existence is a probationary stage and those who fail the probative stage are born as blacks. 5. Adam's fall was a good thing because otherwise there would be no human race. 6. Christ is divine but only in the sense that all men are divine. 7. Resurrection is a right earned by Christ for all Mormons. 8. Justification* is not by faith* but by good works* and through belief in Joseph Smith. 9. The Mormon Church is the only

true church in Christian history. 10. Baptism* by immersion* is essential for salvation*. 11. The Lord's Supper* is administered weekly but water is substituted for wine. 12. Christ will reign over the earth in a literal millennium* from two capitals: Jerusalem* and Independence, Missouri. 13. Hell* is a place where the devil, his angels*, and nonbelievers will be consigned. 14. The dead may receive baptism and absolution* for their sins. 15. There are three heavenly kingdoms: the celestial, the terrestrial, and the telestial.

Mormons put great emphasis on missionary work, which explains their phenomenal growth in recent years. Each member is expected to tithe* strictly and to devote some time to proselytization. Local churches are called wards, but ceremonies, such as marriages and baptisms for the dead, can be performed only in temples. There are a few breakaway groups in the United States, the largest being the Reorganized Church of Jesus Christ of Latter-Day Saints*, headquartered in Independence, Missouri.

Mornay, Philippe de (1549–1623) Also, Seigneur de Plessis-Marly; Duplessis-Mornay. French Huguenot* leader. Originally a Roman Catholic, he adopted Protestantism* upon his father's death in 1559 through his mother's influence. He traveled widely and on returning to France escaped the St. Bartholomew's Day Massacre*. He fled to England, but returned in 1573 and shortly thereafter entered the service of Henry IV of Navarre as soldier, diplomat, and adviser. In 1589 he was appointed governor of the Huguenot stronghold of Saumur, where he founded the famous academy in 1603. For nearly a decade he was the principal representative of Huguenot interests and champion of toleration and was known as the "Huguenot pope." He was instrumental in drafting the Edict of Nantes* in 1598. When Henry IV converted to Catholicism* in 1893, he lost much of his influence but continued in royal service until 1600.

morning prayer See MATINS.

Morning Star of the Reformation Title of John Wycliffe*.

Morris, Leila Naylor (1862–1929) American hymn

writer and composer. An active worker in the Methodist Episcopal Church, she wrote more than 1,000 hymn texts as well as numerous tunes, although she became blind at the age of 51. Some of her well-known compositions include "Nearer, Still Nearer," "Sweeter as the Years Go By," "What If It Were Today?" and "Stranger of Galilee."

Morris, Leon Lamb (1914–) Australian Anglican biblical scholar. Ordained a priest in 1939, he pastored and taught in Australia before becoming principal of Ridley College, Cambridge (1963–1979). He lectured and preached extensively, especially on the Atonement* and on pastoral care for the flock. He was largely instrumental in setting up The Evangelical Alliance Relief Fund (TEAR*) in Australia. Among his books are *The Apostolic Preaching of the Cross* (1955), *Commentary on the Gospel of John* (1971), *Theology of the New Testament* (1986), *The Epistle to the Romans* (1988), and *Commentary on the Gospel of Matthew* (1993).

Morrison, Charles Clayton (1874–1966) American leader of the Disciples of Christ* and editor of the *Christian Century*. A pacifist, he opposed U.S. entry into the two world wars. He was one of the founding members of the National Council of Churches and World Council of Churches*.

Morrison, Robert (1782–1834) First Protestant missionary in China. Of Scottish parentage, he became a member of the LMS* in 1804, was ordained and sent to Canton in 1807. Here he learned Mandarin Chinese and became a translator to the East India Company. His life work was the *Chinese Dictionary* in six volumes (1821), which remained the standard reference on Chinese language for over a century. It was followed by the publication of the first Chinese Bible in 21 volumes in 1823. In 1818 he founded the Anglo-Chinese College in Malacca.

morrow Mass In Medieval England, an early Mass*.

morse Clasp or band fastening a cope* across the chest.

Morse, Jedediah (1761–1826) American Congregational* missions leader. He was instrumental in

organizing the Trinitarian General Association of Massachusetts Clergy whose meeting in Bradford in 1810 created the American Board of Commissioners for Foreign Missions* (ABCFM), and he was also a principal founder of the Andover Theological Seminary* (1808), the New England Tract Society (1808), and the American Bible Society* (1816). He was the secretary of the Society for Propagating the Gospel among the Indians. In 1805 he founded a magazine, the *Panoplist,* which later became the organ of the ABCFM and was renamed the *Missionary Herald* in 1820.

mortal sin Also, grave sin; sin unto death. The most serious category of sin, involving a deliberate and willful act of turning away from God or frustrating his purpose. Unless followed by proper contrition* and confession*, it leads to eternal damnation and the loss of grace* (1 John 5:16). Compare venial sin.

mortification In ascetical theology*, subjugation and denial of bodily passions and appetites, principally through fasting*, penance*, and abstinence. In Romans 8:13 and Colossians 3:3–5 Christians are bidden to mortify the works of the flesh as they have died with Christ in baptism*.

Moschus, John (c. 550–619 or 634) Also known as Eukratas. Writer. In about 575 he entered the Monastery of St. Theodosius, near Jerusalem*.

Robert Morrison

He later traveled widely to monasteries in Mount Sinai, Antioch*, Egypt, Cyprus*, and Rome*. His *Pratum Spirituale* is the record of his travels, including a large collection of monastic anecdotes.

Moscow Capital of Russia. It became the headquarters of the Russian Orthodox Church* in 1326 when Metropolitan Peter of Kiev* took up residence there. Peter began work on the first Dormition Cathedral, Uspenskii Sobor. Other major churches in Moscow include the Annunciation Cathedral (1489), the Kremlin Cathedral of St. Michael the Archangel (1505–1509), Cathedral of the Savior, rebuilt in the 1990s after being demolished by Stalin, and the Cathedral of Basil the Blessed (1555–1560). With the fall of Constantinople*, Moscow became the "third Rome." Moscow was also the center of Russian monasticism*. Many famous Russians are buried in the cemetery of the Virgin of Smolensk Cathedral at Novodevichii Monastery.

Moses bar Kepha (c. 815–903) Syrian Orthodox (Jacobite) bishop of Mosul for 40 years from about 863. He is one of the preeminent writers in Syriac* literature who wrote commentaries on most books of the Bible.

Moses of Chorene (fifth or eighth centuries) Armenian historian. He was a pupil of Mesrob and author of the *History of the Armenians,* a standard history of the formation and growth of the Armenian nation and church.

Moses of Ethiopia Ascetic. Leader of a gang of thieves, he was converted at the Monastery of Petra in the Egyptian desert of Scete. There he became an ascetic and was ordained by Theophilus of Alexandria. Later he founded the Monastery of Dar al Baramus. He was murdered in his old age by burglars.

Mosheim, Johann Lorenz von (1694–1755) Lutheran Church historian, noted for his *Institutes of Ecclesiastical History* (1726). He was chancellor of the University of Gottingen from 1747.

Most Catholic Title or term of address of the kings of Spain.

Most Christian Title or term of address of the kings of France.

most reverend Title or term of address of an archbishop and of some other senior church officials.

Most Sacred Title or term of address of the kings and queens of England.

motet Polyphonic musical composition used at the Offertory and the Elevation* of the Mass*, based on a sacred but nonliturgical Latin text. In conventional usage, the term is used for settings of antiphons* and Psalms, but not hymns, canticles*, or anthems. The motet originated as a trope* and was therefore a liturgical genre. In its earliest usage, it designated an upper part with words of its own set against a cantus firmus*. It served as the focal point for the development of the complex medieval structural device known as isorhythm. The medieval motet was sung by a group of solo voices and used as a plainsong* melody, but by the fifteenth century it became choral in style.

The period of the Renaissance was the golden era of the motet. In the early fifteenth century it was the principal genre for Guillaume Dufay*. It reached its highest development under the great sixteenth-century composers, Adriaen Willaert*, Josquin des Prez*, Orlandus de Lassus, William Byrd*, and Giovanni P. de Palestrina*. In the Baroque period the traditional motet was broadened in Protestant countries to apply to sacred compositions in the vernacular. In the seventeenth century it once again included solo voices and instrumental accompaniment. Outstanding composers in this period included Giovanni Gabrieli* and Heinrich Schuetz. In France Marc-Antoine Charpentier* developed the Grand Motet for use in the royal chapel*.

After the Baroque period, classical composers, such as Haydn*, Verdi*, and Brahms*, continued to produce motets. In the twentieth century, Max Reger, Hugo Distler*, and Ernst Pepping* have contributed Protestant motets, and Johann Nepomuk and David and Hermann Schroeder have contributed Latin motets for Catholic service. In France Francis Poulenc* has composed four motets on penitential texts and four Christmas* motets.

mothat Stole* worn by the Ethiopian clergy embroidered with many crosses.

mother church Cathedral church or a church sponsoring other churches or missions.

mother house Center of a religious order with branch houses under it.

Mother of God (Gk., *Theotokos**, strictly, God-bearer) Appellation of the Virgin Mary*.

Mother of the Church Title given to the Virgin Mary* at Vatican Council II* in 1964.

mother superior Office of the head abbess in a convent.

Mothering Sunday Fourth Sunday in Lent*, also known as Laetare Sunday*, when mothers are visited by their offspring or receive cards and gifts.

motif research Theological method developed by the Swedish theologians Gustaf Aulen* and Anders Nygren* emphasizing human incapacity to initiate a true relationship to God. The task of theology is to discern the motif or distinctive themes, such as agape*, in religious traditions.

Mott, John Raleigh (1865–1955) American Methodist leader of the twentieth-century ecumenical movement*. In 1888 he became general secretary of the Student YMCA and chairman of the Student Volunteer Movement for Foreign Missions*. In 1895 he became general secretary of the World Student Christian Federation* which he helped to found. He was instrumental in convening the 1910 Edinburgh Missionary Conference* where he presided at most of the sessions. He went on to become chairman of the International Missionary Council* (1921), Chairman of the Second Life and Work* Conference at Oxford (1937), vice chairman of the Provisional Committee of the World Council of Churches (1938), and copresident of the World Council of Churches* in 1948. He remained the central figure in the ecumenical movement* for over 40 years. His books included *The Evangelization of the World in This Generation* (1900). He shared the Nobel Peace prize in 1946.

Mottlingen movement Swabian Pietist revival movement begun by Friedrich Stanger (1855–1935) in 1909 in Mottlingen, Wurttemberg, under the motto, "The Ark of Salvation." Stanger practiced a ministry of faith healing*. Banned by the Nazis, it experienced a resurgence after World War II.

motu proprio (Lat., of his own accord) Letter addressed by the pope to the whole church or a diocese* or a particular person under his own signature and on his own initiative.

motwa (lit., a seat) Assyrian liturgical anthem, the text of which varies according to the day of the week.

Moulton, James Hope (1863–1917) British New Testament scholar, author of *Grammar of New Testament Greek* (1929) and *Vocabulary of the Greek Testament, Illustrated from the Papyri and other Non-literary Sources* (1930).

mourners' bench Also, anxious bench. Area in front of an evangelistic meeting where those who responded to the preacher's altar call* gathered to mourn over their sins.

movable feast Annual ecclesiastic feast that does not fall on a fixed date on the calendar but varies according to preset rules.

John R. Mott

movement prayer Congregational or liturgical dance used to accompany communal prayer.

Mozarabic Chant Music used in the Mozarabic Rite* of which only two chant traditions have been preserved, those of Toledo and Leon. The neumes* in which the others are written cannot be read today.

Mozarabic Rite Ancient Spanish liturgy in use in the Iberian Peninsula from the earliest times to the eleventh century. The liturgy was compiled in the centuries before the Moorish Conquest in 711 by national councils and the Spanish Church Fathers* and bishops, such as Isidore*, Leander, Ildefonsus, Eugenius II, and Julian*. The Mozarabic Rite was replaced by the Roman Rite* after the Christian reconquest, but it was allowed to survive in certain pockets, such as Toledo*, especially through the efforts of Ximenez de Cisneros*.

The Mozarabic Rite is closely related to the Gallican with some traces of Byzantine and North African influences. Its distinctive features include the use of the Trisagion* in Greek, a chant known as the *Sacrificium* (corresponding to the

Mozarabic Rite

Offertory) followed by two prayers, the *Missa* or *Oratio Admonitionis* and the *Illatio,* the recitation of the Nicene Creed* before or after the Lord's Prayer*, and the division of the host* into nine parts, of which seven are arranged in the form of a cross. There is also a distinction between the Secular Office consisting of only the vespers* and the mattins* and the Monastic Office with 12 offices by day and 12 by night. The principal service books were the Psalter, *Liber Canticorum, Liber Hymnorum, Liber Antiphonarium, Liber Orationum, Liber Missarum* corresponding to the Sacaramentary, and *Liber Ordinum** containing votive masses* and ordination rites. It was suppressed by Pope Gregory VII* in 1080.

Mozarabs Designation of Christians under Moorish rule in Spain.

Mozart, Wolfgang Amadeus (1756–1791) Austrian composer. His father, Leopold, was composer to the ruling archbishop of Salzburg*. A remarkable prodigy, he began composing church music as a teen. Among these works are a coronation Mass*, two vesper services, the *Miseracordias Domini,* and the Munich kyrie*. He wrote only three more sacred works after he left Salzburg in a dispute with the archbishop. They were an unfinished Mass in C Minor, *Ave Verum,* and the *Requiem,* which other composers finished after his death.

mozetta/mozzetta Cape with a small hood worn by the pope, cardinals, abbots, and other ecclesiastical dignitaries. The color of the hood—violet, red, or black—indicates the rank of the wearer and the occasion.

mqablana (Syr., veil) In the Assyrian Church*: 1. Sanctuary* door between the holy place and the nave*. 2. Humeral veil worn by the deacon who holds the paten* when the priest administers the Communion*.

MRA Moral Re-Armament*. See also OXFORD GROUP.

Msgr. Monsignor.

m'sham-shono In the Maronite Church, a deacon.

m'sham-shonoitho In the Maronite and Jacobite churches, vessel in which the celebrant's* fingers may be washed or the wine and water at the offertory may be mixed.

m'sone In the Jacobite tradition, special shoes worn as part of eucharistic vestments by the clergy.

Mueller, Carl Frank (1892–1982) American organist and composer. His most popular anthems were "Create in Me a Clean Heart, O God" and "Surely the Lord Is in This Place."

Muggeridge, Malcolm (1903–1990) English writer. He was editor of the influential British humor journal, *Punch* (1953–1957). He was past middle age when he was converted, but became one of the most fervent Christian apologists in the twentieth century. Among his books are *Jesus Rediscovered* (1969), *Something Beautiful for God* (1971) on Mother Teresa, *Jesus: The Man Who Lives* (1975), and an autobiography, *Chronicles of Wasted Time* (2 vols., 1972/73).

Muhlenberg, Henry Melchior (1711–1787) "Patriarch of American Lutheranism." Born in Einbeck, Germany, and ordained in 1739, he was called in 1741 to serve the United Lutheran Congregations of Pennsylvania. He landed in America in 1742 and immediately set about to revitalize the declining Lutheran Church. Constantly traveling, he established numerous congregations in the colonies. He summoned the first Lutheran synod* in America in 1748 to supervise the churches planted by him. He recruited and trained pastors and shepherded the Lutheran Church in its formative years.

Muhlenberg, William Augustus (1796–1877) Episcopal leader and hymn writer. He founded an industrial community in New York State named St. Johnland. He also established the first Episcopal school in the United States and its first order of Episcopal deaconesses.

Muller, George (1805–1898) Prussian-born British prayer-warrior and philanthropist. Converted in 1825, he came to London in 1829 to train for missionary service among Jews. Here he met Henry Craik, a disciple of A. N. Groves* of the Plymouth Brethren*, and began a joint ministry with him at Gideon Chapel and later at Bethesda Chapel in Bristol. In 1834 he formed the Scriptural Knowledge Institution for Home and Abroad to circulate Bibles and to stimulate missionary work. Next year he began the orphanage with which his name will always be associated. To maintain this orphanage he received neither salary nor solicited funds, but always relied on the power of prayer to bring him support at the right time. With Groves*, Craik, and Robert Chapman, he became the leading representative of the Independent Brethren, the moderate wing of the sect that split from the exclusivist wing represented by J. N. Darby*.

multiplication evangelism Evangelism* and discipling of small numbers of believers with a view to training them as disciplers*, thus multiplying exponentially.

Mumford, Bernard ("Bob") C., Jr. (1930–) American pastor and Bible teacher. Converted and Spirit-baptized at the age of 24, he formed—together with Derek Prince, Don Basham*, and Charles Simpson—the Holy Spirit Teaching Mission that focused on the areas of discipleship, shepherding, and submission. In 1986 he moved to California, where he established Lifechangers.

mundatory White linen used to wipe the vessels after the Eucharist* or Mass*.

Henry M. Muhlenberg

Munich City in Germany. It is the site of the Jesuit College*, a bastion of the Counter-Reformation*, built after 1581 with the support of Duke Wilhelm V. The Church of St. Michael was consecrated in 1597. After the dissolution of the Jesuit Order, it became the court church. It contains the celebrated statue of St. Michael.

Munificentissimus Deus Apostolic constitution* issued by Pope Pius XII* in 1950 defining the doctrine of the Assumption of the Blessed Virgin Mary*, so named from its opening words.

Munkacsy, Mikhail von (1844–1900) Birth name: Michael Leo Lieb. Hungarian painter, noted for such paintings as *Christ Before Pilate* and *Ecce Homo*.

Munster, Sebastian (1489–1552) German Franciscan monk who became one of the great scholars of the Reformation* and Lutheran court preacher at Heidelberg. From 1529 until death he taught at Basel*. He edited the first Hebrew Bible* in Germany and also published Hebrew and Aramaic grammars.

Muntzer, Thomas (c. 1489–1525) Also, Munzer. German radical reformer. He participated in Luther's Disputation at Leipzig* and began preaching at Zwickau with Luther's approval. Here he became associated with a radical fringe group called Zwickau Prophets* and he turned against Luther whom he abused as "Brother Fattened Swine," "Dr. Liar," and "Pope of the Lutheran Scripture Perverters." Muntzer's theology was apocalyptic and mystical, fusing violence and suffering as means to usher in a new age. He tried to stir up opposition to Luther and the secular princes in Prague*, Allstedt, and Muhlhausen, calling for the abolition of private property and the establishment of the true gospel through the use of force. To counter Roman Catholic persecution, Muntzer formed a Christian league. For his role in the Peasants' Revolt, he was captured, tortured, and executed. Although his social revolutionary ideas were discredited, his theological emphasis on the inspiration* of the Holy Spirit* influenced the Anabaptists*.

munus triplex (Lat., threefold office) The threefold office of Jesus Christ as prophet*, priest, and king.

Muratori, Ludovico Antonio (1672–1750) Italian scholar known as the father of Italian history. He discovered the Muratorian Canon* in 1740. After his ordination in 1695 and after obtaining his doctorate, he took the post of archivist and librarian at the court of Modena and provost* of Santa Maria della Pomposa. His extensive corpus included *Rerum Italicarum Scriptores* (25 vols., 1723–1751), *Antiquitates Italicae Medii Aevi* (6 vols., 1738–1748), and *Liturgia Romana Vetus* (2 vols., 1748).

Muratorian Canon Oldest extant list of New Testament books, compiled in Latin before 200 in Rome*, discovered by Ludovico Muratori*. It contains all the present New Testament writings except Hebrews, James, the Epistles of Peter, and one Epistle of John. Spurious letters, like the Letter to the Laodiceans and the Letter to the Alexandrians, both in the Marcionite canon*, are rejected. Catholic Epistles* are accepted and so is the apocryphal *Wisdom of Solomon*. The *Revelation* of John is accepted, and also the *Apocalypse of Peter*. *The Shepherd** may be read privately, but not in worship.

Murder in the Cathedral (1935) Verse play by T. S. Eliot*, commissioned by the Canterbury Festival of 1935, a reenactment of the murder of Thomas Becket*.

Murillo, Bartolome Esteban (1618–1682) Spanish painter. He spent most of his working life in Cadiz, Seville*, and Madrid. As a member of a religious brotherhood, Murillo's paintings are marked by tenderness for the suffering and the poor. He portrayed the gospel in human terms. He is celebrated as the painter of the *Immaculate Conception* of which he painted 20 versions, none of them alike. Among his best known works are: *Martyrdom of St. Andrew, Prodigal Son, Vision of St. Anthony, Birth of the Virgin, Moses,* and *The Miracle of Loaves and Fishes.*

muronitho In the Jacobite Rite, crozier or pastoral staff* designed as two intertwined serpents with a ball mounted by a cross between them.

Murray, Andrew (1828–1917) South African Dutch Reformed* pastor. Ordained in 1848, he served in Bloemfontein (1840–1860), Worcester (1860–

1864), Cape Town (1864–1871), and Wellington (1871–1906). A theological conservative, he opposed the liberal trends in the Dutch Reformed Church*. In 1874 he founded the Huguenot Seminary and in 1877 the Mission Institute at Wellington. He was influenced by reading William Law* to adopt a mystical and devotional theology which he promoted in his frequent evangelistic tours and addresses before the Keswick* and Northfield conventions and the Bible and Prayer Union. Although not a Pentecostal, he was deeply influenced by the Methodist holiness tradition and through his books helped to shape South African Pentecostalism*. He wrote over 250 pietist books of which the most popular were *Abide in Christ, With Christ in the School of Prayer* (1885), *The New Life* (1891), *Absolute Surrender* (1895), *The Spirit of Christ* (1888), *The Second Blessing* (1891), *The Full Blessing of Pentecost* (1907), and *Divine Healing* (1900).

Murray, John Courtney (1904–1967) American Jesuit theologian. His writings focused on religious freedom, and he was instrumental in drafting the Declaration on Religious Freedom (1965) at Vatican Council II*.

muscular Christianity Charles Kingsley's* term for a form of Christianity that flexes its muscles in the social and political marketplace, as opposed to a Christian faith that is spiritual and contemplative.

Musculus, Wolfgang (1497–1563) Also, Mauslein. German reformer. He entered a Benedictine monastery at the age of 15, but left it in 1527 after reading Luther*. At Strasbourg*, he became Bucer's* secretary and later a preacher at Augsburg. Here he was involved in the struggle over the Lord's Supper* and the relationship of the secular powers to the church. Since he could not be reconciled to the Interim of Charles V, he left Augsburg and began teaching at the old Franciscan College in Bern. Musculus supported the right of the magistrates at Bern to control the churches and to maintain discipline. Among his works are commentaries, translations of Church Fathers*, and *Common Places* (1560).

Mustair Benedictine monastery in the eastern canton of Graubunden, Switzerland, founded in 780. Originally the monastery church was small with a single nave*, but it was replaced in 1490 by a hall church with a bell tower* and the residence of the abbess, known as the Planta Tower. Mustair achieved fame in 1947–1952 when layers of limewash and overpainting were scraped away to reveal a sequence of extraordinary frescoes* dating from the ninth century.

Myconius, Friedrich (1490–1546) Lutheran reformer of Thuringia. He entered the Franciscan Order* in 1510, but influenced by Luther*, left it in 1524 to become preacher at Gotha. He played a leading part in the Reform movement and was present at the conferences at Marburg (1529), Wittenberg* (1536), Schmalkalden (1537), Frankfurt and Nuremberg (1539), and Hagenau (1540). His main work was *Historia Reformationis* (1715), a valuable source on the Reformation* in Thuringia.

Myconius, Oswald (1488–1552) Original name: Geisshausler. Swiss reformer and humanist. From 1523 he collaborated with Zwingli* in Zurich* and succeeded J. Oecolampadius* at Basel*. He was a moderate who favored a compromise* with Lutherans on consubsantiation* and distrusted the Zwinglian tendency to coopt secular authorities in church affairs.

myroblytes (Gk., myrrh-gushing) Title of several Orthodox saints* whose relics* produce an aromatic liquid with healing properties. The most famous myroblytes are Demetrios of Thessaloniki, Nylos of Kynouria, and Barbaros. Certain icons also are believed to have the same property. A parallel phenomenon is eiodia, or fragrance that emanates from certain relics.

myron In the Eastern churches*, chrism* consecrated by patriarchs* or heads of autocephalous* churches.

mystagogia 1. Instruction in the mysteries* of the faith before baptism* and part of the initiation into Christian life. 2. In the Byzantine Church*, the Eucharist*.

mystagogue One who initiates another into or interprets mysteries*.

mysteries Truths not accessible to human reason, used of the sacraments* and of the hidden purposes of God. In the New Testament, a secret plan of God made known by revelation*.

Mysteries of the Rosary The 15 subjects of meditation associated with the 15 decades of the Rosary*. They are divided into groups of five corresponding to three chaplets of which the Rosary is composed, known as the joyful, sorrowful, and glorious mysteries*.

mysterium Institution narrative in the eucharistic prayer recited silently by the priest.

mysterium tremendum et fascinans (Lat., fearful and fascinating mystery) Description of the numinous*, popularized by Rudolf Otto*.

mystery play Also, miracle play*. Vernacular religious drama of the later Middle Ages, such as the Corpus Christi* plays in England and passion plays* in France, staged during the Holy Week*, Whitsuntide*, and Easter*. Typical subjects were the harrowing of hell*, life of the Virgin Mary*, Antichrist*, and the last judgment or the lives of the saints*. Performances usually took place out of doors, sometimes on wagons used as movable stages. Some of the plays were presented in cycles, as for example, York* (48 plays), Towneley (32 plays), Chester (25 plays), and Coventry* (42 plays). They were eventually suppressed in Protestant countries. The most famous mystery play is the Passion Play* at Oberammergau*.

mystic recitation Parts of the Byzantine Liturgy said in a low voice.

mystical body The church considered as the body of Christ.

Mystical Rose Designation of the Virgin Mary*.

mystical theology Branch of theology dealing with physical and contemplative states in which the divine is apprehended in terms that cannot be translated into language. Dionysius the Pseudo-Areopagite* was the first to use the term, which he defined as the "darkness of unknowing" and as a "revelation in silence." According to later Byzantine writers, it is the last stage of spiritual progress, called unitive. Mystical theology affirms that God is essentially unknowable, since he is totally the other, and that human faculties are incapable of plumbing the depths of his mystery, but that the soul can dissolve itself in an ineffable union with God. Some theologians have held that such a state is only the sanctifying grace* of the Holy Spirit* in operation. Most mystical theology has been strongly influenced by neo-Platonism.

Mystics of St. Victor Religious school in the Abbey of St. Victor outside Paris where Peter Lombard* and Hugh of St. Victor* taught.

mzamrono In the Syrian tradition, a singer, a member of a minor order*.

Nn

nabedrennik In the Byzantine tradtion, an oblong piece of rich stiff material suspended from the hip of a priest, signifying the sword* of the Spirit or the towel used by Jesus at the Last Supper.

NAE National Association of Evangelicals*.

nafur One of the three silk veils used to cover the eucharistic vessels in the Maronite Church.

Nag Hammadi Town in Central Egypt on the western bank of the Nile River about 40 miles north of Luxor where a Coptic Gnostic library was unearthed in 1945–1946 in a cemetery. It consists of 13 papyrus* codices totaling over 1,100 pages. Ten manuscripts are in Sahidic* Coptic and three in a sub-Akhmimic dialect. They were probably written in the first half of the fourth century. They contain in whole or in part 53 works, most of them translated from Greek. Three were known

Nag Hammadi Manuscripts

previously: *The Sophia of Jesus Christ, The Sentences of Sextus,* and the *Apocryphon of John*.* There are duplicates of three texts: *The Letters of Eugnostos the Blessed, The Egyptian Gospel,* and *The Gospel of Truth*. All the manuscripts are in the Coptic Museum in Cairo. The manuscripts are of great importance for the study of various forms of Gnosticism*, such as Valentinian, Basilidian, and Sethian. They also illuminate the relationship between Christian Gnosticism and its pagan and Jewish predecessors.

Nahum of Ochrid (830–910) Serbian monk and translator. He was a disciple of Sts. Cyril and Methodius* who founded a famous monastery, subsequently named after him, on Lake Ochrid in Macedonia*. He translated liturgical and patristic texts into Church Slavonic*.

naidrion Small chapel in a Byzantine monastic house, which may be a part of a larger monastic community.

name of Jesus The name above all names in the New Testament by which the power of Christ is invoked to perform miracles, cast out devils, and baptize believers. From the fifteenth century the devotion to the holy name has been popularized by the Franciscans, St. Bernardino of Siena*, and Giovanni Capistrano*.

Name of Jesus, Feast of the Feast, celebrated January 2. It was originally granted to the Franciscans in

1530 for commemoration on January 14 and prescribed in 1721 for observance by the universal church on the second Sunday after Epiphany*. The Office and the Mass* were composed by Bernardino dei Busti and included the hymns, *Jesu Dulcis Memoria, Jesu Rex Admirabilis,* and *Jesu Decus Angelicum.* It was suppressed in 1969.

Nantes, Edict of Agreement signed between Henry IV of France and the Huguenots* after Henry converted from Protestantism* to Roman Catholicism*, to bring to an end the wars of religion. It codified and enlarged rights granted by prior agreements, such as the Edict of Poitiers of 1577 and the Convention of Nerac of 1578, permitting the free exercise of religion, judicial and civil equality, and grant of state subsidy to Protestant pastors and troops. The Protestants also retained control of over 200 towns. The edict was revoked by Louis XIV in the Edict of Fontainebleau in 1685.

naos (Gk., temple) 1. Church building. 2. Person indwelt by the Holy Spirit*.

napqa (lit., one who has left the world) Chaldean monk of the Antonian Congregation of St. Hormisdas, founded by Gabriel Dambo in 1808. The monks wear a black gown and black turban.

narrative theology 1. Branch of theology concerned with eternal truths expressed in narrative or story form in the Bible. Of relatively recent origin, it has built on the recognition of the important place occupied by narratives of various kinds in Scripture. 2. Post-modern form of theology stressing personal story over abstract doctrine as a medium of theology.

Narses/Narsai (c. 399–c. 503) Poet and theologian of the Church of the East* and head of the celebrated School of Edessa from 437. He fled Edessa* because of the hostility of Nestorians and founded another school at Nisibis*. His extensive commentaries on the Old Testament have been lost, but his large number of hymns have gained him the epithet of "Harp of the Spirit."

narthex Vestibule or antechamber of a church, separated from the nave* by rails or columns,

originally a place for catechumens* who were not admitted into the sanctuary proper. Distinguished from exonarthex*, or porch opening on to a street.

Nasrani Designation of Christians in Malabar, India, and some parts of West Asia, a corruption of Nazarene*.

natalitia (Lat., birthday) The death days of Christian martyrs* in the sense of their birth into eternal life*. Sometimes used in the sense of an important anniversary.

National Association of Evangelicals Organization of American Evangelical churches founded in 1942 in St. Louis by Ralph T. Davis and J. Elwin Wright and other leaders. It began as a counterforce to the liberal Federal Council of Churches* and as an alternative to the Fundamentalist American Council of Christian Churches. Its doctrinal position was reflected in its motto, "Cooperation without Compromise." Among its subsidiary groups are the Evangelical Foreign Missions Association*, National Religious Broadcasters*, World Relief, and National Sunday School Association.

National Conference of Catholic Bishops Ecclesiastical organization of U.S. Catholic bishops for the exercise of their joint pastoral ministry, founded in 1966. It is the ecclesiastical counterpart of the bishops' civil arm, the U.S. Catholic Conference.

National Conference of Christians and Jews Organization founded in New York City in 1928 to promote increased collaboration and understanding between Christians and Jews and to reduce anti-Semitism in national life. It is now known as the National Conference for Community and Justice.

National Council of Churches of Christ in the USA (NCCC) Cooperative ecumenical agency representing 33 Protestant and Orthodox denominations, founded in Cleveland, Ohio, in 1950, as the successor to the Federal Council of Churches* of Christ in America, founded in 1908. It describes itself as "a community of Christian communions which, in response to the gospel revealed in the Scriptures, confess Jesus Christ, the incarnate Word of God*, as Savior and Lord." Churches that remain outside NCCC include the Roman Catholic Church, Southern Baptists, Lutheran Church-Missouri Synod, as well as all Pentecostal, Holiness, Evangelical, and Fundamentalist churches. Its principal areas of concern include social justice, evangelism, Christian unity, the struggle against racism, international peace and understanding, and civil rights. Among its major accomplishments is the publication of the Revised Standard Version* in 1952. One important NCCC ministry is the Church World Service*, an international network of relief and development agencies. Its funds make up 85 percent of NCCC budget.

National Covenant Legal covenant drawn against Charles I by Scottish Presbyterians in the Greyfriars* churchyard in Edinburgh* in 1638 in answer to the royal attempt to impose the *Book of Common Prayer** on the Scottish Church. The subscribers pledged to defend the Presbyterian religion and the freedom of the church. The document was signed by over 300,000 people, who were thereafter known as the Covenanters*.

National Day of Prayer Day set aside in the United States on October 1 every year by a resolution of U.S. Congress in 1952 for prayer and a just and durable peace under divine guidance.

National Religious Broadcasters (NRB) Arm of the National Association of Evangelicals*, representing religious radio and television stations and programs in the United States, founded in 1943. NRB is one of the most powerful media organizations and for the past 25 years, the president and/or vice president of the United States have regularly appeared at its annual convention in Washington, D.C.

Nativity 1. Birth of Christ. 2. Feast celebrating the birth of Christ. 3. Artistic representation of the birth of Christ. 4. Birth of John the Baptist or the Virgin Mary*.

Nativity, Church of the Magnificent church built in Bethlehem* by Constantine* in the fourth century. It is one of the holiest Christian shrines in Israel.

Nativity of St. John the Baptist Feast celebrated on June 24 to commemorate the birth of St. John the Baptist, one of the earliest feasts on the Christian calendar.

Nativity of the Blessed Virgin Feast observed on September 8 to commemorate the birth of the Virgin Mary*.

natural theology Branch of theology that deals with knowledge about God that is obtained through the exercise of the senses and human faculties without recourse to or belief in direct revelation* or prophecy*. Distinguished from revealed theology*. Many Christians have rejected the possibility of natural theology because in a fallen state human beings are incompetent to derive fundamental truths through observation or study of nature alone. Romans 1:18, however, suggests that human beings may derive some intimations of the working of divinity but without any certainty or clarity and, worse, they may be led to confuse the created nature with the Creator and thus become pantheists or animists. Natural theology was favored by Deists in the eighteenth century who were unhappy with revealed religion. They replaced the God of the Bible with a "being" who is the immanent ground of all life.

A major resource for natural theologians is the Gifford Lectures* established by Lord Gifford in the nineteenth century. Natural theology also figures prominently in medieval Scholasticism*

Nativity

which offered a series of arguments as proofs of the existence of God as a supplement to revelation, however, and not as a replacement or repudiation. These arguments include the ontological argument developed by St. Anselm* and the cosmological, teleological, and moral arguments developed by Aquinas*. None of these arguments is conclusive proof for the truth of Christianity and the gospel.

Naumburg Cathedral Cathedral in Naumburg, Germany, first built in 1042 and rebuilt in the thirteenth century. It is noted for its eight reliefs on the choir screen* on biblical themes as well as sculptures of the benefactors of the church.

Naumburg Convention A conference in 1561 of 12 German Protestant princes and theologians to establish doctrinal unity, especially on the Eucharist*. It agreed to accept the Augsburg Confession* in both the *Invariata,* or unaltered, form, and the *Variata*, or altered, form along with Melanchthon's* *Apology* of 1531. Theological conflicts, however, continued and ended in the Formula of Concord*.

navagadik In the Armenian tradition, a mild fast.

Navarette, Juan Fernandez (1526–1579) Spanish religious painter, noted for his *The Baptism, The Nativity, The Burial of St. Lawrence,* and other paintings.

nave (Lat., *navis,* ship) Central part of the church extending from the vestibule to the chancel* in some communions, commonly separated from the sanctuary by a screen* and from the aisles by pillars or columns. It is reserved for the laity.

navicula Boat* for carrying incense for replenishing the censer*.

Navigators, The Organization promoting Bible study and memorization, witness, and fellowship, founded by Dawson Trotman* in 1943 with 2 Timothy 2:2 as his guiding principle. It is headquartered in Colorado Springs, Colorado. It emphasizes one-to-one discipleship and has developed principles of Bible memorization, prayer, meditation, witnessing, and Bible study. Naviga-

tors branches are found in over 70 countries, some of them with their own boards. It operates especially on university campuses. NavPress is its publishing arm.

Nayler, James (c. 1618–1660) English Puritan who joined the Quakers* and became their principal spokesman by 1655. His followers were deluded into thinking that he was a Messiah and the Lord God of Sabaoth, and he staged a reenactment in Bristol of Christ's triumphal entry into Jerusalem*. For this act of blasphemy*, he was branded in the forehead, his tongue was bored through, he was whipped through the streets, and jailed. He repented within a year and was released.

Nazarene 1. In the New Testament, appellation of Jesus Christ. 2. Person who is a native or resident of Nazareth in Palestine. 3. In the early church, a Christian, especially a member of a herterodox group of this name. 4. Early Jewish Christian in Syria. 5. Any of a group of nineteenth-century German artists who specialized in Christian art.

Nazarene, Church of the International denomination formed through the merger of 15 Wesleyan Holiness movement groups at Pilot Point, Texas, in 1908. Until 1919 it was called the Pentecostal Church of the Nazarene, but the term *Pentecostal* was dropped in that year because of its association with glossolalia*, which is not accepted by

Nave

the Holiness churches*. The church had its origin in 1906 in Glasgow, Scotland, through the ministry of George Sharpe when it was called the Pentecostal Church of Scotland. The church emphasizes missions, Christian education and communication, and hospitals. Nazarene theology is rooted in the Wesleyan tradition, and it fosters sanctification* and holy living as a work of grace. Members are required to tithe*, keep the Lord's Day*, and renounce alcohol, tobacco, theater, cinema, ballroom dancing, and gambling. The government of the church combines a congregational system with a superintendent and a general assembly that meets every four years.

Nazarenes, Gospel of the Also, Gospel According to the Hebrews. Aramaic Gospel used by the Jewish Christians in the early period.

NCC National Council of Churches.

Ne Temere Decree announced by Pope Pius X* in 1907 placing special restrictions on a mixed marriage. The non-Catholic spouse is required to raise the children in the Catholic faith and may not interfere with the religion of the other. Mixed marriages should preferably be celebrated by a Roman Catholic priest.

Neale, John Mason (1818–1866) Anglican scholar and hymn writer. Although born in an Evangelical family, he was converted to the High Church* movement and helped to found the Cambridge Camden (later Ecclesiological) Society whose goal was to revive Anglo-Catholic traditions in worship and architecture. From 1846 until his death he was the warden of Sackville College in East Grinstead. Here he founded in 1854 the Sisterhood of St. Margaret for the education of girls and the care of the sick on the model of St. Francis de Sales's Visitation and St. Vincent de Paul's Sisters of Charity.

Neale excelled as a scholar and a hymn writer. He is the author of *A Commentary on the Psalms* (4 vols., 1860–1874), *The History of the Holy Eastern Church* (5 vols., 1847–1873), and *Essays on Liturgiology and Church History* (1863), in addition to many children's stories. A scholar in 20 languages, he translated 94 of the 105 hymns in *The Hymnal Noted* (1852–1854). Among the

hymns he translated were "All Glory, Laud and Honor," "Art Thou Weary," "Good King Wenceslaus," "O Come, O Come, Immanuel," "O Happy Band of Pilgrims," "Jerusalem the Golden," "Ye Choirs of New Jerusalem," and "Of the Father's Love Begotten." In the *English Hymnal* more than one tenth of the hymns were his own or his translations. He also compiled *Hymns for Children* (1842–1846), *Medieval Hymns and Sequences* (1851), and *Hymns of the Eastern Church* (1862).

Neander, Joachim (1650–1680) German Pietist hymn writer, the first important poet of the German Reformed Church. He wrote some 60 hymns collected in a volume published in 1680. They included two hymns well-known in their English translation: "All My Hope on God Is Founded" and "Praise to the Lord, the Almighty."

Neander, Johann August Wilhelm (1789–1850) Original name before conversion: David Mendel. German historian of Jewish origin. Converted in 1806, he was professor of church history in Berlin for nearly four decades from 1813. He is considered the arch-opponent of liberal theologians like D. F. Strauss* and the founder of modern Christian historiography. Among his classic works are *General Church History* (6 vols., 1826–1852) and *History of the Planting and Training of the Christian Church by the Apostles* (2 vols., 1887–1888), in addition to lives of Christ (in answer to Strauss), Bernard of Clairvaux*, Chrysostom*, and Tertullian*.

nebrid An Ethiopian archdeacon or rector* of a cathedral.

Nectarius (1605–c. 1680) Patriarch of Jerusalem* (1661–1669). He opposed both Catholicism* and the Calvinism* of his predecessor, Cyril Lucar*. He took an active role in the Synod of Jerusalem in 1672 which repudiated Cyril Lucar and approved the confession of Peter Mogila*.

Nee, Watchman (Nee Shu-Tsu) (1903–1972) Chinese leader of the "Little Flock." Converted at age 17, he changed his name to To-Sheng or "God's Watchman." He was influenced by the writings of J. N. Darby* and also by the Holiness and Keswick* movements. He published a three-volume work on sanctification*, *The Spiritual Man* (1968). He also began to establish local centers of worship, known as the Little Flock, headquartered in Shanghai. Eventually there were more than 700 such assemblies, and they became the nucleus of the house churches* under the Communist regime. In 1952 Nee was arrested, and he died in prison in 1972. His books, *Sit, Walk, Stand* (1961) and *The Normal Christian Life* (1969) have sold widely.

Watchman Nee

Neeshima, Yuzuru (1843–1890) Japanese Christian leader. Born of Samurai stock, he was converted while a sailor in Boston. He returned to Japan, where he was commissioned a missionary by the Congregational Church*. In 1875 he founded in Kyoto the first Christian school in Japan, calling it Doshista.

nefka diyakon In the Ethiopian tradition, a subdeacon who reads the Epistles.

negative theology 1. Also, apophatic theology*; via negativa*. Theological approach that describes God by negating his limits or likeness to human attributes, virtues, or qualities. Compare cataphatic theology*. 2. Theological approach that focuses on points of disagreement with opposing viewpoints rather than on affirming or explaining its own positions.

Neill, Stephen Charles (1900–1984) Anglican missionary bishop and scholar. He was elected

bishop in Tirunelvely, India, in 1939 and served in that capacity until 1944. He worked for the World Council of Churches* from 1947 to 1954, editing the monumental *History of the Ecumenical Movement, 1517–1948* (1954). From 1962 to 1967 he was professor of missions at Hamburg and from 1969 to 1973 professor of religious studies at Nairobi. During this time he wrote the *Concise Dictionary of the Christian World Mission* (1971). Of his total output of over 100 books, the most notable is his two-volume *History of Christianity in India*.

nekrosimon Troparion* for the dead.

Neo-Caesarea, Council of Cappadocian council held probably in the early fourth century which passed 15 canons on questions of marriage and discipline.

neo-Calvinism Revival of Calvinist ideas, especially a return to Calvinist orthodoxy regarding key doctrines, such as predestination*. Neo-Orthodoxy* was in part a renewal of Calvin's thought.

neo-Catholicism Anglican or Protestant theology oriented toward Roman Catholicism* and emphasizing tradition, episcopacy*, and ritual.

neo-Chalcedonianism Definition of Chalcedon* as modified in the light of the teaching of Cyril* of Alexandria* and expounded by John the Grammarian and Leontius of Jerusalem*. It identified the second person of the Trinity* as identical with the hypostasis* of the Incarnate Christ.

neo-Evangelicalism Resurgence of Evangelical activity in the 1960s and 1970s represented by Fuller Theological Seminary*, Carl F. H. Henry* and *Christianity Today**, the National Association of Evangelicals*, Campus Crusade for Christ*, and the Inter-Varsity Missionary Conference at Urbana. See NEW EVANGELICALISM.

neo-martyr Saint* martyred after the end of the Roman persecutions.

Neonomianism Radical Arminian doctrine proposed by Richard Baxter* whereby good works* and morality are necessary conditions for salvation*.

neo-Orthodoxy Theology that recovers the distinctive ideas and themes of the orthodox theologians of the Reformation* and reverses the liberalism* of the nineteenth and early twentieth centuries. In contrast to the historical quest of the liberals, neo-Orthodoxy emphasized the transcendence and "otherness" of God, the reality of sin, the uniqueness of Christ as a mediator* between God and humanity, and the redeeming power of revelation*. Neo-Orthodoxy carried forward the premises of dialectical theology* or crisis theology* and was first expressed in Karl Barth's* *Commentary on the Romans* where the risen Christ is the fullness of God seen through the eyes of faith*. Barth expanded his teaching beyond that of the verbal inspiration* of the Scriptures to point to the subjective and personal appropriation of the revelation of God in Christ. Other major neo-Orthodox theologians include Emil Brunner*, whose central motif was personal encounter* with God, and Rudolf Bultmann* and Friedrich Gogarten* who reinterpreted the Scriptures in radical terms of existentialism* and a remythologizing hermeneutic.

neo-Pentecostalism Charismatic renewal* in mainline churches* that introduced to a larger audience many of the classic Pentecostal doctrines and practices and crossed traditional doctrinal lines.

neophyte (Gk., newly planted) Newly baptized Christian monk, nun, or priest; novice*.

neo-Scholasticism Also, neo-Thomism. Renewed interest in the scholastic thought of St. Thomas Aquinas* and other scholastic theologians, promoted by Pope Leo XIII's letter, *Aeterni Patris*. Leo urged philosophers to "combat the speculative and practical errors of modern philosophy" by reappropriating the teachings of the major Christian writers from the Middle Ages, such as Thomas Aquinas*. Neo-Thomists are principally interpreters of medieval thought or builders of Thomistic systems. Among the most able neo-Thomists are Etienne Gilson*, Jacques Maritain*, Martin Grabmann, Pierre Mondonnet, Maurice De Wulf, Bernard Lonergan*, and Desire Mercier*.

Neresheim Abbey in Neresheim, Germany, founded in 1095 by Count Hartmann and Countess Adalheid von Dilingen-Dyburg as a canonical monastery and converted in 1106 to a Benedictine monastery. Its Romanesque church was consecrated in 1119. However, during the next five centuries, the monastery suffered depredations and devastation. But in 1745 Balthasar Neumann drew up plans to renovate the abbey. His son, Ignaz, completed the work, and it was consecrated in 1792. The ceiling frescoes* and the decorative painting are the work of Martin Knoller. The monastery was dissolved in 1802, and despite the patronage of King Friedrich, it went into decline. In 1966 it was closed.

Nerezi Church of St. Panteleimon at Nerezi, near Skopje in Macedonia*, built by a member of the Byzantine Comnenos dynasty in 1164. It has five domes, the corner domes being square and the central one an octagon.

Nerses IV, St. (1102–1173) Birth name: Klayetsi. Armenian catholicos* (1166–1173). He promoted closer relations with the Byzantine Church*. He wrote extensively and is best known for his poems on the destruction of Edessa* and the history of salvation*. Feast day: August 3 (Armenian Church*); August 13 (Western Church*).

Nerses of Lampron, St. (1153–1198) Armenian bishop and theologian. He was bishop of Tarsus for many years. He was an active proponent of union with the Roman and Greek churches. Feast day: Third Monday after Assumption (Armenian Church*); July 17 (Western Church*).

Nerses the Great, St. (c. 326–373) Armenian catholicos*. A descendant of Gregory the Illuminator*, he married a princess, but after her death entered the church and became catholicos in 353. He identified the Armenian Church* with the people and, at the Council of Ashtishat* in about 365 he instituted a number of reforms of worship, marriage, and the sacraments*. He built schools and hospitals and trained evangelists. He came into conflict with the court and was exiled and later poisoned on the king's orders. Feast day: November 19.

nesaha-abat (Ge'ez, father of penance) In the Ethiopian Church, a confessor-priest.

neshkar (lit., wafer) In the Armenian Rite*, the wafer*.

Nestor, St. (d. 250) Bishop of Pamphylia and martyr* who was crucified in the Decian persecutions*. Feast day: February 26.

Nestorian Church When the Council of Ephesus* anathematized Nestorius* and his supporters, they formed a separate church based in Persia with a great theological school at Edessa*, where a school of Nestorian theology developed under Ibas. Later the center of Nestorian theology moved to Nisibis* in the school founded there by Barsumas, a pupil of Ibas. The patriarch* of the Nestorian Church resided at Seleucia-Ctesiphon* on the Tigris, "by the waters of the River of Babylon," a standard phrase used in the patriarch's epistles to the faithful. His seat moved to Baghdad after the Arab Conquest. In the Middle Ages, the Nestorian Church was one of the largest in the world, extending from modern Baghdad to Beijing in China, with thousands of bishops and missionaries. The church was wiped out in the Mongol invasions of the thirteenth and fourteenth centuries, but a remnant survives in the mountains of Kurdistan and in the United States. See also ASSYRIAN CHURCH; CHURCH OF THE EAST.

Nestorianism Heresy which was condemned at the Third Ecumenical Council at Ephesus* in 431. It rejected the traditional Alexandrian theology that Jesus Christ was a single person, truly man and God, that the two natures remain fused in their union within one person. Nestorius* abhorred the concept of the divine nature undergoing suffering or change, and he wanted to hold the two natures separate, distinct, and unaltered. There is still controversy over whether he was as clearly heretical as his opponents maintained.

It was impossible, Nestorius argued, for God to change, suffer, and be tempted. To solve this problem, Nestorius advanced the theory that Jesus combined in himself two distinct elements, the divine and the human, and the result was a conjunction, not a union, in the person of Jesus Christ. The human Christ had the Spirit of the Godhead bestowed upon him while the divine took upon himself the form of a servant. Thus

Mary was not Theotokos* or the Mother of God, but Christotokos*, or Christ-bearer. In trying to separate the divine and the human in Christ, Nestorius erred by not defining the bond that held the two natures together.

Nestorius (c. 351–c. 451) Heresiarch*. Born of Persian parents, Nestorius studied under Theodore of Mopsuestia* and became a monk and presbyter* at Antioch*. His fame as a preacher led Emperor Theodosius to elevate him in 428 to the throne of the patriarch* of Constantinople*. Soon he was embroiled in the controversy bearing his name. At the Council of Ephesus* he was anathematized as a heretic and deposed. The emperor exiled him to his monastery at Antioch* and later to the Great Oasis in Egypt, where he died, but not before writing an autobiographical refutation of the charges against him.

Neumann, St. John Nepomucene (1811–1860) American bishop. A Bohemian immigrant, he was bishop of Philadelphia*. In 1963 he became the first Roman Catholic priest to be beatified. Feast day: January 5.

Neumann, Therese (1898–1962) Stigmatic Bavarian visionary. Having lost her eyesight and her mobility in 1918/19, she regained her eyesight in 1923 and her ability to walk in 1925. During Lent* 1926 she began to have visions of the Passion* and received the stigmata* which remained visible and bled on Fridays. She is said to have had no solid food after 1922 and no nourishment of any kind except Holy Communion* after 1927. She is also credited with the ability during her visions to read people's minds and to discern the authenticity of relics*.

neume 1. Sign employed in early plainsong* to indicate melody. 2. In plainsong, a prolonged group of notes, sung to a single syllable, especially at the end of the hallelujah* and in the responsories of the Mass*.

Ne'us Crestiyan (lit., young Christian) In the Ethiopian tradition, a catechumen*.

Neutral Text Name given to a text of the Greek Testament derived from the Alexandrian but free from later admixture and corruption. The two leading representatives of the Neutral Text are the Codex Vaticanus* and the Codex Sinaiticus*.

Nevin, John Williamson (1803–1886) American theologian, professor at the Western Theological Seminary and the German Reformed Church Seminary, and the originator of the Mercersburg theology*. He advocated the real mystical presence* of Christ in the Eucharist*.

Nevius, John Livingston (1829–1893) American missionary to China who devised the Nevius Method of mission work. The four principles of the method were: 1. Each Christian missionary should support himself by his own work and witness. 2. Indigenous Christians should be able to take responsibility and carry on the work if foreign missionaries leave. 3. Churches should be built in the native style and with indigenous resources. 4. Churches should exercise great care in choosing the right people for the mission field*.

New American Bible First official Catholic translation of the Bible into English, replacing the Douay-Reims Version (1970, 1987).

New American Standard Bible English translation of the Bible by 58 translators who adopted a conservative approach to their work. (1963, 1970).

New Apostolic Church Breakaway church founded in 1863 by Heinrich Geyer excommunicated by the senior apostle of the Catholic Apostolic Church*. It was less millennial than the parent group and was led by a patriarch* regarded as the visible incarnation of Christ on earth. It flourished in Nazi Germany and has spread to many parts of the world.

new birth Fact of being born again* or being born from above and of the Spirit on the basis of John 3:3, where Jesus tells Nicodemus, "Unless one is born again, he cannot see the kingdom of God."

new covenant 1. The new covenant for human salvation instituted by the work of Christ and sealed by his sacrificial blood. 2. The New Testament as distinct from and as the fulfillment of the Old Testament (Jer. 31:3).

New Delhi Assembly The Third Assembly of the World Council of Churches* held in New Delhi in 1961 with the theme, "Jesus Christ, Light of the World." It was attended by 577 delegates and 1,006 participants. The assembly approved merger of the World Council of Churches with the International Missionary Council* and the addition of two churches, including the Russian Orthodox Church*. It overwhelmingly approved the Trinitarian formula which stated that "The WCC is a fellowship of churches which confess the Lord Jesus Christ as God and Savior according to the Scriptures, and therefore seek to fulfill together their common calling to the glory of the one God, Father, Son, and the Holy Spirit."

New England theology Revisionist Calvinism* formulated by Jonathan Edwards*, who introduced the concept of inclined will to modify strict Calvinism. In his work, *Freedom of the Will,* Edwards taught that the Holy Spirit* inclines the human will so that it responds positively to divine grace*. He thus struck a middle ground between older Calvinists who rejected revivals* and Arminians who denied predestination*. New England theology was further developed after Edwards's death by his son, Jonathan Edwards, Jr., Joseph Bellamy, Timothy Dwight*, and Nathaniel Taylor*, all of whom emphasized the reasonableness of Christianity and the natural powers of the human will. By the nineteenth century, it had abandoned all pretense of historic Calvinism and had become a humanist manifesto.

New English Bible New translation of the Holy Bible in bold and less archaic English, the first such completely new translation since the Authorized Version* in 1611. The New English Bible was considered too literary and rested in part on unrepresentative scholarship. The New Testament was published in 1961 and the whole Bible in 1970.

New Evangelicalism Conservative Evangelical movement from the 1940s to the 1960s to reform Fundamentalism* and restore the vitality and influence of Christianity in society. The term was coined by Harold John Ockenga*, cofounder of Fuller Theological Seminary*, who called it "progressive Fundamentalism with a social message." It sought to rid Fundamentalism* of its anti-cultural and anti-intellectual image. The movement received considerable boost from the rise of Billy Graham* as an international preacher and the foundation of the National Association of Evangelicals*, Youth for Christ*, and *Christianity Today* under the editorship of Carl F. H. Henry*. Beside Ockenga and Henry, New Evangelicalism was promoted by a number of brilliant theologians, including Edward J. Carnell*, Donald Bloesch*, J. I. Packer*, and John Stott*. By the 1960s and 1970s it came to be called simply Evangelicalism*, and the next two decades saw it diversify into many special interest movements. Yet, the network of scholars and seminaries that still carries the Evangelical message remains influential in American politics and religion.

New Fire Lighting and blessing of the new fire at the opening of the Paschal Vigil*. Light from the church lamps was preserved from Good Friday* or Maundy Thursday* until the beginning of the vigil* on Saturday evening. The lamps were brought back into the church and from them all other lamps and candles were lighted.

New Hampshire Confession (1833) Baptist confessional* statement espousing a moderate Calvinism*.

New Haven theology Theological position associated with Timothy Dwight* and Nathaniel Taylor*. It represented a further departure from Calvinism* than New England theology. Sometimes known as Taylorism, it was a form of Calvinism shorn of all its essentials and designed to provide a rational basis for the revivalism* of the Second Great Awakening*. In contrast to the Calvinism of Samuel Hopkins*, known as "Consistent Calvinism*," which emphasized total divine sovereignty and human depravity, New Haven theology postulated voluntary sin as a moral disposition or tendency. The satisfaction aspect of the Atonement* was replaced by a governmental theory under which universal salvation* was possible. Taylor made concessions to reason in order to reduce the appeal of the Unitarians and to support experiential religious conversion. The New Haven theology was a powerful engine for revival and reform in the first half of the nineteenth century, particularly through the efforts of Taylor's fellow Yale graduate, Lyman Beecher*.

New Hermeneutic Interpretative approach of Rudolf Bultmann* and his followers who explored the relationship of language to meaning and events in their study of the New Testament.

New Jerusalem Heavenly city awaiting the believers and the redeemed, described in Revelation.

New Jerusalem, Church of the Also, Swedenborgians. Sect organized in 1787 by the followers of Emanuel Swedenborg*. Swedenborg never preached a sermon nor did he have disciples. At his death he left 20 volumes of his works in Latin which were translated into many languages and gained adherents in many countries. These adherents organized their first church under Robert Hindmarsh, a Methodist in London. The first general conference of the sect was held in London in 1789. In 1792 a church was established in Baltimore, Maryland, and in 1817 the General Convention of the New Jerusalem met in Philadelphia*. Another branch of the church established its headquarters at Bryn Athyn, Pennsylvania. The church has its own liturgy and observes baptism* and the Lord's Supper*. There are seminaries at Bryn Athyn, Cambridge, Massachusetts, and Islington, London. There is a Swedenborg Foundation in New York with an active publishing program.

New Lights New England Congregational* preachers who supported revivals, especially the Great Awakening* of the 1740s when converts were "new-lighted" by the Spirit of God, and they experienced sudden and dramatic conversions* with mystical overtones.

New martyrs Title given to the Orthodox martyrs* who were killed by Muslims or Communists. According to the Koran, all apostates* from Islam, non-Muslims who insult Islam, and those who seek to convert Muslims are put to death.

Among those regarded as new martyrs are: Monk Makarios (d. 1507) and tailor John of Ionnina, for defying the Muslim rulers by proclaiming the gospel; Philothei (d. 1589), leader of Christian revival movement; Kosmas Aitolos* (d. 1779) and Theodore Sladich (d. 1788), for disturbing religious peace; Patriarch Cyril VI* (d. 1821) and Gregory V* (d. 1821), killed in reprisal against Christian rebels; Thomas Paschidis (d. 1890) and Chrysostom of Smyrna (d. 1922), for questioning Muslim hegemony; Demetrios Doukas of Philadelphia* (d. 1657), for returning to Christianity after having embraced Islam; Michael Mavroudis (d. 1544), Chrestos the Albanian (d. 1748), and George of Ioannina (d. 1838), for breaking Muslim law; Akylina of Chalkidike (d. 1764), for refusing to marry a Muslim; Zlata of Moglena (d. 1795) and Panteleimon Dousa, a child of 12 (d. 1848), in retaliation against Christians; Ahmet (d. 1582), Hasan (d. 1814), Constantine the Turk (d. 1819), and Boris the Pomak (d. 1913), for converting from Islam to Christianity.

Under the Bolsheviks in the Soviet Union, millions of new martyrs were added to the rolls. Only a few of these names are recorded. They include Vladimir Bogoiavlenskii, metropolitan* of Kiev*, Veniamin Kazanskii, and Seraphim Chichagov. During World War II the Nazis killed many Christians, such as Archbishop Gorazd Pavlik, of Prague*, and Plato Jovanovic (d. 1941). The number of anonymous new martyrs runs into millions. Of these the Arab rulers have killed 7 million, the Turks at least 15 million, the Soviets 2 million, Chinese Communists 400,000, and the lesser Communist regimes about 200,000.

new measures Style of revivalism* followed by Charles Finney* that highlighted the place of human effort as a catalyst in revivals. These included placing public pressure on individuals for making a decision on conversion, sustained prayer, lay participation, and the anxious bench*.

New Revised Standard Version English translation of the Bible, published in 1989. A revision of the Revised Standard Version* (1952) particulary in order to incorporate inclusive language.

New Rome Designation of Constantinople* by Constantine the Great* as the Eastern capital just as Rome* was the Western capital.

New School/New Side Presbyterians favoring revivalism* in the first half of the nineteenth century. It originated in the Second Great Awakening* during the early part of the nineteenth century which brought together pro-revival Presbyterians and Congregationalists. It was part of a broader Evangelical movement until it came under attack from the Old Side or Old School Presbyterians. The two sides were soon engaged in skirmishes over the theological innovations of the New School, especially departures from Calvinist orthodoxy by Samuel Hopkins*, Nathaniel Taylor*, Albert Barnes*, and Lyman Beecher*. The New School also favored a more lax interpretation of confessionalism* and church discipline*. From 1837 until 1869 the New School existed as a separate denomination. However, the New School became more doctrinally conservative after the Auburn Declaration* of 1837 and in 1852 the Plan of Union with Congregationalists was terminated.

New Testament The 27 books of the Bible proclaiming the new covenant* of Jesus Christ. It includes the four Gospels, Acts, Epistles, and the Book of Revelation.

New Testament criticism Investigation of the date, authorship, composition, and other elements of the New Testament as historical and literary texts. The term has a generally negative connotation because many of the scholars who engage in such criticism are hostile to the orthodox doctrines of the faith, or seem influenced in their work by skeptical or anti-supernaturalist convictions, or reach conclusions based on inappropriate techniques. New Testament criticism may be divided into five categories, each of which has evolved into a separate discipline: textual, linguistic, historical, literary, and redaction.

Textual criticism*, or lower criticism*, is the primary level which seeks to determine the original words, particularly as they have been altered in the course of the transmission of the text from one language to another or from one copyist to another in the centuries before printing. Linguistic criticism is concerned with matters of grammar and philology, idiosyncracies of usage, relationship of words to one another, connotations and nuances, and idiomatic expressions peculiar to one language. It also traces the migration of ideas from Aramaic to Hebrew to Greek to Latin.

Historical criticism is cultural criticism because it involves placing words, events, and ideas in their cultural context and also relating allusions and references to their original sources. Literary criticism*, or higher criticism*, builds on the results of textual or lower criticism and deals with issues of authorship, sources, composition, literary form, date and place and time of writing. Redaction criticism* examines the peculiar style of each New Testament writer and the ideas and beliefs that motivated him.

New York Bible Society Second oldest Bible society* founded in the United States in 1809 and incorporated in 1866. It has provided the millions of immigrants who landed in New York with the Scriptures in their mother tongue. It sponsored the New International Version (NIV) in 1978.

Newbigin, James Edward Lesslie (1909–1998) Missionary bishop and theologian. After a short period as a Student Christian Movement* secretary, he was ordained and in 1936 went as a missionary of the Church of Scotland* to India. When the Church of South India* was formed, he became one of its first bishops. In 1959 he left India to become general secretary of the International Missionary Council* but returned to India to become bishop of Madras in 1965. During his later years he taught and pastored in Birmingham, England. Newbigin's writings cover many subjects, reflecting his interest in missiology*, ecclesiology*, and apologetics. They include *The Household of God* (1953), *Foolishness to the Greeks* (1986), and *The Gospel in a Pluralist Society* (1989). His later writings helped to direct Christian attention to mission to the post-Christian West.

Newman Club Roman Catholic organization for college-age youth.

Newman, John Henry (1801–1890) English cardinal. He was born into an Evangelical family. At Oxford University, he was converted to Tractarianism* under the influence of E. B. Pusey*, J. Keble*, and R. H. Froude who revealed to him the critical mission of the church as an instrument of God. In 1823 he was appointed vicar* of St. Mary's, the University church in Oxford. There he began a campaign to reconcile the Church of England* with the Church of Rome through a se-

ries of tracts known as *Tracts for the Times*. The series came to an end with Tract No. 90 by which time he had serious doubt about the apostolicity* of the Church of England. He also published a study of an earlier heresy in *The Arians of the Fourth Century* which convinced him of the role of heresy in destroying faith.

In 1843 Newman resigned St. Mary's and two years later was received into the Roman Catholic Church. In the same year he published his *Development of Christian Doctrine*. His early career in the Catholic Church was undistinguished until in 1864 he published his autobiography, *Apologia pro Vita Sua*, in response to a personal attack on him by Charles Kingsley*. In 1870 he published *Grammar of Assent* in defense of the faith and in 1879 he was made cardinal. Although a prince of the church, Newman's opposition to papal infallibility* was not well received at the First Vatican Council*. He also came under criticism for his description of faith* as more a matter of intellectual assent to theological propositions than the working of divine grace*. He was also a hymn writer, and among his best-loved hymns is "Lead, Kindly Light."

Newman's influence on the church, both Anglican and Roman Catholic, has been great. He is conceded even by Protestants as one of the keenest minds of his generation and also an able theologian whose views were developed in treatises, such as *Lectures on the Prophetical Office of the*

John Henry Newman

Church (1837) and *Lectures on Justification* (1838). His ideas on education, liberty of conscience, the authority of the Bible, and the role of the episcopate* were validated by the Second Vatican Council*. In 1991 he was declared venerable*.

Newton, Benjamin Wills (1807–1899) Plymouth Brethren* leader. He began his ministry in Plymouth through the influence of J. N. Darby*. Later he and Darby fell out over prophecy* and church order*. In 1847 he was accused of heresy but recanted. He left Plymouth in that year and ministered in Bayswater, London, for many years.

Newton, John (1725–1807) English hymn writer and divine. A sailor on slaving ships, he was converted during a particularly violent storm and thereafter dedicated his life to Christ. He gave up the sea in 1764 and accepted the curacy of Olney, where he collaborated with William Cowper* in compiling the *Olney Hymns* (1779). It included the perennial favorite, "Amazing Grace," as well as other well-loved hymns, as "How Sweet the Name of Jesus Sounds" and "Glorious Things of Thee Are Spoken." Next year he was appointed rector* of St. Mary, Woolnoth, London. He had great influence in Evangelical circles, especially on William Wilberforce*, Hannah More*, and George Whitefield*.

Newton, Sir Isaac (1642–1717) English scientist and theologian who believed that his every discovery was communicated to him by the Holy Spirit*. Although unorthodox in his beliefs, regarding the Trinity* and infant baptism*, he contributed almost as extensively to church history and chronology as he did to his scientific interests. His belief in God rested on the admirable beauty and order of the natural world. He shared millenarian interests with the Cambridge Platonists* and wrote *Observations on the Prophecies of Daniel and the Apocalypse of St. John* (1733).

Niagara conferences Meetings dedicated to Bible study at Niagara-on-the-Lake, Ontario, during the closing decades of the nineteenth century, marking the beginning of the Bible conference movement. The first meeting held in Chicago in 1875 was attended by Nathaniel West, James H. Brookes*, W. J. Erdman, and H. M. Parsons. They,

along with A. J. Gordon*, met again the next year at Swampscott, Massachusetts, as the "Believers' Meeting for Bible Study." They continued to meet annually in Niagara-on-the-Lake from 1883 to 1897. The methods of the Bible readings and the topics discussed during the conference suggest the influence of the Plymouth Brethren* and anticipated twentieth-century Fundamentalism*.

Nicaea Town in Bithynia* in Asia Minor, close to Constantinople*, now Isnik in Turkey.

Nicaea, First Council of The First Ecumenical Council held in Nicaea, Bithynia*, in Asia Minor in 325, convoked by Emperor Constantine* to settle the Arian heresy. Of the attending bishops, about 225 in number, almost all were from the East and only four or five bishops represented the Western Church*. One of the Western bishops, Hosius* of Cordoba, presided over the council. To condemn Arianism*, the bishops sought a formula* to define orthodoxy*. The result of this effort was the creed of Nicaea, but it is not what is today known as the Nicene Creed* (the Niceno-Constantinopolitan Creed*). The creed was signed by almost all the bishops. Arius and his friends were thereupon

Council of Nicaea

anathematized and banished along with two bishops who refused to sign the creed. The council also dealt with the Melitian Schism* and the date of Easter*.

Nicaea, Second Council of Seventh Ecumenical Council convened by Irene, the widow of Constantine V, in 787 to deal with the issue of iconoclasm*. It tried to resolve the conflict between Emperor Leo and Constantine V on the one hand and the patriarch* of Constantinople* and the pope on the other over the issue of veneration* of images and icons of Christ and the saints*. The council met in eight sessions over a month and was attended by over 300 prelates, mostly from the West. It condemned the iconoclastic position and accepted as lawful the veneration* but not the adoration or worship of images. In addition, the council promulgated 22 disciplinary decrees.

Nicene Creed Creed issued in 325 by the First Council of Nicaea, the earliest and one of the shortest of the many Christian creeds approved by councils of bishops in the fourth and fifth centuries. It was the first to use the term *homoousios**. The emphases of the creed are on: 1. the sonship of Christ as distinct from the Logos*. 2. Ousia*, or being, shared by the Son and the Father. 3. The use of *begotten* in contradistinction to the Arian term, *made*. 4. The use of the words, "and became man." It had nothing after "and in the Holy Spirit" apart from a series of anathemas* against Arius's errors.

Niceno-Constantinopolitan Creed Creed agreed upon at the First Council of Constantinople* in 381 which enlarged the faith but not the actual creed of Nicaea, 325. Its authenticity is sometimes doubted by scholars because there is no mention of the creed in the four canons of the Council of Constantinople*, it is not mentioned in any documents until the Council of Chalcedon*, and it omits any reference to the *ousias* clause in the Nicene Creed*. Its second section on the person

Nicene Creed

We believe in one God the Father, the Almighty, maker of heaven and earth, of all that is seen and unseen;

We believe in one Lord, Jesus Christ, the only Son of God, eternally begotten of the Father,

God from God, Light from Light, true God from true God, begotten not made, one in being with the Father,

Through Him all things were made, For us men and for our salvation.

He came down from heaven, by the power of the Holy Spirit.

He was born of the Virgin Mary and became man,

For our sake He was crucified under Pontius Pilate; He suffered, and was buried.

On the third day He rose again in fulfillment of the Scriptures;

He ascended into heaven and is seated at the right hand of the Father.

He will come again in glory to judge the living and the dead.

And His kingdom will have no end.

We believe in the Holy Spirit, the Lord and giver of Life who proceeds from the Father.

With the Father and the Son He is worshiped and glorified.

He has spoken through the Prophets.

We believe in one holy catholic and apostolic church.

We acknowledge one baptism for the forgiveness of sins.

We look for the resurrection of the dead and the life of the world to come. Amen.

of Christ and third section on the Holy Spirit* are both much longer than in the Nicene Creed. In both the Eastern and Western churches*, the creed is used in the Eucharist*, and in the East it is used as a baptismal creed. In the Middle Ages the Filioque* clause was added to it in the West.

Nicephoros Callistus (c. 1256–1335) "Xanthopoulos." Byzantine historian and monk. His principal work is a church history which narrated in 18 books the history of the world from the birth of Christ to 610.

Nicephorus, St. (c. 758–829) Historian, confessor*, and patriarch*. He represented the emperor at the Second Council of Nicaea but later abandoned his office to found a monastery on the Propontis. He was recalled to Constantinople* and made patriarch by Emperor Constantine VI and his mother Irene. In return for this favor, the emperor asked him to rehabilitate the priest Joseph, who blessed the emperor's adulterous marriage. Nicephorus gave in to this demand, and it remained as a stain on his reputation. When Emperor Leo V began his campaign against iconoclasm*, Nicephoros opposed him and was thereupon deposed and banished. Here he spent his time writing the authoritative works on history that he is famous for: *Apologeticus Major* and *Apologeticus Minor; Historia Syntomos,* a history of Byzantium*; and *Chronographia*. In 847 he received the title of Confessor of the Faith. Feast day: June 2 (Greek Church); April 13 (Latin Church).

Niceta, St. (d. 414) Ecclesiastical writer. He was the author of *Explanatio Symboli,* a source for the history of the Apostles' Creed; *De Diversis Apellationibus* on the titles of Christ; *De Ratione Fidei* against Arianism*; and *De Spiritu Sancto* against the Pneumatomachi*. Feast day: June 22.

Nicetas Acominatos (1155/57–1217) Byzantine scholar, author of the *Treasury of Orthodoxy* in 27 books (1204–1210), a valuable source on the councils held between 1156 and 1166.

niche Recess in the wall of a church for a statue.

Nicholas I, St. (d. 867) Pope from 858. Royal by birth, Nicholas was one of the most forceful of early medieval popes and asserted papal authority over all who tried to diminish it, particularly Photius*, patriarch* of Constantinople*, Archbishop John of Ravenna, and Hincmar* of Reims. He invited Sts. Cyril and Methodius* to visit Rome* and tried to bring the Bulgars into the Catholic fold. Feast day: November 13.

Nicholas V (1389–1455) Pope from 1447. Birth name: Thomas Parentucelli. He was one of the first and probably the best of the Renaissance popes, and his personal life was blameless. He restored many ruined churches and founded the Vatican Library*. He decreed the jubilee* of 1450 and sent out legates to France and Germany to reform abuses. After the fall of Constantinople* in 1453, he made vain efforts to mobilize Christian princes against the Turks. He put down the revolt of Stefan Porcaro in Rome* against the papal regime and restored order in the states of the church.

Nicholas Cabasilas See CABASILAS/CAVASILAS, NICOLAUS.

Nicholas, Henry (1502–c. 1580) Also, Hendrik Niclaes. Founder of the Familists* sect.

Nicholas of Cusa (1401–1464) German philosopher and cardinal. He held a number of high positions in the Roman Catholic Church after obtaining a doctorate in canon law* in 1423. He was dean of St. Florin's in Coblenz, and was sent by Pope Eugenius IV* on a number of diplomatic missions to Constantinople*, Mainz*, Frankfurt, Nuremberg, and Vienna*. In 1448 Pope Eugenius V* made him cardinal and in 1450 he was made papal legate* in Germany, but was forced by the opposition of Duke Sigismund of Austria to flee in 1457. He built a hospital in Cusa, where he established his library. He was very learned and is considered a precursor of the Renaissance. He wrote a number of books on theology, sciences, geography, law, philosophy, and mysticism, the chief of them being *De Docta Ignorantia* (1440), *De Coniecturis* (1442), *Idiota* (1450), and *De Pace Fidei* (1453). His most famous work is *De Concordantia Catholica,* a plan for the reform of the church and empire.

Nicholas of Flue, St. (1417–1487) Swiss ascetic, known as Brother Klaus, the patron saint* of Switzerland. In 1467, influenced by the Friends of God*, he left his wife and 10 children to become a hermit in the Alps, where he lived for 19 years with no food except the Eucharist*. His reputation for sanctity* attracted many visitors from all over Europe who sought his advice. He was beatified in 1669 and canonized in 1947. Feast day: March 21; September 25 (in Switzerland).

Nicholas of Lyra (c. 1270–1349) Biblical expositor. He was a Franciscan minister of the provinces of France and Burgundy. He is best known for his two biblical commentaries, *Postillae Litterales* (1332–1333) and *Postillae Morales* (1339). His commentaries were often used as Sunday sermons. They went into over 100 editions between 1471 and 1600.

Nicholas of Myra, St. (fourth century) Legendary saint who morphed into Santa Claus* in the nineteenth and twentieth centuries. He is the patron saint* of Greece, Sicily, Russia, youth, and sailors. According to tradition, he was the bishop of Myra in Lycia and was imprisoned during the Diocletian persecution*. His cult* became popular in the West from about the eleventh century. His symbol is three bags of gold, the dowry he gave to three destitute children. Feast day: December 6.

St. Nicholas of Myra

Nicholas of Torentino (1245–1305) Augustinian friar* and miracle worker who is credited with over 300 miracles. He is the patron saint* of Lima, Peru, and Antwerp, Netherlands.

St. Nicodemus of the Holy Mountain

Nicholson, William Patteson (1876–1959) Irish evangelist. Converted in 1896, he was ordained as an evangelist in the Presbyterian Church. He became a powerful revivalist* whose crusades in Ulster, Glasgow, Cambridge*, Australia, and South Africa drew thousands.

Nicodemus, Gospel of Apocryphal work, dating from the fourth century, consisting of the *Acts of Pilate** and *Descent of Christ* into the underworld.

Nicodemus of the Holy Mountain, St. (c. 1749–1809) Greek monk and writer. He lived in Mount Athos* for most of his life, writing a number of devotional works. Among them were *Philocalia* and *Pidalion*. He also published the Greek edition of the *Spiritual Exercises** of Ignatius Loyola*. Feast day: July 14 (Eastern Church*).

Nicolai (c. 1835–1912) Birth name: Ivan Kasatkin*. Russian Orthodox missionary to Japan and founder of the Orthodox Church of Japan. Arriving in Japan in 1861, he acquired a knowledge of Chinese and Japanese and began clandestine evangelization, since Christianity was a banned religion. He gained three secret converts before returning to Russia to found the Orthodox Mission. When the legal prohibition of Christianity was lifted in 1873, he moved to Tokyo, where he built a church. He was created archbishop in 1906. Although his work experienced a setback during the Russo-Japanese War of 1904–1905, his church had 30,000 members at his death. See also KASATKIN, NICOLAI IVAN DMITRIYEVICH.

Nicolai, Philipp (1556–1608) German composer. From his *Freden-Spiegel des Ewigen Lebens* (1599) came three monumental German hymns for which he wrote both the text and the tune, of which *Wachet Auf, Sleepers Awake,* and *How Brightly Shines the Morning Star* are the best-loved. *Wachet Auf* is considered the greatest of all chorales. Many composers, including Bach* and Mendelssohn*, have used these words and melodies in their compositions.

Niebuhr, Helmut Richard (1894–1962) Neo-Orthodox theologian, minister, and professor of Christian ethics at Yale University from 1931 to 1962. Turning away from his early liberalism*, he became the voice of the left wing of neo-Orthodoxy*, seeking for the restoration of Reformation* ideals in American culture. Among his books were *Social Sources of Denominationalism* (1929), *The Kingdom of God in America* (1937), *The Meaning of Revelation* (1941), *Christ and Culture* (1951), and *Radical Monotheism and Western Culture* (1961). In his works Niebuhr presents an integrative vision and helpful typologies for analyzing the paradox of faith*.

Niebuhr, Reinhold (1892–1971) Neo-Orthodox* theologian who served for 32 years as professor at Union Theological Seminary*, New York. He helped found Americans for Democratic Action, the National Council of Churches*, and New York's liberal party, and he considered himself a Socialist for a while. In 1941 he founded the influential *Christianity and Crisis* as a vehicle for his liberal ideas. He coined the term *Christian Realism* to distinguish his ideas from liberal theology as well as Barthianism. Among his 17 major books were *Moral Man and Immoral Society* (1932), *The Nature and Destiny of Man* (1941), *Faith and His-*

tory (1949), and *Christian Realism and Social Problems* (1953).

Niemoller, Martin (1892–1984) German Lutheran pastor. Ordained in 1924, he was appointed in 1931 as pastor at Berlin Dahlem. Although he at first welcomed National Socialism, he was alarmed by the pagan attitudes of Nazi rule and joined Bon-

Martin Niemoller

hoeffer* and Franz Hildebrandt in opposing Hitler. He supported the Confessing Church* in opposition to Nazi-led churches and also formed and became president of the Pastors' Emergency League in 1933. In 1937 he was arrested and sent to a concentration camp, where he remained until 1945. After the war he became a symbol of the healing process in German society. He served as a president of the World Council of Churches* from 1961 to 1967.

nihil obstat (Lat., nothing hinders) Formula approving the publication of a book after receiving ecclesiastical clearance that nothing in it is contrary to Roman Catholic doctrine.

Nihilianism Christological doctrine that Christ's human nature was an illusion. It was defended by theologians, such as Peter of Poitiers, but condemned by Pope Alexander III* in 1170 and 1177.

Nikon (1605–1681) Patriarch* of Moscow*, considered the greatest in the Russian church. He became a monk at the Solovetsky Monastery after the early deaths of his three children and after separating from his wife, who became a nun. He became hegumen* or abbot of the Kozheozerski Community in 1643 and later archimandrite* of the Novospasskiy Monastery in Moscow. He was promoted by Czar Alexis to the patriarchate in 1652 and allowed to exercise considerable power as regent in the czar's frequent absences from Moscow*. Nikon made many reforms in the Orthodox Liturgy, bringing it into conformity with Greek and Ukrainian liturgies, but aroused the opposition of a traditionalist group who called themselves "Old Believers*." As a result Nikon was deposed and exiled to a remote monastery, but was pardoned before his death.

Patriarch Nikon

Nikon the Metanoeite, St. (c. 930–1000) Greek monk, itinerant preacher, and saint*. He is known for his missionary work among non-Christian native Greeks in Lacedaimon, pagan Slavs, and apostates* to Islam in Crete. He died in the monastery he had established near Sparta. Feast day: November 26.

Nil Sorsky, St. (1433–1508) Russian monk and mystic. During a visit to Mount Athos* he trained himself in the contemplative prayer life of Hesychasm*. Returning to Russia, he founded a hermitage near Beloozero, where he introduced and wrote the rule for the Russian monastic institution known as the *skete** guided by a spiritual father known as *staretz*.

Niles, Daniel Thambyrajah (1908–1970) Tamil evangelist and ecumenical leader. He gave the keynote address at the founding of the World Council of Churches* in 1948 and was one of its six presidents in 1968. He wrote 45 hymns and many books, including *Preaching the Gospel of the Resurrection* (1953).

Nilus the Ascetic (d. c. 430) Bishop of Ancyra. He was a disciple of St. John Chrysostom* who became the founder and superior* of a monastery near Ancyra. His many writings on ascetic and moral subjects include *De Monachorum Praestantia, De Monastica Exercitatione, De Voluntaria Paupertate,* and a collection of 1,061 letters.

nimbus Halo* or light placed in Christian art around the head of Jesus Christ, the Virgin Mary*, or the saints*. Compare aura*, halo.

Nine Saints Nine monks from Syria who helped in the fifth century to evangelize* Ethiopia, translate the Bible into Ge'ez*, and introduce monasticism*. Their names were Al, Shema, Aragawi, Garima, Pantaleon, Leqanos, Afsie, Gougo, and Yemata.

Ninety-Five Theses, The Summons to academic debate that became, unintentionally, the first public declaration of the Reformation* nailed by Luther* to the door of the Castle Church in Wittenberg* in 1517. They were hardly radical and were not designed to force a breach with the papacy. The more important theses were: that penance* implies repentance*, not priestly confession*; that mortification* of the flesh is a useless exercise unless accompanied by inward repentance; that the merits of Christ alone avail for the forgiveness of sins, not the works prescribed by the church; that the pope has no power of the keys, and that the real treasure of the church is the gospel of the grace* of God in Jesus Christ.

Nineveh, Fast of Pre-Lenten three-day fast, observed in all the Eastern churches*, except the Byzantine. In the Armenian Church*, it is called aratshavoratz*.

Luther's Theses

Ninian, St. (fifth or sixth century) "Apostle of Scotland." He was largely responsible, along with St. Columba*, for the conversion of Picts in East Scotland. His monastic base at Whithorn in southwest Scotland became a center of training and mission. His tomb at Whithorn was a medieval shrine. Feast day: September 16.

Nino, St. (d. 330) Missionary and apostle who began the conversion of Georgia to Christianity. According to Rufinus*, she was a Cappadocian slave who performed many miracles to convert Queen Nana and King Mirian of Georgia. She built the first Georgian church at Mtskheta, near Tbilisi. Feast day: January 14.

Nisibis City in Asia Minor, transit point of the caravans between east and west in the ancient world. It became a Christian center at an early date. The city's first bishop was Jacob, celebrated by Ephraem* in his *Carmina Nisibena*. He also founded the School of Nisibis, where Ephraem taught. But the School of Nisibis began properly

with Narsai* after the closure of the School of the Persians at Edessa* in 489. The most famous metropolitan* of Nisibis in the fifth century was Barsumas, who ensured the triumph of Nestorianism* in Persia.

nithi mar (Syr., "let him come, O my lord") In the Assyrian Church*, invocation* of the Holy Spirit* upon the Holy Communion*.

Nitrian Desert Also, Desert of Scete*; Nitrian Valley; (Arab.) Wadi al Natrun. Region between Alexandria* and Cairo west of the mouths of the Nile River, where Christian monasticism* flourished in the fourth century. The first monastic settlement in the desert, which runs diagonally across the tip of the Libyan Desert, was by Amun, one of the Tall Brothers*. At the time of Macarius the Egyptian, there were more than 5,000 monks living in the area in lauras or clusters of cells. Their teaching and lives are recorded in *Apothegmata Patrum* and related works. Four monasteries still survive.

Wadi al Natrun in the Nitrian Desert

NIV New International Version.

'nkar In the Armenian Church*, ikons.

nobis quoque (Lat., to us also) Eleventh section of the Roman canon* beginning, "To us sinners, your servants, also grant some part . . . with all your saints."

Noble Guard Papal bodyguard consisting of 77 men commanded by a Roman prince. They were instituted by Pope Pius VII* in 1801 but were disbanded in 1970.

Nocturn 1. In the medieval church, the service of

prayer held at night. 2. In the contemporary Roman Catholic Church, the night office of mattins* or one of its three divisions. In the 1568 Roman Breviary*, there were three nocturns* on Sundays and major feasts. Nocturns generally consist of groups of Psalms with an antiphon* for each psalm, followed by a versicle*, Pater Noster*, a short prayer, and readings from the Bible, the Lives of the Saints, or a homily* on the Gospel of the day, followed by a responsory*.

node Knob in the stem of a chalice*.

Noel (Fr., Christmas) 1. Christmas*, the Yuletide. 2. Christmas carol of the same name. 3. Expression of Christmas spirit or joy.

noetic Relating to the mind or intellect.

nolo episcopare (Lat., I do not desire to become bishop) Formula expressing reluctance to accept nomination to an ecclesiastical office.

nomen sacrum Sacred name of God, either as a sacred monogram or as a name.

nominal Christian Formal member of a church who does not take the demands of Christian discipleship seriously.

Nommenson, Ludwig Ingwer (1834–1918) German missionary to Indonesia, known as the "Apostle of the Bataks." He went to Sumatra in 1857 and was able to convert many Barak chiefs. He used the pivotal influence of the tribal chiefs for the expansion and upbuilding of the church. By the time he died there were over 180,000 Baraks converted as a result of his labors.

Nomocanon In the Eastern Church*, a collection of ecclesiastical canons and imperial laws arranged topically. The earliest nomocanon* was compiled by John Scholasticus.

Nonconformity Non-Anglican Protestants, such as Methodists*, Presbyterians*, Baptists*, Pentecostals*, and Congregationalists*, who did not belong to the national Church of England*. The term is not much used in Scotland where it refers to Episcopalians and others outside the national

Presbyterian Church of Scotland*. Term first used in the Act of Uniformity* in 1662 and the penal acts following the Restoration. Nonconformists were known earlier as dissenters* and later as free churchmen.

None The last of the Little Hours of the Divine Office* appointed to be recited at the ninth hour, or at 3:00 P.M.

noqusho In the Syrian Rite, a tongueless bronze cup struck with a metal rod during important moments in the liturgy.

Norbert, St. (c. 1080–1134) German founder of the Premonstratensians*. Born of a noble family, he gave up his position at the imperial court, distributed his goods to the poor, received ordination, and became an itinerant preacher. In 1182 he founded a community in Premontre which eventually became the Premonstratensian Order. Norbert was made archbishop of Magdeburg in 1126. He was canonized by Gregory XIII* in 1582. Feast day: June 6.

norma normans (Lat., the rule ruling) The Holy Scripture as "the only rule and norm according to which all doctrine and teachers must be appraised and judged".

norma normata (Lat., the rule ruled) The creeds and confessions that are standards in a church, but are subservient to Scripture.

Norris, J. Frank (1877–1952) Fundamentalist Baptist minister. His first pastorate* was the McKinney Avenue Baptist Church in Dallas, Texas. Later he moved to the First Baptist Church, Fort Worth, Texas (1909–1952), serving simultaneously as pastor of Temple Baptist in Detroit, Michigan (1935–1948), and president of Baptist Bible Seminary (1939–1950). During this period, he emerged as a leader of the hardcore Fundamentalists. In his papers, especially *The Fundamentalist,* he attacked Catholics, liberals, opponents of inerrancy*, and others.

North India, Church of Church founded in 1970 through the merger of the Council of Baptist Churches, the Church of the Brethren*, the

Methodist Church, and the United Church. The church combines Episcopal*, Presbyterian*, Baptist*, and Congregational* elements in its doctrine and practice.

Northern Thebaid Constellation of monasteries in Russia's northern provinces, an icy wilderness.

Northfield conferences Bible conferences held in Northfield, Massachusetts, during the latter part of the nineteenth century under the leadership of D. L. Moody* which eventually led to the founding of the Student Volunteer Movement*.

Norwich Famous English Cathedral of the Holy and Undivided Trinity, founded as a monastic church under the Rule of St. Benedict* by Bishop Herbert of Losinga in 1096. It is a Norman building with a fifteenth-century spire* and vaulted roofs. It was destroyed by fire in 1171 and destroyed by a mob in 1272. It has one of the longest naves* in England and one of the finest central towers. It includes the Jesus Chapel, the Bauchun Chapel, and St. Luke's Chapel. The late Norman Bishop's throne is in the basilican* position behind the altar.

notes of the church (Lat., *Notae Ecclesiae*) The four identification marks according to the Niceno-Constantinopolitan Creed* of unity, holiness, catholicity, and apostolicity. In post-Reformation controversy, Roman Catholic theology has added others, such as magisterium* (the church has the exclusive authority to teach and govern), infallibility* (the church cannot err in matters of faith and morals, and indefectibility* (the church will endure until the end of time). 2. See also MARKS OF THE CHURCH.

Notes on the New Testament (1755) One of John Wesley's principal works, regarded as a doctrinal standard in the Methodist Church. The *Notes* manifest his Evangelical doctrines and his Arminianism*. It relied on prior work of J. A. Bengel*.

notitia (Lat., understanding) Intellect as one of the components of faith*.

Notker Labeo (c. 950–1022) Also, Notker the German; Notker III of St. Gall. He was the most no-table German vernacular writer of his time who translated the Psalms into Old High German.

Notker "the Stammerer," Balbulus (c. 840–912) Benedictine monk, librarian, and master of the school in the monastery* of St. Gall in Switzerland. He is the author of many literary works, including the *Liber Hymnorum,* a life of St. Gall*, a martyrology*, and a life of Charlemagne*.

Notre Dame, Paris Cathedral Church of Paris, built in the Early Gothic* style, on the Ile de la Cite, the heart of Paris and the central point in France. All geographical distances are measured from here. It is the unofficial national church of France. Its construction was begun in 1163, and it was consecrated in 1182. The west front was added in 1200–1220. The church is large enough to accommodate 9,000 people. The church was desecrated during the French Revolution when the Feast of Reason was celebrated in it in 1793, and it was returned to the Roman Catholic Church in 1802. The same name is used for many other Roman Catholic cathedrals, churches, and institutions throughout the world.

nouvelle theologie (Fr., new theology) French Catholic theological movement of the 1940s that sought to return to biblical and patristic sources, reintegrate pastoral experience with theology, and challenge the rationalistic exegesis* of the

Cathedral of Notre Dame, Paris

Scriptures. Vatican Council II* adopted many of its theological premises.

Nouwen, Henri Josef Machiel (1932–1996) Dutch-born American Roman Catholic theologian. Ordained priest in 1957, he has served as professor in Notre Dame*, Yale, and Harvard. He has written extensively on Christian spirituality and Catholicism. The best known of his books are *With Open Hands* (1971), *The Wounded Healer, Ministry in Contemporary Society* (1972), *Out of Solitude: Three Meditations on Christian Life* (1974), *The Way of the Heart* (1980), *Making All Things New* (1981), *Love in a Fearful Land* (1985), *The Road to Daybreak* (1988), *In the Name of Jesus* (1989), and *Bread for the Journey* (1997). The last decade of his life was spent in l'Arche* community in Canada, ministering among the handicapped.

Novalis (1772–1801) Pseudonym of Friedrich Leopold Freiherr von Hardenberg. Lyric poet whose Pietistic background was reflected in his poems. In *Die Christenheit oder Europa* (1799) he attacked the Reformation* for the loss of mystical piety in worship and the Enlightenment for its worship of reason. His own religious beliefs tended toward Catholicism* and mysticism. His chief works were *Hymns to the Night* (1800), *Die Lehrlinge zu Sais,* and *Heinrich von Ofterdingen.*

Novatian (third century) Roman presbyter* and early author of dogmatic literature in Latin. He led the conservative or rigorist party that opposed Pope Cornelius* and his efforts to welcome lapsed Christians back into the fold after the end of the Decian persecutions* (249–250). He was consecrated rival bishop of Rome. He also wrote the first Latin work in defense of the orthodox doctrine of the Trinity*. He died as a martyr* during the Valerian persecution in 257–258.

Novatianism Doctrine associated with Novatian* that opposed readmission to the church of those who had lapsed from the faith under duress during the imperial persecutions. In all respects, Novatianists were strongly orthodox and Trinitarian*, but were nevertheless excommunicated. The Novatian sect survived until the fifth century.

Novello, Vincent (1781–1861) Church musician. He was one of the founders of the London Philharmonic Society and the Choral Harmonists Society. He was instrumental in publishing new editions of sacred music and also compiling music collections, including *A Collection of Sacred Music* (2 vols., 1811), *Twelve Easy Masses* (3 vols., 1816), and *Purcell's Sacred Music* (5 vols., 1828–1832).

novena Period of nine days of private and public devotion by which special favors were sought from Jesus Christ, the Virgin Mary*, or any of the saints*.

Novgorod Russian city on the River Volkhov, an ancient Christian center on the trade route from Scandinavia to Constantinople*. It has many fine medieval churches, including the Cathedral of the Divine Wisdom (1045–1050), Transfiguration Church (1374), Church of St. Nicolas (1113), Church of St. Procopius (1529), and the Church of Our Savior at Nereditsa (1198).

novice New member of a religious order on probation for a period of one year. Generally, only postulants* are made novices. During the novitiate*, the novice lives under a novice-master, separate from the rest of the community, while enjoying the privileges and indulgences* of the order. The novice is free to leave just as the order is free to expel him or her.

novitiate 1. State of being a novice*. 2. Place where a novice lives.

Noyes, John Humphrey (1811–1886) Religious and social reformer. He developed anti-Calvinist ideas of human perfection* and declared himself sinless in 1834, whereupon he was dismissed from the ministry and from Yale University. He developed two Utopian communities, at Putney, Vermont (1840–1848), and Oneida, New York (1848–1881), where he tried to apply his ideas of biblical communism, multiple marriages, population control, and open love. He taught that sex was perfect love.

NRB National Religious Broadcasters*.

NT New Testament.

Nubia Ancient region situated along the Nile River between northern Sudan and southern Egypt from the confluence of the White and Blue Niles at Khartoum and the first cataract at Aswan. It was evangelized by the third century and remained Christian well into the Muslim era.

number of the beast Number 666* assigned to the beast in Revelation 13:18.

numinous Mystical elements in the experience of the holy that inspire awe, clarified especially by Rudolf Otto*.

nun Woman consecrated to the service of the Lord and who has professed vows of perpetual chastity*, poverty, and obedience. Term properly applied to women living in cloistered communities distinguished from sisters* who live in less restricted environments.

Nunc Dimittis (Lat., now may be dismissed) Song of Simeon welcoming the Christ child in the temple (Luke 2:29–32) from the first two words in the Latin version, used as an evening canticle* in the worship services in the Western and Eastern churches* since the fourth century. It is also part of the final devotions in the Liturgy of St. Chrysostom* and at the Candlemas* Procession in the Roman Rite*.

nuncio Permanent diplomatic representative of the Holy See* accredited to a civil government with ambassadorial status.

nuptial mass Mass* following a wedding conferring blessings on the married couple.

Nuremberg Declaration German Old Catholic declaration drafted by 14 German Catholic professors at a meeting in 1870 to protest the decrees of the First Vatican Council*. It formed the manifesto of the Old Catholic movement.

Nygren, Anders (1890–1977) Swedish theologian and philosopher of religion. He developed a form of dialectical theology* focused on religious motifs through his works, such as *Agape and Eros, Essence of Christianity,* and *Meaning and Method.*

Oo

O. Cart. Carthusian Order.

O Salutaris Hostia (Lat., O Saving Victim) Words that begin the last two stanzas of the hymn *Verbum Supernum Prodiens* written by Thomas Aquinas* for the feast of Corpus Christi*.

O Sapientia First of the O Antiphons, sung on December 17, marking the beginning of the second part of Advent*.

Oak, Synod of the Illegitimate synod* held in 403 at the Oak, a suburb of Chalcedon, by an anti-St. John Chrysostom* faction to remove him from office. After Chrysostom was condemned on several fabricated charges, he was deposed and exiled, but the emperor was forced to recall him within a few days because of popular outrage.

O-Antiphons Also, Greater Antiphons. Antiphons* sung before and after Magnificat* at vespers* on the seven days preceding Christmas eve*, beginning with "O Sapientia" and ending with "O Emmanuel."

oath Formal and solemn affirmation of the truth of a statement, in which God may be called upon to be the witness. Several Christian groups, such as the Anabaptists*, Mennonites*, and Quakers*, oppose the use of oaths as unscriptural in literal obedience to the words of Jesus (Matt. 5:33–37; James 5:12). Prohibition of oaths is included in the Mennonite Confession of 1963.

obedientiary Official in a medieval monastery appointed by the abbot.

Oberammergau Town in upper Bavaria where a celebrated passion play* is held every decade in a special theater, based on a script written by J. A. Daisenberger in 1860. It is performed by over 700 villagers and lasts for over seven hours.

Oberammergau

Oberlin, Jean Frederic (1740–1826) Alsatian Lutheran minister who became well-loved because of his social philanthropy. He built schools, roads, and bridges and established factories, stores, and savings-and-loans. He embraced the ideals of the French Revolution as representing the application of Christian principles. His work in promoting human welfare was much admired around the world. Oberlin College in Ohio was named in his honor.

Oberlin theology Theological system associated with Charles G. Finney* and Asa Mahan*, both presidents of Oberlin College, Ohio, combining Calvinist and Arminian elements. It emphasized an attainable and moderate form of perfection* as outlined in Mahan's *Scripture Doctrine of Perfection* (1839) and Finney's *Lectures on Systematic Theology* (1846). According to Finney, human beings are capable of growing toward perfection* through obedience and faith*, although they may not achieve absolute perfection. Thus individual justice and social justice were valid goals of Christian evangelism.

obex (Lat., hindrance) In Roman Catholic theology, a specific impediment to receiving spiritual grace*.

objective Christianity In Kierkegaardian thought, detached and impersonal Christianity, required to be proven scientifically, in contrast to subjective Christianity.

oblate (Lat., *oblatus,* offered) Originally, child dedicated to a monastery by parents for monastic upbringing. The term is now used in certain Roman Catholic communities, as the Oblates Regular of St. Benedict*, Oblates of Charles Borromeo*, and Oblates of Mary Immaculate*.

Oblate Sisters of Providence First Congregation of African-American religious women founded in 1829 with the help of the Sulpician priest, James Hector Joubert (1777–1843), to meet the needs of refugees from Haiti and San Domingo in the 1790s. They were later under the direction of the Redemptorists*, Jesuits*, and Josephite Fathers. They run a number of schools, including St. Frances' Academy in Baltimore.

Oblates of Mary Immaculate (OMI) Also, Oblates of St. Charles. Congregation of men founded by Charles Joseph de Mazenod* in 1816 in Aix-en-Provence, France. The Oblates take a fourth vow of perseverance* until death, in addition to the three regular ones of obedience, poverty, and chastity*. They are also involved in parochial* and mission work, clergy education in seminaries, and care of Marian* shrines.

Oblates of St. Francis de Sales Religious community of priests and brothers* founded in 1871 in Troyes, France, by Louis Brisson. They are involved in education, foreign missions, and pastoral ministry.

Oblates Regular of St. Benedict The Oblates of Mary founded by St. Frances of Rome* in 1425 affiliated with the White Benedictines or Olivetans of Santa Maria Nuova, later the Oblate Congregation of Tor de' Specchi. They follow the Rule of St. Benedict*.

oblati (Lat., offered; sing., oblatus) Lay persons who, in the Middle Ages, gave themselves and their property to a monastery and became its members, but without taking vows.

oblation Bread and wine offered for consecration in the Eucharist* in certain churches or any other material gift presented by believers. Also, more widely of spiritual sacrifices of heart and life.

obsecration (Lat., to ask on sacred grounds) Fervent petition* calling upon God to grant a request, specifically, a section of the litany* in which petitions are introduced with the words, "by the Sacred Heart of Jesus."

Observants/Observantines Members of the Franciscan Order* who follow literally the original Rule of St. Francis. The movement started in the fourteenth century, as a reaction against the decline in religious discipline in the order. In 1517 they were separated from the Conventuals and recognized as the true order of St. Francis*. In the sixteenth century they were further divided into the Reformed*, the Recollects*, and the Discalced* or the Alcantarines, all of whom were merged into the single Order of Friars Minor* in 1897.

OC Cistercian Order.

Occam's/Ockham's Razor Philosophical maxim of William of Ockham*, sometimes called the "Law of Parsimony." It states, "It is futile to do with more elements what can be done with fewer."

occasional offices In the *Book of Common Prayer**, services of baptism*, confirmation*, matrimony*, visitation of the sick, communion of the sick, burial of the dead, commination as distinct from communion*, morning prayer, and evening prayer.

occasionalism View propounded by Arnold Geulinex, a Dutch Roman Catholic who later joined the Reformed Church, that every event in the universe is caused by God's direct intervention.

Occom, Samson (1723–1792) Native American preacher of the eighteenth century. Converted during the Great Awakening* in 1740, he served as minister to the Montauk Indians of Long Island and as missionary to the Oneidas. He helped Eleazar Wheelock* raise funds in Great Britain for the Indian school that later became Dartmouth College, New Hampshire. He established the Indian town of Brotherstown in 1784 and published an Indian hymnal.

Ocean Grove Town in New Jersey founded and governed by the Methodists through the Ocean Grove Camp Meeting Association.

Ochino, Bernardino (1487–1564) Italian reformer. He entered the Franciscan Observants* in 1504, becoming a Capuchin in 1534 and vicar general* of the Capuchin Order from 1538 to 1542. He was a great preacher of whom it was said by Charles V that he could make the stones weep. Influenced by Juan de Valdes* to question the role of the church in salvation*, he attacked the Inquisition* in one of his sermons and was summoned to Rome to explain his Protestant sympathies. He escaped to Geneva* and was welcomed by Calvin*. Thereafter he moved frequently, first to Augsburg, then to Basel*, Strasbourg*, and London where Thomas Cranmer* became his patron. Here he published tracts attacking both the Catholic Church and Calvinist doctrine of predestination*. On Mary's accession to the throne, he fled England and returned to Zurich* from where he was expelled because of his book *Thirty Dialogues* (1563) in which he expressed unorthodox views on the Trinity* and on monogamy. He moved to Cracow before finally settling down in Moravia.

Ockeghem, Johannes (c. 1410–1497) Franco-Flemish musical composer who was the master of the counterpoint. He spent much of his life at the French court where he wrote ten complete masses, a small number of motets*, such as *Alma Redemptoris Mater** (Mother Nurturer of the Redeemer), and secular chansons. He was one of the first to write in five voice-parts and he had the ability to write a "seamless web" of polyphonic voices.

Ockenga, Harold John (1905–1985) American Evangelical leader. After serving pastorates* in Pittsburgh and Boston, Ockenga became president of the National Association of Evangelicals* in 1942. In 1947 he became founding president of Fuller Theological Seminary* while remaining pastor of Park Street Congregational Church in Boston. In 1950 he was one of the earliest sponsors of a Billy Graham Crusade. Subsequently, with Graham*, he helped to found *Christianity Today**. From 1970 to 1979 he was president of Gordon-Conwell Theological Seminary*.

Ockham See WILLIAM OF OCKHAM/OCCAM.

O'Connor, Flannery (1925–1964) American Roman Catholic novelist. In her two novels, *Wise Blood* (1952) and *The Violent Bear it Away* (1960), she gave expression to her brooding Catholic faith that melded her artistic vision and her fervent religious convictions. Her grotesque situations and characters demonstrated the presence of evil and darkness in the world, illuminated by a supernatural grace* that somehow redeemed the horror and the degradation.

octavarium Collection of lessons, supplementary to those of the Breviary*, for use in the second and third nocturns* of the mattins* of octaves* of local observance.

octave Eighth day after a Christian festival and also of the whole eight-day period.

October devotions Devotions to the Virgin Mary* during the month of October.

Octoechos See OKTOECHOS.

oculi Third Sunday in Lent* from the first word of the introit* of the day.

Odes of Solomon Collection of poetical devotional verse dating from the second century. Despite hints of Gnostic influences, it has been called the earliest extrabiblical Christian songbook.

Odilo, St. (c. 962–1049) Fifth abbot of Cluny* (999–1049). He was responsible for the expansion of the Cluniac Order*, initiating a building program and centralizing control of the daughter houses by the main monastery. He introduced the observance of All Souls Day* on November 2. He sold the treasures of the monastery to aid the poor during the famine of 1033. Feast day: January 1 or 2.

odium theologicum (Lat., theological hatred) Hatred engendered by theological differences and conflicts.

Odo of Cluny, St. (879–942) Abbot of Cluny*. He was admitted by St. Berno to the monastery of Baume in 909, but next year he was placed in charge of the monastery school. He succeeded Berno as abbot of Cluny. He raised Cluny to the high position it held in the next centuries and also completed the building of the Church of Sts. Peter and Paul. He wrote an epic on the redemption and 12 choral antiphons* in honor of St. Martin. Feast day: November 18.

odor of sanctity Fragrant odor believed to be miraculously exuded by the bodies of saints* after death, associated with their personal holiness*.

Oecolampadius, Johannes (1482–1531) Birth name: Hussgen. German reformer of Basel*. A brilliant philologist, he was called in 1515 to minister at Basel, where he met Erasmus* and assisted him in the publication of the Greek New Testament. He moved to Augsburg, where he became a Lutheran. In 1522 he accepted the position of a court chaplain* but returned to Basel as lecturer. He promoted the Reformation* cause throughout Switzerland by his writings and through participation in the disputations of Baden (1526) and Bern (1528). At the Colloquy of Marburg* (1529) on the eucharistic doctrine, he sided with Zwingli* against Luther*. He also supervised the removal of all images from churches in Basel. He was an able patristic scholar.

Johannes Oecolampadius

oecumenical council See ECUMENICAL COUNCIL.

oecumenical patriarch See ECUMENICAL PATRIARCH.

offertory 1. Gifts, especially of money, dedicated during worship to God's service. In some churches, offering of bread and wine brought to the altar by a group of the laity to be consecrated by the celebrant while a chant is sung. 2. In the Eastern Church*, the cutting up and arranging of the bread at the prothesis* at the outset of the whole service while the elements* are solemnly brought to the altar at the Great Entrance*. 3. In the Protestant* traditions, music which accompanies the presentation of tithes and offerings as an act of worship.

Office, Divine The daily public prayer of the medieval Western and later Catholic church, recited at fixed times, called the Liturgy of the Hours. The monastic offices of the hours of the night and day were adopted in the early church. These were mattins* and lauds*, prime*, terce*, sext*, none*, vespers*, and compline*. St. Benedict* based the office of his rule on these hours, and included in them responsories, antiphons*, hymns, canticles*, Bible readings, and Psalms. On saints' days, the legends displaced Bible readings. The

Liturgy of the Hours issued by Paul VI* in 1971 re-ordered the offices. It provides for an Office of Readings* which may be said at any time during the day, lauds, a midday office, vespers, and compline said before retiring. In addition, there are Psalms, Bible readings, and readings from the fathers of the church. Offices generally begin with hymns. In lauds and vespers there is a short responsory* after the reading, and they also include prayers. All priests and deacons as well as the religious are obliged to recite the offices daily.

office hymns Hymns sung as a part of the Divine Office*. The hymns of the little hours and compline* are the same throughout the year, while those of the other hours vary according to the feast and the season. The 1971 Breviary* places hymns before Psalms in all the offices. The most commonly used office hymns* are "O Blest Creator of Light" at Sunday vespers*, "Before the Ending of the Day" at compline*, and "Of the Glorious Body Telling" at Corpus Christi vespers*.

office of readings Office that replaced mattins* in the 1971 Breviary*. It may be said at any time of the day. It consists of a versicle* and response, a hymn, three Psalms, with antiphons*, two lessons or readings, responsories, and the collect* of the day.

offices of Christ Threefold role of Christ as messianic prophet*, high priest, and king.

officiant Clergyman who leads a worship service or directs an ecclesiastical ceremony.

officium pastorum (Lat., office of the shepherds) Medieval Spanish play in three parts: appearance of the shepherds, the angel's announcement, and adoration of the shepherds.

OFM Order of Friars Minor.

OFM Cap. Capuchin Order.

Ohrid Town in Macedonia* on Lake Ohrid, an important center of early Christianity in the Balkans, and possibly the seat of an archbishopric in the sixth century. It became an important cen-ter of Slav culture as a result of the work of Clement* and Naum, disciples of Sts. Cyril and Methodius*. It became the capital of the Bulgarian Empire under Tsar Samuel (976–1014) and for a brief time a patriarchate*, and later an autocephalous* archbishopric. The archbishop of Ohrid is the head of the Macedonian Orthodox Church.

Oktoechos (Gk., of the Eight Tones) Also, paracletice. Byzantine Rite* liturgical book containing the liturgical propers (prayers assigned to particular Sundays and feasts) of the mobile cycle whose dates depend each year on the date of Easter*, throughout the liturgical year* except for the cycles of Lent*, Easter*, and Pentecost*. So called because the proper texts for each day of the week are arranged according to eight musical tones. The cycle takes eight weeks to complete, one week per tone, and is repeated throughout the year from All-Saints' Day on the first Sunday after Pentecost* until fully replaced in Lent*. It overlaps with the monthly Menaion* propers for the Divine Office* and complements the Triodion* and Pentecostarion*.

Olav, St. (c. 995–1030) Birth name: Olav Haraldsson. Patron saint* of Norway and king from 1016 to 1028. He was converted from a predatory life and baptized at Rouen*. He became king in 1016. He was instrumental in evangelizing Norway. However, his enemies combined to dethrone him and force him to flee to Russia. When he tried to regain his kingdom in 1030, he was killed in the Battle of Stiklestad. After death, he was venerated as a martyr*, and his shrine at Nidaros at Trondheim was a famous place of pilgrimage* in the Middle Ages. Feast day: July 29.

Old Believers Dissident* group of Russian Orthodox believers, also known as Roskolniki, or those in schism*. They broke away from the Russian Orthodox Church* in protest over the reforms of Patriarch Nikon* that brought the Russian Church into conformity with the rest of the Orthodox Church. Because they adhere to pre-Nikon traditions and practices, they call themselves starovery*, or "adherents of the old rite" of which "Old Believers"* is a rough English translation. Their leader was Avvakum*, who was exiled in 1664. Thousands of his followers suffered the same or worse fate. They, in turn, regarded their persecutors as the Antichrist*. Open persecution lasted until the reign of Peter the Great and was renewed during the reign of Nicholas I* (1825–1855). Penal laws against them remained on the statute books until 1903. There are two distinct groups within Old Believers: Popovtsy, those with priests, and Bezpopovtsy, those without priests. Both groups embody the Pietist traditions in the Orthodox Church.

old calendar Old style or Julian calendar*, devised by Julius Caesar in 46 B.C., followed by all Orthodox churches up to 1918 and followed now by the churches of Russia, Jerusalem*, Serbia, and Bulgaria and by the monasteries of Mount Athos*.

Old Catholics 1. Roman Catholics who refused to accept the doctrine of papal infallibility* proclaimed at the First Vatican Council* of 1870. 2. Roman Catholics who accept the Declaration of Utrecht* (1889) rejecting papal infallibility, immaculate conception*, and other doctrines. 3. Dutch Catholics, known as the Church of Utrecht, who separated from the Roman Catholic Church in 1724 in support of Jansenism*. Old Catholics recognize the first seven councils and retain the seven sacraments*, but they make auricular confession* voluntary and absolution* a ceremonial declaration of forgiveness. They hold firmly to apostolic succession* with its threefold office of deacon, priest, and bishop. Vernacular is used in all services. The governing body is the synod* which elects the bishop. From the outset, Old Catholics had close relations with the Church of England*.

Old Church Slavonic See CHURCH SLAVONIC.

Old Fashioned Revival Hour Classic evangelistic radio program begun in 1937 by Charles Fuller* and broadcast over Mutual Broadcasting System and later CBS.

Old Latin See VETUS LATINA.

Old Lights New England Congregationalists who opposed revival during Great Awakening*. They were led by Charles Chauncy and other rational-

ists, supported by the near-Unitarian divinity faculties of Harvard and Yale.

Old Order Amish Conservative Amish Mennonite group in America who since 1850 have opposed all forms of modernization. They continue to wear eighteenth-century dress and resist modern inventions, such as cars. Because they worship in private homes, they are sometimes called "house Amish" while the more progressive among them are called "church Amish." They use German in worship services and speak a German dialect known as Pennsylvania Dutch.

old Roman chant Musical repertory considered a precursor of the Gregorian chants* to which it is closely related.

Old Roman Creed An earlier and shorter form of what became the Apostles' Creed*, used as the baptismal creed of the church of Rome.

Old School theology Traditional nineteenth-century Calvinism* upheld by theologians, as Archibald Alexander* and Charles Hodge*. Opposed to New School theology which supported revivalism*.

Old Syriac Version Syriac* translation of the Christian New Testament used in the Syriac-speaking church before the Peshitta* appeared in the fifth century. There are two known versions, the Curetonian and the Sinaitic, both discovered in the nineteenth century.

Old Testament Hebrew Scriptures of the Jews forming the first part of the Bible. In Jewish tradition, it is divided into three parts: the Law (Torah or the Pentateuch), the Prophets, and the Writings. Christian tradition divides it into three parts: Historical, Didactic, and Prophetic Books.

older churches Mainline* denominations of Europe and North America, as distinguished from the so-called younger churches* of the Third World.

Oldham, Joseph Houldsworth (1874–1969) Missionary statesman and ecumenical leader. Associated as a young man with the British Colleges Christian Union, YMCA*, and SCM, he was appointed organizing secretary of the World Missionary Conference* which met in Edinburgh* in 1910. He helped to restore relations with German Christians after World War I. As joint secretary of the International Missionary Council* in 1921, he did outstanding work in Africa. He organized the Oxford Conference* of 1937 and the Utrecht Conference of 1938 which set up the provisional committee for a World Council of Churches*. During World War II he was secretary of the Council on Christian Faith and the Common Life and the Christian Frontier Council.

Olevianus, Caspar (1536–1587) German Reformed* theologian. He became a preacher and teacher at Trier* after studying theology at Geneva* and Zurich*. At the invitation of the Calvinist elector Frederick III he went to Heidelberg, where he was one of those principally responsible for the Heidelberg Catechism*. After Frederick's death he labored successfully to spread Calvinism* in the Hesse-Nassau region.

Olga, St. (d. 968) Russian princess. Wife of the pagan Duke of Kiev*, she was converted to Christianity, taking the baptismal name* of Helena. She was the first Russian to be baptized and canonized. Her grandson was Vladimir*, who Christianized Russia. Feast day: July 11.

Olier, Jean-Jacques (1608–1657) French founder of the Society and Seminary of Saint-Sulpice*, Paris. Converted on a pilgrimage* to Loreto*, he was ordained priest in 1633, and he came under the influence of Vincent de Paul*. He founded a seminary at Vaugirard in 1641. In 1642 he became parish priest of St. Sulpice in 1642 and introduced a number of reforms. He transformed the seminary into a Society of St. Sulpice, a community of secular priests without religious vows. He is the author of a number of works on Christian life, including *La Journée Chretienne* (1655), *Catechisme Chretien pour la Vie Intérieure* (1656), *Introduction à la Vie et aux Vertus Chretiennes* (1658), and *Lettres Spirituelles* (1672).

Oliva Former Cistercian abbey, also known as Mount Olive, to the north of Gdansk, in Poland, founded in 1170. The Romanesque and Early

Gothic* basilica* was built in the thirteenth and fourteenth centuries. The west facade, flanked by two slender towers, was refashioned in Rococo style in 1771 when pinnacles were added to the tower. The palace of the former abbots was built between 1754 and 1756 and the monastery between the thirteenth and fourteenth centuries. The monastery contains the historic Hall of Peace where the Peace of Oliva was signed in 1660. In the Middle Ages, it was repeatedly ransacked and destroyed by vandals, the Prussians in 1224 and 1234, the Poles in 1243 and 1245, the Teutonic Knights in 1252, the Hussites* in 1433, and a local mob in 1577.

Olivetan (c. 1506–1538) Birth name: Pierre Robert. Bible scholar and reformer. A cousin of John Calvin*, he translated the Bible into French (1535). In his later years, he helped Calvin* in preaching Reformation* themes at Geneva*.

Olivetans Popular name of The Congregation of Our Lady of Mount Olivet, founded in the fourteenth century by Giovanni Tolomei at Monte Oliveto, near Siena. They are a branch of the Benedictine* Order who follow the rule strictly. They wear a white habit. The congregation includes the Abbey of Bec*.

ombrellino In the Western Church*, a small canopy* of white silk carried over the Blessed Sacrament* when it is carried from one place to another.

omega Last letter of the Greek alphabet. See also ALPHA AND OMEGA.

omega point Concept, first stated by Teilhard de Chardin*, that Jesus Christ is the source of all matter and that all things are biologically evolving toward unity with him.

OMF Overseas Missionary Fellowship.

omologia (lit., confession) In the Coptic Rite, the profession or confession* of faith that precedes the reception of the Holy Communion*.

omophorion In the Orthodox Church, long scarf worn by bishops, originally of wool, and now of white embroidered silk or velvet, about ten inches wide, falling loosely around the shoulders. It corresponds to the pallium* in the Roman Catholic

Omophorion

Church. During worship service, the larger omophorion is worn until the end of the Epistle and the shorter one is worn from the Cherubicon* until the end of the service.

omphalos (Gk., navel) Central point in a Byzantine church.

Oneida Community Christian communist and utopian society founded in 1848 at Oneida, New York, by John Humphrey Noyes* (1811–1886). They were also known as Perfectionists from their belief that human beings could attain true sinlessness, even as Christ. However, they opposed monogamy and advocated open marriage. It broke up in 1880 and was succeeded by a joint-stock community to promote their handicrafts.

Oneness Pentecostalism Also, Jesus Only*. Originally, New Issue. Form of Pentecostalism* known as the United Pentecostal Church International, founded in 1914, that rejected the doctrine of the Trinity* and insisted on rebaptism* solely in the name of the Lord Jesus Christ, whose name subsumed all the three persons of the Godhead. It challenged the traditional Trinitarian* doctrine with a modalistic view of God and a revelational theory of the sufficiency of the name of Jesus*.

onion-dome Spheroid dome coming to a point, typical of Russian Orthodox churches*.

onitha dh'qanke In the Assyrian Rite, the anthem of the sanctuary consisting of verses from the Psalms and the Gloria.

Oost, Jacob van (1601–1671) Flemish religious painter, noted for his *Descent from the Cross*.

OP Order of Preachers*.

Open Brethren See PLYMOUTH BRETHREN.

open communion Holy Communion* or Mass* in which all Christians, irrespective of denominational affiliation, may participate, as distinguished from a closed communion* in which only members of the same denomination or congregation may participate.

Open Doors with Brother Andrew Ministry run since 1955 by Brother Andrew, a Dutchman, helping Christians who are persecuted for their faith. It has over 20 offices around the world distributing Bibles and providing leadership and pastoral training.

opera ad extra (Lat., works to the outside) Also, notae externae. Activities and effects by which the Trinity* is manifested outwardly. They include creation, preservation*, and government of the universe as a function of the Father; redemption* as a function of the Son; and inspiration*, regeneration*, and sanctification* as a function of the Holy Spirit*.

opera ad intra (Lat., works to the inside) Also, notae internae. Immanent and intransitive activities of the Trinity* or actions which the three persons of the Trinity exercise toward one another, such as the eternal generation* of the Son and the Procession of the Holy Spirit*.

Operation Mobilization This international missions organization traces its roots to the mid-1950s, when Dorothy Clapp, a New Jersey homemaker, was offering prayer and Christian literature which led to changed lives in a local high school. One of the students reached was George Verwer*, who received a copy of the Gospel of John from the Clapps and made a public commitment to Christ at age 16 in a Madison Square Garden meeting led by Jack Wyrtzen and Billy Graham*. In 1957 Verwer was joined by friends in distributing Bible portions in Mexico—supported in prayer and financially by others "at home." Subsequently, he attended Maryville College and Moody Bible Institute* (where he met future wife, Deena), and has remained a key organizational leader. Today, over 3000 OM'ers are working in 83 countries to advance the cause of Christ, embracing self-professed core values: knowing and glorifying God, living in submission to God's Word, being people of grace and integrity, serving sacrificially, loving and valuing people, evangelizing the world, reflecting the diversity of the body of Christ, interceding through prayer, and esteeming the church.

Optina Monastery and skete* in north Russia. Established in the fifteenth century, it was closed for a while in the eighteenth century. In 1800 the community was reorganized under Feofan the Cossack with Avraami as abbot. Among the celebrated staretz* of the monastery were Anthony and Moses Putilov, Leonid Nagolkin, Makarii Ivanov, Amvrosii Grenkov, Anatolii, Osip Litovkin, Varsonofii Plekhankov, and Nektarii. The monastery was linked to the Shamordino Convent.

Opus Dei (Lat., the work of God) 1. Divine Office* in the Benedictine* lexicon expressing their belief that prayer is the work of God. 2. Roman Catholic organization founded in Madrid in 1928 by the Blessed Josemaria Escriva (1902–1975). It has four branches: one for men, another for women, a Society of the Holy Cross* for priests, and a Personal Prelature of the Holy Cross. It has extraordinary influence on public affairs in many Catholic countries because many of its lay members hold important positions in government, industry, and the professions.

opus operantis See EX OPERE OPERANTIS.

opus operatum See EX OPERE OPERATO.

ora pro nobis (Lat., pray for us) Portion of a litany* to the Virgin Mary*.

Oracle of the Church Title of St. Bernard of Clairvaux*.

oracles of God Various ways in which God speaks to the church: Incarnation, Scripture, prophecy, preaching, and the sacraments. In Reformation* theology, used especially of Scripture.

Oral Roberts University Prayer Tower Building located on the Oral Roberts University campus in Tulsa, Oklahoma, dedicated to prayer. The bold, futuristic 200-foot structure, made mostly of steel and glass, was erected in 1967. Prayer counselors man the building 24 hours a day, responding to prayer requests worldwide.

Orange, councils of Early synods held at Orange in what is now southern France, one in 441 and the other in 529. The first under St. Hilary of Arles* was attended by 16 bishops and enacted 30 canons* concerning church discipline*. The second condemned semi-Pelagianism* and by canonizing nearly all of Augustine's teaching on grace* and election* was of great significance in Western theology.

orant (Lat., praying one) 1. Ancient Eastern position of prayer, standing with arms outstretched sideways, or bent at the elbow with the hands at shoulder level and palms facing forward or upraised, rather like a modern Charismatic. 2. Figure with extended arms in the attitude of prayer found in the early Christian catacombs.

orarion In the Eastern Church*, the deacon's narrow stole* worn over the left shoulder, hanging straight down back and front, sometimes passed down below the right arm and attached once more to the left shoulder. He holds it in his hand during prayers and crosses it around him during Communion.

Orate, Fratres (Lat., Pray Brethren) Call addressed by the celebrant to the people at Mass*, immediately after the offertory.

oratio (Lat.) Sermon or prayer.

Oratorians Name of two associations of secular priests. 1. Italian oratory* founded by Philip Neri* in Rome* in 1564 as an informal association of priests who live communally, without vows. It included creative artists such as Palestrina* and scholars such as Cesare Baronius* and Giovanni Dominico Mansi. Newman* introduced them to England in 1847. 2. French oratory founded by Pierre de Berulle* at Paris in 1611 as the Oratory of Jesus Christ. Governed by a superior general*, it trained priests in seminaries. The oratory was dissolved during the French Revolution but was reestablished in 1852 as the Oratory of Jesus Christ and the Immaculate Mary. Many of its members have been distinguished for their holiness* and scholarship.

oratorio Dramatic and elaborate musical setting for a libretto with soloists, chorus, and orchestra without dramatic action, scenery, or special costumes. The best known oratorio composers are Giocomo Carissimi* (1605–1674), who wrote *Jephte;* George Frederick Handel*, whose works include *Saul* (1738), *Israel in Egypt* (1738), *Samson* (1741), and *Messiah* (1741); and Felix Mendelssohn*, who wrote *St. Paul* (1836) and *Elijah* (1846). Among the more important modern oratorios are Edward Elgar's* *Gerontius* (1900) and *Apostles* (1903); William Walton's *Belshazzar's Feast* (1931); and Benjamin Britten's* *War Requiem* (1961).

oratory (Lat., *oratorium,* place of prayer) Place where the Mass* is celebrated other than a parish* church. There are three types of oratorios: public, open to all communicants; semipublic, open to a particular community who may or may not exclude others, and private or domestic.

Order of Preachers See DOMINICANS.

Order of St. Basil the Great Byzantine Rite* monastic order in the Ukrainian and Belorussian Catholic churches. A Roman branch was established in the 1920s.

order of salvation (Lat., *Ordo Salutis*) Order or sequence in which salvation* becomes effective, generally acknowledged as consisting primarily of three steps: regeneration*, justification*, and sanctification* but also including faith*, repentance*, and glorification. Based especially on Romans 8:28–30. Contrast salvation history.

Orders, Holy Offices or ranks of ministry, especially the episcopate*, presbyterate*, and diaconate and also sometimes including clerical orders, such as subdeacon, acolyte*, exorcist*, lector*, cantor*, and porter or doorkeeper*. The New Testament speaks of the fivefold ministry of apostles, prophets*, teachers, evangelists, and pastors, but in addition there are references to elders, overseers, deacons, and proclaimers (Acts 6:1–7; 13:1–3; 15:22–24; Rom. 12:4–8; 1 Cor. 12:28–30; 1 Tim. 3:1–13, 1 Pet. 5:1–5). All candidates* to the holy orders need to be designated, commissioned, and consecrated in a liturgical service of ordination. Much recent theology has favored a functional rather than official approach to ordained ministry. The term *order (ordo)* comes from Roman imperial society.

ordinal 1. Manual for the conduct of divine services* in accordance with the variations in the ecclesiastical year. 2. Book of regulations and the order of service.

ordinance 1. Religious rite. In the Baptist churches, baptism* and the Lord's Supper* are ordinances rather than sacraments*. 2. Rite for the administration of a sacrament*.

ordinand One being ordained into a ministry or one who is a candidate* for an ordination.

Orarion

Cuffs

Orarion

ordinariates 1. Administrative division of a particular Roman Catholic diocese or archdiocese. 2. Group of members of an Eastern rite in communion with the pope who are subject to the personal jurisdiction of an appointed prelate. 3. Body of Roman Catholic chaplains serving military forces headed by a bishop.

ordinary Regular and permanent jurisdiction of an archbishop, bishop, or priest where he may teach, govern, administer sacraments*, and exercise executive power.

Ordinary of the Mass (Lat., *Ordo Missae*) Invariable part of a Mass* as distinguished from the variable parts called the Proper. Sometimes it is combined with the canon* and termed the Ordinary and the Canon of the Mass*. It consists of preparatory prayers, the kyrie*, Gloria in Excelsis* and the Creed, the Sanctus*, the Canon, the Lord's Prayer*, Fraction* and Agnus Dei*, Communion and post-Communion devotions and, until 1965, the last Gospel.

Ordinary Time The liturgical year* outside Advent*, Christmas*, Lent*, and Easter*. There are two periods of ordinary time. The first is the five to eight weeks between Epiphany* and the beginning of Lent*. The second is the 23 to 27 weeks between Pentecost* and the Solemnity of Christ the King*, the final Sunday of the liturgical year*.

ordination Commissioning of a person for the work of the ministry by the prayer of and laying on of hands* by duly authorized persons. See LAY-ING ON OF HANDS.

Ordines Romani Ancient collections of ceremonial directions for the performance of the Roman Rite* from which the *Caeremoniale Romanum**, the *Caeremoniale Episcorum**, and the *Pontifical* are descended. They are dated from the eighth to the tenth centuries.

Ordo Salutis See ORDER OF SALVATION.

oremus (Lat., let us pray) Bidding to a prayer in a Latin liturgical service.

organized church Body of Christian believers

joined in formal and legal organization with membership rolls, constituting the visible church.

Oriental Orthodox Churches Lesser Eastern Churches*, consisting of the Armenian, Syrian (including Malabar), Coptic, and Ethiopian churches which do not subscribe to the canons of the Council of Chalcedon*. Nominally, they are Monophysite in doctrine, although this is more a disagreement on terminology than substance.

orientation Construction of a church so that the communion table and pulpit are at the east end.

Origen (c. 185–c. 254) Birth name: Origenes Adamantius. Greek Father of the Church and Alexandrian theologian ranking with St. Augustine* as one of the greatest figures in Christian history. Born in Egypt and raised by Christian parents, he studied under Clement* in the Catechetical School of Alexandria* and became head of the same school at the age of 18 after the martyrdom of his father. As head of the Catechetical School for 28 years, he gained renown for his teaching and his ascetic life. Many flocked to hear him, especially in his travels, including members of the imperial family. His lectures were copied and published with the help of a wealthy convert.

During the Caracallan persecution in 215, he was invited to preach in Palestine although he was still a layman. Since this was a breach of ecclesiasti-

Origen

cal discipline, his bishop, Demetrius, disapproved. From 218 to 230 he devoted himself almost entirely to writing. In 230 he went once again to Palestine and was ordained priest. Demetrius thereupon deposed him from his teaching position and in effect exiled him. Origen established a new school at Caesarea* in Palestine* and continued to preach and write. In 250 during the Decian persecution*, he was put in chains, tortured, placed in stocks, and confined to a dungeon. Although released, he survived the ordeal only by a few years.

Origen was one of the earliest Bible commentators, one of the first textual critics of the Bible, and one of the first to construct a doctrinal framework for the Christian faith. The number of his works range from 8,000 according to Epiphanius*, to 2,000 according to Pamphilius*, and 800 according to Jerome*. Most of them have been lost, and only fragments survive. His most important works are the *Hexapla*, *De Principiis,* and *On Prayer. Hexapla* is a six-column edition of the Old Testament in Hebrew, Greek, Greek versions of Aquila, Symmachus, the Septuagint, and Theodotion. *De Principiis* is his seminal work of theology in four books. Book I deals with the Trinity*, Book II with the material world and the fall and redemption* of man, Book III with good and evil and the freedom of the will, and Book IV with biblical hermeneutics*. He also wrote a treatise, *Contra Celsum,* against the pagan philosopher Celsus*.

Origenism Body of theological doctrines associated with Origen. Origen was a scholar who constructed a scripturally valid universe in which the invisible coexisted with the visible and the spiritual and mystical with the corporeal, and the task of the Christian was to navigate through these opposing camps to attain perfection*. His thought was deeply imbued with Platonism. Origen affirmed the doctrine of the Trinity* and the unity of the Godhead. The Son is eternally generated from the Father and manifests all his attributes. The Holy Spirit* is also eternal, but Origen is somewhat unclear about his nature and relationship to the other persons in the triune Godhead.

Some of Origen's speculations, although bold, proved controversial and resulted in attacks on his orthodoxy*. Origenist controversies lasted almost from his lifetime until the sixth century. He held that God is finite because if he were other-

wise, he could not think himself, that the created world has always existed, because without a creation God could not be omnipotent, that although all spirits were created equal, some fell into sin, and so became demons, but in the final Apocatastasis, all creatures, even the devil, will be saved, that the soul purified by the wisdom of the Word will participate in the deity of Christ, and that all souls are pre-existent. These doctrines were condemned twice, once at the Council of Alexandria* convened by Theophilus in 400, and then at the Second Council of Constantinople* in 553. Theophilus called Origen "the hydra of heresies." Nevertheless, Origen is a seminal thinker who was the first to present Christianity as a coherent theological system.

original righteousness Counterpart of original sin*, representing the original human condition before the Fall, gratuitously bestowed on man by God (Gen. 1:31). It included freedom from lust, incorruptibility, immortality*, and impassibility*. In Roman Catholic theology, original righteousness was a *superadditum bonum,* an additional gift that Adam lost in the Fall.

original sin Corrupt state of created beings since the Fall of Adam; a sinful condition in which the creatures are alienated from their Creator. The scriptural basis of the doctrine is the Pauline* teaching that "through one man [i.e., Adam] sin entered the world" (Rom. 5:12–21; 1 Cor. 15:22). The term, used often in Calvinistic and Augustinian theology as well as Covenant theology* and indeed throughout Western theology, has a panoply of meanings: the natural tendency or impulse of human beings to sin from their birth, the fact that they are conceived in sin, the inherited component of evil that is traced back through all the generations back to Adam's disobedience and the curse that followed, and the universality of sinfulness that envelopes a person from the moment of birth. All personal sins of human beings are ascribed to the corporate liability to sin inherited from Adam. Later theologians have taught that Adam's sin was imputed to his race, just as Christ's righteousness is imputed to his believers.

orison 1. Prayer. 2. Anthem in the form of a prayer sung at the close of a service of worship.

orkiolion In the Byzantine Rite*, vessel for the hot water that is added to the wine in the chalice* just after the fraction*.

orletz (lit., the eagle) In the Byzantine Rite*, small circular rug with the image of an eagle* flying over a battlemented city. A bishop stands on this rug during certain services.

orphaned mission Missionary outreach cut off from their home base of support.

orphrey Embroidered band on ecclesiastical vestments.

Orr, James (1844–1913) Scottish theologian. As professor of church history at the United Presbyterian Divinity Hall and later at the United Free Church College in Glasgow, he defended orthodoxy* in *The Christian View of God and the World,* creationism* in *God's Image in Man* (1905), the virgin birth* in *The Virgin Birth of Christ* (1907), resurrection in *The Resurrection of Jesus* (1908), and biblical trustworthiness in *Revelation and Inspiration* (1910). He was also the editor of the *International Standard Biblical Encyclopedia* (1915).

Orthodox Church See EASTERN ORTHODOX CHURCH.

Orthodox Presbyterian Church Conservative denomination led by J. Gresham Machen* that broke away from the Presbyterian Church in 1936. It believes in scriptural inerrancy*. It was at first called the Presbyterian Church of America.

orthodoxy 1. Right "opinion" in matters of doctrine and faith*. In theology, it generally includes Trinitarian* and Christological belief.
2. **Orthodoxy** Descriptive note of the churches of the Byzantine Rite* under or associated with the ecumenical patriarch* of Constantinople*. Orthodoxy is based on the seven ecumenical councils ending with the Council of Nicaea* in 787, the local councils of Constantinople* (1341 and 1351), Jassy* (1642), and Jerusalem* (1672). In many theological areas, the liturgical texts used in the church, rather than the canons of councils, are the guiding documents. Orthodoxy attaches great importance to conciliar authority and to the epis-

copacy*, while at the same time allowing an active place to the laity. It acknowledges the sanctity* of the seven sacraments* or mysteries*. Baptism* is performed by immersion*. Chrismation*, the equivalent of confirmation* in the Western Church*, is administered immediately after baptism, and children are taken to Communion from infancy. Transubstantiation*, although undefined, is accepted as part of the mystery of the Eucharist*. The veneration* of icons is universal as are prayers to the Virgin Mary* and the saints*. The assumption of the Virgin Mary* is not a dogma*, yet is approved. Intercession for the departed is common, although purgatory* is denied. Monasteries* are as important as churches in the Orthodox tradition, and bishops are generally drawn from the ranks of monks or celibate clergy. On the other hand, parish* priests may marry before ordination but may not remarry.

Orthodox worship is distinguished by congregational participation. Laymen, both readers* and cantors*, play a larger role in the conduct of services than their counterparts do in the West. Services are always in the vernacular of the country, making the worshiper thoroughly at home in the audible parts of the holy liturgy, although in countries like Russia and Greece, the liturgical language varies from the common language. On the other hand, the sanctuary and the nave* are separated by a solid screen*, creating a distance between the priest and the congregation. The reception of the Holy Communion* by the adult

Triumph of Orthodoxy

laity is infrequent. The entire worship is sung, but only the choir takes part in the singing. The Holy Eucharist* is celebrated according to three liturgies: Liturgy of St. James*, Liturgy of St. Basil* the Great, and the Liturgy of St. John Chrysostom*.

The four principal divisions of the liturgy are: Prothesis* or the preparation; Enarxis* or the introductory office of prayer and praise; Synaxis* or the Liturgy of the Word* or the Liturgy of the Catechumens; and Eucharist* proper. The Synaxis comprises the entrance rite, readings from the Scriptures, and the common prayers of the church. The Eucharist proper begins after the dismissal* of the catechumens* and comprises seven parts: Prayers of the Faithful, Great Entrance* with offerings, kiss of peace* and the creed, anaphora or eucharistic prayer, the breaking of bread*, Communion, and Conclusion. The Great Entrance comprises five acts, the first four of which are covered by the singing of the almost invariable offertory chant, the cherubikon, or the hymn of the cherubim, a long secret private preparatory prayer of the priest; censing of the altar; the actual entrance; censing of the offerings; and a litany* leading to a prayer over the offerings.

The eucharistic prayer or anaphora* is of the Antiochene pattern, the greater part of which is said secretly. Its order is Introductory Dialogue, Preface*, Sanctus* and Benedictus*, post-Sanctus*, Narrative of the Institution, Anamnesis, epiclesis*, Diptychs*, Doxology*, and final Amen. Communion is in both kinds* administered together with a spoon, the bread having been placed in the chalice*. The Byzantine Liturgy is unsurpassed for color, clarity, and coherence.

Orthodoxy, Feast of the Feast established in 843 to celebrate on the first Friday in Lent* the final downfall of the Iconoclastic party, the restoration of icons, and the triumph of the church over all heresies. On this day, two lists are read, one of condemned heretics, and the other of saints* and pious emperors.

orthopraxis/orthopraxy (Gk., *orthos*, right + praxis*, practice) Right practice as distinct from orthodoxy, or right beliefs, especially as a basis for recognition or communion.

orthros (lit., daybreak) In the Eastern Church*, the morning office, corresponding to the mattins* and lauds* in the West.

Orvieto Cathedral built by Pope Urban IV in Orvieto, Italy, to house the miraculous bleeding Host of Bolsena*, founded between 1195 and 1230. The most notable features of the cathedral are the rectangular cross-ribbed vaulted choir by Giovanni di Bonini, frescoes* by Ilario, relief of biblical scenes on the pillars of the three-storied facade carved by Andrea Pisano and Vitale Maitani, and the casket holding the priceless relic* by Ugolino di Vieris.

Orvieto Cathedral

OSA Augustinian Order.

OSB Order of St. Benedict.

Osborn, Tommy Lee (1923–) Missionary and faith healer. He was converted at the age of 12 and called to preach at 14. He and his wife, Daisy, went to India in 1945 but was invalided and forced to return. In 1948 they began a ministry of healing evangelism and thereafter conducted highly successful crusades* in over 40 countries, including the United States, Puerto Rico, Venezuela, Kenya, Indonesia, Holland, Chile, and Switzerland. The Osborn Foundation is headquartered in Tulsa, Oklahoma.

OSD Order of St. Dominic*.

Osek Cistercian monastery at Osek in the north BohemIan mountains in the Czech Republic, erected between 1206 and 1220. Raided and plundered in the religious wars of the fifteenth and sixteenth centuries, the monastery became bankrupt and was dissolved by Pope Gregory XIII* in 1580. After Bohemia again became Catholic at the end of the wars, Osek came to life again. Between 1712 and 1718 the monastery Church of the Assumption was rebuilt in Baroque style by the architect, Ottavio Broggio. Among the great artists and sculptors who worked on the project were Franz Anton Kuen, Edmund Johann Richter, Giacomo Antonio Corbellini, Wenzel Lorenz Reiner, Johann Jakob Steinfels, and Michael Willmann.

Osiander, Andreas (1496/8–1552) German reformer of Nuremberg. He was ordained priest in 1520 and revised the Vulgate* on the basis of the Hebrew text. At the Colloquy of Marburg* in 1529 he sided with Luther* and Melanchthon* against Zwingli* and Oecolampadius* regarding the Lord's Supper*. He also attended the Diet of Augsburg. After the Augsburg Interim* (1548) he left Nuremberg to become professor at Königsburg, where he published *De Justificatione* (1550). He opposed Luther's doctrine of justification* by faith*, maintaining that Christ's righteousness was not merely imputed to the believer but was infused, or transferred.

Osservatore Romano Newspaper in Italian published daily except on Sundays by the Vatican*, founded in 1861. It publishes the official text and authorized translations of encyclicals* and papal documents and speeches, announcements, and appointments of bishops.

ostension Elevation of the chalice* after consecration by the priest.

ostensory/ostensorium 1. Receptacle showing objects of religious devotion to the faithful. 2. Monstrance* used for the exposition of the Blessed Sacrament*.

Ostian Way (Lat., *Via Ostiensis*) Ancient imperial road which led from Rome* to the seaport of Ostia, on the left bank of the mouth of the Tiber, about 14 miles from Rome. On the west side lies the Church of St. Paul's Outside the Walls*, the traditional site of the resting place of the remains of St. Paul*.

ostiary 1. Church doorkeeper*. 2. Member of the lowest of the minor orders*.

ostrich eggs Symbol of the Resurrection.

Ostrog Bible First full text of the Bible in Church Slavonic* named after Prince Constantine of Ostrog. It was produced by the Ostrog Circle of Orthodox scholars including Cyril Lukaris. The translation employed classical Church Slavonic while following closely Greek textual traditions. A landmark in Slavic biblical history, it was as influential on subsequent editions of Russian Bibles as the King James Version* was on later English Bibles.

Oswald, St. (c. 605–642) King of Northumbria and martyr*. He was converted to the Christian faith by the monks of St. Columba* at Iona*. He was restored to the throne that had been stolen by Edwin after defeating the British king Cadwallon in 634. With the help of St. Aidan*, he established Christianity throughout his kingdom. In the eighth year of his reign he was killed in battle. He is honored as a martyr*. Feast day: August 5.

Oswald, St. (d. c. 992) Archbishop of York* who promoted the revival of monasticism* in England before the Norman Conquest and helped to found a number of monasteries, including Ramsey. He introduced the Benedictine Rule into England and promoted many reforms of the clergy. Feast day: February 28.

OT Old Testament.

otpust In the Byzantine Rite*, a dismissal hymn sung at the end of the vespers* just before the bread is blessed.

Otterbein, Philip William (1726–1813) German Reformed* pastor and cofounder of the United Brethren in Christ*. After ordination in 1749 he emigrated to the American colonies, where he served a number of German Reformed congregations as pastor. While pastor at York*, he teamed with Martin Boehm* to hold a series of evangelistic meetings out of which came the United Brethren in Christ in 1789.

Otto, Rudolf (1869–1937) German Protestant theologian. He was professor of systematic theology at Breslau and Marburg. His *Idea of the Holy* (1923) developed the concept of the numinous* as an element of religious consciousness. Among his other works was *The Kingdom of God and the Son of Man* (1938).

Otto, St. (1062/3–1139) Apostle of Pomerania and bishop of Bamberg*. He was responsible for the founding of over 20 monasteries and the building of a cathedral. In 1124 he went on a missionary journey to the Pomeranians, who had agreed to accept the Christian faith as a condition of the peace they made with Duke Boleslas III of Poland in 1120. He converted many of the most important towns. He was canonized in 1189. Feast day: September 30.

Ottobeuren Benedictine monastery, called the Swabian Escorial* and the Gateway to Heaven, founded in 764 in the foothills of the Alps in Germany. The whitewashed monastic buildings built from 1711 to 1725 are arranged around three courtyards. The massively proportioned cathedral was principally the work of Johann Michael Fischer*. The interior was decorated by the best artists of the time. Johann Jakob and Franz Zeiller did the paintings, Johann Michael Feichtmayer the stucco, and Johann Christian the sculptures.

Our Father The Lord's Prayer*.

Our Lady The Virgin Mary*.

Our Lady of Sorrows Marian* title recalling her seven sorrows*.

Our Lady of the Rosary Marian* title focusing on the recitation of Ave Marias* in the Rosary*.

Our Lady of the Snows Catholic liturgical feast, now known as the Dedication of the Basilica of St. Mary Major* (Santa Maria Maggiore), celebrated

August 5. It recalls the miraculous mid-summer snowfall in Rome* during the pontificate* of Liberius* when, according to tradition, the Virgin Mary appeared to a Roman couple and instructed them to build the basilica*.

ourar In the Armenian tradition, the diaconal stole* with three crosses generally worn over the left shoulder with the free ends falling in the front and behind.

ousia (Gk., substance or nature) Defining term of the Christological controversies of the early church clarifying the relationship of the Father to the Son. *Homoousion,* the term in the Nicene Creed*, expressed the essential unity of the Godhead in which the Father and the Son shared the same nature or substance. Semi-Arians, on the other hand, used the term *homoiousion,* expressing the notion of like or similar substance.

outreach Extent and range of evangelistic efforts directed toward non-Christians or nominal Christians.

Overbeck, Johann Friedrich (1789–1896) German religious painter responsible for the revival of Christian art in the nineteenth century. He is best remembered for such paintings as *Christ's Agony in the Garden* and *The Triumph of Religion in the Arts.*

Overseas Missionary Fellowship (OMF) International and interdenominational fellowship founded in 1865 by J. Hudson Taylor* as the China Inland Mission* by which name it was known until 1965. Following the closure of the People's Republic of China to missionary work, OMF now works in ten East Asian countries. It has been one of the greatest of the faith missions in modern times.

overture Formal submission of a proposal or communication from a presbytery* to the general assembly* or vice versa.

Owen, John (1616–1683) Outstanding Reformed* theologian. He was dean of Christ Church, Oxford,* and university vice chancellor and chief architect of Oliver Cromwell's state church. He helped to compose the Savoy Declaration* of

Faith and Order. After the restoration, he lost his positions, but emerged as the leading nonconformist voice and defender of the rights of his fellow dissenters. A prolific writer, he remains still a powerful theological voice to reckon with.

Owen, St. Nicholas (c. 1550–1606) English martyr*. He was a carpenter who built a number of priests' hiding places in country houses and thus saved the lives of many Roman Catholics during the Elizabethan persecution. He was arrested, imprisoned, tortured, and killed. He was canonized in 1970 as one of the forty martyrs* of England and Wales.

ox, winged Symbol of St. Luke* in Christian art.

Oxford English city whose ecclesiastical history begins with a convent founded in the eighth century by the father of St. Frideswide. About 1122 the convent was taken over by the Augustinian Canons*. During the Middle Ages Oxford was part of the Diocese of Lincoln, but in 1542 Henry VIII elevated it as the See of Oxford with the Oseney Cistercian Abbey as the cathedral church. In 1546 the seat of the bishopric was transferred to King's (formerly Cardinal's) College founded by Thomas Wolsey on the site of St. Frideswide's Priory. The priory* church thereupon became the cathedral church and the college was renamed Christ Church*. The University of Oxford has its origins in the schools attached to parishes in the town. In 1214 the papal legate, Nicholas de Romanis, drew up a constitution for the schools and named the bishop of Lincoln as its first chancellor. In the thirteenth century Balliol and University colleges were founded. In 1571 the university was incorporated by Act of Parliament. Oxford University has played a major role in the development of the Church of England*, as witnessed by such leaders as Hugh Latimer*, John Fell, Robert South, and such movements as the Oxford movement*.

Oxford Cathedral Christ Church*, smallest cathedral in England, originally built in the eighth century as St. Frideswide's nunnery which was burned down by the Danes in 1002. It was rebuilt around 1170. One impressive feature of the cathedral is the fan-vaulting* of the choir.

Oxford Conference The second conference of the Life and Work* branch of the ecumenical movement* held at Oxford in 1937. It was attended by 425 delegates from all countries except Nazi Germany. The meeting agreed to merge Life and Work* with Faith and Order*. The first combined meeting of the two bodies was held at Amsterdam in 1948 as the World Council of Churches*.

Oxford Group Original name of Moral Re-Armament* (MRA) founded by Frank Buchman* in 1921 as a moral and spiritual "expeditionary force" for transforming societies and catalyzing change through education and reconciliation. Part of its work was in securing personal conversion through the four techniques of confession*, surrender, guidance, sharing, as well as group involvement and witnessing. It promoted four absolute standards of life: absolute purity, absolute unselfishness, absolute honesty, and absolute love. MRA's early successes were due to its effective use of visual and dramatic media, including films and musicals. It has an international center at Caux in Switzerland.

Oxford movement Also, Anglo-Catholic movement; Ritualist movement; Tractarianism*. Nineteenth-century movement within the Church of England* to return to the pre-Reformation doctrines, rituals, and practices and to restore the integrity of the Christian church assailed by the liberal establishment. It was so called because many of its leaders, especially J. H. Newman*, J. Keble*, and E. B. Pusey*, were all members of Oriel College, Oxford, in the 1820s. The movement began with Keble's sermon on "National Apostasy" delivered at St. Mary the Virgin, Oxford, in 1833, against a Parliament bill to reduce the number of bishoprics* of the Church of Ireland*. Keble's colleagues soon came out with the *Tracts of the Times,* contributed by many who shared his views on the erosion of orthodoxy* in the Church of England.

From 1840 the movement, under Newman*, began to display pro-Catholic sympathies. In 1841 he published Tract No.90 in which he argued for a Catholic interpretation of the Thirty-Nine Articles*. Public condemnation of this tract led to Newman's withdrawal from the movement in 1843. A similar fate awaited W. G. Ward's *The Ideal* *of a Christian Church* in 1845. In the same year, Newman joined the Roman Catholic Church, and this marked the virtual end of the movement as a force in the Church of England*.

Oxyrhynchus Papyri Fragments of Greek papyri* discovered at Oxyrhynchus, one of the chief cities of ancient Egypt, by B. P. Grenfell and A. S. Hunt and others in 1897. The most important documents in this cache, before the seventh century, are the *Sayings of Jesus,* which are similar to the Coptic Gospel of Thomas*, and a Christian hymn with musical notation, the oldest known piece of Christian music.

Ozanam, Antoine Frederic (1813–1853) French scholar and founder of the Society of St. Vincent de Paul*, an association of laymen ministering to the poor. From 1844 he was full professor at the Sorbonne*. In 1849 he published his most influential work, *La Civilisation Chretienne Chez le Francs.* Politically, he was a liberal and cofounded *Ere Nouvelle* in 1848 as a magazine of Catholic socialism.

Gospel of St. Thomas

Pp

Pachelbel, Johann (1653–1706) German Baroque organist-composer. His entire career was spent as a church organist. A Lutheran by birth and training, he, nevertheless, assimilated Roman Catholic musical traditions. The majority of his organ works were composed for the Lutheran Liturgy*, including 70 chorale preludes and 95 fugues. Most of his nonliturgical organ music was intended for use in church. He also produced a significant number of sacred vocal works, including 13 Magnificats*, 11 cantata-like compositions, and 11 motets*.

Pachomius St. (c. 287–346) Egyptian founder of community-life Christian monasticism*. Born to pagan parents, he was converted and baptized after his discharge from the army. He founded a monastery in 320 at Tabennisi in the Thebaid* near the Nile River, where his reputation for holiness* attracted hundreds. At his death Pachomius was the abbot general* over nine monasteries for men and two for women. His rule formed basis for the later monastic rules of St. Basil*, John Cassian, St. Caesarius of Arles*, and St. Benedict*. Feast day: May 9 (Coptic Church*); May 14 (Western Church*); May 15 (Eastern Church*).

Pacific Garden Mission One of the most celebrated urban evangelical rescue missions in Chicago founded in 1877 by Sarah Dunn Clarke and her husband Colonel George Rogers Clarke. It was originally called Clarke's Mission. In 1880 the Clarkes purchased the Pacific Beer Garden, a tawdry beer joint, and at the suggestion of Dwight L. Moody* renamed it the Pacific Garden Mission. It purchased a former brothel known as the White House in 1922, two more buildings to the north in 1941, and the Loyola Hotel in 1955. The mission operates a number of specialized ministries, including a night shelter for the homeless, a shelter for women, an outreach for servicemen, and a radio program called "Unshackled."

Packer, James Innell (1926–) Anglican Evangelical theologian. He taught at Tyndale Hall, Bristol, and then was professor of historical and systematic theology* at Regent College, Vancouver, Canada. He is one of the most influential Christian apologists and theologians in the Evangelical Re-

J. I. Packer

formed* and Puritan tradition in the twentieth century. His work has proved popular because of its clarity and vigor. Among his works are *"Fundamentalism" and the Word of God* (1958), *Evangelism and the Sovereignty of God* (1961), *Knowing God* (1973), *Knowing Man* (1979), *Rediscovering Holiness* (1992), and *Concise Theology: A Guide to Historic Christian Beliefs* (1993). He also pursued Christian unity on a biblical basis, as in Evagelicals and Catholics Together.

Paderborn Hall-church in Westphalia in Germany, built by Charlemagne*. Five earlier buildings preceded the present cathedral. The three-naved hall measures 105 feet and is one of the largest in Germany. Among the church's finest features are the Paradise Portal on the south side and the Red Portal on the north side.

padre (Span., father) Term of address for a priest or chaplain*.

paedobaptism Infant baptism*.

paenula Chasuble*. It was the name of the Roman cloak from which the chasuble is derived.

pahk In the Armenian tradition, fasting on Wednesdays and Fridays.

pain benit Blessed bread, distributed to the congregation after the Mass*, corresponding to the antidoron* in the Eastern Orthodox Church*.

Paissi Velichkovskii (1722–1794) Of Jewish and Ukrainian descent, he became a monk in 1741 at Medvedka Monastery and settled at Athos* in 1746. Driven out by the Turks, he and his followers moved to Dragomirna and to Neamt in Moldavia, then the largest Orthodox monastery.

pakegh Conical hat worn by Armenian clerics.

pakila Outermost eucharistic vestment worn by Assyrian and Chaldean clerics.

pala Large altarpiece in which the action, the figures, and the scenes are treated in one space and take place in a single continuum. Distinct from ancona*, which consists of several pictures united

in a single frame, or a polyptych* which consists of a central picture with a number of smaller pictures grouped around it.

Pala d' Oro

Palatine Of or relating to the Vatican*, especially to the Vatican palace.

Palatine Guard Papal militia corps created in 1850 and disbanded in 1870.

Palau, Luis (1934–) Argentine evangelist. He founded the Luis Palau Evangelistic Team in the early 1960s and began a series of crusades* that has taken him throughout Latin America, North America, and Europe. He operates radio and television programs and has published over 40 books in Spanish and English.

Palestine Exploration Fund Society and foundation established in London in 1865 to provide "for the accurate and systematic investigation of the archeology, topography, geology and physical geography, natural history and manners and customs of the Holy Land*." It funded the pioneer work of Sir Charles Warren in Jerusalem*.

Palestrina, Giovanni Pierluigi da (c. 1525–1594) Italian composer, regarded as the first Catholic Church musician. In 1551 Pope Julius III* appointed him musical instructor at the Capella Giulia of St. Peter's* with the title of magister capellae. From 1554 to 1560 he was maestro della capella of St. John Lateran and from 1561 to 1567 he held a similar post at Santa Maria Maggiore*. In 1571 he was

Giovanni Pierluigi da Palestrina

appointed choirmaster of St. Peter's*, a post he held until his death. For the Roman Catholic Church Palestrina represents the best of sacred music and, although austere and of limited emotional range, his works are deeply spiritual and his disciplined techniques have influenced generations of religious composers. Palestrina left over 250 motets*, including many on texts taken from the *Song of Solomon*. As a composer of masses he has no equal. Of the 100 that he wrote, the best known are the *Aeterna Christi Munera, Assumpta est Maria, Missa Brevis**, and *Missa Papae Marcelli*. Among his most performed works are *Sicut Cervus* and *Stabat Mater**.

Paley, William (1743–1805) Anglican scholar who was one of the chief proponents of natural theology*. He sought to prove the existence of God from evidences in nature in his books *Natural Theology* (1802) and *Evidences of Christianity* (1794). He was an active apologist for the Church of England* when religious beliefs were being eroded by Deism*.

palimpsest (Gk., rubbed again) Parchment* from which the writing has been erased so that another

text may be entered. Many biblical manuscripts were palimpsests. The original text can often be read by modern techniques.

palitsa In the Byzantine tradition, vestment that is similar to the epigonation*, worn on the right hip.

Palitsa

pall 1. Sacred cloth, usually a square piece of cardboard covered with linen, placed over the chalice* at Mass*. 2. Cloth, usually black, purple, or white velvet, spread over a coffin.

Palladio (1508–1580) Birth name: Andrea della Gondola. Italian architect. One of his earliest churches was at Maser, and his next was San Francesco della Vigna in Venice*. In 1566 he began San Giorgio Maggiore facing the Doge's palace across the lagoon. It has been called "the most beautiful church in the world." His third church was the Redentore, begun in 1576.

Palladius (c. 363–425) Bishop and historian. He entered monastic life at the age of 23 and went to the Nitrian Desert*, where he became acquainted with many of the great monastic communities. Returning to Palestine, he was consecrated bishop of Helenopolis by his friend John Chrysostom,* and was later exiled to Egypt by anti-Chrysostom factions. In addition to *Historia Lausiaca* (419–420), a celebrated chronicle of early monasticism*, he wrote a biography of Chrysostom.

Palladius, Peter (1504–1560) Danish Reformation* leader. He studied under Luther* and Melanchthon* before being named bishop in 1557. He helped introduce Lutheranism* into Denmark, Norway, and Iceland, translated

Luther's *Shorter Catechism**, and assisted in the translation of the Bible.

pallium White circular band, marked with six purple or black crosses, with two strips hanging from it, worn over the shoulder by the pope, archbishops, and certain bishops. It is made from the wool of lambs blessed on St. Agnes's day after being placed overnight on the tomb of St. Peter* in the Vatican basilica*. It is the symbol of papal and metropolitan authority.

Pallottini Fathers Official name: Society of the Catholic Apostolate. Society of Roman Catholic fathers, lay brothers*, sisters*, and associates founded in 1835 by St. Vincent Pallotti (1795–1850), formerly known as the Pious Society of Missions.

Palm Sunday Also, Passion Sunday*. Sunday beginning Holy Week*, commemorating Jesus' triumphal entry into Jerusalem* and marking the beginning of the Holy Week. The distinctive ceremony of Palm Sunday services is the blessing of palms and a procession reenacting the biblical events on this day.

Palmarum Title for the sixth Sunday in Lent*, called the Sunday of the Passion.

palmatorium See BUGIA.

palmer Pilgrim* who carried a palm as a memento of a visit to the Holy Land*.

Palmer, Phoebe Worrall (1807–1874) Methodist lay revivalist*. By 1835 she and her sister Sarah Worrall Lankford Palmer (1806–1896) had become vigorous exponents of Wesleyan perfectionism* or entire sanctification*. Her sanctification theology consisted of three simple steps: Consecrating or presenting one's body as a living sacrifice to God, believing God keeps his promise to sanctify what is thus consecrated, and bearing witness to what God has done. She also popularized the idea of Pentecostal Spirit baptism* available to every believer. She edited the magazine *Guide to Holiness,* published over 10 books, including the *Way of Holiness* (1845), and took part in over 100 camp meetings* and revival campaigns in the United

States, Canada, and the United Kingdom. Her concept of lay ministry was one of the ideas that triggered the awakening of 1858. She was also ac-

Phoebe Palmer

tive in promoting women's ministries and urban ministries.

Pamphilius, St. (c. 250–310) Christian martyr*. He founded a Christian school at Caesarea* in Palestine and restored the library of Origen*, copying biblical manuscripts, especially the *Hexapla**. Arrested under Maximin Daza, he spent 15 months in prison and was beheaded in 310. His devoted pupil, Eusebius* of Caesarea, wrote his life's story. Feast day: February 16 (Eastern Church*); June 1 (Western Church*).

Panagia (Gk., all holy) Title of the Virgin Mary* in the Eastern Church*, especially in reference to the oval medallion worn on the breast suspended on a chain by Orthodox bishops.

Panagia

Panagia Nikopia (Gk., all-holy bringer of victory) Title applied to icons of the Virgin Mary* and child enthroned.

panagiarion In the Eastern Church*, a paten* set on a high foot, instead of being flat.

panague Armenian episcopal pectoral cross, oval in shape and decorated with precious stones.

pan-Christian Encompassing all Christian denominations.

panentheism (Gk., everything in God) Doctrine that God includes the world as a part, though not the whole, of his being. Unlike pantheism*, it holds that he is more than the universe, although he penetrates the entire universe.

Pange Lingua Title of two famous Latin hymns, both beginning with "Pange Lingua," one a Passiontide* hymn written by Venantius Fortunatus* and the other a Corpus Christi* hymn written by Thomas Aquinas*.

panikhida (Gk., all-night vigil*) Memorial services for the deceased sung at a funeral or anniversary of a death.

Pannenberg, Wolfhart (1928–) German Protestant theologian. A student of Karl Barth*, he has worked on developing a theology of revelation*. His first work in this field was *Jesus—God and Man* (1968), a defense of the historicity of the Resurrection in the context of apocalyptic thought. His *Systematic Theology* (3 vols., 1988–1993) presents a complete exposition of major Christian doctrines.

panniculus Small morsel of bread, like the bread of the Eucharist*.

Pannonhalma Ancient Benedictine abbey near Gyor in Hungary founded in 996 by the Grand Prince Geza. Its patron saint* was Martin* of Tours*. It was twice rebuilt in 1137 and 1224. In 1241 it was fortified as a defense against invading Mongols. In the following centuries the abbey became rich and powerful. In 1575 it was destroyed by fire and the monks moved out, and in 1594 it was captured by the Turks. The Benedictines* returned in 1638, and the rebuilding of the abbey began in the seventeenth century. The medieval cloister* is approached through the Porta Speciosa, the magnificent southern entrance ornamented with fantastic symbolic carvings of the late Gothic* period. The great Refectorium was built by the Carmelite* Martin Witwer, and in 1730 Antonio Fossati decorated it with biblical frescoes*.

pannychis In the Byzantine tradition, a vigil*, especially an all-night vigil for the dead.

Panormitis Monastery of the archangel* Michael at Panormitis in Symi in the Dodecanese, Greece, built in 1783.

Pantaenus, St. (d. c. 190) First known head of the famous Catechetical School of Alexandria*. He was the teacher of Clement* (who succeeded him in 190) and of Alexander. Eusebius* states that he preached the gospel in India. Feast day: June 22 (Coptic Church*); July 7 (Western Church*).

Pantaleon, St. (d. 305) Martyr*. Physician at the court of Emperor Galerius, who was martyred under Diocletian. In the Middle Ages, he was honored as a patron saint* of physicians, and he was also one of the auxiliary saints*. Feast day: July 27.

pantheism Belief that God and the universe are one and that God is the combined manifestation of all the forces and phenomena in the existing universe. It holds that everything there is constitutes a unity and that this unity is divine. Pantheists deny the distinction between God and creatures found in Christianity. Term coined by John Toland*.

Pantocrator Christ in majesty as the judge of the world. As normally portrayed in church decoration, his countenance is severe and he is heavily bearded and long-haired. His right hand is raised in blessing or pointing to the Gospel that is held in his left hand.

Paolo, San Fuori le Mura (St. Paul's Outside the Walls) Basilica of St. Paul the apostle in Rome*. Nearby is an ancient catacomb* in which St.

Paul* is believed to have been buried, but his remains were transferred to a large basilica* of the same size and shape as the original St. Peter's* begun by the Emperor Valentinianus I in about 386 and continued by his successors, Theodosius, Arcadius, and Honorius. It was burned down in 1823 and restored on the same plan and reconsecrated in 1854.

Papa (Ital., father) 1. Term of address for the pope. 2. Term of address originally for any senior bishop, then later for an Eastern Orthodox* priest.

papa angelicus Traditional belief, as recorded by Telesphorus* of Cozenza in the fourteenth century, that a coming pope would usher in a new age of apostolic faith and zeal.

papacy Office of the pope as the vicar* of Christ*, keeper of the keys and successor of St. Peter*, and head of state of the Vatican*. Also used of the whole complex of papal power and splendor.

papal blessing Benediction or blessing bestowed by the pope. On solemn occasions, cardinals and bishops may be delegated to bestow the blessing.

Papal flag National standard of Vatican City State consisting of two equal-sized vertical stripes of yellow and white, with the insignia of the papacy on the white stripe.

Pantocrator

Papal insignia Triple crown or tiara* over two crossed keys*, one gold and one silver, tied with a red cord and two tassels.

papal Mass Pontifical High Mass* over which the pope presides and in which the Gospel and the Epistle are sung in both Latin and Greek.

Paphnutius, St. (d. c. 360) Egyptian monk, disciple of St. Anthony. He was so mutilated in the persecution by Maximin Daza (305–313) that his seared eye was kissed by Constantine*, and his body became an object of veneration*.

Papias (c. 60–c. 130) Bishop of Hierapolis in Phrygia who is reported by Irenaeus* to have been a "man of long ago," who was a companion of St. John the Evangelist and Polycarp* and to have known Aristion* and the daughters of Philip* the apostle. His work, *Expositions of the Oracles of the Lord* in five books, survives only in quotations and contained many oral traditions of the first century, including traditions regarding the writings of the Gospels.

Papini, Giovanni (1881–1956) Italian author. After many years as a secular philosopher, he was converted to Catholicism* and wrote the immensely popular *The Story of Christ* in 1923. It was followed by a less popular *Life of Augustine*.

papist Derogatory term used by Protestants for a Roman Catholic.

papyri/papyrus Ancient manuscripts made of papyrus, of which large numbers, mostly fragments, have survived in Egypt's dry climate. See PAPYROLOGY.

papyrology Study of papyri* as writing materials. The original form of a written work was the scroll or volumen consisting of a number of strips pasted together to form a strip of any length, which was then rolled up so that the writing was on the inner, usually more protected and smoother surface. But by the first century B.C. Romans bound parchment* sheets together to form rudimentary books or membranae to which Paul* refers in 2 Timothy 4:13. Christians were pioneers in this innovation, and very soon the codex*, as the book-form was called, became the most widely used format for Christian Scriptures. The papyrus-codex became the distinctive form of Christian manuscripts as distinct from the parchment* scroll of Judaism and the papyrus* scroll of the pagan world.

Papyrus

Parabalani Association of men at Alexandria*, attested in the fifth century, devoted to looking after the sick and burying the dead. Although they were listed among the clergy and they functioned under a bishop, they had neither orders nor vows. They were not permitted to be present at public gatherings or theaters. They also served as bodyguards for bishops.

parabema Also, parekklesia. Chapel or recess in an Orthodox church containing altars.

parable Narrative and didactic technique used in the New Testament by Jesus Christ consisting of an extended metaphor or simile drawn from real life that stimulates reflection by transferring meaning from the symbolic to the real. By posing an analogy, its meaning may be couched in enigmatic terms that can only be interpreted allegorically.

parachurch Of or relating to groups that carry out specific missions, ministries, or social services outside denominational structures and boundaries.

Paraclete Johannine* term for the Holy Spirit*, variously translated as the helper, intercessor, consoler, counselor, advocate, comforter, instructor, or one called alongside to help.

paradenomination Service agency which develops its own distinct and separate church life, offering its members worship facilities, and resembling a new or separate denomination.

paradiscus (lit., house of oblation) In the Jacobite Church*, place where the Blessed Sacrament* may be reserved.

Paradise Lost Epic poem by John Milton*, written about 1667, describing events in Genesis, particularly the fall of Adam and Eve. It was the first original non-dramatic work to be written in English in blank verse.

paragraph Bible Common modern practice of publishing Bible text in paragraphs rather than verses. Two editions of the King James Version* were brought out in paragraphs in 1838 and 1853, and the Revised Version* of 1881 also followed this arrangement.

parainesis/paraensis (Gk., moral instruction) Biblical exhortation containing ethical prescriptions about Christian life and conduct.

paraklesis Service of intercession to Jesus Christ, the Virgin Mary*, and the saints*, usually sung during the fortnight before the feast of the Dormition*.

parakletike (Gk., [Book] of Supplication) Byzantine Rite* liturgical book, also known as the oktoechos*.

parallel church In the Roman Catholic Church, suppressed but ongoing underground liberal or activist groups within the church.

paraman Part of the monastic habit of a Greek monk on which is embroidered the inscription, "I bear the wounds of the Lord on my body."

paraments Ornamental church hangings or garments and altar furnishings made from textiles.

paramoni (lit., to wait) In the Eastern Orthodox Church*, celebrations on the eves of Christmas* and Theophany* in which the Great or Royal Hours are recited.

parastasa In the Byzantine Rite*, the great requiem* service said after the evening service.

parathronos In the Greek tradition, a less ornate episcopal throne than the thronos*.

paratorium Sacristy* or vestry* used as a place of preparation.

Paray-le-Monial French place of pilgrimage* where St. Margaret Mary Alacoque* had a vision of Christ and established the cultus* of the Sacred Heart of Jesus*. It was founded in 977 as a Benedictine monastery, and in 999 it became a dependency of the Abbey of Cluny*. Its Priory church of Notre Dame*, a notable example of Burgundian Early Romanesque, was built from the eleventh to the twelfth centuries. It is a scaled-down version of Cluny, and although simple and modest, is a masterpiece of awe-inspiring grandeur. In 1875 the church was renamed Notre Dame de Sacre Coeur.

parchment Animal skin on which manuscripts were commonly written in the ancient world.

parclose Screen* or set of railings at the east end of the aisle of a church for enclosing a chantry* altar for requiems* and a few seats for family members.

pardon Indulgences sold by church officers, or pardoners*, in return for money for building purposes or for crusades.

pardoner Medieval Roman Catholic hawker of indulgences* granting remission of temporal punishment for sins in return for money or donations for church-approved causes.

parekklesion Additional small chapel, either attached to a main church, or free-standing

alongside, with its own altar flanked by prothesis* and diaconicon*, the whole separated by an iconostasis*.

paremii/paremia In the Byzantine Rite*, lessons from the Old and New Testaments relating to the feast being celebrated.

parenthesis In dispensationalist theology, the present or Church Age*, considered as a parenthesis in God's plan for human history.

Parham, Charles Fox (1873–1929) Pioneering Pentecostal leader. In 1900 he established a Bible school in Topeka, Kansas, where he taught the apostolic faith regarding the baptism of the Holy Spirit*, including speaking in tongues* as its initial sign. In 1901 one of his students, Agnes Ozman, experienced the blessing and sign. Another of his students, William J. Seymour*, a black Holiness evangelist, took the new message to Los Angeles where, at Azusa Street, it made history. However, the Azusa Street Revival* dealt a blow to Parham's prominence in the new movement. The final blow came when Parham was arrested in 1907 on charges of sodomy. Although the charges were eventually dropped, he never recovered his leadership and died comparatively unknown among the later generation of Pentecostals.

Paris Evangelical Missionary Society Missionary society founded in Paris in 1822 under the influence of C. G. Blumhardt and Mark Wilks. It was active in Lesotho, Zambia, Tahiti, Madagascar, Loyalty Islands, and New Caledonia.

Paris, Twila (1958–) American contemporary Christian singer. Most of her songs are original and have won many awards. They include "For Every Heart," "He Is Exalted," "We Will Glorify," "Lamb of God," and "Faithful Men."

parish (Gk., *paroikia*, district) Local area served by a local congregation led by a priest or pastor. In the Middle Ages, the parish was also a unit of civil administration with priests, constables, church wardens, overseers of the poor, and elected vestries. In Episcopal churches, a parish is a subdivision of a diocese*. In established or national churches, the parish system represents the availability of the ordinances of religion to every inhabitant of the nation. In Roman Catholic usage, parish is used of the local church community.

parish clerk Church official in the Church of England* who assists the priest by leading the responses of the congregation and sometimes in reading the Epistle. In three-decker pulpits, he was assigned the lowest.

parishioner Member of a parish*.

Parker, Horatio William (1863–1919) American composer of church music, noted for his collection *Hora Novissima*, based on a poem by Bernard of Cluny*. He restored liturgical propriety to church music.

Parker, Joseph (1830–1902) English Congregational* preacher. He ministered at the City Temple, where he enjoyed a reputation equal to Spurgeon* and Henry Liddon*. He never strayed from the evangelical truths enshrined in the Apostles' Creed*. His discourses were published in the 25 volumes of the *People's Bible*.

Parker, Matthew (1504–1575) Archbishop of Canterbury* from 1559. Ordained in 1527, he became chaplain* to Queen Anne Boleyn in 1535. Under Edward VI he was appointed dean of Lincoln

Matthew Parker

Cathedral in 1552 but was ousted during Mary's reign. On Elizabeth's accession he was named archbishop of Canterbury in 1559. He enforced the Settlement of Religion and consecrated and trained all the new bishops. Throughout the 1560s he contended with the Puritans*, who were growing in numbers. He donated his valuable library to Corpus Christi College, Cambridge.

Parker, Peter (1804–1888) First medical missionary to China. He was sent by the American Board to China in 1834, and in 1835 he opened an eye hospital in Canton, the first Christian hospital in the Far East. In 1838 he helped to organize the Medical Missionary Society in China and opened a hospital in Macao. He helped the United States negotiate its first treaty with China in 1844 after the First Opium War. In 1845 he left the mission field* for U.S. diplomatic service.

Parker Society Society established in 1840 under the leadership of the Earl of Shaftesbury and other prominent Evangelicals to issue the works of the early writers of the Reformed Church, such as Matthew Parker and Thomas Cranmer*.

parlatorium Room in a monastery set apart for conversation and consultation.

Parmigianino, Francesco (1503–1540) Most famous member of a family of painters in Parma called Mazzuoli. He developed into a highly sophisticated Mannerist painter. His best paintings are the *Mystic Marriage of St. Catherine* (1525), *Vision of St. Jerome* (1527), *Madonna and Child with St. Margaret and the Saints* (1529), *Madonna and Child with St. Mary Magdalene and St. Zachariah* (1535), and *Madonna and Child with Angels* (1535).

parochial Of or relating to a parish* as in parochial church council.

parochial school School, generally elementary, run by a parish* or controlled by a religious group.

Paroissien Prayer books in French designed for use by the laity published in France in the seventeenth century. In addition to devotional exercises, they contained translations of the masses and vespers* for Sundays and feasts.

Parousia (Gk., presence or arrival) Second Coming* or the return of Christ to earth in glory to judge the living and the dead.

parson Clergyman, rector*, or vicar*.

parsonage Minister's residence; rectory*.

parthenogenesis (Gk., *parthenos**, virgin + genesis, birth) The Virgin birth* and strictly, virginal conception.

Parthenos (Gk., virgin) Designation of the Virgin Mary*.

particle Small piece of communion bread* given to each communicant.

Particular Baptists Calvinist Baptists who believed that Christ's atonement* is reserved and limited to the elect*. The first Particular Baptist Confession was published in 1644. Among notable Particular Baptists were William Carey*, John Bunyan*, and Charles Spurgeon*. See also GENERAL BAPTISTS.

particular church In Roman Catholic usage, the local church.

particular confession Form of confession for specific needs and occasions.

particular judgment Divine judgment of each individual soul immediately on death. It is prior to and distinct from the general judgment on the last day.

particular redemption See LIMITED ATONEMENT.

Particularism Calvinist doctrine in which particular individuals are singled out by God for salvation* and others are passed over.

parvis 1. Court in front of a cathedral, especially when surrounded by a colonnade. 2. Church porch or portico.

parvitas materiae (Lat., smallness of matter) In scholastic moral theology*, a venial sin* that involves only a slight moral lapse.

pasbans In the Armenian tradition, small strips of brocade worn on each wrist used to wipe the hands during the liturgy.

Pascal, Blaise (1623–1662) French writer and scientist. He was converted twice, first at Rouen* in 1646 when he came into contact with the Jansenists, secondly, definitively, in 1654, following a miraculous vision when he discovered "the God of Abraham, Isaac and Jacob and not of the philosophers and men of science." He carried the memorial of this experience on his person for the rest of his life. His two chief works are *Lettres Provinciales* and *Pensées*. The former consisted of

Blaise Pascal

18 letters attacking the Jesuits*, especially their theory of grace* known as Molinism* and their moral theology* known as probabilism*. *Pensées* consisted of notes he left at his death toward a broad Christian apology. Pascal's theology was Christ-centered and based on the heart rather than reason. He held that only faith can rescue human beings from their wretched condition.

Pascha (Heb., passover) Easter*, in early church celebration embracing the Crucifixion as well as the Resurrection of Jesus Christ.

Paschal II (d. 1118) Pope from 1099. Birth name: Ranierus. Much of his papacy was spent in the investiture controversy* with Emperor Henry V. Henry took the pope prisoner and at Ponte Mammalo extorted concessions from him which Paschal later condemned. His councils at Lateran* and elsewhere enacted important canons.

Paschal Of or relating to Passover or Easter*.

Paschal Annotinum Anniversary of a baptism*, commemorated with prayer and thanksgiving.

Paschal Babylon, St. (1540–1592) Franciscan lay brother*. He entered the Franciscan Order* in response to a miraculous vision. At the convent he practiced extreme mortification* and was particularly devoted to the cult of the Blessed Sacrament*. He was canonized in 1690, and in 1897 he was declared the patron of eucharistic congresses and associations. Feast day: May 17.

Paschal candle Large candle lighted throughout the Easter* season in Roman Catholic churches. During the Paschal Vigil Service*, the celebrant blesses the new fire* and then marks the candle with the sign of the cross, the Alpha and Omega* in Greek, and the date of the year, places five grains of sand on the cross, and lights the candle from the new fire. The deacon carries the lighted candle through the church, making three stations during which Lumen Christi (Light of Christ) is sung. When the celebrant and the deacon reach the sanctuary, all lights are lit and the exultet* is sung. The candle remains in the sanctuary until Whitsuntide* when it is taken to the baptistery and lighted at all baptisms throughout the year.

Paschal controversies Controversy from the second to the eighth centuries regarding the date for celebrating Easter*. The earliest dispute in the second century concerned whether the Pascha* should be celebrated on the same day as the Jewish Passover, 14 Nissan, regardless of the day of the week, or only on the following Sunday. See also QUARTODECIMANISM. Once this was resolved in favor of Sunday Pascha, there remained questions about the calculation of the date. These have been of stubborn complexity because of divergent regional traditions, different calendrical systems, and inconsistent computation tables. As a result, although the Western churches observe a common Easter, the Orthodox, following the Julian calendar* rather than the Gregorian calendar*, may be up to five weeks later.

Paschal lamb Christ as the Lamb of God* sacrificed for the sins of the world, as foreshadowed in the sacrifice of a perfect lamb at the first Jewish Passover in Egypt (1 Cor. 5:7).

Paschal Vigil Service Easter* celebration during the night of Holy Saturday* and Easter Sunday morning. It consists of two parts. The first part is the ceremony revolving around the Paschal candle* followed by Old Testament and New Testament readings and a homily*. The second part is the blessing of the baptismal font* by lowering the Paschal candle and raising it again. In the Byzantine Rite*, the Easter service consists of mattins* and the liturgy of Easter Day.

Paschalion Table used for establishing the date of Easter*.

Paschaltide Passiontide* or Easter* season.

Paschasius, St. Radbertus (c. 790–c. 860) Carolingian theologian. His chief work was *De Corpore et Sanguine Domini* (831/2) on the Eucharist* maintaining the real presence* of Christ. His other works include a life of Abbot Adelard, a commentary on St. Matthew, and a commentary on the Book of Lamentations.

paskha In the Byzantine tradition, an Easter* food made of sweetened curds mixed with butter, cream, eggs, and various dried fruits and nuts, decorated with almonds and glace cherries. On one side the letters XB, standing for "Christ is risen," are outlined.

Passau Cathedral in Passau, Germany, founded in the ninth century as the mother church of the eastern Danube and as a bulwark against Byzantium*. The present cathedral was built in the seventeenth century to replace one that was destroyed by fire. The architect was Carlo Lurago, the stucco work was done by Giovanni Battista Carlone and Paolo d'Aglio, and the paintings by Carlo Antonio Bussy and Carpoforo Tencalla. The cathedral contains the largest organ in the world.

passibile Able to undergo suffering or pain; liable to change as a result of external pressures or circumstances. Considered as one element of Christ's humanity. Thus, possibility.

Passion 1. Agony and death of Jesus Christ on the cross. 2. Oratorio* based on the Lord's death on the cross.

passion bearers Martyrs in the Eastern Orthodox Church*, as Boris and Gleb*, the first canonized saints* of Rus and the sons of Prince Vladimir*; the Serbian John Vladimir; Maria of Bizye; John Joasaph IV; Laskaris; and most recently, Tsar Nicholas II, and other members of the Romanov family murdered by the Bolsheviks.

passion play Religious drama built around Christ's Passion* and usually played at Paschaltide*. The most famous passion play is that at Oberammergau*.

Passion Sunday Fifth Sunday in Lent* marking the beginning of Passiontide*.

Passion Week See HOLY WEEK.

Passional Various Latin liturgical books*, especially the series of lections from the lives or acts of the saints* read at mattins* on their feast day or a book containing the narratives of the Lord's Passion from the four Gospels.

Passionists Popular name for the Congregation of Discalced Clerks of the Most Holy Cross and Passion of Our Lord Jesus Christ, founded in 1737 by Paul of the Cross* at Monte Argentario, Italy. They take a fourth vow in addition to the regular three, to further the memory of Christ's Passion*. They wear a black habit bearing the emblem of a white heart inscribed *Jesu XPI Passio*, surmounted by a cross. Their chief activities are missions and retreats.

passions Detailed contemporary accounts of the early Christian martyrdoms.

Passiontide Last two weeks of Lent* from Passion Sunday to Holy Saturday*. During this period it was customary to veil all pictures, crucifixes, and images in the church in purple and for the Gloria Patri* to be omitted from the Psalms, the introit*, and the venite*.

Passover Lamb 1. Lamb sacrificed at the Jewish Feast of Passover. 2. Christ as the eternal sacrificial lamb* of the Atonement*.

pastophorion In the Eastern Church*, the sacristy* adjoining the apse* used for the reservation* of the sacrament*.

pastor (Lat., pastor, shepherd [of souls]) Title of minister or clergyman in charge of a local Protestant church. It is one of the five ministries specifically mentioned in Ephesians 4:11, the other four being apostle, prophet*, evangelist, and teacher.

Pastor Aeternus Opening words of the First Dogmatic Constitution on the Church of Christ issued by the First Vatican Council* of 1870, defining papal infallibility*.

Pastoral Epistles The epistles of Paul to Timothy* and Titus*. So called because they are written by Paul* in his capacity as pastor to these two individual church leaders and not because they deal with responsibilities of pastors.

pastoral letter 1. In Episcopal churches, a letter from the bishop of a synod* to all believers in his jurisdiction. 2. In nonliturgical churches, a letter from the minister to his congregation.

pastoral prayer In Protestant churches, a long introductory prayer at the beginning of the service combining adoration, confession*, supplication, thanksgiving, and intercession.

pastoral staff The crosier*.

pastoral theology Branch of theology concerned with the practical application of Scriptures to the care of souls and the pastor's duties as a shepherd. It is a three-sided discipline involving God, the pastor, and his or her congregation. Much of pastoral theology is laid down in Paul's epistles that outline the pastor's personal commitment to Christ and his service, driven by compassion for his flock*. Paul* gives the details of the mode of government and couples them with solemn warnings and exhortations. It includes the art of preaching and the science of homiletics*. More recently it has also expanded into counseling.

Pastoralia Branch of theology dealing with the office of the local minister or priest, especially the methods of worship, the administration of sacraments*, preaching, the care of sick and dying, and the application of moral theology* to the lives of the parishioners* or members.

pastorate Office, state, jurisdiction, or tenure of a pastor.

pastorium Residence of a pastor; parsonage*.

patarag Armenian eucharistic liturgy, a modified version of the Liturgy of St. Basil*.

pataragamaduitz Armenian book containing liturgical texts.

paten In the Western Church*, metal plate, usually silver or gold, from which consecrated bread is dispensed during the Eucharist*. It corresponds to the discus* in the Eastern Church*.

Pater Noster (Lat., Our Father) 1. The Lord's Prayer*. 2. The rosary* bead used in reciting the Lord's Prayer*.

Paten and Host

pateressa In the Greek Orthodox Church, the bishop's staff*.

paterika/paterikon (fem., materikon) In the Eastern Orthodox* tradition, collections of sayings and deeds relating to the Church Fathers* or ascetic holy men.

Paterines Lay reform movement in North Italy in the eleventh century directed against clerical corruption and simony*. They played an important role in church-state politics in Milan* until the twelfth century.

Paternians Sect* in the early church which taught that the lower part of the body was not created by God. They made this doctrine an excuse for lives of flagrant sexual abuse.

pathora (lit., table) In the Syrian Church, the altar or sanctuary.

pathuro d'haiye In the Jacobite Rite, the altar or table of life.

Patmos Small island of the Sporades group in the Dodecanese in the Aegean Sea off the coast of Asia Minor to which John, author of Revelation,

Theologos Monastery

was exiled under Domitian, and where he received his vision in a grotto* on the hillside. Under the Romans, it was a penal colony. There is a monastery, the Theologos Monastery, in the middle of the island under the control of the patriarch* of Constantinople*.

patmucan In the Armenian Church*, priestly vestment corresponding to the sticharion*.

Patnit, Joachim de (c. 1475–1524) French religious painter noted for such paintings as *St. Jerome, The Temptation of St. Anthony, The Baptism of Christ, The Flight into Egypt,* and *St. John of Patmos.*

Paton, John Gibson (1824–1907) Scottish missionary to Vanuatu, formerly the New Hebrides. In 1857 he was ordained by the Reformed Presbyterian Church of Scotland as a missionary to the New Hebrides. He and his wife first served Aneityum and then Tanna in the island group. After the death of his wife in childbirth in 1859, he became a traveling ambassador and moved to the island of Aniwa as a missionary of the Presbyterian Church of Victoria. In the 1880s he made Melbourne in Australia his headquarters and also traveled widely. His *Autobiography* is a classic of missionary literature.

Paton, William (1886–1943) British missionary organizer and writer. He went to India for the YMCA* and was instrumental in the formation of the National Christian Council of India, Burma, and Ceylon as its general secretary. Subsequently he became the joint secretary of the International Missionary Council* and the editor of its journal, *International Review of Missions.* He helped to prepare missionary conferences at Jerusalem* (1928) and Madras (1938) and was one of the architects of the World Council of Churches*. He wrote extensively on missions and the world church. Among his books are *Jesus Christ and the World's Religions* (1916) and *The Church and the New Order* (1941).

patriarch Title of the bishops of the five chief sees*: Rome*, Alexandria*, Antioch*, Constantinople*, and Jerusalem*. Of these the first three are the oldest and were recognized by the Council of Nicaea* in 325. The other two were recognized at the Council of Chalcedon* in 451. In addition, the title is used by the heads of certain Orthodox autocephalous* churches, as Serbia, Russia, Romania, Bulgaria, and Georgia. The title is used as an honorific by the Roman Catholic bishops of Venice* and Lisbon. In the Byzantine Church*, the patriarch is assisted by numerous officials, as mega sakellarios or great treasurer; chartophylax* or chancellor; protonatarios or chief secretary; kastrensios or official in charge of the patriarchal insignia; hypomnematographos or secretary who writes the minutes of the synod*; hieromnemon, who edits and monitors the liturgical books*; and protosynkellos, who witnesses all acts of the patriarch.

patriarchate Office or jurisdiction of a patriarch*.

Patrick, Prayer of St. Poetic prayer, called "Lorica" (Celt., invoking protection), attributed to St. Patrick*, which runs as follows:

Power of God for my upholding,
Wisdom of God for my guidance,
Eye of God for my foresight
Against incantations of the false prophets,
Against black laws of paganism,
Against false laws of heresy,
Against encompassment of idolatry,
Against spells of women and smiths and druids,
Against all knowledge forbidden the human soul.

Patrick, St. (d. 460 or c. 490) "Apostle of Ireland." Patrick was the son of a deacon and Roman magistrate and was brought up as a Christian in Britain or Scotland. At 16 he was taken captive by Irish marauders and became a slave in East Antrim. After six years of indentured labor, he escaped to his homeland, but obedience to an earlier vision prompted him to return to Ireland in about 430 or 460. He traveled the length and breadth of Ireland for the next 30 years and had

St. Patrick

great success in converting Irish chieftains, ordaining clergy, and founding monasteries. He broke the power of paganism in Ireland. While his teaching was orthodox, the Irish church developed in practice largely isolated from the church of mainland Europe. Toward the end of his life, he wrote in Latin a moving account of his spiritual pilgrimage* called *Confessions*. His Feast day on March 17 is celebrated by the Irish all over the world.

Patrick's Cross Cross similar to St. Andrew's Cross*, but red on a white background.

Patrimony of St. Peter Temporal possessions of the Holy See*. Historically, the Patrimony of St. Peter goes back to the land given to the Holy See in perpetuity by Pepin the Short in 754 and 756. The papal states were lost by the Holy See in 1870 during the Italian Risorgimento. Under the Lateran Treaty* of 1929, an autonomous Vatican state was created over which the pope acts as the head of state.

Patripassianism See MONARCHIANISM; SABELLIANISM.

patristic age Period lasting roughly from the end of the first century to the death of the last of the Church Fathers*. There are no generally agreed upon dates for the close of the patristic age.

patristic conferences International conferences on Patristic Studies held at Oxford every four years since 1951.

patristics Branch of theology dealing with the writings of the patres or the Fathers of the Church* during what is known as the patristic age*. The writings of the patres are important in the study of heresies and the evolution of Christian doctrines and creeds. Less precisely it refers to the study of all early Christian sources and history.

patrology 1. Systematically arranged manual of patristic literature. 2. Study of the life and works of the early Christian Fathers. See also FATHERS OF THE CHURCH.

patron saint Special intercessor and protector in heaven* of a particular place, church, city, county,

profession, person, or organization. Patron saints correspond to the titular deities of Roman religion.

Patteson, John Coleridge (1827–1871) English founder of the Melanesian Mission and first bishop of Melanesia who was martyred on the island of Nukapu in 1871. He founded a college on Norfolk Island for the training of Melanesian boys.

Patti, Sandi (1956–) American singer and recording artist, known as the voice of contemporary Christian music. Her first work, *Sandi's Song* (1979), led to work with the Bill Gaither Trio. Her work bridges the gap between the Christian and secular world by a blend of contemporary styles and ministry-oriented texts.

Paul III (1468–1549) Pope from 1534. Birth name: Alessandro Farnese. Although immoral in his personal life and given to worldly pleasures, he presided over the Counter-Reformation* efforts and promoted a renewal of the church. During his reign many of the great religious orders, as the Jesuits*, were founded. He also established the Congregation of the Roman Inquisition*. He called the Council of Trent* in 1545 but suspended it three years later.

Paul V (1552–1621) Pope from 1605. Birth name: Camillo Borghese. His papacy was clouded by disputes with the city of Venice* and with England. Blameless in character, he promoted the work of the congregations devoted to education and care of the sick and to missionary work in North America and Africa. He completed the building of St. Peter's* and expanded the Vatican Library*. He vigorously enforced the decrees of the Council of Trent*.

Paul VI (1897–1978) Pope from 1963. Birth name: Giovanni Battista Montini. Ordained in 1920, he held office in the papal secretariat of state for 30 years from 1922. He was named archbishop of Milan* in 1954 and was elevated cardinal by Pope John XXIII*. In 1963 he was chosen to succeed John XXIII as pope. The central event of his papacy was Vatican Council II* of which he convened the second, third, and fourth sessions. He established a number of post-conciliar commissions, such as the Secretariat for Promoting Christian Unity* and the Secretariat for Non-Christian Religions and for Non-Believers.

Among his far-reaching reforms were the publication of a new missal in 1970, accompanied by a new lectionary* and a new Breviary* in 1971 and the introduction of the vernacular in the Mass* and Office. At the close of Vatican Council II*, he proclaimed an extraordinary jubilee*, or Holy Year*, from January 1 to Whitsunday*, 1966. He declared the Virgin Mary* to be the Mother of the Church*, and also proclaimed the first women, St. Teresa of Avila* and St. Catherine of Siena*, as doctors of the church*. He established a permanent Synod of Bishops with deliberative as well as consultative powers and convened a number of episcopal synods on social and economic justice, evangelization, priesthood, and catechesis*.

Pope Paul VI* was one of the most ecumenical of modern popes. He met with Athenogoras, the ecumenical patriarch*, and in a historic gesture issued a joint declaration expressing mutual regret for the schism* of 1054. He also met with two archbishops of Canterbury*, Ramsey and Coggan, and addressed the United Nations General Assembly in 1965 and the World Council of Churches* in Geneva* in 1969. He expanded the College of Cardinals* while restricting the right to vote in papal elections to cardinals under 80. His many encyclicals were generally conservative, shoring up traditional doctrines and opposing newfangled innovations.

Paul, Acts of St. Second-century apocryphal Greek account of the life of St. Paul* compiled in Asia Minor and merging a number of other similarly apocryphal accounts, such as the Martyrdom of St. Paul*, the Acts of Paul and Thecla*, and a Third Epistle of St. Paul to the Corinthians.

Paul and Thecla, Acts of St. Apocryphal work, popular in the early church and extant in Latin, Syriac*, Armenian, Slavonic, and Arabic. It described how Paul* converted Thecla, a heathen woman, and consequently was beaten. Thecla was condemned to death by burning, but was saved.

Paul, Apocalypse of St. Apocryphal account of St. Paul's journeys in heaven* and hell*. It is preserved in Greek, Latin, Coptic, Syrian, Armenian, Georgian, and Slavonic versions.

Paul, Martyrdom of St. Apocryphal account of the death of St. Paul* dating from the second part of the second century. It narrates the story of the sentence of death passed on Paul by Emperor Nero and the conversion of his two executioners, Longus and Cestus.

Paul of Samosata Heresiarch*. He became bishop of Antioch* in 260. He is reported to have taught a form of dynamic Monarchianism* according to which the Logos* was merely an attribute of the Father, constituting his power and reason. He was an Adoptionist in his Christology*, holding that in the Incarnation* the Logos descended on and dwelt in the man Jesus. His teaching was condemned at two, possibly three, synods of Antioch and he was deposed.

Paul of the Cross, St. (1694–1775) Birth name: Paul Francis Danei. Founder of the Passionists*. He was one of the most famous preachers and spiritual directors of his time, noted for his stirring meditations on the Passion*. Many miracles also have been attributed to him. In 1720 he was inspired by a vision to found a religious order in

St. Paul of Thebes and St. Anthony

honor of the Passion of our Lord. He drew up its rules. After being ordained in 1725 by Benedict XIII, he went to Monte Argentario, where he opened the first Passionist retreat* in 1737. In 1744 he moved to a second house near Vetralla as superior general*. By the time of his death, he had established over 12 monasteries in Italy with headquarters in the Church of Sts. John and Paul in Rome*. Feast day: April 28.

Paul of Thebes, St. (d. c. 340) Also, Paul the Hermit. According to Jerome, the first Christian hermit, who lived to be over 113. St. Anthony is said to have visited him on his deathbed and buried him. Feast day: January 15.

Paul, St. (d. c. 65) Birth name: Saul. "Apostle to the Gentiles." Writer who wrote most of the New Testament outside the Gospels. He was a Jewish Pharisee of the tribe of Benjamin, born in Tarsus in Cilicia* and educated under Gamaliel in Jerusalem, and a Roman citizen who spoke and wrote in Greek. He was present at the martyrdom of Stephen* and was commissioned by the high priest to arrest converts at Damascus*. On the road to Damascus he was converted in 33. After a short stay in Arabia, he spent most of his life in missionary travels in Asia Minor, Greece, Italy, and possibly Spain. Luke's narrative ends with his captivity in Rome*, and Eusebius* dates his martyrdom by beheading under Nero near the Ostian* in Rome.

The *Acts of St. Paul** describes him as "a man of small stature, with a bald head and crooked legs, in a good state of body, with eyebrows meeting and nose somewhat hooked." Paul was a brilliant writer and theologian who transmitted the radical message of the new messianic faith in a way that helped Christians break away from their Jewish roots. His epistles, the writings that he left behind, show him to be a many-faceted person, at times filled with anguish, affliction, tears, and pain (2 Cor. 1:4; 6:4–6), beside himself (2 Cor. 5:13), fighting within and without (2 Cor. 7:5), bold (2 Cor. 1:12), humble (2 Cor. 10:1), boastful (2 Cor. 11), warm and tender (2 Cor. 2:4; Phil. 1:7–8; 2:12; 4:1), and joyful and hopeful (2 Cor. 2:4; 4:16; 7:16; Phil. 1:4).

Many of the theological concepts and doctrines that have evolved through the centuries are a result of Paul's clear and lucid presentation of the gospel. A man of extensive learning, he used terms and analogies drawn from law, government, sports, philosophy, and commerce. Paul was an urban missionary who took the gospel to some of the most populated areas of the Roman Empire where he established a network of coworkers and colleagues. Surprisingly, his effectiveness had little to do with the length of time he spent in a local community. A brief stay in Thessalonica yielded great results, while a visit of 18 months and three letters to Corinth* were less successful. Paul was not only one of the earliest Christian missionaries; he was the first theologian of the church. He was not a systematic theologian, but rather developed his ideas in response to situations. This explains how he was able to reconcile apparent contradictions.

For example, in Galatians, he emphasized discontinuity with Jewish roots but in Romans he

St. Paul

spoke of continuity with Jewish traditions. His Christology* and ecclesiology* developed along parallel lines, but in both Christ is the centerpiece. Successive writers from Marcion* to Augustine* to Luther* have borrowed heavily from him to construct the lexicon of Christian faith. Justification* by faith in Christ and viewing the church as the body of Christ* are among the unique insights that he has left for all believers. A joint Feast of Saints Peter and Paul is observed on June 29 and the Feast of the Conversion of St. Paul on January 25.

Paul the Deacon (c. 720–c. 800) Also, Paulus Levita or Warnefridi. "Father of Italian History." About

760 he became a monk at Monte Cassino*. He was until 785 in the court of Charlemagne*. Among his great historical works are *Historia Gentis Langobardorum* in five books, a valuable source for the Lombard history for this period, and *Historia Romana*. He also produced a collection of homilies and a life of St. Gregory.

Paula, St. (347–404) Roman widow who founded a Christian community in Rome* and helped Jerome*. When he established two monasteries in Bethlehem*, she headed the one for women. Feast day: January 26.

Paulicians Heretical dualist sect originating in the Near East in the seventh century appearing like a recrudescence of Manichaeism. Its principal features were rejection of the Old Testament, mariolatry*, images, infant baptism*, Communion, monasticism*, and the Veneration of the Cross*. They distinguished between two gods, one good and the other evil, the latter being the ruler of the material world. Like the Manichaeans, they considered matter to be evil, although they formally repudiated Manichaeism. As a result, they denied the reality of Christ's body and of Christ's redemptive work. They honored the Gospels, especially Luke, and Paul. Their founder was probably Constantine Sylvanus of Mananali, near Samosata, who was stoned to death, but his persecutor, Simeon, was converted only to be martyred later. They were persecuted bitterly under Theodora* and Basil*, and, although their leaders, Carbeas and Chrysocheir, received help from the Muslims, they were decimated over time.

In the tenth century, remnants of the sect found their way to Europe, especially the Balkans. They spread to France and Italy by the twelfth century, merging with other heretic sects like the Bogomils*, Cathari*, and the Albigenses*. They influenced some Radical Reformers in the sixteenth century and a copy of their doctrinal manual, *The Key of Truth,* was circulating in Russian Armenia in the nineteenth century.

Pauline Of or relating to St. Paul* and his writings.

Pauline Monastery Monastery built by the Hungarian monastic order of the Paulines* in 1309 at Lindenberg, near Buda in Hungary. It was dedicated to St. Laurence* and from 1381 housed the remains of the hermit Paulus of Thebes. It was abandoned after the Turkish conquest and rebuilt in Pest, Hungary, only after the Turks had been expelled. The rebuilding took place between 1725 and 1742, and the consecration in honor of the Virgin Mary* and the two hermit saints, Paul* and Anthony*, took place in 1748. The Pauline Order was dissolved in 1786 and the monastery subsequently became a seminary and, after 1805, the theological faculty of Budapest University.

Pauline privilege Privilege established in canon law* as conceded by St. Paul* (1 Cor. 7:15) to a Christian married to a heathen to divorce and remarry a Christian if the non-Christian partner wished to separate or objected to the practice of Christian faith.

Paulines Popular name of the Society of St. Paul for the Apostolate of Communications, a congregation of priests and brothers* who work in the media, founded in Alba, Italy, in 1914 by James Alberione. They are the largest international Catholic publishing organization, with branches in 26 countries.

Paulines, the Paul's letters.

Paulinism Theological perspectives developed from the writings of St. Paul* in the New Testament.

Paulinus of Nola, St. (353/5–431) Latin poet and bishop of Nola in Italy. Born to a noble family, he was converted while married to a Spanish noblewoman. Soon after, he renounced the world, took a vow of poverty and continence, was ordained, and was made bishop of Nola. His letters to some of the most famous Christians of his day, as Augustine*, Jerome*, Ambrose*, and Martin of Tours*, have survived. He is also considered among the foremost Latin poets of the patristic period. Feast day: June 22.

Paulinus of York, St. (d. 644) English monk. He was one of the second band of missionaries sent to England by Gregory* the Great. He was the first apostle from within England to Northumbria, where he converted many people and founded the see* of York*. He also founded a church at Lincoln in Nottinghamshire. Bede* describes him as a "tall, dark man . . . his presence being venerable and awe-inspiring." Feast day: October 10.

Paulists The Society of Missionary Priests of St. Paul the apostle founded in 1858 in New York City by Isaac Thomas Hecker*, Augustine Hewit, George Deshon, and Francis Baker, all former Redemptorist priests. Their purpose was the conversion of America. To overcome anti-Catholic bias, they advocated discarding nonessential foreign and Roman traditions and encouraged rapid Americanization of immigrants. Hecker founded the *Catholic World* and the Paulist Press, as the society's publishing arm.

Pavia Carthusian monastery, the Certosa di Pavia, to the north of Pavia, Italy, established in 1396 by Giovanni Galeazzo Visconti as an act of contrition*. Although the first monks moved in by 1398, building work continued until 1542. Work on the three-aisled church in the form of a Latin cross started in 1453. On the right side there are 11 chapels, on the left side 6, with a further 2 at the end of the transept* and an imposing dome above the center of the crossing*.

pax/pax brede Also, osculatorium. Small plate of ivory, metal, or wood, with a representation of the Crucifixion or other religious scene on the face and a projecting handle at the back used at Mass* for conveying the kiss of peace*.

Pax Christi (lit., Peace of Christ) International Roman Catholic peace movement, with headquarters in Antwerp, founded in 1935, by a small French group led by Bishop Pierre Theas of Lourdes*.

pax Dei (Lat., peace of God) Also, Truce of God*. Immunity of churches, clerics, and members of religious orders from attack or danger during time of war.

Pax Romana World organization of Roman Catholic students, also called the International Movement of Catholic Students.

peace churches Mennonite*, Brethren*, and Friends* church bodies that are pacifist in their theology and oppose war, conscription, and participation in the military.

Peace of the Church See MILAN, EDICT OF.

Peale, Norman Vincent (1898–1993) Reformed Church in America* pastor and promoter of positive thinking*. Ordained into the Methodist Episcopal Church in 1922, he held pastorates* in Brooklyn and Syracuse before taking over the Marble Collegiate Church, New York City, founded in 1628. Here he spent the rest of his career, combining his ministry with active writing and counseling. Peale's positive thinking was a Pollyannish mixture of psychiatry and psychology promising confident living and peace of mind. In addition to writing, he ran a psychiatric clinic, hosted a radio program called "The Art of Living," and published *Guideposts,* an inspirational monthly magazine with circulation in the millions. For many years, he also had a television program, "What's Your Problem?" His books include *The Power of Positive Thinking* (1952), *The Art of Living* (1937), *A Guide to Confident Living* (1948), and *The Art of Real Happiness* (1950).

Pec Monastery in the Patriarchate of Pec on the left bank of the Bistrica River in the Kosovo* region. From 1346 it was considered the mother of Serbian churches. It has a complex of four churches of which the oldest is the Holy Apostles Church, founded in 1230, and the others were the Church of St. Demetrios founded in 1320, the Church of the Virgin, and the Church of St. Nicholas, both founded between 1330 and 1337. After the fall of Serbia to the Ottomans, Pec fell into disrepair until 1557, when it was reestablished. It was abolished in 1766 and then established again in 1920.

pectoral cross Cross suspended by a chain over the neck of a bishop, abbot, or cardinal and worn over the breast.

Peculiar People 1. The apostle Peter's* designation for Christians (1 Pet. 2:9). 2. Scriptural name for Christians appropriated by the Quakers* and by the Tractarians as well as by small sects in England and the United States.

pedilavium (Lat., washing of the feet) Liturgical washing of the feet on Maundy Thursday*. During the ceremony, 12 men are led into the sanctuary while antiphons* are sung and the celebrant solemnly washes and dries the feet of each in turn (John 13).

Peeters, Flor (1903–) Belgian organist, one of the most prolific composers of organ music in the twentieth century. He was for over half a century organist of the Metropolitan Cathedral of St. Rombaut in Malines, Belgium. His 500 organ compositions reveal his love for the Gregorian Chant* which he blends with twentieth-century harmonies and rhythms within a contrapuntal setting. In addition, he composed a number of sacred choral works, motets*, psalm settings, masses, a *Te Deum,* and a magnificat*. His published works include *Little Organ Book* (1957), *30 Short Chorale-Preludes* (1959), and *213 Hymn Preludes for the Liturgical Year* (1959–1964).

Peguy, Charles Pierre (1873–1914) French Catholic writer. He abandoned his Catholic faith and turned to socialism as a panacea for human ills until 1908 when a new awareness of Catholic spirituality* brought him back to the fold, although he never gave up socialism or his anticlerical views. He celebrated Catholicism* in *Mystery of the Charity of Joan of Arc* (1910), *The Portico of the Mystery of the Second Virtue* (1911), *The Mystery of the Holy Innocents* (1912), and *Eve* (1913).

Pelagianism Doctrinal system associated with Pelagius* and others, based on the inherent created goodness and innocence of human beings, the efficacy of the human will to achieve salvation*, and sinless perfection* without divine help. It opposed the Augustinian doctrine of original sin* and predestination*. It held that every soul is created sinless, that the will is absolutely free, and that the grace* of God is universal but not indispensable. It taught that infants were baptized for sanctification*, not forgiveness. Pelagius and his friend, Celestius*, were anathematized by Pope Zosimus* in 418, and Pelagianism was con-

demned at the Council of Ephesus* in 431. After the death of Pelagius, the heresy was kept alive by Julian of Eclanum. It found a favorable climate in Britian for some years. Pockets of the heresy flourished in Dalmatia and central Italy for some time.

Pelagius (d. c. 424) Birth name: Morgan. Heresiarch* and initiator of Pelagianism*. A native of Britain, he took residence in Rome* before 405. He fled to Africa when Rome was sacked by the Goths in 410. He died in Egypt in 424.

Pelagius

Pelagonitissa Iconographic palladium of the town of Ohrid* in Macedonia*, showing the Virgin holding lovingly the Christ child.

pelican Symbol of Christ's redeeming work and the Eucharist*, because of the pelican's supposed habit of piercing her breast and feeding her young with her blood.

Pella City south of the Sea of Galilee* and the Sea of Jordan to which the Christian Jews of Jerusalem* fled in response to an oracle before the outbreak of the Jewish revolt in 66 A.D. The event is recorded by Eusebius*.

Peloubet, Francis Nathan (1831–1920) American writer of Sunday school* lessons. Ordained in 1857, Peloubet pastored in numerous churches in Massachusetts. In 1874 he began writing the Sunday school lessons for which he is best known. In 1883 he resigned his pastorate* to devote himself entirely to writing. He also wrote Bible commentaries and edited a Bible dictionary.

penal substitution See SUBSTITUTIONARY ATONEMENT.

penance (Lat., *paenitentia,* punishment) Atonement* for post-baptismal sins by some form as satisfaction* adequate to the sin on the ground that it is better to be punished in this world than in the next. Its rationale was that such punishment controlled and sometimes eradicated the sin that caused the sinner to stumble and shielded the sinner from further temptations. Implicit in this doctrine was the right of the church to intercede for sinners and the powers of its ministers to absolve. Penance generally consisted of prayers, fasts, continence, pilgrimages*, floggings, and imprisonment. However, the church, while insisting on penance, also encouraged a system of commutation by the payment of money which, in turn, led to the sale of indulgences*.

The Second Vatican Council* revised the rites and formulas of the sacrament* of penance, emphasizing reconciliation and rehabilitation rather than confession*, judgment, and punishment. It provided for three rites: 1. Reading a short passage of Scripture. 2. A service of penitence, including prayers, Psalms, Bible readings, and a sermon followed by confession* and absolution*. 3. A service similar to the second but without confession*. Theologians also distinguish between culpa (guilt) and poena (punishment) and between poena damnationis and poena temporalis. Culpa and poena damnationis could be absolved through contrition* and absolution, whereas poena temporalis required penance on the part of the sinner or its equivalent drawn from the treasury of merit*.

Penderecki, Krzysztof (1933–) Polish avant-garde religious composer. Among his outstanding religious works are *Psalmy Dawida* (1958) for chorus and percussion; *Psalmus* (1961); *The St. Luke Passion* (1965), for soloists, chorus, and orchestra; *Urenia* (1971), on the burial and Resurrection of Christ; *Magnificat* (1974), for soloists, mixed chorus, and orchestra; and *Te Deum* (1979), for soloists, chorus, and orchestra. His opera on *Paradise Lost** was performed in Rome before the pope.

penitential books Books containing directions for confessors, including a list of sins with a set of graded penances for each. Some of the widely used penitential books were those by confessors such as Alan of Lille, Raymond of Penafort*, and Burckard of Worms*, though earlier this literature developed extensively in Celtic lands.

penitential orders Roman Catholic orders emphasizing penance* or asceticism* and emphasizing care of the ill.

Penitential Psalms Psalms 6, 32, 38, 51, 102, 130, and 143, considered suitable for penitential use and designed to promote contrition*.

penitentiary In the Roman Catholic Church, a cleric charged with the administration of the sacrament* of penance*. A canon penitentiary is a member of the cathedral chapter* who has special powers in this regard, while a major penitentiary is a cardinal who presides over a tribunal, deciding cases relating to penance* and indulgences*.

penitents Persons subject to a system of public penance*. In some contexts they might wear a special robe, have close-cropped hair, and worship apart from the rest of the congregation.

Penn, William (1644–1718) English Quaker* and founder of Pennsylvania. For his nonconformist views he was expelled from Christ Church, Ox-

William Penn

ford*, and was imprisoned many times. He made many missionary journeys in the 1660s, advocating religious freedoms. In 1681 he secured a charter for Pennsylvania from Charles II because of a debt owed to his father by the king. He later added Delaware to his dominion. The colony of Pennsylvania was his "Holy Experiment" in religious freedom, and his just treatment of Indians was at variance with the practice in the other colonies. Among his many works were *Primitive Christianity* (1696), *No Cross, No Crown* (1669), and *Christian Quaker and his Divine Testimony Vindicated* (1673).

Pennsylvania spirituals Revival songs popular in bush-meetings during the Second Great Awakening* among German-speaking Methodists.

penqitho In the Syrian Rite, a liturgical book containing texts for the vespers*, nocturns*, mattins*, and terce* for Sundays, the greater feasts, and the season of Lent*.

pensile table 1. List noting the miracles that have taken place at a shrine or church. 2. Tablet containing the names of the benefactors of a church or shrine.

Pentarchy (Gk., rule of five) Rule of the universal church by the five patriarchs* of Rome*, Constantinople*, Antioch*, Alexandria*, and Jerusalem*.

Pentecost (Gk., fiftieth) 1. Jewish feast day known as shabuoth observed 7 weeks or 50 days after the sixteenth of Nisan, the Feast of Passover. 2. Feast observed on the seventh Sunday after Easter* commemorating the descent of the Holy Spirit* as described in Acts 2:1.Also known as Whitsun.

Pentecostal churches Protestant churches that subscribe to the Pentecostal faith. Modern Pentecostalism* began in the United States as an outgrowth of the Holiness movement*. In 1901 a Bible school called Bethel College was started in Topeka, Kansas, by Charles F. Parham*, who preached Spirit baptism as indispensable for holiness*. His students carried this message across the South and one of them, William J. Seymour*, an African-American, brought the teaching in

1906 to Los Angeles, where he founded the Apostolic Faith Gospel Mission on Azusa Street. Despite his unimpressive appearance and lack of preaching abilities, the revival that he sparked on Azusa Street had reverberations throughout the Christian world. Azusa Street became the birthplace of modern Pentecostalism*. It was carried to many countries within almost a few decades; Thomas Ball Barratt* carried it to Norway, Alexander A. Boddy to England, Pandita Ramabai* to India, and Willis C. Hoover* to Chile.

As opposition to Pentecostalism from mainline* denominations grew, Pentecostals began to establish their own denominations. Of these the most important were the Assemblies of God*, the Church of God in Christ*, the Church of God (Tomlinson*), the International Church of the Foursquare Gospel, and the United Pentecostal Church International. Of these, the largest is the Assemblies of God, based in Springfield, Missouri. It is very active in foreign missions and has extensive facilities for training ministers. The Church of God in Christ is the largest and most influential black Pentecostal body. A great number of the healing ministries and media ministries in the world belong to the Pentecostal movement. The post World War II period witnessed the appearance of a spate of independent Pentecostal

Pentecost

groups, such as the New Order of the Latter Rain and Wings of Healing.

Within every major denomination, including the Episcopal, Roman Catholic, Lutheran, and Methodist churches, there are Charismatic groups that share in the explosive growth of Pentecostalism. Originally, the religion of the poor, it has become increasingly middle class and diverse in its racial mix. The five largest churches in the world are Pentecostal. By 2000 Pentecostals numbered over 100 million around the globe. Lesslie Newbigin* has described Pentecostalism as the "third wave* of Christianity." Whereas the Catholic and Orthodox traditions emphasize continuity, orthodoxy*, and the sacraments*, and Protestantism* emphasizes the centrality of the Scriptures, the Pentecostals have added the gifts of the Spirit*.

Pentecostalism Worldwide movement based on the belief that Christians in every age may receive the baptism in the Spirit* and the same Charismatic gifts of the Holy Spirit* as did the first Christians on the day of Pentecost* in Jerusalem*. These gifts include speaking in tongues* or glossolalia*, prophecy*, physical healing, and exorcism*, the exercise of all of which are given to the believer in an experience known as baptism in the Holy Spirit*, an experience distinct from conversion* and baptism*. Pentecostalism distinguishes between the indwelling of the Holy Spirit as a source of saving faith and the outpouring of the Spirit which empowers for Christian ministry and witness. Pentecostalism also has a strong millennial element and teaches the plenary inspiration* of the Bible and instantaneous sanctification*. In some ways it has a strong affinity with Montanism* of the second century and is strongly restorative in its efforts to revive the spontaneity of worship and fullness of gifts that were marks of the Apostolic Age*.

Pentecostalism as it has spread around the world in the twentieth century is associated with joyous forms of worship, characterized by physical expressions, such as clapping of hands, raising of hands, and, in rare cases, dancing. In addition to what has come to be called "classic Pentecostalism," there are neo-Pentecostal or Charismatic movements within mainline churches* of which the Catholic Charismatics are the best known.

Pentecostarion (Gk., Book of the Five Days) In the Eastern Church*, a liturgical book containing the variable portions of the services for the season between Easter* and the Sunday of All Saints. It is also known as the Flowery or the Festal Triodion.

people of God Also, Holy People. Body of Christian believers, based on 1 Peter 2:9–10: "[You] who once were not a people but are now the people of God." This approach to the church became common in the biblical theology movement* and is used prominently in documents of the Second-Vatican Council*.

Pepping, Ernst (1901–1981) German composer. His *Choralsuite* (1929) was the beginning of a career that was spent largely in church music. In 1931 he published a cycle of six motets*. In 1934 he accepted the position at the Spandau Church Music School and, over the course of the next several years, composed more than 250 settings for his *Spandauer Chorbuch* (1934–1941). Another collection appeared in 1959 as the *Neues Choralbuch,* arranged according to the church year*. Compositions based on original melodies also occupy an important place in Pepping's works, such as *Prediger-Motette* (1937), considered one of his finest works, *Passionsbericht des Matthaeus* (1950) for a capella chorus, and the Gospel motet *Das Weltgericht* (1958). In addition Pepping also composed considerable organ music.

Pepuzians See MONTANISTS.

per saltum (Lat., through a leap) Skipping a grade when promoting a person in a particular hierarchy*, as for example, when a priest is ordained without being a deacon.

pere (Fr., father) Term of address in French for a priest.

peregrinatio (Lat., pilgrimage) Journey to the Holy Land* or to the tombs of Christian saints* and martyrs*. The first recorded Christian pilgrimage* was that of a Cappadocian bishop named Alexander in 200 to Palestine or possibly Melito of Sardis, a generation earlier.

Perfectibilists Original name of the Illuminati* founded by Johann Weishaupt in Bavaria.

perfection 1. Quality, state, or condition of being complete, mature, and whole. 2. Lacking nothing in goodness or excellence. 3. Freedom from faults, defects, and flaws. 4. Quality of Christlikeness.

perfectionism Theological teaching that moral perfection* is not merely an ideal for a Christian to strive for, but is attainable in this life in the light of the Scriptures (Matt. 5:48; 1 Cor. 2:6; Eph. 4:13; Phil. 3:15; Col. 1:28; 4:12; Heb. 6:1; 1 John 4:18). In the early church and the Middle Ages, perfection* was the goal of the monks and nuns as well as the mystics, and their attainment of this goal was in direct proportion to their asceticism* and self-renunciation. In Protestantism*, the major advocate of perfectionism was John Wesley*, who was himself influenced by Jeremy Taylor* and William Law* as well as the Mennonites*. For Wesley perfection was received through faith and confirmed by the Holy Spirit*. Some Wesleyans do not use the term *perfection,* preferring *entire sanctification** as somehow less threatening. In the United States, the Oberlin theologians Charles Finney* and Asa Mahan* upheld perfectionism. Wesley's perfectionism was carried forward by the American Holiness movement* out of which sprang the Church of the Nazarene*, the Wesleyan Church, and some forms of Pentecostalism*.

Pergamum Town about 50 miles north of Smyrna in Asia Minor, site of one of the seven churches in Revelation.

pergola Chancel screen* separating the chancel* or sanctuary from the nave*.

perichoresis (Gk., interpenetration) In Trinitarian* theology, intimate union, mutual indwelling, and mutual interpenetration of the three members of the Trinity* with one another so that each is always in the other two. See also CIRCUMINCESSION.

pericope (Gk., section) Passage from Scriptures appointed to be read in church services. In New Testament scholarship, a unit within the Gospel narrative.

periodeuta/periodeutes In the Syrian Church, supervisor of the clergy.

peristera In the Byzantine tradition, a dove* with outstretched wings usually made of silver and containing a wooden or silver casket.

peristerion Hanging tabernacle or pyx* in the shape of a dove*, suspended over a high altar for reserving the Blessed Sacrament*.

peritus (Lat., expert) Consultant to an ecclesiastical body with special expertise in canon law* or theology.

permanent deacon Ordained deacon in an Episcopal church who remains a deacon throughout life and does not seek ordination as a priest.

permissive will of God Doctrine that God sometimes allows certain things to happen that are outside his ideal plan or economy, contrasted with his directive or prescriptive will.

Perpetua, St. (d. March 7, 203) North African martyr*. She was arrested with four fellow catechumens*, including St. Felicitas. They were baptized and joined by their catechist* Saturus, and all the five died in the amphitheater. *The Passion of Perpetua* recounting the story of their martyrdom was very popular in the Middle Ages. Feast day: March 7.

perpetual adoration Ceaseless worship of the Eucharist* in which a person or persons sit or kneel before it at all times. It is maintained by many Catholic congregations, such as Lugo Cathedral in Spain and Stillwater, Minnesota.

perpetual deacon Also, permanent deacon. Deacon who does not aspire to become a priest.

perpetual virginity Doctrine that the Virgin Mary* remained a virgin all her life.

persecution Systematic and officially sanctioned attempt to extirpate a religion through harassment, imprisonment, execution, and violence directed against its members. The Christian church is unique in that it has suffered persecution in some part of the world every year since its beginning. The gospel warns Christians to expect persecution but also assures them that they will grow through and despite persecution. Even today in many countries, such as Saudi Arabia, being a Christian is a capital offense. Throughout history, many Christians have abandoned their faith during times of persecutions, particularly in Muslim countries, but a remnant have survived.

In Christian history there have been four major eras of persecution:

1. Roman emperors: Nero (64), Domitian (90–96), Trajan (98–117), Hadrian (117–138), Marcus Aurelius (161–180), Septimus Severus (202–211), Maximinus the Thracian (235–236), Decius (149–251), Valerian (257–260), Diocletian and Galerius (303–311). Of these the Decian persecution* and the Diocletian persecutions were the most severe.

2. Muhammad and Islam (mid-seventh century to the present): Muhammad, an illiterate Bedouin from Mecca, established in the seventh century a religion, now known as Islam, that from the beginning was dedicated to the extirpation of Christianity. Roman persecutions pale in comparison to the brutal persecution and oppression of Christians under Islam. Muhammad himself is the most successful Antichrist* in history, because while other evil empires have come and gone, Islamic colonialism has endured. Muslim Arabs and Ottoman Turks, although culturally inferior to all the races they have conquered, have imposed their language and religion on their hapless subjects and stolen not only their lands but their identities. Thus Egyptians, Berbers, Phoenicians, Syrians, and Nubians are all now known as Arabs, speak Arabic, and prostrate toward Mecca. During the past 14 centuries, Muhammad's followers have killed more than 38 million Christians, forcibly converted another 42 million, and destroyed the Christian church in Arabia, Syria, Iraq, Yemen, Lebanon, Palestine, Egypt, Nubia, Libya, Tunisia, Algeria, Morocco, Albania, Persia, Afghanistan, and Central Asia.

3. Pagan emperors of China and Japan (sixteenth to nineteenth centuries): The worst persecution was in Japan under the Shogun Iyeyasu (1542–1616), who killed hundreds of thousands of Japanese Christians.

4. Communist rulers of Soviet Union and China (1917–1989 in the Soviet Union; 1949 to the present in China): Lenin and his Bolsheviks unleashed a reign of terror against the Orthodox Church that lasted nearly 70 years. By the time the Soviet Union collapsed, more than 6 million Christians were killed, including hundreds of thousands of priests and bishops, thousands of churches, monasteries, and seminaries were destroyed, two generations were taught to hate the church, and thousands of believers were sent to prisons and gulags.

perseverance In the doctrine of predestination*, the gift of continuing to endure to the end in full obedience to the commands of the Lord. Such a gift is part of the package of salvation* and is part of the path foreordained by God for his elect. As a gift, perseverance is free, and not tied to human efforts. It was Augustine* who first clearly elaborated a doctrine of perseverance. It was taken up in the Reformed* tradition by Calvin*, John Owen*, and numerous others who built it as one of the pillars of their theology.

persuasion Denomination or sect adhering to a particular system of religious beliefs; confession*.

Perth, Articles of Five articles forced upon the Church of Scotland* by James I in 1618. They included kneeling at the Lord's Supper*, confirmation*, and other High Church* observances.

Perugino, Pietro Vannucci (c. 1448–1523) Italian painter of the Umbrian school. In 1482 he painted the *Delivery of the Keys to St. Peter* in the Sistine Chapel*, the first of many such frescoes. Among his other masterpieces were the *Adoration of the Holy Child* (1491), the *Vision of St. Bernard* (1494), *Charge to St. Peter,* the *Lamentation* (1495), and the *Crucifixion* (1496). Later he began the fresco* cycle in the Sala del Cambio in Perugia.

Peshitta (Syr., simple or current) Version of the New Testament written for Syriac-speaking Christians. It is believed to be of multiple authorship, but Rabbula*, bishop of Edessa*, appears to have been the coordinator. The New Testament did not include the Revelation or the four lesser Catholic Epistles—2 Peter, 2 and 3 John, and Jude.

Peter, Acts of St. Apocryphal book including the Martyrdom of St. Peter. It recounts many legends about St. Peter*, including the healing of his paralytic daughter, the Quo Vadis incident, and his being crucified head downwards.

Peter, Apocalypse of St. Apocalyptic account of the second-century vision granted by the Lord to the apostle. It was accepted as Scripture by Clement* of Alexandria and the Muratorian Canon*. There is a Coptic and Ethiopian version.

Peter Canisius, St. (1521–1597) Jesuit theologian, responsible for the success of the Counter-Reformation* in South German lands. A vigorous champion of Roman Catholicism*, he founded a Jesuit colony at Cologne* and preached in Bavaria, Vienna*, and Prague* against the Reformers. He compiled a number of catechisms*, of which *Summa Doctrinae Chistianae* or *Catechismus Major* was published in 1554 and went through over 100 editions. As provincial* of Upper Germany from 1556, he was responsible for the founding of colleges at Augsburg, Munich*, and Innsbruck, and for extending Jesuit influence to Poland. He was canonized in 1925 when he was also declared to be a doctor of the church*. Feast day: December 21.

Peter Chrysologus, St. (d. c. 450) Bishop of Ravenna*. He was noted as a preacher, hence his name which means "golden worded." He viewed Eutychianism* with some favor but asserted the supremacy of the Roman See in matters of doctrine. In 1729 he was declared a doctor of the church*. Feast day: July 30.

Peter Claver, St. See CLAVER, PETER.

Peter Comestor (c. 1100–1178/79) Biblical scholar, known as *Magister Historiarum*. He became dean of the Cathedral of Troyes* in 1147, and in 1167 chancellor of Notre Dame* in Paris. His most famous work is *Historia Scholastica*, a history of the world from creation to ascension. It was the standard work on biblical history in the Middle Ages.

Peter Damian, St. See DAMIAN, ST. PETER.

Peter de Bruys (d. c. 1131) Opponent of the church. He taught that infant baptism* was invalid, that church buildings were unnecessary, that the cross should be despised, not venerated, that there was

no real presence* of Christ in the Communion, and that prayers for the dead were worthless. He rejected large parts of the Scriptures and the authority of the church. His teachings were condemned a number of times, especially by the Second Lateran Council* in 1139. He was thrown to the flames by a mob infuriated at his publicly burning the crosses. His followers came to be known as Petrobrusians.

Peter Fourier, St. (1565–1640) After 30 years as a parish priest he joined the Augustinian Canons*. Together with Mother Alix le Clerq, he founded the Congregation of Augustinian Canons of Our Lady. Feast day: December 9.

Peter, Gospel of St. Apocryphal Gospel discovered at Akhmim in Egypt in 1886/7. Its existence is cited by Origen* and Serapion, bishop of Antioch*. It has a strong anti-Jewish and probably Docetic bias. Among apocryphal Gospels it has attracted close scholarly interest.

Peter, Letter to Philip of St. Coptic document of the Nag Hammadi* Library recounting a gathering of the apostles on the Mount of Olives after the Resurrection and before the ascension.

Peter, Liturgy of St. Mass* combining elements from the Byzantine and Roman rites*. The canon* is that of the Roman Mass*.

Peter Lombard (c. 1100–1160) Master of Sentences. In 1141 he became a canon* at Notre Dame* and in 1159 was elected bishop of Paris. His fame rests principally on his great work, *Book of Sentences* (*Libri Quatuor Sententiarum*), completed in 1157 or 1158. The book is a thesaurus of doctrines with a wealth of citations from Church Fathers* and eminent theological authorities such as Anselm*, Peter Abelard*, Hugh of St. Victor*, the *Decretum* of Gratian*, *Summa Sententiarum,* and Ivo of Chartres*. The work is divided into four books: Trinity*, creation and sin*, Incarnation* and sacraments*, and the last four things.

Regarding sacraments he was one of the first to distinguish them from sacramentals and to establish that they are not merely visible signs but channels through which grace* flows. Lombard's work marked the culmination of medieval scholastic pedagogy. By the thirteenth century it had become required reading for all theological students. Hundreds of commentaries were written on it until the seventeenth century. Despite its popular acceptance, some of the doctrines advanced in the book were attacked as heterodox, particularly Lombard's Christological nihilism, or the teaching that Christ's humanity was nothing, and his views on the Trinity*.

Peter Martyr, St. (c. 1200–1252) Also known as Peter Veronensis, from Verona*. Dominican preacher and inquisitor. Born into a Catharist family, he grew up as a Catholic and entered the Dominican Order in 1220/1. He emerged as a powerful controversialist against the Cathari* and was appointed inquisitor of Milan* and Como. He and a companion were assassinated between Milan and Como. As he died he prayed for his murderer and wrote the first words of the creed on the ground where he lay in his own blood. Feast day: June 4.

St. Peter Martyr

Peter Martyr Vermigli (1499–1562) Anglicized form of Pietro Martire Vermigli. Italian reformer. He joined the Augustinians and became their abbot at Spoleto in 1530 and prior* of St. Petrus-ad-aram in Naples in 1533. Here he fell under the influence of Martin Bucer* and Zwingli* and was forced to flee and take refuge in Zurich*, Basel*, and Strasbourg*, where he was appointed professor of theology. From 1547 to 1553 he was in England where, as regius professor of divinity at Oxford, he was consulted on the *Book of Common Prayer** and was named one of the commissioners for the reform of canon law*. In 1553 he went back to Strasbourg but spent his last years teaching in Zurich*. The Commonplaces compiled from his learned biblical commentaries after his death gave him a wide influence.

Peter Nolasco, St. (c. 1180–c. 1249) Founder of the Mercedarians* of the Order of Our Lady of Ransom. Between 1218 and 1234 he established the Mercedarians with the help of Raymond of Penafort*. The order worked in Spain and Africa to ransom Christians held captive by the Muslims. He was canonized in 1628. Feast day: January 28.

Peter of Alcantara, St. (1499–1562) Spanish Discalced Franciscan. He was ordained priest in 1524 and became provincial* of the Franciscan conventuals in 1538. In 1557 he became commissary general* of the reformed conventuals and founded the convent of El Pedroso del Acim. In 1560 St. Teresa* met him and she noted her admiration for his asceticism* in her *Life*. He drew up the constitution for the province of St. Joseph*, emphasizing prayer and penitence. His *Tratado de la Oracion y Meditacion* (1556) is a celebration of contemplative life* grounded in prayer, penitence, and poverty. Feast day: October 19.

Peter of Alexandria, St. (d. 311) Bishop of Alexandria from 300 and martyr*. He was imprisoned during the Diocletian persecution* and administered the church from prison and drew up rules for readmission of the lapsed Christians into the church. The usurpation of his office by Melitius of Lycopolis caused the Melitian Schism*. Peter excommunicated Melitius* in 306. He returned after the Edict of Tolerance but was beheaded in the persecution of Maximin in 311. Eusebius* described him as a model bishop both for his knowledge of the Scriptures and holiness*. Feast day: November 24 (Eastern Church*); November 26 (Western Church*).

Peter, Preaching of St. Document dating from the second century, emphasizing the superiority of Christianity over pagan religions and Judaism.

Peter, St. Prince of the apostles; disciple; the first bishop of Rome*; brother of St. Andrew*; also known as Cephas. Original name: Simon. A fisherman by profession and somewhat unlettered, he is nevertheless acknowledged as the first among apostolic equals. He received the promise of the Lord that "thou art Peter, and on this rock will I build my church," together with the keys of the kingdom* and the power of loosing and binding, which in later centuries formed the basis of the Catholic Church's claim for primacy. After the Resurrection, he was the first apostle to whom the Lord appeared and at the Sea of Tiberias, he received the charge to feed his sheep.

    After the ascension, Peter took over the leadership of the fledgling church before Paul* appeared. He gave the main sermon on the day of the Pentecost*, he was the first apostle to perform a miracle in the name of Jesus*, and throughout Acts he was the greatest miracle worker. He opened the church to the Gentiles by admitting Cornelius, and he headed the first council at Jerusalem*. Peter was reported at Rome at the same time as Paul*. He is traditionally believed to have been the first bishop of Rome and suffered martyrdom under Nero, being crucified head downwards. Papias* says that the Gospel of Mark was written as the memoirs of Peter. His tomb is in St. Peter's*, Rome. Feast day: June 29.

Peter the Chanter (d. 1197) Medieval theologian and ethicist. He was precentor at Notre Dame* in Paris from 1183 to 1197, when he became dean of Reims*. He was the author of *Summa de Sacramentis* and *Verbum Abbreviatum*. In the Lateran Council* of 1215, his ideas were influential in outlawing the use of ordeals in the administration of justice.

Peter the Fuller (d. 488) Monophysite theologian. He became bishop of Antioch* in 470 but was deposed and reinstated twice in the next 12 years. He is chiefly remembered for the addition of the words to the Trisagion*, "Who wast crucified for us," which was approved by the Second Council of Constantinople* in 553.

Peter the Hermit (1050–1115) Preacher of the First Crusade*. After the Council of Clermont* in 1095, Peter raised a force of 20,000 that arrived at Constantinople* ahead of the First Crusade and, after many reverses, entered Jerusalem* with the main army. On his return to Europe, he became prior* of the Augustinian monastery of Neufmoutier (Huy), which he had helped to found.

Peter the Venerable (1092 or 1094–1156) Eighth abbot of Cluny*. After being prior* at Vezelay and Domene he was elected abbot of Cluny in 1122. During a 34-year tenure as abbot he drew up detailed constitutions and introduced financial and educational reforms. He traveled extensively in England, Spain, Italy, and Germany, and wrote against heretics and Muslims.

Peterborough Benedictine monastery and cathedral founded in 655 at Peterborough, England. It was over 120 years in building and was consecrated only in 1237. It is a magnificent building, the most perfect Norman cathedral in England. Since the monks of Peterborough owned their own quarry, they used the same ivory-colored stone throughout the construction.

Peter's Chains, Feast of Feast, also called Feast of St. Peter Ad Vincula, observed on August 1 marking

Crucifixion of Peter

the dedication of the basilica* where the chains that allegedly bound St. Peter* (Acts 12:3, 6) are preserved.

Peter's Pence Lay contributions sent to the pope by Roman Catholic congregations. Formerly, an ecclesiastical tax in England paid to the pope from 787 to 1534.

Petite Eglise (Little Church) French and Belgian Catholics who refused to accept the Concordat of 1801 between Napoleon I and the pope. Persecuted under the Bourbons, most of them returned to the Catholic fold, but a small remnant has survived, mostly in Vendée, where they are called Illumines.

petition 1. Prayer or supplication. 2. Form of prayer requesting special favors.

Petri, Olavus (1493–1552) Swedish reformer. After the Diet of Vasteras in 1527 ended the Roman ascendancy of the Swedish Church, Olaus prepared the first service book in Swedish, a Swedish Mass, and a collection of songs. He also translated the New Testament and Luther's works and laid the groundwork for revised religious instruction.

Petrine 1. Of or relating to St. Peter* and his theology. 2. Of or relating to the paper office.

pew Bench or a compartment containing seats for worshipers in a church.

phaina In the Assyrian tradition, vestment similar to a chasuble*, resembling a headless cope* and ornamented with many crosses. It is not fastened at the neck.

Phanar Official residence and court of the ecumenical patriarch* of Constantinople* in the Greek quarter of the City on the Golden Horn.

Phaneromene Greek icons of the Virgin Mary*, usually discovered through visions and dreams and associated with healings and miracles. Such icons are highly revered.

phanon In the Greek Orthodox Rite, maniple*.

phelguth-m'shamshono In the Maronite Church, a half deacon, or a minor order of subdeacon.

phelonion In the Eastern Church*, the chasuble*, a vestment gathered up in front, similar to a cape.

Phelonion

Patriarchs* wear phelonions embroidered with crosses. Since 1453 the phelonion has been replaced by the sakkos*.

Philadelphia 1. City in the Roman province of Asia, site of one of the seven churches in the Revelation. 2. City in Pennsylvania founded by William Penn*.

Philaret Drozdov (1782–1867) Metropolitan of Moscow*. Ordained in 1809, he lectured in theology and philosophy until 1818 when he was elected to the Holy Synod*, made bishop of Jaroslav (1820), archbishop (1821), and metropolitan* of Moscow (1826). He was liberal in outlook and sympathetic to Protestant reforms. He is the author of an Orthodox catechism*.

Philaret, Theodore Nikitich Romanov (c. 1553–1633) Patriarch of Moscow* and father of the first Romanov tsar. Under his cousin, Theodore I, the last tsar of the House of Rurik, he was a soldier and diplomat. He was confined by Boris Godunov to the Antoniev Monastery, but was released and elevated in 1605 as metropolitan* of Rostov by Pseudo-Dimitri I and four years later made patriarch* of All Russia by Pseudo-Dimitri II. He was imprisoned by the Poles from 1610 to 1618 but when the Poles were expelled by Philaret's son, Mikhail, the founder of the House of Romanovs, he was restored under the Truce of Deulino in 1619. Thereafter he was the virtual ruler of Russia, even though his son Mikhail was the tsar. He was instrumental in founding the patriarchal library and in establishing a seminary in every diocese*.

Phileas of Thmuis (d. c. 316) Martyr and first known bishop of Lower Egypt. He and three of his fellow bishops in the company of a Roman official, Culcianos, were executed during the Diocletian persecution*.

philia (Gk., friendship, love) Wholesome, natural affection among friends. Combined with *adelphos* (Gk., brother), as in *Philadelphia*, it connotes warm Christian fellowship or brotherly love.

Philibert, St. (d. 684) Founder and first abbot of Jumieges*. He founded the Monastery of Jumieges on land given to him by Clovis II. Later he retired to the Island of Her, where he established another monastery. Feast day: August 20.

Philip Benizi, St. (1223–1285) Italian monk. He entered the Servite Order at Monte Senario, becoming its prior general* in 1267. He attended the Council of Lyons*. He appears in Andrea del Sarto's frescoes. Feast day: August 23.

Philip, Gospel of Gnostic treatise in Coptic discovered at Nag Hammadi*. It contains sayings attributed to Jesus.

Philip, John (1771-1851) South African missionary. Converted by Robert and James Haldane, he was pastor at Aberdeen when he accepted a call from LMS* to go to South Africa. He became a doughty defender of native rights, and helped to protect the Xhosa, Khoi or Hottentot, Sotho, and Zulus.

Philip Neri, St. (1515–1595) "Apostle of Rome."

Founder of the Congregation of the Oratory. He experienced a miraculous and ecstatic vision in 1544. In 1548 he became a cofounder of the Confraternity of the Holy Trinity for caring for the sick and the poor and the pilgrims who came to Rome*, a work which eventually led to the founding of the Trinity Hospital. He was ordained in 1551 and went to live in a religious community at San Girolamo where he held spiritual conferences at the Oratory of Girolamo. Out of these conferences sprang the Congregation of the Oratory. His gentleness and piety made him one of the respected figures in Rome. He was canonized by Gregory XV in 1622. Feast day: May 26.

Philip of Moscow, St. (1507–1569) Birth name: Theodore Kolyshov. He became a monk in the remote monastery at Solovetsk under the name of Philip and was elected abbot in 1547. He was appointed metropolitan* of Moscow* and primate* of the Russian Orthodox Church* under Tsar Ivan the Terrible. Rebuked by Philip, Ivan had him imprisoned, dragged from place to place in chains, and finally smothered to death. Under Tsar Theodore, his body was found to be incorrupt and translated to Solovetsk. He was canonized in 1636. Feast day: January 9.

Philip, St. One of the 12 apostles. In John 1:43–51 he is described as from Bethsaida. He is reputed to have been crucified. Feast day: May 3 (Western Church*); November 14 (Eastern Church*).

Philip the Evangelist In the New Testament, one of the seven men chosen to serve the early church because they were reported to be "full of faith and the Holy Spirit" (Acts 6:5). Following the stoning of Stephen, many Christians scattered from Jerusalem, and Philip became an evangelist in Samaria, preached the gospel, worked miracles, and brought many to faith in Christ (Acts 8:5–8). His most notable convert was the Ethiopian eunuch, an official under Candace, the queen of the Ethiopians (Acts 8:37). Later Philip preached in Azotus and Caesarea*. He was in Caesarea when Paul passed through the city on his last journey to Jerusalem (Acts 21:8). Luke notes that Philip had four virgin daughters who prophesied (Acts 21:9).

Philippists Followers of Philip Melanchthon*,

sometimes known as Crypto-Calvinists and Synergists.

Philips, Dirk (1502–1568) Anabaptist leader in the Netherlands. A Franciscan who became an Anabaptist* in 1533, he was one of the most learned among the Mennonite leaders. His *Enchiridion* was translated into many languages.

Philip's Lent In the Eastern Church*, Lent* observed from November 15 to December 24, corresponding to Advent* in the Western Church*.

Philocalia/Philokalia (Gk., love of what is beautiful) Name of two books: 1. *Philocalia of Origen,* an anthology of writings of Origen compiled by St. Basil the Great* and Gregory of Nazianzus*. 2. *Philocalia of Saints Macarius Notaras and Nicodemus of the Holy Mountain,* first published at Venice* in 1782, a collection of ascetic and mystical writings on the Hesychasm* and the Jesus Prayer*.

Philocalian calendar The Liberian Catalog* compiled by the Chronographer of A.D. 354*, illuminated by the artist Furius Dionysius Philocalus.

Philomena, St. Virgin martyr* whose loculus* was found in the catacomb* of St. Priscilla* in Rome*, containing an ampulla* of blood. She came to be venerated as a saint* until 1961 when her feast day was suppressed.

philon Black woolen cloak worn by an Armenian priest.

Philoxenian Version The Syriac* version of the New Testament made from Greek in 508 for Philoxenos of Mabbug* by Polycarp*. Unlike the Peshitta*, it contained the four lesser Catholic Epistles* and the Book of Revelation.

Philoxenos of Mabbug (c. 440–523) Birth name: Xenaya. Monophysite theologian. He was appointed bishop of Hierapolis or Mabbug in 485. One of the most learned Syrian theologians, he was the spokesman of Monophysitism* in Antioch*. His writings include *Discourses on Christian Life,* a Syriac* version of the New Testament, and works on the Incarnation*. He spent his last days in exile.

phoenix Symbol of the Resurrection in Christian art.

Phoenix

phokh In the Armenian Rite*, verse of an antiphon*.

Phos Hilaron In the Eastern Church*, hymn sung at hesperinos* or vespers* during the lighting of the lamps.

Photian Schism Schism* between the Greek and Latin churches during the patriarchate of Photius*, the ecumenical patriarch* who was installed in place of Ignatius, deposed by Emperor Michael III in 858. Rome maintained that Ignatius was still patriarch and declared Photius deposed. This assertion of papal authority over the East offended the Greek Church. The breach was widened by the efforts of Latin missionaries to bring Bulgaria, then being Christianized, under the authority of the pope. Photius also revived Greek objections to the introduction of the Filioque* clause in the creed. In 867 a council at Constantinople* deposed and excommunicated the pope in retaliation and declared him anathema. Photius was the first important ecclesiastic to disavow the primacy of Rome and to assert the equality of all the five patriarchates of the Christian world.

Photinus (fourth century) Heretic and bishop of Sirmium (344–351). He taught a form of Sabellianism* which denied the preexistence of

Christ*. His teachings were condemned at the Council of Sirmium* in 347 and 351 and again at the First Council of Constantinople* in 381.

photisomenai In the Byzantine Church*, catechumens* admitted to the final stage of the preparation for baptism*.

Photius (c. 810–c. 895) Patriarch of Constantinople*. His reign was troubled by dissension between Latin and Greek churches over the deposition of Patriarch Ignatius, his predecessor, the introduction of the Filioque* clause in the Nicene Creed* and claims to jurisdiction over Bulgaria (whose khan Boris* had become a Christian), Sicily, Calabria, and Illyricum. He died in exile in the monastery of Armeniaki. His scholarly output

Patriarch Photius

consists of *Amphilochia,* dealing with doctrines; *Bibliotheke* or *Myriobiblion,* a description of several hundred books with analyses and extracts; *Treatise on the Holy Spirit;* and *Lexicon.* Photius is important in the history of the relations between Western and Eastern churches* because his insistence on the equality of the five patriarchates and his opposition to the Filioque clause made the schism* deep and unbridgeable. Feast day: February 6 (Orthodox Church).

photogogicka Lenten alternative for the Hymn of Light.

phrumiur In the Maronite Rite*, an introductory prayer said before a sedro*.

phyletism Ecclesiastic nationalism, such as Gallicanism*.

Physician, The Beloved Epithet of St. Luke*.

piano, abito Ordinary cassock* with colored piping buttons and sash worn by Roman Catholic

prelates. It is red for cardinals, purple for bishops, and black for others.

Piarists Roman Catholic order, Regulares Pauperes Matris Dei Scholarum Piarum, founded by Jose Calasanze in 1622 for the free education of young boys. In 1597 he opened the first free elementary school in Europe to educate street children in Rome*. In 1622 it gained the privileges of mendicant orders*, especially the right of members to work or beg for their living, and by 1631 the order was working in Germany, Poland, Hungary, and other places. It flourished in the seventeenth century, especially in Spain and its imperial possessions. Calasanze was canonized in 1767.

pie Rubrics in the Sarum Breviary containing instructions for the recitation of the Divine Office*.

pier Central pillar dividing a church into two.

Pierce, Robert Willard ("Bob") (1914–1978) American evangelist and founder of World Vision*. He came to Christ through the Church of the Nazarene* and started an evangelistic ministry at 33. As his ministry broadened, he was ordained a Baptist minister. After dropping out of church work for two years, he joined Youth for Christ* of which he became vice president in 1945. In 1947 he made his first evangelistic trip to Asia which inspired him to found World Vision in 1950. After his retirement in 1967, he led Food for the World, which he rebuilt as Samaritan's Purse.

Piero della Francesca (1410/20–1492) Italian painter. Between 1452 and 1459 he painted his major work, the fresco* cycle in San Francesco, Arezzo, of the *Legend of the True Cross.* Before 1460 he painted the *Flagellation of Christ.* Another unusual work is the fresco of the *Madonna del Parto,* painted between 1450 and 1455. The *Madonna and Child with Saints and Federigo of Montefletro* was painted for the Church of San Bernardino in Urbino. One of his last works was the *Resurrection.* He was the most cerebral of Renaissance artists, and his works are rich with theological significance.

Pierson, Arthur Tappan (1837–1911) Presbyterian minister and writer. He was a student of prophecy*, missionary history, and dispensationalism*. From 1891 to 1893 he was a minister at Spurgeon's Tabernacle in London. He was also a leader in the Bible Conference movement and the Student Volunteer Movement*, a consulting editor for the Scofield Bible*, and a lecturer at the Moody Bible Institute* and at Keswick.

Pieta Representation of the Virgin Mary* mourning the dead body of Christ which she holds in her lap. The most famous Pieta is that by Michelangelo* in the Vatican*.

Pieta

Pietism Protestant movement in the seventeenth and eighteenth centuries emphasizing the need for inner devotion and active commitment. It began as a reaction against the formalism of Protestantism*, chiefly in Lutheran Germany. It was born in the life and works of Philipp J. Spener*, whose book *Pia Desideria* (1675) outlined the six goals of a Christian life: 1. Intensified study of the Bible. 2. Fuller exercise by the laity of their spiritual priesthood. 3. Emphasis on the heart and not the head in matters of faith*. 4. Charity in doctrinal controversies which should be directed toward winning hearts and not in proving who is right. 5. Reorganization of theological studies in seminaries. 6. Revival of preaching as a proclamation of the personal truths embedded in the gospel.

Spener's teachings had a dramatic impact at the Leipzig University where A. H. Francke* led a group for prayer and Bible study and was expelled for doing so. Later Francke wrote an influential book with the title *Pietas Hallensis: or, a Public Demonstration of the Footsteps of a Divine Being Yet in the World*. Francke made Halle the center of the movement and he represented radical Pietism which, with its emphasis on the work of the Holy Spirit*, was the heir to the great German mystical traditions. Spener himself represented the more moderate wing of Pietists.

In the Netherlands, Pietism was represented by William Teellinck (1579–1629), Jadocus van Lodensteyn (1620–1677), and the Brakels, Theodore Gerardi (1608–1669) and his son Willem (1635–1711). The outstanding representatives of German Pietism were Theodore Untereyck (1635–1693), Friedrich Adolph Lampe (1683–1729), Johann Albrecht Bengel* (1687–1752), and Johann Caspar Lavater (1741–1801). In Scandinavia, Pietism was promoted by Hans Nielsen Hauge* (1771–1824), a lay evangelist. The radical branch of Pietism was represented by Johann Conrad Dippel (1673–1734), Gottfried Arnold* (1666–1714), and Hochmann von Hochenau* (1670–1721).

Pietism was introduced into America by Henry Melchior Muhlenberg* and Theodore J. Frelinghuysen*. The tradition was carried forward by William Tennent, Sr. and his son Gilbert Tennent*, Philip William Otterbein, Martin Boehm*, Alexander Mack*, and August Gottlieb Spangenberg*. In course of time, Pietism influenced every facet of Protestantism*, including its theology, hymnody*, worship, and fellowship. The influence of Pietism can be seen in such diverse movements as Wesleyanism and the Holiness movement*. The hymns of Paul Gerhardt* did much to spread Pietism. Philanthropic activities and foreign missions were two major thrusts of Pietism. Wherever they went Pietists were active in founding orphanages, schools for the poor, hospitals, widows' homes, and Bible schools*.

Many early Pietists established religious communities in order to separate themselves from the world. Among them were Ephrata and Bethlehem, both in Pennsylvania, and Harmony, Indiana. Two Pietists, Bartholomaeus Ziegenbalg* and Heinrich Plutschau*, were among the first missionaries to India who established the Danish-Halle Mission in Tranquebar. Another Pietist, Count von Zinzendorf*, Spener's godson, created the Moravian Church.

Pighi, Albert (c. 1490–1542) Dutch theologian and humanist. He was an opponent of Luther* and champion of papal infallibility*. At Ratisbon* in

1541 he took part in the efforts at reunion with the Protestants. He later engaged in controversy with Calvin*.

Pilate, Acts of Apocryphal account of the trial, death, and Resurrection of Jesus Christ to which is attached another document called Descent of Christ into Hades. The two are sometimes known as *Gospel of Nicodemus**.

pilgrim 1. Traveler to a holy place or shrine. 2. Sojourner in a foreign land. 3. See PILGRIM FATHERS. 4. Christian viewed as on a pilgrimage to heaven*.

Pilgrim Fathers Also, Pilgrims. Puritan founders of Plymouth Colony in Massachusetts who sailed from Holland and England on the *Mayflower* in 1620. Chief among them were John Smyth, Thomas Helwys, and William Bradford*, later governor of the Plymouth Colony.

pilgrimage Journey to a shrine as an act of religious devotion or to discharge a vow* or obligation. The principal centers of Christian pilgrimage have varied from age to age according to Christian traditions, although all would include the Holy Land*. In the Roman Catholic Church, Marian* shrines are popular destinations.

Pilgrimage of Etheria/Egeria Record of pilgrimage* to the Holy Land* in the fifth century by Etheria, a nun. The manuscript was discovered in 1884. Etheria identifies the traditional sites in the Holy Land: Mount Zion, Calvary, Bethlehem*, Gethsemane*, and the Mount of Olives.

Pilgrimage of Grace Revolt in northern England in 1536–1537 against the ecclesiastical policies of Henry VIII, especially his suppression of monasteries and the abolition of papal supremacy. It was led by Robert Aske and other members of the northern aristocracy, such as Sir Thomas Darcy. It was put down brutally after about 200 executions.

Pilgrim's Progress Full title: *The Pilgrim's Progress from This World to That Which Is to Come*. Allegorical work written by the Puritan writer John Bunyan*, while in prison, recounting the adventures of the hero Christian in journeying from the City of Destruction to the heavenly Jerusalem.

The first part was printed in 1678. The second part, published in 1684, narrates the similar journey of Christiana, Christian's wife. It remains one of the most durable devotional classics.

Pilgrim's Way Ancient English road followed by medieval pilgrims to the tomb of Thomas a Becket* at Canterbury*.

Pillar of Fire, the Holiness group founded by Mrs. Alma White in 1901, originally called the Pentecostal Union.

pillar saint See STYLITE.

pilonion Sleeveless black cloak worn by the Armenian clergy.

pinco In the Jacobite Rite, a linen purificator* used to clean the priest's fingers during the liturgy.

pinka In the Assyrian Rite, a paten* or both the paten and the chalice*.

Pinkham, Daniel (1923–) American composer of choral music. He was for many years music director of the King's Chapel in Boston. Among his contributions to church music are four cantatas

John Bunyan

of which one is for Christmas*, one for Easter*, and one for Ascension. His liturgical works include a requiem*, a Magnificat*, a Stabat Mater*, and a Passion according to St. Mark*. Other religious compositions include *Daniel in the Lion's Den* (1973), *The Passion of Judas* (1976), *When God Arose* (1979), and *The Conversion of Saul* (1981). His organ music includes *Psalms* (1983), *Blessings* (1977), and *Epiphanies* (1978).

pirmo In the Jacobite tradition, a censer* with short chains to which bells are attached. It is swung in the Byzantine fashion along its entire length.

Pisa 1. Cathedral in Pisa, Italy, built by Buscheto. Work on the cathedral began in 1095 and it was consecrated in 1118, but work continued into the fourteenth century. In 1595 a fire destroyed most of the interior. 2. Construction of the famous

Cathedral of Pisa

Leaning Tower designed by Bonnano began in 1174, but when the third story was reached, the building began to tilt and was therefore abandoned. The work was resumed and the remaining storys were completed in the next 90 years. In 1350 Tommaso Pisano added the belfry and corrected the floor level of the final story. It is one of the architectural marvels of the world.

Pisa, Council of Council convoked in 1409 to end the Great Schism*. It was attended by eight of Gregory XII's cardinals as well as Avignonese cardinals, and 500 members representing the Western Church* except Scotland, Scandinavia, Hungary, Castile, Aragon, Naples, and Germany. The council deposed both existing popes, Gregory XII and Benedict XIII, as heretics and schismatics and elected

Alexander V* as new pope. The council is not recognized as ecumenical by the Roman Catholic Church because it was not convened by the pope. It did not end the Great Schism, but it paved the way for the Council of Constance* in 1415.

Pisano, Nicola and Giovanni (1220–1284 and 1245–1314, respectively) Father and son, Italian sculptors. **Nicola's** major work is his *Last Judgment*. The pulpit in Siena Cathedral* marks the emergence of **Giovanni** as a sculptor. It contains several scenes from the New Testament. He followed it with two other pulpits, Sant'Andrea, Pistoia, and the Pisa* Cathedral. Giovanni also did several Madonna* and Child groups for the Pisa Baptistery, the Arena Chapel in Padua, and Prato Cathedral.

piscina (Lat., bowl) Small bowl, often richly decorated, with drain in a niche* on the side wall of a

Piscina

church, near the altar, intended for washing the priest's hands, the chalice*, and the paten* after the Mass*.

pistic Of, relating to, or exhibiting faith*.

Pistis Sophia Third-century Sahidic* work recording conversation between Jesus and certain disciples at the end of a 12-year sojourn on the earth after Resurrection, ascribed to various Gnostic sects. It narrates the deliverance of Pistis Sophia, the female embodiment of wisdom, from a demon called self-will and purports to be a revelation of esoteric mysteries* by which human beings may escape the present world that is doomed to destruction.

Pistoia, Synod of Roman Catholic synod* held in 1786 under the presidency of Scipione de Ricci to uphold Jansenist doctrines. It reaffirmed Jansenism*, adopted the Four Gallican Articles*, urged the use of vernacular, and called for liturgical and catechetical revision, reorganization of the clergy and the episcopate*, just distribution of church goods, and the promotion of personal piety. Rome condemned many of the proposals, and Ricci was forced to recant.

Pistology Branch of theology dealing with faith* and belief.

Pius II (1405–1464) Pope from 1458. Birth name: Enea Silvio de' Piccolomini. During his six-year papacy, he tried to organize a crusade against the Turks, who had captured Constantinople* in 1453 and then menaced Europe. He put himself at the head of the crusaders in 1463, but died soon afterwards at Ancona.

Pius IV (1499–1565) Pope from 1559. Birth name: Gian Angelo Medici. His greatest achievement was the successful conclusion of the Council of Trent*. He published a new Index in 1564, prepared the Roman Catechism*, and reformed the Sacred College*.

Pius V, St. (1504–1572) Pope from 1566. Birth name: Michele Ghislieri. As pope he continued to practice the rigorous asceticism* of the Dominican Order to which he had belonged and also introduced the papal habit of wearing the white cassock* of that order. His papacy was marked by completion of the Roman Catechism* (1566), the reform of the Breviary* (1568) and the Missal* (1570), and the publication (1570) of a new complete edition of the works of Thomas Aquinas*, who was declared a doctor of the church* in 1567. The highlight of his reign was the defeat of the Turks at Lapanto in 1571 by the combined papal, Venetian, and Spanish fleets. Feast day: April 30.

Pius VI (1717–1799) Pope from 1775. Birth name: Giovanni Angelico Braschi. His pontificate* was marked by continuing struggle against anti-Catholic movements and secular rulers, as Joseph II of Austria. He was the pope during the French Revolution, and he denounced the Civil Consti-

tution and the Declaration of the Rights of Man. Thereupon Napoleon Bonaparte invaded the papal states and imposed severe terms of peace. He was deposed as head of state, taken first to Florence* and then across the Alps, where he died. This was the lowest point in the history of the papacy in modern times.

Pius VII (1742–1823) Pope from 1800. Birth name: Luigi Barnaba Chiaramonti. His pontificate* covered the Napoleonic years which brought much

Pope Pius VII

humiliation to the papacy. After the fall of Napoleon, he returned to the Vatican* and reestablished his authority over the papal states. He restored the Jesuit Order in 1814. His reign marked the steady resurgence of the papacy after the nadir that it reached during the time of his predecessor.

Pius IX (1792–1878) Pope from 1846. Birth name: Giovanni Maria Mastai-Ferretti. His pontificate* of more than 32 years was the longest in the history of the Vatican*. Politically, his reign marked the loss of all papal dominions and the triumph of Risorgimento. The Law of Guarantees of 1871 took away his sovereignty over the papal states, and the pope's authority was henceforward confined to the Vatican*. Ecclesiastically, his reign was one of the most momentous and eventful. The hierarchy* was restored in England (1850) and in the Netherlands (1853), and concordats were concluded with many European and American countries. The two most important events in his reign were the definition of the immaculate conception* of the Virgin Mary* in 1854 and the convocation of the First Vatican Council* in

Pope Pius IX

1869–1870 which approved the doctrine of papal infallibility*. His *Syllabus of Errors** sounded the clarion call against rationalism, religious liberalism*, and materialism.

Pius X, St. (1835–1914) Pope from 1903. Birth name: Giuseppe Melchior Sarto. From the beginning he intended to be a spiritual rather than political pope, yet anti-Catholic measures in France and

Pope Pius X

Portugal forced him to oppose both governments. He enforced the purity of Catholic doctrine against the modernists and liberals. He reorganized the Curia*, prepared a new code of canon law*, encouraged early and frequent communion, and reformed the liturgy. His *Motu Proprio* of 1903 restored the Gregorian Chant* to its preeminence in the liturgy. He reformulated Catholic social policy and laid down the principles of Catholic Action* in his encyclical*, *Il Fermo Proposito* (1905).

Pius XI (1857–1939) Pope from 1922. Birth name: Achille Ambrogio Damiano Ratti. The principal goal of his pontificate* was "the restoration of all things in Christ," as symbolized by the institution of the Feast of Christ the King*. He encouraged lay participation in the church and condemned con-

Pope Pius XI

traception. Many of his encyclicals* dealt with social problems, as *Quadragesimo Anno* (1931), or education, as *Divini Illius Magistri* (1929). The most important political event of his reign was the Lateran Treaty* of 1929 with Mussolini, establishing the Vatican City state. He opposed both Nazism and Fascism but supported Franco in Spain. The number of Catholic missionaries doubled during his pontificate. He was the first pope to use radio for communication. The jubilee* in 1925 was the occasion for a number of canonizations*, including those of Teresa of Lisieux* and Peter Canisius*.

Pius XII (1876–1958) Pope from 1939. Birth name: Eugenio Pacelli. His pontificate* was clouded by

World War II. He prepared the way for the Second Vatican Council* through his encyclicals on the renewal of biblical studies and the liturgy. He adopted a moderate position in the church's ef-

Pope Pius XII

forts to combat modern ideologies. He approved a limited use of the historical-critical method for biblical studies (*Divino Afflante Spiritu,* 1943), a modest beginning for the liturgical movement* (*Mediator Dei,* 1947), and a theology that encouraged positive relations with nonbelievers (*Mystici Corporis,* 1943). In 1950 he proclaimed the Assumption of the Blessed Virgin Mary* into heaven* in his encyclical*, *Munificentissimus Deus*. During his reign the number of Catholic dioceses* rose from 1096 to 2048.

Placebo (Lat., I will please) Traditional title of the vespers* for the dead.

plague saints Nineteen saints* who may be invoked for protection from plague. Of these the most prominent are St. Roch*, St. Sebastian*, Sts. Cosmas and Damian*, St. Anthony Abbot, St. Borromeo*, St. Christopher*, St. Genevieve*, St. George*, and St. Francesca Romana.

plainsong Also, Gregorian Chant*; plainchant. Traditional ecclesiastical music of the Latin Rite* known as the Gregorian Chant, derived from the music of many medieval rites, such as Ambrosian, Mozarabic*, and the Old Roman. Plainsong is entirely monophonic and sung in unison with free rhythm. Its tonal organization is based on scales corresponding to the white notes of the piano, especially the notes D, E, F, and G. The repertory of the plainsong grew after the Middle Ages. In the nineteenth century, medieval traditions were restored through the efforts of the monks of Solesmes* under the leadership of Dom Joseph Pothier (1835–1923) and his successors. Most plainsong chants are contained in the Gradual for the Mass*, Antiphonal for the Choral Office, Manuale, Pontifical*, and the Processional.

plainsong Mass Mass in which the composer has based each section of the ordinary* upon the liturgically appropriate Gregorian Chant*.

plan of salvation Summary of the basic truths of the gospel and steps necessary to becoming a Christian, as presented in the Four Spiritual Laws*, "Steps to Peace with God," and other gospel tracts.

plane tree Broad-leaved tree symbolizing the grace* of Christ in religious art.

planeta The chasuble*.

planeto plicata Folded chasuble* used in place of the dalmatic* during Advent* and Lent*.

plantatio ecclesiae (Lat.) Church planting as the goal of missions.

Plantin Bible Bible printed by Christopher Plantin, Dutch printer, especially the Antwerp Polyglot Bible in eight folio volumes, 1569–1572. He and his successors printed many carefully crafted editions of the Missal*, Breviary*, and other liturgical books*.

plashtschanitza In the Byzantine tradition, area near the sanctuary where the table used for requiem* services and the requiem stand are kept along with memorials.

Platytera Iconographic type of the Virgin Mary* with her arms outstreched, the Christ child in a medallion encompassed by her bodily form or with her hands held in front of her, the palms facing outward.

plenary council Regional church council of archbishops and bishops presided over by a papal legate*.

plenary indulgence In the Roman Catholic Church, indulgence* that remits the entire punishment due to a person's sins, and that may be applied personally or to the profit of souls in purgatory*. Its efficacy depends on the state of the sinner's soul. The conditions of the grant are the recitation of certain prayers, or devotional exercises, the use of the sacrament* of penance*, and the reception of the Holy Communion*. The abuse of such indulgences was one of the sparks that lit the Reformation*.

plenary inspiration Theory that states that God is the author of the Bible, that the writers of the Bible are inspired in all that they wrote in matters of content, and that the accuracy of transmissions was also monitored and superintended by divine inspiration*.

plenary Mass Musical setting for both the proper and the ordinary of the Mass*, such as the requiem*.

pleroma/plerosis Fullness or completeness, as an attribute of the Godhead and as applied to fullness of divine revelation* in the Incarnation*. For Gnostics, it meant the divine and celestial dimension, once full and intact, and now moving toward restoration. Its opposite is kenoma, the present world where the souls are consigned to perdition.

Plough Monday In England, the first Monday after Epiphany* when prayers are offered for farmers.

pluriform church Church which accepts differences of doctrinal emphases among members as healthy and normal.

Plutschau, Heinrich (1677–1747) Pietist missionary. He was a cofounder with Ziegenbalg* of the Halle-Danish Mission in Tranquebar, on the east coast of southern India, the first Protestant mission in India.

pluvial Cope.

Plymouth Brethren Also, the Brethren. Christian religious body established in Dublin about 1827 and in Plymouth in 1830. Early leaders of the movement were J. N. Darby*, John Gifford Bellett, Samuel P. Tregelles, and A. N. Groves*. The movement in its early days was a protest against the formalism and sectarianism* of the established churches*. Plymouth Brethren teachings combine Calvinist, Pietist, Puritan, and Millennialist elements. They normally have no organized ministry. They believe in the inerrancy* of the Bible and emphasize the priesthood of all believers*. Each church or assembly is autonomous and has no prescribed order of worship. Assemblies are Christ-centered and marked by a zeal for evangelism and prophetic utterances.

Despite their emphasis on unity, Plymouth Brethren have had their share of divisions. Controversies over the human nature of Christ and church government produced the first division between the Open Brethren* representing the mainstream and the Exclusive Brethren* representing the Darbyist group. Within the latter there developed a Needed Truth faction which sought to develop formal rituals and practices of church government. One small faction follows the extremist teachings of James Taylor*. From the beginning the Brethren have placed great emphasis on evangelization. Its missionary outreach*, known as Christian Missions to Many Lands, covers several large countries, including India, where mission work began in the nineteenth century.

Among the Open Brethren, places of worship are called "gospel halls" chapels, or churches, and among the Exclusive Brethren, the "meeting room." They are Evangelical in doctrine and practice, leaning for the most part toward Calvinism* rather than Arminianism*. They observe both sacraments of baptism* and the Lord's Supper*. Communion services* are held every Sunday morning. The bread is usually an entire loaf passed from hand to hand, each communicant breaking off a small piece and eating it. The cup*, similarly, is passed from hand to hand, each communicant drinking a portion.

pneumatikos (lit., the ghostly father) In the Byzantine tradition, priest who hears confessions.

Pneumatology (Gk., *pneuma*, spirit + logos, study) Branch of theology dealing with the Holy Spirit*, especially his divine attributes and nature and relationship to the Father and the Son, and his work.

Pneumatomachi (Gk., fighters against the Spirit) Fourth-century group that denied the deity of the Holy Spirit*. The sect* was led by Eusthathius* of Sebaste, Macedonius of Constantinople, and Marathonius of Nicomedia. They were condemned by Pope Damasus in 374 and by the First Council of Constantinople* in 381.

Poblet Cistercian monastery of Santa Maria at Poblet in Catalonia in Spain, built by the Catalan king Ramon Berenguer IV. The monastery complex is a fortress ringed by three walls. The fifteenth-century Porta Daurada, the Golden Gateway, leads to the second wall and its portal, named in honor of Isabella and Ferdinand of Castile and Aragon. The third wall dating from the fourth century is guarded by 13 towers. The church is entered through the King's Gate, which dates from the fourteenth century. The alabaster altar built by Damia Forment has four tiers.

Pocket Testament League Group founded in 1893 in Birmingham, England, by Helen Cadbury as a Bible club. It eventually became a worldwide movement covering 33 countries and distributing millions of copies of the Gospel of John.

poderis Vestment that reaches to the feet, as cassock*, alb*, or surplice*.

podriznik In the Russian Church, the inner rason* or a close-fitting cassock* worn by the clergy.

poimenics Pastoral theology.

Poissy, Colloquy of Conference held in 1561 in Poissy, France, between French bishops and Protestant Reformers, led by Beza*. Although it failed to reach agreement, it paved the way for the edict of toleration of 1562.

Poitiers Notre Dame le Grande, cathedral dedicated to St. Hilary of Poitiers* whose remains are buried in it, in Poitiers, a city in France on the way to Santiago de Compostela*. Its construction began in the second half of the eleventh century and was completed by the middle of the twelfth.

Pokrov Feast of the Holy Protection introduced into Russia by Andrei Bogoliubskii of Vladimir* and commemorated on October 1.

pokrovy In the Byzantine tradition, the three veils used to cover the paten* and chalice*. The third veil, known as the aer* or vosdukh*, covers both the paten and the chalice.

Polanus, Amandus (1561–1610) Professor of theology at Basle* and one of the leading theologians of Protestant orthodoxy*. In his *Substance of Christian Religion* (1609) he emphasized that the literal sense is the only true and genuine sense of each passage in the Scripture. He established the glory of God as the true test of scriptural interpretation.

polemical theology Theology developed in conscious opposition to the doctrinal systems of other churches.

polemics Study of theological controversies and rebuttal of errors and heresies.

political theology Precursor of liberation theology*, emphasizing greater influence on the political process by theologians and theological ideas. Representatives of political theology argue that all theology is political in nature even when it is not so stated explicitly. Often, political theology is ideological and has a Marxist coloring, concerned with power relationships in society. Proponents of the social gospel*, as Rauschenbusch* in the United States, have explored the political dimensions of various theological doctrines. Even Reinhold Niebuhr*, a critic of the social gospel, tried to imbue political thinking with theological ideas. Evangelical Christians generally have opposed political theology, but the political scope of the gospel has been acknowledged by a number of important strains within the Evangelical community. The theocratic vision of Puritan New England has been revived by the so called Religious Right in the latter half of the twentieth century.

polity Form of church government adopted by a denomination.

Pollock, Algernon James (1864–1957) Plymouth Brethren* leader. He left a career in banking to enter the ministry and spent the rest of his life traveling the world as an evangelist and teacher. He edited the *Gospel Messenger* for many years.

Polluiuolo, Antonio del and Piero (c. 1432–1498 and c. 1441–1496, respectively) Italian brothers and artists. Their works include the celebrated *Martyrdom of St. Sebastian* (1475) and two papal monuments in St. Peter's*.

Polycarp, St. (c. 69–c. 155) Greek bishop of Smyrna, martyr*, and Church Father*. Irenaeus* reports that Polycarp was a contemporary of the apostles and had been ordained by them. He is thus a link between the Apostolic Age* and the age of the great Christian writers that followed. Ignatius visited him about 110 and wrote to him afterwards. He visited Rome* about 155 and met with Bishop Anicetus. He also confronted Marcion* at Rome. Soon after his return he was arrested during a pagan festival. Declaring that he

Like his friend Ignatius before him, Polycarp, elderly bishop of Smyrna, sought to imitate Christ in his death. "If we suffer for the sake of his name, let glorify him," wrote Polycarp in a letter to the Philippians. One February afternoon in 155 or 156, Polycarp entered a crowd stadium and refused yet again to blaspheme Jesus. As Polyca foresaw in a dream, the rabble demanded that he be burned a Confident that Jesus would give him the power to endure the without moving, he asked not to be nailed to his wooden pyr

St. Polycarp

had been "a Christian for 86 years," he refused to recant and was publicly burned. The *Martyrdom of Polycarp* which recounts his death is the earliest extant *Acta* of a martyr. Feast day: February 23.

polychoral Music composed for two or more choirs, as in Venetian music.

polychronion In the Byzantine Rite*, chant sung at the end of a pontifical liturgy wishing the bishop long life.

polyeleos 1. Chandelier directly beneath the central dome of a church, lit at the Great Entrance* on major feasts and at funerals. Around a polyeleos hangs a great metal circle, decorated with icons, normally including the 12 apostles, and surmounted by candles. 2. Part of the office of mattins* for Sundays, some saints' days, and major feasts when Psalms 134 and 135 are sung.

Polyglot Bible Single Bible containing the text in a number of languages in parallel columns. Origen's *Hexapla** in Hebrew and five Greek versions was the first. Other examples are the *Complutensian Polyglot** in six volumes (1522); Christopher Plantin's *Biblia Regia* (8 vols., 1569–1572); the *Antwerp Polyglot* (10 vols., 1629–1645), edited by J. Morinus; and *Biblia Sacra Polyglotta* (6 vols., 1653–1657).

polykandelon In the Byzantine Church*, a branched candlestick containing lamps of oil.

polykerion In the Byzantine Church*, a many-branched candlestick.

polyphony Music composed in more than one voice-part.

polyptych Picture, relief, or altarpiece made up of more than three parts, of which the central part is a large picture flanked by smaller pictures to the left and right.

polystavrion In the Greek Orthodox Church, a white phelonion* or liturgical cape with a decoration of black crosses.

pomata In the Byzantine tradition, four squares sewn on the mandyas* representing the four Gospels and embroidered with the symbols of the four evangelists.

pome Vessel of precious metal, shaped like a ball,

filled with hot water during winter and used to warm the hands of the priest during service.

pomegranate In Christian art, symbol of the Resurrection.

pompon Ornamental ball of cloth material attached to the top of a biretta*.

Pomposa Benedictine abbey of Pomposa on the estuary of the Po in Italy affiliated with the archbishopric of Ravenna*. Under Abbot Guido of Ravenna, the abbey became a major spiritual center. However, decline set in during the fourteenth and fifteenth centuries, and by the seventeenth century it was abandoned. The church is an outstanding example of Italian Romanesque. It is a triple-aisled pillared basilica* with a nine-tiered 157-foot-high tower, built in the ninth century. The church is famous for its murals and frescoes*.

pontifex maximus (Lat., supreme pontiff*) Title of the pope. Originally the title of the high priest of the ancient Roman religion, it was adopted by the Roman emperors until the fall of the Western Empire.

pontiff Title of the pope. Originally the title of a member of the Pontifical College, the group of high priests in ancient Rome*.

pontifical 1. Of or relating to the pope. 2. Pontificale book of rites or offices, other than a pontifical Mass*, to be performed by a pope or bishop. The earliest pontifical was the Romano-Germanic Pontifical which was replaced by the pontificals of the Roman Curia* in the twelfth century, which itself gave way to the compilation by William Durandus. The most recent revision is that by the Second Vatican Council*. 3. Vestments of a prelate* celebrating pontifical Mass. These are buskins* (silk leg-coverings), sandals, gloves, dalmatic*, tunicle*, ring, pectoral cross, mitre*, and pastoral staff*.

pontifical Mass Special High Mass*, usually celebrated by a pope, cardinal, bishop, abbot, or certain other prelates.

pontificals/pontificalia Insignia or pontifical* vestments of a bishop, abbot, cardinal, or pope.

pontificate Office or tenure of a pontiff*.

Pontigny Cistercian monastery in Pontigny, near Auxerre* in Burgundy, France, founded in 1114. Nothing is left of the monastic buildings.

Poole, Matthew (1624–1679) English Protestant biblical commentator, author of *Synopsis Criticorum Aliorumque Sacrae Scripturae Interpretum* (5 folio vols., 1669–1676). His *Annotations upon the Holy Bible* was completed by his friends after his death.

Poor Clares The Second Order of St. Francis founded by him and St. Clare* about 1213. Cardinal Ugolino (later Gregory IX*) placed Clare and her nuns under the strict Rule of St. Benedict* to which were added severe ascetic practices such as complete silence, perpetual fasting, and lying on boards. Some of these rules were eased by Francis in 1224 and by Urban IV in 1263. Those who follow the stricter rule were known as Clarisses and those who follow the relaxed rules as Urbanists. In 1436 the reform of St. Colette* brought most of the houses back to the original Rule of St. Francis, and they are thus known as Colettines*. The Capuchinesses were added to the Poor Clares in the sixteenth century, making the Colettines, Urbanists, and Capuchinesses the three main branches of the order. Poor Clares are sworn to poverty, penance*, fasting, and manual work and wear a dark frieze habit with no cord or girdle*, black veil, and cloth sandals on bare feet.

Poor, Preference for the Cardinal tenet of liberation theology*, that the Incarnation* has a special relevance for the materially poor, implying that the gospel is primarily designed to redeem believers from economic poverty.

pope (Lat., papa, father) Title of the bishop of Rome*. The title was originally applied to any bishop. In the Coptic Church*, it is applied to the patriarch*. In the Eastern Orthodox Church*, it is applied to any parish priest. The full title of the Roman Catholic pope is "bishop of Rome, vicar* of Jesus Christ*, successor of the prince of the apostles, supreme pontiff* of the universal church, patriarch* of the West, primate* of Italy, archbishop and metropolitan* of the Roman

Popes of the Twentieth Century

Leo XIII (1878–1903)
Pius X, St. (1903–1914)
Benedict XV (1914–1922)
Pius XI (1922–1939)
Pius XII (1939–1958)
John XXIII (1958–1963)
Paul VI (1963–1978)
John Paul I (1978)
John Paul II (1978–)

province, and sovereign of the state of the City of Vatican." There have been approximately 266 popes since St. Peter*. (See the Appendixes for a list of these popes.)

Pope, William Burt (1822–1903) English Wesleyan divine. A tutor at Didsbury Wesleyan College, he wrote the authoritative textbook on Wesleyan dogmatic theology, *Compendium of Christian Theology* (3 vols., 1875–1876).

popery Derogatory name applied by some Protestants to the Roman Catholic Church and its practices and doctrines.

poppy In religious art, symbol of Christ's Passion*.

poprazdnestvo (lit., after-feast) In the Byzantine tradition, period that follows the celebration of a feast.

Porres, St. Martin de (1579–1639) Peruvian Dominican who was the first American black to be canonized. He is the patron saint* of work for interracial justice and harmony. Feast day: November 5.

Porta Clausa (Lat., closed door) Title of the Virgin Mary* with reference to Ezekiel 44:2: "This gate shall be shut; it shall not be opened, and no man shall enter by it; because the LORD God of Israel has entered by it, therefore it shall be shut."

Porta Coeli (Lat., Gate of Heaven*) In the Roman Catholic Church, title of the Virgin Mary*.

Portiuncula Small chapel, also known as Santa Maria degli Angeli, in the plain below Assisi* dating from the eleventh century. It was St. Francis's favorite church and the headquarters of his order during his lifetime. The chapel and the cell in which St. Francis died are enclosed by a sixteenth-century church destroyed by an earthquake in 1832 and again in 1996 but since restored. The Portiuncula indulgence* can be gained by anyone visiting the church.

Port-Royal Cistercian abbey of nuns founded in 1204 which emerged in the seventeenth century as the main center of Jansenism*. The original monastery, about 17 miles from Paris, was called Port-Royal des Champs. In 1625 the community was transferred to Paris to a new monastery called Port-Royal de Paris. In 1665 the nuns who refused to sign a formulary condemning the five Jansenist Propositions were transferred back to Port-Royal des Champs, where they were kept as prisoners. In 1706 the aging nuns refused to accept yet another papal condemnation of Jansenism, and the abbey was suppressed. In 1710 the buildings were razed.

St. Martin de Porres

porurar Stole* similar to the Byzantine epitrachelion* worn by Armenian priests. It is generally made of expensive silk or brocade with attached jewels.

positional holiness State of being holy or sanctified as a result of being in Christ (1 Cor. 1:2; 3:1–3).

positive confession Also, "name it and claim it." Prosperity doctrine popularized by several American televangelists under the inspiration of Essek William Kenyon* (1867–1948). It is based on the biblical premise that since faith is a confession*, anything that is confessed with the mouth can be realized. This teaching has been espoused by many popular evangelists, especially Jim Bakker*, Kenneth Hagin*, Kenneth Copeland*, Robert Tilton, Charles Capps, Frederick K. C. Price, and others, almost all of them Pentecostal.

positive theology Branch of theology dealing with historical facts and traditions as distinct from natural theology*, which deals with universal unwritten principles and laws. It is sometimes called "historical theology*."

positive thinking Pop psychology developed by Norman Vincent Peale* (1898–1993) emphasizing perpetual optimism in the face of the problems of life. It makes no reference to sin or evil. A variant called "possibility thinking" was developed by Robert H. Schuller* (1926–).

posokh In the Byzantine tradition, crozier or pastoral staff* carried by bishops and archimandrites as a symbol of their authority.

post-Christian 1. (*adjective*) In secular usage, of or relating to a worldview that ignores the reality and relevance of the Christian church or finds that reality passe. 2. (*noun*) Disaffiliated, backslidden, or lapsed Christian. 3. Suggestive description of much of the Western world that seems to be rejecting the Christian faith that has so powerfully shaped its history.

postcommunion In the Roman Mass*, the final prayer in the Eucharist* following the Communion. It is similar in structure to the collect*.

postconciliar Of or relating to events taking place after the Second Vatican Council*.

post-conversion experience Baptism of the Holy Spirit* that follows initial conversion experience.

postdenominationalism Trend among smaller independent churches away from denominational labels and affiliations and toward a noncreedal church order*.

postil Gloss on a scriptural text or a homily* on the Gospel or Epistle for the day.

postlude Music after the ending of a worship service.

postmillennialism/postmillenarianism Belief that the return of Christ will take place after the millennium, a period of peace and prosperity representing the triumph of the gospel and the full operation of the Holy Spirit* (Rev. 20). Evil will not be totally eliminated but will be muted. The period will close with the Second Coming* of Christ, the resurrection of the dead, and the last judgment*. It is often dismissed by its critics as the Christian version of the secular idea of material progress. But the idea was actually formulated by the Puritan theologians in the seventeenth century and continues to be popular in Reformed* circles.

post-modern theology Contemporary theology that tries to respond to the rejection of modernity as shaped by the tradition of the Enlightenment and that rejects all claims to an exclusive and objective truth or set of values. Post-modernity is a complex phenomenon to which theologians respond in different ways.

postnaya triod In the Byzantine tradition, a set of choir books including the office of St. Gregory Palamas*. Also known as the Fasting Triodion because it is used during the Great Fast* of Lent*.

post-Sanctus Prayer in the eucharistic liturgy following the Sanctus*. It survives in the Mozarabic Rite*.

post-tribulationism Eschatological doctrine that the

church will endure a time of suffering during the tribulation period until the return of Jesus Christ at the end of that period.

postulant Candidate for a monastic order living in a religious house under the supervision of a superior* for a probationary period before formally entering the novitiate*.

potent Cross of Jerusalem* formed by four tau crosses joined by the foot.

poterion In the Coptic Church*, a chalice*, also called kas*, usually a silver bowl with small and straight sides, long stem, round knop*, and a circular foot. Also called potir in the Byzantine Church*.

Pothinus, St. (c. 87–c. 177) Also, Potheinos. Martyr* and first bishop of Lyons. A disciple of Polycarp*, he probably introduced Christianity into south Gaul. He was martyred at the age of 90. Feast day: June 2.

pothurhaye In the Jacobite tradition, the altar which stands clear of the east wall of a church to permit processions to pass around it. It has three steps in Syria and one step in Malabar.

Poulenc, Francis (1899–1963) French composer. A leading pop composer, he was led to return to his Roman Catholic faith through the accidental death of a friend in 1935. His first religious work, *Litanies a la Vierge Noire* (Litanies to the Black Virgin of Rocamadour), came out in 1936. His most compelling masterpiece may well be the *Dialogues of the Carmelites* (1956), an opera in three acts about the martyrdom of a group of nuns executed during the French Revolution for refusing to abjure their vows. The first of his liturgical compositions was *Mass in G* (1937). It was followed by four penitential motets* and four Christmas* motets as well as his large-scale sacred compositions: *Stabat Mater** (1950), *Gloria* (1959), and *Sept Repons des Tenebres* (Office for Holy Saturday, 1961).

Poullart-des-Places, Claude Francois (1679–1709) Founder of the Congregation of the Holy Ghost (Spiritans). A small community of students he led

at the Jesuit College* in Paris was the foundation of the Congregation of the Holy Ghost involved in rural domestic as well as foreign missions.

Poussin, Nicolas (1594–1665) Greatest of the French classical painters. Among his religious paintings are the *Martyrdom of St. Erasmus* (1628), *Seven Sacraments* (1637–1642), *Return from the Flight into Egypt* (1628–1629), *Lamentation Over the Dead Christ* (1628), *Massacre of the Innocents* (1630–1601), *Madonna on the Steps* (1648), *Madonna with the Basin* (1650), and *Ecstasy of St. Paul* (1650). Poussin's works are not grandiose, but they stimulate the mind and understanding.

Poverello (Ital., the poor one) Epithet of St. Francis of Assisi*.

poverty Vow voluntarily renouncing the right of ownership and independent use of property, one of the monastic vows and evangelical counsels.

poyas In the Byzantine tradition, girdle* worn over the sticherion*. It is made of soft black material in the case of non-monastic clergy and of leather in the case of monastic clergy.

practical theology Branch of theology concerned with such disciplines as Christian education, homiletics*, liturgy, and pastoral care.

practicing Christian Also, professing Christian. Christian who participates actively in the worship rites of a Christ-centered church and takes the church's doctrinal standards and mandates seriously.

praeconium (Lat., announcement) Liturgical announcement or solemn proclamation.

praeparatio (Lat., preparation) Fourth Sunday in Advent*.

Praepositinus (c. 1140–c. 1210) Theologian and liturgist*. He was in charge of the cathedral school* in Mainz* from 1194 to 1203 and chancellor of the cathedral in Paris from 1206 to 1209. His principal work is the *Summa Theologica*, a classical work in scholastic theology. Following Peter Lombard*, the work is divided into four books, dealing with God, the creation and fall, Incarnation*, and the sacraments*. His minor works include *Summa Super Psalterium, Summa Contra Haereticos,* and *Tractatus de Officiis,* a book on the liturgical year*.

Praetorius, Michael (1571–1621) German composer. His work was primarily for the Lutheran liturgy. Most of his compositions appear in the nine-volume work, *Musae Sioniae* (1605–1619).

Prague Capital of the Czech Republic and location of the Gothic* cathedral of St. Vitus*. It is built on the Hradcany, the rock that forms the royal citadel of Prague, where a small Wenceslas rotunda had been built at the turn of the first millennium. Work on the cathedral began in 1344 under the architect Peter Parler and was not completed until 1929. The cathedral includes a number of chapels, as the Wenceslas Chapel, Chapel of the Holy Cross, Vladislav Oratory, Waldstein Chapel, and the Nepomuk Chapel. The Golden Door contains a magnificent Venetian gold mosaic of the last judgment* and a bronze statue of St. George* slaying the dragon.

Prague is also the location of the Premonstratensian monastery of Strahov, founded in 1140 by Prince Vladislav II. Work on the conventual Church of the Assumption, a basilica*, began in 1143. In 1258 a fire destroyed all the buildings, but by 1263 it was rebuilt. Toward the end of the seventeenth century Jean Baptist Mathey refashioned the interior in Baroque style, Georg Wilhelm Neunherz painted the frescoes*, Josef Lauermann and Franz Plazer built the high altar, and Johann Anton Quittainer did the decorative carvings on the side altars. The founder of the Premonstratensian Order, Norbert* of Xanten, is buried here in the chapel of St. Ursula.

Prague, Infant of Eighteen-inch high statue of the child Jesus donated by Princess Polixena to Our Lady of Victory Church in Prague* in 1628.

Praise and Worship Interdenominational Christian renewal movement, emerging notably after the mid-1940s, expressing worship in forms (especially musical) sensitive to contemporary culture. In American Protestantism*, the heritage of gospel music* and meetings (often associated with revival* and Sunday evening services) brought a spontaneity and informality particularly favored by young people following World War II. In 1948 a "Singing Youth for Christ" songbook was published by YFC*, with a foreword citing 1 Corinthians 14:15: "The components of any spiritual experience are *heart* and *mind* . . . These songs . . . will stimulate your thoughts, turning them to Calvary and the Christ of God." Included were hymns from Watts* and Newton*, gospel songs from Bliss* and Crosby*, together with collected choruses such as Daniel Iverson's "Spirit of the Living God, Fall Afresh on Me" (1934) and Seth Sykes's "Thank You, Lord, for Saving My Soul" (1940). Also among these was Alfred B. Smith's "For God So Loved the World," a scripture song from 1941, the year in which he founded the influential Singspiration Inc.

In 1955, California music minister Ralph Carmichael was invited to lead music at the annual YFC convention, utilizing styles which, after a decade of growing acceptance, would lead to his 1964 *Lexicon Music* and the score for Billy Graham's film "The Restless Ones" (including "He's Everything to Me"). During the 1960s, the Jesus Movement often involved meetings with extended musical preparation ("worship") anticipating focused biblical instruction ("teaching"). This concept became influential organizationally through churches such as Calvary Chapel in Costa Mesa, California, and the collections (favoring acoustic guitar and/or piano) of Maranatha! Music (1971). In this decade, world cultures were represented, as "I Have Decided to Follow Jesus" (Assam, India), "Kumbaya" (Angola, Africa) and Taize songs (France) became favorites. Personal theological concerns including community (Peter Scholtes, "They Will Know We Are Christians by Our Love," 1966), eschatology (Larry Norman, "I Wish We'd All Been Ready," 1969), evangelism (Kurt Kaiser, "Pass It On," 1969), and simple, scriptural lifestyle (Karen Lafferty, "Seek Ye First the Kingdom of God," 1972) found common expression.

Traditional folk songs and spirituals such as "Lord, I Want to Be a Christian," "God Is So Good," and "He Is Lord" (all anonymous) were found at evangelical Bible camps, Roman Catholic folk masses, and charismatic healing services alike. In very different idioms, however,

Steven Schwartz's rock-oriented "Godspell" (1971) and Bill and Gloria Gaither's country gospel "Alleluia! A Praise Gathering for Believers" (1973) represented an emerging pattern. Today, periodicals such as *Worship Leader* and *Contemporary Christian Music* chronicle the movement. (See Appendix, "Chronology of Christian Music.")

praise service Worship service in which the focus is on praising God through songs and hymns and other expressions of gratitude, thanksgiving, and adoration. Its popularity is largely due to the Charismatic movement.

praise the Lord Common exclamatory phrase among Protestant Christians, equivalent of "hallelujah."

Praise to the Holiest in the Highest Hymn by John Henry Newman*, originally part of his poem, "The Dream of Gerontius*," set to music by Edward Elgar*. The hymn celebrates Christ's incarnation*.

Praxeas (c. 200) Heretic. Leader of Patripassian Monarchians who declared that God the Father also suffered the agony of crucifixion. Before the end of his life, he recanted. Tertullian* wrote an important treatise on the Trinity* against him.

praxis In liberation theology*, religious faith directed toward making the present world a better place, emphasizing social and political involvement, even at the cost of doctrinal purity. The word is now used much more widely with reference to theologically-determined practice or action.

prayer Fellowship and communion with God involving adoration, worship, praise, thanksgiving, supplication, petition*, confession*, repentance*, meditation, dedication, and intercession*. Christian prayer is addressed to God as Father through and in the name of Jesus Christ, his Son, and is based on the confidence that he hears his children. Prayer* is drawn partly from the urgency of human needs and partly from the promise and challenge of God's Word. Personal prayer is shaped by the awareness of God's presence. Corporate prayer is the living breath of the church.

Through prayer the church resists the assaults of Satan* (Matt. 26:41; Eph. 6:13–20), receives the gifts of grace* (Acts 4:31), seeks deliverance, healing, and restoration for the saints (Eph. 6:18; James 5:15; 1 John 5:16), supports evangelization (Col. 4:3–4), and hastens the return of the Lord (Rev. 22:20).

prayer breakfast Breakfast combined with extended time in group and personal prayer, a common ritual in political and business circles.

prayer chain Network of praying Christians activated by calls for intercessory prayer from those in need.

prayer cloth Cloth prayed over by a holy person and laid on those who are sick to transmit divine healing powers (Acts 19:11–12).

prayer meeting Traditional midweek prayer services held in Protestant churches with lay participation. Such prayer meetings are a common feature of Evangelical churches.

prayer of quiet See CENTERING PRAYER.

prayer of the heart See CENTERING PRAYER.

prayer tower Special building or room in a building set aside for prayer. The most prominent example is the Prayer Tower on the Oral Roberts University complex in Tulsa, Oklahoma.

prayer warrior Person noted for fervent prayers and especially gifted in intercessory prayers.

prazditchinaya mineya In the Byzantine Church*, service book that contains an abridged version of other books, such as the festal menaion.

preacher Person who preaches the gospel; often used as a title for a clergyman.

preaching Proclamation of the Word of God* with authority, both in a church service and as part of evangelistic meetings. In the Roman Catholic and Orthodox traditions, only ordained priests may preach, but in most Protestant denominations anyone called upon to preach may do so.

prebend In the Church of England*, portion of a church endowment earmarked for support of members of a chapter*; benefice*.

prebendary Anglican canon* who holds a prebend* or benefice* providing his income.

precentor 1. In the Old Foundation cathedrals of the Church of England*, official, ranking next to the dean in the chapter*, in charge of the singing of the church choir or congregation. In the New Foundation cathedrals, minor canon* or chaplain*. 2. In churches which use no musical instruments, a singer who leads congregational singing, particularly in Scottish Presbyterianism.

precept 1. In moral theology*, a solemn obligation, as contrasted with counsel, a matter of persuasion. 2. Matter of obligation established by God or by a superior* for those in religious communities who have taken a vow of obedience.

preceptory Community established on one of the provincial estates of Knights Templar, corresponding to the commandery among Hospitallers*.

preces (Lat., prayers) In the Roman Catholic Church, brief prayers of intercession* said responsively with an opening phrase delivered by a minister and a concluding phrase by the congregation.

preces feriales In the Roman Catholic Church, a short series of prayers said on ferial days consisting of Kyrie eleison*, the Lord's Prayer*, versicles, and responses. In the 1971 Breviary* they have been replaced by a series of intercessions* said every day at lauds* and vespers*.

prechastiye In the Byzantine tradition, the order of receiving Holy Communion*. After the priest breaks the consecrated bread, he puts the particles* in the chalice*, covers it, and puts the spoon on top. Then he and the deacon go out through the holy doors* to the soleas. Administering the Communion, the priest says, "The servant of God partakes of the holy precious body and blood of our Lord and God and Savior Jesus Christ unto the remission of sins and unto everlasting life." The deacon wipes the communicant's lips with a napkin.

Precisian Puritan, on account of the rigid and punctilious observance of external religious rules by Puritans*.

precious blood Blood of Jesus Christ poured out for the salvation* of sinners. In the Roman Catholic Church, the Feast of the Most Precious Blood is celebrated on July 1.

predella 1. Platform on the top step to an altar on which the priest stands. 2. Lowest piece of a reredos*, immediately above an altar; the strip of paintings at the base of an altarpiece.

predestination Divine and unalterable determination of the salvation* or damnation of human beings even before they are created. It expresses one aspect of divine sovereignty whereby the Creator not only creates but also foreordains. It became a subject of theological controversy when pitted against the humanistic and Pelagian doctrine of free will* because they are in theory irreconcilable. Neither predestination nor unlimited free will* has been established to everyone's satisfaction, but the sovereignty of God is such an overarching concept in Christian theology that it leaves only marginal room for the operation of human will in such a way as to cancel divine determinism and foreknowledge. Predestination has the imprimatur of two of the most brilliant minds in Christian history: Augustine* and Calvin*.

Augustine laid out the classic formulation of predestination when he taught that: 1. Human will is enslaved to sin*. 2. Grace* is needed to choose God. 3. Grace is enduringly available only to the elect* of God. Augustine was only reaffirming scriptural teachings, especially Romans 8:28–30 where Paul* talks of the salvation of those "who are called according to His purpose." In Ephesians 1:3–14 Paul talks of election "according to the measure of Christ's gifts." In John 10:29 Jesus tells the Jews that "no one is able to snatch [My sheep] out of My Father's hand." The Augustinian position was upheld by the Synod of Orange in 529. However, when Gottschalk* tried to extend this doctrine to mean that God actively willed the nonelect to be damned, the Synod of Quiercy* in 849 rejected it as unscriptural.

The Scholastics tried to reconcile predestination with reason, but with only a measure of success. For them, predestination could coexist with apparent human free will because God was outside time, and for him all things are present and there is no past and future. But this solution was attacked by Duns Scotus*, William of Ockham*, and others who questioned how God's love can be harmonized with his predetermination and how God can be sovereign if he cannot change his own will. Augustinians held that predetermination was a requisite for an ordered universe. Generally, the Reformers were Augustinians and viewed the church as a community of the elect rather than as a community of sinners in need of salvation. Calvin rejected belief in the universal saving will of God. But a reaction to Calvinism* set in as Arminius* and his followers dismissed predestination as robbing Christianity of its evangelical element.

John Wesley*, the fiery Methodist preacher, espoused Arminianism* because missionary work was meaningless if people are already predetermined to be saved or condemned. George Whitefield*, an equally great evangelist, however, remained a Calvinist to the end. Meanwhile, the controversy raged in the Catholic Church as well. The Council of Trent* leaned toward a semi-Pelagian position. Luis de Molina* formulated a doctrine known as Molinism*, which tried to give free will a role in personal salvation, while Cornelius Jansen* promoted a very rigid form of Augustinianism*. Jesuits* favored the former and Dominicans* the latter. The controversy overflowed into science and social sciences when it was discovered that there are scientific laws that are as deterministic as predestination in affecting human genes and conduct. If heredity and environment have rigid laws, how can human beings be punished for actions or conduct over which they have no control? Thus, predestination remains not so much a doctrine as a mystery.

predestination, double Doctrine that God both predestines or elects some people to salvation* and condemns others to perdition, both by eternal decrees. The latter is often called reprobation*.

predestination, single Doctrine that God predestines and elects some to salvation* while those who are not saved condemn themselves because

of their sin and unbelief. The unsaved are passed over in an act known as preterition*.

predprazdnestvo In the Byzantine tradition, period that precedes a great feast. In the case of Christmas*, it is five days.

preevangelism Evangelistic effort to soften the mind of the listeners and prepare them to be receptive to the message of the gospel. It may include works of charity, miracles, and education.

preexistence of Christ Trinitarian* doctrine that Jesus Christ is the Son of God who existed eternally before his Incarnation*, coequal with the Father.

preexistence of souls Doctrine that the human soul or spirit exists before conception and birth, a view propagated from Platonism by Origen*, in opposition to both Creationism* and Traducianism*.

Preface Introduction to the central portion of the Eucharist*, beginning with Sursum Corda* and ending with Sanctus*.

prefecture apostolic In the Roman Catholic Church, district of a missionary territory in its initial stage of ecclesiastical organization.

preferential option for the poor In liberation theology*, love for and service to the poor as a privileged class in the gospel. The poor are the special wards of Christ, and the Christian message has a special relevance to them.

prelacy 1. In Episcopal churches, system of church government by prelates, such as bishops. 2. Office and tenure of a prelate*. Often used in a derogatory sense, of authoritarian, autocratic rule.

prelate High Church* official, as a bishop. Those having episcopal authority are called major prelates, and those who have quasi-episcopal authority, such as abbots, vicars general*, vicars*, and prefects apostolic, are called minor prelates.

prelate nullius Prelate* ordained by the pope and having ordinary jurisdiction over a territory that is not a bishopric* or diocese*. Thus, prelature nullius.

prelates of honor Class of Catholic priests commonly called monsignors* who may wear ecclesiastical garb similar to that of a bishop.

prelature 1. Prelacy. 2. Body of prelates.

prelest Spiritual death in which there is no remembrance of God and the mirage of the world is mistaken for reality.

premillenarian One who believes in the imminent return of Christ, to be followed by a thousand years of peace during which he reigns over the earth.

premillennialism Chiliastic belief that holds that Christ will come a second time before his 1000-year reign. It was the common view of early Christians before Origen* and Augustine*. Modern theological scholars, such as J. N. Darby*, W. E. Blackstone, and C. I. Scofield* have elaborated it into a prophetic time sequence consisting of the rapture* of the saints, the first resurrecton*, tribulation, second advent* before the millennium*, the brief release of bound Satan*, the second resurrection*, and the last judgment* afterward.

Premonstratensians Also, White Canons, from the color of their habit. Community founded by Norbert* (therefore also known as Norbertines) at Premontre, near Laon, in 1120. They adhered to the Augustinian Rule with certain monastic features adopted from the Cistercians*. Houses were arranged into regional and national circaria, constituting the Grand Congregation under the abbot of the mother house* at Premontre. Premonstratensians played an important role in the evangelization of Germany east of the Elbe.

preparatio evangelica (Lat.) Preparation for the gospel, especially laying the groundwork for potential converts to be receptive to the message of the gospel. Used particularly of the providential readiness of the Roman world for the first expansion of the church.

preparation In the Western Church*, the Rite of Entry consisting of greeting, address, act of penitence, and absolution* with which the Mass* begins.

preparatory service Worship service designed to prepare communicants for the reception of the Lord's Supper*.

Presanctified, Mass of the Shortened form of the eucharistic liturgy without consecration and using a host* previously consecrated for Communion. In the Byzantine Rite*, it is celebrated on Wednesdays and Fridays in normal weeks and on Monday, Tuesday, and Wednesday in the Holy Week*. The ceremony consists of readings, which do not normally include the Gospel, litanies, the Great Entrance*, Lord's Prayer*, and Communion. In the Latin Church, it is restricted to Good Friday*. It consists of the Veneration of the Cross*, after which the ciborium* containing the Hosts consecrated on Maundy Thursday* is brought from the altar of repose* to the high altar, followed by the Lord's Prayer*, the embolism*, a pre-Communion prayer, invitation to Communion, Communion, collect*, and dismissal*.

presbyter (Gk., *presbuteros,* older person) 1. Official in the New Testament church, serving as an elder or bishop (Acts 20:17, 28; Titus 1:5–9; 1 Pet. 5:1–4). 2. Member of a governing board of a Presbyterian congregation. 3. Priest.

presbyterate Office of a presbyter* or a body of presbyters.

Presbyterian 1. Member of a Presbyterian church. 2. Relating to the Presbyterian Church or its system of government by presbyters.

Presbyterianism Form of ecclesiastical polity* in which the church is governed by presbyters. This form of government is drawn from New Testament models as interpreted by John Calvin*, and consists of three or four levels in ascending order: session*, presbytery*, synod*, and general assembly*. Several churches do not have both synod and general assembly. A session, also known as consistory*, represents the local church and includes ministers and elders; a presbytery (also known as colloquy* or classis*), comprises representatives from a group of sessions; a synod* includes a number of presbyteries and may function also as a court of appeal; and a general assembly consists of ministers and elders, elected in equal numbers by the presbyteries. It meets annually but has no legislative or punitive powers (except in the Presbyterian Church of the United States).

Calvin placed great importance on the office of elders which he considered one of the four main ministries of the church along with pastors, teachers, and deacons. Ministers, also known as teaching elders and moderators*, are elected and in many churches, both men and women may be ordained. The only national Presbyterian church is that of Scotland. The doctrinal foundation of Presbyterianism is the Westminister Confession with the two Westminster Catechisms* of 1647. In the United States, the Presbyterian Church USA has adopted its own *Book of Confessions** (1967). It contains the Nicene* and Apostles'* creeds, the Scots Confession*, the Heidelberg Catechism*, the Second Helvetic Confession*, the Westminster Confession*, the two Westminster Catechisms, the Barmen Declaration*, and the Confession of 1967* to which a brief statement of faith was added in 1991. Confessional* standards are interpreted with some laxity in many Presbyterian churches. There is also a wide variance in liturgical practice, but, after many centuries, there is a revival of interest in sacraments*. Presbyterianism belongs to the Reformed* tradition issuing from the sixteenth-century Reformation*.

presbytery/presbyterium 1. Alliance of Presbyterian churches through ministers and elders that oversees a district, ordains and dismisses ministers, and serves as a court. 2. Place at the eastern portion of the chancel* of a church or cathedral reserved for the clergy of high rank or officiating priests. 3. Residence of a Roman Catholic priest.

Presentation of Christ in the Temple The Feast of the Purification of the Blessed Virgin Mary* or Candlemas*, observed on February 2.

Presentation of the Blessed Virgin Mary Feast commemorating the legend of the presentation of the Virgin in the temple when she was three years old as related in the apocryphal Book of James, observed November 21. Pope Sixtus V* made its ob-

servance universal in the Roman Catholic Church in 1585. In the Eastern Church*, it is one of the Twelve Great Feasts*.

Presentation of the Lord Candlemas*.

preservation 1. The continual activity of God whereby he maintains in existence the things which he has created along with the forms, properties, and powers with which he has endowed them. 2. In Calvinist theology, special divine grace* extended to the elect* by which their faith* is sustained and their salvation* is assured.

presiding bishop Head of the Episcopal Church in the USA elected by the General Convention* or similar position in other Episcopal churches.

presiding elder District superintendent in a Methodist church.

Prester John Legendary king of Ethiopia or Central Asia, the subject of numerous medieval legends. He was possibly a Nestorian prince of Asia or a ruler of Ethiopia.

prestol In the Byzantine tradition, the sanctuary.

Presuppositionalism System of Christian apologetics pioneered by Cornelius Van Til*. He held that the Bible never sets out to prove the truth of

Presbytery (2)

God's existence or of the gospel by human reason. Rather, it presupposes God. God is not someone whose existence may be questioned or denied, because he is necessary to the existence of all the facts, including the faculties of human beings. God proved by reason is always less than the true God. The Christian task is not to prove but to proclaim and to open the eyes of those who are blind.

preterition (Lat., a passing by) Calvinist infralapsarian doctrine that not all human beings are elected by God for salvation* and that some are passed over and allowed to sin* and be condemned.

pretiosa Short addition to the office of prime*.

Pretribulationism Eschatological doctrine which teaches that Christians will escape the coming Great Tribulation* by virtue of being raptured or removed from the earth.

prevenient grace See GRACE, PREVENIENT.

Price, Charles Sydney (c. 1880–1947) Healing revivalist*. Born in England, he moved first to Canada and then to the United States. He became a Pentecostal in 1920 and launched a successful independent healing ministry in 1922, holding meetings in the United States, Canada, and Europe.

prichasten In the Byzantine tradition, communion verse or hymn sung after the priest elevates the consecrated bread.

pricket Stand containing one or more upright spikes on which votive candles are fixed.

prie-dieu 1. Private kneeling desk or bench with a high back. In the Roman Catholic Church, desk used by a prelate* when kneeling before the Blessed Sacrament*, or before a high altar. It is covered by a large red silk cloth when used by a cardinal and a green cloth when used by other prelates. On penitential days or funerals its color is violet, and on Good Fridays* it is undraped.

Prierias, Sylvester (1456–1527) Birth name: Sylvester

Mazzolini. Dominican opponent of Martin Luther*. He entered the Dominican Order at Savona in 1471. He served in various academic and ecclesiastical positions at Bologna*, Venice*, Padua, Milan*, Verona*, Genoa, and Cremona and also held the posts of inquisitor at Brescia, Milan, and Rome*. He wrote a number of works on logic, theology, homiletics*, spirituality*, and hagiography*, including *Rosa Aurea* (1503), a collection of sermons, and *Summa Silvestrina* (1514) on moral theology*. He wrote four polemical works against Luther, *Dialogus de Potestate Papae* (1518), *Replica ad Fratrem Martinum Lutherum* (1518), *Epitoma Responsionis ad Lutherum* (1519), and *Errata et Argumenta Martini Luteris* (1520).

priest Ordained clergyman who represents God before his people and represents people before their God. He also performs certain rites and ritual obligations and administers the sacraments*. In the New Testament, Christian ministers are never called priests. The High Priest is Christ Jesus (Heb. 5:10). The New Testament also speaks of the general priesthood by which all believers are priests and perform a priestly function of ministering to God and fellow believers.

priesthood of all believers 1. Priestly status sanctioned in 1 Peter 2:5 to all believers who thus have the ability to minister and communicate directly to God and hear from him. Like all priests, they have the right to approach the holy of holies* rather than wait in the outer court. 2. In Luther's* theology, the right and responsibility of all Christians to intercede with God for one another.

Primasius (sixth century) Bishop of Hadrumetum in North Africa and author of a commentary on the Revelation. He supported Pope Vigilius* during the Three Chapters controversy*.

primate Chief bishop of a territory. The archbishop of Canterbury* is the primate of All England, and the archbishop of York* is the primate of England.

primatial Of or relating to primate* or archbishop.

prime First canonical hour, celebrated at 6:00 A.M.

primer Devotional book for laymen in the Middle Ages.

Primitive Baptists Baptist churches that have adopted a rigid predestinarianism and an opposition to missions and church auxiliaries, such as Bible societies, Sunday schools*, and seminaries. Their church order* is characterized by simple, monthly worship meetings, closed communion*, refusal to accept members without Primitive Baptist immersion*, and untrained and unsalaried ministers. There are four main groups of Primitive Baptists: Absoluters, Old Liners, Progressive Primitive Baptists, and National Primitive Baptists.

primitive church Period in church history when the apostles were alive, that is, extending from about 100.

Primitive Methodist Church One of the three Methodist churches—the others being Wesleyan and United Methodists—which united in 1932. It developed out of the work of Hugh Bourne*, Lorenzo Dow, and William Clowes*, who had initiated evangelistic movements outside official Methodism*. During most of the nineteenth century it successfully engaged in widespread evangelism in Britain, Australia, New Zealand, and Africa. The Primitive Methodists were actively associated with the trade union and labor movements, especially among miners.

Primitive Rule Carmelite* Rule laid down in 1209 by Albert of Vercelli, the Latin patriarch* of Jerusalem*. One of the most rigorous monastic rules, it prescribed absolute poverty, solitude, and total abstinence from meat. Those Carmelites who live under this rule are known as Discalced*.

primus Presiding bishop in the Scottish Episcopal Church who is addressed as "most reverend*."

Prince of Peace Title given to Jesus Christ in Isaiah 9:6.

prince of the church Cardinal of the Roman Catholic Church.

Princeton theology Conservative Calvinism* revived by a series of able theologians who taught at the Presbyterian Seminary at Princeton, New Jersey. These theologians included Archibald Alexander* (1772–1851), founding professor of the school; his two sons, James Waddell Alexander (1804–1859) and Joseph Addison Alexander (1809–1860); Charles Hodge* (1797–1878); his son, Archibald Alexander Hodge* (1823–1886); Benjamin Breckinridge Warfield* (1851–1921); and Gresham Machen*. They upheld Reformed* confessionalism*, biblical inerrancy*, and the role of the Holy Spirit* in religious experience. The main tenets of Princeton theology were outlined in Charles Hodge's *Systematic Theology*.

prior Head or deputy head of a monastery. Under the Benedictine* Rule, the claustral prior is the deputy prior concerned with discipline. In the Cluniac Order*, the conventual prior is the head of a monastery, and the obedientiary* prior is the ruler of a dependent priory*.

prioress Head or deputy head of a house of nuns.

priory Religious house presided over by a prior* or prioress*. They are divided into conventual or self-governing priories and obedientiary* or dependent priories. In medieval England there were also cathedral priories.

priory nullius Priory* that is not dependent on a diocese* but on the pope.

Prisca Latin version of the canons of certain Greek councils, namely those of Nicaea*, Sardica, Ancyra, Neocaesarea, Gangra*, Antioch*, Chalcedon, and Constantinople*.

Priscilla (first century) Also, Prisca. Christian woman, mentioned six times in the New Testament, wife of Aquila*, a Jew of Pontus, a tentmaker* by profession. She and her husband aided St. Paul* and Apollos*. Feast day: February 13 (Eastern Church*); July 8 (Western Church*).

Priscillian (d. 385) Heretical bishop of Avila, Spain. He was influenced by Gnosticism* and began teaching the heresy later known as Priscillianism, a form of Manichaeism*. His followers included a few bishops, and he was consecrated bishop of

Avila. Eight canons of the Council of Saragossa were directed against him. In 381 he was exiled to France, and on his appeal to the emperor was found guilty of using magic arts and sentenced to death by beheading with six other fellow heretics. They were the first persons to suffer death as heretics in the history of Christianity. Priscillianism was condemned again at the Council of Toledo* in 400 but survived until the end of the sixth century. According to later research, Priscillianism has been misrepresented as Manichaean and was in fact a movement for spiritual renewal through asceticism* and the gift of prophecy.

Prison Epistles Books of the New Testament attributed to Paul* while he was in prison. These include Ephesians, Philippians, Colossians, and Philemon.

Prison Fellowship Ministries Parachurch* organization devoted to ministering to prisoners, ex-prisoners, and their families, founded by Charles Colson* in 1976. Colson himself had been in prison for his part in the Watergate conspiracy.

pritvor In the Byzantine Church*, the inner vestibule at the western end of the church where, in the early church, catechumens* and penitents* were expected to remain during part of the liturgy.

privileged altar Formerly, an altar on which a plenary indulgence* could be obtained for a soul in purgatory* through the celebration of a Mass* on it.

Pro Oriente Movement to promote understanding between Roman Catholic Church and Orthodox churches, founded by Cardinal Franz Konig in 1946.

Probabiliorism (Lat., *probabilior,* more likely) Principle of moral theology* that in matters where the legitimacy or illegitimacy of a course of action is not easily determined, it is lawful to follow the choice favoring liberty only when it is more probable than the choice favoring law. Opposite of probabilism*.

probabilism Principle of moral theology* that when the legitimacy or illegitimacy of a course of action is in doubt, the choice favoring liberty should be followed even when the choice favoring law is more probable. The principle was attacked as too lax, thus making freedom easily abused. Competing principles included rigorism*, which holds that only if the less safe opinion is most probable is it acceptable, and laxism*, which maintains that any slightly probable opinion could be followed with a good conscience. A modified form of probabilism was advanced by St. Alphonsus Liguori* as equiprobabilism*, which was officially accepted by the Roman Catholic Church.

probationer In the Presbyterian and Methodist churches*, person who, having completed theological studies, is authorized to preach the Word, but not yet administer the sacraments*. Subsequent ordination is dependent upon satisfactory fulfillment of probation.

procathedral Church used temporarily as a cathedral.

process theology Also, bi-polar theism; panentheism*. Branch of theology that studies the process of evolution of God as well as his creation and the change and progress that result from such an evolution. It is a theistic mode of theology that emphasizes relationships and becoming rather than the static concepts of nature and being. The key element in process theology is the event. Reality is seen as a process, not a state. It is a concrescence of all past events, all of which are stored, inherited, and remembered. Every event modifies prior events as well as succeeding events. This affective nature of God reflects his consequent aspect that supplements his creative aspect. Thus Incarnation* is an event that is part of divine becoming and God's need for relationship. But, by the same token, every event is a divine act and in this sense an incarnation in its own right. All events, including human actions are a revelation* of his character and as a result there is no distinction between special and general revelation.

On the other hand, because every event is self-determined, no revelation completely represents him. The future is never fully known and cannot be predicted even by God. A human being is a series of separate events, each autonomous not only in relation to all others but also in reference to God. Each event is preserved as a reality in God's memory bank, and this spells out the idea of eternity*. Nothing is forgotten but continues to resonate throughout aeons. Influential process theologians include A. N. Whitehead, C. Hartshorne, S. M. Ogden, J. B. Cobb, P. N. Hamilton*, and W. N. Pittenger.

procession Ecclesiastical march.

Procession of the Holy Spirit Distinguishing attribute of the Holy Spirit* eternally united with the Father and the Son in the Trinity*, making him a person and not a creature. It was developed at length by the Cappadocian Fathers* and played a role in the Christological debates of the early centuries. In the Western Church*, the Double Procession* of the Holy Spirit from the Father and the Son is embodied in the Filioque* clause in the Niceno-Constantinopolitan Creed*. This clause was interpolated at the Council of Toledo* in 539 and was sanctioned by Pope Benedict VIII in 1017. It was the single most important cause of the East-West Great Schism* in 1054.

processional 1. March of the choir or the officiating minister into the chancel* at the beginning of a worship service or on festival days. It is of two kinds: festive and penitential. The order of procession in the Roman Catholic Church is the thruifer, cross-bearer, candle-bearers, subdeacon, deacon, celebrant, choir, clergy, bishop. Banners* are often carried to dramatize the event. In the Eastern Orthodox Church*, a procession, called the lity*, may carry relics* and icons. In parish* churches, it goes only to the narthex*, but in monasteries, it goes around the outside of a church. Processions are held on Sunday eve vespers*, Good Friday*, Holy Saturday*, and at the beginning of mattins* in the Midnight Easter Vigil. 2. Hymn sung in such a processional. 3. Book of hymns for such a processional.

processional cross Cross leading an ecclesiastical procession*.

processional hymn Hymn sung during the procession* of the choir into the chancel*.

Proclus, St. (d. 446 or 447) Patriarch* of Constantinople* from 434. He promoted the orthodox cause against the Nestorians and wrote the *Tome of St. Proclus,* an exposition of the doctrine of two natures in Christ. He may also have written the introduction to the Trisagion*. He was also a brilliant preacher. Feast day: October 24 (Western Church*); November 20 (Eastern Church*).

Procopius, St. (d. 303) Martyr. He was a lector* at the church of Scythopolis who became the first Christian martyr* in the Diocletian persecution* when he refused to sacrifice to the gods. Feast day: July 8.

proctors of the clergy In the Church of England*, the elected representatives of the clergy who, with ex officio members, constitute the lower houses of the convocations of Canterbury* and York*.

procurator Also, syndic or cellarer*. In monasteries and other religious communities, official in charge of the temporal goods of the house. In some churches, he is a senior adviser on legal questions.

proem In the Syrian tradition, an introductory prayer following the shuraya* or initial antiphon*. The proem forms part of the hussoyo, which also includes the m'bass'yono bokhil and the sedro* or long prayer. Also called proemia in the Maronite Church.

proeortia In the Byzantine tradition, the period of one to five days that precedes a Feast of Our Lord* or of the Blessed Virgin Mary*. A troparion* sung as part of the preparation services is known as proeortion.

professing Christians Those who publicly confess and acknowledge their Christian faith and consider themselves Christians in the New Testament sense.

profession 1. That which is believed in or confessed as a creed*. 2. Act of taking vows when entering a religious order.

profession of faith Public statement of faith by a person on joining a church.

progressive revelation Doctrine that divine revelation*, given by God and recorded by the Scriptures, is a continuing and incremental process in which later revelation is built on earlier ones.

prokeimenon/prokeimena (Gk., lying before) In the Byzantine Rite*, verses from the Psalter sung at the beginning of a series of readings from Scriptures or after Phos Hilarion* at vespers*. It is the equivalent of the Western gradual*.

Prokhanov, Ivan Stepanovich (1869–1935) Leader of the Russian Evangelical Christian movement. He established Evangelical Christians as a separate denomination which by 1914 had a membership of 30,000. He edited 10 songbooks for which he contributed 600 poems and translated 400 hymns from English and German. After the Bolshevik Revolution in 1917, he fled Russia and settled in the West.

prolegomena (Gk., things said beforehand) Topics and issues addressed before the main discussion in a work. Often, the method of theology as opposed to its contents.

prolepsis (Gk., anticipation) Anticipation of future events, especially the representation of a future event as already real and accomplished. Thus, proleptic.

prolife Of or relating to protection of the unborn fetus; opposed to abortion and prochoice programs.

prolocutor Title of the president and chairman of each of the lower houses of the convocations of Canterbury* and York*.

Promise Keepers American Christian men's organization dating its beginnings to a 1990 meeting in which Colorado football coach Bill McCartney and Dave Wardell asked 70 friends to prayerfully pursue mutual discipleship, personal outreach, and seek God's favor for national revival. Promise Keepers was born at a conference the following July (1991), attended by 4,200 men. The next summer, it was 22,000. Then in 1993, more than 50,000 men filled the Colorado University football stadium to sing ("Let the Walls Fall Down"), pray, and hear keynote speakers. Their teachings were outlined in *Seven Promises of a Promise Keeper* (1994), emphasizing relationships between each man and God, mentors, integrity, family, church, brothers, and world. In the mid-1990s, large stadium conferences across the United States invited men to deeper Christian commitment and relationships of love and reconciliation. Later in the decade, a policy change that no longer charged admission to these events led to financial retrenchment and strategic planning, leading to smaller meetings and continued communication of core values in print and media.

promotor fidei (Lat., promoter of the faith) Also, devil's advocate*. Official of the Congregation of Rites who carefully and skeptically examines positive as well as negative evidence for a candidate's beatification* or canonization*.

promotor justitiae (Lat., promoter of justice) In the Roman Catholic Church, the priest charged with testing with a critical eye local evidence adduced on behalf of a candidate for beatification* or canonization*.

pronaos Enclosed portico in a Byzantine church in which catechumens* and audientes* gather.

prone 1. Vernacular office inserted into the High Mass* after the Offertory on Sundays and other feast days. It consists of announcements of ensuing feasts and fasts, and of banns* of marriage and ordination. 2. Expository sermon.

pronuncio Diplomatic envoy of the pope in a foreign country where Roman Catholics are in a minority.

proof text Text of Scripture quoted to prove or support a theological doctrine.

propaganda In the Roman Catholic Church, the propagation of faith or evangelization.

Propaganda, Sacred Congregation of Renamed Congregation for the Evangelization of the Nations in

1988. Office within the Vatican* secretariat for the direction and administration of Roman Catholic missionary activity, and the coordination of the work of various missionary orders, created by Gregory XV in 1622. It lays down standards for training missionaries; runs the seminary, Collegium Urbanum; prints materials in hundreds of languages; and prepares multimedia presentations and programs.

Proper/Proper of the Mass Part of the Eucharist* and Offices that vary according to the feast and the season as distinguished from the invariable Ordinary* or Order of the Mass*. The Proper of Saints is the proper for festivals with a fixed date; the Proper of Time is the proper for Sundays, ferias, and festivals with no fixed date; the Common of Saints is the proper for saints with the same feast days.

prophecy Message conveyed by a prophet* acting on behalf of God in any given situation. In the New Testament, prophecy is a gift of the Spirit for the edification* of the body of believers.

prophet 1. Spokesperson for or messenger of God who foretells events that God in his foreknowledge has transmitted to him or her or declares the oracles of God* for the edification* of the church. The message may be one of admonition or one of consolation* and comfort. In contrast to teaching which is bound by tradition, prophecy* has the character of a revelation*. 2. Order of ministers, next to the apostles, and above evangelists, teachers, and pastors, within a local congregation, with the special gift of prophecy (1 Cor. 12:28). The gift is exercised during worship service, communicating the inspired Word and spiritual truths and warnings and edifying the body. Unlike mystical and cryptic utterances in a trance, prophetic utterances are always rational and clearly understood. 3. Seer or visionary who interprets God's will or plan in any setting.

propitiation 1. Appeasing divine anger by a sacrifice that atones for a sin or offense against God. 2. In the New Testament, restoring the holy relationship between the Creator and his creation through the atoning sacrifice of Christ that satisfies the needs of divine justice.

propositional revelation God's self-revelation as preserved in scriptural statements, rejecting claims that restrict it to God's action.

propositional theology Branch of theology that treats the Bible, called "inscripturated revelation," as a record of propositions or declarations about God, given by God himself. It begins with the premise that revelation* is essentially the divine communication of rationally comprehensible truths to humanity. Because they are rationally comprehensible, they can be put into language and stated as propositions. Propositional theology takes these revealed propositions or truths and synthesizes, analyzes, and deduces conclusions from them. Christ is considered the ultimate reality and the ultimate proposition because he is rationally comprehensible. Propositional theology insists upon the absolutely nonnegotiable, unchanging, and essential character of the Christian faith. A Christian needs to hold to the fundamentals—such as the verbal inerrancy of the Bible*, the deity of Christ, the virgin birth*, substitutionary atonement*, and the physical resurrection and bodily return of Christ—because these are literal scriptural propositions.

prose Hymn without regular meter, also known as sequence, sung or spoken in Mass*.

proselyte Convert from one religion to another. Thus, proselytize.

proseucha Small Byzantine chapel or oratory*.

prosfarin In the Coptic tradition, large veil or corporal* used to cover the offerings at the start of the service as part of the enarxis*. It is lifted just before the anaphora*. It is made of white or colored silk with a cross embroidered in the middle and tiny bells at the corners.

prosfonesis In the Coptic tradition, diaconal direction to the congregation to stand or sit.

prosfori In the Coptic tradition, the Eucharist*.

proskomide (Gk., offering) In the Eastern Church*, preparation of the bread and wine for the Eucharist* which takes place before the beginning of the service on a table known as the prothesis*.

proskynesis/proskynema (Gk., veneration) Veneration* offered to icons* and other sacred objects, especially the act of making the sign of the cross before them. It is less than worship or latria*.

proskynetarion In the Byzantine tradition, the folding desk on which the icon of the feast being celebrated is displayed and to which proskynesis* is offered.

prosopon (Gk., person) Each member of the Trinity* as a distinct person; personhood of each of the members of the triune Godhead. See also HYPOSTASIS.

prosperity cult Popular teaching that interprets certain Christian tenets and New and Old Testament promises as a road to material wealth, without any attendant commitments or obligations. See also FAITH MOVEMENT; POSITIVE CONFESSION.

Prosphora In the Eastern Church*, the altar bread in the form of five round leavened cakes each divided by a cross into four quarters. From each of the cakes, particles* are cut out in honor of the Virgin Mary*, the apostles, saints*, and the living and dead communicants to be prayed for. Only the principal particle* is consecrated, and the others are distributed among the congregation as the antidoron*.

prostrates Member of an order of penitents* in the early church.

Protei Anastasis In Byzantine Liturgy, Great Resurrection, traditional name of the Paschal* service celebrated on the Great Sabbath*, now superseded by the mattins* of the Resurrection. It is a vesper liturgy focusing on Christ's triumph over hades. The clergy discard the somber vestments they have used in Lent* and robe themselves in Paschal* gold or white. The priest scatters laurel leaves about the altar, and the congregation beat on the stalls to celebrate the collapse of the brazen gates of hades before the triumphant Christ. Oil is forbidden on this Saturday, but bread and wine are blessed. Dried fruit is distributed with the antidoron* and eaten with the wine.

Protestant (*adjective*) Of or relating to a church that separated from the Roman Catholic Church in the sixteenth and seventeenth centuries during the Reformation* or a church that follows the traditions established during the Reformation. (*noun*) Member of a Protestant church.

Protestant principle Justification* by faith* as the single most important tenet or principle of the Protestant Reformation*. Sometimes called the material principle* of Protestantism* in distinction from the formal principle which is the sole and sufficient authority of the Bible.

Protestant work ethic Moral and social values associated with Anglo-Saxon Protestantism in the seventeenth and eighteenth centuries, especially hard work, a sense of moral responsibility for one's actions, thrift, and a love of liberty and learning. Max Weber argued that capitalism grew and thrived on these qualities, which are often traced back especially to the Calvinist Reformation*.

Protestantism Movement, considered the "second wave of Christianity," that broke away from the Roman Catholic Church in Europe in the sixteenth and seventeenth centuries. Its name is derived from *Protestatio,* a statement issued by 5 reforming princes and 14 cities of the Holy Roman Empire at the Diet of Speyer* in 1529. The term *Protestatio* did not imply a mere protest, but a confession*. For the early Reformers, Protestantism was not so much a revolution as a revival of the faith and practices of the early church.

The five marks of the Protestant Church may not apply to all churches falling under this rubric*, but they express the driving theological convictions of the early Reformers: 1. The authority of the Scriptures as the definitive guide to faith and practice. They uphold the doctrine of *Sola Scriptura**, which means that only traditions and liturgical practices that are consistent with the Scriptures are acceptable. 2. Justification* by faith*. For Luther* and his associates, justification by faith constituted the capstone of Christian faith. Whereas the Catholic faith teaches that the grace* of God must be supplemented by human merits and sacramental grace, Protestants teach that every believer is justified by faith and the righteousness of Christ is imputed to the believer. 3. Regenerative power or consecration by baptism* and the efficacy of the Lord's Supper*. The latter is accepted not as a sacrifice in which there is transusbtantiation of the elements*, but as a memorial in which the Lord is present in some form for believers to feed upon. 4. Priesthood of all believers*. 5. Ministry. Most Protestant denominations accept at least three orders of ministers: bishop (superintendent), pastor, and deacon.

Protestant denominations number in the thousands, and they vary widely in structure, theology, and forms of worship. Some denominations are close to Catholic and Orthodox traditions, and others are close to Unitarianism*. The eight principal streams of modern Protestantism are Episcopal or Anglican*, Methodist*, Presbyterian* (including Calvinist or Reformed*), Lutheran*, Congregational*, Baptist*, Holiness*, and Pentecostal*. Within each of these denominations there are warring liberal and conservative or evangelical factions that sometimes merge and at other times split. Among the most prominent Protestant theologians of the late twentieth century are Wolfhart Pannenberg*, Jurgen Moltmann*, John R. Stott*, Thomas F. Torrance, J. I. Packer*, and E. Jungel.

Protevangelium 1. Apocryphal infancy narrative also known as the *Book of James,* written after 150. 2. In covenant theology*, the first proclamation of the gospel as found in Genesis 3:15.

prothesis (Gk., setting forth) In the Eastern Church*: 1. Table on which the Eucharist* is prepared. 2. By extension, the chamber in which the table is placed on the left of the apse* of the church, on the opposite side of the diaconicon*. 3. Preparation of the bread and wine for the Eucharist*, equivalent to the Western offertory. The number and form of the loaves vary. In one form, there are five small loaves, three stamped with the words IC.XC.NI-KA (Jesus Christ conquers), one marked with a triangular seal for the Theotokos*, and one marked with nine triangles. In the second form, one large loaf is stamped with five seals in the shape of a cross. In the third form, there are two small loaves, one marked with the seal of the lamb or amnos, and one stamped with the other four seals.

At the table the priest raises the bread and consecrates them, cuts the lamb* from the center and makes four incisions, cutting deeply in the form of a cross. He then cuts one fraction* for the Theotokos* which he then places to the north of the lamb and nine particles* from the third seal to the south of the lamb, arranging them in nine ranks called tagmata to represent the saints*, prophets*, apostles, holy bishops, martyrs*, and ascetics. The other two seals are used to cut commemorative particles for the living and the dead, including the founders of the church, the bishop, and the priest himself. The particles are arranged in a circular discus*, symbolizing the world, with the lamb in the center, surrounded by members of the church, his mystical body*. The priest covers the discus with the asteriskos* or star and covers both chalice* and discus with three veils. He then censes them and says the Prayer of Offering.

protodeacon Senior deacon in the Byzantine Church*, similar to the archdeacon in the West.

protoiereus In the Byzantine tradition, an archpriest, the highest rank attainable by a married priest.

Protevangelium of James

protology Doctrine of first things, as opposed to eschatology*, the doctrine of last things*.

protomartyr Title of St. Stephen*, the first martyr* of the Christian church. Also applied to the first Christian martyrs in a country.

protonotary apostolic Also, prothonotary. 1. Member of the College of Notaries attached to the papal court. 2. Chief secretary to a patriarch* in the Eastern Orthodox Church*.

protopope/protopapas Rank in the Eastern Orthodox Church* comparable to that of dean in the Western Church*.

protopresbyter (Lat., the first presbyter) Byzantine Rite* archpriest, an honorary title, similar to a monsignor*. In the Russian Orthodox Church*, it is the highest title conferred on a non-monastic priest.

protopsaltes In the Byzantine tradition, the principal cantor*.

protos Chairman of the committee that represents the 20 principal monasteries on Mount Athos*.

Prousiotissa Ancient icon of the Hodegetria* preserved in the Prousa Monastery in the Agrapha region in central Greece.

province Group of territorially contiguous dioceses* under the ecclesiastical jurisdiction of an archbishop.

provincial Superior* of a religious order, having administrative duties but responsible to the abbot or superior general*.

Provincial Letters Series of 18 letters written by Blaise Pascal* during 1656–1657 in defense of Antoine Arnauld*, then on trial before the theological faculty of the University of Sorbonne* for his Jansenist views. They are considered a classic of French literature because of the brilliance of Pascal's style. They were placed on the Index by the Roman Catholic Church soon after publication.

provolution Progress of the church from its present state to its eschatological future centered in the establishment of the kingdom of God* through a series of paradigms. Term devised by Jurgen Moltmann*.

provost Dean of a cathedral or collegiate church. In the early church he was next in dignity to the abbot of a monastery.

Prudentius, Aurelius Clemens (c. 348–c. 410) Christian Latin poet. Among his works are *Peristephanon* (Martyr's Crowns) and *Psychomachia* (Spiritual Combat). His best known hymn-poem is "Of the Father's Love Begotten," most often sung as plainsong*. He was a layman, unlike nearly all Latin Fathers of the church.

psak In the Armenian tradition: 1. Marriage crown or garland. 2. Cross* hung on a red and white thread and suspended around a newly baptized child's neck.

psali In the Coptic Rite, a liturgical office in honor of the Virgin Mary*.

Psalm One of the sacred poems in the Book of Psalms in the Old Testament, often set to music.

psalm tone Melody used for chanting psalms. In the Roman Catholic Church, there is a psalm tone, or reciting tone, for each of the church modes, plus a special irregular tone, called the *tonus peregrinus**.

psalmellus Precentor or cantor* of worship music in a church.

psalmody Music of the metrical psalms* sung in Protestant churches from the sixteenth century. Metrical psalms formed one of the foundations of the Reformation* and the major source of Protestant devotion. Opposed to elaborate liturgy and suspicious of nonscriptural music, Calvin* adopted the Psalms as virtually the only source for church music.

psalter Book of Psalms used in worship from the early centuries, normally from translations of the Bible, as in the *Book of Common Prayer**. Among the earliest Protestant psalters was the *Geneva Psalter** of 1562. The first English psalter was the *Sternhold and Hopkins Psalter* (1562), which was bound along with the Authorized Version* of the Bible. The *Ainsworth Psalter** of 1612 accompanied the Pilgrims to America. Psalm-singing became a focal point in the religious services of

Illuminated Psalter

Baptists*, Methodists*, and other dissenters*. In 1719 Isaac Watts* established the trend of free paraphrase of the Psalms. A new version of the *Psalms of David* (1696) by Nahum Tate and Nicholas Brady presented the Psalms as poetry. In the American colonies, *The Ravenscroft Psalter* of 1621 offered four-voice settings for psalm tunes. In 1640 the first American Psalter, *The Bay Psalm Book**, was printed and later revised in 1651 as *The New England Psalm Book.*

Psalterion (Gk., Book of Psalms) In the Eastern Orthodox Church*, book containing the Psalms, arranged according to their normal liturgical use, together with canticles* from the Old and New Testaments. It is divided into kathismata or sessions, according to which the Psalms are read in Divine Office*.

psaltes In the Byzantine Church*, psalmist or cantor* who is expected to know the typicon*

and be able to sing all the congregation's sung part of the service.

Pseudepigrapha Scriptural writings ascribed to someone other than their real author, specifically works not included in the Greek canon* of the Old Testament. Among them are Book of Enoch, Assumption of Moses, Books of Baruch, and the Psalms of Solomon.

pseudodoxy False belief or opinion.

p'shto (lit., extension) In the Syrian Rite, priestly outstretching of the arms during the great intercessory anaphora*.

Psilanthropism (Gk., mere-man-ism) Heresy that Christ was only a man inspired by the Holy Spirit*, held by Theodotus the Cobbler, Paul of Samosata*, and others.

psychopannychy See SOUL SLEEP.

psychosabbaton/psychosabbata (Gk., soul Sabbath) Saturday set apart in the Byzantine Calendar as day of prayer for the faithful departed believers. Designated as psychosabbata are the Saturdays before the Sunday of the Last Judgment, Pentecost*, and the second, third, and fourth Saturdays of Lent*.

PTL 1. Praise the Lord. 2. Jim Bakker's* erstwhile and ill-fated television ministry.

Pulcheria (399–453) Roman empress. She was the daughter of the Emperor Arcadius and the elder sister of the Emperor Theodosius. She became empress in 450 and convoked the Council of Chalcedon*. As a defender of orthodoxy*, she condemned both Nestorianism* and Monophysitism*.

pulpit Elevated platform, often with enclosed sides and a rest or stand for reading, from which the minister or priest delivers the sermon. In the early church, bishops preached from their chair or cathedra*, and later from the ambo* and the roodloft. Pulpits are not found in Eastern Orthodox* churches.

pulpitum Stone screen* in a cathedral or

monastery that separates the choir from the nave*.

Purcell, Henry (1659–1695) English composer. Organist of Westminster Abbey* from 1679 until his death, and organist at the Chapel Royal from 1682. One of his most famous works is *Te Deum* and *Jubilate in D* which was regularly performed in St. Paul's Cathedral*. He also composed a complete setting for the morning and evening service in B flat and an evening service in G minor. He excelled in full anthems and verse anthems, often with string accompaniments with the words nearly always from the Old Testament. They included "In Thee, O Lord, Do I Put My Trust," "Rejoice in the Lord Always," "O Sing unto the Lord," and "My Beloved Spake." Purcell is considered one of the foremost English composers of sacred music.

purgative First of the three stages of spiritual growth or mystical ascent, marked by purification of the soul before it moves to illumination* and union with God.

purgatory (lit., place or means of purification) In Roman Catholic theology, a state or place of purification prior to admission to heaven*, where souls are made fit for heaven through expiatory suffering. Here the souls of the departed are cleansed of their unforgiven venial sins* and satisfy divine justice by receiving such punishment as is still due their remitted mortal sins*. It is not a period of probation, but rather a cleansing process for those who are already partakers of divine grace*, but who, for reason of imperfection, are not qualified to receive the beatific vision*. It is for that mass of partially sanctified Catholics who have died in fellowship with the church. It is based on two premises: that not all souls are worthy of heaven at the moment of death and that some of their ill deeds may be reversible through the intercession of the living. There are purgatorial societies or confraternities* whose sole purpose is to assist in every possible way those in purgatory through their prayers and gifts. The doctrine, which also provided a basis for the development of indulgences*, was taught by Gregory the Great*, Bonaventura*, and Aquinas*. It was professed at the Second Council of Lyons* (1274), the Union of Florence (1445), and the Council of Trent* (1545–1563). The Old Testament apocryphal text most often cited in support is 2 Maccabees 12:39–45.

Purification of the Blessed Virgin Mary Also, Presentation of the Lord*. Feast on February 2 commemorating the purification of the Virgin Mary* in the temple as recorded in Luke 2:21–39.

purificator Small piece of white linen to cleanse the chalice* after Holy Communion*.

Puritan ethic Attitudes and values associated with seventeenth-century Puritans*, such as industriousness, discipline, honesty, moderation, thrift, and self-sufficiency. See also PROTESTANT WORK ETHIC.

Puritanism Reformed* theological beliefs of the Puritans* in the sixteenth and seventeenth centuries. Puritanism emphasized the purity of biblical worship and polity* and inner transformation from death in sin to life in Christ, based on faith*. Although Puritanism did not neglect the great theological issues, they were more concerned with practical piety and keeping the Sabbath holy. To a greater degree than other theological sys-

Pulpit

tems, Puritanism tried to create a righteous civil society along with a church polity*.

The great Puritan theologians included William Ames* (1576–1633), author of *Marrow of Theology* (1623), Thomas Cartwright* (1535–1603), Dudley Fenner (c. 1558–1587), Walter Travers (c. 1548–1643), Robert Browne* (c. 1550–1633), John Greenwood (d. 1593), Francis Johnson (1562–1618), Henry Smith (c. 1550–1591), Richard Greenham (c. 1535–c. 1594), Richard Rogers (c. 1550–1618), William Perkins (1558–1602), Richard Sibbes (1577–1635), Thomas Goodwin (1600–1680), John Owen* (1616–1683), and beyond England, Thomas Boston* (1677–1732), and Jonathan Edwards* (1703–1758).

Puritans In the sixteenth and seventeenth centuries, English Protestants who first sought to purify the Church of England* from corrupt and unscriptural practices and later separated from the established church* and became very hostile to it. They attacked as "popish," superstitious, anti-Christian, and idolatrous such practices as vestments, surplices*, rochets, organs, signs of the cross, ecclesiastical courts*, and the episcopacy*. Both before and after the failure of the Commonwealth, many of the Puritans emigrated to other countries, especially the English North American colonies. The Puritan legacy was mainly an emphasis on practical holiness* and keeping the Sabbath.

purple Color symbolizing penitence. It is the liturgical color of the seasons of the Septuagesima*, Lent*, and Advent*, Rogation* and ember days*, except at Pentecost*, and most vigils*. In the Western Church*, purple is the proper color of cassocks and birettas worn by prelates.

Pusey, Edward Bouverie (1800–1882) Leader of the Oxford movement*. In 1828 he was appointed regius professor of Hebrew and canon* of Christ

E. B. Pusey

Church, Oxford*, where he became acquainted with Keble* and Newman* and where he contributed to the *Tracts for the Times* on fasting* and baptism*. When Newman left for the Roman Catholic Church, Pusey became the unofficial leader of the Tractarians. He continued to support the revival of rituals and the real presence* of Christ in the Eucharist*, founded sisterhoods, encouraged private confession*, and vehemently opposed the inroads of liberalism* into the Church of England*. His efforts to reconcile the Church of England and the Church of Rome failed to materialize. Pusey was also instrumental in the publication of the Oxford Library of the Fathers*. Pusey House at Oxford commemorates him.

pyx (Gk., box-wood vessel) Small box made of wood, gold, or silver in which the Blessed Sacrament* is carried to the sick. It is wrapped in a small corporal* and placed in a pyx-bag hung around the priest's neck.

Qq

Q (Ger., *quelle*, source) Symbol of the document which, according to pioneering studies by Sir John Hawkins, Adolf Harnack*, and Burnett Streeter*, is the source of much material in the Gospels of Matthew and Luke not found in the Gospel of Mark.

qadisha aloho (lit., you are holy God) In the Syrian tradition, the opening words of the Trisagion* which is sung in eight tones.

Qala'at Sima'an The martyrium* church of St. Simeon Stylites* in northern Syria built on the site of the 64-foot pillar on which Simeon lived for 40 years. The church was constructed in 475–491 by Emperor Zeno on a cruciform* plan with an octagonal court in the center enclosing the pillar.

qaltha/qalyatha (Syr., little songs or short portion) In the Assyrian Church*, anthem and psalm said after the hulala* at the night service before the motwa*.

qami In the Ethiopian Church*, priestly vestment corresponding to the sticharion*.

Qandeila In the Assyrian Church*, ceremonial lamp required to be kept burning in the sanctuary at all times.

qanke Sanctuary* in a Chaldean church.

qanona In the Assyrian tradition, audible conclusion to a silent prayer, sometimes accompanied by a clash of cymbals.

qaruqtho In the Jacobite tradition, the black tarbush decorated with seven crosses worn by secular priests.

qaruya In the Assyrian Church*, the reader* who is part of the third order* of deacons. He reads the Old Testament and the Acts during the liturgy.

qaryana In the Assyrian Rite, lectionary* that contains the text of the Epistles and the Gospels.

qasisho Maronite priest.

qatismata In the Jacobite tradition, chants sung during the fraction* of the consecrated bread.

qdhush qushshi In the Assyrian Church*, the holy of holies* or the sanctuary.

qeidar Purification service in the Ethiopian Church over those who have not observed Lent* and other ecclesiastical ordinances*.

qene In the Ethiopian Church, brief religious poems often improvised or composed by individual cantors* or dabtara*. Unlike liturgical chants, they are never printed.

qerelos Canons* or collections of theological texts in the Ethiopian Church.

qidist In the Ethiopian Church, the sanctuary or the holy of holies*.

qilitha In the Assyrian Church*: 1. Monastery or cell. 2. Residence of a patriarch*, metropolitan*, or bishop.

Qiryana In the Assyrian Rite, a book of lessons.

qole d'matalto In the Syrian Rite, canticles* sung during the prothesis*.

qolo (lit., voice or tune) In the Syrian tradition, chants sung during the liturgy after a passage from the holy Scriptures is recited.

qomos Official in the Ethiopian Church who adjudicates and settles disputes among the clergy.

q'roito In the Syrian tradition, an invocation*.

quaddish In the Syrian Rite, the Sanctus* which is part of the Anaphora* and concludes the Preface*.

Quadragesima The 40 days of Lent*.

Quadragesima Sunday First Sunday in Lent*.

Quadratus, St. (second century) Earliest known apologist of the Christian faith. His *Apology* (c. 120–130) was addressed to Emperor Hadrian. Only one fragment survives. Feast day: May 26.

quadriga (Lat., set of four) Set of four types of biblical interpretation*: literal, allegorical, moral, and anagogical.

Quadrilateral, Lambeth See LAMBETH QUADRILATERAL.

Quadrilateral, Wesleyan Four sources of authority in Wesleyan thought: Scripture, tradition, Holy Spirit* or experience, and reason.

Quaker Member of the Society of Friends*, so named because Quakers tremble or quake at the Word of God*. Quaker theology contains both Puritan* and Anabaptist* elements. Quakers reject all sacraments* but emphasize the universal Inward Light as sufficient for spiritual enlightenment. They enjoin nonviolence, strict equality, and disuse of all conventional forms of address. They believe the true church worships in silence and waits on the Holy Spirit* to inspire ex tempore prayers, sermons, and testimonies. Ministers are unpaid and unordained, and may be men or women. Largely due to the influence of Joseph John Gurney (1788–1847), nearly half of all Quakers are Evangelicals*. The Richard Declaration of 1887 is the standard statement of Evangelical Quaker belief. The non-evangelical Quakers are more active in philanthropic ministries and peace work. See also SOCIETY OF FRIENDS.

Quaker meeting Friends' worship service with extended periods of silence.

Quarant'Ore (Ital., forty hours) Forty-hour devotion commemorating the 40 hours between Christ's death and Resurrection. It consists of a night and day vigil* before the Blessed Sacrament* exposed on a monstrance* on the altar.

Quarles, Francis (1592–1644) English religious poet. In 1630 he published his first book of poems, *Divine Poems,* followed by *Divine Fancies* in 1632. He also published two emblem books, *Emblems* (1635) and *Hieroglyphikes of the Life of Man* (1638), and *Enchiridion* (1640), a collection of meditations.

Quarr Abbey Modern Benedictine monastery near Ryde in the Isle of Wight, built in 1912 on the site of an original Cistercian monastery founded in 1131 or 1132. It is now an independent house of the Solesmes* Congregation.

Quartodecimanism (Gk., fourteenth) Celebration of Easter* on 14 Nisan, the day of the Jewish Passover irrespective of the day of the week. The practice was mostly limited to Asia Minor, where it survived into the fifth century. It probably reflected the earliest Christian practice and illustrated early Christianity's problematic relationship with its Jewish origins.

Quasimodo Sunday Low Sunday.

quasisha Priest in the Assyrian Church* of the East.

qubbtho In the Jacobite tradition, curtains that hang from the canopy* over the altar.

qublat-as-salaam In the Coptic tradition, the kiss of peace*.

qudashe In the Assyrian and Chaldean rites, anaphoras* or hallowings. Also, quddosho in the Maronite Church.

quddasa (Syr.) In the Church of the East*: 1. Liturgical sanctification* of any object or building. 2. Communion or Eucharist*.

qudsho (lit., holy place) In the Jacobite tradition, the sanctuary with one or three altars with two candles and a crucifix on the gradines. It is separated from the nave* by a curtain. The altar stands away from the wall to permit processions to pass around it. The sanctuary also contains two episcopal thrones.

quecone In the Armenian tradition, a musical instrument topped by a cherub's figure with bells attached.

Queen of Heaven In Roman Catholic theology, the Virgin Mary*.

quenat In the Ethiopian tradition, girdle* given to an Ethiopian novice* by a superior*.

Quercia, Jacopo della (c. 1374/5–1438) Italian sculptor. His greatest work was a series of 15 reliefs to decorate the main door of San Petronio, Bologna*. Among his other works were a *Madonna and Child* (1406) and an altarpiece of the *Madonna and Child and Four Saints* (1416–1422).

Quesnel, Pasquier (1634–1719) French Jansenist theologian. In 1672 he produced his major work, *Reflexions Morales,* with comments on every verse of the New Testament. In 1708 it was condemned by Pope Clement XI*. It was condemned again

five years later in the bull* *Unigenitus.* Quesnel's 101 Propositions, a summary of Jansenist doctrines, taught that grace* is irresistible, without grace human beings are incapable of good, and that all acts of a sinner, including prayer and attendance at Mass*, are sins.

Qui Pridie (Lat., who the day before) Fourth section of the Roman canon*, beginning the consecration of the bread and wine.

Quicunque Vult (Lat., whosoever wishes [to be saved]) Athanasian Creed*, from its opening words.

Quiercy, synods of Several synods held at Quiercy, near Laon, especially that in 838 which condemned Amalar of Metz, that in 849 to condemn the double predestination* doctrine of Gottschalk*, a monk of Fulda*, and that in 857/58 which partially rehabilitated Gottschalk.

quiet time Time set apart for prayer and meditation.

Quietism Theological principle that holds that: 1. Human effort contributes nothing to the achievement of perfection*. 2.The soul's highest attainment is the passive and mystical contemplation of the divine through passive prayer. 3. There is no need for a human response to God's grace*. 4. The intellect, will, and emotions must be renounced to achieve spiritual union with the infinite. Once the will is annihilated, sins cease to be sins. 5. Once the soul achieves union with the divine, it can never be lost. 6. Renunciation of self and desire is possible only by disregarding distractions, such as thoughts of heaven* and hell*. Spiritual exercises and the ordinances* of the church are superfluous when one is in the presence of God. The resulting state is called a mystic death or a form of nirvana. The three chief exponents of Quietism were Francois Fenelon*, Miguel de Molinos*, and Madame Guyon*. Quietism was condemned by the Roman Catholic Church.

Quinquagesima (Lat., fiftieth) Sunday that falls roughly 50 days before Easter* but mostly used of the Sunday itself.

Quinquarticular (Lat., five points) Five articles or points summarizing Arminianism*.

Qumran Site on the northwest end of the Dead Sea, eight miles south of Jericho, where the Dead Sea Scrolls* were discovered in 1947.

Quo Vadis? Legendary question, *Domine, Quo Vadis?* ("Lord, where are you going?") asked by St. Peter* when he met Christ on the Appian Way* when fleeing from Rome*. The Lord answered, "I am going to be crucified again." Reproached by this answer, Peter turned back and was martyred at Rome.

Quod Libet Academic exercise in medieval universities, held twice a year, before Christmas* and Easter* in which a master theologian fielded any questions raised by his student body or participants. The answers were then written down and published.

quoroyo In the Maronite tradition, minor order of reader* or lector*.

quqelion In the Syrian Rite, a chant of psalms typically interspersed with hallelujahs.

qurara In the Coptic tradition, cruet* for holding wine during the liturgy. Wine is poured into the chalice* from the right side and water from the left.

Quo Vadis?

rab kahni In the Assyrian Church*, a bishop directly under the patriarch*.

rab kumre In the East Syrian Church, an archpriest who ranks next after the bishop in a diocese* and who may act on his behalf.

raban/rabbantha (lit., the great one) Chaldean or Assyrian term for a monk.

Rabanus, Maurus (c. 780–856) Archbishop of Mainz*. Entering the Abbey of Fulda* as a child, he became its abbot in 824 and remained as abbot for 18 years. Forced to retire, he returned as archbishop of Mainz in 847, holding important synods in 847, 848, and 852. He wrote commentaries on nearly every book of the Bible, hymns, a revised martyrology*, works on grammar, two penitentials, chronology, treatises on ecclesiastical law* and practice, a handbook for the clergy, and about 100 poems. His *De Rerum Naturis* is an encyclopedic view of Christian belief and practice. Feast day: February 4.

Rabbula (c. 350–435) Syrian theologian. Converted about 400, he became bishop of Edessa* in 411. He supported the orthodox position of Cyril of Alexandria* at the Council of Ephesus* in 431 and attacked Nestorianism*, especially Theodore of Mopsuestia*. He translated into Syriac* Cyril's *De Recta Fide* and wrote many hymns in the Jacobite Liturgy.

Rabbula Gospels Codex* written by Rabbula*, a calligrapher, at the Monastery of St. John at Zagba in Mesopotamia in 586. It is the earliest known extant Syriac* manuscript and the earliest to have a colophon giving the name of the scribe and a date. It has 26 illuminated pages of which seven are full page and show Christ with short hair. The work is in Syriac*.

Rabbula Gospels

rabdos Properly, poimantike rabdos. In the Byzantine Church*, a crozier with a small orb on the top supporting a cross. On the side two arched serpents face each other.

Raccolta (lit. collection) Roman Catholic prayer book containing devotions which earned indulgences*. In 1968 it was supplanted by *Enchiridion Indulgentiarum.*

Racovian Catechism The first statement of Unitarianism* drawn up by Valentin Schmalz and Johannes Volkel on the basis of early drafts of F. P. Sozzini* and published in Polish in 1605 in Rakow, Poland. Among its eight sections, it dealt with Christ as "a man who, by his marvelous life and resurrection, was raised to divine power."

Rader, Paul (1879–1938) American evangelist. Soon after conversion, he began a lifelong association with Christian and Missionary Alliance* (CMA). He succeeded A. B. Simpson* in 1919 as president of CMA, and he also served as president of the Nyack Missionary Training Institute. A pioneer in the use of radio for evangelism, he began broadcasting as early as 1922 from the Chicago Gospel Tabernacle, which he founded. In 1926 he established the Maranatha Bible and Missionary Conference in Michigan.

Radical Orthodoxy Emerging theological school that tries to restore the primacy and autonomy of biblical truths. It starts from the premise that all secular forms of knowledge derive their authority from political power and are therefore subjective. Only absolute and transcendent truth can make knowledge more than a prop for power. It is not merely the transcendent and supernatural nature of ultimate truth that distinguishes it from secular knowledge. The ways of knowing the truth are also different. Symbol, ritual, narrative and allegorical thinking all lead seekers to a truth "that is beyond all understanding." Secular philosophical systems are not only inadequate, but incoherent, without the perspectives of theology. Among the leaders of the movement are John Milbank, Graham Ward, and Catherine Pickstock.

Radical Reformation Third wave* of the Protestant Reformation (the first two being those associated with Luther* and Calvin*) which rejected national churches and advocated a highly varied radical return to the practices of the early church. Among the radical groups were Anabaptists*, Mennonites*, and Melchiorites. Radical reformers were distinguished by a number of emphases, such as sanctification* rather than justification*, emotion rather than intellect, desire to be separate from the world, a pure and holy church, believer's baptism*, a non-creedal approach in doctrinal matters, evangelism, and religious freedom. The more orthodox sought simply to be New Testament Christians with little place for the Old Testament and a restorationist impulse.

radical theology Nontraditional theology exemplified by liberation theology*, death of God theology*, and liberal theology characterized by a rejection of transcendence and an abandonment of the institutional church. It calls for a new morality of love and generally supports a radical social ethic. It is reflected in popular eccentric theologians such as John Arthur Robinson* and Bishop Spong.

radonitsa In the Byzantine tradition, ceremony held on the Tuesday of the second week after Easter* when the faithful visit the graves of their departed relatives and scatter pashka, or blessed Easter food, on the graves.

Rahner, Karl (1904–1984) Roman Catholic theologian. He entered the Jesuit Order in 1922 and was ordained in 1932. He was professor of dogmatic theology at Innsbruck (1949–1964), Munich* (1964–1967), and Munster (1964–1971), and a peritus* at the Second Vatican Council*. Rahner has left a large body of works which attempts to construct a revised system of Thomist metaphysics using the existentialist idiom of Martin Heidegger. His chief works are *Spirit in the World* (1968), *Horer des Wortes* (1941), *Foundations of Christian Faith* (1978), *Theological Investigations* (22 vols., 1961–1992), and the editing of *Lexicon fur Theologie und Kirche* (10 vols., 1967–1975) and the encyclopedia, *Sacramentum Mundi* (6 vols., 1968–1970).

Raikes, Robert (1735–1811) Founder of the Sunday school* movement. He started the first Sunday (Sabbath) school in Ashbury, Berkshire, in 1780 as a way to educate poor and illiterate children. The idea spread through England and Wales and into America through the Methodists.

ra'is a-shamamish In the Coptic Church*, an archdeacon who may act as the diocesan vicar general*.

Ramabai, Pandita (1858–1922) Indian Christian reformer. Born as a Hindu Brahmin, she became a Sanskrit scholar and was given the title of Pandita. Meeting some Christians, who introduced her to the Bible, she went to England and was converted and baptized with her young daughter. In 1886 she went to America and on her return wrote *The High Caste Hindu Woman* (1887), recounting her life and faith. She opened a boarding school in Bombay (1889) and later Poona, where a Pentecostal revival followed in a few years. She established a mukti (salvation) mission and translated the Bible into Marathi.

ramban In the Syro-Malankarese* Rite, a clerical order between a priest and a bishop.

ramcha In the Assyrian Church*, Prayer of the Evening or Prayer of the Dusk, one of the two compulsory offices, the other being sapra*, or the Morning Office.

Ramm, Bernard (1916–1992) American Baptist scholar and theologian. He taught at a number of theological schools, especially at California Baptist Theological Seminary (1959–1974), and the American Baptist Theological Seminary of the West (1978–1986). He was an influential theologian who defended the historic Christian faith and steered a middle way between Fundamentalism* and modernism*. His publications include *Special Revelation and the Word of God* (1961), *The Evangelical Heritage* (1973), *After Fundamentalism* (1983), and *An Evangelical Christology* (1985).

ramsa (Syr., evening) In the Syrian church, vespers*.

Ramsey, Arthur Michael (1904–1988) Archbishop of Canterbury* (1961–1974) He was appointed professor of divinity at Durham* in 1940 and thereafter rose quickly: regius professor of divinity at Cambridge in 1950, bishop of Durham in 1952, archbishop of York* in 1956, and archbishop of Canterbury in 1961. As primate* of All England, he traveled widely and promoted closer relations with Orthodox and Roman Catholic churches. He wrote extensively but was most influential in his writings on prayer and spirituality*. Among his books are *The Resurrection of Christ* (1945), *The Glory of God and the Transfiguration of Christ* (1949), *Sacred and the Secular* (1965), *God, Christ and the World* (1969), and *Be Still and Know: A Study in the Life of Prayer* (1982).

Rance, Armand-Jean le Bouthillier de (1626–1700) Abbot of La Trappe*. He was ordained as a priest in 1651 but led a worldly life, until the sudden death of Mme de Monbazon in 1657 caused him to forsake the world, join the Cistercian monks of Strict Observance, and become regular abbot of La Trappe in 1664. His reforms emphasized manual labor rather than study, and penitence rather than physical austerity.

Ranke, Leopold von (1795–1886) Protestant German historian. Professor of history at the University of Berlin from 1825, he gained fame for his magisterial history of the papacy.

Raphael (1483–1520) Birth name: Raffaello Sanzio. Italian painter, the most famous of the Renaissance period. At Florence* he worked under the tutelage of some of the greatest painters of the age: Michelangelo*, Leonardo da Vinci*, and Fra Bartolommeo*. Among the great paintings that he left as his legacy are the *Transfiguration, Crucifixion, Coronation of the Virgin, St. Peter Released from Prison, Agony in the Garden, Temptation of Eve, Espousals of the Virgin,* and *Disputa.* He did

Robert Raikes

numerous Madonnas, including the *Sistine Madonna*, Madonna del Granducca, Ansidei Madonna,* and *Madonna della Sedia.*

rapture (Lat., *raptus,* caught up) Bodily transport of living believers to heaven* at the time of Christ's Second Coming*, based on 1 Thessalonians 4:14–17 where Paul* states that in addition to the resurrection of the righteous dead, "we who are still alive and remain shall be caught up together with them in the clouds to meet the Lord in the air." In dispensationalist theology there is a pretribulation rapture* before the Second Coming.

rasam In the Coptic Rite, consignation, which consists of signing the consecrated bread and the chalice* with the intincted bread. The particle* is then dropped into the chalice.

Raskolniki (Russ., schismatics) Also, Old Believers*. Splinter sect of the Russian Orthodox Church* that refused to accept the reforms of the patriarch Nikon*. They never smoked, used an eight-pointed cross, and crossed themselves with only two fingers.

rason In the Byzantine tradition, long, black gown with wide sleeves worn by Eastern Orthodox* clergy. The inner rason or anterion* resembles a cassock*, while the outer rason is worn over the inner rason and has wider sleeves.

rasophore Also, ryasonosets. In the Byzantine tradition, lowest grade of monks, below the stavrophore*.

ratio studiorum (Lat., method of studies) Jesuit scheme of studies issued in 1599 on which was based the success of Jesuit secondary education from the sixteenth to the eighteenth centuries. It called for study of Latin, Greek, philosophy, and theology.

rationale 1. Liturgical vestment sometimes worn by bishops over their shoulders instead of the pallium*. 2. Gold ornament worn by bishops on the breast over the chasuble* when celebrating Mass*.

Ratisbon, Colloquy of See REGENSBURG, CONFERENCE OF.

Ratramnus (ninth century) Carolingian theologian. His most important work was *De Corpore et Sanguine Domini* (843), which contradicted later church teaching on transubstantiation*. In *De Praedestinatione* (849–850) he accepted Gottschalk's belief in double predestination*. His opinions were condemned at the Synod of Vercelli in 1050. His teachings influenced the Protestant Reformers in the sixteenth century.

Ratzinger, Joseph (1927–) German Catholic theologian and cardinal. He served as professor of theology at the universities of Bonn (1959–1963), Munster (1963–1966), Tubingen (1966–1969), and Regensburg (1969–1977) and as theological adviser at Vatican Council II*. In 1977 he was named archbishop of Munich and later, in the same year, elevated as cardinal. In 1981 he was appointed prefect of the Congregation for the Doctrine of the Faith where he has led the effort to maintain doctrinal orthodoxy in the post-Vatican Council II*church.

Rauschenbusch, Walter (1861–1918) Father of the social gospel*. He served for 11 years as pastor of the Second German Baptist Church near Hell's Kitchen in New York City, where he developed a strong social conscience and a theology that met human needs. Returning to teach at the Rochester Seminary, he wrote *Christianity and Social Crisis* (1907), examining social concerns in a theological setting. It became one of the most influential Christian books of the pre-World War I years. He followed it with *Christianizing the Social Order* (1912), *The Social Principles of Jesus* (1916), and *A Theology for the Social Gospel* (1917).

Ravenna Italian city that became the most important Western outpost of Byzantine rule. It played a major role in the history of Christianity in Italy and was also a bastion of Christian art. The fifth-century cathedral, now Sant'Orso, was dedicated to the Resurrection but was rebuilt in 1734. The Baptistery of the Orthodox, or of Bishop Neon (c. 440–450), is an octagonal, tower-like brick building. Sant' Apollinare Nuovo was originally built for the Arian Theodoric in 500–514 but was rededicated in its present name in 560. San Vitale was begun by Theodoric's daughter, Amalasuntha, and paid for by the banker Julianus Argentarius and is said to have cost 26,000 gold solidi. It was dedicated in 547/48. Sant'Apollinare in Classe was also built by Argentarius between 532 and 536.

Raymond Nonnatus, St. (c. 1204–1240) Mercedarian missionary. He was sent to North Africa to ransom Christian slaves at Algiers but was imprisoned by the Muslims. Patron saint* of midwives. Feast day: August 31.

Raymond of Penafort, St. (c. 1180–1275) Spanish canonist. In 1216 he was appointed professor of law at Bologna*, but he returned to Spain and entered the Dominican convent at Barcelona in 1222 and, with Peter Nolasco*, helped to found the Mercedarians*, an order dedicated to redeeming Christian captives in Moorish lands. Here he wrote his *Summa de Casibus Poenitentiae,* a work that shaped the Catholic theology and practice of penance*. In 1230 he was called to Rome* where Pope Gregory IX* appointed him chaplain* and penitentiary* and charged him with organizing the papal decretals* subsequent to Gratian*, a work he completed in four years. In 1236 he returned to Spain as general* of his order, and in this capacity revised the Dominican Constitutions. After resigning his position in 1240, he dedicated his last years to the conversion of Jews and Muslims, setting up schools for the study of Hebrew and Arabic. He was canonized in 1601. Feast day: January 7.

raza (Syr., mystery) In the Syrian Church, the most solemn part of the Eucharist*.

RC Roman Catholic.

reader See LAY READER.

reading desk Pulpit desk or lectern*.

real presence In eucharistic theology, the actual and physical, rather than the symbolic, presence of the blood and the body of Christ in the sacrament*. This doctrine is distinguished from transubstantiation*, but its meaning is not constant, sometimes suggesting a spiritual or sacramental rather than a material presence.

Realism Eucharistic understanding that rejects a purely symbolic view and leans to an objective

presence of Christ's body or blood, however such language is interpreted.

realized eschatology See ESCHATOLOGY, REALIZED.

reatus (Lat., guilt) Sin* that has to be purged by confession* and absolution* and by an act of atonement* and reparation*.

rebaptism Later baptism of a person who was already baptized as an infant, perhaps using a different mode or means of baptism*, as immersion*. Rebaptism has also occurred in Christian history when one body, e.g. the Donatists and earlier Cyprian's church in North Africa, rejected baptism conferred by others as invalid for one reason or another. Conditional rebaptism is used by Roman Catholics.

recapitulation Summing up or summary: 1. Christ's passage through every stage of human life, from birth to death, recapitulating each stage so that he might save all. See also IRENAEUS. 2. Incarnation* as the summing up the previous revelations* of God in past ages.

Received Text (Lat., *textus receptus,* received text) Greek text of the New Testament, such as published by Erasmus* in 1516, and underlying most later editions and translations, roughly the same as the Byzantine Text*.

receiving countries Countries that receive missionaries.

recension (Lat., *recensio,* a reviewing) Revision of an earlier biblical text by an editor or of any written work by the original author or a later writer.

reception Informal process by which conciliar or papal pronouncements are accepted by the entire church as being in conformity with Scripture and tradition. Innovations in ecclesiastical policy need to be received well by the faithful before they can become legitimate and binding on the clergy and the laity.

receptionism In eucharistic theology, the teaching that while the bread and the wine remain unchanged after consecration, the communicant who has faith receives them as the true body and blood of Christ. A non-believer receives only bread and wine.

recessional Procession of choir and clergy out of the chancel* after a church service, usually accompanied by a hymn.

recidivism Falling back into the same sin from which a person was saved, possibly because of the persistence of old habits or the severity of the temptation.

recluse Person consecrated to God who withdraws from the world and secludes himself or herself purposefully like a hermit.

recollection 1. Stage in the interior life when the soul collects itself in prayer by not allowing worldly concerns to distract it. 2. In the life of Christian mystics, a spiritual exercise by which the soul regains its focus by turning its attention to God.

Recollects 1. The Franciscan Recollects, a reformed branch of the Franciscan Observants* founded in France in the sixteenth century which merged with the Observants in 1897. 2. The Augustinian Recollects, a strict branch of the Augustinian Hermits founded in Spain in 1589, active as missionaries in Peru and the Philippines. In 1912 they were constituted into an independent order under a prior general*.

Reconstructionism Also, theonomy*. Conservative movement dating from the 1960s to reconstruct society along the lines set forth in the Mosaic Law. Its three main leaders are Rousas John Rushdoony, Greg Bahnsen, and Gary North. It aims to restore not only the moral law but also the judicial law of Old Israel.

rector 1. Anglican or Episcopal clergyman entitled to the whole tithes of a parish*. 2. Elected officer of certain universities, usually the president. 3. In the Roman Catholic Church, head of a seminary or Jesuit house or priests with the care of certain types of churches.

rectory Residence of a rector*.

recusancy Refusal to accept or submit to an ecclesiastical authority, especially refusal to attend the services of the Church of England* or obey the Act of Uniformity*. It was used as a penal term in England in the seventeenth and eighteenth centuries against Roman Catholics and dissenters*. Thus, recusant.

red In religious art, the color of martyrdom and the Holy Spirit*. In church liturgy, it is the color of the Pentecost* season and of martyrs' festivals.

red hat Flat crowned red hat with two clusters of 15 tassels worn by a cardinal.

red letter Bible Bible in which the words of Jesus are printed in red.

red letter day Feast or saint's day marked in red in liturgical calendars.

Red Mass Votive mass* of the Holy Spirit celebrated with red vestments, at the opening of councils and synods.

redaction criticism Study of the editorial processes used by biblical authors and their use of prior materials, as the use of the Marcan text by Matthew and Luke.

Redditio Symboli (Lat., giving back the symbol) Public recitation of the Apostles' Creed* on Maundy Thursday* by the candidates for baptism to whom the creed was taught the previous Sunday. Attested in the fourth and fifth centuries.

redeem Regain possession of something that was lost; save, rescue, or deliver. Applied in the New Testament to the saving act at Calvary by which Christ redeemed his people through his blood. Thus, redeemer.

redemption 1. Act of a redeemer who rescues someone else from loss or bondage; deliverer. 2. Aspect of the salvation* of his people by Jesus Christ through his own substitutionary sacrifice on the cross as payment or ransom. Jesus' healing ministry also was part of his redemptive work.

Redemptoristines The Order of the Holy Redeemer, a religious congregation* of contemplative nuns who intercede for sinners, founded by Alphonsus Maria de Liguori* in 1731 and approved in 1750.

Redemptorists Congregation of the Most Holy Redeemer founded in 1732 by St. Alphonsus Maria de Liguori* and approved in 1749. It does mission work among the poor. They entered the United States in 1832 and England in 1843. They are governed by a rector* major who resides in Rome*.

reduction 1. In South American Catholic history, the act of resettlement by missionaries of Native Americans in villages or compounds for acculturation or control. 2. The settlement itself.

reed In Christian art, a symbol of Christ's Passion*.

Rees, Thomas Bonner (1911–1970) English evangelist. Converted in his teens, Rees conducted crusades* in northern Ireland, where thousands were converted. He also conducted a number of mass rallies and campaigns in major British cities and in the United States (where he went more than 50 times). He founded three conference centers, including Hildenborough Hall. He is the author of *Breakthrough,* a handbook on home evangelism. His brother **Dick Rees** was similarly an evangelist, largely within the Church of England*.

Re'esa-Daber In the Ethiopian Church, an archimandrite*.

refectory Dining room in a monastery, convent, or seminary.

Reformation Mass movement climaxing in the sixteenth century in Christian Europe resulting in a vast religious revival and renewal and also the breakup of the monolithic Western Church* into two main bodies, Roman Catholic and Protestant. It coincided with an intellectual resurgence known imprecisely as the Renaissance and also the rise of nationalism among the various ethnic groups. By the fourteenth century, the Roman Catholic Church itself was in a state of serious decline, plagued by systemic corruption in the hierarchy* and monastic orders that various Reformers like Savonarola* were unable to correct from

within. Other contributory causes prepared the way for a challenge to the church's authority and magisterium* at every level: the loss of papal power resulting from the Babylonian Captivity*, the Great Schism*, lax discipline in the monastic orders, the rise of humanism as an anti-clerical ideology, the persistent discontent of the lower class against the church as expressed by the Lollards* in England, the Hussites* in Bohemia, and the Waldenses* in the Alps, and the invention of printing which made unauthorized translation and publication of Bibles practical.

Martin Luther* was the catalyst of the Reformation, and he had all the personal qualities of a man born for the right cause at the right time. However, he had no desire to lead a new religious movement or break away from the Catholic Church. He was forced to do so as a result of papal intransigence and a series of missteps and miscalculations on the part of Luther's Catholic antagonists. By 1521 when Luther refused to recant, the rupture was complete and by 1529, when the imperial diet convened at Speyer, six German princes and representatives of 14 major cities made their "Protestation" as adherents of Lutheranism*. By the time of Luther's death the movement had spread throughout Germany and Scandinavia.

Meanwhile, the mantle of leadership fell on two other brilliant leaders: Zwingli* and Calvin*. They helped the Reformation to spread westward through the Swiss cantons, France, Netherlands, and Scotland. Calvinism* triumphed in Scotland primarily through John Knox*, who was instrumental in committing the national state church to Reformed* religion. In England, Reformation came not through religious leaders but through the Tudor monarchs. The Church of England* took shape in the sixteenth century as a non-Roman church but not entirely Protestant. Later, in the following centuries, the Anglican Church took the message of the Reformation to the American colonies and British colonies and possessions in every continent.

An important part of the Reformation belongs to the Radical Reformers, who continued the struggle not only for restoring the primitive church but also for religious liberty. The most prominent among these were the Anabaptists*, Mennonites*, Hutterites*, and Schwenckfelders.

Meanwhile, The Catholic Church itself underwent a reformation of its own, called the Counter-Reformation*, and set its own house in order primarily in response to the Protestant

Monument to the Reformation in Geneva

threat. A reformed and chastened papacy, the Council of Trent*, the Roman Inquisition*, and the establishment of the Jesuits* in 1540 and the Oratory of Divine Love in 1517—all helped to stanch the erosion of papal authority and to bring renewal into the church.

Reformation Day October 31, celebrating the nailing of Martin Luther's Ninety-Five Theses* to the door of the Wittenberg* Church on that day in 1517.

Reformed Protestant in the Calvinist tradition as distinct from Protestant in other traditions. Within the Calvinist tradition, Reformed sometimes designates continental origins whereas Presbyterian designates Anglo-Saxon origins.

Reformed Church in America Also, Dutch Reformed Church*. It came with the original Dutch settlers to New Amsterdam (later, New York), and its first congregation was organized in 1628 by Jonas Michaelis. When T. J. Frelinghuysen* arrived in the colonies in 1720 at the time of the Great

Awakening*, the church broke its ties to Netherlands and became a local denomination with its own *coetus* or assembly. Queen's College (now Rutgers) was founded in New Jersey for training ministers, and Hope College was founded in Michigan in 1866 for the same purpose. During the nineteenth century the church spread westward, but it is centered in Michigan in the Grand Rapids area. It is Calvinistic in theology and Presbyterian in government.

Although the Reformed churches have been accused of neglecting the Eucharist*, their liturgies all emphasize its importance. The central feature of the Reformed worship is the weekly Communion. There are no lectionaries, and sermons are preached at every service. Vestments are abandoned for cassock* and bands, black gown, and scarf. The bidding prayer is expanded into a long didactic exhortation.

Reformed Theological Seminary One of the ten largest seminaries in North America, located in Jackson, Mississippi. It was founded in 1966 as a Presbyterian and Reformed* institution, emphasizing training for the ministry, application of the Bible to all aspects of life, and evangelism. In 1989 a second campus was established in Orlando, Florida. In addition, partnerships for advanced studies were established in Korea, Scotland, and Brazil.

Reformed theology Theological tradition that emerged from the work of Zwingli*, Calvin*, Bucer*, Vermigli*, Musculus, Knox*, and other Reformers as distinct from Lutheran theology. Its key elements include divine sovereignty in election*, assurance of salvation*, godly discipline, the proper ordering of polity and worship, and the Christian ordering of society.

reformer Any of the leaders of the Protestant Reformation*.

Refreshment Sunday Also, Laetare Sunday*; Mothering Sunday*. Fourth Sunday in Lent*, so called perhaps in reference to the feeding of the five thousand.

refrigerium 1. Refreshing and cooling in both moral and physical senses. In the moral sense, it is used to describe the beatitude in paradise. 2. Charitable meal served to the poor on the birthdays of martyrs*.

regeneration Spiritual rebirth caused supernaturally by the Holy Spirit*. Some Christian groups believe that regeneration takes place through or is symbolized by baptism* or justification* (John 1:12; 3:1–10; Gal. 4:23–29; James 1:15–18; 1 Pet. 1:3, 23; 1 John 2:29). Regeneration, decision for Christ*, conversion*, and being born again* are commonly used as synonyms. However, R. A. Torrey* defined regeneration as the new life entering the inner person whereas conversion refers to the outward state of restoration and baptism of the Spirit to the empowerment for Christian service.

Regensburg Cathedral in Regensburg, Germany, built between 1250 and the fifteenth century on the site of an old Romanesque basilica* that had been destroyed by fire. Work was halted in 1525 and resumed only in 1618. It was renovated in the nineteenth century and again in the 1980s. Its interior is considered one of the most beautiful examples of German Gothic* in which the stained glass windows and the elaborate tracery shine in mystical colors. The Chapel of All Saints is entered through the cloister* on the northeast.

Regensburg, Conference of Meeting on reunion in 1541 between German Protestants and Catholics at Regensburg* (Ratisbon*) sponsored by Emperor Charles V. The Protestant spokesmen were Melanchthon*, Bucer*, Pistorius, and Cruciger* with John Calvin* also present. The Catholic side was represented by Eck*, Julius von Pflug, and Johann Gropper. The basis of the discussion was a 23-article statement drawn up by Bucer and Gropper, later called the Regensburg Book. The conference reached an impasse on the teaching authority of the church and the Eucharist* but produced an agreed statement on justification*. The meeting ended with the Interim of Regensburg.

Reger, Max (1873–1916) German composer of organ music. Although a devout Roman Catholic, he was so moved by his love for the Lutheran chorale that he joined Arnold Mendelssohn as a

leader in the revival of Protestant church music. Most of his fantasias were composed on Protestant chorale melodies. His greatest sacred composition was his setting of Psalm 100 for chorus, organ, and orchestra.

Regina Coeli (Lat., Queen of Heaven) Eastertide* anthem to the Virgin Mary*, from its opening words.

Regions Beyond Missionary Union (RBMU) Nondenominational foreign mission agency that traces its roots to the East London Institute for Home and Foreign Missions founded in 1873 by Irish evangelist H. Grattan Guinness. The American branch is known as RBMU International. The society sponsors frontier evangelism and the training of national church leaders in Irian Jaya, Kalimantan, Congo, Cameroon, Philippines, Chile, and Peru.

Regnum Papal tiara* or triple crown.

regula Book of rules, regulations, and customs of a religious house.

regula fidei Also, rule of faith*. Doctrinal norms that govern Christian search for truth, especially in determining what language to use and what traditions to respect. They ensure that Christian ideas are expressed in apostolic terms.

regular Roman Catholic priest attached to a religious order and bound by vows of religion* and living in a community. Distinguished from a secular who lives in the world.

Regular Baptists Calvinistic Baptists in America opposed to the evangelistic fervor of the Great Awakening*. Regular Baptists were more orderly in worship, supported trained and salaried ministers, and discouraged women from public ministry. Although most Regular and Separatist Baptist congregations merged by 1800 on the basis of the Philadelphia Confession of 1742, scattered Regular Baptist congregations survive.

Reichenau Small island in the western arm of Lake Constance, site of a medieval Benedictine monastery founded by St. Pirminius in 728 as

Augea Dives. There are three other churches in Reichenau: the pillared basilica* of St. George* in Oberzell built between 890 and 896, the minster* of Saint Mary and Mark in Mittelzell, and the monastery church of St. Peter and St. Paul in Unterzell. Reichenau was an important monastic center, noted for its manuscript collections.

Reichenau Monastery

Reid, Thomas (1710–1796) Scottish philosopher. Born near Aberdeen, Scotland, Reid attended Marischal College. Taught by George Turnbull, he came to regard common language as factually-based and representative of the common convictions of humankind. Entering the Presbyterian ministry at New Mychar in 1737, he subsequently read David Hume's *Treatise of Human Nature* and was appalled at his countryman's skepticism. Like Kant in Germany, who was "awakened from his dogmatic slumbers" by Hume, Reid committed himself to a direct philosophical response. Believing that Hume's logic was virtually unassailable, yet his conclusions were absurd and undermined the cognitive capacity by which Christian truth must be considered, Reid contended that Hume's assumptions about the nature of knowledge must be false. Objects, not ideas, must be immediately given to the mind. Accordingly, in 1764 Reid's *Inquiry into the Human Mind* was published, establishing him as the Scottish "defender of common sense." In his two most famous works, *Essays on*

the Intellectual Powers of Man (1785) and *Essays on the Active Powers of the Human Mind* (1788), Reid proposed alternatives to Hume's epistemology and moral relativism, respectively.

Reims One of the oldest French episcopal sees* in the old capital of Remi in Gaul, founded in the third century by St. Sixtus. Its power grew under Bishop Imbetausius, who took part in the Council of Arles in 314; under St. Remigius*, who baptized Clovis*; and under Hincmar*. From the middle of the tenth century, the kings of France were crowned at Reims, as was Charles VII in the presence of St. Joan of Arc* in 1429. Its Gothic* cathedral was begun in 1211 and completed in the fourteenth century. It is considered the most beautiful cathedral in France. The influence of Reims is seen in most European cathedrals. It was a pioneer in such innovations as tracery windows,

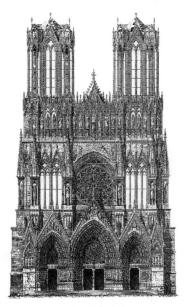

Reims Cathedral

the use of round pillars, and delicate structures, placing rose windows* in the tympana, or gables above the west doors, and moving the statuary inside. Until 1914 it had 2,303 sculptures, most of which were destroyed in the two world wars. The tomb of St. Remigius* in the former Benedictine abbey of St. Remi is a place of pilgrimage*.

Reims-Douai Bible See DOUAI-REIMS BIBLE.

relational theology Type of liberal theology that focuses on interpersonal relationships rather the divine-human relationship. Sin* is the wrong interaction, and holiness* is the right interaction. Christian relationship, therefore, consists of the right relationships with God, others, and oneself. Love is seen as the central note of Christianity because it is the menstruum of right relationships. It was silent on the fact that right relationships can be accomplished only through real spiritual changes in the relator. Its foremost exponents were Harry Emerson Fosdick* and Norman Vincent Peale*.

relator 1. Roman Catholic official who oversees canonization* or beatification*. 2. One of the parties in a relationship.

relic Object of religious veneration*, as the material remains of a saint* after death or sacred bones of a martyr*.

religion 1. Institutionalized system of beliefs relating to a quest for and knowledge of God and the supernatural. 2. Systems of practices and observances relating to a worship of God or gods. 3. System of moral and ethical values and practices designed to undergird them. 4. Practice of personal devotion to a deity.

religionless Christianity Genuine, biblical Christianity without religious trappings; a term coined by Dietrich Bonhoeffer*. What Bonhoeffer meant by the phrase is not always clear.

Religionsgeschichte Schule History of Religions School. A group of German biblical scholars who interpreted Christianity on the basis of the comparative study of other earlier or contemporary religions. Major scholars of this school included Ernst Troeltsch*, Richard Reitzenstein, Hermann Gunkel*, Wilhelm Bousset, and Johannes Weiss*.

religiosity Excessive or affected religious zeal, especially an outward display of religious piety.

religious Member of a religious institute, congregation, or order bound by a public vow to observe the counsels of poverty, obedience, and chastity*.

religious frontier/distance Line of demarcation between one religion and another, or between a Christian evangelist and the target population.

Religious Tract Society Former name of United Society for Christian Literature*, founded in England in 1799 for the production, publication, and dissemination of Christian tract literature.

reliquary Receptacle for relics*, such as caskets, capsules, and ampullae, made of precious metals and richly decorated. For larger relics, shrines were built.

Reliquary

Rembrandt, Harmensz (1606–1669) Also Harmenszoon van Rijn. Dutch painter. By age 25, he was one of the most famous painters in the Netherlands. Hundreds of his paintings dealt with scriptural subjects, 90 on the Passion* alone, and they are not only imaginative but are done with spiritual insight. The most famous of his paintings are *Disciples at Emmaus* (1648), *Return of the Prodigal Son* (late 1660s), *Peter Denying Christ* (1660), *Nativity* (1646), *Holy Family with Angels* (1645), *The Risen Christ Appearing to Magdalene* (1638), *Raising of Lazarus* (1632), *Descent from the Cross* (1633), *Christ Healing the Sick* (1649), and the *Three Crosses* (1660). Rembrandt created a new Protestant iconography* in which, unlike the earlier Catholic paintings, Christ was humanized. There are no haloes or aureoles, and visions of saints* are totally absent.

Remigius/Remi, St. (d. c. 533) "Apostle of the

Franks." He was elected bishop of the metropolitan see* of Reims at the age of 22. His baptism of Clovis* with 3,000 of his subjects after the Battle of Tolbiac was a turning point in ecclesiastical history. He directed missions to the Morini and the Arians of Burgundy and founded four new bishoprics* in Gaul. His remains are at the Abbey of St. Remi. Feast day: October 1.

Remonstrance Statement of Arminianism* drawn up in 1610 by a close friend of Arminius*, Johannes Uitenbogaert, and signed by 44 Arminian leaders known as remonstrants. It contained five articles drawn from Arminius's* *Declaratio Sententiae* summarizing the Arminian doctrines. It repudiated key Calvinist doctrines, such as sublapsarianism* and supralapsarianism* and also the doctrines which stated that Christ died only for the elect* and that grace* was irresistible and indefectible. The contra-Remonstrants opposed to the Remonstrance gained the sympathy of William of Orange and condemned Arminianism* at the Synod of Dort* (1618–1619). Some 200 Remonstrant ministers were ousted from their pulpits, and many more exiled. The ousted ministers began the Remonstrant Brotherhood and founded a seminary at Amsterdam in 1630. Over the course of the next two centuries the Remonstrants steadily lost members to Deism* and Socinianism*.

Renan, Joseph Ernst (1823–1892) French humanist. A professor of Hebrew at the College de France, he is best known for his attack on Christ in his *Life of Jesus* (1863) and *History of the Origins of Christianity* (7 vols., 1863–1881).

renewal Movement within churches seeking enhanced devotion and faithfulness to Jesus Christ and a fresh commitment to evangelism.

Reorganized Church of Jesus Christ of Latter-Day Saints Mormon* church which followed Joseph Smith's* son rather than Brigham Young* and is now headquartered in Independence, Missouri. It differs doctrinally from the official Mormon Church, especially on polygamy (which it rejects) and the nature of God.

reparation In moral theology*, making amends through prayer and penance* for damage done to God through offenses against him.

repentance Contrition, the acknowledgment and condemnation of one's own sins together with a turning back toward God. Springing from a disinterested love of God, it includes sorrow, confession*, and a determination not to sin again.

Repose, Altar of Altar to which the Blessed Sacrament* is taken in procession after the evening Mass* of Maundy Thursday* and reserved for Holy Communion* on Good Friday*.

Reproaches, the Set of reproofs addressed by Christ on the cross to his people as part of the Good Friday Liturgy*. They consist of 12 verses sung by two choirs during the Veneration of the Cross*.

reprobation Predestination to condemnation.

requiem (Lat., rest) Mass* offered for the dead, so called from the first word of the introit*. The Paschal candle* is placed at the head of the coffin, and the officiating priest may wear black or any other color. The opening section of the requiem uses traditional Gregorian Chant* melodies with orchestral accompaniment.

reredos Elaborate rich silk or jeweled decoration or screen* behind and above an altar in the chancel* of a church and usually under the east window. Sometimes carved wooden panels and sculptured stone or alabaster figures take the place of screens.

res sacramenti (Lat., the thing of the sacrament) Also, res signata (the reality signified). That to-

Reredos

ward which a sacrament* points. In the Eucharist* it is the real presence of the blood and body of Christ.

res tantum (Lat., the reality alone) In sacramental theology*, grace* conferred by a sacrament* and hence its ultimate goal or purpose.

rescript Papal response to a question about judicial or ethical matters.

reservation Practice of keeping the consecrated bread (and the wine) for reception at a later date or time or to be administered to the sick and the dying or those absent from the Eucharist*. In the early church the host* was carried about by the faithful on their persons. But they were later placed in the church, in an aumbry* in the wall, in a pyx* hanging over the altar, or a tabernacle on the altar, or in a separate chapel. In the Eastern Church*, the reserved sacrament is used for the Communion of the sick as well as for the Liturgies of the Presanctified* in Lent*.

reserved sin Sin* set apart for being dealt with by a bishop, based on the gravity of the offense and the magnitude of the contemplated punishment.

residential see Diocese* or other jurisdiction with a resident bishop.

resistible grace Arminian doctrine that God's saving grace* is universally offered but may be refused by anyone through the exercise of his or her free will*.

response Liturgical statement said or sung antiphonally by the choir and congregation following a statement by the celebrant or worship leader.

responsory Liturgical chant of alternating versicles and responses taken from the Scripture, said or sung at the Mass*, Offertory, and in the canonical hours*.

restitution 1. Restoration or reparation* to a wronged person. 2. Divine restoration of all things to their pristine order and purpose.

Restoration movement Nineteenth-century Christian movement spearheaded by Barton Stone* and Alexander Campbell* to restore the purity of New Testament Christianity by maintaining the authority of the Bible as the only guide to faith and practice. They coined the phrase, "When the Bible speaks, we speak; when the Bible is silent, we are silent." The Disciples of Christ* trace their origin to this movement.

restorationism 1. Universalist heresy that believes ultimately all human beings will be saved. It accepts the reality of hell*, but denies its finality. See also APOCATASTASIS. 2. Belief that the church should in every respect reproduce the life of the New Testament churches. This conviction inspired some sixteenth-century radicals and later movements, including some latter-day Pentecostals and Charismatics.

resurrection body New and incorruptible body received by those who are raised from the dead by the power of God (1 Cor. 15:35–54). It, however, maintains the continuity and identity of the human person.

resurrection, first Physical resurrection of believers that precedes the physical resurrection of unbelievers (Rev. 20:5).

resurrection life Power of Jesus Christ's resurrection transmitted to his followers, endowing them with a glorious new existence (Phil. 3:10).

retable Shelf, also known as gradine*, or set of panels behind the altar in a church. See also REREDOS.

retreat Period of spiritual rest and renewal during which a group of believers withdraws from routine life and seeks new direction and pace through prayer and meditation.

retrochoir Part of a church or cathedral lying behind the presbytery* which can be reached from the choir aisles.

Rev. Reverend.

revealed theology Theological tenets revealed by the Scriptures as opposed to natural theology*, which seeks to derive its knowledge of God from the natural world and human reason.

Reveil, Le (Fr., The Awakening) Evangelical revival* which began in French-speaking Switzerland in the early nineteenth century and spread to France and Netherlands by 1825. Its leaders emphasized the orthodox Reformed* doctrines, especially the authority of the Bible, the sovereignty of God, repentance*, justification* by faith in Christ, and personal commitment. It was led by numerous Swiss, French, and Dutch revivalists*, including Cesar Malan, Francois Gaussen, and Merle d'Aubigne* in Geneva*; Alexandre Vinet* in Vaud; Felix Neff, Henri Pyt, Adolphe and Frederic Monod* in France; and Willem Bilderdijk, Isaak da Costa, and Guillaume Groen van Prinsterer in the Netherlands.

revelation 1. Divine act of making known things that were hidden before, and the truth that is revealed in the process. General or natural revelation consists of intimations of the divine in nature and in the Scriptures. Special or historical revelation deals with God's dealings with Israel, leading to the fact of Christ, his death on the cross, Resurrection, ascension, and the apostolic testimony of his atonement* revealing God in history. Much of the truth that is revealed can be grasped only through faith*, and they are set down in the Scriptures and in the doctrines of the church. 2. The Book of Revelation.

Revelation of St. John, Book of Also, the Apocalypse. The last book in the New Testament attributed to St. John the beloved apostle or St. John the Elder in the Island of Patmos* some time before the end of the first century. Its eschatological meaning has never been fully deciphered.

revelator One who reveals something.

reverend Title of respect used in addressing clergymen. Archbishops are styled "most reverend*," bishops and the moderator* of the General Assembly* of the Church of Scotland* as "right reverend," and deans as "very reverend."

Revised English Bible Revision (1989) of the New English Bible* in which archaic expressions such as "thou" were abandoned in favor of more modern usage.

Revised Standard Version (RSV) Revision of the King James Version* of the Bible by scholars commissioned by U.S. churches and published in 1952.

Revised Version Revision of the Authorized Version* of the Bible produced by British and American scholars, 1880–1890. Sometimes called the English Revised Version to distinguish it from the Revised Standard Version*.

revival Spiritual renewal or God's quickening visitation* of his people caused by the Holy Spirit* through the proclamation of the gospel. It results in deeper religious experience, mass conversions, and a greater fervor for holy living and evangelism over a wide region. It is essentially a corporate rather than personal occurrence. Some of the great revivals in history appear to have happened without any prior signs or even a causative agent. Examples are the Great Awakening* in America, the Great Welsh Revival* of 1904–1905, and the East African Revival. Some revivals, more limited and short-lived, follow crusades* or evangelistic campaigns.

The major theologian of revival is Jonathan Edwards* who, after the Great Awakening of 1740, wrote *The Distinguishing Marks of a Work of the Spirit of God* (1741) and *Thoughts on the Revival of Religion in New England in 1740* (1742). He viewed revivals as cyclical works of grace* that recur periodically like the breaking of waves on the shore, and as God's principal means of extending his kingdom. Charles Finney* saw a correlation between corporate prayer, repentance*, and revival and was responsible for a significant shift in Christian thought that viewed revivals as happenings that could be arranged by appropriate means, and even announced in advance.

revivalism Evangelistic practice of promoting through crusades* and preaching large-scale conversions for the purpose of influencing and sanctifying an entire society.

revivalist Evangelist or leader of a revival*.

reviviscence In sacramental theology*, a sacrament* that is delayed in its action because of the resistance of the recipient but, nevertheless, achieves its purpose over the course of time. Also, according to Augustine*, the return of the forgiven sins upon the sinner, if repentance* proves only momentary.

rhantismos In the Byzantine tradition, the ceremony of sprinkling, as part of the blessing of the waters*. During the ceremony, the priest dips a cross into the water three times and a branch of basil is thrown into the water.

rhantistron In the Byzantine tradition, an aspergil used to sprinkle holy water*.

rhema Special word or message from God based on the Bible that has unique significance to an individual or group.

Rhema Bible Training Center Seminary founded by Kenneth Hagin* in 1974 to train people in the Pentecostal ministry. The campus is located in Broken Arrow, a suburb of Tulsa, Oklahoma.

rhodostagma In the Byzantine tradition, rosewater used to sprinkle people and things during the Holy Week* ceremonies.

rhythmical office Form of Divine Office* in the Middle Ages in which all parts except songs and lessons were put into metre or rhyme. The best known rhythmical offices were written by St. Odo* and St. Odilo*, abbots of Cluny*, and Fulbert, bishop of Chartres*.

Ribera, Jose de (1591–1652) Spanish Baroque painter who blended Spanish realism with Italian style as in *Nativity of Jesus Christ* and *The Penitent Magdalene*. His paintings expressed the theology of the Counter-Reformation*.

Ricci, Matteo (1552–1610) Italian Jesuit missionary to China. He joined the Jesuits* in 1571 and was sent in 1578 to Goa and in 1582 to Macao where he learned Mandarin Chinese. He settled in Beijing in 1601 and won over the imperial court by displaying his knowledge of astronomy and science. He adopted the dress and etiquette of the Chinese literati. He tried to Confucianize Christ-

ian theology, especially in his book, *The True Meaning of the Lord of Heaven*. He did not regard Confucianism as inconsistent with the Christian faith and assimilated many of its features and

Matteo Ricci

rites. While he won some converts, his methods proved controversial and caused the China Rites controversy*.

rice Christian Convert to Christianity in the Third World who is motivated not by personal conviction or faith* but by a desire for food, medical services, or other benefits.

Rice, John R. (1895–1980) Baptist Fundamentalist, evangelist, and editor. He was pastor of the Fundamentalist Baptist Church in Dallas (1932–1940) and editor of the influential journal, *The Sword of the Lord* (1934–1980). He is known for his opposition to modernism*, Communism, liberalism*, civil rights, smoking, movies, and alcohol.

Rice, Luther (1783–1836) Baptist educator and promoter of missions. Ordained as a Congregationalist missionary, he embarked for India in 1812, but en route became a Baptist. Returning in 1813, he promoted Baptist interest in missions and was responsible for the formation in 1814 of the General Convention of the Baptist Denomination in the United States for Foreign Missions, also known as the Triennial Convention, as well as the

Baptist General Tract Society in 1824. His preaching led to the foundation of several Baptist colleges, beginning with Columbian College in Washington, D.C., in 1821.

Richard of Chichester, St. (1197–1253) After serving as chancellor of the University of Oxford and chancellor of Canterbury*, he became bishop of Chichester in 1224. Many cures were attributed to his shrine in Chichester which was destroyed by Henry VIII. Feast day: April 3.

Richard of Middleton (c. 1249–?) Franciscan philosopher and theologian. He was the author of a celebrated commentary on the Sentences of Peter Lombard*.

Richard of St. Victor (d. 1173) Victorine spiritual writer and theologian. He became prior* of the Abbey of St. Victor in Paris in 1162. His chief work is *De Trinitate*, on the Trinity*. He wrote extensively on spiritual life and scriptural exegesis*. He listed six steps to spiritual perfection*, beginning with the study of nature and culminating in ecstasy*. He also wrote *Liber de Verbo Incarnato, De Statu Interioris Hominis, De Emmanuele*, and *Adnotationes Mysticae in Psalmos*.

Richard, Timothy (1845–1919) English missionary to China. He went to China with the China Evangelization Society in 1870 and later joined the Baptist Missionary Society. Like Ricci, he tried to adapt Christianity to Chinese culture and planned to win the allegiance of the intelligentsia through an ambitious publications program under the imprint of the Christian Literature Society. He founded a university in Taiyuan, the Shansi capital, with the Boxer Rebellion* indemnity money.

rida Chasuble* worn by Maronite priests.

riddels Tall curtains at the sides of an English-style altar, hung at right angles to the dorsal*.

Ridley, Nicholas (c. 1500–1555) English reformer and martyr*. In 1540 he became chaplain* to the king and master of Pembroke. Seven years later he was consecrated bishop of Rochester and in 1550 was transferred to London. Ridley helped to com-

pile the *Book of Common Prayer** of 1549 and directed its revision in 1552. He was active in carrying through Henry VIII's reforms. On the accession of Queen Mary, he was deposed and imprisoned and, with Latimer*, burned at the stake. As the fires were lit, Latimer cried out, "Be of good cheer, Master Ridley, and play the man. We shall this day light such a candle by God's grace in England as I trust shall never be put out."

Nicholas Ridley

Riemenschneider, Tilman (c. 1460–1531) German woodcarver and sculptor who specialized in wood and stone, especially altarpieces. Among his most notable works are *Altar of the Blessed Sacrament* in St. Jacobus, *Rothenburg ob der Tauber,* the tomb of Rudolph von Scherenberg, carvings in the Wurzberg Cathedral, and the tomb of Henry II and his queen Cunigunde in Bamberg* Cathedral.

Rievaulx Cistercian abbey in North Yorkshire in England dedicated to the Virgin Mary*, founded in the twelfth century. For the next three cen-

Rievaulx Abbey

turies, it gained a reputation as a center of learning and devotion. Today the abbey lies in ruins.

Right to Life Also, pro-life. Movement opposed to the taking of innocent human life at any time from conception to natural death. It is opposed to abortion, euthanasia, and other liberal-supported measures.

Rigorism Also known as Tutiorism*. Puritanism* or formalism in which the letter of the law is observed through extreme self-denial.

Rila Monastery in the Rhodope Mountains of Bulgaria, originally founded by John of Rila in the tenth century. The oldest part of the present monastery is the stone tower built in 1335 with a Transfiguration Chapel on its top floor. The main Church of the Virgin was built in the nineteenth century. The gilded iconostasis* contains 36 panels painted by the Zograph brothers. It was a center of Bulgarian cultural revival in the thirteenth century and is now a national monument.

Rimsky-Korsakov, Nikolai Andreyevich (1844–1908) Russian composer. His religious works include eight settings of the divine liturgy of St. John Chrysostom*, traditional Orthodox liturgical chants, and the *Easter Festival Overture*.

ring shout African-American religious musical form that used a shuffling step while chanting, clapping, or praying.

RIP Requiescat in Pace; May he or she rest in peace, used as a form of prayer for the dead.

ripidion (Gk., fan) Byzantine-rite flabellum* or liturgical fan* of wood or metal, also called hexapterygon, or six-winged, because it symbolized and often bears the image of the six-winged seraphim worshiping before the throne of God. They are often carried in processions.

rish-m'shamshono In the Maronite Church, a cleric, similar to an archdeacon in the West, who supervises church property.

rish-qoleh In the Syrian Rite, the tune in which a hymn is to be sung.

rite 1. Order of service for a particular sacrament* or a liturgical event. 2. Ritual process that includes several rites. 3. Pattern of worship service in a particular denomination, such as Coptic, Greek Orthodox, Malabar, or Syrian.

Rites, Congregation of Sacred Department of the Roman Catholic Curia* responsible for the Liturgy of the Latin Rite* and the canonization* of saints*, created in 1588 to carry out the directives of the Council of Trent*. Its twofold responsibility covered the liturgy of the church, indulgences* and dispensations, as well as canonization*, beatification*, and veneration* of relics*. It was composed of some 20 cardinals divided into three sections. In 1969 the congregation was divided into a Congregation for the Causes of Saints* and a Congregation for Divine Worship.

Ritschl, Albrecht (1822–1889) German Protestant theologian. He began his career in 1848 as a student of the Tubingen School, but by 1857 he had completely abandoned it. Ritschl's theology differentiated religious experience from every other form of experience because God is apprehended by faith, not reason, and faith rests not on intellectual or philosophical assumptions but on value judgments. He further taught that Christ's redemptive work was directed to the church and that personal salvation* and justification* are achieved in and through the community. The goal of the kingdom of God* is to fully integrate all of humanity in it. The kingdom of God* is primarily social, and the individual cannot experience salvation outside the church as a community of believers. He rejected the concept of the penal wrath of God and Christ's death on the cross as a propitiation*.

Ritschl's chief works were *Das Evangelium Marcions und das kanonische Evangelium des Lukas* (1846), *Die Entstehung der altkatholischen Kirche* (1858), *The Christian Doctrine of Reconciliation and Justification* (3 vols., 1870–1874), *Die christliche Volkommenheit* (1874), *Die Christliche Lehre von der Rechtfertigung und Versohnung* (3 vols., 1870–1874), *Geschichte des Pietismus* (3 vols., 1880–86), *Theologie und Metaphysik* (1881), *Gesammelte Aufsatze* (2 vols., 1893–1896), and *Instruction in the Christian Religion* (1901). The theology that grew out of his teachings, called Ritschlianism, in-fluenced many succeeding theologians, such as Adolf Harnack*, Ernst Troeltsch*, Julius Kaftan, William Herrmann, and Ferdinand Kattenbusch.

ritual 1. Properly, the prescribed words of a liturgical function. 2. The accompanying ceremony.

ritual masses Masses for use when sacraments* are included in the Eucharist*, as at baptism*, confirmation*, ordination, and weddings.

Rituale Romanum Official service book of the Roman Rite* containing prayers and formulas for administering sacraments* other than the Mass* and the Divine Office*. The first edition appeared in 1614.

ritualism 1. Emphasis on religious ceremony, often in a derogatory sense. 2. Movement in the Church of England* to restore Catholic forms of worship.

Ritus Servandus Former name of *Instructio Generalis* attached to the Roman Missal, containing ceremonial for the Mass.

River Brethren European Mennonites* and Anabaptists* who fled to the United States in the seventeenth century and settled by the Susquehanna River in Pennsylvania, led by John and Jacob Engle. They are divided into Brethren in Christ*, Old Order Brethren, and the United Zion Church. Members practice foot washing and triune immersion*.

Robber Synod See EPHESUS, ROBBER COUNCIL OF.

Robbia, Luca Della See DELLA ROBBIA, LUCA.

robe Garb worn by clergymen*. Its color and shape are determined by the status and rank of the wearer.

Robert, St. (c. 1027–1111) Abbot of Citeaux* and Molesme. He founded a monastery at Molesme based on the strictest Benedictine principles, but left it in 1098 to found the famous house at Citeaux, which became the mother house* of the Cistercian Order. Robert returned to Molesme in 1100. Feast day: April 29.

Roberts, Evan John (1878–1951) Welsh revivalist*. A blacksmith and coal miner in his youth, he experienced visions and an intense outpouring of the Holy Spirit*. In 1904 he began to hold prayer meetings* at his home church. These meetings sparked a revival* that swept across Glamorganshire. The fervor of the Holy Spirit* that fell upon the crowds was spontaneous, and the people prayed, testified, confessed, or sang as the Spirit moved them. Soon Roberts extended the meetings to other parts of Wales. The revival is said to have led to over 100,000 conversions. But the physical stress of the campaigns broke Roberts, and he retired from public life.

Roberts, Granville Oral (1918–) American Pentecostal evangelist and university founder. Healed of tuberculosis during services held by George Moncey in 1935, he became an evangelist in 1936. In 1947 he received the gift of healing and started an independent program which eventually became the Oral Roberts Evangelistic Association in 1948. For the next several decades he traveled around the country and the world holding healing services. He made early use of radio and expanded into television in 1954. He started Oral Roberts University in 1965 and expanded it in the 1970s to include graduate-level programs in medicine and law. The university incorporates a City of Faith and a Prayer Tower. In 1968 Roberts joined the United Methodist Church. That same year he stopped holding evangelistic meetings, although his television specials continued.

Robertson, Archibald Thomas (1863–1934) American Baptist scholar in Greek and New Testament. He established his scholarly reputation with 45 books, including grammars, commentaries, and historical and biographical studies. He is best known for his *Grammar of the Greek New Testament in the Light of Historical Research* (1914), *A Harmony of the Gospels* (1922), *An Introduction to Textual Criticism* (1925), and *Word Pictures of the New Testament* (1930).

Robertson, Marion Gordon "Pat" (1930–) American Christian educator and televangelist. He was ordained in the Southern Baptist ministry soon after conversion and thereafter established himself as a Charismatic leader. After seminary Robertson purchased in 1959 a small UHF television station in Norfolk, Virginia, which eventually became the Christian Broadcasting Network*. Over the years, he has established other organizations to advance the cause of Charismatic Christianity: Regent University, founded in 1978, and Operation Blessing, a worldwide humanitarian relief agency, founded in 1978. He is also the host of the television talk show, "700 Club" (1968–), which made him one of the best known personalities in American media. To mobilize Christians as an influential bloc in public life, he established the Christian Coalition in 1989. He is the author of numerous books, including *Shout It from the Housetops* (1972) and *The Secret Kingdom* (1982).

Robinson, John Arthur Thomas (1919–1983) Anglican theologian and bishop. As suffragan bishop of Woolwich, he published the highly controversial yet popular *Honest to God* (1963). Many of his heterodox ideas were drawn from Tillich*, Bultmann*, and Bonhoeffer*.

Roch/Rocco, St. (c. 1295–1327) Healer. During an outbreak of plague in northern Italy, he cured many people by the sign of the cross. A miraculous cross was discovered on his body after his death. He is invoked against plague, and his relics* in Venice* are venerated. Feast day: August 16.

rochet White surplice-like linen vestment with either close-fitting or loose sleeves.

rock In religious art, the symbol of St. Peter* according to Matthew 16:18.

Roermond Cistercian convent in Roermond, Netherlands, founded by Count Gerhard V of Geldern in 1224. The convent was entirely rebuilt in the nineteenth century by the architect P. G. H. Cuypers in neo-Gothic* style.

Rogate Fifth Sunday after Easter*.

rogation Litany of prayer.

Rogation Days Also, Rogationtide. Special days of prayer for three days before Ascension Day* when prayers are offered for the harvest, the fruits of the earth, and the work of human hands.

Rogation Sunday Sunday before Ascension Day*.

Rogers, John (c. 1500–1555) Editor of Matthew's Bible* and first English Protestant martyr* under Mary. In 1537 under the name of Thomas Matthew he published the first complete version of the Bible in English, known therefore as Matthew's Bible*. For preaching Protestant doctrine, he was burned at Smithfield.

Rolduc Abbey in Rolduc, in the Netherlands, founded in 1104 by Albertus of Antoing. The triple-naved Romanesque basilica* was consecrated in 1108 but destroyed by a fire in 1123. It was rebuilt and reconsecrated in 1209. There were later additions in the thirteenth and seventeenth centuries. Nothing is left of the convent, but most of the nineteenth- and twentieth-century additions remain.

roll Written list of names of church members kept by a local church.

Rolle, Richard (1295–1349) Hermit. He was noted not only as a mystic but as one of the first religious authors to write in English as well as Latin. Among his many popular books were *Meditations on the Passion* and *The Forme of Perfect Living*. He had great influence on the Lollards*.

Roman Breviary Form of the Daily Office for the Roman Catholic Church, published in 1570 and in use until replaced by the Liturgy of the Hours in 1970.

Roman Catechism Properly, *Catechismus ex Decreto Concilii Tridentini* (1566), a doctrinal exposition of creeds*, sacraments*, and prayers for the use of parish priests issued under papal authority.

Roman Catholicism Apostolic faith taught by the Roman Catholic Church headed by the pope as the vicar* of Christ, the supreme pontiff* and the patriarch* of the West. It regards itself as the custodian of the deposit of truth handed down directly from Jesus Christ through St. Peter* in an unbroken line of succession. On the doctrinal side, this truth is enshrined in the canons of the ecumenical councils as well as the Council of Trent* and the two Vatican councils of modern times. It upholds the orthodox and biblical doctrines regarding the Trinity*, Incarnation*, and salvation*, and it prides itself on having defended the gates of faith vigilantly for 2000 years. It is an exclusive faith that proclaims that there is no salvation outside the church. It also encompasses special extra-biblical doctrines regarding the structure and rights of the church, the intercession of the saints* and Virgin Mary*, and the functions of the pope and the councils.

Roman Catholicism is built on an episcopal* system of government in which the supremacy of the pope and his infallibility in matters of faith and doctrine are fundamental. Pope Paul VI* defined the Roman Catholic Church as "Christ's extension and continuation . . . a single complex reality, the compound of a human and a divine element." Hence the church is incapable of sinning or being wrong in belief. The function of the hierarchy* is to mediate the seven sacraments* that govern the entire life of Roman Catholics from birth to death. The major sacraments include baptism*, Eucharist*, confirmation*, holy orders*, penance*, extreme unction*, and matrimony*. In addition, there are other symbolic rites known as Sacramentals and traditional extra-liturgical* exercises, such as the Benediction of the Blessed Sacrament, the Rosary*, and the Stations of the Cross*. Saints play a large role in the liturgical calendar of the Catholic Church, and numerous canonizations* are added to the calendar every year. Sacraments are the channels through which the grace* of God flows to the recipient. When administered with the right intention, in the right form and using the right matter, they work *ex opere operato**, that is, without reference to the communicant or the celebrant.

The focal point of the traditional Roman Catholic worship is the Mass*, which is viewed as a propitiatory sacrifice of Christ. Catholics believe in transubstantiation* in which the substance of the bread and wine become in fact the body and blood of Christ. Priesthood is a sacred ministry and priests are shepherds who alone have the right to offer sacrifice and forgive sins. Next to the priesthood, religious orders constitute the bulwark of the church. They range from well-known multinational orders like Jesuits*, Dominicans*, and Franciscans to lay congregations like Little Brothers and Little Sisters. The sacrament of penance* is tied to the auricular confession* of sins to a priest. Sins may be mortal or venial, and their expiation* requires absolution* and the imposition of penance which may be commuted through indulgences* in which the benefits of a heavenly treasury of merit* may be set to the sinner's account even after death. Catholics believe in purgatory* as a preliminary purification for heaven*.

The most prominent feature of Roman Catholicism is the cult of the Virgin Mary*. Mary was not only conceived without sin, but she ascended bodily into heaven where she sits as a co-mediatrix* and coredemptrix*. Devotion to Mary is one of the most popular and universal of Catholic exercises.

Since the Second Vatican Council*, a process of renewal, called *aggiornamento**, has brought incremental reforms into a church set in the rock of tradition. Pope John XXIII*, in his opening address to the Second Vatican Council, said that while "the substance of the ancient doctrine of the deposit of faith is one thing, the way it is presented is another." There is also a strong ecumenical interest in the emerging New Catholicism which views non-Catholics as separated brethren rather than heretics. The vernacular has been introduced in many countries into liturgical worship and the Missal* and the Breviary* have been made more relevant to the needs of modern believers. Renewal is also evident in the toleration, and even encouragement, of Charismatic Catholicism, in which Pentecostal practices are adopted without change in a Catholic setting. There is a strong emphasis among Catholic Charismatics on baptism in the Spirit and speaking in tongues* and healing without giving up traditional devotions to the Virgin Mary* and the saints*.

Roman Catholicism is found among all but a dozen of the 191 countries of the world. Brazil is the largest Catholic country. Roman Catholic worship remains warm and devout, although it is designed with the priest in mind rather than the congregant. A corpus of rubrics dictates every movement and word of the celebrant. What is lacking in liturgical worship is made up for by a great variety of popular devotions, expositions of the Blessed Sacrament*, the rosary*, and processions of the Stations of the Cross*. The earthly liturgy is considered the counterpart of the heavenly. It is the summit of the church's activity and the manifestation of all its power.

Roman collar Stiff clerical collar* fastened at the back of the neck.

Roman Congregations Executive departments of the Roman Curia* responsible for the administration of the Roman Catholic Church. Established by Sixtus V* in 1588, their original number of 14 was reduced to 11 in 1917 and nine in 1967. The principal congregation is the Holy Office*, now styled Congregatio de Doctrina Fidei. Each congregation comprises cardinals under a cardinal prefect assisted by a group of diocesan bishops and a panel of consultors. Its official organ is the *Acta Apostolicae Sedis**.

Roman Martyrology Official martyrology* of the Roman Catholic Church compiled by a commission of ten scholars and issued in 1584 by Gregory XIII*.

Roman Psalter Text of the biblical Psalter, believed to have been produced by Jerome*, used in Roman churches until the time of Pope Pius V* when it was replaced, except at St. Peter's*, Rome, by the Gallican Psalter*.

Roman Rite Roman Catholic Liturgy*.

Romanos, St. (c. 540) "Melodus." Greek religious poet and composer of kontakion*, the metrical sermon chanted to music. He composed over 80 kontakions, many of them considered gems of literature.

Rome "The Eternal City." City in Central Italy in the compartimento of Latium, the capital of Italy, including the independent state of Vatican City, the center of the Roman Catholic Church. It is situated on both banks of the Tiber River about 15 miles from its mouth. The papal quarter, known as the Leonine, including Vatican City, is on the right bank. Rome has over 400 churches, of which St. Peter's*, built 1506–1526, is the preeminent one. There are several other churches that are places of pilgrimage*: San Giovanni (905) in Laterano; Santa Maria Maggiore* (fourth and fifth

centuries); Santa Croce in Gerusalemme (1743), founded in the fourth century in the imperial palace of St. Helena*; San Lorenzo Fuori le Mura (sixth century) where St. Lawrence* is buried; and San Sebastiano Fuori le Mura (sixth century), on the Appian Way* over the catacombs*; and St. Paul's Outside the Walls*.

Of the other churches, some were erected on ancient foundations and some are early Christian basilicas*: *San Pietro in Vincoli* (c. 400). Also, Basilica Eudoxiana. It contains the tomb of Pope Julius II*, with a statue of Moses by Michelangelo*. *Santa Maria delle Pace* contains the Sibyls of Raphael*. *Santa Maria delle Vittoria* contains the statue of St. Teresa* by Bernini. *St. Agnese* (fourth century), where the lambs that provide wool for the archepiscopal pallia are blessed. *St. Clemente* (twelfth century) in the hands of the Irish Dominicans* *Sts. Cosmas and Damiano* (528), formerly an imperial building built by Vespasian. *St. Francesca Romana* (ninth century) in the Forum. Formerly the Temple of Venus. *The Gesu** (1568–1575), principal church of the Jesuits*, where Ignatius Loyola* is buried. *Sts. Giovanni and Paolo* (fourth century), on the Celian Hill. Here St. Paul of the Cross*, founder of the Passionists*, is buried. *St. Gregorio Magno* (sixth century), on the Celian Hill, close to the site of a monastery established by St. Gregory* the Great.

*St. Maria in Ara Coeli** (fourteenth century), on the site of ancient Roman citadel and the Temple of Juno Moneta. *St. Maria in Cosmedin.* Also, Bocca della Verita (sixth century). On the site of ancient Temple of Fortune. *St. Maria ad Martyres* (seventh century). The first pagan temple in

The City of Rome

Rome to be turned into a Christian church. It contains the tomb of Raphael. *St. Maria Sopra Minerva* (fifteenth century), on the ruins of an

Porta S. Paulo

ancient temple of Minerva. It is the only Gothic* church in Rome. *St. Prassede* (ninth century), on the Esquiline. A column in the Chapel of St. Zeno is believed to be that to which Christ was bound. *St. Pudenziana* (fourth century), near the foot of the Esquiline. A table in the church is believed to be that on which St. Peter* celebrated Mass*. *Sts. Quattro Coronati* (fourth century), where the bodies of the Quattro Coronati are buried. *St. Sabina* (fifth century), on the Aventine, one of the most impressive Roman basilicas*. *St. Stefano Rotondo* (fifth century), on the Celian Hill, not far from the Lateran*. It is the largest circular church in existence and contains the episcopal throne of St. Gregory.

Romero, Oscar Arnulfo (1917–1980) Archbishop of San Salvador. He was ordained priest in 1970 and archbishop of San Salvador in 1977. A conservative when he was named primate*, he turned increasingly liberal and was instrumental in the overthrow of the then dictator, also named Romero. He was assassinated by his enemies in 1980 while celebrating Mass*.

Romuald, St. (c. 950–1027) Born in Ravenna*, the son of a duke, he abandoned the world for the life of a hermit. He moved from place to place, founding small monasteries or hermitages. Emperor Henry II put all the monasteries in the region, including Monte Amiata and Camaldoli, under his control. In art he appears in white robes as a Camaldolensian and in black robes as a Benedictine*.

rood 1. Cross* or crucifix, especially a large one formerly set in stone. 2. Cross or crucifix, built of timber, decorated with carvings and statues, part of the screen* that divides the nave* from the choir.

rood light Oil or taper light placed in front of a rood* in medieval times. Oil with a wick was kept in a rood-bowl or cresset, and the taper was placed on a pricket*.

rood loft Loft or gallery over the rood screen in a medieval church used for a display of the rood and for the reading of the gospel and the epistle.

rood screen Arch, screen*, or latticework separating the nave* or the chancel*.

Rorate Fourth Sunday in Advent*, so called from the first word of the Latin introit* for the day.

Rorem, Ned (1923–) American composer. His church music includes works for the soloists well as for the chorus. Among the former are *A Psalm of Praise, A Song of David* (both 1945), *A Cycle of Holy Songs* (1951), *A Christmas Carol* (1952), and *The Lord's Prayer* (1957). Music for the church choir includes *Miracles of Christmas* (1959), *Praises for the Nativity* (1970), *Praise the Lord O My Soul* (1982), unaccompanied choral works as *Christ the Lord Is Risen Today* and *Sing My Soul of His Wondrous Love* (1955), *O Magnum Mysterium* (1978), and *Three Christmas Choruses* (1978). Also com-

Rood Screen

posed for church service are *Prayers and Responses* (1960), *Proper for the Votive Mass of the Holy Spirit* (1966), *Canticles* (1971), and *Missa Brevis** (1974).

Rosary (Lat., rose garden) 1. String of 150 small beads and 15 larger ones divided into 15 sets used by Catholics in prayer. Each set of beads represents a mystery on which to meditate as the prayers are recited. 2. Prayer in which 15 decades of Hail Marys* are recited, each decade* being preceded by the Lord's Prayer* and followed by the Gloria Patri*. Five decades make a corona* or chaplet*, the third part of the Rosary. It is comparable to the Jesus Prayer* in the Eastern Church*. It is called kombologion or komboschoinion in Greek and vervitza, chotki, or liestovka in Russian.

Rosary Confraternity Dominican brotherhood* for the propagation of the Rosary*.

Rosary, Servite Rosary* used in the Servite Order with seven sections in memory of the Seven Sorrows* of the Blessed Virgin Mary*.

rose In Christian art, symbol of purity or martyrdom.

Rose, Mystical Emblem of the Virgin Mary* with five or seven petals to signify her joys.

Rose of Lima, St. (1586–1617) Peruvian Dominican nun, the first saint* to be canonized in the Americas. She is the patroness of South America and the Philippines.

Rose Window

Rose window Circular window, the mullions of which form petal-like openings, usually found in the west front of Gothic* cathedrals. So called because of its likeness to the rose and its petals. Its size increased in the middle of the twelfth century with the development of Gothic architecture. The largest examples extend over the entire width of the nave* and always under a circular arch.

rose without thorns In Christian art, symbol of the Virgin Mary*.

Rosminians The Fathers of Charity, founded in 1828 by Antonio Rosmini-Serbati (1797–1855), who engage in works of charity, teaching, preaching, and literary pursuits. There are two grades, presbyters and bishop coadjutors*. A women's branch, the Sisters of Providence, was founded in 1831/32.

Rossano Gospels Sixth-century manuscript now in Rossano Cathedral, Calabria, Italy, written in Greek

Rossano Gospels

in gold and silver letters on purple vellum. It contains nearly all of Matthew and Mark. There are 15 illuminated pages, three of which are full page.

Rossetti, Christina Georgina (1830–1894) Younger sister of Dante Gabriel Rossetti* and Maria Francesca Rossetti. A member of the Pre-Raphaelite Brotherhood, she wrote many poems that deal with Christian subjects and express deep Christian faith. She also wrote Christian books, among them *Seek and Find* (1879) and *Time Flies: A Reading Diary* (1885).

Rossetti, Dante Gabriel (1828–1882) Painter, poet, and cofounder of the Pre-Raphaelite Brotherhood. In the early period of his life, his poetry abounded with Christian themes, expressing devotion to the Virgin Mary*. Of his paintings *The Girlhood of Mary Virgin* (1849) and *Ecce Ancilla Domini* (1850) convey the magic and spiritual beauty of medieval art.

Rostock Massive three-aisled Marienkirche in Rostock, Germany, built in the thirteenth century. The church had 40 altars. Nothing of the old cathedral survives.

Rosy Sequence Part of the hymn, "Jesu, Dulcis Memoria,"* used as a sequence for the Feast of the Name of Jesus* in the Sarum Gradual.

rota Appeal tribunal for judging cases brought before the Holy See*.

Rotislav (d. 870) Prince of Moravia, considered the founder of the Czech and Slovak Orthodox Church. He invited the brothers, Cyril and Methodius*, to Greater Moravia from Constantinople* in 862. Their efforts were opposed by the Roman Catholic German clergy who, after the death of Cyril, had Rotislav tortured and executed.

Rouault, Georges (1871–1958) French painter who restored the stained-glass windows of Chartres*. His Christ figures, especially the long series of the Holy Face, the Crucifixion, and Christ Mocked, have a rough, muted dignity that make him one of the most important religious artists of the twentieth century. Some of his stained-glass windows are at the church at Plateau d'Assay, near Chamonix.

Rouen City in France, the seat of a bishop since the third century. It has one of the most beautiful cathedrals in France. Work on the cathedral began in the thirteenth century and was completed in the sixteenth century. It has seven towers including the Tour Romain on the north end, the Butter Tower on the west front, four towers on the corners of the transepts*, and the central tower above the crossing*.

royal doors 1. Central doors leading from the narthex* into the nave* of a Byzantine church. 2.

The holy doors* or the beautiful gates in the middle of the iconostasis*.

Royaumont Cistercian abbey at Royaumont, France, founded by St. Louis in 1228. The monastic buildings were erected in the thirteenth century. The abbey church is now in ruins.

r'shom koso In the Syrian Uniat Church, Liturgy of the Presanctified* celebrated on Good Friday* morning and on the weekdays of Lent* after vespers*.

RSV Revised Standard Version*.

Rubens, Sir Peter Paul (1577–1640) Flemish painter of the Counter-Reformation*. In Rome* in 1606 he painted the altarpiece for the Chiesa Nuova. Returning to his native Antwerp, he was appointed court painter to the Spanish governors of the Netherlands. His first great commissions were for the Antwerp Cathedral—the *Raising of Lazarus* (1610) and *Descent from the Cross* (1611–1614). Thereafter he painted traditional subjects: *St. Ignatius Loyola Healing the Possessed* (1619), *Adoration of the Magi* (1624), *Mystic Marriage of St. Catherine* (1628), *Assumption* (1626), *Last Judgment* (1616), *Christ and Doubting Thomas* (1613–1615), *Flight into Egypt* (1614), and *Lamentation over the Dead Christ* (1614). His decoration for the Jesuit church in Antwerp consisted of 39 ceiling paintings, commissioned in 1620. They were lost when the church burned down in 1718. Many of his large compositions were engraved and widely disseminated.

Rublev, Andrei (c. 1360/70–c. 1430) Russian monk and artist. His icons and frescoes adorn the Cathedral of the Annunciation in the Kremlin and the Cathedral of the Dormition in Vladimir*. His *Ascension* and *Trinity* are in the Tretyakov Museum in Moscow*. About 1400 he moved to the Andronikov Monastery and worked as an assistant to Theophan the Greek.

rubric Ceremonial or ritual direction printed in red at the beginning of service books or in the course of the text.

Rufina Kokoreva (1872–1937) Russian monastic

founder and miracle worker. She entered the Pokrov Convent of Verkhoturie in 1900 and in 1911 was appointed abbess of a convent in Cherdyn. In 1919 she and her nuns along with 150 orphans were evacuated by the White Army, and she moved to Manchuria in 1923. Here she established the Convent of the Tikhvin Mother of God in Harbin in 1924, followed by another convent in Shanghai in 1927.

Rufinus (fourth or fifth century) "The Syrian." Palestinian presbyter* and author of the treatise *On the Faith*. He taught that infants were baptized not for forgiveness but to inherit the kingdom and that Adam might have become immortal had he not fallen. He opposed Origenism* and influenced the beginnings of Pelagianism*.

Rufinus, Tyrannius/Turranius (345–411) Monk and historian. Generally, Rufinus of Aquileia. He was a friend of some of the most notable Christians of his day, including Jerome*, Melania the Elder*, and Didymus the Blind*. Although a writer in his own right, he is best remembered for his translations. His most important translation was that of Origen's *De Principiis,* the only complete text of Origen now surviving. It was a vindication of Origenism* that brought him into conflict with Jerome. He also translated some works of Basil the Great* and Gregory of Nazianzus*, the *Historia Monachorum*, and the *Ecclesiastical History* of Eusebius*. His Commentary on the Apostles' Creed is the earliest continuous Latin text of the Apostles' Creed* as used at Rome*.

rule (Lat., *regula,* norm, measure) Regulations prescribed for the daily life and conduct of members of religious communities. Many rules were named after the saints* who founded the great religious orders. The Rule of St. Pachomius was written for the monks of the Egyptian desert, and it prescribed strict, almost military discipline, hard manual labor, and constant study of the Scriptures. All monks in the Orthodox tradition follow the Rule of St. Basil* as modified by St. Theodore of Studios*. In the Roman Catholic tradition, there are three main rules: The Rule of St. Augustine* is followed by the Austin Friars*, the Augustinian Canons*, Dominicans*, and Servites*. The Rule of St. Benedict* set the pattern for Western monasticism* and was adopted by Benedictines*, Camaldolese*, Cluniacs, and Vallumbrosans*. It enjoins strict obedience to the abbot or abbess, the Opus Dei*, abstinence from meat, and a day divided between manual work, prayer, and study. The original Rule of St. Francis, written by St. Francis in 1209 and approved by Pope Honorius* in 1223, enjoins chastity*, obedience, and communal poverty. Carmelites*, Carthusians*, and Jesuits* follow their own constitutions.

rule of faith Doctrinal standard adopted by a denomination, generally expressed as a creed*. In particular, a summary of church teaching as handed down by the apostles presented by early Christian writers, such as Irenaeus*.

ruler Former name of choir leaders in cathedrals.

Ruotsalainen, Paavo (1777–1852) Finnish Pietist leader, one of the greatest in Finland's church history. He united the two branches of Pietism*, thus making it a powerful force for revival.

rural dean In the Church of England*, the bishop's deputy in the deanery*.

rushma In the Assyrian Rite, the seal on the eucharistic bread.

rushmo In the Syrian Rite, consignation of the consecrated bread following the fraction*. Each portion of the broken bread is partially dipped in the chalice* and anointed.

Russell, Charles Taze (1852–1916) Founder of Jehovah's Witnesses*. His theological opposition to the doctrines of the Trinity* and eternal punishment* led him to form the Jehovah's Witnesses as a sect* to promote his heretical ideas. He was also obsessed with fixing a date for the Second Coming*, which he asserted would be in 1884 and, when that did not materialize, in 1914. He was proved wrong both times. In 1884 he set up Zion's Watchtower Tract Society in Pittsburgh to produce literature for his followers. The sect's theology is contained in the six volumes of his *Studies in the Scriptures* (1886–1904) plus a seventh volume on the Revelation.

Russian Orthodox Church National church of Russia, an independent Eastern Orthodox Church* dating from the conversion of Prince Vladimir* of Kiev* in 988. Its traditions are drawn largely from the Greeks. The first Greek missionaries to the Slavs, Cyril and Methodius*, devised the so called Glagolitic* alphabet, the forerunner of the Cyrillic* alphabet used in Russia today. Cyril's translations laid the foundation for Old Church Slavonic* used in the Russian Liturgy. For the first 700 years as a Christian nation, Russia borrowed heavily from Greek theology and patristics*. The centuries-long isolation of Russia from the outside world was felt even more by the Russian Church. The first original Russian spiritual writer was Ilarion, the Greek metropolitan* of Kiev* (1037–1054), who produced a confession* of faith. The fall of Constantinople* to the Turks in 1453 had the beneficial effect of energizing the Russian Church. Moscow* took on the mantle of Byzantium* as the "third Rome"* and Russian rulers took the title of Tsar (from Caesar), and appropriated the Byzantine double eagle*.

The patriarchy of Moscow was established in 1589. In 1581 Prince Konstantin Ostrozhsky (1526–1608) brought out the Ostrog Bible*, the first complete Bible in Slavonic. After the sixteenth century, Protestant influences began to penetrate Russia and received a mixed reaction. On the one hand, it stimulated the real flowering of Russian Orthodox theology in the nineteenth century, but on the other it offended Russian nationalistic sensibilities. In the seventeenth century, Peter Mogila* wrote the great *Confession of Faith* that is considered a landmark in Russian church history. It was translated and revised by Melitios Syrigos (d. 1667), and was accepted in this form at the Synod of Jassy* in 1643. Mogila also published a *Small Catechism* and a liturgical handbook called *Euchologion,* both containing traces of Protestant doctrines.

Tsar Peter the Great (1682–1721), in his efforts to promote the westernization of Russia, directed theologian Feofan Prokopovich to draft a new church constitution. Called the *Ecclesiastical Regulations,* the new constitution of 1721 abolished the patriarchate* and created the Holy Synod* in its stead, thus bringing the church thoroughly under imperial control. In 1765 the first theological work in Russian appeared. Called *Orthodox Teaching, or a Brief Christian Theology,* it was written by Platon Levshin. But the greatest influences on the Russian church during this period were not those of theologians but of monks and ascetics, who branded the Russian religious mind forever with their mysticism, sanctity*, and spirituality*. Two monks stand out: St. Tikhon of Zadonsk* and Paisssi Velichkovski. Velichkovski gave a new impetus to the Hesychastic tendencies in the Orthodox Church by publishing the devotional handbook, the *Philocalia,* in Slavonic, which popularized the Jesus Prayer*.

The nineteenth century was the golden age of Russian Orthodoxy, exemplified by St. Seraphim*

Church Kizhi

Millennium of Russian Orthodox Church

of Sarov, Metropolitan Filaret, and theologian Aleksei Khomyakov*. Khomyakov inspired the Slavophil movement which is still strong in Russia. Contributing to the Orthodox renaissance were writers like Dostoevsky* and theologians and philosophers like Vladmir Solovyov* and Nikolai Berdyaev. The Russian Revolution of 1917 virtually wiped out the Orthodox Church. Thousands of churches were destroyed or desecrated, hundreds of thousands of priests were killed or exiled, and Christian theological works were suppressed. Yet the church survived seventy years of barbaric persecution and has been restored to its former place at the center of Russia's national life.

Ruthenian Churches Uniat churches* in Polish Galicia, Slovakia, and Hungary with smaller communities in the United States, Canada, Brazil, and Argentina. The Ruthenian Liturgy is based on the Byzantine Rite* with certain Latin modifications.

Ruysbroeck, Jan van, Blessed (1293–1381) Properly, Ruusbroec. Dutch mystic. In 1343 he retired to a hermitage near Brussels where he was joined by others. In 1350 this community became a com-munity of canons regular* with Ruysbroeck as prior* and was transformed within a few years into the celebrated devotio moderna* with which were associated the Brethren of the Common Life* and the Canons Regular* of Winchester*. His many devotional works, written in powerful Flemish, have been translated into many languages. They include *Spiritual Espousals, The Kingdom of the Lovers of God, The Book of Supreme Truth, The Mirror of Eternal Salvation, The Seven Steps of the Ladder of Spiritual Love, The Sparkling Stone,* known also as *The Treatise of the Perfection of the Sons of God,* and *The Book of the Spiritual Tabernacle.* He was beatified in 1908. Feast day: December 2.

Ryrie, Charles R. (1925–) Dispensationalist leader. As a professor at Dallas Theological Seminary* and later the Philadelphia College of the Bible, he attacked neo-Orthodoxy* and promoted dispensationalism*. Among his literary output, the most important works are *The Basis of the Premillennial Faith* (1953), *Biblical Theology of the New Testament* (1959), *Balancing the Christian Life* (1969), and the *Ryrie Study Bible* (1976).

Ss

SA Salvation Army.

sa'aure (lit., visitors) In the Assyrian Church*, clergy not ordained as bishops but with jurisdiction over many parishes.

sabanon In the Byzantine Church*, linen cloth worn by a bishop to protect his vestments against spills.

Sabas, St. (439–532) Hermit and monastic founder. He entered a monastery at the age of eight. From 457 he lived as a hermit in a desert between Jerusalem* and the Dead Sea, and founded a large lavra* (now called Mar Saba). As his fame spread, he founded a number of monasteries. He was a defender of the orthodox faith against Origenism* and Eutychianism*. Feast day: December 5.

Sabbatarianism Doctrine that the Fourth Commandment is a moral law that applies to Christians and that the Jewish laws against the secular use of the Sabbath apply to Sunday for Christians. Strict observance of Sundays was a characteristic feature of Puritanism* and many forms of Protestantism*. The Lord's Day Observance Society was formed in 1831 to enforce the cessation of secular activities on the day set apart for the Lord.

Sabellianism Also, Modalistic Monarchianism*; Patripassianism*. Third-century heresy propounded by Noetus of Smyrna, his disciple Epigonus, Sabellius, and Praxeas*. Sabellianism was an attempt to solve the contradictory problem posed in maintaining both the unity of God and the divinity of Christ. It held that there were not really three persons in the Trinity*, but the Son and Holy Spirit* were only temporal modes or manifestations of the one God, who may reveal himself as one or the other. Its implication was that it was the Father himself who suffered on the cross. Because it believed that the Father suffered on the cross, it is also called Patripassianism*. and because it believed that God is strictly unitary, it is called Monarchianism*.

sabori In the Serbian Orthodox Church*, council of elders.

sacco benedetto (Ital., blessed sack) Yellow linen robe with two crosses, and painted over with flames and devils, worn by those going to the stake after condemnation by the Inquisition*. Jews wore a St. Andrew's Cross* in red in back and front.

sacerdotalism (Lat., *sacerdos*, priest) 1. Authority to administer the sacraments* endowed through ordination. 2. Excessive clerical domination in a society. 3. Approach to the ministry of the church in priestly categories.

sacra conversazione (Ital., holy conversation) One of the most popular forms of Madonna* and Child with Saints, perfected in the works of Fra Angelico*, Dominico Venezione, Fra Filippo

Lippi*, Giovanni Bellini*, Titian*, and Raphael*. In this form several saints* or angels* are grouped together around the Madonna* and the Child, some talking or gesturing and some meditative.

Sacra Conversazione

sacra rappresentazione Sacred drama of the Middle Ages the Italian mystery play*.

Sacra Via See VIA DOLOROSA.

sacral (Lat., *sacrum,* sacred) Or or relating to the sacred or that which is set apart for God.

sacrament Action using material means and verbal formulae by which believers partake in, commemorate, or respond to the mystery of Christ and through which he communicates and relates to his people. It is a channel or a sign of grace* or, in the words of St. Augustine*, grace made visible. From early times different views have been held of the relation between the material elements and the spiritual realities they signify, of the number of sacraments, and of the criteria for regarding something as sacraments. By the twelfth century, with Peter Lombard*, theologians accepted as sacraments only those that were explicitly or implicitly instituted by Christ and by this criteria, seven sacraments were acknowledged as meeting the test. They were baptism*, confirmation*, Eucharist*, penance*, extreme unction*, orders and matrimony*. All other symbolic rites came to be called sacramentals. Three of the sacraments—baptism, confirmation, and orders—have a permanent effect and may not be repeated.

In the Middle Ages, a distinction was made between the matter and the form of the sacraments. Emphasis was laid on the right intention, without

which, the act ceases to be efficacious, although official Catholic teaching is that the validity* of the sacraments is independent of the worthiness or unworthiness of the celebrant or the participant. Since the Second Vatican Council*, there is a growing awareness that sacraments are not mechanical means to holiness*, but evidence of the faithfulness of Christ. Some Protestant traditions, on the grounds that sacrament is not a biblical category, prefer to use the term *ordinance**. Nearly all Protestant churches hold to only two sacraments—baptism and Holy Communion* or Lord's Supper* or Eucharist—as instituted directly by Christ (and hence dominical).

sacrament house Shrine-like receptacle for the reservation* that developed from the aumbry*.

sacrament of reconciliation New name for confession*, officially called penance*.

sacramental In Roman Catholicism*, spiritual sign instituted by the church whose efficacy rests not on the power of the rite itself, but in the power of custom as mediated by the church. Sacramentals include blessing of the holy oils*, sign of the cross, or grace at meals*. Unlike sacraments* which engage the redeeming power of Christ, sacramentals are effective only through the intermediation of the church. Sacramentals are of two classes: those closely associated with sacraments (e.g., the blessing of the ring in marriage) and those connected with social or professional activities (e.g., the blessing of the waters*).

sacramental healing Use of outward signs or symbols in physical healing, including laying on of hands*, anointing with oil and Holy Communion*.

sacramental theology Branch of theology dealing with the administration and value of sacraments. It defines humans as sacramental beings because they are vessels of God's blessing who can attain sanctity* through participation in Christ-ordered sacraments. Christ himself is the primary sacrament*. The church is a sacrament in so far as it is the believer's connection to the holy. In this sense the church is a continuation of the Incarnation*. Sacraments and proclamation of the Word are the means by which the church fulfills its divinely ordained function. Both the Roman Catholic and Orthodox churches administer seven sacraments.

sacramentalism Attachment of exaggerated importance to sacraments*, either linking personal salvation* too rigidly to the correct performance of sacramental rituals or viewing sacraments as the primary if not the sole means by which grace* is mediated and received.

Sacramentarians Theologians, such as Zwingli* and Oecolampadius,* who denied the real presence* of Christ in the Eucharist* and maintained that the bread and wine in the Eucharist were the blood and body of Christ only in a sacramental or metaphorical sense. Pejorative word coined by Martin Luther*. Thus, sacramentarianism.

Sacramentary Liturgical book used until the thirteenth century for the celebration of the Mass*. It contained the Canon of the Mass* and the proper collects*, prefaces*, and other prayers used throughout the year, ordination formularies and blessings. It was replaced by the Missal* and Pontifical*.

sacraments, dominical Two sacraments instituted by Jesus Christ in the New Testament: baptism* and the Lord's Supper*.

sacramentum tantum (Lat., the sacrament only) In sacramental theology*, the external sign and symbol, as the bread and wine in the Eucharist*.

sacrarium Basin or sink in the sacristy* used for cleaning the eucharistic vessels and for the disposal of ashes, oil, or water.

sacred (Lat., *sacer,* holy) That which is consecrated and revered as holy or set apart for the use of God or hallowed by association with supernatural manifestations.

Sacred College Former name of the College of Cardinals*.

Sacred Harp American oblong tunebook, compiled by Elisha James King and Benjamin Franklin White, published in 1844 and revised a number of times since. It is the most widely used tunebook, containing a variety of hymn tunes, including Psalms, anthems, and folk tunes.

Sacred Heart of Jesus In the Roman Catholic Church, worship of and devotion to the physical heart of Jesus, traced back to the cult of the wound in the side. The devotion was confined to a small number of mystics until the sixteenth century, when it became a general practice encouraged by the Carthusians*, Jesuits*, and Visitandines. The theological and liturgical groundwork for the devotion was provided by St. John Etudes while the visions of Margaret Mary Alacoque* made the practice universally popular. In 1765 Pope Clement XIII* authorized the Mass* and the office of the feast on the Friday after Corpus Christi*. In 1856 Pius IX* extended the feast to the universal church and Leo XIII* raised it to a double of the first class or the most solemn feast on the Roman calendar and ten years later consecrated all mankind to the Sacred Heart.

Sacred Heart of Mary Devotion to the heart of the Virgin Mary* begun in the seventeenth century by St. John Etudes and closely linked to the cult of the Sacred Heart of Jesus*. An office was authorized in 1857, and in 1942 Pius XII* consecrated the world to the Immaculate Heart of Mary* and established a universal feast on August 22.

Sacred Orders Three primary orders of priest, deacon, and subdeacon.

sacrifice Offering, especially of a live gift to a deity, a practice characteristic of early Judaism as well as many other religions. In the New Testament, the sacrifice of the Paschal lamb* was abolished by the eternal sacrifice of Jesus Christ on the cross (Mark 10:45; 1 Cor. 5:7; Eph. 5:2). The Eucharist* is considered in Catholic theology a sacrifice in some sense, but most Protestants view it as only a sacrifice of praise and thanksgiving. Sacrifices may be propitiatory by which the deity is appeased or they may be expiatory by which the sacrificer's sins are removed or blotted out. Christ's sacrifice is interpreted in the New Testament in language which some people see as propitiatory and others as expiatory.

sacrilege Desecration or irreverent treatment of something sacred or dedicated to God.

sacring bell Also, sanctus bell*. Bell rung at Mass*, especially at the elevation* of the elements* and before Communion.

sacristan Sexton* or church official in charge of the sacristy*.

sacristy Room annexed to a church or chapel for keeping sacred vessels, liturgical books*, a basin for washing hands, a prie-dieu*, and vestments used in divine worship. See also VESTRY.

saddaya In the Syrian Church, a priestly head-covering.

saghavart Cap or crown worn by Armenian priests during the celebration of the liturgy.

saghmos jaschou The Psalm of Dinner Time recited before the Old Testament lesson in the Armenian Liturgy.

Sahak the Great (c. 350–438) Armenian catholicos* from 387. He was the last descendant of Gregory the Illuminator*. His intercession led to the end of the Persian king Yezdegerd's persecution of Christians. In 425 he was deposed for political reasons but continued to have great influence over the Armenian Church. He was active in the creation of the Armenian alphabet and translated the Scriptures into Armenian.

sahal Large golden plate used in the Ethiopian Church* for distributing the Holy Communion*.

Sahdona (seventh century) Also, Martyrius. Bishop of Mohoze and writer, author of *The Book of Perfection,* one of the classics of Syriac* literature.

Sahidic One of the dialects of Coptic, also known as Thebaic. It was the principal literary dialect from the fourth to the tenth centuries and has an extensive body of biblical and Christian literature.

said service Service that is entirely spoken, although with a few hymns, as distinct from a sung service in which the liturgy is sung or chanted.

saint (Lat., *sanctus,* holy) 1. In the New Testament, a believer consecrated to God in Jesus Christ. 2. Person whose life is characterized by intense sanctity and devotion. 3. Person who has attained an exceptional degree of holiness* or spiritual power or who has performed miracles and who has been declared to be one by the church after a process of beatification* and canonization*.

Four Saints

St. Albans English town and see*, known in ancient times as Verulamium, the reputed site of the martyrdom of St. Alban*.

St. Bartholomew's Day Massacre Massacre of French Protestants (Huguenots*) beginning August 24, 1572, that marked the beginning of renewed fighting in the Wars of Religion. The massacre was the result of intense political rivalry between the Protestants led by Gaspard de Coligny and the Catholics led by the Guises and Catherine de Medicis. When an attempt to assassinate Coligny failed, Catherine persuaded her son, King Charles IX, to order the death of all Protestant leaders then in Paris for the wedding of Henry of Navarre. Thousands were slaughtered by the time the killings were halted in October.

St. Davids City in southwest corner of Wales with a Norman cathedral and a Welsh monastery founded by St. David*, the patron of Wales. The

Shrine of St. David was one of the most popular destinations for pilgrims in the Middle Ages.

St. Ephraem Monastery Syriac Orthodox monastery founded in 1894 by Mar Juilus Yeshue Cicek in Glane/Losser near Enschede, Netherlands. It is the seat of the Syriac Orthodox Archdiocese of Central Europe with a large cathedral of the Virgin Mary*.

St. Ephraem Monastery Syriac Orthodox monastery founded by Patriarch Ignatius Zakka I Iwas in Ma'arat Sayidnaya, near Damascus*, in 1996. It houses a theological seminary, the patriarchal residence, a convent, and a youth center.

St. Gabriel Monastery Syriac Orthodox monastery founded in 397 by St. Shmuyel of Eshtin and his disciple Shem'un of Quartmin, near Turabdin, in modern-day Turkey. It is the oldest surviving Syriac Orthodox monastery.

St. Gallen Baroque Benedictine monastery in St. Gallen, Switzerland, founded by St. Gall* (c. 550–645). Between 830 and 867 the imposing monastic complex was built. It consisted of three churches, the Gallus crypt, and St. Michael Chapel with its domed roof. From the end of the ninth century, it was famous for its scriptorium*

St. Gallen Cathedral

and its library whose holdings of 100,000 volumes included the *Psalter Aureum* with its text inscribed in gold. The abbey was rebuilt between 1748 and 1767. The magnificent rotunda has eight massive pillars supporting the smooth-vaulted cupola which is painted with the Holy Trinity*, saints*, and monks—the work of Christian Wenziger. The monastery still houses its famous library.

Saint Hubert Abbey in the Ardennes, in Belgium founded in 687 by Pepin of Herstal. It contains the relics* of St. Hubert*, apostle of the Ardennes. The crypt was consecrated in 1081. In 1526 Saint Hubert was destroyed in a fire and rebuilt in late Gothic* style. Around 1690 the huge basilica* with five aisles stood at the center of a fortified monastery. In 1700 the facade with its two bell towers* was rebuilt in Baroque style by Celestin de Jongh (1726–1760).

St. John's Abbey Benedictine monastery in Collegeville, Minnesota, founded in 1856, an important center of the liturgical movement*. It operates St. John's University, the Liturgical Press, and publishes the journal, *Worship*.

St. Mark's Church See SAN MARCO.

St. Mary Major See SANTA MARIA MAGGIORE.

St. Patrick's Cathedral Premier Roman Catholic church in America, on Fifth Avenue in New York City. It is a Gothic* structure in the form of a Roman Cross.

St. Patrick's Day March 17. When the Irish commemorate St. Patrick* and celebrate their heritage with parades and other festivities.

saint, patron Saint declared as the tutelary guardian of a particular profession or field or one whose aid may be invoked in special circumstances. The Roman Catholic Church has declared many patron saints. (See the Appendixes for a list of these saints.)

St. Paul's Cathedral, London The largest church in England, built about 607. It is 517 feet long, 364 feet high, and covers an area of 3.5 acres. It was destroyed by fire in 1087 and 1666. The present cathedral was built after the second fire by Sir Christopher Wren*, who preserved the classic

St. Paul's Cathedral

style. In the crypt, which is considered to be the largest in Europe, are the Chapel of the Most Excellent Order of the British Empire as well as the tombs of some of the most celebrated Englishmen, including Lord Nelson, Duke of Wellington, and Wren himself.

St. Paul's Outside the Walls, Rome One of the major basilicas* on the Ostian Way* built over the relics* of St. Paul* by Constantine*, rebuilt by Emperor Honorius, destroyed by fire in 1823, and rebuilt again in 1854.

St. Peter's, Rome Sixteenth-century church rebuilt over an older one erected by Constantine* on the site where it is believed that Peter* died and was buried. It is the largest church in the world, 619 feet long and 390 feet high, and contains the remains of 130 popes. The high altar is built over the supposed burial place of St. Peter. Work on the new building began under Pope Nicholas V* in the fifteenth century and was completed in 1614 and consecrated by Urban VIII* in 1626. Six great architects worked on the basilica*: Bramante*, Raphael*, Peruzzi, Sangallo*, Michelangelo*, and Carlo Maderno*. The dome was designed by Michelangelo, and the immense bald-

achino* over the high altar is the work of Bernini*, who also laid out St. Peter's Square in front of the church.

St. Peter's Church

St. Thomas Christians See MALABAR CHRISTIANS.

St. Vladimir's Orthodox Theological Seminary One of the more important theological seminaries run by the Orthodox Church in America in Crestwood, New York. It opened in 1905 in Minneapolis and was transferred in 1913 to Tenafly, New Jersey. After World War II, it moved to new buildings rented from the Union Theological Seminary*, New York City. The arrival from Europe of several outstanding Orthodox scholars, including George P. Fedotov*, Nicholas S. Arseniev, Eugene Spektorsky, Nicholas O. Lossky, Alexander Schmemann*, and John Meyendorff*, helped the development of the seminary as a graduate school of theology. Under the leadership of Georges Florovsky*, who served as dean from 1945 to 1955, a pan-Orthodox theological curriculum was implemented. In 1961 the seminary moved to new buildings in Crestwood, New York.

Saint-Chapelle The pearl of French churches in Paris, built in the thirteenth century by Louis IX. The chapel is divided into an upper and a lower church. Among its special features are the statues of the 12 apostles, of which three have survived. During the French Revolution the church suffered heavy damage. For a while it served as a meeting hall, grain store, and public archives. Since then it has been restored to its pristine greatness.

Saint-Cyran, Abbe de (1581–1643) Birth name: Jean Duvergier de Hauranne. French Jansenist theologian and spiritual adviser. At Louvain he met Cornelius Jansen*, a fellow admirer of St. Augustine*. His defense of Agnes Arnauld led to his imprisonment at Vincennes in 1638. He influenced the Jansenist movement primarily through Mere Angelique and Antoine Arnauld*. He was a devout man whose spiritual ideas resembled those of St. Francis de Sales*, and his reliance on grace* became a standard theme in French devotional literature. John Wesley* translated many of his letters.

St.-Denis Benedictine abbey at St. Denis north of Paris, founded about 625 by Abbot Suger*. It contained the reputed shrine of St. Denis and was one of the richest and most important places of pilgrimage* in France where the kings of France were traditionally buried. Here St. Joan of Arc* hung up her arms in 1429 and Henry IV became a Catholic in 1593. It was dissolved and sacked during the French Revolution but restored under Napoleon III and turned into a national monument.

St.-Germain-des-Pres Famous abbey in Paris on the south bank of the Seine founded in the sixteenth century and named after St. Germanus*. In the seventeenth century it became a Maurist center.

sainthood Quality or condition of being a saint.

Saint-Sulpice, Society of See SULPICIANS.

sakkos In the Eastern Church*, an embroidered liturgical vestment, comparable to the dalmatic*, with side slit sleeves, usually fashioned with tiny bells, worn instead of the phelonion* by all bishops.

salam Also, sh'lomo. (Arab.) Peace, conveyed by a clasp of the hands during the service.

Salamanca City in Spain, known as Little Rome, site of an ancient university and a magnificent cathedral. The old cathedral was built in the twelfth century and a new cathedral was built on it starting in 1513, and not completed until the eighteenth century. Its 361-foot-high tower is modeled on that of Toledo Cathedral. Nicholas Florentino painted the frescoes* on the vaulting*

of the choir depicting the last judgment*, as well as 53 panels on the retable* behind the high altar. In the lower center of the retable is Virgende la Vega, patron saint* of Salamanca.

Salesbury, William (c. 1520–c. 1584) Welsh New Testament translator. As required by the Act of 1563, work began on a translation into Welsh of the *Book of Common Prayer** and the New Testament, with Salesbury in the lead role. It was a great achievement and formed the basis of all subsequent translations.

Salesians Society of St. Francis of Sales*, founded in Turin* by St. John Bosco* in 1859 for the Christian education of poor boys and young men and to train them for the ministry. The society spread to several parts of the world and is now the third largest Catholic order in the world. A sister congregation of Daughters of Our Lady Help of Christians* was founded in 1872 for similar work among girls.

salib (lit., the cross) In the Jacobite Rite, arrangement of the broken consecrated particles* of the bread in the form of a cross.

Salisbury English town, site of an ancient cathedral built in 1266. It is completely dominated by 365-foot tall, narrow windows. Its 394-foot spire*

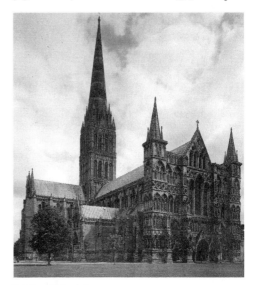

Salisbury Cathedral

is the highest in England. The most beautiful part of the church is the Lady Chapel*, built in 1220, celebrated by the paintings of Thomas Constable.

Salisbury/Sarum Rite A modification of the Roman Rite* used in the cathedral church of Salisbury*. A directory of cathedral statutes, customs, and services was compiled by Richard Poore. By 1457 Sarum was in use throughout England, Wales, and Ireland, and it provided the Reformers with a model for the first *Book of Common Prayer**.

Sallman's "Head Of Christ" This classic example of "Protestant iconography" began as a head-and-shoulders charcoal drawing of Jesus, sketched by American artist Warner Sallman in 1924. Seen on the cover of a denominational magazine, its popularity led to subsequent rendering as an oil painting in 1940. In this form, over 500 million prints have been distributed. A primary archive of Sallman's other works (including "Christ at the Heart's Door," 1942) is at Anderson University, Indiana.

salos Form of asceticism* in which an ascetic presents himself as a holy fool. In Russia, he was known as *yurodivy*.

saltire X-shaped cross on which St. Andrew* was reportedly crucified.

salutary act In Roman Catholic theology, a human action that leads toward justification* or, in the case of those who are justified, an action that contributes to the attainment of a beatific vision*.

salvation 1. Central act in the life of a Christian by which he or she is brought into a right relationship with God through the redemptive grace* of Jesus Christ, forgiven of sins, adopted as the child of God, and given eternal life*. 2. Sum total of the benefits bestowed on believers by God and the full range of divine activity encompassing justification*, redemption*, reconciliation, regeneration*, sanctification*, and final glorification*. It is the gift of God and is entirely wrapped up in the person of Jesus Christ.

Salvation Army International Christian organization for evangelistic and social work, founded by William Booth* in 1865 as Christian Mission in East London. It adopted its present name in 1878. It is organized on military lines with "soldiers"* in standard uniforms and a general* at its head, elected by a high council comprised of commanders and leading officers. The army is divided into national territories, which are, in turn, divided into provinces and divisions. It follows and promotes theologically orthodox, Evangelical, and biblical Christianity, believing in the doctrine of the Trinity*, the salvation* of believers by faith* through grace*, the immortality* of the soul, the Resurrection of the body, final judgment, and a personal holiness* experience which can be subsequent to conversion.

However, the Salvation Army does not observe the sacraments of baptism* or the Lord's Supper*. Outreach* takes place partly through large, open-air meetings with brass bands and banners*. Converts are expected to share their testimony and to repent for their sins. Salvation Army has become the premier Christian relief agency in the world, engaged in all kinds of relief work, care of criminals and alcoholics, as well as providing soup kitchens and night shelters. Its massive social program consists of homes for female victims of white slave traffic, discharged prisoners, and homeless men and women. It also runs inexpen-

Salvation Army Bell Ringer

sive food depots, employment exchanges, missing persons bureaus, farm colonies, soup kitchens, hospitals, home industries, schools, and lifeboats for fishermen.

salvation by grace Doctrine that salvation* is given as a gift of grace* without any merit*, worthiness, or effort on the part of the recipient.

salvation by works Doctrine that salvation* is earned as a result of the recipient's good works* and meritorious acts of piety by which God is pleased.

salvation, order of See ORDO SALUTIS.

salvator mundi (Lat., savior of the world) Devotional image of Christ blessing and, in some instances, holding an orb in his hand.

Salve Regina (Lat., Hail, Queen) One of the oldest and most popular antiphons* to the Virgin Mary*, dating from the eleventh century, used at compline* and after Low Mass*.

salvific That which leads or contributes to salvation*.

Salzburg Austrian city, site of St. Rupert Cathedral built on the initiative of Archbishop Wolf Dietrich von Raitenau and his successor, Marcus Sittikus Count Hohenems. It was completed after the end of the Thirty Years' War. Above the nave* rises the great central dome and the two angular towers with their lantern-topped cupolas. The modern bronze doors were built by Giacome Manzu and Ewald Matare. The cathedral has three altars dedicated to the Resurrection, the vision of St. Francis, and the Miracle of Snows.

samdanion In the Byzantine Rite*, candlesticks on the altar.

Samuel, Mar Athanasius Yeshue Samuel (1907–1995) Syriac Orthodox metropolitan*, the first owner of the Dead Sea Scrolls*. He made his monastic profession at St. Mark's Syriac Orthodox Monastery in Jerusalem* in 1927 and was ordained to the priesthood in 1932. In 1946 he was consecrated as metropolitan* of Jerusalem*. In 1947 he acquired the Dead Sea Scrolls from Bedouin boys who had found them in caves in Qumran*. The event catapulted him into worldwide fame and is retold in his autobiography, *Treasure of Qumran: My Story of the Dead Sea Scrolls* (1967). In 1952 he emigrated to the United States and was named Syriac Orthodox archbishop of the United States and Canada. Beside his autobiography, he has written or edited a number of liturgical publications.

San Juan Capistrano Town in California, site of a historic Spanish mission to which swallows come each year on St. Joseph's Day in spring and depart on the anniversary of the death of St. John Capistrano* in the fall.

San Juan de la Pena Benedictine monastery in Aragon, Spain, located beneath a picturesque overhanging cliff of pink rock on the spot where the hermit Juan built his tiny oratory* in the eighth century. The monastery was a favorite hiding place for Christians persecuted by the Moors. Its single-naved upper church, consecrated in 1094, leads to the tenth-century lower church. The twelfth-century cloister* has an arch of rock as its roof. It includes a fifteenth-century chapel dedicated to St. Victoria and a sixteenth-century San Voto chapel.

San Marco, Venice Basilica San Marco, in St. Mark's Square, Venice*, described by Napoleon as the "drawing room of Europe." It is one of the most celebrated churches in Europe, built in the second half of the eleventh century and consecrated in 1094 to house the relics* of St. Mark*, which had

Basilica San Marco

been brought to Venice from Alexandria*. Known as the Golden Church (Chiesa d'Oro), San Marco is a unique example of Byzantine* architecture arranged in the form of a Greek cross* with five domes. A free-standing campanile* in front of the cathedral is crowned by a statue of the archangel* Gabriel. Within the central arch stand four horses of gilded copper dating from the third or fourth century B.C. and looted from Constantinople* by the Venetians in 1204. The Zeno Chapel has a superb paradise vaulting* with Tintoretto's* mosaic depicting the last judgment*. The mosaics in the interior of the church cover over an acre, and about 500 columns rise from the floor. The golden retable*, Pala d'Oro, in the presbytery, has 80 enamel panels embedded with precious stones.

San Zeno Three-aisled basilica* dedicated to St. Zeno*, in Verona*, Italy, built between 1118 and 1135. The main chapel of choir was rebuilt in the fourteenth century in Gothic* style, and the campanile* on the south side was completed in 1178.

sanbenito Penitential garment ordered to be worn by convicted heretics by the Inquisition*. It was normally yellow with one or two crosses, except in the case of those handed over to the secular authorities to be burned, in which case it was black with painted flames and demons.

Sancta Sophia (Gk., *Hagia Sophia;* Holy Wisdom) Church at Constantinople* dedicated to holy wisdom built under Justinian* by Anthemius of Tralles* and Isidore of Miletus, consecrated in 538. It is a perfect example of Byzantine* architecture. Its chief feature is the enormous dome, pierced by 40 windows, that crowns the basilica*. In 1453 the church was converted into a mosque

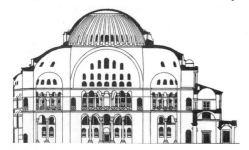

Hagia Sophia

by the Turks and reconverted into a museum in 1935.

sanctification Act, process, or experience of consecration and purification by which a person is made holy and acceptable to God through the supernatural working of the Holy Spirit*. It also involves separation from the impurities and pollution of the world and a renunciation of sins. It is the total process by which the justified are renewed in the spirit. While justification* is Christ for us with the Father, sanctification is Christ in us by the Spirit. Wesley* distinguished between initial sanctification*, which is regeneration*, and entire sanctification*, which is the continual infilling of the Holy Spirit*. Positional sanctification is sometimes designated as an act and progressive sanctification as a process.

sanctity Holiness*, sacredness, or saintliness.

sanctorale Part of a Missal*, lectionary*, or Breviary* containing the variable parts of the Mass* or offices specific to the festivals of particular saints*.

sanctuario (Ital., holy place) Church containing relics* or venerated objects, and thus a place for pilgrimage*.

sanctuary 1. Church building, i.e., the part set apart for the worship of God. 2. Holy space for gathered worship. 3. Portion of a church containing the communion table, altar, pulpit, etc. 4. Asylum in a church or religious building as a right under civil law. Christian sanctuaries were recognized in Roman law in 399 and reaffirmed in 419 and 431. Under Justinian* the right was limited to persons not guilty of major crimes and was available under canon law* and civil law. Henry VIII limited it to seven cities of refuge. The practice was common until the time of the French Revolution.

sanctum sanctorum Holy of holies*, sometimes applied to the altar.

Sanctus Hymn of praise beginning "Holy, Holy, Holy, Lord God of Hosts," sung during the Eucharist*. The Sanctus* and the Benedictus* form part of the eucharistic prayers.

sanctus bell See SACRING BELL.

Sanctus candle In the Roman Catholic Church, additional candle on the epistle side* of the altar, lighted at the Sanctus* and left burning until after Communion.

sandarus Variety of Coptic incense with a strong odor.

Sanday, William (1843–1920) British biblical scholar. He was professor at Oxford from 1882 and held the Lady Margaret chair of divinity from 1895. His major works are: *The Authorship and Historical Character of the Fourth Gospel* (1872), *The Gospels in the Second Century* (1876), *Inspiration* (1893), *Outlines of the Life of Christ* (1905), *Christologies, Ancient and Modern* (1910), and *Personality in Christ and in Ourselves* (1911).

Sandemanians Sect founded by John Glas (hence also known as Glasites*) which flourished from 1725 until 1900. They were named after John Sandeman (1718–1771), Glas's son-in-law. Their doctrinal feature was that the finished work of Christ is all that is needed for salvation*. They practiced infant baptism* and foot-washing*. Strict obedience was enforced (including control over the finances of members), and the disobedient were excommunicated. Some of their doctrines are set forth in Sandeman's book, *Some Thoughts on Christianity* (1762). See also GLASITES.

Ira D. Sankey

Sangallo Family of Florentine architects. **Giuliano** (c. 1443–1516) built Sta Maria delle Carceri at Prato and the Pazzi Chapel, both in Florence*. **Antonio the Elder** (1455–1534) Guiliano's brother, built San Biagio at Montepulciano and Sta Maria dell'Anima in Rome*. **Antonio the Younger** (1485–1546) built most of the Farnese Palace. His design for the rebuilding of St. Peter's* was rejected by Michelangelo*.

Sankey, Ira David (1840–1908) American hymn writer and song leader who shared D. L. Moody's* ministry from 1870. His songs are compiled in *Sankey and Moody Hymn Book*.

Santa Claus Caricature of St. Nicholas of Myra*, an American corruption of the Dutch form of his name, used for the commercial exploitation of Christmas* in modern times. In popular mythology, he is a corpulent old man, decked in red, carrying gifts for children in a sleigh driven by reindeer, one of which is named Rudolph.

Santa Cruce, Florence Franciscan monastery in Florence*, Italy, built between 1295 and 1442. It has the largest of all Franciscan churches. Some of the greatest artists of the time, including Donatello*, Giotto*, and Benedetto da Maiano, contributed to the decoration of the church. The monastic buildings are to the left of the church. The first cloister* was built by Arnoldo di Cambio and the Capella Pazzi by Brunelleschi*.

Santa Maria Maggiore, Rome Basilica* on the Esquiline Hill founded by Pope Liberius*. The present structure was erected under Sixtus III. It is the largest of the 80 churches in Rome* dedicated to the Virgin Mary*.

Santiago de Compostela Celebrated cathedral of St. James* in the northern Spanish city of Compostela, one of Europe's greatest pilgrimage* centers. It is believed to hold the relics* of the apostle, St. James the Elder, who was beheaded in Jerusalem* in 44 and whose bones were brought to Compostela by his disciples Athanasius* and Theodorus. In 813 a small church was built in the place to which a hermit named Pelago was guided by a star. It was replaced by a Carolingian church in the ninth century. In 997 the city and the church were captured and destroyed by the Moorish caliph Al Mansur. Work on a new cathedral started in 1128, and the Baroque facade was completed between 1738 and 1750. The interior is approached through the Portico de la Gloria, the Doors of Glory, on which the figure of St. James* greets every pilgrim*.

Santiago, Order of Military order under the patronage of St. James* founded in 1170 for the expulsion of the Moors and the protection of pilgrims to the Holy Land*. Its constitution and rules followed the pattern of the Templars* with the exception that the knights were allowed to marry.

santo Religious image carved on a panel of cottonwood or pine in the American Southwest.

santo bambino Wooden statue covered with jewels of the infant Jesus in the Church of Santa Maria in Anacoeli, Rome*. Every Christmas eve* the statue is brought from its private chapel next to the sacristy* to a ceremonial Baroque throne before the high altar. During the vigil Mass's *Gloria,* the veil is removed and the statue is paraded to a nativity crib where it receives gifts from the children of Rome until Epiphany*. Carved by a Fran-

ciscan friar* in Jerusalem* in the fifteenth century, it is credited with miraculous works.

Santiago de Compostela Cathedral

sanwartha Amice-like vestment worn by Chaldean and Nestorian bishops and priests.

sapra (Syr., dawn) In the Syrian Church, mattins*.

Saragossa Aragonese town in Spain, site of La Seo Cathedral, also called San Salvador, built between 1190 and 1550. It was built over an early Christian church that had been converted into a mosque under the Moors. The Gothic* figure of Christ on the gilded cupola of the baldachin dates from the twelfth century and the sculptures of the Virgin Mary* and St. John from the sixteenth century. The Capilla Mayor, or principal chapel, has an alabaster altar.

Sardica/Serdica, Council of Council summoned in 343 by emperors Constans and Constantius at the request of Pope Julius* to determine the orthodoxy* of Athanasius*, Marcellus of Ancyra, and Asclepas of Gaza, deposed at the Council of Tyre* in 335. Nearly 170 bishops met in Sardica (the modern Sofia) under the presidency of Hosius* of Cordova, but the synod* was divided from the outset with the 70 or so Easterners refusing to sit

Santa Maria Maggiore

with the Western majority. The synod confirmed the restoration of Athanasius*, acquitted Marcellus of heresy, and restored Asclepas, while at the same time deposing all Arian bishops. It also set the date of Easter* for the following 50 years and reiterated that the hypostasis* of the Father and the Son was one.

sarkavak In the Armenian tradition, a deacon.

Sarum Rite See SALISBURY/SARUM RITE.

sarx (Gk., flesh) Sinfulness as a human condition and as a liability of the flesh (Gal. 5:17, 19; Eph. 2:3).

Satan (Heb., *satanas*, adversary, demon) Chief of the devils and demons. He is referred to in the Bible by several names, such as prince of this world (John 12:31; 14:30; 16:11), adversary (Matt. 4:10; 1 Pet. 5:8), evil one (John 17:15), great red dragon (Rev. 12:3), serpent (Rev. 12:9), abaddon (Rev. 9:11), apollyon or destroyer (Rev. 9:11), beelzebub or lord of the flies (Matt. 12:24), belial (2 Cor. 6:15), god of this world (2 Cor. 4:4), ruler of this world (John 12:31), prince of the power of the air (Eph. 2:2), enemy (Matt. 13:28; 1 Pet. 5:8), tempter (Matt. 4:3), murderer (John 8:44), liar (John 8:44), accuser (Rev. 12:10). His purposes are spelled out in the Bible: he seeks to destroy, dominate, and deceive God's people. In the Book of Revelation, he is finally vanquished by Christ and thrown into the lake of fire* (Rev. 20:2, 10).

satisfaction Full repayment of a debt owed or reparation* for an injury committed, used in reference to the atonement* of Jesus Christ on the cross. In Catholic moral theology*, it is an element of penance* and follows contrition* and confession* toward obtaining absolution*.

Sattler, Michael (c. 1490–1527) Early Anabaptist leader who left the Benedictine* Order to join the Swiss Brethren* in 1525. He presided at the conference at which the German and Swiss Anabaptists* adopted the Schleitheim Confession* of which he was probably the author. Shortly afterward, he and his wife were arrested, tried, condemned, and executed.

saturation evangelism In-depth evangelism.

Saturday of Light In the Coptic Church*, Holy Saturday* when the liturgy is celebrated as on Good Friday* and a procession circles the church while the choir sings the "Song of the Three Children."

Sava, St. (c. 1175–c. 1235) Also, Sabas. Patron saint* of Serbia. Third son of the Serbian monarch Stephen Nemanya, the founder of modern Serbia. He retired in 1191 to Mount Athos*, where his father joined him. Together, they founded the Monastery of Khilandari which became a center of Serbian culture. He returned to Serbia to become the archimandrite* of the monastery of Studenica*. In 1230 he went on a pilgrimage* to

St. Sava

the Holy Land*, where he built the Monastery of St. John at Jerusalem* and a hospice for Serbian pilgrims. He built many churches and organized the autonomous Serbian Church and was consecrated its first archbishop. Feast day: January 14 (Serbian Church).

saved Redeemed from the bondage of sin by the blood of Christ into everlasting life. See SALVATION.

Savigny, Abbey of Monastery founded in 1093 in Savigny, Normandy, by Vitalis of Mortain. As its reputation grew, daughter monasteries were founded in the twelfth century in France, England, and Ireland. In 1147 it was absorbed by the Cistercian Order, although retaining some of its peculiar features, such as wearing the grey habit. It was dissolved during the French Revolution.

Savior In the New Testament, Jesus Christ, the Holy One*, who saves his people from sin and destruction and is the source of salvation*.

Savonarola, Girolamo (1452–1498) Italian reformer. He entered the Dominican Order in 1475 and soon came to be known as a fiery preacher. He became prior* of San Marco*, Florence*, in 1491 and began Jeremiads* against the corrupt state and church of his time. He secured the independence of San Marco from the Reformed Congregation of Lombardy in 1493 and launched a new congregation of which he became the vicar general*. When the French king Charles VIII invaded Italy, Savonarola interceded with him to spare Florence. When the Medici boss of Florence, Piero, left, Savonarola established a republican government similar to that of Venice*. Under his administration, he initiated tax reform, aided the poor, reformed the courts, and turned the fun-loving Florentines into ascetics through stern laws, including censorship. His radical prophecies and condemnations alarmed the Vatican*, and in 1495 he was summoned to Rome by Pope Alexander IV* to explain his incendiary rhetoric. When

Girolamo Savonarola

Savonarola refused, the pope forbade him to preach and also removed him from the position of vicar general* of an independent San Marco.

In 1497 Savonarola was excommunicated, but he declared the excommunication* to be invalid because the pope was not even a Christian, and he continued to defy the pope by preaching. In the same year he published his apologia, *Triumphus Crucis,* defending the authenticity of his revelations. But as he began to lose popular support and the Florentine authorities abandoned him, he was arrested, condemned for schism* and heresy, hanged, and burned at the age of 46. After his death he was venerated by some as a martyr*.

Savoy Declaration The first basic English Congregational* statement of doctrine and church government, produced at a meeting in 1658 in Savoy Palace, London. It is similar to the Westminster Confession* since most of the clergymen who drafted it were also at Westminster. It was the governing document of the New England Congregationalists.

sawdust trail In a revival meeting, lines of those answering a preacher's altar call at the end of the service to commit their lives to Christ and to accept him as their Savior. Term first used by Billy Sunday* with reference to trails of sawdust used by lumberjacks to find their way back to camp from the woods.

Saxon alb White linen vestment, similar to a surplice*, worn over a black robe or talar* at the Holy Communion*. It is a German sleeveless version of the rochet*.

Saxon Confession Protestant confession* of faith drawn up by Philip Melanchthon* in 1551 at the emperor's request to be presented to the Council of Trent*. It followed the main outlines of the Augsburg Confession*. It asserted that the Scriptures were the only foundation of the church, that the Apostles' Creed* was the only sure doctrinal bedrock of the church, and that the sacramental character* of the eucharistic gifts was confined to their use in worship service.

Saybrook Platform Confessional* document produced in 1708 by the Congregational* churches of

Connecticut that reaffirmed the Savoy Declaration* in matters of church polity* and doctrine and replaced the Cambridge Platform* of 1648.

Sayers, Dorothy Leigh (1893–1957) English detective writer and popularizer of theology. During World War II, she was a member of a group that included C. S. Lewis*, Charles Williams*, J. R. R. Tolkien, and Owen Barfield. A medievalist, she produced an impressive translation of the *Divine Comedy**. She established herself as a major Christian writer with a series of plays, of which *The Zeal of Thy House* (1937) and *The Devil to Pay* were for the Canterbury Festival and *The Man Born to Be King* was a radio play on the Life of Christ. *The Mind of the Maker* was a Christian apology that explained the doctrine of the Trinity*.

sayings of Jesus Although used generally of Jesus' teaching, it is used particularly of the extracanonical sayings of Jesus, the *Agrapha,* or the collected sayings of Jesus, the *Logia**, in the Gospel of Thomas* and other documents discovered at Oxyrhynchus*.

Scala Sancta (Lat., holy stairs) Stairway in Rome* said to have been used by Jesus after his trial. It was brought from Jerusalem* by St. Helena*. Pilgrims go up the stairs on their knees.

Scalabrini Fathers Congregation of the Missionaries of St. Charles Borromeo*, founded in Italy in 1887 by John Baptist Scalabrini. The congregation provided priests and established churches and schools for Italian immigrants in America.

scallop Symbol of pilgrimage*, from the scallop shell, known as St. James's Shell, worn on the caps of medieval pilgrims to the tomb of St. James*.

scamnum Seat without back or arms on the epistle side* of the sanctuary for the clergy.

scapular (Lat., *scapulare,* shoulder blades) Monastic garment consisting of a piece of cloth, 24 to 18 inches wide, worn over the shoulders and hanging down in front and behind with its two ends falling almost to the ground. It denotes the yoke of Christ and is worn by the monks at night and when doing manual labor.

Scarlatti, Alessandro (1660–1725) Italian composer. He was the most important Italian composer of oratorios* after Carissimi*. About half of 20 extant oratorios deal with biblical subjects. The remainder of his church music consists of about 80 motets*, 10 masses, a number of cantatas, two Magnificats*, and one Passion*.

Scete, Desert of Region with several salt lakes, west of the Nile Delta, halfway between Alexandria* and Cairo, now known as Wadi-al-Natrun. Macarius the Egyptian settled here in 330, and a monastic community formed around him. From then on, it was the most important Christian monastic center. Four monasteries are still active here: St. Macarius, St. Pshoi, Silurians, and Abraham.

Schaeffer, Francis August (1912–1984) American theologian. He was ordained in the Reformed Presbyterian Church in 1938 and served as pastor in Pennsylvania and Missouri before going in 1955 to Switzerland, where he founded L'Abri Fellowship* which became a Christian retreat* center and think tank. Similar communities developed in four other countries. He defended Evangelicalism* against deviant modern culture and tried to equip Christians in the struggle to survive in an increasingly hostile world. Among his two dozen books were *Escape from Reason* (1968), *Pollution and the Death of Man* (1970), and *How Should We Then Live?* (1976).

Schaff, Philip (1819–1893) American theologian and church historian. Invited in 1844 to become professor of church history and biblical literature in the German Reformed Church Seminary at Mercersburg, Pennsylvania, he became the leading spirit behind the Mercersburg school of theology. In 1870 he moved to Union Theological Seminary*, New York. He was also active in the ecumenical movement*, working through the Evangelical Alliance*. His great legacies are his books, including the *History of the Christian Church* (7 vols., 1858–1892) and *The Creeds of Christendom* (3 vols., 1877). He also edited the *Schaff-Herzog Encyclopedia of Religious Knowledge* (1844), the patristic series known as the *Nicene and Post-Nicene Fathers,* and helped to prepare the American Standard Version* of the Bible. In

1888 he founded the American Society of Church History and served as its first president.

Schall, Johann Adam (1591–1666) German Jesuit missionary to China. He arrived in Macao in 1619 as a Jesuit missionary and succeeded Ricci in Beijing. Through his skills as an astronomer he gained the favor of the first Manchu emperor, who made him the chaplain* of a chapel within the imperial palace. However, he provoked the jealousy and enmity of the courtiers who accused him of being a Portuguese spy. He was arrested but was spared execution by an amnesty.

Scheeben, Matthias Joseph (1835–1888) German Catholic theologian. He was professor of dogma at the Seminary of Cologne from 1860. He developed the doctrine of the supernatural in *Die Herrlichkeiten der göttlichen Gnade* (1863). In *Mysterien des Christenthums* (1865) he tried to build a unified Christian doctrine viewed as a supernatural realm with the Trinity* at its center. His *Handbuch der katholischen Dogmatik* (1873–1887) was a work of profound erudition based on Thomist principles. He was a vigorous defender of papal infallibility*.

Scheffler, Johann (1624–1677) Birth name: Angelus Silesius*. Polish hymn writer. A Lutheran in his youth, his interest in mysticism led him to become a zealous Roman Catholic monk. Most of his hymns were written when he was a Lutheran. They include "Thee Will I Love, My Strength, My Tower" and "O God, of Good th' Unfathomed Sea."

Scheidt, Samuel (1587–1654) German composer. He is one of the first great masters of the organ-chorale, and he wrote many choral concertatos based on Lutheran chorales. His *Tabulatura Nova* (1624) is the first great collection of organ music, and his *Görlitz Tabulaturbuch* (1650) is the first important collection of chorales in four-part harmony.

schema (Gk., dress) Byzantine Rite* monastic habit of monks and nuns. The small schema is the mandyas* or monastic mantle. The great schema is the cross-covered cap or scapular* worn by monastic clergy in Eastern churches*.

schematologion In the Byzantine tradition, a parchment* manuscript.

Schereschewsky, Samuel Isaac (1831–1906) Missionary. Born of Jewish parents in Lithuania, he was converted through reading the New Testament. Emigrating to the United States, he was baptized in a Baptist church, and he joined the Protestant Episcopal Church. From 1859 he served as a missionary in Shanghai, becoming bishop of Shanghai in 1877. Four years later he was struck down with paralysis, but despite this handicap, translated the entire Bible into Wen-li, typing with one finger. He also helped to found St. John's University in 1880.

Schein, Johann Hermann (1586–1630) Early Baroque Lutheran musician who contributed to the development of chorale concertato. He published a chorale book with just the melodies and the continuo bass.

Schillebeeckx, Edward Cornelis Florentius Alfons (1914–) Belgian theologian. He entered the Dominican Order in 1934. From 1958 he was professor of dogmatics and the history of theology in the University of Nijmegen. His writings were investigated several times by the Congregation of the Doctrine of the Faith for challenging Catholic teachings, and he was denied the status of a peritus* at the Second Vatican Council*. His early works explored the many aspects of Christology*, while his later works focused on the existential nature of religious experience and the role of the church in the world. He has also worked on the sacraments*, ecclesiology*, and hermeneutics*. His major works are *Jesus* (1979), *Christ, the Sacrament of the Encounter of God* (1963), *Christ* (1980), *The Church with a Human Face* (1985), and *The Church: The Human Story of God* (1990).

schism (Gk., *schisma*, division) Separation of one church from another generally on nondoctrinal issues. It is disputed whether schism entails loss of orders and affects the validity of schismatic ordination and administration of sacraments; Augustine* argued against the Donatists that the sacraments* could have no saving effect if one remained in schism. Notable schisms in church history include the Donatist Schism, Acacian

Schism*, and Great Schism* between the Latin and the Greek churches and the Avignon* Schism.

Schlatter, Adolf (1852–1938) German Protestant theologian who was a forerunner of Barth*. He held that biblical exegesis* was the only solid foundation for systematic theology*. His writings include *Der Glaube im Neuen Testament* (1885), *Die Theologie des Neuen Testaments* (2 vols., 1909), and *Das Christliche Dogma* (1911).

Schleiermacher, Friedrich Daniel Ernst (1768–1834) German theologian. Although brought up as a Pietist, he rejected traditional Pietism* and adopted a liberal, Romantic attitude toward religion. He was professor of theology and dean of faculty at the new university at Berlin. From 1809 he was minister at Berlin's Dreifaltigkeitskirche, where he preached regularly. His collected sermons fill ten volumes. He also wrote extensively on systematic theology*, hermeneutics*, and philosophy. His chief works were *On Religion* (1799), *The Christian Faith* (1821), *Einleitung ins Neue Testament* (1845), and *Das Leben Jesu* (1846) where he steered clear of both orthodoxy* and rationalism. Rather, he sought to analyze the roots of religious knowledge and experience.

Schleiermacher identified religion with feeling and intuition rather than dogma*. He defined religious experience as absolute dependence on God and sin as an act of presumption and independence. Jesus Christ was portrayed not as God the redeemer, but as a person who, because of his sense of total dependence on God, was able to mediate the redemptive awareness of God to humanity. He focused on man rather than God and on feeling rather than faith*. He was one of the most important influences on the liberal Protestantism* that emerged in the nineteenth century. His ideas were developed by his followers who made up a school known as mediating theology. The Christology* of Adolf von Harnack*, Albrecht Ritschl*, Ernst Troeltsch*, and a number of other liberal theologians was inspired by Schleiermacher.

Schleitheim Confession Confession of faith adopted by the Anabaptists* in 1527. Its seven articles, authored by Michael Sattler*, dealt with baptism*, the Lord's Supper*, church discipline*, ministry, nonresistance, and nonconformity*.

Schmalkaldic Articles Also, Smalcald Articles*. Doctrinal statement drawn up by Martin Luther* in 1537. It consisted of three parts: a statement of the doctrine of the creeds, a section on the office and work of Christ, and a section on 15 doctrines on which further discussion would take place. These include sin*, law, repentance*, ordination* and the call*, the gospel, baptism*, the sacrament* of the altar, the Keys, confession*, excommunication*, celibacy*, the church, justification* and good works*, monastic vows, and human traditions.

Schmemann, Alexander (1921–1983) Orthodox theologian and dean of St. Vladimir's Theological Seminary*, New York. Born in Estonia, he emigrated to the United States in 1951 to succeed George Florovsky* as dean of St. Vladimir's. Through his books, particularly *An Introduction to Liturgical Theology* (1966), *The Historical Road to Eastern Orthodoxy* (1966), and *Eucharist* (1968), he established himself as one of the most prominent Orthodox theologians.

Schola Cantorum (Lat., school for singers) School for training singers to aid Christian worship, first begun in Rome by Pope Gregory I*. Such schools continue to exist as cathedral choir schools.

Schola Cantorum

Scholastica, St. (c. 480–c. 543) Sister of St. Benedict of Nursia* and the first Benedictine* nun. She established a convent at Plombariola, a few miles from Monte Cassino*. She is invoked against storms. Feast day: February 10.

Scholasticism System of Christian theological philosophy and speculation in the Middle Ages often characterized by opposing schools of interpretation and analysis. The major branches of Scholasticism included specifically Christian systems, such as Thomism* and Augustinianism* as well as systems borrowed from elsewhere and given a Christian coloring, such as Averroism and Aristotelianism. It often applied Aristotelian categories to the Christian revelation and attempted to reconcile reason and faith*. The scholastic method of inquiry was to discover the inner unity and truth in all things by applying rules of logic and exposing internal and external contradictions. It tried to open the lid of reality by uncovering the structure of reasoning and language, and by doing so it was a precursor of the humanism that followed on its heels in the sixteenth century.

Originally Scholasticism was a teaching device developed in universities from the eleventh century, and it applied to all branches of knowledge. However, as secular scholars abandoned the method, it became increasingly theocentric* and its scope became more narrowly defined. The greatest Scholastics* were Peter Lombard*, Albertus Magnus*, Alan of Lille, Bonaventura*, Aquinas*, Duns Scotus*, and William of Ockham*. The major schools of Scholasticism included Empiricism, Mystical Scholasticism, Nominalism, and Realism*. After the Reformation*, a Protestant Scholasticism developed and found its full expression in Calvinism*.

scholia Marginal comments on manuscripts, often made by medieval scholars.

schoolmen Teachers of scholastic philosophy at the medieval European universities, known as schools, who were engaged in investigating truth by logical discussion, a method known as dialectic.

schoorchar In the Armenian tradition, the chasuble*, which resembles a Western hoodless cope* but with a tall, stiff, embroidered collar called varkas*.

Schubert, Franz (1797–1828) German composer. His church music hews closely to liturgical texts. Among his best are two settings of the offertory *Salve Regina* for soprano and orchestra (1815,

1819). Three of his unusual religious compositions are *Lazarus* (1820), which Albert Einstein called "a perfect work of art"; a Mass for organ, wind instruments, and a mixed choir; and Psalm 92 in Hebrew for baritone and mixed chorus. He has also created six complete settings of the Mass ordinary and a short *Requiem* (1818). The first four Masses—Mass in F, Mass in G, Mass in B-Flat, and Mass in C—were composed between 1814 and 1816. Mass in A-Flat was composed between 1819 and 1822 and Mass in E-Flat in 1828.

Schuller, Robert Harold (1926–) Televangelist and Reformed Church in America* minister. In 1955 he began a drive-in church in Orange Grove, California, which grew within the next 25 years into the massive Crystal Cathedral*. From 1970 he also began broadcasting over television his Sunday worship service known as the "Hour of Power" which, by the 1980s, had an international audience. He preaches a success-oriented brand of pop theology called possibility thinking (similar to Norman Vincent Peale's* positive thinking*) directed at creating self-esteem. Through his Institute for Successful Church Leadership, he has trained hundreds of pastors and church leaders.

Crystal Cathedral

Schultz-Marasauche, Roger (1915–) French founder and prior* of the Taize community*. After acquiring a house in Taize, near Cluny*, in France he began sheltering Jews and other refugees fleeing the Nazis. In 1944 he was joined by his first brothers*. In 1949 the first seven brothers, all from different Protestant backgrounds, committed themselves for life to communal living and celibacy*. Since 1969 Taize has included Roman Catholics as well. Members, scattered over all continents, support themselves by their work and share the living conditions of the poor. Weekly interdenominational meetings in the Church of Reconciliation bring together youth from various countries, those in the summer drawing up to 6,000 participants at a time. Songs from Taize are used in groups and parishes around the world. Taize has been visited by Pope John Paul II* in 1986 and three archbishops of Canterbury*. Brother Roger has won numerous awards, including the Templeton Prize and the German Peace Prize in 1974 and the Karlspreis in 1988.

Schutz, Heinrich (1585–1672) Also known as Henricus Sagittarius. The greatest Lutheran composer of the seventeenth century. A student of Giovanni Gabrieli*, Schutz's enormous output was entirely sacred. He was kapellmeister* at the court in Dresden for 55 years. Here he wrote *Kleine Geistliche Konzerte* (in which he set the Psalms for solo voices and organ), *Symphoniae Sacrae,* and *Geistliche Chormusik* (scriptural motets). He also wrote the oratorio*, *The Story of Christmas,* the *Seven Words from the Cross,* and three Passions.

Schwabach, Articles of Lutheran confession* of 1529, probably composed by Luther* which formed the basis of the first part of the Augsburg Confession* of 1530 and the Wittenberg Concord* of 1536. Its 17 articles were directed against Calvinists, Zwinglians, and Anabaptists* and reasserted the real presence* of Christ in the Eucharist*.

Schwarmer (Ger., *Schwarmerei,* enthusiasm) Early Protestants who emphasized personal experience over the Word and the sacraments. It was Luther's* derogatory label for Anabaptists*, other radicals, and even mainstream reformers whom he distrusted.

Schwartz, Carl August Ferdinand (1817–1870) Jewish Christian missionary. Converted and baptized in 1837, he worked in Constantinople*, London, Amsterdam, and Berlin. In Amsterdam (1849–1864) he founded with Isaac da Costa the Scottish Seminary for Mission at Home and Abroad (1852–1860) and the Netherlands Society for Israel (1861). In London (1864–1870) he founded the Hebrew Christian Alliance (1865) and edited *The Scattered Nation* (1866). In 1858, on his way to the pulpit, he was stabbed by a Jew, but recovered.

Schwartz, Christian Friedrich (1726–1760) Missionary to India. He was called to India by Benjamin Schultze, a former missionary who had worked in Tranquebar and completed the Tamil translation of the Bible. Fluent in Tamil, he arrived in India in 1750. He was stationed in his early years at the Danish-Halle mission in Tranquebar. From here he opened other mission centers in Sri Lanka, Tiruchirapally, and Tanjavore. He gained the favor of the British as well as Hindu and Muslim native rulers.

Schweitzer, Albert (1875–1965) German theologian, medical missionary, and musician. From 1905 he studied medicine after completing studies in theology and becoming an expert musician. He felt the call* to the mission field* and went to Gabon in Africa to found a hospital at Lambarene*. He devoted the rest of his life to this hospital, which became one of his legacies to the world. Schweitzer was the heir to the German Protestant tradition of critical and historical theology* that was already in decline when he arrived on the scene. His principal Christological works are *The Mystery of the Kingdom of God* (1901) and *The Quest for Historical Jesus* (1910), which interpreted Christ in terms of a "thoroughgoing" or "consistent" eschatology*. Schweitzer taught that Christ's ministry was guided by an "interim ethic"* or by the world-negating expectation of the imminent end of the world and the establishment of a kingdom of God* on earth and that his death was an attempt to fulfill this apocalyptic vision. In 1911 he applied similar eschatological principles to the study of St. Paul* in *Paul and his Interpreters,* and later he completed his study of St. Paul in *Die Mystik des Apostels Paulus* (1930).

Schweitzer was uncertain about orthodox Christian doctrines and dogmas, but his own life exemplified a form of discipleship that made Christian dogmas become real. In 1921 he published his reminiscences, *On the Edge of the Primeval Forest,* and two years later summed up his philosophy of "reverence for life" in *Kulturphilosophie* (1923). He was awarded the Nobel Prize in 1952.

Schwenckfeld, Caspar von Ossig (1490–1561) Silesian sect founder. Although he was an early follower of Luther*, he had serious disputes with Reformation* leaders on many key Protestant doctrines, such as the Lord's Supper* and church discipline*. As a result he was forced to leave Silesia and later Strasbourg*. He provoked an anathema against him by a convention of Evangelical theologians led by Melanchthon* in 1540 for his assertion of the deification of the humanity of Christ. Schwenckfeld held that Christ was begotten and not created and that God is the Father of Christ's humanity. He withdrew from the Lutheran Church after 1540 and established a community of followers known later as Confessors of the Glory of Christ or Schwenckfelders. Persecution forced them to emigrate to Pennsylvania by 1734.

Science and Health with Key to the Scriptures Book by Mary Baker Eddy*, considered the textbook of Christian Science*.

scientia media (Lat., mediate knowledge) Foreknowledge of God mediated by certain intermediate human events. It was a term coined by the Jesuit theologian, Luis de Molina*, in an attempt to reconcile God's knowledge of future events with human free will* that may change the outcome of those events.

scintilla animae (Lat., spark of the soul) Term used by mystical writers to designate the element in the soul that achieves union with God.

SCM Student Christian Movement*.

Scofield, Cyrus Ingerson (1843–1921) American dispensationalist scholar. After serving in the Confederate Army, he was ordained to serve as a pastor in Dallas. He moved to Massachusetts to serve in D. L. Moody's church in East Northfield in 1885, but returned to Dallas in 1902. In 1909 he edited the *Dispensational Premillennial Bible* for which he is famous.

Scofield Reference Bible Highly influential dispensationalist Bible edited by Cyrus Ingerson Scofield*, begun in 1900 and published by Oxford University Press in 1909. The revised New Scofield Reference Bible was published in 1967. Although dispensationalism* denies that spiritual gifts* operate today, the influence of the Scofield Reference Bible on Pentecostalism* has been enormous.

Scopes trial Sensational trial in 1925 of John T. Scopes, a young Tennessee high school science teacher, accused of teaching Darwinian evolution contrary to state law. The trial pitted William Jennings Bryan*, a three-time Democratic nominee for the U.S. presidency, against Clarence Darrow, one of the leading criminal lawyers of the day and an avowed atheist. Scopes was found guilty and fined $100, but the trial had the ironic effect of turning public opinion against Creationism*.

Scots Confession Confession of the Scottish Reformed Church from 1560. Compiled by John Knox* with five other colleagues, it was ratified by the Scottish Parliament in 1647. Its theology is broadly Calvinistic with ideas borrowed from a number of other Reformers. Among the doctrines that it affirmed are justification* by faith* and election*. The kirk* is defined as an assembly of the elect* outside of which there is no salvation*.

Scott, Peter Cameron (1867–1896) American founder of the Africa Inland Mission*. Soon after conversion, he sailed to West Africa in 1890 under A. B. Simpson's International Missionary Alliance. Returning to the United States, he joined with A. T. Pierson*, C. E. Hurlbut, and others to form the Africa Inland Mission in 1895. The same year Scott sailed for Zanzibar and Mombasa and during the first year established four mission stations*. However, after traveling 2,600 miles, Scott succumbed to fever and dysentery within a year.

Scott, Walter (1796–1861) Early leader of the Restoration movement*. Born in Scotland, he emigrated to the United States in 1818. In Pittsburgh he pastored a group called the "Kissing Baptists" because they practiced the holy kiss*. Later, he became an evangelist for the Mahoning Baptist Association and is reported to have converted about 1,000 persons every year for the next three decades. It was Scott who created the Restoration movement's five-finger exercise setting forth the order of salvation*—faith*, repentance*, baptism*, remission of sins, and the gifts of the Holy Spirit*. His work was rewarded with a great revival.

Scottish Realism School of philosophy, also known as Scottish Common Sense, which was widely influential in early American Presbyterianism* through John Witherspoon* and other immigrants. It began with Thomas Reid* (1710–1796) who, after serving as minister and academic in and around Aberdeen, was professor of moral philosophy at Glasgow (1764–1796). Reid responded to the skepticism of David Hume (1711–1776), appealing to intuitive beliefs as matters of common sense, especially beliefs concerning the external world and God's existence. Others associated with this school include Dugald Stewart, Sir William Hamilton, and James McCosh.

scotula See BUGIA.

screen Partition in a church dividing the nave* from the chancel*.

scriptorium Room in a monastery set apart for the scribes to copy manuscripts and equipped with the necessary materials, such as parchment* and pens.

Scripture 1. The Bible; books of the Old and the New Testaments or either of them. 2. Passage or text from the Bible.

Scripture Gift Mission International service mission that distributes free copies of the Scripture*, in whole, part, or selections, in about 300 languages. It was founded in 1888 in Birmingham, England, by William Walters.

Scripture Union International and interdenominational Evangelical youth and Bible-reading movement founded in England in 1867 as the Children's Special Service Mission. Its basic activities are children's evangelism and youth work and vacation camps. It publishes Bible-reading aids, graded Sunday school* lesson aids, story books for children and youth, training literature and discussion group aids, and audiovisual materials.

Scroggie, William Graham (1877–1958) Scottish minister and author. He left his business and entered the ministry after listening to Spurgeon*. He held pastorates* in London, Halifax, Sunderland, and Edinburgh*. In the 1930s he traveled to North America as an evangelist and Bible teacher to promote the Deeper Life theme of Keswick*.

scroll Manuscripts, especially of the Bible, wound in a roll.

scruples (Lat., pebble or sharp stone). Doubt or hesitation of an over-sensitive conscience from fear of sin.

scrutiny 1. Formal examination of candidates* for church membership or for ordination. 2. Election of a pope by ballot in the College of Cardinals*.

Scudder, Ida Sophia (1870–1960) Missionary doctor and founder of the Christian Medical College and Hospital in Vellore, India. She was born in Ranipet in Madras, where her father, John Scudder, was in the North Arcot Mission of the Dutch Reformed Church* of America. In 1893 she received a call* to become a missionary. She went back to the United States to study medicine and returned to India in 1900 to open a hospital in Vellore, followed by a nursing school and a medical college.

SDA Seventh Day Adventists.

Seabury, Samuel (1729–1796) First bishop of the Protestant Episcopal Church in the United States. Ordained in 1753, he served as missionary in New Brunswick and as rector* in Jamaica and Westchester, New York, where he also practiced medicine. As a Tory, he was imprisoned during the American Revolution. He was chosen bishop by Connecticut Episcopal clergymen and consecrated in

1784 at Aberdeen by Scottish bishops because he was unwilling to take the oath* of allegiance to the United States. He became the presiding bishop of the new Protestant Episcopal Church in 1789.

Seagrave, Gordon S. (1896–1965) "Burma Surgeon." American Baptist missionary who served as a doctor in the remote regions of Myanmar.

seal of confession Absolute obligation in canon law* not to reveal anything said by a penitent during confession* or act of penitence. It binds not only the confessors but also persons who may have overheard or interpreted the confessions.

season Special religious period, such as Advent* or Lent* or period of exceptional blessing in church ministry or set aside for special prayer or other religious exercises.

seasonal assistant Short-term Christian personnel serving abroad, for six months or less.

se-baptism Baptism* of oneself, such as that performed by John Smyth when he established the first congregation of Baptists* in Amsterdam in the seventeenth century.

Sebaste, forty martyrs of Forty Christian soldiers of the Thundering Legion who were martyred at Se-

Forty Martyrs of Sebaste

baste, Armenia, during the Licinian persecution in 320. They were left naked on the ice of a frozen pond. Feast day: March 9.

Sebastian, St. Roman martyr* killed during the Diocletian persecution*. According to legend, he was shot by arrows. In art he is represented as a man pierced by many arrows. Feast day: January 20.

St. Sebastian

Second Adam Christ as the head of a new race of people liberated from sin who escape the legacy of the first Adam by being united with Christ (Rom. 5:1–14; 1 Cor. 15:45).

Second Advent See SECOND COMING.

second baptism See REBAPTISM.

second birth Also, new birth; rebirth. Regeneration* through the Holy Spirit* to new life from being dead in sin. Baptism* dramatically portrays this experience, but views differ on its actual relation to the second birth.

second blessing In Holiness theology, sanctification* as a second definite work of grace received by faith*, the first being justification*.

Second Coming Biblical teaching that Jesus Christ

will return in glory to judge the living and the dead and to consummate the purposes of God for his people and the world. While most Christians believe in the certainty and finality of his return, they are divided on its nature, manner, and outcome. Some believe there will be a millennial reign of Christ on earth before the last judgment* and that it will be followed, according to the *Revelation,* by the binding of Satan* and the resurrection of the saints who will rule with him over a temporal kingdom of peace, plenty, and righteousness. In the nineteenth century, a new element, dispensationalism*, was added through the Plymouth Brethren* movement which held that the Second Coming will follow the restoration of Israel in the last days*. Millennialism is a prominent feature of American Evangelicalism* in the twentieth century.

Second Great Awakening National revival in the United States that followed the Revolutionary War between about 1787 and 1825. The revival in the East was centered in the colleges along the Atlantic coast, such as Hampden-Sydney, Yale, Amherst, Dartmouth, and Williams, and was marked by restraint and order. The revival in the West, by contrast, was exuberant, as was to be expected in frontier territories. Among the major centers were three Presbyterian churches pastored by James McGready* in Logan County, Kentucky, and Cane Ridge, Kentucky, where Barton Stone* was the revivalist*. The revival served to counter the spiritual decline and the corresponding rise in Deist influence in the early years of the republic.

Second London Confession Baptist confession* of faith drawn up in 1677 revising the First London Confession of 1644. Like the Savoy Declaration* of 1658, it was an adaptation of the Westminster Confession*, reaffirming its Calvinism*. Adopted by the Philadelphia Baptist Association in 1707, it became the doctrinal standard of the Baptist churches until it was superseded by the New Hampshire Confession* of 1832.

second resurrection In premillennial theology, resurrection of unbelievers and unregenerate sinners at the end of the millennial period.

second wave Charismatic movement as representing the second wave of the Pentecostal movement. Thus, Second Waver.

second work of grace Second crisis in Christian experience, following conversion*, baptism*, or new birth*. For Roman Catholics it is confirmation* following baptism, for Wesleyans it is entire sanctification*, and for Pentecostals and Charismatics it is the baptism of the Holy Spirit*. Some Protestants believe that the second work of grace forgives and removes original sin* whereas the first work of grace forgives and removes acts of sin. Other Protestants reject the notion entirely, believing that all the Christian needs is given an initial union with Christ.

Secret Prayer said or sung by the celebrant at Mass* after the offering of bread and wine. Formerly, it was said silently. It varies with the Proper. In the 1970 Roman Missal it is called Oratio Super Oblata.

Secretariat for Promoting Christian Unity Vatican* office created by Pope John XXIII* to facilitate collaboration with Eastern Orthodox* and other Christian churches and to promote common programs and ventures. Its first president was Cardinal Augustin Bea*.

Secretariat of State Office in the Roman Curia* vested with the oversight of the Roman Catholic Church under the direction of the holy father*.

secretarium Room near the entrance of a cathedral, distinct from the sacristy*, for the vesting of the bishop or celebrant prior to the opening procession of the Mass*.

sect Dissenting religious group within organized religion whose adherents follow a special set of teachings or practices and reject the mainstream or traditional church. Unlike a cult*, a sect may hold orthodox beliefs, like the Plymouth Brethren*, but although sociologists use it as a technical category, the term is more generally used pejoratively. Sects are divided into several categories: conversionist sects that emphasize being born again*, millennial sects that anticipate an immediate millennium*, separatist sects that advocate separation and isolation from the world, thaumaturgical sects that emphasize divine signs and wonders, and reformist sects that seek to reconstruct society. A church-sect typology was developed by Ernst Troeltsch*.

sectarianism 1. Overzealous attachment or loyalty to a sect*. 2. Presence of diverse religious groups in a place or epoch.

sectary In seventeenth- and eighteenth-century England, Protestant dissenters* such as Anabaptists*. Used derogatively.

secular clergy In Roman Catholicism, priests living in the world as distinguished from regular clergy who are members of religious orders living according to a rule. Secular clergy are not bound by vows and may possess property, yet they must obey their bishops and must be celibate.

secular theology Term, coined by Dietrich Bonhoeffer*, focusing on a Christianity that is engaged and fully interactive with the world, as opposed to ascetical theology* which promotes a retreat from the world.

secularism Term coined in the mid-nineteenth century by G. J. Holyoake to describe a system of values and beliefs based only on the present and visible world without any reference to God and the supernatural. Later, the term came to denote a deliberate effort to exclude religion from public life and the shaping of social policy.

secularization 1. Transfer from ecclesiastical to civil possession and use. 2. Divesting of spiritual and eternal significance and subjection to profane and mundane influences. 3. Exclusion of religious values and their replacement with a system of impersonal and utilitarian social ethics guided not by divine ordinances but by temporal well-being.

sedalen In the Byzantine Church*, the short troparion* sung at the end of each psalter division during mattins* or orthros*.

sede vacante (Lat., the see being vacant) Period during which a diocese* is without a bishop.

sedia gestatoria Formerly, the portable throne on which the pope used to be carried by 12 uniformed footmen on ceremonial occasions.

sedilia Seats, usually three in number, on the south side of the chancel* where the celebrant, deacon, and subdeacon sit during certain parts of the service. In medieval times, they were usually richly carved stone benches built into a wall, surmounted by arches or canopies.

Sedlec Cistercian monastery in Sedlec, Czech Republic, founded in 1142–1143. Its church was built between 1280 and 1320. It was destroyed in the fifteenth-century Hussite Wars and in 1601 the monks abandoned the place. After 1700 the monastery was renovated and restored.

sedro (lit., order) In the Syrian Church, a penitential prayer recited at the start of the Liturgy of the Faithful when it is called the sedro of the Entrance.

Sedulius (fifth century) Christian poet, author of *Paschale Carmen,* on the life of Christ. He also wrote a prose version, *Opus Paschale.*

see Properly, the seat or throne of a bishop in the cathedral of the diocese*. By extension, the power, authority, and jurisdiction of a bishop.

See, Holy Official name for the Vatican State, as the principal see in the Roman Catholic Church.

Seekers Small seventeenth-century sect of independent Quietists who held that there was no true church and that the Antichrist* was dominant in the world. They had many affinities with the Quakers*. One of their preachers, Bartholomew Legate, was burned at Smithfield for Arian heresy in 1612, and many of his followers were absorbed by the Quakers.

Seelenabgrund (Ger., ground of the soul) In mystical theology*, the spark of the soul or conscience within each individual.

Segerelli, Gerard (d. 1300) Founder of the medieval group known as the Apostolici*. He and his followers lived on alms and preached penance* without rule or vows. For his attacks on the institutional church, he was arrested, tried, and executed.

Segovia Three-aisled cathedral in the Spanish city of Segovia, built by Juan Gil de Hontanon and consecrated in 1768. Its tower was originally the tallest in Spain at 344 feet, but it was struck by lightning and reduced to its present height of 289 feet. However, its dome is one of the highest in Spain at 220 feet. The nave* is 344 feet long and 164 feet wide. Close to the ambulatory are seven polygonal chapels of which the most distinctive are the Capilla Mayor, built in 1614, and the Chapel of Christo del Consuelo.

Segundo, Jean Luis (1925–) Uruguayan theologian. A prominent exponent of liberation theology*, his works include *The Liberation of Theology* and *Jesus Christ, Yesterday and Today*.

sehnsucht Sense of longing for the infinite, a German word popularized by C. S. Lewis*.

Seleucia, Council of See ARIMINUM.

Seleucia Ctesiphon Ancient twin cities on the Tigris River of which the first was founded by Seleucus I Nicator in 312 B.C. and the latter by the Persians. It was the capital of the Nestorian Church* from the third until the seventh century. Several synods of bishops were held there from about 325 onwards.

semandron (Gk., bell) In the Byzantine Church*, long bar of wood or metal struck with a hammer or mallet to produce a musical sound, used in monasteries to summon the monks to worship. Under Ottoman rule, it replaced the forbidden bells. The wooden hand semandron, called the talanton, the iron semandron, and the large wooden semandron are the principal varieties of the semandron.

semi-Arianism Theological position closer to orthodoxy* than Arianism*. It was held by Basil of Ancyra*, Macedonius of Constantinople, George of Laodicea, Eusthathius* of Sebaste, and Eleusius of Cyzicus. They preferred homoiousios to homoousios*, but represented a reconstructive impulse.

semidoubles Until 1955, feasts in the Roman Catholic Church which ranked below doubles and above simple feasts.

seminarian 1. Clergyman educated in a seminary. 2. Seminary priest. 3. Seminary student.

seminary School or college devoted to the training of clergy.

Semipelagianism Theological position misleadingly so called, as though midway between Augustinianism* and Pelagianism*. It holds that while salvation* is effected by grace*, the first step toward salvation was through human will and that grace intervened only with human assent. Its foremost exponent was John Cassian*, who developed it to counter Augustine's* extreme form of predestinationism in which human will had no role. It was in reality a moderate Semi-Augustinianism*.

sending countries Countries which send out missionaries, or which send out far more foreign missionaries than they receive.

Senfle, Ludwig (c. 1486–1543) Swiss composer. He was Kapellmeister* at the imperial court until 1519 and then at the court of Duke Wilhelm of Bavaria. Senfle composed seven settings of the Mass* ordinary, a cycle of Magnificats* for each mode, and a considerable number of motets*. Although he was a Roman Catholic, he had sympathies for the Reformers, having met Luther* in 1518.

seniorate Ecclesiastical geographical division within some Reformed* denominations in Eastern Europe, corresponding to a presbytery*.

senkessar (Ge'ez) In the Ethiopian Church*, a form of synaxarion*, or a collection of brief daily commemorations* of the lives and martyrdoms of the saints*.

Senlis Cathedral of Notre Dame in Oise, France, consecrated in 1191. In the thirteenth century the magnificent South Tower and the west front were completed. Work on the cathedral ceased for a hundred years and was resumed only in the fourteenth century. In 1504 the entire church was destroyed in a fire. Rebuilding began immediately and was completed in 1560. The building represented a turning point in Marian* devotion that

Senlis Cathedral

was then sweeping Europe. In the tympanum*, Christ and Mary are enthroned, and there are scenes depicting the death, burial, and ascension of the Virgin Mary*.

Sens, Council of Council held in 1141 to hear charges of heresy against Abelard* by Bernard of Clairvaux*. In 1121 Abelard had been forced to burn his works on the Trinity* on the ground that he was teaching Tritheism* or three gods. At Sens, Abelard refused to defend himself and appealed the case to Innocent II. But the pope declared Abelard a heretic and condemned him to perpetual silence and banishment. Other councils were held in Sens in 601, 833, 845, 1225, 1461, and 1485.

sensata Feast of the Immaculate Conception in the Ethiopian Catholic Church.

sensus fidei (Lat., sense of faith) Intuitive knowledge of the truth of God possessed by the whole church as a community of faith. The concept states implicitly that church teaching is guided by the corporate and universal faith of the people of God and as such assumes a Roman Catholic ecclesiology. The Second Vatican Council* taught that "the body of the faithful as a whole, anointed as they are by the Holy One, cannot err in matters of belief," and "is in universal agreement in matters of faith and morals." It forms part of the theology of the laity and supplements the magisterium* of the church.

sensus plenior (Lat., fuller sense) Deeper meaning of the words of the Scripture not fully understood even by its human authors.

sentences Short expositions of Christian doctrines in which the authors studied words and their literal meaning (litera), plain meaning (sensus), and underlying meaning (sententia). Collections of sentences, such as that by Peter Lombard*, were very popular in the Middle Ages.

Sentences Title of the book by Peter Lombard*, the most commented upon book in the Middle Ages. It was a topical arrangement of the teachings of the Church Fathers* with a discussion by Lombard.

senwarta In the Assyrian tradition, a white handkerchief as part of priestly vestments.

Separate Baptists Baptists in the United States who reject Calvinism* and accept no creeds or ordinances* other than baptism*, the Lord's Supper*, and foot-washing*. They are highly Evangelical and moderately Calvinist. They allow women to preach, practice nine rites, and reject paid ministry.

separatists Protestants who left the Church of England* in the sixteenth and seventeenth centuries, such as the Quakers*, Pilgrims*, Baptists*, and Presbyterians*. Also used more generally of those who on principle or other grounds depart from a majority church.

Septuagesima (Lat., seventieth) Third Sunday before Lent*, about 70 days before Easter*.

sequence 1. Hymn sung between the gradual* and the Gospel in certain services. 2. Text of a chant sung before the hallelujah* of the Mass*. The five sequences that are in use are *Victimae Paschali** at Easter*, *Veni, Sancte Spiritus** at Whitsun, *Lauda*

Zion at Corpus Christi*, *Dies Irae** at All Souls*, and *Stabat Mater** at the feast of the Seven Sorrows* of the Blessed Virgin Mary*.

Serampore Trio The three leaders of the Serampore mission: William Carey*, Joshua Marshman*, and William Ward*.

Seraphic Doctor Epithet of St. Bonaventura*.

Seraphic Father St. Francis.

Seraphic Hymn The Sanctus*, "Holy, Holy, Holy," sung by the seraphim (Isa. 6:3).

Seraphic Order Franciscan Order*, so called after St. Francis's vision in which he saw a seraph from heaven* impress the stigmata* on his body.

Seraphim of Boiotia (1527–1602) Founder of the Savior Monastery near Levadeia, Greece. He was a renowned staretz* who lived as a hermit before joining the Sagmation Monastery. He traveled through the Ottoman-ruled Balkans, praying for the oppressed Christians under Turkish rule. Feast day: May 6.

Seraphim of Sarov, St. (1759–1833) Birth name: Prokhor Moshnin. Russian monk and staretz*. He entered the Monastery of Sarov at the age of 19. From 1794 to 1825 he lived in total seclusion, first as a hermit in a nearby forest and then in a cell in his monastery. He emerged from this cell eight years before his death and became a spiritual adviser to a stream of disciples and followers. He is the last of the saints* canonized by the Russian Orthodox Church*. Feast day: January 2.

Serapion of Thmuis (d. c. 362) Bishop of Thmuis in Egypt, and superior* of a colony of monks. As a friend of Athanasius*, he supported him in his theological struggle with Arians. He wrote a treatise *Against the Manichaeans* and a sacramentary* called *Euchologion*. Feast day: March 21.

Serbian Orthodox Church One of the earliest Christian churches in the Balkans, the result of a Christian mission sponsored by emperors Heraclius (610–641) and Basil (867–886). In 886 disciples of Sts. Cyril and Methodius*, particularly Clement

and Naum, started working among the southern Slavs. From Preslav and Ohrid*, they helped to bring the Slavs into the Orthodox fold. Between 1169 and 1196 the grand zupan Stefan Nemanja united Serbian lands, including Kosovo*, and founded a dynasty which lasted 200 years. His son Vukan and elder brother Miroslav wrote two of the earliest illuminated lectionaries.

The ancient Serbian institution of sabori* (elders) was brought into the church as an administrative body. Toward the end of his life Nemanja left his throne to his second son, Stefan, and became a monk at Studenica* and his queen Anna took the veil at the Monastery of the Virgin at Toplica. Nemanja, now Monk Symeon, went to Athos* with his youngest son Sava and founded the monastery at Hilander*, which became an important center of Orthodox spirituality*. Nemanja's mausoleum in the Monastery of the Virgin at Studenica* is one of the holiest shrines in Serbia. In 1219 Sava* was appointed the first autocephalous* archbishop of Serbia by Emperor Theodore I Lascaris. Sava's reign as head of the Serbian Church was one of its most formative eras. His Nomocanon* (krmcija) served as both the civil and ecclesiastical constitution for Serbia. Although firmly Orthodox, both Sava and King Stefan maintained cordial relations with Rome

St. Seraphim of Sarov

and Roman Catholic churches, and monasteries were built in the kingdom. Stefan himself received his crown from Pope Honorius III*. In 1346 the Serbian archbishopric was raised to a patriarchate as the Patriarchate of Pec* which was recognized by Constantinople* in 1375.

In 1389 the Serbian army led by Prince Lazar was defeated by the Turks at Kosovo Polje. Soon after the battle, Lazar was canonized and Kosovo itself became a symbol of Serbian national pride. The Patriarchate of Pec, extinct from 1459, was reestablished in 1557 under an agreement with the Ottomans. Having achieved a degree of autonomy, the Serbian Church assumed the role of a mediator in both ecclesiastical and secular matters and helped to preserve the national and confessional* identities. At the same time, the Turks continued to brutalize the population by instituting the devshirme, by which the healthiest Christian male children were taken by force, converted as Muslims, and trained as janissaries. Scores of churches were converted into mosques. In 1713 the Serbian Church was reorganized with the creation of a metropolitanate at Sremski-Karlovci.

The modern Serbian state was established after World War I, but Serbs had to undergo two more bloodbaths, first under the Nazis in World War II and then from U.S. and NATO forces in 1999. Serbia's historic churches include Bogorodica Ljeviska at Prizren, St. Nikita, Staro Nagoricino*, Gracanica*, Decani*, Pec*, and Lesnovo*. Its great monasteries include Ravanica, Ljubostinja, Kalenic, Manasija, Studenica*, Zica*, Mileseva*, Sopocani*, and Arilje.

Serenity Prayer Prayer composed by Reinhold Niebuhr* as follows: "God grant me serenity to accept the things I cannot change, courage to change the things I can, and wisdom to know the difference. Living one day at a time, enjoying one moment at a time, accepting hardship as the pathway to peace. Taking as He did, this sinful world as it is, not as I would have it, trusting that He will make all things right if I surrender to His will. That I may be reasonably happy in this life, and supremely happy with Him forever in the next."

Sergius (d. 638) Patriarch* of Constantinople* from 610 and the champion of Monothelitism*.

In an effort to bring Monophysites back into the fold, Sergius devised a compromise in which Christ had two natures but only one activity or will. The doctrine was promulgated by the Emperor Heraclius in his famous *Ecthesis* of which Sergius was the author. Two synods held in Constantinople in 638 and 639 approved this teaching, which was, however, condemned by the Third Council of Constantinople* in 681. He is the author of the famous Greek hymn, *Akathistus,* in honor of the Virgin Mary*, sung during Lent*.

Sergius, St. (d. 701) Pope from 687. He baptized Caedwalla, king of the West Saxons, in 689 and consecrated St. Willibrord* as bishop of the Frisians. He made many liturgical innovations, such as the singing of the Agnus Dei* in the Mass*. Feast day: September 6.

Sergius, St. (c. 1314–1392) Birth name: Bartholomew. The greatest Russian mystic and saint*. He founded near Radonezh the famous monastery of the Holy Trinity, the first of over 40 monasteries that he founded in the course of his life. He played a major role in Russian history, helping to save Russia from four civil wars and inspiring Prince Dmitri to save Russia from the Tartars in 1380. He was canonized before 1449. He is

St. Sergius of Radonezh

the patron of Moscow* and all Russia. Feast day: September 25.

Serious Call to a Devout and Holy Life Devotional book by William Law*, published in 1728. It is said to have had more influence as a spiritual guide than any except *Pilgrim's Progress*. It is a forceful exhortation to lead a Christian life to its fullest moral and ascetic potential and to animate every human activity by the love of God and the desire to glorify him through the exercise of the virtues of temperance, humility, and self-denial.

Seripando, Girolamo (1492/3–1563) Cardinal. Ordained in 1513, he became general* of the Augustinian Order from 1539 to 1551. After Luther* left the order, Seripando initiated a series of reforms and organized a visitation of the whole order. He was a legate to the Council of Trent* in 1561, where he took a moderate position. He was made cardinal in 1561.

sermo generalis Ceremony in the Inquisition* at which the final decision in the trial of heretics was pronounced with great solemnity, after a short sermon, from which the name was derived.

sermon (Lat., *sermo,* discourse, teaching, oracle) Also, homily*. Religious discourse delivered in a church as part of a worship service. The biblical purpose of a sermon is to offer salvation* under the power of the Holy Spirit* and to equip and strengthen the congregation. In most Reforma-

tion* traditions, it is an essential, and even the central, act of worship without which no sacrament* can be administered.

Serra, Junipero (Miguel Jose) (1713–1784) Franciscan missionary to Mexico and present-day Southwestern United States. Born in Majorca, Spain, he emigrated to Mexico City in 1750 and worked there until 1767. When the Franciscans replaced Jesuits* in Baja (Lower) California, Serra was appointed *presidente* for the region. He joined the expedition into Alta (Upper) California led by Gaspar de Portola which, in 1769, established Mission San Diego, the first of nine missions Serra planted in the region. More than 6,000 Native Americans were baptized as a result of his work.

servant Status of a leader. Christ fulfilled the role of a suffering servant*. Luther* described Christians as the servants of all (Matt. 20:27; Mark 10:42–45; 2 Cor. 4:5).

server Assistant to the celebrant, usually a layman, at the Eucharist* or Mass*, who makes responses, brings the bread and wine to the altar, washes the celebrant's hands, and rings the sacring bell* at the elevation*.

Servetus, Michael (1511–1553) Spanish theologian and physician. He espoused radical theological ideas on the Trinity*, which he believed was a

Junipero Serra

Michael Servetus

stumbling block to the conversion of Jews and Muslims. In 1531 he published his first book on the subject, *De Trinitatis Erroribus Libri VII* in which he attacked the doctrine of Trinity* as unbiblical. To escape the persecution that followed, he began a second career as a physician and discovered the circulation of blood through the pulmonary system. At the same time he was writing his chief work, *Christianismi Restitutio* (1553), which not only continued to attack the Trinity* and other orthodox doctrines such as infant baptism*, but also developed unorthodox views of the Incarnation* while proposing a Christocentric* pantheism* drawn from Cabalistic and Neoplatonic ideas. He was arrested and condemned in Geneva* and burned. He is highly regarded by the Unitarians.

service 1. Public act of devotion and praise to God. See also DIVINE SERVICE. 2. Act of help or assistance to another.

service bulletin Printed order of worship distributed to a congregation as they enter the sanctuary.

Service of the Word 1. Liturgy of the Word* as the first half of the Eucharist*. 2. Service of reading and preaching without the celebration of the Holy Communion*.

Servites Also, Servants of Mary. Order of the Servants of the Blessed Virgin Mary*, founded in Florence* in 1240. They wear black, follow the Rule of St. Augustine*, and are devoted to the Sorrowful Virgin. Its most influential member in the early days was St. Philip Benizi* (1233–1285). The Second Order of Servite nuns is principally a contemplative order with a growing missionary activity. The Third Order founded by St. Juliana Falconieri in 1306 devote themselves to the relief of the sick and the poor and the training of the young.

servus servorum Dei (Lat., the servant of God's servants) Title of the pope used in official documents, first used by Gregory* the Great.

sesle In the Jacobite tradition, cymbals which, together with noqusho*, are sounded to mark the more solemn moments in the liturgy, such as the Sanctus*, Institution, Epiclesis*, and Elevation*.

session 1. Board of elders governing a Presbyterian church, called kirk-session* in Scotland. Its members are lay ruling elders, a teaching elder, and the minister. 2. Christ's appearance seated on the right hand of God as the sovereign high priest pleading the virtue of his atoning sacrifice on behalf of his people.

Seton, St. Elizabeth Ann Bayley (1774–1821) The first American-born Roman Catholic saint*. Of Protestant religious background, she was converted to Roman Catholicism* in Rome* where she had gone with her husband, the physician Richard Bayley. In 1809 she took vows as a nun and began forming a religious congregation* known as the Sisters (or Daughters) of Charity. She went on to found St. Joseph's College and the first Catholic free school in the United States at Emmitsburg, Maryland. She was canonized in 1975. Feast day: January 4.

seven champions of Christendom The seven most popular patron saints* in the Middle Ages: St. George*, St. Andrew*, St. David*, St. Patrick*, St. James of Compostela, St. Denis of Paris, and St. Anthony of Padua*.

seven churches of Asia The churches of Asia Minor to whom John wrote in Revelation: Ephesus*, Smyrna, Pergamum*, Thyatira*, Sardis, Philadelphia, and Laodicea*.

seven deacons Men appointed to help the apostles: Stephen*, Philip*, Prochorus, Nicanor, Timon, Parmenas, and Nicolas. Often called simply the Seven, especially by scholars who do not view them as deacons, in the light of their role in evangelism.

seven deadly sins Seven besetting sins of believers: pride, covetousness, lust, envy, gluttony, anger, and sloth.

seven gifts of the Holy Spirit Gifts listed in Isaiah 11:2: wisdom, understanding, counsel, fortitude, knowledge, piety, and fear of the Lord.

seven sacraments Baptism*, confirmation*, Eucharist*, penance*, extreme unction*, ordination*, and matrimony*.

seven sleepers of Ephesus According to legend, seven Christian young men who died in a cave during the Decian persecution* about 250 and were said to have been resurrected under Emperor Theodosius about 450.

Seven Sorrows of Mary Seven sorrows of Mary honored on the Friday after Passion Sunday* and on September 15. They are her sorrows at the prophecy of Simeon, flight into Egypt, absence of Jesus in the temple, finding him going to the cross, standing at the cross, descent of Jesus from the cross, and his burial at the sepulchre.

seven virtues The three theological virtues of faith, hope, and charity and the four cardinal virtues of justice, prudence, temperance, and fortitude.

Seventh Day Adventists Christian denomination that grew out of the millennial prophecy of William Miller*, who predicted the return of Christ between March 21, 1843, and March 21, 1844. When the prediction did not materialize, Miller reset the date to October 22, 1844, a date that came to be known subsequently as the "great disappointment." Miller's followers who survived this disappointment constituted themselves into an apocalyptic group. Among the prominent leaders of this group were Hiram Edson, who saw new visions of Christ's return, Joseph Bates, James White, and Ellen G. White*. Ellen White had visions requiring the group to scrupulously observe the Sabbath from sundown Friday to sundown Saturday. One of her books, *Steps to Christ,* was translated into 85 languages and sold millions of copies. The early Adventists were concentrated in New England, but the Westward expansion dispersed them over the new territories. The denomination was formally founded in 1863 in Battle Creek, Michigan.

Adventism* teaches that the end of the age will occur when the gospel message has been preached throughout the world, when the righteous living will be gathered into heaven* where they will spend the millennium* while Satan* rules the earth for the same period. At the end of this period Christ will descend with his saints, destroy Satan and his cohorts, and create a new earth with New Jerusalem* as its center. It also teaches soul sleep*, mandatory tithing, free will*, the deity of Christ,

and believer's baptism* by immersion*. Holy Communion* is observed four times a year preceded by a foot-washing* service. Emphasizing that the body is the temple of the Holy Spirit*, Seventh Day Adventists insist on hygiene and proper nutrition, abstain from foods forbidden in the Old Testament, such as ham, pork, and shellfish, and do not smoke or drink. They oppose secret societies, card playing, gambling, worldly entertainments, such as dancing, theater, and motion pictures, and the use of jewelry and cosmetics. They operate parochial schools* and conduct an extensive publishing program with the periodical, *Review and Herald* as their flagship, support a large medical system with hospitals and clinics, and operate Loma Linda University in California.

Seventh Day Baptists 1. Baptist sect, founded in 1672, which observes Saturday as their Sabbath. 2. Monastic community in Ephrata, Pennsylvania, founded in 1732 by Peter Becker, who also founded the Dunkers*.

Severinus, St. (d. 482) "Apostle of Austria." He came to Noricum Ripense during the Barbarian invasions of Europe. For 30 years he evangelized the lands around Comagene and Astura, founding monasteries at Boiotro and Faviana. When Rome* abandoned the region, he took charge, gaining the friendship and respect of the poor as well as the barbarian leaders. He is the patron saint* of vine dressers. Feast day: January 8.

Severus (c. 465–538) Monophysite theologian and patriarch* of Antioch*. He became a monk soon after 488 and was made patriarch of Antioch in 512. On Justinian's* accession, he was deposed in 518 and excommunicated by a synod* in Constantinople* in 536. He was the leading Monophysite theologian of the moderate school, and his theology is widely accepted in the Syrian Orthodox Church*. His literary remains include treatises, liturgical writings, 125 homilies, and 400 letters.

Severus ibn al-Muqaffa (c. 905–c. 987) Coptic bishop and Christian writer in Arabic. Among his more than 20 works is *A History of the Councils.*

Seville City in Spain, site of the magnificent Cathedral of Santa Maria built between 1402 and

1506 on the site of the former Great Mosque of Seville. It is the largest Gothic* cathedral in the world and the third largest Christian church after St. Peter's,* Rome, and St. Paul's,* London. Some parts of the mosque are still preserved, as the minaret, the Orange-Tree Courtyard and La Giralda, the 318-foot bell tower* on which there is a 12-foot figure of Fides (faith). Nine sculptured doorways lead into the cathedral. The five aisles have a total width of 249 feet and a length of 384 feet. The roof height is 131 feet, reaching 184 feet at the crossing*. Other notable features are the decorative grill in the choir, the choir stalls* with their superb wood carving, and the alabaster chapels on the outer walls of the choir. The cupola-roofed Renaissance Capilla Royal is the royal burial chapel dedicated to King Ferdinand. In the middle of the chapel stands the Virgen de los Reyes, the patron saint* of Seville.

sexagesima (Lat., sixtieth) Second Sunday before Lent*, about 60 days before Easter*.

sext Second of the three daytime hours of liturgical prayer, prayed at the sixth hour (i.e., about 12:00 noon).

sexton Church officer or caretaker with various duties. He was traditionally the assistant to the parish clerk* who did the cleaning, rang the bell, and dug graves. He combined the duties of fossor, doorkeeper*, and sacristan*.

Seymour, William Joseph (1870–1922) Prominent Pentecostal leader and pastor of the Azusa Street Mission where modern Pentecostalism* was born. Born to slaves, he was illiterate and also blind in his left eye. He was initiated into the Pentecostal experience by Charles Parham* in whose Bible school he had enrolled. In 1906 he was invited to pastor a church in Los Angeles. Here, in the home of Richard Asberry, he experienced Holy Spirit* baptism accompanied by glossolalia*, an event that brought hundreds to his services. To accommodate the large crowds, he rented a dilapidated stable and warehouse at 312 Azusa Street. On April 18, 1906, the *Los Angeles Times* reported "a weird babble of tongues" amid "wild scenes" in the mission. Soon Azusa Street was the scene of a pilgrimage* from around the world.

By the end of 1906 Seymour officially incorporated his ministry as the Pacific Apostolic Faith Mission* and began publishing *Apostolic Faith*. The Azusa Street meeting continued for three years, three times a day, seven days a week, attended by people of virtually every race, nationality, and culture. Seymour's style of leadership was one of meekness. He often sat with his head covered behind the rough shoe boxes used as a makeshift pulpit. Seymour's leadership was soon challenged by a number of his colleagues, especially by William H. Durham, whose followers organized the Assemblies of God* in 1914. By 1914 Azusa Street Mission had become a small black church.

shabbuqto In the Jacobite tradition, a crozier, the head of which has two intertwined serpents with a small orb between them and a cross at the top. When held by the bishop during the liturgy, it must not touch the floor.

shabho'a (lit., set of seven) In the Assyrian Church*, one of the seven-week periods into which the church year* is divided.

shabto damyokhto (lit., week of rest) In the Maronite Church, Easter* week.

shahara One of the minor orders* in the Assyrian Church*.

Shakers Full name: The United Society of Believers in Christ's Second Appearing*. Also, the Millennial Church*. Communistic sect that had its origin in a group called the "Shaking Quakers" in Bolton, Lancashire, England, founded by James and Jane Wardley in 1747. After the death of the founders, the sect was taken over by Ann Lee*, later known as Mother Ann, who was honored as the "female principle in Christ." Persecution forced the fledgling group to emigrate in 1774 to the United States, where Mother Ann settled in New Lebanon, New York. The group grew with influx from other revivalist groups. By 1784 Shaker communities were found in New York, Massachusetts, Connecticut, and as far west as Kentucky and Indiana. Membership peaked in the decade before the Civil War when it reached 6,000 in 18 different settlements.

After Mother Ann's death the mantle passed on to James Meacham and Lucy Wright, who made the Shakers a tightly organized group. The informal name "Shakers" by which the group is commonly known is a reference to the physical shaking which they displayed under the influence of spiritual exaltation and which later developed into formal ritual dances. Their cardinal tenets were: celibacy as the way to holiness*, separation from the world, simplicity as a way of life, confession* to the elders before admission, strict code of dress and personal behavior, ban on tobacco and alcohol, and use of herbal medicine as a supplement to spiritual healing*. They were organized in large families within each community, with a hierarchical form of government and a strict discipline, and full members owned all goods in common. Shakers are now nearly extinct but are still remembered for their simple and austere furniture that reflected their lifestyle.

shamamout In the Armenian Church*, an introit* marking the start of the enarxis*. Like the Byzantine monogenes*, its text varies according to the day and season of the year.

shamashuta (lit., herald) In the Assyrian Church*: 1. The book of deacons. 2. The office of deacon.

shamlach In the Coptic tradition, a long white band of linen or silk up to six meters in length embroidered with gold crosses at the ends, worn twisted around the head like a turban with one end hanging down the back. It is worn by priests and archpriests, while bishops and patriarchs* wear the ballin, a type of amice*.

shamrock National symbol of Ireland, selected by St. Patrick* because it represented the Trinity*.

shamsha In the Assyrian Church*, a deacon.

shapik In the Armenian tradition, an alb-like vestment, usually made of silk or velvet.

sharakan In the Armenian tradition, a book of hymns of canticles*.

sharing countries Countries which both send and receive large numbers of missionaries and personnel.

shauthophutho In the Syrian tradition, the Holy Communion*.

Shea, George Beverly (1909–) Canadian-born evangelistic singer, associated with the Billy Graham Evangelistic Association* from the beginning. He has recorded 49 albums of hymns and spirituals. Two of his favorites are "I'd Rather Have Jesus" and "Then Sings My Soul."

Shedd, William Greenough Thayer (1820–1894) American theologian. He taught at the theological seminaries in Auburn, Andover, and New York (Union). His *Dogmatic Theology* (3 vols., 1888–1894) was a classic study of conservative and Calvinistic theology. He defended orthodoxy* against C. A. Briggs of Union Theological Seminary*. His other works included *History of Christian Doctrine* (1863) and *Homiletics and Pastoral Theology* (1869).

Sheen, Fulton John (1895–1979) Born Peter Sheen. American Catholic prelate*. An enthralling preacher with a theatrical style, he won huge audiences for his radio program, "the Catholic Hour" (1930–1952), the television series, "Life Is Worth Living" (1952–1965), and for his many books, such as *Peace of Soul* (1949). From 1950 until 1966 he was national director of the Society for the Propagation of the Faith.

Sheer Thursday Maundy Thursday*, so called from the old meaning of sheer, "free from guilt."

shehimo In the Jacobite tradition, the daily office.

Sheldon, Charles Monroe (1857–1946) Congregational* minister and reformer. He began his ministry in Waterbury, Vermont, but moved in 1899 to the Central Congregational Church in Topeka, Kansas. Later, he was associated with the magazine *Christian Herald*, first as editor-in-chief (1920–1925) and later as contributor (1925–1946). Throughout his life, he worked hard for social and religious reform, especially for civil rights, world peace, and prohibition. But he is best known as the author of *In His Steps**, a book that sold millions of copies over the years. In addition, he wrote some 50 books, hundreds of articles, poems, hymns, and plays.

Shenouda III (c. 1921–) Coptic patriarch* from 1971. Birth name: Nazir Gayyid. He became a monk in 1954 at the monastery of the Syrians at the Wadi al-Natrun and 17 years later was elected pope of Alexandria and 117th patriarch* of the See of St. Mark*. When tensions between Copts and Muslims escalated in 1981, he was exiled by the Egyptian government to the Monastery of St. Bishoi and was released only in 1985.

Shenouti (d. c. 466) Also, Shenudi. Abbot of Athribis in Egypt. He entered the White Monastery near Schag, about 50 miles downstream from Nag Hammadi*, where he became abbot about 388. He presided over one of the largest monastic communities in Egypt at that time, consisting of 2,200 monks and 1,800 nuns. He enforced a severe discipline, although he allowed older monks to live apart as hermits. He attended the Council of Ephesus*, where he played an important role in the defense of orthodoxy*. Feast day: July 1.

Shepherd, The Treatise written by Hermas*, so called because its contents were communicated to Hermas by an angel* in the form of a shepherd. The work consists of 5 visions, 12 mandates, and 10 similitudes. It throws considerable light on the beliefs of the early Jewish Christians and the simple piety of some Roman Christians. In the early centuries *The Shepherd* was included among the Scriptures.

shepherding movement Movement in Charismatic circles for stimulating greater discipleship by making each member responsible for monitoring the spiritual growth of one or more of their peers. Church elders keep a close watch on the conduct and lifestyles of all members. The original movement began with the Christian Growth Ministries founded in Fort Lauderdale, Florida, by the Holy Spirit Teaching Mission (1969) led by six men, Derek Prince, Bob Mumford*, Charles Simpson, Don Basham*, Ern Baxter, and John Poole, who were propagating a doctrine of delegated authority and covenant loyalty. The goal of the movement is to bring moral accountability and spiritual maturity into the church and to shield members from becoming a prey to wrong teaching and practice. The movement has a national network of followers who form pyramids of

sheep and shepherds. They also taught the need for proper covering or subjection to authority as a biblical mandate. Many Covenant churches* still follow the practice. Shepherding churches are often characterized by strong community, zeal, obedience, and vibrant worship, and sometimes by oppressive authoritarianism, almost cultic in character. See also DISCIPLING MOVEMENT.

Sheppard, Hugh Richard Lawrie (Dick) (1880–1937) High-profile Anglican vicar*. He was vicar of St. Martin's-in-the-Fields from 1914 to 1926 and later dean of Canterbury* and canon* of St. Paul's*. As a social reformer and pacifist, he founded the Peace Pledge Union.

sher'ata gecawe Ethiopian lectionary* containing the texts of the Psalms and Gospels for vespers*.

sher'ata keddase Book of the Oblation used by Ethiopian Catholics.

S'Hertogenbosch St. Janskerk, a five-aisled basilica*, in S'Hertogenbosch in the Netherlands built from 1360 to 1419. In the first half of the fifteenth century the north and south transepts* were added and in 1498 to 1497 Alard Duhamel built the side-aisles as well as the Chapel of the Sacrament. Much of the original furnishing has been lost. The surviving treasures include the choir stalls*, carved Renaissance pulpit, a copper font, candelabra, and a triptych* altar.

Shield of Orthodoxy Declaration of the Synod of Jerusalem*, 1672, which defined the Orthodox doctrines on sacraments*, transubstantiation*, and the infallibility of the church.

ship Ancient symbol of the church in religious art.

shkinta In the Assyrian tradition, table below the steps leading to the sanctuary on which is placed a wooden cross and a Bible. When receiving Communion, communicants kiss the shkinta and leave an offering.

shlika Also, the apostle. In the Assyrian tradition, the text of the Epistles found in the East Syrian lectionary*.

sh'lomo In the Syrian tradition, the kiss of peace* that consists of taking the offered hands between one's own and then touching one's face or forehead.

sh'mash (lit., minister) In the Syrian tradition, vessel used for cleaning the vessels after Communion or cleaning the hands.

shordion In the Coptic tradition, the stole* worn in different styles according to the status of the wearer. In the case of a subdeacon, the free end is tucked into the band or zinnar* in front, but in the case of deacons and priests it is allowed to hang outside.

Shorter Catechism Presbyterian catechism* written in 1647 in the form of questions and answers covering all theological doctrines drawn up at the Westminster Assembly* for "those of weaker faith." It begins with the famous question, "What is the chief end of man?" and gives the answer, "Man's chief end is to glorify God and to enjoy him forever." It exerted a deep and extensive influence in cultures dominated by the Presbyterian tradition.

shoure In the Coptic tradition, heavily ornamented censer* with tiny bells.

shrift (Old Eng.) Confession and absolution*.

shrine (Lat., *scrinium*, chest) Sacred image kept in a church or in any holy place, especially one that is the object of pilgrimages*. More broadly, memorial tableau that becomes a center of commemoration and devotion.

shrive (Old Eng.) To hear a confession* of sin, prescribe a penance*, and absolve from guilt.

Shroud of Turin Shroud preserved since 1578 in Cathedral of Turin, Italy, said to be the linen cloth in which Joseph of Arimathea wrapped the body of Jesus after it had been taken down from the cross. It appears to bear the faint features of a man's features, although it is not established that it is the authentic face of Christ. The first historical reference to the shroud is in 1360 at Lirey in the diocese* of Troyes in France.

Shrove Tuesday Day immediately preceding Ash Wednesday*, so named because it is a day for shriving, confession*, and absolution*.

Shrovetide The one to three days before Lent* set apart for confession* of sins.

shubboho In the Assyrian tradition, short anthem that precedes the priest's Communion.

shunning In Mennonite usage, the penalty that those excommunicated by the church were to be shunned by others.

shunoyo In the Jacobite tradition, Feast of the Dormition of the Virgin* celebrated on August 15.

shuraya (lit., the beginning) In the Assyrian tradition, the antiphon* that precedes the prayer before the apostle, similar to the Byzantine prokeimenon*.

shurjar Chasuble* shaped like a cope* worn by Armenian priests.

shushepo In the Jacobite and Assyrian traditions: 1. Small hand cross with a veil. 2. The three veils covering the sacred vessels during the liturgy. Those that cover the paten* or chalice* are known as the huppoyo, and that which covers both is known as kletho.

Shroud of Turin

shvot Coptic episcopal pastoral staff* with two serpents entwined at the top on either side of a small round sphere mounted by a cross.

Si quis (Lat., if anyone) Notice given in a parish* church that a resident intends to offer himself for ordination, and calling on anyone who knows a just cause or impediment thereto to declare it before the bishop.

siamidha (Syr., laying on of hands) In the Assyrian Church*: 1. Ordination or consecration. 2. Book containing the service of ordination. 3. Prayer said at the laying on of hands*. 4. Consecration of a church.

Siberia Orthodoxy was introduced into Siberia along with Russian conquest and colonization. Patriarch Filaret of Moscow* created the Tobolsk diocese* to coordinate the Christianization of Siberia. Metropolitan Filioque Leshchinskii built over 37 monastic missionary outposts for this purpose. In 1793, the first Orthodox missionary group reached Alaska. This group included the monk Herman, the patron saint* of Alaska. Innokentii Veniaminov continued evangelization of the native people of Alaska and Siberia. In 1870 he founded the Orthodox Missionary Society. Work on the translation of Christian texts began in the eighteenth century and has continued into the twentieth.

Sic et Non (Lat., yes and no) 1. Method of argument used by medieval theologians in which contradictory passages of Scripture are presented in order to stimulate the resolution of the contradictions. 2. Title of Abelard's famous work using this method.

sic transit gloria mundi (Lat., thus passes the glory of the world) Words addressed to a new pope at his coronation when symbols of worldly pomp are burned before him.

sidesmen In the Church of England*, assistants to church wardens elected by the annual parochial meeting. Their duties include showing worshipers to their seats and taking up the offering.

Siena Santa Maria Assunta, cathedral in Siena, Italy. The lower part of the marble facade was designed by Giovanni Pisano* between 1284 and 1299. The dome over the crossing* was erected by the monks of San Galgano between 1259 and 1264.

Si-Gan-Fu Stone Also, Sian-Fu Stone. Inscription in Chinese and Syriac* dated between 779 and 781 discovered at Si-Gan-Fu in 1625 by Jesuit missionaries. The stone is 7.5 feet high and 3 feet wide. Set up by a Nestorian synod of 779, it describes the fortunes of the Nestorian Christians since Alopen* visited the Emperor T'ai Tsung, particularly the establishment of monasteries under Emperor Kao-tsung and the establishment of a bishopric in 650. Later, there were conflicts with Buddhists and persecutions, but by the first part of the eighth century, Catholicos Selibhazekha became metropolitan* of China. The stone also contains a confession* of faith using much Chinese idiom.

sign In Scriptures, any one of the following: a physical mark (Gen. 4:15), a warning (Num. 16:38), a monument (Josh. 4:6) an ensign (Ps. 74:4) a reminder (Deut. 6:8), a portent (Isa. 20:3), a signature (2 Thess. 3:17), or a miracle, as in signs

Si-Gan-Fu Stone

and wonders (John 4:54). In the New Testament, a sign may be a physical healing, a confirmation of personal salvation* or prophecy*, or an indication of the advent of eschatological events.

sign of the cross Tracing the cross in outline with a motion of the hand. The traditional way is to take the right hand from the forehead to the center of the chest, then from shoulder to shoulder, and then back to the center of the chest. In the West the chest is crossed from left to right and in the East from right to left. In Chalcedonian churches it is made with three fingers and in the Monophysite churches with two.

signation Signing of the cross, especially in baptism*, when the baptisand is "marked with the cross of Christ forever."

Signatura, Apostolic Highest tribunal of the judicial system of the Roman Catholic Church.

Sigtuna Foundation and center of Christian missions in Sweden, located since 1984 in Uppsala*. It was founded in 1915 by M. Bjorkquist, later bishop of Stockholm.

Silent Night! Holy Night! Best-loved Christmas carol* written by the Austrian Joseph Mohr*. It was first sung on Christmas Eve 1818 when (because of an organ breakdown) organist Franz Gruber* was asked to set the text to music for choir, two voices, and guitar. The carol was translated into English by John Freeman Young in 1863.

SIM International Evangelical foreign mission agency formed in 1982 through the merger of Sudan Interior Mission* (founded in 1893) and Andes Evangelical Mission, founded in 1907. In 1989 SIM added Asia to its mission fields* through a merger with the International Christian Fellowship.

simar Black cassock* with cape, purple sash, buttons, and piping worn by a bishop.

Simeon, Charles (1759–1836) Anglican evangelical leader. He was converted to Evangelical Christianity through his friendship with John and Henry Venn*. He ministered in the Holy Trinity

Church in Cambridge from 1782 until his death and was also a fellow of King's College. He helped found the Church Missionary Society* and London Jews Society, later Church Mission to the Jews. His sermon outlines were published in 21 volumes. He influenced and set standards for generations of Evangelical leaders.

Simeon Stylites (c. 390–459) The most famous of the pillar ascetics. Born in Cilicia*, he became an anchorite* in Antioch*. From 423 he began living on a pillar at Telanissus (Dair Sem'an) and continued to do so until his death. The height of the pillar was gradually increased until it reached 60 feet. After his death a monastery and a church were built on the site of the pillar. Feast day: September 1 (Eastern Orthodox*); January 5 (Syrian Orthodox*).

Simeon the New Theologian, St. (949–1022) Byzantine mystic, the greatest of the Byzantine mystical writers. In 977 he entered the Studios* Monastery in Constantinople* and later became abbot of the Monastery of St. Mamas. In 1005 he was forced to resign and four years later exiled. Although his sentence was revoked, he remained in retirement for the rest of his life. His ascetical practices shaped the development of Hesychasm*. The Eucharist* had a central place in his teaching.

Simon Magus Sorcerer who appears in Acts 8:9–24 as one who professed Christianity and was baptized but later was rebuked by Peter* for trying to obtain spiritual powers for money. Later he was regarded as the fountainhead of Christian heresies.

Simon, Richard (1638–1712) Biblical scholar and father of Old Testament criticism. In his *Histoire Critique du Vieux Testament* (1678), he argued that Moses was not the author of the Pentateuch. For this he was expelled from his order, the French Oratory.

Simon the Less, St. One of the 12 apostles, called in Matthew 10:4 and Mark 3:18 "the Canaanite." The apocryphal Passion of Simon and Jude narrates his martyrdom in Persia.

simony Deliberate use of monetary incentives to purchase or acquire spiritual gifts* or offices, so called from Simon Magus, the sorcerer who tried to do so (Acts 8:9–24).

Peter and Simon Magus

simpatizante In Latin America, a person sympathetic to Protestantism* but unable to make public profession or seek church membership.

simple feast Feast of the lowest rank having no second vespers* and only one nocturn* with three lessons at mattins*.

Simplicius, St. (d. 483) Pope from 468. During his reign Monophysitism* spread throughout the East, and he worked hard to contain it. He established several new churches, including the St. Stefano Rotondo on the Celian Hill. Feast day: March 2 or 10.

Simpson, A. B. (1843–1919) Founder of the Christian and Missionary Alliance*. Originally a Presbyterian minister, he became an Evangelical after receiving a miraculous healing and founded the Christian and Missionary Alliance* in 1887 with a strong emphasis on sanctification* and the Great Commission*. He coined the term *Fourfold Gospel* to exalt Christ as Savior, sanctifier, healer, and coming king.

Simul Justus et Peccator (Lat., at the same time righteous and a sinner) Martin Luther's description of a Christian as never ceasing to be sinful while justified before God. The Christian never outlives repentance* and justification*.

simultaneity In Kierkegaardian thought, the state for a Christian of being present with and in Christ in a state of constant interaction.

simultaneous audible prayer Prayer in tongues* by an entire congregation aloud and at the same time during worship services.

sin 1. Act or thought that deliberately violates divine law and offends holiness*. 2. Falling short of the mark of righteousness required of a believer. 3. Any of the various failings and shortcomings as well as lusts and evil desires to which the human race is subject as a result of original sin*. Divided into mortal sin and venial sin in theology. See also ACTUAL SIN (a violation of the moral order) and HABITUAL SIN (the condition that results from repeated actual sins).

Sinai, Church of Smallest independent church of the Orthodox Communion ruled by the archbishop of Mount Sinai who is also the abbot of the Monastery of St. Catherine*. It consists of the monastery and some dependencies. Its independence dates from 1575, confirmed in 1782. Its archbishop is consecrated by the patriarch* of Jerusalem*. The monastery library was the source of the famous Codex Sinaiticus* and has a rich collection of manuscripts, icons, and other early Byzantine* treasures. The monastery church dates from the reign of Justinian* and was built by Stephen of Aila.

sindon In the Byzantine tradition, liturgical veil, handkerchief, or cloth.

sindonology Science of the study of the Shroud of Turin*.

singing in the Spirit 1. Singing in tongues*. 2. Spontaneous and unrehearsed music.

siniyah In the Jacobite tradition, the linen purificator* used to gather up the particles* of the consecrated bread during the liturgy.

Sinodos Ethiopic collection of canons, the first

two sections of which are also known as Sinodos Alexandrina, dating from the fifth century. It contains four discrete documents: the Apostolic Church Order, *Apostolic Tradition**, part of the Apostolic Constitutions*, and the apostolic canons*.

Siricius, St. (d. 399) Pope from 384. His letter to Himerius of Tarragona is the first papal decretal. He held a synod* in Rome* in 386 which passed nine canons on ecclesiastical discipline. Feast day: November 26.

Sirmium, Council of Council convened by Emperor Constantius, an Arian sympathizer, in 357 to overthrow the decrees of the Nicaean Council*. It deleted the reference to ousios and substituted a baptismal Trinity* and a subordinate, begotten Son. Its doctrinal formula* is therefore known as the Blasphemy of Sirmium.

sister 1. A nun. 2. A female church worker, often as a term of address.

Sisters for Christian Community Noncanonical community of women founded in 1970 by Lillanna Kopp. It is not subject to any control by the Vatican* or local bishops. There is no presiding officer, motherhouse, rule, or constitution. Each member is self-supporting and responsible for her own living arrangements.

Sisters of Holy Cross Congregation founded by Father Basil Moreau in Le Mans, France, in 1841, with an independent congregation at Notre Dame, Indiana. They are involved in education, health, and missions.

Sisters of Loreto at the Foot of the Cross Congregation founded in 1812 by three women from Kentucky: Mary Rhodes, Christina Stuart, and Nancy Havern. The sisters* were notable in opening schools in sparsely settled territories in the American Southwest.

Sisters of Mary of the Presentation Congregation founded in Broons, France, in 1828 by Mother St. Louis Le Marchand and Father Joachim Fleury. At various times, the sisters* were persecuted by the anticlerical French governments.

Sisters of Mercy Also, Sisters of Charity. Any of a number of Roman Catholic women's religious orders, such as the sisterhood founded in Dublin in 1827 by Catherine McAuley*, that founded by Vincent de Paul* in 1634, or those founded by Mgr. Marechaux, canon E. J. Triest, Mary Aikenhead, Mgr. Zwissen, and Madame Mole de Champlatreux. All U.S. Congregations of Mercy, 18 independent congregations, and nine provinces are affiliated with the Federation of the Sisters of Mercy of the Americas.

Sisters of Notre Dame de Namur Congregation founded in 1803 by Julie Billiart in Amiens*, France, and later moved to Namur, Belgium. Now headquartered in Rome*, the sisters* are active in many countries of the world.

Sisters of Providence Name of several congregations in France, Belgium, Netherlands, and Canada. In the United States they have congregations in Holyoke, Massachusetts; Seattle, Washington; and St. Mary of the Woods, Indiana.

Sisters of St. Dominic Apostolic religious communities of women affiliated with the Order of Preachers* founded in 1205 by St. Dominic*. The goal of the order is to "contemplate and give others the fruits of contemplation." In the 1990s there were 148 congregations, including 36 in the United States.

Sisters of St. Joseph Congregations of women religious founded at LePuy, France, in 1661, dedicated to the Holy Trinity. The constitutions, rules, and maxims of perfection of the order were prepared by Father Jean Pierre Medaille. The first U.S. branch was established in St. Louis, Missouri, in 1836.

Sisters of the Holy Name of Jesus and Mary Order of nuns established in 1843 in Quebec, Canada, under Eulalie Durocher, later known as Mother Marie-Rose.

Sisters, Servants of the Immaculate Heart of Mary Order of nuns founded in 1845 in Monroe, Michigan, by Louis Florent Gillet and Mother Teresa Maxis Duchemin. They are involved in education and health.

Sistine Of or relating to popes bearing the name *Sixtus.*

Sistine Chapel Main chapel in the Vatican* used by the pope as his private chapel. It is used for important papal ceremonies and also for the election of new popes. The chapel is noted for its frescoes* by Michelangelo*, particularly his *Last Judgment* covering the altar wall. It was built by Sixtus IV*.

Sistine Chapel

Sistine Madonna One of Raphael's most famous altarpieces, now in Dresden, showing the Virgin Mary* and child floating on the clouds of heaven between Pope Sixtus II* and St. Barbara*. It has been called the "sublimest lyric of the art of Catholicity*."

Sitz im Leben (Ger., place in life) Principle in biblical criticism* that determines the meaning of a text or story within the cultural context of the time and place or the mode or purpose of the text's transmission.

Six Articles Articles imposed by the Religion Act of 1539 called, disparagingly, the whip with six strings, to contain the spread of the Reformation* in England. It maintained six Catholic doctrines:

transubstantiation*, Communion in only one kind, clerical celibacy*, monastic vows, private masses, and auricular confession*.

Six Points Six High Church* practices introduced into the Church of England* through the efforts of the Oxford movement*. They include eastward position, eucharistic vestments, mixed chalice*, altar lights, unleavened bread* at the Eucharist*, and incense.

666 See NUMBER OF THE BEAST.

Sixtus II, St. (d. 258). Bishop of Rome* from 257. He suffered martyrdom under the second edict of Emperor Valerian and was buried in the catacomb* of St. Callistus*. Feast day: August 7.

Sixtus IV (1414–1484) Pope from 1471. Birth name: Francesco delle Rovere. He was one of the most corrupt and extravagant of the medieval popes, and his energies during the 13-year pontificate* were devoted to the furtherance of his family interests and to political manipulation. However, he was a friend of the arts and scholarship. He founded the Sistine* Choir, built the Sistine Chapel*, and enlarged the Vatican Library*.

Sixtus V (1521–1590) Pope from 1585. Birth name: Felice Peretti. His pontificate* was devoted to the reform of the church and the papal states. He fixed the number of cardinals at 70 and established 15 congregations. He was also a patron of art and scholarship. He rebuilt the Lateran Palace and the Vatican Library* and finished the cupola of St. Peter's*. He also oversaw a new edition of the Vulgate*.

S.J. Society of Jesus*.

skete Small Russian monastic community, generally dependent on a lavra*.

skeuphylaion In the Byzantine tradition, area to the right of the altar where the sacred vessels and vestments are stored.

ski In the Armenian tradition, the chalice*.

Skobtsova, Mother Maria (1891–1945) Born Elizaveta

Iur'evna Pilenko to a privileged family, she became a socialist revolutionary, but fled the Soviet Union in 1920 and settled in Paris in 1923. In 1930 she became the secretary of the Russian Student Christian Movement*. Under the guidance of Sergius Bulgakov*, Metropolitan Evlogii, and other emigres, she became a nun in 1932. She was one of the founders of Orthodox Action, an independent Christian social action organization. Because of her work to aid Jews, she was deported to the death camps by the Nazis and died in the gas chamber in Ravensbruch.

Skoptsi/Skoptsy (Russ., eunuchs) Russian sect whose members emasculated themselves in obedience to Matthew 19:12. They condemned sex and engaged in severe ascetical practices. Their early leaders were Akulina Ivanova and Blochin.

skouphos In the Byzantine tradition, a small brimless cap worn by monks under their veils. The skouphos and the veil are collectively called perikephalaia in Greek and shlem in Slavonic.

skrizhali (lit., the tables of the Law) In the Byzantine Church*, the squares of velvet sewn on a bishop's mantle at the neck, symbolizing the four evangelists.

skufya In the Russian Orthodox Church*, black pointed cap worn by priests, corresponding to the biretta*.

Skufya

slain in the Spirit Pentecostal phenomenon in which the believer falls down being overtaken by the Holy Spirit*, also known as "falling under the power," "overcome by the Spirit," and "resting in the Spirit." This practice is particularly associated with the Toronto Blessing* and the ministries of Kathryn Kuhlman*, Kenneth Hagin*, and Charles and Frances Hunter. Characteristics of the blessing include a loss of feeling and control,

lack of sensation, holy laughter* or weeping, and making of strange noises. The experience may last from a few seconds to a few minutes or hours.

Slava Also, Krsno Ime. Feast of the family patron saint* among the Serbian Orthodox Church*. Slava refers to the glory of the patron saint of the family. Krsno Ime refers to the sign of the cross made when a believer receives a Christian name*. The ceremony includes blessing of the cross-loaf, a round loaf of bread decorated with five bread stamps placed in a cross-shaped pattern and kollyba, a dish of cooked wheat mixed with sugar and ground walnuts. Slava is distinct from Imendan, or the feast day of an individual's christening*.

sleepless lamp In the Byzantine tradition, lamp that burns perpetually in the apse* behind the altar.

Sleidanus, Johannes (1506–1556) First historian of the Reformation* whose *Commentarii de Statu Religionis et Rei Publicae Carolo V Caesare*, published in two volumes in 1555, is valuable as an eyewitness document of the Reformation*.

Slessor, Mary (1848–1915) Scottish missionary to West Africa. Converted in her teens, she sailed for Nigeria in 1876 and worked among the Ibo almost continuously until her death. She was fluent in the native languages and became a trusted arbiter in disputes of all kinds. She began the Helen Waddell Institute to train Africans in the useful trades and to engage in medical work. She was instrumental in making the Ibo one of the most Christianized tribes in Africa.

Slovak Rite Rite used by Byzantine Catholics in the Slovak Republic.

slutha dlilya (lit., prayer at night) In the Assyrian Rite, the night office which may be combined with shara or lauds* and slutha dsafra or prime*.

sluzhebnik In the Byzantine Rite*, service book that contains the fixed parts of the three liturgies of St. Basil*, St. John Chrysostom*, and the Liturgy of the Presanctified* together with an abridged euchologion* containing common services, such as baptism, penance*, and unction*.

Smalcald Articles See SCHMALKALDIC ARTICLES.

Small Euchologion In the Eastern Orthodox Church*, book containing five minor sacraments*, the funeral offices, occasional offices*, and blessings.

small group movement Transdenominational movement of groups or cells who meet together for Bible study, prayer, and faith-sharing as a means of renewal.

Smith, Chuck (1927–) Pastor and leader in the Jesus People* movement in Southern California in the 1970s and 1980s. After serving in churches in Arizona and Southern California, he was called to the Calvary Chapel* in Costa Mesa, California. Under his pastorate*, the church grew to 25,000 members and received national attention as one of the centers of the Jesus People movement. His mass baptisms brought thousands into the fold. The church established a Bible college and spawned over 700 affiliate congregations across the United States and the world. Smith is also a well-known broadcaster.

Smith, Hannah Whitall (1832–1911) American Quaker*, author of *The Christian's Secret of a Happy Life*. She was converted in 1858 under the influence of Plymouth Brethren* and experienced a new life in Christ based on Romans 6:6. She and her husband committed their lives to Christ and moved to England, where their interdenominational meetings devoted to biblical exposition led to the founding of the Keswick Convention* in 1874.

Smith, Joseph (1805–1844) Founder of Mormonism and a prophet* of the Church of Jesus Christ of Latter-Day Saints*. He is said to have experienced a conversion at the age of 15 and subsequently to have received a direct revelation* from God engraved on golden plates. He translated and published the contents of these tablets as the *Book of Mormon*ned in 1830. He followed it up with *A Book of Commandments* in 1833 (later republished as *Doctrine and Covenants* in 1835). Both these

books form the scriptures of the Mormon Church. He claimed divine sanction for his own polygamy, which so incensed his neighbors in Carthage, Illinois, that they lynched him in 1844.

Smith, Wilbur Moorehead (1894–1976) Presbyterian Fundamentalist teacher. Beginning in 1917, Smith served congregations in Delaware, Maryland, Virginia, and Pennsylvania. He began a teaching career in 1937 at Moody Bible Institute*, leaving it ten years later to move to Fuller Theological Seminary*, where he taught until the inerrancy* controversy forced him out in 1963. He spent his last years as a teacher at Trinity Evangelical Divinity School. He was also the author of a dozen books and edited the 38 annual volumes of *Peloubet's Select Notes on the International Bible Lessons for Christian Living*.

Smolny Convent The Cathedral of the Assumption of the Virgin in St. Petersburg, Russia, built in the form of a Greek cross*, with four onion-domed towers enclosing a central dome. It was built by Francesco Rastrelli at the instance of Empress Elizabeth I. The cathedral was completed by Stasov between 1832 and 1835. Although intended as a convent, the monastery became a boarding school for girls of noble birth.

snake handling Physical handling of snakes as a means of demonstrating the truth of Mark 16:18; Luke 10:19, and Acts 28:3–5. The practice is limited to Pentecostal communities in some southern U.S. states. Sometimes, the practice extends to fire contact and drinking of poison.

sobor In the Russian Orthodox Church*, a church council or synod*.

sobornost (Russ., *sobor*, assembly) 1. Special characteristic of the Russian Orthodox Church* denoting conciliarity* and the organic unity of believers within the fellowship of the church. 2. Principle of spiritual unity and religious community based on a free commitment to a tradition of catholicity* interpreted through the ecumenical councils of the Orthodox Church. The word cannot be adequately translated by any one English word. It has been taken up in recent ecumenical reflections. See KOINONIA.

sobranya Worship meeting of the Doukhobors*.

Social Creed of the Churches Statement adopted in 1912 by the Federal Council of Churches of Christ* (U.S.A.). It opposed capitalistic exploitation of the working class and urged social legislation.

social gospel Prominent theological movement in North America in the nineteenth and early twentieth centuries emphasizing social improvement over the propagation of the gospel. It corresponded to the Christian socialist movement in the United Kingdom and focused on correcting the injustices and exploitation suffered by the working poor, championed the rights of labor, and criticized the excessive individualism of capitalist society. It also provided an avenue for the do-gooders in Christian churches by ascribing Christian virtue to the public display of compassion for the poor in and of itself.

The father of the social gospel was Washington Gladden (1836–1918), a Congregational* minister and prolific author. Other spokesmen for the movement included Josiah Strong, secretary of the American Evangelical Alliance; economist Richard T. Ely, author of *Social Aspects of Christianity* (1889) and *The Social Law of Service* (1896); and Walter Rauschenbusch*, who became the prophet of the movement. Because advocates of the social gospel did not belong to any denomination exclusively, it did not have a homogeneous theology, but it shared many affinities with liberal theology, especially a view of Christ as a source of ethics only, an exaggerated view of human brotherhood*, a utopian view of human nature, and a certainty that progress was inevitable. Two world wars helped to deflate the social gospel, but it survives in many churches in one form or another.

social holiness In Wesleyan theology, holiness* in its interpersonal and societal relationships, as distinguished from ascetical holiness.

Socialism, Christian See CHRISTIAN SOCIALISM.

Society for Promoting Christian Knowledge See SPCK.

Society for the Propagation of Gospel [in Foreign Parts] See SPG.

Society of Biblical Literature North American association of biblical scholars founded in 1880 by Frederic Gardiner, Charles A. Briggs, and Philip Schaff*. It publishes the *Journal of Biblical Literature*.

Society of Brothers (Bruderhof) Intentional Christian community founded in 1920 in Sannerz, Germany, by Eberhard Arnold* and inspired by the Hutterite leader, Christoph F. Blumhardt. Later, after the rise of Hitler forced them out of Germany, the society established colonies in Paraguay, Uruguay, and the United States. The society is based on the Sermon on the Mount, and fosters hospitality, pacifism, and frequent worship.

Society of Friends See QUAKER.

Society of Jesus See JESUITS.

Society of St. John the Evangelist Oldest men's religious community in the Church of England*, popularly known as the Cowley Fathers*, founded by R. M. Benson* in 1865. The society has branches in India, the United States, Canada, and Africa where they conduct retreats and promote ecumenical activities. See also COWLEY FATHERS.

Society of St. Vincent de Paul International Roman Catholic association of lay persons seeking to help the poor founded by Frederic Ozanam* (1813–1853) in 1833. It currently operates in 112 countries and has over 800,000 members.

Society of the Divine Word Missionary congregation of priests and lay brothers* exempt from clerical control, founded in 1875 at Steyl in the Netherlands by Blessed Arnold Janssen* (1837–1909) and approved by the pope in 1905. The generalate* is located in Rome*. Members include both brothers* and priests whose main work is evangelization. There are branches in Argentina, West Africa, United States, Papua New Guinea, Japan, Philippines, Britain, and other European countries. It focuses on countries where the gospel has not been preached at all or only insufficently and is involved in education and the dissemination of Christian literature.

Society of the Holy Cross (Lat., *Societas Sanctae Crucis*) Anglo-Catholic society of clergy founded in 1855 by C. F. Lowder and others to foster a stricter rule for the clergy. It was instrumental in the liturgical revision of the *Book of Common Prayer** and in the revival of sacramental confession*.

Society of the Sacred Heart Community of sisters* devoted to religious and academic education, founded in France by Madeleine Sophie Barat* in 1800.

Socinianism Heresy founded by Lelio Francesco Maria Sozzini* (1525–1562) and his nephew Fausto Paulo Sozzini* (1539–1604) which was the forerunner of modern Unitarianism*. The former was a Sienese lawyer who became an anti-Trinitarian early in life and traveled through Italy, Switzerland, France, England, and the Netherlands, propagating his views. Fausto followed in his uncle's footsteps, writing and teaching against the Trinity* and the deity of Christ. After wandering through Italy, France, Hungary, and other countries, he settled in Poland, where he spread moderate Unitarian ideas among the upper classes. See also UNITARIANISM.

Faustus Sozzini

Socrates Scholasticus (380–450) Ecclesiastical historian. Socrates's work, divided into seven books and covering the period from 306 to 439, is a continuation of Eusebius* and is arranged chronologically.

sodality (Lat., *sodalis,* companion) Catholic guild or confraternity* organized for specific religious purposes.

Soderblom, Nathan Lars Olof (1866–1931) Archbishop of Uppsala* and Swedish liberal theologian. A primate* of the Lutheran Church of Sweden, he was awarded the Nobel Peace Prize in 1930 and was active in the ecumenical Stockholm Conference* of 1925. Among his books, the best known is *The Living God* (1931).

Soga, Tiyo (c. 1829–1871) First African ordained minister of the United Presbyterian Church in South Africa, translator of the Bible and *Pilgrim's Progess** into Xhosa.

Soissons, Council of 1. Council held about 1092 against Roscelin, the Nominalist theologian who was accused of Tritheism*. 2. Council held in 1121 to censure* and burn Peter Abelard's* work, *Theologia Summi Boni.*

Sojourners Community of Christians committed to radical discipleship, founded in Chicago by Jim Wallis in 1971 as the People's Christian Coalition. It moved to Washington, D.C., in 1975 and changed its name as well as the name of its magazine to *Sojourners* to reflect the belief that Christians are an alien society of God's people. It challenges contemporary establishment on a number of social and economic issues and attempts to create a discipleship of believers committed to social peace, justice, reconciliation, and equality.

Sola Fide (Lat., faith alone) Phrase summarizing the Reformation* doctrine of justification* as received by faith* alone.

Sola Gratia (Lat., grace alone) Phrase summarizing the Reformation* doctrine of the grace* of God as the exclusive agent of salvation*.

Sola Scriptura (Lat., scripture alone) Phrase summarizing the Reformation doctrine that the Bible alone is the ultimate authority of faith and life.

Solafidianism Doctrine based on *Sola Fide** as established in Romans 4:5, Galatians 2:16, 3:11, and Ephesians 2:8.

soldier In the Salvation Army*, a converted person over age 14 enrolled as a member after signing the Articles of War.

solemn High Mass High Mass* sung with the aid of a deacon and subdeacon.

solemnitas/solemnity In the Roman Catholic Church, feast of the greatest importance. Its observance begins with first vespers* on the evening of the preceding day. Some solemnities have their own vigil Mass*. All Sundays throughout the year are solemnities. Easter* and Christmas* are the two greatest solemnities.

Solesmes Benedictine monastery dedicated to St. Peter* in Sarthes, France, founded in 1010. It was constituted an abbey in 1837 with Dom Prosper Gueranger* as its first abbot. It is a center of the liturgical movement* in France and has been a powerful influence in the revival and development of liturgical music, especially the Gregorian Chant*.

Solovyov, Vladimir Sergeevich (1853–1900) Russian philosopher and theologian. In 1877 he became a friend of Feodor Dostoevsky*, whose religious ideas he shared. From the early 1880s he worked for a union of the Roman Catholic* and Russian Orthodox churches* in the hope of the eventual creation of a universal ecumenical church. Because of his Roman Catholic sympathies, he is known as the "Russian Newman." In his philosophy, he evidenced a disturbing influence of pantheism* and Gnosticism*. He espoused the ideal of Sophia* as eternal wisdom and the eternal feminine principle and argued the existence of a world soul. In the early 1880s he was forbidden by the Holy Synod* to write on theology. His chief works are: *Lectures Concerning Godmanhood* (1878), *The History and the Future of Theocracy* (1886), *La Russie et l'Eglise Universelle* (1889), and *Three Conversations* (1899–1900).

Solus Christos (Lat., Christ alone) Phrase summarizing the Reformation* doctrine that Jesus Christ is the only mediator* and Savior for sinful humanity.

Solzhenitsyn, Alexander (1918–) Russian writer. Although a convinced Marxist, he was arrested by the Soviet Secret Police for critical comments about Stalin and sentenced to eight years in prison. This formed the setting of his novel, *The First Circle* (1968) and *One Day in the Life of Ivan Denisovich* (1968). During his imprisonment he became an ardent Christian. Released with terminal cancer after Stalin's death in 1953, he made a miraculous recovery, which is recorded in *Cancer Ward* (1953). Although his books were banned from the Soviet Union, he won the Nobel Prize for Literature in 1970. The publication of *August 1914* (1971) and *The Gulag Archipelago* (1973) led to his exile in the West. He moved first to Switzerland and later to Vermont, U.S.A., where he settled down until the late 1980s, when he returned to Russia. The liberal West has never been able to accept his greatness as a Christian writer or his strictures about its decadence.

Alexander Solzhenitsyn

Somaschi Order of clerks regular* who follow the Rule of St. Augustine*, founded in 1532 by St. Jerome Emiliani* at Somasca in northern Italy to work among the poor and destitute.

sonata de chiesa Church sonata, one of the two principal types of instrumental music in the Baroque period. The trio sonata was usually composed of two violins and violincello and sona sonata, usually for solo violin and violincello.

Sophia (Gk., wisdom) 1. Principle of wisdom, based

on presentation of personified wisdom in the Old Testament Wisdom books, but developed especially by Gnostic systems and in some modern radical feminist theology*, almost as female divinity. 2. Attribute of Jesus Christ and a title applied to him by St. Paul* in 1 Corinthians 1:24.

Sophronius, St. (c. 560–638) Patriarch* of Jerusalem* from 634. He had the misfortune to witness the capture of Jerusalem by the Arabs under Caliph Omar in 637. He upheld the Chalcedonian doctrine of two natures. In addition to sermons and poems, he wrote lives of Cyrus and John, Alexandrian martyrs*. Feast day: March 11.

Sopocani The Holy Trinity Church at Sopocani in southwestern Serbia, founded about 1256 by King Uros I. It was demolished by the Turks some time after 1389, rebuilt in the fifteenth century, destroyed by the Turks again in 1689, and restored in 1926. It was rebuilt in 1975.

Sorbonne College of the Old University of Paris, originally known as the Collegium Pauperum Magistrorum, founded about 1257 by Robert de Sorbon, confessor* of St. Louis. It was approved by Pope Clement IV in 1268. In the Middle Ages it was the most famous theological faculty in Europe, and although it subscribed to Gallicanism*, defended the Roman Catholic Church against the Reformers and the Rationalists of the eighteenth century. It was suppressed in 1793 after the French Revolution, and although revived under Napoleon, was finally abolished in 1885. The name *Sorbonne* continues to be applied to the university as a whole.

Sorin, Edward Frederick (1838–1893) Founder and first president of the University of Notre Dame. A Frenchman by birth, he was ordained in 1838 and joined the Congregation of the Holy Cross* in 1840. Next year he was sent to the United States to establish the congregation in Vincennes, Indiana. In 1842 he founded the University of Notre Dame near South Bend. Sorin was instrumental in developing the thoroughly American character of the university. As the congregation's superior general* from 1868 to 1893, he moved its international headquarters from France to the United States. Sorin also founded six other institutions of Catholic higher education.

soros In the Byzantine tradition, chapel used to house the relics* of saints*.

Sorrowful Mysteries In Roman Catholic devotion, second chaplet* of the Rosary*, consisting of five decades: the agony in Gethsemane, the scourging, the crowning with thorns, the carrying of the cross, and the crucifixion.

soteriology (Gk., *soteria,* salvation) Branch of theology dealing with salvation*, including atonement*, grace*, original sin*, redemption*, repentance*, justification*, regeneration*, adoption, initial sanctification*, and final glorification*.

soul One of the facets of a human being, particularly that which is designed for fellowship with God. It is often identified with spirit. Theological anthropology now generally focuses on a unitary view of humanity, rather than a three-part (soul, body, and spirit) or two-part (soul and body) division into different elements. It affirms that the whole person is made in God's image and views the immortality* of the soul as quite possibly an alien Greek intrusion. The Greek word, *psyche,* often translated as *soul* in the King James Version, should often be rendered *life.*

soul competence Baptist doctrine that each person is capable of interpreting scriptural doctrines in the light of personal circumstances.

soul sleep Also, psychopannychy*. Period between death and the final resurrection in which the soul is in an unconscious state. This has been a matter of controversy in Christian circles.

soul-winning Evangelism* as a means of rescuing souls from eternal damnation and bringing people to personal acceptance of and belief in Jesus Christ as Lord and Savior. Thus, soul-winner.

sourb astvats (Arm., holy God) Trisagion* in the Armenian Liturgy. On feast days of the cross and on fasting days, "who was crucified for us" is inserted in the hymn.

soutane (Lat., underneath) Cassock*, as part of a priest's vestments.

South India, Church of Church formed in 1947 through the union of the Anglican Church (or Church Missionary Society*) of India, Burma, and Ceylon with four dioceses* of Madras, Tinnevelly, Travancore and Cochin, and Dornakal, the South India province of the Methodist Church, and the South India United Church, itself a merger of Presbyterian*, Congregational*, and Dutch Reformed* bodies. It is doctrinally based on the Lambeth Quadrilateral* with a united, episcopally ordained ministry.

Southern Baptist Convention The largest evangelical denomination in the United States. It is a voluntary organization of Baptist churches with no legal claim or authority over them. Baptists* originally were confined to New England, and they spread rapidly to the South after the Great Awakening* when Shubal Stearns won thousands of southerners to Christ. In 1814 Baptist churches of the South joined with others to form the Triennial Convention. In the 1840s, relations between the northern and southern members of the Triennial Convention soured, and in 1845 member churches in the eight southern states voted to form the Southern Baptist Convention. During the Civil War black Baptist churches withdrew. There were also disputes between the anti-mission Calvinists and the evangelistic General Baptists*. Generally, Southern Baptists have had fewer splits and controversies than other denominations.

Southern Baptist beliefs are centered around the primacy of the Bible as the sole norm for faith and practice, adult baptism by immersion*, democratic church polity*, and religious liberty. There is a heavy emphasis on evangelism and missions. Some of the twentieth-century's most influential preachers were Southern Baptists.

Southern Christian Leadership Conference (SCLC) Black organization founded in 1955 by Martin Luther King* to coordinate local, nonviolent struggle for civil rights in the South. It encouraged voter registration projects, mass demonstrations, and civil disobedience. After King's death, Ralph D. Abernathy succeeded as SCLC leader.

Southwell, St. Robert (c. 1561–1595) Roman Catholic poet and martyr*. He entered the Society of Jesus* in 1580 and was made the prefect of studies in the English College* in Rome*. In 1586 he was sent on a secret mission to England and gained many conversions. He spent much of his time hiding among Catholic friends using disguises and assumed names. He was betrayed, imprisoned for three years, and then hanged and quartered as a traitor. He was beatified in 1929 and was among the forty martyrs* of England canonized in 1970. Southwell was a poet of note, and many of his poems written in prison express deep Christian piety. Feast day: February 21.

Sowerby, Leo (1895–1968) American composer. He spent much of his life as an Episcopal church organist and choirmaster. In 1946 he was awarded the Pulitzer Prize for his *Canticle of the Sun**. One of his finest works was his Passiontide* cantata, "Forsaken of Man" (1940). He served on the Hymnal Commission of the Episcopal Church and on the Joint Commission on Church Music and was associated with the school of church music at the Washington, D.C. Cathedral.

Sozomen (d. after 450) Ecclesiastical historian and author of *Historia Ecclesiastica*, a history in nine books covering 325 to 425, heavily dependent on Socrates*.

Sozzini, Fausto Paulo See SOCINIANISM.

Sozzini, Lelio Francesco Maria See SOCINIANISM.

Spafford, Horatio Gates (1828–1888) American hymn writer who wrote the incomparable hymn, "It Is Well with My Soul" (1873) after the tragic death at sea of his four daughters on the ill-fated *Ville du Havre* that sank off the shores of England. It was set to the familiar tune by Philip Bliss*. In 1881 Spafford established the American Colony in Jerusalem*.

Spalatin, Georg (1484–1545) Birth name: Burkhardt. German reformer and one of Luther's early disciples. As adviser and chaplain* from 1516 to Frederick III, elector of Saxony, he helped introduce Lutheranism* throughout Saxony. He was one of the theologians who assisted Melanchthon* in drafting the Augsburg Confession* of 1530.

Spangenberg, Augustus Gottlieb (1704–1792) German Moravian bishop and missionary. Born in Germany, he became Zinzendorf's assistant in 1733. He worked in the United States from 1735 to 1739, from 1744 until 1748, and from 1754 to 1762. The last 30 years of his life were spent in missionary activities in Europe. In his *Idea Fidei Fratrum,* he set forth his vision of Christian piety. He is remembered for the theme song he wrote for the American Moravian Church and for the motto he left them, "Together we pray, together we labor, together we suffer, and together we rejoice."

sparrow In Christian art, symbol of divine providence based on Matthew 10:29.

Spasimo, La (Ital., agony) Representation of the Virgin Mary* fainting beside the cross, or on the way to Calvary.

SPCK Society for Promoting Christian Knowledge*, founded by Thomas Bray and four laymen in 1698. It has three divisions: SPCK Worldwide, which makes Christian books available outside the United Kingdom; publishing; and bookselling. It is the third oldest publisher in the United Kingdom.

speaking in tongues See GLOSSOLALIA.

spear In the Eastern Church*, small dagger-like instrument used to cut particles* from the altar bread.

special grace Grace known only by the elect* of God. Distinct from common grace*.

species Form or kind, with reference to the material elements* used in the sacraments*, especially the bread and the wine in the Eucharist*.

Speculum Humane Salvationis (Lat., Mirror of Human Salvation) One of the most important and popular typological books in the Middle Ages, written about 1324, probably by a Dominican.

Speculum Majus (The Great Mirror) Greatest of the late medieval encyclopedias compiled by the Dominican, Vincent of Beauvais*. In four parts it attempted to codify all human knowledge, summarizing the works of some 450 authors, both pagan and Christian.

Spener, Philipp Jakob (1635–1705) German Pietist leader. As a Lutheran minister from 1666, he introduced *Collegia Pietatis,* or schools of piety for Bible study and Christian fellowship. In 1675 he published *Pia Desideria,* considered the seminal document of Pietism*. It contained his six "simple proposals," including an intensified study of the Bible, a fuller exercise by the laity of their spiritual priesthood, emphasis on practical piety rather than intellectual knowledge, charity in reli-

Philipp Jakob Spener

gious controversies, revival of theological studies in seminaries, and revival of preaching. While he remained loyal to the Lutheran tradition, he wanted to infuse it with a passion for holiness*. Spener's movement, supported by the elector of Brandenburg, the future King Frederick I of Prussia, made a deep impact, and in 1694 the University of Halle was founded largely as a result of his labors. But Spener also provoked considerable opposition, and in 1695 he was charged with 283 counts of heretical teaching. In 1698 Spener withdrew to devote his last years to pastoral work.

Speyer Also, Spires. Imperial cathedral in Speyer, Germany, the burial place of Salic and Hohenstaufen emperors. Four emperors, three empresses, and four kings lie in the imperial vault. The original St. Dagobert's Cathedral was built in the seventh century. Then in 1030 Konrad II began to erect the present cathedral, which was completed in the twelfth century. During the War of the Palatine Succession (1689), the cathedral was laid waste, but it was restored by Napoleon.

Speyer, Diet of 1. Imperial assembly in Speyer, Germany, in 1526 which granted each prince the power to determine the religion of his subjects. 2. Conference in Speyer, Germany, in 1529 which passed legislation ending tolerance of Lutherans in Catholic districts. Two more diets were held here, in 1542 and 1544.

SPG Society for the Propagation of the Gospel [in Foreign Parts]*. An Anglican society founded in 1701 by Thomas Bray and his associates to assist the SPCK* in missionary work, especially in the evangelization of non-Christian subjects of the British Empire. In 1965 it merged with the [Anglican] Universities' Mission to Central Africa to form the United Society for the Propagation of the Gospel*.

spiration Process by which the Holy Spirit* originates from the Father and, in most Western theology, from the Son. The Son is begotten of the Father, but the Holy Spirit proceeds through spiration or outbreathing. See also FILIOQUE.

spire Slender church tower topping a steeple. It is usually developed from the cornice and may be pierced with ornamental openings, enriched with crockets, and interposed with open lantern. One of the finest spires* is at Chartres* where the south spire rises to 350 feet and the north spire to 380.

spirit 1. Holy Spirit*. 2. One of the aspects of the human personality. 3. Member of an order of supernatural beings outside time and space.

Spirit, Fruits of the Evidences of the working of the Holy Spirit* in the life of a believer. As listed in Galatians 5:22–23, they are love, joy, peace, longsuffering, kindness, goodness, faithfulness, gentleness, and self-control.

Spirit of Truth Holy Spirit* as one who points to Jesus Christ as the truth, the life, and the way of salvation* (John 15:26).

spiritual director In the Roman Catholic, Anglican, and other traditions, person whose ministry is to guide a fellow believer into deeper Christian faith*.

Spiritual Exercises, The (1541) Book by Ignatius Loyola* designed as a manual for retreat* masters. It details an individually structured week-by-week program of spiritual study and prayer lasting for about a month. The first week concentrates on sin, the second on the life of Christ, the third on the Passion, and the fourth on the Resurrection.

Spiritual Franciscans Franciscan group, also known as Zealots, who wished to maintain poverty as a rule of life for Franciscans. They held to a rigid adherence to St. Francis's rule of poverty and resisted papal attempts to mitigate the rule. Complete renunciation of property was seen by the Spiritual Franciscans as constituting the foundation for a perfect ascetic life.

spiritual gifts Five gifts of the Holy Spirit* that enable Christians to minister to fellow Christians. These are: working of miracles, gifts of healing, gifts of helpers, gifts of government, and gifts of faith. There are 14 gifts concerning the Word of God*: apostleship, prophecy*, discernment of spirits, teaching, exhortation, word of wisdom*, word of knowledge*, tongues*, interpretation of tongues*, evangelism, service, contributing to the needs of the church, acts of mercy, and giving aid (Rom. 4; 1 Cor. 12; Eph. 4).

spiritual healing Also, faith healing*; divine healing*. Healing by spiritual means, exclusive of scientific and medical interventions. It is one of the gifts of the Holy Spirit*, and it may be exercised by any believer. Spiritual healing may be by prayer, holy oil*, laying on of hands*, or through sacramental exercises, such as unction* and Eucharist*, or through pilgrimages*. In the early church, the expansion of the church was accompanied by miraculous acts of healing. According to Tertullian*, Christians healed the lepers, gave sight to the blind, restored the paralytics, exorcised the demons, and raised the dead. Some of the greatest saints* in the Middle Ages were also healers. The tradition continued among the

Protestants, particularly the Quakers*, German Pietists, and the Pentecostals.

spiritual song 1. Musical form referred to in Colossians 3:16. 2. Nonliturgical revival song or hymn. 3. Folk songs of African-American traditions or folk melodies of the frontier or New England. Also called Spirituals or Negro Spirituals*. Examples include "Swing Low, Sweet Chariot" and "Lord, I Want to Be a Christian."

spiritual warfare Constant struggle between the flesh and the spirit, between good and evil, between hope and despair, between faith* and unbelief, and between carnality and spirituality* in a believer. Spiritual warfare is waged on three fronts: personal, corporate, and cosmic. In all three cases the war is waged against unseen enemies, principalities and powers, and evil in high places.

spiritual works of mercy Seven good works* expected of the believer: Converting the sinner, instructing the ignorant, counseling the doubtful, comforting the sorrowful, bearing wrongs patiently, forgiving injuries, and praying for the living and the dead.

spirituality 1. Properly, the indwelling* of the Holy Spirit* and the active operation of New Testament spiritual gifts* in the sanctified life of the believer. 2. Subjective experience of God expressed in prayer, meditation, contemplation, and mysticism. 3. Characteristic set of spiritual practices and beliefs of a group, denomination, or monastic order, as, for example, Jesuit spirituality. 4. Highly developed interior religion associated with certain devotional practices of ascetics, and others especially called by God. 5. In New Age usage, human religiosity associated with the occult.

Spirituals, Negro Indigenous musical genre developed by black slaves in the eighteenth and nineteenth centuries. Among their characteristic features are a call and response*, complex rhythmic structure and syncopation, ornamented melodic lines, improvised harmonization, bodily gestures and movements such as dancing, clapping, swaying, foot-tapping, and moaning. Words drawn

from well-known hymns were improvised and constantly modified. Tunes were simple, repetitive, and pentatonic. Sometimes they contained code words whose meanings were known only to blacks.

Spirituals, White Songs and hymns popular among whites in nineteenth-century revival meetings, often based on secular songs and melodies on which Christian lyrics were superimposed.

Spitta, Karl Johann Philipp (1801–1859) Lutheran hymn writer. Converted about 1825, he took holy orders* and began writing hymns. The compilation of his hymns, *Psalter und Harfe* (1833–1843), remained for many years the standard collection of German hymns.

sponsor 1. Godparent at the baptism* of a Christian child. 2. Person who during the rite of Christian initiation, stands as witness to the candidate's moral character, faith, and intention.

Sproul, Robert Charles (1939–) Presbyterian pastor and theologian. He taught at Westminster College, Gordon College, and the then Conwell School of Theology before becoming president of Ligonier Ministries in 1971. After 1980 he served as professor of systematic theology and apologetics at Reformed Theological Seminary*, Jackson, Mississippi. Sproul is one of the notable exponents of Reformation* theology in his over 30 books, including *God's Inerrant Word* (1975), *Classical Apologetics* (1984), *God's Will and the Christian* (1984), *The Holiness of God* (1985), *Surprised by Suffering* (1989), and *Doubt and Assurance* (1993).

Spurgeon, Charles Haddon (1834–1892) "The Prince of Preachers." He preached his first sermon in 1850 at the age of 16. Four years later he moved to Southwark, where his sermons drew such a crowd that a new church seating 5,000 had to be built for him. During his 38-year ministry he built up a congregation of 6,000 and added 14,692 members to the church. He was a strong Baptist and Calvinist and unyielding in his insistence on God's sovereignty and man's obedience. As a preacher he had no peer. His clear voice, mastery of the language, and sure grasp of the Scriptures and personal commitment to Christ made his ministry one of the most powerful in the Anglo-Saxon world. Spurgeon's College trains students to preach the gospel. Compilations of his sermons are still used as are his devotional books, such as *Morning and Evening.*

Spy Wednesday Wednesday after Palm Sunday*, so named for Judas's betrayal of Christ on that day.

Spyridion, St. (d. 348) Miracle worker and bishop of Tremethius in Cyprus*. He attended the Council of Nicaea* and the Council of Sardica*. He is the patron of the island of Corfu, where his church at Kerkyra attracts a large number of pilgrims. Feast day: December 12 (Eastern Church*); December 14 (Western Church*).

squint Hole or slit cut through the wall of medieval churches to enable persons, such as lepers, to see the altar from the outside.

srbaran In the Armenian tradition, raised sanctuary approached by seven steps.

srbasathsouthiun In the Armenian tradition, hagiology* of the saint* whose festival is being commemorated.

srbitsch In the Armenian tradition, a fine linen purificator*.

srboutheanch In the Armenian Rite*, the oblation*, or bread and wine presented at the offertory.

S.S.D. Sacrae Scripturae Doctor. Doctorate in sacred scripture granted by a Roman Catholic institute.

S.S.L. Sacrae Scripturae Licentiatus. Licentiate in sacred scripture, granted by a Roman Catholic institute.

St. Saint.

Stabat Mater Dolorosa (Lat., the sorrowful Mother was standing) Ancient Latin hymn on Mary's sorrows during the Passion, used during the Holy Week*.

staff 1. In Christian art, a symbol of religious pilgrimage* and of St. Christopher*, St. Jerome*, and St. John the Baptist. 2. Wooden walking stick, used as a symbol of authority in many African indigenous churches. 3. Bishop's crosier*.

stag In Christian art, symbol of Christian hope.

Stainer, Sir John (1840–1901) English composer and organist of St. Paul's Cathedral*, London. From 1889 to 1899 he was also professor of music at the University of Oxford. His principal works are oratorios and cantatas, among them *St. Mary Magdalen* (1887), *The Crucifixion* (1887), and *The Story of the Cross* (1893) as well as anthems, including "Lead Kindly Light," "O Clap Your Hands," and "I Saw the Lord."

stake In Mormon* usage, a regional division of the church.

stall Permanent seat for the clergy in a church choir or chancel*.

Stams Cistercian monastery in Stams, Austria, built in 1273 in memory of King Konradin, the last of the Hohenstaufen line, by his mother Elizabeth. In 1593 the monastery was burned down, only to be rebuilt in the seventeenth century. The new building was completed in 1615. Between 1729 and 1732 the building underwent further alterations. Among the monastery's impressive features are the massive, free-standing altar; the pulpit by Andreas Kolle; the Rose Grill in the Heiligenblut Chapel, created by Bernhard Bachnetzer; the broad staircase with wrought ironwork; and the Bernhardi Room decorated with frescoes* by Anton Zoller and Michael Huber.

Stanford, Sir Charles Villiers (1852–1924) English composer considered one of the most formidable musical talents of the twentieth-century English church. From 1873 to 1882 he was organist at the Trinity College, Cambridge, and from 1883, professor of composition at the Royal College of Music. His anthems and settings of morning, evening, and Holy Communion* services are comparable to the great European masters. Among his best known anthems are "The Lord Is My Shepherd" and 'Ye Choirs of New Jerusalem."

Together with Hubert Parry and Edward Elgar* he launched a new era in church music.

Stanislaus, St. (1030–1079) Also, Stanislaw. Patron of Poland. He became bishop of Cracow in 1072 but soon came into conflict with King Boleslaw II, who murdered him with his own hand while Stanislaus was offering Mass*. He was canonized in 1253. Feast day: April 11.

starchestvo In the Russian Orthodox Church*, eldership exercised by priests, monks, and lay people, in relation to a disciple, fellow monk or a younger believer through formal counsel, prayer, or guidance. It was practiced in the great monasteries of Optina* and Valaam*.

staretz/startsy (Russ., elder). Monk or layperson who is revered for his personal holiness* and whose advice and blessings are much sought after. Among the Greeks the equivalent is gerontas, or elder. Among the celebrated startsy are Seraphim* of Sarov, John of Kronstadt (d. 1908), Isidor of Gethsemane (d. 1908), Gabriel of Eleazar (d. 1915), Silouan Antonov (d. 1938), and Michael Pitkevich (d. 1962) in Russia; Symeon Popovic* and Justin Popovic (d. 1979) in Serbia; and George Karslidis (d. 1959), Porphyrios of Oropos (d. 1991), Jacob Tsalikis of Euboia (d. 1991), Paisios Eznepidis of Athos* (d. 1994), and Nikodemos the Hagiorite (d. 1809) in Greece.

Staro Nagoricino The Church of St. George near Kumanovo in Macedonia* built in 1313 by King Stefan Uros II Milutin. The monastery was active until the nineteenth century.

Staroslav Alternative name for Church Slavonic*, the liturgical language of the Russian Orthodox Church*.

Starovery Russian name for Old Believers*.

state church Established national church with a constitutional status and receiving direct financial support from secular authorities.

stated clerk Permanent officer with administrative responsibilities in the Presbyterian Church.

station 1. Representation of the Passion. 2. A Catholic fast.

station collect Prayer said at a station in a procession. See also STATION, NO. 1.

station days Certain days on which the pope formally celebrated Mass* in the so-called "station churches" in Rome*. These stations, marked in the Old Roman Missal, were 84 in all, held at 40 different churches, of which 45 were basilicas*. These churches included Santa Maria Maggiore*, St. John Lateran, and Santa Sabina.

stational liturgy Processional liturgy used in public processions going through urban streets.

stations of the cross A series of 14 pictures and carvings representing incidents in the last journey of Christ from Pilate's house to his burial. They are commonly arranged in time sequence on the walls of a church and are designed for devotion and meditation, especially during Lent* and Passiontide*. The 14 incidents are: 1. Christ is condemned to death. 2. He receives the cross. 3. He falls to the ground. 4. He meets his mother. 5. Simon of Cyrene is made to carry the cross. 6. His face is wiped by Veronica*. 7. He falls again. 8. He meets the women of Jerusalem*. 9. He falls a third time. 10. He is stripped of his clothes. 11. He is nailed to the cross. 12. He dies on the cross. 13. His body is taken down from the cross. 14. His body is laid in the tomb.

status confessionis 1. Condition or situation in which the church must address a specific theological or social issue, often at great risk to itself. 2. Article of faith* or morals that is definitive.

stavkirke Architecturally distinctive church buildings in central Europe, particularly Norway, with a pagoda-like structure. Out of a known 322 churches, only 34 still exist. They are also called "mast churches," because they are built of tall pine masts, arranged as a frame to support the sloping roofs rising in tiers, one above the other. The high nave* is open to the roof, the aisles are narrow, and the walls are thick timber planks held together with diagonal crossbeams.

Stavriotes Crypto-Christians in the Ottoman Empire who outwardly conformed to Islam while secretly remaining Christians.

Stavkirke, Norway

stavropegion Byzantine monastery that is independent of a bishop and is directly under a patriarch*.

stavrophore (lit., crossbearer) Superior grade of Byzantine monks who take four vows: poverty, chastity*, obedience, and stability.

stavros In the Byzantine Rite*, the sign of the cross which is made by a bishop or priest with the right hand in blessing. The thumb and the first two fingers are joined to represent the Trinity*. The sign is made from right to left, and not from left to right as in the West.

stavrosimon Byzantine troparion* on the Crucifixion.

stavrotheotokion Byzantine troparion* in honor of both the cross and the Virgin Mary*.

STD Doctor of Sacred Theology.

Stebbins, George Coles (1846–1945) Composer, hymn writer and music evangelist. He served as music director in a number of churches in Chicago and Boston, before joining Moody*, with whom he worked for 25 years as music leader in crusades*. With James McGranahan and Ira D. Sankey* he edited *Gospel Hymns*, which sold over 10 million copies. Stebbins also compiled the *Northfield Hymnal* (1904). Many of his hymns have endured, including "Have Thine Own Way," "Jesus Is Tenderly Calling," "I've Found a Friend," and "Take Time to Be Holy."

steeple Church tower, consisting of a spire-like, tapering structure, surmounting a church. It is generally topped by a cross.

Stein, Blessed Edith (1891–1942) Carmelite* nun. Jewish by birth, she studied under Edmund Husserl and became an authority on phenomenology. She was received into the Roman Catholic Church in 1922 and entered the Carmelite Order in 1934 under the name of Teresa Benedicta of the Cross. During the war she escaped to the Netherlands but was captured by the Nazis and put to death in the gas chamber. She was beatified in 1987. Feast day: August 9.

Stephanus See ESTIENNE (STEPHANUS).

Stephen ad Duwaihi (1630–1704) Maronite scholar who was elevated as Maronite patriarch* in 1670. He helped to establish the Order of St. Anthony and compiled many historical works, including a history of the Maronite Church.

Stephen bar Sudayle (fifth century) Monophysite monk of doubtful orthodoxy*. His sole surviving work is the *Book of Hierotheus* in Syriac* dealing with cosmology and eschatology*.

Stephen Harding, St. (d. 1134) Third abbot of Citeaux* and cofounder of the Cistercian Order. He became a monk at Molesme and then transferred to Citeaux and was elected abbot in 1109. After Bernard* joined the monastery, Harding drew up the constitution of the order, *Carta Caritatis*, and established a system of regular visitations and general chapters. Feast day: April 17.

Stephen of Perm (1340–1396) Russian apostle to the Zyrians, a Finnish people living near Perm. He invented the Zyrian alphabet and translated the Scriptures and liturgical works into that language.

Stephen, St. (d. c. 35) Protomartyr* and the first deacon. He incurred the enmity of the Sanhedrin who, without a formal trial, stoned him to death for blasphemy*, an event witnessed by Saul, the future St. Paul* (Acts 6, 7, and 8).

Stephen, St. (975–1038) The first king of Hungary who helped to convert Hungarians to Christianity. He was canonized in 1083. Feast day: August 15; August 20 (Hungary).

Stern, Henry Aaron (1820–1885) German-born missionary to the Jews. A Jew by birth, he received Christian baptism in London in 1840. He served as a missionary in many out-of-the-way places, including Baghdad, Iran, Kurdistan, Constantinople*, and Ethiopia. For four years from 1860 to 1864 he was imprisoned in Ethiopia. On release he returned to London, where he continued to work as an evangelist, bringing many Jews to a saving knowledge of the Lord.

steward In the Methodist Church, overseer of the temporal affairs of the church, serving in the capacity of an executive secretary.

stewardship 1. Management of a property by a servant on behalf of its owner; by extension, the faithful administration of one's talents and gifts for the glory of God. 2. Systematic pledging and giving to a church or parachurch* organization a certain percentage of one's income, generally a tithe*, representing a discharge of one's financial obligations to the Lord's work.

sticharion In the Eastern Church*, ankle-length, colored liturgical tunic, similar to the alb*. It is worn by all Byzantine clergy. That worn by bishops has red and white bands called potamoi. Also called stoicharion in the Coptic Church*.

sticheron In the Eastern Church*, brief liturgical hymn attached to a verse of a Psalm or other scriptural passage.

stichos In the Byzantine Rite*, a short verse taken from the Psalms that introduces the sticheron*.

stigma/stigmata Visible or invisible wound, similar to that of the Passion of Christ, on the human body, particularly on the hands, side, shoulder, chest, or back. It is usually accompanied by pain or afflictions, like blindness or lameness without organic causes, and nearly total abstinence from food and sleep. It tends to bleed periodically, most often on Fridays and during Lent* and Passiontide*, and resists medical treatment but never becomes septic. It may or may not be accompa-

Stigmatization of St. Catherine of Siena

nied by a divine revelation. Stigmatization is not a cause for canonization*. Of the over 300 Catholics who have been stigmatized, only some 60 are saints* or beati. St. Francis of Assisi* was the first to receive the stigmata, and of the others most were women, such as St. Catherine of Siena* (who had invisible stigmata), St. Catherine of Genoa*, Anna Katharina Emmerick*, Therese of Avila, Julian of Norwich*, St. Gemma Galgani*, and Therese Neumann*. Thus, stigmatic.

Stigmatines Congregation of the Sacred Stigmata founded in 1816 by Gaspare Bertoni in Verona*, Italy. They arrived in the United States in 1905.

stikhar In the Slavonic tradition, alb-like vestment worn by readers, subdeacons, and deacons.

stipend Salary or allowance of pastors and clergymen*.

stipes Stone support of the altar mensa*.

stock In the Roman Catholic Church, one of three small metal vessels containing the holy oils*.

Stikharion

Stockholm Conference Ecumenical gathering, officially known as the Universal Christian Conference on Life and Work*, which met in 1925 in Stockholm, Sweden, under the guiding spirit of Archbishop Soderblom*. It was attended by 600 official delegates from 37 countries, including the Orthodox Church.

stole Liturgical vestment consisting of a long colored strip. Priests wear it around the neck with its ends falling straight down in front. Deacons wear it like a sash over the left shoulder, its ends being fastened together under the right arm. When hearing confessions it is generally purple, but the color varies on other occasions. In the Eastern Church* it is called an orarion* or epitrachelion* which is worn on top of the sticharion*. In the West it was called an orarium until the eleventh century.

Stone, Barton Warren (1772–1844) American frontier Presbyterian evangelist. He set forth his Arminian beliefs in his *Last Will and Testament of the Springfield Presbytery* (1804). Later he organized the Christian Church, which merged in 1832 with Alexander Campbell's Disciples.

Stonehouse, Ned Bernard (1902–1962) Presbyterian biblical scholar. He taught for most of his career at the Westminster Theological Seminary, Philadelphia*. He was also one of the founders of the Orthodox Presbyterian Church* and one of its most respected leaders. The range of his schol-

Barton W. Stone

arship is evident in his numerous works, especially *Origin of the Synoptic Gospels* (1963), *The Witness of Matthew and Mark to Christ* (1944), and *The Witness of Luke to Christ* (1951).

stool of repentance High stool in a Scottish Presbyterian church on which grievous sinners were required to sit as a penance*.

storefront church Small church located in a mall or shopping center, generally serving the urban poor.

Stott, John Robert Walmsley (1921–) Anglican theologian, evangelist, and author. He became rector* of All Souls, London, in 1950 and it became the most influential evangelical center over the next 25 years. He restored Evangelicalism* to its former vigor through university missions, conferences for clergy and other initiatives, and a series of books, including *Basic Christianity* (1958), *Issues Facing Christians Today* (1984), *The Cross of Christ* (1986), and *The Contemporary Christian* (1992). *I Believe in Preaching* (1982) summed up his ideas on the proclamation of the gospel. After his retirement from All Souls in 1975, he founded the London Institute of Contemporary Christianity.

stoup Basin near the entrance of a church containing holy water* with which the faithful may sprinkle or cross themselves. They are richly ornamented, either built into a wall or standing on a socle.

Stowe Missal Early Mass book of the Irish Church enclosed in a cumdach*, or a case of precious metal, containing the Gospel of St. John, an Ordinary and Canon of the Mass*, propers for three special masses, an office of Baptism and Visitation of the Sick, a treatise on the Mass*, and three Irish spells. Formerly in the Stowe House, it is now in the library of the Royal Irish Academy at Dublin.

Strachan, Robert Kenneth (1910–1965) Protestant missionary leader. He took over as general director of the Latin America Evangelization Crusade, which later became the Latin America Mission started by his parents, Harry and Susan Strachan. He initiated the Evangelism-in-Depth movement and helped establish the School of World Mission at Fuller Theological Seminary*.

Stralslund St. Nicholas, the rich Hanseatic red-brick church in Stralslund, Germany. Work on the church began in 1270 and was completed by the end of the fourteenth century. The twin towers, originally topped with Gothic spires*, were destroyed in a fire, but were rebuilt in 1662. The Altar of the Bergen Traders dates from 1500 and the Baroque High Altar by Andreas Schluter from 1700. An ambulatory leads to a ring of chapels around the choir.

Strasbourg/Strassburg City in France. It was an important center of the Reformation* under

Stoup

Bucer*.The present cathedral at Strasbourg was preceded by an older cathedral founded in the first century. The new cathedral was built between 1015 and 1050. The transept* and the choir were rebuilt after 1176, and the Romanesque nave* was rebuilt after 1250. A fire in 1298 destroyed the tower once again. In the fourteenth century Meister Erwin began the work of reconstruction. Under two master-masons, Ulrich of Esslingen and Johann Hultz, the tower was rebuilt. The new facade was compared to a piece of floating lace made of stone, and it was considered the "eighth wonder of the world."

stratchitza In the Byzantine tradition: 1. Altar covering. 2. Linen cloth worn by a bishop to protect his vestments.

Strauss, David Friedrich (1808–1874) German theologian. He achieved notoriety with his *Life of Jesus Critically Examined* (2 vols., 1835–1836), which dismissed the New Testament as myth created by the disciples to fulfill the legends and prophecies of the Old Testament and the miracles of Jesus as fables. His sequel, *Christliche Glaubenslehre* (2 vols., 1840–1841), and his second, *Life of Jesus,* went on to describe Christianity as incompatible with modern knowledge and ruled out the supernatural. He ended his life as an evolutionary pantheist and Darwinian.

Stravinsky, Igor (1882–1971) Russian-American composer. One of the twentieth-century's greatest composers. Although sacred works form only a small portion of his opus, they form a major contribution to modern religious music. They include *Symphony of the Psalms* (1930), *Mass* (1948), *Babel* (1944), *A Sermon, A Narrative and A Prayer* (1960–1961), *Threni; id est, Lamentationes Jeremiae Prophetae* (1958), *Canticum Sacrum* (1956), and *The Flood* (1962) and such songs as *Paternoster* (1926) and *Ave Maria* (1934). Some of his musical pieces evoke and are redolent of the liturgies of the Russian Orthodox Church*.

Streeter, Burnett Hillman (1874–1937) English biblical scholar. He studied the sources of the four Gospels, emphasizing the priority of Mark, "Q," and Proto-Luke in his *Four Gospels: A Study of Origins* (1924).

Strong, Augustus Hopkins (1836–1921) Baptist theologian. Ordained in 1861, he held pastorates* in Massachusetts and Ohio and was elected president of the Rochester Theological Seminary (1872–1912). He was president of the American Baptist Missionary Union (1892–1895). His major achievement was his *Systematic Theology* (3 vols., 1886).

Studd, Charles Thomas (1862–1931) English missionary leader, he was converted in 1878 and volunteered for missionary service as one of a group of students known as the Cambridge Seven*. He sailed for China with the China Inland Mission* in 1885 and gave away his fortune to Christian causes. Returning home in 1894, he helped found the Student Volunteer Mission movement. After pastoring in India from 1900 to 1906, he left for Africa in 1910, where he founded the Heart of Africa Mission in 1912 which became the Worldwide Evangelization Crusade*.

Studenica Monastery in the Ibar Valley in southwestern Serbia, built between 1186 and 1196 by Stefan Nemanja, the founder of the medieval Serb state. In 1196 Nemanja took monastic vows with the name Symeon and joined his youngest son Sava on Mount Athos*, where in 1198 they founded the Monastery of Hilander*. Symeon died in 1199, and his relics* were brought to Studenica. The monastery was badly damaged under Ottoman rule, and only two of the monastery churches survive.

Student Christian Movement The British section of the World Student Christian Federation* founded by John R. Mott* in 1895 as a fellowship of students who "desire to understand the Christian faith and to live the Christian life." Gradually, it became an interdenominational movement with ecumenical goals. It operates in schools as well as universities and runs a publishing house under the imprint, Student Christian Movement Press. Its weakness in doctrine in recent years has led to open questioning of its Christian identity.

Student Volunteer Movement for Foreign Missions Movement enlisting Christian college students for foreign missions. It grew out of a summer Bible study conference in 1886 at Mount Her-

mon, Massachusetts, presided over by D. L. Moody*, where students like Robert P. Wilder pleaded for recruiting more college students as foreign missionaries. In response, the Student Volunteer Movement was formed with John R. Mott* as chairman, a position he held for the next 30 years. The motto of the movement was "the evangelization of the world in this generation." The movement peaked in 1920 when 6,890 attended its convention in Des Moines, Iowa. It declined thereafter, merging with the National Student Christian Federation in 1959 which became the University Christian Movement in 1966. In 1969 it disbanded. In the 80 years of its existence, more than 20,000 of its members became foreign missionaries.

Studios/Studion Monastery in Constantinople*, dedicated to St. John the Baptist, founded in 463 by the former Roman consul, Studios. Its monks followed the Rule of Acoemetae* and recited the psalmody* continually day and night. They were zealous champions of orthodoxy* and the decrees of Chalcedon. About 799 its abbot, St. Theodore*, introduced a new rule based on St. Basil* requiring stricter discipline, manual work, exclusion of women, and poverty. From this time it became the center of Eastern monasticism* and the model for the monasteries of Mount Athos*, producing many of the hymns and icons of the Greek Church as well as supplying copyists for the ancient manuscripts. It was destroyed by the Crusaders in 1204, rebuilt in 1290, again destroyed by the Turks in 1453, and its church was converted into a mosque for some time. The Rule of St. Theodore of Studios* was revived in 1906 by A. Szeptyckij, metropolitan* of Lvov in the Ukraine*.

studium generale Higher educational institutions in the Middle Ages that attracted students from many countries and evolved into universities.

Stumpf, Johannes (1500–1578) Swiss Protestant historian and theologian. He was a resolute defender of Zwingli's view of the Eucharist* and published the first biography of Zwingli*. His *Swiss Chronicle* was published in 1548.

Stundists Russian Evangelical sect that flourished

in the Ukraine* from about 1858 to 1862 under the influence of Lutheran, Reformed*, and Mennonite preachers. It was so called because they gave designated hours (stunden) for Bible study and prayer. It freed itself from the Reformed connection and became Russian in character. The majority linked up with the Russian Baptists, and were called Stundo-Baptists to distinguish them from the Baptist group founded by J. G. Oncken. They now form part of the All Russian Council of Evangelical Christians and Baptists.

Sturm, St. (d. 779) Apostle of Germany. A disciple of St. Boniface*, he became a Benedictine* and founded the monastery at Fulda*.

Stylite (Gk., pillar) Solitary hermit, also known as pillar saint*, who lived on top of a pillar in Syria, Mesopotamia, Egypt, and Greece. The pillars which varied in height had a platform and a hut in which the hermit could sleep or a parapet against which he could lean. Food was provided by disciples who would lift it up the pillar by means of ropes. While Stylites spent most of their time in prayer and fasting, they would often address the crowds gathered at the foot of the pillar and mediate theological controversies. St. Simeon Stylites* was the most famous Stylite.

St. Simeon Stylites

SU Scripture Union.

Suarez, Francisco de (1548–1617) Spanish theologian, considered the greatest of the Jesuit theologians. He was ordained in 1572 and taught in various Spanish universities and in the Roman College until 1616. His writings formed a system of scholastic thought called Suarezianism, which held that the individual is the focus of divine care, that matter has pure potential, and that there is a conceptual, not real, distinction between essence and existence. He wrote extensively and made original contributions to theology, political theory, and philosophy.

In his first work, *De Verbo Incarnato* (1590), he tried to reconcile the Thomist view of redemption* as the final cause of the Incarnation* with that of Duns Scotus*. His *De Mysteriis Vitae Christi* (1592) and *Disputationes Metaphysicae* (1597) combined the teachings of Aristotle with that of Thomas Aquinas*. In *Varia Opuscula Theologica* (1599) and *De Vera Intelligentia Auxilii Efficacis* (1605), he devised a system called congruism* to solve the paradox of human freedom and God's sovereignty. He taught that God does not control human freedom but rather disposes an individual to salvation* by giving congruent graces which, in his foreknowledge, he supplies to enable human beings to draw near to him. In 1608–1609 he published *De Virtute et Statu Religionis* on the state of religion and in 1612 his key work on natural and international law, *De Legibus*.

His political ideas are based on the natural rights of people, all of whom are equal before God, and he repudiated the divine right of kings. His last great work was the three-part treatise on grace*, *De Necessitate Gratiae* (1619), *De Gratia Habituali* (1619), and *De Gratia Actuali* (1651). He was called by Paul V* "Doctor Eximius et Pius," and by his peers "the Teacher of Europe, as also of the Whole World."

sub specie aeternitatis (Lat., under the form of eternity*) In its essential or universal form or nature; seen from the perspective of eternal life*.

Sub Tuum Ancient prayer translated as follows: "We fly to thy patronage, O Holy Mother of God; despise not our petitions in our necessities; but deliver us from all danger, O ever glorious and blessed Virgin."

subapostolic Of or relating to the period between the death of John, the last of the apostles, and the deaths of their immediate associates and disciples, roughly between 75 and 150.

subcintorium Ecclesiastical vestment, similar to the maniple*, formerly worn by the popes on the left side, attached to the girdle* when celebrating a solemn pontifical Mass*.

subdeacon Formerly a church official who ranked the lowest of the three Major Orders*. He prepared the bread, wine, and vessels, chanted the Epistle, presented the chalice* and the paten* at the offertory, and removed the vessels from the altar after the Communion. In the Roman Catholic Church, the office was suppressed in 1972. In the Eastern Church*, it exists as a minor order*.

subdiaconate Order of subdeacons.

Subiaco Congregation Congregation of Benedictine monks, formerly known as the Cassinese Congregation* of the Primitive Observance, founded in 1851 by Peter Casaretto within the Cassinese Congregation. It became a separate congregation in 1872 and was officially renamed Subiaco Congregation after the town some 40 miles east of Rome* where St. Benedict* retired before his death.

subintroductae Also, agapetae. In the early church, nuns who lived with monks in spiritual marriage. It was forbidden by the canons of the Council of Elvira*, Ancyra, and Nicaea*.

sublapsarianism Also, infralapsarianism; postlapsarianism. Calvinist doctrine that God created human beings with the possibility of the Fall and had foreknowledge of that fall, and in view of that fall, elected some human beings to salvation*, leaving the rest to perish. Contrasted with supralapsarianism*.

submersion Also, total immersion*. Form of baptism* in which the water covers the candidate's body completely as was the custom in the New Testament and in the early church (Rom. 6:3–11).

subordinationism Early tendency in theology which places the Son, even as divine, as subordinate to the Father and the Holy Spirit* as subordinate to both. This was widely held in the early church, and was voiced by such otherwise diverse theologians as Origen*, Justin Martyr*, Irenaeus*, and Clement of Alexandria* who so emphasized the oneness of God the Father as to deny the equality of the three persons of the Trinity*. This heresy was dealt with in the struggle against the Arians, who held that the Son was not God by nature but was a favor of the Father and was created by the Father outside time.

subsellia 1. Lower range of stalls for acolytes* and choristers* in a cathedral. 2. Seats for the deacon and subdeacon in a sedilia*.

subsistence Personal mode of existence of each of the three persons in the Trinity*. In the Godhead there is one substance but three subsistences*.

substance 1. In Christian theology, the underlying single essence of the three persons of the Trinity*. 2. In eucharistic literature, the underlying nature of the eucharistic species* as contrasted with their accidents.

substitutionary atonement Doctrine that Christ died on the cross as a substitute for the death of sinners, so that those who believe in him may have eternal life*. One form of it emphasizes penal substitution, whereby Christ's death, bearing God's wrath in judgment, took the punishment due sinners.

subunists Bohemian sect in the fifteenth century practicing Communion in one kind, so called from the Latin term, *sub una specie*, under one kind. They were opposed by the more moderate Utraquists or Calixtines* who took Communion in both kinds*.

suburbicarian dioceses Seven ancient dioceses* in the immediate vicinity of Rome*: Albano, Frascati, Ostia, Palestrina, Porto and Santa Rufina, Sabina and Poggio Mirteto, and Velletri.

succentor Deputy to the precentor who is generally a minor canon*.

Suceava Rumanian city noted for its churches and monasteries.

Sudan Interior Mission (SIM) Missionary society founded in Canada in 1893 to evangelize* the interior of Africa between the Sahara and the Equator by W. Gowans, T. Kent, and R V. Bingham*. On the death of Gowans and Kent, Bingham established the first station at Patigi on the Niger. There were few converts until 1908, when hundreds of Yagbas joined the church at Egbe. In the decades that followed, SIM's work expanded to Nigeria, Ghana, Burkina Faso, Niger, Ethiopia, Somalia, and the Sudan where it is involved in medical work, education, and publishing. Its periodical *African Challenge* is widely circulated, and its radio station ELWA broadcasts to all Africa. Now merged with SIM International.

sudarium (Lat., handkerchief) Offertory veil covering the offerings received from the people. Also, the veil covering the hands of a subdeacon or clerk* taking sacramental vessels to and from the altar.

sudra In the Assyrian Church*, a cotton alb-like vestment decorated with three black or red crosses on the shoulder, worn by a reader*.

Suenens, Leo Josef (1904–1995) Belgian cardinal and leader of the Charismatic movement in the Catholic Church. Made cardinal in 1962, he served as moderator* of the Second Vatican Council* and received the Templeton Prize in 1976. Among his books on the Charismatic movement is *A New Pentecost?* (1974).

suffering church Persecuted church in nations in which Christianity is officially proscribed and in which the enemies of the gospel are apparently able to harass and weaken it, but not completely destroy it. Churches in all countries under the heel of Islam as well as churches in Communist countries constitute the suffering church in the twentieth century.

Suffering Day Good Friday*.

Suffering Servant Title applied to Jesus Christ based on Isaiah 52:13, 53:12.

sufficient grace See GRACE, SUFFICIENT.

suffragan bishop Auxiliary bishop in a diocese* who does not have the right of succession, in contrast to the bishop coadjutor* who does. Originally, a bishop who could be counted on for casting his suffrage or vote with the metropolitan* in a synod*.

Suger (1081–1151) Abbot of St. Denis, near Paris, from 1122 until his death. He initiated the rebuilding program that converted St. Denis from a dilapidated building into one of the finest examples of Gothic* architecture.

Suicer, Johann Kaspar (1620–1684) Swiss Reformed* theologian. He taught Latin, Greek, and Hebrew at Zurich* from 1644. He is known for his magnum opus, *Thesaurus Ecclesiasticus e Patribus Graecis Ordine Alphabetico* (2 vols., 1682), a work of remarkable scholarship still used today.

Suidbert, St. (d. 713) Anglo-Saxon bishop and missionary. As a Benedictine monk-priest in the Monastery of Rathmelsigi, Ireland, he accompanied Willibrord* on his mission to Frisia, where his companions elected him district bishop. His evangelistic activity was concentrated in the region of the present city of Utrecht*. Later, he evangelized the Germanic tribe of the Bructeri. Toward the end of his life, he founded the monastery known as Kaiserswerth*. Feast day: March 1.

Sullivan, Arthur S. (1842–1900) English composer, author of the famous hymn, "Onward Christian Soldiers," as well as oratorios*, cantatas, and anthems. He was a partner in the Gilbert and Sullivan operas for which he wrote the operattas, while W. S. Gilbert wrote librettos.

Suloqo In the Syrian Rite, Ascension Thursday.

Sulpicians The Society of St-Sulpice founded in 1642 by J. J. Olier* in the parish* of St. Sulpice in Paris. They are secular priests who train parish clergy but take no special vows and are permitted to own property. They are devoted to prayer and asceticism*, live a common life and share spiritual exercises*. The society has spread to North America where, in 1791, the order founded St. Mary's Seminary in Baltimore, the oldest Roman Catholic seminary in the United States, now a pontifical* university.

summa Medieval encyclopedia or compendium, used as handbook in the schools.

Summa Theologiae Principal theological treatise by St. Thomas Aquinas*, one of the most famous works in the Middle Ages. It is divided into three parts: the first part deals with God as Creator, the second part with God as the end of man and man's return to God, and the third part with Christ as the way of man's return to God.

Sumner, John Bird (1780–1862) Archbishop of Canterbury* from 1848 to 1862. He was a noted Evangelical and opposed the Oxford movement*. He avoided theological controversy. His writings include, in addition to several volumes of sermons, *Apostolical Preaching* (1815) and *The Evidence of Christianity* (1824).

Sundar Singh, Sadhu (1889–c. 1929) Indian Christian mystic. He was converted through a vision and was baptized. Disinherited by his Sikh father, he donned the saffron robes of a *sadhu* or holy man and became an itinerant preacher. He traveled widely in Asia and Europe. He disappeared during a trip to evangelize Tibet.

Sunday The Lord's Day* as the day of worship for Christians. From the time of Constantine*, it has been the traditional day of rest in a week and in most Christian countries increasingly viewed as the Christian Sabbath and enshrined in civil legislation.

Sunday school Bible-based school held in churches mainly to provide religious instruction to children. The movement began in Gloucester, England, in 1780 when Robert Raikes* established a small school to care for local illiterate and neglected slum children. The movement spread rapidly, first throughout England, and then to North America, and the Continent. The Sunday School Union was founded in 1803.

Sunday, William ("Billy") Ashley (1862–1935) American evangelist. A professional baseball player, he was converted through the Pacific Garden Mission*. From 1896 he held crusades in almost every American city and preached to over 100 million, of which 1 million "hit the trail," or were saved. He combined dramatic preaching with superb

Billy Sunday

advance planning. He was a strong Fundamentalist, and he preached an uncompromising message, although couched in rough language.

sunhadus In the Assyrian Rite, the Breviary* containing services for the seven canonical hours*. The four obligatory ones are: 1. Ramsha or evening. 2. Suba'a or compline*. 3. Slutha Dlilya* or night office. 4. Shahra or vigil*.

supara In the Assyrian tradition, a monastic tonsure*.

super oblata In the liturgy of the Roman Catholic Church, prayer over the eucharistic offering.

supererogation Better works (as distinguished from good works*) over and beyond that required by scriptural and ecclesiastical ordinances*. These works produced merits that were deposited in a common account in the church.

superfrontal Band of fabric that extends across the front of an altar from the mensa* over the frontal*.

superintendent In Protestant churches, a church official who holds the same position as a bishop in traditional Episcopal churches. The superintendent has authority over the clergy and congregations within a province, exercises discipline, especially excommunication*, and serves as the church's administrative officer. In some churches there are general superintendents over superintendents.

superior Head of a religious organization or congregation. Head of an order of nuns is known as mother superior*.

supernal Heavenly.

superpersonal Term applied by C. S. Lewis* to the personal or Trinitarian* nature of God.

superpopulum (Lat., over the people) Prayer of blessing said over the people at the conclusion of a Mass*.

supersessionism Teaching that the New Testament supersedes the Old Testament and that Christianity supersedes Judaism.

suppedaneum 1. Platform or predella* of an altar. 2. Footrest on a crucifix which supports the feet.

supplices te Ninth section of the Roman canon* beginning, "We humbly beseech you, Almighty God."

supra quae Eighth section of the Roman canon* beginning, "Upon which look with favor and accept."

supralapsarianism Form of Calvinism* that holds that God created mankind with the intention of saving some and not saving others and then allowed the Fall to bring this intention to pass.

Election* takes place above or before, without reference to the Fall. Critics contend that the doctrine made God the author of sin. The problem is an abstruse one involving logic rather than theology or chronology. Contrasted with sublapsarianism* or infralapsarianism*.

Supremacy, Act of 1. The Supremacy of Crown Act of 1534 under which Henry VIII of England and his successors assumed the title of "the only supreme head in earth of the Church of England." 2. Act of Supremacy of 1558, the first act of Elizabeth I by which the English monarch became "the only supreme governor of the realm . . . in all spiritual and ecclesiastical things or causes temporal."

surcingle Girdle* or cincture* around the waist to keep the cassock* in place.

surdzar In the Armenian Church*, priestly vestment of rich material. In the Eastern churches*, it has a more conic shape, the front cut away above the waist or divided down the front and clasped at the neck.

Surin, Jean Joseph (1600–1665) French mystic. For 20 years from 1636 he served as the exorcist* at the community of Ursuline nuns at Loudun. He wrote a number of spiritual works, including *Catechisme Spirituel* (1657), *Les Fondements de la Vie Spirituelle* (1667), and *Dialogues Spirituels* (1704–1709).

surplice White liturgical vestment with wide sleeves worn over the cassock*. It is the distinctive dress of the lower clergy and of priests outside the Mass*. The modern surplice*, known as the cotta*, is much shorter than the medieval one.

Sursum Corda (Lat., lift up your hearts) In the eucharistic liturgy, words addressed by the celebrant to the congregation immediately before the Preface*.

Suso, Blessed Henry (c. 1300–1366) Swabian mystic. He entered the Dominican friary at Constance when he was 13 and had a deep conversion experience at 18. He became a student of Meister Eckhart* and later returned to Constance as a prior*. At 40 he left his ascetical mode of life to become a preacher, teacher, adviser, and confessor*. Among his devotional books are *The Life of the Servant,* the *Little Book of Truth,* and the *Little Book of Eternal Wisdom,* all of which were widely read in the fourteenth and fifteenth centuries and translated into many European languages, including English. Feast day: January 23.

suspension Disciplinary measure against ministers or clergy in many churches, normally debarring them from exercising some or all of their official functions either indefinitely (sine die) or for a specific period. See also CENSURE.

sutafe In the Ethiopian Rite, Holy Communion* received in a fixed order starting with bishops and priests, newly baptized infants, deacons, male faithful, and female faithful. When a communicant receives the sacrament*, he or she places a hand over the mouth until it is consumed.

Sutton, Christopher (c. 1565–1629) English devotional writer whose *Godly Meditations upon the Most Holy Sacrament of the Lord's Supper* (1601) defended the doctrine of Christ's presence in the Eucharist*.

suyakha (Syr., the conclusion) Extra psalm, said on some days at the evening service before the royal anthem, and at the night service.

Swaggart, Jimmy Lee (1935–) Television evangelist. Ordained by the Assemblies of God*, he went on to establish one of the largest Pentecostal ministries which included a worldwide television ministry, the Family Worship Center, Jimmy Swaggart Bible College, a music recording company, and the magazine, *The Evangelist.* His ministry was characterized by a fiery brand of old-time Pentecostal preaching during which he would cry, shout, dance, run, and sing. His downfall began in 1987 when he was embroiled in the controversy over Jim Bakker's* PTL* ministry. Shortly thereafter he was defrocked by the Assemblies of God* for conduct considered inappropriate for a minister. He continued to preach defiantly and eventually returned to broadcasting on a limited scale.

Swain, Clara (1834–1910) The world's first woman missionary doctor and founder of the first hospital for women in Asia. Sent to India in 1869 by the Methodist Women's Foreign Missionary Society, she was assigned to Bareilly, the birthplace of Indian Methodism*. Here, on land donated by a local potentate, she built the Clara Swain Hospital.

Swedenborg, Emanuel (1688–1772) Originally, Swedborg. Swedish scientist, philosopher, and theologian. He abandoned his early scientific pursuits into minerals and mineral kingdom to study theology. He experienced strange dreams and visions which increased in frequency after 1739. During this spiritual crisis he received a vision of Jesus Christ, and the rest of his life was devoted to the interpretation of his visions. His main exegetical works were *Heavenly Secrets* (8 vols., 1749–1756),

Emanuel Swedenborg

Jimmy Swaggart

The Earths in the Universe (1758), *The New Jerusalem and the Heavenly Doctrine* (1758), *Heaven and Hell* (1758), *Divine Love and Wisdom* (1763), *Apocalypse Revealed* (1766), and *The True Christian Religion* (1771). Although he denied the Trinity* and vicarious atonement*, he upheld several other principles of orthodox theology, such as heaven* and hell*, Jesus Christ as the manifestation of the eternal, invisible, and timeless God, Second Coming*, and the establishment of a New Jerusalem*. He envisaged a spiritual world in which the living and the dead constituted one single being. He did not attempt to gain converts, but his followers organized themselves after his death as the New Jerusalem Church*.

Sweelinck, Jan Pieterszoon (1562–1621) Dutch composer. He served for 44 years as organist at the Oude Kirk in Amsterdam, even though Calvinists did not permit the organ to be used during church service. His greatest achievement was the polyphonic setting of the Psalter. The *Cantiones Sacrae,* a collection of his sacred music published in 1619, consists of 37 motets*. Approximately 70 keyboard compositions by Sweelinck are extant; none of them were published during his lifetime.

Sweet, William Warren (1881–1959) Methodist scholar known as "the dean of historians of Christianity in America." He taught at Ohio Wesleyan (1911–1913), DePauw University (1913–1927), and the Divinity School of the University of Chicago (1927–1946). His works include *Religion on the American Frontier* (1931–1946), *The Story of Religion in America* (1930), and *Religion in Colonial America* (1942).

Swiss Brethren Pioneer Anabaptist group who later formed part of the Mennonites*. They believe in believer's baptism* and non-resistance. Their dogmatic source is the seven articles of the Schleitheim Confession*. Their early leaders included Michael Sattler*, Conrad Grebel*, and Georg Blaurock*. The majority emigrated to Germany, the Netherlands, and the United States.

Swiss Guard Corps of 100 military guardians of the Vatican* instituted by Pope Julius II* on the basis of an agreement with the Swiss cantons of Zurich* and Lucerne to supply 250 men. The uni-

form of the guard was designed by Michelangelo* and consists of tunic, breeches, and stockings of wide red, yellow, and dark blue stripes.

sword In Christian art, a symbol of martyrdom or of the sword of the Spirit (Eph. 6:17).

Sword of the Spirit Roman Catholic social movement founded by Card A. Hinsley in 1940 to unify international Catholic social efforts by prayer, study, and action, and to promote justice.

syen In the Byzantine tradition, a canopy suspended over the altar.

Syllabus of Errors Eighty theses condemned as erroneous and heretical in the encyclical* *Quanta Cura* issued by Pope Pius IX* in 1864. The syllabus was arranged under ten headings: 1. Pantheism*, naturalism, and absolute rationalism. 2. Moderate rationalism. 3. Indifferentism and false tolerance in religious matters. 4. Socialism, Communism, secret societies, Bible societies, and liberal clerical associations. 5. The church and its rights. 6. The state and its relation to the church. 7. Natural and Christian ethics. 8. Christian marriage. 9. Temporal power of the pope. 10. Modern liberalism*.

Pope Pius IX

Sylvester I, St. (d. 335) Pope from 314. He oversaw the building of St. Peter's* Basilica as well as St. John Lateran. Feast day: December 31.

Sylvester II (c. 940–1003) Pope from 999. Birth name: Gerbert. He was a distinguished scholar in his own right as well as a dedicated churchman who opposed simony* and upheld clerical celibacy.

Sylvestrines Minor monastic order following the Rule of St. Benedict*, emphasizing poverty and founded by Sylvester Gozzolini (1177–1267) in 1231. Their mother house* is in Rome*, where their abbot-general* resides, and they wear a blue habit.

symbolics Branch of theology that studies and compares formal creeds and confessions as theological statements of faith.

symbolum 1. Military pass or password. 2. Creed of the church as the equivalent of a password for entry into the Christian church.

Symeon Popovic (1855–1941) Montenegrin staretz* and theologian. He joined the Pecherskaya Lavra in the Ukraine*. Back in his native Montenegro, he worked to revive monasteries and opened a theological academy. In 1896, he became a hermit in Podgorica. His disciples founded the Dormition Monastery.

Symmachus, St. (d. 514) Pope from 498. His election was followed by bloody conflict with his rival, archpriest Laurentius, which lasted until 507. During the latter part of his reign, Symmachus was engaged in the defense of orthodoxy* against the Henoticon* of Zeno and also the Manichaeans and the Arians. His liturgical innovations included the singing of "Gloria in Excelsis*" on Sundays and feasts of the martyrs. Feast day: July 19.

synapheia (Gk., conjunction) Combination of two natures in Jesus Christ as distinct from henosis, or union of two natures. The term is characteristic of Nestorian emphases.

Synapte In the Eastern Church*, prayer in the form of a litany*, consisting of short petitions said by the deacon to which the choir or the congregation respond with Kyrie eleison*.

Synaxarion (Gk., Book of the Assembly) In the Eastern Church*: 1. Short narrative of a saint* or a feast appointed to be read at the early morning service of orthros*. 2. **Greater Synaxarion.** Book in which these passages are arranged according to the calendar. 3. **Lesser Synaxarion.** Book listing the feasts to be observed every day with appropriate biblical lessons.

Synaxis 1. In the Eastern Church*, an assembly for public worship and prayer when the Eucharist* is celebrated. Also called Liturgical Synaxis. In the Western Church*, a non-eucharistic service, consisting of prayers and reading from the Scriptures and Psalms. Also called aliturgical synaxis. 2. Gathering or synod* of elder monks in a monastery. 3. Collection of short prayers.

syncellus (Gk., person who shares a cell with another) In the Byzantine Church*, an ecclesiastic who lived with a bishop in order to bear witness to the purity of a bishop's life.

Syndesmos (Gk., uniting bond) World fellowship of Orthodox youth, founded in 1953.

Synergism Cooperation of the divine and the human for salvation*, regeneration*, and sanctification*. In Lutheran theology, it is defined as "the human will assenting to and not resisting the Word of God*."

synod 1. General church council. 2. Representative body of a diocese* or province. 3. In the Presbyterian Church, an assembly intermediate between the presbytery* and the general assembly*.

synodical 1. Of or relating to a synod* or its decrees. 2. Of or relating to government of a church by a synod.

Synodicon 1. Collection of synodical* acts. 2. Liturgical text read in the Eastern Church* on the Feast of Orthodoxy.

Synoptic Gospels The first three Gospels of the

New Testament—Matthew, Mark, and Luke—the narratives of which are similar in many respects.

Synoptic problem In New Testament studies, questions relating to the similarities, differences among, and sources of the Synoptic Gospels* generally resolved by viewing Mark as the source of Matthew and Luke and the dependence of Matthew and Luke also on a lost source referred to as Q*.

syntagma Collection of laws and commentaries written by Matthew Blasteres, a fourteenth-century monk of St. Basil*.

Synthronon Semicircle of seats around the apse* of a Byzantine church, reserved to the clergy. In the center was the bishop's throne, a little higher than other seats.

Syriac Language belonging to the East Aramaic group. It was originally the dialect of Edessa*, one of the great centers of Christianity. As a literary language, it flourished from the second to the thirteenth centuries. It is still used as a liturgical language in the Jacobite (West Syriac) and Assyrian (East Syriac) churches. Three distinct scripts, all of them cursive, were used. The oldest is Estrangelo, and the other two are named for the two divisions of the Syrian Church, Nestorian in the East and Jacobite or Serta in the West with separate systems of vowel notation. Syriac literature is almost entirely Christian. There exists several translations of the Bible in Syriac, such as Diatessaron, Old Syriac Version*, Peshitta*, and Syro-Hexapla*, all of them extremely valuable because of the natural accuracy of Syriac translators. Among the more important Syriac writers are Aphraates*, St. Ephraem Syrus,* Philoxenos*, Jacob of Edessa*, Isaac of Nineveh*, Moses bar Kepha*, and Bar Hebraeus.* Jacob of Sarug* and Narsai* are preeminent poets.

Syriac/Syrian Orthodox Church (Until 2000, the Syrian Orthodox Church) One of the Lesser Eastern Churches*, often called Jacobite (after Jacob Baradaeus) because of its Monophysite beliefs and its opposition to the Council of Chalcedon*. Its liturgical language is Syriac*, and its official calendar is Julian* except in India. Its current head, the 122nd patriarch* of Antioch*, resides at

Damascus*, having been driven out by the Turks from Antioch after World War I. The church has between 300,000 and 400,000 members in 20 archdioceses* in the Middle East, Europe, North America, and Australia. Since the sixteenth century, almost half of the Syriac Christians of Malabar, India, have belonged to the Syriac Orthodox Church. Numbering over one million, they have a separate catholicos*, but their relations with the Antiochene Church have not always been happy.

The church traces its roots to the original patriarchate of Antioch, one of the four (later five) patriarchates of the early Christian church, established by St. Peter* who is considered the first patriarch (33–40) of the Syriac Orthodox Church. About the year 70 the martyr* St. Ignatius, known as "the Enlightened," became the third patriarch, succeeding Euodius. In his honor each patriarch since 1293 has carried the ecclesiastical name of Ignatius. The Council of Nicaea* confirmed the ecclesiastical jurisdiction of the See of Antioch as covering all territory between the Mediterranean Sea and the Persian Gulf and extending into India. Around the middle of the fourth century a Catholicate of the East was established at Seleucia-Ctesiphon* to serve the faithful in Persia and Iraq, but it later fell to Persian political persecution and conflicts with the Assyrian Church of the East. In 628 a new Catholicate was established in Mesopotamia by Patriarch Athanasius I, and its jurisdiction was expanded to include all of Arabia, Persia, and Afghanistan. After the patriar-

Jacob Baradeus

chates of Alexandria and Antioch rejected the decisions of the Council of Chalcedon (451), a season of imperial persecution followed.

In 512 Severus the Great*, the patriarch of Antioch, was deposed by Justinian*. By 544 only three bishops remained. At this time, the monk Jacob Baradeus* won over the Empress Theodora* to the Monophysite side. With her help and the support of Theodosius, the patriarch of Alexandria, Baradeus set out to restore the persecuted churches. He traveled in rags (hence his name) all over the Middle East, Asia Minor, and Ethiopia, rebuilding the church. During his travels, he ordained over 100,000 priests and deacons and consecrated 27 bishops and one patriarch, Paul II. In gratitude, the Syriac Orthodox Church is often called the Syriac Jacobite Church*.

During the following centuries, the seat of the patriarchate was moved to the Monastery of Mar Barsuma, near Malatya, in present-day Turkey and thence to Diyarbakir, Turkey, and Za'faran* Monastery, outside of Mardin, Turkey. Syriac Christians did not experience serious persecution from the Muslim rulers in the early centuries. In 1236 the See of Antioch had 20,000 parishes and hundreds of monasteries and convents. It administered great educational institutions, such as the famous schools of Antioch, Nusaybin, and Edessa*. Many of the illustrious scholars of this age were Jacobites, including Gregory Bar Hebraeus, Dionysius bar Salibi*, Jacob of Edessa*, Philoxenos of Mabbug*, Jacob of Sarug*, and Ephraem the Syrian*. But after the twelfth century the history of the church was clouded with persecutions and massacres on a scale unmatched until then. Mongols, Kurds, and Ottomans decimated the church, killing millions, forcibly converting others, and destroying thousands of churches and monasteries. The holocaust has lasted well into the middle of the twentieth century.

The faith of the Syriac Orthodox Church is based directly on the holy Scripture as embodied in the Nicene Creed*. The church professes the oneness of God and acknowledges and believes that he subsists in three distinct persons: the Father, the Son, and the Holy Spirit*. The Holy Trinity is professed as one God, of one essence and one Godhead. Jesus Christ is professed to be the only begotten Son of God who was incarnate

by the Holy Spirit of the Virgin Mary*, taking upon himself our humanity. He is of one nature, being fully God and fully man without mixture or confusion. It condemns Eutychianism* which affirmed one nature, in Christ, but only one of divinity, not of humanity. Christ's true Godhead and humanity were united at his Incarnation*. He is acknowledged as Lord and Savior, having suffered in the flesh and having died upon the cross to save mankind from the bondage of sin. He rose victoriously on the third day, ascended into heaven* and is seated at the right hand of God the Father and he will come again in glory to judge all mankind, both living and dead. Christ is professed as head of the church and the church's foundation.

The Holy Spirit proceeds from the Father and is the giver of life, inspirer of the Scriptures, and the sanctifier of the church and the holy sacraments*. The Virgin Mary* is truly the bearer of God (yoldath aloho). The church observes seven canonical stations as the liturgy of the hours. They are ramsho (vespers*), soutoto (compline*), lilio (mattins*), safro (lauds*), tloth sho'een (terce*), felgeh dyawmo (sext*), and tsh' sho'een (none*). The weekday office is found in shimo, which contains the ferial cycle. The dominical cycle of hours is found in fenquitho, a book of hours for Sundays and feast and fast days supplemented by husoyo, a book of supplicatory prayers. The church observes seven sacraments*: baptism*, chrismation*, Holy Eucharist*, penance*, marriage, priesthood, and anointing of the sick of which the first four are necessary for salvation* and the first two and priesthood can be received only once. The baptismal font* is considered both a womb and a tomb. Candidates* for priesthood are permitted to marry, but they must marry prior to their ordination to the diaconate. Bishops are chosen from the monastic clergy.

The eucharistic liturgy of the Syriac Orthodox Church is among the richest in all Christendom*, with more than 80 anaphoras. The principal liturgy is that of St. James, but the Liturgies of the Twelve Apostles, St. Peter*, Dionysius bar Salibi*, and St. John the Evangelist are also used. The liturgy is referred to as rozae qadeeshae or the holy mysteries* and the Eucharist as qurbono or sacrifice. The church believes in transubstantiation*. The bread for the Eucharist* is made from leavened bread mixed with salt and oil. The words, "who was crucified on our account," are added to the Trisagion* in the liturgy, and the sign of the cross is made with one finger.

Dayre d'Zafran Monastery

Syrian Catholics Uniat offshoot of the Syrian Orthodox Church* dating from 1783 when Mar Michael Garweh, archbishop of Aleppo, brought a small group of Syrian Orthodox faithful into the Uniat fold. The seat of the patriarchate* is in Beirut.

Syro-Chaldeans Chaldean Christians* of the ancient Church of the East*, now in communion with Rome.

Syro-Hexapla Translation into Syriac* of the Greek text of the Septuagint contained in Origen's *Hexapla* made in 616–617 by Paul, the Syrian Orthodox bishop of Tella in Mesopotamia.

Syro-Malankarese Catholic St. Thomas Christians* who submitted to Rome in 1930 and who use the West Syrian Rite*.

systematic theology Branch of theology drawing upon the whole of Scripture, relating various portions to one another so as to form a coherent system. It employs biblical, historical, and philosophical resources to illuminate the practical applications of God's truth.

Szentgotthard Cistercian abbey in Hungary, on the River Raab. The church, a triple-naved basilica* in the Provencal style, was consecrated in the name of the Virgin Mary*. However, in 1570 the complex was blown up by the Imperial general Tieffenbach. A century later in 1677 the archbishop of Kalosca had the church rebuilt. In 1740 a new program of rebuilding began, and the new church was completed by 1764. It had paintings by Matthias Gusner and decorative frescoes on the victory over the Turks at Szentgotthard in 1666 by Istvan Dorffmeister.

Tt

tabak In the Coptic tradition, circular mat made of silk and backed by a coarse material with one embroidered cross and several smaller crosses, used to cover the chalice*.

tabieh Soft, round, quilted, dark-blue turban used by the Maronite clergy.

tablitho In the Syrian Church, consecrated wooden tablet used by the patriarch* as a liturgical altar on which the paten* and the chalice* are placed.

Taborites Radical Hussites* who rejected transubstantiation*, purgatory*, saints*, relics*, and the priesthood. They were also millenarians who believed in an imminent Second Coming* of Christ and the establishment of a just social order. In 1419, 40,000 Taborites gathered on a hill named Tabor, hence their name. Under the leadership of John Zizka*, they defied the imperial Crusades against them, but after Zizka's death in 1424 they were beaten at the Battle of Lipany and their leader, Procopius, was killed.

Tabot Ark of the Covenant, found in the sanctuary of Ethiopian Orthodox churches.

tabula ansata (Lat., *ansa*, handle) Horizontal rectangle with handle-like projections in which an inscription was framed.

tailasan In the Coptic tradition, amice-like vestment, a long band of white linen worn by priests and deacons twisted around the head.

Tait, Archibald Campbell (1811–1882) Archbishop of Canterbury* from 1868 to 1882. He was a Broad Church* advocate who opposed Anglo-Catholicism* and ritualism*, yet was sympathetic to Evangelicalism*. He presided over the Second Lambeth Conference* in 1878.

Taize community Religious community near Cluny* in France founded in 1940 by Roger Schultz-Marasauche*, its prior*. It is made up of members from the Roman Catholic, Orthodox, and Protestant traditions who go in small groups to different countries to live and work and share the gospel. Its weekly meetings are attended by up to 6,000 participants, most of them young adults. Songs from Taize are popular in many countries. See also SCHULTZ-MARASAUCHE, ROGER-LOUIS.

Brother Roger Schultz-Marasauche

Takayama, Justus Ukon (1552–1615) Japanese Christian feudal lord. He was baptized in 1564 by Irmao Lourenco, the first Japanese Christian. As lord of Takatsuki Castle, he built a church and seminary in the center of his territory, a large church in Kyoto, and a seminary in Azuchi. Takayama converted many of his subjects, and through him many other feudal lords also became Christians. He declined to abandon his faith when Toyotomi Hideyoshi banished missionaries in 1587 and Tokugawa Ieyasu banned Christianity. In 1614 Takayama and 350 other Christians were banished from the land and exiled to the Philippines.

takhshephtho In the Jacobite Rite, a petition* in a litany*.

Takla-Haymanot (c. 1215–1313) Ethiopian Orthodox* monk and leader of renewal and mission. After nine years as a monk in Dabra Hayq monastery of Iyasus-Mo'a, he relocated to the monastic school at Dabra Damo in Tigre* province. Here he attracted a dedicated following including Ar'ayana Saggahu, Madhanina Egzi, and Bartolomewos. After helping to revive monasticism* in Tigre, he returned to his homeplace of Shawa. He established the great center of Christian learning, now known as Dabra Libanos. It marked the turning of the tide of Muslim expansion and the consolidation of Christianity in the kingdom.

taksad'husaye (lit., rite of mercy) In the Assyrian Rite, book containing rites and prayers of penance* and absolution*.

taksad'mada In the Assyrian Rite, the Book of Baptism, usually bound with the Taksa, a liturgical book containing the anaphoras*.

taksad'syamida In the Assyrian Rite, book containing the ordination ceremonies.

talar Black gown of European clergy, similar to the cassock*.

Talbot, Louis Thomson (1889–1976) Evangelical minister and president of the Bible Institute of Los Angeles. He pastored in churches in Illinois, Iowa, Minneapolis, Ontario, before becoming pastor of the Church of the Open Door (1932–1948) and president of the Bible Institute, Los Angeles (1932–1952). After 1952 he became chancellor of Biola College (now Biola University). The Talbot Seminary was named in his honor. Among his many books are *God's Plan for the Ages* (1936), *The Prophecies of Daniel in the Light of Past, Present and Future Events* (1940), and *Christ in the Tabernacle* (1942).

Tall Brothers Four monks—Dioscoros, Ammonius, Eusebius*, and Euthymius*—excommunicated by Theophilus, bishop of Alexandria,* in 401 for Origenism*. Thereupon they took their case to Constantinople*, where Chrysostom's reception of them contributed to his fate at the Synod of the Oak* in 403.

tallia (lit., youth) In the Jacobite Rite, arrangement of the broken and consecrated particles* after the fraction*.

Tallis, Thomas (c. 1505–1585) Great English composer before Byrd*, with whom he was granted a 21-year license by Queen Elizabeth to print music in the realm. From 1540 until his death he was organist at the Chapel Royal. His major work was his motet*, *Spem in Alium,* written for eight choirs of five parts each, building up to a 40-part climax. He wrote both Catholic and Anglican works. The former consists of three Latin masses, 30 motets, six settings of responsories for major feasts, seven hymns, and two lamentations. The latter consists of three Anglican services, 20 anthems, and some Psalm settings. Two of Tallis's most sumptuous works are his Catholic ones: *Missa Puer Natus est Nobis* and the antiphon* *Gaude Gloriosa Dei Mater* (Rejoice, Glorious Mother of God) in six voices.

Tambaram Conference Missionary conference convened by the International Missionary Council*, which met at Tambaram* in Tamil Nadu, India, in 1938. It was attended by 471 delegates from 69 different countries under the chairmanship of John Mott*.

Tana Monastic center in Ethiopia in the western highlands containing 38 islands, many with monasteries.

tanaretz In the Armenian tradition, a married parish priest.

Tantum Ergo (Lat., only therefore) Opening words and title of a eucharistic hymn at the Benediction of the Blessed Sacrament*.

tanurta In the Assyrian tradition, oven set aside for baking the bukhra or bread used in the liturgy.

tarwodho In the Jacobite Rite, the communion spoon.

Tasso, Torquato (1544–1595) Italian Christian poet, made poet laureate by Clement VIII*. His great achievement was his epic poem, *Jerusalem Delivered.*

Tatian (c. 110–172) Christian apologist, ascetic, and author of the *Diatesseron*. Born in Assyria, he came to Rome* about 150 and was converted and later became a pupil of Justin Martyr*. He wrote his apology for the Christian faith, *Address to the Greeks,* about 160. After Justin's death, he returned to Syria, where he founded a school promoting encratite asceticism*.

Tau cross T-shaped cross, especially that used by the Egyptian monks, as St. Anthony the Great*.

Tauler, John (c. 1300–1361) German Dominican mystic. He was famous as a preacher and a spiritual teacher. A friend of Henry Suso* and Meister Eckhart*, his sermons and writings reveal a kind of mysticism that had a great appeal to the lay Christian and not merely the religious, using imagery drawn from everyday life. During the Black Death he devoted himself to serving the sick.

Taverner, John (c. 1490–1545) English composer. His church music includes eight Masses Ordinary, three Magnificats*, and 25 motets*, most of them votive antiphons*.

taylasan In the Coptic Church*, cylindrical cap of vestment material surmounted by a cross, worn by priests.

Taylor, James Hudson (1832–1905) Pioneer British missionary to China. A Methodist by background, he was converted at 17 and heeded a call* to go to China. He landed in Shanghai at age 22 as agent of the Chinese Evangelization Society. When the society failed, he continued alone for many years, adopting Chinese dress and carrying the gospel to the closed inland regions. Ill health forced him to return to England in 1860. When China was opened to Westerners, he founded the China Inland Mission* in 1865 with 24 missionaries, two for each unreached province.

Taylor returned to China in 1866 and in the next 35 years helped transform China into a vast mission field*. By 1895 he led 641 missionaries, about half of all Western missionaries in China. He also laid down the five principles that guided the successful evangelization of China by all missionaries who followed him: Dependence on God for supplies; sensitivity to the native customs, including adoption of Chinese dress; direction of the mission by field personnel, not from home; efficient administration; and prayer support from the home base. His books include *China: Its Spiritual Needs and Claims* (1865), *A Retrospect* (1894), and *Union and Communion* (1894).

Taylor, Jeremy (1613–1667) Anglican divine, known as "the glory of the English pulpit," "the Shakespeare of Divines," and "the Spenser of Prose." His fame rests on his devotional writings, especially *The Rule and Exercise of Holy Living* (1650) and *The Rule and Exercise of Holy Dying* (1651).

Hudson Taylor

Among his other books are *The Liberty of Prophesying* (1647), a plea for toleration; *The Golden Grove* (1655), a collection of sermons; and *Unum Necessarium* (1655).

Taylor, Kenneth Nathaniel (1913–) Bible translator and publisher. After service on the InterVaristy Christian Fellowship, he served with many publishers, including *His* magazine, Good News Publishers, and Moody Press. In the 1950s he wrote a paraphrased Bible and formed his own company, Tyndale House, to publish it. In 1971 the complete Living Bible* appeared under the Tyndale imprint. Millions of copies of this popular translation have been sold.

Taylor, Nathaniel William (1786–1858) Founder of New Haven theology*. He contributed to the rise of Evangelical theology by modifying Calvinism* and opening it to revivalism*. He modified Calvinism by making human beings free moral agents and not merely inheritors of original sin* and by describing God as a benevolent moral governor.

Tbilisi martyrs One hundred thousand martyrs slaughtered by the Muslim ruler of Khwarezm in 1227 after defeat of the Georgian armies and the surrender of Tbilisi.

TBN Trinity Broadcasting Network, one of the principal American Christian television broadcasting organizations, founded in 1973 and based in California. It is headed by Paul Crouch* and is Pentecostal in orientation.

Tchaikovsky, Pyotr Ilych (1840–1893) Russian composer. Among his religious works are a unified setting of the Liturgy of St. John Chrysostom* (1878), *Vesper Service* (1881–1882), a *Hymn in Honor of St. Cyril and Methodius* (1885), and a series of nine sacred works for mixed chorus.

tchasoslov Byzantine Book of Hours containing the hours and some Psalms.

tchetz In the Byzantine tradition, a reader*.

tchinovnik In the Byzantine Rite*, pontifical* service book containing fixed portions of the liturgies as celebrated by a bishop.

Te Deum (Lat., Thee Lord) Early Christian hymn beginning "We Praise Thee, O Lord," commonly ascribed to St. Ambrose* and St. Augustine*, but probably written by St. Niceta*, bishop of Remesiana. Of the hymn's 21 verses, the first 9 are an ascription* of praise and the next 12 a confession of faith.

Te Igitur (Lat., Thee Therefore) Opening words of the Canon of the Mass*. It offers intercession for the entire church, the pope, the diocesan bishop, and all the faithful.

team ministry Pastoral care shared by a team consisting of a main pastor, known as the team rector*, and one or more lay or ordained coministers.

TEAR Fund The Evangelical Alliance Relief Fund, the largest emergency relief and development fund operating under Christian auspices in the United Kingdom. It was established in 1968 by the Evangelical Alliance* and grew rapidly under the vigorous leadership of George Hoffman (1968–1969).

Teen Challenge U.S. evangelistic program started by David Wilkerson* in 1958 to organize and inspire street evangelism. It developed a successful drug rehabilitation program and also programs for inner-city children and youth.

tegula Slab with which a loculus* was sealed in a catacomb*, often with inscriptions or other means of identification.

Teilhard de Chardin, Pierre (1881–1955) French Jesuit philosopher and paleontologist. He was ordained in 1911. He left for China in 1922 as a consultant to a geological survey where he helped to discover Pithecanthropus and Sinanthropus. He returned to France after World War II and was soon embroiled in the controversy surrounding his seminal work, *The Phenomenon of Man*. He was forbidden by his order from writing on religious subjects or from accepting the professorial chair at the College de France. He moved to the United States, where he worked until his death with the Wenner Gren Foundation for Anthropological Research.

In his writings Teilhard de Chardin tried to offer a unique synthesis of science and religion. He saw the universe as an evolutionary process moving toward more complex natural systems and higher levels of consciousness through several critical thresholds during which leaps to new paradigms are made. One such threshold was the appearance of rational self-consciousness and the emergence of what he called the noumenon. Evolution is now directed by human consciousness as much as it is by natural laws. The whole movement is teleological and sacramental because evolution is an ascent toward God in a process of "Christification." Among his other books is *The Divine Milieu* (1957), a devotional summary of his ideas.

Tekawitha, Blessed Kateri (1656–1680) Native American holy woman, known as the "Lily of the Mohawks." She was baptized in 1676 and thereafter lived a life of prayer and penance*. She was beatified in 1980. Feast day: July 14.

Blessed Kateri Tekawitha

telaria Crossbar to which the frontal* or antependium* of the altar is attached.

Telemann, George Phillip (1681–1767) German composer. He served as Kapellmeister* in a number of cities, including Hamburg. He composed 1,043 church cantatas, 46 passions, 6 passion oratorios, 11 masses on chorale tunes, 4 short masses, 2 Magnificats*, 17 Psalm settings, and 26 motets*.

teleology (Gk., *telos,* end) 1. Science of ultimate design or purpose. 2. Fact or character of being directed toward a goal or shaped by a purpose.

Telesphorus (d. c. 137) Bishop of Rome* from about 127. He suffered death by martyrdom. Feast day: January 2 or 5.

televangelism Evangelism* through the electronic media, especially televised religious services and evangelistic crusades*. In the United States, the Christian Broadcasting Network* and the Trinity Broadcasting Network (TBN*) are among the networks devoted exclusively to televangelism. Thus, televangelist.

Templars See KNIGHTS TEMPLAR.

Temple, Frederick (1821–1902) Archbishop of Canterbury* from 1896 to 1902. Ordained in 1846 he became successively principal of Kneller Hall, a training school for schoolmasters, headmaster of Rugby School, bishop of Exeter, bishop of London, and archbishop of Canterbury. He presided over the Lambeth Conference* in 1897. A liberal in outlook, he had conflicts with the High Church* wing of the Anglican* Church.

Temple, William (1881–1944) Archbishop of Canterbury* from 1942 to 1944. Son of Frederick Temple*, he was appointed bishop of Manchester in 1921, archbishop of York* in 1929, and archbishop of Canterbury in 1942. Temple was an accomplished scholar and theologian who combined learning with social awareness. He was for many years president of the Workers Education Association. He was also an ecumenist who promoted the formation of the British Council of Churches* and the Church of South India*. Among his many books that reflected his passion for social justice was *Christianity and Social Order* (1942).

Temporale Section of a Missal*, lectionary*, or Breviary* containing variable parts of the masses, offices, and other services for a whole year.

tempus clausum (Lat., closed time*) In the Roman

Catholic church, certain penitential or other seasons in a Christian year* when marriages may not be celebrated. It includes the period from the first Sunday in Advent* to Epiphany* and from Ash Wednesday to Easter*.

ten Boom, Corrie (Cornelia) (1892–1983) Dutch evangelist and author. Born into a Calvinist home, ten Boom assisted the Jews in escaping the Germans during World War II. Betrayed by two fellow Dutchmen, she was arrested and imprisoned until the end of the war. Thereafter she established a rehabilitation home for victims of concentration camps in Darmstadt, Germany. With the royalties of her bestseller, *The Hiding Place* (1971), she founded Christians Incorporated to support the work of multiracial missionaries.

ten martyrs Ten statues of modern Christian martyrs* of various churches placed in 1998 on the west front of the Westminster Abbey* in niches vacant from the Reformation*. They are Maximilian Kolbe*, a Franciscan monk in Poland killed by the Nazis in place of a Jew in Auschwitz in 1941; Manche Masemola of South Africa, killed by her pagan parents at age 14 in 1928; Archbishop Janani Luwum of Uganda, killed by Idi Amin; Russian Orthodox Grand Duchess Elizabeth, killed by the Bolsheviks in 1918; American civil rights leader, Martin Luther King, Jr.*; Archbishop Oscar Romero* of El Salvador, killed by right-wing assassination squads; German Lutheran Dietrich Bonhoeffer*; Presbyterian Esther John, killed by a fanatic in Pakistan in 1960; Lucian Tapiedi, an Anglican in Papua New Guinea murdered in 1942; and Wang Zhiming, an evangelical pastor in South China, executed in 1973.

tenebrae (Lat., darkness) Special form of mattins* and lauds* for Wednesday, Thursday, and Friday of the Holy Week* during which 14 out of 15 candles are extinguished one by one.

Tennent, Gilbert (1703–1764) American Presbyterian minister who took a leading part in the Great Awakening* and the New Side* movement. He is remembered for his sermon, "The Danger of an Unconverted Ministry." George Whitefield* called him the "Son of Thunder."

tent meeting Also, camp meeting*. Crusade held by an itinerant preacher in a large tent. Charles Finney* was among the earliest preachers to use tent meetings. Billy Graham* held his first crusade* in a tent, and Oral Roberts* once claimed that he had the largest tent.

tentmaker A Christian worker in a self-supporting ministry who earns his livelihood in a secular occupation. The term refers to St. Paul's* profession that he combined with his ministry so as not to burden his churches.

terbroutiun Armenian book of canticles* and office hymns*.

Terce, Sext, None Little hours of the Divine Office* recited at the third, sixth, and ninth hours, respectively. Each office consists of three Psalms, preceded by Pater, Ave Maria*, versicle*, and hymn followed by responsory*, prayer, and concluding versicles.

Teresa, Mother (1910–1997) Birth name: Agnes Gonxha Bojaxhiu. Nun and founder of the Missionaries of Charity. Born of Albanian parents in Macedonia*, she joined the Sisters of Loreto* in 1928 and was sent to Darjeeling in India to begin her novitiate* under the name of Teresa. From 1929 to 1948 she was in Calcutta as a teacher in St. Mary's School, but she left the order in that year as she felt a call* to serve the poorest of the poor.

Mother Teresa

Adopting a blue-edged sari as her habit, she lived in the slums among the destitute and the dying, caring for the homeless and the hopeless with an intensity and devotion that made her a legend in her own lifetime. In 1948 she founded the Order of the Missionaries of Charity and became an Indian citizen. She received honors from around the world, including the Padma Ratna from the government of India and the Nobel Peace Prize in 1979. Her funeral in 1997 was attended by hundreds of thousands of people, including heads of state.

Teresa of Avila, St. (1515–1582) Properly, St. Teresa of Jesus. Carmelite* mystic. She entered the Carmelite Convent of the Incarnation at Avila in 1553. Seeking a life of perfection*, she began to have visions and to hear divine voices. Among her spiritual experiences was a mystical piercing of the heart by a spear of divine love. She was much influenced by St. John of the Cross*, Peter of Alcantara*, her confessor*, and Domingo Báñez*, a Dominican priest. To lead a more mortified life, she founded the convent under the original (Discalced*) Carmelite* Rule, St. Joseph's at Avila, in 1562. Here she wrote her great work, *The Way of Perfection*, as a manual for her nuns. She followed it with an autobiography, *Life* (1562), *Book of Foundations*, and *The Interior Castle*. At the same time, her contemplative life* deepened until she felt she had reached a state of "spiritual marriage." She managed to combine a contemplative

St. Teresa of Avila

life of the highest order with a tireless organizing ability and a passion for reform. She was canonized in 1622 and declared a doctor of the church* in 1970. Feast day: October 15.

Teresa of Lisieux, St. (1873–1897) Birth name: Marie Francoise Therese Martin. Also known as the "Little Flower of Jesus*" and "Theresa of the Child Jesus." Carmelite* nun and mystic. At 13 she had a conversion experience that led her to enter the Carmelite convent in Lisieux at 15. Seriously ill with tuberculosis, she wrote her autobiography, *L'Histoire d'un Ami*, which established her cult as a miracle worker. Benedict XV* said of her *Little Way* that "it contained the secret of sanctity for the entire world." She was beatified in 1923 and canonized in 1925 and proclaimed the patroness of foreign missions and copatroness (with Joan of Arc*) of France. Feast day: October 1.

Terminism 1. Teaching that the grace* of God is not infinite and that it is available only for a certain period of time. This belief was held by the German Pietists, who were opposed to deathbed conversions. 2. Nominalism.

terna List of three candidates proposed to fill an office for an ecclesiastical vacancy.

territory In the Salvation Army*, a country or region under a territorial commander.

Tersanctus Sanctus* repeated thrice, as "Holy, Holy, Holy," sung or recited in the eucharistic liturgy.

Tersteegen, Gerhard (1697–1769) German Protestant hymn writer and devotional writer. After conversion at the age of 20, he began a ministry of teaching as a spiritual director* to a group of friends. In 1729 he published his collection of poems and hymns under the title *Geistliches Blumen-Gartlein inniger Seelen*. He also published a series of biographies of Catholic mystics, *Auserlesene Lebensbeschreibungen heiliger Seelen*. His fame and influence spread over Northern Europe; and his cottage, Pilgerhutte, became a major retreat* center. He conducted extensive correspondence with mystics and Quietists, including Madame Guyon*. His remarkable hymns survive in German and many other languages, including English. The two best known of them were translated by John Wesley* as "Thou Hidden Love of God" and "Lo, God Is Here."

tertianship In the Jesuit Order, the third year of probation beyond the two years of the novitiate* before admission to final vows. It includes 30 days of spiritual exercises* and a study of the Jesuit constitutions.

tertiary Lay person who belongs to a third order* in a monastic system, after monks and nuns. Tertiaries are found among the Franciscans, Augustinian Hermits, Dominicans*, Servites*, and Carmelites*. They are bound by the order's discipline but take no vows.

Tertullian (c. 160/70–c. 215/20) Birth name: Quintus Septimius Florens Tertullianus. "Father of Latin Theology." African Church Father. Converted to Christianity before 160, he probably served as a lay catechist and teacher. Around 206 he became a supporter of Montanism*, though probably without leaving or being ejected from the Catholic church. He led a group increasingly critical of episcopal leadership. Tertullian wrote extensively from 196 to 212 in Greek and Latin, but many of his Greek works have been lost, including *Ecstasy, Paradise, Fate, The Hope of Believers, Flesh and Soul,* and *Against the Apellians.* His 31 extant Latin books make up the first and most significant corpus of Latin Christian literature. These writings fall into three categories: Apologetics, moral and disciplinary instruction for Christians, and theological works.

In *Apologeticum* and other apologetical works, he attacked pagan superstitions, appealed for toleration of Christians as useful citizens of the state, and rebutted charges of immorality levied against Christians. His main works of moral instruction were *De Spectaculis, De Corona Militis, De Idololatria,* and *De Paenitentia* in which he extolled Christian martyrdom with the memorable dictum, "The Blood of the Martyrs is the Seed of the Church," and pleaded with Christians to shun the contamination, corruption, and idol worship of pagan society. His theological writings consisted of both refutation of heresy and exposition of sound doctrine. In *De Praescriptione Haertico-*

rum, he argued that there is only one holy, apostolic, catholic, and episcopal church which alone possesses the authentic tradition of Christ and the apostles and the authority to interpret Scriptures. In his works against heresy, he attacked the

Tertullian

Gnostics, the Docetists, Marcionists, Valentinians, and Hermogenes. In *De Baptismo* he discussed baptism*; in *Prayer* he produced one of the earliest expositions of the Lord's Prayer*, and in his work *Against Praxeas* he established the orthodox definition of the Trinity*. In *De Anima* he espoused Traducianism*, which held that the human soul is transmitted by parents to children, thus laying the foundation for Augustine's doctrine of the original sin*.

Tertullian found in Montanism a congenial home for his beliefs on the indwelling* of the Holy Spirit*, millennial expectations, prophetic gifts, asceticism*, and a rigorous application of the doctrine of perfection*. Many of his later works are Montanist, such as *De Monogamia, De Exhortatione Castitatis, De Jejunio,* and *De Pudicitia*. Montanism accentuated his natural ascetic inclinations. Tertullian was the most brilliant theologian of his time, skilled in rhetoric and logic, and a master of the Latin language. His terminology provided the base for the Trinitarianism and Christological ideas of the following centuries, and he did much to guide the dogmatic development of the nascent church. His ideas and language have had a great influence on the evolution of early Christianity, in recognition of which he is called the "Father of Latin Theology."

tesebhotho In the Syrian Liturgy, hymn of praise honoring Christ the king sung on major feasts before the Gospel at the liturgy and vespers*.

teshbota Assyrian post-communion hymn of thanksgiving.

teshmeshto In the Jacobite Rite, Psalms recited before entry into the sanctuary.

Testament of Our Lord Jesus Christ in Galilee Also, Epistle of the Apostles*. Apocryphal Syriac* work (probably written by Jacob of Edessa*) of the fourth or fifth centuries. It is a translation from Greek; and there are Ethiopic, Arabic, Coptic, and Latin versions. It purports to give a postresurrection discourse of the Lord to his disciples with a section on the imminent apocalypse and detailed prescriptions for church order*, services, ministry, and catechumenate* as well as prayers. Later it was incorporated in the Clementine Octateuch used in the Monophysite churches of Syria.

testimony Brief personal account or narrative, either written or spoken, by an individual Christian concerning how he or she became a Christian and how Christ has worked in his or her life.

testimony meeting A gathering where attendees are invited to share their personal religious experiences in the presence of the entire assembly. It is a Puritan practice that was revived in the Great Awakening* and has continued to the present day.

teston In the Byzantine Rite*, a vessel containing the water used for washing the altar on Holy Thursday*.

Tetramorphs Four figures—a man, a lion*, an ox, and an eagle*—from Revelation 4:6–7 representing the Four Evangelists, according to an interpretation dating from the second century.

Tetrapolitan Confession Protestant confession* of faith drawn up by Martin Bucer* and Wolfgang Capito* at the Diet of Augsburg (1530) and pre-

sented by Jakob Sturm in the name of the cities of Strasbourg*, Memmingen, Lindau, and Constance and hence called the Four-City Confession. It embodied the convictions, especially on the Lord's Supper*, of Protestants unable to agree wholly with Luther*.

tetravela In the Byzantine tradition, curtains hung between the four columns of the kiborion* above the altar.

Tewkesbury Abbey Benedictine abbey founded in 1087 in Tewkesbury, England, by Robert Fitzhamon with Giraldus, abbot of Cranborne. The magnificent abbey church was consecrated in 1121 and remodeled in the early fourteenth century.

textual criticism Comparison and evaluation of the different readings of the manuscripts of the Bible in order to construct the history of the text through its various stages and to establish, as far as possible, the original, or ur-text.

Textus Receptus (Lat., received text) Greek text of the New Testament that forms the basis of the Authorized Version* of the English Bible. It was also the text followed by Theodore Beza*, Eras-

Tetramorphs

mus*, and the Complutensian Polyglot*. Compare Received Text*.

thaborstand Movable platform on which the monstrance* may be placed during exposition of the Blessed Sacrament*.

Thaddaeus, St. Apostle mentioned in Matthew 10:3 and Mark 3:8, sometimes identified with Addai*, one of the Seventy who was sent to Abgar, but more often with Jude. See also JUDE, ST. Feast day: August 21.

thalassa In Coptic churches, altar cavity down which rinsing from the ablutions* and ashes are disposed of.

Thanksgiving Day Annual national holiday in the United States for expressing thanks to God, first proclaimed by George Washington in 1789. Lincoln's proclamation of 1863 made it an annual observance and a 1941 act of the U.S. Congress fixed its observance on the fourth Thursday of November. The original Thanksgiving of the Pilgrims* was instituted by Governor William Bradford* after the first harvest in Plymouth Colony in 1621.

thaumaturgus (Gk., wonder-worker) Title applied to any number of saints* reputed to have performed miracles, especially Gregory Thaumaturgus* and Bernard of Clairvaux*.

Th.D. Doctor of Theology.

theandric acts Acts performed by Jesus Christ as God-Man, as distinct from acts of God and acts of man, a term coined by Dionysius the Pseudo-Areopagite*. It formed the Christological dogma* of the Monothelites and Monophysites, who taught one will and one nature in Christ. It was also used in an orthodox sense by Maximus the Confessor* and others.

Theatines Religious order founded in Rome* in 1524 as Clerks Regular of Divine Providence by two members of the Roman Oratory of Divine Love, St. Cajetan* and Gian Petro Carafa (afterwards Pope Paul IV), to reform the church and rid it of corruption and to combat heresy. The Theatines were not allowed to have any property

or to beg. They followed a very austere rule, and they adopted the habit of secular clergy with the exception of white socks. It was one of the orders most involved in the Counter-Reformation*.

Thebaid The cradle of Christian monasticism* in the upper part of the Nile Valley, named after the ancient city of Thebes. The first monastic settlement in this region was by St. Paul of Thebes*, and it was later inhabited by St. Antony the Great and Pachomius*.

Theban Legion, the Christian legion from the Thebaid* massacred according to tradition in the persecution under Maximian at St. Maurice-en-Valais.

Theban Legion

Theism Theological system which postulates a transcendent God who is the creator of the universe, an immanent God who sustains it, and a personal God who is able to communicate with and redeem* his creation. Christian theism is also monistic or monotheistic. Theism is usually contrasted with Deism*, the fashionable view in the Enlightenment and the modern world, that God is a higher power or force with only minimal involvement in the affairs of the world.

themelining Protestant non-liturgical practice of relating every element in a worship service to a theme. All non-thematic materials are eliminated in an attempt to channel the focus of the worship hour toward one goal.

theocentric Having God as the central concern of an institution or individual.

theocracy 1. Administration of a society or state under the immediate direction of God. 2. Government or political rule by priests or clergy as the representatives of God. Thus, theocratic.

theodicy 1. Vindication of the justice of God, especially in ordaining or permitting evil, vice, pain, and suffering. 2. Branch of theology that treats of the nature and government of God and the destiny of the soul.

Theodora I (c. 500–548) Queen of the Byzantine emperor, Justinian I*. After a notorious career as an actress, she became a Christian and married Justinian in 523, and they were crowned together in 527. She adopted a pro-Monophysite stand which led to the Three Chapters controversy*. She showed much heroism during the insurrection at Nika in 532.

Empress Theodora

Theodore of Mopsuestia (c. 350–428) Antiochene theologian. He was ordained presbyter* by Flavian* about 383 and made bishop of Mopsuestia in Cilicia* in 392. He was a brilliant scholar noted for his erudition and literary skills, but his reputation suffered as the mentor of Nestorius* with whom his name is forever associated and with whom he was condemned at the Council of Ephesus*, and anathematized in the first of the Three Chapters* by Justinian* and the Second Council of Constantinople*. Although only some of his works survive, modern scholars have been able to reestablish his doctrinal integrity and his opposition to the major heretics of the day, such as Apollinaris*, Arius*, and Eunomius*. While his terminology was imprecise, his contributions to Christology* were more orthodox than his enemies acknowledged, and his biblical commentaries used critical methods with great insight.

Theodore of Studios, St. (759–826) Byzantine abbot. He became monk in 787 and abbot in 794 of the Saccudion monastery in Bithynia*. When the monastery was exposed to Muslim attacks, he transferred to Studios* in Constantinople* which then became a center of monastic reform. He had lifelong conflicts with the imperial court, first over the adulterous marriage of Constantine VI and then over the iconoclastic policy of Leo V. He was exiled a number of times and ill-treated, and never returned to his monastery, but spent his last years on the Peninsula of Tryphon. He was instrumental in enlarging the community to 600 monks and promoting the development of minuscule script. He is considered one of the greatest leaders of Byzantine monasticism* who vigorously defended the independence of the church and sought to reform monastic life through his own austerities and iron will. He is the author of *Catecheses,* a treatise on icons entitled *On the Holy Images* and many hymns. Feast day: November 11.

Theodore of Tarsus, St. (c. 602–690) Archbishop of Canterbury*. He was an Asiatic Greek monk in Rome* when he was consecrated by Pope Vitalian* in 668 as archbishop of Canterbury. He reformed the government of the church by dividing dioceses* and extending the episcopate*. He held two great synods* in Hertford in 672 or 673 and in Hatfield in 679. He unified the English church and established the authority of the see of Canterbury. His writings include *Iudicia, Laterculus Malalianus,* as well as commentaries on the Pentateuch and the Gospels.

Theodore Sladic (d. 1788) Serbian Orthodox new martyr* born in Bosnia. Arrested and condemned as an agitator by the Ottomans, he was burned at Moshtanica Monastery with 150 followers.

Theodoret (c. 393–c. 458) Bishop of Cyrrhus in Syria. He entered monastic life in 416 and was elevated to the bishopric seven years later. In the Christological controversies of the time, he took a moderately Antiochene position that Christ had two natures, united in one person, but not in one essence. At the Council of Ephesus*, he opposed Cyril*, and this led to his deposition and exile at the Robber Council of Ephesus* in 449. He was restored at the Council of Chalcedon* in 451, but only after he condemned Nestorius*. His works as an exegete and theologian include biblical commentaries, collection of biographies of monks, and a church history.

Theodosian Collection Collection of canonical documents ascribed to one Theodosius the Deacon. It includes a number of ancient epistles and canons and may be dated about 420.

Theodosius of Kiev, St. (1002–1074) Birth name: Theodosius Pechersky. Russian monastic founder. He founded the Pecherskaya Lavra, or the cave monastery of Kiev*. Called "St. Benedict of Russia," he gave Russian monasticism* its first rule. Feast day: May 3.

Theodosius the Coenobiarch, St. (423–518) Monk. In 455 he went to the Monastery of the Theotokos of the Kathisma between Jerusalem* and Bethlehem*. To avoid being made hegumen*, he retired to the Monastery of Metopa and thence to the solitude of the Grotto of the Magi, where he lived for 38 years in continual prayer. The locality is still called Dejr Dosi (Monastery of Theodosius). Feast day: January 11.

theody Hymn praising God.

theologaster Shallow theologian, especially one who pretends to have theological wisdom.

theologia crucis (Lat., theology of the cross) Knowledge of God derived from the study of the Crucifixion where God takes on an unlikely guise, as a suffering human, thus confounding human reason and expectation. Contrasted with *theologia gloria**, theology of glory*. Term devised by Martin Luther*.

Christ on the Cross

Theologia Germanica Anonymous German spiritual work written by a priest of the Teutonic Order in the late fourteenth century. It teaches self-renunciation as the way for union with God. It was much admired by the Pietists and translated into many languages. Luther* admired it so much that he published a complete edition in 1518, stating in a preface that "no book, except the Bible and St. Augustine*, has come to my attention from which I have learned more about God, Christ, man and all things."

theologia gloriae Antithesis of theology of the cross. Martin Luther's dismissive term for any theology that presumed an easy access to God revealed in divine power, especially in scholastic theology.

theologian 1. Scholar or expert in theology. 2. Candidate* for Roman Catholic priesthood engaged in his theological course of study.

theological notes Positive degree of authority attached to a theological proposition or thesis. Its purpose is to safeguard the faith by distinguishing between binding doctrines and theological opinions. The Council of Trent* systematized gradations of theological notes and censures in the works of Melchior Cano* and Francisco Suarez*, based on the degree of conformity with or opposition to divine revelation*. A doctrinal proposition was considered de fide* definita, of defined faith, if it was solemnly defined by the pope or an ecumenical council. Teachings that border on the faith are called proxima fidei, and those that are theologically certain as theologice certa. The lowest level of authority is that of a probable opinion.

Christ in Glory

theological virtue Also, supernatural virtue. One of the three basic spiritual graces—faith, hope, and charity—with which a Christian is endowed so that he or she may find harmony and fulfillment in the service of God.

theologism Excessive theological speculation, especially the extension of theological speculations beyond their normal scope.

theologoumenon Theological statement or concept that is more individual opinion than authoritative doctrine.

theologue Student preparing for full-time work in religion.

theology 1. Interpretation of religious faith, practice, or experience. 2. Organized body of knowledge dealing with God; intellectual discipline employing a variety of categories and methodologies to study the nature of God. 3. Study and analysis of traditional religious doctrines, as apologetics, dogmatic theology, natural theology*, systematic theology*, or practical theology*. 4. Systematic study of God in relation to the world, especially dealing with the arguments for the existence of God, divine nature and attributes, and related doctrines of the Trinity* and Incarnation*, as Christology*, eschatology*, and soteriology*. 5. Historical, exegetical, and comparative study of religious beliefs, as patristics* and symbolics*. 6. Coherent body of theological ideas developed by a theologian with a characteristic emphasis or method, as Calvinist theology, Thomist theology, Wesleyan theology, Arminian theology. 7. Sum of beliefs held by a person or group regarding matters of religious faith or of ultimate concern. 8. Course of study in a seminary including Scripture, church history, homiletics*, canon law*, and moral and dogmatic theology. 9. Science of divinely revealed religious truths.

theology of glory Branch of theology concerned with divine power and magnificence rather than the Incarnation*, the cross, and the Atonement*. See also THEOLOGIA GLORIAE.

theology of the cross Branch of theology concerned with the significance of the cross, especially its scandal, humiliation, and suffering and its implications for the salvation* of the world. Contrasted with the theology of glory*. See also THEOLOGIA CRUCIS.

theomachist One who resists God or divine will.

theomonism Metaphysical monism holding that the universe is governed by one divine spirit.

theomorphic Possessing divine form or quality.

theomorphism Condition of being formed in the image of God. Thus, theomorphic*.

Theomusicology Branch of musicology that studies sacred music. Term coined by John Michael Spencer.

theonomy State of being subject to the authority and rule of God as the ultimate ground of being*. Thus, theonomic. See also RECONSTRUCTIONISM.

Theopaschite Adherent of a sixth-century sect of Monophysites who held that in Christ's Passion*, God suffered. Distinguished from Patripassian, one who confounds the persons of the Father and the Son.

theopathy Mystical ecstasy* or tense absorption in religious devotion, especially the experience of divine illumination*.

Theophan the Recluse, St. (1815–1894) In Russian, Feofan. Birth name: George Vasilievich Govorov. Spiritual writer. He taught in various theological seminaries until 1859, when he was consecrated bishop of Tambov. He retired in 1866 and spent the rest of his life as a monk and as a hermit in the monastery of Vyshi. He popularized the use of the Jesus Prayer* among the Russian Orthodox faithful and translated into Russian Greek spiritual writings, including *Philocalia* and *Unseen Warfare* by Nicodemus of the Holy Mountain*. He was canonized in 1988. Feast day: January 10.

theophany 1. Temporary physical manifestation or revelation of God to an individual, as distinct from a vision. Distinguished from Incarnation*. 2. In the Eastern Church*, Epiphany*.

Theophilus (late second century) Christian and bishop of Antioch*. In his *Apology,* addressed to a pagan friend, he distinguished between two phases of Logos*: the Logos Endiathetos that is innate in God and the Logos Prophorikos, that is his creative element. He considered Christ as the Second Adam* by whose obedience mankind is saved. He was the first to use the term *triune* to describe the Godhead.

theophoroi (Gk., God-bearing) Believers within whom God dwells.

Theopneustos (Gk., God-breathed) Of the Holy Bible, breathed out by God and thus, according to 2 Timothy 3:15–17, able to teach salvation* and train in godliness.

theosis (Gk., making divine) In Eastern Orthodox* theology, deification, salvation* as a process in which believers become united with Christ and partake of his nature. Based on 2 Peter 1:4, it is Orthodoxy's leading view of salvation, promising freedom from death and corruption. Sometimes called "divinization," it echoes the ancient saying, "Christ became as we are that we might be as He is" (see 2 Pet. 1:3–4).

Theotokarion In the Byzantine Rite*, liturgical book containing the canons of the Theotokos*. They are divided into eight series, each of which comprises seven canons, one for each day of the week.

theotokia In the Coptic Rite, office in honor of the Virgin Mary*, divided into four parts: psali* or invitation, hymn, lobsh or explanation, and tarh or commentary.

theotokion In the Eastern Church*, hymn ascribing praise to the Virgin Mary* as the Mother of God and forming the final troparion* of a canonical ode. See STAVROTHEOTOKION.

Theotokos (Gk., the one who gave birth to God) Description of the Virgin Mary*, first applied by the Greek Fathers* by about 300. In 429 it was attacked by Nestorius* and his followers as incompatible with the humanity of Christ and replaced with Christotokos*. But its use was upheld in the Councils of Ephesus* (431) and Chalcedon* (451). In Latin the corresponding terms are *Dei Genitrix* (Mother of God) not *Deipara** (Bearer of God). Neither Greek nor Latin Fathers characteristically used the Latin *Mater Dei,* the basic word for "Mother of God."

thermarion In the Eastern Church*, a vessel for the warm water used in the eucharistic rite for mixing with the species* of consecrated wine and in the washing of altars at the dedication.

Thermi Convent on Lesbos and place of pilgrimage* where numerous martyrs* were killed in two groups by Turkish marauders, including the nun Olympia and her associate Euphrosyne in 1235 and the monks Raphael and Nicolas, Irene, and many villagers.

theurgy Manipulation of the supernatural through certain rites, deeds, and incantations.

Thielicke, Helmut (1908–1986) German pastor and theologian. Before and during World War II, he opposed Hitler. His vast body of works includes *Theological Ethics* (4 vols.) and *The Evangelical Faith* (3 vols.). He was doctrinally conservative, affirming most traditional creedal statements.

Thiessen, Henry Clarence (1883–1947) Evangelical Bible scholar. Thiessen taught at Dallas Theological Seminary* (1931–1935) and at Wheaton College* (1935–1946) before becoming president of Los Angeles Baptist Seminary. He wrote authoritative works, including *Introduction to the New Testament* (1943) and *Introductory Lectures in Systematic Theology* (1949).

Thiman, Eric Harding (1900–1975) English organist and composer of anthems and cantatas, as *The Last Supper* (1925) and *The Temptation of Christ* (1925), and organ compositions, as *44 Hymn Tunes Freely Harmonized.*

third orders Religious organizations affiliated to one of the mendicant orders*, distinguished from the first and second orders, namely men and women. They were established in the twelfth century when Pope Alexander III* gave married penitents* a special status in which only obedience, not continence, was required.

Third Rome In the Russian Orthodox Church*, Moscow* considered as the third great center of Christianity after Rome* and Constantinople*.

third wave Extension of the Pentecostal movement (the first wave) and the Charismatic movement (the second wave), a term coined by Peter Wagner*. Some of the distinctive features of the third wave are: 1. Belief that the baptism of the Holy Spirit* occurs at conversion* rather than as a second work of grace*. 2. Expectation of multiple fillings of the Holy Spirit subsequent to the

new birth*. 3. Less emphasis on speaking in tongues* than in traditional Pentecostal churches*. Speaking in tongues is not considered the initial physical validation of baptism of the Holy Spirit but rather as a prayer language or as a ministry gift. 4. Ministry under the power and anointing of the Holy Spirit as applicable to a body of believers, especially in praise and worship, rather than as an individual spiritual experience. 5. Greater ecumenism* than in traditional Pentecostalism* and a desire to avoid divisiveness at any cost by yielding on the adiaphora. The third wave accepts all the manifestations of the Holy Spirit, including the power to cast out devils, prophecy*, and healing. Thus, Third Wavers.

Third World Theologies Theological systems devised by Asian, African, and Latin American theologians seeking to express biblical concepts in the context of their distinctive worldviews and cultures. Some of them, like liberation theology*, border on or tend toward heterodoxy*. Concepts of oppression, poverty*, racism, social justice, and cultural diversity animate their discussions.

Thirty-Nine Articles Set of doctrinal statements of the Anglican Church replacing the Ten Articles* of 1536, the Bishops' Book* of 1537, the Six Articles* of 1539, the King's Book of 1543, and the Forty-Two Articles* of 1553. They do not constitute a creed*, but are short dogmatic tenets defining the Anglican position vis-à-vis Catholic, Calvinist, and Anabaptist teachings. Some of them are vague because they avoid narrow definition. Among the major issues it dealt with are the Eucharist*, the place of the holy Scriptures in salvation*, creeds, general councils, and predestination*. Since 1975 all Church of England* clergy have been required to acknowledge the Thirty-Nine Articles as one of the historic formularies that undergird the Anglican tradition. They represent a divided Protestantism, more Reformed* than Lutheran.

thistle In religious art, symbol of sorrow and of Christ's suffering.

Tholuck, Friedrich August Gottreau (1799–1877) German Pietist theologian and professor of theology at Halle. His first work, *The Doctrine of Sin and* *the Propitiator* (1823), helped check the spread of Rationalism in Germany. Tholuck wrote commentaries on Romans (1824), John (1827), the Sermon on the Mount (1833), Hebrews (1836), and the Psalms (1843); an essay on hermeneutics*, *The Merits of Calvin as an Interpreter of the Holy Scriptures;* and numerous devotional works, as *Hours of Christian Devotion, Light from the Cross,* and *Festal Chimes.* As a champion of biblical conservatism, he attacked D. F. Strauss* and other Rationalists. He was the foremost exponent in his day of *Vermittlungstheologie** (theology emphasizing personal piety and downplaying confessionalist dogma*).

thom (lit., a plate) In the Coptic Rite, a small mat that covers the top of the chalice* and on which the paten* is placed.

Thomas à Becket, St. (c. 1118–1170) Archbishop of Canterbury* from 1162. As chancellor to Henry II, he became good friends with the king and a partner in his drinking and carousing. When Theobold died in 1162, Henry appointed Thomas as archbishop although the latter was still in minor orders* and had to be ordained priest, bishop, and archbishop in a single day. As primate*, Thomas changed from a courtier to an ar-

Thomas Becket's Martyrdom

dent churchman. He resigned his secular offices and adopted a pious lifestyle.

Henry wished to recover the royal authority lost to the church during the reign of his predecessor, Stephen, particularly the authority to prosecute in royal courts clergymen* who had already been tried and convicted in church courts. When Thomas refused to go along with the royal proposal, Henry issued the Constitutions of Clarendon, claiming plenary authority over the church. Thomas reluctantly agreed to the Constitutions, but later recanted and fled to the Continent. He returned to England and in 1170 was murdered by four knights, who carried out Henry's implied wish to be rid of him. Universal outrage over the assassination forced Henry to do penance* at Avranches, France, and to grant the church the powers that he had sought to take away. Thomas was canonized in 1173. His shrine was one of the principal places of pilgrimage* in medieval England until its destruction in 1538 by Henry VIII. Feast day: December 29.

Thomas a Jesu (1564–1627) Spanish spiritual author. After entering the Carmelite* Order in 1587, he taught at Seville* and was prior* at Saragossa* and provincial* at Old Castile. His mystical works, *De Contemplatione Divina* (1622) and *Divinae Orationis Methodus* (1623), presented the teachings of St. Teresa*.

Thomas à Kempis (c. 1380–1471) Birth name: Hemerken or Hammerlein. German mystic. He was educated in a school operated by the Brethren of the Common Life* and entered the Augustinian Convent of Mount St. Agnes. He was ordained a priest in 1413. All his writings are of a devotional nature, but his fame rests on *The Imitation of Christ**.

Thomas, Acts of Apocryphal account of the apostle Thomas*, represented as Christ's twin and the guardian of a secret gospel. It recounts 13 wonderful deeds of the apostle and ends with his martyrdom. In its symbolism and teachings the work is semi-gnostic, most clearly expressed in its two famous hymns, "The Marriage Song," praising the "daughter of light," and "The Song of the Pearl" or the "Hymn of the Soul," describing the soul sought by the Savior to be freed from earthly bondage. It was probably compiled in Syriac*, but it exists in Greek, Latin, Ethiopic, and Armenian versions.

Thomas, Apocalypse of Manichaean eschatological document dated from the fourth century. The book, of which two recensions* exist, borrows from the canonical Book of Revelation and describes the end-time events according to a seven-day timetable.

Thomas Aquinas, St. (c. 1225–1274) "Doctor Communis"; "Doctor Angelicus." Doctor of the church*, Dominican philosopher, and theologian. At the age of five, he was given by his parents to the Benedictine abbey of Monte Cassino*. He began his theological studies at the University of Naples and continued them at the University of Paris and Cologne*. In 1256 he became master of theology and served as a regent master at the Do-

St. Thomas Aquinas

minican Priory of St. Jacques. In Paris he wrote his first major work, *Summa Contra Gentiles*, for the use of Dominican missionaries. He returned to Italy in 1259 and by 1261 was in Orvieto, where he wrote several works at the urging of Pope Urban IV and began the first part of his masterpiece, *Summa Theologiae*.

In 1268 Aquinas returned to Paris, where he remained until 1272. During this period, the most productive of his life, he completed the second part of *Summa Theologiae* and held disputations on the soul, the rights of mendicants, and the use of Aristotle in theology. In 1272 he returned to Italy and settled at his own priory*

near Naples to work on the third part of *Summa Theologiae* and where he died at the Cistercian abbey of Fossanuova.

Thomism*, as his theology came to be called, emphasizes human reason even in the construction of faith. While his treatises are essentially Aristotelian and empirical, and he held that all knowledge starts with the sense perceptions and the facts of the natural world, he was equally Augustinian. Also fundamental to his thought is the antithesis between potency and act, matter and form, essence and existence, immanence and transcendence. For Thomas theology was a science just as much as philosophy, even though he acknowledged the role of revelation*. The fundamental truths are the Trinity* and the Incarnation*, but all doctrines are synthesized into a single discipline covering worship, morals, and spiritual practice. His moral theology* is practical, dealing with happiness which is achieved through the soul's faculties and powers directed by virtue and guided by law and grace*. In doing so Thomas emphasized the role of Christ's humanity in the Incarnation which had a causal relationship to the work of redemption*. The work of redemption is continued through the sacraments* of which the Eucharist* was the highest.

Although many of his teachings have been attacked and condemned, the Roman Catholic Church has given Thomism its imprimatur* as an authentic and official expression of its doctrine. In 1880 he was declared the patron of Catholic universities, and in 1974 he was declared a model for theologians. Thomism was revived in the fifteenth century and again in the twentieth century in the form of neo-Thomism. Feast day: January 28.

Thomas, Book of One of the Coptic documents discovered at Nag Hammadi* in 1946, originally written in Greek, purporting to convey the secret message of Jesus to Judas Thomas on ascetic ethics and eschatology*.

Thomas, Gospel of Apocryphal gospel, originally written in Greek about 150, conveying a syncretist version of pithy sayings and parabolic discourses of Jesus, some of which have similarities with the canonical Gospels. A Coptic version dating from about 350 was found among the papyri* at Nag Hammadi* in 1945/46 and is now at the Coptic

Museum in Cairo. It is the most discussed text from Nag Hammadi, with relevance to the tradition of the teachings of Jesus.

Gospel of Thomas

Thomas, Infancy Gospel of Apocryphal writing extant in two Greek recensions* as well in Armenian, Ethiopic, Georgian, Latin, Syriac*, and Slavonic versions recording alleged miracles performed by Jesus Christ in his childhood, most of them exaggerated folk tales with no theological value.

Thomas Nelson Largest Christian publisher in the world, located in Nashville, Tennessee. Founded in England in 1798, its American branch was acquired in the 1970s by Sam Moore, a Lebanese immigrant, who began his career selling Bibles door to door. Today, it includes a number of subsidiaries, including Word.

Thomas of Marga (ninth century) Nestorian historian. In 832 he entered the monastery of Beth Garmai and was consecrated bishop of Marga in 850 and later metropolitan* of Beth Garmai. He is well-known for his *Book of Governors,* a history of his monastery and the Nestorian Church*.

Thomas, St. Apostle. He is mentioned in all the Gospels. In John he is further identified as Didymus* or Twin, and he is shown as doubting the Resurrection unless he could touch the wounds of the risen Lord (John 20:25–28). After Christ's appearance to him, he exclaimed, "My Lord and my God," and was thus the first to confess Christ's divinity. There are a number of apocryphal documents with his name. According to some of them, he evangelized the Parthians. According to others, he went to India, where the Syrian Christians of

St. Thomas* claim descent from those converted by his labors. At least three places claim to be where he was martyred or where his last remains were buried: Mylapore, India, Edessa*, Syria, and Ortona in Abruzzi, Italy. Feast day: July 3 (Western Church* and the Syrian Church); October 6 (Greek Church).

Thomism Theology of St. Thomas Aquinas* viewed as a system.

Thompson, Francis (1859–1907) English Catholic poet. He was educated for the priesthood, but was never ordained. He ended up as a drug addict and was rescued from destitution by Wilfred and Alice Meynell*, who cared for him for the rest of his life. His first volume of poems, published in 1893, contained the well-known "Hound of Heaven" for which he is still remembered. It was followed by *Sister Songs* (1895) and *New Poems* (1897).

Thompson, Randall (1899–1984) American composer of choral music. His sacred vocal music ranks among the best composed in the twentieth century. It includes an anthem *Alleluia* (1940) for four-voice chorus, the *Mass of the Holy Spirit* (1957), a *Requiem* (1958), and a *Passion* (1965), as well as extended settings of biblical texts such as a *Peaceable Kingdom* (1936).

Thorn Monastery in Thorn, near Limburg, Netherlands, founded in 985. In the twelfth century, it was transformed into a nunnery for noble ladies who did not take the vows but committed themselves for a limited period of time to live in accordance with the Rule of St. Augustine*. In the fifteenth century chapels were added to the nave* in the north and south. The baroque altar by Franz Xaver Bader was created in 1769.

Thorn, Colloquy of Conference held in Thorn, West Prussia, in 1545 under the auspices of King Vladislav IV of Poland and aimed at religious peace.

Thorndike, Herbert (1598–1672) Anglican High Church* theologian. His principal work is *An Epilogue to the Tragedy of the Church of England* (1659) in which he defended transubstantiation* and proposed a unified Christendom* on the basis of the first six general councils. In his *Discourse of the Government of Churches* (1641) he defended the apostolic origin on episcopal* government.

Thoronet, Le Monastery in Le Thoronet in Provence, France. Its Church of Our Lady of the Flowers is large, with a nave* 134 feet long, 28 feet wide, and 53 feet high. By about 1200 the church, cloister*, and monastic buildings were completed.

Thorvaldsen, Bertel (1770–1844) Danish sculptor. His most famous religious works are *Christ and the Apostles* (1821–1842) in the Frue Kirke in Copenhagen, the tomb of Pope Pius VII* in St. Peter's* (1830), and the *Entrance of Christ into Jerusalem.*

Three Chapters controversy Controversy over the three subjects condemned by an edict of Emperor Justinian* in 543/44 to conciliate the Monophysites. The three chapters were the writings of Theodore of Mopsuestia*, the writings of Theodoret* of Cyrrhus against Cyril of Alexandria* and in defense of Nestorius*, and the letter of Ibas of Edessa to the Persian Bishop Mari of Hardascir. While the Eastern Church* generally accepted the edict, the West rejected it as contrary to the decrees of Chalcedon. The Fifth Ecumenical Council of Constantinople condemned the edict. Pope Vigilius* accepted the council's decision, but parts of the Western Church*, notably Milan* and Aquileia*, refused to follow the pope and broke off communion with Rome for half a century.

Three Holy Hierarchs Three Greek Church Fathers*: John Chrysostom*, Basil the Great*, and Gregory* the Theologian of Nyssa. The Feast of the Three Hierarchs is observed in the Greek Church on January 30.

Three Hours' Service Service on Good Friday* commemorating the Lord's Passion from noon until 3:00 P.M. when the seven words from the cross are the basis of meditation and devotions.

threefold ministry Pattern of ordered ministry evident as early as Ignatius* consisting of one bishop, several presbyters*, and several deacons.

Originally the ministry of a local congregation, it has been adapted in most Episcopal churches on an area basis.

threefold way Three stages of mystical experience moving from purgation to illumination* and union.

throniyon In the Jacobite Church*, an episcopal throne in the sanctuary with its back to the screen* on the north side and facing west or south.

thronos (Gk., throne, seat) In Eastern churches*, the principal altar at the east end. In the Byzantine Church*, it may also mean: 1. The antimension* because it has direct contact with the consecrated bread and wine. 2. High-backed episcopal chair at the back of the apse* to the rear of the altar where the bishop sits.

Thundering Legion See SEBASTE, FORTY MARTYRS OF.

thurible (Lat., *thus,* incense) Also, censer*. Metal vessel for the ceremonial burning of incense. It consists of a container suspended on chains which can be swung back and forth.

thurifer Person who carries the thurible* in a service, usually accompanied by a boy carrying the incense boat.

Thurneysen, Eduard (1888–1974) Swiss theologian and pastor. As a close friend and coworker, he collected, edited, and published the sermons of Karl Barth*.

Thyatira City in ancient Lydia, now in modern Turkey, one of the seven churches addressed in the Revelation. In the beginning of the third century, it was a stronghold of Montanism*.

thymaterion Byzantine censer* with a short chain and attached bells.

thyra (Gk., door) One of the doors in a Byzantine church, the royal door, holy door*, or deacon's* door.

tiara Papal crown resembling a beehive. Also

called camelaucum*, it has three coronets, one on top of another and two lappets* hanging down at the back. It was worn by the pope or carried in front of him on important ceremonial occasions.

Papal Tiara

Tiepolo, Giambattista (1696–1770) Venetian artist, finest exponent of Rococo. His first major works were the Udine frescoes for the palace of the patriarch* of Aquileia*. It was followed by a series of paintings on a grandiose scale: *Institution of the Rosary* with the adjoining panels of the *Glory of St. Dominic* (1738–1739) and the *Coronation of the Virgin* (1755), the *Virgin and Child with St. Catherine of Siena, Rose of Lima, Agnes of Montepulciano** (1748), *Communion of St. Lucy* (1748), and *St. Thecla Interceding for the Plague-Stricken of Este* (1758–1759). His last religious pictures were painted in Spain, where he went in 1762.

Tigre 1. Semitic Ethiopian language, spoken in northern Ethiopia, Eritrea, and Sudan. 2. Northern highland province of Ethiopia, where the ancient kingdom of Axum* was located. 3. A member of the Tigre tribe.

Tikhon of Zadonsk, St. (1724–1783) Russian bishop and spiritual writer. He took monastic vows in 1758 and within five years was named bishop of Voronezh. He resigned in 1767 and settled in the Zadonsk Monastery. He was canonized in 1861. Feast day: August 13.

Tikhon, St. (1866–1925) Birth name: Vasili Ivanovich Belavin. He was the first patriarch* of the Russian Orthodox Church* after the restoration of the patriarchate* which had been abolished under Peter the Great. He was elected as patriarch in 1917, the year the Bolsheviks seized power. During the ensuing years, the most difficult for the church in its history, he helped keep the church alive, although deeply persecuted. In 1923 he was forced to sign a declaration of loyalty to the Bolshevik government and thereafter allowed to live for the next two years in the Don Monastery in Moscow*. He was canonized in 1989. Feast day: October 9.

Tilak, Narayan Vaman (c. 1862–1919) Marathi hymn writer and poet. A high-caste Brahmin, he abandoned Hinduism and was converted to Christianity and baptized in 1895. He was ordained in 1904 and began preaching and writing. He wrote hundreds of bhajans or hymns in Marathi. At his death, he left unfinished a life of Christ in verse called *Chritayan*. Two years before his death he left mission work and established a Christian ashram* at Satara.

Tillich, Paul (1886–1965) American Protestant theologian of German origin. He taught successively at Marburg and Dresden. In 1933 he fled Nazi Germany and settled in the United States, where he taught at Union Theological Seminary* in New York (1933–1955), Harvard Divinity School (1955–1962), and the University of Chicago (1962–1965). Tillich was an existentialist theologian whose methodology, called the method of correlation, argues for a partnership between philosophy and theology. In his most important work, *Systematic Theology* (3 vols., 1951–1963), God is interpreted as the ground of being* and Christ as the new being. Faith* is transcribed as ultimate concern or the courage to affirm oneself in the face of non-being. Tillich's epistemology considers myths and symbols as signs that point to ultimate reality. Among his other works are: *The Protestant Era* (1936), *The Interpretation of History* (1936), *The Courage to Be* (1952), *Love, Power, and Justice* (1954), *Dynamics of Faith* (1957), and *Theology of Culture* (1959).

time setting Calculation or determination of the day of Christ's Second Coming*, a prominent exercise in Adventism*.

timkat In the Ethiopian Church calendar, festival of the Epiphany* when the waters are blessed. During the celebration the clergy perform a dance with the koboro* (drum) and mekamia* (crutches) to the accompaniment of chanting.

Timothy I (728–823) Patriarch of the East from 780. He began his patriarchate* at a time when the Muslims had established their ascendancy in Mesopotamia. He moved his center from Ctesiphon to Baghdad and created six new metropolitan provinces: Damascus*, Armenia, Rai, Dailam, Turkestan (Kashgar), and Tibet (Tangut). Timothy was a great missionary-statesman who enlisted some of the greatest Christian missionaries to expand the Assyrian Church* throughout Central Asia. Among them were the Arab martyr* Shubhal-Ishu, Yab-alaha the scribe, Qardagh the bookbinder, and Elijah of Moqan.

Timothy Associate of Paul*, of both Jewish and Gentile descent. Paul called him his "fellow laborer" and "beloved son." Timothy went with Paul on his second missionary journey and led the Ephesus Church as bishop. Two of Paul's Pastoral Epistles* are addressed to him. According to tradition, he was stoned to death at Ephesus*. Feast day: January 24.

Timothy Aelurus (d. 477) Monophysite patriarch* of Alexandria, named aelurus, or weasel, because of his small stature. He became patriarch in 457 but was exiled by Leo I*. In exile he propagated Monophysitism* with his writings. He held that Christ is by nature God and became man only through divine dispensation* or oikonomia. However, he held that Christ's body was of the same substance as all human bodies. He is venerated as a saint in the Coptic Church*. Feast day: July 31 (Coptic Church*).

Tintern Abbey Magnificent abbey on River Wye in England founded in 1331 by Cistercian monks. It was dissolved in 1536 and is now in ruins. It inspired one of William Wordsworth's finest poems.

Tintoretto, Jacopo (1518–1594) Birth name: Jacopo Robusti. Venetian painter, noted for such luminous paintings as *Miracle of St. Mark* and *Last Supper*. Most of his religious paintings were done for the Scuola di San Rocco in Venice*, as its official painter. He completed a series of 64 canvases to cover the entire walls and ceilings of their meeting hall. The lower hall has a series of scenes from the life of the Virgin Mary* and 12-foot high pictures of St. Mary Magdalene and St. Mary of Egypt*. On the upper floor are 17-foot-high scenes from the life and passion of Christ, including an enormous crucifixion. Among his other works are *The Last Supper* and *Entombment of Christ*, both in San Giorgio Maggiore, and *St. George and the Dragon*.

tippet Broad black scarf worn by Anglican clergy over the surplice*.

Tischendorf, Lobegott Friedrich Konstantin von (1815–1874) New Testament textual critic. As a professor in the theological faculty at Leipzig, he devoted much of his time searching out unpublished ancient manuscripts and publishing them as well as critical editions of the Greek New Testament. His most famous discovery was the Codex Sinaiticus* at St. Catherine's Monastery in Sinai. He also edited other important manuscripts including Codex Ephraemi Rescriptus, Codex Amiatinus*, and Codex Claromontanus.

Tissot, James Joseph Jacques (1836–1902) French biblical illustrator. He was a painter of fashionable women, but on conversion, devoted himself to illustrating the life of Christ for which purpose he went to Palestine. His *Vie de Notre Seigneur Jesus-Christ* (1896) is a series of some 350 watercolors.

tistole nieratikon In the Coptic Rite, ecclesiastical vestments.

Titcomb, Everett H. (1884–1968) American composer of anthems based on biblical texts, such as "Behold Now, Praise the Lord." The popular hymn-anthem, "The Lord's My Shepherd," features both a scriptural text and a traditional hymn tune. Among other works that best reflect Titcomb's range as a composer are *Eight Short Motets* (1934), a group of pieces for a capella chorus for use during the great church festivals of the year, and a powerful English setting for the *Te Deum* (1944).

Titelouze, Jehan (c. 1562–1633) French composer of organ music, organist at the Cathedral of Rouen* from 1588 until 1633. In the twelve *Hymnes de l'Eglise* of 1623 he used the plainchant melody. His collection entitled *Le Magnificat* (1626) offers eight cycles of versets.

tithe One-tenth of income devoted to the work of the Lord and paid to a church or any other ministry. While an Old Testament principle, it is not a legal requirement for a Christian, but rather expresses the disciples' mandate to give cheerfully and proportionately.

Titian (1487–1576) Birth name: Tiziano Vecellio or Vecelli. Venetian painter. He was a pupil of Georgione, whom Titian admired. After Bellini's death, he became the acknowledged leader of the Venetian school. His long life enabled him to produce a body of work of unparalleled range and variety. His religious paintings glow and sparkle with a wide range of hues. Among the most famous of his paintings are *Tribute Money* (1515), *Assumption* (1518), *St. Peter Martyr* (1528–1530), *Crowning with Thorns* (1542), *Ecce Homo* (1543),

Titles of Christ

Alpha and Omega (Rev. 22:13)
Bread of Life (John 6:35)
Bridegroom (Mark 2:19)
Good Shepherd (John 10:11)
Head of the Body (Col. 1:18)
High Priest (Heb. 5:10)
Just One (Acts 3:14)
Lamb of God (John 1:29)
Light of the World (John 8:12)
Logos (John 1:1)
Lord (Rom. 10:9)
Master (Luke 8:24)
Prophet (Matt. 21:46)
Redeemer (Luke 24:21)
Savior (Titus 3:7)
Servant (Luke 22:26)
Son of God (Matt. 14:33)
Son of Man (Matt. 8:20)
The Firstborn (Col. 1:15)
The Resurrection (John 21:23)
The Vine (John 15:1)
The Way, the Truth and the Life (John 14:6)

St. Sebastian (1570–1575), *Entombment* (1525), and *Annunciation* (1574).

title (Lat., titulus) Particular ministerial charge or office. Normally a precondition for ordination and carrying stipend* or the equivalent.

Titles of Christ Names given to Christ in the Bible.

titular 1. Of or relating to the oldest churches in Rome*. 2. Of or relating to churches dedicated to God, a mystery (as the Holy Trinity*), a saint*, a sacred object or relic* (as the Holy Cross) or a sacred event (as the ascension or the nativity). A fixed altar in a church also may have a title or dedication. 3. Of or relating to a see* in Muslim-held countries where Christian communities have died out.

titulus (Lat., title) 1. Title of Christ affixed to the top of the cross, Jesus Nazarenus Rex Iudeorum (Jesus of Nazareth, king of the Jews). 2. Church that can provide a living for a priest because it has land or an endowment.

Titus Associate of Paul*. A Greek convert, he took charge of the church in Crete and was its first bishop. One of the Pastoral Epistles* is addressed to him. Feast day: August 25 (Greek and Syrian churches); January 26 (Roman Catholic Church).

t'litho (lit., elevation) In the Syrian tradition, posture and tone during prayer, such as g'hontho, which indicates a low voice and inclined head.

Toland, John (1670–1722) Irish deist. He converted from Roman Catholicism* to Anglicanism* before becoming an atheist. He rejected the miracles of the New Testament as well as the divine inspiration* of the Bible. His book, *Christianity Not Mysterious,* was influential among eighteenth-century deists, but is now forgotten.

Toledo City in Spain, site of a great cathedral, built between 1226 and 1493 in the reign of Ferdinand III. The principal facade has three Gothic* portals: Puerta del Perdon in the center, Puerto del Infierno on the left, and Puerto del Juicio on the right. The 295-foot tower was built between 1380 and 1440 in pure Gothic* style. The nave* consists of five large aisles. The Capilla Mayor, or principal chapel, is located at the end of the central aisle.

Toledo, Councils of Eighteen councils between 400 and 702 and 10 councils between the eleventh and sixteenth centuries held in Toledo in the Visigothic Kingdom in Spain. The early councils were assemblies of bishops called to deal with ecclesiastical affairs. One of the most important was the Third Council summoned in 589 by King Recared after his conversion from Arianism*. It recognized the orthodox creeds and established orthodox Christianity as the official state religion.

Toledo, Rite of Mozarabic Rite*.

tolerati (Lat., tolerated) In canon law*, excommunicated persons with whom the faithful may have some form of communication and contact. Distinguished from vitandi*.

Tolstoy, Leo (1828–1910) Russian novelist and reformer. He was the author of two of the greatest Russian novels, *War and Peace* and *Anna Karenina*. His religious beliefs were heterodox, and he was deeply critical of the Orthodox Church, which excommunicated him in 1901. He denied the key tenets of orthodoxy*, particularly the Incarnation*, Resurrection*, Trinity*, and personal immortality*, and focused solely on the Sermon on the Mount as a moral teaching. While denying the divinity of Christ, he continued to express admiration for his person and teachings, such as the kingdom of God*, non-violence, and love of one's neighbor and one's enemies.

Tomar The former castle of the Order of the Knights of Christ, in Tomar, Portugal. It originally belonged to the Knights Templar. The Knights of Christ reached the acme of its power in the fifteenth century under Prince Henry the Navigator who died in 1460. The order was founded in 1317 by King Dinis for "the defense of the faith, the fight against the Moors, and the expansion of the Portuguese monarchy." The architect who left the most indelible impress on the building was Joao do Castilho. Almost three quarters of the space inside the church is occupied by the prayer hall, now the choir.

Tome of Leo Also, Epistola Dogmatica. Letter addressed by Leo I* to the Patriarch Flavian* of Constantinople* in 449, explaining the Catholic doctrine of Incarnation*. Endorsed by the Council of Chalcedon* in 451, it was the most important Western contribution to fifth-century Christological debates.

Tome of St. Damasus Collection of canons presented by Pope Damasus I* to bishops at a Roman synod dated between 369 and 382. It consists of the Nicene Creed* of 325 together with 24 anathemas against schismatics and heretics, including Sabellians, Eunomians, Macedonians, Melitius of Antioch*, and Apollinarians.

Tomkins, Thomas (1572–1656) English Renaissance composer. He composed over 100 anthems printed in *Musica Deo Sacra,* most of them based upon texts drawn from the Book of Psalms. The full anthems are written for between 3 and 12 voice-parts. His forty-one verse anthems were intended for use in the great feast days of the church year*. Among the five services by Tomkins, the finest is probably the third.

Tomlinson, Ambrose Jessup (1865–1943) Church of God leader. He was converted in 1892. He joined the Pentecostal Church of God in Tennessee and rose to become general overseer of the denomination from 1902 to 1923. His authoritarian administration created factions, and the church became fragmented into four large denominations and 40 smaller splinter groups.

tonary Liturgical book in which chants are classified by church mode.

tonatsouyts (Arm., feast-indicator) Typikon or directory of feasts in the Armenian Liturgy.

tongues See GLOSSOLALIA.

tonsure Shaving of the hair of a priest or monk as a symbol of ordination. In the Middle Ages, Roman or coronal tonsure was required of all ordinands* in which only a fringe of hair was left around the head. Celtic practice had been to shave the front of the head. In contemporary practice, tonsure is purely symbolic and involves cutting a few strands of hair.

tonus peregrinus (Lat., wandering tone) Irregular psalm tone* that differs from the traditional eight psalm tones by changing its reciting tone after the mediation.

Topeka Revival Revival in Topeka, Kansas, in 1901 marking the birth of the Pentecostal movement. It was a product of the ministry of Charles F. Parham*, who had established a Bible school in 1900 at an unfinished mansion called "Stone's Folly." At the New Year's service in 1900 Parham's students received the baptism of the Spirit and spoke in tongues*.

Toplady, Augustus Montague (1740–1778) Anglican Calvinist hymn writer. Although he was converted through a Methodist lay preacher, he became a vigorous Calvinist, opposed to John Wesley*. His doctrinal writing included *Historical Proof of the Doctrinal Calvinism of the Church of England* (2 vols., 1774). But his principal claim to fame is the perennial hymn "Rock of Ages." His other hymns included "A Debtor to Mercy Alone," "A Sovereign Protector I Have," and "From Whence This Fear and Unbelief?"

Torgau Book, The (1570) Also known as the Belgic Book; Solid Declaration; the Formula of Concord*. Twelve articles prepared by James Andreae, Martin Chemnitz*, Nicholas Selneccer, Andreas Musculus, Christopher Carnerus, and David Chytraeus as common ground for doctrinal harmony. The 12 articles dealt with original sin*; free

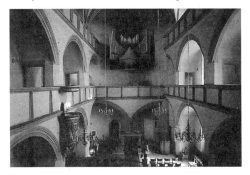

Torgau

will*; righteousness of faith before God; good works*; law and the gospel; third use of the law; Lord's Supper*; person of Christ; descent of Christ into hell*; church rites; predestination* and election*; factions, heresies, and sects.

Toronto Blessing Form of religious ecstasy*, primarily characterized by ecstatic manifestations, such as mass fainting, or falling backwards, accompanied by speaking in tongues*, weeping, or uncontrollable laughter, interpreted as evidence of the working of the Holy Spirit*. It was first observed in the Airport Church in Toronto, then part of the Vineyard network. By 2000 it had attracted an estimated two million visitors from around the world. The original meetings began under Vineyard pastors John Arnott and Randy Clark.

Torquemeda, Juan de (1388–1468) Spanish theologian. He entered the Dominican Order in 1404 and was made cardinal in 1439 and granted the title of "Defender of the Faith*." He was one of the leading defenders of papal authority. He led the negotiations with the Greek Orthodox Church which led to a short-lived decree of unity in 1439. His major work is *Summa de Ecclesia* (1448), a treatise on the church. He was also an authority on canon law* and wrote a commentary on the *Decretum Gratiani*.

Torquemeda, Tomas de (1420–1498) Spanish inquisitor general and nephew of Cardinal Torquemeda*. Of Jewish origin, he entered the Dominican Order at Valladolid and became prior* of Segovia. In 1482 he founded a new Reformed* priory* at Avila which admitted only those of pure Spanish blood. For many years he was confessor* to Ferdinand V and Isabella. When the Spanish Inquisition* was founded, he became its first grand inquisitor or inquisitor general in 1483. He made the Inquisition a powerful force in the repression of conversos*, or nominally converted Jews. He shaped the practices and procedures of the Inquisition through his series of instructions that were collected together and published in 1484 as *Ordinances*. He was also instrumental in the expulsion of Jews from Spain in 1492.

Torrey, Reuben Archer, Sr. (1856–1928) American evangelist and Bible scholar. Ordained in 1878, he began a lifelong association with D. L. Moody*, serving as the first superintendent of the Moody Bible Institute*. He went on several foreign crusades* with Moody between 1902 and 1921. From

R. A. Torrey

1912 to 1924 he was dean of the Bible Institute of Los Angeles and from 1915 also pastor of the Church of the Open Door there. He wrote numerous devotional and theological works, including *How to Work for Christ* and *The Person and Work of the Holy Spirit*.

total depravity Human condition following Adam's Fall which imparted to all his descendants an inclination toward evil and an incapacity to do good except through the Spirit of God's grace* given freely to believers. It is distinguished from the scholastic belief that human nature consists of both natural gifts, as reason, and supernatural gifts, such as love of God, and that only the latter was lost at the Fall. Total depravity, on the other hand, holds that all aspects of human beings, including both reason and human will, were corrupted at the Fall and therefore human beings are totally depraved. It does not mean that they are as bad as they can be. It is a key tenet of Calvinism*, making election* absolutely necessary for salvation*, but it was taught by almost all the mainline Reformers.

tote In the Coptic Rite, box or ark in which the chalice* stands during the liturgy.

Toulouse 1. Saint-Romain, the Eglise des Jacobins, in Toulouse, France, the mother church of the Dominicans*, founded in 1215. By 1294 the Gothic* tower was completed. Of the monastery buildings, the cloister*, the chapel house, and the Chapel of St. Anthony have all survived. 2. Cathedral of Saint-Sernin in Toulouse, France, France's last surviving Romanesque church, built between 1060 and the twelfth century. The five-aisled church was on the pilgrim road to Santiago de Compostela* in Spain, and St. James* was venerated here. The figure of St. James appears on the south portal, Porte-Miege-Ville, built around 1119. In the ambulatory is the marble relief, the Majestas Domini, with the symbols of the evangelists.

Tourette, Le Dominican monastery at Le Tourette, France, designed by Le Corbusier. It is built on three levels, church, cloister*, refectory*, and chapter house* at ground level, sleeping and work cells on the top level, and the library, study rooms, lecture rooms, common rooms, and chapel in the middle level. The large church stands next to the main building but separate from it.

Tournus Abbey and cathedral of St. Philibert*, in Tournus, overlooking the River Saone, France, built between 937 and 1019. Above the portico is the St. Michael's Chapel. The triple-aisled basilica* has a square crossing* in the large transept* and a choir with an ambulatory and a ring of chapels. In the crypt beneath the apse* is the Notre Dame la Brune, a statue of Virgin Mary* in cedar wood dating back to the twelfth century.

Tours French city famous as a monastic and educational center in the Middle Ages. Its most famous landmark is the Basilica of St. Martin of Tours*.

Tours, Battle of (732) Also, the Battle of Poitiers. Battle in which Charles Martel*, the king of the Franks, won a decisive victory over the Muslim invaders from Spain and thus saved Europe from the Muslim menace. It was the first major defeat suffered by the Arabs for a century.

Townsend, William Cameron (1896–1982) Bible translator and missiologist. In 1917 he received an appointment to sell Bibles in Central America, only to find that 60 percent of the people could not read Spanish and that Bibles were not available in most Indian languages. In 1934 he established Camp Wycliffe in Arkansas as a training center for missionaries who wanted to translate the Bible into other languages. Out of this small beginning emerged the Summer Institute of Linguistics (SIL) and Wycliffe Bible Translators* (WBT). With 3,700 members by 1982, when Townsend died, SIL/WBT is now the largest independent Protestant missionary agency in the world.

Tozer, Aiden Wilson (1897–1963) American Christian and Missionary Alliance* (CMA) pastor, author, and editor. Converted at seventeen, he held CMA pastorates* in West Virginia, Ohio, and Indiana before moving to Southside, Chicago, where his 31-year ministry attracted national attention. He was also for thirteen years the editor of *The Alliance Weekly*. His legacy consists of forty books of which the best known is *The Pursuit of God* (1948). Among his other books were *Wingspread* (1943), *The Divine Conquest* (1950), and *The Knowledge of the Holy* (1961). Tozer taught an intense spirituality* based on intimate worship, contemplation of God, prayer, hymns, practical holiness, discipline, and being filled with the Spirit.

tract 1. Literature of religious propaganda*, longer than a handbill and shorter than a treatise, often published and distributed by Protestant sects as well as cults. Evangelicals* have relied heavily on tracts. The Religious Tract Society* was founded by George Burder and others in 1799 to promote the use of tracts in evangelism. 2. Scripture portion sung before the Gospel at Mass* on certain penitential days instead of hallelujah*.

Tractarianism Name of the Oxford movement* in England when the *Tracts for the Times* were being published. The first three tracts were published in 1833. Tract writers included J. H. Newman*, E. B. Pusey*, R. H. Froude, R. I. Wilberforce, R. W. Church, J. B. Mozley, and I. Williams. The last

issue was Tract No. 90 in 1841 by Newman* which tried to put a Roman Catholic cast on the movement.

tractatus (Lat.) Exegetical writing, commentary on the Holy Scriptures.

tractoria Letters containing the decisions of councils transmitted by the pope to the church at large.

traditio clavium (Lat., handing over of the keys) Giving of the keys. Christ giving the keys to the kingdom of heaven* to St. Peter* (Matt. 16:13–20).

traditio legis Handing over of authority from Christ to the apostles, a common theme of early Christian art on catacomb* walls and on sarcophagi.

traditio symboli (Lat., handing over of the creed) Course of instruction administered to adult candidates for baptism* including the transmittal of the creeds* of the church for memorizing. At baptism, they were required to profess this creed. See also REDDITIO SYMBOLI.

traditio-historical criticism Also, history of traditions method. Study of the development and oral transmission of texts and themes in the cultural context of the creating community. It is similar to form criticism* which uses more literary methods. The pioneer of this method was Hermann Gunkel*, whose work was continued by Rudolf Bultmann* and Martin Dibelius.

tradition (Lat., *traditio*, handing on, transmission) 1. Gospel record contained in Scripture as well as the revelations and oracles of God* confirmed by apostolic and prophetic testimony. 2. Accumulated teachings, wisdom, and heritage of the church. Apostolic tradition* is defined and enshrined in the church which is also its custodian. In Roman Catholicism*, tradition is built up through the magisterium* of the church which helps to clarify the mysteries* of the gospel. Tradition gives the church continuity, stability, and unity. The authority of tradition extends to the institutions, doctrines, and sacraments of the church. 3. Usually traditionalism. Human traditions, customs, rites, dogmas, liturgical practices, and beliefs that are accepted uncritically. 4. Central beliefs crystallized and preserved in the great creeds of the church and handed down from one generation to the next. 5. The process of transmission of the central beliefs of the Christian church. 6. Unwritten or oral beliefs and practices drawn from Scripture and followed as normative by a denomination or sect.

traditors (Lat., *traditores*, those who handed over, traitors) African Christians who surrendered copies of the Bible during the Diocletian persecution* to save their lives. The controversy over attitudes to this offense gave rise to the Donatist split.

Traducianism Belief that parents transmit the soul as well as the physical body of their offspring. Traducianism was advocated by some of the Church Fathers*, as Tertullian*. Augustine* found support in it for his doctrine of original sin* but never decided finally between it and creationsim*.

Traherne, Thomas (1637–1674) English metaphysical poet whose pantheism* was expressed in the prose work *Christian Ethics* as well as two books published only in the twentieth century: *Poems* (1903) and *Centuries of Meditation* (1908).

transcendental Thomism Philosophical and theological approach that combines the scholastic thought of Thomas Aquinas* with a wide range of modern philosophy on the nature of the human subject. Karl Rahner's theology particularly views the most basic truths of Christianity from the point of view of the human subject without sacrificing Catholic doctrines of revelation* and grace*. The church is presented as a symbolic sacrament for history and the world. Transcendental Thomism is represented by many modern theologians, as Pierre Rousselot, Joseph Marechal*, Maurice Blondel*, Gustav Siewerth, Johann Baptist Lotz, Bernhard Welte, Bernard Lonergan*, and Hans Urs van Balthasar*.

transenna/transennae In ecclesiastical architecture, a wall, usually of marble pierced with holes en-

abling the congregation to see through the grating and, sometimes, to pass a handkerchief or napkin called brandea* through the openings.

transept Transverse arms of a church running north and south from the center, or near the east end of a nave*, to form a cross.

transfinalization Eucharistic doctrine, a refinement of transubstantiation*, that the elements* on being consecrated change their final purpose and acquire a new function as spiritual food.

transignification Eucharistic doctrine, an alternative to or redefinition of transubstantiation*, according to which the elements* acquired new meaning and significance on being consecrated, although their substance remains the same.

Transitorium Prayer in the Ambrosian Rite* corresponding to the communion anthem in the Roman Rite*.

translation (Gk., *methestemi*, change) 1. Change of a text from one language to another. Translation first from Hebrew and Greek to Latin, and then from Latin to all the languages of the civilized world greatly enhanced the spread of Christianity. 2. Transfer of the relics* of a saint* from one location to another. 3. Transfer of the date of a feast when its observance interferes with a particular season, as the Holy Week*. 4. Transfer of a cleric from one ecclesiastical office to another.

transubstantiation Conversion of the substance of the bread and the wine in the Eucharist* to the actual physical substance of the body and blood of Jesus Christ, although the accidents or appearances remain the same. It was fixed as dogma* by the Fourth Lateran Council* in 1215 when it became the central feature of the Mass*. The Council of Trent* confirmed the doctrine as central to the celebration of the Eucharist* and proclaimed it as a mystery.

trapeza In the Byzantine and Coptic churches, altar. Also called ma'idah in Coptic.

Trappistine Sisters Cistercian Nuns of the Strict

Observance, an order of Cistercian women founded in Tart, France, in 1796 by Dom Augustin Lestrange.

Trappists Order of Reformed Cistercians or Cistercians of Strict Observance, an order of monks of the reform instituted by Armand Jean Le Bouthillier de Rance*, abbot of La Trappe*, a Cistercian abbey near Soligny, France. It is one of the strictest of Catholic orders whose monks take a vow of silence and abstain from meat, eggs, and fish. The Trappist habit is white with a black scapular* and cowl*. The order of nuns is called Trappistine*. After being expelled from France during the French Revolution, they returned to La Trappe* in 1817. In 1898 they recovered possession of their Citeaux Abbey which had been secularized.

Tre Fontane Trappist monastery some three miles south of Rome* at the traditional site of St. Paul's* martyrdom.

Tre Ore Trinity Prayer or Three-Hour Prayer, a group prayer including elements of both public and private prayer forms. It is composed of one hour of adoration, one hour of journaling, and one hour of sharing insights and reflections with others in the group.

treasury (lit., house of the holy thing) In the Assyrian tradition, recess in the north wall of the sanctuary where sacred vessels are stored.

treasury of merits Supererogatory merits acquired by Christ and the saints* from which merits are dispensed under certain conditions to sinners in need of them. This Roman Catholic belief was rejected by the Reformers, who declared the gospel to be the treasury of the church.

treboution (lit., the Book of Choir Boys) Armenian book containing text of the portions of the liturgy sung by the choir.

Trecanum In the Gallican Liturgy, the title of the Communion chant.

trefoil Choir of a church with three rounded apses*.

trendle Circular object or wheel hung in a church on which candles may be placed.

Trent, Council of The Nineteenth Ecumenical Council, according to Roman Catholic reckoning, held at Trent, Italy, from 1545 to 1563. It is the high water mark of the Counter-Reformation*. The council met in three stages: 1545 to 1547, 1551 to 1552, and 1562 to 1563. The first stage consisted of eight sessions, attended at first by a small assembly composed of 3 legates, 1 cardinal, 4 archbishops, 21 bishops, and 5 generals of orders. The third session reaffirmed the Niceno-Constantinopolitan Creed*, the validity of both Scriptures and unwritten traditions as sources of truth, the sole right of the church to interpret the Bible, and the authority of the text of the Vulgate*. The other sessions defined justification*, merit*, and the theology of the sacraments*.

During the second stage, six sessions were held (9 to 14) when decisions were reached on Eucharist*, penance*, extreme unction*, and transubstantiation*. During the third stage, the council abandoned any effort at conciliating the Protestants, and the Jesuits* dominated the sessions 15 through 25. The council reached agreement on the eucharistic Communion in one kind, the doctrine of the Mass*, Orders, matrimony*, purgatory*, invocation* of saints, the veneration* of saints and images, indulgences*, the Index, clerical seminaries, and provincial and diocesan synods. The conciliar reforms failed to satisfy the Protestants or the

Assembly of the Council of Trent

die-hard Catholics, but the council helped the renewal of the Catholic Church in its struggle with Protestantism* in the centuries ahead. The council ended its deliberations on December 4, 1563, and a summary of the council's work called the Tridentine Creed was issued in 1564.

trental Thirty masses for the repose of a deceased person.

Triad See TRINITY.

triadikon Byzantine troparion* honoring the Holy Trinity*.

triangle In Christian art, symbol of the Trinity*.

Tribulation, Great In dispensationalist theology, a seven-year period of great suffering prior to the Second Coming* of Jesus Christ and the beginning of the millennium*. "For then there will be great tribulation, such as has not been from the beginning of the world until this time, no, nor ever shall be" (Matt. 24:21–22). There are differing views on the status of the church during the Great Tribulation*. They are pre-, mid-, and post-tribulationism*, depending on whether the church endures none, some, or all of the tribulation.

trichora Church of which the east end or altar area is designed with three apses* placed around a central domed space.

trichotomy Body, soul, and spirit constituting a human being as a tripartite entity (1 Thess. 5:23).

Tridentine Of or relating to the Council of Trent* and its decrees.

Triduum (Lat., three days) Three days set apart for devotion preparatory to the celebration of an ecclesiastical feast or seeking the aid of a saint*.

Triduum Sacrum Last three days of the Holy Week*: Maundy Thursday*, Good Friday*, and Holy Saturday*.

Trier 1. Oldest German city, after Augsburg, founded by Augustus around 15 B.C. on the Moselle River. 2. Cathedral in Trier, Germany, a

double basilica*, first built in 326 and then rebuilt in 1035. The most valuable relic* in the cathedral is the Holy Robe, a seamless garment supposedly

Trier Cathedral

worn by Christ, made from a brown* fabric and wrapped in a Byzantine silk cloth. The Andreas Altar in the Badisches Bau between the choir and the north walk of the cloister* was created in the tenth century.

triforium 1. Arcaded passage or gallery with three openings in the interior elevation of a nave* above the aisle of a church. 2. Part of a wall between the arcade of a nave and the clerestory*, or between the gallery and the clerestory. It may have open or blind arcades facing the nave*.

trikerion Candlestick with three lights, representing the Trinity*, used by Greek bishops to bless the congregation.

Trikerion

Trinitarian Person who believes in the doctrine of the Holy Trinity*, as opposed to a Unitarian.

trinitarian formula Ancient formula*, "In the name of the Father, the Son and the Holy Spirit," used in baptism*, dedication, and other services and prayers.

Trinitarians Order of the Most Holy Trinity founded at Cerfroid, Meaux, in 1198 by John of Martha and Felix of Valois, following an austere Augustinian Rule and wearing a white habit and a cross flory on the scapular* and cloak. They devoted themselves to ransoming Christian captives, taking a vow to sacrifice their own liberty to do so. By the fifteenth century there were 800 Trinitarian houses. The Barefooted Trinitarians date from 1596 and the Barefooted Trinitarian Sisters from 1612.

Trinity Central tenet of Christian theology in which the Father, the Son, and the Holy Spirit* constitute one, personal, and triune God. It is defined in the Athanasian Creed* as follows: "We worship one God in Trinity and Trinity in Unity; neither confounding the persons, nor dividing the substance." Trinity was a neologism that was first used in its Greek form, *trias,* by Theophilus* of Antioch (c. 180), but the doctrine had been adumbrated in both the Old Testament and the New Testament (Matt. 28:19). In the days of Tertullian* and Origen*, the categories and language of theology struggled to elucidate the concept for which there was no precedent. It was at the Councils of Nicaea* and Constantinople* that the doctrine of the Trinity began to take shape, and the Cappadocian Fathers* were the first to place a dogmatic face on what had been until then a mystery.

The three persons in the Trinity were accepted as coequal, eternally self-existent, and mutually indwelling through circumincession*. In the Eastern Orthodox Church*, the official doctrine, which received its clearest exposition in the works of St. John of Damascus*, is the Procession of the Holy Spirit from the Father alone. In the Western Church*, the doctrine, as clearly formulated by St. Augustine* in *De Trinitate* and by St. Thomas Aquinas*, laid the emphasis on the unity of the substance of Godhead and the coequality of the three persons of the Godhead. The Procession of

the Holy Spirit* was attributed to both the Father and the Son. See also FIORETTI.

Trinity College College in the University of Dublin founded in 1591 which has a valuable collection of ancient Christian manuscripts, including *Book of Kells** and *Book of Armagh**.

Trinity Sunday Sunday after Pentecost*, dedicated to the Trinity*.

Triodion (Gk., three odes) In the Byzantine Rite*, liturgical book containing variable portions of the services from the fourth Sunday before Lent* until the Saturday before Easter*, so named because during this season the canons contain only three odes instead of the usual nine. In the Slavonic churches, it is called the Fasting Triodion, as distinguished from the Flowery Triodion or Pentecostarion*.

triple candlestick In the Western Church*, three candles mounted on a pole successively lighted in the course of the procession up to the altar on Holy Saturday*. In the Eastern Church*, it is used for episcopal blessings when the bishop holds one in each hand.

Trinity

triple tiara Ceremonial tiara* encrusted with precious metals worn by the pope on formal occasions.

triptych Painting made up of three parts or panels, in which the two wings close over the central part. Sometimes there is a predella* below the central part to enable the wings to swing easily.

triquetra Ornamental device made up of three interlaced ovals, symbolizing the Trinity*; enclosed in a circle, representing eternity*.

Trisagion (Lat., thrice holy) Ancient Christian liturgy beginning "Holy God, holy and mighty, holy and immortal."

triskelion In the Byzantine tradition, a portable lectern* from which the Gospel may be read.

Tritheism Belief in three gods, as distinguished from belief in Trinity*. Tritheists argue that there are three substances in the Trinity. Early Tritheism advocated by a sixth-century Monophysite sect was condemned by the Third Council of Constantinople* (680–681). In the Middle Ages Nominalists like Roscellinus of Compiegne and the Realist Gilbert de la Porree* were accused of tritheism. Both were condemned at the Council of Soissons* in 1092 and the Council of Reims in 1248. Gilbert influenced Joachim of Fiore*, whose doctrine was condemned at the Fourth Lateran Council* in 1215.

triumphalism Brash confidence in the ultimate victory of the Christian church over the forces of evil, as determining one's approach to evangelism, history, and theology. Sometimes applied pejoratively to believers who emphasize Christian successes to the exclusion of problems, difficulties, and reverses.

triune immersion Also, trine immersion*. Immersion in the water three times, as practiced in Eastern Orthodox* and some Protestant churches.

Troeltsch, Ernst (1865–1923) German theologian and religious sociologist. Author of the influential *The Social Teaching of the Christian Churches* (2 vols., 1912) in which he interpreted the social de-

velopment of Christianity as a product of social and environmental factors and propounded an influential distinction between sect and church.

troichen In the Byzantine Rite*, a stanza or verse honoring the Trinity*.

troparion In the Eastern Church*, a stanza of religious poetry, applied particularly to the Apolytikion, or the troparion* of the day.

trope Poetic phrases or sentences set to music interpolated into the chants of the Mass* and some chants of the Divine Office*. They were designed to increase the solemnity of the occasion by interpreting or explaining the text.

troper Liturgical book containing tropes* and sequences and other accretions to the Roman Liturgy.

trophy of the cross Cross surmounted by a Chi-Rho monogram encircled by a wreath.

tropology Figurative interpretation of the Scriptures that emphasizes the text's moral teachings.

Trotman, Dawson Earle (1906–1956) American founder of the Navigators*. Converted in 1926, he did street evangelism by promoting Bible memorization. In 1934 he organized the Navigators as a a ministry to sailors, with the motto, "To Know Christ and to Make Him Known." He described the Navigators as a self-reproducing ministry (based on 2 Tim. 2:2), emphasizing Bible memorization, small-group Bible study, evangelism, and discipleship. Known as the "Apostle of the Follow-Up," Trotman assisted Billy Graham* and many Evangelical mission agencies and churches in counseling new converts. In the 1990s the Navigators had more than 3,500 workers in 90 countries.

Trotter, Isabella Lilias (1858–1928) English missionary to North Africa. She gave up a successful career as a painter in London to go to North Africa as a missionary. She arrived in Algiers in 1888 and for next 40 years devoted herself to preaching the gospel and translating the Scriptures.

Trotter, Mel (1870–1960) Evangelist. Converted at the Pacific Garden Mission* in Chicago, he moved to Grand Rapids and established over 60 rescue missions. During World War I he preached to soldiers at the front.

Troyes Cathedral of Saint-Pierre-et-Saint-Paul, in Troyes, France. The forerunner of the present cathedral was destroyed by fire in 1188. The second church was built between 1208 and 1640. The massive 220-foot facade is the work of Martin Chambiges. The magnificent stained glass required over 400 years to complete.

truce of God In medieval times, a suspension of hostilities ordered by the church on Sundays or during certain seasons, as Advent* and Lent*.

Trullan Synod Synod held in 692 in the imperial palace at Constantinople*, so called because it was held in the *troullos,* or a bowl-shaped council chamber. The council defined the practice of the Eastern Orthodox Church*. It sanctioned the marriage of the clergy, made the patriarch* of Constantinople equal to the pope in power and privileges, and prohibited fasting on Saturdays in Lent*. Its decrees helped to widen the breach between the Greek and Latin churches. Because it was held to complete the work of the fifth and sixth councils, it was also known as Quinisext, the fifth-sixth.

trumus In the Syrian tradition, the altar.

Trzebinic Cistercian convent in Trzebinic, Poland, founded in 1203 by Heinrich II and his wife Hedwig. The Hedwig Chapel was built in 1269, and it has a carving of the coronation of Mary on its portal tympanum*. In 1741 the church was rebuilt in Baroque style.

Tsalota-Hawaria Collected liturgical prayers in the Ethiopian Church.

tsarskiya vrata (lit., royal doors*) In the Byzantine church, the central opening of the iconostasis* also called svyatya vrata, or holy doors*, through which gifts are brought during the liturgy. Women and laymen may not pass through these doors.

tsatskoths skih In the Armenian Rite*, the second veil in addition to the kogh* used to cover the chalice* during the liturgy.

tschi In the Coptic Rite, reception of the Holy Communion*.

Tserkovnost (Russ., sense of the church) Belief that salvation* is universal and that a person can be saved only in communion with others.

Tsomedeggwa In the Ethiopian Church*, chants for Lent* but not for the Holy Week*.

Tubingen The University of Wurttemberg, founded in 1477, which became a center for Lutheran orthodoxy* in the sixteenth century. At least two theological schools had their origin here, the first founded by G. C. Storr based on the authority of the Bible and the second founded by F. C. Baur*, which sought to interpret the early Christian church on the basis of a supposed conflict between Paul* and Peter*, Petrinists or Jewish Christians, and Paulinists or Gentile Christians. Baur's pupils included D. F. Strauss* and A. Ritschl*.

tukas razi In the Assyrian Rite, the point in the liturgy when the remains of the Blessed Sacrament* are consumed.

tukkoso dh'q'say w'rushmo (lit., order of breaking and signing) In the Jacobite Rite, the recitation of the catholic prayer of general intercession.

Tukutendereza (Luganda, We Praise You, Jesus) Theme song of East African revivals.

TULIP Acronym and mnemonic tool for the five points that emerged as the defining tenets of developed Calvinism* at the Synod of Dort*: total depravity*, unconditional election*, limited atonement*, irresistible grace*, and perseverance* of the saints.

tunica talaris Alb* or cassock*.

tunicle In the Western Church*, the outer liturgical garment of the subdeacon, similar to the dalmatic*, but without colored stripes and having narrower sleeves. Formerly it was worn by the bishop under his dalmatic and chasuble*.

Tur Abdin (lit., mountain of the servants of God)

Center of Syrian Orthodox Christianity in south-eastern Turkey noted for many ancient monasteries, such as Mar Gabriel at Kartmin, founded in 394, and Deir Za'faran*, near Mardin, founded before the sixth century and until the end of World War I, the seat of the Syrian Orthodox patriarch* of Antioch*.

Turgama (lit., the interpretation) Assyrian book of doctrinal hymns sung before the Gospel or Epistle, attributed by Ebed Jesu to Bar Sauma.

turikes In the Byzantine tradition, Cheese Week which starts seven weeks before Easter* and follows the meat fast week.

Turin Italian city on the Po River, the capital of Piedmont in northwest Italy. It was Christianized around 250. It is the home of the Shroud of Turin*.

Turretin, Francis (1623–1687) Calvinist theologian, known as the foremost interpreter of Calvinism*. His *Institutio* (1688) is a standard Presbyterian textbook. He created a precise and complete doctrinal framework for Calvinism in *Formula Consensus Helvetica* (1675).

turris Pyx* or reliquary* in the form of a tower.

Tutiorism Also, Rigorism*. System of moral theology* which states that in doubtful cases, the safer opinion, or the one with greater moral certainty, must be followed. Many Jansenists maintained Tutiorist doctrines until it was condemned by the Holy Office* in 1690.

Tutu, Desmond (1931–) South African bishop and ecumenist. He was ordained as an Anglican priest in 1961. In 1967 he was made bishop of Lesotho and next year general secretary of the South Africa Council of Churches. He later occupied the see* of Johannesburg before becoming the archbishop of Cape Town and the primate* of South Africa. His theology is ecumenical rather than Evangelical. He was awarded the Nobel Peace Prize in 1984, chiefly for his stance against apartheid. After its demise, he chaired the Truth and Reconciliation Commission.

Twelfth Night Epiphany* eve, 12 days after Christmas*, concluding the Christmas season.

Twelve Great Feasts In the Byzantine Church* calendar, the eight Feasts of our Lord and four Feasts of the Theotokos. The Feasts of Our Lord are Nativity, Epiphany*, Purification of the Virgin, Palm Sunday*, Ascension, Pentecost*, Transfiguration, and Exaltation of the Cross*. The Feasts of the Theotokos are Nativity, Presentation, Annunciation, and Dormition*.

Twelve, the Group of 12 disciples chosen by Jesus at the beginning of his ministry.

tympanum Front surface of a triangular or semi-circular gable above a doorway, usually filled in medieval churches with elaborate carvings.

Tympanum

Tyndale, William (c. 1494–1536) English reformer and Bible translator. Unable to undertake the translation of the Bible in his native country because of the opposition of the established church*, Tyndale left England, never to return. He began the printing of the first translation of the New Testament in Cologne* in 1525 but faced enormous odds and misfortunes, such as a shipwreck, loss of manuscript, betrayal by his coworkers, harassment by secret agents, and police raids on his printer. It was completed and published at Worms in 1525. Tyndale also translated sections of the Old Testament and wrote extensively on theology. His translation, made directly from Greek and Hebrew, was lucid and crisp and was influential on both the Authorized Version* and the Revised Version. In 1535 he was arrested and imprisoned, and next year he was strangled and burned at the stake at Brussels.

William Tyndale

typica In the Byzantine Rite*, service of prayer and praise, interspersed between sext* and none*, on days when there is no celebration of the liturgy.

Typicon (Gk., the Ordinances) In the Eastern Church*, a liturgical manual with directions on how the services are to be recited during the ecclesiastical year.

typoi/typos Diversity of forms of administration and governance, liturgical expressions, spiritual and devotional traditions, and canonical discipline within a church, fellowship, or ecclesiastical allegiance, without any disagreement on faith, doctrine, and mission.

Typos Imperial edict issued by Constans II and drafted by Paul, patriarch* of Constantinople*, in 647 or 648 superseding the *Ecthesis**. It condemned both Monothelite and Dyothelite beliefs. The refusal of Pope Martin I* to accept it led to his deposition.

Tyre, Synod of Synod held in Tyre (modern-day Lebanon) in 335. It was convoked by Emperor Constantine* to deal with Arianism*, which had been declared anathema at the Council of Nicaea* in 325. The Synod of Tyre was railroaded by Arian bishops into upholding Arius* and condemning Athanasius*. The synod is not therefore recognized as a proper church council.

Tyrrell, George (1861–1909) English modernist theologian. Of Evangelical background, he converted to Roman Catholicism* in 1879 and next year entered the Jesuit Order. Under the influence of Friedrich Von Hugel* and Henri Bergson*, he moved away from Catholic orthodoxy and left the Jesuits* in 1906 and was excommunicated in 1907. Toward the end he flirted with near apostasy* and was denied a Catholic burial. Some of his earlier works show a strong attraction to the devotional aspects of Catholicism*.

tzvyetnaya triod Byzantine book, called the Flowery Triodion, containing the order of service from Easter* to Pentecost*.

Uu

Ubertino of Casale (1259–1330) Franciscan preacher and leader of the Spiritual Franciscans*. In 1305 he wrote *Arbor Vitae Crucifixae Jesu Christi,* one of the seminal works in Franciscan mysticism. In 1310 he defended the spririals on their poverty in a debate at Avignon*. In 1325 he was accused of heresy and transferred to a Benedictine house. Dante mentions him in Canto 12 of *Paradiso.*

ubiquity Omnipresence. Lutheran doctrine that Christ not only in his divinity but also in his inseparable humanity is omnipresent. It is a key element in the Lutheran teaching which holds that the omnipresent human nature of Christ is locally present in the Holy Communion*.

UBS United Bible Societies.

Uchimura, Kanzo (1861–1930) Founder of the Japanese nondenominational movement called mukyokai and author of a 22-volume Bible commentary.

UFM Unevangelized Fields Mission, an international nondenominational foreign missionary agency founded as a faith mission* in London in 1931. Over the next half century UFM incorporated a number of other mission agencies, including the World Christian Crusade in 1949, the Alpine Mission to France in 1962, and the Mexican Indian Mission in 1971. UFM also has developed mission fields* in Haiti, Guyana, Indonesia, Quebec, South Africa, and the Philippines.

UIODG Ut in Omnibus Deus Glorificatur, "that God may be glorified in all things." One of the mottoes of the Benedictine Order.

Ukraine Ukraine was the first home of Christianity in the region called Rus. It was at Kiev* that Vladimir I* was converted and led his people to the Orthodox faith. Kiev was destroyed in 1240 by the Mongols. The metropolitan* of Kiev moved his residence to Vladimir* in 1299 and then to Moscow* in 1326. Nevertheless, the patriarch of Constantinople* consecrated in 1375 a Bulgarian monk, Cyprian, as metropolitan of Kiev, Russia, and Lithuania. The fall of Constantinople in 1453 reinforced the claim of Rome over the Ukrainian Church. Under the Union of Brest-Litovsk in 1596 the Ukrainian hierarchy* joined Rome. The union was renounced when Russia annexed Ukraine in 1686, although the Uniats continued to flourish in Austrian-held Galicia. Three times in the twentieth century (1917–1930, 1941–1945, and since 1989) the Ukrainian Church has tried to regain its independence. In 1921 the Ukrainian Autocephalous Orthodox Church (UAOC) was created, but it was twice wiped out by the Bolsheviks. In 1989 following the collapse of the Soviet Union, it was revived again when Ioann Bodnarchuk of Zhytomir and Metropolitan Mstyslav Skrypnik became its leaders.

Meanwhile, Patriarch Aleksei II of Moscow named Volodymyr Sabodan, an ethnic Ukrainian, as metropolitan of Kiev and head of the Ukrainian Orthodox Church of the Moscow Patriarchate

(UAOC-MP). A third group led by Filaret Deny-senkov established the Ukrainian Orthodox Church of the Kiev Patriarchate (UAOC-KP). UAOC and UAOC-KP merged in 1992 with Mstyslav as head, but, on his death, the merger came apart. Ukraine thus has two patriarchs of Kiev and three Orthodox churches: UAOC, UAOC-KP, and UAOC-MP. The last is the largest with 6,300 parishes. In western Ukraine, the Greek Catholic Church is the second largest with 3,151 parishes.

Ukrainian Uniat Church The Ukrainian Catholic Church, formerly known as the Ruthenian Church, exists mostly in western Ukraine*. It was brought into the Latin fold under the Union of Brest-Litovsk in 1596 by which Ukrainians were allowed to retain their traditional creeds and rites, including Communion in both kinds*, feasts, married clergy, and ordination of bishops without mandate of Rome. The union became a dead letter when Russia absorbed Ukraine and suppressed Catholicism* throughout the empire by an imperial decree in 1839. The church was severely persecuted under the Czars and the Soviets. Joseph Kuntsevych, the monk who became bishop of Vitebsk in 1617, archbishop of Pskov in 1618, and led the Catholic resistance to the Czars, was murdered in 1623. An underground Catholic Church continued to exist for the next 300 years.

In 1963 Metropolitan Josephat Slipy assumed the title of patriarch* of Kiev and Halych and all Rus. In 1989 the church was formally reestablished with its traditional eparchies. By 1993 over 1,350 parishes were registered as Catholic. In 1990 the Cathedral of St. George in Lviv was returned to the Ukrainian Catholic Church. In 1991 Cardinal Liubachivsky came from Rome to assume the leadership of the church. Another Ukrainian community, the Podcarpathian Ruthenians, was brought into communion with Rome in 1646 by the Union of Uzhorod. It is part of the eparchy* of Mukachevo subject to the Hungarian hierarchy*. Ukrainian Uniats have their own college, the Ruthenian College, founded in 1897 in Rome.

Ulm Cathedral in Ulm, Germany. Its 528-foot spire* is the highest church tower in the world. Begun in 1392 by Ulrich Ensinger and continued by Matthaus Boblinger and Burkhard Engleberg,

it was completed only in the nineteenth century. In the sixteenth century the cathedral became a Protestant church, and some of the old furnishings were destroyed.

Ulphilas/Ulfilas (c. 311–383) Apostle of the Goths. A Goth from Cappadocia*, he was consecrated bishop in about 341 by the Arian bishop of Nicomedia, Eusebius*. He translated the Bible into the Gothic language. Through his influence the Goths remained Arian for many centuries.

ultradispensationalism Movement within dispensationalism* which believes that the church began the day after Pentecost* as described in Acts 13 or 28. Acts 28 dispensationalism was championed by Ethelbert W. Bullinger (1837–1913), who held that the mark of the church is Spirit baptism. They therefore do not practice water baptism (which they associate with the pre-church era) or the Lord's Supper*. Acts 13 dispensationalism was taught by Charles F. Baker and Cornelius R. Stam. According to them, the church began with the missionary journeys of Paul*. They accept the Lord's Supper but not water baptism.

Ultramontanism (lit., beyond the mountains, that is, the Alps) Roman Catholic movement in Western Europe that favored centralization of authority in the Roman Curia* and opposed national or

Ulm Cathedral

diocesan independence. It was partly a reaction to the excesses of the French Revolution and to the discredited Gallicanism* and partly a desire for the restoration of the strong moral values represented by the church. Disillusionment with the Rationalism of the Enlightenment and the growing power of the state also contributed to Ultramontanism. It served as a magnet for the conservative elements in the church who were alarmed by the growing theological liberalism*. The movement was spearheaded by Catholic leaders, as Cardinal Manning, Joseph de Maistre, and Louis de Bonald*.

Umilenie Russian form of the icon of the Virgin Mary* known as Eleousa*, showing her and the Christ child in a tender and affectionate mode.

una sancta (Lat.) One and holy, two of the four marks* of the church.

Unam Sanctam Papal bull* issued by Pope Boniface VIII* in 1302 affirming the spiritual authority of the pope and the unity of the church. It declared that there is one holy, catholic, and apostolic church outside which there is neither salvation* nor remission of sins. It further affirmed that anyone who did not acknowledge the pope as the successor of St. Peter* and the vicar of Christ* was outside the church, and thus a heretic.

Unamuno, Miguel de (1864–1937) Spanish Catholic writer. A religious man who called himself a Catholic, he was a mystic and rebel at heart whose books expressed his spiritual despair. Two of his religious works are *The Tragic Sense of Life* (1926) and *The Agony of Christianity* (1928).

unaya In the Assyrian Rite, congregational response or refrain to a reading of the Psalms.

unchurched Those who do not belong to or participate in a Christian church or denomination.

unconditional election The Augustinian doctrine that the election* of some people to salvation* on the basis of God's sovereign choice rather than on human merit*. The stronger view, known as double predestination*, holds that God elects some for salvation and damns others, while the more

moderate view, known as single predestination*, holds that God only elects some for salvation while others are passed over and left in their sin. While most Reformers agreed on the elect, views differed on the non-elect.

uncreated light Also, the light of Tabor*. In Hesychasm* the mystical light of God's visible presence received by the soul that has been purified by ascetic devotions.

unction 1. Anointing with oil by a priest or bishop on any of a number of occasions, such as baptism* and confirmation*. 2. Also, extreme unction*. Sacrament of anointing the sick and those at the point of death. The sacrament* may be administered to all who are ill, more than once if necessary, and to old people who are weak but not ill. Blessed oil is anointed on the forehead and hands after which the sick person may receive Communion. In the Greek Church the rite is called Euchelaion* and may be received even by those who are not ill as a preparation for Communion. 3. Metaphorically, remarkable anointing by the power of the Holy Spirit*, especially in preaching.

unde et memores Seventh section of the Roman canon*, beginning "wherefore, Lord, we, your servants, as also your holy people, remembering the blessed Passion of Christ."

underground church 1. Suppressed church that functions clandestinely, particularly by meeting in house churches*. 2. Any new alternative ecclesial community* that tries to supplant the institutional church. It is essentially ecumenical with minimum doctrinal content.

Underhill, Evelyn (1875–1941) Birth name: Mrs. Hubert Stuart Moore. English Anglican mystic. She had a conversion experience in 1911 and thereafter devoted her life to spiritual writings with a pronounced interest in mysticism and Roman Catholic and Orthodox liturgical worship. Her first book, *Mysticism,* appeared in 1911 followed by *Mystic Way* in 1913, *Practical Wisdom* in 1915, *Essentials of Mysticism* in 1920, and *Worship* in 1937. She published two books, *The Spiral Way* and *The Path of Eternal Wisdom,* under the pseudonym John Cordelier. She also translated *The Cloud of Unknowing, The Scale of Perfection* by W. Hilton*, and devotional classics by Ruysbroeck*. In the U.S. Episcopal Church she is commemorated on June 15.

Unger, Merrill F. (1909–1980) Old Testament scholar. He began his teaching career at Gordon Divinity School and later taught at Dallas Theological Seminary* and pastored at Buffalo, New York, Dallas, and Baltimore. Many of his books continue to be used today, including *Unger's Bible Dictionary* (1957) and *Introductory Guide to the Old Testament* (1951).

Uniat/Uniate churches Eastern Christian churches in communion with Rome while retaining their own liturgies, liturgical languages and ecclesiastical customs, vestments and rites, such as Communion in both kinds*, married clergy, and baptism* by immersion*. There are four groups of Uniat churches*:

1. **Antiochene Rite***, of which the most important are the Maronites*, the Syrians, and the Malankarese. The Maronites are the oldest Uniats, who renounced their original Monothelitism* and united with Rome* in 1182. The Syrians united in Rome in 1783 under the leadership of Mar Michael Garweh, having renounced their Monophysitism*. The Malankarese separated from the Syrian Orthodox (Jacobite) Church* of Malabar under the leadership of Mar Ivanios in 1930.

2. **Chaldean Rite,** of which the most important groups are the Armenians, Chaldeans, and Malabar Christians*. The Armenians united with Rome (1198–1291, 1741) under the patriarch* of Cilicia*, the Chladeans or former Nestorians (1551 and 1830), and the Malabar Christians (before 1599).

3. **Alexandrine Rite,** of which the most important groups are the Copts and the Ethiopians. The Coptic Uniats date from 1741 and the Ethiopian Uniats from 1839.

4. **Byzantine Rite***, of which the most important Uniats are the Ruthenians of East Galicia, now called the Ukrainian Catholic Church, and Sub-Carpathian Russia dating from the Union of Brest-Litovsk (1595–1596) and the Rumaics and the Rumanians of Transylvania (1701). There are also small Uniat groups: Hungarians (1595), Serbs (1611), Melchites* (1724), Bulgars (1860), and Greeks (1860).

Union of Messianic Jewish Congregations Transdenominational American fellowship of over 60 Messianic Jewish congregations. It is Charismatic in orientation and includes many Assemblies of God* congregations.

Union Theological Seminary Nondenominational theological seminary, affiliated with Columbia University, in New York City, founded in 1836. It has been from the beginning a moderate and liberal institution without denominational ties. Its faculty has included over the years some great theological scholars, including Edward Robinson, Henry Boynton Smith, Philip Schaff*, Francis Brown, Arthur C. McGiffert*, Henry Sloane Coffin, Henry P. Van Dusen, Reinhold Niebuhr*, Paul Tillich*, James Muilenburg, Wilhelm Pauck, Cyril C. Richardson, John Knox, John C. Bennett, Daniel D. Williams, Roger L. Shinn, Raymond Brown*, and Beverly Harrison.

Unists Also Subunists*. Bohemian Hussites*, who practiced Communion under one kind, in opposition to the Utraquists, who practiced Communion under both kinds.

Unitarianism Heretical Christian tradition that affirms monotheism* but rejects both the Trinity* and the divinity of Christ. Its modern exponents are united by no single set of beliefs but generally represent a free-thinking liberalism*. In the early church there were intimations of anti-Trinitarianism* among the Arians, Paulicians*, and Monarchians. But organized Unitarianism dates from the Reformation* period when it was established in Poland, Hungary, and England.

In the fifteenth and sixteenth centuries Unitarian ideas were propagated by Martin Cellarius, Johannes Reuchlin, Michael Servetus*, and Bernardino Ochino*. In Poland, Unitarians were led by George Blandrata and Fausto Sozzini* who were instrumental in the publication of the Racovian Catechism*. Blandrata also was responsible for the spread of Unitarianism in Hungary, where he converted King Sigismund. In England

John Biddle (1615–1662) is considered the "Father of Unitarianism," and a century later the scientist Joseph PrIestley lent his skills to further Unitarianism. The first Unitarian coventicle was founded by Theophilus Lindsey in 1774. In the eighteenth century Unitarian views were fashionable among all dissenting congregations. In 1853 the Hibbert Trust was founded to promote liberal theology, and in 1888 Manchester College was founded under the sect's auspices. In America, King's Chapel, Boston, was the first to turn itself into a Unitarian congregation in 1785. Over the course of the next century many congregational churches in eastern Massachusetts adopted Unitarian beliefs.

In the writings of William Ellery Channing*, Ralph Waldo Emerson, and others, Unitarianism is presented as nothing more than a bundle of ethical precepts*. Many prominent Americans like Thomas Jefferson were antitrinitarians. In 1805 Henry Ware, a liberal, was appointed to the chair of the Harvard Divinity School, and he turned the school permanently into a Unitarian bastion. The American Unitarian Association was founded in 1825 and the National Conference of Unitarian Churches in 1865. In 1961 the American Unitarian Association joined with the Universalist Church of America* to form the Unitarian Universalist Association. Unitarianism has steadily lost ground in the twentieth century.

United Bible Societies Federation of 70 Bible societies worldwide founded in Elfinsward in England in 1964. It works in 180 countries to print, translate, and distribute Bibles.

United Church of Canada Canada's largest Protestant denomination, founded in 1925, through the merger of the Methodist Church, the Congregational Union, the Council of Local Union Churches (comprising 3,000 congregations), and about two-thirds of the Presbyterian Church. The church was enlarged later by the addition of the Wesleyan Methodist Church of Bermuda and the Canada Conference of the Evangelical United Brethren*. The new denomination was the first modern church formed by the union of diverse Christian traditions. The United Church has a strong Presbyterian polity* and is governed by a general council presided over by a moderator*.

Central boards in Toronto administer the various ministries, and there are corresponding boards at the conference, presbytery*, and local church levels. The United Church theology is generally liberal or radically skeptical with a strong commitment to ecumenism* and social issues. The Renewal Fellowship represents the Evangelical element within the church.

United Free Church of Scotland Church formed in 1900 by the union of the United Presbyterian Church* and the Free Church of Scotland. In 1929 it joined the Established Church of Scotland except for a small group that still uses the original name.

United Pentecostal Church Pentecostal nontrinitarian church, the result of a merger in 1945 between the Pentecostal Church and the Pentecostal Assemblies of Jesus Christ. It believes in water baptism in the name of Jesus*, and not in the name of the Father, the Son, and the Holy Spirit*.

United Presbyterian Church Scottish church formed in 1847 through the union of the United Secession Church and the Relief Synod. The former had been formed in 1820 through the fusion of the New Lichts of the Burghers* and the Antiburghers*. The latter had been formed in 1761. In 1900 the United Presbyterians merged with the Free Church of Scotland to form the United Free Church of Scotland*.

United Reformed Church Reformed church in the United Kingdom formed in 1972 through the union of the Congregational Church of England and Wales and the Presbyterian Church of England. It was joined later by the Disciples of Christ in Britain.

United Society for Christian Literature British society founded in 1935 through the merger of Religious Tract Society*, Christian Literature Society for India and Africa, and the Christian Literature Society for China. It works closely with Feed the Minds, a charity founded in 1964 that sponsors Christian media projects.

United Society for the Propagation of the Gospel Missionary society formed in 1965 through the merger of the Society for the Propagation of the Gospel [in Foreign Parts]* (founded in 1701) and the Universities' Mission to Central Africa* (founded in 1857).

United Society of Believers in Christ's Second Appearing Official name of the Shakers*.

United States Center for World Mission Evangelical Foreign Missions Center in Pasadena, California, begun in 1976 by Ralph and Roberta Winter. It represents more than 70 mission agencies targeting the unreached people of the world.

unitha/unyatha In the Assyrian Church*, an anthem as in unitha d'bim, anthem of the bema* sung during Holy Communion*; unitha d'eewangaliyun, anthem of the Gospel; unitha d'qanki, anthem of the sanctuary; and unitha d'raze, anthem of the holy mysteries*.

Unity Heretic religious movement begun by Charles and Myrtle Fillmore in 1889, following a miraculous healing received by the former. They have no sectarian or denominational ties. Their headquarters is in Unity Village in Lee's Summit, Missouri, where the Unity School of Christianity is located. They believe in assorted ideas, such as positive thinking*, health, happiness, and prosperity. They teach that God is a principle, that Jesus was the perfect expression of that principle, and that all human beings will become like Christ through a series of reincarnations.

Universal Doctor Epithet of Alain de Lille* and Albertus Magnus*.

Universalism 1. Belief that all human beings will eventually be saved. 2. Religious system emphasizing the universal Fatherhood of God and universal salvation*.

Universalist Church of America North American sect that believes in the final reconciliation of all human beings with God. It was created in eighteenth-century America, the first congregation was organized in 1779, and the first creed* was adopted in 1790. The Winchester Platform of 1803 emphasized the perfectibility of all human beings, the ultimate salvation* of all created beings,

and the humanity of Christ. Early leaders included John Murray*, Hosea Ballou*, and Elhanan Winchester. In 1961 it merged with the American Unitarian Association to form the Unitarian Universalist Association.

Universities' Mission to Central Africa See UNITED SOCIETY FOR THE PROPAGATION OF THE GOSPEL.

unleavened bread Bread without leaven used in the Eucharist* by the Roman Catholic Church and the Church of England*.

unmixed chalice Ancient Armenian eucharistic custom of using pure wine unmixed with water, signifying that Jesus had only one nature.

unreached Of or relating to nonevangelized ethnic, linguistic, or other groups without contact with Christians or without knowledge of the gospel.

Uppsala Town in Sweden, the site of the largest cathedral in Sweden (1287–1435) and whose archbishop bears the title primate* of Sweden. It was made into an ecclesiastical province separate from Lund in 1164, and the see was transferred from Old Uppsala to its present site under Archbishop Folke (1274–1277). The University of Uppsala is the center of a Low Church* and liberal theology.

Uppsala Cathedral

Uppsala Assembly 1. National Assembly of the Church of Sweden held in Uppsala* in 1592 which firmly adopted the Lutheran Reformation* as the basis of the Swedish national church. 2. Fourth Assembly of the World Council of Churches* held in Uppsala in 1968. It was attended by 704 delegates of whom 3 percent were from developing countries.

urara/uraro In the Syrian Church, stole* worn by priests and deacons. In the Armenian Church*, it is called the urar.

Urban II, Blessed (c. 1035–1099) Pope from 1088. Birth name: Odo of Lagery. He presided over the Council of Clermont* (1095) which launched the First Crusade* and the Council of Bari (1098) where he attempted an unsuccessful reconciliation of the Greek and Latin churches. Feast day: July 29 or 30.

Urban V (1309/10–1370) Pope from 1362. Birth name: Guillaume de Grimoard. Frenchman. He was the best of the Avignon* popes. In 1367 he returned to Rome* and two years later received Emperor John V Paleologus back into communion. Disregarding the warnings of St. Bridget*, who foretold his early death if he left Rome, he returned to Avignon in 1370 and died soon afterwards. His plans for a crusade against the Turks did not materialize.

Urban VI (1318–1389) Pope from 1378. Birth name: Bartolommeo Prignano. His pontificate* was marked by a series of rash actions attributed to his mental derangement. His plan to establish an

Pope Urban II Preaching the Crusades

Italian majority in the College of Cardinals* led to the French cardinals revoking his election and electing in his stead Clement VII* (Robert of Geneva) as antipope. Thus began the Great Schism* in the West. Urban had six of his cardinals tortured and five of them executed for conspiracy. Among the few acts of his reign that had spiritual relevance were his decree appointing the Holy Year* to be celebrated every 33 years and extension of the Feast of the Visitation of the Blessed Virgin Mary* to the whole church.

Urban VIII (1568–1644) Pope from 1623. Birth name: Maffeo Barberini. He was a gifted classical scholar and poet in his own right. He strenuously promoted missions by founding the Urban College of Propaganda in 1627. He approved new religious orders, such as the Visitation (1626) and St. Vincent de Paul's Lazarists* (1632). His liturgical reforms included revisions in the Breviary*, revision of the Missal* and the Pontifical*, and reduction in the number of feasts of obligation. His decrees codified the procedure for canonization*. He appointed Bernini* as the architect of St. Peter's* as well as his own tomb in the basilica*.

urbi et orbi (Lat., to the city and the world) Phrase used in papal bulls* as well as in papal blessing* pronounced from the balcony of St. Peter's*.

Urbs Beata Jerusalem Hymn of rare beauty, of unknown authorship, sung at the vespers* of church dedication. It celebrates the praises of heavenly Jerusalem.

urgeschichte (Ger., prehistory) In dialectical theology*, events that foreshadowed the Incarnation* from the perspective of later faith.

Urmarcus (Ger., original Mark) Supposed early and lost draft of Mark's Gospel.

uroro rabbo In the Syrian Church, the great stole* corresponding to the Byzantine omophorion*.

Ursinus, Zacharias (1534–1583) German reformer and theologian. His best known work is the Heidelberg Catechism* of 1562 which he composed with Caspar Olevianus* under the guiding spirit of Melanchthon*. From 1561 until 1568 he lectured on dogmatics* at the University of Heidelberg. At Neustadt he wrote *Admonitio Christiana,* a rebuttal of the Formula of Concord*.

Ursula, St. (Date unknown) Legendary martyr*, a British princess, supposedly killed with 11,000 virgins at Cologne* during the Maximian persecutions. Feast day: October 21.

Ursulines Oldest teaching order of women in the Roman Catholic Church, founded in Brescia in 1535 by St. Angela Merici*. Appoved by Paul III* in 1544, its simple vows were drawn up by Charles Borromeo* and introduced in 1572 by Gregory VIII. From the seventeenth century, Ursulines became noted for their educational work. The order spread beyond Europe into the New World and the Far East. Most houses are autonomous, but are affiliated with regional and international unions. Since the Second Vatican Council*, Ursulines leading an active life (as opposed to a contemplative life*) are free of the obligation of strict enclosure.

use In liturgiology*, a local modification of the standard Roman Rite*, such as Sarum use. All except the Mozarabic use in Toledo* and the Ambrosian use in Milan* were abolished by the Council of Trent*.

usher Person who conducts congregants to their seats in a church and also takes up the offerings during worship service.

Usuard, Martyrology of One of the most popular medieval martyrologies, compiled by Usuard (d. 875), a Benedictine monk who was commissioned by Charles the Bald. It became the basis for the Roman Martyology.

Utica, martyrs of Group of 153 early African martyrs who, according to legend, were thrown alive during the persecution of Valerian into slaking quicklime (c. 258) at Utica, 35 miles from Carthage*, and their bodies reduced to a mass of white powder. Later accounts fix their number at 300 and the place at Carthage. Feast day: August 24.

Utraquism (Lat., both) Doctrine that the laity, like the clergy, should receive the Holy Communion* in both kinds or species*, bread and wine. It was held by the moderate faction of the Hussites* who were opposed to the radical Hussites known as the Taborites*. Thus, Utraquist.

Utrecht Dutch city noted since the seventh century as an important episcopal see*. In the seventeenth century, it was an important center of Jansenism*. It contains a fourteenth-century cathedral. The transept* was built around the middle of the fifteenth century. In 1674 the nave* was destroyed by a terrible storm, and whatever remained was demolished between 1826 and 1847. The fourteenth-century tower stands today on the west side of the Cathedral Square. In 1580 Utrecht became Protestant.

Utrecht, Declaration of Old Catholic profession of faith* drawn up by an assembly of Old Catholic bishops at Utrecht* in 1889. It accepts the creeds of the ecumenical councils up to 1000, but rejects the First Vatican Council*, the dogma* of the immaculate conception*, papal infallibility*, and the Syllabus of 1864 but adheres to the theology of the Eucharist* and the real presence* without mention of propitiation* or transubstantiation*.

Vv

vacation Bible school Two-week-long instruction period held in many Protestant churches in which religious teaching is combined with summer activities.

Vaison, Council of Either of two church councils held at Vaison, France. The first was held in 442 and enacted 10 canons and the second was held in 529 and enacted 5 canons. The second dealt with matters concerning the Mass* and required regular prayers for the pope.

Valaam Monastery Celebrated Russian monastery founded by the Greek monks Sergei and German. It was sacked and burned a number of times but always rebuilt. It was in ruins until 1988 when it was returned to the Orthodox Church.

Valdes, Juan de (c. 1499–1541) Spanish reformer. He was influenced by Protestant ideas, although he remained a Catholic throughout life. His *Dialogue on Christian Doctrine* provoked the wrath of the Inquisition*, and he left for Italy where he became chamberlain* to Pope Clement VII*. Later, after Clement's death, he became spiritual adviser to Lady Giulia Gonzaga and wrote *Christian Alphabet* (1536) based on his discussions with her. Among his other works are *110 Considerations,* commentaries, and translations of parts of the Bible into Spanish. His emphasis on personal religion and disregard for ecclesiastical authority anticipated Protestant ideas. His followers, including Bernardino Ochino* and Peter Martyr Vermigli*, left the church after Valdes's death.

Valence, Council of Any of seven councils held in Valence on the Rhone River in France in 374, 585, 592, 890, 1100, 1209, and 1248.

Valentine, St. Roman priest beheaded by Claudius about 270. His connection with love is not clear. Feast day: February 14.

Valentinus (second century) Gnostic theologian and founder of the Valentinian sect. His disciples claimed that he had been taught by Theodas, a pupil of St. Paul*. He came about 136 to Rome*, where his episcopal ambitions were unfulfilled. He thereupon seceded from the church and went east. He was one of the most influential of the Gnostics, with a large following in the East and the West. His theology was constructed from ideas borrowed from Greek and pagan mythologies and cosmologies. From the Primal Ground of Being emanated 30 aeons that comprise the spiritual world or pleroma*. The offspring of Sophia*, the last of the aeons, was the demiurge* who is the Yahweh of the Old Testament and who rules the world through his archons and imprisons Gnostic spirits in their physical bodies. Christ is another of the 30 aeons who unites with the man Jesus at his conception or baptism to bring human beings the saving gnosis* or knowledge through which redemption* is effected and through which the imprisoned divine spark in believers is liberated.

Human beings are divided into three classes: the pneumatics who realize the gnosis and return to the pleroma; the psychics or Christians without gnosis, who attain a lower realm; and the non-spiritual hylics, who are doomed to perdition. Some of the writings of Valentinus or his pupils, especially the *Gospel of Truth,* have been discovered in the Coptic texts from Nag Hammadi*.

validity In sacramental theology*, one of the characteristics of a proper sacrament*, the others being fruitfulness (efficacy) and regularity. It denotes the fact that certain conditions have been fulfilled before a sacrament is performed. The three formal conditions ensuring the validity* of a sacrament are: the person ministering the sacrament is properly ordained, the liturgy used is appropriate, and the intention of the celebrant is proper.

Valignano, Alessandro (1539–1606) Jesuit missionary. He joined the Society of Jesus* in 1566 and seven years later was named superintendent of all Jesuit missions in the Far East. He consolidated the work of Francis Xavier* in India. From Macao he organized a mission into China and encouraged Matthew Ricci in his translation of the gospel into Chinese. To train native Christians, he founded colleges in Macao, Nagasaki, and Arima.

Vallumbrosan Order Contemplative order established by John Gualbert* about 1036 with a mother house* at Vallombrosa, near Florence*. He incorporated many of the elements of the Rule of Benedict'*, including poverty, strict enclosure, and perpetual silence. The order had a lay branch, the Conversi*, who did manual work. The mother house was burned in 1527, plundered in 1808, suppressed in 1866, but restored in 1849. The order has produced a number of noted writers, artists, and scientists.

Van Dyck, Anthony (1599–1641) Flemish painter. He was a disciple of Rubens* and worked for him for two years. In 1632 he became a court painter to Charles I of England by whom he was knighted.

Among his notable religious paintings is *Christ Crowned with Thorns.*

Van Eyck, Hubert and Jan (d. 1426 and d. 1441, respectively) Flemish brothers who painted the famous Ghent altarpiece in the Cathedral of St. Bavon in Ghent. It is a very large polyptych* of 12 oak panels arranged in 2 layers, the outer panels painted on both sides, with a total of 24 scenes. The panels on the inside lower tier depict the Adoration of the Lamb, while other panels show Christ enthroned between St. John the Baptist and the Virgin Mary*, the Annunciation, and other biblical scenes.

Van Til, Cornelius (1895–1987) Reformed Christian and author of *The Defense of the Faith* (1955). He was ordained in the Christian Reformed Church* in 1927 and joined Westminister Theological Seminary in 1929 and taught there until 1975. He wrote over 20 books in addition to course syllabi. He attempted to prove that all human reasoning presupposes God and thus cannot be autonomous.

varapochumn In the Armenian Rite*, the Feast of the Assumption*, also known as the Dormition* on the Sunday nearest to August 15.

Vardan Mamikonian, St. (d. 451) Armenian general and martyr*. He was the commander of the Armenian forces that fought against the Persians who attempted to extirpate Christianity from Armenia. Vardan and most of his troops fell at the Battle of Avarair in 451. Feast day: Thursday before Lent*.

Variata Edition of the Augsburg Confession* prepared by Melanchthon* in 1540. It toned down the Lutheran doctrine of the real presence* to accommodate Zwinglian and Calvinistic teachings and was therefore rejected by Lutherans. See also INVARIATA.

varkas Armenian vestment similar to an amice* worn over the shapik*.

vartabed Armenian order of clergy who are celibate priests regarded as hieromonks or doctors of the church*. They are not permitted to hear confessions but may teach and preach with authority. The order is divided into several grades. There are differences among the grades in the crosier* they carry and the philon* or cloak they wear.

vartavar (lit., the festival of roses) Armenian feast commemorating the transfiguration of Jesus.

Vatican Modern papal residence in Rome* located on the ancient Mons Vaticanus. The first papal residence was erected by Pope Symmachus* (495–514), but it did not become the principal residence of the pope until the return of the popes from Avignon* in 1377. The buildings have been extensively renovated since the fifteenth century so that little of the older building before that period remains. Sixtus IV* erected the Sistine Chapel*, Innocent VIII the Belvedere*, and Paul III* the Sala Regia. The present palace was completed by Clement VIII* and the Braccio Nuovo by Pope Pius VII* in 1821. The Vatican along with the Castel Gondolfo* and the Lateran* form part of the principality of the Vatican State. It also contains the Vatican Museum and the Vatican Library*.

Vatican Council, First The Twentieth Ecumenical Council convoked by Pius IX* and held in Rome* in 1869–1870. It was attended by over 700 delegates of whom the majority were the conservative Ultramontanes, represented by William George Ward*, Cardinal Manning, and Louis Veuillot* who wanted to shore up papal authority and support papal infallibility*. The liberal minority was represented by John Cardinal Newman* and J. J. I. von Dollinger. The assembly passed a revised constitution on faith, *Dei Filius,* deploring atheism, materialism, and pantheism*. But the most important task of the council was its approval of papal infallibility* by a vote of 533 to 2, most of the minority having abstained from voting. The definition made clear that the claim of papal infallibility was "not from the consent of the church," but it restricted the exercise of the right to those occasions when the pope speaks ex cathedra*, in the discharge of the office of pastor and doctor of all Christians, and he defines a doctrine regarding faith or morals to be held by the universal church by virtue of his supreme apostolic authority. War brought the council to a sudden end before it could deal with other aspects of ecclesiology.

Vatican Council, Second The Twenty-First Ecumenical Council convoked by Pope John XXIII* and held in Rome* from 1962 to 1965. Its immediate task was aggiornamento* or the modernization of the teaching, organization, and discipline of the church. Members of the council were assisted by several thousand perituses, or experts in theology, canon law*, and church history. The council held four sessions. The first session lasted from October 11 to December 8, 1962. Within six months of the closing of the session John XXIII died and was succeeded by Pope Paul IV. The second session lasted from September 29 to December 4, 1963. Among the important measures it enacted were a new constitution on the sacred liturgy, a decree on the Instruments of Social Communication, and the revival of the diaconate as a separate and permanent order.

The third session lasted from September 14 to November 21, 1964, and enacted the Dogmatic Constitution of the Church, the Decree on Ecumenism, and the Decree on the Eastern Catholic Churches. The pope proclaimed the Virgin Mary* to be the Mother of the Church*. The concluding session lasted from September 14 to December 8, 1965. It enacted new decrees on the bishop's pastoral office in church, appropriate renewal of the

Assembly at Vatical Council I

religious life, priestly formation, Christian education, dogmatic constitution on divine revelation*, apostolate* of the laity, religious freedom, the ministry and life of priests, missionary activities, and relationship with non-Christian religions. On the whole it enacted four constitutions, nine decrees, and three declarations.

The most enduring legacies of the council were the replacement of Latin with the vernacular in the Latin Liturgy, extension of Communion in both kinds* to the laity, opening the window of dialogue with Orthodox, Anglican, Lutheran, Methodist, and other churches, the introduction of a married diaconate, and a shift in emphasis in the church's concern toward social and political issues. The council did not heal the breach between the conservative establishment and the progressives within the Catholic Church, but it helped to define the issues clearly and helped to focus attention on the problems the church faces in an increasingly secular and godless world. It also helped to reduce the antagonism between the Catholic Church and the Orthodox and Protestant communions.

Vatican Library   See BIBLIOTECA APOSTOLICA VATICANA.

Vatican Radio   Broadcasting station founded in 1931 by Pope Pius XI*, designed by Guglielmo Marconi and supervised by him until his death in 1937. The Vatican Television Center was founded in 1983 by Pope John Paul II*.

Vaughan Williams, Ralph (1872–1958) English composer. Although not a professing Anglican, a large part of his musical output was religious music of which the most outstanding was his oratorio*, *The Holy City,* and the Christmas cantata, *Hodie.* He was the editor of *The English Hymnal* (1906, 1933), and coeditor of the *Songs of Praise* and *The Oxford Book of Carols.* Among his most popular hymns is the perennial "All Hail the Power of Jesus' Name." Another of his impressive creations was Mass in G Minor. He wrote several compositions based on *Pilgrim's Progress*,* culminating in the full-scale opera, *A Morality* (1951). He is considered the greatest single force in Protestant music in the English-speaking world in the twentieth century.

vaulting   The greatest achievement of Gothic* church architecture, the pointed arch-shape achieved by means of supporting ribs in a variety of increasingly complex configurations: rib and cross-rib, groin, hip, fan, net, palm, and star-vaulting.

veghar (Arm., hood) Distinctive hood worn by Armenian celibate clergy. The hood is a black cone pointed on top. The catholicos* of all Armenians wears a jeweled cross in front of the hood.

veil   Liturgical cloth covering various objects, as the chalice* and the ciborium*. All crucifixes, statues, and pictures are veiled during Lent* and Passiontide*.

veil, to take the   To take vows as a nun and enter a convent. In most orders, the veil of the professed sister* is black, and that of the novice*, white. In the post-Vatican Council II* era, most veils have been dropped.

velichanie   Byzantine hymn known as the Exaltation.

Velichkovsky, St. Paisy (1722–1794) Ukrainian monk and spiritual director*. In 1746 he became a monk on Mount Athos*, where his community grew so large that he transferred it to Moldova. At Dragomirna and later at Neamt, he founded a large monastery. He and his monks produced revisions and translations of the Greek and Latin Fathers, and he started a spiritual revival in the Hesychast tradition. Feast day: November 15.

velikaya ekteniya   In the Byzantine Rite*, a litany* recited by the deacon or the celebrant from the holy doors* of the iconostasis* during mattins* or orthros*.

velorio (Span., wake) Prayer service for the dead or in honor of a saint*, popular among Hispanics.

velothyron   In the Byzantine tradition, veil hung behind the holy doors* of the iconostasis* concealing the upper part of the central doors. It is drawn aside during certain parts of the liturgy.

Venantius Fortunatus (530–c. 600) Latin Christian poet and hymn writer, author of *Pange Lingua,*

Gloriosi Proelium, the Latin office hymn used at mattins* and lauds* during Passion Week*. His prose works include 11 books of *Miscellanea* and *Vita St. Martini.*

venerable 1. Anglican title for an archdeacon. 2. Roman Catholic title for a candidate for canonization* who has reached a particular stage in the process. 3. Title of honor bestowed on a person of great sanctity* and achievement, as the Venerable Bede*.

Venerable Bede, the See BEDE, ST.

veneration 1. Feeling of awe and respect excited by the dignity, sacredness, superiority, wisdom, or hallowed association of a person. 2. In traditions that use images or icons and acknowledge saints*, reverence paid to them as distinct from worship offered only to God.

Veneration of the Cross Also, Creeping to the Cross. Ceremony of the Latin Rite for Good Friday in which clergy and congregants solemnly venerate a crucifix at the entrance to the sanctuary. A similar ceremony, consisting of a solemn procession and elevation of the cross, takes place in the Eastern Church* on Holy Cross Day on September 14 and on the third Sunday in Lent*.

Veni, Creator (Lat., Come Creator) Ninth-century hymn to God the Holy Spirit* attributed to Rabanus Maurus*. It is used widely at ordinations.

Veni, Sancte Spiritus (Lat., Come Holy Spirit) Thirteenth-century hymn known as the Golden Sequence* in Catholic and Anglican worship for Whitsuntide*, attributed to Stephen Langton*.

Veni, Veni Emmanuel (Lat., O Come, O Come Emmanuel) Eighteenth-century Advent* hymn, a versification of the O-Antiphons*.

venial sin Minor or light sin (as distinguished from grave sin) that can be forgiven or remitted by penitence, fasting, almsgiving, and prayer. It does not need to be confessed before one takes Holy Communion* and does not deprive the soul of sanctifying grace*.

Venice City on the Adriatic in Italy, on the isle of Olivolo, later known as Castello. The Patriarchate of Venice was established in 1451. It contains the famous Church of San Marco*. Other churches in Venice include the Franciscan Santa Maria Glorioso for which Titian* painted an *Assumption*

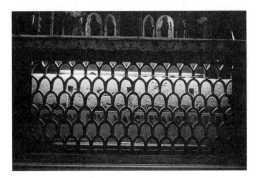

Church of San Marco

and the Dominican Sts. Giovanni e Paolo with the tombs of the Doges. It is the location of the convent of the Armenian Benedictine Congregation of the Mechitarists. The San Giorgio Maggiore, Benedictine abbey, dating from 982, was rebuilt by Andrea Palladio*, the most important architect of the sixteenth century, in 1566. After Palladio's death, the work was completed by Vincenzo Scamozzi. Baldassare Longhena added the great staircase, the abbot's lodgings, and the library in the seventeenth century.

Venite (Lat., O Come) Admonition to come into the presence of the Lord during worship service. It appears in the Latin version of Psalm 95, often used at mattins*, or *O Come, All Ye Faithful,* the majestic Latin nativity hymn attributed to John F. Wade (1751).

Venn, Henry (1796–1873) Evangelical Anglican clergyman. He served as secretary of the Church Missionary Society* (CMS) from 1841. He was one of the most influential mission statesmen in the nineteenth century. During his years with CMS eight new bishoprics* were added overseas, the number of non-British missionaries grew from 9 to 148, and 498 missionaries were sent out. He was also the author of *The Complete Duty of Man.* His father **John Venn**

(1759–1813) was a founder of the Church Missionary Society*.

venturum (Lat., what shall come) The present as influenced by a power that is yet to come.

verarkou Sleeved mantle worn over the blue cassock* of married Armenian priests.

Verbiest, Ferdinand (1623–1688) Belgian Jesuit missionary to China. A trained astronomer and mathematician, he became assistant to J. A. Schall* and later succeeded him as president of the Imperial Board of Astronomy. He was a friend and teacher of Emperor Kang Hsi. He founded in Beijing a seminary for training native priests and missionaries.

verbum visibile Visible Word of God*, definition of sacrament* by St. Augustine*.

Verdi, Giuseppe (1830–1901) Italian composer. His Roman Mass* of 1874 is one of his best librettos. His other religious music included a Pater Noster* (1880), and an aria for soprano and strings entitled "Ave Maria*," both based on Dante. His Four Sacred Pieces includes a Stabat Mater* written for a four-part chorus and orchestra.

Henry Venn

verger 1. Caretaker of a church. 2. Person who carries the verge or mace* before a dignitary or heads a procession in Anglican worship.

Veritatis Splendor Encyclical* issued by Pope John Paul II* in 1963 on Catholic ethical teachings condemning homosexuality, contraception, and artificial insemination. It reaffirmed the inviolability of human life.

Vermigli, Pietro Martire See PETER MARTYR VERMIGLI.

Vermittlungstheologie (Ger., mediation theology) School of liberal theology in nineteenth-century Germany that tried to combine traditional Protestantism* with modern historical and scientific scholarship. Among its chief representatives were J. A. W. Neander*, F. A. G. Tholuck*, I. A. Dorner*, R. Rothe, H. L. Martensen, and W. Beyschlag.

Verona City in Italy whose association with Christianity goes back to the third century when St. Euprepius became its first bishop. Its patron is St. Zeno*. An important synod* was held here in 1184. In 1818 it was made a suffragan of Venice*. Its main cathedral houses an *Assumption* by Titian*. St. Zeno Maggiore and the Dominican church St. Anastasia* are also ancient churches that go back to the twelfth and thirteenth centuries, respectively.

Verona Fathers Popular name for the Comboni Missionaries of the Heart of Jesus, a religious missionary society founded by the Blessed Daniele Comboni* in 1867. The Comboni Missionary Sisters were founded by him in 1871. Both societies work in Africa and the Americas.

Veronese (c. 1528–1588) Birth name: Paolo Cagliari. Venetian decorator. He painted numerous religious subjects, including many for the Church of San Sebastiano. His *Feast in the House of Levi* (1573) incurred the wrath of the inquisitor.

veronica Legendary handkerchief or veil with which St. Veronica* wiped Jesus' face during his passion*.

Veronica, St. Woman of Jerusalem* who, according to legend, wiped Jesus' bleeding face with a handkerchief or veil on which the image of a

St. Veronica

human face was imprinted forever. Although not included in the official list of saints, her feast day is July 12.

Verrocchio, Andrea Del (1435–1488) Italian sculptor of *David* and other works, and painter of *The Madonna and the Child, The Baptism of Christ,* and *Crucifxion with Saints.*

verse Short portion of a hymn or of a chapter of the Bible.

verset Short organ piece that replaces a verse of Gregorian Chant* in the service.

versicle Short sentence taken from the Psalms said or sung antiphonally in Christian worship with a response by the choir or congregation.

version Translation of the Bible, as the Vulgate*, Septuagint, Douai Version, Authorized or King James Version*, or the Revised Standard Version*.

Verwer, George (1938–) American founder and director of Operation Mobilization* (OM, 1962, originally Send the Light, 1958) which mobilizes thousands of young people in cross-cultural mis-

sion. He has led OM to target less-evangelized countries through literature distribution and the use of ships.

vesica piscis (Lat., bladder of fish) Mandonla,* or an upright, almond-shaped aureole* enclosing a figure, such as Christ enthroned.

vesper lights Branched candlesticks used for the office of vespers*, as distinct from eucharistic lights* or single candlesticks.

Vesperale 1. Book of prayers and music used at vespers*. 2. Cloth covering the white altar-cloth when no service is being held.

vespers Also known as lucernarium* because candles were lit during its celebration. Evening Daily Office of the Roman Catholic Church preceded by none* and followed by compline*. It is the oldest of the seven Daily Offices and, together with the lauds*, is the most important Day Office and is celebrated with great solemnity. It consists of a hymn, the reading of Psalms, a New Testament canticle*, the Magnificat* (during which the altar is censed), intercessions, the Lord's Prayer*, a collect* and concluding versicles, and a blessing. In the Orthodox Church*, where it is called hesperinos*, it is the first service of the liturgical day. It consists of singing of the Psalms, litanies, troparia and the singing of the Phos Hilanon*, scriptural readings, more litanies, prayers and troparia, and the Nunc Dimittis*. On Sundays and feast days there is a procession with incense. In the Lent* a prayer by Ephraem Syrus is recited.

vestments Traditional and distinctive dress worn by the clergy when leading worship. Vestments come in many shapes, sizes, and colors. In the Roman Catholic Church, subdeacons use tunicle*; bishops, priests, and deacons wear the alb*, surplice*, amice*, chasuble*, dalmatic*, girdle*, maniple*, and stole*; while bishops wear additional vestments, such as the mitre* and pallium*. Special prayers are recited while these vestments are put on. The shape, material, and color of these vestments are also regulated and have specific symbolic significance. In the Orthodox Church*, similar vestments are worn except for the dalmatic and the tunicle*. But they use certain vestments, such as the epigonation* and epimanikion, for which there are no equivalents in the West. From the Reformation* onwards, Protestants generally have rejected most medieval vestments, especially because of their sacerdotal and sacrificial associations. Ministers mostly wear gowns that signify their teaching office.

Choir Gown

vestry (Lat., *vestiarium*, robing room) 1. Room in or attached to a church in which the vestments and vessels used in liturgical services are kept and in which the clergy put on their robes. 2. Governing body of a parish church, since parishioners* formerly used to meet in this room to transact the business of the parish*. In the Episcopal Church in the United States and in Scotland, every parish has a vestry* consisting of the incumbent*, two wardens, and a number of vestrymen.

vetus Latina Latin translations of the Bible preceding Jerome's Vulgate*. No complete manuscripts of these translations have survived.

Veuillot, Louis (1813–1883) French Roman Catholic writer. Converted to an active Catholic faith in 1839, he became editor of *L'Universe,* the most powerful Catholic journal in France (1843–1860;

1867–1874) and a champion of Ultramontanism*. Veuillot was a formidable enemy of liberal Catholicism* and strove to restore the Catholic Church to its pre-revolution glory. He was one of the steadfast supporters of the doctrine of papal infallibility* during the First Vatican Council*.

Vexilla Regis (Lat., banner of the king) Latin hymn by Venantius Fortunatus* celebrating the mystery of Christ triumphant on the tree of the cross, sung at vespers* during the Holy Week* and on the Exaltation of the Holy Cross.

Vezeley Benedictine monastery of Sainte-Madeleine at Vezeley, France, the starting point of one of the four great pilgrim routes to Santiago de Compostela*. The original monastery, containing the alleged remains of Mary Magdalene, was founded in 860 and consecrated in 878. Later it was destroyed by the Normans. A new basilica* was built in 1096 and consecrated in 1104. In 1120, the church burned down, burying 1,000 pilgrims who were at prayer. In the same year reconstruction began and was completed by 1215. It was at Vezeley that Bernard of Clairvaux* issued the call for the Second Crusade* in 1146. In 1569 the church was plundered by the Huguenots*, and in 1789 the French Revolution dealt it a deathblow. What survived was struck by lightning in 1811. However, in the nineteenth century, Prosper Mer-

Vezeley Monastery

imee, as inspector of ancient monuments, initiated a rebuilding which was completed between 1840 and 1859.

via antiqua (Lat., the old way) In scholastic theology, theological approach of Thomas Aquinas*, Duns Scotus*, and other theologians of the High Middle Ages, as contrasted with the via moderna*, or the modern way of later theologians, such as William of Ockham* and Gabriel Biel*.

Via Crucis Way of the Cross. 1. See VIA DOLOROSA. 2. Devotion in the Roman Catholic Church commemorating the events of Christ's Passion* presented through the Stations of the Cross*.

Via Dolorosa Traditional route in Jerusalem* followed by Christ from the judgment hall of Pilate to Calvary, marked by 14 Stations of the Cross*.

Via Eminentiae (Lat., way of eminence) Theology that describes the Creator by superlatives drawn from or based on creaturely attributes, such as creatures having power but God being omnipotent.

via media (Lat., the middle way) Used in many contexts, particularly to commend moderation between two extremes. Anglicanism is often treated as a via media, originally as a form of Protestantism between Rome and the radicals, more recently between Rome and other Protestants.

via moderna (Lat., the modern way) See VIA ANTIQUA.

via negativa (Lat., the negative way) Theology that describes the Creator in terms that negate creaturely attributes, such as comparing creatures who are finite, against God who is infinite. See APOPHATIC THEOLOGY.

via positiva (Lat., the positive way) Theology that describes the Creator and the creatures in terms of qualities that they both possess, though to different degrees, such as love.

Vianney, St. Jean-Baptiste Marie (1786–1859) Popularly known as Cure d'Ars*. In 1818 he was appointed parish priest at Ars, where he gained worldwide fame through his dedication and simple life. In 1855, more than 20,000 visitors came to see him. He was canonized in 1925 and made the patron of parish priests. Feast day: August 4.

Viaticum (Lat., provision for a journey) Holy Communion* given to those in danger of immediate death.

viator (Lat., wayfarer) Christian as a wayfarer or pilgrim* in a strange land journeying home.

Viatorian Fathers Clerics of St. Viator, an order founded in 1835 by Louis Joseph Querbes in Lyons, France, to promote religious education.

vicar (Lat., *vicarius,* substitute or representative) 1. In the Anglican and other Protestant churches, parish priest, perpetual curate*, or a minor cathedral official. 2. Representative of Christ, as in vicar of Christ.

vicar apostolic 1. Church official to whom the pope delegates responsibility in a territory, generally in missionary fields, where a formal diocese* has not yet been established. 2. Titular* bishop appointed in a territory where the church has become extinct as in Turkey and North Africa or where a bishop is unable to carry out his functions, as in some Communist countries.

vicar forane In the Roman Catholic Church, clergyman with limited jurisdiction in a diocese*.

vicar general 1. Representative of a bishop, usually an archdeacon. 2. In the Church of England*, any deputy of the archbishop of Canterbury* and the archbishop of York*.

vicar of Christ Title of the Roman pontiff* used in conjunction with the title, vicar of St. Peter.

vicariate castrensi Military chaplain*.

vicarious Of or relating to an act performed on behalf of or instead of another person, so that the benefits of that act accrue to the latter. In reference to Christ's Passion*, it is often used as a synonym for substitutionary.

vicarious faith Doctrine that one might have faith* on behalf of another, as for example, parents on behalf of their children or a spouse on behalf of a mate.

victimae paschali (Lat., to the paschal victim) In the Western Church*, the Easter* sequence composed by Wipo*.

Victor I (d. 198) Pope from 189. A North African by birth, his name is associated with the Quartodeciman* controversy. He deposed Florinus for defending the Valentinian heresy and excommunicated Theodotus, the founder of Dynamic Monarchianism*.

Victoria, Tomas Luis de (1548–1611) Spanish composer. He became maestro di capella* at the German College in Rome* in 1573 and was ordained priest in 1575. Returning to Spain as chaplain* to the Dowager Empress Maria, he became maestro of the choir of the Madrid Convent, where she lived. His compositions consisting entirely of sacred music are ranked among the greatest music of the Renaissance. His liturgical music includes 20 settings of the Mass Ordinary and two masses for the dead. Unlike Palestrina, Victoria achieves clarity of structure through frequent cadences and tonal use of harmony. Justly famous is his music for the Holy Week*, including 9 lamentations, 18 responsories, and 2 passions that have been performed in the Sistine Chapel* for 300 years. He also composed 18 Magnificats*, 13 antiphons*, 8 polychoral* Psalms, and more than 32 hymns.

Victorines Canons regular* of the Abbey of St. Victor in Paris founded in 1108 by William of Champeaux, teacher of Abelard*. Although never very large, they count among their numbers some of the greatest medieval scholars and mystics, including Adam of St. Victor*, Hugh of St. Victor*, Richard of St. Victor*, and Walter of St. Victor. The abbey was secularized at the time of the French Revolution.

Victorinus Afer, Caius (Fabius) Marius (fourth century) North African philosopher and theologian. He was a teacher in Rome* when he was converted and devoted his life to Christian writing, including a treatise against the Arians and a short work on the Trinity*. Strongly Neoplatonic, he had a great influence on Augustine* and anticipated many of the latter's theological positions.

Vidi Aquam Anthem traditionally sung at Eastertide* during the sprinkling of the congregation at Mass* on Sundays.

Vieira, Antonio (1608–1697) Portuguese theologian. He entered the Society of Jesus* in 1623 and was appointed preacher of the royal chapel* in 1644. In 1652 he was sent to Brazil, where he became a champion of American Indians against Spanish exploitation. This resulted in opposition from the colonists, and he was recalled to Portugal. He was imprisoned by the Inquisition* for two years. In 1669 he went to Rome* to plead his own case as well as the cause of the New Christians, or Jews converted to Christianity. Here his fame as a preacher led Queen Christina of Sweden to invite him to be her confessor*. In 1675 he returned to Portugal and in 1681 to Brazil, where he spent the remainder of his life. From 1688 to 1691 he was vicar general* of Brazil. In his theology Vieira was a chiliast who believed in the imminent triumph of Christianity throughout the world.

Vienna Capital of Austria, site of Stephansdom, Cathedral of St. Stephen. The original church was erected between 1230 and 1260. In 1359 Rudolf II laid the foundation stone of the new Gothic cathedral. In 1439, the Steffl, the richly ornamented, slender, soaring spire* was topped out. Much of the church was destroyed during World War II but restored immediately thereafter.

Vienne, Council of Fifteenth Ecumenical Council convoked by Pope Clement V* and which met from October 16, 1311 until May 6, 1312. The council agreed to the demand of Philip IV to suppress the Templars*. The council also condemned the Beghards* or Beguines* and issued a number of canons dealing with church reform.

vigil (Lat., watch) Service of prayer and devotion the night before an ecclesiastical feast. Originally vigils were popular because of the belief that the Second Coming* would take place at night and because of the examples in Acts 12:12 and 16:25. There was also a tradition of greeting the evening with a hymn and prayer from which the Cathedral Vigil and the Paschal candle* seem to have developed. The custom of spending the whole night in prayer seems to have been common in Egyptian and Western monasteries, and has gained popularity among many Evangelical Christian communities. In the Eastern Church*, vigil services consisting of vespers*, apodeipnon*, midnight office, and orthros* are celebrated with great solemnity and may last up to 15 hours. A shorter all-night vigil may be held on Saturday evenings.

vigil light Light shining perpetually before a shrine or statue.

Vigilius (d. 555) Pope from 537. He was involved in the Three Chapters controversy* in which he vacillated, and was excommunicated by a council at Carthage*. His loyalty to Chalcedon was subjected to pressures he could not resist.

Vignola (1507–1573) Birth name: Giacomo Barocchio or Barozzi. Italian architect. He wrote a book on the five orders of architecture. After the death of Michelangelo* he was named architect of St. Peter's*, and he also designed the Escorial* in Spain.

Vilmar, August Friedrich Christian (1800–1868) German Lutheran theologian. He broke with the liberal rationalism of his youth to become a leader of the political and theological conservatives. In 1855 he was named to the chair of theology at Marburg. His principal theological work was *Die Theologie der Tatschen wider die Theologie der Rhetorik* (1856) in which he identified the institutional church with the body of Christ* and described it as a firewall against the encroachments of secularism*. Many of his works appeared posthumously, including *Die Augsburgische Konfession* (1870), *Die Lehre vom geistlichen Amt* (1870), *Christliche Kirchenzucht* (1872), *Pastoraltheologie* (1872), *Dogmatik* (1874), *Theologische Moral* (1871), *Collegium Biblicum* (6 vols., 1879–1883), and *Predigten und Geistliche Reden* (1876).

vimpa Veil worn over the shoulders and hands by

an attendant who holds the crosier* at episcopal functions.

Vincent de Paul (1581–1660) Founder of the Lazarists* and the Sisters of Charity. Ordained priest in 1660, he was captured by the Barbary pirates and was for two years a slave in Tunisia. Following his conversion, he served as almoner*, pastor, and chaplain*. In 1617 he heeded a call* to serve the poor and founded the Confraternity of Charity. As chaplain of the galleys he did much to help the prisoners. In 1622 St. Francis de Sales gave him charge of the Visitation Order* in Paris. In 1625 he founded the Congregation of the Mission, popularly known as Lazarists* or Vincentians. The first of the seminaries that he founded grew out of the College des Bons-Enfants, a school for young boys. In 1633 he cofounded with St. Louise de Marillac the Sisters of Charity, a congregation of women who were not enclosed and who took no final vows. In 1638 he established a home for foundlings. During the Wars of the Fronde, he organized relief work. Canonized in 1737, he was named in 1885 the patron of works of charity. In 1833 the Society of Vincent de Paul* was founded in his honor. Feast day: September 27.

Vincent Ferrer, St. (1350–1413) Dominican preacher, known as the "Angel of Judgment." He entered the Order of Preachers* in 1368 and in 1379 became prior* at Valencia. Here he wrote his best known work, *De Vita Spirituali*. He worked hard to end the Great Schism*. He was canonized in 1455. Feast day: April 5.

Vincent of Beauvais (c. 1194–1264) French Dominican encyclopedist. His main work, *Speculum Maius,* consisted of 80 books in three sections, *Speculum Naturale, Speculum Doctrinale,* and *Speculum Historiale.* It was the most complete and extensive encyclopedia produced in the Middle Ages. The cost of the encyclopedia was underwritten by Louis IX.

Vincentian Canon Test of religious orthodoxy* laid down by Vincent of Lerins, a monk of Lerins*, Gaul, in the fifth century. In his *Commonitorium* he states that what was Catholic was *quod ubique, quod semper, quod ab omnibus creditum est* (what has been believed everywhere always, and by all), a threefold test of universality, antiquity, and consent. He held that in relation to Scripture the role of tradition was chiefly as a guide to interpretation.

vincible ignorance The opposite of invincible ignorance*. Ignorance caused by partial knowledge or neglect in acquiring information necessary to avoid transgressions.

Vinet, Alexandre Rudolph (1797–1847) Swiss Reformed theologian and historian, known as the "Schleiermacher of French Protestantism." He taught at Basel and at Lausanne. He was an ardent defender of freedom of religion and separation of church and state* and advocated a personal religion without dogma*. He placed great importance on a good conscience and right conduct. In 1845 he took a leading part in the founding of the Free Church in the Canton of Vaud. His principal works include *Etudes sur Blaise Pascal* (1848), *Discours sur Quelques Sujets Religieux* (1831, 1841), and *Essai sur la Manifestation de Convictions Religieuses* (1842).

Vineyard Christian Fellowship Group of more than 250 churches led by John Wimber* until his death in 1996. The movement began as a home fellowship in Anaheim, California, and later became a church in association with Chuck Smith's Calvary Chapel*. In 1983 it joined a group of six churches called Vineyards, led by Kenn Gulliksen. The Vineyard Christian Fellowship is a full Pentecostal church with heavy emphasis on the gifts of the Spirit*.

Vingren, Adolf Gunnar (1879–1933) Swedish Pentecostal missionary and a founder of the Assemblies of God* in Brazil. Originally Baptist when he arrived in Brazil in 1910, he received the baptism of the Holy Spirit* and left with 18 others to form a small Pentecostal congregation. Between 1930 and 1931 they went south and founded large congregations in Rio de Janeiro, Sao Paulo, Porto Alegre, and other places.

Virgen de Pilar (Span., Virgin of the Pillar) Statue of Mary and the Christ child atop a six-foot pillar in the Church of the Virgin of the Pillar in Zaragoza, Spain. According to tradition, the statue was miraculously given to St. James* the apostle.

Virgilius of Salzburg, St. (c. 700–784) "Apostle of Carinthia." Irish monk considered one of the most learned men of his age. He served as abbot of the monastery of Aghaboe. In 743 he went to the court of Pepin, who sent him to Bavaria as bishop of Salzburg*, where he had conflicts with Archbishop Boniface* who tried to have him branded as a heretic. By 772 he had completed the conversion of the Alpine Slavs, and in 774 he dedicated the first cathedral at Salzburg and established a famous scriptorium* there. He was canonized in 1233. Feast day: November 27.

Virgin Birth More precisely, Virgin Conception. Doctrine that Jesus was conceived supernaturally by the power of the Holy Spirit* upon the Virgin Mary* without a human father (Matt. 1:18; Luke 1:35). It has been a consistent doctrine of orthodox theology, and its denial is one of the key tests of heresy. Belief in the Virgin Birth is a corollary of the Incarnation* and of belief in the divinity of Christ. It is also taught in the Apostles' Creed* and the Nicene Creed* and the Reformation Confessions.

Virgin Mary Theotokos*, Mother of God; Christotokos*, Mother of Christ. In the New Testament she figures in the birth stories of Jesus Christ in Matthew 1–2 and Luke 1–2. She remains in the background during Jesus' public ministry, but she reappears at the foot of the cross (John 19:25) and in the Upper Room at Jerusalem* (Acts 1:14). A number of Roman Catholic doctrines relate to her: perpetual virginity, asserted in the apocryphal *Book of James* and accepted by Church Fathers* such as Clement of Alexandria*, Irenaeus*, and Athanasius*; Bodily Assumption of Mary, formulated first by Gregory of Tours*; and Immaculate Conception of the Blessed Virgin Mary*, formulated by Eadmer* and Duns Scotus* and upheld by the Franciscans* and the Jesuits*.

In the Roman Catholic Church, she is called the "Queen of Heaven*" and "Fountain of Grace." There are continuing efforts to secure a papal declaration of Mary as the mediatrix of all graces and coredemptrix*, a description popularized by

St. Alphonsus Liguori*. The mariology* of the Orthodox Church is similar to that of the Roman Catholic Church, but it denies the immaculate conception* of the Virgin Mary* and does not dogmatically subscribe to her bodily assumption. Her veneration* is ranked as hyperdulia*, below that of latria* due to God and above that of dulia*, due to the saints. Belief in the efficacy of her intercession is universal outside the Protes-

Virgin of the Don

tant churches and dates from the third or fourth centuries. Liturgical devotions in the Western Church* include the Little Office of Our Lady* as well as the Saturday Mass* and Office. Popular piety is expressed in Hail Mary*, Rosary*, Angelus*, May and October devotions*, and pilgrimages* to Lourdes*, Fatima*, and other places where her apparitions have been recorded.

In the Orthodox Church, Marian* devotion is expressed in the Acathistus hymn and short prayers known as Theotokia*. Feasts in her honor include Feast of the Assumption* on August 15, Immaculate Conception on December 8, Annunciation of the Lord on March 25, Presentation of Christ* on February 2, Visitation on July 2 or May 31, Solemnity of Holy Mary, the Mother of God on January 1, Seven Sorrows of the Blessed Virgin Mary* on September 15, Presentation of St. Mary in the Temple on November 21, Dedication of the Basilica of St. Mary on August 5, and Our Lady of Mount Carmel on July 16. A number of religious orders are dedicated to her, including the Ecumenical Society of the Blessed Virgin Mary*, Loreto, and Walsingham*.

The earliest recorded apparition of the Virgin Mary* is that of St. Gregory the Illuminator* in about 270. Modern apparitions include those of Lourdes in France, Fatima* in Portugal, La Salette* in the Alps near Grenoble (Virgin of the Alps, 1846), Knock* in Ireland (1879), Beauraing* (1932–1933) and Banneux (1933) in Belgium, and Medjugorje* in Yugoslavia (1981). All the apparitions, except that in Knock, were to children.

virginity, perpetual Doctrine, first developed by Origen*, that the mother of Jesus, remained a virgin throughout her life and had no other children other than Jesus.

Virgo inter virgines (Lat., Virgin among virgins) Devotional image showing Virgin and Child seated among a group of female virgin saints: Agatha*, Agnes, Catherine*, Dorothy*, Lucy*, and others, often in a garden setting.

Virgo Inter Virgines

virtualism Word used, not altogether happily, to express the doctrine that the virtue or power of Christ's body and blood is received through the Holy Communion*, although the physical elements* of bread and wine remain unchanged.

visible church The church as a visible society of professing Christians as distinct from the invisible church, a spiritual community of believers whose membership is known only to God.

visica 1. Oval-shaped border for ecclesiastical seals. 2. Aureole.

visitation 1. Periodic ecclesiastical inspections of the temporal and spiritual affairs of a local church or a diocese*. 2. Divine blessing bestowed or punishment inflicted on a person. 3. The Virgin Mary's visit to Elizabeth before the birth of St. John the Baptist. 4. Catholic feast commemorating the Virgin Mary's visit to Elizabeth, observed on July 2 and known as the Visitation of Our Lady*.

Visitation of Our Lady See VISITATION, NO. 4.

Visitation Order Also, Visitandines. Order of female contemplatives founded in 1610 by St. Francis de Sales and St. Jane Frances de Chantal*. Originally, it had simple vows. Only the novices* were enclosed, while the sisters* went out on works of mercy*. But this feature was not included in the constitution approved by Pope Urban VIII* in 1626. Under the new constitution in 1987, each house is under the jurisdiction of the diocesan bishop. The house at Annecy is the mother house*.

Visser't Hooft, Willem Adolf (1900–1985) Dutch ecumenical leader. He was successively general secretary of the World Alliance of the YMCA, general secretary of the World Student Christian Federation*, and general secretary of the World Council of Churches* (1948–1966). He was one of the foremost ecumenical statesmen of modern times. He was the author of *None Other Gods* (1937) and other books.

Willem A. Visser't Hooft

Vitalian (d. 672) Pope from 657. His pontificate* coincided with the Monothelite controversy, but he maintained good relations with the Eastern Church* and with the Eastern emperor Constans II.

vitandi (Lat., persons to be avoided) Excommunicated persons with whom members of the church are debarred from having any intercourse or communication. Compare tolerati*.

Vitoria, Francisco de (c. 1483–1546) Spanish Dominican theologian and philosopher. He taught in Paris, Valladolid, and Salamanca*. In his chief works, *De Indis, De Jure Belli,* and *De Potestate Civili,* he pioneered ideas, later developed by Francisco de Suarez* and Hugo Grotius*, which form the basis of international law. He also developed the theory of the just war* and criticized the disregard of justice in the Spanish treatment of Indians in the New World.

Vitus, St. (c. fourth century) South Italian martyr* who was killed probably during the Diocletian persecution*. He is invoked against sudden death, hydrophobia, and the convulsive disorder known as chorea or St. Vitus's Dance. He is one of the 14 auxiliary saints*. Feast day: June 15.

Vivaldi, Antonio (1675–1741) Italian composer. His numerous sacred works include seven masses, Psalms, hymns, antiphons*, motets*, and a Magnificat*. His oratorios include *L'Adorazione delli tre re Magi* (1722).

Vladimir City in northeastern Russia, a metropolitan see* by 1300. It has two outstanding twelfth-century churches, Cathedral of the Dormition and St. Dimitri.

Vladimir, Our Lady of Holiest Russian icon, the Palladium of Vladimir and, from 1315, of Moscow*, now in the Tretyakov Museum. It is a glykophilousa* Madonna* type.

Vladimir, St. (956–1015) Prince of Kiev* responsible for the Christianization of Russia. He came to power about 980. Although his grandmother, St. Olga*, was a Christian, he investigated all religions before adopting Eastern Orthodoxy around 988. Two years later he proclaimed Christianity as the faith of his realm, ordered all his subjects to be baptized, and erected many churches and monasteries. He was canonized by the Russian Church as equal to the apostles. Feast day: July 15.

Vladimir's Baptism

vladyka Term of respect in addressing Slavonic bishops.

vocation 1. Call* of God to the people of God* for a life of faith, obedience, and service. 2. Luther's doctrine that all Christians, not just priests, have a divine calling*.

Voetius, Gisbertus (1589–1676) Dutch Reformed* theologian and the first Protestant to attempt a comprehensive theology of mission. His ideas on mission were spelled out in *Selectae Disputationes Theologicae* (5 vols., 1648–1669) and in *Politica Ecclesiastica* (3 vols., 1663–1676). He emphasized that only apostles and assemblies, such as synods, had the right to send out missions, not parachurch* groups.

voghjouyn (Arm., greeting) Kiss of peace* in the Armenian Liturgy. The standard greeting is "Christ has been revealed among us," and the response is "Blessed is the revelation of Christ."

Volotovo Pole The Dormition Church at Volotovo Pole near Novgorod*, built in 1352. It was completely destroyed during World War II.

Volto Santo (Ital., Holy Face) Representation of the face of Christ, showing him standing against the cross, rather than hanging from it, clad in ankle-length tunic, or collobium.

voluntary Organ piece composed or improvised for the service of worship which it generally introduces or follows.

Volunteers of America Evangelical social welfare organization founded in 1896 at New York City, by Ballington Booth*, son of Salvation Army* founder, William Booth*. It retains the quasi-military structure of the Salvation Army and holds nondenominational Protestant services and Bible classes, distributes Christian literature, comforts the aged in hospitals, and serves prisoners through the Volunteer Prisoners League.

von Hugel, Baron Friedrich (1852–1925) Roman Catholic liberal theologian. Born in Florence*, he lived most of his life in England (1876–1925). He became a Roman Catholic after a religious crisis in Vienna*. Being a keen student of science, philosophy, and history, he gravitated to liberal Catholicism* and became friends with some of the most liberal Catholic modernists, such as Alfred Loisy* and George Tyrrell*. In 1904 he founded the London Society for the Study of Religion and during the next 17 years wrote a number of studies on religion, including *The Mystical Element of Religion as Studied in St. Catherine of Genoa and her Friends* (1908), *Eternal Life* (1912), *Essays and Addresses on the Philosophy of Religion* (1921), and *The Reality of God* (published posthumously, 1931). "The Baron," as he was called, was very influential in religious circles within and without the Roman Catholic Church. He contributed seminal ideas to religious thinking on the relationship of Christianity to history, culture, and time (eschatology*). He saw the institutional, intellectual, and mystical branches of religion forming an integral whole.

Vondel, Joost Van Den (1587–1679) Dutch Catholic poet and dramatist, called "the Dutch Shakespeare.* The first of his biblical dramas was *Jerusalem Destroyed* (1619). It was followed by *St. Ursula* (1639), *Brothers, The Sons of Saul* (1639), *Joseph in Dothan* (1640), *Joseph in Egypt* (1640), *Peter and Paul* (1641), *Solomon* (1648), *Lucifer* (1654), *Jephtha* (1659), *King David in Exile* (1660), *King David Restored* (1660), *Samson* (1660), *Adam in Exile* (1664), and *Noah* (1667). His own religious views changed from Calvinism* to Arminianism* to Roman Catholicism*. In 1641 he joined the Roman Catholic Church and wrote a number of poems with a Catholic theme: *Mysteries of the Altar* (1645), *John the Evangelist* (1662), *The Glory of the Church* (1663), and the tragedy, *Mary Stuart* (1646).

Vos, Geerhardus (1862–1949) Presbyterian theologian and author. Born in the Netherlands, he immigrated to the United States. In 1893 he became the first professor of biblical theology at Princeton and taught there until his retirement in 1932. As a conservative Reformed* scholar, he was one of the first to expound the progressive character of God's special and redemptive revelation*. He interpreted the Bible as an ongoing history of redemptive acts culminating in the Incarnation*. Vos's contributions to biblical studies included *Biblical Theology* (1948), *The Teaching of Jesus Concerning the Kingdom of God and the Church* (1903), and *Pauline Eschatology* (1930).

vosdukh In the Byzantine Rite*, the aer* or third veil covering both the paten* and the chalice*.

votary A person consecrated by a vow.

votive Dedicated to the honor of God or in fulfillment of a vow made to God.

votive candle Burning candle, usually set in a glass container, placed before a statue or an icon*.

votive masses Fifteen masses in the Roman Missal, including those of the Trinity*, the Holy Spirit*, the Blessed Sacrament*, the Virgin Mary*, angels, St. Joseph*, the apostles, St. Peter* and St. Paul*, and all saints*. Forty-six masses for various occasions are designed to encourage popular piety and may be said at the discretion of the celebrant on any day on which there is no feast or obligatory memoria*. Ritual masses are designed for particular needs, such as marriage.

votive offering Offering of gratitude or devotion to God or a saint*.

votum Apostolic blessing* from Philippians 4:7 said by the minister at the conclusion of a sermon.

vow Solemn voluntary promise made to a deity not actually required as a duty, but made in expectation of a blessing or a favor or in discharge of a commitment or obligation. The most common vows outside a monastic profession are those to go on a pilgrimage*, vows of chastity*, vows dedicating property, or in obedient surrender of one's life to God's service. There is a distinction in canon law* between simple and solemn vows and between temporary and perpetual vows.

vows of religion Promises by a member of a Catholic religious order requiring poverty, chastity*, and obedience. Some orders require a fourth vow.

Vulgate, the The ancient Latin version of the Bible based on the work of St. Jerome* declared by the Council of Trent* in 1546 as the only authentic Latin text of the Scriptures. It was commissioned in 382 by Pope Damasus. Jerome's translation did not meet with acceptance at first, but it was copied, edited, and corrected throughout the Middle Ages, leading to further transcriptional errors and contamination. The oldest known manuscript containing the whole Vulgate is the Codex Amiatinus*. After the invention of printing, a number of printed editions followed, beginning with the famous Mazarin or Gutenberg Bible* of 1456. A revised text was issued in 1592 by Clement

St. Jerome

VIII* with some 3,000 corrections. Known as the Clementine Edition*, it was approved as the authorized edition and its text was declared unalterable. In 1908 a new commission, headed by Aidan Gasquet, was appointed by Pope Pius X* to produce a new edition under the auspices of the Benedictine abbey of St. Jerome in Rome*.

Ww

Wace, Henry (1836–1924) English scholar and dean of Canterbury*. Ordained in 1861, he held a number of ecclesiastical positions, including principal of King's College and royal chaplain* before being named dean of Canterbury in 1903. He is best known for his collaboration with William Smith in the monumental *Dictionary of Christian Biography* (4 vols., 1880–1886) and with Philip Schaff* in the second series of *Nicene and Post-Nicene Fathers* (14 vols., 1890–1900). He was a strong Evangelical.

wafer Cracker-like disc used instead of bread in the Eucharist* in many churches.

Wagner, C. Peter (1930–) Missionary and authority on church growth. Ordained in 1955, Wagner served many years as a missionary in Latin America before joining the Fuller Theological Seminary* in 1971 as professor of world mission and later as Donald A. McGavran professor of church growth. He also designed and taught, with John Wimber*, the course on signs and wonders and popularized the third wave* concept in Pentecostal studies. Wagner has been a founding member of the Lausanne Committee for World Evangelization and has coedited the first three *Unreached Peoples* annuals. In 1985 he became the founding president of the North American Society for Church Growth.

Walafrid Strabo (c. 808–849) "Walafrid the Squinter." Poet and biblical exegate. He was the abbot of Reichenau* (839–849). His literary works include poems, exegetical writings, lives of saints* in verse and prose, and sermons.

Walburga/Walpurga, St. (c. 710–779) Sister of St. Willibald and St. Wynnebald and abbess of Heidenheim. On St. Wynnebald's death, she took over the direction of his monastery at Heidenheim. Her feast day falls on February 25, but is popularly believed to be on May 1, thus explaining its name as Walpurgis Night, an old pagan feast commemorating the beginning of summer.

Waldenses Also, Vaudois; Waldensians. Several possibly interrelated groups, all tracing their origin to Peter Waldo* or Valdes of the twelfth century. Before the twelfth century, they were known as the First Reformation. At first Waldo was approved by the Roman Catholic Church as an itinerant preacher. But when he broke the church's ban on unofficial preaching, the Council of Verona in 1184 condemned and excommunicated him and expelled him from Lyons, and included his followers among the Cathars, Humiliati*, and others as heretics. The Albigensian-Waldensian crusade in 1210 drove them out of their major strongholds. Because most of Waldenses at this time had adopted voluntary poverty, they were known as "the Poor Men of Lyons."

The marks of the Waldensian Church were emphases on the Sermon on the Mount and the gospel; a rigorous asceticism*; a Donatist aversion to receiving communion from corrupt clergy; belief in visions, prophecies, spirit-possession and Chiliasm*; aversion to images and episcopal hierarchy*; and a concern for social renewal. After the death of Waldo, the movement was split between the Poor Lombards and the Poor Lyonnais, and one splinter group returned to the Catholic fold. In the thirteenth century, the Waldenses spread beyond France into the Holy Roman Empire, where their clergy were known as the Barbes and their followers as friends.

Their common beliefs included distrust of Roman Catholic priests, and doubts regarding prayers for the dead and purgatory*. Some Waldenses continued to distrust the church's rites but nevertheless continued to receive the sacraments* and to meet and travel in secret to avoid persecution. By the mid-fifteenth century the Waldenses were able to establish contacts with the Hussites* in Bohemia, then in revolt against Rome*. They also began to take an interest in the emerging Protestant Reformation*, but not all Protestant doctrines received the approval of the Waldenses. However, in course of time the Waldenses lost their separate identity and were absorbed by the Protestant denominations. The only exception is in the Alpine Valleys in Piedmont-Savoy in Italy, where they continue to flourish as an independent Reformed Church.

Its liberties are guaranteed by the Albertine Statute of Emancipation in 1848. The church is headed by a moderator* elected for a seven-year term, an executive board called Tavola, and an annual synod*. Although small, it supports missions, schools, orphanages, hospitals, homes for the aged, and a publishing house.

Waldenstrom, Paul Peter (1838–1917) Swedish theologian and churchman. Ordained in 1864, he led a revival emphasizing a salvation* that came from a personal commitment to Christ. He resigned from the national church in 1882 and took over the leadership of the National Evangelical Association, founded in 1856. In 1878 he organized the Swedish Mission Covenant based on Congregational* principles. In 1905 he took over the direction of the Swedish Mission Society. His devotional books are widely read.

Waldo, Peter (c. 1140–1217) Also, Valdes. Wealthy merchant of Lyons, France, who gave away all his possessions to become an itinerant preacher proclaiming the gospel. Forbidden to preach without ecclesiastical permission, he nevertheless continued to preach. In 1180 he subscribed to a profession of Catholic belief, but shortly thereafter he ignored the church's ban on unofficial preaching and was condemned, excommunicated, and expelled from Lyons. See also WALDENSES.

Wallace, Lewis (1827–1905) American lawyer, Civil War general, and writer, noted for his novel *Ben Hur*, a novel of Rome under Nero.

Wallin, Johan Olaf (1779–1839) Archbishop of Sweden and prolific hymn writer. As a member of the commission to revise the Swedish hymnbook, he contributed over 100 original hymns and translated and adapted many more. Among his best known hymns is "The Angel of Death."

Walsh, James Anthony (1867–1936) Cofounder of the Maryknoll Priests and Brothers. Ordained in 1892, he became a tireless speaker for missions and founded the Catholic Foreign Mission Bureau to stimulate vocations. In 1906 he teamed with Mary Josephine Rogers to launch *Field Afar*, an illustrated missionary magazine that later became the official organ of Maryknoll. In 1910 Walsh met with Thomas Frederick Price, and they worked out a plan to establish a foreign mission seminary. The plan was approved by the American hierarchy* in 1911, and it became a reality when the Propaganda Fide approved in 1912 the plan to start the Catholic Foreign Mission Society of America* and to open a seminary in Maryknoll*, near Ossining, New York. The first Maryknoll missionaries left for China in 1929. In 1920 Walsh and Rogers founded the Foreign Mission Sisters of St. Dominic*, known as the Maryknoll Sisters.

Walsingham Ancient English shrine and place of pilgrimage*, known as the "English Loreto." It is a replica of the Holy House of Nazareth founded in 1061 by Richeldis de Faverches, a local noblewoman who received a vision of the Virgin Mary* and the command to erect the building. Numerous miracles were recorded here until it was destroyed in 1538. It was revived in 1922 with Anglican, Roman Catholic, and Orthodox chapels attached to the shrine.

Walther, Carl Ferdinand (1811–1887) American Lutheran theologian. Ordained in 1837, he was influenced by Pietism* and joined the *Erweckungsbewegung,* the Lutheran Confessional movement. He joined Pastor Martin Stephan in emigrating to the United States. He took an active role in deposing Stephan for his autocratic tendencies and moral turpitude. In 1849 he became professor of theology at Concordia Seminary and later its president. He was the first president of the Evangelical Lutheran Synod of Missouri, Ohio, and other states (Lutheran Church-Missouri Synod) and the first president of the Evangelical Lutheran Syndical Conference of North America, founded in 1872, a federation of confessional* churches. He was an outstanding preacher whose published sermons filled 14 volumes. He wrote extensively on law and the gospel and on pastoral theology*.

Walvoord, John F. (1910–) Presbyterian author and pastor. He was president of Dallas Theological Seminary from 1952 to 1986 and the leader of dispensationalist theologians. He is the author of over 20 books and served on the committee of the New Scofield Reference Bible.

wandering Jew Medieval legend recounted by Matthew Paris* of a servant of Pilate named Cartaphilius who gave Jesus a blow when he was led out of the palace for crucifixion. In a later story he was a cobbler, named Ahasuerus, who refused Jesus permission to sit down and rest and who taunted Jesus Christ on his way to the cross. Both legends agree on the sentence passed by Jesus on the offender, "Thou shall wander on the earth till I return." He is the subject of a number of novels, such as those by Eugene Sue, George Croly, A. W. Schlegel, and Edgar Quinet.

wangel In the Ethiopian Rite, the liturgical Gospel.

war, just Theory of war which seeks to define when and how war should be waged by Christian rulers and their armies. It was first formulated by Augustine* and later developed by Aquinas*. According to the theory, a just war can be undertaken only if three conditions are met: (1) It is defensive and is waged for the common good and in defense of the peace of the realm. (2) It is charita-

ble and waged in a spirit of benevolence and magnanimity toward the vanquished. (3) It is waged for a lawful purpose or goal.

waraguir In the Armenian tradition, two curtains in front of the altar that conceal the altar when drawn.

Ward, Mary (1585–1645) English founder in 1609 of the Institute of the Blessed Virgin Mary* organized on Jesuit lines, subject directly to the pope. The institute did not receive papal approval and was suppressed in 1631. Subsequently, she secured the approval of Pope Urban VIII*, and it survives in three branches.

Ward, William (1769–1823) Associate of William Carey*. He reached India in 1800 and for the next 23 years proved an indispensable member of the Serampore Trio* as a practical administrator, printing press manager, and counselor.

warda Collection of Assyrian hymns sung after the Gospel or during the distribution of the Holy Communion*.

Ware, Timothy Kallistos (1934–) Greek Orthodox bishop and Oxford University lecturer in Eastern Orthodox* studies. In 1966 he became a monk under the monastic name of Kallistos and was ordained priest in the same year. In 1982 he was ordained titular bishop of Dioclea. He is widely respected as a leading authority on the Eastern Orthodox Church* on which he has written extensively, including *The Orthodox Church* (1963) and *The Orthodox Way* (1979).

Warfield, Benjamin Breckinridge (1851–1921) American Presbyterian scholar. He served as professor in Western Theological Seminary in Allegheny and at Princeton Theological Seminary. An accomplished linguist, he was an authority on patristics* and New Testament criticism* and also a strict Calvinist who upheld the Westminster Confession*. His principal works include *An Introduction to the Textual Criticism of the New Testament, The Lord of Glory, The Plan of Salvation, The Acts and Pastoral Epistles,* and *Counterfeit Miracles,* as well as numerous important extended essays, including one on "Inspiration"

(1881). He was the ablest conservative theologian of his age.

B. B. Warfield

Warneck, Gustav Adolf (1834–1910) German Protestant missiologist. In 1874 he founded *Allgemeine Missionszeitschift*, the oldest German missiological journal, and in 1879 began sponsoring annual missions conferences. In 1885 he helped form the German Protestant Missions Committee and served as its secretary until 1901. From 1896 to 1908 he occupied the first university chair in missiology at Halle. His writings inspired the Edinburgh Conference* of 1910 and the formation of the International Missionary Council* in 1921. His writings on missiology* fill five volumes of his *Evangelische Missionslehre* (1892–1903). His major works include *Modern Missions and Culture: Their Mutual Relations* (1879) and *Outline of a History of Protestant Missions from the Reformation to the Present Times* (1882). His son, **Johannes Warneck** (1867–1944), was a missionary in Indonesia, working among the Batak people in Sumatra.

Warner, Anna Bartlett (1827–1915) Hymn writer. She is the author of *Hymns of the Church Militant* (1858) and *Wayfaring Hymns, Original and Translated* (1869). Among her best-loved songs are "Jesus Loves Me," "We Would See Jesus," "For the Shadows Lengthen," and "One More Day's Work for Jesus."

Washington Cathedral The Cathedral Church of St. Peter and St. Paul, Washington, D.C., known as the National Cathedral. It is the seat of the Episcopal bishop of Washington. The diocese* was founded in 1893 and the foundation stone laid in 1907 and it was completed in 1990. It is a cruciform* building in fourteenth-century Gothic* style with a central tower 301-feet high and two west towers each 235-feet high.

Watch Tower Bible and Tract Society See JEHOVAH'S WITNESSES.

watch-night service Service held on New Year's eve as a preparation for the New Year, especially as an alternative to the wild revels associated with secular celebrations.

water-buffalo theology Theology conveyed in simple terms understandable to local cultures. Term devised by Japanese theologian Kosuke Koyama (b. 1929).

Watts, Isaac (1674–1748) Hymn writer. He served as pastor of a nonconformist church in London from 1702 until his death. He is now best remembered for his hymns which first appeared in *Hymns and Spiritual Songs* in 1707. Earlier he had published *Horae Lyricae* (1706) followed by *Divine Songs for Children* in 1715 and *The Psalms of David Imitated in the Language of the New Testament* in 1719. Among his most memorable hymns are "When I Survey the Wondrous Cross," "O God, Our Help in Ages Past," "Joy to the World," "Jesus Shall Reign," and "There Is a Land of Pure Delight."

Wattson, Paul James Francis (1863–1940) Ecumenist and founder of the Society of the Atonement. After ordination as an Episcopal priest, he founded in 1898 the Society of the Atonement at Graymoor, New York, to work toward unity between Protestant churches and the Roman Catholic Church. In 1903 he began publication of *The Lamp* and in 1909 inaugurated a period of prayer called Church Unity Octave. The Graymoor Community was received corporately into the Roman Catholic Church in 1909, and Wattson was reordained a Catholic priest in 1910.

Way of the Pilgrim Nineteenth-century Russian story of a wandering pilgrim* who recited the Jesus Prayer* and lived the life of a holy fool. The manuscript was found on Mount Athos* by the abbot of a monastery in Kazan.

Way, The Early name for Christianity (see Acts 9:2).

WCC World Council of Churches*.

Wearmouth and Jarrow Twin Benedictine abbeys between the Tyne and the Wear in Northeast England—St. Peter at Wearmouth founded in 674 and St. Paul at Jarrow founded in 682—both founded by Benedict Biscop*. It soon became one of the great centers of Christian learning, and the celebrated library at Jarrow contained a vast collection of manuscripts. The Codex Amiatinus* was written at Jarrow in the seventh century. See BEDE, ST.

WEC World Evangelization Crusade*.

Weddase Amlak (Ge'ez, Praise to God) Prayer book in the Ethiopian Church.

Weddase Maryam (Ge'ez, Praise of Mary) Collection of seven prayers, one for each day of the week, in honor of the Virgin Mary*.

wegheret In the Ethiopian tradition, a linen collar worn over the shoulders of a monastic superior*.

Weigel, Gustave (1906–1964) American Jesuit theologian and ecumenist. He taught at the Catholic University in Santago de Chile and Woodstock College in Maryland. From 1954 he was at the forefront of the Roman Catholic renewal movement in the United States. He helped to prepare Vatican Council II's* Decree on Ecumenism.

Weil, Simone (1909–1943) French essayist and mystic. Of Jewish birth, she espoused Christianity, although she was never baptized. Her many books include *Waiting for God, The Need for Roots,* and *Gravity and Grace.*

Weingarten Monastery in Weingarten, Germany, originally founded in 920 by the Guelf Count Heinrich in Altdorf, north of Lake Constance. Since 1090, the monastery is the repository of a relic* called the Precious Blood of Christ. The building of a new basilica* began in 1124, but it was destroyed by fire in 1215. In its place was built the Church of St. Martin and St. Oswald between 1715 and 1724. It was the largest Baroque church in Germany with a 384-foot nave* and 141-foot transept*.

Weiss, Johannes (1863–1914) German Protestant New Testament critic. Son of **Bernhard Weiss** (1827–1918), the conservative theologian, he taught at Gottingen, Marburg, and Heidelberg where he represented the comparative religion approach to the study of the Bible. His most influential book was *Jesus' Proclamation of the Kingdom of God* (1892), offering an eschatological interpretation of the message of the New Testament. It marked the end of the older liberal school which had limited the New Testament to a system of ethics or inward spiritual experience. He later expounded the principle of form criticism* which was later developed by Rudolf Bultmann*. His monumental study of early Christian history and literature, *Das Urchristentum,* was published posthumously.

Wells One of the largest and most magnificent cathedrals in England in Wells, built in the twelfth century. The magnificent west front has 293 medieval figures.

Welsh Bible The Welsh New Testament first appeared in 1567, translated by William Salesbury*, who also produced the Welsh Prayer Book in collaboration with Richard Davies, bishop of St. Davids*. It served as the basis of the complete Bible published in 1588 by William Morgan*, bishop of St. Asaph, with the help of Edmund Prys. A second revision by Richard Parry and John Davies was published in 1620.

Welsh Revival Major spiritual revival that broke out in Wales in 1904. It began in November 1903 in a church served by Joseph Jenkins at New Quay on Cardigan Bay. Among the first converts was Evan Roberts*, a miner-blacksmith turned evangelist who so influenced the course of the revival as to make his name synonymous with it. The revival included distinctive features, such as long hours of singing, praying in concert, frequent interruptions by worshipers, and the Hwyl—a spontaneous half-sung, half-spoken hymn of thanks or penitence. The three main Pentecostal bodies in the United Kingdom—the Elim Pentecostal Church, the Assemblies of God*, and the Apostolic Church—credit the Welsh Revival for their early leaders and inspiration.

Weltenberg Monastery at Weltenberg, Germany, on the Danube where the river narrows, built by Duke Tassilo in 760. In the eighteenth century, Abbot Maurus Bachl initiated a building program which turned Weltenberg into a spectacular divine theater. Bachl hired two creative artists, Cosmas Damian Asam*, architect and builder, and Egid Quirin Asam*, sculptor and stucco artist. Beginning 1714 they created a vast monastic complex, including the church of St. George* and St. Martin*. The initial consecration took place in 1718.

Wenceslas, St. (c. 907–c. 929) Patron of Bohemia. Bohemian king noted for his piety who was murdered by his brother. His relics* were translated to the Church of St. Vitus at Prague*. The Crown of Wenceslas is the symbol of Czech independence. Feast day: September 28.

werabereouthiun In the Armenian Rite*, the Great Entrance* that proceeds around the altar by way of the rear.

Wesley, Charles (1707–1788) "The Sweet Singer of Methodism*." Methodist hymn writer. The sixteenth or seventeenth son of Samuel and Susanna Wesley and brother of John Wesley*, he joined his brother John in a mission to Georgia in the American colonies. On his return he came under the influence of the Moravians and was converted three days before his brother, on Whitsunday*, 1738, and soon after composed his first hymn, "Where Shall My Wandering Soul Begin." He began evangelism with an untiring zeal and became a powerful field preacher. In 1756 his itinerant ministry came to an end as he settled first in Bristol and then in London, and began writing hymns. He was the most prolific of all hymn writ-

ers, writing more than 5,000 (by some accounts 7,270), including some of the most lyrical in the

Charles Wesley

English language. His best loved hymns include "Jesus, Lover of My Soul," "Hark, the Herald Angels Sing," "Love Divine, All Loves Excelling," and "Lo! He Comes with Clouds Descending."

Wesley, John (1703–1791) Founder of Methodism*. He was the fifteenth child of Samuel and Susanna Wesley and brother of Charles Wesley*. He was ordained in 1728. At Oxford, the Wesley brothers and George Whitefield* formed a religious soci-

John Wesley

ety known as the "Holy Club"* whose members met regularly for prayer, Bible study, and devotional and charitable exercises. Both brothers accepted a call* to join a mission to the colonists and Indians in Georgia, in North America. On return from Georgia, the brothers met Peter Boehler*, a Moravian who led them to Christ. Reading Luther's preface to Romans kindled in him a fire for evangelism that was never to be extinguished. Wesley believed himself to be an apostle commissioned by God to evangelize* England and to "spread holiness over the land."

In April 1739 Wesley began, at the instigation of Whitefield*, open-air preaching, "the strange way of preaching in the fields," as he described it. It enabled him to reach the mass of common people outside the churches where he was not welcome. To disciple his converts, he organized societies which gathered and conserved his harvest of souls. Thus was born the Methodist Church as the direct outcome of his crusades*. He broke with the Moravians and also the Calvinists (of whom Whitefield was one). At first limited to England, he extended his journeys to Scotland and Ireland, and later North America, where he deputed Thomas Coke* to superintend the fledgling church. His global vision was expressed in his saying, "The world is my parish." He is said to have traveled 200,000 miles and preached over 40,000 sermons. He attracted large audiences wherever he went, but also considerable hostility from the established churches and from those opposed to his stern moral teachings.

Although Wesley never formally left the Church of England*, Methodism developed its own constitution and traditions. The Wesleyan theological legacy was the pursuit of Christian holiness* and perfection* combined with justification* by faith*. He emphasized liturgical prayer, eucharistic devotion, and free worship.

Wesley, Samuel Sebastian (1810–1876) English composer and organist. Grandson of Charles Wesley*, he was an organist at a number of cathedrals, as Hereford, Exeter*, Winchester*, and Gloucester*. He wrote some of the finest church music of his generation, including "The Wilderness," "Blessed Be God the Father," "Thou Will Keep Him in Perfect Peace," and Cathedral Service E.

Wesleyan Methodists See METHODIST CHURCHES.

Wessel (1419–1489) Also known as Gansfort. Often confused with John of Wesel. Biblical humanist, member of the Brethren of the Common Life*, he was known as the "Master of Contradictions" because he attempted to combine Nominalism with mysticism. He was a forerunner of the Reformation* who anticipated Luther* in his substitution of the Bible for the church councils as the ultimate arbiter in spiritual matters. He attacked fasting*, indulgences*, and ritualism*. While he accepted transubstantiation*, he held that Christ is present in the elements* only to believers.

West of Scotland Manifestations Pentecostal manifestations, such as miracles, healing, and speaking in tongues*, in the Gareloch region of Scotland. Two key figures associated with these manifestations were Mary Campbell* and Margaret Macdonald. The resulting revival led to the founding of the Catholic Apostolic Church*.

West Syrian Rite Also, Syro-Antiochene Rite. Liturgical tradition of the Syrian Orthodox Church* of Antioch and Malabar, India.

Westcott, Brooke Foss (1825–1901) Bishop of Durham*. As regius professor of divinity at Cambridge, he prepared a critical edition of the Greek New Testament (1881) followed by commentaries on St. John's Gospel (1881), Epistles of St. John (1883), and the Epistle to the Hebrews (1889). In 1890 he was consecrated bishop of Durham. The Cambridge Clergy Training School and the Cambridge Mission to Delhi owe much to his vision and guidance. Among his major works are *The Gospel of Life* (1892), *History of the Canon of the New Testament* (1855), *Introduction to the Study of the Gospels* (1860), and *History of the English Bible* (1868).

Western Church The Roman Catholic Church and the Protestant and other churches that seceded from it as distinguished from the Eastern Orthodox Church* and the Lesser Eastern Churches*.

Western Text Type of Greek text of the New Testament dating from the second century, marked by characteristics such as changing the text to make the meaning clearer by omitting or inserting words, clauses, or sentences. In certain cases words and phrases are assimilated and harmonized in similar and parallel passages in the interest of consistency. Its chief representatives are the Codex Bezae* for the Gospels and Acts and Codex Claromontanus for the Epistles, the Old Latin* version, and the Curetonian Syriac that is not all Western, as this text-type was first called. It was the preferred text of the Western, and one or two Eastern, Church Fathers*, such as Marcion*, Tatian*, Justin*, Irenaeus*, Hippolytus*, Tertullian*, and Cyprian*. See also ALEXANDRIAN TEXT; NEUTRAL TEXT.

Westminster Abbey Unique national cathedral of the Church of England*, founded about 616 as a Benedictine abbey. It was rebuilt by Edward the Confessor* and rededicated in 1065. After the canonization* of Edward the Confessor in 1161, his relics* were translated to a shrine in the abbey. A Lady Chapel* was built at the east end. Henry III began construction of the present church in French style in 1245, and the western towers designed by Christopher Wren* were added in 1745. Its rich stalls are appropriated to the knights and squires of the Bath and over each are suspended a

Westminster Abbey

sword and a banner*. Probably the best known part of the abbey is the Henry VII Chapel, built between 1503 and 1512. The abbey was granted exemption from the jurisdiction of the bishop of London and the archbishop of Canterbury*. Since the time of William the Conqueror, it has been the chapel of coronation for the monarchs of England. The coronation chair incorporates the Stone of Scone from Scotland. Numerous kings and national figures are buried here. The south transept* is the famous Poets' Corner. Until 1395, the House of Commons frequently sat in the chapter house*.

Westminster Assembly Assembly convened by Long Parliament consisting of 121 divines, 10 lords, and 20 commoners that met from 1643 to 1649 to give advice and guidance to the civil authorities for the promotion of unity and uniformity in the work of the Reformation*. The Church of Scotland* was asked to send commissioners and appointed four ministers and ten elders. The major accomplishment of the assembly was the preparation of the Westminister Confession of Faith, the *Larger* and *Shorter Catechisms*, the Form of Church Government, and the Directory for Public Worship. It also examined and approved Rouse's metrical version of the Psalter. The Westminster Standards were adopted by the Church of Scotland* by a special act in 1647.

Westminster Catechisms The *Larger* and *Shorter Catechisms* compiled in 1647 by the Westminster Assembly*. The *Larger Catechism** is a restatement and practical amplification of the Westminister Confession. The *Shorter Catechism** uses the question-and-answer form to teach the essentials of Christian faith. It includes the famous question and answer: "What is the chief end of man?" "Man's chief end is to glorify God and to enjoy him forever."

Westminster Cathedral The cathedral of the Roman Catholic archbishop of Westminster, England, dedicated to the precious blood* of our Lord Jesus Christ, completed in 1903.

Westminster Confession The profession of Presbyterian faith and a creedal standard for all Presbyterian churches, drawn up at the Westminster Assembly*. Two-thirds of the 33 chapters in the confession deal with doctrine. It emphasized the sovereignty of God and election* to salvation*, taught covenant theology*, and the observance of the Sabbath on the Lord's Day*, but avoided disputed issues, such as sublapsarianism*.

Westminster Standards Comprehensive term for the formularies produced by the Westminster Assembly*.

Weyden, Roger van der (c. 1400–c. 1464) Flemish painter who was among the first to use oil paint. His paintings include *Virgin and Child with Saints, Adoration of the Magi, St. Luke Painting the Virgin, The Crucifixion, Saint Gregory at Prayer, The Descent from the Cross,* and *The Last Judgment.*

Weymouth New Testament *The New Testament in Modern Speech,* subtitled "An Idiomatic Translation into Everyday English from the Text of the Resultant Greek Testament." It was prepared by Richard Francis Weymouth (1822–1902), English Baptist headmaster of Mill Hill School.

Wheaton College Independent Evangelical liberal arts college, originally founded in Wheaton, Illinois, as Illinois Institute in 1848 by Wesleyan Methodists* with the support of Congregationalists. The land was donated by William Wheaton, one of the founders of the town of Wheaton. Evangelical leaders educated at Wheaton include Billy Graham*, Carl F. Henry*, Edward J. Carnell*, Kenneth Taylor*, Harold Lindsell, and Leighton Ford*. The Billy Graham Center* is located here.

Wheaton Declaration Statement adopted by the Congress on the Church's Worldwide Mission at Wheaton College* in Illinois in 1966, convened by the interdenominational Foreign Mission Association and the Evangelical Foreign Missions Association*. It dealt with ten areas of missiology*: syncretism, neo-universalism, proselytism, neo-Romanism, church growth, foreign missions, Evangelical unity, evaluating methods, social concern, and a hostile world.

wheel Symbol of St. Catherine of Alexandria* who was martyred, according to tradition, by being tortured while tied to a wheel.

Wheelock, Eleazar (1711–1779) Congregational* minister and founder and first president of Dartmouth College. During his first year as pastor in Lebanon, Connecticut, an awakening* broke out in his church, and Wheelock took part in the Great Revival* in New England. He received from Col. Joshua More a gift of a house and a schoolhouse in his parish* which he named More's Charity School. It was later moved to Hanover, New Hampshire, and under a 1769 charter transformed into Dartmouth College.

Whitby, Synod of (663/64) Synod called at Streanshalch (Whitby) in Yorkshire, England, by King Oswy of Northumbria to settle the differences of observances between the Celtic practices as represented in the traditions of Columba* and Lindisfarne* and the continental or Roman practices as represented in the traditions of Augustine* and Paulinus*. The synod decided in favor of the latter, thus bringing the English church as a whole more fully into the mainstream of European Christendom.

Whitby Abbey

white In Christian art, symbol of light, joy, purity, innocence, and holiness. It is used at Christmastide*, Eastertide*, and on Trinity Sunday*.

White, Ellen Gould (1827–1915) Seventh-Day Adventist leader. Through her preaching and writing, she guided the Seventh Day Adventist movement in its early days in the formulation of its key doctrines on eschatological and prophetic ministry and health practices. In 1855 she and her husband, Elder James White, moved to Battle Creek, Michigan, where they established the church headquarters.

White Fathers Popular name of the Society of Missionaries of Africa, a Roman Catholic religious order founded by Charles-Martial Allemand-Lavigerie*, cardinal and archbishop of Algiers, in 1869, composed of secular priests and bishop coadjutor* brothers* living in community without vows and dedicated to the conversion of Africans. They wear a white tunic and a cloak or burnous with a rosary around the neck. They are the most numerous of Roman Catholic missionaries working in Africa.

White Friars Carmelite friars*, from their white cloaks and scapulars.

White Ladies Sisters of the Presentation of Mary, a teaching order founded at Theuyts, Ardeche, France, in 1796 by Marie Rivier for the education of young girls.

White Monks Cistercian monks, so called from their white habit.

White Sisters 1. Congregation of the Missionary Sisters of Our Lady of Africa founded by Charles-Martial Allemand-Lavigerie in 1869, on the same rules as the White Fathers*. 2. Congregation of the Daughters of the Holy Ghost, founded in 1706 at Plerin in Brittany, moving to St. Brieuc in 1834.

Whitefield, George (1714–1770) English evangelist. He came under the influence of the Wesley brothers in 1736, was ordained, and followed the Wesleys

George Whitefield

to Georgia in the American colonies. He began preaching at open-air meetings from early 1739. He broke with the Wesleys over their Arminian beliefs in 1741 and thereafter devoted himself to travel and preaching, delivering up to 20 sermons a week. He visited Scotland 14 times and America 7 times, helping to inspire the Great Awakening*. In his later years, he was associated with the Countess of Huntingdon and her Connexion* as well as her theological college at Trevecca. Although not original or profound, he was a prince among preachers, with a gifted voice and a range of rhetorical skills, able to grip the attention of his listeners.

Whitgift, John (1532–1604) Archbishop of Canterbury* (1583–1604). Ordained in 1560, he served as master of Trinity College* (1567), vice-chancellor (1570), dean of Lincoln* (1571), and bishop of Worcester (1577) before being named by Elizabeth I as archbishop of Canterbury. He was a fervent supporter of episcopacy and ritual uniformity and did much to promote administrative reforms. To unify the church against Puritans, he imposed the articles of loyalty to the established church.

Whitsunday Feast of the Descent of the Holy Spirit* upon the apostles at Pentecost*. It ranks after Easter* as the greatest festival in the Christian calendar. Its name comes from the white robes worn by the newly baptized on that day. Its liturgical color is red.

Whitsuntide Day of the Pentecost* and the first two or six days that follow.

Whittier, John Greenleaf (1807–1892) American Quaker* poet and abolitionist. In his old age he wrote religious verse, some of which reveal his fervent Christian faith.

Whittingham, William (1524–1579) Bishop of Durham*. He took a leading part in the production of the Geneva Bible*. As a supporter of John Knox*, he was an exile in Geneva* until 1560, but on his return to England was made dean of Durham in 1563.

wholly other In Kierkegaardian theology, God as absolutely transcendent in every respect.

Wichern, Johann Hinrich (1808–1881) Founder of the German Innere Mission*. Beginning with a mission to the poor and underprivileged children of Hamburg known as Rauhes Haus (Rough House), Wichern established a number of charitable services which were consolidated as the Innere Mission* under the auspices of the Evangelical churches in 1848.

Wies, Die Famous pilgrimage* church in the countryside below the Bavarian Alps, and one of the masterpieces of Rococo architecture. It was built by Dominikus Zimmermann (1685–1766) to house a miraculous statue of Christ of the Flagellation.

Wigglesworth, Smith (1859–1947) English evangelist. Born into a poor family, he had no education and never learned to read until he was an adult. He received the Pentecostal experience in 1907, but his healing ministry had begun earlier. His healing methods were rough, but he had intense compassion for suffering people, often praying and weeping over them.

wila In the Assyrian tradition, veil that hangs before the sanctuary door leading west out of the sanctuary.

Wilberforce, William (1759–1833) English philanthropist and statesman. An Anglican layman, an Evangelical leader, and a prominent member of the Clapham Sect*, he championed foreign missions and was instrumental in putting an end to the slave trade. He helped to found the British and Foreign Bible Society* and the Church Missionary Society*.

Wilbur, John (1774–1856) Quaker* preacher who opposed the teachings of Joseph Gurney, Elizabeth Fry's brother, and Elias Hicks, and defended the traditional Quaker emphasis on the Inner Light*. His followers, known as the Wilburites, broke away in 1845 to become the Religious Society of Friends*.

Wiley, Henry Orton (1877–1961) Church of Nazarene* theologian. As author of *Christian Theology* (3 vols., 1941), he is regarded as one of the leading Wesleyan theologians of the twentieth century. He was also instrumental in revising the Nazarene *Manual of Discipline*. He was president of Pasadena College for 29 years (1910–1916, 1926–1949) and Northwest Nazarene College, Nampa, Idaho (1917–1926).

Wilkerson, David Ray (1931–) Evangelist and founder of Teen Challenge*. As narrated in his book *The Cross and the Switchblade* (1963), he began his ministry as a street evangelist ministering to gang members and drug addicts. His success led to the founding of Teen Challenge in 1958. To train graduates of Teen Challenge to enter full-time Christian ministry, he founded Teen Challenge Bible Institute in Rhinebeck, New York. In 1987 he cofounded the Times Square Church in New York City together with his brother, Don, and Robert Philips.

Willaert, Adriaen (1490–1562) Flemish composer. In 1527 he was elected maestro di cappella* at St. Mark's in Venice*, becoming a composer of both instrumental and vocal music. He wrote over 175 motets* and 9 masses and contributed greatly to the rise of Venice to musical leadership.

William of Malmesbury (c. 1090–1143) English monastic historian, author of *Gesta Regum Anglorum* and *Gesta Pontificum Anglorum*. The latter covered English church history from the end of the sixth century.

William of Ockham/Occam (c. 1285–1347) "Venerabilis Inceptor." Medieval scholastic theologian. He entered the Franciscan Order* about 1310. In the struggle between the Spiritual Franciscans* and Pope John XXII*, he sided with the Spirituals, and was censured for heresy. His most important work is the *Summa Logicae*, which he completed at Avignon*.

The most complete account of Ockham's thought is presented in his *Commentary on the Sentences* of which he revised and edited only the first book. He was a vigorous and independent logician in the Augustinian-Franciscan tradition. He popularized the principle of Ockham's Razor* which stated that "what can be done with fewer assumptions is done in vain with more." He opposed the Thomist system of Aristotelian logic (called the via antiqua*) with the via moderna* or Nominalism under which no universals existed but only individual things.

Ockham resolutely opposed anything that limited God's sovereignty and omnipotence. Moral order is dependent on divine will, but God's omnipotence and omniscience cannot be philosophically proved and thus must be accepted by faith. The traditional proofs of God's existence are not scientifically provable, and therefore there is no relationship between philosophy and theology. Ockham's theology was based on intuition rather than abstraction, singulars rather than universals, and induction rather than deduction.

William of St. Thierry (c. 1080–1148) Scholastic philosopher. He entered the Benedictine abbey of St. Nicasius of Reims and was later elected abbot of St. Thierry. His prolific output included ascetical and didactic works, as *De Natura et Dignitate Amoris* and *De Contemplando Deo,* on the relationship between knowledge and love; *De Natura Animae et Corporis,* on the relationship of the body and the soul; two treatises on faith, *Speculum Fidei* and *Aenigma Fidei; De Sacramento Altaris* on the Eucharist*; and a study of Romans. He began but did not complete a biography of his lifelong friend, Bernard of Clairvaux*.

Williams, Charles Walter Stansby (1886–1945) English writer, noted for his fiction with Christian themes, such as *Taliesin through Logres* (1938), *He Came Down from Heaven* (1937), *Descent of the Dove* (1939), and *Forgiveness of Sins* (1942).

Williams, John (1796–1839) "Apostle of Polynesia." Missionary of the London Missionary Society and martyr*. In 1817 he sailed for the Society Islands and in 1818 settled on Raiatea. In 1822 he visited the Cook Islands and claimed the discovery of Rarotonga. In 1839 he landed at Vanuatu (formerly New Hebrides), where he and his fellow missionary, John Harris, were killed by the natives. Two years before his death he wrote the classic *Narrative of Missionary Enterprises in the South Sea Islands.*

Williams of Pantecelyn, William (1717–1791) Welsh Methodist leader and hymn writer. He was converted under the ministry of Howell Harris and

joined the Church of England*. Denied ordination, he became a Methodist. Between 1744 and 1791 he published over 90 books, mostly poetry, of which the most outstanding are his long poems, *Views of Christ's Kingdom* (1756) and *Life and Death of Theomemphus* (1764, 1781). His hymns, published in 24 books, were not only contributions to Evangelical literature but also practical aids to the work of revival.

Williams, Roger (1603?–1683) Founder of Rhode Island. In 1631 he emigrated from England to Boston. He served as pastor and teacher in the Pilgrim Colony until 1635 when he was banished because of his theological views. He fled to Providence in 1636 and bought land from the Indians to found Rhode Island. He secured a charter for the colony from the king and became the colony's president until 1657. His view that church and state* must be separate and all citizens have freedom of conscience is part of his legacy.

Williams, Sir George (1821–1905) Founder of the Young Men's Christian Association. He was converted through the preaching of Charles Finney*. Gathering 12 young men to meet together in prayer in his room in 1844, he founded the YMCA*, which later spread around the world.

Williams, William ("o'er Wern") (1781–1840) Welsh preacher. Considered with John Elias* and Christmas Evans* as one of the three greatest Welsh preachers. He led the last revival of Welsh Methodism* with his quiet and persuasive preaching.

Willibrord, St. (658–739) Anglo-Saxon missionary and "Apostle to the Frisians." In 690 Willibrord and 11 companions sailed to Frankish Frisia to begin evangelization. In 695 he was made archbishop of a new Frankish church province with its center at Utrecht*. He also established the famed monastery at Echternach*, near Luxembourg. Much of the region, including Denmark, Heligoland, and Thuringia, was Christianized by the time of Willibrord's death. Feast day: November 7.

Wimber, John (1934–1998) Founding pastor of the Vineyard Christian Fellowship*. Converted in

1963, he served as pastor at Yorba Linda and then as an associate of C. Peter Wagner* of the Fuller Evangelistic Association. In 1977 he left Fuller to establish the Anaheim Vineyard and launch the "signs and wonders" ministry that had a profound effect on thousands of Charismatics. During the mid-1980s he taught a very popular course at Fuller Theological Seminary* called "The Miraculous and Church Growth."

wimple Cloth wound around the head, framing the face, and gathered into folds beneath the chin, worn by nuns as part of their habit.

Wimple

Winchester Fifth-ranked English bishopric*, after Canterbury*, York*, London, and Durham*, it was established by King Cenwealth of Wessex about 648. Its famous cathedral was rebuilt a number of times, most recently in the seventeenth century. It was first consecrated in 1093, but the massive tower collapsed in 1101 and had to be rebuilt.

Winchester Bible Bible in the library of the Winchester Cathedral, one of the great examples of medieval illumination*, begun in 1160 but never completed.

Windesheim Augustinian house established in Windesheim, near Zwolle, in the Netherlands, in 1387 under the direction of Florentinus Radewijns by six of Gerard Groote's disciples. Its constitution was approved in 1395. By the fifteenth cen-

tury it formed with three other Dutch monasteries the Congregation of Windesheim. It was joined in 1413 by the seven houses of the Groenendael Congregation and in 1430 by the Congregation of Neuss. The monks of Windesheim were the chief representative of the *devotio moderna** movement and included among their numbers many saints*, such as Thomas à Kempis*, Johannes Mauburnus, and Johannes Vos.

Wipo of Burgundy (d. c. 1050) Burgundian monk, author of both the text and tune of the Latin sequence, *Victimae Paschali Laudes*. Its drama is the story of the three Marys and is used during the Mass* on Easter* and daily through the following week, or at mattins* on Easter day.

Wishart, George (c. 1513–1546) Scottish reformer and martyr*. He was the first to translate the Helvetic Confession* into English. In Scotland, he boldly preached the gospel and ministered to those sick and dying of the plague. He was responsible for converting John Knox*. Seized for preaching heresy, he was condemned to death and burned at the stake.

Witherspoon, John (1723–1794) Presbyterian minister and educator. Born in Scotland, he served as pastor in various parishes from 1745 to 1768. As a

Winchester Cathedral

defender of traditional Reformed* orthodoxy*, he supported Thomas Reid's* Common Sense Realism, which held that the fundamental truths of Christianity are consistent with common sense. In 1768 he accepted an invitation from the New Side* Presbyterians to serve as the president of the College of New Jersey in Princeton. After the American Revolution, he helped to reorganize the Presbyterian Church and was instrumental in the establishment of the General Assembly* of which he was the first president. He was a delegate to the Continental Congress and was the only clergyman to sign the Declaration of Independence.

George Wishart

witness (*noun*) 1. Public testimony by word or deed to one's Christian faith. 2. Person who testifies in public to the power of the gospel or proclaims the good news of salvation through Jesus Christ. (*verb*) To provide such testimony in public.

Witnesses See JEHOVAH'S WITNESSES.

Wittenberg The "Cradle of the Reformation" in Germany, famous for its university (founded in 1502) and its Schlosskirche to whose doors Luther* affixed his Ninety-Five Theses*. The Augustinian monastery where Luther lived as a monk is now the Lutherhaus Museum. Both Luther and Melanchthon* are buried at Wittenberg, and the first Luther Bible was printed here.

Wittenberg, Concord of (1536) Agreement reached by Lutheran and Zwinglian theologians in their dispute over the Eucharist*. Those signing the accord included Luther*, Melanchthon*, and Bucer*. However, the concord collapsed because the Zwinglians refused to accept it.

Women's Aglow Fellowship Interdenominational worldwide evangelistic outreach* founded in 1967 in Seattle, Washington. Its central goals are to share worship, witness for Christ, work for unity among believers, and encourage women to participate fully in the local church.

Woodworth-Etter, Maria Beulah (1844–1924) Holiness-Pentecostal evangelist. Converted at the age of 13, she began holding revivals around 1888, first under the auspices of the United Brethren and later as a Pentecostal. People who attended her protracted meetings often fell in the Spirit, were healed of physical ailments, were prophesied to, or received visions. Some of her meetings were attended by 20,000 people or more. She also planted many churches, including the Lakeview

Maria Beulah Woodworth-Etter

Christian Center in Indianapolis. Among her many books is *Marvels, Miracles, Signs and Wonders* (1922).

Word of God Holy Scriptures as God's written word presenting Christ, the living or Incarnate

Word. The Word of God is the subject of preaching or proclamation of the gospel.

word of knowledge 1. Knowledge about a person or future event communicated supernaturally for the purpose of edification* or as a caution. 2. Ability to receive such knowledge as a gift of the Holy Spirit*.

word of wisdom One of several charismata* mentioned by Paul* in 1 Corinthians 12:8, a word of revelation* given by the Holy Spirit* to provide guidance to the community of believers at a particular time of need, often applying scriptural wisdom to the situation. It provides illumination* to the listener who receives it as the Word of God*.

words of administration Words used to accompany the giving of the elements* of the Eucharist*, based on the words of Jesus at the Last Supper*.

Words of Institution Words used by Jesus Christ in instituting the Lord's Supper* (1 Cor. 11:23–25).

worker-priest French Roman Catholic priest who for missionary purposes spent a part of each weekday as a worker in a secular job, generally in a factory. The experiment of allowing priests to work in factories was initially supported by the Roman Catholic Church. But many of these priests began to stray from their vocations, and the practice was halted in 1954.

works Good activities demonstrating love of God and fellow human beings done as a result of grace* and as directed by the Holy Spirit* (Rom. 2:3–10).

works of mercy Deeds done from a spirit of love reflecting the grace and compassion of God. The seven works of corporal mercy are to feed the hungry, give drink to the thirsty, clothe the naked, visit the prisoner, shelter the stranger, visit the sick, and bury the dead. The seven works of spiritual mercy are to correct the sinner, teach the ignorant, counsel the doubtful, comfort the sorrowful, bear wrongs patiently, forgive all injuries, and pray for the living and the dead.

World Alliance of Reformed Churches Oldest international Protestant confessional* body, founded in London in 1875 under the title, Alliance of Reformed Churches Throughout the World Holding the Presbyterian System. The Alliance is a consultative and advisory body promoting cooperation and understanding among member churches. At the Nairobi General Council in 1970 it merged with the International Congregational Council. In 1990 it had 150 member churches with over 60 million members.

World Congress on Evangelism Global ecumenical assembly sponsored in West Berlin in 1966 on the tenth anniversary of the magazine *Christianity Today** and associated with the Billy Graham* crusades. The congress drew attendees from more than 100 countries. The papers were published as *Let the Earth Hear His Voice.*

World Council of Churches (WCC) The principal interdenominational body representing Christian churches throughout the world with the exception of the Roman Catholic Church and a few separatist churches. The basis of membership is stated as: "A fellowship of churches which confess the Lord Jesus Christ as God and Savior according to the Scriptures and therefore seek to fulfill together their common calling to the glory of the one God, Father, Son and Holy Spirit." The WCC was founded in 1948 at Amsterdam when 147 churches from 44 countries resolved to form a common body. It was a merger of two earlier movements, Life and Work* and Faith and Order*, and its origin goes back to the World Missionary Conference* at Edinburgh* in 1910. In the early 1990s it had a membership of 322

Seven Corporal Works of Mercy

churches with headquarters in Geneva*. As reorganized in 1992, WCC has four program units: 1. Unity and renewal, including faith and order*, worship, theological education, and the laity. 2. Mission, education, and witness, including education and health. 3. Justice, peace, and creation. 4. Sharing and service, including inter-church aid and refugees.

World Day of Prayer Movement of Christian women gathering to pray on the first Friday of March. It began in 1887 as a domestic initiative by Mary Ellen James and was made worldwide in 1890 through the efforts of Helen Barrett Montgomery and Lucy Peabody. In 1927 it was officially named World Day of Prayer with the motto, "Informed Prayer and Prayerful Action."

World Evangelical Fellowship International alliance of Evangelical bodies founded by the International Convention of Evangelicals which met in the Netherlands in 1951 led by Harold J. Ockenga* and J. Elwin Wright. Its membership includes 57 autonomous national and regional Evangelical bodies. It is assisted by four commissions on theology, missions, women's concerns, and church renewal.

World Home Bible League International and interdenominational Bible distribution agency founded by William and Betty Chapman as an extension of the American Home Bible League, founded in 1938. It distributes Bibles and Bible study materials through local churches in 95 countries in over 200 languages. It works closely with Wycliffe Bible Translators*. In the first 50 years of its ministry, it distributed over 250 million Bibles, New Testaments, and portions of the Bible.

World Literature Crusade (WLC) Evangelical interdenominational agency dedicated to placing gospel tracts and other forms of literature in every home in the world, founded in Canada in 1946. It works through the Every Home Crusade in each of the 43 countries in which WLC is active. In countries with high illiteracy, the printed word is supplemented by gospel recordings and pictorial tracts. WLC also targets high schools, universities, hospitals, prisons, maritime personnel, and the blind

for whom braille messages are made. The work is supported by a 24-hour-a-day prayer chain of committed Christians.

World Missionary Conference See EDINBURGH MISSIONARY CONFERENCE.

World Student Christian Federation Federation of 40 autonomous Christian student groups, founded in Sweden in 1895. Its stated purpose is to "lead students to accept the Christian faith in God—Father, Son, and Holy Spirit—according to the Scriptures and to live together as true disciples of Jesus Christ."

World Vision International Christian relief and development organization founded in 1950 by Robert ("Bob") Pierce*. He was inspired to found World Vision after his first evangelistic trip to Asia as a vice president of Youth for Christ*. Its initial mandate was to care for Asian orphans. Children remain its primary focus and concern. It also responds to humanitarian emergencies caused by natural disaster or war. Today it operates in nearly 100 countries with a budget of almost one billion dollars.

Worldwide Church of God Denomination founded in 1933 by Herbert W. Armstrong (1892–1986) as the Radio Church of God. Armstrong taught seventh-day Sabbatarianism*, rejected the doctrine of the Trinity*, and emphasized obedience to the Law of Moses. Under the leadership of his successor, Joseph Tkach, Sr. (d. 1995) and Tkach's son Joseph, the denomination underwent a drastic doctrinal change and affirmed an Evangelical faith.

Worldwide Evangelization Crusade (WEC) Movement founded in 1913–1914 by C. T. Studd*, one of the Cambridge Seven*. It is an international and interdenominational faith mission* with some 1,500 partners in 50 countries. The Christian Literature Crusade*, started by Kenneth Adams in 1941 as a branch of WEC, is now a major movement in its own right.

Worms Cathedral in the historic city of Worms, Germany. The first Early Romanesque church was consecrated in 1018, but it collapsed two years later. The present cathedral of St. Peter* dates between 1150 and 1220.

Worms, Diet of (1521) Celebrated imperial diet held in the Bischofshof at Worms, Germany, at which Martin Luther* defended his doctrines before Emperor Charles V. Luther refused to recant and ended his answer with the words, *Hier stehe ich ich kan nicht anders. Gott hef, mir. Amen* ("I can do no other. God help me. Amen."). Six days later, his teachings were formally condemned by the Edict of Worms.

worship (Anglo-Saxon, worth-ship) 1. Sense of veneration* and adoration toward God. 2. Act, process, or instance of expressing such veneration through performing a religious exercise or ritual.

Worship, Directory of Public Directory for the public worship of God compiled by the Westminster Assembly* in 1645 to replace the *Book of Common Prayer**. It contained general instructions, rather than set forms of service, for the Holy Communion*, baptism*, visitation of the sick, marriage, and burial.

wounds, the five sacred Wounds in Jesus' feet, hands, and side. Devotion to the wounds developed in the Middle Ages under the influence of St. Bernard* and St. Francis of Assisi*. The church and the sacraments* are said to have sprung from the wounds on the side. The devotion was adopted by some Protestant Pietist groups and by Zinzendorf* and his followers.

Wrede, William (1859–1906) German theologian. He taught New Testament in the University of Breslau and was a prominent member of the History of Religions School. In his *Das Messiasgeheimnis in den Evangelien* (1901) he argued that Mark's Gospel carried a strong theological agenda couched in terms of Christ's messianic secret*, and in *Paulus* he maintained that St. Paul* was the real founder of Christian doctrine.

Wren, Sir Christopher (1632–1723) British architect. He was one of the founders and from 1680 to 1682 president of the Royal Society. He built 52 churches in London, including St. Paul's Cathedral*, with which his name is forever associated.

WSCF World Student Christian Federation*.

Wurttemberg Confession Protestant confession of faith in 35 articles compiled by Johann Brenz* on the model of the Augsburg Confession* for presentation to the Council of Trent* in 1552. It formed the basis of the Thirty-Nine Articles* of 1563.

WWJD "What Would Jesus Do?" A popular Christian question in dealing with ethical and moral issues often appearing on bumper stickers, bracelets, and jewelry. Initially popularized by Charles Sheldon's best-selling nineteenth-century classic, *In His Steps*.

Wycliffe Bible The first translation of the entire Bible into English (c. 1380–1392) done chiefly by Nicholas of Hereford and John Purvey. It was based on the Vulgate*, and never printed.

Wycliffe Bible Translators Organization dedicated to the production of translations of the Bible in languages that have none. It was founded in 1934 by L. L. Legters and W. Cameron Townsend* who started Camp Wycliffe in Arkansas as a summer school in descriptive linguistics for pioneer missionaries. In 1942 this organization was split into two divisions. The Summer Institute of Linguistics represents the scientific branch of the work, and it is nonsectarian. Wycliffe Bible Translators*

Sir Christopher Wren

is the religious division, working with churches and missionaries. Another division, Jungle Aviation and Radio Service, provides transportation and communication services.

Wycliffe/Wyclif, John (c. 1329–1384) English reformer. "The Morning Star of the Reformation*." He was rector* in three benefices* from 1361 to 1384 and established early a reputation as a

John Wycliffe

philosopher. He reacted against the prevailing skepticism of Scholasticism* that tended to separate the natural and the supernatural. He distin-

guished the eternal, ideal church from the visible, corrupt, and material church. He maintained that the Bible was the sole basis of doctrine and attacked papal authority, the institution of monasteries, and the doctrine of transubstantiation*. These positions were condemned at the Black Friars* Council in 1382 and again in 1388, 1397, and finally at the Council of Constance* in 1415. He inspired the translation of the Bible which was undertaken by his followers. He anticipated the Protestant Reformation* by over a century, and his ideas had a lasting influence on the Continental Reformers, especially on John Hus*. By order

Wycliffe Bible

of the Council of Constance in 1428, his remains were exhumed and burned and the ashes were thrown into the Swift River.

Xx

Xanten Romanesque cathedral built by St. Norbert* in Xanten, Germany. It was converted to the Gothic* style beginning in 1263. The conversion dragged on until the middle of the sixteenth century. On the pillars of the central aisle the baldachins cover 28 statues, sculpted by various masters between 1300 and 1500. The high altar contains the casket holding the relics* of St. Victor. The superb panels by Barthel Bruyn depict events in the life of St. Victor and St. Helena*.

xenoglossy Form of glossolalia* consisting of the ecstatic utterance of a known foreign language by a person who had no previous knowledge of that language.

xenolalia A variant of glossolalia* in which the speaker speaks in a known foreign language which he or she has never learned.

xenophagia (lit., dry nourishment) 1. Form of fasting practiced by Montanists* consisting of eating only dry food. 2. Among modern Roman Catholics, strict fast lasting from Monday through Thursday of the Holy Week* in which one may eat only bread, salt, onions, garlic, herbs, and water.

Ximenez/Jimenez de Cisneros, Francisco (1436–1517) Scholar, inquisitor, and patron of learning. He served as a priest in Uzeda and Siguenza, but gave it up to become an Observantine friar*. In 1492 he accepted the offer of confessor* to Queen Isabella and in this position was influential in affairs of state. He rose quickly to become provincial* of the Franciscans in Castile in 1494 and archbishop of Toledo* and primate* of Spain in 1495. In this office he also functioned as the high chancellor of Castile. On the death of Isabella, the resignation of Ferdinand, and the death of their heir, Philip of Burgundy, Ximenez found himself the virtual ruler of Castile. In 1507 he was made cardinal and the inquisitor general, the position by which he is principally known. But he was a great patron of learning and a dedicated servant of the church. In 1500 he founded out of his private income the University of Alcala and helped to translate and publish many devotional classics as well as the *Complutensian Polyglot**. At Toledo he revived the Mozarabic Rite* and endowed a chapel in the cathedral where it could survive.

Yy

yaysmavurk (lit., this very day) Armenian Synaxary or Menologion* containing versions of the lives of saints* and homilies for Sunday feasts.

year, liturgical See CHURCH YEAR.

yefe tsamie qob Tall, white hat worn by an Ethiopian monk.

Yew Sunday Palm Sunday*, so called because yew branches are carried in procession on this day.

YFC Youth for Christ*.

YMCA Young Men's Christian Association. A lay, interdenominational, and interconfessional organization serving young men and bringing them through its various activities to a knowledge of Jesus Christ. Founded by George Williams* in London in 1844, the basis of its faith is the 1855

YMCA Symbol

Paris Declaration. The World Alliance of YMCAs has its headquarters in Geneva*. Its principal outreach is through its hostels, but it also provides sports and leisure activities, training for the unemployed, drug counseling, and summer day camps. Its symbol is a red triangle. Its specifically Christian mission has become blurred over the years.

York City and see* in Great Britain. Known as Eboracum, it was the military headquarters of Roman Britain. A bishop of York is mentioned in the Acts of the Council of Arles in 314. After the original Christian community was destroyed by the Saxons, it was restored in the seventh century when St. Paulinus* was consecrated bishop of York in 625. He baptized the Northumbrian king, Edwin, in 627. In 664 Wilfrid was consecrated bishop, and he introduced Roman usages and Benedictine monasticism*. Under Egbert*, York was raised to an archbishopric and its archbishops came to be the primates of the Northern province. In the eleventh century, York contended with Canterbury* for precedence in authority. The dispute was finally settled in the fourteenth century when Innocent VI decided that the archbishop of Canterbury would have precedence as the primate* of All England while the archbishop of York would be the primate of England. In the Middle Ages the city contained over 40 churches, 9 religious houses, and 16 chapels.

York Cathedral Minster, dedicated to St. Peter, in York, England. It is the largest medieval cathedral in northern Europe. The nave* was built between 1291 and 1360. The choir which, following the English custom, is longer than the nave, was built in the second half of the fourteenth century. The work of John Thornton of Coventry, it is remarkable for its large window, 33 feet by 75 feet, which

York Cathedral

takes up the east wall.

York use Ancient Catholic rite used in northern England and named after York*.

Young, Brigham (1801–1877) Founder of the Mormon* settlement in Utah and successor to Joseph Smith* as leader of the Mormon Church. Joining Joseph Smith's sect in 1832, he led the group to Kirtland, Ohio, became an apostle in 1835, and chief of the twelve apostles in 1838. After Joseph Smith's death, he led the Mormons from Nauvo, Illinois, to Salt Lake City in 1847, and organized the State of Deseret. In 1850 he became governor of the territory of Utah. He was instrumental in building the Mormon Temple in Salt Lake City and the University of Utah.

Young Life Interdenominational and evangelical outreach to high school youth, founded by John Rayburn in 1940. It ministers to half a million young people in 40 countries. It is headquartered in Colorado Springs, Colorado.

younger churches Newer or relatively recent denominations of the Third World, as distinct from the older churches* of Europe and North America.

Youth for Christ Organization founded in 1945 by Torrey Johnson, George Beverly Shea*, and Douglas Fisher at Winona Lake, Indiana, to promote teenage evangelism, high school Bible clubs, and programs to prevent juvenile delinquency. The first Youth for Christ rally was conducted by Paul Guiness in 1934 in Brantford, Ontario. Its creed describes the organization as "geared to the times and anchored to the rock."

Youth—with a Mission Nondenominational parachurch* organization working to evangelize* youth around the world. It was founded by Loren Cunningham in 1960 and incorporated in 1961. Its methods include street meetings, door-to-door evangelism, music, drama, urban evangelism, Olympic evangelism, and mercy service. It owns two mercy ships, *Good Samaritan* and *Anastasia*. For purposes of evangelism, the world is divided into three regions, consisting of areas, nations, and districts. Each region has its own council, but the authority is decentralized among more than 300 autonomous centers, each with its own separate funding and constitution. There are two international offices, one in Hawaii, where the Pacific and Asia Christian University is located, and the other in Amsterdam, where the School of

Brigham Young

Urban Missions is located. There are no salaried employees, and each person must raise his or her own funding.

yuqno In the Jacobite tradition, an icon.

yule Christmas.

yule log Traditional custom on Christmas eve* of carrying to the hearth a large, freshly cut log. On Christmas eve, the master of the house would put the log on the hearth, sprinkle it with oil, salt, and mulled wine, and utter suitable prayers. Although the custom has died out, it is sometimes used symbolically in Protestant worship services.

Yves, St. (c. 1253–1303) Priest and lawyer of Brittany. Patron saint* of lawyers. Feast day: May 19.

Y–WAM Youth—with a Mission*.

YWCA Young Women's Christian Association. Originally two separate organizations, both founded in Britain in 1855 by Emma Roberts and Lady Kinnaird. They united in 1877, and the first World Committee of the YWCAs met in London in 1894. Its symbol is a blue triangle. There is very little Christian about YWCA except the "C" in its name.

Zz

Zagorsk Monastery city in Zagorsk, northeast of Moscow*, originally built between 1340 and 1345 by Sergei of Radonezh. After Sergei's death, the Cathedral of the Trinity was built over the wooden church erected earlier over his grave. The monastic complex includes several other churches: the golden-domed Nikono Chapel, dating from 1548; the Church of the Holy Ghost, built between 1476 and 1477; the Church of the Dormition of Mary, built on the orders of Ivan IV between 1559 and 1583; the Church of Sosima and Savvati, built between 1635 and 1638; the Church of Sergei, built between 1686 and 1692; the Chapel of the Fountain, the gate church of St. John the Baptist, built between 1692 and 1699; and the Church of the Icon of the Virgin of Smolensk, built between 1746 and 1748.

Zagorsk Monastery

zahawariat In the Ethiopian Rite, the anaphora* of the apostles.

Zahn, Theodore (1838–1933) German Lutheran biblical scholar. He taught at the universities of Gottingen (1868–1877), Kiel (1877–1878), Erlangen (1878–1888 and 1892–1909), and Leipzig (1888–1892). He was one of the greatest scholars of his day. In an age when liberal theology was in the ascendant, he was a staunch defender of orthodoxy*. His principal work was a 12-volume study of the canon of the New Testament (*Geschichte des neutestamentlichen Kanons,* 2 vols., 1888–1892; *Forschungen zur Geschichte des neutestamentlichen Kanons,* 10 vols., 1881–1920). He also wrote seven commentaries on the New Testament and a two-volume introduction to the New Testament. His studies in the field of patristics* included *Marcellus von Ancyra* (1867), *Der Hirt des Hermas untersucht* (1868), *Ignatius von Antiochien* (1873), and *Acta Joannis* (1880).

Zakaryas (c. 1845–1920) Ethiopian prophet* who led a mass conversion of Muslims into the Orthodox Church. Born of Muslim parents, he was baptized at Dabra Tabor in 1910, assuming the Christian name* Newaya Krestos (property of Christ). His dialectical skills led to the conversion of many Muslim dignitaries. By the time of his death thousands of Muslims had converted to Christianity.

zatik In the Armenian calendar, Easter*.

zenar In the Ethiopian tradition, the girdle* enclosing the alb* or kamis.

zena-zil Ethiopian musical instrument that produces a rattle-like sound.

zende In the Syrian Church, a pair of richly ornamented cuffs fastening the sleeves of the priestly sticharion*.

Zeno, St. (c. 362–375) Bishop of Verona*. He was an African by birth. His sermons were collected and published in *Tractatus*. Feast day: Arpil 12.

zeon (Gk., hot water) In the Byzantine Rite*, small metal container for hot water poured into the chalice* before the reception of the Holy Communion*.

Zeon

Zephyrinus, St. (d. 217) Pope from 198. He is commemorated as a martyr*. Feast day: August 26.

Zernov, Nicholas (1898–1980) Russian scholar. Leaving Russia after the Russian Revolution, he settled in England in 1934. From 1934 to 1947 he was secretary of the Fellowship of St. Alban and St. Sergius*. From 1947 to 1966 he was Spalding lecturer of Eastern Orthodox* culture in the University of Oxford. Among his many books are *Eastern Christendom* (1961) and *Russian Religious Renaissance of the Twentieth Century* (1963).

zewd In the Ethiopian tradition, crown used by priests.

zezle In the Jacobite Rite, cymbals which, together with the noqusho*, a type of gong, are sounded at the sanctus*, institution, epiclesis*, and blessing before Holy Communion*.

zhamagirk (Arm., Book of Hours) Breviary* or liturgy of the hours.

Zica Monastery of the Savior at Zica in Serbia built by Stefan I, brother of Sava*. Its most famous relic* was the hand of St. John the Baptist, now at Siena. Zica was heavily bombed and damaged during World War II.

Ziegenbalg, Bartholomaeus (1682–1719) German cofounder with H. Plutschau* of the first Protestant mission to India and the first to translate the New Testament into an Indian language. Converted at 16, he accepted along with H. Plutschau a call to go to Tranquebar, a Danish settlement on the Coromandel coast. There, braving local and official opposition, they established a complex of facilities that included schools, orphanages, printing press, and training schools, a model that came to be known as the "Tranquebar Method." Ziegenbalg also produced the first translation of the New Testament into Tamil (1714).

zimarra See SIMAR.

zinnar In the Coptic tradition, a girdle*. Originally imposed on Christians as a mark of shame and humiliation by the mad caliphs.

Zinzendorf, Count Nikolaus Ludwig Graf von (1700–1760) Founder of the Moravian Brudergemeine or Moravian Brethren*. A deeply Pietist youth, he became interested in foreign missions after meeting the Danish-Halle missionaries to India. While in the civil service in Saxony, he purchased an estate at Berthelsdorf in 1722 and invited a group of Bohemian Protestant refugees (Unitas Fratrum) to form a Christian community called Herrnhut* and from 1727 devoted his full time to the development of this community. He broke with the Pietists and began to teach a heart religion growing from a deeply mystical and experiential faith and promoting ecumenical relationship with other confessions and worldwide evangelism. When the Pietists and the Lutherans dismissed his ideas, he formed a separate sect with himself as its bishop. The Moravian evangelistic fervor was expressed in missions to the Caribbean in 1734. He also sent missionaries to Holland, Baltic provinces, England, and the American colonies. Zinzendorf's last years were spent as a pastor at Herrnhut*. For some time, he had considerable influence on Evangelicals, especially John Wesley*. His hymns, prayers, and poems still inspire his followers.

Count Nikolaus von Zinzendorf

zinzgha Armenian musical instrument consisting of two bronze plates struck against each other like cymbals at certain high points of the liturgy.

Zitomislic Monastery on the River Neretva between Mostar and Medjugorje* in Herzegovina built between 1566 and 1602/03. The first Orthodox theological school was opened in the monastery in 1858. In 1941 the entire community of monks was killed by the Croat Ustase, and parts of the monastery were burned. It was restored, but the complex was again burned by the Croats in 1992.

Zizka, John (d. 1424) Founder of the Taborites*, the most radical of the followers of John Hus*. Zizka was a brilliant soldier, and his army defeated the imperial troops. The group disintegrated after his death.

Zoe (Gk., life) Renewal movement in the Greek Orthodox Church, emphasizing prayer, Bible reading, worship, and personal devotions.

zone Girdle worn by priests of the Byzantine Rite* over the sticharion* and the epitrachelion*.

zoodochos (Gk., life-receiving) 1. Tomb of Christ which received the body of Christ. 2. Zoodochos Pege. Shrine and monastery outside Constantinople*. 3. One of the titles of the Virgin Mary*.

Zosimus, St. (d. 418) Pope from 417. He revoked Pope Innocent I's condemnation of Pelagius* and Celestius* and readmitted them to communion in 417. Then, under pressure from African bishops, he reversed himself. Feast day: December 26.

zqifutho (lit., the cross) In the Jacobite Rite, arrangement of the particles* of broken consecrated bread to resemble the Crucifixion.

Zuart'noc' The seventh-century rotunda Church of the Guardian Angels near Etchmiadzin*, Armenia, built between 646 and 652 by Catholicos Nerses III. It was one of the great achievements of medieval Armenian architecture.

Zuccaro, Federigo (1542–1609) Italian painter who decorated cathedrals in Florence* and Rome*.

Zuccaro, Taddeo (1529–1566) Italian painter to Pope Julius III* and Paul IV. With his brother Federigo*, he painted frescoes* in the Vatican*.

zucchetto Small, round skullcap worn by Catholic clergy during Mass*. Its color indicates the grade of the wearer. The pope wears white; the cardinals, red; bishops, violet; and others, black.

zumara (lit., the song) In the Assyrian Rite, preparatory rite preceding the reading of the Gospel.

Zumarrage, Juan de (1468–1548) Spanish Franciscan who became the first bishop of Mexico. He published some of the earliest books printed in the Americas. He also built the first high school and seminary in the Western Hemisphere.

zunnar In the Syrian and Maronite churches, girdle* worn over the alb*. Called zunnara in the Assyrian Church*.

Zurbaran, Francisco de (1598–1662) Spanish painter. Most of his paintings were done for religious houses and consisted of austere pictures of saints*. About 1630 he was appointed as painter to Philip IV, who described him as the "king of painters." His numerous commissions resulted in a painting of *Bonaventura, Apotheosis of St. Thomas Aquinas;* many paintings for the Carthusians* at Xeres; 13 on Jerome for the Hieronymites* at Guadalupe; and a series on great founders of religious orders, from Elias to Loyola*, for the Capuchins* at Castellon. Among his other noble paintings are *The Martyrdom of St. Serapion* (1628), *St. Margaret* (1631), *St. Francis* (1635–1640, 1639), *Saint on His Bier* (1639), and *Adoration of the Magi* (1638).

Zurich City in Switzerland that was a stronghold of Zwinglian Protestantism* during the Reformation*. It was also a birthplace of Anabaptist* radicalism.

Zurich Consensus Creed of the Reformed Churches reconciling the views of John Calvin* and Heinrich Bullinger*, head of the Swiss Reformed Church and successor to Zwingli*, on the doctrine of the Lord's Supper*. The first nine articles declare that the Lord's Supper is not a mere symbol, but a testimony of seal and grace* as well as spiritual communion with Christ.

zuyoho In the Jacobite Rite, elevation* of the paten* and chalice*, one after the other, during the liturgy.

Zwemer, Samuel Marinus (1867–1952) American "Apostle to Islam." He was an early leader in the Student Volunteer Movement*. At seminary he and James Cantine planned to start a mission to the world's most difficult field in Muslim countries. From 1890 he worked in the Arabian Peninsula under the aegis of the Dutch Reformed Church*. In 1911 he founded the periodical *The Moslem,* now *The Muslim World*, and edited it for 40 years. From 1913 to 1929 he worked out of Cairo, traveling throughout the Islamic world. From 1929 he taught at Princeton Theological Seminary and at the Missionary Training Institute at Nyack, New York.

Zwettl Cistercian monastery at Zwettl in lower Austria, founded in 1137. The Gothic* buildings were largely destroyed by the Hussites*. The surviving buildings include the monastery chapel dating from 1218, the cloister* (1180–1240), and the chapterhouse (1159–1180). Zwettl represents a mixture of architectural styles, passing from Romanesque to Gothic* to Baroque.

Zwickau Prophets Group of early Anabaptists* who tried to establish a religious community at Zwickau in Saxony in the sixteenth century. They were led by Nicholas Storch, Thomas Drechsel, and Marcus Stubner. Influenced by the teachings of the Waldensians and the Taborites*, they preached a radical theology that rejected infant baptism*, professional ministers, and the institutional church. They claimed to be under the direct influence of the Holy Spirit* and to receive revelations through visions and dreams, and they declared the imminent return of Christ. They were expelled from Zwickau and later from Wittenberg*.

Zwingli, Ulrich (Huldreich) (1484–1531) Swiss reformer. Ordained a priest in 1506, he became a friend of Erasmus* and a student of Greek and Hebrew. In 1518 he was elected preacher at the Old Minster in Zurich*, where he remained for the rest of his life. In 1519 he initiated the Reformation* in Switzerland with his attacks on purgatory*, invocation of

Ulrich Zwingli

saints*, and monasticism*. In 1522 his conflict with the ecclesiastical authorities escalated with the publication of his first tract, *Von Erkiesen und Fryheit der Spysen,* followed by a second, *Architeles.* Zwingli's rejection of the authority of the pope, the Mass*, images and pictures, fasting, church music, and clerical celibacy* received the full support of the City Council which legalized the Reformation in 1523.

Zwingli's views on the sacraments* represented a far more radical break with tradition than did the Lutheran position. Yet, at the same time, he broke with his most ardent followers, Felix Manz* and Conrad Grebel*, over the issue of infant baptism*. In 1529 he met Luther* and Melanchthon* at the Marburg Conference but failed to reach an agreement with them on doctrine He died in a battle against the Roman Catholic Forest Cantons. Zwingli is remembered as the first of the Reformed* theologians and his theological positions came to be known as Zwinglianism*.

Zwinglianism Tenets developed by Zwingli* on the Eucharist*. Against Luther*, Zwingli maintained that it is only the communicant's* faith that makes Christ present in the Eucharist and that there is no physical presence or any transformation of the elements*. He also maintained that there is no distinction between the Old Testament law and the gospel and that the civil authorities had the right to legislate in religious matters.

Zwischen den Zeiten (Ger., Between the Times) Influential neo-Orthodox theological journal founded by Friedrich Gogarten*, Karl Barth*, and George Merz, which was published from 1923 to 1933.

zymite In the Greek Orthodox Rite, priest who celebrates the Holy Eucharist* with unleavened bread*.

Christian Centuries

THE FIRST CENTURY (1–100): THE AGE OF THE APOSTLES

Status of the Christian church
On the day of the Pentecost: About 4,000 members. At the end of the first century: 0.6 percent of the population of the then known world is Christian, 70 percent non-white, 28 percent evangelized. The Scriptures are available in 6 languages.

Popes of the century
St. Peter (d. before 66), Linus (66–78), Anacletus (79–91), Clement I (91–101)

Christians of the century
St. Paul, St. Peter, St. John, St. Stephen, St. Mark, St. Luke, St. Matthew

1. The birth of Christ is the great watershed in human history, but it was not a cosmic event like an exploding supernova, but rather the gentle cry of an infant in the Judean night. For the next 2,000 years and beyond, that cry would reverberate through the corridors of time, changing human lives, as no other before or since.

2. The world was at peace when Christ was born. Octavian, later Emperor Caesar Augustus, was at the zenith of his power, and his legions kept peace in the largest empire in history up to that time. It extended from Armenia and Arabia in the east, Nubia and Carthage in the south, Gaul in the north, and Spain in the west. Outside of Rome, there were only two great powers, China and India, but they were outside the pale of known civilization.

3. Christianity began not with the birth of Christ, but with his resurrection. The New Testament, like all testaments, became effective only with the death of the testator. It is not so much Christ's message that forms the foundation stone of Christianity as his atoning sacrifice and his resurrection.

4. The event that transformed a small band of apostles and their immediate followers into the largest missionary enterprise in the world at that time was the Pentecost. On this day the Holy Spirit was poured down on this motley crowd of believers, and they were emboldened to attempt audacious things, challenging the established religions of Greece and Rome.

5. Christianity spread like a conflagration, a fire from heaven that consumed the pagan cultures of the day. Within two decades of Calvary, Christianity had spread to three continents: Paul, Peter, and possibly James took it to Europe; Mark took it to Africa; St. Thomas took it to India; and the other apostles took it to some of the smaller countries in the Middle East. By the end of the first century, there were Christians in Egypt, Nubia, Armenia, France, Italy, Spain, Greece, Cyprus, Germany, Britain, Mesopotamia, Persia, India, Illyria, Dalmatia, Asia Minor, Albania, Carthage, Libya, and all of North Africa.

6. Within seven years of Calvary, Christians were called by that name for the first time in Antioch. In Roman usage, the suffix -ian implied the property of, and the term Christian meant, in its original sense, one who belonged to Christ rather than someone who simply believed in him.

7. The three decades after Calvary were dominated by a man who was not even one of the twelve apostles—Paul, formerly Saul, the learned Jew from Cilicia. Paul was a towering figure in all except the physical sense, a brilliant intellect, a gifted writer, and a tireless worker. Two-thirds of the New Testament came from his pen. His epis-

tles form the foundation of Christian theology. Known as the "Apostle of the Gentiles," Paul almost singlehandedly took the gospel to the non-Jewish world and made it a global rather than an ethnic religion.

8. Within a few years of Calvary, Christianity had its first martyr—the protomartyr Stephen. Stephen set the pattern that will last through the centuries. The blood of the martyrs would become the seed of the church, and millions of Christian martyrs would give their lives for their faith.

9. Open persecution of Christians began in Palestine under King Herod Agrippa, who beheaded James the Great, one of the first apostles, in Jerusalem. Soon, as Christianity spread to other provinces of the Roman Empire, it brought on Christians the imperial wrath. In the first century, both Nero and Domitian persecuted the new religion and put many Christians to the sword or threw them to the lions.

10. By the end of the first century, Christianity had cut its links to Judaism. Christians were ousted from all synagogues. The temple of Solomon in Jerusalem, in fulfillment of the prophecy of Jesus, was destroyed by the Romans, and the Jews were expelled from their native land after the suppression of their final revolt against Rome in A.D. 70. For the next nineteen centuries, Jews and Christians would remain hostile to each other.

11 The four Gospels, all of Paul's epistles, and most of the other epistles in the New Testament were completed by the end of the first century.

THE SECOND CENTURY (100–200): AGE OF THE CHURCH FATHERS

Status of the Christian church
At the end of the second century, the world is 3.4 percent Christian, 68 percent of them non-white, 32 percent evangelized. The Scriptures are available in 7 languages.

Popes of the century
Evaristus (101–109), Alexander I (109–116), Sixtus I (116–125), Telesphorus (125–137), Hyginus (138–142), Pius I (142–155), Anicetus (155–166), Soter (166–74), Eleutherius (174–189), Victor I (189–198)

Christians of the century
St. Ignatius, St. Polycarp, Tertullian, Justin Martyr, Hermas, Tatian, Irenaeus, Clement of Alexandria

1. At the turn of the first century, the last of the surviving apostles, John, was an exile on the island of Patmos, where the angel of the Lord parted the veil of the future and revealed to him the mysteries of things to be. His Apocalypse, couched in enigmatic language, spoke of cosmic cataclysms that defy human understanding. The Apocalypse was to become the last chapter of the New Testament, and he ended the great drama of which he had been such a faithful witness with the words, "Even so, come, Lord Jesus."

2. A new generation of saints and martyrs took up the torch of faith even as the last of the apostles passed from the scene. The greatest among these were Ignatius of Antioch and Polycarp, bishop of Smyrna, who was burned at the stake. Other Church Fathers were defining the faith that had been handed down from the apostles, creating a *consensus patrum* that was to develop later. Irenaeus of Lyons, student of Polycarp, emerged as one of the earliest Christian theologians. His *Against Heresies* was the first attempt to defend orthodoxy.

3. The fledgling church was being beset by heretics even by the beginning of the second century. The most formidable of these heretics was Marcion of Sinope, who was a brilliant theologian. He was the first to realize the radical nature of the Christian revelation and to break away completely from Judaism. He considered the Jehovah of the Old Testament as a demiurge who was not only inferior to the Father of Jesus Christ, but, in fact, evil. Marcion rejected most of the Old Testament and accepted only the Pauline Epistles in the New Testament. By doing so, he prompted the church to determine the authenticity of each of the books of the Bible. The Gnostics also emerged as a serious threat to orthodoxy. They followed a forerunner of Manichaeism that posited a struggle between a god of light and a god of darkness and offered knowledge (gnosis) as the path of salvation.

4. By the end of the second century, the church

recognized twenty-three books of the New Testament as canonical. At this time, these books came to be called Scripture. Other New Testament writings were received more slowly. Doubts persisted about Hebrews, Jude, 2 Peter, 2 and 3 John, and Revelation. Certain books not included in the modern New Testament were considered canonical by some churches, but rejected by others. These included the Epistle of Barnabas and the *Shepherd of Hermas.*

5. By the second century, two of the seven major sacraments of the Roman Catholic Church —baptism and Eucharist—had been accepted as the defining marks of a Christian life. The other five sacraments, including extreme unction, confirmation, ordination, marriage, and monastic consecration, were being incorporated as divine services. Baptism was originally adult baptism, but paedobaptism, or the baptism of infants, was becoming increasingly the norm. The Eucharist was being celebrated on Sundays as prescribed by Paul rather than on the Sabbath, as the early Christians did.

6. By the end of the second century, Christianity was sweeping the Empire, posing a threat to the imperial religion. Tertullian wrote, "There is no nation indeed which is not Christian." Hermas wrote, "The Son of God has been preached to the ends of the earth." And Justin Martyr wrote that "Christ has been proclaimed to every race of men." Christianity spread to present-day Morocco, Bulgaria, Portugal, Romania, Arabia, and Austria.

7. The second century saw the birth of Christian literature. Among the notable works was the *Didache*, an important document describing Christian beliefs, practices, and church government. Justin Martyr wrote his *Apology*, introducing the branch of theology known as apologetics. Another classic is the *Shepherd of Hermas* by the subapostolic writer Hermas.

8. In 132 the Jews revolted again under Bar Kokeba, leading to the second destruction of Jerusalem by the Romans in 134. Almost the entire Jewish population of Palestine were either killed or exiled, and they were not to return to their native land until modern times.

9. The second century witnessed even more brutal persecutions of Christians under Septimus Severus and Marcus Aurelius. The number of martyrs throughout the Roman Empire were in the thousands. The church was planted on blood, and it was being watered with blood.

THE THIRD CENTURY (200–300): THE GREAT PERSECUTIONS

Status of the Christian church
At the end of the third century, 10.4 percent of the world's population is Christian, 65.7 percent of them non-white, 36 percent evangelized. The Scriptures are available in 10 languages.

Popes of the century
Zephyrinus (198/9–217), Callistus I (217–222), Urban I (222–230), Pontian (230–235), Anterus (235–236), Fabian (236–250), Cornelius (251–253), Lucius I (253–254), Stephen I (254–257), Sixtus II (257–258), Dionysius (260–268), Felix I (269–274), Eutychian (275–283), Caius (283–296), Marcellinus (296–304)

Christians of the century
St. Anthony the Great, Origen, St. Gregory the Illuminator, Cyprian of Carthage, Gregory Thaumaturgus, Hippolytus, Novatian, Dionysius the Great

1. By 200 the Scriptures were translated into seven languages, including Syriac and Coptic. The edition of the four Gospels in a continuous narrative, compiled by Tatian about 150 to 160, began to circulate widely in Syriac-speaking churches where it became the standard text until the fifth century when it was replaced by the four separate Gospels we have today.

2. The third century saw the birth of Christian monasticism in Egypt. St. Anthony the Great, born in the middle of the century, was the first Desert Father to go into the Wadi el Natrun as a hermit to launch the great wave of asceticism that would reach its full flowering in the fourth century.

3. In the early third century, Christian theology was taken to new heights by two theologians based in Alexandria. By the end of the second century, Alexandria was the site of a great school of catechumens of which Clement of Alexandria was the head from 190. He was an authority on Greek phi-

losophy, and he was able to fashion a theology rooted in the best hellenic traditions. Clement was among the first to describe Christ as the Logos, the Word of God. After Clement came Origen, the greatest of the Alexandrian theologians. He taught in Alexandria for 28 years. He was a very prolific writer and left behind him some 2,000 works about which Jerome wrote, "Who could ever read all that Origen wrote?" Origen's writings included commentaries on most books of the New Testament. Origen was killed in the Decian persecution.

4. The Decian persecution began in the middle of the century. Decius issued a decree requiring all citizens to sacrifice to an image of the emperor and to obtain a certificate called *libellus* attesting to their obedience. Those who failed to obtain a *libellus* were tortured and beheaded, a fate that befell most of the bishops and church leaders. Valerian, who succeeded Decius as emperor, issued another decree in 257: "The most sacred emperors Valerian and his son Gallienus command that there shall be no meetings of Christians in any place, and that they shall not frequent the cemeteries. If anyone fails to observe this beneficial precept, he shall be beheaded." Those who were killed included Cyprian of Carthage, one of the greatest of Christian theologians. The persecution ended in 261 when Emperor Gallienus issued his edict of toleration.

5. The end of the third century marked the bloodiest persecutions against Christians. In 298, during pagan sacrifices at a temple in Antioch, the priests accused Christians of disrupting their ceremonies. Roman troops were called in, and they unleashed a persecution that lasted more than seven years and left hundreds of thousands dead. Diocletian, the senior emperor, had been at first tolerant of Christians during the first 20 years of his reign, as his wife and daughter were probably Christians. But Galerius, the junior emperor, was opposed to the new religion. In 300, as some Christians refused to serve in the imperial legions, Galerius ordered all Roman soldiers to offer sacrifices to the pagan gods. Three years later, further edicts ordered the destruction of churches, the confiscation of Scriptures, and the arrest of bishops and theologians. In 304 the edict was extended to all citizens of the empire. As Galerius redoubled his efforts to stamp out Christianity, Lactantius wrote, "There is another cause why God permits persecutions to be carried out against us, that the people of God may be increased."

6. In the third century North Africa and Carthage, its principal city, were among of the most heavily Christianized areas of the Roman Empire. It was the first Latin-speaking church and produced some of the greatest of the Church Fathers, including Tertullian and Augustine.

7. In the third century the first church buildings began to take shape as rectangular-shaped basilicas. Previously Christians met in homes or in underground hiding places. Archeological excavations in Dura-Europos, on the eastern frontier of the Roman Empire, discovered the remains of the earliest surviving Christian church, about 250. It had an altar, a chair, a baptistery, and room for some sixty people.

8. The third century saw the establishment of the first Christian kingdom and the first national church. St. Gregory the Illuminator (257–332) went to Armenia and persuaded King Tiridates, who was then persecuting the church, to embrace Christianity. The king then encouraged all his people to follow him, the first time such a national conversion had taken place. Armenia is the oldest Christian nation in the world.

THE FOURTH CENTURY (300–400): IMPERIAL CONVERSION

Status of the Christian church
At the end of the fourth century, 12 generations after Christ, 17.1 percent of the population of the known world is Christian, 64 percent of them non-white, 39 percent evangelized. The Scriptures are available in 11 languages.

Popes of the century
Marcellus I (306–308/9), Eusebius (310), Militiades (311–314), Silvester (314–335), Mark (336), Julius I (337–352), Liberius (352–366), Damasus (366–384), Siricius (384–399), Anastasius (399–401)

Christians of the century
Eusebius of Caesarea, Constantine the Great, Ambrose of Milan, Jerome, Basil the Great, St. John Chrysostom, Pachomius, Athanasius

1. The fourth century is remembered as the century when the church emerged from its catacombs and became an established religion in the Roman Empire. The central event in the century took place not in a church or a palace, but on a bridge, Milvian Bridge, outside Rome, where Emperor Constantine the Great defeated his rival Maxentius in 312. At that battle, following instructions received in a dream the previous night, Constantine fought under the sign of the cross that was subsequently modified into the labarum standard. Although he was baptized only near his death in 337, Constantine favored Christianity for the rest of his life. He built several basilicas, including St. Peter's, used Christian symbols on his coinage, and declared Sunday the official rest day. In 313 he and fellow-emperor Licinius issued the Edict of Milan, ending the persecution against Christians.

2. However, Christianity did not become the state religion until much later. In the interim, Julian the Apostate, who came to power in 361, tried to restore paganism and renewed the persecution of Christians. However, he was killed in battle in the third year of his reign. On his deathbed, according to tradition, he acknowledged the triumph of Christianity by saying, "Thou hast won, pale Galilean." His successors, Jovian and Flavius Theodosius, favored Christianity. In 380 Theodosius made Christianity the official religion of the empire and in 391 he closed down all pagan temples. "It is our will," he decreed, "that all the peoples we rule shall practice that religion that Peter the Apostle transmitted to the Romans."

3. Almost at the same time that Christianity had succeeded in overcoming the pagan empire, the first of the many serious theological dissensions that were to plague the church in the succeeding centuries broke out. In 319 Arius, a Libyan presbyter, began to preach a heresy that denied the divinity of Christ, the cardinal tenet on which Christianity is founded. Although Arius was silenced and exiled, the heresy gained support in Antioch and other places. The celebrated opponent of Arianism was Athanasius the Great, who had succeeded Alexander as bishop of Alexandria in 328. His tenacity as the champion of orthodoxy earned him the sobriquet, *Athanasius Contra Mundum.*

4. The rise of Arian heresy was the occasion for one of the defining events in Christian history, the First Ecumenical Council at Nicaea. It was convened by Constantine, who ordered 1,800 bishops to meet at Nicaea (modern-day Iznik in Turkey). Between 220 and 250 bishops actually attended under the presidency of Hosius, the venerable bishop of Cordoba. The council not only condemned Arius, but they drew up the central statement of the Christian faith, now known as the Nicene Creed. The creed defined the Trinity and affirmed that Jesus was of one substance with the Father and that he was true God of true God. Arianism, however, survived in pockets of the Empire, especially among the Goths. The Second Ecumenical Council of Constantinople reaffirmed the Nicene Creed.

5. The fourth century also saw the birth of Christian history. Eusebius of Caesarea, kown as the "Father of Church History," wrote the first major historical work on Christianity, *Ecclesiastical History,* in ten books.

6. The fourth century was the golden age of Egyptian monasticism. The Egyptian Desert at this time contained the largest concentration of monks at any time or place in history, living as hermits or in cenobitic monasteries. The most famous of these monks was Pachomius, who founded the Monastery of Tabennisi.

7. Christianity continued to expand into all parts of the known world. By the end of the fourth century, it had spread to Belgium, Switzerland, Edessa, Hungary, Ethiopia, and Luxembourg. Nestorian missionaries carried the gospel to parts of Northern India and Afghanistan as a preliminary to their eventual evangelization of Central Asia and China. The first Christians arrived in Ireland.

8. In the fourth century, Christian liturgy and the special vestments associated with it began to take shape. Bishops began to wear purple, and the clergy began to wear a cloak of fine material during the celebration of the Eucharist.

9. Constantine moved the capital of the Roman Empire to Byzantium and renamed it Constantinople in 330.

10. The canon of the New Testament was finally agreed upon in 367. The present twenty-seven books were listed both in the Easter Letter of Athanasius in the East and the Synod of Carthage in the West.

11. In 381 the First Council of Constantinople was held under Emperor Theodosius I to unite the church on the basis of the Nicene Creed. It ratified the work of the Council of Nicaea, condemned Apollinarianism, and endorsed the Niceno-Constantinopolitan Creed.

THE FIFTH CENTURY (400–500): THE GREAT COUNCILS

Status of the Christian church
At the end of the fifth century, 16 generations after Christ, 22.4 percent of the world population is Christian, 61.9 percent non-white, 42 percent evangelized. The Scriptures are available in 13 languages.

Popes of the century
Innocent I (402–417), Zosimus (417–418), Boniface I (418–422), Celestine I (422–432), Sixtus III (432–440), Leo I (440–461), Hilarus (461–468), Simplicius (468–483), Felix III (483–492), Gelasius I (492–496), Anastasius II (496–498)

Christians of the century
Augustine of Hippo, St. Patrick, Leo the Great, Jerome, Cyril of Alexandria, Theodore of Mopsuestia, Theodoret of Cyrrhus

1. The fifth century is known to church as the post-Nicene Age. In the Council of Nicaea, the church had passed another landmark. Christianity had become the established religion of the Roman Empire, but the lands outside the imperial borders still beckoned Christian missionaries. The church had successfully defused the first challenge to orthodoxy posed by Arius. But it still had to contend with many more heresies before the century ended.

2. The first of these heresies was Nestorianism. Nestorius, the patriarch of Constantinople, taught that there are two distinct natures in Jesus Christ, the divine and the human, and Mary, as the mother of the human Jesus was not entitled to the title Theotokos, or Mother of God. This was opposed to the orthodox teaching that the incarnate Christ was a single person, at once God and man. The Third Ecumenical Council was summoned by Emperor Theodosius II and held at Ephesus in 431 to condemn Nestorianism. The Council of Ephesus also condemned Pelagianism, a heresy formulated by the British Pelagius and his associate Celestius. Pelagianism denied the original sin and held that man can achieve salvation through his own efforts.

3. The next great heresy to trouble the church was Monophysitism, also called Eutychianism after its early advocate Eutyches. Monophysitism was a reaction to Nestorianism and held that Jesus Christ had only a divine nature and not a human nature. Many variant forms of this heresy developed over the centuries. To condemn this heresy, the Council of Chalcedon was held in 451 in Chalcedon, a city in Asia Minor. The council drew up a statement of faith known as the Definition of Chalcedon and affirmed Pope Leo's Tome. However, the Definition of Chalcedon proved unacceptable to the churches of Alexandria and Antioch, both of which to this day uphold a moderate form of Monophysitism. One of the great champions of Monophysitism was Jacob Baradeus, and the Syrian Orthodox Church is thus known as the Jacobite Church.

4. The towering figure of the fifth century was St. Augustine, bishop of Hippo, whose *City of God* and *Confessions* are not only theological but literary classics. Augustine's ideas dominated Christian theology for centuries just as Aristotle did Greek philosophy. Augustine introduced the term *predestination* into the currency of Christian thought, and it passed through Roman Catholic Scholasticism to influence John Calvin and the Reformers of the sixteenth century. During his struggle against Pelagianism and the doctrine of human free will, Augustine wrote a massive vindication of Christianity against its pagan critics. The 22 books of the *City of God* appeared in installments and portrayed Christianity as the heavenly city whose gates are open to all believers. Augustine wrote more than 1,000 works in all, including 242 books.

5. Meanwhile, in Jerusalem, the monk and scholar Jerome (Hieronymus) completed the translation of the Old and New Testaments into Latin after working on it for 22 years. The Vulgate, as his work came to be known, was the only Bible used in the Latin Church for the next 1000 years. Jerome was a prolific writer. Beside the translation of the Bible, he was active in many of the controversies of the day.

6. Christianity continued to spread to the farthest corners of the known world. In the fifth century, many more countries were added to the those evangelized earlier, including western North Africa, Isle of Man, San Marino, Liechtenstein, Caucasus, and Ireland. The gospel was brought to the Irish by St. Patrick, whose work as the apostle of Ireland spanned 30 years. The Franks became part of the Christian world when Clovis, their king, was converted and baptized in 496.

7. The fifth century is particularly significant for the Roman Catholic Church as it marked the consolidation of its influence. St. Leo I, also known as Leo the Great, became pope in 440. A great defender of orthodoxy, his *Tome* was accepted by the Council of Chalcedon. He also increased the power of his office by persuading Attila the Hun to spare Rome and by securing concessions when the Vandals took Rome. He was the first to use the title, once reserved for the emperors, Pontifex Maximus, the Supreme Pontiff.

8. In 404 the imperial residence was established away from Rome in Ravenna, in northeast Italy. The city provided a safe haven for the Western emperor and went on to grow in wealth and importance until it fell to the Goths in 492.

9. In the East, the Nestorian Church was growing rapidly in Persia, Arabia, and Central Asia.

THE SIXTH CENTURY (500–600): THE GOLDEN AGE OF THE EASTERN CHURCH

Status of the Christian church
At the end of the sixth century, 19 generations after Christ, 21 percent of the world population is Christian, 59 percent of them non-white, and 39 percent evangelized. The Scriptures are available in 14 languages.

Popes of the century
Symmachus (498–514), Hormisdas (514–523), John I (523–526), Felix IV (526–530), Boniface II (530–532), John II (532–535), Agapetus I (535–536), Silverius (536–537), Vigilius (537–555), Pelagius I (556–561), John III (561–574), Benedict I (575–579), Pelagius II (579–590), Gregory I (590–604)

Christians of the century
St. Columba, St. Benedict of Nursia, Dionysius Exiguus, Emperor Justinian, St. Augustine of Canterbury

1. The year 500 is generally reckoned by historians as the beginning of the Dark Ages that lasted until 1000. But for the Christian church, from which the dark cloud of Roman persecution had just lifted, the sixth century was anything but dark. It was specially significant for the Eastern churches for which this would be the last full century of free growth before the dark night of Islam would envelop them, seemingly forever.

2. For both the Nestorian Church, an outcast church after the Council of Ephesus, and the Monophysite churches of Egypt, Syria, Ethiopia, and Armenia, outcasts after the Council of Chalcedon, this was a century of growth. Shut out of the West, all these churches grew in the only direction in which they could—toward the east and south. Nestorians gained hundreds of thousands of converts in Central Asia. The Monophysites spread throughout the Middle East. This included the Arabian Peninsula, including Yemen, and across the Arabian Sea into Malankara in India, where the St. Thomas Christians formed a Christian beachhead. There were reports of Christians in the modern Sri Lanka. Syrian Orthodox Nine Saints founded a monastery in Ethiopia and thus brought the Ethiopians into the Monophysite fold. Jacob Baradaeus is reported to have ordained 100,000 priests to minister to the expanding number of Christians in Syria and Mesopotamia. Justinian sent missionaries to Nubia who converted its king. Nestorians sent missionaries to the Huns. In Egypt the number of bishoprics grew to 168.

3. In the West, too, there was growth, although less conspicuously. Scotland was evangelized by Columba, who founded the celebrated Iona Monastery in the Inner Hebrides. The monastery became famous for its learning and was a popular center for pilgrimage until the Reformation.

4. Monasticism spread during this century to the West. The man responsible for bringing monastic institutions and ideals to the West was St. Benedict of Nursia, called the "Father of Western Monasticism." Repelled by the licentiousness of the society of his day, he withdrew from the world and retired to a cave at Subiaco about 500.

Here he lived as a hermit for some years, but as a community of monks gathered around him, he moved to Monte Cassino, where he founded the order of Benedictines and composed the rule named after him.

5. Toward the end of the century, in 574, Gregory, a high-ranking Roman official, resigned his post, gave all his wealth to the poor, and entered the Holy Orders. In 590 he was elected pope. Known as Gregory the Great, he instituted reforms in the church and sent St. Augustine to reevangelize England after the invasion of the Anglo-Saxons. Gregory also fostered the growth of monasticism and promoted liturgical music. His name is so closely linked with plainsong that it is commonly known as the Gregorian Chant. He is the fourth and the last of the traditional doctors of the church. He was canonized immediately after his death. Among the many reforms of St. Gregory was the institution of the Gregorian Calendar which established the leap year.

6. The Christian era, which firmly established the birth of Christ as the great dividing line of history, was born in this century. The Christianization of the calendar was an achievement that the world owes to a humble Scythian monk, Dionysius Exiguus, whose somewhat inaccurate arithmetic does not diminish the epic nature of his work. The Christian Era that he devised, each year of which is called Anno Domini (Year of Our Lord), has now become universal. Despite the many attempts by anti-Christians throughout the course of history to abandon it, Dionysius's work will probably last until the end of time as a lasting testimony.

7. The Second Council of Constantinople, the Fifth Ecumenical Council, was held in the middle of the century in 553. It was convoked by the Emperor Justinian, to resolve the so called "Three Chapters controversy" and thus bring back the Monophysite churches into the mainstream.

8. Justinian himself was one of the greatest of the Roman emperors. He and his queen, Theodora, worked tirelessly to advance orthodox Christianity. He closed the ancient schools of philosophy in Athens, had 70,000 persons baptized in Asia Minor, built the Hagia Sophia in Constantinople and the magnificent basilica at Ravenna, and established the legal system now known as the Code of Justinian.

9. The Arian Visigoths of Spain were converted to Catholicism, which was then declared the state religion.

10. Cosmas Indicopleustes, the Nestorian geographer, completed his *Topographia Christiana*, in 12 books.

THE SEVENTH CENTURY (600–700): THE ANTICHRIST FROM ARABIA

Status of the Christian church
At the end of the seventh century, 23 generations after Christ, the world is 22 percent Christian, 54 percent of them non-white, 31 percent evangelized. The Scriptures are available in 15 languages.

Popes of the century
Sabinian (604–606), Boniface III (607), Boniface IV (608–615), Adeodatus I (615–618), Boniface V (619–625), Honorius I (625–638), Severinus (640), John IV (640–642), Theodore I (642–649), Martin I (649–654), Eugene I (655–657), Vitalian (657–672), Adeodatus II (672–676), Donus (676–678), Agatho (678–681), Leo II (682–683), Benedict II (684–685), John V (685–686), Conon (686–687), Sergius I (687–701)

Christians of the century
St. Aidan, Alopen

1. Christ spoke of the Antichrist who one day will come with the sword to destroy his church. All the apostles and those who followed them speculated on the nature of the Antichrist, and many looked to Rome as the place where the Antichrist will appear. But before the Antichrist appeared, it was expected that many small antichrists will rise to trouble the church and try to decimate it. In the seventh century, one finally appeared, not from the West, as many had prophesied but from the East, from the city of Mecca in Arabia.

2. Muhammad (his name sometimes spelled as Mohammad or Mahmud) was an illiterate Bedouin who, toward the beginning of the century, reported receiving visions from the angel Gabriel (or possibly some Jew called Gabriel), who also dictated the book known as the Koran or Quran. The theology that the Koran outlines is

heavily borrowed from Judaism, and thus adamantly monotheistic and extraordinarily legalistic and rigid. But it was well suited to the genius of the desert, and it inspired his band of wild Arabian fanatics to embark on the Jihad, one of history's most enduring and most brutal proselytization missions by the sword. Through the next several centuries, this sword would decimate most of the Christian world in Asia and Africa as well as the Iberian Peninsula, but the rest of Europe would escape, at least until the fifteenth century.

3. Muslims, as the followers of Mohammad came to be known, swept across Palestine, Syria, Egypt, Libya, North Africa, and the Iberian Peninsula in one of the swiftest campaigns in military history. The Arabs, though culturally inferior to all the nations they conquered, soon imposed their religion and their language on the conquered peoples. So complete was the Arabicization of the peoples of the Middle East and North Africa that these Hamitic peoples consider themselves even to this day as "Semitic" Arabs, rather than as what they truly are: Berbers or Egyptians or Libyans or Phoenicians.

4. Between 688 and 691, the Caliph Abd-al Malik desecrated the temple mount by building the Dome of the Rock on it. The beautiful columns in the shrine are adorned with crosses, indicating those that were plundered from Christian churches.

5. As Christianity entered into its long eclipse in the lands of its origin and early growth, it continued to expand into Europe, China, Mongolia, Indonesia, and Niger. The list of newly Christianized countries included Netherlands and Andorra in Europe. The conversion of England was completed under Wilfrid as Sussex and the Isle of Man, the last strongholds of paganism, fell. The Synod of Whitby aligned the nascent church with Rome for the next nine centuries.

6. The oldest Anglo-Saxon translations and paraphrases of the Bible were made by Caedmon and Aldhelm.

7. Eastern and Western churches drifted further apart because of differences in church practices and doctrine. The Eastern Church allows its clergy to be married, as long as they are married before ordination. In the West, clerical celibacy is not only a desirable norm but is enforced as an ordinance.

8. Nestorians continued their vast missionary enterprise, particularly under Patriarch Yeshuyab, who had moved his capital to Seleucia-Ctesiphon. One million Persian Christians now belonged to the Nestorian Church. Alopen, a Nestorian missionary from Syria, traveled to China by foot and reached the capital, Chang'an, in 635. The Nestorian bishop of Merv converted some Turkish tribes. Nestorians also reached Mongolia and Indonesia. At this point, the territorial extent of the Nestorian Church was greater than that of the Western Church.

9. The Third Council of Constantinople—the Sixth Ecumenical Council—was held in 680 to condemn Monothelitism.

THE EIGHTH CENTURY (700–800): FRANKISH CHRISTIANITY

Status of the Christian church
At the end of the eighth century, 26 generations after Christ, 22.5 percent of the world population is Christian, 51 percent of them non-white, 31 percent evangelized. Scriptures are available in 15 languages.

Popes of the century
John VI (701–705), John VII (705–707), Sisinnius (708), Constantine (708–715), Gregory II (715–731), Gregory III (731–741) (Zacharias (741–752), Stephen II (752), Stephen III (752–757), Paul I (757–767), Stephen IV (768–772), Hadrian I (772–795)

Christians of the century
Bede, Boniface (Winifrith), Charles Martel

1. In 711 the Muslim Moors who had captured Carthage in 697 invaded Spain and Portugal, their first foothold in Europe. But in 732 Charles Martel saved European civilization and the Christian church by decisively beating the Muslims at the Battle of Tours, the first reverse the Arabs had suffered in almost 100 years.

2. The Arab conquests in the Middle East and North Africa were paralleled by the continued expansion of Christianity in Europe. Pepin, the son of Charles Martel, united the Franks and thus founded the first Christian empire in north-

ern Europe. At the request of Pope Stephen II, Pepin invaded Italy to defend it against the Lombards. Pepin gave the conquered lands to the church (called the Donation of Pepin) which established the papal states. Charlemagne, the son of Pepin, extended his empire through military conquests to cover all of present-day France, Germany, and Italy. He forced the German Saxons to convert.

3. In 722 St. Boniface, the "Apostle of the Germans," felled the Oak of Thor at Geismar, Hesse, marking the end of German paganism. He evangelized south and central Germany.

4. In 720 Bede the Venerable, known as the "Father of English History," translated the Gospel of John into English and later wrote *Ecclesiastical History*. Later, in 1899, Leo XIII declared him a doctor of the church.

5. The eighth century saw the beginning of the iconoclastic controversy that troubled the Eastern Church for a century. Emperor Leo III, the Isaurian, condemned the veneration of sacred images and relics as unbiblical and as the chief obstacle to the conversion of Jews and Muslims. Pope Gregory III condemned iconoclasm and supported the veneration of icons. In 754 a council of 300 Byzantine bishops endorsed iconoclasm, but the council was condemned by the Lateran Synod of 769.

6. The Second Council of Nicaea (the Seventh Ecumenical Council) was convened in 787. It strongly condemned iconoclasts. The council is the last of the ecumenical councils accepted by both Western and Eastern churches.

7. The Nestorian patriarchal see was moved from Seleucia-Ctesiphon to Baghdad.

8. The first missionaries from Ireland reached Iceland.

THE NINTH CENTURY (800–900): THE CAROLINGIAN RENAISSANCE

Status of the Christian church
At the end of the ninth century, 28 generations after Christ, 20 percent of the world population is Christian, 41 percent of them non-white; 26 percent of them evangelized. The Scriptures are available in 17 languages.

Popes of the century
Leo III (795–816), Stephen V (816–817), Paschal I (817–824), Eugene II (824–827), Valentine (827), Gregory IV (827–844), Sergius II (844–847), Leo IV (847–855), Benedict III (855–858), Nicholas I (858–867), Hadrian II (867–872), John VIII (872–882), Marinus I (882–884), Hadrian III (884–885), Stephen IV (885–891), Formosus (891–896), Boniface VI (896), Stephen VII (896–897), Romanus (897), Theodore II (897), John IX (898–900)

Christians of the century
Anskar, Sts. Cyril and Methodius

1. In 800 Charlemagne was crowned Roman emperor by Pope Leo III. Charlemagne encouraged all monasteries and churches to teach reading and writing. He appointed Alcuin as his adviser to oversee the founding of schools and scriptoria. His advocacy of ecclesiastical reforms and patronage of letters earned for his reign and the following centuries the description of the Carolingian Renaissance. After Charlemagne's death, his empire was split among his three sons.

2. Christian missionaries continued to evangelize central and northern Europe. Anskar, a monk from Flanders, known to later generations as the "Apostle of the North," took the gospel to Sweden and Denmark. In central Europe, Bavaria and Moravia were evangelized in a twin-pronged effort from the East and the West.

3. The Slavs, one of the most important peoples of eastern Europe, had not yet had the gospel preached to them. This was the task that the two brothers St. Cyril and St. Methodius, the "Apostles to the Slavs," undertook in 860 when they went on an imperial diplomatic mission to the Khazars, north of the Caucasus. In 862 Emperor Michael III entrusted them with a mission to the Moravians. Before leaving Constantinople, St. Cyril invented the Glagolitic alphabet and thus became the founder of Slavic literature. In 1980, the brothers were declared by Pope John Paul II to be the Patrons of Europe.

4. In 846 Muslims invaded Italy and even sacked Rome. This represented the zenith of their power which would begin its decline over the next few centuries.

5. In 857 communion between the Western and

Eastern churches was again suspended following what is known as the Photian Schism. Photius, who is venerated as a saint in the Orthodox Church, had been appointed patriarch of Constantinople in 858, succeeding Ignatius, who had been deposed. Pope Nicholas I, meeting in a synod at Rome, annulled the deposition of Ignatius and reinstated him as patriarch. This act gave great offense to Photius who, in turn, anathematized the pope. The Fourth Council of Constantinople condemned the Photian Schism. Although the dispute became moot after the death of Ignatius when Photius once again became the rightful patriarch, it had lasting consequences and contributed to the final break between the two churches.

6. The heavy hand of Arab Muslim oppression began to weigh down on the ancient Christian church in Egypt and all of North Africa. Christian education was prohibited, the heavy jiziya was levied on all dhimmis, as Christians and Jews were called under the caliphs, with the sole purpose of forcibly converting them to Islam. The celebration of Christian festivals, including Sunday worship and Christmas, was banned; no new church buildings were permitted and old ones were demolished; and all Christians were ordered to wear five-pound crosses around their necks.

7. In 864 Boris, the king of the Bulgars, was baptized. By 870 all of Bulgaria had been Christianized and a Bulgar had been consecrated as an archbishop. Meanwhile, the Serbs of Narenta Valley were baptized through the efforts of Emperor Basil I.

8. Severe persecutions against the Nestorian Church broke out in China. Thousands of churches and monasteries were destroyed.

THE TENTH CENTURY AND THE END OF THE FIRST MILLENNIUM (900–1000): SLAV CHRISTIANITY

Status of the Christian church
At the end of the first millennium, 32 generations after Christ, 18.7 percent of the world population is Christian, 39 percent of them non-white, 25 percent evangelized. The Scriptures are available in 17 languages.

Popes of the century
Benedict IV (900–903), Leo V (903), Sergius III (904–911), Anastasius III (911–913), Lando (913–914), John X (914–928), Leo VI (928), Stephen VIII (928–931), John IX (931–935), Leo VII (936–939), Stephen IX (939–942), Marinus II (942–946), Agapetus II (946–955), John XII (955–964), Leo VIII (963–965), Benedict V (964), John XIII (965–972), Benedict VI (973–974), Benedict VII (974–983), John XIV (983–984), John XV (985–996), Gregory V (996–999), Silvester II (999–1003)

Christians of the century
Vladimir of Kiev, Abbot Odo, Stephen of Hungary

1. The tenth century was a landmark in the history of Christianity. At this point more than 50 percent of the original homelands of the Christian faith had been submerged under the flood of Islam. All of North Africa and most of the Middle East were now part of what eventually came to be called the "Fertile Crescent" where Islam was supreme. As a result Christianity had become a purely Western or European religion. Whereas until now, white Christians were in a minority, they became a majority in this century and would remain so until the twentieth century.

2. As the century began, the first Christian missionaries reached Norway, the northernmost point of the expansion of Christianity in Europe. In 999 Leif Ericson converted to Christianity, and the next year he brought the gospel to his father's colony in Greenland. In neighboring countries, the conversion of Northmen was under way in Denmark, Norway, and Sweden.

3. The most significant event of the century was the conversion of Russia. The conversion began in 954 when Olga, the regent of Kiev, was baptized. In 987, Vladimir, the grand duke of Kiev, followed his grandmother Olga by being baptized. Wanting to embrace the purest form of Christianity, he sent emissaries to many countries. Those sent to Constantinople came back with glowing reports of the worship service in Hagia Sophia, the great cathedral built by Justinian. "We knew not," they said, "whether we were in heaven or on earth. For on earth there is no such splendor or such beauty, and we are at a loss

to describe it. Only we know that God dwells in the church among men, and that their worship surpasses the worship of all other places. We cannot forget their beauty." Vladimir was baptized in 988 and next year he ordered all Kievans to be baptized. In 991 the whole population of Novgorod was baptized by a bishop from Crimea. Within five centuries, Moscow was to become the "Third Rome," succeeding Constantinople that had prided itself as the "Second Rome."

4. In Egypt, Caliph El Hakim began one of the worst persecution of Christians since Diocletian. He destroyed thousands of churches and forced hundreds of thousands of Christians to convert to Islam. The number of Coptic bishops was reduced to 110. In North Africa, most of the Berbers were forced to apostasize.

5. Moravia became a part of the Western Church by the early part of the tenth century, along with Bohemia under Boleslav II. To the north of Moravia, Poland converted to the Latin form of Christianity when the Duke of Mieszka was baptized with his wife. The first Polish bishopric was established at Poznan. Meanwhile, in Hungary, the Magyars were converted under Stephen I, the saintly king. In 997, as the century drew to a close, Prussians, the last remaining pagans in Europe, were brought into the Christian fold.

6. Muslims continued to advance into Europe. Sicily was subjugated after 75 years as well as some coastal areas in southern Italy.

7. Monasticism rose in the West much later than in the East, but by the tenth century it was flourishing in Italy, France, Spain, and England. In France, William, duke of Aquitaine, founded the Benedictine Abbey of Cluny which became the center of monastic resurgence under Abbot Odo. Cluniacs adopted the strict Benedictine Rule, emphasizing personal spiritual life, long choir offices, and solemn worship. In the next century, the influence of Cluny reached its height with over 1,000 houses spread all over western Europe. The magnificent church at Cluny (which was desecrated during the French Revolution) was the largest church in Europe at that time, over 555 feet in length.

8. Otto I, the Great, the founder of the Holy Roman Empire, was crowned by Pope John XII in 962. This empire would last for another 900 years.

THE ELEVENTH CENTURY (1000–1100): THE GREAT SCHISM

Status of the Christian church
At the end of the eleventh century, 35 generations after Christ, 19 percent of the world population is Christian, 37 percent of them non-white, 25 percent of them evangelized. The Scriptures are available in 19 languages.

Popes of the century
John XVII (1003), John XVIII (1004–1009), Sergius IV (1009–1012), Benedict VIII (1012–1024), John XIX (1024–1032), Benedict IX (1032–1044, 1045, 1047–1048), Silvester III (1045), Gregory VI (1045–1046), Clement II (1046–1047), Damasus II (1048), Leo IX (1048–1054), Victor II (1055–1057), Stephen X (1057–1058), Nicholas II (1059–1061), Alexander II (1061–1073), Gregory VII (1073–1085), Victor III (1086–1087), Urban II (1088–1099)

Christians of the century
St. Stephen Harding, St. Bruno

1. On Saturday, July 16, 1054, as afternoon prayers were about to begin, Cardinal Humbert, legate of Pope Leo IX, strode up to the altar in the Cathedral of Hagia Sophia in Constantinople and placed on it a parchment excommunicating the patriarch of Constantinople, Michael Cerularius. He then marched out of the church, shaking the dust from his feet. This incident is said to mark the beginning of the schism between the Latin and Greek churches, a division that still persists. The incident was provoked by the fact that the Norman rulers of southern Italy, formerly under Byzantine Rule, replaced Greek bishops with Latin bishops. Patriarch Cerularius retaliated by closing down all Latin churches in Constantinople. However, the break was not complete, and both churches would continue negotiations on and off, and the Great Schism would become effective only centuries later.

2. Pope Urban II issued a call in 1096 for a vast Christian army for a crusade against the Muslim armies of the Antichrist. The crusade, so called because the Crusaders wore crosses, was the first Christian response to four centuries of Muslim assaults against Christianity, the brutal oppression of believers, and the destruction of churches

in Asia and Africa. The purpose of the Crusaders was to liberate the Holy Land from the infidels, reopen Jerusalem to pilgrims, and to stem the tide of the Seljuk Turks, then poised to take over Asia Minor and Constantinople. The Crusades took the form of a series of military expeditions, the first four of which lasted until 1204 and are numbered in conventional order.

The First Crusade lasted from 1097 to 1099, and it mobilized over 70,000 people. They captured Jerusalem in 1099 and set up the Latin Kingdom of Jerusalem under Godfrey of Bouillon. In the same year the Latin patriarchate of Jerusalem was established. Between 1204 and 1291 further expeditions were organized but with diminishing success until the last Latin possessions in the Holy Land fell to the Muslims in 1291.

3. In 1073 Hildebrand was invested as pope. His papacy, which lasted twelve years, is noted for his reforms and the moral revival of the church. He opposed simony, sexual immorality of the clergy and lay investiture, or the practice of lay rulers choosing bishops. He met considerable resistance from Henry II of Germany who, however, submitted to him at Canossa.

4. In 1071 the Turkish hordes under Alp Arslan overwhelmed the Byzantines at Manzikert in Anatolia. This battle marked the darkest chapter in Byzantine history, next to the fall of Constantinople, which would take place in 1453. The Byzantine defeat opened the floodgates to the Turks (whose name means appropriately "robber" in Turkic), who then swept through Asia Minor within the next four centuries and menaced Europe until modern times.

5. Even as the Muslims were strangling the church from Morocco to Afghanistan, the Nestorian Church had become the largest in the world with 250 dioceses stretching across Asia, including such forbidding places as Tibet and Sinkiang. There were 15 Nestorian metropolitan provinces within the Arab caliphate, and its authority extended as far as Malabar in India and Beijing in China. In northern Mongolia, Nestorians converted over 200,000 Keraits, including their prince. Nestorians constituted over 60 percent of the population in Syria, Iraq, and Khorasan.

6. The eleventh century saw the ultimate triumph of Christianity in Europe. The Norman Conquest of Britain in 1066 brought the British Isles fully into the Christian fold. The Norman reconquest of Sicily from the Arabs was completed in 1091. Iceland, the farthermost western European country, was Christianized and many monasteries and abbeys were established. The Patriarchate of Constantinople had 624 dioceses around eastern Mediterranean, and the Orthodox Church now included all of Russia. Christian kingdoms emerged in Denmark, England, Hungary, Norway, Poland, Sweden, and Scotland. Nubia, present-day Sudan, was completely Christianized, and the Nubian king erected many churches and monasteries.

7. New monastic orders followed the Benedictines. The first was the Carthusians. The ultrastrict monastery of Grand Chartreuse was founded near Grenoble in France in 1084. Carthusian houses, called charterhouses, spread throughout Europe. The most popular of the new orders was the Cistercians, which was founded in 1098 in the monastery at Citeaux in Burgundy in eastern France.

THE TWELFTH CENTURY (1100–1200): THE CRUSADES

Status of the Christian church

At the end of the twelfth century, 39 generations after Christ, 19.4 percent of the world population is Christian, 35 percent of them non-white, 26 percent evangelized. The Scriptures are available in 22 languages.

Popes of the century

Paschal II (1099–1118), Gelasius II (1118–1119), Callistus II (1119–1124), Honorius II (1124–1130), Innocent II (1130–1143), Celestine II (1143–1144), Lucius II (1144–1145), Eugene III (1145–1153), Anastasius IV (1153–1154), Hadrian IV (1154–1159), Alexander III (1159–1181), Lucius III (1181–1185), Urban III (1185–1187), Gregory VIII (1187), Clement III (1187–1191), Celestine III (1191–1198)

Christians of the century

Peter Abelard, Peter Valdes, St. Bernard, Thomas à Becket

1. The twelfth century witnessed two crusades as the Christian West made desperate attempts to

dislodge the Muslims from their stolen possessions. The Second Crusade was preached by St. Bernard of Clairvaux in response to the Muslim conquest of Edessa, the ancient Christian city in Asia Minor and crusader capital. It was led in 1147 by Louis VII of France and Emperor Conrad of Germany. It failed to relieve the besieged Christian garrisons, and after 30 years in 1187 it was overcome by the army of Saladin, who captured Jerusalem and overran a great part of the Latin kingdom. The disaster provoked the Third Crusade of 1189–1192, led by Emperor Frederick Barbarossa, Richard I of England, and Philip II of France. It captured Cyprus, Acre, and Jaffa, but Jerusalem itself remained in the hands of Saladin.

2. In 1174, the early precursors of the Reformation appeared in Europe. One of the most influential was a man called Peter Valdes, who inspired the Waldensian heresy. Valdes was a rich merchant of Lyons who underwent a personal conversion and gave all his wealth to the poor. His ministry was approved at first by Pope Alexander III on condition that he refrain from preaching except at the invitation of the clergy. However, Valdes and his followers broke the church's ban on unofficial preaching and, in 1182 or 1183, they were excommunicated and expelled from Lyons. The Council of Verona in 1814 declared them schismatic and pertinacious and included them with the Cathars as heretics. The condemnation only seemed to have helped the movement which was now spread by lay preachers, called the "Poor Men of Lyons," all over Europe.

3. In 1162 Henry II of England elevated his close friend and drinking companion, Thomas a Becket, as archbishop of Canterbury and primate of England. Shortly thereafter, Becket opposed Henry's attempts to exert royal authority over the church and fell out of the king's favor. He paid a price for his independence when he was killed by the king's knights when celebrating Mass. Miracles were soon recorded at Becket's tomb, and a widespread cultus developed. In 1173 he was canonized, and his shrine remained one of the principal centers of English pilgrimage until the Reformation.

4. The Knights Templars, one of the most powerful of the medieval military orders, was founded in 1119 by Hugh de Payens, a knight of Champagne, along with eight companions with the express purpose of protecting pilgrims to the Holy Land from Muslim bandits. In 1129 the order was approved by the Council of Troyes, and its rules were drawn up by St. Bernard. The new order gained the support of the papacy which, in a series of bulls, granted it many privileges. The Templars fought valiantly in the Second Crusade, but after the fall of Acre, generally lost their influence. Their wealth led to their downfall as Philip the Fair, the king of France, coveted their riches and sought to confiscate their possessions. The order was finally suppressed in 1312.

5. The twelfth century was the golden age of the Cistercian Order. In 1112, a young French nobleman named Bernard knocked on the doors of the recently founded monastery of Citeaux and asked to be admitted to the cloisters. Three years later, he was asked by the abbot Stephen Harding to choose a place for a new monastery. Bernard established a house at Clairvaux, which soon became the focal point of the Cistercian Order. Bernard's place in Western monasticism has never been rivaled in medieval or modern ages.

6. After the Seventh Ecumenical Council, there were no more universal councils, but the Roman Catholic Church continued to hold councils of the Western Church, some of which were called Lateran councils after the Lateran palace in Rome where they were held. Three Lateran councils were held in the twelfth century. The first of these ended the Investiture controversy, and the third restricted the right to elect popes to the newly formed College of Cardinals.

7. In 1121 Peter Abelard, the scholastic theologian, published one of the most influential books of the Middle Ages, *Sic et Non* (Yes and No), which was a textbook for students of theology for over four centuries. It was a collection of apparently contradictory statements from the Bible and the Church Fathers on a large number of questions and was intended to help the reader to reconcile these contradictions.

8. The eleventh century saw the expansion of the Jacobite Church of Syria. At the close of the century, it had over 20 metropolitan sees and 103 bishoprics in Syria, Iraq, and the Holy Land.

THE THIRTEENTH CENTURY (1200–1300): THE AGE OF SCHOLASTICISM

Status of the Christian church
At the end of the thirteenth century, 42 generations after Christ, 22 percent of the world population is Christian, 36 percent non-white, 27 percent evangelized. The Scriptures are available in 25 languages.

Popes of the century
Innocent III (1198–1216), Honorius III (1216–1227), Gregory IX (1227–1241), Celestine IV (1241), Innocent IV (1243–1254), Alexander IV (1254–1261), Urban IV (1261–1264), Clement IV (1265–1268), Gregory X (1268–1276), Innocent V (1276), Hadrian V (1276), John XXI (1276–1277), Nicholas III (1277–1280), Martin IV (1281–1285), Honorius IV (1285–1287), Nicholas IV (1288–1292), Celestine V (1294), Boniface VIII (1294–1303)

Christians of the century
St. Francis of Assisi, St. Thomas Aquinas, Yabalaha III, Henry of Uppsala, St. Dominic

1. In the thirteenth century, a new class of academic theologians had become influential in defining Christian beliefs and practices. In the West they were known as Scholastics and the theological studies they undertook as Scholasticism. One of the foremost architects of Scholasticism was St. Thomas Aquinas, also called the "Angelic Doctor," the Dominican monk who taught at Paris and was considered one of the most brilliant minds of the age. His *Summa Theologiae*, published in 1255, is one of the seminal works of philosophy. It was the first to define theology as a science or as an ordered body of knowledge with its own laws. He treated sacred doctrine as a single discipline at a time when it was often presented in a fragmented way, obscuring its connection with the practice of piety. In Thomas's teaching, theology embraced the whole life of the church, including worship, morals, and spiritual practice.

2. The thirteenth century witnessed the zenith of papal power. Pope Innocent III claimed the right of the pope to choose rulers and oversee their moral conduct. In 1231 the Papal Inquisition was established when Gregory IX appointed full-time papal inquisitors drawn from the Dominican and Franciscan orders.

3. Three crusades were launched in the thirteenth century. The Fourth Crusade was launched in 1202 by Innocent III to defeat Egypt, but under the influence of Boniface of Montserrat and the Venetians, it was deflected from its original purpose and ended in Constantinople, which it sacked for three days. A Latin Empire was established here in 1204, but its net result was a weakening of the Eastern Empire against Muslim expansion and a lingering residue of bitterness that poisoned the relations between Eastern and Western churches for centuries. In 1212 the Children's Crusade ended in disaster as all its juvenile combatants either died at sea or were sold into slavery. The Fifth Crusade, the largest ever, was launched in 1217. Jerusalem was recovered through negotiation by Frederick II and was once again in Latin hands from 1229 to 1244. The next crusade under Louis IX, also against Egypt, failed after a promising beginning. The Latin states were slowly overrun, and in 1291 the last remaining Christian possessions were overrun. The concept of crusades was sometimes extended to cover the extirpation of heretics, such as the Albigenses and the Cathari.

4. In 1266 the church failed one of the greatest evangelistic opportunities as it ignored a call from the Mongol leader, Kublai Khan. The Khan wrote to the pope: "Send me 100 teachers skilled in your religion . . . and so I shall be baptized, and then all my barons and great men, and then their subjects. And so there will be more Christians here than there are in your parts." Only two Dominicans were sent, but they turned back. In 1278 another team of five Franciscans were sent, but then it was too late; the great Khan was dead.

5. The thirteenth century saw the founding of two of the most influential Roman Catholic orders: the Franciscans and the Dominicans. St. Francis of Assisi is the quintessential Catholic saint. Son of a rich cloth merchant of Assisi, he was so moved, while on a pilgrimage to Rome, by the plight of beggars outside St. Peter's that he became one himself, and then overcame his fear of leprosy by embracing a leper. One day while attending Mass in the church of the Portiuncula in the plain below Assisi, he heard the Lord calling him to a life of self-denial and service. He dis-

carded his staff and shoes, put on a long garment girded with a cord, and gathered a few followers who eventually became the mendicant order of Franciscans. Francis's generosity, his simple and unaffected faith, and his passionate devotion to God, men and women, and nature have made him one of the most beloved saints of modern times.

St. Dominic, a contemporary of St. Francis, also gave away all his goods to the poor and founded a monastic order for the preaching of the gospel. The Dominican Order was distinguished by the fact that they adopted not only personal but corporate poverty and each community was supported not by income or properties but by alms. The Dominicans were also active in education and scholarship.

6. Christianity continued to expand in some of the smaller countries. In 1219 the independent Serbian Orthodox Church was founded. Finland was converted through Birger Jarl Magnusson and the English bishop, Henry of Uppsala. All Prussians were baptized, and pagan worship was eradicated from their country.

7. Two councils were held in this century. Lyons I, the Thirteenth Ecumenical Council, was convoked in 1245 by Innocent IV to deal with what he called the "Five Wounds of the Church": the bad lives of the clergy, the danger of the Muslims, the Greek schism, the invasion of Hungary, and the deposition of Emperor Frederick II. Lyons II, the Fourteenth Ecumenical Council, was convoked in 1274 by Gregory X to bring about union with the Greek Church, the reform of morals, and the liberation of the Holy Land.

THE FOURTEENTH CENTURY (1300–1400): THE AGE OF BABYLONIAN CAPTIVITY

Status of the Christian church
At the end of the fourteenth century, 47 generations after Christ, 21 percent of the world population is Christian, 11 percent of them non-white, 24 percent evangelized. The Scriptures are available in 26 languages.

Popes of the century
Benedict XI (1303–1304), Clement V (1305–1314), John XXII (1316–1334), Benedict XII (1334–1342), Clement VI (1342–1352), Innocent VI (1352–1362), Urban V (1362–1370), Gregory XI (1370–1378), Urban VI (1378–1389), Boniface IX (1389–1404)

Christians of the century
John Wycliffe, Ramon Lull, St. Catherine of Siena

1. The "Babylonian Captivity" was a strange term that recalled the bondage of the Jews to Nebuchadnezzar, and it threatened to divide the Western Church. It was first used by Petrarch and other writers to describe the exile of the popes in the French city of Avignon from 1309 until 1377. Clement V was the first pope to make his residence in Avignon. A puppet of King Philip the Fair of France, he favored the French and convened the Council of Vienne that abolished the Order of the Knights Templar and gave their valuable property to the French king. Six other popes followed Clement, all of them Frenchmen.

Meanwhile, antipopes were installed in Rome, prompting the later Avignon popes, as Urban V, to seek a return to Rome. Matters came to a head in 1378 when St. Catherine of Siena issued a personal appeal to Pope Gregory XI to resume residence in Rome. He did, but in the face of continuing hostilities in the papal states, returned to Avignon, where he died. His death led to a period of major disturbances in the papacy known as the Great Schism when there were two or three popes at a time. The College of Cardinals elected an Italian pope Urban VI, the first in nearly 70 years, but later denied the validity of the election and chose the Frenchman Clement VII instead. Urban remained in Rome, but Clement went back to Avignon. The schism continued until 1417.

2. In 1321 Dante Alighieri wrote the epic allegorical poem, *The Divine Comedy*, one of the top ten masterpieces in literary history. *The Divine Comedy* is an allegory divided into three parts. In "Inferno," the poet Virgil guides Dante through nine concentric circles of hell. In "Purgatory," Virgil guides him up a nine-tiered mountain upon which saved souls work off their sins before entering paradise. In the final book, "Paradise," Beatrice (the woman Dante idolized all his life) and St. Bernard of Clairvaux lead him through the nine concentric circles of heaven, where he meets the saints of God. Dante's vision captured in lapidary language the beauty and the poetry of medieval theology.

3. Wycliffe appeared toward the end of the century, but he was a man far ahead of his times. Called the "Morning Star of the Reformation," Wycliffe left his stamp on his age. Although considered a reformer, he remained a Catholic all his life and opposed the prevailing skepticism of his contemporaries. As a theologian he sought inspiration in the Bible and the Fathers rather than in the dry speculation of the Scholastics. In his *De Veritate Sacre Scripturae* and other books, he maintained that the Bible was the sole criterion of doctrine to which no ecclesiastical authority might lawfully be added. "For as much as the Bible contains Christ," he wrote, "that is all there is necessary for salvation, it is necessary for all men, not for priests alone." Despite the church's disapproval, he worked together with other scholars to translate the first complete English Bible, using a handwritten copy of the Vulgate. The second edition of this translation, published after Wycliffe's death, became known as the "Wycliffe Bible."

4. Between 1348 and 1351 the Bubonic Plague, also known as Black Death, killed 33 percent of all Europeans, or about 60 million people. People blamed the plague on the Avignon papacy, Jews, or the immoral life of the princes.

5. The fourteenth century saw the apogee of the Nestorian Church in Asia and its extermination. As the century opened, a large portion of Persia was still Christian. Geographically, the Nestorian Church flourished over a wider area than the Roman Catholic Church. There were 25 metropolitans (each with six to 12 suffragan bishops) under the patriarch at Baghdad and 250 dioceses spread across China, India, Kashgar, Samarkand, Afghanistan, and Turkestan with a total membership of over 15 million. But beginning in 1358, Tamarlane (or Timur the Lame), the Muslim Mongol emperor, known to Christians as the "Scourge of God," began his campaign of murder and pillage that wiped out Christian civilization from the entire region. In Isfahan alone he had 70,000 skulls piled up, and in Baghdad, another 90,000. Meanwhile, Christianity was being extirpated from other countries in Asia and Africa. The Mameluk Dynasty of Egypt ordered the closure and destruction of all Christian churches between 1301 and 1321. The Ming Dynasty of China banned Nestorian Christianity from Mongolia

and replaced it with Buddhism. Bulgaria fell to the Turks in 1396, signaling the rise of Ottoman power in the Balkans and another five centuries of Muslim oppression of the Christian church.

6. As a result of Muslim persecutions, the non-European percentage of Christians rapidly shrank. White Europeans now constituted more than two-thirds of all Christians, and that percentage would continue to rise for the next three centuries. With the baptism of Jagiello, king of the Lithuanians, all of Europe had become Christian.

THE FIFTEENTH CENTURY (1400–1500): THE FALL OF CONSTANTINOPLE

Status of the Chrisitan Church

At the end of the fifteenth century, 49 generations after Christ, 19 percent of the world population is Christian, 8 percent of them non-white, 21 percent of them evangelized. Printed Scriptures are available in 12 languages.

Popes of the century

Innocent VII (1404–1406), Gregory XII (1406–1415), Martin V (1417–1431), Eugene IV (1431–1447), Nicholas V (1447–1455), Callistus III (1455–1458), Pius II (1458–1464), Paul II (1464–1471), Sixtus IV (1471–1484), Innocent VIII (1484–1492), Alexander VI (1492–1503)

Christians of the century

Joan of Arc, Christopher Columbus, Savonarola, Thomas à Kempis

1. The Crusades had failed. The Arab tide had weakened and subsided by the fifteenth century. But the Muslim Jihad against Christians continued with the Turks as the successors to the Arabs, invading Byzantium, the citadel of Eastern Christianity. Ever since the tenth century, the newly converted Muslim Turks continued to move from their Central Asian homelands into Armenia, Cilicia, Anatolia and into Thrace and Bulgaria. Brutal and inhuman warriors trained to pillage and kill, the nomadic Turks had only one goal: to extend the Ottoman power to the farthest corners of the world, dispossess the original inhabitants of the lands they conquered, convert them to Islam, and

spread terror throughout the known world. Every square inch of the Ottoman Empire was stolen from other peoples. The zenith of their power was the siege and conquest of Constantinople, the jewel of the Eastern Empire, in 1453, considered the darkest year in the Byzantine calendar. The first act of the conquering Turks was to convert the magnificent Hagia Sophia into a mosque. Over the next five hundred years the Turks would kill over 10 million Christians, convert over 20,000 churches into mosques, and forcibly convert over 25 million Christians to Islam.

2. The year 1450 is generally regarded as the beginning of the Renaissance. The term itself is significantly vague because it is not clear what exactly the Renaissance ushered in. There was a renaissance of learning, as printing became a means of communicating knowledge faster, and there was a renaissance of arts and culture as the fine arts and literature gained a notable momentum in this century. This was also the beginning of the great age of geographical discoveries.

3. In 1492 one of the most momentous events in human history took place when Christopher Columbus, a Genoan by birth, accepted a commission from their Most Catholic Majesties, Ferdinand and Isabella of Castile, Leon, and Aragon to sail across the Atlantic. The expedition discovered the New World and added two continents to human civilization. This single act expanded the Christian world by more than half and compensated for the loss of the Middle East, North Africa, and Asia Minor to the Muslims. Christopher Columbus was a devout Catholic who considered himself an apostle of the gospel and his expeditions as divinely ordained. Before the end of the century Vasco da Gama sailed around the Cape of Good Hope to reach Kozhikode in India. In 1493 Pope Alexander VI issued a bull dividing the New World between Portugal and Spain and assigning Africa and Asia to Portugal. The Treaty of Tordesillas of 1494 between Spain and Portugal confirmed the provisions of the bull.

Immediately afterwards, the great Roman Catholic orders, the Jesuits, Franciscans, and Dominicans, took the challenge and carried the cross to the unknown lands that beckoned them. As a result of their efforts, the first Christians are reported in lands with strange names: Senegal, Guinea-Bissau, Mauritania, Haiti, Dominican Re-

public, Kenya, and Equatorial Africa. By a strange coincidence, 1492 also marked the final reconquest of Spain from the Moors, as Granada, the last Muslim stronghold, fell to the Christians.

4. The Council of Florence in 1438 affirmed the primacy of the pope over general councils. It declared union between Western and Eastern churches, but its decree was not accepted by the Eastern Orthodox Church. The Council of Constance rejected Wycliffe's teachings and burned John Hus at the stake as a heretic.

5. In 1431 Joan of Arc, a French peasant girl during the Hundred Years' War, began to see visions and hear voices asking her to save France from the Burgundians and their English allies. She led a successful military expedition that saved Orleans, and she was present at the coronation of Charles VII at Reims. Later she was taken prisoner, tried for heresy, and burned. In 1456 the verdict was reversed, and she was canonized as a saint. Over the centuries she became an icon for Gallic pride and one of the patron saints of France.

6. In 1453–1455 Johann Gutenberg made history when he printed, with the help of a loan from Banker Johann Fust, the 42-line Mazarin Bible, known to later generations as the Gutenberg Bible. It was the first printed book in the history of Europe, and it set in motion a revolution in communications and the transmission of knowledge that continues to this day. Fust and Peter Schoeffer produced in 1457 the first dated book, a beautiful psalter. More people could now afford to buy and read Bibles, a fact that encouraged more translations into European vernaculars. The first High German printed Bible appeared in 1466, the first Italian and Dutch printed Bibles in 1477, and the first Spanish and French printed Bibles in 1478 and 1487, respectively. The widespread printing of Bibles was one of the contributory causes of the Reformation.

7. In 1497–1498 the Dominican friar Savonarola began to preach reform, encouraging the people of Florence to burn luxury items and return to a humbler life. He sold church property and gave the proceeds to the poor. For a while, he was the ruler of a theocratic republic. Soon he was embroiled in a conflict with Pope Alexander VI and was excommunicated, hanged, and burned.

8. The Great Papal Schism ended as Martin V was elected pope. This would be the last schism within the Catholic Church.

9. In 1455 one of the enduring classics of Christian literature, Thomas à Kempis's *The Imitation of Christ*, appeared. Thomas was a member of the celebrated medieval order, the Brethren of the Common Life.

10. Although the Inquisition as an institution had atrophied by the fifteenth century, it was revived in 1477 by Ferdinand and Isabella of Spain who were initially concerned about the problem of Marranos, or nominally converted Jews. In 1478 they obtained permission from Sixtus IV to set up a new Inquisition, backed by royal authority. Initially limited to Castile, it was gradually extended by 1484, in spite of papal objections, to Aragon and later all lands subject to the Spanish monarchy. It soon became a highly centralized organization, especially after the appointment of Tomas de Torquemeda as the inquisitor general in 1483. Although the Inquisition has acquired a certain notoriety, it was considered by contemporaries as more benign than secular courts of the period.

11. In 1480 Russia expelled Mongol Muslim rulers and became a Christian state. Earlier, in 1448, the Russian Orthodox Church became an autocephalous patriarchate.

THE SIXTEENTH CENTURY (1500–1600): THE REFORMATION

Status of the Christian church
At the end of the sixteenth century, 52 generations after Christ, 20.7 percent of the world population is Christian, 14 percent of them non-white, 24 percent of them evangelized. Printed Scriptures are available in 36 languages.

Popes of the century
Pius III (1503), Julius II (1503–1513), Leo X (1513–1521), Hadrian VI (1522–1523), Clement VII 1523–1534), Paul III (1534–1549), Julius III (1550–1555), Marcellus II (1555), Paul IV (1555–1559), Pius IV (1559–1565), Pius V (1566–1572), Gregory VIII (1572–1585), Sixtus V (1585–1590), Urban VII (1590), Gregory XIV (1590–1591), Innocent IX (1591), Clement VIII (1592–1605)

Christians of the century
William Tyndale, Erasmus, Martin Luther, John Calvin, Huldreich Zwingli, Philip Melanchthon, Martin Bucer, Ignatius Loyola, St. Francis Xavier, Claudio Aquaviva, Matteo Ricci, Menno Simons

1. The central event of the sixteenth century was the breakup of the monolithic Western Church through the Reformation. The Reformation was not a single act nor was it an event inspired or led by a single person, but before the century ended Germany, Scandinavia, Iceland, the Netherlands, and England had broken away from Rome and established national churches that did not subscribe to the Roman Catholic traditions or acknowledge the pope as their head.

2. A series of Bibles published within a few years of one another heralded the Reformation. Erasmus, a scholar and humanist, published in 1516 a Greek translation of the New Testament. Later editions of his Greek text formed the basis or the *textus receptus* of translations by Martin Luther, William Tyndale, and the Authorized, or King James, Version. Erasmus paved the way for the Reformation by his merciless satires on the doctrines and institutions of the church, but he himself had no desire to break away from Catholicism. In 1525 William Tyndale made an English translation of the New Testament from Greek without permission and smuggled copies into England, for which act he was burned at the stake. In 1537 Matthew's Bible (produced by John Matthews, an alias for John Rogers) became the first English-language Bible published with royal permission.

3. In 1517, a German Augustinian monk named Martin Luther ignited an ecclesiastical revolution by posting his manifesto known as the Ninety-Five Theses on the door of the Schlosskirche in Wittenberg, henceforth known as the "Cradle of the Reformation." Luther declaimed primarily against the practice of selling indulgences. He had no plans to start a Reformation but only a more modest and worthy goal of ridding the church of its corruption. The posting of the Ninety-Five Theses is generally considered the birth of the Reformation. Ironically, Luther was harking back to St. Augustine, one of the most revered of the

Church Fathers, in defense of his theses. In 1518 Luther defended his position in the Heidelberg Disputation and he won over several of his fellow monks, including the Dominican Martin Bucer. In the same year he was tried in his absence in Rome on charges of heresy and summoned before Cardinal Cajetan at Augsburg. Refusing to recant, Luther fled, but he met his opponents again in 1519 at the Leipzig Disputation at which Luther denied both the primacy of the pope and the infallibility of the general councils.

In 1520 Luther published three seminal works outlining his theology. In the first, *An Appeal to the German People,* he opposed the celibacy of the clergy, masses for the dead, and many other Catholic practices. This was followed by *The Babylonian Captivity of the Church* in which he attacked all sacraments other than baptism and the Eucharist, the doctrine of transubstantiation, and the division between clergy and laity. In the final work of the trilogy, Luther called for the liberation of a Christian from the bondage of works and affirmed the sufficiency and authority of the Scriptures and salvation by faith alone. In 1520 the pope condemned Luther in his bull, *Exsurge Domine.* Luther replied by burning the bull. This was followed by his excommunication in 1521.

4. Two other streams flowed into the Reformation to make it a surging flood. In Switzerland John Calvin and Ulrich (or Huldreich) Zwingli advocated an even more radical version of Christianity. In 1536 John Calvin published his *Institutes of Christian Religion,* which became the foundation of Calvinism. Zwingli was the most radical of the three Reformation leaders. He denied transubstantiation, reduced the importance of the Eucharist to mere symbolism, and opposed the invocation of the saints, monasticism, purgatory, and icons. Calvin and Zwingli also promoted a more theocratic view of the gospel, encouraging civil authorities to intervene more actively in religious affairs.

5. By 1529 the word *Protestantism* became accepted as the name for the churches that broke away from Rome during the Reformation. The central tenets of Protestantism common to all the churches that came under the rubric were the acceptance of the Bible as the only source of revealed truth, the doctrine of justification by faith alone, and the priesthood of all believers.

6. In 1534 Henry VIII, England's dissolute monarch, seeking divorce from his Catholic queen, was led through a series of events having nothing to do with theology, to place himself as the head of a national church by the Act of Supremacy. The new "Church of England," now known as the Anglican Church, accepted many of the Protestant tenets but retained much of the Catholic ritual and ceremony. Its doctrinal basis is the Thirty-Nine Articles adopted in 1563. These articles were not a statement of Christian doctrine in the form of a creed, but rather short and vague summaries of dogmatic tenets. They combined both High Church or Catholic teachings and Low Church or radical teachings, and both strands continue to coexist in the Anglican Church today.

In 1549 the Church of England issued The Book of Common Prayer as its official service book. It contains the daily offices of Morning and Evening Prayer, the forms for administration of the sacraments, and other public and private rites. In 1555 Queen Mary Tudor reversed the Reformation and reestablished Catholicism, but Protestantism returned permanently with the accession of Queen Elizabeth in 1558. In 1570 the pope excommunicated Elizabeth, and relations between Rome and Canterbury were strained until the nineteenth century. In 1560 John Knox began the Reformation in Scotland. In the British Isles only Ireland remained faithful to the Catholic Church.

7. In 1525 the "Radical Reformation" was born. The early forerunners of this movement were the Anabaptists, predecessor to the Brethren and the Mennonite churches which teach believer's adult baptism, separation of church and state, and presbyterian or democratic church government. In 1535, Anabaptist extremists took over Munster and were slaughtered. Later, under Menno Simons, the sect became an influential community, and many emigrated to North America.

8. Throughout the sixteenth century, Protestants tried to codify their beliefs in a series of confessions or creeds. In 1530 the Augsburg Confession was adopted by the Lutherans. In 1562 the Heidelberg Catechism was issued, and it remained the most widely held doctrinal statement for centuries. The Formula of Concord of 1577 was the last of the classical Lutheran formulas of faith.

9. Meanwhile, the Catholic Church, rather than becoming weakened by the rise of Protestantism, was entering a period of unusual growth. One evidence was the celebrated Council of Trent held between 1545 and 1563. The council, the Nineteenth Ecumenical Council on the Roman calendar, began what is known as the Counter-Reformation, and it is the most impressive embodiment of the renewal of the Catholic Church under pressure. The decrees of the council, known as the Profession of the Tridentine Faith, or the Creed of Pius IV, affirmed the traditional beliefs of the Catholic Church but condemned the sale of indulgences, nepotism, and clerical immorality. It ordered the revision of the Vulgate. Based on the work of the council, Pope Pius V founded the Congregation of the Index in 1571 and issued the Roman Catechism in 1566, the Breviary in 1568, and the Missal in 1570.

10. Closely following on the Council of Trent, Catholic scholars from Oxford, led by Gregory Martin, translated the Douay-Rheims Bible from the Latin Vulgate, while in exile in France. It would remain the version of the Bible in use among English-speaking Roman Catholics for three centuries.

11. In 1540 the Society of Jesus, better known as Jesuits, founded by Ignatius Loyola and his nine companions, was approved by Paul III. Among the more immediate goals of the society were the propagation of the faith and the promotion of Christian piety. Hardly had the society been approved when St. Francis Xavier established it in Japan and Manuel de Nobriega in Brazil. Peculiar to the Jesuits is a special vow to travel anywhere in the world that the pope may order. Some other features distinguish the Jesuits from other religious orders: they are bound by vows not to accept any position in the hierarchy except under direct order of the pope, and they have no distinctive habit. The most characteristic institutions of the society, however, were the great humanist schools and universities which they have established all over the world. By 1581, under Claudio Aquaviva, the fifth Jesuit general, the number of Jesuits increased to 13,000.

12. After many centuries of evangelistic inertia, worldwide expansion of Christianity began again under Catholic auspices. Magellan took the gospel to the Philippines. Mass conversion of Mexican Indians began under Cortes on the orders of the Spanish monarch. The first Spanish missionaries reached Florida, California, and Texas. The first permanent Catholic community was founded in St. Augustine, Florida, in 1565. St. Francis Xavier carried the gospel to Goa, Travancore in South India, Malacca in the East Indies, China, and Japan. Meanwhile, the first Protestant mission was founded in Tranquebar, India, in 1575.

13. In 1503 Pope Julius II commissioned Michelangelo to paint the Sistine Chapel. The foundation stone of St. Peter's Basilica was laid in 1506.

14. In 1598, the Edict of Nantes granted freedom of worship to French Protestants, known as Huguenots, after 30 years of persecution. This edict would be revoked by Louis XIV in 1685.

THE SEVENTEENTH CENTURY (1600–1700): THE AGE OF CHRISTIAN EXPANSION

Status of the Christian church
At the end of the seventeenth century, 56 generations after Christ, 21.7 percent of the world population is Christian, 15 percent of them non-white, 25.2 percent are evangelized. Printed Scriptures are available in 52 languages.

Popes of the century
Leo XI (1605), Paul V (1605–1621), Gregory XV (1621–1623), Urban VIII (1623–1644), Innocent X (1644–1655), Alexander VII (1655–1667), Clement IX (1667–1669), Clement X (1670–1676), Innocent XI (1676–1689), Alexander VIII (1689–1691), Innocent XII (1691–1700)

Christians of the century
Alexander de Rhodes, Philipp Spener, John Eliot, George Fox

1. In 1601 the Jesuit missionary and scholar, Matthew Ricci, began evangelization of China by adopting the dress and customs of the land and incorporating Confucian traditions, such as ancestor worship. It sparked the prolonged and damaging Chinese Rites controversy that troubled missionary work in Asia and Africa until it was condemned by Clement XI in the eighteenth

century. By 1692 when the Chinese emperor officially allowed Christianity to be practiced in his realm, the number of Christians numbered over 300,000.

2. In 1611 King James I of England commissioned 54 scholars to undertake a new Bible translation which took six years to complete. The scholars used the Bishops' Bible and Tyndale's Bible as well as available Greek and Hebrew manuscripts. The result was the King James Version or the Authorized Version whose majestic and evocative cadences made it the popular Bible in the world for the next 300 years.

3. In 1603 the Dutch Reformed theologian, Jacobus Arminius, caused the first dissension within Calvinism by setting forth, on the basis of the Epistle to the Romans, doctrines that denied predestination and affirmed human ability to choose Christ and Christ's atoning death for all people and not merely for the elect. In 1618 the Dutch Reformed Synod of Dort denounced Arminianism with five points of Calvinism, known by their mnemonic initials, TULIP: total depravity, unconditional election, limited atonement, the irresistibility of grace, and the final perseverance of the saints.

4. Under James I, successor to Queen Elizabeth, the Puritan dissidents, known officially as nonconformists, became more restless. Describing themselves as separatists, they wanted to establish their own commonwealth, built on Calvinist ideas and untainted by the flaws, especially the episcopacy, of the Church of England. They first went to Holland, where they found themselves to be strangers or "Pilgrims." They returned to England and in 1620 set sail from Plymouth on a ship named *Mayflower* for the New World. Though they had intended to head for Virginia, a storm swept them off course and they landed in Plymouth Rock, Massachusetts. One pilgrim described the new land as "a hideous and desolate wilderness." But more than the wilderness, the pilgrims feared the possible anarchy of an unregulated and ungodly community. To create an orderly government under God, 41 pilgrims, huddled aboard the wind-tossed vessel and signed the Mayflower Compact. In it they agreed that the colony they were about to found would be for the glory of God and the advancement of Christianity.

5. The first decades of the seventeenth century marked one of the bloodiest persecutions against Christians in modern times. The mission of St. Francis Xavier had converted hundreds of thousands of Japanese to Christianity, and Christians formed a sizable segment of the Japanese population. However, by 1587, under the suspicion that the missions were preparing the way for foreign conquest, Christianity was proscribed. From 1596 to 1598 the first wave of persecution claimed the lives of 26 Japanese Christians who were crucified. In 1613 it broke out again under shogun Iyesu, and by 1640 several thousands suffered martyrdom for their faith. Then all foreigners were banned from Japan under pain of death. The proscription against Christianity was not lifted until 1859, and complete freedom of religion was not allowed until 1890.

6. From 1618 to 1648 Europe was ravaged by the last of the religious wars, known as the Thirty Years' War. Europe had by this time become a crazy quilt of Catholic, Lutheran, and Calvinist territories. Bohemia, a strongly Protestant territory, was under the Catholic Holy Roman Empire. In 1618 some Protestant rebels stormed the royal palace in Prague and threw the rulers out the window. This act, called the Defenestration of Prague, caused severe reprisals from Emperor Ferdinand II who, with the help of Spanish forces, routed the rebels in the Battle of the White Mountain in 1620. Bohemia was declared officially Catholic, and the Protestants were forced to leave. Among those that left was Jan Amos Comenius, the great educational innovator, who was a pastor of the Unity of the Brethren (Unitas Fratrum). Comenius finally settled in Leszno, Poland, where he published his seminal books on education. Meanwhile, the war raged on until the Peace of Westphalia in 1648. It is estimated that Germany lost half its population in the war.

7. Two of the greatest works of Christian literature appeared in this century. John Milton, the blind English poet, completed his epic *Paradise Lost* in 1667. In 1678 John Bunyan, while in prison as a nonconformist, published his well-loved classic, *Pilgrim's Progress,* an allegorical masterpiece that is as relevant today as when it was written.

8. In 1608, a separatist group of nonconformists fled to Holland under the leadership of John Smyth. From the Mennonites Smyth

learned that only adult baptism was biblical, and he conducted the first adult baptism of believers. In 1610 Smyth tried to merge his group with the Mennonites but without success. Another splinter group led by Thomas Helwys took their beliefs about adult baptism back to London, where they founded the first Baptist church. Arminian Baptists became known as General Baptists and Calvinist Baptists as Particular Baptists. In 1639 Roger Williams founded the first Baptist church in the New World at Providence, Rhode Island.

9. In 1643 the English Parliament summoned an assembly at Westminister Abbey to draft a "confession of faith for the three kingdoms." After 27 months of deliberations, the assembly created the Westminster Confession (1646), the Shorter Westminster Catechism (1647), and the Larger Catechism (1648), all of them founded on Calvinism. The Confession expounded in 33 chapters all the leading articles of the Christian faith from the creation of the world to the last judgment. Although it reaffirmed predestination, it recognized two covenants, the covenant of law and the covenant of grace. The observance of Sunday as the Lord's Day was made a cardinal tenet. The confession remains to this day the most authoritative definition of Presbyterianism.

10. In 1647 an English radical preacher named George Fox heard an inner voice that told him: "There is only one, even Jesus Christ, who can speak to thy condition." Fox called it the Inner Light, and it became the central doctrine of a new group that he founded, known as the Society of Friends, although originally it was called "Children of the Light." Fox spent some time in jail because of his teachings, and when he was brought before Justice Bennett, he warned the judge to "tremble at the Word of God." "You are the tremblers, the quakers," the judge replied, and the name stuck. The Quaker movement reflected the religious ferment of the seventeenth century. Fox emphasized the immediacy of Christ's teachings, holding that ordained ministers, sacraments (even baptism and Communion), and church buildings were unnecessary. Quakers have no church services, but only meetings. They renounced oath-taking, dressed simply, ate sparingly, and abhorred war.

11. By the seventeenth century, the Lutheran Church has lost much of its early zeal for personal piety. The man who revived it was Philipp Jakob Spener, who led the great renewal of Protestantism known as Pietism. In 1675, he published the classic *Pia Desideria* (Pious Desires) which presented a six-point plan for kindling personal piety in Christians. First, he wanted Christians to have a deeper, more life-affecting understanding of the Scriptures. He also wanted them to take their personal priesthood as believers seriously and waste less time in sterile controversies and polemics over minor theological doctrines. Spener instituted devotional circles for prayer and Bible study groups. Pietism also gave a boost to hymnody. Hymn writers like Paul Gerhardt, Joachim Neander, and Gerhard Tersteegen produced great hymns that would later be translated into English Methodist hymnbooks. The practical aspects, especially the warmth, of Pietism would have far-reaching effects. It has been particularly influential in the development of American Evangelical Christianity.

12. In 1698–1701 the world's first two non-Catholic mission societies were formed under the aegis of the Church of England: the Society for the Promotion of Christian Knowledge (SPCK) and the Society for the Propagation of the Gospel in Foreign Parts. The Society of Foreign Mission was founded in Paris in 1660. In 1613 *De Procuranda Salute Omnium Gentium* by Thomas a Jesu urged the conversion of the entire world to Christ. In 1622, Vatican created the Congregation de Propaganda Fide to direct Roman Catholic missionary efforts.

13. In 1685 Louis XIV of France revoked the Edict of Nantes, forcing the large-scale exodus of Huguenots from France.

14. In 1629 Cyril Lucar, the Orthodox patriarch of Constantinople, befriended Protestants and presented the earliest copy of the Bible in Greek, now known as Codex Alexandrinus, to Charles I of England.

THE EIGHTEENTH CENTURY (1700–1800): THE AGE OF PROTESTANT REVIVALS

Status of the Christian church

At the end of the eighteenth century, 59 generations after Christ, 23.1 percent of the world population is Christian, 14 percent of them non-white, and 27.2 percent evangelized. Printed Scriptures are available in 67 languages.

Popes of the century

Clement XI (1700–1721), Innocent XIII (1721–1724), Benedict XIII (1724–1730), Clement XII (1730–1740), Benedict XIV (1740–1758), Clement XIII (1758–1769), Clement XIV (1769–1774), Pius VI (1775–1799)

Christians of the century

John Wesley, Charles Wesley, George Whitefield, Isaac Watts, John Newton, Jonathan Edwards, Junipero Serra, William Carey, Robert Raikes, Nicholas Zinzendorf

1. In 1729 John Wesley and his brother Charles began a "Holy Club," at Oxford University which their detractors named "Methodists" because they searched for personal holiness methodically. That search led the brothers on a missionary journey to Georgia in the American colonies in 1735. When they returned to London they went to a Moravian meeting at which someone read from Luther's Commentary on the Romans. That night John Wesley wrote, "About a quarter before nine, while he was describing the change which God works in the heart through faith in Christ, I felt my heart strangely warmed. I felt I did trust in Christ, Christ alone for salvation; and an assurance was given me that He had taken away my sins, even mine, and saved me from the law of sin and death." Out of that conversion experience grew the worldwide Methodist Church. John Wesley began preaching in open fields, because the Anglican churches were closed to him. For the remaining 63 years of his life, he traveled 250,000 miles on horseback, preached over 40,000 sermons, and wrote hundreds of books and letters.

Another member of the Holy Club, George Whitefield, was converted around the same time, and together they led England and America into a new age of revival. Methodism became successful because it appealed primarily to the lower classes that were ostracized by the mainline churches. As the church grew John Wesley assigned circuits or districts, and each Methodist society was broken down into fellowship classes and prayer bands. The brothers, especially Charles, had no intention of breaking away from Anglicanism. Instead they wanted to reform the church from within. In 1771 John Wesley sent Francis Asbury to preach in America. The American Methodist Church became a separate entity in 1784. Although overshadowed by his brother, Charles also had great impact on Methodism. He wrote some of the sweetest hymns in the English language, some 5,000 in all, including the unforgettable "Jesu, Lover of My Soul," "Hark the Herald Angels Sing," "O for a Thousand Tongues," and "And Can It Be."

2. The eighteenth century indeed was the age of great hymns. One of the first to write hymns that could be sung as part of a church service was Isaac Watts, who published his *Hymns and Spiritual Songs* in 1709. He based some of his songs on the Psalms, such as Psalm 98 which formed the basis of "Joy to the World." Watts wrote more than 600 hymns, among them the evergreen classics, "When I Survey the Wondrous Cross" and "O God Our Help in Ages Past," which earned him the name of "Father of English Hymnody." In 1764, another perennial favorite, "Amazing Grace," was written by John Newton, a former slave trader who was converted while his ship was battered by a storm in the North Sea. Later, in 1779, John Newton collaborated with William Cowper, the emotionally troubled English poet, to produce *Olney Hymns.*

3. Just as the spiritual fervor of the Puritan Commonwealth seemed to die out in America, Jonathan Edwards, a New England pastor, ignited a revival that swept New England and most of the 13 colonies. Drinking deeply from the wells of Calvinism, Edwards preached the necessity of a new birth, mixing fire and brimstone messages with pleas for changed lives and increased devotion. In the winter of 1734 and through the years that followed, a great change came over the church at Northampton that Edwards pastored. "The Spirit of God began extraordinarily to set in," Edwards wrote. "The town seemed to be full of the presence of God. It never was so full of love and so full of joy."

The revival was taken to New Jersey by Theodore Frelinghuysen, a pastor who came from a distinguished Dutch family, and by Gilbert Tennent and his brothers. Towering above them all was George Whitefield, the most striking and eloquent orator of the Evangelical Revival. Tirelessly crisscrossing the colonies, he was the guiding spirit behind the Great Revival. It is estimated that 80 percent of the colonists heard Whitefield at one time or another. The Second Great Awakening took place almost half a century later, in 1792. The movement was parallel to the Continental Pietism and the English Evangelicalism.

4. In 1769 Father Junipero Serra, a Spanish Franciscan missionary, founded the first of the nine Californian missions in San Diego, thus bringing the gospel to the west coast of North America for the first time. He was instrumental in the settlement of what is California today.

5. In 1741–1742 George Frederic Handel, a German composer, wrote *Messiah*, the most-performed oratorio in the world. Handel came from the German Pietist family, and he conveyed a deep evangelistic message in the oratorio, which was first performed before an audience that included the king of England.

6. 1793 is a landmark in the history of Christian missions. In that year William and Dorothy Carey set sail on a ship to India on what was the first Protestant missionary effort, apart from the Tranquebar mission. Even as a young man Carey was obsessed with the Great Commission, in which Jesus Christ charged his followers to go into all the world and proclaim the gospel to every living creature. Three weeks after publishing his thesis, "An Enquiry into the Obligations of Christians to Use All Means for the Conversion of Heathens," he issued the call for missionaries to "go into all the world," and cited the words that remained the motto of his life, "Expect great things from God; attempt great things for God." In 1800 the couple reached Calcutta, the capital of the English possessions in Bengal, and moved to Serampore, the Danish colony, where they gained their first convert. In the next 34 years Carey, whose wife had by now succumbed to mental illness, translated the Bible into 44 languages and started several schools and mission stations that began the evangelization of northern India.

7. In 1721 Peter the Great abolished the patriarchate and appointed the Holy Synod headed by an oberprocurator to head the Russian Orthodox Church. The church would remain under state control until 1917. In 1700 Peter the Great ordered the Christianization of Siberia, expanding the territorial extent of Christianity.

8. In 1780 one of the most beloved of Christian institutions had its genesis in the Gloucester kitchen of one Mrs. King where a roomful of children were taught the Bible every Sunday from 10:00 to 12:00 in the morning and from 1:00 to 5:00 in the afternoon. It was the pet project of Robert Raikes, editor of the *Gloucester Journal,* who publicized it in his journal. Soon a number of prominent Christians, including John Wesley and Queen Charlotte, applauded the idea. To extend the effort to all England, Raikes founded, with the help of William Fox, the Society for the Support and Encouragement of Sunday Schools in Different Counties of England. Within a century the movement had become worldwide and a part of Sunday services.

9. In 1722 a group of Moravians, who had been expelled from their homeland by Catholics, appeared at the door of Count Nikolaus Ludwig von Zinzendorf in Dresden seeking asylum. Zinzendorf was a wealthy and devout Lutheran who had been planning to open his vast estates to a community based on principles of Christian piety. Thus the noble and the asylees were bound in a common bond. Zinzendorf welcomed other Moravians into the new community which he called Herrnhut, which meant the "Lord's Watch." By 1726 the Herrnhut grew to be 300 strong, and next year common worship services and a 24-hour-a-day prayer vigil were instituted. In 1732 the Moravians began sending out missionaries to all the new unreached colonial lands, including West Indies, Greenland, Lapland, Suriname, South Africa, Guyana, Algeria, and Ceylon. Zinzendorf, meanwhile, revived the *Unitas Fratrum,* the original Moravian Church. After being expelled from Saxony by his political enemies, Zinzendorf began his missionary travels to the American colonies and England, establishing Moravian communities everywhere. By the time he died in 1760, more than 226 missionaries were serving in Moravian communities around the world.

10. The French Revolution of 1789 was one of the catastrophic events that periodically punctuate European history. The French revolutionaries, like revolutionaries throughout modern history, were hostile to Christianity, and they attacked and pillaged the magnificent cathedrals and monasteries for which France was justly famous,

killed thousands of priests and monks, converted Notre Dame into a temple, and instituted the cult of reason. Fortunately, the Jacobins, as the more radical of the revolutionaries were called, were ruined by their own excesses and were, before the end of the century, suppressed by Napoleon, who then would dominate French history for the next two decades.

11. In 1746 widespread and severe persecution of Christians began in China, lasting 38 years.

THE NINETEENTH CENTURY (1800–1900): THE AGE OF THE GREAT MISSIONARIES

Status of the Christian church
At the end of the nineteenth century, 62 generations after Christ, 34.4 percent of the world population is Christian, 18 percent non-white, 51.3 percent evangelized. Printed Scriptures are available in 537 languages.

Popes of the century
Pius VII (1800–1823), Leo XII (1823–1829), Pius VIII (1829–1830), Gregory XVI (1831–1846), Pius IX (1846–1878), Leo XIII (1878–1903)

Christians of the century
John Nelson Darby, David Livingstone, Adoniram Judson, Charles Finney, D. L. Moody, Charles Spurgeon, Hudson Taylor, Charles-Martial Allemand Lavigerie, William Booth, John Henry Cardinal Newman, Feodor Dostoevsky, Soren Kierkegaard, John Keble, George Muller

1. The nineteenth century represented the best and worst of times for the Christian church. In Europe, still the bastion of Christianity, the church was being battered by a host of ideologies, including modernism, scientific rationalism, humanism, and deism (Marxism was still nascent). But after 19 centuries, the Great Commission was being taken seriously by all the major denominations, and marked progress was being made toward the conversion of entire continents. To accomplish this awesome task God raised the most remarkable constellation of Christian leaders found in any century. They included John Nelson Darby, Adoniram Judson, David Livingstone, Charles Finney, D. L. Moody, Charles H. Spur-

geon, and Hudson Taylor among Protestants and Charles-Martial Allemand Lavigerie among Catholics. These were not great theologians or church fathers but "doers"—men and women who braved all kinds of dangers to bring the gospel to all nations.

2. The Congregation for the Propagation of the Faith, reestablished by Pope Pius VII, spurred Roman Catholic missionary efforts in Ethiopia, Mongolia, and North Africa. Under the auspices of the congregation in 1868, Charles-Martial Allemand Lavigerie founded the Society of Missionaries for Africa, popularly known as the White Fathers. As cardinal and primate of Africa, Lavigerie was instrumental in persuading the colonial powers to abolish slavery.

3. Nineteenth-century revivalism was the typified by three men: D. L. Moody of Chicago, Charles Finney of Oberlin, and Charles H. Spurgeon of London. Dwight Lyman Moody was a successful businessman who abandoned his business in 1860 to enter evangelistic work. In 1865 he met his lifelong associate, Ira David Sankey, and for the next several decades the two toured America and the British Isles. In 1893 he organized a mission in connection with the World Fair and Columbian Exposition out of which grew the Bible Institute Colportage Association and the Moody Institute. In 1865 Moody founded the nondenominational Northfield conferences, which emphasized holiness, missions, evangelism, and the spirit-filled life.

Charles Grandison Finney underwent a powerful conversion experience in 1821 and three years later began his spectacular rise to prominence as a revivalist preacher. Almost singlehandedly, he introduced the concept of revivalist crusades in America. He popularized the so called "new measures," including protracted meetings, during which all secular activities ceased in the area for several days, the anxious bench for sinners, prayer meetings, public prayer for individuals by name, and a dramatic pulpit style. Later, with Asa Mahan, Finney became a proponent of Oberlin perfectionism.

Charles Haddon Spurgeon, called the "Prince of Preachers," was such a powerful preacher that a new 20,000-seat Metropolitan Tabernacle in London had to be built to accommodate his growing audience. His sermons and meditations are still read today. The 1870s were the heyday of British evangelists. Beside Spurgeon, there were Henry Drummond (1851–1897), Wilson Carlisle (1847–1942), and Gipsy Smith (1860–1947).

4. In 1840 a young Scot, David Livingstone, decided to forsake a medical career and devote his life to the gospel in Africa, then known as the "Dark Continent." By the time he died in 1873, that continent was dark no more because of him. Singlehandedly, he evangelized half a continent, a feat that has never been equaled since. Livingstone was also one of the century's great explorers. His discovery of the lakes of Shirwa, Nyasa, and Bangweulu and the basin of the Upper Nile are part of the annals of geography. When he died in 1873 he was given a hero's burial in Westminster Abbey.

5. In 1853 James Hudson Taylor heard the call to be a missionary and sailed for China. Despite many obstacles, he founded in 1865 the China Inland Mission which was the premier missionary organization in the Celestial Empire. A man of indomitable faith and great personal courage and devotion, he carried his missionary work into the very heart of China. By 1895 the China Inland Mission had a force of 641 missionaries working in every province.

6. In 1865 one of the world's most unusual Christian groups was formed when William Booth, a freelance evangelist, began working among the destitutes of London. Gradually his work was named The Christian Mission, and he was aided by his wife Catherine, herself a gifted preacher. They combined evangelism with social work, including the supply of free meals to the hungry. Military terminology was then in vogue ("Onward Christian Soldiers" was written about this time) and Booth's meetings were advertised as "The Hallelujah Army Fighting for God," which was later shortened to the Salvation Army. Booth himself was titled "General," and military titles and uniforms were used for all echelons in the Salvation Army. During the next 35 years, Booth traveled 5 million miles, preached 60,000 sermons, and enlisted 16,000 officers in his army. When he died in 1912, the world mourned; 150,000 people filed past his coffin and 40,000 attended his funeral. Vachel Lindsey, the American poet, wrote a special poem in honor of the occasion, called "General William Booth Enters Heaven."

7. One of the most important pontificates of the nineteenth century was that of Pius IX. Ironically, it was during his reign that the Vatican lost all its temporal possessions to the Risorgimento and the pope became a virtual prisoner of the Vatican as a result of King Victor Emmanuel's Law of Guarantees. But the pontificate was one of the defining moments in the history of modern papacy. In 1854 the pope issued the controversial dogma of immaculate conception which stated that "from the first moment of conception the Blessed Virgin Mary was, by the singular grace and privilege of Almighty God, and in view of the merits of Jesus Christ, Savior of mankind, kept free from all stain of original sin."

In 1869–1870 Pius IX convoked the First Vatican Council to deal with a variety of subjects, including faith and dogma. It was the Twentieth Ecumenical Council and the first in the nineteenth century. This council adopted the dogma of papal infallibility. The dogma stated that the pope is free from error when he speaks ex cathedra, that is when he speaks as the supreme pastor and doctor of all Christians, and when he defines a doctrine regarding faith and morals to be held by the universal church.

8. In 1833 a group of scholars at Oxford began publishing a series of pamphlets with the somewhat undistinguished title of *Tracts for the Times*. It was begun by John Henry Newman, and it soon gained many articulate supporters, including Edward Pusey, John Keble, R. H. Froude, and Robert Wilberforce. The purpose of the *Tracts* was to defend the catholic and apostolic elements in the Church of England against liberal and humanist attack. And it decried what Pusey described as the "National Apostasy." After the publication of the *Tracts* was suspended in 1841, a number of members of the movement, now called the Oxford Movement, joined the Catholic Church and Newman himself was later elevated as a cardinal. The Oxford Movement left a permanent impress on the Church of England, especially by fostering monasticism, a higher order of worship and patristic scholarship.

9. In 1816 the Christianization of African-Americans took an important step forward when the first free black church was founded in Philadelphia by Richard Allen. Called the African Methodist Episcopal Church, it was soon fol-

lowed by other black churches, such as the African Methodist Episcopal Zion Church in 1821.

10. In 1895 the struggle between Christian conservatives and liberals intensified when the conservative Evangelical Alliance published *The Fundamentals,* setting forth the five fundamentals of faith. They were the inerrancy of Scripture, the deity of Jesus, virgin birth, the substitutionary atonement of the cross, Jesus's physical resurrection, and his imminent return.

11. In 1844 Christian scholasticism was dealt its death blow by the *Philosophical Fragments,* written by a young Danish philosopher, Soren Aabye Kierkegaard, considered the father of modern existentialism. Although he wrote extensively, his major influence did not begin to felt until the twentieth century. Kierkegaard is responsible for subjectifying modern theology. God is not an object, he maintained, but a living actual being, who, in the person of Jesus Christ, confronts us to save us. God is not reachable or knowable through reason, but only through a leap of faith. This leap required full commitment, a rejection of the world's and the church's value systems. Kierkegaard also castigated the Lutheran Church for its emphasis on form as opposed to substance and spirit and for its comfortable dalliance with the world system. Some of Kierkegaard's greatest books followed, especially *Either/Or.*

12. The nineteenth century witnessed another phenomenon that has continued into the twentieth: the fragmentation of the Protestant church into sects and micro-denominations, based sometimes on personality and sometimes on doctrine. The American blacks, as noted, were among the first to form separate denominations. In 1830 John Nelson Darby, a relative of Admiral Nelson, became the leading spirit behind the Plymouth Brethren, a radical (for the times) group that tried to divest themselves of all unbiblical accoutrements. Communion was celebrated weekly and there were no ordained ministers or a fixed order of worship. The Brethren also believed in pacifism and the importance of prophecy and apocalypticism. Another member of the Plymouth Brethren was George Muller, who founded a faith orphanage, that is, an orphanage that never sought funding but trusted God to provide its needs. Muller's work was a testimony to the simple faith of the Brethren. Soon, rifts

arose among the Brethren, and they split into Exclusive Brethren and Open Brethren and then into further smaller groups.

The Campbells, Thomas and his son Alexander, were Irish Presbyterians who emigrated to the United States—then, as now, a fertile ground for new sects. Affiliated at first with the Baptists, the Campbells worked for what they called "a restoration of the ancient order of things." Eased out of the Baptist church for their radical ideas, Alexander Campbell joined with Barton Stone to found the Disciples of Christ, now a major denomination. The sect is important because they espoused one of the most elementary and simplest forms of the gospel.

13. Meanwhile, even as Christianity expanded, the blood of the martyrs continued to flow to be transformed into the seeds of the church. In 1831, 1843, and 1846 there were largescale massacres of Assyrians by the Muslim Kurds. Queen Ranavalona tried to eradicate Christianity in Madagascar by killing large numbers of Christians from 1835 to 1861. In 1843 millions were killed in China as the Great Peaceful Heavenly Kingdom (Tai Ping Tien Kueh) that began as a quasi-Christian sect with a Hakka founder strongly influenced by the New Testament, was suppressed. In Uganda some 250 Anglican and Catholic Christians were executed by King Mwanga at Namugongo. In 1885 a violent persecution against Christians broke out in Indochina, resulting in the martyrdom of 100,000 Catholics, including 115 priests. In 1895 the Turks, who over the centuries have killed over 10 million Christians, massacred 850,000 Armenians, including 1,200 burned alive in Urfa Cathedral. The massacre of Christians has become the longest and the bloodiest holocaust in history, lasting from the first century to the twentieth.

14. Driving much of the global evangelism was the translation and publication of the Bible in hundreds of non-Western languages and the founding of the early Bible societies. The German Bible Society and the British and Foreign Bible Society were founded in 1804, the Russian Bible Society in 1810, and the American Bible Society in 1816. The American Tract Society was founded in 1825. In 1817 Robert Moffat completed his Tswana Bible. In 1817 Robert Morrison, the first Protestant missionary in China, translated the Bible into Chinese.

15 Similarly, the nineteenth century was the birth period of some of the great parachurch organizations that came into full blossom in the twentieth century. In 1844 the Young Men's Christian Association was formed in London followed by the World Evangelical Alliance in 1846, the Scripture Union in 1879, the Student Volunteer Movement for Foreign Missions in 1888, and the Christian Endeavor movement in 1895. The Keswick covention began in England. It would be associated with the Deeper Christian Life movement.

16. In 1858 a young French peasant girl named Bernadette Soubirous received 18 apparitions of the Blessed Virgin Mary at Massabielle Rock, near Lourdes. The Virgin who manifested herself as the Immaculate Conception, revealed her presence by supernatural occurrences (such as a miraculous spring of water) and commands (as the building of a church). Over the course of the next century Lourdes would become a synonym for healing and miracles.

THE TWENTIETH CENTURY (1900–2000): THE AGE OF EXPECTANCY

Status of the Christian church

At the end of the twentieth century and the close of the Christian Bimillennium, 67 generations after Christ, 33.0 percent of the world population is Christian, 51 percent of them non-white, 78.4 percent of them evangelized; that is, they have been exposed to the gospel at least once in their lifetime. Printed Scriptures are available in over 2,000 languages.

Popes of the century

Pius X (1903–1914), Benedict XV (1914–1922), Pius XI (1922–1939), Pius XII (1939–1958), John XXIII (1958–1963), Paul VI (1963–1978), John Paul I (1978), John Paul II (1978–)

Christians of the century

Dietrich Bonhoeffer, Billy Graham, Mother Teresa, Cameron Townsend, C. S. Lewis, Brother Roger Schutz

1. Theologians divide the ages of the church into the church militant and the church triumphant. After 2,000 years, the church is still in its first age, still struggling to survive and to spread against a host of enemies from within and without. Striking a balance sheet at 2000, a momentous divide in human history, Christians make up about 33 percent of the world's population. Roman Catholics make up roughly half of this number; the Orthodox Church and the 20,000 Protestant denominations account for the remaining.

The hideous persecutions have not ceased; in fact, the Diocletian and Decian persecutions under the Roman Empire pale into insignificance when compared to the bloody massacres of Christians in the twentieth century under Communism and Islam. Muslims continue to be, as they have for the past 13 centuries, the principal enemies of the gospel, oppressing Christians in every country under their dominion. More than 600,000 Armenians and 200,000 Greeks were killed by the Turks in a blood bath during World War I. More than 5 million Christians perished under Lenin and Stalin and another 3 million when the Communists took over China in mid-century. There were other scattered outbursts of violence against Christians, as during the Boxer Rebellion in China in 1900 when 50,000 Christians were slaughtered. But the church strangely has managed to survive and to flourish. The gates of hell, to claim the biblical promise, have not prevailed against it.

Another notable statistic is that by the middle of the twentieth century, a great transition took place; from the tenth to the twentieth centuries, Europeans constituted the majority of Christians, unlike the first six centuries when non-Europeans were in the majority. The tide turned again around 1980 when, as a result of mass conversions in the Third World, especially Africa, non-Europeans again became the majority. This trend will continue as Europe becomes more and more apostate and the Third World more open to the gospel.

The Bible is available in nearly 1,900 languages. There are over 3 billion copies of the Bible in print, more than any other book in the world. In terms of territorial extent, the Christian church is close to fulfilling the Lord's command to go to every country and to every tribe. There are only four countries in the world without a

Christian presence (Saudi Arabia, Yemen, Afghanistan, and Maldives), all of them Muslim. There are rumblings of the end, but nothing visible, nothing certain. It is still the Age of Expectancy, a church still waiting for its bridegroom.

2. The central event of twentieth-century Christianity was the survival of the Russian Orthodox Church under the Bolsheviks for over 75 years. The extirpation of Christianity was one of the principal goals of Lenin, Stalin, and Khrushchev. They used every means in their power to wipe out the Orthodox Church, converting tens of thousands of churches into museums, sending thousands of priests into Siberian gulags, banning baptisms and other sacraments, bell ringing, and the celebration of Christmas and shutting down seminaries and monasteries. Khrushchev promised that by 1971 the last Christian priest in Russia would be put on display as a relic. Yet, it was Khrushchev and the Communists who eventually bit the dust, their empire dismantled and their vaunted Marxist ideology exposed and discredited. The Orthodox Church has emerged from this dark chapter of history as a phoenix and as the very embodiment of the soul of the great Russian people.

3. In 1906 an illiterate black preacher, William Seymour, went to Los Angeles to start a church. He rented a run-down warehouse in the seedy part of town in a street called Azusa. There, he began holding services without any fanfare, sometimes covering his face with a brown paper shopping bag. His audience, which grew larger day by day, began to be boisterous, praying in strange tongues under the guidance of the Holy Spirit. This was the beginning of the modern phenomenon known as Pentecostalism. Within weeks, Azusa Street services were in the front pages of national newspapers as miracles and healings were reported amidst the speaking in tongues. The Azusa phenomenon was soon replicated not only in many other cities in the United States, but in far countries, such as England, Chile, and India. Within eight years, the first Pentecostal denominations were founded, including Assemblies of God, Church of God, and the Four-Square Gospel. Pentecostalism would leave a permanent impress on the Christian faith, and Pentecostal churches would become the

fastest-growing denomination in the world before the end of the century.

In the 1960s and 1970s the so called "Jesus Movement" provided a rich harvest of souls and many of its members eventually ended as Pentecostal church planters and evangelists. Later the Catholic Church would welcome the second Charismatic wave of the movement. Led by Cardinal Suenens of Belgium, the Charismatic movement spread to Europe and then to many countries in Asia and Africa. Long-time Pentecostal leader David du Plessis worked for many years as an unofficial ambassador bringing together Pentecostals, Charismatics, and mainline churches. Charismatics and Pentecostals have become one of the most dynamic expressions of Christianity in the twentieth century, effectively reaching out to those not touched by more traditional churches.

4. The twentieth century has witnessed a remarkable recovery from the liberalism and agnosticism of the nineteenth century. The horrors of two world wars and seven decades of Marxism-Leninism have convinced thinking men and women that the socialist and humanist utopias of endless progress and prosperity cannot be sustained by unregenerate human nature. The magisterial voice of the church is once again heard in the twentieth century as the custodian of the conscience of humanity. Not only has atheism been shrinking as an ideology and as an ideal, but even Christian liberalism has been shriveling despite an entirely materialistic cultural environment. Unitarian churches have dwindled and may soon entirely disappear. The great liberal theologians of the nineteenth century and the early part of the twentieth century have lost much of their influence in the seminaries. Orthodoxy, as represented by Karl Barth and his school, has become the dominant influence by the end of the twentieth century.

5. Similarly, the twentieth century has produced some of the great crusaders and preachers in history. The list is led by Billy Graham, who, since 1948, has preached to more people, both in person and on radio and television, than any evangelist in history. The other great itinerant evangelists include Billy Sunday, the "baseball preacher," the Latin American Luis Palau, and the German Reinhard Bonnke. Not only are more

crusades being held today than ever before, but they are larger. The World Evangelization Crusade in South Korea was attended by 16.5 million people.

6. In 1934, some 550 years after the death of John Wycliffe, Cameron Townsend founded the Wycliffe Translators, for the translation of the Bible into all languages of the world. By 1914 the Bible had been translated into only 600 languages, but by 1999, the number of Bible translations had risen to nearly 2000.

7. The twentieth century was also the century of ecumenism. Ecumenism is the fulfillment of Christ's directive that all his believers should form one, indivisible body. The first steps in this direction were taken at the Edinburgh Conference of 1910 presided over by John R. Mott. It was followed by the Oxford and Edinburgh conferences in 1938. These conferences had led to the founding of two movements: Life and Work and Faith and Order, both of which were merged through the founding, in 1948, of the World Council of Churches. The council is defined as a "fellowship of churches which confess the Lord Jesus as God and Savior according to the Scriptures and therefore seek to fulfill together their common calling to the glory of the one God, Father, Son and Holy Spirit." The council comprises 322 member churches from every continent and country. The Roman Catholic Church, the only major non-member, has the status of an observer and actively participates in many of the WCC agencies.

8. The major event in twentieth-century Catholic history was the convocation of the Second Vatican Council in 1962 by Pope John XXIII. The council's goal was *aggiornamento*, or "bringing the church up to date." It is significant that of the more than 2,000 delegates, more than one-fourth were from Africa and Asia. Without making any sweeping changes in the structure or the mission of the church, the council cut away some deadwood and set a new course for Catholicism. Latin was no longer the sole language of the liturgy, but the Mass may be said in native languages. Both the clergy and the laity were accepted as people of God, each with their share of ministerial functions. The council document, "On Divine Revelation," emphasized that Scripture and tradition were the primary basis of divine truth. In the Decree on Ecumenism, non-Catholic Christians were called "separated brethren" and not heretics.

Within six years, after the death of John XXIII and his successor, John Paul II, a new pontiff of Polish origin, would give meaning and substance to the decrees of the council. One of the most traveled and most popular of modern popes, John Paul II would preside over the church during the final decades of the twentieth century, and bring extraordinary luster to his apostolic office.

9. For nineteen centuries, the only means of preaching of the Word was through sermons and open-air meetings. In the early part of the twentieth century, technology added broadcasting as another means, one never envisioned by the apostles. In 1921, a year after Westinghouse began radio broadcasting, the church service of Calvary Episcopal Church in Pittsburgh was broadcast over KDKA. Others followed in the next two years, notably Paul Rader broadcasting for 14 hours every Sunday (when regular broadcasting was suspended) on WJBT, R. R. Brown, on WOW, Omaha, and the Moody Bible Institute on WGES, Chicago. In 1928 Donald Grey Barnhouse became the first radio preacher to buy time on CBS to air his service from Philadelphia's Tenth Presbyterian Church. In 1930 HCJB in Quito, Ecuador, became the world's first Christian-owned missionary radio station. Within the next 70 years, Christian media grew phenomenally until it now blankets the world.

In the 1960s and 1970s, Billy Graham, Rex Humbard, Oral Roberts, Pat Robertson, and Bishop Fulton Sheen blazed the trail into television. At least two Christian television networks, Christian Broadcasting Network (CBN) and Trinity Broadcasting Network (TBN), have global affiliates. Without Christian radio and television, it is doubtful whether Evangelical and Pentecostal Christianity would have spread as wide and as fast as they have during the past half century.

10. The media also helped to bring into focus the lives and works of some of the modern heroes of the faith. One was C. S. Lewis, an icon among Protestants, who is unusual in that he was an Oxford don who brought clarity to basic theological propositions. Another was Mother Teresa, an Albanian nun who adopted India as her home and worked among the destitute and the dying. Still another was Dietrich Bonhoeffer, a Lutheran pas-

tor who defied Hitler and paid for it with his life. It is a powerful testimony to the Christian faith that twenty centuries after Calvary, it can still produce men and women of the same caliber and devotion as the apostles.

11. The center of gravity of the Christian world has shifted from the First World to the Third World. Christianity is in serious decline in Europe outside Russia. The missionary thrust is now being slowly reversed as missionaries from the Third World, including Korea, Africa, and India, are carrying the gospel to Europe and other parts of the world.

12. The two millennia of Christian history end with the same hope as that of the aged apostle John, an exile on the rocky isle of Patmos, as he wrote his last words in the Book of Revelation: "Even so, come, Lord Jesus! . . . Amen."

Chronology of Evangelization

31   Jesus commissions first the 12 disciples to go to the tribes of Israel and later the 70 disciples to go to the 70 nations of the world.

33   Jesus gives the Great Commission to all believers, "Go into all the world and make disciples," emphasizing seven mandates: receive, go, witness, proclaim, disciple, baptize, train.

34–100   The 12 apostles cover the known world with the Good News: Paul through Asia Minor, the Balkans, Cyprus, Syria, Eastern Mediterranean, and Rome; Peter to Rome; James to Spain; Bartholomew to Armenia; Thomas to India.

36   Martyrdom of Stephen. The church grows through martyrdom as well as signs and wonders.

100   As the age of the apostles comes to a close, Christian communities are planted over all parts of the Roman Empire and house churches are found in urban areas.

140   Hermas writes, "The Son of God . . . has been preached to the ends of the earth."

150   Justin Martyr founds a catechetical school in Rome and documents signs and wonders among the faithful. "There is not one single race of men," he wrote, "whether barbarians or Greeks, or whatever they may be called, nomads or vagrants or herdsmen dwelling in tents, among whom prayers and giving of thanks, are not offered through the name of the Crucified Jesus."

156   Montanism begins as a charismatic, millennial, prophetic, and apocalyptic movement that was over 19 centuries ahead of its time. Its most famous member was Tertullian. Persecuted by the established church, it goes underground.

205   First Christian theologian, Clement of Alexandria, writes, "The whole world, with Athens and Greece, has already become the domain of the Word."

c. 220   Origen writes, "The Gospel of Jesus Christ has been preached in all creation under heaven, to Greeks and barbarians, to the wise and foolish . . . it is impossible to see any race of men which has avoided accepting the teaching of Jesus"; "The divine goodness of our Lord and Savior is equally diffused among the Britons, the Africans and other nations of the world"; and "The preaching of the Gospel through the whole Oikumene shows that the church is receiving divine support." He, however, acknowledges that the gospel has not reached the Chinese or the Ethiopians and to some people even in the Roman Empire.

270   Itinerant monks join missionaries in spreading the gospel.

303–310   Over half a million Christians are martyred in the ten Roman persecutions, the last under Diocletian, yet the church flourishes.

313 Constantine legalizes Christianity throughout his empire.

378 Jerome estimates that 1.9 million Christians had been martyred up to his time.

c. 410 Total episcopate in North Africa, including Egypt, Numidia, and Mauretania, reaches 1,200 bishops.

Honoratus at Lerins trains notable missionary bishops.

c. 510 Irish peregrini or Exultantes Christi (wandering hermit-preachers) embark as missionary pilgrims for Christ converting most of Europe during the next 400 years.

547 Cosmas Indicopleustes, Nestorian merchant missionary, completes his *Topographia Christiana*, a global survey of the Christian world, in 12 books.

c. 550 Nestorian monasticism is organized and reformed by Abraham of Kashkar, to serve as engine of evangelization in the East.

635 Nestorian missionary, Alopen, one of the greatest missionaries of all time, reaches Chinese capital and translates the Scriptures into Chinese.

c. 700 End of the patristic age.

c. 780 The entire Saxon race is baptized under the imperial edict of Charlemagne.

1000 The end of the first millennium inspires belief in the imminent end of the world.

The Catholic Apostolic Church of the East, considered outcast Nestorians by the West, is now the largest in the world, with 250 bishoprics and millions of adherents.

1095 The Western Church leads the first of eight crusades to liberate the Holy Land from the infidels.

1209 Francis of Assisi tries to convert the sultan of Egypt.

1215 New mendicant orders, including the Franciscans and Dominicans, add thousands of preachers to the contingents of missionaries from Lapland to China.

1266 Mongol ruler, Kublai Khan, requests the pope: "Send me 100 men skilled in your religion . . . and so I shall be baptized and then all my barons and great men, and then their subjects. And so there will be more Christians here than in your parts." By the time two Dominicans and five Fransicans are sent in response to this request, the great Khan was dead.

1399 Catalan Dominican preacher, Vincent Ferrer, preaches to thousands and converts 25,000.

1450 Gutenberg prints the first Bible, making possible the widespread dissemination of the Bible.

1455 Thomas à Kempis writes the *Imitation of Christ*, that would bring millions to a closer relationship with Jesus Christ.

1492 Christopher Columbus discovers the New World, adding two new continents for evangelization.

Within the next 50 years millions of American Indians would be baptized.

c. 1520 Martin Luther writes, "The Gospel will always be preached . . . It has gone out through the length and breadth of the world." But he and John Calvin taught that the Great Commission applied only to those called to the apostolic ministry of preaching and teaching, whereas the Anabaptists claimed that it was binding on every Christian.

1523 Ignatius Loyola founds the Society of Jesus for "the Defense and Propagation of the Faith through Preaching." In time, it will grow into a powerful missionary organization in all continents.

1580 Discalced Carmelite Sisters devote themselves to prayer for the evangelization of the world.

1588 Hadrian Saravia becomes one of the

first non-Catholic advocates of foreign missions.

1613   Spanish Discalced Carmelite monk, Thomas a Jesu, writes *De Procuranda Salute Omnium Gentium,* envisaging conversion of the entire world to Christ.

1622   Pope Gregory XV sets up Sacred Congregation for the Propagation of the Faith.

1648   Spanish Jesuit Ildefonso de Flores calculates the number of Christian martyrs until then at 11 million.

1680   Christian Brothers founded in Reims to teach Christian doctrine to the poor and working class.

1685   Russian Orthodox Church sends first missionaries to China.

1698   First Anglican missionary society formed: Society for the Promotion of Christian Knowledge.

1700   First evangelistic campaigns in Germany by Ernst Christoph Hochmann von Hochenau.

1701   Society for the Propagation of the Gospel [in Foreign Parts] is formed in London.

1703   Spiritans or Holy Ghost Fathers founded for the conversion of the heathen.

1705   The first foreign mission society in Germany, the Lutheran Danish-Halle Mission, sends Bartholomew Ziegenbalg, Heinrich Plutschau, and Christian Schwartz to Tranquebar, India, as pioneer missionaries.

1710   Canstein House Printing Press is founded in Halle, Germany, together with the first Bible society by Count Karl von Canstein.

1725   The Great Awakening breaks out in the American colonies under Jonathan Edwards and T. J. Frelinghuysen.

1732   Moravians send out missionaries to St. Thomas, West Indies.

1736   Moravians send missionaries to Greenland.

1743   Russian Orthodox Church sends missionaries to Kamchatka.

1780   Deutsche Christentumsgesellschaft (Christendom Society) is founded in Germany.

1782   Concerts for Prayer and World Mission is initiated by Jonathan Edwards.

1784   Russian Orthodox Missions reach Alaska.

1785   Evangelistic awakenings spread in Wales.

1787   Society of the United Brethren for Propagating the Gospel among the Heathen is founded in Pennsylvania.

1792   William Carey publishes *An Enquiry into the Obligations of Christians, to Use All Means for the Conversion of the Heathens* and then sets sail for India under the auspices of the Particular Baptist Society for Propagating the Gospel among the Heathen, thus beginning the modern era of Protestant world missions. He serves 41 years in Bengal and translates the Bible into 35 languages.

1795   London Missionary Society is founded.

1800   Kentucky mass revival follows camp meetings.

1802   Massachusetts Baptist Mission Society is formed for the evangelization of frontier communities.

1804   British and Foreign Bible Society is founded.

1806   The Haystack Prayer Meetings at Williams College inspire the foundation of the American Board of Commissioners of Foreign Missions in 1810. In 1961 it was renamed United Church Board for World Ministries.

1815   Italian priest Caspar del Bufalo founds Missioners of the Most Precious Blood for evangelization of the world through charitable works. The Basel Mission is founded in Germany.

1818   *The Conversion of the World, or the Claims of 600 Millions and the Ability and Duty of the Churches Respecting Them* by G. Hall and S. Newell calls for 30,000 missionaries to convert the heathen.

1819   Missionary Society of the Methodist Episcopal Church is organized; reorganized in 1964 as the Board of Global Ministries of the United Methodist Church.

1825   Bombay Missionary Union is founded.

1826   Glasgow City Mission is founded as the first of 50 city missions in the United Kingdom.

1828   Karl Gutzlaff, a Lutheran, begins work in the Far East, especially the Dutch East Indies, Siam, southern China, and Hong Kong.

1829   Christian Brethren send A. N. Groves and others as first missionaries to Baghdad and later India. Renamed as Christian Missions in Many Lands.

1837   The Board of Foreign Missions of the Presbyterian Church is established "to aid in the conversion of the world." In 1958 it became the Commission on Ecumenical Mission and Relations with the goal of "making the Lord Jesus Christ known to all men."

1841   CMS General Secretary Henry Venn requires all missionaries to complete annual questionnaires recording church growth statistics. He propounds three self-goals of mission to make churches become self-supporting, self-governing, self-propagating.

1844   First Young Men's Christian Association is founded in London.

1845   Southern Baptist Convention is formed as an independent denomination. It founds the Board of Domestic Missions (later Home Mission Board) and Foreign Mission Board.

1846   Evangelical Alliance is formed in London by 800 Christians representing 52 confessions.

1850   British Quaker millionaire Robert Arthington donates millions to reach unreached peoples by supplying these peoples with copies of the New Testament.

1854   First Union Missionary Convention is held in New York under the leadership of Alexander Duff. Duff is later appointed first chair of evangelism and evangelical theology at New College, Edinburgh.

1855   World Alliance of YMCAs is founded in Paris with headquarters in Geneva.

1857   Mass evangelism era begins as U.S. evangelist D. L. Moody begins crusades with singer and composer Ira Sankey. Moody preached to 750,000 people during his lifetime.

1859   Society of St. Francis of Sales (Salesians of Don Bosco) is founded for the Christian education of youth.

1861   Woman's Union Missionary Society of America for Heathen Lands is founded in New York. Russian Orthodox Church begins evangelism in Mongolia and Japan.

1862   The Congregation of the Immaculate Heart of Mary is founded.

1865   Christian Revival Association is founded in London by Methodist evangelist William Booth. In 1878 it is renamed as Salvation Army. Its emphasis is stated as "the supremacy of evangelism in fulfilling the Lord's Great Commission . . . To work to the end that every man and woman and child has the opportunity to hear the good news of the Gospel."

1867   Archbishop of Canterbury C. T. Longley convenes the first decennial Lambeth Conference of all bishops of the Anglican Communion.

1870   Orthodox Missionary Society is organized in Russia by metropolitan of Moscow, I. Veniaminov.

1872   Salesian Sisters is founded in Italy for world mission by prayer and works of charity.

1873   East London Institute for Home and Foreign Missions formed. It would be renamed Regions Beyond Missionary Union in 1900.

1875   The World Alliance of Reformed Churches is founded.

1876   The World Methodist Council is founded.

1877   First General Foreign Missions Conference is held in Shanghai with 473 missionaries from 20 Protestant missionary societies.

1880   A. T. Pearson publishes "A Plan to Evangelize the World" in *The Missionary Review,* calling for an ecumenical council to oversee global evangelization.

1881   United Society of Christian Endeavor is formed in the United States. In 1895 it would become the World Christian Endeavor.

1887   Christian and Missionary Alliance is organized by A. B. Simpson. It would later have one of the largest contingents of missionaries per capita.

1888   Student Volunteer Movement for Foreign Missions is organized with the motto: "The evangelization of the world in this generation."

1890   Scandinavian Alliance Mission of North America is founded for worldwide evangelism and church planting; in 1949 it would be renamed The Evangelical Alliance Mission (TEAM).

1892   Student Voluntary Missionary Union is begun in England.

1893   Sudan Interior Mission is begun as Africa Industrial Mission. In 1982 it would be renamed SIM International,

which expanded its operations to Latin America.

1894   Young Women's Christian Association (YWCA) is founded.

1897   Association of Pentecostal Churches in America (later, the Church of the Nazarene) begins foreign missions.

1898   Russian Orthodox Church send missionaries to Korea.

1899   Gideons International begins free distribution of Bibles. Over the next century it would distribute over half a billion free Bibles.

1900   John R. Mott publishes the influential classic, *The Evangelization of the World in This Generation,* and names the twentieth century, "the Christian Century."

1901   Charles F. Parham opens Bethel Bible School near Topeka, Kansas, teaching his students about the infilling of the Holy Spirit as evidenced by speaking in tongues. The gifts of the Holy Spirit are restored to the church and are reinforced by Latter Rain teaching.

Consolata Missionary Fathers is founded in Turin.

1902   Young People's Missionary Education Movement is founded by 15 denominational boards in the United States to enlist missionaries.

1903   All Nations Flag Church (Church of God of Prophecy) is founded. In 1911 it would begin overseas work in the Bahamas.

1904   Revival sweeps Wales under the ministry of Evan Roberts.

1906   First General Conference of Missionaries to the World of Islam is held in Cairo under the leadership of Samuel Zwemer.

Laymen's Missionary Movement is launched as foreign missions auxiliary agency.

1910   World Missionary Conference, precursor of the World Council of

Churches, is held in Edinburgh and presided over by John R. Mott.

Church of God (Cleveland) initiates world evangelism program by sending out missionaries to Bahamas, Egypt, and Cuba.

1912 In the first attempt by a mission body to reach systematically every home in an entire nation, Oriental Missionary Society reaches 10.3 million homes in Japan.

1913 English missionary C. T. Studd founds Christ's Etceteras (later, Worldwide Evangelization Crusade).

1915 Elim Foursquare Gospel Alliance and Revival party begun in Britain by Pentecostal healer G. Jeffreys, who also founds World Revival Crusade.

1917 Interdenominational Foreign Missions Association of North America founded by a number of evangelical organizations.

1918 Aimee Semple McPherson founds Worldwide Evangelism as part of her International Church of the Foursquare Gospel.

Interchurch World Movement of North America launched to "conquer the world for Christ." Supported by 34 major U. S. denominations, the movement fails.

1919 International Missionary Council is launched with preliminary conference in Crans, Switzerland.

Mennonite Central Committee is formed in Akron, Pennsylvania. General Council of Cooperating Baptist Missions is organized. It would be renamed Baptist Mid-Missions in 1953.

1923 Million Testaments Campaign founded in Philadelphia by G. T. B. Davis.

1926 Lighthouse of International Foursquare Evangelism is begun by Aimee Semple McPherson for training in missiology and evangelism.

1927 First World Conference on Faith and Order meets in Lausanne, France.

Association of Baptists for Evangelism in the Orient is formed.

1928 World Fundamental Baptist Misionary Fellowship is founded in Texas. It is later renamed as the World Baptist Fellowship Mission.

1929 Congregationalist missionary Frank C. Laubach begins "Each One Teach One" method in the Philippines. In 1950 he would describe his method in *Literacy As Evangelism.*

1930 Movement for World Evangelization (Mildmay Movement) founded in London.

World Council for Life and Work succeeds the Stockholm Conference.

International Missions (originally the India Mission) is founded in the United States by B. Davidson.

Foundation Farthest Out is begun as a world belt of prayer around the world.

1931 Unevangelized Fields Mission (UFM) is founded in London. Renamed UFM International in 1985.

Worldwide Prayer and Missionary Union is founded in Chicago.

Radio Vatican is inaugurated by Pope Pius XI.

1933 The Navigators is founded. It is a one-on-one discipling agency that specializes in memorization of the Bible and multiplication of believers.

1934 W. Cameron Townsend begins Wycliffe Bible Translators for Scripture translation by professional linguists with overseas work under the name of Summer Institute of Linguistics. In 1959 it adopts the slogan, "Two Thousand Tongues to Go."

First Youth for Christ rally is held in Brantford, Ontario, under Paul Guiness.

1935   World Revival Crusade founded by Pentecostal leader G. Jeffreys.

World Intercessors, the Prayer Circle of Oriental Missionary Society, is begun as a worldwide prayer movement for evangelization.

1936   Student Foreign Missions Fellowship is begun in the United States. It holds triennial mass conventions.

1937   Child Evangelism Fellowship is founded.

1938   Fourth World Missionary Conference and meeting of the International Missionary Council in Tambaram, Madras, India. It summoned the churches "to unite in the supreme work of world evangelization until the kingdoms of this world become the kingdom of our Lord."

Gospel Recordings is founded to produce gospel records in every known language and dialect.

World Home Bible League is founded in Chicago.

1939   Worldwide Signs Following Evangelism is begun under United Fundamentalist Church.

Young Life, an interdenominational outreach to youth, is founded by Jim Rayburn.

1941   The first base ecclesial communities are formed in Brazil to promote grassroots evangelism among the poor.

The first Bible correspondence course, Emmaus Bible School, is founded in Toronto.

1942   Ling Liang Worldwide Evangelistic Mission is founded in Shanghai to send Chinese missionaries to the uttermost parts of the world.

New Tribes Mission is begun in the United States to evangelize primitive tribes around the world.

1943   National Religious Broadcasters of North America is formed as official broadcasting arm of the National Association of Evangelicals.

Global Outreach Mission is founded in Buffalo.

Conservative Baptist Foreign Mission Society is formed in Wheaton, Illinois.

1944   Youth for Christ International is founded.

1945   Evangelical Foreign Missions Association is formed "to give all men everywhere the privilege of hearing and receiving the message of salvation."

1946   First Urbana Conference is held.

Conference of Bible Societies at Haywards Heath in the United Kingdom creates the United Bible Societies (UBS) as a federation and fellowship of 13 autonomous Bible societies from Europe and North America.

World Literature Crusade begins in Canada for radio outreach and expands into systematic tract distribution through Every Home Crusades.

Egede Institute of Missionary Study and Research is founded in Oslo to promote scholarly research in missiology.

Associacion Misionera Evangelica Nacional (AMEN, National Evangelical Missionary Association) is begun as a home mission in Peru.

1947   Fifth meeting of the International Missionary Council in Whitby, Toronto. It coins the phrase, "Expectant Evangelism."

Lutheran World Federation (LWF) is founded "to bear united witness before the world to the gospel of Jesus Christ as the power of God for salvation." Two years later it would form the LWF Commission on World Missions.

Fuller Theological Seminary is founded in Pasadena, California.

World Revival Prayer League (National Christian Women's Prayer League) is founded in Japan.

Oral Roberts Evangelistic Association is founded in Tulsa, Oklahoma, with its own foreign missions program.

1948 First World Congress on World Evangelization convened by Youth for Christ International at Beatenberg, Switzerland. It is led by Billy Graham.

World Council of Churches (WCC) is inaugurated in Amsterdam with 144 member churches.

International Council of Christian Churches (ICCC) is founded as an anti-ecumenical and fundamentalist alternative to WCC.

Christian Crusade (Christian Echoes National Ministry) moves to Tulsa, Oklahoma. It plans to send one million scripture portions in hydrogen-filled balloons into Eastern Europe.

1949 T. L. Osborn Evangelistic Association is founded for mass evangelism, utilizing native workers.

World Gospel Crusades (Every Creature Crusade) is founded for mass evangelization through print and broadcast media.

Survey Application Trust produces the first *World Christian Handbook,* edited by K. Grubb, with church membership statistics by denomination for every country.

Cursillos de Cristianidad is begun in Spain by Bishop J. Hervas as a crash course on Christianity, including three-day retreats. The movement spreads to Latin America, the United States, and Britain.

1950 Billy Graham Evangelistic Association is founded.

Help Open Paths to Evangelize (HOPE) is founded.

World Vision is founded. By 2000 it would become one of the largest

philanthropic organizations in the world working in over 90 countries and effectively using computers and new technology.

Full Gospel Business Men's Fellowship International (FGBMFI) is founded by dairy magnate Demos Shakarian.

Baptist Bible Fellowship International is founded.

Missionaries of Charity is begun in Calcutta by Mother Teresa, one of the icons of the age. Within the next 45 years, the order would spread to 80 countries.

Worldwide Missions International is begun in Nigeria.

1951 First World Congress of the Lay Apostolate aims to mobilize all Catholics to reach the lost.

1952 Worldwide Revival Movement is launched in Ireland by W. E. Allen.

Billy Graham Evangelistic Association founds World Wide Pictures to make Christian motion pictures.

1953 Worldwide Evangelization Crusade begins work in Java, Indonesia, and founds Batu Bible School.

World Committee for Christian Broadcasting is founded. Later, in 1968, it would become the World Association for Christian Communication.

1954 The Second Assembly of the World Council of Churches meets in Evanston, Illinois.

MAP International is begun as an interdenominational evangelical service agency providing medical assistance.

World Missionary Evangelism is begun as a nondenominational service agency in Dallas, Texas.

New Life League World Missionary Society is begun in Waco, Texas.

1955 Midnight Call Missionary Work is founded in Zurich, Switzerland.

1956   Charismatic, neo-Pentecostal renewal begins among Episcopal and Protestant churches, and then becomes part of a worldwide movement.

Belgian Charismatic Cardinal Suenens publishes *The Gospel to Every Creature* on evangelism.

1957   Assemblies of God unveils Global Conquest program "for the rapid evangelization of the world." In 1967 its name would be changed to the Good News Crusades.

Nights of Prayer for Worldwide Renewal launched by Anglican clergyman, G. S. Ingram.

Send the Light (later Operation Mobilization) is founded as an interdenominational youth agency sending short-term missionary workers.

1959   Southern Baptists develop long-term emphasis on "Sharing Christ Around the World," and approve its slogan of Bold Mission.

First nationwide Evangelism-in-Depth campaign organized in Nicaragua. Later it would spread to Latin America and Japan and become incorporated into evangelization strategies.

1960   Congress on World Missions meets in Chicago.

Baptist International Missions is founded.

Youth with a Mission (YWAM), an outgrowth of the Jesus movement, begins as an evangelical-charismatic sending agency. Within the next 20 years it would become the world's largest evangelistic agency.

1961   World Missionary Press is founded in New Paris, Indiana.

Third Assembly of the World Council of Churches is held in New Delhi, India.

First Christian television station is opened in Virginia Beach, Virginia, by M. G. "Pat" Robertson.

The Sixth International Student Missionary Convention meets in Urbana, Illinois.

World Radio Missionary Fellowship inaugurates HCJB-TIV in Quito, Ecuador, as pioneer missionary telecaster.

Karl Barth writes, "The Great Commission is truly the most genuine utterance of the risen Jesus."

1962   Haggai Institute for Advanced Leadership Training begins courses in Singapore to train missionary leaders from the Third World.

New Life for All begins a 10-year campaign in Nigeria; later spreads to other African countries.

1963   Missiologist Donald D. A. McGavran begins *Church Growth Bulletin,* renamed in 1979 as *Global Church Growth.*

Evangelical Missions Quarterly is founded.

1966   Evangelical Congress on "The Church's Worldwide Mission," meets in Wheaton, Illinois, and signs the Wheaton Declaration, "covenanting together for the evangelization of the world in this generation."

World Congress on Evangelism is held in Berlin.

World Vision founds Missions Advanced Research and Communication Center (MARC) as a research and publication agency, using the tools of technology for advancing the gospel.

1967   International Correspondence Institute is founded by the Assemblies of God offering Bible courses by mail.

Millions attend Crusade for World Revival in Seoul.

1968   The Fourth Assembly of the World Council of Churches is held in Uppsala, Sweden.

Association for World Evangelization is founded in Portland, Oregon.

1969   Pentecostal evangelist Jimmy Swaggart launches radio ministry, Camp Meeting Hour, followed three years later by a television ministry, following God's directive to carry out the Great Commission by means of radio and television. Twenty years later the ministry would collapse engulfed by a sex scandal.

World Evangelism Foundation is founded in Texas by Baptist missionaries to promote Partnership Evangelism.

1970   Hal Lindsay's *The Late Great Planet Earth* inspires widespread interest in eschatology and conversions among its ten million readers.

Evangelistic ship *Logos* begins missionary voyages visiting large ports with books and other evangelistic tools. In 1988 the ship is lost at sea. In 1977 its sister ship Doulos joins the endeavor.

1972   International Catholic Charismatic Renewal Office is founded as International Communications Office in Ann Arbor, Michigan.

1973   Presbyterian Church launches Mission to the World.

First Annual Summer Institute of World Mission is held in Seoul.

Global Missionary Evangelism is begun in Pensacola, Florida.

Trinity Broadcasting Network is launched in southern California as a Pentecostal television station "to get the gospel to every living human being on planet earth."

World Film Crusade is founded in Florida.

1974   International Congress on World Evangelization is held in Lausanne, Switzerland, on the theme, "Let the earth hear his voice." By 1980 it develops into the Lausanne Movement directed by the Lausanne Committee for World Evangelization.

EXPLO-74, the Second Training Congress on Evangelism, is held in Seoul, with one rally drawing 1.5 million people.

Discipling a Whole Nation (DAWN) Conference in the Philippines plans for seven million more churches by 2000.

Presbyterian Order for World Evangelism is begun in Pasadena, California, as a support agency.

1975   Full Gospel World Mission Association is established in Seoul.

Fifth Assembly of World Council of Churches is held in Nairobi.

New Life International begun as evangelical charismatic service agency in Fresno, California. In 1984 it would be renamed Total World Evangelization Vision.

Genesis Project is begun to produce the entire Bible on film in 33 years.

World Evangelical Fellowships Missions Commission is set up in Seoul.

1976   Gabriel Olasoji World Evangelism, founded in Ibadan, Nigeria, holds crusades in 25 nations.

U.S. Center for World Mission is founded in Pasadena, California.

Church Growth International seminars begun in Seoul by P. Yonggi Cho.

First Chinese Congress on World Evangelization meets in Hong Kong.

Lausanne Intercession Advisory Group sets Pentecost Sunday as annual day of prayer for world evangelization.

1977   First Conference on the Charismatic Renewal in the Christian Churches is held in Kansas City.

Bill Bright's Here's Life, World announces goal to saturate the world with the gospel by 1980.

1978   International Conference on the Charismatic Renewal in the Catholic

Church meets in Dublin, led by Cardinal Suenens.

1979   First Norwegian Conference on World Evangelization is held in Drammen, Norway.

Anglican renewal agency, Sharing of Ministries Abroad (SOMA), holds its first international conference in Singapore.

Campus Crusade for Christ produces Jesus film. Dubbed in nearly 300 languages, the film is seen by billions of people.

Billy Graham calls for 120,000 missionaries by 2000 at Urbana conference.

1980   First World Missionary Conference on Mission and Evangelism is held in Melbourne, Australia, on the theme, "Thy Kingdom Come."

Consultation on World Evangelization meets in Pattaya, Bangkok.

16.5 million attend World Evangelization Crusade in Seoul.

Third Wave of renewal in the Holy Spirit begins in 40 major evangelical churches.

1981   World Evangelization Strategy Work Group is formed by the Baptist World Alliance.

1982   World Satellite Evangelism begun in Tulsa, Oklahoma, to reach closed countries; forms a global media task force in 50 nations.

Institute on World Evangelism is established in Atlanta, Georgia, by the World Evangelism Committee of the World Methodist Council.

1983   World Baptist Congress on Urban Evangelism is held in Niteroi, Brazil.

First International Conference for Itinerant Evangelists in Amsterdam is attended by 3,800 evangelists from 132 nations.

Sixth Assembly of the World Council of Churches is held in Vancouver, Canada.

Lumen 2000 launched as Catholic global television evangelism agency based in Dallas and Vatican City.

Committee on the Holy Spirit and Frontier Missions is formed in California.

New Focus is founded in San Bernardino, California, to promote evangelism during sports events, especially the Olympic games.

1985   Youth Congress on World Evangelization meets in Stuttgart, Germany.

Interchurch Consultation on Future Trends in Christian World Mission meets in Maryknoll, New York, to discuss unfinished tasks of world evangelization.

International Consultation on Missions is convened in Jos, Nigeria.

Maranatha Christian Ministries unveil World Ambassadors, a plan to evangelize foreign non-Christian students in the United States.

Global Network of Centers for World Mission is formed with 30 members.

Campus Crusade for Christ holds EXPLO-85, a global Christian training teleconference.

Association of International Mission Services (AIMS) is formed with 75 member agencies.

1986   Assemblies of God unveils plans to reach all world cities by 2000.

International Conference for Equipping Evangelists is held in Sacramento, California.

Second International Conference for Itinerant Evangelists meets in Amsterdam.

Presbyterian Church announces Decade of Evangelism, 1990–2000.

U.S. Society for Frontier Missiology is founded in Colorado Springs, Colorado.

Intercontinental Broadcasting Network is begun in Virginia Beach, Virginia.

1987 Pope John Paul II creates new office in Rome, Evangelization 2000, to plan for the Decade of Evangelization.

International Conference of Evangelical Bible Societies is founded with 10 member agencies.

World Literature Crusade changes name to Every Home for Christ.

North American General Congress on the Holy Spirit and World Evangelization meets in New Orleans.

Adopt-a-People is begun to link North American churches and mission agencies with unreached people groups.

Worldwide Prayer Crusade is initiated by the Vatican.

International Global Missions Conference in Dallas is attended by 20 mission agencies.

Decade of Harvest inaugurated by the Assemblies of God to reach all human beings by 2000. A similar program, Decade of Destiny, is launched by Church of God (Cleveland).

Advance Ministries, a mission sending agency serving independent Charismatic churches, is begun with Mennonite support.

1988 World Wesleyan Conference on Witness and Evangelism is held on the 250th anniversary of John Wesley's conversion.

1989 Global Consultation on World Evangelization meets in Singapore, and Second World Conference on World Mission and Evangelism meets in San Antonio, Texas.

Lausanne II, or the Second International Conference on World Evangelization, is convened in Manila.

1990 Decade of Universal Evangelization begins with around-the-world prayer events.

1991 Global Congress of Charismatic Leaders for World Evangelization is held in Brighton.

Seventh Assembly of the World Council of Churches meets in Canberra, Australia.

Pan Orthodox Ecumenical Council meets, the first since 787.

Tentmakers International Exchange holds second international conference in London.

Quadrennial World Assembly of the International Fellowship of Evangelical Students is held in Wheaton, Illinois, on the theme, "the Cross of Jesus."

Sixth World Youth Day is held in Katowice, Poland, attended by John Paul II and 1.3 million students.

1992 Third Latin American Congress on Evangelization is held in Quito, Ecuador.

The Sixteenth Triennial Pentecostal World Conference convenes in Oslo, attended by 12,500.

Fifth Conference on Faith and Order (WCC) is held in Santiago de Compostela, Spain.

1994 World Holy Spirit Conference convenes in Seoul, Korea.

First World Conference of the World Assemblies of God Fellowship is held in Seoul, Korea.

1995 Revival erupts in Assemblies of God Church in Brownsville, Pensacola, Florida.

1996 Third World Missionary Conference on World Mission and Evangelism is held in Salvador, Bahia, Brazil.

1997 Promisekeepers hold mass rally for national repentance in Washington, D.C., attended by 1.5 million men.

John Paul II visits Cuba.

1998   World Conference on Intercession, Spiritual Warfare, and Evangelism is held in Guatemala City.

The First National Conference on Fasting and Prayer is held in Houston, Texas, attended by 1.8 million.

Ten million believers in 150 countries join March for Jesus.

1999   World Conference on Deliverance: Equipping the Church for Revival is held in Colorado Springs.

First International Consultation on Discipleship is held in Eastbourne, England.

Source: World Christian Encyclopadia

Chronology of Christian Music

Century	Form	Person/Contribution	Example
c. ninth	Organum	Liturgical chant (cantatus firmus) accompanied by one or more additional voices at interval of fourth or fifth	
	sequence/trope	Practice of setting a free text to melismatic passage	
twelfth	Mass	Leonin writes earliest musical setting of Mass.	
fourteenth	Mass	Guillaume Machault First polyphonic (more than one voice) setting of ordinary	Messe de Notre Dame
fifteenth	Mass, Motet, Hymn, Antiphon	New techniques developed by John Dunstable in England, Johannes Ockenghem in Netherlands, and Josquin des Pres in Belgium	
sixteenth	Mass, Motet Magnificat Concerto Oratorio Monody Choral Music	Orlando Lassus perfects the motet form; Giovanni Perluigi (Palestrina) gives church music its distinct form; Adrian Willaert develops polychoral style with divided chorus in opposite galleries; Andrea and Giovanni Gabrielli develop concerto style with instruments and voices Opera on sacred text utilizing chorus, solo, or both with no action, scenery, or costumes; San Felippo dei Neri institutes popular service in oratory; Laude (devotional songs) provide basis for semi-dramatic works on sacred theme; Claudio Monteverdi's compositions include melodic writing in recitative style. --a narrative text sung by solo voice with chordal accompaniment; Christopher Tye writes first English motet, syllabic, more chordal with straightforward rhythm; Thomas Tallis, founder of cathedral music, Latin masses, and motets; William Byrd develops the verse anthem, including solo and choral sections.	Penitential Psalms (1565)

seventeenth	Cantata	Cantata is developed in Italy as a smaller version of the oratorio. Giacomo Carissimi's cantatas consist of two or more arias with recitative, no chorus.	Jephte (c. 1650)
	Verse Anthem	Henry Purcell in England adds instrumental sections to chorus and solo sections.	
	Dramatic Concertato	Heinrich Schultz develops dramatic concertato with instruments and voices.	Symphoniae Sacra (1629–1650) Seven Words of Christ on the Cross (1664) Passion Settings (1666)
seventeenth/ eighteenth	Chorale, Cantata	Dietrich Buxtehude institutes evening concerts in sacred music during Advent. J. S. Bach writes cantatas for specific services including chorus, solo recitative, arias, duets.	Wachet Auf In Dulci Jubilio
	Oratorio	George F. Handel composes dramatic oratorios based on biblical texts.	Israel in Egypt (1738) Messiah (1741) Jephtha (1751)
	Mass	Haydn, Mozart, Beethoven, Schubert, and Bruckner compose concert settings for Mass.	
eighteenth		Joseph Haydn	Seven Last Words (1785) Creation (1798)
		Wolfgang A. Mozart	Solemn Vespers (1780) Requiem (1791)
nineteenth		Ludwig von Beethoven	Christ on the Mount of Olives (1803) Missa Solemnis (1818–1823)
		Felix Mendelssohn	St. Paul (1836) Elijah (1846)
		Hector Berlioz	Requiem (1837) Te Deum (1848–1849) L'Enfance du Christ (1854)
		Johannes Brahms	A German Requiem (1857–1868)
		Anton Bruckner	Te Deum (1884)
		Giuseppi Verdi	Requiem Mass (1874)
		Claude Debussy	The Prodigal Son (1884)
		Gabriel Faure	Requiem (1887)

		Cesar Franck	The Beatitudes (1899)
		Charles Stanford	
		Charles H. H. Perry	
		Charles Ives	Psalm 67
twentieth		Arthur Honneger	Symphonic Psalm King David (1923)
		Francis Poulenc	Gloria (1961)
		Ralph Vaughan Williams	Hodie (1954)
		William Walton	Belshazzar's Feast (1931)
		Benjamin Britten	A Ceremony of Carols (1942) Festival Te Deum (1945)
		Andrew Lloyd Webber	Requiem (1984)
		John Rutter	Requiem (1978)
		Igor Stravinsky	Symphony of Psalms (1930) Mass (1948)
		Leo Sowerby	Forsaken of Man
		Randall Thompson	Peaceable Kingdom (1936)
		Leonard Bernstein	Chichester Psalms (1965) Mass (1972)
		Krzysztof Penderecki	Passion According to St. Luke (1965)

Century	Form	Person/Contribution	Example
Congregational Music			
third	Hymnody	Clement of Alexandria writes earliest extant hymn.	Shepherd of Tender Youth
fourth		Ambrose of Milan encourages congregational singing.	O Splendor of God's Glory
		Gregory the Great. The Schola Cantorum codifies chant and hymn tunes.	Father, We Praise Thee
eighth to thirteenth		Many classic hymns belong to this period.	Come, Ye Faithful; All Glory, Laud and Honor
thirteenth to fifteenth	Carol	Carol is developed as a musical form.	In Dulci Jubilo; O Sons and Daughters of the King
		St. Francis of Assisi develops practice of singing nativity songs around manger.	
sixteenth	Metrical Psalmody	The Psalms are set to meter or verse. Martin Luther versifies Psalms, translates Latin hymns to German, encourages original hymns for congregational worship, and adapts quality folk songs and Latin chant. German congregations begin singing in unison.	A Mighty Fortress Is Our God
		John Calvin versifies Psalms set to music with the help of poet Clement Marot. In 1549 Thomas Sternhold in England does similar versification. John Hopkins enlarges Psalter in 1562 to include all Psalms. John Merbecke sets service of Holy Communion in four-part harmony. Methods are devised to change pitch in verses of variable length. English Psalters reach the New World.	
seventeenth		Bishop Thomas Ken	All Praise to Thee My God this Night
eighteenth		Isaac Watts versifies Psalms in free verse and collects original hymns.	Hymns and Spiritual Songs; Psalms of David Imitated
		Charles Wesley writes 6,000 Christ-centered hymns collected in two volumes. Moravian missionaries introduce classical hymns into the English colonies. William Billings publishes collections of Psalms.	*New England Psalm Singer*, When Jesus Wept

nineteenth		Gospel music and white spirituals emerge.	Amazing Grace; What Wondrous Love
		Negro Spirituals	Swing Low, Sweet Chariot
		Oxford movement in England prompts a return to Catholic traditions in music. John Keble, Edward Caswall, and John M. Neale write and translate hymns.	Jesus, the Very Thought of Thee; All Glory, Laud and Honor
		The blind Fanny Crosby writes over 8,000 gospel hymns.	To God Be the Glory Blessed Assurance
		Ira Sankey composes tunes for Moody crusades.	Hiding in Thee
		Philip Bliss composes hymns with Maj. Whittle.	When Peace Like a River
		Homer Rodehaver teams with Billy Sunday.	Then Jesus Came
twentieth		Cliff Barrows and George Beverly Shea make music a part of Billy Graham crusades.	
		Ken Modema composes songs of social justice.	

Contemporary Christian Music	
Style	**Performing Artist or Group**
Inspirational Praise	Sandi Patti, Steve Green, Larnelle Harris, Evie Tornquist, Bill and Gloria Gaither, Keith Green
Rock *Formula of two bars in blues or ballad style.* *Marked by beat, physical movement, and high decibel.*	Stryper, Petra, Larry Norman, Steve Taylor, Audio Adrenaline, Rez Band, 77s, Undercover
Contemporary *Softer sound than rock, mostly solo.*	Imperials, Amy Grant, Twila Paris, Michael Card, First Call. Russ Taff, Michael W. Smith, White Heart, Rick Cua, Petra
Southern Gospel *Usually quartet harmonies, family groups.* *Lyrics rely heavily on clever phrase turns.*	Hemphills, The Cathedrals, Florida Boys, Nelsons
Traditional Black Gospel *Emphasis on rhythm.*	Aretha Franklin, Shirley Caesar, Al Green
Contemporary Black Gospel *Combines elements of rock with rhythm and blues.*	The Winans, The Clark Sisters, Andrae Crouch
Source: *Gladys Christiansen, Contemporary Christian Music Magazine*	

English Versions of the Bible

Date	Name of Version	Translated/Published by
1380	Wycliffe Bible	Nicholas Hereford and Wycliffe (revised by John Purvey)
1525/26	New Testament	William Tyndale
1535	First complete Bible in English	Miles Coverdale
1537	The Matthew Bible	John Rogers (revised by Richard Taverner)
1539	The Great Bible	Miles Coverdale for Thomas Cromwell
1560	Geneva Bible	William Whittingham
1568	Bishops Bible	Matthew Parker and others
1582	Reims New Testament	Gregory Martin, William Allen, and others
1609–1610	Douay Old Testament	Gregory Martin and others
1611	Authorized (King James)	54 scholars and translators
1718–1719	New Testament	Cornelius Nary
1729	Greek and English New Testament	William Mace
1730	New Testament	Robert Witham
1745	Primitive New Testament	William Whiston
1749–1772	Revised Douay-Reims	Richard Challoner
1755	Revised Authorized Version	John Wesley
1764	New Testament	Richard Wynne
	Bible	Anthony Purver
1768	New Testament	E. Harwood
1770	New Testament	John Worsley
1833	New Testament	Rodolphus Dickinson
1858	New Testament	Leicester Ambrose Sawyer
1862	Old and New Testaments	Robert Young
1869	New Testament	Henry Alford
	Old and New Testaments	Robert Ainslie
1871	New Testament	J. N. Darby
1872	New Testament	J. B. Rotherham
1875	New Testament	Samuel Davidson
1885	Revised Version (RV)	
1890	Bible	J. N. Darby
1895	Current English New Testament	Fenton
1898–1901	Twentieth Century New Testament	20 lay scholars
1901	American Standard Edition of RV	American scholars
1902	Emphasized Bible	Joseph Bryant Rotherham
1903	Bible in Modern English	Fenton
	New Testament in Modern Speech	R. F. Weymouth
1907	Moulton's Modern Reader's Bible	Richard G. Moulton
1913	New Testament	James Moffatt
1923	New Testament	J. M. P. Smith
	Riverside New Testament	W. G. Ballantine
1924	Old Testament	James Moffatt
	New Testament	Helen B. Montgomery
1927	Old Testament	Edgar Goodspeed

1935	Westminister New Testament	Catholic scholars
1937	New Testament	C. B. Williams
	New Testament	F. A. Spencer
1941	New Testament in Basic English	S. H. Hooke
1945	Berkeley New Testament	Gerrit Verkuyl
	New Testament	R. A. Knox
1946	Revision of RV	International Council of Religious Education
1947–1957	New Testament	J. B. Phillips
1948	The Letchworth New Testament	T. F. and R. E. Ford
1949	Bible in Basic English	S. H. Hooke
	Old Testament	R. A. Knox
1952	Plain English New Testament	C. K. Williams
1952	Revised Standard Version	Corporate
1954	New Testament	J. A. Kleist and J. L. Lilly
1954	Authentic New Testament	H. J. Schonfield
1956–1959	Expanded Translation of Greek New Testament	K. S. Wuest
1957	Holy Bible	George M. Lamsa
1958	Amplified New Testament	F. E. Siewert & Lockman Foundation
	New Testament in Modern English	J. B. Phillips
1959	Berkeley Bible	Gerrit Verkuyl
1961	The New English Bible	Corporate; C. H. Dodd and others
1962	Amplified Old Testament	F. E. Siewert and Lockman Foundation
1962–1971	The Living Bible	K. N. Taylor
1963	New Testament in the Language of Today	W. F. Beck
1963	New American Standard Bible	Evangelical scholars
	Holy Name Bible	A. B. Traina
1964	Anchor Bible	William F. Albright and David N. Freedman
1965	The Amplified Bible	Frances E. Siwert
1966	Good News for Modern Man	American Bible Society
	Jerusalem Bible	Catholic scholars
	Living Scriptures	Jay P. Green
1968–1969	New Testament	William Barclay
1970	New English Bible, Old Testament	Corporate
	New American Bible	Confraternity of Christian Doctrine
	Mercier New Testament	Kevin Condon
1971	Living Bible	Tyndale House
	New American Standard Bible	Lockman Foundation
1972	New International Version, New Testament	International Bible Society
1973	Common Bible	Zondervan
	Translators New Testament	British and Foreign Bible Society
1974	New Testament in Everyday English	Don J. Klingensmith
1976	Complete Good News Bible	American Bible Society
1979	New International Version	International Bible Society
1982	The Reader's Digest Bible	Reader's Digest
	New King James Version	Thomas Nelson; Arthur L. Farstad and others
1985	The Word	World Bible Translation Center
1985	New Jerusalem Bible	Henry Wansbrough
1988	New Testament	Hugo McCord
1989	God's New Covenant	Heinz W. Cassirer
	Revised English Bible	Oxford Univ. Press/Cambridge Univ.Press
1998	New Living Bible	Tyndale

Chronology of the Electronic Church

1921 Calvary Episcopal Church in Pittsburgh broadcasts for the first time (KDKA) a Christian worship service. A Baptist radio broadcast follows.

1922 The first Pentecostal broadcast by Aimee Semple McPherson.

1923 The number of radio stations run by churches increase to ten. Charles E. Fuller makes his first radio broadcast. By 1937 it will blossom into the "Old-Fashioned Revival Hour" over the Mutual Network.

1925 Moody Bible Institute launches WMBI in Chicago, the nation's oldest listener-supported station.

1928 The number of radio stations run by churches increase to 60. Donald Grey Barnhouse becomes the first preacher to purchase radio network time for his "The Bible Study Hour." It entered national syndication in 1949 and moved to NBC in 1956.

1929 "The Catholic Hour" produced by the National Council of Catholic Men is first heard over NBC radio network. Its principal speaker from 1930 to 1952 was Bishop Fulton Sheen.

1930 "The Lutheran Hour" is broadcast over station WHK in Cleveland, Ohio, by Lutheran Church, Missouri Synod. Within a year it has an audience of 5 million, growing to 30 million by 1965.

1931 Radio Vatican is inaugurated by Pope Pius XI and entrusted to the Jesuits.

1939 "Back to the Bible" is first radiocast from Lincoln, Nebraska, by Theodore Epp.

1941 "The Baptist Hour" begins under the auspices of the Southern Baptist Radio and Television Commission. Its main speaker was M. E. Dodd. By 1990 it became the fifth top-rated weekly religious radio broadcast.

1943 National Religious Broadcasters of North America is founded by the National Association of Evangelicals.

1946 World Literature Crusade begins radio outreach.

1947 "Back to God Hour" begins on the Mutual Radio Network emceed by Harry Schultze, Peter Eversveld, and Joel Nederhood.

1948 The first Christian children's radio program, "All Aboard for Adventure," is begun.

1950 Billy Graham begins broadcasting on ABC radio.

1951 Billy Graham begins television broadcasts and starts Hour of Decision radio program; by 1978 it claims 20 million listeners. The first Christian children's television program, "Bible Puppets," is launched.

1952 "Life Is Worth Living," a Catholic television program hosted by Bishop Fulton Sheen, debuts on the Old DuMont network.

1953 Rex Humbard and Oral Roberts begin telecasts weekly. World Committee on

Christian Broadcasting is founded in Britain.

1955   World Conference on Missionary Radio begins in the United States.

1956   Jerry Falwell begins "Old-Time Gospel Hour" from his church in Lynchburg, Virginia. A weekly television show would follow in 1971.

1958   Harold Camping begins the Family Stations group. These stations were financed solely through the contributions of listeners rather than by advertising.

1959   "Davey and Goliath," one of the best-known children's religious programs, begins production. In 1961 it was syndicated nationally by the United Lutheran Church.

1961   M. G. "Pat" Robertson founds the first religious television station in the United States, WYAH in Tidewater, Virginia. Later it became the Christian Broadcasting Network (CBN).

World Association for Christian Broadcasting is founded. In 1968 it became the World Association for Christian Communication.

World Radio Missionary Fellowship inaugurates HCJB-TV in Quito, Ecuador, as pioneer missionary broadcaster.

1969   Pentecostal evangelist Jimmy L. Swaggart begins radio ministry, "Camp Meeting Hour."

1970   Robert Schuller begins "Hour of Power" television program from his drive-in church at Garden Grove, California. Later, he would build the Crystal Cathedral.

1971   Lester Sumrall begins LeSea Broadcasting.

1972   Swaggart begins television ministry. Before it collapsed in 1987, its telecasts were beamed through 3,200 stations in 15 languages and were viewed by 50 million people in 45 countries.

1973   Trinity Broadcasting Network (TBN) is launched by Paul Crouch as a Pentecostal station. At the same time, Jim Bakker starts PTL Club as part of TBN.

1974   Jim Bakker splits with TBN and starts his own "PTL Club" in Charlotte, North Carolina. Within four years it was syndicated and satellite-cast over the United States and many other parts of the world.

1978   Frederick K. C. Price begins his "Ever Increasing Faith" program on TBN.

1979   James D. Kennedy launches the "Coral Ridge Hour," a television worship hour from his Coral Ridge Baptist Church of Fort Lauderdale, Florida.

1981   Mother Angelica kicks off the Eternal Word Television Network (EWTN), the first denominational cable-TV service to be licensed by the FCC.

1982   Pope Paul II inaugurates Vatican Television.

1986   Intercontinental Broadcasting Network begins in Virginia Beach, Virginia.

1987   PTL Ministries collapse in a sex and financial scandal; later Jim Bakker is convicted of fraud and sentenced to prison. Global Rosary for World Peace and World Evangelization prayed by John Paul II at the Vatican and is beamed to a television audience of 1.5 million.

1988   Jimmy Swaggart's ministries collapse after his sexual wrongdoings are exposed.

2000   The number of Christian radio and television stations worldwide reaches 4,000.

U.S. Denominations

Note: In the following entries, the term *orthodox* is used to mark adherence to the following 12 cardinal tenets of the Christian faith: Plenary and verbal inspiration and inerrancy of the Bible, Trinity, deity of Christ, virgin birth, substitutionary and atoning death of Christ on the cross, resurrection of the dead, justification by faith, salvation by grace, baptism, eternal punishment of the wicked and nonbelievers in hell, last judgment and Second Coming.

ADVENT CHURCHES

Advent Christian Church. Founded in 1860. Among its doctrines is conditional immortality as preached by George Storrs and Charles F. Hudson. It maintains the Aurora University.

Church of God General Conference. Founded in 1888 and refounded in 1921. Among its doctrines are the establishment of a literal kingdom of God in Jerusalem and the sonship of Jesus Christ.

Seventh Day Adventist. *See dictionary article.* Founded about 1846. Among its early leaders were Joseph Bates, Ellen Harmon White, Hiram Edson, Frederick Wheeler, and S. W. Rhodes. Its doctrines are evangelical, conservative, and orthodox, except for the observance of Saturday as Sabbath. Redemption is through the total atoning work of Jesus Christ.

Amana Church Society. *See dictionary article.*

Apostolic Christian Church of America. Founded about 1832. Its creed teaches salvation by grace through faith in Jesus Christ, regeneration and the direction of the Holy Spirit.

Apostolic Overcoming Holy Church of God. Founded in 1916 by Bishop W. T. Phillips. Its creed teaches sanctification and holiness, the deity of Christ, the final resurrection of the dead, last judgment and the Second Coming.

Armenian Church. *See dictionary article.*

Assyrian Church of the East. *See dictionary article.*

BAPTIST CHURCHES

American Baptist Association. (Also, Landmarkers) Founded in 1905 as the Baptist General Association. Their creed teaches the verbal inspiration of the Bible, triune God, virgin birth, deity of Christ, substitutionary and atoning death of Christ, premillennial Second Coming, eternal punishment of the wicked, and bodily resurrection.

They also believe in the complete autonomy of the local church.

American Baptist Churches USA. Founded in 1907 as the Northern Baptist Convention, renamed as American Baptist Convention in 1950 and as American Baptist Churches USA in 1972. They are less conservative than Southern Baptists, but hold orthodox doctrines, as the plenary inspiration and validity of the Scriptures, the lordship of Christ, adult baptism, immortality, and redemption from sin through the atoning work of Jesus Christ. They emphasize evangelism and the Great Commission.

Baptist Bible Fellowship, International. Group of evangelical, independent Baptist churches. They are ultraconservative and prescribe strict moral codes for their members.

Baptist General Conference. Founded in Rock Island, Illinois, in 1852 through the labors of Gustaf Palmquist, a Swedish immigrant. It is theologically conservative and evangelical and maintains an active foreign mission program. The conference runs Bethel College and Seminary and publishes *The Standard*.

Baptist Missionary Association of America. Organized at Little Rock, Arkansas, in 1950 as the North American Baptist Association and renamed in 1968. It is a fundamentalist denomination, emphasizing orthodox doctrines. They hold as unscriptural open communion, alien baptism, modernism, and tongues. It subscribes to the Landmark tenet that Baptist churches are not Protestant, but date back to Christ and the apostles.

Central Baptist Association. Founded in 1956. Its heritage is Primitive Baptist, including two resurrections of the dead, one for the just and the other for the unjust.

Conservative Baptist Association of America. Founded in 1920 as the Fundamentalist Fellowship and renamed in 1947. Theologically, it is orthodox and fundamentalist, but maintains the autonomy of the local church and its accountability to Christ alone.

Duck River Associations of Baptists. Founded in 1825 but split in 1843 into two groups, one known as Missionary Baptists and the other as Separate Baptists (Baptist Church of Christ) founded in 1843. Theologically, they are liberal Calvinists.

Free Will Baptists. Founded as two groups: a Southern group founded by Paul Palmer in 1727 at Chowan, North Carolina, and a Northern group founded by Benjamin Randall in 1780 in New Durham, New Hampshire. They merged as the National Association of Free Will Baptists at Nashville, Tennessee, in 1935. Theologically, it is Arminian, teaching free grace, free will, and free salvation. It practices open communion and footwashing.

General Association of Regular Baptist Churches. Founded in 1932 when 22 Baptist churches of the American Baptist Convention left that body as a protest against modernist and liberal tendencies. They hew to orthodox doctrines as spelled out in the New Hampshire Confession and oppose fellowship or cooperation with bodies that teach unscriptural doctrines.

General Baptist. The General Baptist Church claims its name from the English church of that name and traces its origins from John Smyth, Thomas Helwys, and Roger Williams. It reached the United States through the work of Benoni Stinson who, in 1823, established the Liberty Baptist Church in Evansville, Indiana. Their confession of faith is similar to that of Free Will Baptists.

General Conference of the Evangelical Baptist Church. Founded in 1935 as the Church of the Full Gospel. Its doctrines are Arminian, Wesleyan, and premillennial.

National Baptist Convention of America. Founded in 1895, it is the second largest black Baptist denomination. It is a splinter group of the National Baptist Convention.

National Baptist Convention, U.S.A. Founded in 1895 it is the largest body of black Baptists.

National Missionary Baptist Convention of America. Founded in 1988 when it split from the National Baptist Convention, U. S. A.

National Primitive Baptist Convention. Founded in 1907, it is the black counterpart of the Primitive Baptist churches.

North American Baptist Conference. Founded by German immigrants from 1840 through 1851. They follow the usual Baptist theological positions, especially as adumbrated in the New Hampshire Confession.

Primitive Baptist. The most orthodox and exclusive of all Baptists, Primitive Baptists are not organized in the conventional sense and have no administrative bodies of any kind. No minister, association, or convention has authority over the churches. They oppose money-based missions, although they support evangelism, and Sunday schools, although they support religious training of children. Theologically, they are strongly Calvinist, believing in total depravity, election, and perseverance of saints. Ministers are not required to be trained in seminaries.

Progressive National Baptist Convention. Founded in 1961 as a splinter group of the National Baptist Convention. It was the home denomination of Martin Luther King, Jr. and Ralph Abernathy.

Reformed Baptist. A fellowship of churches, not all of whom call themselves Reformed or Baptist. They adhere to the five points of Calvinism, the doctrines of the Synod of Dort, and the Philadelphia Confession.

Separate Baptists in Christ. They trace their origins to George Whitefield and the eighteenth-century conflict between the Old Lights and New Lights. Mildly Calvinist, they reject all creeds and confessions as well as the "election, reprobation and fatality" of Calvinism. They do not claim to be Protestants.

Seventh Day Baptist General Conference. It is the only Baptist group that observes the Sabbath on Saturday. They were first organized as a separate body in North America at Newport, Rhode Island, in 1671.

Southern Baptist Convention. *See dictionary article.* It is the largest and perhaps one of the most conservative and orthodox of the Baptist churches. The Southern Baptist heritage is more Calvinist and, at the same time, more evangelical. Its International Mission Board is one of the most active in the nation. The term *Southern* is a misnomer because its members are found throughout the country and its North American Mission Board has missionaries in all 50 states.

United Baptist. A merger of several groups of Separate and Regular Baptists, some of whom were Arminian and some Calvinist. The earliest group was in Richmond, Virginia, in 1887. Their theology is a mixture of grace (Calvinism) and free will (Arminianism).

United Free Will Baptist Church. Founded in 1901 as an offshoot of the Free Will Baptists.

Berean Fundamental Church. Founded in the 1930s by Pastor Ivan E. Olsen in North Platte, Nebraska. It is strongly Bible-centered and evangelistic.

Bible Fellowship Church. Founded in 1858, it has Mennonite roots.

Bible Protestant Church. Founded in 1939 when one-third of the Eastern Conference of the Methodist Protestant Church withdrew to protest the proposed union with the liberal Methodist Episcopal Church. Doctrinally, it is very conservative and orthodox.

Bible Way Church, Worldwide. Founded in 1957 when 70 black Pentecostal churches withdrew from the Church of Our Lord of the Apostolic Faith.

BRETHREN. *See dictionary article.*

Brethren Church (Ashland). Founded in 1882, it is the Arminian wing of the Progressive Dunker movement and is therefore sometimes known as Progressive Brethren.

Brethren in Christ Church. It began as a group called River Brethren about 1778. The denomination opposes war, and its theological positions are entirely orthodox. The church has two well-known institutions of learning: the Messiah College and Niagara Christian College.

Church of the Brethren. The original Church of the Brethren was founded in 1708 at Schwarzenau, Germany. It has Reformed, Anabaptist, and Pietist roots. It moved to the United States between 1719 and 1729 under the leadership of Alexander Mack, Sr. when it was known as German Baptist Brethren or Dunkers. Although noncreedal, it holds orthodox doctrines. Among its distinctive practices are foot-washing and baptism by threefold immersion. As a peace church, it is very active in worldwide relief programs.

Church of the United Brethren in Christ. Founded in 1767. It insists on scriptural living by all its members, and condemns the use of alcoholic beverages and membership in secret societies. It is active in evangelism and church aid.

Fellowship of Grace Brethren Churches. It was born out of the 1881–1883 split in the Brethren and a further split in 1939 when the more Calvinist Grace group split from the more Arminian Ashland group. Its statement of faith is entirely scriptural and orthodox.

Old German Baptist Brethren. Founded in 1881 when the Old Order Dunkers left the Church of the Brethren because the latter was not conservative enough. It opposes Sunday schools, salaried ministers, missions, higher education, church societies, military service, worldly adornments and entertainment, alcoholic beverages, secret societies, oaths, and lawsuits. On issues on which the Scriptures are silent, an annual conference determines the church's position.

Christadelphian. Founded by John Thomas, who came to the United States from England in 1844. Its theology is both Unitarian and Adventist, denying the deity of Christ but but holding on to Scriptural inerrancy and Millennarianism.

Christian and Missionary Alliance. *See dictionary article.*

Christian Catholic Church. Organized in 1896 by John Alexander Dowie who founded Zion City, Illinois. Doctrinally, it teaches evangelical orthodoxy. Dowie emphasized faith healing which remains a strong element in its theology.

CHRISTIAN CHURCH, THE (THE STONE-CAMPBELL MOVEMENT)

Christian Church (Disciples of Christ). Founded by four pioneers—Barton Stone, Thomas Campbell, Alexander Campbell, and Walter Scott—it is a rugged American frontier denomination. Stone (whose church at Cane Ridge, Kentucky, was the center of the famous Kentucky Revival), the Campbells, and Scott deemphasized denominations and church affiliations and tried to restore New Testament Christianity without creeds, clerical titles, and privileges. They emphasized the importance of faith, repentance of sin, and baptism. The Disciples are Christ-centered and Bible-centered.

Christian Churches and Churches of Christ. A loose grouping of independent churches that broke away from the Disciples over issues such as the use of instrumental music. Otherwise they are as orthodox as the Disciples.

Churches of Christ. The largest of the three principal bodies that grew out of the Restoration movement. Holding to its tenet, "to speak where the Bible speaks and to be silent where the Bible is silent," it acknowledges no written creed or confession of faith. Doctrinally, it is conservative and orthodox. The church is believed to be the bride of Christ, and the Bible is regarded as all-sufficient. Worship services are simple without instrumental music.

Christian Church of North America General Council. Pentecostal body similar to the Assemblies of God.

Christian Congregation. Founded in 1887 in Indiana, it is pacifist and noncreedal, and opposes abortion, violence, warfare, and capital punishment.

Christian Union. Founded in 1864 in Greenfield, Ohio, it emphasizes the unity of the Church of Christ, the Bible as the only rule of faith and practice, and good fruits in the life of the believer.

Church of Christ (Holiness) U.S.A. Black church emphasizing holiness founded in 1894 by C. P. Jones in Alabama and Mississippi.

CHURCH OF GOD. *See dictionary article.*

Church of God, The (Huntsville, Alabama). Offshoot of the Tomlinson group of Cleveland. It carries on the legacy of Homer Tomlinson, who crowned himself in the major capitals of the world. It places heavy emphasis on preparing for the return of Christ and the reestablishment of the kingdom of God in Israel.

Church of God, The Original. Founded in 1886 after a split among the followers of Richard G. Spurling. Its doctrines are Wesleyan and Pentecostal and include speaking in tongues, divine healing, repentance, justification, and regeneration.

Church of God (Anderson, Indiana). It began in 1880 as a nondenominational movement seeking to establish the New Testament as the rule of faith and practice. It is not related to other Church of God bodies derived from the Holiness movement and it is not Pentecostal. Its teachings are orthodox.

Church of God (Cleveland, Tennessee). It was formed in 1882 in the wake of a major Holiness revival. Split in the church over the autocratic rule of A. J. Tomlinson led to the breakaway of Church of God (Cleveland, Tennessee) in 1923 under F. J. Lee. Its doctrines blend Holiness and Protestant tenets; baptism in the Holy Spirit, speaking in tongues, and divine healing are accepted as integral elements of the creed.

Church of God (Seventh Day). Born of the Adventist movement, it broke away from other Adventist groups by rejecting Mrs. White's visions. In 1933 it divided into two groups, one in Stanberry, Colorado, and the other in Salem, West Virginia. They reunited partially in 1949, but subscribe to slightly different beliefs regarding apostolic succession and the physical identity of the church.

Church of God by Faith. Organized in 1914 at Alachua, Florida, it emphasizes many Pentecostal doctrines, such as speaking in tongues and baptism of the Holy Spirit.

Church of God in Christ. Founded in 1897 in Memphis by ministers C. H. Mason and C. P. Jones after they were rejected by Baptists for preaching entire sanctification, healing, and baptism of the Holy Spirit and the evidential speaking in tongues.

Church of God in Christ (International). Group that broke away from Church of God in Christ. Both bodies hold the same Pentecostal doctrines.

Church of God of Prophecy. It is a classical Pentecostal and Holiness church founded by A. J. Tomlinson. Its official teachings include entire sanctification, Holy Spirit baptism, and speaking in tongues. It also subscribes to all orthodox beliefs.

Church of God, Holiness. Founded in Atlanta, Georgia, in 1914 under the leadership of K. H. Burrus. Theologically, it espouses orthodox doctrines. Further, it believes in the work of the Holy Spirit subsequent to conversion and in present and ultimate perfection.

Church of Jesus Christ. Any one of more than 20 independent groups. The largest, headquartered in Cleveland, Tennessee, was founded in 1927 under the leadership of M. K. Lawson. All of them hold common doctrinal beliefs, especially justifi-

cation by faith, free will, baptism by immersion, and premillennial Second Coming.

Church of Our Lord Jesus Christ of the Apostolic Faith. Founded in 1919 at Columbus, Ohio, by R. C. Lawson. Doctrinal emphases are on Second Coming, priesthood of believers, and baptism of the Holy Spirit.

Church of the Nazarene. *See dictionary article.* Body of Wesleyan heritage, as modified by the Holiness revival of the nineteenth century. It was formed through the merger in 1907–1908 of three independent Holiness groups: the Association of Pentecostal Churches of America, Church of the Nazarene, and the Holiness Church of Christ. Until 1919 it was known as the Pentecostal Church of the Nazarene, but opposition to Pentecostalism among Nazarenes led to the name being changed to Church of the Nazarene. The core doctrines are justification by faith and the sanctification of believers, especially entire sanctification as a second work of grace subsequent to regeneration.

Churches of Christ in Christian Union. Group that broke away from Christian Union in 1909. They are highly evangelistic and hold frequent camp meetings and revivals.

Churches of God, General Conference. Founded by John Winebrenner, a Reformed Church pastor whose evangelistic zeal proved unpopular in his home denomination. In 1825 he severed relations with the Reformed Church to found an independent Church of God in Harrisburg, Pennsylvania. It is Arminian in theology and holds the Bible as the sole rule of faith and practice.

Congregational Bible Churches. Pentecostal movement dating back to 1922 but organized under the present name in 1977 when the Light of the Way Open Door Church merged with the Independent Holiness Church. Its articles of faith are the same as those of the Assemblies of God.

Congregational Christian Churches, National Association. Founded in 1955 by a group of churches wishing to preserve historical Congregational forms of belief and worship. They did not join the merger of the General Council of Congregational Churches with the Evangelical and Reformed Church as the United Church of Christ in 1957.

Congregational Holiness Church. Founded in 1921, it is trinitarian in belief and Pentecostal in practice and Congregational in polity.

Conservative Congregational Christian Conference. Founded in 1935 through the efforts of H. B. Sandline, a Congregationalist pastor in Hancock, Minnesota. The first congregation was organized in Chicago in 1948. Its statement of faith is conservative, orthodox, and evangelical. It is active in the areas of missions, church planting, and Christian education.

Coptic Orthodox Church. *See dictionary article.*

EPISCOPAL CHURCH, *See dictionary article.*
See also, ANGLICANISM.

Reformed Episcopal Church. Group that broke away from the Protestant Episcopal Church in 1873. It differs from the parent church in certain respects, especially regarding the Lord's Supper and baptism. Worship is liturgical.

Evangelical Free Church. Church formed through the merger in 1950 of the Swedish Evangelical Free Church and the Evangelical Free Church Association of Danish and Norwegian churches. It has an aggressive church planting and foreign missions program.

Foursquare Gospel, International Church of the. *See dictionary article.*

Friends. *See dictionary article.*

Latter-Day Saints (Mormons). *See dictionary article.*

LUTHERAN. *See dictionary article.*

American Lutheran Church. Formed in 1960 through the merger of the American Lutheran Church (German), Evangelical Lutheran Church (Norwegian), and the United Evangelical Lutheran Church (Danish). In 1963 a fourth body, the Lutheran Free Church (Norwegian), joined the common denomination.

Apostolic Lutheran Church of America. Also called the Church of Laestadius. It was formerly known as the Finnish Apostolic Lutheran Church of America. The church accepts the first three ecumenical councils and emphasizes the confession of sins, absolution, and regeneration.

Church of the Lutheran Brethren. Independent Lutheran body made up of autonomous congregations accepting basic Lutheran teachings. Worship is nonliturgical, and preaching is evangelical.

Evangelical Lutheran Church in America. Formed in 1988 through the union of the Lutheran Church in America, the American Lutheran Church, and the Association of Evangelical Lutheran Churches. It is the largest U.S. Lutheran body. The Lutheran Church in America was the oldest, dating back to the 1660s when the Dutch ruled New York.

Evangelical Lutheran Synod. Formed in 1918 by a minority group that did not join other groups that merged into the Norwegian Lutheran Church.

Free Lutheran Congregations, Association of. Independent, conservative and Pietist body, founded in 1962.

Lutheran Church-Missouri Synod. Second largest Lutheran body, founded by German immigrants in Missouri in 1847. The group is strongly devoted to confessional Lutheranism and has long been a leader in evangelical communications.

Wisconsin Evangelical Lutheran Synod. The third largest Lutheran group in the United States, it was organized in 1850 in Milwaukee as the German Evangelical Lutheran Synod of Wisconsin. It subscribes to orthodox confessional Lutheranism, but opposes fellowship with churches that are not in full doctrinal agreement.

MENNONITE. *See dictionary article.*

Beachy Amish Mennonite Churches. Amish Mennonites who separated from the more conservative Old Order Amish. They follow a milder discipline.

Church of God in Christ, Mennonite. Formed in 1859 by John Holeman, who preached new birth,

Holy Ghost baptism, and condemnation of worldly and apostate members.

Conservative Mennonite Conference. Formed in 1910, it is an autonomous affiliation of congregations that subscribe to the 1963 Mennonite Confession of Faith and 1991 Mennonite Statement of Theology.

Evangelical Mennonite Church. Formerly the Defenseless Mennonite Church, founded about 1865 under the leadership of Henry Egly.

Fellowship of Evangelical Bible Churches. Formerly known as the Evangelical Mennonite Brethren, its membership consisted of Russian immigrants.

General Conference Mennonite Church. The more liberal wing of Mennonite tradition, it is very active in relief and developmental work.

Hutterian Brethren. *See dictionary article.*

Mennonite Brethren Churches, General Conference. Organized in 1860 by Dutch and German Mennonites. It is Pietistic in orientation.

Mennonite Church. The largest Mennonite group in the United States. It was founded in Germantown, Pennsylvania, in 1683 by Dutch and German immigrants. Its statement of faith is the Dordrecht Confession as amplified by the Christian Fundamentals of 1921.

Old Order Amish Church. Founded by Amish immigrants during 1720–1740. Its members wear distinctive garb and worship in private homes.

Old Order (Wisler) Mennonite Church. Named for Bishop Jacob Wisler, who protested the use of English and the introduction of Sunday Schools in the parent church.

METHODIST. *See dictionary article.*

African Methodist Episcopal Church. *See dictionary article.*

African Methodist Episcopal Zion Church. *See dictionary article.*

Christian Methodist Episcopal Church. Black group founded in 1870 as Colored Methodist Episcopal Church. The present name was adopted in 1954.

Congregational Methodist Church. Splinter group of the Methodist Episcopal Church, South.

Evangelical Methodist Church. Organized in 1946 in protest against modernism and liberalism in the Methodist Church. It is Arminian in theology and Wesleyan in doctrine.

Free Methodist Church of North America. Conservative body founded by B. T. Roberts in 1860. Doctrinally, Free Methodists seek to restore pristine Wesleyanism, and they emphasize the virgin birth, deity of Christ, vicarious atonement of Christ, and entire sanctification.

Primitive Methodist Church U.S.A. Founded in England in 1807, it was brought to the United States in 1829. It accepts modified Wesleyan articles of religion.

Southern Methodist Church. Doctrinally the same as the Methodist Episcopal Church, it seeks "to perpetuate the faith of John Wesley."

United Methodist Church. The largest Methodist body in the nation, formed in 1939 through the merger of the Methodist Episcopal Church, Methodist Episcopal Church, South, Methodist Protestant Church, and Evangelical United Brethren. Its theological basis was adopted in 1988 and restates classic Wesleyan doctrines.

Missionary Church. This group is made up of two groups that merged in 1969: the Missionary Church Association (1889) and the United Missionary Church (1883). Both had a Mennonite heritage and were born out of the Holiness revivals of the 1800s.

Moravian. *See dictionary article.*

New Apostolic Church of North America. Offshoot of the Catholic Apostolic Church of Great Britain, organized in North America by Preuss and Schwarz. It accepts the Apostles' Creed, the authority and inspiration of the Bible, laying on of hands, and the gifts of the Holy Spirit. The church is governed by apostles, as in apostolic times.

Old Catholic Churches. These churches in the United States are an outgrowth of the Old

Catholic movement in Europe which rose as a protest against the doctrine of papal infallibility. Although it rejects papal infallibility, the doctrine of immaculate conception , the compulsory celibacy of priests, and the Filioque clause in the Nicene Creed, it has kept all other doctrines, creeds, customs, and liturgies of the Roman Catholic Church, particularly apostolic succession of bishops and priests through laying on hands. The three main branches of the Old Catholic Church are the Mariavite Old Catholic Church, Old Roman Catholic Church (English Rite), and North American Old Catholic Church.

Orthodox Churches. *See dictionary article.* The principal branches of Orthodoxy in the United States are: Albanian Orthodox Church in America, American Carpatho-Russian Orthodox Greek Catholic Church, Bulgarian Eastern Orthodox Church, Greek Orthodox Archdiocese of North and South America, Romanian Orthodox Episcopate of America Russian Orthodox Church (*see dictionary article*), Serbian Eastern Orthodox Church in the U.S.A. and Canada, Syrian Orthodox Church of Antioch, and Ukrainian Orthodox Church of the U.S.A.

Pentecostal Churches. *See dictionary article.*

ASSEMBLIES OF GOD. *See dictionary article.*

Independent Assemblies of God. A Holiness group of Swedish origin with an extensive missionary program, especially in Brazil.

Pentecostal Assemblies of the World. "Jesus Only" Pentecostal movement.

Pentecostal Church of God. Founded in Chicago in 1919, it is evangelical and Pentecostal in doctrine and practice.

Pentecostal Free-Will Baptist Church. Founded in 1959, it espouses both Pentecostal and Baptist beliefs.

Pentecostal Holiness Church, International. Formerly called Fire-Baptized Holiness Church, it was founded in 1898 at Anderson, South Carolina, by a number of Holiness associations. Although Methodist theological standards prevail, it be-

lieves in divine healing and Holy Spirit baptism attested by the speaking in other tongues. Worship services are characterized by joyous demonstrations.

United Pentecostal Church, International. Founded in 1945 by Jesus Only Pentecostals who withdrew from the Assemblies of God. They water baptize in the name of Lord Jesus Christ, not in the name of the Father, Son, and Holy Spirit.

Plymouth Brethren. *See dictionary article.*

PRESBYTERIAN. *See dictionary article.*

Associate Reformed Presbyterian Church. It is a union of the Covenant or Reformed branch and the Seceder branches. It follows the Westminster Confession.

Bible Presbyterian Church and **Orthodox Presbyterian Church.** Formed in 1936 by a group of dissenters under the leadership of J. Gresham Machen against the growing liberalism of the Presbyterian Church in the U.S.A. First known as the Presbyterian Church of America, the name was changed (after an injunction was brought against the use of the name by the parent body in 1938) to Orthodox Presbyterian Church. In 1983, an internal split led to the creation of the Bible Presbyterian Church. Both are thoroughly fundamentalist and strongly Reformed. They oppose all forms of social gospel and liberation theology and refuse to cooperate with those who compromise on the orthodox doctrines of historic Christianity. The Orthodox Presbyterian Church has published the *Trinity Hymnal* to supplement the Westminster Confession of Faith.

Cumberland Presbyterian Church. Founded in 1810 as an outgrowth of the great revival of 1800 by three ministers: Finis Ewing, Samuel King, and Samuel McAdow. The group disavows predestination.

Evangelical Presbyterian Church. Formed in 1981, it is a conservative denomination. It is Presbyterian in polity, Reformed in theology, and evangelical in action. It emphasizes world missions and church planting.

Presbyterian Church in America. Founded in 1973 as the National Presbyterian Church in opposition to the prevailing liberalism of the parent church, the Presbyterian Church in the United States. In 1982 it was joined by the Reformed Presbyterian Church, Evangelical Synod. It is firmly committed to the Westminster Confession of Faith and the Catechisms.

Presbyterian Church (U.S.A.). Born in 1983 through the merger of the two largest American Presbyterian churches: United Presbyterian Church in the U.S.A. and Presbyterian Church in the United States. Both churches trace their origins to the first American presbytery founded in Philadelphia in 1706. The first general synod met in 1729 and adopted the Westminster Confession of Faith together with the Larger and Shorter Catechism. Under prominent preachers, as William Tennent, Sr., the church grew, aided by the revivalism of the Great Awakening. Even disputes between the New Side and the Old Side during the Great Awakening and the New School and the Old School in the early 1800s did not slow the pace of expansion. Marcus Whitman drove the first team and wagon over the South Pass of the Rockies into the great Northwest, heralding a vast building program of churches, schools, colleges, and seminaries. Princeton and Union Theological Seminaries were among the scores of seminaries built between 1812 and 1836.

Its doctrinal position is found in the *Book of Confessions* with these creeds and/ or catechisms: the Nicene Creed, the Apostles' Creed, the Scots Confession of 1560, the Heidelberg Catechism, Westminster Confession of 1647, the Shorter and Larger Catechism of 1647, the 1934 Barmen Declaration, the Confession of 1967, and Brief Statement of Faith.

Reformed Presbyterian Church of North America. Founded in 1798 under the name of Reformed Presbytery. The first synod was constituted in Philadelphia in 1809. It emphasizes the inerrancy of Scriptures and the lordship of Jesus Christ. No instrumental music is permitted in worship services, and members may not join secret societies.

Second Cumberland Presbyterian Church in the United States. A black group founded in 1869 as the Colored Cumberland Presbyterian Church. It follows the Westminster Confession with some reservations.

REFORMED. *See dictionary article.*

Christian Reformed Church in North America. Originally founded in 1847, it was affiliated with the Reformed Church in America until 1857, when it broke away to form the Holland Reformed Church. The present name was adopted after the influx of English-speaking members.

Reformed Church in America. Founded in 1614 by the Dutch in their colony of New Amsterdam and Albany. Their doctrinal standards are the Belgic Confession, the Heidelberg Catechism, and the Canons of Dort. Worship is semi-liturgical with an optional liturgy. Baptism and the Lord's Supper, the only recognized sacraments, are obligatory.

Roman Catholic Church. *See dictionary article.* Roman Catholicism reached the New World long before Protestants. Outside the 13 colonies, Western Christian presence was entirely Catholic. French and Spanish explorers, *voyageurs*, and colonizers, as Marquette, Cartier and Joliet, were Roman Catholic, and a number of missionary groups such as the Sulpicians, Recollects, Jesuits, and Capuchins were active in North and South America. New France reaching down the valley of Mississippi from Quebec to Louisiana became a vicariate apostolic in 1658. In 1634 Roman Catholic founded the colony of Maryland. But in most of the Protestant-dominated colonies, Roman Catholics were discriminated against in matters of religion. In 1696 there were only seven Catholic families in New York. Eighty years later, they still had no church and had to travel to Philadelphia to attend Mass.

At the time of the American Revolution there were fewer than 25,000 Roman Catholics in the 13 colonies, and they were under the jurisdiction of the vicar apostolic of London. After the Revolution John Carroll was named prefect apostolic of the church. Baltimore became the first American diocese in 1789 and an archdiocese in 1808. The first plenary national councils were held in Baltimore in 1852, 1866, and 1884. Archbishop John

McCloskey of New York became the first American cardinal in 1875.

Salvation Army. *See dictionary article.*

Syrian Orthodox Church of Antioch. *See dictionary article*. A lesser Eastern church belonging to the Monophysite non-Chalcedonian confessional group.

Triumph the Church and Kingdom of God in Christ International. Founded in 1902 by E. D. Smith. It teaches that all justified believers are cleansed from sin through the shed blood of Christ, that entire sanctification is instantaneous, and that a second work of grace and baptism by fire are obtained through faith.

United Church of Christ. Formed through the merger of the United Church of Christ, the Congregational Churches, the Christian Church—Evangelical Synod, and the Reformed Church. The first two bodies merged in 1931 to form Congregational Christian Churches, and they were joined in 1957 by the latter two. The union was consummated in 1961 with the adoption of a constitution. The church has its roots in the congregational traditions of English Protestantism and the Evangelical and Reformed traditions of German Protestantism. All of Colonial New England from the time of the Plymouth Colony to the nineteenth century was Congregational. Jonathan Edwards played a leading role in the Great Awakening which began in 1734.

Congregationalism left two significant marks on American religious history in the field of missions and of education. The Mayhews, David Brainerd, and John Eliot were among the earliest missionaries to the Native Americans. Congregationalists also helped to found in 1810 the American Board of Commissioners for Foreign Missions which sent out hundreds of missionaries to more than 30 countries. In the field of education, Congregationalists founded Harvard (1636), Yale (1707), Dartmouth (1769), Williams, Amherst, Bowdoin, and Middlebury, and 41 other colleges and universities.

Wesleyan Church, The. Formed through the merger in 1968 of the Wesleyan Methodist Church of America, founded 1843, with the Pilgrim Holiness Church, founded 1897. The church upholds Wesleyan doctrines and teaches entire sanctification.

World Council of Churches Membership

AFRICA

African Christian Church and Schools
African Church of the Holy Spirit
African Israel Church
African Protestant Church
Baptist Community of Western Congo
Christian Protestant Angola Church
Church of Jesus Christ in Madagascar
Church of Jesus Christ on Earth by His
    Messenger Simon Kimbangu
Church of the Brethren in Nigeria
Church of the Lord Aladura
Church of the Province of Burundi
Church of the Province of Central Africa
Church of the Province of Kenya
Church of the Province of Nigeria
Church of the Province of Rwanda
Church of the Province of Southern Africa
Church of the Province of Tanzania
Church of the Province of the Indian Ocean
Church of the Province of West Africa
Community of Disciples of Christ
Community of Light
Episcopal Baptist Community
Episcopal Church of the Sudan
Ethiopian Evangelical Church Mekane
    Jesus
Ethiopian Orthodox Tewahedo Church
Evangelical Church of Cameroon
Evangelical Church of the Congo
Evangelical Community (Congo)
Evangelical Congregational Church in Angola
Evangelical Lutheran Church in Namibia
Evangelical Lutheran Church in Southern
    Africa
Evangelical Lutheran Church in Tanzania
Evangelical Lutheran Church in Zimbabwe
Evangelical Pentecostal Mission of Angola
Evangelical Presbyterian Church, Ghana

Evangelical Presbyterian Church in Southern
    Africa
Evangelical Presbyterian Church of Togo
Lesotho Evangelical Church
Lutheran Church in Liberia
Malagasy Lutheran Church
Mennonite Community
Methodist Church, Ghana
Methodist Church in Kenya
Methodist Church in Zimbabwe
Methodist Church, Nigeria
Methodist Church of Southern Africa
Methodist Church, Sierra Leone
Moravian Church in Southern Africa
Moravian Church in Tanzania
Presbyterian Church in Cameroon
Presbyterian Church in the Sudan
Presbyterian Church of Africa
Presbyterian Church of Cameroon
Presbyterian Church of East Africa
Presbyterian Church of Ghana
Presbyterian Church of Rwanda
Presbyterian Church of Southern Africa
Presbyterian Community
Presbytery of Liberia
Protestant Church of Algeria
Protestant Methodist Church, Ivory Coast
Protestant Methodist Church of Benin
Reformed Church in Zimbabwe
Reformed Church of Equatorial Guinea
Reformed Church of Zambia
Reformed Presbyterian Church in Southern
    Africa
Union of Baptist Churches of Cameroon
United Church of Zambia
United Congregational Church of Southern
    Africa
United Evangelical Church, Angola
Uniting Reformed Church in Southern Africa

ASIA

Anglican Church in Aotearoa, New Zealand, and
    Polynesia
Anglican Church of Australia
Associated Churches of Christ in New Zealand
Bangladesh Baptist Sangha
Baptist Union of New Zealand
Batak Christian Community Church
Batak Protestant Christian Church
Bengal-Orissa-Bihar Baptist Convention
China Christian Council
Christian Council of Central Sulawesi
Christian Evangelical Church in Minahasa
Christian Protestant Church in Indonesia
Church of Bangladesh
Church of Ceylon
Church of Christ in China
Church of Christ in Thailand
Church of North India
Church of Pakistan
Church of South India
Church of the Province of Burma
Churches of Christ in Australia
East Java Christian Church
Evangelical Christian Church in Halmahera
Evangelical Christian Church in Irian Jaya
Evangelical Christian Church of Sangir Talaud
Evangelical Methodist Church in the Philippines
Holy Catholic Church in Japan
Indonesia Christian Church GKI
Indonesia Christian Church HKI
Japanese Orthodox Church
Javanese Christian Churches
Kalimantan Evangelical Church
Karo Batak Protestant Church
Korean Christian Church in Japan
Korean Methodist Church
Malankara Orthodox Syrian Church
Mar Thoma Syrian Church of Malabar
Methodist Church
Methodist Church in India
Methodist Church in Malaysia
Methodist Church in Singapore
Methodist Church of New Zealand
Methodist Church, Upper Burma
Myanmar Baptist Convention
Nias Protestant Christian Church
Pasundan Christian Church
Philippine Episcopal Church

Philippine Independent Church
Presbyterian Church in Taiwan
Presbyterian Church in the Republic of Korea
Presbyterian Church of Aotearoa New Zealand
Presbyterian Church of Korea
Presbyterian Church of Pakistan
Protestant Christian Church in Bali
Protestant Church in Indonesia
Protestant Church in Sabah
Protestant Church in South-East Sulawesi
Protestant Church in the Moluccas
Protestant Church in Western Indonesia
Protestant Evangelical Church in Timor
Samavesam of Telugu Baptist Churches
Simalungun Protestant Christian Church
Toraja Church
United Church of Christ in Japan
United Church of Christ in the Philippines
United Evangelical Lutheran Churches in India
Uniting Church in Australia

CARIBBEAN

Church in the Province of the West Indies
Methodist Church in Cuba
Methodist Church in the Caribbean and the
    Americas
Moravian Church, Eastern West Indies Province
Moravian Church in Jamaica
Moravian Church in Suriname
Presbyterian Church in Trinidad and Tobago
Presbyterian Reformed Church in Cuba
United Church in Jamaica and the Cayman
    Islands
United Protestant Church

EUROPE

Autocephalic Orthodox Church in Poland
Baptist Union of Denmark
Baptist Union of Great Britain
Baptist Union of Hungary
Bulgarian Orthodox Church
Catholic Diocese of the Old Catholics in
    Germany
Church in Wales
Church of England
Church of Greece
Church of Ireland
Church of Norway

Church of Scotland
Church of Sweden
Czech Hussite Church
Ecumenical Patriarchate of Constantinople
Estonian Evangelical Lutheran Church
Euro-Asiatic Federation of the Unions of
    Evangelical Christians-Baptists
European Continental Province of the Moravian
    Church (Netherlands)
Evangelical Baptist Union of Italy
Evangelical Church in Germany
Evangelical Church of Czech Brethren
Evangelical Church of the Augsburg and Helvetic
    Confessions in Austria
Evangelical Church of the Augsburg Confession
    in Poland
Evangelical Church of the Augsburg Confession
    in Romania
Evangelical Church of the Augsburg Confession
    in the Slovak Republic
Evangelical Church of the Augsburg Confessions
    of Alsace and Lorraine
Evangelical Lutheran Church
Evangelical Lutheran Church in Denmark
Evangelical Lutheran Church of Finland
Evangelical Lutheran Church of France
Evangelical Lutheran Church of Iceland
Evangelical Lutheran Church of Latvia
Evangelical Methodist Church of Italy
Evangelical Presbyterian Church of Portugal
Evangelical Synodal Presbyterian Church of the
    Augsburg Confession in Romania
Georgian Orthodox Church
Greek Evangelical Church
Latvian Evangelical Lutheran Church Abroad
Lusitanian Catholic Apostolic Evangelical
    Church
Lutheran Church in Hungary
Mennonite Church
Mennonite Church in the Netherlands
Methodist Church, Great Britain
Methodist Church in Ireland
Mission Covenant Church of Sweden
Moravian Church in Great Britain and Ireland
Netherlands Reformed Church
Old Catholic Church of Austria
Old Catholic Church of Switzerland
Old Catholic Church of the Netherlands
Old Catholic Mariavite Church in Poland
Orthodox Autocephalous Church of Albania

Orthodox Church in the Czech Republic
Orthodox Church in the Slovak Republic
Orthodox Church of Finland
Polish Catholic Church in Poland
Presbyterian Church of Wales
Reformed Christian Church in Slovakia
Reformed Christian Church in Yugoslavia
Reformed Church in Hungary
Reformed Church of Alsace and Lorraine
Reformed Church of France
Reformed Church of Romania
Reformed Churches in the Netherlands
Remonstrant Brotherhood
Romanian Orthodox Church
Russian Orthodox Church
Scottish Congregational Church
Scottish Episcopal Church
Serbian Orthodox Church
Silesian Evangelical Church of the Augsburg
    Confession
Slovak Evangelical Church of the Augsburg Con-
    fession in Yugoslavia
Spanish Evangelical Church
Spanish Reformed Episcopal Church
Swiss Protestant Church Federation
Union of Welsh Independents
United Free Church of Scotland
United Protestant Church of Belgium
United Reformed Church of the United
    Kingdom
Waldensian Church

LATIN AMERICA

Baptist Association of El Salvador
Baptist Convention of Nicaragua
Bolivian Evangelical Lutheran Church
Church of God
Church of the Disciples of Christ
Episcopal Anglican Church of Brazil
Evangelical Church of Lutheran Confession in
    Brazil
Evangelical Church of the River Plate
Evangelical Methodist Church in Bolivia
Evangelical Methodist Church in Uruguay
Evangelical Methodist Church of Argentina
Evangelical Methodist Church of Costa Rica
Free Pentecostal Mission Church of Chile
Latin American Reformed Church
Methodist Church in Brazil

Methodist Church of Chile
Methodist Church of Mexico
Methodist Church of Peru
Moravian Church in Nicaragua
Pentecostal Church of Chile
Pentecostal Mission Church
Salvadorean Lutheran Synod
United Evangelical Lutheran Church
United Presbyterian Church of Brazil

MIDDLE EAST

Armenian Apostolic Church
Church of Cyprus
Coptic Orthodox Church
Episcopal Church in Jerusalem and the Middle
    East
Greek Orthodox Patriarchate of Alexandria and
    All Africa
Greek Orthodox Patriarchate of Antioch and All
    the East
Greek Orthodox Patriarchate of Jerusalem
Holy Apostolic Catholic Assyrian Church of the
    East
National Evangelical Synod of Syria and
    Lebanon
Synod of the Evangelical Church of Iran
Synod of the Nile of the Evangelical Church
Syrian Orthodox Patriarchate of Antioch and All
    the East
Union of the Armenian Evangelical Churches in
    the Near East

NORTH AMERICA

African Methodist Episcopal Church
African Methodist Episcopal Zion Church
American Baptist Churches
Anglican Church of Canada
Canadian Yearly Meeting of the Religious Society
    of Friends
Christian Church (Disciples of Christ)
Christian Methodist Episcopal Church
Church of the Brethren
Estonian Evangelical Lutheran Church
    Abroad

Evangelical Lutheran Church in America
Evangelical Lutheran Church in Canada
Friends General Conference
Friends United Meeting
Hungarian Reformed Church in America
International Council of Community Churches
International Evangelical Church
Moravian Church in America (Northern
    Province)
Moravian Church in America (Southern
    Province)
National Baptist Convention of America
National Baptist Convention, USA
Orthodox Church in America
Polish National Catholic Church
Presbyterian Church (USA)
Presbyterian Church in Canada
Progressive National Baptist Convention
Protestant Episcopal Church in the USA
Reformed Church in America
United Church of Canada
United Church of Christ
United Methodist Church

PACIFIC

Church of Melanesia
Congregational Christian Church in American
    Samoa
Congregational Christian Church in Samoa
Cook Islands Christian Church
Evangelical Christian Church in New Caledonia
    and the Loyalty Isles
Evangelical Church of French Polynesia
Evangelical Lutheran Church of Papua New
    Guinea
Kiribati Protestant Church
Methodist Church in Fiji
Methodist Church in Samoa
Methodist Church in Tonga
Presbyterian Church of Vanuatu
Tuvalu Christian Church
United Church in Papua New Guinea and the
    Solomon Islands
United Church of Christ-Congregational in the
    Marshall Islands.

Popes of the Roman Catholic Church

There have been approximately 266 popes since St. Peter:

Pope:	Dates:	Nationality
Peter	d. before 66	Galilean
Linus	c. 66–c. 78	Italian
Anacletus	c. 79–c. 91	Italian
Clement I	c. 91–c. 100	Italian
Evaristus	c. 100–c. 109	Italian
Alexander I	c. 109–c. 116	Italian
Sixtus I	c. 116–c. 125	Italian
Telesphorus	c. 125–c. 137	Greek
Hyginus	c. 137–c. 140	Greek
Pius I	c. 140–c. 154	Italian
Anicetus	c. 154–c. 166	Greek
Soter	c. 166–c. 175	Italian
Eleutherius	175–189	Greek
Victor I	189–198	African
Zephrynus	198–217	Italian
Callistus I	217–222	Italian
Hippolytus (antipope)	217–c. 235	Italian
Urban I	222–230	Italian
Pontian	230–235	Italian
Anterus	235–236	Greek
Fabian	236–250	Italian
Cornelius	251–253	Italian
Novatian (antipope)	251	Italian
Lucius I	253–254	Italian
Stephen I	254–257	Italian
Sixtus II	257–258	Italian
Dionysius	259–268	Italian
Felix I	269–274	Italian
Eutychianus	275–283	Italian
Caius	283–296	Italian
Marcellinus	296–304	Italian
Marcellus I	306–309	Italian
Eusebius	310	Italian
Militiades	311–314	African?
Sylvester I	314–335	Italian
Mark	336	Italian
Julius I	337–352	Italian
Liberius	352–366	Italian
Felix II (anitpope)	355–365	Italian
Damasus I	366–384	Italian
Ursinus (antipope)	366–367	Italian
Siricius	384–399	Italian
Anastasius I	399–401	Italian
Innocent I	402–417	Italian
Zosimus	417–418	Greek
Boniface I	418–422	Italian
Eulalius (antipope)	418–419	Italian
Celestine I	422–432	Italian
Sixtus III	432–440	Italian
Leo I	440–461	Italian
Hilarus	461–468	Italian
Simplicius	468–483	Italian
Felix III	483–492	Italian
Gelasius I	492–496	African
Anastasius II	496–498	Italian
Symmachus	498–514	Italian
Laurentius (antipope)	498, 501–505	Italian
Hormisdas	514–523	Italian
John I	523–526	Italian
Felix IV	526–530	Italian
Boniface II	530–532	Italian
Dioscorus (antipope)	530	Italian
John II	532–535	Italian
Agapetus I, St.	535–536	Italian
Silverius, St.	536–537	Italian
Vigilius	537–555	Italian
Pelagius I	556–561	Italian
John III	561–574	Italian
Benedict I	575–579	Italian
Pelagius II	579–590	Italian
Gregory I, St.	590–604	Italian
Sabinianus	604–606	Italian

Boniface III	607	Italian	Marinus I	882–884	Italian
Boniface IV, St.	608–615	Italian	Hadrian III, St.	884–885	Italian
Deusdedit or			Stephen VI	885–891	Italian
Adeodatus I	615–618	Italian	Formosus	891–896	Italian
Boniface V	619–625	Italian	Boniface VI	896	Italian
Honorius I	625–638	Italian	Stephen VII	896–897	Italian
Severinus	640	Italian	Romanus	897	Italian
John IV	640–642	Dalm.	Theodore II	897	Italian
Theodore I	642–649	Greek	John IX	898–900	Italian
Martin I, St.	649–654	Italian	Benedict IV	900–903	Italian
Eugenius I, St.	655–657	Italian	Leo V	903	Italian
Vitalian, St.	657–672	Italian	Christopher (antipope)	903–904	Italian
Adeodatus II	672–676	Italian	Sergius III	904–911	Italian
Donus	676–678	Italian	Anastasius III	911–913	Italian
Agatho, St.	678–681	Italian	Lando	913–914	Italian
Leo II, St.	682–683	Italian	John X	914–928	Italian
Benedict II, St.	684–685	Italian	Leo VI	928	Italian
John V	685–686	Syrian	Stephen VIII	928–931	Italian
Conon	686–687	Italian	John XI	931–935	Italian
Theodore (antipope)	687	Italian	Leo VII	936–939	Italian
Paschal (antipope)	687	Italian	Stephen IX	939–942	Italian
Sergius I, St.	687–701	Syrian	Marinus II	942–946	Italian
John VI	701–705	Greek	Agapetus II	946–955	Italian
John VII	705–707	Greek	John XII	955–964	Italian
Sisinnius	708	Syrian	Leo VIII (antipope)	963–965	Italian
Constantine	708–715	Syrian	Benedict V	964	Italian
Gregory II, St.	715–731	Italian	John XIII	965–972	Italian
Gregory III, St.	731–741	Syrian	Benedict VI	973–974	Italian
Zacharias, St.	741–752	Greek	Boniface VII (antipope)	974, 984–985	Italian
Stephen II (antipope)	752	Italian	Benedict VII	974–983	Italian
Stephen II	752–757	Italian	John XIV	983–984	Italian
Paul I, St.	757–767	Italian	John XV	985–996	Italian
Constantine (antipope)	767–769	Italian	Gregory V	996–999	Saxon
Philip (antipope)	768	Italian	John XVI (antipope)	997–998	Italian
Stephen III	768–772	Italian	Sylvester II	999–1003	French
Hadrian I	772–795	Italian	John XVII	1003	Italian
Leo III, St.	795–816	Italian	John XVIII	1004–1009	Italian
Stephen IV	816–817	Italian	Sergius IV	1009–1012	Italian
Paschal I, St.	817–824	Italian	Benedict VIII	1012–1024	Italian
Eugenius II	824–827	Italian	Gregory (antipope)	1012	Italian
Valentine	827	Italian	John XIX	1024–1032	Italian
Gregory IV	827–844	Italian	Benedict IX	1032–1044	Italian
John (antipope)	844	Italian	Sylvester III	1045	Italian
Sergius II	844–847	Italian	Benedict IX	1045	Italian
Leo IV, St.	847–855	Italian	Gregory VI	1045–1046	Italian
Benedict III	855–858	Italian	Clement II	1046–1047	Saxon
Anastasius (antipope)	855	Italian	Benedict IX	1047–1048	Italian
Nicholas I, St.	858–867	Italian	Damasus II	1048	Bavarian
Hadrian II	867–872	Italian	Leo IX, St.	1048–1054	Alsatian
John VIII	872–882	Italian	Victor II	1055–1057	Swabian

Stephen X	1057–1058	French		Martin IV	1281–1285	French
Benedict X (antipope)	1058–1059	Italian		Honorius IV	1285–1287	Italian
Nicholas II	1059–1061	French		Nicholas IV	1288–1292	Italian
Alexander II	1061–1073	Italian		Celestine V, St.	1294	Italian
Honorius II (antipope)	1061–1072	Italian		Boniface VIII	1294–1303	Italian
Gregory VII, St.	1073–1085	Italian		Benedict XI	1303–1304	Italian
Clement III (antipope)	1080,			Clement V	1305–1314	French
	1084–1087	Italian		John XXII	1316–1334	French
Victor III	1086–1087	Italian		Nicholas V (antipope)	1328–1330	Italian
Urban II	1088–1099	French		Benedict XII	1334–1342	French
Paschal II	1099–1118	Italian		Clement VI	1342–1352	French
Theodoric (antipope)	1100–1102	Italian		Innocent VI	1352–1362	French
Albert (antipope)	1102	Italian		Urban V	1362–1370	French
Sylvester IV (antipope)	1105–1111	Italian		Gregory XI	1370–1378	French
Gelasius II	1118–1119	Italian		Urban VI	1378–1389	Italian
Gregory VIII (antipope)	1118–1121	Italian		Clement VII (antipope)	1378–1394	Italian
Callistus II	1119–1124	French		Boniface IX	1389–1404	Italian
Honorius II	1124–1130	Italian		Benedict XIII (antipope)		
Celestine II (antipope)	1124	Italian			1394–1417	Italian
Innocent II	1130–1143	Italian		Innocent VII	1404–1406	Italian
Anacletus II (antipope)	1130–1138	Italian		Gregory XII	1406–1415	Italian
Victor IV (antipope)	1138	Italian		Alexander V (antipope)	1409–1410	Italian
Celestine II	1143–1144	Italian		John XXIII (antipope)	1410–1415	Italian
Lucius II	1144–1145	Italian		Martin V	1417–1431	Italian
Eugenius III	1145–1153	Italian		Clement VIII (antipope)	1423–1429	Italian
Anastasius IV	1153–1154	Italian		Benedict XIV (antipope)		
Hadrian IV	1154–1159	English			1425–1430	Italian
Alexander III	1159–1181	Italian		Eugenius IV	1431–1447	Italian
Victor IV (antipope)	1159–1164	Italian		Felix V (antipope)	1439–1449	Italian
Paschal III (antipope)	1164–1168	Italian		Nicholas V	1447–1455	Italian
Callistus III (antipope)	1168–1178	Italian		Callistus III	1455–1458	Spanish
Innocent III (antipope)	1179–1180	Italian		Pius II	1458–1464	Italian
Lucius III	1181–1185	Italian		Paul II	1464–1471	Italian
Urban III	1185–1187	Italian		Sixtus IV	1471–1484	Italian
Gregory VIII	1187	Italian		Innocent VIII	1484–1492	Italian
Clement III	1187–1191	Italian		Alexander VI	1492–1503	Spanish
Celestine III	1191–1198	Italian		Pius III	1503	Italian
Innocent III	1198–1216	Italian		Julius II	1503–1513	Italian
Honorius III	1216–1227	Italian		Leo X	1513–1521	Italian
Gregory IX	1227–1241	Italian		Hadrian VI	1522–1523	Dutch
Celestine IV	1241	Italian		Clement VII	1523–1534	Italian
Innocent IV	1243–1254	Italian		Paul II	1534–1549	Italian
Alexander IV	1254–1261	Italian		Julius III	1550–1555	Italian
Urban IV	1261–1264	French		Marcellus II	1555	Italian
Clement IV	1265–1268	French		Paul IV	1555–1559	Italian
Gregory X	1268–1276	Italian		Pius IV	1559–1565	Italian
Innocent V	1276	French		Pius V, St.	1566–1572	Italian
Hadrian V	1276	Italian		Gregory VIII	1572–1585	Italian
John XXI	1276–1277	Portuguese		Sixtus V	1585–1590	Italian
Nicholas III	1277–1280	Italian		Urban VII	1590	Italian

Gregory XIV	1590–1591	Italian	Benedict XIV	1740–1758	Italian
Innocent IX	1591	Italian	Clement XIII	1758–1769	Italian
Clement VIII	1592–1605	Italian	Clement XIV	1769–1774	Italian
Leo XI	1605	Italian	Pius VI	1775–1799	Italian
Paul V	1605–1621	Italian	Pius VII	1800–1823	Italian
Gregory XV	1621–1623	Italian	Leo XII	1823–1829	Italian
Urban VIII	1623–1644	Italian	Pius VIII	1829–1830	Italian
Innocent X	1644–1655	Italian	Gregory XVI	1831–1846	Italian
Alexander VII	1655–1667	Italian	Pius IX	1846–1878	Italian
Clement IX	1667–1669	Italian	Leo XIII	1878–1903	Italian
Clement X	1670–1676	Italian	Pius X, St.	1903–1914	Italian
Innocent XI	1676–1689	Italian	Benedict XV	1914–1922	Italian
Alexander VIII	1689–1691	Italian	Pius XI	1922–1939	Italian
Innocent XII	1691–1700	Italian	Pius XII	1939–1958	Italian
Clement XI	1700–1721	Italian	John XXIII	1958–1963	Italian
Innocent XIII	1721–1724	Italian	Paul VI	1963–1978	Italian
Benedict XIII	1724–1730	Italian	John Paul I	1978	Italian
Clement XII	1730–1740	Italian	John Paul II	1978–	Polish

Patron Saints of the Roman Catholic Church

Patron Saint:	Patron Saint of:
St. Matthew	accountants, bankers, tax collectors, and bookkeepers
St. Genesius	actors, secretaries
St. Bernardino of Siena	advertising
Our Lady of Loreto	airmen
St. Joseph of Cupertino	air travelers
St. John Berchmans	altar boys
St. Rene Goupil	anaesthetists
St. Andrew	anglers, fishermen
St. Francis of Assisi	animals, ecologists, merchants
Apostle St. Thomas	architects
St. Luke	artists
St. Dominic	artists
St. Sebastian	athletes
St. Francis de Sales	authors and journalists, the deaf
Our Lady of Loreto	aviators
St. Elizabeth of Hungary	bakers
Sts. Cosmas and Damian	barbers, druggists, surgeons
St. Anthony of Padua	barren women, lost articles, travelers
St. Anthony Abbot	basket makers, butchers, gravediggers
St. Alexis	beggars
St. Dunstan	blacksmiths
St. Raphael	the blind
St. Julian the Hospitaller	boatmen
St. Peter Celestine	bookbinders
St. John of God	booksellers
St. Augustine of Hippo	brewers, printers
St. Stephen	bricklayers
St. Nicholas of Myra	brides, children
Archangel Gabriel	broadcasters, clerics, messengers, postal employees, radio, telecommunications, television
St. Anthony	brushmakers, domestic animals
St. Vincent Ferrer	builders
St. Fiacre	cabdrivers
St. Joseph	carpenters, church, fathers of families, the dying, workers
St. Charles Borromeo	catechists
St. Vincent de Paul	charities
St. Gerard Majella	childbirth, expectant mothers
St. Dominic Savio	choirboys
St. Gabriel of the Sorrowful Mother	clerics
St. Vitus	comedians, dancers, epileptics
St. Lawrence	cooks
St. Giles	cripples
St. Apollonia	dentists
St. Jude	desperate situations
St. Martha	dieticians
St. Zita	domestic servants
Sts. Maurice and Lydia	dyers
St. Emygdius	earthquakes
St. John Bosco	editors
St. Frances Cabrini	emigrants
St. Ferdinand III	engineers
St. Lucy	eye trouble
St. Raymond Nonnatus	midwives, the falsely accused
St. George	farmers, scouts
St. John the Baptist	farriers
St. Florian	firemen

St. Dorothea	florists, gardeners	teachers
St. John Gualbert	foresters	St. Mark	notaries
St. Barbara	founders, gunners, miners, stonemasons	St. Agatha	nurses
		St. John Chrysostom	orators, teachers
The Holy Innocents	foundlings	St. Jerome Emiliani	orphans
St. Anastasius the Fuller	fullers	St. John Vianney	parish priests
Joseph of Arimathea	funeral directors, tinmakers	St. Nicholas	pawnbrokers
		St. Catherine of Alexandria	philosophers
St. Agnes	girls	St. James the Great	pilgrims, rheumatics
St. Dunstan	goldsmiths, metalworkers	St. Bartholomew	plasterers
St. Michael	grocers, paratroopers, policemen, radiologists	St. David	poets
		St. Dismas	prisoners
		St. Leonard	prisoners of War
St. Martin de Porres	hairdressers	St. Joseph Cafasso	prisons
St. Teresa of Avila	headaches	St. Bernardino of Siena	public relations
St. John of God	heart patients	St. Ignatius Loyola	retreats
St. Camillus de Lellis	hospitals	St. Cuthbert or Brendan	sailors
St. Amand	hotelkeepers, innkeepers, wine merchants	St. Bridget	scholars
		St. Albert	scientists
		St. Claude	sculptors
St. Anne	housewives, cabinet makers, women in labor	St. Dunstan	silversmiths
		St. Cecilia	singers
		St. Lidwina	skaters
St. Hubert	hunters	St. Bernard of Menthon	skiers
St. Maurice	infantrymen, swordsmiths	St. Marculf	skin disease
		St. Louise de Marillac	social workers
St. Martha	innkeepers	St. Joan of Arc	soldiers
St. Roch	invalids	St. Benedict	speleologists
St. Eloi	jewelers	St. Clement	stonecutters
St. John Capistrano	jurists	St. Thomas Aquinas	students
St. Thomas More	lawyers	St. Homobonus	tailors
St. Ambrose	learning	St. Clare	television
SS Crispin and Crispinian	leatherworkers	St. Alphonsus Liguori	theologians, vocations
St. Jerome	librarians	St. Blaise	throat sufferers
St. Venerius	lighthouse keepers	St. Peter of Alcantara	watchmen
St. Dunstan	locksmiths	St. Paul of Thebes (St. Paul the Hermit)	weavers
St. Valentine	lovers	St. Paula	widows
St. Catherine of Alexandria	maidens	St. Vincent of Saragossa	winegrowers
St. Monica	married women, mothers	St. Amand	wine merchants
St. Albert the Great	medical technicians	St. Adjutor	yachtsmen
St. Dymphna	the mentally ill	St. Aloysius Gonzaga	youth workers
St. Arnulf of Metz	millers		
St. Francis Xavier	missions		
Our Lady of Grace	motorcyclists	**The following are patron saints of nations:**	
St. Christopher	motorists		
St. Bernard of Menthon	mountaineers	Rose of Lima	Americas
St. Gregory the Great	musicians, singers,	Our Lady of Lujan	Argentina

St. Gregory the Illuminator	Armenia	St. Peter Baptist	Japan
Our Lady Help		Sts. Joseph and Mary	Korea
of Christians	Australia, New	St. Casimir	Lithuania
	Zealand	St. Willibrord	Luxembourg
St. Joseph	Belgium	St. Paul	Malta
Nossa Senhora de Aparecida	Brazil	Our Lady of Guadalupe	Mexico
SS Joseph and Anne	Canada	St. Olav	Norway
St. James the Greater	Chile	Michael the archangel	Papua New Guinea
St. Joseph	China	Our Lady of Assumption	Paraguay
St. Peter Claver	Colombia	St. Joseph	Peru
St. Wenceslas	Czech Republic	Sacred Heart of Mary	Philippines
St. Asgar	Denmark	Our Lady of Czestochowa	Poland
St. Dominic	Dominican Repub-	St. Francis Borgia	Portugal
	lic	St. Sergius of Radonezh	Russia
Sacred Heart	Ecuador	St. Ansgar	Scandinavia
St. George	England	St. Andrew	Scotland
Sts. Benedict,		St. Sava	Serbia
Cyril, and Methodius	Europe	Our Lady of Sorrows	Slovakia
St. Henry	Finland	Our Lady of the	
Sts. Denis and Joan of Arc	France	Assumption	South Africa
St. Boniface	Germany	St. James	Spain
St. Nicholas	Greece	St. Lawrence	Sri Lanka
St. Willibrord	Netherlands	St. Bridget	Sweden
St. Stephen	Hungary	Immaculate Conception	United States
St. Thorlac	Iceland	Blessed Virgin Mary	Uruguay
St. Thomas	India	Our Lady of Coromoto	Venezuela
St. Patrick	Ireland	St. David	Wales
St. Francis of Assisi	Italy	St. Gertrude	West Indies

Feast Days of Saints and Other Notables of the Church

JANUARY

1	St. Basil the Great (Eastern Church)
1	St. Fulgentius of Ruspe
1/2	St. Odilo
2	St. Basil the Great (Western Church)
2	St. Gregory of Nazianzus (Western Church)
2	St. Macarius of Alexandria (Western Church)
2	St. Seraphim of Sarov
3	St. Genevieve
4	St. Angela of Foligno
4	St. Elizabeth Ann Bayley Seton
5	Pope Telesphorus
5	St. John Nepomucene Neumann
5	Simeon Stylites (Syrian Orthodox Church)
7	St. Lucian of Antioch (Western Church)
7	St. Raymond of Penafort
8	St. Severinus
9	St. Philip of Moscow
10	St. Gregory of Nyssa (Eastern Church)
10	St. Theophan the Recluse
11	St. Theodosius the Coenobiarch
12	St. Ailred
14	St. Hilary of Poitiers
14	St. Kentigern
14	St. Nino
14	St. Sava (Serbian Church)
15	Macarius of Egypt (Western Church)
15	St. Paul of Thebes
17	St. Anthony the Great
19	St. Macarius of Alexandria (Eastern Church)
20	Henry of Uppsala
20	St. Euthymius
20	St. Sebastian
21	St. Agnes

21	St. Maximus the Confessor (Eastern Church)
21	St. Maximus the Greek
21	St. Meinrad
23	Blessed Henry Suso
24	Babylas (Western Church)
24	St. Francis of Sales
24	Timothy
25	St. Gregory of Nazianzus (Eastern Church)
25	St. Paul
26	St. Alberic
26	St. Paula
26	Titus (Roman Catholic Church)
27	St. Angela Merici
28	Isaac of Ninevah
28	St. Ephraem the Syrian (Eastern Church)
28	St. Peter Nolasco
28	St. Thomas Aquinas
30	St. Hippolytus (Eastern Church)
31	St. John Bosco
31	St. Marcella

FEBRUARY

1	Ignatius of Antioch
1	St. Bridget
2	St. Jeanne de Lestonnac
3	St. Anskar
3	St. Barsumas
4	Isidore of Pelusium
4	St. Maurus Rabanus
5	St. Agatha
5	St. Amandus
6	Phobius (Orthodox Church)
6	St. Barsanuphius
6	St. Dorothy (suppressed 1969)
8	St. John of Matha

9	St. Jerome Emiliani	20	St. Cuthbert
10	St. Scholastica	21	St. Nicholas of Flue
11	St. Blaise	21	Serapion of Thmuis
12	St. Melitius of Antioch	28	John of Capistrano
13	Elias III	30	St. John Climacus
13	Priscilla (Eastern Church)	31	St. Benjamin
14	St. Auxentios the Persian		
14	St. Cyril and Methodius (Western Church)		
14	St. Valentine		
15	St. Ethelbert		

APRIL

16	St. Pamphilius (Eastern Church)
17	St. Mariamne
18	St. Bernadette
18	St. Leo I (Eastern Church)
19	Mesrob (Armenian Church)
21	St. Peter Damian
21	St. Robert Southwell
22	St. Margaret of Cortona
23	St. Polycarp
26	St. Nestor
27	St. Gregory of Narek
28	St. Oswald

APRIL

1	Mary of Egypt (Eastern Church)
1	St. Melito
2	Mary of Egypt (Western Church)
2	St. Francis of Paola
3	St. Joseph the Hymnographer
3	St. Richard of Chichester
4	St. Benedict the Black
4	St. Isidore of Seville
5	Blessed Juliana of Liege
5	St. Vincent Ferrer
7	John Baptist de la Salle
7	St. Hegesippus
11	St. Gemma Galgani
11	St. Stanislaus
12	St. Zeno
13	St. Benezet
13	St. Nicephoros (Latin Church)
14	St. Elmo
17	St. Stephen Harding
19	St. Alphege
20	St. Agnes of Montepulciano
21	St. Anselm
21	St. Beuno
21	St. Januarius (Eastern Church)
23	St. George
24	St. Egbert
25	St. Mark
28	St. Louis Marie Grignion de Montfort
28	St. Paul of the Cross
29	St. Hugh of Cluny
29	St. Robert
30	St. Catherine of Siena
30	St. James the Great (Eastern Church)
30	St. Pius V

MARCH

1	St. David
1	St. Suidbert
2	St. Simplicius
4	St. Casimir
6	St. Colette
7	St. Felicity
7	St. Perpetua
8	St. John of God
9	Forty martyrs of Sebaste (Eastern Church)
9	St. Catherine of Bologna
9	St. Frances of Rome
9	St. Gregory of Nyssa (Western Church)
9	Macarius of Egypt (Eastern Church)
10	Forty martyrs of Sebaste (Western Church)
10	Macarius
11	St. Sophronius
12	St. Gregory I (Eastern Church)
14	St. Benedict of Nursia (Eastern Church)
15	St. Clement Mary Hofbauer
15/16	St. Aristobulus
16	St. Jean de Brebeuf
18	St. Edward
20	Blessed John of Parma

MAY

2	St. Boris
3	St. James the Less (Western Church)
3	St. Philip (Western Church)

3	St. Theodosius of Kiev
4	St. Florian
5	St. Hilary of Arles
6	St. John the Apostle
6	Seraphim of Boiotia
7	St. John of Beverley
8	Julian of Norwich (Anglican Church)
9	St. Christopher (Eastern Church)
9	St. Pachomius (Coptic Church)
10	Comgall
10	St. John of Avila
11	Sts. Cyril and Methodius (Eastern Church)
12	St. Germanus
14	St. Pachomius (Western Church)
15	St. Pachomius (Eastern Church)
16	St. Brendan
16	St. John of Nepomuk
17	St. Paschal Babylon
19	St. Dunstan
19	St. Yves
20	St. Alcuin
20	St. Bernardino of Siena
20	St. Ivo of Chartres
21	St. Arsenius the Great
21	St. Helena (Eastern Church)
25	St. Bede
25	St. Gregory VII
26	St. Augustine of Canterbury (Anglican Church)
26	St. Philip Neri
26	St. Quadratus
27	St. Augustine of Canterbury (Catholic Church)
28	St. Germanus
30	St. Joan of Arc

JUNE

1	St. Justin Martyr
1	St. Pamphilius (Western Church)
2	St. Blandina (Western Church)
2	St. Nicephorus (Greek Church)
2	St. Pothinus
3	St. Clotilda
4	St. Peter Martyr
5	St. Boniface of Germany
6	St. Norbert
9	St. Columba

9	St. Cyril (Eastern Church)
9	St. Ephraem the Syrian (Western Church)
11	St. Barnabas
11	St. Bartholomew (Eastern Church)
12	St. Leo III
13	St. Anthony of Padua
15	St. Vitus
16	St. Benno
17	St. Alban
17	St. Botulph
19	St. Boniface
19	St. Jude (Eastern Church)
20	Nicolaus Cabasilas
21	St. Aloysius Gonzaga
22	St. Niceta
22	St. Pantaenus (Coptic Church)
22	St. Paulinus of Nola
22	Sir Thomas More
27	St. Cyril (Western Church)
27	St. Ladislaus
28	St. Irenaeus (Western Church)
29	St. Peter

JULY

1	St. Shenouti
2	St. Juvenaly of Alaska
3	St. Thomas (Western Church)
4	St. Andrew of Crete
5	St. Athanasius the Athonite
7	St. Pantaenus (Western Church)
8	Priscilla (Western Church)
8	St. Procopius
9	St. John Fisher
11	St. Benedict of Nursia (Western Church)
11	St. Olga
13	James of Voragine
14	Blessed Kateri Tekawitha
14	Camillus of Lellis
14	St. Nicodemus of the Holy Mountain (Eastern Church)
15	Jacob of Nisibis
15	St. Bonaventura
15	St. Vladimir
17	St. Leo IV
17	St. Margaret of Antioch (Eastern Church)
17	St. Nerses of Lampron (Western Church)
19	St. Symmachus
20	Aurelius of Carthage

20	St. Margaret of Antioch (Western Church)	24	Kosmas Aitolos
21	St. Laurence of Brindisi	24	Martyrs of Utica
23	St. Bridget of Sweden	24	St. Bartholomew (Western Church)
23	St. John Cassian (Eastern Church)	25	St. Joseph Calasanctius
25	St. Christopher (Western Church)	25	Titus (Greek and Syrian churches)
25	St. James the Great (Western Church)	26	St. Zephyrinus
26	St. Blandina (Eastern Church)	27	Monica
27	St. Pantaleon	28	St. Augustine of Hippo
29	Basil Preobrazhenski	31	St. Aidan
29	St. Olav	31	St. Raymond Nonnatus
30	Blessed Urban II		
30	St. Peter Chrysologus		
31	Blessed Giovanni Colombina		
31	St. Ignatius Loyola (Coptic Church)		
31	Timothy Aelurus		

AUGUST

SEPTEMBER

1	St. Alphonsus Liguori	1	St. Giles
1	St. Peter Julien Eymard	1	Simeon Stylites (Eastern Orthodox Church)
2	St. Eusebius	2	St. John the Faster (Eastern Church)
3	St. Merses IV (Armenian Church)	3	St. Gregory I (Western Church)
4	St. Jean-Baptiste Marie Vianney	4	Babylas (Eastern Church)
5	St. Oswald	4	Dioscorus
6	St. Roch	6	St. Sergius
7	St. Sixtus II	8	St. Adrain
8	St. Cajetan	9	Peter Claver
8	St. Dominic de Guzman	10	St. Finnian
9	Blessed Edith Stein	13	John Chrysostom (Western Church)
10	St. Laurence	14	St. Cyprian
11	St. Clare	16	Pope Cornelius
12	Pope Innocent XI	16	St. Euphemia
13	St. Hippolytus (Western Church)	16	St. Ninian
13	St. Maximus the Confessor (Western Church)	17	St. Hildegard of Bingen
13	St. Nerses IV (Western Church)	17	St. Robert Bellarmine
13	St. Tikhon of Zadonsk	19	St. Januarius
14	St. Maximilian Kobe	20	St. Agapetus
15	St. Joseph Calasanz	20	St. Martin I
15	St. Stephen	21	St. Matthew (Western Church)
17	St. Hyacinth	22	St. Catherine of Genoa
18	St. Helena (Western Church)	23	St. Linus
19	St. John Eudes	25	St. Sergius
20	St. Bernard of Clairvaux	25/26	St. Lancelot Andrewes
20	St. Philibert	26	Charles Garnier
21	St. Frances de Chantal Jane	26	Gabriel Lalemant
21	St. Thaddaeus	26	Noel Chabenel
23	St. Giovanni Capistrano	26	St. Isaac Jogues
23	St. Irenaeus (Eastern Church)	26	St. Jean de Brebeuf
23	St. Philip Benizi	26	St. Jean Lalande
		26	St. Rene Goupil
		27	St. Adamnan
		27	Vincent de Paul
		28	St. Julia Eustochium
		28	St. Wenceslas

29	St. Hripsime (Western Church)
30	St. Jerome
30	St. Otto

OCTOBER

1	St. Remigius
1	St. Teresa of Lisieux
4	St. Ammon
4	St. Francis of Assisi
6	St. Bruno of Germany
6	St. Thomas (Greek Church)
9	Dionysius the Areopagite
9	St. Dionysius of Paris
9	St. James the Less (Eastern Church)
9	St. Tikhon
10	Blessed Daniele Comboni
10	St. Francis Borgia
10	St. Paulinus of York
11	St. Bruno
13	Edward the Confessor
15	St. Lucian of Antioch (Eastern Church)
15	St. Teresa of Avila
16	Hugh Latimer
16	St. Margaret Mary Alacoque
17	St. Etheldreda
18	St. Luke
19	St. Peter of Alcantara
21	St. Hilarion
21	St. Ursula
23	St. Anicius Manlius Torquatus Severinus Boethius
23	St. James
23	St. John Capistran
24	St. Proclus (Western Church)
25	Forty martyrs of England and Wales
25	St. Alexander Briant
25	St. John Boste
25	St. John of Beveley
25	Sts. Crispin and Crispinian
27	St. Frumentius
28	St. Demetrius of Rostov
28	St. Jude (Western Church)

NOVEMBER

3	St. Hubert
4	Charles Borromeo
5	St. Martin de Porres

7	St. Willibrord
8	Elizabeth of the Blessed Trinity
8	Fur Crowned Martyrs
10	St. Leo I (Western Church)
11	St. Martin (Western Church)
11	St. Menas
11	St. Theodore of Studios
12	St. Joseph of Polotsk
12	St. Martin (Eastern Church)
13	John Chrysostom (Eastern Church)
13	St. Abbo of Fleury
13	St. Nicholas I
14	St. Gregory Palmas
14	St. Philip (Eastern Church)
15	St. Albertus Magnus
15	St. Paisy Velichkovsky
16	Gertrude the Great
16	St. Edmund of Abingdon
16	St. Matthew (Eastern Church)
17	Dionysius the Great
17	St. Elizabeth of Hungary
17	St. Gregory of Tours
17	St. Gregory Thaumaturgus
17	St. Hilda
17	St. Hugh of Lincoln
18	St. Odo of Cluny
19	St. Nerses the Great
20	St. Bernward
20	St. Edmund
20	St. Proclus (Eastern Church)
21	St. Clement of Rome (Western Church)
21	St. Gelasius I
22	St. Cecilia
23	St. Alexander Nevski
23	St. Columbanus
24	St. Peter of Alexandria (Eastern Church)
24/25	St. Clement of Rome (Eastern Church)
25	St. Catherine of Alexandria
25	Mesrob (Western Church)
26	St. Nikon the Metanoeite
26	St. Peter of Alexandria (Western Church)
26	St. Siricius
27	St. Virgilius of Salzburg
28	St. Benedict Joseph Labre
29	St. Cuthbert Mayne

DECEMBER

2	Blessed Jan van Ruysbroeck
4	St. Barbara

4	St. Damasus I	14	St. Spyridion (Western Church)
4	St. John of Damascus	21	St. Francis Xavier
5	St. Sabas	21	St. Peter Canisius
6	St. Nicholas of Myra	22	Jacopone da Todi
7	St. Ambrose	22	St. Frances Xavier Cabrini
9	St. Peter Fourier	26	St. Zosimus
12	St. Finnian	29	St. Thomas a Becket
12	St. Spyridion (Eastern Church)	30	St. Macarius
13	St. Lucy	30	St. Melania the Younger
14	St. John of the Cross	31	St. Sylvester I

Liturgical Books

ROMAN CATHOLIC

In the Middle Ages more than 100 books were used in Roman Catholic worship. In the Mass there were four principal books: the Sacramentary, the Antiphonale Missarum, the Lectionary, and the Missal. For the Divine Office there were four principal books: the Psalter, the Antiphonal, the Hymnal, and the Breviary.

The Council of Trent standardized the liturgical books into seven classes: 1. The Breviarum Romanum called the Liturgy of the Hours since 1971, including the Pontificale Romanum and Rituale Romanum. 2. Missale Romanum, including Ritus Servandus or directions for celebration of the Mass. 3. Lectionarium. 4. Martyrology. 5. Graduale Romanum. 6. Antiphonale, and 7. Caeremoniale Romanum, containing rubrical directives.

EASTERN ORTHODOX

The Orthodox Church uses several different sets of liturgical books:

1. Euchologion (Book of Prayers) exists in two forms. The Great Euchologion contains the fixed parts, or ordinary, of vespers, mattins, the eucharistic liturgy, the Liturgy of the Presanctified, and the six remaining sacraments. The Small Euchologion or Agiasmatarion (Book of Blessings) contains funeral offices and occasional blessings.
2. Liturgikon or Hieratikon is an altarbook containing the priest's part in vespers, mattins, and other services.
3. Archieratikon (Book of the Bishop) corresponds to the Western Pontifical.

Another set of books, nine in number, deals with the Divine Office:

1. Horologion (Book of Hours)
2. Oktoechos (Book of Eight Tones) also known as Parakletike (Book of Supplication) contains the variable parts of the daily offices throughout the week.
3. Triodion (Book of Three Odes), containing propers for Lent.
4. Pentekostarion (Book of the Five Days) contains propers for Eastertide and Pentecost.
5. Menaia (Book of the Months) contains propers for the fixed feasts throughout the year.
6. Eirmologion (Book of the Eirmoi) contains the text of anthems known as Eirmoi.
7. In addition, three books cover the Bible. The Evangelion (Book of the Gospels); Apostolos (Book of the Apostles), containing Acts and Epistles; Psalterion (Book of the Psalms), containing the Psalms and the Canticles.
8. Synaxarion (Book of the Assembly) or Menologion (Book of Remembrance) contains brief lives of saints.
9. Typicon (Book of Ordinances) contains rules and rubrics governing celebration of services throughout the year.

ANGLICAN CHURCH

Book of Common Prayer.

BAPTISTS

The use of liturgical books was condemned by Baptists as the invention of the man of sin. They rejected prescribed liturgies and the use of books of any kind in worship. However, the use of hymn books became common from the seventeenth century. Other service books may not be used at all because there is no prescribed liturgy and each Baptist church is autonomous. More recently, service books may be used by the clergy but not by the congregation. These books are compiled by private individuals, such as John Skoglund's *Minister's Worship Manual.* Baptists use the Baptist church hymnal for worship songs.

CHRISTIAN CHURCH (DISCIPLES OF CHRIST)

The authorized liturgical book is *Christian Worship: A Service Book,* largely the work of G. Edwin Osborn. Authorized hymnals include the first *Hymnal* published by Alexander Campbell in 1834 and *Hymns of the United Church,* 1924.

CONGREGATIONAL CHURCHES

Congregationalists use a variety of service manuals, including *Directory of Public Worship* (1644), John Hunter's *Devotional Services for Public Worship* (1882), W. E. Orchard's *Divine Service, The Book of Congregational Worship* (1920), *A Manual for Ministers* (1936), *A Book of Public Worship Compiled for the Use of Congregationalists* (1948), *Prayers and Services for Christian Festivals* (1951), *A Book of Services and Prayers* (1959), *A Book of Worship for Free Churches* (1948), *The Lord's Day Service* (1954), and *Services of Word and Sacrament* (1956). Hymnals include *Congregational Praise, Pilgrim Hymnal,* and *Hymnal Containing Complete Orders of Worship.*

LUTHERAN CHURCHES

The oldest Lutheran worship manuals are *Formula Missae* of 1523 and *Deutsche Messe* of 1526. The first American liturgy (in German) was adopted by the Ministerium of Pennsylvania in 1748, but an English version was approved in 1860. Since 1957 the *Service Book and Hymnal* is used for the Eucharist, mattins, vespers, baptism, confirmation, confession, burial, and matrimony.

METHODIST CHURCHES

In the United States, the first Methodist manual was the *Sunday Service with Other Occasional Services, 1784.* It underwent many revisions, most notably as the *Ritual.* The true liturgy of Methodism is found in its hymnal, and the principal hymnal is the *Methodist Hymnal,* issued in 1935. It was followed by the *Book of Worship for Church and Home* (1944, 1964). In England Methodists used *The Sunday Service, Order of Administration of the Sacraments, Book of Public Prayers and Services, Book of Offices,* and *Order for Morning Prayer* together with the *Methodist Hymn-Book.*

PENTECOSTAL CHURCHES

Pentecostal churches are experiential rather than liturgical, and liturgy is looked upon as quenching the free flow of the Holy Spirit. The emphasis is on the exercise of charismatic gifts. As a result, liturgical practices are looked down upon and therefore much impoverished.

PLYMOUTH BRETHREN

Brethren do not use liturgical books to any extent but use hymns extensively. Exclusive Brethren use *Hymns for the Little Flock,* 1856. Open Brethren use *The Believer's Hymn Book, Hymns of Light and Love, Hymns for Christian Worship Service, Christian Praise,* and *Hymns of Faith.*

REFORMED CHURCHES

Presbyterian churches variously use the *Book of Common Order,* the *Westminster Directory,* or the *Worship-Book.*

ARMENIAN CHURCH

The Armenian Church uses eight principal liturgical books:

1. Badarkamaduitz or Korhtadedr (The Book of Oblation)
2. Book of Ordinations
3. Djachotz or Tschaschotz (The Book of Noon), a lectionary
4. Donatsoitz (Indicator of Feasts), calendar similar to the Byzantine Typicon

5. Haysmavurk (This Very Day), containing abridged lives of saints
6. Jamarkik or Breviary
7. Mashdotz Ritual, containing text and rubrics for the administration of the sacraments and blessings
8. Sharagan or Terbroutiun (Book of Choir Boys), containing canticles for office hymns

COPTIC CHURCH

The Coptic Church has nine principal liturgical books:

1. Hulaki or Euchologion, containing three separate parts: Book of the Three Anaphoras of St. Basil, St. Gregory the Theologian, and St. Cyril; Book containing all the holy prayers including ordinations, blessing of religious habits, enthroning of bishops, and consecration of chrism, churches, altars, vessels, and vestments; Book of the Services and mysteries.
2. Diakonikon, exclusively for the use of deacons
3. Synaxar or Martyrology, containing lives of the saints
4. Difnari or Antiphonary, with two alternative hymns and chants for each saint's day
5. Kutmarus or Katameros, a lectionary
6. Pontifical or Book of Priestly Offices
7. Egbiyah or Horarium or Breviary
8. Psalmodia, containing odes or canticles from the Old Testament together with Theotokia or Office of Our Lady
9. Kitab al Pasca or Office of the Holy Week

ETHIOPIAN CHURCH

The Ethiopian Church has six principal liturgical books.

1. Sher'ata Keddase or Mashafa Keddase, a missal containing the text of many anaphoras
2. Mawase'et or Antiphonary
3. Sher'ata Gecawe, a Lectionary containing the Psalms and Gospels for vespers
4. Pontifical

5. Ritual
6. Mashafa Sa'atat, a Breviary

ASSYRIAN CHURCH

Of the numerous liturgical books in the Assyrian Church, the following 14 are the most important:

1. Taksa corresponding to the Byzantine Euchologion, containing the three anaphoras of Sts. Addai and Mari, Theodore of Mopsuestia, and Nestorius. It is bound with Taksa d'mada or baptismal rite and the Taksa d'syamida or ordination rite.
2. Shamashutha, a diaconal
3. Karyane, a lectionary. When it contains the Epistles, it is called Shliha and when it contains the Gospels, it is called Iwangaliyuna.
4. Turgama (Interpretation), a collection of verses sung in the form of hymns
5. Kashkul, choirbook containing various chants sung on weekdays
6. Gazza, containing various hymns, antiphons, and collects for those feasts that do not fall on Sundays
7. Warda, hymnbook dating from the twelfth century
8. Baootha d'Ninwaye or Nocturn of the Ninevites, a collection of hymns used during the Ninevite Fast
9. Hudra or Kudra (circle) containing variable chants for the office on Feasts of Our Lord and during the Ninevite Fast
10. Sunhadus, a Breviary containing text for vespers (ramcha), compline, midnight office (lilia), and the morning office (sapra)
11. Dauida or Psalter
12. Kthawa d'Burrakha (The Blessing), contains rites for weddings
13. Taksa d'Kahnutha, used for burial of the clergy; Taksa d'Anaida, used for burial of the laity
14. Taksa d'Husaya (Rites of Mercy), provides service for the reconciliation of penitents
15. Kdam Wadathar (Before and After), contains extracts from the Psalter
16. Abu-Halim, contains concluding prayers for Sunday nights

JACOBITE CHURCH

The Jacobites or West Syrians have six principal liturgical books:

1. Annafura (Kthobo Dkhourobo), the Missal, contains 64 anaphoras; the one most used is St. James
2. K'tobo d'Teshmeshto, the diaconal
3. Ewanghelion or the Book of Gospels
4. Egroto Dashlihe (Epistle of the Apostles), contains other lessons used in the Liturgy
5. Penquitho, contains the office of vespers, mattins, and terce
6. Shehimo, office book for ordinary commemorations

Most Important Books and Authors in Christian Literature

Books	Authors
Address to the Greeks	Tatian
Adornment of the Spiritual Marriage, The	John of Ruysbroeck
Against Celsus	Origen
Against Eunomius	St. Basil
Against Heresies	St. Irenaeus
Agape and Eros	Anders Nygren
Anxiety and the Christian	Hans Urs von Balthasar
Apologia Pro Vita Sua	John Henry Cardinal Newman
Apology for the True Christian Divinity, An	Robert Barclay
Apology	Athenagoras
Apology, The	Aristides
Apology, The	Tertullian
Apostolic Tradition, The	St. Hippolytus
Art and Scholasticism	Jacques Maritain
Attack on Christendom	Soren Kierkegaard
Ascent of Mount Carmel	St. John of the Cross
Ascent to Truth	Thomas Merton
Ascetic Life, The	St. Maximus the Confessor
Autobiography Alacoque	St. Margaret Mary
Autobiography of a Hunted Priest	John Gerard
Babylonian Captivity of the Church	Martin Luther
Basic Christian Ethics	Paul Ramsey
Basic Christianity	John Stott
Basic Verities	Charles Peguy
Bazaar of Heraclides, The	Nestorius
Benjamin Minor and Benjamin Major	Richard of St. Victor
Bloody Tenent of Persecution, The	Roger Williams
Bondage of the Will, The	Martin Luther
Book of Sentences	Peter Lombard
Call of All Nations, The	St. Prosper of Aquitaine
Catechetical Lectures, The	St. Cyril of Jerusalem
Catholicism	Henry de Lubac
Christ and Culture	H. Richard Niebuhr
Christ and Society	Charles Gore

Books	Authors
Christ and Time	Oscar Cullmann
Christ of Faith	Karl Adam
Christian Directory, A	Richard Baxter
Christian Discourses	Soren Kierkegaard
Christian Doctrine	J. S. Whale
Christian Doctrine of Justification and Reconciliation	Albrecht Ritschl
Christian Dogmatics	Hans Lassen Martensen
Christian Faith, The	Friedrich Schleiermacher
Christian Message in a Non-Christian World	Hendrik Kraemer
Christian Mysticism	William Ralph Inge
Christian Nurture	Horace Bushnell
Christian Pastor	Washington Gladden
Christian System, The	Alexander Campbell
Christian Understanding of God, The	Nels Ferre
Christianity and Liberalism	John Gresham Machen
Christianity and Paradox	Ronald W. Hepburn
Christus Victor	Gustaf Aulen
Church Dogmatics	Karl Barth
Church of the Word Incarnate	Charles Journet
City of God, The	St. Augustine
Cloud of Unknowing, The	Unknown
Come, Let Us Worship	Godfrey Diekmann
Commentary on the Apostle's Creed	Rufinus of Aquileia
Commentary on Galatians	Ragnar Bring
Commentary on the Summa Theologica	St. Cajetan
Commonitory, The	St. Vincent of Lerins
Confessions	St. Augustine
Cost of Discipleship, The	Dietrich Bonhoeffer
Cur Deus Homo	St. Anselm of Canterbury
Dark Night of the Soul, The	St. John of the Cross
De Corpore Christi	William of Ockham
De Doctrina Christiana	St. Augustine
De Regno Christi	Martin Bucer
De Religione Laici	Edward Herbert, First Lord of Cherbury
De Trinitate	St. Augustine
De Veritate	St. Thomas Aquinas
De Viris Illustribus	St. Jerome
Decades, The	Johann Heinrich Bullinger
Declaration of Faith, A	St. Gregory Thaumaturges
Declaration of Sentiments, The	Jacob Arminius
Defense of the True and Catholic Doctrine of the Sacrament, A	Thomas Cranmer
Degrees of Knowledge	Jacques Maritain
Destiny of Man	Nikolai Berdyaev
Devotions Upon Emergent Occasions	John Donne
Dialogue Between the Soul and the Body, The	St. Catherine of Genoa

Books	Authors
Dialogue of Catherine of Siena	St. Catherine of Siena
Dialogue of Comfort Against Tribulation, A	St. Thomas More
Dialogues	St. Gregory the Great
Dialogues, The	Theodoret of Cyrus
Dialogues of Sulpicius Severus	Sulpicius Severus
Diary of David Brainerd	David Brainerd
Didache, or The Teaching of the Twelve Apostles	Unknown
Didactica Magna	Johannes Amos Comenius
Discourse Concerning the Holy Spirit	John Owen
Discourse on the Priesthood	St. John Chrysostom
Discourses upon the Existence and Attributes of God	Stephen Charnock
Divine Comedy, The	Dante Alighieri
Divine Imperative, The	Emil Brunner
Divine Institutes, The	Lucius Caecilius Firmianus Lactantius
Divine Milieu, The	Pierre Teilhard de Chardin
Divine Names, The	Dionysius the Pseudo-Areopagite
Divine Relativity, The	Charles Hartshorne
Doctor Dubitantium	Jeremy Taylor
Dogmatics	Emil Brunner
Ecce Homo	Sir John Robert Seeley
Ecclesiastical History	Eusebius of Caesarea
Ecclesiastical History of the English Nation	St. Bede
Ecclesiastical Ordinances	John Calvin
Edmund Campion	Evelyn Waugh
Eirenicon, An	Edward B. Pusey
Enchiridion Militis Christiani	Desiderius Erasmus
Enchiridion on Faith, Hope and Love, The	St. Augustine
Epistle of Barnabas, The	Unknown
Epistle to Diognetus, The	Unknown
Epistle to the Philippians	St. Polycarp of Smyrna
Epistle to the Romans, The	Karl Barth
Epistles of St. Ignatius of Antioch, The	St Ignatius
Essay on the Development of Christian Doctrine, An	John Henry Newman
Everlasting Man, The	Gilbert Keith Chesterton
Faith and History	Reinhold Niebuhr
Faith and Knowledge	John Hick
Faith, Hope and Charity	St. Augustine
Faith of the Christian Church, The	Gustaf Aulen
First Apology and The Second Apology, The	Justin Martyr
First Epistle of Clement to the Corinthians, The	St. Clement of Rome
Five Theological Orations	St. Gregory Nazianzus
Following of Christ, The	Gerard de Groote
Form of the Personal, The	John Macmurray
Foundation of Christian Doctrine	Menno Simons
Fountain of Wisdom, The	St. John of Damascus

Books	Authors
Freedom and the Spirit	Nikolai Berdyaev
Freedom of the Christian	Martin Luther
Freedom of the Will	Jonathan Edwards
God in Christ	Horace Bushnell
God Was in Christ	Donald M. Baillie
God's Grace and Man's Hope	Daniel Day Williams
Gospel and the Church, The	Alfred Loisy
Grace Abounding to the Chief of Sinners	John Bunyan
Grammar of Assent	John Henry Newman
Grand Inquisitor	Fyodor Dostoevsky
Great Catechism, The	St. Gregory of Nyssa
Great Christian Doctrine of Original Sin Defended, The	Jonathan Edwards
Hind and the Panther, The	John Dryden
History of the Councils	Karl Joseph von Hefele
History of the Development of the Doctrine	
of the Person of Christ	Isaac August Dorner
History of the Reformation in Scotland	John Knox
Homilies on the Statues	St. John Chrysostom
Homo Viator	Gabriel Marcel
Hound of Heaven The	Francis Thompson
Hymns of Ephraem the Syrian, The	Ephraem the Syrian
Hymns of St. Ambrose	St. Ambrose
Idea of a Christian Society, The	T. S. Eliot
Idea of Christ in the Gospels, The	George Santayana
Idea of the Holy, The	Rudolf Otto
Imitation of Christ, The	Thomas à Kempis
In His Steps	Charles M. Sheldon
Incarnation of the Word of God, The	St. Athanasius
Institutes of the Christian Religion, The	John Calvin
Institutes of the Monastic Life, The	John Cassian
Instructions in Favor of Christian Discipline	Commodianus
Interior Castle, The	St. Teresa of Avila
Introduction to the Devout Life	St. Francis of Sales
Invitation to Pilgrimage	John Baillie
Jerusalem Delivered	Torquato Tasso
Jesus the Lord	Karl Heim
John Ploughman's Talks	Charles Haddon Spurgeon
Journal of Francis Asbury, The	Francis Asbury
Journal of George Fox, The	George Fox
Journal of John Wesley, The	John Wesley
Journal of John Woolman, The	John Woolman
Journals of George Whitefield	George Whitefield
Journals of Henry Melchior Muhlenberg, The	Henry Melchior Muhlenberg
Journey of the Mind to God, The	St. Bonaventura

Books	Authors
Keys of the Kingdom of Heaven, The	John Cotton
Kingdom of Christ, The	Frederick Denison Maurice
Know Thyself	Peter Abelard
Ladder of Divine Ascent, The	St. John Climacus
Ladder of Perfection	Walter Hilton
Lectures on Calvinism	Abraham Kuyper
Lectures on Godmanhood	Vladimir Solovyev
Lectures on Preaching	Phillips Brooks
Lectures on Revivals of Religion	Charles Grandison Finney
Letters	St. Basil
Letters	St. Bernard of Clairvaux
Letters	St. Jerome
Letters and Extant Fragments of the Works of Dionysius	Dionysius the Great
Life of Antony, The	St. Athanasius
Life of Columba	Adomnan
Life of St. Martin, The	Sulpicius Severus
Life of St. Teresa of Avila, The	Teresa of Avila
Little Book of Eternal Wisdom	Blessed Henry Suso
Little Flowers of St. Francis, The	Unknown
Living God, The	Nathan Soderblom
Living Word, The	Gustaf Wingren
Loci Communes Rerum Theologicarum	Philipp Melanchthon
Longer Rules and The Shorter Rules, The	St. Basil of Caesarea
Lord, The	Romano Guardini
Lord's Prayer, The	St. Gregory of Nyssa
Love of God, The	St. Francis de Sales
Love of Learning and the Desire for God	Jean Leclerq
Love, the Law of Life	Toyohiko Kagawa
Magdeburg Centuries, The	Matthias Flacius
Magnalia Christi Americana	Cotton Mather
Meaning of God in Human Experience, The	William Ernest Hocking
Meaning of Revelation, The	H. Richard Niebuhr
Meditations on the Life of Christ	Unknown Franciscan monk and St. Bonaventura
Martyrdom of St. Polycarp	St. Polycarp
Mere Christianity	C. S. Lewis
Mind's Road to God, The	St. Bonaventura
Monologion	St. Anselm of Canterbury
Much Abused Letter, A	George Tyrrell
Mystical Element of Religion, The	Baron Friedrich von Hugel
Nature and Destiny of Man, The	Reinhold Niebuhr
Nature, Man and God	William Temple
Nature of Faith, The	Gerhard Ebeling
Nature of the Atonement, The	John McLeod Campbell
Necessity of Reforming the Church	John Calvin

Books	Authors
Octavius	Minucius Felix
Of Learned Ignorance	Nicholas of Cusa
On Ecclesiastical Unity	John Gerson
On First Principles	Origen
On the Christian Faith	St. Ambrose
On the Divine Names	Dionysius the Pseudo-Areopagite
On the Duties of the Clergy	St. Ambrose
On the Holy Trinity	Anicius Manlius Severinus Boethius
On the Resurrection of the Dead	Athenagoras
On the Steps of Humility and Pride	St. Bernard
On the Theology of Death	Karl Rahner
On the Trinity	St. Augustine
On the Trinity	St. Hilary of Poitiers
On the Unity of the Catholic Church	St. Cyprian of Carthage
Ordinatio: Oxford Commentary on the Sentences of Peter Lombard	Johannes Duns Scotus
Orthodoxy	G. K. Chesterton
Our Calling	Einar Billing
Our Experience of God	H. D. Lewis
Panarion	St. Epiphanus of Salamis
Parables of the Kingdom	Charles Harold Dodd
Paradise Lost	John Milton
Pastoral Care	St. Gregory I
Path to Rome	Hilaire Belloc
Pensees	Blaise Pascal
Person and Place of Jesus Christ, The	Peter Taylor Forsyth
Phenomenon of Man	Teilhard de Chardin
Pilgrim's Progress	John Bunyan
Plain Account of Christian Perfection	John Wesley
Plan of Salvation, The	Benjamin Warfield
Poems of Gerard Manley Hopkins	Gerard Manley Hopkins
Practice of the Presence of God, The	Brother Lawrence
Prayer	George Arthur Buttrick
Preces Privatae	Lancelot Andrewes
Priest to the Temple, A	George Herbert
Prologion	St. Anselm of Canterbury
Quest of the Historical Jesus, The	Albert Schweitzer
Reality of Faith, The	Friedrich Gogarten
Refutation of All Heresies	St. Hippolytus
Religio Medici	Sir Thomas Browne
Retracing the Arts to Theology	St. Bonaventura
Revelations of Divine Love, The	Lady Julian of Norwich
Rule and Exercise of Holy Living and Holy Dying, The	Jeremy Taylor
Rule of St. Benedict, The	St. Benedict of Nursia

Books	Authors
St. Francis of Assisi	G. K. Chesterton
Saints' Everlasting Rest	Richard Baxter
Scale of Perfection	Walter Hilton
Screwtape Letters	C. S. Lewis
Selected Letters	Baron Friedrich von Hugel
Selected Writings on the Spiritual Life	Saint Peter Damian
Serious Call to a Devout and Holy Life	William Law
Sermons and Treatises	Johannes Eckhart
Seven Epistles of Ignatius, The	St. Ignatius of Antioch
Seven Storey Mountain, The	Thomas Merton
Shepherd, The	Hermas
Short and Clear Exposition of the Christian Faith	Ulrich Zwingli
Sic et Non	Peter Abelard
Soliloquy on the Earnest Money of the Soul	St. Hugh of St. Victor
Spiritual Espousals	Blessed John Ruysbroeck
Spiritual Exercises	Ignatius of Loyola
Steps of Humility, The	St. Bernard
Story of a Soul	St. Therese of Lisieux
Stromata, or Miscellanies, The	St. Clement of Alexandria
Summa Contra Gentiles	St. Thomas Aquinas
Summa Theologiae	St. Thomas Aquinas
Systematic Theology	Charles Hodge
Systematic Theology	Augustus Hopkins Strong
Systematic Theology	Paul Tillich
Theologia Germanica	Unknown
Theology of the New Testament	Rudolf Bultmann
Thophilus to Autolycus	Theophilus of Antioch
Tome	St. Leo
Training in Christianity	Soren Kierkegaard
Treatise of Reformation Without Tarrying for Any	Robert Browne
Treatise on Christian Liberty	Martin Luther
Treatise on the Church	John Hus
Treatise on the Four Gospels	Joachim of Fiore
Treatise on the Holy Spirit	St. Basil
Trialogus	John Wycliffe
True Christianity	Johann Arndt
True Humanism	Jacques Maritain
Unity of Church	Cyprian
Vision of God: The Christian Doctrine of the Summum Bonum, The	Kenneth E. Kirk
Way of Perfection, The	St. Teresa of Avila
Way to Christ	Jakob Boehme
Wisdom of God, The	Sergei Bulgakov
World of Silence	Max Picard
Worship	Evelyn Underhill

Major Theologians

Name	Nationality	Major Works	Comments
Abelard, Peter (1079–1142)	French	*Christian Theology*	
Adam, Karl (1876–1966)	German	*The Spirit of Catholicism*	
Adam of Marsh (d. 1258)	English	*Commentaries on Canticles and Hebrews*	Doctor Illustris
Alain of Lille (c. 1128–1203)	French	*Regulae Caelestis Iuris*	Universal Doctor
Albertus Magnus (1193–1280)	German	*Summa de Creaturis*	
Alexander of Hales (c. 1186–1245)	English	*Commentary on Sentences*	
Althaus, Paul (1886–1966)	German	*Christian Truth*	
Altizer, Thomas Jonathan Jackson (1927–)	American	*The Gospel of Christian Atheism*	
Alves, Rubem Azevedo (1933–)	Brazilian	*Theology of Human Hope*	Liberation
Ames, William (1576–1633)	English	*Medulla Theologiae*	
Anselm (1033–1109)	English	*Monologion*	
Antoninus (1389–1459)	Italian	*Summa Theologica Moralis*	
Apollinarius of Laodicea (c. 310–90)	Greek	Most of his works are now lost	Heretic
Arminius, Jakobus (1560–1609)	Dutch	*Lectures on Predestination*	Founder of Arminianism
Arnauld, Antoine (1612–1694)	French	*On Frequent Communion*	
Arndt, Johann (1555–1621)	German	*Four Books on True Christianity*	
Arnold, Gottfried (1666–1714)	German	*Unparteiische Kirchen-und Ketzer-Historie*	
Athanasius (c. 296–377)	Egyptian	*De Incarnatione*	
Augustine (354–430)	North African	*The City of God, Confessions*	
Aulen, Gustaf Emmanuel Hildebrand (1879–1978)	Swedish	*Faith of the Christian Church*	
Baillie, Donald McPherson (1887–1954)	Scottish	*God Was in Christ*	
Baillie, John (1886–1960)	Scottish	*Our Knowledge of God, and the Life Everlasting*	
Balthasar, Hans Urs von (1905–1988)	Swiss	*The Glory of the Lord* (7 vols.); *Theologik*	
Barclay, Robert (1648–1690)	Scottish	*Apology for the True Christian Divinity*	

Barth, Karl (1886–1968)	Swiss	*Church Dogmatics*	
Basil, St. (330–379)	Greek	*On the Holy Spirit*	
Baur, Ferdinand Christian (1792–1860)	German	*Lectures on the History of Christian Dogma*	
Bavinck, Herman (1854–1921)	Dutch	*Reformed Dogmatics*	
Beck, Johann Tobias (1804–1878)	German	*Lectures*	
Berdyaev, Nicolai Aleksandrovich (1874–1948)	Russian	*Destiny of Man*	
Berengar (c. 999–1088)	French	*De Sacra Coena*	
Berkhof, Hendrikus (1914–)	Dutch	*Christian Faith*	
Berkhof, Louis (1873–1957)	American	*Systematic Theology*	
Berkouwer, Gerrit Cornelis (1903–1998)	Dutch	*Studies in Dogmatics*	
Berulle, Pierre de (1575–1629)	French	*Discours de l'etat et des Grandeurs de Jesus; Vie de Jesus*	
Beyschlag, Willibald (1823–1900)	German	*Neutestamentliche Theologie*	
Boesak, Allan (1946–)	South African	*The Finger of God*	
Boff, Clodovis (1944–)	Brazilian	*Theology and Praxis*	
Boff, Leonardo (1938–)	Brazilian	*Church: Charism and Power*	
Bonaventura (1221–1274)	Italian	*Life of St. Francis*	
Bonhoeffer, Dietrich (1906–1945)	German	*The Cost of Discipleship*	
Bonino, Jose Miguez (1924–)	Argentine	*Revolutionary Theology Comes of Age*	
Boston, Thomas (1676–1732)	Scottish	*Human Nature in Its Fourfold Estate*	
Bradwardine, Thomas (1290–1349)	English		
Bruce, Alexander Balmain (1831–1899)	Scottish	*The Humiliation of Christ*	
Brunner, Heinrich Emil (1889–1966)	Swiss	*The Mediator; The Divine Imperative*	
Bulgakov, Sergei N. (1871–1944)	Russian	*The Orthodox Church*	
Bultmann, Rudolf (1884–1976)	German	*Theology of the New Testament*	
Bushnell, Horace (1802–1876)	American	*Christian Nurture; God in Christ*	
Calvin, John (1509–1564)	French	*Institutes of the Christian Religion*	Founder of Calvinism
Campbell, John McLeod (1800–1872)	Scottish	*The Nature of the Atonement*	
Campbell, Reginald John (1867–1956)	English	*The New Theology*	
Canisius, Peter (1521–1597)	German	*Summa Doctrinae Christianae*	
Carnell, Edward John (1919–1967)	American	*An Introduction to Christian Apologetics*	
Carol, Juniper (1911–1990)	American	*Why Jesus Christ?; De Corredemptione B.V.M.*	
Carter, Charles W. (1905–)	American	*A Contemporary Wesleyan Theology*	
Cassander, Georg (1513–1566)	Belgian	*On the Duty of Pious Men Who Love Public Tranquillity in Dissent over Religion*	
Catharinus, Ambrosius (1484–1553)	Italian	*Opuscula Magna*	
Chao, Tzu-ch'en (1888–1979)	Chinese	*An Interpretation of Christianity; A Life of Jesus*	
Chemnitz, Martin (1522–1586)	German	*De Duabus Naturis in Christo*	

Childs, Brevard Springs (1923–)	American	*Old Testament Theology in Canonical Context*
Clarke, William Newton (1841–1912)	American	*Outline of Christian Theology*
Cobb, John Boswell, Jr. (1925–)	American	*Living Options in Protestant Theology*
Cocceius, Johannes (1603–1669)	German	*Summa Doctrinae de Foedere et Testamento Dei*
Comblin, Jose (1923–)	Belgian	*The Holy Spirit and Liberation*
Cone, James Hal (1938–)	American	*A Black Theology of Liberation*
Courayer, Pierre Francois le (1661–1776)	French	*Dissertation sur la Validite des Ordinations des Anglais*
Cox, Harvey Gallagher (1929–)	American	*The Secular City*
Cremer, August Hermann (1834–1903)	German	*Die paulinische Rechtfertigungslehre*
Cullmann, Oscar (1902–)	German	*Christ and Time; Salvation in History; The Christology of the New Testament*
Cyril of Alexandria (c. 375–444)	Egyptian	*That Christ Is One, Dialogues on the Holy and Consubstantial Trinity*
Daille, Jean (1609–1685)	French	*Traite de l'employ des Saints Peres*
D'Ailly, Pierre (1350–1420)	French	*Tractus super Reformatione Ecclesia*
Daly, Mary	American	*Beyond God the Father*
De Lubac, Henri (1896–)	French	*Catholicism; The Supernatural; Sources of Revelation*
De Maistre, Joseph (1753–1821)	French	*On the Pope*
Denney, James (1856–1917)	Scottish	*The Death of Christ*
Didymus the Blind (c. 313–398)	Egyptian	*On the Holy Spirit, On the Trinity*
Dillistone, Frederick William (1903–)	English	*The Christian Understanding of the Atonement*
Dodd, Charles Harold (1884–1973)	English	*The Apostolic Preaching and Its Development*
Dorner, Isaac August (1809–1884)	German	*Geschichte der Protestantischen Theologie*
Dunn, James D. G. (1939–)	American	*Christology in the Making; Baptism in the Holy Spirit*
Duns Scotus, John (c. 1266–1308)	Scottish	*Treatise on the First Principle*
Dussel, Enrique (1934–)	Argentine	*Ethics and the Theology of Liberation*
Ebeling, Gerhard (1912–)	German	*Word and Faith, The Study of Theology*
Eck, Johannes (1486–1543)	German	*De Primatu Petri adv. Ludderum Libri III, Enchiridion*
Edwards, Jonathan (1703–1758)	American	*Freedom of the Will*
Ellul, Jacques (1912–)	French	*The Technological Society*
Erigena, John Scotus (810–877)	Irish	*On Predestination*
Erskine, Thomas (1788–1870)	Scottish	*Internal Evidence for the Truth of Revealed Religion*
Farmer, Herbert Henry (1892–1981)	English	*The World and Religion*
Fiorenza, Elisabeth Schussler (1938–)	American	*In Memory of Her; Bread, Not Stone Feminist*
Forsyth, Peter Taylor (1848–1921)	Scottish	*The Person and Place of Christ*

Fuchs, Ernst (1903–1983)	German	*Studies of the Historical Jesus*	
Galilea, Segundo (1928–)	Chilean	*Following Jesus; The Way of Living Faith Liberation*	
Galot, Jean (1919–)	Belgian	*La Redemption; La Coeur du Christ; La Personne du Christ*	
Gerson, Jean (1363–1423)	French	*The Mountain of Contemplation*	
Gilkey, Langdon (1919–)	American	*The Maker of Heaven and Earth*	
Gogarten, Friedrich (1887–1967)	German	*Christ and Crisis; Demythologizing and History*	
Gollwitzer, Helmut (1908–)	German	*The Existence of God as Confessed by Faith*	
Gottschalk (c. 803–869)	German	*The Ecologue of Theodolus*	
Gregory of Nazianzus (330–389)	Greek	*Theological Addresses*	
Gregory of Nyssa (c. 330–395)	Greek	*Catechetical Orations*	
Gregory Palamas (c. 1269–1359)	Greek	*Triads in Defense of the Holy Hesychasts*	
Gutierrez Merino, Gustavo (1928–)	Peruvian	*Theology of Liberation*	
Hallesby, Ole Krisstian (1879–1961)	Norwegian	*Prayer; Why I Am a Christian*	
Hamann, Johann Georg (1730–1788)	German	*Golgotha and Schlebimini*	
Harnack, Adolf von (1851–1930)	German	*What Is Christianity? History of Dogma*	
Haroutinian, Joseph (1904–1968)	American	*God with Us*	
Harvey, Van Austin (1926–)	American	*The Historian and the Believer*	
Headlam, Arthur Cayley (1862–1947)	English	*Romans*	
Heiler, Friedrich (1892–1967)	German	*Prayer*	
Heim, Karl (1874–1958)	German	*God Transcendent*	
Hendry, George Stuart (1904–)	American	*The Gospel of the Incarnation, The Holy Spirit in Christian Theology*	
Henry, Carl F. H. (1913–)	American	*The Uneasy Conscience of Modern Fundamentalism*	
Hermann, Johann William (1846–1922)	German	*The Communion of the Christian with God*	
Hilary of Poitiers (c. 315–367)	French	*On the Trinity*	
Hodge, Charles (1797–1878)	American	*Systematic Theology* (3 vols)	Calvinist
Hodgson, Leonard (1889–1969)	English	*For Faith and Freedom*	
Hoekema, Anthony Andrew (1913–1988)	Dutch	*Saved by Grace; The Bible and the Future*	
Hofmann, Johann Christian Konrad von (1830–1877)	German	*Prophecy and Fulfillment*	
Holland, Henry Scott (1847–1918)	English	*Logic and Life; Creed and Character; God's City*	
Hromadka, Josef Luki (1889–1969)	Czech	*Thoughts of a Czech Pastor*	
Hugh of St. Victor (died 1142)	French	*De Sacramentis Christianae Fidei*	
Jacobs, Henry Eyster (1844–1932)	American	*A Summary of the Christian Faith; The Elements of Religion*	
Jansen, Cornelius Otto (1585–1638)	French	*Augustinus*	Founder of Jansenism

Jenkins, David Edward (1925–)	English	*The Glory of Man*	
John of Damascus (675–749)	Greek	*Feast of Wisdom*	Last of the Greek Church Fathers
Jungel, Eberhard (1932–)	German	*God the Mystery of the World*	
Kaftan, Julius Wilhelm Martin (1848–1926)	German	*The Essence of Christian Religion*	
Kachler, Martin (1835–1912)	German	*The So-Called Historical Jesus and the Historic, Biblical Christ*	
Kirk, Kenneth Escott (1866–1954)	English	*The Vision of God*	
Knox, John (1900–)	American	*The Death of Christ*	
Koyama, Kosuke (1929–)	Japanese	*Waterbuffalo Theology*	
Krauth, Charles Porterfield (1823–1883)	American	*The Conservative Reformation and Its Theology*	
Kuenen, Abraham (1828–1891)	Dutch	*Historisch-Kritisch Onderzoek* (3 vols)	
Kung, Hans (1928–)	Swiss	*The Structures of the Church; Infallible? An Inquiry*	
Kuyper, Abraham (1837–1920)	Dutch	*Calvinism*	
Lampe, Geoffrey William Hugo (1912–1980)	English	*God as Spirit*	
Lanfranc (c. 1010–1089)	Italian	*On the Body and Blood of the Lord*	
Lecerf, Auguste (1872–1943)	French	*Introduction to Reformed Dogmatics*	
Lehmann, Paul Louis (1904–)	American	*Ethics in a Christian Context*	
Leontius of Byzantium (480–543)	Greek	*Three Books Against the Nestorians and Eutychians*	
Lindbeck, George Arthur (1923–)	American	*The Nature of Doctrine*	
Lipsius, Richard Adelbert (1830–1892)	German	*Die Apokryphen Apostelgeschichten und Apostellegenden* (4 vols.)	
Lonergan, Bernard Joseph Francis (1904–1985)	Canadian	*Method in Theology*	Roman Catholic
Lossky, Vladimir (1903–1958)	Russian	*Essay on the Mystical Theology of the Eastern Church*	
Machen, John Gresham (1881–1937)	American	*Christianity and Liberalism*	
Mackintosh, Hugh Ross (1870–1936)	Scottish	*Types of Modern Theology*	
Macquarrie, John (1919–)	Scottish	*Jesus Christ in Modern Thought; Principles of Modern Theology*	
Mansel, Henry Longueville (1820–1871)	English	*The Limits of Religious Thought Examined*	
Marmion, Columba (1858–1923)	Irish	*Christ, the Life of the Soul; Christ in His Mysteries*	
Marty, Martin Emil (1928–)	American	*The New Shape of American Religion*	

Matthews, Shailer (1863–1941)	American	*The Social Teaching of Jesus*	Liberal
Maurice, John Frederick Denison (1805–1872)	English	*The Kingdom of Christ*	
Maximus the Confessor (580–662)	Greek	*Quaestiones ad Thalassium*	
Mbiti, John S. (1931–)	Kenyan	*Bible and Theology in African Christianity*	
McClain, Alva J. (1888–1968)	American	*Bible Truths; The Greatness of the Kingdom*	
McFague, Sallie (1933–)	American	*Speaking in Parables: A Study of Metaphor and Theology*	
McIntosh, Douglas Clyde (1877–1948)	Canadian	*The Problem of Religious Knowledge*	
Meland, Bernard Eugene (1899–)	American	*The Realities of Faith*	
Melville, Andrew (1545–1622)	Scottish	*Commentary on Romans*	
Miguez, Bonino Jose (1924–)	Argentine	*Doing Theology in a Revolutionary Situation*	
Miranda, Jose Porfirio (1924–)	Mexican	*Marx and the Bible*	Liberation
Moberly, Robert Campbell (1845–1903)	English	*Ministerial Priesthood*	
Molina, Luis de (1536–1600)	Spanish	*The Concord of Free Will with the Gift of Grace*	
Moltmann, Jurgen (1926–)	German	*Theology of Hope; The Crucified God; Church in the Power of the Spirit*	
Murray, John (1898–1975)	Scottish	*Commentary on Epistle to the Romans*	
Neibuhr, Reinhold (1892–1971)	American	*The Nature and Destiny of Man*	
Newman, John Henry (1801–1890)	English	*Essay on the Development of Christian Doctrine*	
Nicole, Pierre (1625–1695)	French	*Logique de Port Royal; La Perpetuite de la foi de l'Eglise catholique Touchant la Eucariste*	
Niebuhr, Helmut Richard (1894–1962)	American	*The Meaning of Revelation; Christ and Culture*	
Nunez, Emilio Antonio (1923–)	El Salvadoran	*Liberation Theology*	
Nygren, Anders (1890–1978)	Swedish	*Agape and Eros*	
Ogden, Schubert Miles (1928–)	American	*The Reality of God*	
Oman, John Wood (1860–1939)	Scottish	*The Natural and the Supernatural*	
Origen (185–254)	Egyptian	*Hexapla; De Principiis*	
Orr, James (1844–1913)	Scottish	*The Christian View of God and the World*	
Otto, Rudolf (1869–1937)	German	*The Idea of the Holy*	
Packer, James Innell (1926–)	English	*Knowing God; Rediscovering Holiness; Fundamentalism and the Word of God*	
Padilla, Carlos Rene (1932–)	Colombian	*Mission Between the Times*	
Pannenberg, Walter (1928–)	German	*Revelation and History; Jesus—God and Man*	
Paschasius, Radbertus (785–860)	French	*On the Body and Blood of Christ*	
Pelagius (died c. 410)	English	*On Nature; Letter to Demetrius*	Founder of Pelagianism
Peter Lombard (c. 1095–1169)	Italian	*Sentences*	
Pfleiderer, Otto (1839–1908)	German	*Paulinism; The Development of Theology since Kant*	

Philaret, Drozdov (1782–1867)	Russian	*Catechism*	
Prosper of Aquitaine (390–463)	French	*Pro Augustino Responsiones; Capitula Caelestiana*	
Pusey, Edward Bouverie (1800–1882)	English	*Scriptural Views of Holy Baptism*	
Rabanus, Maurus (776–856)	German		
Rahner, Karl (1904–1984)	German	*The Foundations of Christian Faith*	
Ramm, Bernard (1916–1992)	American	*An Evangelical Christology*	
Ratramnus (ninth century)	French	*De Anima; De Nativitate Christi*	
Rhee, Jong-Sung (1922–)	Korean	*Systematic Theology*	
Richardson, Alan (1905–1975)	English	*An Introduction to the Theology of the New Testament*	
Ritschl, Albrecht Benjamin (1822–1889)	German	*The Christian Doctrine of Reconciliation and Justification* (3 vols.)	
Ruether, Rosemary Radford (1936–)	American	*Faith and Fratricide; Sexism and Gold-Talk Feminist*	
Rutherford, Samuel (c. 1600–1691)	English	*Lex Rex; The Divine Right of Church Government and Excommunication*	
Sabatier, Louis Auguste (1839–1901)	French	*The Religion of Authority and the Religion of Spirit*	
Sabatier, Paul (1859–1928)	French	*Life of St. Francis*	Calvinist
Schaeffer, Francis (1912–1984)	American	*The God Who Is There; How Shall We Then Live?*	
Schebeen, Matthias Joseph (1835–1888)	German	*Dogmatics; The Mysteries of Christianity*	
Schillebeeckx, Edward Cornelis Florentius Alfons (1914–)		*Jesus; Christ the Sacrament*	
Schlatter, Adolf (1852–1939)	Swiss	*The Church in the New Testament Period*	
Schleiermacher, Friedrich Daniel Ernst (1768–1834)	German	*The Christian Faith*	
Schmemann, Alexander (1921–1983)	Russian	*Introduction to Liturgical Theology*	
Schmucker, Samuel Simon (1799–1873)	American	*Elements of Popular Theology*	
Schweitzer, Albert (1875–1965)	German	*The Mysticism of Paul the Apostle*	
Segundo, Juan Luis (1925)	Uruguayan	*Jesus of Nazareth: Yesterday and Today* (5 vols.)	
Severus of Antioch (c460–538)	Syrian	*Philalethes*	
Sobrino, Jon (1938–)	Spanish	*Christology at the Crossroads*	
Soderblom, Nathan (1866–1931)	Swedish	*The Living God; The Religion of Luther*	
Solle, Dorothee (1929–)	German	*Thinking About God*	
Solovyov, Vladimir Sergyevich (1853–1900)	Russian	*Russia and the Universal Church*	
Song, Choan-Seng (1929–)	Taiwanese	*Third-Eye Theology; The Compassionate God*	
Strauss, David Friedrich			

(1808–1874)	German	*The Life of Jesus Critically Examined*
Strong, Josiah (1847–1916)	American	*Our Country*
Suarez, Francisco (1548–1617)	Spanish	*De Mysteriis Vitae Christii; Varia Opuscula Theologica;* *De Vera Intelligentia Auxulii Efficacis*
Taylor, Nathaniel William (1786–1858)	American	*Lectures on the Moral Government of God*
Teilhard de Chardin (1881–1955)	French	*Phenomenon of Man*
Tertullian (160–220)	North African	*De Spectaculis; De Corona Militis; De Paentitentia*
Theodore of Mopsuestia (350–427)	Syrian	*Commentary on the Minor Prophets*
Theodoret of Cyrrhus (393–466)	Syrian	*Compendium of Heretical Fables*
Thielicke, Helmut (1908–1985)	German	*The Evangelical Faith* (3 vols)
Thiessen, Henry Clarence (1883–1947)	American	*Introduction to the New Testament*
Tholuck, Friedrich August Gottreau (1799–1877)	German	*Doctrine of Sin and the Reconciler*
Thomas Aquinas (1225–1274)	Italian	*Summa Theologica;* *Summa Contra Gentiles*
Thurneysen, Eduard (1888–1974)	Swiss	*Revolutionary Theology in the Making; Das Wort Gottes und die Kirche*
Tillich, Paul Johannes (1886–1965)	German	*Systematic Theology* (3 vols.)
Torrance, Thomas Forsyth (1913–)	Scottish	*Theological Science*
Tracy, David (1939–)	American	*Blessed Rage for Order; The Analogical Imagination*
Troeltsch, Ernst (1865–1923)	German	*The Absoluteness of Christianity*
Tyrrell, George (1861–1909)	Irish	*Christianity at the Crossroads*
Vahanian, Gabriel (1927–)	Armenian	*The Death of God: The Culture of Our Post-Christian Era*
Van Dusen, Henry Pitney (1897–1975)	American	*One Great Ground of Hope*
Van Til, Cornelius (1895–1987)	Dutch	*The Defense of the Faith; A Christian Theory of Knowledge*
Vilmar, August Friedrich Christian (1800–1868)	German	*Die Theologie der Tatsachen wider die Theologie der Rhetorik*
Vitoria, Francisco de (1485–1546)	Spanish	*De Indis; De Iure Bellis, De Potestate Civli*
Vogel, Heinrich R. G. (1902–1989)	German	*Gesammelte Werke*
Vos, Geerhardus (1862–1940)	German	*Biblical Theology*
Walvoord, John Flipse (1910–)	American	*The Rapture Question; The Millennial Kingdom*
Ware, Timothy Kallistos (1934–)	Greek	*The Orthodox Church*
Warfield, Benjamin Breckinridge (1851–1921)	American	*The Lord of Glory*
Weber, Otto (1902–1966)	German	*Foundations of Dogmatics*
Weigel, Gustav (1906–1964)	American	*The Modern God*
Welch, Claude (1922–)	American	*Protestant Thought in the Nineteenth Century*
Wiley, Henry Orton (1877–1961)	American	*Christian Theology*

William of Ockham (1280–1349)	English	*Summa Logicae*
Williams, John Rodman (1918–)	English	*The Era of the Spirit; The Gift of the Holy Spirit Today; The Pentecostal Reality*
Wingren, Gustav (1910–)	Swedish	*Creation and Gospel: The New Situation in European Theology*
Zwingli, Ulrich (1484–1531)	Swiss	*Eine kurze christliche Einleitung; Responsio Brevis*

APPENDIX 14

Notable Christian Missionaries

Name and Dates	Nationality & Sending Agency	Main Mission Field
Abeel, David (1804–1846)	American ABCFM	China
Abel, Charles William (1863–1930)	English LMS	Papua New Guinea
Abrams, Minne F. (1859–1912)	American-Methodist	India
Acosta, Jose D. (1540–1600)	Spanish Jesuits	Peru
Acquaviva, Rudolf (1550–1583)	Italian Jesuit	India
Adalbert (d. 705)	English	Germany
Adalbert of Prague (956–997)	Czech	Slavs
Adeney, David Howard (1911–1994)	British CIM	China and East Asia
Aea, Hezekiah (1835–1872)	Hawaiian	Marshall Islands
Agnew, Eliza (1807–1883)	American ABCFM	Sri Lanka
Aidan (d. 651)	Irish	Britain
Alcina, Francisco Ignacio (1610–1674)	Spanish Jesuit	Philippines
Aldersey, Mary Ann (1797–1868)	British	China
Aleni, Giulio (1582–1649)	Italian Jesuit	China
Alexander, William P. (1805–1884)	American ABCFM	Hawaii
Allan, George (1871–1941)	New Zealander Evangelical	Bolivia
Allen, David Oliver (1799–1863)	American ABCFM	India, Western
Allen, Horace Newton (1858–1932)	American Presbyterian	Korea
Allen, Young John (1836–1907)	American Methodist	China
Allouez, Claude Jean (1622–1689)	French Jesuit	North America
Allshorn, Florence (1887–1950)	English CMS	Uganda
Alopen (seventh century)	Persian Nestorian	China
Altham, John (1589–1640)	English Jesuit	Maryland
Amadeus, Mary (1846–1919)	Irish Catholic	Native Americans
Amiot, Jean Joseph (1718–1793)	French Jesuit	China
Anchieta, Jose de (1534–1597)	Portuguese Jesuit	Brazil
Andel, H. A. van (1875–1945)	Dutch Reformed	Java
Anderson, John (1805–1855)	Scottish Church of Scotland	India, South
Anderson, William (1769–1852)	English LMS	South Africa
Anderson, William (1812–1895)	Scottish Presbyterian	Jamaica; Nigeria
Anderson, William H. (1870–1950)	American Seventh Day	Africa
Andrade, Antonio de (1580–1634)	Portuguese Jesuit	India; Tibet
Andre, Louis (1631–1714)	French Jesuit	North America
Ansgar (801–865)	French Catholic	Scandinavia
Anthing, F. L. (1818–1883)	Dutch Lutheran	Indonesia
Anzer, Johann Baptist von (1851–1903)	German SVD	China

Name and Dates	Nationality & Sending Agency	Main Mission Field
Appenzeller, Henry Gerhard (1858–1902)	American Presbyterian	Korea
Arbousset, Jean Thomas (1810–1877)	French PEMS	Lesotho; Tahiti
Armstrong, Hannah Maria (1842–1919)	Canadian Baptist	Burma
Armstrong, Richard (1805–1860)	American ABCFM	Hawaii
Armstrong, William Frederick (1849–1918)	Canadian Baptist	Burma; India
Arnot, Frederick Stanley (1858–1914)	Scottish Plymouth Brethren	Africa, Central
Arriaga, Pablo Jose de (1564–1622)	Spanish Jesuit	Peru
Arthur, John William (1881–1952)	Scottish Church of Scotland	Kenya
Ashmore, William (1824–1909)	American Baptist	China
Atkinson, Maria W. (1879–1963)	American Church of God	Mexico
Augouard, Prosper Philippe (1852–1921)	French CSSP	Africa, Central
Avison, Oliver R. (1860–1956)	American Presbyterian	Korea
Aylward, Gladys (1902–1970)	British	China
Azevedo, Ignacio de (1527–1570)	Portuguese Jesuit	Brazil
Bach, Thomas John (1881–1963)	Swedish TEAM	Venezuela
Bachmann, J. Traugott (1865–1948)	German Moravian	East Africa
Baedeker, Friedrich William (1823–1906)	German Evangelical	Russia
Bagby, William Buck (1855–1939)	American Southern Baptist	Brazil
Bailey, Wellesley (1846–1937)	Irish	India
Baird, William M. (1862–1931)	American Presbyterian	Korea
Baker, Amelia Dorothea (1802–1888)	German CMS	India, South
Bakker, Dirk (1865–1932)	Dutch Reformed	Java, Central
Baldaeus, Philippus (1632–1671)	Dutch Reformed	Sri Lanka
Baldwin, Elizabeth (1859–1939)	American ABCFM	South Pacific
Ball, Dyer (1796–1866)	American ABCFM	China
Ball, Henry Cleophas (1896–1989)	American AG	Latin America
Ballantine, Henry (1813–1865)	American ABCFM	India, Western
Baller, Frederick William (1852–1922)	British CIM	China
Barclay, Thomas (1849–1935)	Scottish Presbyterian	Taiwan
Barreira, Balthazar (1531–1612)	Portuguese Jesuit	Angola; Sierra Leona
Bartel, Henry Cornelius (1873–1975)	Polish Mennonite	China
Barton, John (1836–1908)	Anglican CMS	India
Barzaeus, Gaspar (1515–1553)	Dutch Jesuit	Hormuz; Goa
Barzana, Alonso de (1528–1598)	Spanish Jesuit	Peru
Bataillon, Pierre Marie (1810–1877)	French Marist	Southwest Pacific
Bates, M. Searle (1897–1978)	American Disciples of Christ	China
Baughman, Burr (1910–)	American Methodist	Malaya and Sarawak
Bax, Jacques (1825–1895)	Belgian CICM	Mongolia
Becker, Carl (1894–1990)	American AIM	Zaire
Becker, Christoph Edmund (1875–1937)	German Catholic	Assam, India
Belcourt, Georges Antoine (1803–1874)	Canadian Catholic	Ojibwa Indians
Belksma, Johannes (1884–1942)	Dutch Reformed	Indonesia
Bell, L. Nelson (1894–1973)	American Presbyterian	China
Bender, Carl Jacob (1869–1935)	German Baptist	Cameroon
Bennett, Cephas (1804–1885)	American Baptist	Burma
Bentley, William Holman (1885–1905)	English Baptist	Congo
Berg, Daniel (1884–1963)	American Assemblies of God	Brazil

Name and Dates	Nationality & Sending Agency	Main Mission Field
Bergmann, Wilhelm (1899–1987)	German	New Guinea
Berkeley, Xavier (1861–1944)	English Catholic	China
Bermyn, Alphonse (1853–1915)	Belgian Catholic	Mongolia
Berthoud, Paul (1847–1930)	Swiss Free Church	South Africa; Mozambique
Beschi, Constanzo Giuseppe (1680–1747)	Italian Jesuit	India
Besson, Pablo Enrique (1848–1932)	Swiss Baptist	Argentina
Betanzos, Domingo de (1480–1549)	Spanish Dominican	Espanola; Mexico
Bettelheim, Bernard Jean (1811–1870)	Hungarian	Ryukyu Islands
Bettendorf, Johann Philipp (1625–1698)	German Jesuit	Brazil
Beyzym, Jan (1850–1912)	Polish Jesuit	Madagascar
Biard, Pierre (1567–1622)	French Jesuit	North America
Bickel, Luke Washington (1866–1917)	American Baptist	Japan
Bickersteth, Edward (1850–1897)	Anglican CMS	India; Japan
Bicknell, Henry (1766–1820)	English LMS	Tahiti
Bill, Samuel Alexander (1864–1942)	British Presbyterian	Nigeria
Bingham, Hiram (1789–1869)	American ABCFM	Hawaii
Bingham, Hiram, Jr. (1831–1908)	American Congregational	Micronesia
Bird, Mary Baker (1807–1880)	British Methodist	Jamaica
Bird, Mary Rebecca Stewart (1859–1914)	English CMS	Persia
Birkeli, Otto Emil (1877–1952)	Norwegian	Madagascar
Bishop, Artemus (1795–1872)	American ABCFM	Hawaii
Bisseux, Isaac (1807–1896)	French PEMS	South Africa
Black, William (1760–1834)	English Methodist	Nova Scotia
Blackmore, Sophia (1857–1945)	Australian Methodist	Singapore; Malaysia
Bliss, Daniel (1823–1916)	American ABCFM	Lebanon
Boardman, George Dana (1801–1831)	American Baptist	Burma
Boberg, Folke Anders Adrian (1896–1987)	Swedish Pentecostal	Mongolia
Bodding, Paul Olaf (1865–1938)	Norwegian	India
Bohner, Heinrich (1842–1905)	German Basel Mission	Ghana
Bohnisch, Frederick (1710–1763)	German Moravian	Greenland
Boismenu, Alain de (1870–1953)	French Catholic	Papua New Guinea
Bolanos, Luis (1549–1629)	Spanish Franciscan	Paraguay
Bolotov, Ioasaf (c. 1761–1799)	Russian Orthodox	Alaska
Bompas, William Carpenter (1834–1906)	Anglican CMS	Canada
Bonaventura de Sardegna (c. 1600–1649)	Spanish Capuchin	Congo
Boniface (c. 675–754)	English Catholic	Germany
Bonjean, Ernest Christophe (1823–1892)	French Catholic	Sri Lanka
Bonnand, Clement (1796–1861)	French Catholic	India
Boone, William Jones, Sr. (1811–1864)	American Episcopal	China
Booth, Joseph (1851–1932)	English	Southern Africa
Borghero, Francesco Saverio (1830–1892)	Italian Catholic	Dahomey
Bosshart, Rudolf Alfred (1897–1993)	English CIM	China
Bouvet, Joachim (1656–1730)	French Jesuit	China
Bowen, George (1816–1888)	American ABCFM	India
Bowen, Thomas Jefferson (1814–1875)	American Southern Baptist	Nigeria
Bowley, William (c. 1780–1843)	British CMS	India
Boyce, William Binnington (1803–1889)	British Methodist	South Africa; Australia

Name and Dates	Nationality & Sending Agency	Main Mission Field
Braden, Charles Samuel (1887–1970)	American Methodist	Latin America
Bradley, Dan Beach (1804–1873)	American ABCFM	Thailand
Brainerd, David (1718–1747)	American Presbyterian	Native Americans
Brainerd, John (1720–1781)	American Presbyterian	Delaware Indians
Brand, Evelyn (1879–1974)	British Baptist	India
Brand, Paul Wilson (1914–)	British	India
Braun, Peter (1726–1800)	German Moravian	Antigua
Brebeuf, Jean de (1593–1649)	French Jesuit	Canada
Brent, Charles Henry (1862–1929)	Canadian Episcopal	Philippines
Breton, Raymond (1609–1679)	French Dominican	West Indies
Brett, William Henry (1818–1886)	Anglican SPG	Guyana
Bridgman, Elijah Coleman (1801–1861)	American ABCFM	China
Britto, Joao de (1647–1693)	Portuguese Jesuit	India
Bromilow, William E. (1857–1929)	Australian Methodist	New Guinea
Bronnum, Niels Hoegh (1882–1966)	Danish SUM	Nigeria
Bronson, Miles (1812–1883)	American Baptist	Assam, India
Brooke, Graham Wilmot (1865–1892)	Anglican CMS	West Africa
Broomhall, Anthony James (1911–1994)	English Baptist	China
Brown, Alfred (1803–1884)	English CMS	Maori
Brown, Edith Mary (1864–1956)	English Baptist	India
Brown, Nathan (1807–1886)	American Baptist	Burma; Assam; Japan
Brown, Samuel Robbins (1810–1879)	American Reformed	Japan
Brownlee, John (1791–1871)	Scottish LMS	South Africa
Brubaker, Henry Heisey (1900–1972)	American Brethren	Rhodesia
Bruckner, Gottlob (1783–1857)	German LMS, BMS	Java
Brunton, Henry (c. 1770–1813)	Scottish Edinburgh Miss.	Guinea
Buchanan, Claudius (1766–1815)	Anglican Baptist	India
Buglio, Ludovico (1606–1682)	Italian Jesuit	China
Buker, Raymond Bates, Sr. (1899–1992)	American Baptist	Burma
Buntain, Daniel Mark (1923–1989)	American Assemblies of God	India
Burgess, Paul (1886–1958)	American Presbyterian	Guatemala
Burns, William Chalmers (1815–1868)	Scottish Presbyterian	China
Burton, John Wear (1875–1970)	New Zealander Methodist	Fiji
Burton, William F. Padwick (1886–1971)	English Pentecostal	Africa
Butler, Elizur (1794–1857)	American ABCFM	Cherokee Indians
Butler, Fanny Jane (1850–1889)	English Zenana Missionary	India
Butler, William (1818–1899)	American Methodist	India and Mexico
Buxton, Alfred (1891–1940)	English	Zaire; Ethiopia
Buxton, Barclay Fowell (1860–1946)	English CMS	Japan
Buzacott, Aaron (1800–1864)	British LMS	Cook Islands
Cable, Alice Mildred (1877–1952)	British CIM	Central Asia
Caldwell, Robert (1814–1891)	British LMS	India
Calhoun, Simeon Howard (1804–1876)	American ABCFM	Turkey; Greece; Syria
Callaway, Henry (1817–1890)	Anglican SPG	South Africa
Callenberg, Johann Heinrich (1694–1760)	German Lutheran	Jews
Calvert, James (1813–1892)	British Wesleyan Methodist	Fiji
Cancer de Barbastro, Luis (1510–1549)	Spanish Dominican	Florida

Name and Dates	Nationality & Sending Agency	Main Mission Field
Candidus, Georgius (1597–1647)	German Reformed	Taiwan
Cardoso, Mattheus (1584–1625)	Portuguese Jesuit	Kongo
Carey, William (1761–1834)	British Baptist	India
Cargill, David (1809–1843)	Scottish Methodist	Tonga and Fiji
Carlson, Paul (1928–1964)	American	Zaire
Carneiro Leitao, Melchior M. (1519–1583)	Portuguese Jesuit	China; Japan
Carpenter, Chapin Howard (1835–1887)	American Baptist	Burma; Japan
Cary, Maude (1878–1967)	American GMU	Morocco
Casalis, Eugene (1812–1891)	French PEMS	Lesotho
Case, Isaac (1761–1852)	American Baptist	New England
Case, William (1780–1855)	American Methodist	Canadian Indians
Cassels, William Wharton (1858–1925)	Anglican CIM	China
Castiglione, Giuseppe (1683–1766)	Italian Jesuit	China
Cattaneo, Lazzaro (1560–1640)	Italian Jesuit	China
Cavazzi da Montecuccolo (1621–1678)	Italian Capuchin	Angola
Cespedes, Gregorio (1551–1611)	Spanish Jesuit	Japan; Korea
Chalmers, John (1825–1899)	Anglican LMS	China
Chamberlain, Jacob (1835–1908)	American Reformed	India
Chamberlain, John (1777–1821)	American Baptist	India
Chanel, Pierre Louis (1803–1841)	French Marist	Futuna
Chapdelaine, Auguste (1814–1856)	French PFMS	China
Chaumont, Denis (1752–1819)	French PFMS	China
Chawner, Charles Austin (1903–1964)	American Pentecostal	South Africa
Cheek, Landon Napoleon (1871–1964)	American Baptist	Malawi
Chesterman, Clement Clapton (1894–1983)	English BMS	Zaire
Chestnut, Eleanor (1868–1905)	American Presbyterian	China
Chou Wen-Mo (1753–1801)	Chinese	Korea
Christaller, Johannes Gottlieb (1827–1895)	German Lutheran	Ghana
Christie, Dugald (1855–1936)	Scottish Presbyterian	China
Christoffel, Ernst Jakob (1876–1955)	German	Middle East
Clark, Charles Allen (1878–1961)	American Presbyterian	Korea
Clark, Ephraim W. (1799–1878)	American ABCFM	Hawaii
Clark, Henry Martyn (1857–1916)	English CMS	India
Clark, Robert (1825–1900)	English CMS	Punjab, India
Clarke, John (1802–1879)	English BMS	Jamaica
Classe, Leon (1874–1945)	French Catholic	Rwanda
Clifford, James (1872–1936)	English Brethren	Argentina
Clough, John Everett (1836–1910)	American Baptist	Andhra Pradesh, India
Coan, Titus (1801–1882)	American ABCFM	Hawaii
Cobo, Bernabe (1580–1657)	Spanish Jesuit	Peru
Cochran, George (1833–1901)	Canadian Methodist	Japan
Cochran, Joseph Gallup (1817–1871)	American ABCFM	Persia
Cochran, Joseph Plumb (1855–1905)	American Presbyterian	Persia
Cochrane, Thomas (1866–1953)	Scottish LMS	China
Codrington, Robert Henry (1830–1922)	Anglican	Melanesia
Coillard, Francois (1834–1904)	French PEMS	Central Africa
Colenso, Elizabeth (1821–1904)	British CMS	New Zealand
Collins, Judson Dwight (1823–1852)	American Methodist	China

Name and Dates	Nationality & Sending Agency	Main Mission Field
Columba, St. (c. 521–597)	Irish	British Isles
Columbanus (543–615)	Irish	Europe
Comber, Thomas James (1852–1887)	English Baptist	Cameroons–Congo
Comboni, Anthony Daniel (1831–1881)	Italian Holy Cross	Africa
Condit, Azaubah Caroline (1810–1844)	American Reformed	Southeast Asia
Cook, Albert Ruskin (1870–1951)	English CMS	Uganda
Cook, Gonzalez, Eulalia (1913–)	American Methodist	Cuba
Cook, J. A. B. (1854–1926)	English Presbyterian	Singapore
Coombs, Lucinda L. (1849–1919)	American Methodist	China
Corbett, Hunter (1835–1920)	American Presbyterian	China
Corrado, Alejandro Maria (1830–1890)	Italian Franciscan	Bolivia
Cotta, Anthony (1872–1957)	Catholic	China
Coughlan, Laurence (died 1785)	Irish Methodist	Newfoundland
Couplet, Philippe (1623–1693)	Belgian Jesuit	China
Cousins, William Edward (1840–1939)	English LMS	Madagascar
Couvreur, Seraphin (1835–1919)	French Jesuit	China
Cowman, Charles Elmer (1864–1924)	American C&MA	Japan
Crawford, Daniel (1870–1926)	Scottish Plymouth Brethren	Zaire
Crawford, Isabelle (1865–1961)	American WBHMS	Native Americans
Crawford, T. P. (1821–1902)	American Southern Baptist	China
Creux, Ernest (1845–1929)	Swiss	South Africa
Cripps, Arthur Shearly (1869–1952)	Anglo-Catholic SPG	Rhodesia
Crook, William Pascoe (1775–1846)	English LMS	Marquesas Islands
Crosby, Thomas (1840–1914)	English Methodist	British Columbia
Cross, William (1797–1842)	English Methodist	Tonga; Fiji
Crowe, Frederick (1819–1846)	British Baptist	Guatemala
Cushing, Ellen Windsor (1840–1915)	American Baptist	South Carolina
Cyril (826–869) and Methodius (815–885)	Greeks	Moravia and Slav countries
Dablon, Claude (1619–1697)	French Jesuit	North America
Dahl, Otto Christian (1903–1995)	Norwegian Lutheran	Madagascar
Dahle, Lars Nilsen (1843–1925)	Norwegian NMS	Madagascar
Dalle Perier, Luis (1922–1982)	French	Peru
Dalman, Gustav Hermann (1855–1941)	Dutch Moravian	Jews
Damien of Molokai (1840–1889)	Flemish Catholic	Hawaiian Lepers
Dandoy, Georges (1882–1962)	Belgian Jesuit	India
Daniel, Antoine (1601–1648)	French Jesuit	Canada
Darling, David (1790–1867)	English LMS	South Pacific
Darling, Thomas Young (1829–1909)	English CMS	South India
Dauble, Carl Gustav (1832–1893)	German CMS	India
Davidson, Andrew (1836–1918)	Scottish LMS	Madagascar
Davidson, Hannah Frances (1860–1935)	American Brethren	Rhodesia
Davies, John (1772–1855)	Welsh LMS	Tahiti
Day, David Alexander (1851–1897)	American Lutheran	Liberia
Day, Samuel Stearns (1808–1871)	Canadian Baptist	Andhra Pradesh India
De Smet, Pierre-Jean (1801–1873)	Belgian Jesuits	Native Americans

Name and Dates	Nationality & Sending Agency	Main Mission Field
Dean, William (1807–1895)	American Baptist	Thailand
Deck, John Northcote (1875–1957)	Australian	South Seas
Dennis, Thomas John (1869–1917)	British CMS	West Africa
Depelchin, Henri (1822–1900)	Belgian Jesuit	India
Deyneka, Peter (1898–2000)	Belorussian	Russia
Dick, Amos Daniel Maurice (1894–1979)	American Brethren	India
Dickson, James (1900–1967)	Canadian Presbyterian	Taiwan
Dirks, Heinrich (1842–1915)	Ukrainian Mennonite	Indonesia
Doane, Edward Toppin (1820–1890)	American ABCFM	Pohnpei
Dobinson, Henry Hughes (1863–1897)	Anglican CMS	Niger
Dobrizhoffer, Martin (1718–1791)	Austrian Jesuit	Paraguay
Dodge, Ralph Edward (1907–)	American Methodist	Angola
Dole, Charlotte Knapp (1813–1874)	American ABCFM	Hawaii
Donaldson, Dwight Martin (1884–1976)	American Presbyterian	India; Iran
Donders, Peter (1809–1887)	Dutch Catholic	Suriname
Dorville, Albert (1621–1662)	Belgian Jesuit	China; Tibet
Douglas, Carstairs (1839–1877)	Scottish Presbyterian	China
Drebert, Ferdinand (1890–1981)	Russian Moravian	Alaska
Droese, Ernest (1817–1891)	German CMS	North India
Dubose, Hampden Coit (1845–1910)	American Presbyterian	China
Duchesne, Rose Philippine (1769–1852)	French Catholic	Native Americans
Duff, Alexander (1806–1878)	Scottish Presbyterian	India
Dufresse, Jean-Gabriel-Taurin (1750–1815)	French PEMS	China
Duncan, William (1832–1918)	Anglican CMS	British Columbia
Dunger, George Albert (1908–)	German Baptist	Cameroon
Duparquet, Charles (1830–1888)	French Spiritan	Central Africa
Dwight, Harrison Gray Otis (1803–1862)	American ABCFM	Near East
Dyer, Alfred John (1884–1968)	Australian CMS	Aborigines
Dyer, Samuel (1804–1843)	English LMS	China
Eastman, George Herbert (1881–1974)	English LMS	Cook Islands; Kiribati
Eddy, Mary Pierson (1864–1923)	American Presbyterian	Syria
Edkins, Joseph (1823–1905)	British LMS	China
Edmiston, Althea Brown (1874–1937)	American Presbyterian	Zaire
Edwins, August William (1871–1942)	American Lutheran	China
Egede, Hans (1686–1758)	Norwegian Lutheran	Greenland
Elia, Pasquale d' (1890–1963)	Italian Jesuit	China
Eliot, John (1604–1690)	English Puritan	Native Americans
Elliot, Philip James ("Jim") (1927–1956)	American Plymouth Brethren	Ecuador
Ellis, William (1794–1872)	English LMS	Polynesia
Elmslie, Walter Angus (1856–1935)	Scottish Free Church	Malawi
Elmslie, William J. (1832–1872)	Scottish CMS	Kashmir
Ely, Charlotte Elizabeth (1839–1915)	American Presbyterian	Turkey
Emde, Johannes (1774–1859)	German	Java
England, John (1786–1842)	Irish Catholic	North America
Ewing, James Carruthers Rhea (1854–1925)	American Presbyterian	India
Fabricius, Johann Philipp (1711–1791)	German Lutheran	India

Name and Dates	Nationality & Sending Agency	Main Mission Field
Falkner, Thomas (1707–1784)	English Jesuit	Argentina
Farquhar, John Nicol (1861–1929)	Scottish LMS	India
Farrington, Sophronia (1801–1880)	American Methodist	Liberia
Favier, Pierre-Marie Alphonse (1837–1905)	French Catholic Lazarists	China
Feller, Henriette Odin (1800–1868)	French Protestant	Canada
Fenn, Christopher Cyprian (1823–1913)	British CMS	South India
Fernbaugh, Hettie Luzena (1870–1904)	American Brethren	Morocco
Fielde, Adele M. (1839–1916)	American Baptist	China
Figurovski, Innokentii (1864–1931)	Russian Orthodox	China
Filofei, (1650–1727)	Russian Orthodox	Siberia
Fisch, Rudolf (1856–1946)	Swiss Basel Mission	Ghana
Fisher, Welthy Honsinger (1879–1980)	American Methodist	China
Fisk, Pliny (1792–1825)	American ABCFM	Near East
Fiske, Fidelia (1816–1864)	American ABCFM	Nestorians
Fison, Lorimer (1832–1907)	English Wesleyan	Fiji
Flad, Johann Martin (1831–1915)	German	Ethiopia
Fleming, Archibald Lang (1883–1953)	Anglican CMS	Eskimos
Fleming, John (1807–1894)	American Presbyterian	Native Americans
Fleming, Peter Sillence (1928–1956)	American	Ecuador
Fliedner, Federico (1845–1901)	German Protestant	Spain
Flierl, Johann (1858–1947)	Bavarian Lutheran	New Guinea
Ford, Francis Xavier (1892–1952)	American Maryknoll	China
Forman, Charles William (1821–1894)	American Presbyterian	India
Forsyth, Christina Moir (1844–1919)	Scottish Presbyterian	South Africa
Foucauld, Charles Eugene de (1858–1916)	French Catholic	North Africa
Foucquet, Jean-Francois (1665–1741)	French Jesuit	China
Fox, Charles Elliott (1878–1977)	Anglican	Melanesian
Fox, Henry Watson (1817–1848)	British CMS	India
Frame, Alice Seymour (1878–1941)	American Congregationalist	China
Francis, Mabel (1880–1975)	American C&MA	China
Francke, August Hermann (1870–1930)	German Moravian	Tibet
Fraser, Alexander Gordon (1873–1962)	Scottish CMS	Africa; Sri Lanks
Fraser, Donald (1870–1933)	Scottish Free Church	Africa
Fraser, James Outram (1886–1938)	English CIM	China
Fraser, John Andrew Mary (1877–1962)	Canadian Catholic	China
Fraser, Kenneth (1877–1935)	Scottish CMS	Sudan
Freeman, Thomas Birch (1809–1890)	British Methodist	West Africa
Freinademetz, Joseph (1852–1908)	Austrian Catholic	China
French, Evangeline (1869–1961)	Anglo-French CIM	China
Frey, Joseph Samuel (1771–1850)	German LMS	Jews
Fridelli, Xavier-Ehrenbert (1673–1743)	Austrian Jesuit	China
Friesen, Abraham J. (1859–1920)	German Mennonite	South India
Fritz, Samuel (1651–1728)	German Jesuit	Peru
Frois, Luis (1532–1597)	Portuguese Jesuit	India
Frumentius (c. 300–c. 380)	Tyrian	Abyssinia
Fuller, Jennie (1851–1900)	American C&MA	India
Fulton, Thomas Cosby (1855–1942)	Irish Presbyterian	Manchuria
Furman, Charles Truman (1876–1947)	American Church of God	Guatemala

Name and Dates	Nationality & Sending Agency	Main Mission Field
Gabet, Joseph (1808–1853)	French Catholic	Mongolia
Gairdner, W. H. Temple (1873–1928)	Anglican CMS	Egypt
Gale, James Scarth (1863–1937)	Canadian Presbyterian	Korea
Gall (550–640)	Irish	France; Switzerland
Gamewell, Frank F. Dunlap (1857–1950)	American Methodist	China
Gardiner, Allen Francis (1794–1851)	English CMS	Africa; Latin America
Garnier, Charles (1606–1649)	French Jesuit	New France
Garr, Alfred Goodrich, Jr. (1874–1944)	American Pentecostal	India and China
Gaspais, Auguste Ernest (1884–1952)	French PEMS	Manchuria
Gebauer, Paul (1900–1977)	German Baptist	Cameroon
Geddie, John (1815–1872)	Scottish Presbyterian	New Hebrides
Gerard, Joseph (1831–1914)	French Oblate	South Africa
Gerbillon, Jean-Francois (1654–1707)	French Jesuit	China
Gericke, Christian Wilhelm (1742–1803)	German Lutheran	South India
Geyer, Francis Xavier (1858–1943)	German Catholic	Sudan
Giannecchini, Doroteo (1837–1900)	Italian Franciscan	Bolivia
Gibson, John Campbell (1849–1919)	Scottish Presbyterian	China
Giffen, John Kelly (1853–1932)	American Presbyterian	Egypt; Sudan
Gill, William Wyatt (1828–1896)	English LMS	Cook Islands
Gilman, Franck Patrick (1853–1918)	American Presbyterian	China
Gilmour, James (1843–1891)	Scottish Congregationalist	Mongolia
Glenn, William (1779–1849)	Scottish SMS	Russia
Glover, Archibald Edward (1859–1954)	English CIM	China
Glukharev, Makarii (1792–1847)	Russian Orthodox	Siberia
Gnecci-Soldi, Organtino (1535–1609)	Italian Jesuit	Japan
Gobat, Samuel (1799–1879)	Swiss Lutheran	Abyssinia
Goble, Jonathan (1827–1896)	American	Japan
Goddard, Josiah (1813–1854)	American Baptist	China; Siam
Goforth, Jonathan (1859–1936)	Canadian Presbyterian	China
Gogerly, Daniel John (1792–1862)	English Methodist	Sri Lanka
Goldie, Hugh (1815–1895)	Scottish Presbyterian	Jamaica; Nigeria
Goldie, John Francis (1870–1954)	Scottish	Solomon Islands
Goldsack, William (1871–1957)	Australian Baptist	India
Gollmer, Charles Andrew (1812–1886)	German CMS	Yorubaland
Good, Adolphus Clemens (1856–1894)	American Presbyterian	Cameroon
Goodell, William (1792–1867)	American ABCFM	Near East
Gordon, Andrew (1828–1887)	American Presbyterian	India
Goupil, Rene (1608–1642)	French Jesuit	Canada
Gowans, Walter (1868–1894)	Canadian SIM	Nigeria
Goward, William Edward (1860–1931)	English LMS	Samoa
Graham, James Robert III (1898–1982)	American Presbyterian	China
Graham, John Anderson (1860–1942)	Scottish	Eastern Himlayas, India
Grandin, Vital Justin (1829–1902)	French Catholic	Western Canada
Grant, Asahel (1809–1844)	American ABCFM	Nestorians
Grant, Judith Campbell (1814–1839)	American ABCFM	Nestorians
Grassman, Andrew (1704–1783)	German Moravian	Europe; Greenland
Graybill, Anthony Thomas (1841–1905)	American Presbyterian	Mexico
Green, Samuel Fiske (1822–1884)	American Congregational	Sri Lanka

Name and Dates	Nationality & Sending Agency	Main Mission Field
Grenfell, George (1849–1906)	British BPS	Congo
Griffiths, David (1792–1863)	Welsh LMS	Madagascar
Griswold, Harvey DeWitt (1860–1945)	American Presbyterian	India
Groves, Anthony Norris (1795–1853)	English Plymouth Brethren	India; Baghdad
Grubb, Wilfrid Barbrooke (1865–1930)	Anglican SAMS	Paraguay
Grundler, Johann Ernst (1677–1720)	German Danish-Halle	Tranquebar, India
Guebriant, Jean-Baptiste (1860–1955)	French PFMS	China
Guinness, Henry Grattan (1835–1910)	British Evangelical	Congo
Gulick, Alice (1847–1903)	American ABCFM	Spain
Gulick, Luther Halsey (1828–1891)	American ABCFM	Pacific Islands
Gulick, Orramel Hinckley (1830–1923)	American ABFM	Hawaii
Gulliford, Henry (1852–1937)	British Wesleyan	India
Gurney, Samuel (1860–1924)	American Methodist	Zimbabwe
Gutzlaff, Karl Friedrich (1803–1851)	German Pietist	China
Gwynne, Llewellyn Henry (1863–1957)	English CMS	Sudan
Hagenauer, Friedrich August (1829–1909)	German Moravian	Australian Aborigines
Hahn, Carl Hugo (1818–1895)	German Rhenish Mission	Namibia
Haines, Byron Lee (1828–1890)	American Presbyterian	Pakistan
Hall, Gordon (1784–1826)	American ABCFM	India
Hall, Marian Bottomley (1896–1991)	American Methodist	Korea; India
Hall, Sherwood (1893–1991)	Canadian Methodist	Korea, India
Hallbeck, Hans Peter (1784–1840)	Swedish Moravian	South Africa
Halliwell, Leo Blair (1891–1967)	American Seventh Day Adv.	Brazil
Hambroeck, Antonius (1605–1661)	Dutch Reformed	Taiwan
Hamlin, James (1803–1865)	Anglican CMS	New Zealand
Hanxleden, Johann Ernst (1681–1732)	German Jesuit	India
Hardy, Robert Spence (1803–1868)	British Methodist	Sri Lanka
Harris, George Kaufelt (1887–1962)	American CIM	China
Harris, Merriman Colbert (1816–1921)	American Methodist	Japan
Harrison, Paul Wilberforce (1883–1962)	American Reformed	Middle East
Hartmann, Anastasius (1803–1866)	Swiss Capuchin	India
Hartmann, Maria (d. 1853)	German Moravian	Suriname
Hastings, Eurotas Parmelee (1821–1890)	American ABCFM	Sri Lanka
Hastings, Harry (d. 1951)	Scottish Free Church	Nigeria
Haven, Jens (1724–1796)	Dutch Moravian	Greenland; Labrador
Hawley, Gideon (1727–1807)	American Congregational	Native Americans
Hayward, Victor E. W. (1908–1988)	English BMS	China
Heath, George Reinke (1879–1956)	English Moravian	Honduras
Hebich, Samuel (1803–1868)	German Basel Mission	India
Heckewelder, Johann Gottlieb (1743–1823)	English Moravian	Native Americans
Heine, Carl (1869–1944)	Australian ABCFM	Micronesia
Heinrichs, Marcus (1904–1996)	German Franciscan	China; Japan
Hemans, James H. Emmanuel (1856–1908)	Jamaican LMS	Central Africa
Henriques, Henrique (1520–1600)	Portuguese Jesuit	India
Henry (d. 1156)	English	Finland
Hepburn, James Davidson (1840–1893)	English LMS	Botswana
Herman of Alaska (1756–1837)	Russian Orthodox	Alaska

Name and Dates	Nationality & Sending Agency	Main Mission Field
Hermosillo, Jeronimo (1800–1861)	Spanish Dominican	Vietnam
Herrero, Andres (1782–1838)	Spanish Franciscan	Peru; Bolivia
Herschell, Ridley Haim (1807–1864)	Polish Baptist	Jews
Hetherwick, Alexander (1860–1939)	Scottish Church of Scotland	Malawi
Heurinius, Justis (1587–1652)	Dutch	Dutch East Indies
Heyer, John C. Frederick (1793–1873)	German Lutheran	India
Heyling, Peter (1608–1652)	German	Egypt; Ethiopia
Hiebert, Nikolas Nikolai (1874–1957)	Ukrainian Mennonite	India
Hill, David (1840–1896)	British Wesleyan Methodist	China
Hill, John Henry (1791–1882)	American Episcopal	Greece
Hill, Mary (1791–1847)	English LMS	India
Hinderer, David (1827–1890)	German CMS	Nigeria
Hislop, Stephen (1817–1863)	Scottish Free Church	India
Hitchcock, John William (1882–1919)	Scottish Free Church	Nigeria
Hobson, Benjamin (1816–1873)	English LMS	China
Hodges, Melvin Lyle (1909–1988)	American Pentecostal	Latin America
Hodgson, Thomas Laidman (1787–1850)	English Methodist	Southern Africa
Hoecken, Christian (1808–1851)	Belgian Jesuit	Native Americans
Hoevell, Wolter Robert van (1812–1879)	Dutch Reformed	Dutch East Indies
Hoffman, C. Colden (1819–1865)	American Episcopal	West Africa
Hoffmann, Johannes Baptist (1857–1928)	German Jesuit	India
Hofinger, Johannes (1905–1984)	Austrian Jesuit	Philippines
Hofmeyr, Stefanus (1839–1905)	South African Reformed	Transvaal
Hogg, Alfred George (1875–1954)	Scottish United Free Church	India
Hogg, John (1833–1886)	Scottish	Egypt
Holland, Henry Tristram (1875–1965)	English CMS	India
Holmes, Elkanah (1744–1832)	American Baptist	Native Americans
Hooper, Handley Douglas (1891–1966)	English CMS	Kenya
Hoover, James Matthews (1872–1935)	American Methodist	Borneo
Hore, Edward Coode (1848–1912)	English LMS	Central Africa
Hoste, Dixon Edward (1861–1946)	British CIM	China
Hough, George H. (1788–1859)	American Baptist	Burma
Howard, Leonora (1851–1925)	American Methodist	China
Howe, Gertrude (1847–1928)	American Methodist	China
Howells, George (1871–1955)	Welsh BMS	India
Hoy, William Edwin (1858–1927)	American Reformed	Japan; China
Huc, Evariste-Regis (1813–1860)	French Vincentian	Mongolia; Tibet
Huegel, Frederick J. (1889–1971)	American Lutheran	Mexico
Hueting, Andre (1868–1961)	Dutch NMS	Indonesia
Hulstaert, Gustaf (1900–1990)	Belgian Catholic	Belgian Congo
Hume, Edward Hicks (1876–1957)	American	China
Hume, Robert Allen (1847–1929)	American Congregational	India
Hume, Robert Wilson (1809–1854)	American ABCFM	India
Hunt, Bruce Finley (1903–1992)	American Presbyterian	Korea
Hunt, John (1811–1848)	English Methodist	Fiji
Hunter, George W. (1861–1946)	Scottish CMS	Turkestan
Hyde, John (1865–1912)	American Presbyterian	India
Hynd, David (1895–1991)	Scottish Nazarene	Swaziland

Name and Dates	Nationality & Sending Agency	Main Mission Field
Iglehart, Charles Wheeler (1882–1969)	American Methodist	Japan
Ilminskii, Nikolai Ivanovich (1822–1891)	Russian Orthodox	Muslim Tatars
Ingalls, Marilla Baker (1828–1902)	American Baptist	Burma
Inglis, John (1808–1891)	Scottish Presbyterian	New Hebrides
Innocent Veniaminov (1797–1879)	Russian Orthodox	North America
Intorcetta, Prospero (1625–1696)	Italian Jesuit	China
Isakovich, Nikolai Fedorovich (1798–1874)	Russian Orthodox	Buryat people
Isenberg, Karl William (1806–1864)	German Lutheran	Ethiopia; India
Isherwood, Annie Cecile (1862–1906)	English	South Africa
Iuvenalii (1761–1796)	Russian Orthodox	Alaska
Ivanovskii, Nikolai Ivanovich (1875–1919)	Russian Orthodox	Korea
Jaca, Francisco Jose de (1645–1688)	Spanish Capuchin	Caribbean
Jacobis, Justin de (1800–1860)	Italian Vincentian	Ethiopia
Jaeschke, Heinrich August (1817–1883)	German Moravian	Tibet
Jaffrey, Robert Alexander (1873–1945)	Canadian C&MA	China; Indonesia
James, Leroy Lansing (1837–1909)	American Reformed	Japan
Jameson, William (1807–1847)	Scottish Presbyterian	Jamaica; Nigeria
Jansz, Pieter (1820–1904)	Dutch Mennonite	Indonesia
Janzen, Aaron A. (1882–1957)	American Mennonite	Belgian Congo
Jarlin, Stanislas Francois (1856–1933)	French Vicentian	China
Jefferson, John Clark (1760–1807)	English LMS	Tahiti
Jessup, Henry Harris (1823–1910)	American Presbyterian	Syria
Jeune, Paul de (1591–1664)	French Jesuit	Canada
Jogues, Isaac (1607–1646)	French Jesuit	Native Americans
Johannssen, Ernst (1864–1934)	German Basel Mission	East Africa
John, Christoph Samuel (1747–1813)	German	India
John, Griffith (1831–1912)	Welsh LMS	China
John of Montecorvino (1247–1328)	Italian	China
Johns, David (1796–1843)	Welsh LMS	Madagascar
Johnson, Amelia Dorothea (1820–1904)	English CMS	Kerala, India
Johnson, William A. Bernard (1787–1823)	German CMS	Sierra Leone
Johnson, William Percival (1854–1928)	Anglican UMCA	Central Africa
Jones, David (1797–1841)	Welsh LMS	Madagascar
Jones, Eli Stanley (1884–1973)	American Methodist	India
Jones, Evan (1788–1873)	English BFMB	Cherokees
Jones, George Heber (1867–1919)	American Methodist	Korea
Jones, John Peter (1847–1916)	American Congregational	India
Jones, John Taylor (1802–1851)	American Baptist	Thailans
Jones, Lewis Bevan (1880–1960)	British Baptist	Indian Muslims
Jones, Mabel Lossing (1878–1978)	American Methodist	India
Jowett, William (1787–1855)	English CMS	Malta
Judd, Walter Henry (1898–1994)	American ABFM	China
Judson, Adoniram (1788–1850)	American Baptist	Burma
Julian (sixth century)	Greek Orthodox	Nubia
Jummarti y Espot, Jacinto (1833–1897)	Spanish Catholic	Philippines
Junius de Jonghe, Robertus (1606–1655)	Dutch Reformed	Taiwan

Name and Dates	Nationality & Sending Agency	Main Mission Field
Kahler, Christiane (1800–1871)	German	South Africa
Kalley, Robert Reid (1809–1888)	Scottish	Madeira; Brazil
Kam, Joseph (1769–1833)	Dutch Reformed	Moluccas, Indonesia
Kamma, Freerk Christiaan (1906–1987)	Dutch NMS	New Guinea
Kasatkin, Nikolai (1836–1912)	Russian Orthodox	Japan
Kats, Wilma (1920–1980)	American Reformed	Sudan
Keasberry, Benjamin Peach (1811–1875)	British LMS	Singapore
Keith-Falconer, Ion G.N. (1856–1887)	Scottish	Arabia
Kekela, James (1824–1904)	Hawaiian	Marquesas Islands
Keller, Otto C. (1888–1942)	Canadian Pentecostal	Tanzania; Kenya
Kellersberger, Eugene R. (1888–1966)	American Presbyterian	Congo
Kemp, Johannes T. van der (1747–1811)	Dutch LMS	South Africa
Kempers, John R. (1900–1995)	American Reformed	Mexico
Kendall, Thomas (1778–1832)	English CMS	New Zealand
Keough, George Dorkin (1882–1971)	Irish Seventh-Day Adventist	Middle East
Kerr, George McGlashan (1874–1950)	Scottish Wesleyan Methodist	India
Kerr, John Glasgow (1824–1901)	American Presbyterian	China
Kersten, Christoph (1733–1796)	German Moravian	Suriname
Keysser, Christian (1877–1961)	German Lutheran	New Guinea
Khrisanf (1871–1906)	Russian Orthodox	China
Kidder, Daniel Parish (1815–1891)	American Methodist	Brazil
Kidder, Mary Eddy (1845–1910)	American Reformed	Japan
Kiernander, John Zacharias (1711–1799)	Swedish SPCK	Bengal, India
Kijne, Izaak Samuel (1899–1970)	Dutch Evangelical	New Guinea
Kilbuck, John Henry (1861–1922)	American Moravian	Alaska
Kilham, Hannah (1774–1832)	English Quaker	West Africa
Kilian (640–689)	Irish	Germany (Franconia)
Kincaid, Eugenio (1797–1883)	American Baptist	Burma
King, Jonas (1792–1869)	American Congregational	Greece
Kingsbury, Cyrus (1786–1870)	American ABCFM	Native Americans
Kino, Eusebio Francisco (1644–1711)	Italian Jesuit	Mexico; American Southwest
Kinsolving, Lucien Lee (1862–1929)	American Episcopal	Brazil
Kircherer, Johannes Jacobus (1775–1825)	Dutch LMS	South Africa
Kivebulaya, Apolo (1864–1933)	Ugandan CMS	Pygmies
Klein, Frederick Augustus (1827–1903)	French CMS	Middle East
Kleinschmidt, Johann Conrad (1768–1832)	German Moravian	Greenland
Klinkert, Hillebrandus C. (1829–1913)	Dutch Mennonite	East Indies
Knight-Bruce, George W. H. (1852–1896)	Anglican	Southern Africa
Knoblecher, Ignaz (1819–1888)	Austrian Catholic	Central Africa
Kobes, Aloys (1820–1872)	German Holy Ghost Fathers	Guinea; Senegambia
Koelle, Sigismund Wilhelm (1823–1902)	German CMS	Sierra Leone; Middle East
Krapf, Johann Ludwig (1810–1881)	German Lutheran	Kenya
Kruyt, Albertus Christiaan (1869–1949)	Dutch Reformed	Indonesia
Kuder, John (1906–1990)	American Lutheran	New Guinea
Kugler, Anna Sarah (1856–1930)	American Lutheran	India
Kuhn, Isobel (1901–1957)	Canadian CIM	China

Name and Dates	Nationality & Sending Agency	Main Mission Field
Kulp, Harold Stover (1894–1964)	American Brethren	Nigeria
Lacombe, Albert (1827–1916)	American Catholic	Canada
Lacroix, Alphonse Francois (1799–1859)	Swiss NMS	Bengal, India
Lafitau, Joseph-Francois (1681–1746)	French Catholic	Canada
Lake, John Graham (1870–1935)	American Pentecostal	South Africa
Lalemant, Gabriel (1610–1649)	French Jesuit	Canada
Lalemant, Jerome (1593–1673)	French Jesuit	Canada
Lambert de la Motte, Pierre (1624–1679)	French PFMS	Indochina
Lambie, Thomas A. (1885–1954)	American Presbyterian	Ethiopia
Lamburn, Roger George (1904–1993)	Anglican UMCA	Tanzania
Lambuth, Walter Russell (1854–1921)	American Methodist	China; Japan
Lanneau, Sophie Stephens (1880–1963)	American Southern Baptist	China
Lapsley, Samuel Norvell (1866–1892)	American Presbyterian	Congo
Larsen, Lars Peter (1862–1940)	Danish DMS	India
Las Casas, Bartolome de (1484–1566)	Spanish	South America
Laubach, Frank Charles (1884–1970)	American Congregationalist	Philippines
Laval, Jacques Desire (1803–1864)	French Catholic	Mauritius
Lavigerie, Charles Martial A. (1825–1892)	French White Fathers	North Africa
Lawes, William George (1839–1907)	English LMS	Niue; Papua
Laws, Robert (1851–1934)	Scottish Presbyterian	Malawi
Le Comte, Louis (1655–1728)	French Jesuit	China
Le Roux, Pieter Louis (1865–1943)	Afrikaner Reformed	Zulu people
Lebbe, Frederic-Vincent (1877–1940)	Belgian Catholic	China
Lebuin (d. 780)	Anglo-Saxin Benedictine	Frisia; Westphalia
Lechler, Rudolf (1824–1908)	German Basel Mission	China
Lee, Daniel (1807–1896)	American Methodist	Native Americans
Lee, Jason (1803–1845)	Canadian Methodist	Oregon Territory
Leenhardt, Maurice (1878–1954)	French Reformed	New Caledonia
Legge, James (1815–1897)	Scottish	Malacca; Hong Kong
Lehmann, E. Arno (1901–1984)	German	South India
Lemue, Prosper (1804–1870)	French PEMS	South Africa
Leontiev, Maxim (d. 1698)	Russian Orthodox	China
Lery, Jean de (1534–1611)	French Protestant	Brazil
Leupolt, Charles Benjamin (1805–1884)	German CMS	India
Lewis, Marianne Gould (1820–1890)	English BMS	India
Lewis, Thomas (1859–1929)	Welsh BMS	Cameroons
Leydecker, Melchior (1645–1701)	Dutch Reformed	East Indies
Liddell, Eric Henry (1902–1945)	Scottish LMS	China
Lieberkuhn, Samuel (1710–1777)	German Moravian	Jews
Lievens, Constant (1856–1893)	Belgian Jesuit	India
Liggett, Thomas J. (1919–)	American Disciples of Christ	Argentina; Puerto Rico
Liggins, John (1829–1912)	English Episcopal	Japan
Limbrock, Eberhard Michael (1859–1931)	German Catholic	China
Lindell, Jonathan Luther (1923–1985)	American Lutheran	Nepal
Lindley, Daniel (1801–1880)	American ABCFM	South Africa
Lioba (710–780)	English	South Germany
Lith, Franciscus van (1863–1926)	Dutch Jesuit	Indonesia

Name and Dates	Nationality & Sending Agency	Main Mission Field
Litwiller, John Timothy N. (1928–1971)	American Mennonite	Argentina; Uruguay; Chile
Livingstone, David (1813–1873)	Scottish LMS	South Africa
Livinhac, Auguste Simon (1846–1922)	French White Fathers	Africa
Loayza, Geronimo de (1498–1575)	Spanish Dominican	Peru
Lock, Annie (1877–1943)	Australian	Aborigines
Lockhart, William (1811–1896)	English LMS	China
Lohr, Oscar T. (1824–1907)	German	Central India
Lombard, Eva (1890–1978)	Swiss Basel Mission	India
Long, James (1815–1887)	Irish CMS	India
Long, Retta Jane (1878–1956)	Australian	Aboriginals
Loosdrecht, Antoine van de (1885–1917)	Dutch Reformed	Indonesia
Lorrain, James Herbert (1870–1944)	English Baptist	Mizoram, India
Lourdel, Simeon (1853–1890)	French White Father	Uganda
Louw, Andries Adriaan (1862–1956)	South African Reformed	Rhodesia
Loveless, Sarah (1774–1839)	American LMS	India
Lowe, John (1835–1892)	Scottish LMS	India
Lowrie, John Cameroon (1808–1900)	American Presbyterian	India
Lucas, Bernard (1860–1921)	English LMS	India
Lucas, William Vincent (1883–1945)	Anglican UMCA	Tanzania
Luce, Alice Eveline (1873–1955)	English CMS	India; Hispanics
Luce, Henry Winters (1868–1941)	American Presbyterian	China
Liull, Raymond (1235–1315)	Spanish	Muslims
Luquet, Jean Felix Onesime (1810–1858)	French Catholic	India
Lyall, Leslie Theodore (1905–1996)	English CIM	China
Lyman, David Belden (1803–1884)	American	Hawaii
Lyon, David Willard (1870–1949)	American YMCA	China
Lyons, Lorenzo (1807–1886)	American ABCFM	Hawaii
Mabie, Catherine (1872–1963)	American Baptist	Congo
Mabille, Adolphe (1836–1894)	Swiss PEMS	Lesotho
Macdonald, Andrew B. (1892–1970)	Scottish Free Church	Nigeria
Macdonald, Annie Caroline (1874–1931)	Canadian YMCA	Japan
MacDonald, Duff (1850–1929)	Scottish CSM	Malawi
MacGillivray, Donald (1862–1931)	Canadian Presbyterian	China
Machray, Robert (1831–1904)	Anglican	Canada
Mack, Johann Martin (1715–1784)	German Moravian	North America; Caribbean
Mack, John (1797–1845)	Scottish Baptist	India
Mackay, Alexander Murdoch (1849–1890)	Scottish CMS	Uganda
Mackay, George Leslie (1844–1901)	Canadian Presbyterian	Taiwan
Mackay, John Alexander (1889–1983)	Scottish Presbyterian	Latin America
Mackenzie, Charles Frederick (1825–1862)	Anglican	Central Africa
Mackenzie, Helen Pearl (1913–)	Australian Presbyterian	Korea
Mackenzie, Jean Kenyon (1874–1936)	American Presbyterian	West Africa
Mackenzie, John (1835–1899)	Scottish LMS	South Africa
Mackenzie, John Kenneth (1850–1888)	British LMS	China
Mackichan, Dugald (1851–1932)	Scottish Free Church	India
Maclaren, Albert Alexander (1853–1891)	Anglican	New Guinea
Maclay, Robert Samuel (1824–1907)	American Methodist	China; Japan

Name and Dates	Nationality & Sending Agency	Main Mission Field
MacVicar, Neil (1871–1949)	Scottish Free Church	Southern Africa
Magee, John Gillespie (1884–1953)	American CIM	China
Mailla, Joseph Marie Anne (1669–1748)	French Jesuit	China
Main, David Duncan (1856–1934)	Scottish	China
Makemie, Francis (1658–1708)	Scotch-Irish Presbyterian	North America
Malinke, James Morrison (1893–1982)	English Seventh-Day Adv.	Malawi; Zaire; Zambia
Mamora, Lucius (c. 1920–)	Indonesian	Sarawak
Margil, Antonio (1657–1726)	Spanish Franciscan	New World
Marks, John Ebenezer (1832–1915)	Anglican SPG	Burma
Marquette, Jacques (1637–1675)	French Jesuit	New World
Marsden, Samuel (1764–1838)	Anglican LMS	Maori
Marshman, Joshua (1768–1837)	English BMS	India
Marston, Sarah Hall (1813–1875)	American Baptist	Burma
Martin, Frederick (1704–1750)	German Moravian	Caribbean
Martin, Marie-Louise (1912–1990)	Swiss Reformed	South Africa
Martin, William Alexander P. (1827–1916)	American Presbyterian	China
Martinez, Pedro (1523–1566)	Spanish Jesuit	Florida
Martini, Martino (1614–1661)	Italian Jesuit	China
Marty, Martin (1834–1896)	Swiss Benedictine	Sioux Indians
Martyn, Henry (1781–1812)	Anglican	India; Persia
Mason, Francis (1799–1874)	American Baptist	Burma
Massaja, Guglielmo (1809–1889)	Italian Capuchin	Ethiopia
Mateer, Calvin Wilson (1836–1908)	American Presbyterian	China
Mather, Percy Cunningham (1884–1933)	English CIM	Central Asia
Mather, Robert Cotton (1808–1877)	English LMS	India
Matthews, Daniel (1837–1902)	English	Australian Aborigines
Matthews, Thomas Trotter (1842–1928)	Scottish LMS	Madagascar
Maunsell, Robert (1810–1894)	Irish CMS	New Zealand
Mayhew, Experience (1673–1758)	American Congregational	Native Americans
Mazzuchelli, Samuel (1806–1864)	Italian Dominic	United States
McBeth, Sue L. (1830–1893)	Scottish Presbyterian	Native Americans
McCandliss, Henry M. (1859–1931)	American Presbyterian	China
McCaul, Alexander (1799–1863)	British	Jews
McClure, William Donald (1906–1977)	American Presbyterian	Africa
McCoy, Isaac (1784–1846)	American Baptist	Native Americans
McDougall, Francis Thomas (1817–1886)	Anglican	Sarawak
McDowell, Robert James (1767–1841)	American Reformed	Canada
McFarland, Samuel Gamble (1830–1897)	American Presbyterian	Thailand
McFarlane, Samuel (1837–1911)	English LMS	New Caledonia; New Guinea
McGilvary, Daniel (1828–1911)	American Presbyterian	Thailand
McLaurin, John (1839–1912)	Canadian Baptist	India
McLaurin, John Bates (1884–1952)	Canadian Baptist	India
Mebius, Frederick (1869–1944)	Canadian Pentecostal	El Salvador
Medhurst, Walter Henry (1796–1857)	English LMS	Malaya; Indonesia; China
Meeuwsen, Johanna (1857–1942)	American Reformed	South Africa
Melrose, Margaret (1868–1951)	American Presbyterian	Hainan Island, China
Menard, Rene (1604–1661)	French Jesuit	North America

Name and Dates	Nationality & Sending Agency	Main Mission Field
Mendieta, Jeronimo (1525–1604)	Spanish Franciscan	Mexico
Merensky, Alexander (1837–1918)	German Berlin Mission	South Africa
Merrick, James Lyman (1803–1866)	American Congregational	Persia
Methodius (c815–885)	Greek	Slavs
Miller, Harry Willis (1879–1977)	American Seventh-Day Adv.	China
Miller, Walter Richard Samuel (1872–1952)	English CMS	Nigeria Hausa
Miller, William (1838–1923)	Scottish Free Church	India
Miller, William McElwee (1892–1993)	American Presbyterian	Iran
Mills, Wilson Plumer (1883–1959)	American Presbyterian	China
Milne, Rachel (1783–1819)	Scottish LMS	China
Milne, William (1785–1822)	Scottish LMS	China
Miner, Luella (1861–1935)	American ABCFM	China
Mitchell, John Murray (1815–1904)	Scottish Free Church	India
Moegling, Herrmann Friedrich (1811–1881)	German Basel Mission	India
Moffat, John Smith (1835–1918)	English LMS	South Africa
Moffat, Robert (1795–1883)	Scottish LMS	South Africa
Moffett, Samuel Austin (1864–1939)	American Presbyterian	Korea
Moirans, Epifanio de (1644–1689)	French Capuchin	Caribbean
Molnar, Maria (1886–1943)	Hungarian	Admiralty Islands
Money, Herbert (1899–1996)	Australian Free Church	Peru
Moninger, Mary Margaret (1891–1950)	American Presbyterian	China
Monnier, Henri (1896–1944)	Swiss Seventh-Day Adventist	Rwanda
Monsen, Marie (1878–1962)	Norwegian Lutheran	China
Montesinos, Antonio de (1486–1530)	Spanish Dominican	West Indies
Moody, Campbell Naismith (1866–1940)	English Presbyterian	Taiwan
Moon, Charlotte Diggs (1840–1912)	American Southern Baptist	China
Morales, Juan Bautista de (1597–1664)	Spanish Dominican	China
Morrison, Robert (1782–1834)	English LMS	China
Morrison, William McCutchan (1867–1918)	American Presbyterian	Congo
Motta, Waldomiro (1920–1996)	Brazilian Baptist	Bolivia
Moule, Arthur Evans (1836–1918)	Anglican CMS	China
Moule, George Evans (1828–1912)	Anglican CMS	China
Mouly, Joseph Martial (1807–1863)	French Vicentian	China; Mongolia
Mullens, Joseph (1820–1879)	English LMS	India
Murray, Archibald Wright (1811–1892)	Scottish LMS	Oceania
Murray, William Hoppe (1866–1947)	South African	Malawi
Myers, Estella Catherine (1884–1956)	American Brethren	Central Africa
Nacquart, Charles (1617–1650)	French Lazarist	Madagascar
Nassau, Robert Hamill (1835–1921)	American Presbyterian	Gabon
Nau, Semisi (1866–1927)	Tongan Methodist	Solomon Islands
Neill, Stephen Charles (1900–1984)	Scottish CMS	India
Nelson, Daniel (1853–1926)	Norwegian American Luth.	China
Nerinckx, Charles (1761–1824)	Belgian Catholic	Kentucky
Nesbit, Robert (1803–1855)	Scottish SMS	India
Netsvetov, Iakov Egor (1804–1864)	Russian Orthodox	Eskimos
Neumann, Johann Heinrich (1876–1949)	Dutch	Sumatra
Neuner, Joseph (1908–)	Austrian Jesuit	India

Name and Dates	Nationality & Sending Agency	Main Mission Field
Nevius, John Livingston (1829–1893)	American Presbyterian	China
New, Charles (1840–1875)	British Methodist	East Africa
Newell, James Edward (1852–1910)	English LMS	Samoa
Newton, John (1810–1891)	American Presbyterian	Punjab, India
Nicolayson, John (1803–1856)	German Moravian	Jerusalem
Nielsen, Alfred Julius (1884–1963)	Danish Near East Mission	Syria; Palestine
Nikon the Metanoeite (930–1000)	Greek Orthodox	Greece
Ninian (360–432)	Scottish	Picts, Britons, Scots
Nino, Bernardino de (1868–1923)	Italian Franciscan	Bolivia
Nisbet, Henry (1818–1876)	Scottish LMS	Samoa; Melanesia
Nobili, Robert de (1577–1656)	Italian Jesuit	India
Noble, Robert Turlington (1809–1865)	English CMS	South India
Nobrega, Manoel da (1517–1570)	Portuguese Jesuit	Brazil
Nommensen, Ingwer Ludwig (1834–1918)	German Rhenish Mission	Indonesia
Nott, Henry (1774–1844)	American ABCFM	India
Noyes, Harriet Newell (1845–1924)	American Presbyterian	China
Nunes Barreto, Joao (1510–1562)	Portuguese Jesuit	Morocco; India
Nylander, Gustavus Reinhold (1776–1824)	German Lutheran	Sierra Leone
Odorico de Pordenone (d. 1331)	Italian Franciscan	China
Officer, Morris (1823–1874)	American Lutheran	West Africa
Oldham, William Fitzjames (1854–1937)	English Methodist	India
O'Neill, Frederick W. S. (1855–1952)	Irish Presbyterian	Manchuria
Oveido, Andre de (1518–1577)	Spanish Jesuit	Ethiopia
Owen, Walter Edwin (1878–1945)	Anglican CMS	Kenya; Uganda
Paez, Pedro (1564–1622)	Spanish Jesuit	Ethiopia
Pallu, Francois (1626–1684)	French PFMS	Thailand
Pandosy, Charles (1824–1891)	French Oblates of Mary	Pacific Northwest
Papasarantopoulos, Chrysostom (1903–1972)	Greek Orthodox	Africa
Parker, Peter (1804–1888)	American ABCFM	China
Parrish, Sarah Rebecca (1869–1952)	American Methodist	Philippines
Parsons, Levi (1792–1822)	American ABCFM	Near East
Paton, Francis Hume Lyall (1870–1938)	Scottish Presbyterian	New Hebrides
Paton, John Gibson (1824–1907)	Scottish Presbyterian	New Hebrides
Patrick (390–460)	British	Ireland
Patteson, John Coleridge (1827–1871)	Anglican	Melanesia
Paucke, Florian (1719–1780)	German Jesuit	Paraguay
Payeras, Mariano (1769–1823)	Spanish Franciscan	California
Payne, William Smith (1870–1924)	Irish Plymouth Brethren	Argentina; Bolivia
Pearse, Joseph (1837–1911)	English LMS	Madagascar
Peck, Edmund James (1850–1924)	Anglican CMS	Inuit (Eskimos)
Peery, Rufus Benton (1868–1934)	American Lutheran	Japan
Peet, Joseph (1798–1865)	Anglican CMS	India
Pennell, Theodor Leighton (1867–1912)	Anglican CMS	Pakistan
Perboyre, Jean-Gabriel (1802–1840)	French Vincentian	China
Percival, Peter (1803–1882)	British Wesleyan Methodist	Ceylon; India

Name and Dates	Nationality & Sending Agency	Main Mission Field
Perkins, Justin (1805–1869)	American ABCFM	Persia
Perroton, Marie Francois (1796–1873)	French Catholic	Pacific Islands
Peter of Ghent (1480–1572)	Belgian Franciscan	Mexico
Peterson, Anne Marie (1878–1951)	Danish Lutheran	India
Petitjean, Bernard Thaddee (1829–1884)	French PFMS	Japan
Petitot, Emile (1838–1917)	French Catholic	Canada
Petrie, Irene Eleanora Verita (1864–1897)	English CMS	India
Petter, Rodolphe (1865–1947)	Swiss Mennonite	Cheyenne Indians
Pettitt, George (1803–1873)	English CMS	India
Pfander, Karl Gottlieb (1803–1865)	German Basel Mission	India
Pfanner, Franz (1825–1909)	Bosnian Catholic	South Africa
Phillippo, James Mursell (1798–1879)	English BMS	Jamaica
Phillips, Jeremiah (1812–1879)	American Baptist	Indian Santals
Pickett, Jarrell Waskom (1890–1981)	American Methodist	India
Pigneau, du Behaine Pierre-Joseph-Georges (1741–1799)	French PFMS	Indochina
Pilhofer, Georg (1871–1973)	German Lutheran	Papua New Guinea
Pilkington, George Lawrence (1865–1897)	English CMS	Uganda
Pitkin, Horace Tracy (1869–1900)	American ABCFM	China
Pitman, Charles (1796–1884)	English LMS	Cook Islands
Plasencia, Juan de (d. 1590)	Spanish Franciscan	Philippines
Platt, William James (1893–1993)	British Wesleyan Methodist	West Africa
Plutschau, Heinrich (1677–1752)	German Lutheran	India
Plymire, Victor Guy (1881–1956)	American C&MA	Tibet; China
Polhill, Cecil H. (1860–1938)	English Pentecostal	China
Pollard, Samuel (1864–1915)	British	China
Pompallier, Francois (1801–1871)	French Marist	New Zealand
Ponziglione, Paul Mary (1818–1900)	Italian Jesuit	Native Americans
Pope, George Uglow (1820–1908)	Anglican SPG	India
Popley, Herbert Arthur (1878–1960)	English LMS	India
Porter, Lucius Chapin (1880–1958)	American ABCFM	China
Pott, Francis Lester Hawks (1864–1947)	American Episcopal	China
Pottier, Francois (1726–1792)	French PFMS	China
Pratt, George (1817–1894)`	English LMS	Samoa
Pratt, Henry Barrington (1832–1912)	American Presbyterian	Colombia
Price, Francis Frank Wilson (1895–1974)	American Presbyterian	China
Price, Jonathan David (1796–1828)	American Baptist	Burma
Price, Roger (1834–1900)	Welsh LMS	Southern Africa
Prip, Einar (1868–1939)	Danish	Syria
Proksch, Georg (1904–1986)	Silesian SVD	India
Protten, Christian Jacob (1715–1769)	Danish Moravian	Ghana
Raaflaub, Fritz (1909–1993)	Swiss Basel Mission	Cameroon
Raban, John (1795–1841)	English CMS	Sierra Leone
Rada, Martin de (1533–1578)	Spanish Augustinian	Philippines
Ragland, Thomas Gajetan (1815–1858)	Anglican CMS	South India
Ramsey, Evelyn (1923–1989)	American Nazarene	Swaziland; Papua New Guinea

Name and Dates	Nationality & Sending Agency	Main Mission Field
Ramseyer, Fritz (1840–1914)	Swiss Basel Mission	Ghana
Rankin, Melinda (1811–1888)	American	Latin America
Rauch, Christian Henry (1718–1763)	German Moravian	American Indians
Ravoux, Augustin (1815–1906)	French Catholic	American Northwest
Read, James (1777–1852)	English LMS	South Africa
Rebmann, Johannes (1820–1876)	German Lutheran	East Africa
Reed, George C. (1872–1966)	American GMU	Morocco; Mali
Reed, Mary (1854–1943)	American Methodist	India
Reekie, Archibald Brownlee (1867–1942)	Canadian Baptist	Bolivia
Reeve, William (1794–1850)	English LMS	India
Regis, Jean-Baptiste (1663–1738)	French Jesuit	China
Reichelt, Karl Ludvig (1877–1952)	Norwegian Lutheran	China
Reid, Gilbert (1857–1927)	American Presbyterian	China
Reischauer, August Karl (1879–1971)	American Presbyterian	Japan
Renner, Melchior (1770–1821)	German Lutheran	Sierra Leone
Rhenius, Carl T. Ewald (1790–1838)	Prussian CMS	India
Rhodes, Alexandre de (1593–1660)	French Jesuit	Vietnam
Ricci, Matteo (1552–1610)	Italian Jesuit	China
Rice, Benjamin (1814–1887)	English LMS	India
Richard, Timothy (1845–1919)	Welsh BMS	China
Richards, Henry (1851–1928)	British Baptist	Congo
Richter, Enrique (1652–1695)	German Jesuit	Peruvian Amazon
Ricke, Jodoco (1498–1578)	Flemish Franciscan	Ecuador
Ridley, William (1819–1878)	English Presbyterian	Australian Aborigines
Riedel, Johann Friedrich (1798–1860)	Dutch NMS	Indonesia
Riedemann, Peter (1506–1556)	German Anabaptist	Moravia, Austria
Riggs, Elias (1810–1901)	American ABCFM	Near East
Riggs, Stephen Return (1812–1883)	American Presbyterian	Dakota Indians
Riis, Andreas (1804–1854)	Danish Basel Mission	Ghana
Rijnhart, Susanna (1868–1908)	Canadian Disciples of Christ	Tibet
Ringeltaube, Wilhelm Tobias (1770–1816)	German LMS	South India
Ritchie, John (1878–1952)	Scottish RBMU	Peru
Roberts, Issachar Jacox (1802–1871)	American Baptist	China
Robinson, William (1784–1853)	English Baptist	Bengal; Java; Sumatra
Rocha, Joao da (1565–1623)	Portuguese Jesuit	China
Rodgers, James Burton (1865–1944)	American Presbyterian	Philippines
Rolland, Samuel (1801–1873)	French PEMS	South Africa
Ronning, Halvor (1862–1950)	Norwegian Lutheran	China
Ross, John (1842–1915)	Scottish Presbyterian	Manchuria
Ross, William (1895–1973)	American SVD	New Guinea
Rossel, Jacques (1915–)	Swiss Basel Mission	India
Rottler, John Peter (1749–1836)	German SPCK	India
Rougemont, Francois de (1624–1676)	Belgian Jesuit	China
Rouse, George Henry (1838–1909)	English Baptist	India
Rowlands, John Francis (1909–1980)	English Pentecostal	South Africa
Ruggieri, Michele (1543–1607)	Italian Jesuit	China
Ruiz de Montoya, Antonio (1585–1652)	Peruvian Jesuit	Guarani Indians
Rundle, Robert Terrill (1811–1866)	English Methodist	Saskatchewan

Name and Dates	Nationality & Sending Agency	Main Mission Field
Russell, William Armstrong (1821–1879)	Irish CMS	China
Rycroft, William Stanley (1899–1993)	English Presbyterian	Latin America
Sabatier, Ernst (1886–1965)	French Catholic	Kiribati
Sahagun, Bernardino de (1499–1590)	Spanish Franciscan	Mexico
Saint, Rachel Bradford (1914–1994)	American WBT	Ecuador
Saker, Alfred (1814–1880)	English Baptist	Cameroons
Sale, Elizabeth (1818–1898)	English Baptist	India
Salvado, Rosendo (1814–1900)	Spanish Benedictine	Australia
Sambeek, Jan van (1886–1966)	Dutch White Fathers	Tanzania
San Vitores, Diego Luis de (1627–1672)	Spanish Jesuit	Oceania
Sandegren, Johannes (1883–1962)	Swedish Leipzig Mission	India
Santo Tomas, Domingo de (1499–1570)	Spanish Dominican	Latin America
Sargent, Douglas Noel (1907–1979)	English CMS	China
Sargent, Edward (1816–1889)	English CMS	India
Schafer, Alfons (1904–1958)	German SVD	New Guinea
Schall von Bell, Johann Adam (1592–1666)	German Jesuit	China
Scharer, Hans (1904–1947)	Swiss Basel Mission	Borneo; East Indies
Schauffler, William Gottlieb (1798–1883)	American ABCFM	Near East
Schellenberg, Katharina L. (1870–1945)	Ukrainian Mennonite	India
Scherer, James A. B. (1870–1944)	American Lutheran	Japan
Schereschewsky, Samuel I. J. (1831–1906)	Lithuanian Episcopal	China
Schiller, Karl Emil (1865–1945)	German Evangelical	Japan
Schmelen, Johann Heinrich (1776–1848)	German	Namibia
Schmelzenbach, Harmon F. (1882–1929)	American Nazarene	Swaziland
Schmidt, Georg (1709–1785)	Moravian Brethren	South Africa
Schnarre, Johannes Christian (1791–1820)	German CMS	South India
Schneder, David Bowman (1887–1938)	American Reformed	Japan
Schneller, Johann Ludwig (1820–1896)	German	Syria
Schoenmakers, John (1807–1883)	Belgian Jesuit	Native Americans
Schon, Jakob Friedrich (1803–1889)	German CMS	West Africa
Schrenk, Elias (1831–1913)	German Basel Mission	Ghana
Schreuder, Hans Paludan		
Smith (1817–1882)	Norwegian Missionary Soc.	Zulus; Madagascar
Schultz, Stephan (1714–1776)	German	Jews
Schultze, Benjamin (1689–1760)	Danish-Halle Mission	South India
Schurmann, Johannes (1810–1852)	German LMS	India
Schwartz, Carl August F. (1817–1870)	German Free Church	Jews
Schwartz, Christian Friedrich (1726–1798)	German Lutheran	India
Schwarz, Johann Gottlob (1800–1859)	German NMS	Indonesia
Scott, David Clement Rufelle (1853–1907)	Scottish CSM	Malawi; Kenya
Scranton, William Benton (1856–1922)	American Methodist	Korea
Scudder, Ida Sophia (1870–1960)	American ABCFM	India
Scudder, John (1793–1855)	American ABCFM	India
Seagrave, Gordon S. (1897–1965)	American Baptist	Burma
Sedat, William (1909–1971)	German Nazarene	Guatemala
Sell, Edward (1839–1932)	English CMS	India
Sergeant, John (1710–1749)	American Congregational	Native Americans

Name and Dates	Nationality & Sending Agency	Main Mission Field
Sergii of Valaam (fourteenth century)	Greek	Russia
Serra, Junipero (1713–1784)	Spanish Franciscan	Mexico; California
Severinus (d. 482)	German	Austria
Seward, Sarah Cornelia (1833–1891)	American Presbyterian	India
Shanahan, Joseph (1871–1943)	Irish Holy Ghost Fathers	Nigeria
Sharkey, John Edmund (1821–1867)	Anglo-Indian CMS	India
Shattuck, Corinna (1848–1910)	American ABCFM	Turkey
Shaw, Archibald (1879–1956)	English CMS	Sudan
Shaw, Barnabas (1788–1857)	American Methodist	South Africa
Shedd, William Ambrose (1865–1918)	American Presbyterian	Persia
Shellabear, William G. (1862–1947)	English Methodist	Malaysia; Singapore
Shepherd, Robert Henry W. (1888–1971)	Scottish Free Church	South Africa
Shuck, Jehu Lewis (1814–1863)	American Baptist	China
Shuurman, Barend Martinus (1889–1945)	Dutch Reformed	Java
Sibree, James (1836–1929)	English LMS	Madagascar
Sigfrid (eleventh century)	English	Sweden
Simonton, Ashbel Green (1831–1867)	American Presbyterian	Brazil
Simpson, William Wallace (1869–1961)	American C&MA	China
Skrefsrud, Lars Olsen (1840–1910)	Norwegian Lutheran	India
Slessor, Mary Mitchell (1848–1915)	Scottish Presbyterian	Nigeria
Small, Ann Hunter (1857–1945)	Scottish Free Church	India
Smith, Algernon Charles S. (1890–1978)	English CMS	Rwanda
Smith, Arthur Henderson (1845–1932)	American ABCFM	China
Smith, Eli (1801–1857)	American ABCFM	Armenia; Near East
Smith, George (1815–1917)	English CMS	China
Smith, Henry Light (1888–1924)	American Brethren	India
Smith, John (1790–1824)	English LMS	Guyana
Smith, Stanley P. (1861–1931)	English CIM	China
Smith, William (1806–1875)	English CMS	India
Snow, Benjamin Galen (1817–1880)	American ABCFM	Micronesia
Solano, Francisco (1549–1610)	Spanish Franciscan	Argentina; Peru
Soper, Annie (1883–1976)	English	Peru
Spalding, Henry Harmon (1804–1874)	American ABCFM	Nez Perce Indians
Spaulding, Levi (1791–1873)	American ABCFM	Sri Lanka
Spieth, Andrea Jakob (1856–1914)	German Basel Mission	Togo
Spinner, Wilfrid Heinrich (1854–1918)	Swiss Evangelical	Japan
Spinola, Carlo (1564–1622)	Italian Jesuit	Japan
Springer, Helen E. Rasmussen (1868–1946)	American Methodist	Southern Rhodesia
Springer, John McKendree (1873–1963)	American Methodist	Congo
Stach, Matthew (1711–1787)	Czech Moravian	Greenland
Stahl, Ferdinand Anthony (1874–1950)	American Seventh Day Adv.	Bolivia; Peru
Stallybrass, Edward (1793–1884)	English LMS	Siberia; Mongolia
Stam, John C. (1907–1934)	American CIM	China
Stanway, Alfred (1908–1989)	Anglican CMS	Africa
Stauffacher, John William (1878–1944)	American AIM	Kenya; Belgian Congo
Staunton, John Armitage, Jr. (1864–1944)	American Episcopal	Philippines
Steere, Edward (1828–1882)	Anglican UMCA	Africa
Steidel, Florence (1897–1962)	American Pentecostal	Liberia

Name and Dates	Nationality & Sending Agency	Main Mission Field
Stephen of Perm (1340–1396)	Russian Orthodox	Finno-Ugric Zyryan tribes
Stephens, Thomas (1549–1619)	English Jesuit	India
Stevens, Edwin (1802–1837)	American	China
Stevenson, Marion Scott (1871–1930)	Scottish CSM	Kenya
Stewart, James (1831–1905)	Scottish CSM	South Africa
Stewart, John (1786–1823)	American Methodist	Native Americans
Stirling, Waite Hockin (1829–1923)	English	Patagonia
Stockfleth, Nils Joachim Vibe (1787–1866)	Norwegian Lutheran	Lapps
Stockton, Betsey (1798–1865)	American Presbyterian	Hawaii
Stockwell, Bowman Foster (1899–1961)	American Methodist	Argentina
Stockwell, Eugene Louden (1923–1996)	American Methodist	Latin America
Stosch, Johannes Richard A. (1878–1973)	German Gossner Mission	Bihar, India
Stover, Wilbur B. (1866–1930)	American Brethren	India
Strachan, Harry (1872–1946)	Scottish LAM	Latin America
Strachan, Robert Kenneth (1910–1965)	Scottish LAM	Latin America
Strauss, Hermann (1910–1978)	German	New Guinea
Strehlow, Carl Friedrich T. (1870–1922)	German	Australia
Streicher, Henri (1863–1952)	French White Fathers	Uganda
Stronach, Alexander (1800–1879)	Scottish LMS	China
Stronach, John (1810–1888)	Scottish LMS	China
Stuart, Edward Craig (1827–1911)	Scottish CMS	India; New Zealand
Stuart, John Leighton (1876–1962)	American Presbyterian	China
Sturges, Albert A. (1819–1887)	American ABCFM	Micornesia
Suidbert (d. 713)	Anglo-Saxon	Frisia (Belgium and Netherlands)
Sundkler, Bengt (1909–1995)	Swedish Lutheran	South and East Africa
Sutton, Amos (1802–1854)	British Baptist	Orissa, India
Swain, Clara (1834–1910)	American Methodist	India
Swan, William (1791–1866)	Scottish LMS	Siberia
Takle, John (1870–1939)	British Baptist	Bengal
Talmage, John Van Nest (1819–1892)	American Reformed	China
Taylor, James Hudson (1832–1905)	English CIM	China
Taylor, John Vernon (1914–)	Anglican CMS	Uganda
Taylor, Richard (1804–1873)	English CMS	New Zealand
Taylor, Richard W. (1924–1988)	American Methodist	India
Taylor, William (1821–1902)	American Methodist	Africa
Tellstrom, Carl Ludwig (1811–1862)	Swedish SMS	Saami (Lapp)
Tempels, Placide (1906–1977)	Belgian Franciscan	Africa
Teresa, Mother (1910–1997)	Albanian-Indian Catholic	India
Testera, Jacobo de (d. 1543)	French Franciscan	Mexico
Tewksbury, Elwood Gardner (1865–1945)	American Congregational	China
Thevenoud, Joanny (1878–1949)	French White Fathers	West Africa
Thoburn, Isabella (1840–1901)	American Methodist	India
Thoburn, James Mills (1836–1922)	American Methodist	India; Malaysia
Thomas, John (1796–1881)	English Wesleyan Methodist	Tonga
Thomas, John (1808–1870)	Welsh CMS	India
Thomas, Robert Jermain (1839–1866)	Welsh CMS	China

Name and Dates	Nationality & Sending Agency	Main Mission Field
Thomson, James (1788–1854)	Scottish BFBS	Latin America
Thomson, John Francis (1843–1933)	American Methodist	Argentina; Uruguay
Thompson, Thomas (1708–1773)	Anglican SPG	Africa
Thomson, William Ritchie (1794–1891)	Scottish Presbyterian	South Africa
Thornton, Douglas M. (1873–1907)	Anglican CMS	Egypt
Threlkeld, Lancelot Edward (1788–1859)	English LMS	Tahiti; Australian Aborigines
Thurston, Asa (1787–1868)	American ABCFM	Hawaii
Thurston, Matilda S. (1875–1958)	American Presbyterian	China
Timpany, Americus Vespucius (1840–1885)	Canadian Baptist	India
Tippett, Alan R. (1911–1988)	American Methodist	Fiji
Tisdall, William St. Clair (1859–1928)	Welsh CMS	Muslims
Titus, Murray Thurston (1885–1964)	American Methodist	India
Tollefsen, Gunnerius Olai (1888–1966)	Norwegian Pentecostal	Africa
Tomlin, Jacob (1793–1880)	English LMS	Malacca; Thailand
Torrance, David Watt (1862–1923)	Scottish Free Church	Palestine
Torrance, Thomas (1871–1959)	Scottish CIM	China
Torrend, Jules (1861–1936)	French Jesuit	Africa
Townsend, Henry (1815–1886)	English CMS	Yorubaland
Townsend, William Cameron (1896–1982)	American Presbyterian	Wycliffe Bible Translators
Trasher, Lillian Hunt (1887–1961)	American Pentecostal	Egypt
Trenchard, Ernest Harold (1902–1972)	English Brethren	Spain
Trigault, Nicolas (1577–1628)	Belgian Jesuit	China
Trobisch, Walter (1923–1979)	German	Cameroon
Trollope, Mark Napier (1862–1930)	Anglican	Korea
Trotter, Isabella Lilias (1853–1928)	English	North Africa
Trumbull, David (1819–1889)	American Evangelical	Chile
Tryphon of Pechenga (d. 1583)	Russian Orthodox	Lapps and Samoyeds
Tucker, J. W. (1915–1964)	American Pentecostal	Belgian Congo
Tucker, John Taylor (1883–1958)	English Congregational	Angola
Tucker, John Thomas (1818–1866)	English CMS	India
Turner, George (1818–1891)	Scottish LMS	Samoa
Turquetil, Arsene (1876–1955)	French Oblates of Mary	Canada
Turton, William (1760–1817)	English Methodist	Bahamas
Tyler, Josiah (1823–1895)	American ABCFM	South Africa
Underwood, Horace Grant (1859–1916)	American Presbyterian	Korea
Urios, Saturnino (1843–1916)	Spanish Jesuit	Philippines
Valdivia, Luis de (1561–1642)	Spanish Jesuit	Chile
Valdivieso, Antonio de (d. 1550)	Spanish Dominican	Nicaragua; Costa Rica
Valencia, Martin de (1473–1534)	Spanish Franciscan	Mexico
Valignano, Alessandro (1539–1606)	Italian Jesuit	Japan; China
Van Dyck, Cornelius (1818–1895)	American ABCFM	Syria
Vautrin, Wilhelmina (1886–1941)	American Disciples of Christ	China
Vaz, Joseph (1651–1711)	Goan Catholic	Sri Lanka
Vedder, Hermann Heinrich (1876–1972)	German Rhenish Mission	South-West Africa
Veenstra, Johanna (1894–1933)	American SUM	Nigeria

Name and Dates	Nationality & Sending Agency	Main Mission Field
Venard, Jean Theophane (1829–1861)	French Catholic	Vietnam
Vera Cruz, Alonso de la (1504–1584)	Spanish Catholic	Mexico
Verbeck, Guido Herman F. (1830–1898)	Dutch Presbyterian	Japan
Verbiest, Ferdinand (1623–1688)	Belgian Jesuit	China
Verjus, Henri (1860–1892)	Italian MSC	Papua New Guinea
Vernier, Frederic (1841–1915)	French PEMS	French Polynesia
Vieter, Heinrich (1853–1914)	German Pallotine	Cameroon
Vinco, Angelo (1819–1853)	Italian Catholic	Sudan
Vingren, Adolf Gunnar (1879–1933)	Swedish Pentecostal	Brazil
Vinton, Justus Hatch (1806–1858)	American Baptist	Burma
Visdelou, Claude (1656–1737)	French Jesuit	China
Vories, William Merrell (1880–1964)	American SVM	Japan
Voskamp, Carl Johannes (1859–1937)	German Berlin Mission	China
Waddell, Hope Masterton (1804–1895)	Irish Presbyterian	Nigeria; Jamaica
Wade, Jonathan (1798–1872)	American Baptist	Burma
Wakefield, Thomas (1836–1901)	English Methodist	East Africa
Walker, Thomas (1859–1912)	English CMS	India
Walker, William (1800–1855)	English Wesleyan	Australian Aborigines
Walsh, James Edward (1891–1981)	American Maryknoll	China
Walther, Theodosius (1699–1741)	Danish-Halle	India
Wangerin, Theodora S. (1888–1978)	American Seventh-Day Adv.	Korea
Wanless, William James (1865–1933)	American Presbyterian	India
Ward, William (1769–1823)	British Baptist	Bengal, India
Wardlaw, John Smith (1813–1872)	Scottish LMS	India
Warneck, Johannes (1867–1944)	German Rhenish Mission	Indonesia
Warnshuis, Abbe Livingston (1877–1958)	American Reformed	China
Watson, William (1798–1866)	English CMS	Australian Aborigines
Webster-Smith, Irene (1888–1971)	Irish Quaker	Japan
Weinland, William (1861–1930)	American Moravian	Alaska
Weir, Andrew (1873–1933)	Irish Presbyterian	Manchuria
Westen, Thomas von (1682–1727)	Norwegian Lutheran	Lapps
Weston, Frank (1871–1924)	Anglican	Zanzibar
Wherry, Elwood Morris (1843–1927)	American Presbyterian	North India
White, Andrew (1579–1656)	Spanish Jesuit	Maryland
White, Charlotte Hazen Atlee (d. c. 1830)	American Baptist	India
White, John (1866–1933)	English Wesleyan	Rhodesia
White, Moses Clark (1819–1900)	American Methodist	China
Whitman, Marcus (1802–1847)	American Presbyterian	Native Americans
Widmann, Rosina Binder (1826–1908)	German Basel Mission	West Africa
Wieger, Georges Frederic (1856–1933)	French Jesuit	China
Wilder, Royal Gould (1816–1887)	American ABCFM	India
Wilkes, Paget (1871–1934)	Anglican	Japan
Wilkins, Ann (1806–1857)	American Methodist	Liberia
William of Rubroek (thirteenth century)	French Franciscan	Asia
Williams, Channing Moore (1829–1910)	American Episcopalian	Japan
Williams, Henry (1792–1867)	English CMS	New Zealand

Name and Dates	Nationality & Sending Agency	Main Mission Field
Williams, John (1796–1839)	English LMS	South Pacific
Williams, Ralph Darby (1902–1982)	English Assemblies of God	Central America
Williams, Samuel Wells (1812–1884)	American ABCFM	China
Williams, William Frederic (1818–1871)	American ABCFM	Near East
Williamson, Alexander (1829–1890)	Scottish LMS	China
Williamson, Henry Raymond (1883–1966)	British BMS	China
Williamson, Thomas Smith (1800–1879)	American ABCFM	Dakota Indians
Willibald (700–786)	English	Thuringia
Willibrord, Clemens (657–739)	English Benedictine	Netherlands; Frisia
Willis, John Jamieson (1872–1954)	English CMS	Uganda; Kenya
Willoughby, William Charles (1857–1938)	English LMS	Botswana
Wilson, J. Christy, Sr. (1891–1973)	American Presbyterian	Iran
Wilson, John Leighton (1809–1886)	American Presbyterian	Africa
Wilson, Mary Ann (1784–1868)	British CMS	India
Wilson, Robert Orr (1906–1967)	American	China
Wilson, Samuel Graham (1858–1916)	American Presbyterian	Persia
Winans, Roger (1886–1975)	American Nazarene	Peru
Winslow, Harriet Wadsworth (1796–1833)	American ABCFM	Sri Lanka
Winslow, Miron (1789–1864)	American ABCFM	Sri Lanka; India
Winthuis, Josef (1876–1956)	German Catholic	Papua New Guinea
Wiser, William Hendricks (1890–1961)	American Presbyterian	India
Wolff, Joseph (1795–1862)	German	Jews
Worcester, Samuel Austin (1798–1859)	American	Cherokee Indians
Xavier, Francis (1506–1552)	Spanish Jesuit	Asia
Xenos, Ioannes (c. 970–1027)	Greek	Crete
Yate, William (1802–1877)	British CMS	New Zealand
Yates, Matthew Tyson (1819–1888)	American Baptist	China
Yates, William (1792–1845)	English Baptist	India
Yoder, Charles Frances (1873–1955)	American Brethren	Argentina
Young, George Armstrong (1898–1991)	English Baptist	China
Young, Samuel Hall (1847–1927)	American Presbyterian	Alaska
Zaremba, Felician von (1794–1874)	Polish Basel Mission	Caucasus
Zeisberger, David (1721–1808)	German Moravian	Native Americans
Ziegenbalg, Bartholomaus (1682–1719)	German Pietist	South India
Zimmerman, Johannes (1825–1876)	German Basel Mission	Ghana
Zwemer, Samuel Marinus (1867–1952)	American Reformed	Muslims

100 Most Important Events in Christian History

1. Council of Nicaea (325)
2. Luther posts Ninety-Five Theses (1517)
3. East-West Schism (1054)
4. Vatican II (1962)
5. Conversion of St. Augustine (386)
6. Publication of the Gutenberg Bible (1455)
7. Council of Trent (1545)
8. Council of Chalcedon (451)
9. Completion of *Summa Theologica* by St. Thomas Aquinas (1272)
10. John Calvin publishes *Institutes* (1536)
11. Edict of Milan (313)
12. Jerome completes the Vulgate (406)
13. King James Bible (1611)
14. Diet of Worms (1521)
15. The Great Schism (1378)
16. The Act of Supremacy (1534)
17. Benedict's Monastic rule (540)
18. Athanasius's letter establishes the 27 canons of the New Testament (367)
19. Great Awakening begins (1735)
20. Destruction of Jerusalem by Titus (70)
21. Crusades launched by Pope Urban II (1095)
22. Anabaptist movement (1525)
23. Martin Luther King, Jr. leads march on Washington (1963)
24. Christianization of Russia (988)
25. Conversion of John and Charles Wesley (1738)
26. Paris and Oxford universities founded (c. 1150)
27. Coronation of Charlemagne as Holy Roman emperor (800)
28. Westminster Confession (1647)
29. Passage of Bill of Rights (1789)
30. Gregory the Great's election as pope (590)
31. Collapse of Communism (1988)
32. Augsburg Confession (1530)
33. First Vatican Council (1869)
34. Wycliffe supervises translation of English Bible (c. 1380)
35. Karl Barth writes *Epistle to the Romans* (1919)
36. *Book of Common Prayer* (1552)
37. World Council of Churches is founded (1948)
38. Zwingli becomes people's priest at Zurich (1518)
39. Fourth Lateran Council is convoked (1215)
40. Wilberforce spearheads the abolition of slavery (1807)
41. Origen begins writing (c. 215–220)
42. Treaty of Westphalia (1648)
43. Edict of Nantes (1598)
44. Tyndale publishes New Testament (1525)
45. Monastery of Cluny (910)
46. Hus burned at the stake (1415)
47. Peter and Paul martyred (c. 65)
48. St. Francis of Assisi renounces wealth (1208)
49. Cyril and Methodius embark on mission to the Slavs (864)
50. Colloquy at Marburg (1529)
51. Donatist Schism begins (312)
52. Patrick begins evangelization of Ireland (432)
53. St. Bernard founds monastery at Clairvaux (1115)
54. Athanasius becomes bishop of Alexandria (328)
55. Syllabus of Errors issued by Pope Pius IX (1864)

56. Tertullian begins writing (196)
57. International Missionary Conference at Edinburgh (1910)
58. St. Anthony the Great begins eremetical life (269)
59. Establishment of Spanish Inquisition (1478)
60. William Carey sails for India (1793)
61. Battle of Tours (732)
62. Waldensian movement begins (1175)
63. British and Foreign Bible Society formed (1804)
64. Chinese Church survives the worst of Communist persecutions (1965)
65. Bultmann calls for demythologization of the New Testament (1941)
66. Justin Martyr's *First Apology* (c. 150–155)
67. Publication of *Fundamentals* (1929)
68. Synod of Dort (1618)
69. Public churches begin to be built (c. 230)
70. Kierkegaard writes *Attack on Christendom* (1854)
71. Boniface sets out as missionary (716)
72. Publication of Bede's *Ecclesiastical History* (731)
73. John Knox's final return to Scotland (1559)
74. St. Bartholomew's Day Massacre (1572)
75. Bunyan writes *The Pilgrim's Progress* (1678)
76. Anselm becomes archbishop of Canterbury (1093)
77. Chrysostom consecrated bishop of Constantinople (398)
78. First trial of Galileo (1616)
79. John Keble's sermon initiates the Oxford movement (1833)
80. Columba establishes mission community on Iona (563)
81. Xavier begins mission to Japan (1549)
82. Mayflower Covenant drafted (1620)
83. Bonhoeffer executed (1945)
84. Synod of Whitby (664)
85. Roger Williams establishes Providence, Rhode Island (1636)
86. Francis Asbury assumes leadership of U.S. Methodist congregations (1772)
87. Azusa Street Revival breaks out (1906)
88. Whitefield converted (1735)
89. Richard Allen elected bishop of AME Church (1816)
90. John Smyth is baptized, thus founding the Baptist church (1609)
91. Jesus People phenomenon (1960)
92. William and Catherine Booth found the Salvation Army (1878)
93. Billy Graham debuts in Los Angeles (1949)
94. Irenaeus named bishop of Lyons (177)
95. Triumph of Ambrose (385)
96. D. L. Moody's conversion (1855)
97. Finney leads revival in Rochester, New York (1830)
98. Student Volunteer Movement begins (1886)
99. Niebuhr's *Nature and Destiny of Man* (1941)
100. Medellin Conference ushers in liberation theology (1968)

Source: *Christian History,* Fall 1990

100 Greatest Christians

1. St. Paul (apostle)
2. St. Peter (apostle)
3. St. John (apostle and evangelist)
4. St. Francis of Assisi
5. Ignatius (church father)
6. Martin Luther (Reformer)
7. St. Augustine
8. Origen (church father)
9. David Livingstone (missionary)
10. St. Francis Xavier (missionary)
11. Mark (evangelist)
12. Matthew (apostle and evangelist)
13. Luke (associate of St. Paul)
14. Athanasius the Great (patriarch)
15. Tertullian (theologian)
16. Charles Spurgeon (preacher)
17. St. Patrick of Ireland
18. Jerome (scholar and translator)
19. Gregory the Great (pope)
20. St. Anthony (pioneer of Christian Monasticism)
21. John Wesley (founder of Methodism)
22. St. Teresa of Avila (mystic)
23. Mother Teresa (social worker)
24. St. Anthony of Padua
25. John Wycliffe (Bible translator)
26. John Calvin (Reformer)
27. Hudson Taylor (missionary)
28. Marcion of Pontus (heretic)
29. Joan of Arc (patroness of France)
30. Benedict (monastic founder)
31. John Paul II (pope)
32. Karl Barth (theologian)
33. Nikon (Russian patriarch)
34. Billy Graham (evangelist)
35. William Booth (founder of the Salvation Army)
36. St. Thomas Aquinas (Scholastic Theo.)
37. Innocent III (pope)
38. Gregory Nazianzus (church father)
39. Basil the Great (church father)
40. John Chrysostom (church father)
41. William Carey (missionary)
42. Sts. Cyril and Methodius (apostles to the Slavs)
43. Constantine the Great (emperor)
44. Gregory Palamas (theologian)
45. William Tyndale (Bible translator)
46. John XXIII (pope)
47. Feodor Dostoevsky (Russian writer)
48. Jonathan Edwards (Puritan leader)
49. Dwight L. Moody (preacher)
50. Soren Aabye Kierkegaard (Dan. writer)
51. Leo the Great (pope)
52. Clement of Alexandria (church father)
53. Ignatius Loyola (founder of the Jesuits)
54. St. John of the Cross (mystic)
55. Dominic (founder of the Dominicans)
56. Bernard of Clairvaux (monk and mystic)
57. St. John of the Cross
58. Blaise Pascal (writer)
59. Menno Simons (Mennonite founder)
60. Philip Melanchthon (Reformer)
61. Irenaeus (bishop)
62. John Hus (Czech Reformer)
63. Gregory Abu-l-Faraj Bar Hebraeus (Syriac scholar)
64. Clement of Rome (bishop)
65. Catherine of Siena (mystic)
66. Eusebius of Caesarea (historian)
67. St. Augustine (archbishop of Canterbury)
68. Ambrose (bishop of Milan)
69. Robert Moffat (missionary and Bible translator)
70. John Knox (Reformer)

71. C. S. Lewis (writer and Apologist)
72. Gerard Groote (mystic)
73. Father Damien (missionary to the lepers)
74. Ulrich Zwingli (Reformer)
75. Abraham Kuyper (statesman and theologian)
76. John of Damascus (church father)
77. Toyohiko Kagawa (Japanese leader and Pacifist)
78. Jan Van Ruysbroeck (mystic)
79. St. Sergius (monk)
80. Emil Brunner (theologian)
81. Gregory of Nyssa (bishop)
82. Nikolai Berdyaev (Russian theologian)
83. George Fox (founder of the Quakers)
84. Polycarp (bishop)
85. Thomas à Kempis (mystic)
86. Isaac Watts (hymn writer)
87. Ephraem Syrus (Syriac hymn writer)
88. Charles Finney (preacher)
89. Francis de Sales (founder of the Salesians)
90. Gregory the Illuminator (founder of the Armenian Church)
91. Jacques Maritain (writer)
92. Justin Martyr (Apologist)
93. Isidore of Seville (bishop and encyclopedist)
94. Giovanni Palestrina (composer)
95. Philipp Jakob Spener (Pietist)
96. Anselm of Canterbury
97. John R. Mott (Ecumenist)
98. John Newton (hymnwriter)
99. John Paton (missionary)
100. John Darby (Plymouth Brethren leader)

10 GREAT CHRISTIANS IN THE TWENTIETH CENTURY

1. Karl Barth
2. Billy Graham
3. John Paul II (pope)
4. John XXXIII
5. Martin Luther King, Jr.
6. C. S. Lewis
7. John R. Mott
8. William Seymour
9. Alexander Solzhenitsyn
10. Mother Teresa

Source: *Christian History*

300 Great Hymns of the Christian Church

Hymn	Hymn Writer
A Charge to Keep I Have	Charles Wesley
A Hymn of Glory Let Us Sing	Venerable Bede
A Mighty Fortress Is Our God	Martin Luther
A Wonderful Savior Is Jesus My Lord	Fanny Crosby
Abide with Me	Henry Francis Lyte
According to Thy Gracious Word	James Montgomery
Ah, Holy Jesus	Johann Heermann
Alas and Did My Savior Bleed	Isaac Watts
All Creatures of Our God and King	Francis of Assisi
All for Jesus, All for Jesus	Mary D. James
All Glory Be to God on High	Nikolaus Decius
All Glory, Laud and Honor	Theodulf of Orleans
All Hail the Power of Jesus' Name	Edward Perronet
All My Hope on God Is Founded	Joachim Neander
All Nature's Works His Praise Declare	Henry Ware, Jr.
All People That on Earth Do Dwell	William Kethe
All Praise to Our Redeeming Lord	Charles Wesley
All Praise to Thee, Eternal Lord	Martin Luther
All Praise to Thee, My God, This Night	Thomas Ken
All the Way My Savior Leads Me	Fanny Crosby
All Things Bright and Beautiful	Cecil Francis Alexander
Alleluia, Sing to Jesus	William Chatterton Dix
Almighty God, Thy Lofty Throne	The Psalter
Almighty God Thy Word Is Cast	John Cawood
Am I a Soldier of the Cross	Isaac Watts
Amazing Grace	John Newton
Ancient of Days	William Croswell Doane
And Can It Be?	Charles Wesley
Angels, from the Realms of Glory	James Montgomery
Angels We Have Heard on High	James Chadwick
Another Year Is Dawning	Frances Ridley Havergal
Approach, My Soul, the Mercy Seat	John Newton
Arise, My Soul, Arise	Charles Wesley
Art Thou Weary, Art Thou Languid?	Stephen the Sebaite
As with Gladness, Men of Old	William Chatterton Dix
At Calvary	William Reed Newell
At Even, Ere the Sun Was Set	Henry Twells
At the Lamb's High Feast	Latin Hymn

Hark! the Herald Angels Sing	Charles Wesley
Have Thine Own Way, Lord	Adelaide Addison Pollard
He Giveth More Grace	Annie Johnson Flint
He Leadeth Me	Joseph Henry Gilmore
Here, O My Lord, I See Thee Face to Face	Horatius Bonar
Holy Bible, Book Divine	John Burton
Holy Ghost, with Light Divine	Andrew Reed
Holy God, We Praise Thy Name	Ignace Franz
Holy, Holy, Holy	Reginald Heber
Holy Spirit, Truth Divine	Samuel Longfellow
Hosanna, Loud Hosanna	Jeannette Threlfall
How Firm a Foundation	Unknown
How Great Thou Art	Carl Boberg
How Lovely Is Thy Dwelling Place	Scottish Psalter
How Lovely Shines the Morning Star	Philipp Nicolai
How Sweet the Name of Jesus Sounds	John Newton
I Am His and He Is Mine	George Wade Robinson
I Am Not Skilled to Understand	Dora Greenwell
I Am Thine, O Lord	Fanny Crosby
I Heard the Voice of Jesus Say	Horatius Bonar
I Know That My Redeemer Lives	Samuel Medley
I Know Whom I Have Believed	Daniel Webster Whittle
I Love Thy Kingdom, Lord	Timothy Dwight
I Love to Tell the Story	Arabella Catherine Hankey
I Need Thee Every Hour	Annie Sherwood Hawks
I Sing the Mighty Power of God	Isaac Watts
I Surrender All	Judson W. Van de Venter
I Will Sing of My Redeemer	Philip Paul Bliss
I Will Sing the Wondrous Story	Francis Harold Rowley
If Thou but Suffer God to Guide Thee	Georg Neumark
I'll Praise My Maker While I've Breath	Isaac Watts
Immanuel, to Thee We Sing	Paul Gerhardt
In Christ There Is No East or West	John Oxenham
In Heavenly Love Abiding	Anna Laetitia Waring
In the Cross of Christ I Glory	John Bowring
In the Hour of Trial	James Montgomery
It Came upon the Midnight Clear	Edmund Hamilton Sears
It Is Good to Sing Thy Praises	The Psalter
It Is Well with My Soul	Horatio Gates Spafford
I've Found a Friend, O Such a Friend	James Grindlay Small
Jesus Calls Us	Cecil Frances Alexander
Jesus Christ Is Risen Today	Latin Hymn
Jesus Lives, and So Shall I	Christian Furchtegott Gellert
Jesus Love Me	Anna Bartlett Warner
Jesus Paid It All	Elvina Mabel Hall
Jesus Shall Reign	Isaac Watts
Jesus! The Name High Over All	Charles Wesley
Jesus! What a Friend for Sinners	J. Wilbur Chapman
Jesus, I Am Resting, Resting	Jean Sophia Pigott

Jesus, I My Cross Have Taken	Henry Francis Lyte
Jesus, Keep Me Near the Cross	Fanny Crosby
Jesus, Lead Thou On	Nicolaus von Zinzendorf
Jesus, Lover of My Soul	Charles Wesley
Jesus, My Lord, My God, My All	Henry Collins
Jesus, Priceless Treasure	Johann Franck
Jesus, the Very Thought of Thee	Bernard of Clairvaux
Jesus, Thou Joy of Loving Hearts	Bernard of Clairvaux
Jesus, Thy Blood and Righteousness	Nicolaus von Zinzendorf
Jesus, Thy Boundless Love to Me	Paul Gerhardt
Join All the Glorious Names	Isaac Watts
Joy to the World	Isaac Watts
Joyful, Joyful, We Adore Thee	Henry van Dyke
Just a Closer Walk with Thee	Unknown
Just As I Am	Charlotte Elliott
Lamb of God	James G. Deck
Lamp of Our Feet	Bernard Barton
Lead, Kindly Light	John Henry Newman
Lead On, O King Eternal	Ernest Warburton Shurtleff
Leaning on the Everlasting Arms	Elisha Albright Hoffman
Lenten Hymn	Claudia Frances Hernaman
Let All Mortal Flesh Keep Silence	Liturgy of St. James
Let Thy Blood in Mercy Poured	Greek Hymn
Let Us Break Bread Together	Unknown
Let Us Love, and Sing, and Wonder	John Newton
Lift Up Your Heads, Ye Mighty Gates	Georg Weissel
Like a River Glorious	Frances Ridley Havergal
Lo! He Comes, with Clouds Descending	Charles Wesley
Lo! How a Rose E'er Blooming	Unknown
Lord, It Belongs Not to My Care	Richard Baxter
Lord Jesus Christ, Be Present Now	German Hymn
Lord Jesus Christ, My Life, My Light	Martin Behm
Lord Jesus, Think on Me	Synesius of Cyrene
Lord, Speak to Me	Frances Ridley Havergal
Love Divine, All Loves Excelling	Charles Wesley
May the Grace of Christ, Our Savior	John Newton
May the Mind of Christ, My Savior	Kate B. Wilkinson
More About Jesus	Eliza Edmunds Hewitt
More Love to Thee, O Christ	Elizabeth Payson Prentiss
Must Jesus Bear the Cross Alone	Thomas Shepherd
My Faith Has Found a Resting Place	Lidie H. Edmunds
My Faith Looks Up to Thee	Ray Palmer
My God, How Wonderful Thou Art	Frederick William Faber
My Hope Is Built on Nothing Else	Edward Mote
My Jesus, I Love Thee	William Ralph Featherston
My Savior's Love	Charles Hutchinson Gabriel
Near to the Heart of God	Cleland Boyd McAfee
Nearer, My God, to Thee	Sarah Flower Adams

Rejoice, Ye Pure in Heart	Edward Hayes Plumptre
Rescue the Perishing	Fanny Crosby
Revive Us Again	William Paton Mackay
Rise Up, O Men of God	William Pearson Merrill
Rock of Ages	Augustus Toplady
Savior, Like a Shepherd Lead Us	Dorothy A. Thrupp
Savior of the Nations, Come	Ambrose of Milan
Shepherd of Eager Youth	Clement of Alexandria
Silent Night, Holy Night	Joseph Mohr
Sing Praise to God Who Reigns Above	Johann Jakob Schutz
Sing to the Lord of the Harvest	John Samuel Bewley Marshall
Softly and Tenderly Jesus Is Calling	William Lamartine Thompson
Soldiers of Christ, Arise	Charles Wesley
Songs of Thankfulness and Praise	Christopher Wordsworth
Speak, Lord, in the Stillness	Emily May Grimes
Spirit of God, Descend upon My Heart	George Croly
Stand Up and Bless the Lord	James Montgomery
Stand Up, Stand Up for Jesus	George Duffield, Jr.
Sun of My Soul, My Savior Dear	John Keble
Sweet Hour of Prayer	William W. Walford
Take My Life and Let It Be	Frances Ridley Havergal
Take Time to Be Holy	William Dunn Longstaff
Teach Me, My God and King	George Herbert
Teach Me, O Lord, Thy Holy Way	William T. Matson
Tell Me the Story of Jesus	Fanny Crosby
Thanks to God for My Redeemer	August Ludwig Storm
The Church's One Foundation	Samuel John Stone
The Day of Resurrection	John of Damascus
The First Noel	Unknown
The Friendly Beasts	Unknown
The Head that Once Was Crowned	Thomas Kelly
The Heavens Declare Thy Glory, Lord	Isaac Watts
The King of Love, My Shepherd Is	Henry Williams Baker
The Lord Is King	Josiah Conder
The Lord Jehovah Reigns	Isaac Watts
The Lord's My Shepherd, I'll Not Want	Scottish Psalter
The Old Rugged Cross	George Bennard
The People that in Darkness Sat	John Morison
The Strife Is O'er	Latin Hymn
The Wise May Bring Their Learning	Unknown
Thee Will I Love, My Strength	Johann Scheffler
There Is a Balm in Gilead	Unknown
There Is a Fountain Filled with Blood	William Cowper
There Is a Green Hill Far Away	Cecil Frances Alexander
There's a Wideness in God's Mercy	Frederick William Faber
This Is My Father's World	Maltbie Davenport Babcock
Thou Didst Leave Thy Throne	Emily Elizabeth Steele Elliott
Thy Works, Not Mine, O Christ	Horatius Bonar
'Tis So Sweet to Trust in Jesus	Louisa M. R. Stead

To God Be the Glory	Fanny Crosby
Trust and Obey	John H. Sammis
Turn Your Eyes Upon Jesus	Helen Howarth Lemmel
Under His Wings I Am Safely Abiding	William Orcutt Cushing
Wake, Awake, for Night Is Flying	Philipp Nicolai
Watchman, Tell Us of the Night	John Bowring
We Gather Together	Unknown
We Give Immortal Praise	Isaac Watts
We Give Thee but Thine Own	William Walsham How
We Plow the Fields	Matthias Claudius
We Praise Thee, O God	Julia Cady Cory
We Three Kings of Orient Are	John Henry Hopkins, Jr.
Were You There?	Unknown
What a Friend We Have in Jesus	Joseph Medlicott Scriven
What Child Is This?	William Chatterton Dix
What Wondrous Love Is This?	Unknown
When I Survey the Wondrous Cross	Isaac Watts
When Morning Gilds the Skies	German Hymn
Where Cross the Crowded Ways of Life	Frank Mason North
While the Shepherds Watched Their Flocks	Nahum Tate
Who Is He in Yonder Stall?	Benjamin Russell Hanby
Who Is on the Lord's Side?	Frances Ridley Havergal
Who Is This So Weak and Helpless?	William Walsham How
Wonderful Grace of Jesus	Haldor Lillenas
Ye Servants of God	Charles Wesley
Zion, to Thy Savior Singing	Thomas Aquinas

23 GREATEST HYMNS OF THE CHRISTIAN CHURCH

1.	Amazing Grace	13.	I Surrender All
2.	Old Rugged Cross	14.	I Will Sing of My Redeemer
3.	To God Be the Glory	15.	Just As I Am
4.	When I Survey the Wondrous Cross	16.	Jesus, the Very Thought of Thee
5.	All Hail the Power of Jesus' Name	17.	O, Come, All Ye Faithful
6.	A Mighty Fortress Is Our God	18.	There Is a Fountain Filled with Blood
7.	It's Well with My Soul	19.	All Hail the Power of Jesus' Name
8.	What a Friend We Have in Jesus	20.	Because He Lives
9.	Blessed Assurance	21.	Open My Eyes, Lord
10.	Crown Him with Many Crowns	22.	O, the Deep, Deep Love of Jesus
11.	Great Is Thy Faithfulness	23.	O for a Thousand Tongues to Sing
12.	Hark! The Herald Angels Sing		

Major Creeds of the Christian Church

THE APOSTLES' CREED

I believe in God, the Father Almighty, creator of
Heaven and Earth

And in Jesus Christ, His only Son, our Lord

who was conceived of the Holy Spirit, born of the
Virgin Mary

suffered under Pontius Pilate

was crucified, died, and was buried

He descended into Hell

On the third day He rose again from the dead.

He ascended into Heaven, sits on the right hand
of God, the Father Almighty

From thence He shall come to judge the living
and the dead.

I believe in the Holy Spirit, the Holy Catholic
Church, the Communion of Saints,

the forgiveness of sins, the resurrection of the
body, and life everlasting. Amen.

ATHANASIAN CREED

Whosoever will be saved: before all things it is
necessary that he hold the Catholic faith, which
faith except every one do keep whole and undefiled, without doubt he shall perish everlastingly.
And the Catholic faith is this:

That we worship one God in Trinity, and Trinity in Unity; Neither confounding the Persons,
nor dividing the Substance. For there is one person of the Father, another of the Son: and another
of the Holy Ghost. But the Godhead of the Father,
of the Son and of the Holy Ghost is all one: the
Glory equal, the Majesty co-eternal. Such as the
Father is, such is the Son; and such is the Holy
Ghost. The Father uncreate, the Son uncreate:
and the Holy Ghost uncreate. The Father incomprehensible: the Son incomprehensible: and the
Holy Ghost incomprehensible. The Father eternal, the Son eternal: and the Holy Ghost eternal.
And yet there are not three eternals: but one eternal. As also there are not three incomprehensibles
nor three uncreated: but one uncreated and one
incomprehensible.

So likewise the Father is Almighty: the Son
Almighty: and the Holy Ghost Almighty. And yet
there are not three Almightys: but one Almighty.
So the Father is God, the Son is God: and the
Holy Ghost is God. And yet there are not three
Gods: but one God. So likewise the Father is Lord,
the Son Lord: and the Holy Ghost Lord. And yet
not three Lords: but one Lord. For like as we are
compelled by the Christian verity: to acknowledge every Person by Himself to be God and
Lord: so are we forbidden by the Catholic Religion to say there be three Gods, or three Lords.
The Father is made of none: neither created nor
begotten. The Son is of the Father alone: not
made nor created but begotten. The Holy Ghost
is of the Father and of the Son: neither made, nor
created, nor begotten, but proceeding.

So there is one Father, not three Fathers; one
son, not three Sons; one Holy Ghost, not three
Holy Ghosts. And in this Trinity, none is afore, or
after other: none is greater, or less than another;
but the whole Three Persons are co-eternal together: and co-equal. So that in all things, as is

aforesaid: the Unity in Trinity, and the Trinity in Unity, is to be worshiped. He therefore that will be saved: must thus think of the Trinity.

Furthermore, it is necessary to everlasting salvation: that he also believe rightly the Incarnation of our Lord Jesus Christ. For the right Faith is, that we believe and confess: that our Lord Jesus Christ, the Son of God, is God and Man; God, of the Substance of the Father, begotten before the worlds, and Man, of the substance of His Mother, born in the world; Perfect God, and Perfect Man: of a reasonable soul and human flesh subsisting. Equal to the Father, as touching His Godhead: and inferior to the Father, as touching His Manhood. Who although He be God and Man: yet He is not two but one Christ; One: not by conversion of the Godhead into flesh: but by taking of the Manhood, into God; One altogether; not by confusion of Substance: but by unity of Person.

For as the reasonable soul and flesh is one man: so God and Man is one Christ; who suffered for our salvation; descended into hell; rose again the third day from the dead. He ascended into Heaven, He sitteth on the Right hand of the Father, God Almighty: from whence He shall come to judge the quick and the dead. At Whose coming all men shall rise again with their bodies: and shall give account of their own works. And they that have done good shall go into life everlasting: and they that have done evil into everlasting fire.

This is the Catholic Faith, which except a man believe faithfully he cannot be saved.

Glory be to the Father, and to the Son, and to the Holy Ghost. As it was in the beginning, is now, and ever shall be, world without end, Amen.

NICENE CREED

We believe in one God the Father, the Almighty, maker of heaven and earth, of all that is seen and unseen;

We believe in one Lord, Jesus Christ, the only Son of God, eternally begotten of the Father,

God from God, Light from Light, true God from true God, begotten not made, one in being with the Father,

Through Him all things were made, for us men and for our salvation.

He came down from heaven, by the power of the Holy Spirit.

He was born of the Virgin Mary and became man,

For our sake He was crucified under Pontius Pilate; He suffered, and was buried.

On the third day He rose again in fulfillment of the Scriptures;

He ascended into heaven and is seated at the right hand of the Father.

He will come again in glory to judge the living and the dead.

And His kingdom will have no end.

We believe in the Holy Spirit, the Lord and giver of Life who proceeds from the Father.

With the Father and the Son He is worshiped and glorified.

He has spoken through the Prophets.

We believe in one holy catholic and apostolic church.

We acknowledge one baptism for the forgiveness of sins.

We look for the resurrection of the dead and the life of the world to come. Amen.

Comparative Denominational Chart

Group	Origins	Form of Government	Major Creeds	Sacraments/Ordinances
Roman Catholic	Claims foundation by St. Peter	Episcopal	Nicaea, Constantinople, Chalcedon, Fourth Lateran, Council of Trent, Vatican I and II	Seven sacraments (Infant baptism), Penance, Confirmation, Eucharist (Transubtantiation), Ordination, Extreme unction, (Marriage), Clerical celibacy, Papal authority as vicar of Christ; Magisterium of church; canon laws; veneration of saints and Mary; Apostolic succession, Filioque
Orthodox	Dating from apostolic times. Independant since East-West schism	Episcopal Autocephalous patriarchates	Nicaea Constantinople Chalcedon	All seven sacraments, Celibacy mandatory only for bishops and monks Hesychasm, Holy Spirit proceeds from Father only, Veneration of icons, Apostolic succession
Lesser Eastern Churches	Jacobite, Syrian, Coptic, Ethiopian, Armenian	Episcopal	Ecumenical Councils except Chalcedon	All seven scaraments, Celibacy required only for bishops and monks, Apostolic succession
Assyrian	Second century	Episcopal	Nicaea only	All seven sacraments, Celibacy required only for bishops and monks
Lutheran	1517 Martin Luther posts Ninety-Five Theses	Partly Episcopal, Partly congregational	1530 Augsburg Confession 1577 Formula of Concord	Two sacraments, Infant baptism and Lord's Supper (Consubstantiation). Justification by faith, Liturgical worship.
Reformed	Sixteenth century Calvin, Zwingli	Modified Presbyterian	1558 Gallican Confession, 1561 Belgic Confession, 1563 Heidelberg Catechism, 1566 Second Helvetic Confession, 1619 Canons of Synod of Dort	Infant baptism Lord's Supper
Anabaptist	Multiple origins 1525 Conrad Gregel, Felix Mans, Menno Simons	Congregational	1527 Schleitheim Confession	Believer's baptism, Symbolic Lord's Supper, Footwashing, strict church discipline, Pacifism

Episcopal (Anglican)	1534 Henry VIII	Episcopal	1563 Thirty-Nine Articles, Book of Common Prayer	Infant baptism Holy communion
Presbyterian	1550's Calvin in Geneva, Thomas Cartwright in England, Andrew Melville, 1560 John Knox in Scotland	Presbyterian Plurality of Elders	1648 Westminster Confession	Infant baptism Lord's Supper (spiritual presence only)
Baptist	Multiple origins Sixteenth century Anabaptists, 1609 John Smyth, 1638 Particular Baptists 1638 General Baptists Roger Williams	Congregational	1689 London Confession 1742 Philadelphia Confession 1832 New Hampshire Confession, Generally non-creedal	Believer's baptism by immersion Symbolic Lord's Supper
Methodist	1784 John Wesley 1795 Francis Asbury	Episcopal	(1739) Articles of Religion, Generally non-creedal, Arminian, Perfectionist	Believer's or Infant baptism by sprinkling, pouring, or immersion; Lord's Supper
Disciples of Christ	Barton Stone, Thomas and Alexander Campbell	Congregational	Anti-creedal	Believer's baptism by immersion; weekly Lord's Supper; no instrumental music
Pentecostal	Charles F. Parham, Topeka, Kansas, William Seymour, Azusa Street	Mostly Congregational	Non-creedal Arminian Perfectionist	Believer's baptism by immersion, Lord's Supper, Holy Spirit baptism; Speaking in tongues, healing

Greek and Slavonic Churches: A Comparative Liturgical Glossary

Roman	Greek	Slavonic
Abbess	Hegoumenissa	
Abbot	Archimandrite	Hegumen
	Hegoumenos	
	Kathegoumenos	
Alb	Kamision	Stikhar
	Stikharion	
Altar	Aghia Trapeza	Prestol
	Thronos	Svyathaya
	Thysiasterion	
	Trapeza	
Altar, Canopy of	Kiborion	Syen
	Pyrgos	
Altar Clothes	Antimension	Inditia
	Eileton	Stratchitza
	Endyte	
	Katasarkion	
Altar Stone	Antimension	Antimins
	Kathierosis	
	Thronos	
Anointing of Sick	Euchelion	Eleovastchenie
Archangel	Archistrategos	
Archpriest	Protoiereus	
Asterisk	Asteriskos	Zvyezditza
Baptism	Baptisma	Kretshenia
Baptistery	Baptisterion	
	Kolymbethra	
	Photisterion	
Beatitudes	Makarismoi	
Belfry	Companarion	
	Kodonostasion	
Believer	Pistos	Veroyuschie
Bell	Kodon	
Bishop	Archiereus	Protiere
	Episcopos	
Bishop's Secretary	Syncellus	
Bishop's Throne	Synthronon	
	Thronos	

Roman	Greek	Slavonic
Bread	Prosphora	
Bread, Blessed	Antidoron	
	Eulogia	
Candlestick	Dikeretrikeria	
Branched with Candles	Dibampoulos	
	Kerion	
	Keropegia	
	Polykerion	
Branched with Oil Lamps	Polyelaion	
	Polykandelon	
Double tapered	Dikerion	Dikiri
	Single	Kerostates
	Lampas	
	Manoualion	
	Triple tapered	Trikerion
Cassock	Anterion	Ponriznik
	Rason	
Catechumen	Oglashenniy	
	Triteki	
Censer	Thymaterion	Kadilnitza
Chalice	Potir	
Chasuble	Phailones	Felon
	Phelonion	
	Commixture	Enosisispolnenie
	Smieshevanie	
Communion	Koinonia	Obshcheniye
	Prichashtiye	
Communion Spoon	Labis	Izhitza
Compline	Apodeipnon	Povecherie
Concelebration	Sylleitourgon	Sobornie
Confessor	Epitimion	Duhovnek
	Exagoreutes	
	Pneumatikos	
Confirmation	Meropomazanie	
Credence Table	Predlogenie	
	Zheretvennik	
Creed	Symbolon	
Cross, Sign of the	Stavros	
Crown	Stephanos	Vienetz
Crozier	Dekanikion	Djezl
	Paterissa	Posokh
	Rabdos	
Crucifix	Estavromenos	Raspiate
Cuffs	Epimanikia	Porutchi
	Hypomanika	
Curtain	Belothyron	Zaviesa
	Velothyron	
	Vemothyron	

Roman	Greek	Slavonic
Deacon	Devterevon	Diakon
		Diakonos
Deacon, Senior	Protodeacon	
Diptych	Diptich	
Dismissal	Apolysis	Otpust
Doorkeeper	Pyloros	Dvernik
		Prevratnek
Doors	Basilikos	Vrata
	Pyle	
	Thyra	
Eagle	Aetos	Orletz
	Psathion	
Elevation	Hypsosis	Vozdnosht Shenie
Entrance	Eisodos	Bohod
	Vkhod	
Epiclesis	Epiclesis	Prizivanie
Epigonation	Hypogonation	Nabedrennik
	Palitza	
Epistle	Apostolos	Apostol
Eucharist	Anaphora	Anafora
	Koinonia	
Fans	Exapteryga	
	Ripidia	
	Ripidion	
	Ripisterion	
Fraction	Melismos	Razdroblenie
Girdle	Zonarion	Poyas
	Zone	
	Zoster	
Gospel	Evangelion	Evangelie
	Tetraevangelion	
Icon	Ikon	
Icon Stand	Proskynetarion	
Incense	Thymiama	Ladan
Lauds	Orthros	Khvalitnyi
Lectern	Analogion	
	Diskelion	
	Triskelion	
Marriage	Gamos	Brak
Mattins	Mesonyktion	Polunoshtchnitza
Miter	Mitra	Metra
	Vienetz	
Monastery	Lavra	Rastoyatel
	Skete	
	Stavropegion	
Monastic Ceremony	Apokoukoulismos	

Roman	Greek	Slavonic
Monastic Habit	Analabos	Kamilafka
	Koukoulion	Mantiya
	Mandyas	Paraman
	Megaloschemos	Skhimnik
	Polystavrion	
	Skouphos	
Monk	Calogers	Krestonosets
	Kalogeros	Poslyshnik
	Mikroschemos	Ryasonosets
	Rasosphore	
	Stavrophore	
Monk-Deacon	Hierodeacon	
Monk-Priest	Hieromonk	
Monk, Superior	Archimandrite	
None	Hora Enate	Tchas Devyatie
Pallium	Homophorion	Omophor
	Omophorion	
Parish	Enoria	Prehod
Paten	Discos	
	Diskarion	
Peace, Kiss of	Aspasmos	Tselovanie
Penance	Epitimion	Pokoyanie
	Exomologesis	
	Metanoia	
Precentor	Protopsaltes	Regentchora
Priest	Iereus	Batoushka
	Papas	Svashshtenik
Priest, Senior	Protopapas	
Prime	Hora Prote	Tchas Pierve
Prothesis	Proskomide	Proskomedia
Reader	Anagnostes	Tchetz
Relics	Leipsana	Mostche
Ring, Wedding	Daktylios	
Rosary	Kombologion	Chotki
	Komboschoinion	
	Liestovka	
	Vervitza	
Royal Doors	Belothyron	Zaviesa
Sacristy	Diakonnik	
	Riznitza	
Sanctuary	Hierateion	
Sext	Hora Hekte	Tchas Schiestie
Singer	Psaltes	
	Pevetz	
Sponge	Mousa	Gouba
	Gubka	
Spoon	Labis	Izhitza
	Lzhitza	

Roman	Greek	Slavonic
Sponsors, Baptismal	Anadochoi	
Sponsors, Monastic	Gerontas	Krestnaya Atiets
	Staretz	
Stole	Epitrachelion	Epitrakhil
	Orarion	Orar
	Peritrachelion	
Subdeacon	Hypodiakonos	Eepodiacon
	Ypodiakon	
Tabernacle	Artophorion	Kovtcheg
	Hyrophylakion	
	Peristera	
Terce	Hora Trite	Tchas Triete
Throne	Archieraticos Thronos	
	Cathedra	
	Thronos	
Tonsure	Koura	
	Monachike Houra	
	Apokarsis	
Trisagion	Agios O Theos	Trisyatoe
Unction	Euchelion	Eleosvastchenie
Veils, Chalice	Deuteron Kalymma	
Veils, Paten	Diskokallyma	
	Kalymmata	
	Proton Kalymma	
Veils, Paten and Chalice	Aer	Pokrovy
	Nephele	
Veils, Sanctuary	Belothyron	Zaviesa
	Tetravela	
	Velothyron	
	Vemothyron	
Vespers	Hesperinos	Vetchernya
Vessels for Oils	Albastron	Alavastr

APPENDIX 21

Lesser Eastern Churches: A Comparative Liturgical Glossary

Roman	Armenian	Assyrian	Coptic	Ethiopian	Jacobite
Abbot		Sudra		Mamher	
Alb	Shapik	Kotina	Shento	Kuthino	
			Mappa		
			Marppa		
			Tuniyah		
Altar	Khoran	Trumus	Ma'idah	Meshwa'e	Pathora
	Selan		Manershooushi		Pothur Haye
	Surb		Trapeza		Qudsho
			Thronos		Trumus
					Thronos
Altar Stone	Marmnakal	Tabella	Lax	Tabella	Kethons
	Schouoschphah	T'wilaita	Nakis		Mandil
	Wern		Tabella		Tablith(o)
			Andimissi		
			Lauh		
Amice	Va(r)kas	Birun	Ballin	Ghelab	Masnaphtho
		Sanwartha	Ephout	Hebanie	
			Kidaris	Kesela	
			Palin	Wegheret	
			Shamlah		
			Tailasan		
Anaphora		Kuddasha	Kuddas	Enfora	Kurobho
		Qudashe	Agiasmos	Keddase	Qurobho
			Anafora	Zameshtir	
Anointing of Sick	Henana				
Apse					Beth Diyaqon
					Rose
					Diyoqoniqon
Archdeacon		Arkidyakna	Ra'is a		
			Shammaamishah		
				Nebrid	
Archpriest	Avagueretz	Rab Kumre			
	Kahanayapet				
Asterisk			Dome		
			Kubbah		
Baptistery		Beth Mada			M'amuditho
		Bit Qanki			
Believer	Hhavatathseal		Ethnahti	Ta'amani	M'haimno
Bishop	Episcopos	Efiskufa	Abbas		Episquopo
		Rab Kahni	Anba		Khasvo
					Rakohno
Bread	Neshkar	Bukhra	Korban	H'bst	Buchro

Roman	Armenian	Assyrian	Coptic	Ethiopian	Jacobite
	Surb Khaths	Kaprana	Prosfora	Korban	Katzto
		Malka	Qurban		Paristo
		Melkaita			Tabh'o
Bread, Blessed		M'caprana	Baracah		Burc'tho
			Khubz Moubarak		
Bread, Consecrated	Masn	G'murtho	Asbadikon		
		Lahma	Kedsat		
		Dkudasha	Spoudikon		
		Qudsha			
Cassock	Verarkou				Aba
					Sultana
Cathechumen	Erekah		Katechoumenos	Ne'us Crestiyan	Shomu'o
Censer	Bourwarr		Shoure	Ma'etant	Pirmo
Chalice	Bashak		Poterion	Cenae	Coso
	Ski		Stoicharion	Cewa'e	Kas
Chalice Stand			Cursi Alcas		
			Pitote		
			Thronos nte		
			Pipoterion		
			Tote		
Chasuble	Schoorchar	Ma'apra	Antiforion	Cappa	Phaino
		Paina	Burnus	Kaba	Phaino
		Pakila	Falunyun		Phelono
			Felonion		Rida
			Kouklion		
			Phainolion		
			Phelonion		
Chorpeiscopus		Sa'aure			Kurepisqupo
Chrism	Meron		Myron		
Cleric	Dpir			Kahenat	
Commixture	Kharrnoumn				
Communion	Khaghordouthiun		Tanawal	Sutafe	Shauthophutho
			Tschi		
Communion Spoon			Kokliarion	Myster	Kalb'tho
				Mystheri	Tarwodho
Confirmation			Myron		
Consignation		Rashmo	Rasam	Ataba	Rashmo
Credence Table	Entsaiaran				Kenfo
	Matouthsaran				
Creed	Khavatamch				Haiyimonutho
Crozier			Akaz		Hutro
			Bakteria		Muronitho
			Dikanikion		Shabbuqto
			Shvot		
Cuffs	Bazpan		Kamision	Acmam	Pedhitho
			Cumm	Edjge	Zande
			Cumman		Zende
Deacon	Sarkavak	Shamasha	Diacon		M'Sham-Shono
Deaconess					M'Sham-
					Shonoitho
Diptych		Diupatcin	Diptichon		Diphtucho
			Tarhim		Kanuno
			Touptikon		Qanuno
Dismissal			Massah Wajh		
Doorkeeper	Drpnapan				
Elevation	Werathsouomn				Raf'ah Zuyoho

Roman	Armenian	Assyrian	Coptic	Ethiopian	Jacobite
Entrance	Werabereouthiun				
Epiclesis	Kathschoumn				D'awah
					Kerytho
					K'royotho
Epistle	Arrachealch		Bulus	Pawelos	
Eucharist		Kuddasha	Agiasmos	Enfora	Annaphura
			Anafora	Keddase	Kurbono
			Korban	Zameshtir	Kurobho
			Prosfora		
Fans	Chschoths		Cheroubim		Marwah'tho
	Kashotz		Mirwahah		
			Ripidion		
			Ripisterion		
Fraction	Bekanel		Fosh		Kasyo
			Kism		Tukkoso-
					dh-q'sayo
Girdle	Goti	Zunara	Mintakah	Kamis	Zand
	Kodi	Zunnara	Zinnar	Zenar	Zunar
			Zounarion		Zunnoro
			Zunarion		
Gospel	Avatran	Ewangeliyun	Anjil	Wangel	
		Iwangallyuna	Evangelion		
Icon	Nkar				Yuquo
Incense			Maia		
			Sandarus		
Intercession					Brodiki
					Kathuliki
Lectern					Golgotha
Lessons	Arrachealch			Menbab	Keryana
	Avatran				
	Margarech				
Mats			Pithom		
			Tabak		
			Thom		
Miter	Saghavart		Kham	Zewd	Taj
			Metra		Togho
			Taj		
			Tschrepi		
Monastic Habits	Pakegh			Askema	Eshkim
	Sqem			Wegheret	Jubba
	Veghar				Qubh'ono
					Schema
Monk	Abegha	Naqpa			
		Raban			
Monk-Priest		Raban			
Oven		Tanurta		Bethlehem	
Pallium	Emiphoron	Martuta	Omoforion		Hemnicho
					Homophorion
					Uroro
					Uroro Rabbo
Paten	Maghzma	Pilasa	Diskos	Ained	
		Pinka		Awed	
				Cachel	
				Sahal	
Patriarch			Amba	Abuna	

List of Abbreviations in Evangelism

AACC	All Africa Conference of Churches	FMM	Franciscan Missionaries of Mary
ABCFM	American Board of Commissioners for Foreign Missions	GMU	Gospel Missionary Union
		IMC	International Missionary Council
ABFMS	American Baptist Foreign Mission Society	IVCF	Inter-Varsity Christian Fellowship
ABS	American Bible Society	LAM	Latin American Missions
AG	Assemblies of God	LMS	London Missionary Society
AIM	Africa Inland Mission	LWF	Lutheran World Federation
BCMS	British Churchmen's Missionary Society	M. Afr.	Missionaries of Africa (White Fathers)
BFBS	British and Foreign Bible Society	MCCJ	Comboni Missionaries
BFMR	Baptist Foreign Mission Board	MHM	Mill Hill Missionaries
BM	Basel Mission	MM	Maryknoll Missioners
BMS	Baptist Missionary Society	MMS	Methodist Missionary Society
CEZMS	Church of England Zenana Missionary Society	MSC	Missionaries of the Sacred Heart
CICM	Congregation of Immaculate Heart of Mary	NAE	National Association of Evangelicals
CIM	China Inland Mission (now Overseas Missionary Fellowship)	NMS	Netherlands Mission Society
		NMS	Norwegian Mission Society
CLS	Christian Literature Society	Ocarm	Carmelites
C&MA	Christian and Missionary Alliance	OFM	Order of Friars Minor (Franciscans)
		OFM Cap	Franciscan Capuchins
CMS	Church Missionary Society	OFM Conv	Franciscan Conventuals
CSC	Congregation of the Holy Cross	OM	Operation Mobilization
CSI	Church of South India	OMF	Overseas Missionary Fellowship
CSM	Church of Scotland Mission	OMI	Oblates of Mary Immaculate
CSP	Congregation of St. Paul	OP	Order of Preachers (Dominicans)
CSSP	Holy Ghost Fathers	OSA	Order of St. Augustine (Augustinians)
CSSR	Redemptorists		
CWM	Council for World Mission (formerly London Missionary Society)	OSB	Order of St. Benedict (Benedictines)
		OSU	Order of St. Ursuline (Ursuline Sisters)
EFMA	Evangelical Foreign Missions Association	PCUSA	Presbyterian Church USA
FCSM	Free Church of Scotland Mission	PECUSA	Protestant Episcopal Church in

Roman	Armenian	Assyrian	Coptic	Ethiopian	Jacobite
Peace, Kiss of	Hampuir Srboutian		Sulh	Amcha	Sh'lomo
Priest	Eretz Tanaretz	Kahna Kasha Kasisha	Kassis Kess		Kachicho
Priests, Celibate	Abegha				
Priests, Married	Derders				
Prothesis	Entsaiaran Matouth (soumn) saran	Kubhtha	Proskomide		
Purificator	Srbitsch Thasch-Kinak				Pinco Piyalol Siniyah
Reader		Amura Karuya	Anagnostes Karianjili		Quoroyo
Reliquary		Beth Kaddishe Beth Sadhe			
Sacristy	Avandatoun Sarkanvaganouths	Beth Roze Beth Diyakun Beth Shamasha	Diakonikon		
Sanctuary	Srbaran	Kedush	Erphei Haikal	Beta Makdas Kedest Kedsat Macdan Kedus Magdas Makedes	Madh'bho
Singer	Apir Saghmosergov		Dafteras Mazamer		Mzamrono Psaltu
Sponge					Espugo Gomuro
Stole	Ourar Phakegm Porurar	Urara Uroro	Shordion	Mothat	Bitrashil Hamnikho
Subdeacon	Kisarkavag		Abudiyakun Ypodiakon	Nefka Diyakon Hiupath'aqua	Houpodiacono
Tabernacle		Beth Qurbana			Beth Qurban Paradiscus
Throne, Bishop's		Archieraticos Thronos	Thronos		Throniyon
Tonsure	Supara				Suphora
Trisagion	Erechsbeann Ergsbeann		Ajus		Kadishat Aloho
Unction		Henana			
Veils, Chalice	Tsatskoths Skih		Pitote		Hupp(a)oyo
Veils, Paten				Cedana'awed	Gita Absainiyah
Veils, Paten, Chalice	Kogh	Shushepo	Ibrusfarin Lafafah Prosfarin	Macdan Shoshepa	P'roso
Veils, Sanctuary	Waraguir	Wila	Hijab Katapetasma Sitarah		Qubb'tho

	the USA	SSC	Columbans
PEMS	Paris Evangelical Missionary Society	SUM	Sudan United Mission
PFM	Paris Foreign Missions	SVD	Society of the Divine Word
RBMU	Regions Beyond Missionary Union	SVM	Student Voluntary Movement for Foreign Missions
SA	Salvation Army	TEAM	The Evangelical Alliance Mission
SAGM	South Africa General Mission	TEAR	The Evangelical Alliance Relief Fund
SAMS	South American Missionary Society	UBS	United Bible Societies
SBCFMF	Southern Baptist Convention Foreign Mission Board (now International Foreign Mission Board)	UMCA	Universities Mission to Central Africa
		WBHMS	Women's Baptist Home Missionary Society
SCM	Student Christian Movement	WBT/SIL	Wycliffe Bible Translators/Summer Institute of Linguistics
SDA	Seventh-Day Adventist		
SDB	Salesians of Don Bosco	WCC	World Council of Churches
SIM	Sudan Interior Mission	WEC	Worldwide Evangelization Crusade
SJ	Society of Jesus (Jesuits)		
SM	Society of Mary (Marists)	WF	White Fathers
SMA	Society of African Missions	WMMS	Wesleyan Methodist Missionary Society
SMS	Scottish Missionary Society		
SMS	Swedish Missionary Society	WSCF	World Student Christian Federation
SPCK	Society for Promoting Christian Knowledge		
SPF	Society for the Propagation of Faith	YFC	Youth for Christ
		YMCA	Young Men's Christian Association
SPG	Society for the Propagation of the Gospel	YWAM	Youth with a Mission
SS	Sulpicians	YWCA	Young Women's Christian Association

Bibliography

Anderson, Gerald H. *Biographical Dictionary of Christian Missions.* New York, 1998.

Angeles, Peter A. *A Dictionary of Christian Theology.* San Francisco, 1985.

Apostolos-Cappadono, Diane. *A Dictionary of Christian Art.* New York, 1994.

Appleton, George. *The Oxford Book of Prayer.* New York, 1985.

Atiya, Aziz S. *The Coptic Encyclopedia.* 8 vols. New York, 1991.

Atkinson, David J., and David H. Field. *New Dictionary of Christian Ethics and Pastoral Theology.* Downers Grove, Illinois, 1995.

Attwater, Donald. *A Dictionary of Mary.* London, 1956.

Attwater, Donald. *The Penguin Dictionary of Saints.* New York, 1965.

Babic, Gordana. *Icons.* New York, 1998.

Barker, W. P. *Who's Who in Church History.* Grand Rapids, Michigan, 1977.

Barraclough, Geoffrey. *The Christian World: A Social and Cultural History.* New York, 1981.

Barrett, David B., George Thomas Kurian, and Todd M. Johnson. *World Christian Encyclopedia.* 2d ed. 3 vols. New York, 2000.

Bell, G. K. A. *Documents on Christian Unity.* 4 vols. London, 1924–1958.

Benowitz, June Melba. *Encyclopedia of American Women and Religion.* Santa Barbara, California, 1998.

Berardino, Angelo Di. *Encyclopedia of the Early Church.* Translated by Adrian Walford. 2 vols. New York, 1992.

Bercot, David. *A Dictionary of Early Christian Beliefs: A Reference Guide to More Than 700 Topics Discussed by Early Church Fathers.* Peabody, Massachusetts, 1998.

Bodensieck, Julius. *Encyclopedia of the Lutheran Church.* 3 vols. Minneapolis, 1965.

Bowden, John. *Who's Who in Theology.* New York, 1992.

Brackney, William H. *The Baptists.* New York, 1988.

Brauer, Jerald C. *The Westminster Dictionary of Church History.* Philadelphia, 1971.

Brethren Encyclopedia, The. 3 vols. Philadelphia, 1983–1984.

Brierley, Peter, and Heather Wraight. *Atlas of World Christianity.* Nashville, Tennessee, 1998.

Brownrigg, Ronald. *Who's Who in the New Testament.* New York, 1971.

Burgess, Stanley M., and Gary B. McGee. *Dictionary of Pentecostal and Charismatic Movements.* Grand Rapids, Michigan, 1988.

Butler, Alban. *Lives of the Saints.* Edited and revised by Herbert Thurston and Donald Attwater. 4 vols. Westminster, Maryland, 1981.

Cairns, Earle E. *Christianity Through the Centuries.* Grand Rapids, 1981.

Cameron, Nigel M. de S. *Dictionary of Scottish Church History and Theology.* Downers Grove, Illinois, 1993.

Campbell, Alastair V. *A Dictionary of Pastoral Care.* London, 1987.

Catholic Dictionary of Theology, A. 3 vols. London, 1962.

Chadwick, H., and G. Evans. *Atlas of the Christian Church.* London, 1987.

Chadwick, H., and O. Chadwick. *Oxford History of the Christian Church.* Oxford, England, 1976–.

Child, Heather, and Dorothy Colles. *Christian Symbols, Ancient and Modern.* New York, 1971.

Childress, James F., and John Macquarrie. *The Westminster Dictionary of Christian Ethics.* Philadelphia, 1986.

Christe, Yves. *Art of the Christian World, A.D. 200–1500: A Handbook of Styles and Forms.* New York, 1982.

Clifton, Chas S. *Encyclopedia of Heresies and Heretics.* Santa Barbara, California, 1992.

Cohn-Sherbok, Lavinia. *Who's Who in Christianity.* New York, 1998.

Cooper, J. C. *Cassell Dictionary of Christianity.* New York, 1996.

Coulson, J. *The Saints: A Concise Biographical Dictionary.* London, 1958.

Cross, Frank Leslie. *The Oxford Dictionary of the Christian Church.* Edited by E. A. Livingstone. 3d ed. New York, 1997.

Cully, Iris V., and Kendig Brubaker Cully. *Harper's Encyclopedia of Religious Education.* San Francisco, 1990.

Davidson, James Robert. *A Dictionary of Protestant Church Music.* Metuchen, New Jersey, 1975.

Davies, J. G. *The New Westminster Dictionary of Liturgy and Worship.* Philadelphia, 1986.

Day, Peter D. *The Liturgical Dictionary of Eastern Christianity.* Collegeville, Minnesota, 1993.

Delaney, John J. *Dictionary of Saints.* Garden City, New York, 1980.

Delaney, John J., and James Edward Tobin. *Dictionary of Catholic Biography.* New York, 1961.

Diehl, Catherine Smith. *Hymns and Tunes: An Index.* New York, 1966.

Dilasser, Maurice. *The Symbols of the Church.* Collegeville, Minnesota, 1999.

Douglas, J. D. *New Twentieth-Century Encyclopedia of Religious Knowledge.* 3d ed. Grand Rapids, 1991.

Douglas, J. D. *The New International Dictionary of the Christian Church.* Rev. ed. Grand Rapids, 1978.

Douglas, J. D. *Twentieth Century Dictionary of Christian Biography.* Grand Rapids, Michigan, 1995.

Douglas, J. D., and Philip W. Comfort. *Who's Who in Christian History.* Wheaton, Illinois, 1992.

Douglas, J. D., Walter Ewell, and Peter Toon. *A Concise Dictionary of the Christian Tradition.* Grand Rapids, Michigan, 1989.

Dowley, Timothy. *Atlas of the Bible and Christianity.* Grand Rapids, Michigan, 1997.

Downey, Michael. *The New Dictionary of Catholic Spirituality.* Collegeville, Minnesota, 1993.

Dwyer, Judith A. *The New Dictionary of Catholic Social Thought.* Collegeville, Minnesota, 1994.

Eerdman's Handbook to the History of Christianity. Grand Rapids, Michigan, 1977.

Eliade, Mircea. *The Encyclopedia of Religion.* 16 vols. New York, 1987.

Elwell, Walter A. *Evangelical Dictionary of Theology.* Grand Rapids, Michigan, 1984.

Elwell, Walter A. *Handbook of Evangelical Theologians.* Grand Rapids, Michigan, 1993.

Encyclopedia of Southern Baptists. 4 vols. Nashville, Tennessee, 1958–1982.

Erickson, Hal. *Religious Radio and Television in the United States, 1921–1991.* Jefferson, North Carolina, 1992.

Erickson, Millard J. *Concise Dictionary of Christian Theology.* Grand Rapids, Michigan, 1986.

Fahlbusch, Erwin, et al. *The Encyclopedia of Christianity,* vol. 1. Translated by Geoffrey W. Bromiley. Grand Rapids, Michigan, 1999.

Ferguson, Everett. *Backgrounds of Early Christianity.* 2d ed. Grand Rapids, Michigan, 1993.

Ferguson, Everett. *Encyclopedia of Early Christianity.* 2d ed. 2 vols. New York, 1997.

Ferguson, George Wells. *Signs and Symbols in Christian Art.* New York, 1955.

Ferguson, Sinclair B., and David F. Wright. *New Dictionary of Theology.* Downers Grove, Illinois, 1955.

Fink, Peter E. *The New Dictionary of Sacramental Worship.* Collegeville, Minnesota, 1990.

Fitzgerald, Allan D. *Augustine through the Ages: An Encyclopedia.* Grand Rapids, Michigan, 1998.

Fitzgerald, Thomas E. *The Orthodox Church.* Westport, Connecticut, 1995.

Ford, David F. *The Modern Theologians: An Introduction to Christian Theology in the Twentieth Century.* 2d ed. Cambridge, Massachusetts, 1997.

Freitag, A. *The Twentieth Century Atlas of the Christian World: The Expansion of*

Christianity through the Centuries. New York, 1964.

Gibbon, Edward. *The Decline and Fall of the Roman Empire.* 3 vols. New York, 1932.

Glazier, Michael, and Monika K. Hellwig. *The Modern Catholic Encyclopedia.* Collegeville, Minnesota, 1994.

Glazier, Michael, and Thomas J. Shelley. *The Encyclopedia of American Catholic History.* Collegeville, Minnesota, 1997.

Goddard, Burton. L. *Encyclopedia of Modern Christian Missions.* Camden, New Jersey, 1967.

Gorman, G. E., and Lyn Gorman. *Theological and Religious Reference Materials.* 3 vols. Westport, Connecticut, 1984–.

Hardon, J. A. *Modern Catholic Dictionary.* London, 1981.

Harmon, Nolan B. *The Encyclopedia of World Methodism.* Nashville, 1974.

Harvey, Van A. *A Handbook of Theological Terms.* New York, 1964.

Hawthorne, Gerald F., and Ralph P. Martin. *Dictionary of Paul and His Letters.* Downers Grove, Illinois, 1993.

Hill, Samuel S. *Encyclopedia of Religion in the South.* Macon, Georgia, 1984.

Hillerbrand, Hans J. *The Oxford Encyclopedia of the Reformation.* 4 vols. New York, 1996.

Hunter, Rodney J. *Dictionary of Pastoral Care and Counseling.* Nashville, Tennessee, 1990.

Jockle, Clemens. *Encyclopedia of Saints.* London, 1995.

Johnston, William M. *Recent Reference Books in Religion.* Rev. ed. Chicago, 1998.

Julian, John. *Dictionary of Hymnology: Origin and History of Christian Hymns and Hymnwriters.* 2 vols. Grand Rapids, Michigan, 1985.

Kadel, Andrew. *Matrology: A Bibliography of Writings by Christian Women from the First to the Fifteenth Centuries.* New York, 1995.

Kaufman, Donald T. *The Dictionary of Religious Terms.* Westwood, New Jersey, 1967.

Kazhdan, Alexander P. *The Oxford Dictionary of Byzantium.* 3 vols. New York, 1991.

Kelly, J. N. D. *The Oxford Dictionary of Popes.* New York, 1986.

Kelly, Joseph. *The Concise Dictionary of Early Christianity.* Collegeville, Minnesota, 1992.

Kepple, Robert J., and John R. Meuther. *Reference Works for Theological Research.* 3d ed. Lanham, Maryland, 1992.

Kidd, B. J. *Documents Illustrative of the History of the Church.* 3 vols. London, 1920–1941.

Kirby, James E., Russell E. Richey, and Kenneth E. Rowe. *The Methodists.* Westport, Connecticut, 1996.

Komonchak, Joseph A., Mary Collins, and Dermot A. Lane. *The New Dictionary of Theology.* Dublin, 1987.

Lang, Jovian. *Dictionary of the Liturgy.* New York, 1989.

Latourelle, Rene, and Rino Fisichella. *Dictionary of Fundamental Theology.* New York, 1994.

Latourette, Kenneth Scott. *A History of the Expansion of Christianity.* 7 vols. New York, 1937–1945.

Leonard, Bill J. *Dictionary of Baptists in America.* Downers Grove, Illinois, 1994.

Lewis, Donald M. *The Blackwell Dictionary of Evangelical Biography, 1730–1860.* 2 vols. Cambridge, Massachusetts, 1995.

Lippy, Charles H., and Peter W. Williams. *Encyclopedia of the American Religious Experience.* 3 vols. New York, 1988.

Littell, Franklin Hamlin. *The Macmillan Atlas History of Christianity.* New York, 1976.

Lodi, Enzo. *Saints of the Roman Calendar, Including Feasts Proper to the English-speaking World.* Translated by Jordan Aumann. New York, 1992.

Lossky, Nicholas. *Dictionary of the Ecumenical Movement.* Grand Rapids, Michigan, 1991.

Ludlow, Daniel H. *Encyclopedia of Mormonism.* 5 vols. New York, 1992.

Lueker, Erwin L. *Lutheran Cyclopedia.* Rev. ed. St. Louis, Missouri, 1975.

MacManners, John. *The Oxford Illustrated History of Christianity.* New York, 1990.

Macquarrie, John. *Dictionary of Christian Ethics.* London, 1967.

Martin, Ralph P., and Peter H. Davids. *Dictionary of the Later New Testament and Its Developments.* Downers Grove, Illinois, 1997.

Maxwell-Stuart, P. G. *Chronicle of the Popes.* New York, 1997.

Mayo, J. A. *A History of Ecclesiastical Dress.* London, 1984.

McBrien, Richard P. *The HarperCollins Encyclopedia of Catholicism.* New York, 1995.

McCabe, James Patrick. *Critical Guide to Catholic Reference Books.* 3d ed. Englewood, Colorado, 1989.

McGrath, Alister. *The Blackwell Encyclopedia of Modern Christian Thought.* Cambridge, Massachusetts, 1993.

McKim, Donald K. *Historical Handbook of Major Biblical Interpreters.* Downers Grove, Illinois, 1998.

McKim, Donald K. *Westminster Dictionary of Theological Terms.* Louisville, Kentucky, 1996.

McKim, Donald K., and David F. Wright, *Encyclopedia of the Reformed Faith.* Louisville, Kentucky, 1992.

Mead, Frank Spencer. *Handbook of Denominations in the United States.* New 10th ed. Nashville, Tennessee, 1995.

Meer, Frederik van der, and Christine Mohrmann. *Atlas of the Early Christian World.* Translated and edited by Mary F. Hedlund and H. H. Rowley. London, 1958.

Melton, J. Gordon. *Religious Leaders of America.* Detroit, 1991.

Melton, J. Gordon. *The Encyclopedia of American Religions.* 6th ed. Detroit, 1999.

Melton, J. Gordon. *The Encyclopedia of American Religions—Religious Creeds.* 2 vols. Detroit, 1988–1994.

Menachery, George. *The St. Thomas Christian Encyclopedia of India.* 2 vols., Trichur, India, 1973–1982.

Mennonite Encyclopedia, The. 4 vols. Hillsboro, Kansas, 1955–1959.

Metford, J. C. J. *Dictionary of Christian Lore and Legend.* London, 1983.

Meyer, Elgin S. *The Wycliffe Biographical Dictionary of the Church.* Chicago, 1982.

Miethe, Terry L. *Compact Dictionary of Doctrinal Words.* Minneapolis, 1988.

Muller, Karl. *Dictionary of Mission: Theology, History, Perspectives.* Maryknoll, New York, 1997.

Muller, Richard A. *A Dictionary of Latin and Greek Theological Terms.* Grand Rapids, Michigan, 1985.

Murphy, Larry, J., Gordon Melton, and Gary L. Ward. *Encyclopedia of African American Religions.* New York, 1993.

Murray, Peter, and Linda Murray. *The Oxford Companion to Christian Art and Architecture.* New York, 1996.

Musser, Donald W., and Joseph L. Price. *A New Handbook of Christian Theology.* Nashville, Tennessee, 1992.

Neill, Stephen. *Concise Dictionary of the Christian World Mission.* Nashville, Tennessee, 1971.

Neufeld, Don F. *Seventh-Day Adventist Encyclopedia.* Washington, D.C., 1966.

New Catholic Encyclopedia. 18 vols. New York, 1967–1989.

Newton, Eric, and William Neil. *2000 Years of Christian Art.* New York, 1966.

Noll, Mark A. *Eerdman's Handbook to Christianity in America.* Grand Rapids, Michigan, 1983.

Norris, Kathleen. *Amazing Grace: A Vocabulary of Faith.* New York, 1997.

O'Brien, Thomas. C. *Corpus Dictionary of the Western Churches.* Washington, D.C., 1970

O'Carroll, Michael. *Trinitas: A Theological Encyclopedia of the Holy Trinity.* Wilmington, Delaware, 1987.

O'Carroll, Michael. *Verbum Caro: An Encyclopedia on Jesus, the Christ.* Collegeville, Minnesota, 1992.

Parrinder, Geoffrey. *A Concise Encyclopedia of Christianity.* New York, 1999.

Parry, Ken. *The Blackwell Dictionary of Eastern Christianity.* Oxford, 1999.

Patrinacos, Nikon D. *A Dictionary of Greek Orthodoxy.* Pleasantville, New York, 1984.

Payne, Wardell J. *Directory of African American Religious Bodies.* 2d ed. Washington D.C., 1995.

Peerman, Dean G., and Martin E. Marty. *A Handbook of Christian Theologians.* Nashville, Tennessee, 1984.

Pelikan, Jaroslav. *Jesus Through the Centuries: His Place in the History of Culture.* New York, 1987.

Pelikan, Jaroslav. *The Christian Tradition: A History of the Development of Doctrine.* 5 vols. Chicago, 1971–.

Pelikan, Jaroslav. *The Melody of Theology: A Philosophical Dictionary.* Cambridge, Massachusetts, 1988.

Pfatteicher, Philip H. *A Dictionary of Liturgical Terms.* Philadelphia, 1991.

Poulos, George. *Orthodox Saints: Spiritual Profiles for Modern Man.* 2d expanded ed. 4 vols. Brookline, Massachusetts, 1990–1992.

Poultney, David. *Dictionary of Western Church Music.* Chicago, 1991.

Prokurat, Michael, Alexander Golitzin, and Michael D. Peterson. *Historical Dictionary of the Orthodox Church.* Lanham, Maryland, 1996.

Quasten, Johannes. *Patrology.* 4 vols. Utrecht, The Netherlands, 1950–1986.

Rahner, Karl. *Encyclopedia of Theology: The Concise Sacramentum Mundi.* New York, 1975.

Reid, Daniel G. *Dictionary of Christianity in America.* Downers Grove, Illinois, 1990.

Richard, Taylor S. *Beacon Dictionary of Theology.* Kansas City, Missouri, 1983.

Richardson, Alan, and John Bowden. *A New Dictionary of Christian Theology.* London, 1983.

Richardson, Alan, and John Bowden. *The Westminster Dictionary of Christian Theology.* Philadelphia, 1983.

Rowland, Christopher. *The Cambridge Companion to Liberation Theology.* New York, 1999.

Russell, Letty M., and J. Shannon Clarkson. *Dictionary of Feminist Theologies.* Louisville, Kentucky, 1996.

St. Augustine's Abbey, Ramsgate. *The Book of Saints: A Dictionary of the Servants of God.* 6th ed. London, 1989.

Schaff, Philip. *History of the Christian Church.* 7 vols. New York, 1889–1910.

Shannon, Ellen C. *Layman's Guide to Christian Terms.* New York, 1969.

Sill, Gertrude Grace. *A Handbook of Symbols in Christian Art.* New York, 1975.

Simcox, Carroll Eugene. *A Treasury of Quotations on Christian Themes.* New York, 1975.

Speake, Jennifer. *The Dent Dictionary of Symbols in Christian Art.* London, 1994.

Steeves, Paul D. *The Modern Encyclopedia of Religion in Russia and the Soviet Union.* Gulf Breeze, Florida, 1988–.

Strayer, Joseph R. *Dictionary of the Middle Ages.* 13 vols. New York, 1982–1989.

Sutcliffe, John M. *A Dictionary of Religious Education.* London, 1984.

Van der Bent, A. J. *Historical Dictionary of Ecumenical Christianity.* Metuchen, New Jersey, 1994.

Wace, A. H., and W. C. Piercy. *Dictionary of Christian Biography and Literature to the End of the Sixth Century.* London, 1911.

Wakefield, Gordon S. *The Westminster Dictionary of Christian Spirituality.* Philadelphia, 1983.

Wall, John N. *A New Dictionary for Episcopalians.* Minneapolis, 1985.

Walsh, Michael J. *Dictionary of Catholic Devotions.* San Francisco, 1993.

Walton, Robert C. *Chronological and Background Charts of Church History.* Grand Rapids, Michigan, 1986.

Waltz, Alan K. *A Dictionary for United Methodists.* Nashville, Tennessee, 1991.

Ward, Carol. *The Christian Soucebook.* New York, 1986.

Ware, Timothy. *The Orthodox Church.* Harmondsworth, England, 1963.

Weiser, Franz Xaver. *Handbook of Christian Feasts and Customs: The Year of the Lord in Liturgy and Folklore.* New York, 1958.

West, Edward N. *Outward Signs: The Language of Christian Symbolism.* New York, 1989.

Willimon, William H., and Richard Lischer. *Concise Encyclopedia of Preaching.* Louisville, Kentucky, 1995.

Yearbook of American and Canadian Churches. Nashville, Tennessee, Annual.

Yearbook of the Orthodox Church. Munich, Germany, 1978–.

Yrigoyen, Charles, and Susan E. Warrick. *Historical Dictionary of Methodism.* Lanham, Maryland, 1996.

Zibawe, Mahmoud. *Eastern Christian Worlds.* Translated by Madeleine Beaumont. Collegeville, Minnesota, 1995.

Contributors

David A. Becker
David W. Buschart
David Dorries
Roger Ellsworth
Heather Collins Grattan
Douglas Groothuis
David Hedges
Roger Wayne Hicks
Lavern R. Holdeman
David P. Hustad
Timothy Paul Jones
Seth Kasten
Charles Lawless, Jr.

Gordon Magee
Howard Moffat
R. Bruce Montgomery
Thomas J. Nettles
Christ John Otto
J. A. Reynolds
Ian Shaw
Mozelle Clark Sherman
Wm. H. Swatos
Mark Terry
Carl A. Truman
Peter Wallace
Enoch Wan